Contemporary
Literary Criticism

Guide to Gale Literary Criticism Series

For criticism on	Consult these Gale series
Authors now living or who died after December 31, 1999	*CONTEMPORARY LITERARY CRITICISM (CLC)*
Authors who died between 1900 and 1999	*TWENTIETH-CENTURY LITERARY CRITICISM (TCLC)*
Authors who died between 1800 and 1899	*NINETEENTH-CENTURY LITERATURE CRITICISM (NCLC)*
Authors who died between 1400 and 1799	*LITERATURE CRITICISM FROM 1400 TO 1800 (LC)* *SHAKESPEAREAN CRITICISM (SC)*
Authors who died before 1400	*CLASSICAL AND MEDIEVAL LITERATURE CRITICISM (CMLC)*
Authors of books for children and young adults	*CHILDREN'S LITERATURE REVIEW (CLR)*
Dramatists	*DRAMA CRITICISM (DC)*
Poets	*POETRY CRITICISM (PC)*
Short story writers	*SHORT STORY CRITICISM (SSC)*
Black writers of the past two hundred years	*BLACK LITERATURE CRITICISM (BLC)* *BLACK LITERATURE CRITICISM SUPPLEMENT (BLCS)*
Hispanic writers of the late nineteenth and twentieth centuries	*HISPANIC LITERATURE CRITICISM (HLC)* *HISPANIC LITERATURE CRITICISM SUPPLEMENT (HLCS)*
Native North American writers and orators of the eighteenth, nineteenth, and twentieth centuries	*NATIVE NORTH AMERICAN LITERATURE (NNAL)*
Major authors from the Renaissance to the present	*WORLD LITERATURE CRITICISM, 1500 TO THE PRESENT (WLC)* *WORLD LITERATURE CRITICISM SUPPLEMENT (WLCS)*

ISSN 0091-3421

Volume 132

Contemporary Literary Criticism

Criticism of the Works
of Today's Novelists, Poets, Playwrights,
Short Story Writers, Scriptwriters, and
Other Creative Writers

Jeffrey W. Hunter
EDITOR

Jenny Cromie
Justin Karr
Linda Pavlovski
ASSOCIATE EDITORS

Rebecca J. Blanchard
Vince Cousino
ASSISTANT EDITORS

GALE GROUP

Detroit
New York
San Francisco
London
Boston
Woodbridge, CT

STAFF

Lynn M. Spampinato, Janet Witalec, *Managing Editors, Literature Product*
Kathy D. Darrow, *Product Liaison*
Jeffrey W. Hunter, *Editor*
Mark W. Scott, *Publisher, Literature Product*

Jenny Cromie, Justin Karr, Linda Pavlovski, *Associate Editors*
Rebecca J. Blanchard, Vince Cousino, *Assistant Editors*
Patti A. Tippett, Timothy J. White, *Technical Training Specialists*
Deborah J. Morad, Kathleen Lopez Nolan, *Managing Editors*
Susan M. Trosky, *Director, Literature Content*

Maria L. Franklin, *Permissions Manager*
Mark Plaza, *Permissions Assistant*

Victoria B. Cariappa, *Research Manager*
Tracie A. Richardson, *Project Coordinator*
Barbara Leevy, Robert Waley, *Research Associates*
Nicodemys Ford, Sarah Genik, Ron Morelli, *Research Assistants*

Dorothy Maki, *Manufacturing Manager*
Stacy L. Melson, *Buyer*

Mary Beth Trimper, *Manager, Composition and Electronic Prepress*
Carolyn Fischer, *Composition Specialist*

Michael Logusz, *Graphic Artist*
Randy Bassett, *Image Database Supervisor*
Robert Duncan, Dan Newell, *Imaging Specialists*
Pamela A. Reed, *Imaging Coordinator*
Kelly A. Quin, *Editor, Image Content*

Library of Congress Catalog Card Number 76-46132
ISBN 0-7876-3207-4
ISSN 0091-3421
Printed in the United States of America

10 9 8 7 6 5 4 3 2 1

Contents

Preface vii

Acknowledgments xi

Preface

Named "one of the twenty-five most distinguished reference titles published during the past twenty-five years" by *Reference Quarterly*, the *Contemporary Literary Criticism* (*CLC*) series provides readers with critical commentary and general information on more than 2,000 authors now living or who died after December 31, 1999. Volumes published from 1973 through 1999 include authors who died after December 31, 1959. Previous to the publication of the first volume of *CLC* in 1973, there was no ongoing digest monitoring scholarly and popular sources of critical opinion and explication of modern literature. *CLC,* therefore, has fulfilled an essential need, particularly since the complexity and variety of contemporary literature makes the function of criticism especially important to today's reader.

Scope of the Series

CLC provides significant passages from published criticism of works by creative writers. Since many of the authors covered in *CLC* inspire continual critical commentary, writers are often represented in more than one volume. There is, of course, no duplication of reprinted criticism.

Authors are selected for inclusion for a variety of reasons, among them the publication or dramatic production of a critically acclaimed new work, the reception of a major literary award, revival of interest in past writings, or the adaptation of a literary work to film or television.

Attention is also given to several other groups of writers—authors of considerable public interest—about whose work criticism is often difficult to locate. These include mystery and science fiction writers, literary and social critics, foreign authors, and authors who represent particular ethnic groups.

Each *CLC* volume contains individual essays and reviews taken from hundreds of book review periodicals, general magazines, scholarly journals, monographs, and books. Entries include critical evaluations spanning from the beginning of an author's career to the most current commentary. Interviews, feature articles, and other published writings that offer insight into the author's works are also presented. Students, teachers, librarians, and researchers will find that the general critical and biographical material in *CLC* provides them with vital information required to write a term paper, analyze a poem, or lead a book discussion group. In addition, complete biographical citations note the original source and all of the information necessary for a term paper footnote or bibliography.

Organization of the Book

A *CLC* entry consists of the following elements:

- The **Author Heading** cites the name under which the author most commonly wrote, followed by birth and death dates. Also located here are any name variations under which an author wrote, including transliterated forms for authors whose native languages use nonroman alphabets. If the author wrote consistently under a pseudonym, the pseudonym will be listed in the author heading and the author's actual name given in parenthesis on the first line of the biographical and critical information. Uncertain birth or death dates are indicated by question marks. Single-work entries are preceded by a heading that consists of the most common form of the title in English translation (if applicable) and the original date of composition.

- A **Portrait of the Author** is included when available.

- The **Introduction** contains background information that introduces the reader to the author, work, or topic that is the subject of the entry.

- The list of **Principal Works** is ordered chronologically by date of first publication and lists the most important works by the author. The genre and publication date of each work is given. In the case of foreign authors whose works have been translated into English, the English-language version of the title follows in brackets. Unless otherwise indicated, dramas are dated by first performance, not first publication.

- Reprinted **Criticism** is arranged chronologically in each entry to provide a useful perspective on changes in critical evaluation over time. The critic's name and the date of composition or publication of the critical work are given at the beginning of each piece of criticism. Unsigned criticism is preceded by the title of the source in which it appeared. All titles by the author featured in the text are printed in boldface type. Footnotes are reprinted at the end of each essay or excerpt. In the case of excerpted criticism, only those footnotes that pertain to the excerpted texts are included.

- A complete **Bibliographical Citation** of the original essay or book precedes each piece of criticism.

- Critical essays are prefaced by brief **Annotations** explicating each piece.

- Whenever possible, a recent **Author Interview** accompanies each entry.

- An annotated bibliography of **Further Reading** appears at the end of each entry and suggests resources for additional study. In some cases, significant essays for which the editors could not obtain reprint rights are included here. Boxed material following the further reading list provides references to other biographical and critical sources on the author in series published by Gale.

Indexes

A **Cumulative Author Index** lists all of the authors that appear in a wide variety of reference sources published by the Gale Group, including *CLC*. A complete list of these sources is found facing the first page of the Author Index. The index also includes birth and death dates and cross references between pseudonyms and actual names.

A **Cumulative Nationality Index** lists all authors featured in *CLC* by nationality, followed by the number of the *CLC* volume in which their entry appears.

A **Cumulative Topic Index** lists the literary themes and topics treated in the series as well as in *Literature Criticism from 1400 to 1800, Nineteenth-Century Literature Criticism, Twentieth-Century Literary Criticism,* and the *Contemporary Literary Criticism* Yearbook, which was discontinued in 1998.

An alphabetical **Title Index** accompanies each volume of *CLC*. Listings of titles by authors covered in the given volume are followed by the author's name and the corresponding page numbers where the titles are discussed. English translations of foreign titles and variations of titles are cross-referenced to the title under which a work was originally published. Titles of novels, dramas, nonfiction books, and poetry, short story, or essay collections are printed in italics, while individual poems, short stories, and essays are printed in roman type within quotation marks.

In response to numerous suggestions from librarians, Gale also produces an annual paperbound edition of the *CLC* cumulative title index. This annual cumulation, which alphabetically lists all titles reviewed in the series, is available to all customers. Additional copies of this index are available upon request. Librarians and patrons will welcome this separate index; it saves shelf space, is easy to use, and is recyclable upon receipt of the next edition.

Citing *Contemporary Literary Criticism*

When writing papers, students who quote directly from any volume in the Literary Criticism Series may use the following general format to footnote reprinted criticism. The first example pertains to material drawn from periodicals, the second to material reprinted from books.

Alfred Cismaru, "Making the Best of It," *The New Republic* 207, no. 24 (December 7, 1992): 30, 32; excerpted and reprinted in *Contemporary Literary Criticism,* vol. 85, ed. Christopher Giroux (Detroit: The Gale Group, 1995), 73-4.

Yvor Winters, *The Post-Symbolist Methods* (Allen Swallow, 1967), 211-51; excerpted and reprinted in *Contemporary Literary Criticism,* vol. 85, ed. Christopher Giroux (Detroit: The Gale Group, 1995), 223-26.

Suggestions are Welcome

Readers who wish to suggest new features, topics, or authors to appear in future volumes, or who have other suggestions or comments are cordially invited to call, write, or fax the Managing Editor:

Managing Editor, Literary Criticism Series
The Gale Group
27500 Drake Road
Farmington Hills, MI 48331-3535
1-800-347-4253 (GALE)
Fax: 248-699-8054

Acknowledgments

The editors wish to thank the copyright holders of the excerpted criticism included in this volume and the permissions managers of many book and magazine publishing companies for assisting us in securing reproduction rights. We are also grateful to the staffs of the Detroit Public Library, the Library of Congress, the University of Detroit Mercy Library, Wayne State University Purdy/Kresge Library Complex, and the University of Michigan Libraries for making their resources available to us. Following is a list of the copyright holders who have granted us permission to reproduce material in this volume of *CLC*. Every effort has been made to trace copyright, but if omissions have been made, please let us know.

COPYRIGHTED EXCERPTS IN *CLC*, VOLUME 132, WERE REPRODUCED FROM THE FOLLOWING PERIODICALS:

American Book Review, v. 18, September-October, 1997. Reproduced by permission.—*American Literature,* v. 59, October, 1987. Copyright © 1987 by Duke University Press, Durham, NC. Reproduced by permission.—*The Antioch Review,* v. 40, Fall, 1982; v. 53, Summer, 1995. Copyright © 1982, 1995 by the Antioch Review Inc. All reproduced by permission of the Editors.—*Art History,* v. 14, December, 1991. Reproduced by permission of Blackwell Publishers.—*Artforum,* v. 35, February, 1997. Reproduced by permission.—*Belles Lettres,* v. 8, Spring, 1983; Summer, 1990. Both reproduced by permission.—*The Bloomsbury Review,* v. 13, September/October, 1993 in a review of Alberta by Liz Caile. Copyright © by Owaissa Communications Company, Inc. 1993. Reproduced by permission of the author.—*Books in Canada,* v. xviii, April, 1989 for a review of "The Lovely Treachery of Words" by George Bowering; v. xxii, February, 1993 for a review of "The Puppeteer" by Douglas Glover; v. xxiv, November, 1995 for a review of "A Likely Story: The Writing Life" by Tim Bowling. © 1989, 1993, 1995. All reproduced by permission of the authors.—*British Journal of Aesthetics,* v. 31, April, 1991 in a review of *The Ideology of the Aesthetics* by Colin Lyas. Reproduced by permission.—*The Canadian Forum,* v. lxv, March, 1986 for "Perspectives from Abroad" by Geert Lernout; v. lxxii, July/August, 1993 for "Pulling Strings" by David Wylynko . Copyright © 1986, 1993. All rights reserved. Reproduced by permission by the author.—*Canadian Literature,* n. 128, Spring, 1991 for "The Post-Colonial As Deconstruction: Land & Language in Kroetsch's 'Badlands'" by Dorothy Seaton; n. 128, Spring, 1991 for "What Kroetsch Said: The Problem of Meaning and Language in What the 'Crow Said'" by Kathleen Wall; n. 136, Spring, 1993 for "Heideggerian Elements in Robert Kroetsch's 'Seed Catalogue'" by Douglas Reimer; n. 141, Summer, 1994 for "Framing the American Abroad: A Comparative Study of Robert Kroetsch's 'Gone Indian' and Janet Frame's 'The Carpathians'" by John Clement Ball; n. 146, Autumn, 1995 for "Pizza, Pizza" by Laurie Ricou; n. 149, Summer, 1996 for "Cyberwriting and the Borders of Identity: 'What in a Name' in Kroetsch's 'The Puppeteer' and Mistry's 'Such a Long Journey?'" by David Williams; n. 156, Spring, 1998 for "Talking Writing" by David Creelman. All reproduced by permission of the authors.—*Chicago Tribune,* January 1, 1993. © 1993 Tribune Media Services, Inc. All rights reserved. Reproduced by permission.—*The Christian Science Monitor,* March 6, 1995. © 1995 The Christian Science Publishing Society. All rights reserved. Reproduced by permission from *The Christian Science Monitor.*—*Comparative Literature,* v. 46, Fall, 1994 in a review of *Ideology: An Introduction,* by Christopher Norris. © copyright 1994 by University of Oregon. Reproduced by permission of *Comparative Literature.*—*Contemporary Literature,* v. 25, Winter, 1984; v. xxix, Summer, 1988; v. xxx, Fall, 1989; v. xxxii, Winter, 1991. Copyright © 1984, 1988, 1989, 1991. The Board of Regents of the University of Wisconsin System. All rights reserved. All reproduced by permission.—*Critique: Studies in Contemporary Fiction,* v. xxx, Fall, 1988; v. xxxi, Fall, 1989. Copyright © 1988, 1989 Helen Dwight Reid Educational Foundation. Both reproduced with permission of the Helen Dwight Reid Educational Foundation, published by Heldref Publications, 1319 18th Street, NW, Washington, DC 20036-1802.—*Dissent,* v. 42, Summer, 1995 for "Noam on the Range" by Richard Wolin. © 1995, by Dissent Publishing Corporation. Reprinted by permission of the publisher and the author.—*Essays on Canadian Writing,* v. 35, Winter, 1987; v. 39, Fall, 1989. © 1987, 1989 Essays on Canadian Writing Ltd. Both reproduced by permission.—*The Humanist,* v. 50, November-December, 1990. Copyright 1990 by the American Humanist Association. Reproduced by permission.—*The Journal of Aesthetics and Art Criticism,* v. 49, Summer, 1991. Copyright © 1991 by The American Society for Aesthetics. Reproduced by permission.—*The Journal of Commonwealth Literature,* v. xxviii, 1993; v. xxix, 1994. Reproduced with the kind permission of Bowker-Saur.—*Journal of English and Germanic Philology,* v. lxvi, July, 1967. © 1967 by the Board of Trustees of the University of Illinois. Reproduced by permission.—*Kenyon Review,* v. 9, Summer, 1987. Copyright © 1987 by Kenyon College. All rights reserved. Reproduced by permission of The University of Georgia Press.—*Los Angeles Times Book Review,* February 7, 1988; March 19, 1995; February 15, 1998. Copyright, 1988, 1995, 1998 Los Angeles Times. All reproduced by permission.—*Modern Fiction Studies,* v. 25, Winter, 1979-80; v. 30, Summer, 1984; v. 35, Summer, 1989. © 1979-80, 1984, 1989. All reproduced by permission of The Johns Hopkins University Press.—*Modern*

Noam Chomsky
1928-

(Full name Avram Noam Chomsky) American linguist, nonfiction writer, essayist, lecturer, and critic.

The following entry presents an overview of Chomsky's career through 1999.

INTRODUCTION

Hailed as one of the most brilliant and influential intellectuals of the twentieth century, Noam Chomsky has attracted international renown for his groundbreaking research into the nature of human language and communication. A prolific scholar and professor of linguistics at the Massachusetts Institute of Technology, his work produced what is referred to as the "Chomskyan Revolution," a wide-reaching intellectual realignment and debate with implications that transcend formal linguistics to include psychology, philosophy, and even genetics. Chomsky is also an impassioned political dissenter whose controversial criticism of American society, the mass media, and foreign policy—especially its effects on ordinary citizens of Third World nations—is the subject of many of his books since 1969.

BIOGRAPHICAL INFORMATION

Born in Philadelphia, Chomsky was the oldest of two sons raised by parents William Chomsky, a Hebrew scholar of considerable repute, and Elsie Simonofsky, a Hebrew scholar and author of children's books. A precocious child, Chomsky took an early interest in Semitic languages, Jewish culture, and international affairs, particularly the prewar Zionist movement. After graduating from Central High School in Philadelphia, he attended the University of Pennsylvania, where he studied mathematics, philosophy, and linguistics. There he came under the tutelage of Zellig Harris, a noted professor of linguistics, marking the beginning of Chomsky's career in that field. The school of structural linguistics in which Chomsky took his collegiate training held as its goal the formal and autonomous description of languages without wide reference to the meaning—or semantics—of utterances. Chomsky questioned this approach in his early work as a student at the University of Pennsylvania and broke with it more radically during the early 1950s. After completing his B.A. in 1949, Chomsky remained at the University of Pennsylvania to earn an M.A. in 1951 and a Ph.D. in 1955. He married Carol Schatz, a linguist, in 1945, with whom he shares several children. From 1951 to 1955, Chomsky was supported by junior fellowships from the Society of Fellows at Harvard University, where he was immersed in new developments in mathematical logic, the abstract theory of thinking machines, and the latest psychological and philosophical debates. These ideas led him to develop further his earlier work on generative grammar and to pose new questions that challenged established linguistic scholarship. Chomsky took a teaching position at M. I. T. in 1955, where he has remained as a professor of modern languages and linguistics for more than four decades. He attracted widespread recognition in the academic community with his first book, *Syntactic Structures* (1957). In addition to his important research during the 1960s, Chomsky emerged as an outspoken critic of American military action in Vietnam, the subject of *American Power and the New Mandarins* (1969), and a major figure of the radical Left. He has since published many additional books in the fields of linguistics, social science, psychology, and government policy. Chomsky has received numerous awards and honorary degrees, and has appeared as a visiting professor at major universities throughout the world. He was awarded the prestigious Kyoto Prize in Basic Science in 1988.

MAJOR WORKS

In *Syntactic Structures* Chomsky introduced his pioneering linguistic theories concerning the acquisition and fundamental understanding of language. Refuting the prevailing theories of structuralist linguistics and behavioral psychology, Chomsky posited that language is not limited to a fixed corpus of learned utterances but consists of an infinitely variable system of "transformational-generative grammar." Chomsky adapted this concept from mathematics; generative systems refer to the process of producing an infinite number of proofs from a single postulate through principles of inference. By working with rudimentary sentences and shifting the focus on syntactic processes and systems rather than analysis and classification of specific linguistic units, Chomsky revolutionized the study of language. As Chomsky notes, one's ability to grasp the meaning of an unfamiliar sentence or phrase demonstrates that language is not understood in strictly empirical or inductive terms but functions upon a system of limited rules that facilitates infinite creativity. His mathematically precise description of some of human language's most striking features lead to his belief that language acquisition is an innate ability and that all of the world's languages share certain "deep structures" that are genetically encoded. Chomsky's theories exerted a significant influence beyond the field of linguistics, particularly in related branches of psychology and philosophy. While his research reinforces the philosophical tradition of "rationalism," the contention that the mind, or "reason," contributes to human knowledge beyond what is gained by experience, it opposes "empiricism," the view that all knowledge, including language, derives from external stimuli; Chomsky dismisses the empiricist argument in *Language and Problems of Knowledge* (1987). The basic premises of his theories have also made him one of the most trenchant critics of behaviorism, the view that suggests all human responses are learned through conditioning. Chomsky further developed his linguistic theories in *Current Issues in Linguistic Theory* (1964), *Aspects of the Theory of Syntax* (1965), *Topics in the Theory of Generative Grammar* (1966), *Sound Patterns of English* (1968), co-authored with Morris Halle, *Language and Mind* (1968), *Studies on Semantics in Generative Grammar* (1972), *Knowledge of Language* (1986), and *Language and Thought* (1994).

Chomsky established himself as a forceful political dissenter with *American Power and the New Mandarins*. In this book he levels harsh criticism against the imperialistic values and foreign policy failures that led to American military involvement in Southeast Asia. The book's strongest vitriol is directed toward those so-called "New Mandarins"—the technocrats, bureaucrats, and university-trained scholars who defend America's right to dominate the globe. Chomsky also attacked the undeclared war in *At*

War with Asia (1970), in articles, and from the podium; in the process he became better known for his political views than for his linguistic scholarship. Subsequent Chomsky books on American foreign policy have explored other political hotbeds around the world, including the Middle East in *The Fateful Triangle* (1983), drawing the conclusion that U.S. interests in human rights, justice, and morality are inevitably subordinated to the needs of big business. The very narrowness of public discussion is the subject of *Deterring Democracy* (1991), a book in which Chomsky examines how, regardless of the facts, the American mass media and the United States government conspire to limit the range of opinions that can be widely expressed. Chomsky discusses, for example, the fact that mainstream public opinion embraced only specific kinds of debates regarding the Sandinista government and the Contras in Nicaragua; he shows that the vast majority of lawmakers and reporters disagreed only as to which methods should be employed to rid that country of its communist leaders—no serious attention was given to the debate about whether the Sandinistas or the U.S.-backed Contras would best serve the people of Nicaragua. Chomsky also addresses the American government's "war on drugs." Chomsky examines the U.S. government's propaganda campaign supporting its various "successes" and describes the positive news coverage these victories receive. He concludes that no substantial discussion arises about the effects of this war on the countries involved, and he bitterly denounces the ironic policy of the United States government of threatening trade sanctions against those East Asian countries that block the importing of U.S. tobacco, a product that is proven to be deadly. *Manufacturing Consent* (1988), co-authored with Edward S. Herman, examines the various ways in which news organizations ultimately serve the ideological aims of the government. Chomsky and Herman propose a "propaganda model" of the mass media in the United States; countering the commonly held belief that the mass media tend to respond to rather than create public opinion, the two authors argue that the major American news organizations actively misinform the public about the activities of the United States government. Chomsky has published many other volumes of sociopolitical critique in which he denounces the hypocrisy and prevailing ideology of American culture, the media, and democracy. Among them are *Towards a New Cold War* (1982), *Turning the Tide* (1985), *The Culture of Terrorism* (1988), *Necessary Illusions* (1989), and *World Orders, Old and New* (1994). Many of Chomsky's views and main themes are also outlined in *Chronicles of Dissent* (1992), a collection of interviews conducted with David Barsamian from 1984 to 1991, and *The Chomsky Reader* (1987).

CRITICAL RECEPTION

An independent-minded and enormously gifted thinker, Chomsky is widely recognized as one of the foremost intellectuals of the postwar era. He was named one of the thousand "makers of the twentieth century" by the London *Times* in 1970. A 1993 survey of the *Arts and Humanities*

Citation Index also revealed that he was the most frequently cited living author, ranked eighth on the all-time list behind Plato and Sigmund Freud. Chomsky's highly original work as a linguist, particularly in *Syntactic Structures*, is credited with establishing the scientific study of language and exerting a profound interdisciplinary effect on the social sciences. The wide-reaching influence of his scholarship on contemporary philosophy, psychology, literary criticism, and anthropology has been referred to as the "Chomskyan Revolution," a paradigm shift compared to the intellectual upheavals precipitated by René Descartes, Charles Darwin, Albert Einstein, and Sigmund Freud. Though most scholars praise the novelty and range of Chomsky's thought, he has received criticism for his rationalist perspective and emphasis on the genetic basis of language and learning, which, according to his detractors, reduces human behavior to a series of biologically predetermined activities. Chomsky's anarchist-libertarian political writings have elicited even greater controversy than his linguistic theories. Inevitably, *American Power and the New Mandarins* drew scathing criticism from those who oppose his views and high praise from those who agree with him. Subsequent works such as *The Fateful Triangle* and *Deterring Democracy* similarly received mixed evaluation, with reviewers finding fault in Chomsky's polemical tone and one-sided distortions. While many critics appreciate Chomsky's unwavering commitment to freedom in all its forms—intellectual, political, economic, social, and artistic—others have been less sanguine about the quality and influence of Chomsky's political views; in fact, some have labeled him a pariah and attempted to discredit him on a number of grounds. Branded as a "self-hating" Jew for his criticism of Israeli policies toward the Palestinians, Chomsky also attracted outrage and censure for defending the right to free expression of Robert Faurisson, a French neo-Nazi scholar who wrote an essay denying the historical reality of the Holocaust. Chomsky became increasingly alienated from the mainstream media during the 1970s, but has remained a popular lecturer on college campuses and an icon of radical activism. He was a vocal opponent to the Gulf War in 1991. Despite the mixed reception of his political commentary, Chomsky's major contribution to the study of linguistics and language acquisition remains undisputed.

PRINCIPAL WORKS

Syntactic Structures (nonfiction) 1957

Current Issues in Linguistic Theory (nonfiction) 1964

Aspects of the Theory of Syntax (nonfiction) 1965

Cartesian Linguistics: A Chapter in the History of Rationalist Thought (nonfiction) 1966

Topics in the Theory of Generative Grammar (nonfiction) 1966

Language and Mind (nonfiction) 1968

Sound Patterns of English (nonfiction) 1968

American Power and the New Mandarins (nonfiction) 1969

At War with Asia (nonfiction) 1970

Problems of Knowledge and Freedom: The Russell Lectures (lectures) 1971

Studies on Semantics in Generative Grammar (nonfiction) 1972

Peace in the Middle East? (nonfiction) 1974

The Logical Structure of Linguistic Theory (nonfiction) 1975

Reflections on Language (nonfiction) 1975

Essays on Form and Interpretation (essays) 1977

Human Rights and American Foreign Policy (nonfiction) 1978

Dialogues avec Mitsou Ronat [Language and Responsibility] (nonfiction) 1979

The Political Economy of Human Rights 2 vols. [with Edward Herman; Vol. I: *The Washington Connection and Third World Fascism*; Vol. II: *After the Cataclysm: Postwar Indochina and the Construction of Imperial Ideology*] (nonfiction) 1979

Rules and Representation (nonfiction) 1980

Radical Priorities (nonfiction) 1982

Some Concepts and Consequences of the Theory of Government and Binding (nonfiction) 1982

Towards a New Cold War: Essays on the Current Crisis and How We Got There (essays) 1982

The Fateful Triangle: The United States, Israel, and the Palestinians (nonfiction) 1983

Turning the Tide: U.S. Intervention in Central America and the Struggle for Peace (nonfiction) 1985

Barriers (nonfiction) 1986

Knowledge of Language: Its Nature, Origins, and Use (nonfiction) 1986

Pirates and Emperors: International Terrorism in the Real World (nonfiction) 1986

The Chomsky Reader [edited by James Peck] (nonfiction) 1987

Language and Problems of Knowledge (nonfiction) 1987

Language in a Psychological Setting (nonfiction) 1987

On Power and Ideology: The Managua Lectures (lectures) 1987

The Culture of Terrorism (nonfiction) 1988

Generative Grammar: Its Basis, Development, and Prospects (nonfiction) 1988

Language and Politics [with C. P. Otero] (nonfiction) 1988

Manufacturing Consent [with Edward Herman] (nonfiction) 1988

Necessary Illusions: Thought Control in a Democratic Society (nonfiction) 1989

Deterring Democracy (nonfiction) 1991

Terrorizing the Neighborhood: American Foreign Policy in the Post-Cold War (nonfiction) 1991

Chronicles of Dissent: Interviews with David Barsamian (interviews) 1992

What Uncle Sam Really Wants (nonfiction) 1992

Letters from Lexington: Reflections on Propaganda (nonfiction) 1993

The Prosperous Few and the Restless Many [with David Barsamian] (nonfiction) 1993

Rethinking Camelot: JFK, the Vietnam War, and U.S. Political Culture (nonfiction) 1993

Year 501: The Conquest Continues (nonfiction) 1993

CRITICISM

John Searle (essay date 29 June 1972)

SOURCE: "Chomsky's Revolution in Linguistics," in *New York Review of Books*, June 29, 1972, pp. 16-24.

[*In the following excerpt, Searle provides an overview of Chomsky's theories about language and their impact and influence on the study of linguistics. While hailing the importance of Chomsky's insights into the structure of syntax, Searle finds inadequacies in the semantic component of his linguistic theory.*]

I

Throughout the history of the study of man there has been a fundamental opposition between those who believe that progress is to be made by a rigorous observation of man's actual behavior and those who believe that such observations are interesting only in so far as they reveal to us hidden and possibly fairly mysterious underlying laws that only partially and in distorted form reveal themselves to us in behavior. Freud, for example, is in the latter class, most of American social science in the former.

Noam Chomsky is unashamedly with the searchers after hidden laws. Actual speech behavior, speech *performance,* for him is only the top of a large iceberg of linguistic *competence* distorted in its shape by many factors irrelevant to linguistics. Indeed he once remarked that the very expression "behavioral sciences" suggests a fundamental confusion between evidence and subject matter. Psychology, for example, he claims is the science of mind; to call psychology a behavioral science is like calling physics a science of meter readings. One uses human behavior as evidence for the laws of the operation of the mind, but to suppose that the laws must be laws of behavior is to suppose that the evidence must be the subject matter.

In this opposition between the methodology of confining research to observable facts and that of using the observable facts as clues to hidden and underlying laws, Chomsky's revolution is doubly interesting: first, within the field of linguistics, it has precipitated a conflict which is an example of the wider conflict; and secondly, Chomsky has used his results about language to try to develop general anti-behaviorist and anti-empiricist conclusions about the nature of the human mind that go beyond the scope of linguistics.

His revolution followed fairly closely the general pattern described in Thomas Kuhn's *The Structure of Scientific Revolutions:* the accepted model or "paradigm" of linguistics was confronted, largely by Chomsky's work, with increasing numbers of nagging counter-examples and recalcitrant data which the paradigm could not deal with. Eventually the counter-examples led Chomsky to break the old model altogether and to create a completely new one. Prior to the publication of his **Syntactic Structures** in 1957, many, probably most, American linguists regarded the aim of their discipline as being the classification of the elements of human languages. Linguistics was to be a sort of verbal botany. As Hockett wrote in 1942, "Linguistics is a classificatory science."[1]

Suppose, for example, that such a linguist is giving a description of a language, whether an exotic language like Cherokee or a familiar one like English. He proceeds by first collecting his "data," he gathers a large number of utterances of the language, which he records on his tape recorder or in a phonetic script. This "corpus" of the language constitutes his subject matter. He then classifies the elements of the corpus at their different linguistic levels: first he classifies the smallest significant functioning units of sound, the *phonemes,* then at the next level the phonemes unite into the minimally significant bearers of meaning, the *morphemes* (in English, for example, the word "cat" is a single morpheme made up of three phonemes; the word "uninteresting" is made up of three morphemes: "un," "interest," and "ing"), at the next higher level the morphemes join together to form *words* and *word classes* such as noun phrases and verb phrases, and at the highest level of all come sequences of word classes, the possible *sentences* and, *sentence types.*

The aim of linguistic theory was to provide the linguist with a set of rigorous methods, a set of discovery procedures which he would use to extract from the "corpus" the phonemes, the morphemes, and so on. The study of the meanings of sentences or of the uses to which speakers of the language put the sentences had little place in this enterprise. Meanings, scientifically construed, were thought to be patterns of behavior determined by stimulus and response; they were properly speaking the subject matter of psychologists. Alternatively they might be some mysterious mental entities altogether outside the scope of a sober science or, worse yet, they might involve the speaker's whole knowledge of the world around him and thus fall beyond the scope of a study restricted only to linguistic facts.

Structural linguistics, with its insistence on objective methods of verification and precisely specified techniques of discovery, with its refusal to allow any talk of meanings or mental entities or unobservable features, derives from the "behavioral sciences" approach to the study of man, and is also largely a consequence of the philosophical assumptions of logical positivism. Chomsky was brought up in this tradition at the University of Pennsylvania as a student of both Zellig Harris, the linguist, and Nelson Goodman, the philosopher.

Chomsky's work is interesting in large part because, while it is a major attack on the conception of man implicit in the behavioral sciences, the attack is made from within the very tradition of scientific rigor and precision that the behavioral sciences have been aspiring to. His attack on the view that human psychology can be described by correlating stimulus and response is not an a priori conceptual argument, much less is it the cry of an anguished humanist resentful at being treated as a machine or an animal. Rather it is a claim that a really rigorous analysis of language will show that such methods when applied to language produce nothing but falsehoods or trivialities, that their practitioners have simply imitated "the surface features of science" without having its "significant intellectual content."

As a graduate student at Pennsylvania, Chomsky attempted to apply the conventional methods of structural linguistics to the study of syntax, but found that the methods that had apparently worked so well with phonemes and morphemes did not work very well with sentences. Each language has a finite number of phonemes and a finite though quite large number of morphemes. It is possible to get a *list* of each; but the number of *sentences* in any natural language like French or English is, strictly speaking, infinite. There is no limit to the number of new sentences that can be produced; and for each sentence, no matter how long, it is always possible to produce a longer one. Within structuralist assumptions it is not easy to account for the fact that languages have an infinite number of sentences.

Furthermore the structuralist methods of classification do not seem able to account for all of the internal relations within sentences, or the relations that different sentences have to each other. For example, to take a famous case, the two sentences "John is easy to please" and "John is eager to please" look as if they had exactly the same grammatical structure. Each is a sequence of *noun-copula-adjective-infinitive verb*. But in spite of this surface similarly the grammar of the two is quite different. In the first sentence, though it is not apparent from the surface word order, "John" functions as the direct object of the verb to please, the sentence means it is easy for someone to please John. Whereas in the second "John" functions as the subject of the verb to please; the sentence means John is eager that he please someone. That this is a difference in the *syntax* of the sentences comes out clearly in the fact that English allows us to form the noun phrase "John's eagerness to please" out of the second, but not "John's easiness to please" out of the first. There is no easy or natural way to account for these facts within structuralist assumptions.

Another set of syntactical facts that structuralist assumptions are inadequate to handle is the existence of certain types of ambiguous sentences where the ambiguity derives not from the words in the sentence but from the syntactical structure. Consider the sentence "The shooting of the hunters is terrible." This can mean that it is terrible that the hunters are being shot or that the hunters are terrible at shooting or that the hunters are being shot in a terrible fashion. Another example is "I like her cooking." In spite of the fact that it contains no ambiguous words (or morphemes) and has a very simple superficial grammatical structure of noun-verb-possessive pronoun-noun, this sentence is in fact remarkably ambiguous. It can mean, among other things, I like what she cooks, I like the way she cooks, I like the fact that she cooks, even, I like the fact that she is being cooked.

Such "syntactically ambiguous" sentences form a crucial test case for any theory of syntax. The examples are ordinary pedestrian English sentences, there is nothing fancy about them. But it is not easy to see how to account for them. The meaning of any sentence is determined by the meanings of the component words (or morphemes) and their syntactical arrangement. How then can we account for these cases where one sentence containing unambiguous words (and morphemes) has several different meanings? Structuralist linguists had little or nothing to say about these cases; they simply ignored them. Chomsky was eventually led up claim that these sentences have several different syntactical structures, that the uniform *surface* structure of, e.g., "I like her cooking" conceals several different *underlying* structures which he called "deep" structures. The introduction of the notion of the deep structure of sentences, not always visible in the surface structure, is a crucial element of the Chomsky revolution, and I shall explain it in more detail later.

One of the merits of Chomsky's work has been that he has persistently tried to call attention to the puzzling character of facts that are so familiar that we all tend to take them for granted as not requiring explanation. Just as physics begins in wonder at such obvious facts as that apples fall to the ground or genetics in wonder that plants and animals reproduce themselves, so the study of the structure of language beings in wondering at such humdrum facts as that "I like her cooking" has different meanings. "John is eager to please" isn't quite the same in structure as "John is easy to please," and the equally obvious but often overlooked facts that we continually find ourselves saying and hearing things we have never said or heard before and that the number of possible new sentences is infinite.

The inability of structuralist methods to account for such syntactical facts eventually led Chomsky to challenge not only the methods but the goals and indeed the definition of the subject matter of linguistics given by the structuralist linguists. Instead of a taxonomic goal of classifying elements by performing sets of operations on a corpus of utterances, Chomsky argued that the goal of linguistic description should be to construct a theory that would account for the infinite number of sentences of a natural language. Such a theory would show which strings of words were sentences and which were not, and would provide a description of the grammatical structure of each sentence.

Such descriptions would have to be able to account for such facts as the internal grammatical relations and the ambiguities described above. The description of a natural language would be a formal deductive theory which would contain a set of grammatical rules that could generate the infinite set of sentences of the language would not generate anything that was not a sentence, and would provide a description of the grammatical structure of each sentence. Such a theory came to be called a "generative grammar" because of its aim of constructing a device that would generate all and only the sentences of a language.

This conception of the goal of linguistics then altered the conception of the methods and the subject matter. Chomsky argued that since any language contains an infinite number of sentences, any "corpus," even if it contained as many sentences as there are in all the books of the Library of Congress, would still be trivially small. Instead of the appropriate subject matter of linguistics being a randomly or arbitrarily selected set of sentences, the proper object of study was the speaker's underlying knowledge of the language, his "linguistic competence" that enables him to produce and understand sentences he has never heard before.

Once the conception of the "corpus" as the subject matter is rejected, then the notion of mechanical procedures for discovering linguistic truths goes as well. Chomsky argues that no science has a mechanical procedure for discovering the truth anyway. Rather, what happens is that the scientist formulates hypotheses and tests them against evidence. Linguistics is no different: the linguist makes conjectures about linguistic facts and tests them against the evidence provided by native speakers of the language. He has in short a procedure for *evaluating* rival hypotheses, but no procedure for *discovering* true theories by mechanically processing evidence. . . .

Most of this revolution was already presented in Chomsky's book **Syntactic Structures.** As one linguist remarked.

"The extraordinary and traumatic impact of the publication of *Syntactic Structures* by Noam Chomsky in 1957 can hardly be appreciated by one who did not live through this upheaval."[2] In the years after 1957 the spread of the revolution was made more rapid and more traumatic by certain special features of the organization of linguistics as a discipline in the United States. Only a few universities had separate departments of linguistics. The discipline was (by contrast to say, philosophy or psychology), and still is, a rather cozy one. Practitioners were few; they all tended to know one another; they read the same very limited number of journals; they had, and indeed still have, an annual get-together at the Summer Linguistics Institute of the Linguistic Society of America, where issues are thrashed out and family squabbles are aired in public meetings.

All of this facilitated a rapid dissemination of new ideas and a dramatic and visible clash of conflicting views. Chomsky did not convince the established leaders of the field but he did something more important, he convinced their graduate students. And he attracted some fiery disciples, notably Robert Lees and Paul Postal.

The spread of Chomsky's revolution, like the spread of analytic philosophy during the same period, was a striking example of the Young Turk phenomenon in American academic life. The graduate students became generative grammarians even in departments that had traditionalist faculties. All of this also engendered a good deal of passion and animosity, much of which still survives. Many of the older generation still cling resentfully to the great traditions, regarding Chomsky and his "epigones" as philistines and vulgarians. Meanwhile Chomsky's views have become the conventional wisdom, and as Chomsky and his disciples of the Sixties very quickly become Old Turks a new generation of Young Turks (many of them among Chomsky's best students) arise and challenge Chomsky's views with a new theory of "generative semantics."

II

The aim of the linguistic theory expounded by Chomsky in **Syntactic Structures** (1957) was essentially to describe syntax, that is, to specify the grammatical rules underlying the construction of sentences. In Chomsky's mature theory, as expounded in **Aspects of the Theory of Syntax** (1965), the aims become more ambitious: to explain all of the linguistic relationships between the sound system and the meaning system of the language. To achieve this, the complete "grammar" of a language, in Chomsky's technical sense of the word, must have three parts, a *syntactical* component that generates and describes the internal structure of the infinite number of sentences of the language, a *phonological* component that describes the sound structure of the sentences generated by the syntactical component, and a *semantic* component that describes the meaning structure of the sentences. The heart of the grammar is the syntax; the phonology and the semantics are purely "interpretative," in the sense that they describe the sound and the meaning of the sentences produced by the syntax but do not generate any sentences themselves.

The first task of Chomsky's syntax is to account for the speaker's understanding of the internal structure of sentences. Sentences are not unordered strings of words, rather the words and morphemes are grouped into functional constituents such as the subject of the sentence, the predicate, the direct object, and so on. Chomsky and other grammarians can represent much, though not all, of the speaker's knowledge of the internal structure of sentences with rules called "phrase structure" rules. . . .

At the time of the publication of *Aspects of the Theory of Syntax* it seemed that all of the semantically relevant parts of the sentence, all the things that determine its meaning, were contained in the deep structure of the sentence. The examples we mentioned above fit in nicely with this view. "I like her cooking" has different meanings because it has different deep structures though only one surface structure. "The boy will read the book" and "The book will be read by the boy" have different surface structures, but one and the same deep structure, hence they have the same meaning.

This produced a rather elegant theory of the relation of syntax to semantics and phonology: the two components of the syntax, the base component and the transformational component, generate deep structures and surface structures respectively. Deep structures are the input to the semantic component, which describes their meaning. Surface structures are the input to the phonological component, which describes their sound. In short, deep structure determines meaning, surface structure determines sound. . . .

III

Seen as an attack on the methods and assumptions of structural linguistics, Chomsky's revolution appears to many of his students to be not quite revolutionary enough. Chomsky inherits and maintains from his structuralist upbringing the conviction that syntax can and should be studied independently of semantics; that form is to be characterized independently of meaning. As early as *Syntactic Structures* he was arguing that "investigation of such [semantic] proposals invariably leads to the conclusion that only a purely formal basis can provide a firm and productive foundation for the construction of grammatical theory."[3]

The structuralists feared the intrusion of semantics into syntax because meaning seemed too vaporous and unscientific a notion for use in a rigorous science of language. Some of this attitude appears to survive in Chomsky's persistent preference for syntactical over semantic explanations of linguistic phenomena. But, I believe, the desire to keep syntax autonomous springs from a more profound philosophical commitment: man, for Chomsky, is essentially a syntactical animal. The

structure of his brain determines the structure of his syntax, and for this reason the study of syntax is one of the keys, perhaps the most important key, to the study of the human mind.

It is of course true, Chomsky would say, that men use their syntactical objects for semantic purposes (that is, they talk with their sentences), but the semantic purposes do not determine the *form* of the syntax or even influence it in any significant way. It is because form is only incidentally related to function that the study of language as a formal system is such a marvelous way of studying the human mind.

It is important to emphasize how peculiar and eccentric Chomsky's overall approach to language is. Most sympathetic commentators have been so dazzled by the results in syntax that they have not noted how much of the theory runs counter to quite ordinary, plausible and common sense assumptions about language. The common sense picture of human language runs something like this. The purpose of language is communication in much the same sense that the purpose of the heart is to pump blood. In both cases it is possible to study the structure independently of function but pointless and perverse to do so, since structure and function so obviously interact. We communicate primarily with other people, but also with ourselves, as when we talk or think in words to ourselves. Human languages are among several systems of human communication (some others are gestures, symbol systems, and representational art) but language has immeasurably greater communicative power than the others.

We don't know how language evolved in human prehistory, but it is quite reasonable to suppose that the needs of communication influenced the structure. For example, transformational rules facilitate economy and so have survival value: we don't have to say, "I like it that she cooks in a certain way," we can say, simply, "I like her cooking." We pay a small price for such economies in having ambiguities, but it does not hamper *communication* much to have ambiguous sentences because when people actually talk the context usually sorts out the ambiguities. Transformations also facilitate communication by enabling us to emphasize certain things at the expense of others: we can say not only "Bill loves Sally" but also "It is Bill that loves Sally" and "It is Sally that Bill loves." In general an understanding of syntactical facts requires as understanding of their function in communication since communication is what language is all about.

Chomsky's picture, on the other hand, seems to be something like this: except for having such general purposes as the expression of human thoughts, language doesn't have any essential purpose, or if it does there is no interesting connection between its purpose and its structure. The syntactical structures of human languages are the products of innate features of the human mind, and they have no significant connection with communication, though, of course, people do use them for, among other purposes, communication. The essential thing about languages, their defining trait, is their structure. The so-called "bee language," for example, is not a language at all because it doesn't have the right structure, and the fact that bees apparently use it to communicate is irrelevant. If human beings evolved to the point where they used syntactical forms to communicate that are quite unlike the forms we have now and would be beyond our present comprehension, then human beings would no longer have language, but something else.

For Chomsky language is defined by syntactical structure (not by the use of the structure in communication) and syntactical structure is determined by innate properties of the human mind (not by the needs of communication). On this picture of language it is not surprising that Chomsky's main contribution has been to syntax. The semantic results that he and his colleagues have achieved have so far been trivial.

Many of Chomsky's best students find this picture of language implausible and the linguistic theory that emerges from it unnecessarily cumbersome. They argue that one of the crucial factors shaping syntactic structure is semantics. Even such notions as "a grammatically correct sentence" or a "well-formed" sentence, they claim, require the introduction of semantic concepts. For example, the sentence "John called Mary a Republican and then SHE insulted HIM"[4] is a well-formed sentence only on the assumption that the participants regard it as insulting to be called a Republican.

Much as Chomsky once argued that structuralists could not comfortably accommodate the syntactical facts of language, so the generative semanticists now argue that his system cannot comfortably account for the facts of the interpenetration of semantics and syntax. There is no unanimity among Chomsky's critics—Ross, Postal, Lakoff, McCawley, Fillmore (some of these are among his best students)—but they generally agree that syntax and semantics cannot be sharply separated, and hence there is no need to postulate the existence of purely syntactical deep structures.

Those who call themselves generative semanticists believe that the generative component of a linguistic theory is not the syntax, as in the above diagrams, but the semantics, that the grammar starts with a description of the meaning of a sentence and then generates the syntactical structures through the introduction of syntactical rules and lexical rules. The syntax then becomes just a collection of rules for expressing meaning.

It is too early to assess the conflict between Chomsky's generative syntax and the new theory of generative semantics, partly because at present the arguments are so confused. Chomsky himself thinks that there is no substance to the issues because his critics have only rephrased his theory in a new terminology.[5]

But it is clear that a great deal of Chomsky's over-all vision of language hangs on the issue of whether there is such a thing as syntactical deep structure. Chomsky argues that if there were no deep structure, linguistics as a study would be much less interesting because one could not then argue from syntax to the structure of the human mind, which for Chomsky is the chief interest of linguistics. I believe on the contrary that if the generative semanticists are right (and it is by no means clear that they are) that there is no boundary between syntax and semantics and hence no syntactical deep structures, linguistics if anything would be even more interesting because we could then begin the systematic investigation of the way form and function interact, how use and structure influence each other, instead of arbitrarily assuming that they do not, as Chomsky has so often tended to assume.

It is one of the ironies of the Chomsky revolution that the author of the revolution now occupies a minority position in the movement he created. Most of the active people in generative grammar regard Chomsky's position as having been rendered obsolete by the various arguments concerning the interaction between syntax and semantics. The old time structuralists whom Chomsky originally attacked look on with delight at this revolution within the revolution, rubbing their hands in glee at the sight of their adversaries fighting each other. "Those TG [transformational grammar] people are in deep trouble," one warhorse of the old school told me. But the traditionalists are mistaken to regard the fight as support for their position. The conflict is being carried on entirely within a conceptual system that Chomsky created. Whoever wins, the old structuralism will be the loser.

IV

The most spectacular conclusion about the nature of the human mind that Chomsky derives from his work in linguistics is that his results vindicate the claims of the seventeenth-century rationalist philosophers, Descartes, Leibniz, and others, that there are innate ideas in the mind. The rationalists claim that human beings have knowledge that is not derived from experience but is prior to all experience and determines the form of the knowledge that can be gained from experience. The empiricist tradition by contrast, from Locke down to contemporary behaviorist learning theorists, has tended to treat the mind as a *tabula rasa,* containing no knowledge prior to experience and placing no constraints on the forms of possible knowledge, except that they must be derived from experience by such mechanisms as the association of ideas or the habitual connection of stimulus and response. For empiricists all knowledge comes from experience, for rationalists some knowledge is implanted innately and prior to experience. In his bluntest moods, Chomsky claims to have refuted the empiricists and vindicated the rationalists.

His argument centers around the way in which children learn language. Suppose we assume that the account of the structure of natural languages we gave in Section II is correct. Then the grammar of a natural language will consist of a set of phrase structure rules that generate underlying phrase markers, a set of transformational rules that map deep structures onto surface structures, a set of phonological rules that assign phonetic interpretations to surface structures, and so on. Now, asks Chomsky, if all of this is part of the child's linguistic competence, how does he ever acquire it? That is, in learning how to talk, how does the child acquire that part of knowing how to talk which is described by the grammar and which constitutes his linguistic competence?

Notice, Chomsky says, several features of the learning situation: the information that the child is presented with—when other people address him or when he hears them talk to each other—is limited in amount, fragmentary, and imperfect. There seems to be no way the child could learn the language just by generalizing from his inadequate experiences, from the utterances he hears. Furthermore, the child acquires the language at a very early age, before his general intellectual faculties are developed.

Indeed, the ability to learn a language is only marginally dependent on intelligence and motivation. Stupid children and intelligent children, motivated and unmotivated children, all learn to speak their native tongue. If a child does not acquire his first language by puberty, it is difficult, and perhaps impossible, for him to learn one after that time. Formal teaching of the first language is unnecessary; the child may have to go to school to learn to read and write but he does not have to go to school to learn how to talk.

Now, in spite of all these facts the child who learns his first language, claims Chomsky, performs a remarkable intellectual feat in "internalizing" the grammar: he does something akin to constructing a theory of the language. The only explanation for all these facts, says Chomsky, is that the mind is not a *tabula rasa,* but rather, the child has the form of the language already built into his mind before he ever learns to talk. The child has a universal grammar, so to speak, programmed into his brain as part of his genetic inheritance. In the most ambitious versions of this theory, Chomsky speaks of the child as being born "with a perfect knowledge of universal grammar, that is, with a fixed schematism that he uses, . . . in acquiring language."[6] A child can learn any human language on the basis of very imperfect information. That being the case, he must have the forms that are common to all human languages as part of his innate mental equipment.

As further evidence in support of a specifically human "*facult de langage*" Chomsky points out that animal communication systems are radically unlike human languages. Animal systems have only a finite number of communicative devices, and they are usually controlled by certain stimuli. Human languages, by contrast, all have an infinite generative capacity and the utterances of sentences are not predictable on the basis of external stimuli. This "creative aspect of language use" is peculiarly human.

One traditional argument against the existence of an innate language learning faculty is that human languages are so diverse. The differences between Chinese, Nootka, Hungarian, and English, for example, are so great as to destroy the possibility of any universal grammar, and hence languages could only be learned by a general intelligence, not by any innate language learning device. Chomsky has attempted to turn this argument on its head: in spite of surface differences, all human languages have very similar underlying structures; they all have phrase structure rules and transformational rules. They all contain sentences, and these sentences are composed of subject noun phrases and predicate verb phrases, etc.

Chomsky is really making two claims here. First, a historical claim that his views on language were prefigured by the seventeenth-century rationalists, especially Descartes. Second, a theoretical claim that empiricist learning theory cannot account for the acquisition of language. Both claims are more tenuous than he suggests. Descartes did indeed claim that we have innate ideas, such as the idea of a triangle or the idea of perfection or the idea of God. But I know of no passage in Descartes to suggest that he thought the syntax of natural languages was innate. Quite the contrary, Descartes appears to have thought that language was arbitrary: he thought that we arbitrarily attach words to our ideas. Concepts for Descartes are innate, whereas language is arbitrary and acquired. Furthermore Descartes does not allow for the possibility of *unconscious* knowledge, a notion that is crucial to Chomsky's system. Chomsky cites correctly Descartes's claim that the creative use of language distinguishes man from the lower animals. But that by itself does not support the thesis that Descartes is a precursor of Chomsky's theory of innate ideas.

The positions are in fact crucially different. Descartes thought of man as essentially a language-using animal who arbitrarily assigns verbal labels to an innate system of concepts. Chomsky, as remarked earlier, thinks of man as essentially a syntactical animal producing and understanding sentences by virtue of possessing an innate system of grammar, triggered in various possible forms by the different human languages to which he has been exposed. A better historical analogy than with Descartes is with Leibniz, who claimed that innate ideas are in us in the way that the statue is already prefigured in a block of marble. In a passage of Leibniz Chomsky frequently quotes, Leibniz makes

> . . . the comparison of a block of marble which has veins, rather than a block of marble wholly even, or of blank tablets, i.e., of what is called among philosophers, a tabula rasa. For if the soul resembles these blank tablets, truth would be in us as the figure of Hercules is in the marble, when the marble is wholly indifferent to the reception of this figure or some other. But if there were veins in the block which would indicate the figure of Hercules rather than other figures, this block would be more determined thereto, and Hercules would be in it as in some sense innate, although it would be needful to labor to discover these veins, to clear them by polishing, and by cutting away what prevents them from appearing. Thus, it is that ideas and truths are for us innate, as inclinations, dispositions, habits, or natural potentialities, and not as actions, although these potentialities are always accompanied by some actions, often insensible, which correspond to them.[7]

But if the correct model for the notion of innate ideas is the block of marble that contains the figure of Hercules as "disposition," "inclination," or "natural potentiality," then at least some of the dispute between Chomsky and the empiricist learning theorists will dissolve like so much mist on a hot morning. Many of the fiercest partisans of empiricist and behaviorist learning theories are willing to concede that the child has innate learning capacities in the sense that he has innate dispositions, inclinations, and natural potentialities. Just as the block of marble has the innate capacity of being turned into a statue, so the child has the innate capacity of learning. W. V. Quine, for example, in his response to Chomsky's innateness hypothesis argues, "The behaviorist is knowingly and cheerfully up to his neck in innate mechanisms of learning readiness." Indeed, claims Quine, "Innate biases and dispositions are the cornerstone of behaviorism."[8]

If innateness is the cornerstone of behaviorism what then is left of the dispute? Even after all these ecumenical disclaimers by behaviorists to the effect that of course behaviorism and empiricism require innate mechanisms to make the stimulus-response patterns work, there still remains a hard core of genuine disagreement. Chomsky is arguing not simply that the child must have "learning readiness," "biases," and "dispositions," but that he must have a *specific* set of linguistic mechanisms at work. Claims by behaviorists that general learning strategies are based on mechanisms of feedback, information processing, analogy, and so on are not going to be enough. One has to postulate an innate faculty of language in order to account for the fact that the child comes up with the right grammar on the basis of his exposure to the language.

The heart of Chomsky's argument is that the syntactical core of any language is so complicated and so specific in its form, so unlike other kinds of knowledge, that no child could learn it unless he already had the form of the grammar programmed into his brain, unless, that is, he had "perfect knowledge of a universal grammar." Since there is at the present state of neuro-physiology no way to test such a hypothesis by inspection of the brain, the evidence for the conclusion rests entirely on the facts of the grammar. In order to meet the argument, the anti-Chomskyan would have to propose a simpler grammar that would account for the child's ability to learn a language and for linguistic competence in general. No defender of traditional learning theory has so far done this (though the generative grammarians do claim that their account of competence is much simpler than the diagram we drew in Section II above).

The behaviorist and empiricist learning theorist who concedes the complexity of grammar is faced with a dilemma: either he relies solely on stimulus-response mechanisms, in which case he cannot account for the acquisition of the grammar, or he concedes, à la Quine, that there are innate mechanisms which enable the child to learn the language. But as soon as the mechanisms are rich enough to account for the complexity and specificity

of the grammar, then the stimulus-response part of the theory, which was supposed to be its core, becomes uninteresting; for such interest as it still has now derives entirely from its ability to trigger the innate mechanisms that are now the crucial element of the learning theory. Either way, the behaviorist has no effective reply to Chomsky's arguments.

V

The weakest element of Chomsky's grammar is the semantic component, as he himself repeatedly admits.[9] But while he believes that the semantic component suffers from various minor technical limitations, I think that it is radically inadequate; that the theory of meaning it contains is too impoverished to enable the grammar to achieve its objective of explaining all the linguistic relationships between sound and meaning.

Most, though not all, of the diverse theories of meaning advanced in the past several centuries from Locke to Chomsky and Quine are guilty of exactly the same fallacy. The fallacy can be put in the form of a dilemma for the theory: either the analysis of meaning itself contains certain of the crucial elements of the notion to be analyzed, in which case the analysis fails because of circularity; or the analysis reduces the thing to be analyzed into simpler elements which lack its crucial features, in which case the analysis falls because of inadequacy.

Before we apply this dilemma to Chomsky let us see how it works for a simple theory of meaning such as is found in the classical empirical philosophers, Locke, Berkeley, and Hume. These great British empiricists all thought that words got their meaning by standing for ideas in the mind. A sentence like "The flower is red" gets its meaning from the fact that anyone who understands the sentence will conjoin in his mind an idea of a flower with an idea of redness. Historically there were various arguments about the details of the theory (e.g., were the ideas for which general words stood themselves general ideas or were they particular ideas that were made "general in their representation"?). But the broad outlines of the theory were accepted by all. To understand a sentence is to associate ideas in the mind with the descriptive terms in the sentence.

But immediately the theory is faced with a difficulty. What makes the ideas in the mind into a *judgment?* What makes the sequence of images into a representation, of the *speech act of stating* that the flower is red? According to the theory, first I have an idea of a flower, then I have an idea of redness. So far the sequence is just a sequence of unconnected images and does not amount to the judgment that the flower *is* red, which is what is expressed in the sentence. I can assume that the ideas come, to someone who understands the sentence in the form of a judgment, that they just air somehow connected as representing the speech act of stating that the flower is red in which case we have the first horn of our dilemma and the theory in circular, since it employs some of the crucial elements of the notion of meaning in the effort to explain meaning. Or on the other hand if I do not assume the ideas come in the form of a judgment then I have only a sequence of images in my mind and not the crucial feature of the original sentence, namely, the fact that the sentence *says* that the flower is red in which case we have the second horn of our dilemma and the analysis fails because it is inadequate to account for the meaning of the sentence.

The semantic theory of Chomsky's generative grammar commits exactly the same fallacy. To show this I will first give a sketch of what the theory is supposed to do. Just as the syntactical component of the grammar is supposed to describe the speaker's syntactical competence (his knowledge of the structure of sentences) and the phonological component is supposed to describe his phonological competence (his knowledge of how the sentences of his language sound), so the semantic component is supposed to describe the speaker's semantic competence (his knowledge of what the sentences mean and how they mean what they mean).

The semantic component of a grammar of a language embodies the semantic theory of that language. It consists of the set of rules that determine the meanings of the sentences of the language. It operates on the assumption, surely a correct one, that the meaning of any sentence is determined by the meaning of all the meaningful elements of the sentence and by their syntactical combination. Since these elements and their arrangement are represented in the deep structure of the sentence, the "input" to the semantic component of the grammar will consist of deep structures of sentences as generated by the syntactic component, in the way we described in Section II.

The "output" is a set of "readings" for each sentence, where the readings are supposed to be a "semantic representation" of the sentence; that is, they are supposed to be descriptions of the meanings of the sentence. If, for example, a sentence has three different meanings, the semantic component will duplicate the speaker's competence by producing three different readings. If the sentence is nonsense, the semantic component will produce no readings. If two sentences mean the same thing, it will produce the same reading for both sentences. If a sentence is "analytic," that is, if it is true by definition because the meaning of the predicate is contained in the meaning of the subject (for example, "All bachelors are unmarried" is analytic because the meaning of the subject "bachelor" contains the meaning of the predicate "unmarried"), the semantic component will produce a reading for the sentence in which the reading of the predicate is contained in the reading of the subject.

Chomsky's grammarian in constructing a semantic component tries to construct a set of rules that will provide a model of the speaker's semantic competence. The model must duplicate the speaker's understanding of ambiguity, synonymy, nonsense, analyticity, self-contradiction, and so on. Thus, for example, consider the ambiguous sentence "I went to the bank." As part of his competence the speaker of English knows that the sentence is ambiguous because the word "bank" has at least two different meanings. The sentence can mean either I went to the finance house or I went to the side of the river. The aim of the grammarian is to describe this kind of competence; he describe it by constructing a model, a set of rules, that will duplicate it. His semantic theory must produce two readings for this sentence.

If, on the other hand, the sentence is "I went to the bank and deposited some money in my account" the semantic component will produce only one reading because the portion of the sentence about depositing money determines that the other meaning of bank—namely, side of the river—is excluded as a possible meaning in this sentence. The semantic component then will have to contain a set of rules describing which kinds of combinations of words make which kind of sense, and this is supposed to account for the speaker's knowledge of which kinds of combinations of words in his language make which kind of sense.

All of this can be, and indeed has been, worked up into a very elaborate formal theory by Chomsky and his followers; but when we have constructed a description of what the semantic component is supposed to look like, a nagging question remains: what exactly, are these "readings"? What is the string of symbols that comes out of the semantic component supposed to *represent* or *express* in such a way as to constitute a description of the meaning of a sentence?

The same dilemma with which we confronted Locke applies here: either the readings are just paraphrases, in which case the analysis is circular, or the readings consist only of lists of elements, in which case the analysis fails because of inadequacy; it cannot account for the fact that the sentence expresses a *statement*. Consider each horn of the dilemma. In the example above when giving two different readings for "I went to the bank" I gave two English paraphrases, but that possibility is not open to a semantic theory which seeks to explain competence in English, since the ability to understand paraphrases presupposes the very competence the semantic theory is seeking to explain. I cannot explain general competence in English by translating English sentences into other English sentences. In the literature of the Chomskyan an semantic theorists, the examples given of "readings" are usually rather bad paraphrases of English sentences together with some jargon about "semantic markers" and "distinguishers" and so on.[10] We are assured that the paraphrases are only for illustrative purposes, that they are not the real readings.

But what can the real readings be? The purely formal constraints placed on the semantic theory are not much help in telling us what the readings are. They tell us only that a sentence that is ambiguous in three ways must have three readings, a nonsense sentence no readings, two synonymous sentences must have the same readings, and so on. But so far as these requirements go, the readings need not be composed of words but could be composed of any formally specifiable set of objects. They could be numerals, piles of stones, old cars, strings of symbols, anything whatever. Suppose we decide to interpret the readings as piles of stones. Then for a three-ways ambiguous sentence the theory will give us three piles of stones, for a nonsense sentence, no piles of stones, for an analytic sentence the arrangement of stones in the predicate pile will be duplicated in the subject pile, and so on. There is nothing in the formal properties of the semantic component to prevent us from interpreting it in this way. But clearly this will not do because now instead of explaining the relationships between sound and meaning, the theory has produced an unexplained relationship between sounds and stones.

When confronted with this objection, the semantic theorists always make the same reply. Though we cannot produce adequate readings at present, ultimately the readings will be expressed in a yet to be discovered universal semantic alphabet. The elements in the alphabet will stand for the meaning units in all languages in much the way that the universal phonetic alphabet now represents the sound units in all languages. But would a universal semantic alphabet escape the dilemma? I think not.

Either the alphabet is a kind of a new artificial language, a new Esperanto, and the readings are once again paraphrases, only this time in the Esperanto and not in the original language; or we have the second horn of the dilemma and the readings in the semantic alphabet are just a list of features of language, and the analysis is inadequate because it substitutes a list of elements for a speech act.

The semantic theory of Chomsky's grammar does indeed give us a useful and interesting adjunct to the theory of semantic competence, since it give us a model that duplicates the speaker's competence in recognizing ambiguity, synonymy, nonsense, etc. But as soon as we ask *what* exactly the speaker is recognizing when he recognizes one, of these semantic properties, or as soon as we try to take the seman-theory as a *general* account of semantic competence, it cannot cope with the dilemma. Either it gives us a sterile formalism, an uninterpreted list of elements, or it gives us paraphrases, which explain nothing.

Various philosophers working on as account of meaning in the past generation[11] have provided as with a way out of this dilemma. But to accept the solution would involve enriching the semantic theory in ways not so far contemplated by Chomsky or the other Cambridge grammarians. Chomsky characterizes the speaker's linguistic competence as his ability to "produce and understand" sentences. But this is at best very misleading: a person's knowledge of the meaning of sentences consists in large part in his knowledge of how to use sentences to make statements, ask questions, give orders, make requests, make promises, warnings, etc., and to understand other people when they

use sentences for such purposes. Semantic competence is in large part the ability to perform and understand what philosophers and linguists call *speech acts.*

Now if we approach the study of semantic competence from the point of view of the ability to use sentences to perform speech acts, we discover that speech acts have two properties, the combination of which will get us out of the dilemma: they are governed by rules and they are intentional. The speaker who utters a sentence and means it literally utters it in accordance with certain semantic rules and with the intention of invoking those rules to render his utterance the performance of a certain speech act.

This is not the place to recapitulate the whole theory of meaning and speech acts,[12] but the basic idea is this. Saying something and meaning it is essentially a matter of saying it with the intention to produce certain effects on the hearer. And these effects are determined by the rules that attach to the sentence that is uttered. Thus, for example, the speaker who knows the meaning of the sentence "The flower is red" knows that its utterance constitutes the making of a statement. But making a statement to the effect that the flower is red consists in performing an action with the intention of *producing in the hearer the belief* that the speaker is committed, to the existence of a certain state of affairs, as determined by the semantic rules attaching to the sentence.

Semantic competence is largely a matter of knowing the relationships between semantic intentions, rules, and conditions specified by the rules: Such an analysis of competence may in the end prove incorrect, but it is not open to the obvious dilemmas I have posed to classical empiricist and Chomskyan semantic theorists. It is not reduced to providing us with paraphrase or a list of elements. The glue that holds the elements together into a speech act is the semantic intentions of the speaker.

The defect of the Chomskyan theory arises from the same weakness we noted earlier, the failure to see the essential connection between language and communication, between meaning and speech acts. The picture that underlies the semantic theory and indeed Chomsky's whole theory of language is that sentences are abstract objects that are produced and understood independently of their role in communication. Indeed, Chomsky sometimes writes as if sentences were only incidentally used to talk with.[13] I am claiming that any attempt to account for the meaning of sentences within such assumptions is either circular or inadequate.

The dilemma is not just an argumentative trick, it reveals a more profound inadequacy. Any attempt to account for the meaning of sentences must take into account their role in communication, in the performance of speech acts, because an essential part of the meaning of any sentence is its potential for being used to perform a speech act. There are two radically different conceptions of language in conflict here: one, Chomsky's, sees language as a self-contained formal system used more of less incidentally for communication. The other sees language as essentially a system for communication.

The limitations of Chomsky's assumptions become clear only when we attempt to account for the meaning of sentences within his system, because there is no way to account for the meaning of a sentence without considering its role in communication, since the two are essentially connected. So long as we confine our research to syntax, where in fact most of Chomsky's work has been done, it is possible to conceal the limitations of the approach, because syntax can be studied as a formal system independently of its use, just as we could study the currency and credit system of an economy as an abstract formal system independently of the fact that people use money to buy things with or we could study the rules of baseball as a formal system independently of the fact that baseball is a game people play. But as soon as we attempt to account for meaning, for semantic competence, such a purely formalistic approach breaks down, because it cannot account for the fact that semantic competence is mostly a matter of knowing how to talk, i.e., how to perform speech acts.

The Chomsky revolution is largely a revolution in the study of syntax. The obvious next step in the development of the study of language is to graft the study of syntax onto the study of speech acts. And this is indeed happening, though Chomsky continues to fight a rearguard action against it, or at least against the version of it that the generative semanticists who are building on his own work now present.

There are, I believe, several reasons why Chomsky is reluctant to incorporate a theory of speech acts into his grammar: first, he has a mistaken conception of the distinction between performance and competence. He seems to think that a theory of speech acts must be a theory of performance rather than of competence, because he fails to see that competence is ultimately the competence to perform, and that for this reason a study of the linguistic aspects of the ability to perform speech acts is a study of the linguistic competence. Secondly, Chomsky seems to have a residual suspicion that any theory that treats the speech act, a piece of speech behavior, as the basic unit of meaning must involve some kind of a retreat to behaviorism. Nothing could be further from the truth. It is one of the ironies of the history of behaviorism that behaviorists should have failed to see that the notion of a human action must be a "mentalistic" and "introspective" notion since it essentially involves the notion of human *intentions*.

The study of speech acts is indeed the study of a certain kind of human behavior, but for that reason it is in conflict with any form of behaviorism, which is conceptually incapable of studying human behavior. But the third, and most important reason, I believe, is Chomsky's only partly articulated belief that language does not have any essential connection with communication, but is an abstract formal system produced by the innate properties of the human mind.

Chomsky's work is one of the most remarkable intellectual achievements of the present era, comparable in scope and coherence to the work of Keynes or Freud. It has done more than simply produce a revolution in linguistics; it has created a new discipline of generative grammar and is having a revolutionary effect on two other subjects, philosophy and psychology. Not the least of its merits is that it provides an extremely powerful tool even for those who disagree with many features of Chomsky's approach to language. In the long run, I believe his greatest contribution will be that he has taken a major step toward restoring the traditional conception of the dignity and uniqueness of man.

Notes

1. Quoted in R.H. Robins, *A Short History of Linguistics* (Indiana University Press, 1967), p. 239.

2. Howard Maclay, "Overview," in D. Steinberg and L. Jacobovitz, eds., *Semantics* (Cambridge University Press, 1971), p. 163.

3. Noam Chomsky, *Syntactic Structures* (Mouton & Co., 1957), p. 100.

4. As distinct from "John called Mary beautiful and then she INSULTED him."

5. Cf., e.g., Noam Chomsky, "Deep Structure, Surface Structure, and Semantic Interpretation," in D. Steinberg and L. Jacobovitz, eds., *Semantics* (Cambridge University Press, 1971).

6. Noam Chomsky. "Linguistics and Philosophy," in S. Hook, ed., *Language and Philosophy* (NYU Press, 1969), p. 88.

7. G. Leibniz, *New Essays Concerning Human Understanding* (Open Court, 1949), pp. 45-46.

8. W.V.O. Quine, "Linguistics and Philosophy," in S. Hook, ed., *Language and Philosophy* (NYU Press, 1969), pp. 95-96.

9. I am a little reluctant to attribute the semantic component to Chomsky, since most of its features were worked out not by him but by his colleagues at MIT; nonetheless since he incorporates it entirely as part of his grammar I shall assess it as such.

10. For example, one of the readings given for the sentence "The man hits the colorful ball" contains the elements: [Some contextually definite] (Physical object) (Human) (Adult) (Male) (Action) (Instancy) (Intensity) [Collides with an impact] [Some contextually definite] (Physical object) (Color) [[Abounding in contrast or variety of bright colors] [Having a globular shape]] J. Katz and J. Fodor, "The Structure of a Semantic Theory," in *The Structure of Language,* J. Katz and J. Fodor, eds., (Prentice-Hall, 1964), p. 513.

11. In, e.g., L. Wittgenstein, *Philosophical Investigations* (Macmillan, 1953); J.L. Austin, *How to Do Things with Words* (Harvard, 1962); P. Grice "Meaning," in *Philosophical Review* 1957; J. R. Searle, *Speech Acts, An Essay in the Philosophy of Language* (Cambridge University Press, 1969) and P.F. Strawson, *Logico-Linguistic Papers* (Methuen, 1971).

12. For an attempt to work out some of the details, see J. R. Searle, *Speech Acts, An Essay in the Philosophy of Language* (Cambridge University Press, 1969), Chapters 1-3.

13. E.g., meaning, he writes, "need not involve communication or even the attempt to communicate," *Problems of Knowledge and Freedom* (Pantheon Books, 1971), p. 19.

Bernard Williams (review date 11 November 1976)

SOURCE: "Where Chomsky Stands," in *New York Review of Books,* November 11, 1976, pp. 43-5.

[*In the following review of Chomsky's* Reflections on Language *and Gilbert Harman's* On Noam Chomsky, *William provides discussion of Chomsky's linguistic studies, critical reaction to his theses, and some political implications of his ideas.*]

Since the publication of *Syntactic Structures* nineteen years ago the general shape of Chomsky's position in linguistic theory has become familiar. The subject, as he conceives it, is a branch of cognitive psychology; its basic problem is posed by the human capacity to acquire a natural language, something which Chomsky has insisted we should see as remarkable, with regard both to what the child experiences and to what he acquires. What he acquires is an indefinitely extensive creative capacity to produce and to understand an open-ended set of sentences that he has never heard before. What he is offered by his elders (or rather from them, since Chomsky thinks little importance can be attached to directed language teaching) is evidence, as he has put it, "not only meager in scope, but degenerate in quality." The actual performances the child is exposed to are fragmented and distorted relative to his recognition, apparent in the competence he acquires, of what would be an acceptable sentence of his language.

To explain the gross disproportion between what is acquired (in the form of competence) and what is experienced (in the form of speech) we need to posit a strongly constrained, internal, innate mechanism which, when triggered by the experience of speech, builds a cognitive structure, a grammar of the language, within limits set by very specialized schemata. Any human child, moreover, can learn naturally any human language, so the schemata must be universal, and when Chomsky refers to the properties of the innate mechanism, he often indicates that each of us possesses, indeed knows, the principles of a universal grammar. His model, though cognitive, is also biological, and in the present book, which consists of three lectures given in 1975, together with a long paper which is a revision of one submitted for a *Festschrift,* he particularly favors an embryological analogy, in which development of language is compared to the genetically controlled development of an animal.

As Chomsky has tirelessly pointed out to his critics, the mere idea of an innate component in learning a language is undisputed and uninteresting: the blankest theory of behaviorism requires some innate mechanism, however minimal. The important question concerns how complex and how specific to language acquisition the mechanism is supposed to be. In particular, Chomsky has differed from the empiricist tradition in regarding the mechanism as not simply one that applies a general learning strategy to language. Discussion over the past years, however, has made it clear that this particular difference between Chomsky and the empiricists is ambiguous, and some recognition of the ambiguity can be traced in the present book.

A "general learning capacity" might be defined in terms of some very simple learning theory, such as the traditional empiricist theories of "association" or of "inductive" generalization. In this sense, Chomsky convincingly insists that no one has offered a plausible or even coherent way of representing the learning of language by such empiricist learning theories. But it might also be true that very little that is learned can be represented in these simple empiricist terms; maybe most learning requires innate mechanisms more complex, and with more defined limits, than empiricism traditionally has allowed. If this is so, then the important question for language concerns how specific the capacity for language acquisition is, not the extent to which it is, peculiarly, innate.

The general issue is to some degree, but only to some, independent of what exactly the principles of the grammar of a human language have to be. Chomsky has retained, of course, his original picture of grammatical rules as being "generative." They include transformational rules which turn abstract "deep structures" into "surface structures." These surface structures take on a particular phonological form and emerge as the sentences one actually hears.

But many other more particular aspects of the theory have changed over the years. Above all on the matter of the relations between syntax (how and why a sentence is well formed or, in most everyday senses, "grammatical") and semantics (what a sentence means, what it refers to, what has to obtain for it to be true), Chomsky has abandoned the "standard" theory of *Aspects of the Theory of Syntax* (1965), by which semantic interpretation was applied to deep structure. He now applies semantic interpretation to surface structure, a notable modification of his earlier views. On a verbal matter, Chomsky in these pages proposes giving up the well-known phrase "deep structure" for those initial abstract base sentences to which the transformations are applied. His grounds for doing so are revealing of what he cares most about. He argues that not only these base sentences, but processes applied at the level of surface structure as well, are "deep" in the only interesting sense—namely, expressive of important and hidden human powers.

On the questions of the relations of syntax and semantics, many other positions are possible and have been vigorously discussed. Some expressions of these disagreements about the place of semantics in transformational grammar are to be found in some of the papers collected in the book edited by Gilbert Harman; other papers take the discussion further, into questions about how semantics in general is to be understood and pursued by using a theory of truth, for instance, as proposed by Donald Davidson, or by certain abstract structures of "possible words," advocated here by David Lewis. It is exceptionally difficult for someone like myself, who is not engaged full-time in the technical literature of these subjects (difficult, also, I suspect, for those who are), to have any full sense of how these various approaches relate to one another and to generative grammar, or to understand how far these and other semantic theories exclude one another, or are rather dealing in complementary questions.

Harman's collection, though it contains much good material, is not going to help anyone with this problem. His introduction is useful as far as it goes, but it does not go nearly far enough; and while the book is called *On Noam Chomsky,* in the case of one or two papers it would take someone with a sophisticated understanding of the subject to grasp why the matters discussed bear on issues raised by Chomsky at all.

Even when proposals about the nature of semantics are explicitly related to Chomsky, the size, weight, and exact location of disagreement can remain obscure. Harman valuably reprints John Searle's admirable piece "Chomsky's Revolution in Linguistics," which appeared in this journal in 1972. In it Searle criticizes Chomsky for not associating semantic study with the notion of communicative intention; he urges his own and Grice's theories of speech-acts, which link the meaning of the sentence to the intentions of the speaker, to fill what he sees as a void in the Chomskyan system—the *point* of language. Chomsky, in the present book, replies to Searle, but chiefly to deny, once more, the necessity of communicative intent, and to insist that uses of language can be thoroughly and seriously meant though not intended to influence any hearer.

> As a graduate student, I spent two years writing a lengthy manuscript, assuming throughout that it would never be published or read by anyone. I meant everything I wrote, intending nothing as to what anyone would believe about my beliefs, in fact taking it for granted that there would be no audience.

But how could the existence of such cases possibly be the main issue? One would like to know whether, if what Searle says about the connections of meaning and intention were true, much or any of Chomsky's views would be upset. It might be true that, despite exceptions, language is primarily or centrally connected with intentions to influence hearers' attitudes; and yet some Chomskyan account of the capacities to produce and understand those utterances could also be true.

All through this field, as in other places where exciting work is going on, views which may well be compatible nevertheless struggle with one another. This is because they struggle for attention; the research programs may be compatible in content, but the thought that goes with each of them, "this is the way to go on," excludes the others. This thought may be essential to the researcher—the synoptic peacemaker who pleads for compatibility is up in the observer's balloon, not engaged at the scientific front. In Chomsky's own case, however, a further dimension is involved, and a more important one. He associates his own approach with an affirmation of the depth of the human mind and the value of the individual, and he is suspicious on more than theoretical grounds of many styles of opposing theory.

Chomsky's arguments with his opponents are painstakingly reasoned and academic in tone (though he is unduly given to that polemicists' put-down, "unfortunately," as in, "Unfortunately, X is rather careless in his references," page 218). It is only after technical argument—but still too soon, granted some complexities we shall come to—that he falls back on ideological explanation, associating empiricist opposition to his views with social reaction. But through the laborious and sometimes peripheral self-defense, one can see that he is deeply distrustful and disapproving of some other ways of doing linguistics and the other human sciences, and that his linguistic theories, in their central contentions, have an ideological significance which relates them in some unclear but powerful way to his political and social outlook. This comes to the surface in a few pages of Chomsky's present book, and it gets very brief consideration in the last item in Harman's collection, Dell Hymes's informative review of John Lyons's book on Chomsky in the Modern Masters series (Viking, 1970). It is worth exploring further.

What exactly is involved in the innate component, what principles the language-acquisition device is armed with, are of course technical matters. But whatever they may exactly turn out to be, the more general question comes up of how to describe their presence. Chomsky has favored the terminology of unconscious, innate, *knowledge,* and this has helped to connect his theories with those Rationalist thinkers of the seventeenth century and later whom he has claimed, always with some caution, as his intellectual ancestors. Whether "knowledge" is the right concept, however, is a hard question. Certainly many objections which have been put to Chomsky, such as that, on his principles, a falling stone must know how to fall, entirely miss the point, and ignore the cognitive character of the states governed by Chomsky's innate schemata, as Thomas Nagel well argues in Harman's book. Yet, as Nagel also points out, there remains a long step to accepting the concept of knowledge as applying to the presence of the schemata themselves, and there are theoretical embarrassments in the use of that concept.

There is, for example, the question (raised elsewhere by Harman) of the vehicle by which this knowledge is represented in the mind, a vehicle looking suspiciously like another already mastered language. There is also the related problem that knowledge which is more than merely skill should imply the possession of concepts, and we have no reason to ascribe to the language-learner, at any level, the theoretical concepts of universal grammar. Chomsky's own embryological analogy hardly points unwaveringly in the direction of a model that uses the notion of knowledge. In the present book he suggests that whether we call these potentialities "knowledge" is a verbal question, and he is prepared to let the word go; but how slight a concession this is becomes clear when he agrees to put, in place of "know," the word "cognize."

Chomsky's insistence on a cognitive vocabulary to describe the presence of the innate schemata seems to be sustained by one of his strongest convictions, the power of linguistic theory to reveal the depth of the human mind. It implies an uncovering of lower, but continuously related, levels of human thought, and historically it helps to tie his theory to earlier Rationalist speculations. These however, usually look a less naturalistic view of the mind than Chomsky does—the idea of a cognitive study as a branch of human biology is for Descartes's own system unintelligible. But their views can, like his, be handily opposed to an empiricist outlook, which takes a shallower and more mechanical view of the psychological. That empiricist outlook can, moreover, Chomsky believes, be easily associated with a denial that there is a human nature, and with a manipulative and authoritarian conception of what can be done to human beings.

This opposition between rationalist and empiricist approaches (though, as Hymes says, Chomsky's own theoretical work has transcended it) has great ideological significance for Chomsky. The empiricist conception of human beings as unpredisposed objects for conditioning he associates with potentialities for technological oppression. Chomsky admits that empiricist systems of ideas do, as a matter of historical fact, strongly resist being categorized in the way he requires, since the idea that there is no fixed human nature, but that man is a social product, has very often been associated (for instance, by many Marxists) with "progressive and even revolutionary social thinking," while the opposite view has supported conservative and pessimistic outlooks.

"But a deeper look," he goes on (page 132), "will show that the concept of the 'empty organism,' plastic and unstructured, apart from being false, also serves naturally as the support for the most reactionary social doctrines." "Serves naturally" here is pure ideologists sticky tape, no better than "goes with." Similarly unreliable connections are made when Chomsky goes into historical interpretation:

> Empiricism rose to ascendancy in association with a doctrine of "possessive [sic] individualism" that was integral to early capitalism, in an age of empire, with the concomitant growth (one might almost say "creation") of racist ideology. [Page 130]

In so far as this offers anything except evasive insinuation, it invites a quick answer in any sense in which classical empiricism was "in association with" early capitalism, slavery, etc., so was its near contemporary, classical rationalism. No historical speculations of this sort can effect anything, and Chomsky's other admissions show that he is, or at least has good reason to be, uneasy with them. He is likely to find better ground in certain features of the present. Now, when psychological technology is a conscious weapon of political power, and the notion of human needs as opposed to contingent preferences has been moved by many forces into the center of serious social thought, there really is a case for saying that the spirit of empiricist and, above all, behaviorist outlooks must, apart from their intellectual inadequacies, turn us in the wrong direction. Here Chomsky's negative view, at least, seems to have real power.

But even so, it is more doubtful whether Chomsky's own innatist doctrines can turn us in the right direction: they might even help to do the opposite. For here the question of the specificity of the language capacity, mentioned earlier, takes on a considerable and unexpected ideological significance. Chomsky's claims have always been for the special character of man's capacity for linguistic learning, and part of his evidence for this has precisely been that, the grossly defective apart, men are equal in this capacity, while differing in general intelligence and in their capacities to learn other things, such as physics. But now why should these distributions of innate capacities have any tendency at all to encourage belief in the foundations of libertarian socialism? Chomsky speaks of his hopes for progress toward human self-determination and genuine freedom; but the basic linguistic competence, as he describes it, has no connection with notions of progress at all—it is perfect as it is. What does leave room for progress, and indeed progress toward self-determination and freedom, is man's lexical sophistication and conceptual grasp—but that, precisely, is a linguistic dimension in which men do differ, and in which the results of learning are not the same for all, and the innatist element correspondingly weaker.

Again, why should Chomsky's theory have any power against racism, association with which was one of his more sinister charges against empiricism? In so far as racism has any coherent relation at all to opinions about different intellectual capacities, why should the fact of an equal innate capacity for language acquisition be thought to help against it? No theorist of apartheid is likely to be daunted by being reminded that the African child can effortlessly acquire Xhosa—or, come to that, Afrikaans.

If, on the other hand, the innatist claims are substantially extended from the field of language acquisition into other forms of learning (for instance, as Chomsky seems to speculate at one point, into moral capacities), the charge of their irrelevance to racist issues may decline, but the possibility of an unfortunate and destructive type of belief in their "relevance" might increase. It seems odd that anyone should need reminding at the moment that it is the environmentalist view on matters of "intelligence" which has been identified as the liberal one. The entire question of the ideological significance of such studies is now a notorious moral and intellectual mess, but to accept their ideological significance while cleaving to innatist styles of explanation may not necessarily be the most progressive way out of it.

An important point here is that in the field of language acquisition, Chomsky has good reason to equate what is genetically determined with what is common to the species. That equation may very well hold for all innate human cognitive capacities, but there is no a priori guarantee from the nature of genetics or anything else that it must be so.

The ideological implications of Chomsky's theories are by no means straightforward or unambiguous, and Chomsky himself moves with dangerous speed and simplicity between his theoretical preoccupations and the political ideals for which he has so conspicuously stood up. In fact, the ideological effect of Chomsky's work in language seems to me not so much to support or express distinctively socialist aspirations for society, or opposition to oppression, but rather, a stage further back, to assist a humane revaluation of tough-minded inquiry in the psychological sciences. His work, apart from its spectacular and ongoing effect in linguistics, constitutes the most powerful and encouraging reassurance that a psychological science which is recognizably continuous with the natural sciences does not have to treat human beings as very boring machines.

The recognition that human beings might be scientifically understood but are yet not just machines could well coexist with more than one kind of social or political view, not all equally liberal. But as well as being a vital truth in itself, it is a necessary step to any adequate views on these issues at all, including any adequate liberal views. It is here, in the humane understanding of science itself, rather than in more direct ideological interpretation, that the most general significance of Chomsky's deeply impressive work is likely to be found.

Ian Hacking (review date 23 October 1980)

SOURCE: "Chomsky and His Critics," in *New York Review of Books,* October 23, 1980, pp. 47-50.

[*In the following review of* Rules and Representations *and* Language and Learning, *Hacking provides analysis of Chomsky's linguistic innovations, critical challenges to his*

conclusions, and discussion of Chomsky's debate with Swiss scholar Jean Piaget.]

From time to time, ever since Plato, grammar has been more than the bane of schoolchildren or a topic for scholars. It owes its present prominence outside linguistics to some theses stated twenty-five years ago by Noam Chomsky. There is, he said, a universal grammar common to all human languages. Children are born with it: their inheritance explains the ease with which they pick up the language they hear around them. Universal grammar is like an organ of the body whose structure is genetically determined. It is a characteristic of the human mind and an essential part of the discontinuity between people and beasts.

That is quite an array of paradoxes. How could so arid a subject as grammar be part of the definition of our humanity? When hardly anyone can talk grammatically in more than two languages and when many are deficient in one, what is so universal? There is also a prejudice that Chomsky makes us a little ashamed to confess: grammar is just not the kind of thing one could inherit.

Paradoxes alone did not fuel Chomsky's success. From the start he had a neat definition of grammar as a set of rules that can be mechanically applied to test whether a string of words forms a grammatical sentence. Then he obtained a negative result. Taking a natural and widespread approach to grammar, he cast that approach into a precise form and proved that it is necessarily incapable of providing an adequate grammar for English. This result was important not only for what it said but also because it suggested a new kind of thing to do—that sort of result had not been thought of before.

Then Chomsky did much positive work. He polished up a current idea of grammatical transformation and made it plausible as the main tool for doing grammar. He used an ear-catching phrase: "deep structure." By this he meant that the sentences we use in thinking and speaking are the result of transformations, on structures that underlie the surface arrangement of nouns, verbs, prepositions, and so forth. The speaker is not consciously aware of these structures or the operations upon them; they must be inferred from linguistic abilities. Deep structure added to the appeal of universal grammar, for the "universal" in grammar might be down there at the not-so-conscious level of deep structure, which is why we never noticed it before.

These proposals have since evolved, and *Rules and Representations* is a useful book with which to catch up on the state of the art. The book consists of four lectures (the Woodbridge Lectures at Columbia also given as the Kant Lectures at Stanford) and two related pieces. There is nothing technical in the book but to read it you do need a relish for argument. The lectures might be called "Chomsky Against the Philosophers." Philosophers have much admired him but have also criticized some features of his work. Here he examines their arguments. It is like watching the grand master play, blindfolded, thirty-six simultaneous chess matches against the local worthies. He almost always wins.

There is perhaps some general lesson about reason to be gleaned from this book. Chomsky must be one of the most reasoning of living men. I've heard him called Talmudic but there is nothing ethnic about this: to me he sounds like a Presbyterian preaching double predestinarianism. He runs through arguments again and again, so that some are repeated in the two papers tacked on to the lectures, and were also found in *Reflections on Language* (1975). Chomsky is sometimes a teacher saying, "You haven't quite seen the point, come, let's go over it again, here is the first premise. . . ."

This passion for reason allows one to forgive what would, in another writer, be repetition. But I liked a remark in the second book under review, which derives from a symposium in France featuring a debate between Chomsky and Jean Piaget, the great Swiss pioneer of the genesis of concepts in the child.[1] The philosopher Hilary Putnam starts his contribution to the symposium by noting "the sense of great intellectual power" one gets on reading Chomsky, and then announces with exasperation, "Yet I want to claim that individual arguments are *not good*." Putnam is Chomsky's equal as reasoner, but many attentive readers will be unsure who wins this skirmish. Once argumentation has been pushed to this limit, reason alone will not settle much. What matters is the outcome of the research. All we can hope from arguments is the conviction that the research is well motivated—and that, in this case, we get in abundance.

Chomsky used to say that children have innate knowledge of universal grammar. Philosophers have queried whether this could properly be called "knowledge." Irritated, Chomsky says call it something else; say children "cognize" grammar. What is important for him is that this cognition is a physiological state which will manifest itself in behavior but is not to be defined in terms of behavior. We should not think of cognitive abilities arising from one undifferentiated organ (the brain?) but we should expect a lot of units, or modules, that interact to perform various jobs. Even to produce a single grammatical sentence the brain will employ different modules which may have matured at different stages of development. An infant that has not yet begun to speak still "cognizes" grammar in the sense that it has the appropriate modules which can be triggered by various stimuli as it grows up. If it becomes a feral child growing up alone, it will never mature into speech, but this is just because the appropriate modules have not been triggered.

Such speculations leave untouched many philosophers' questions about knowledge, but in my opinion they are well left untouched, at least here. There are metaphysical questions about knowledge and there are physiological ones. Even the "rules and representations" of Chomsky's

title turn into physiology. What he means by a rule is plain enough from his examples. There should be a rule for forming questions out of declarative sentences, say, take the verb that comes after the first noun phrase and move it up front. ("The man who wore black was ill" becomes "Was the man who wore black ill?") Such a rule works on an analysis of the sentence—it does not say, move the first verb ("wore") but, move the first verb after the noun phrase ("was.")

Deep structure is no longer prominent in Chomsky's work. The rules he examines now work close to the surface of the words we actually utter. I say "close to the surface" because the rules do not act only on the strings of words that we utter or hear, but also on something like echoes of other sentences. The rules involve unuttered "traces" of transformations, and so this development is called *trace theory*. For example, colloquial English can contract "want to" to "wanna"—"Who do you wanna meet?" But though this is a contraction of "Who do you want to meet?" we do not contract "Who do you want to meet Bill?" ("Who do you wanna meet Bill?" is odd). Chomsky explains the difference by saying that questions bear a trace of the declarative sentence. "You want to meet x" is a declarative form whose question is "Who do you want to meet t?" Here the trace t marks the place that the "who" came from. The declarative form "You want y to meet Bill" has the question "Who do you want t to meet Bill?" Here the unuttered trace t comes between "want" and "to," and stops the contraction "wanna." This representation of traces, of echoes just below the level of the uttered surface of words, is what Chomsky calls "S-level."

A sentence may be represented by the words we utter; it may be represented at S-level; it may be represented at deeper levels of analysis. Rules operate on representations, at some level or other. In the above example, the rule operates at the S-level. Such representations are all themselves bits of language. Most grammarians want nothing more than an analysis stated in language. But Chomsky calls himself a psychological realist. For every item of psychology, such as a representation of a sentence, there is to be a corresponding bit of physiology. There must be a representation in the brain, to which a rule, in the brain, applies. Maybe a mechanical analogy will help to explain this.

Take a really old-fashioned calculator, a nineteenth-century difference machine made of brass and steel. Given a sequence of numbers it could calculate, say, the second differences, that is, the differences between the differences between the members of the sequence—not just the difference, for example, between numbers a and b but between *their* difference and the difference between c and d. (This was part of the trick of making tables of logarithms.) Set some numbers on the machine, turn the crank, and it prints out a sequence of second differences. We have a rule expressed in natural languages such as English ("print the sequence of second differences") and output in English, the printout of numbers. But we also have a nonlinguistic version of the rule and the sequence, in the settings on brass and steel. The rule is made incarnate in brass and steel, and so is the sequence of numbers. As you crank it, the machine first arrives at and then operates on a "representation" of first differences in order to calculate the second differences; but there is nothing linguistic about this, it is just an arrangement of brass and steel.

In the same way, Chomsky thinks of representations made incarnate in flesh and blood, and the rules, themselves incarnate, act on these. Doubtless, he says, different modules are employed in connection with different levels of representation. The machine is a poor analogy with Chomsky's thought because it ignores the creative aspect of language use. The difference machine is determined from its initial setting to its final printout while the mind has a lot of freedom. I use the machine to emphasize that representations of sentences need not be anything linguistic, although we can put each representation into a linguistic form: we can produce a blueprint of the first-difference stage of the machine's operations, something linguistic corresponding to the nonlinguistic arrangement of brass and steel.

The idea of flesh-and-blood representations escapes an objection that derives from Wittgenstein and other philosophers. At the very beginning of the lectures Chomsky refers to "the myth of the museum"—the idea that our minds are like museums containing mental objects that we can inspect and that are called meanings. In explaining meanings, so goes the Wittgensteinian argument, it is no use postulating mental objects, like museum specimens, as what we intend. That would invite a regress, for how do we pick out the right mental object? Do we need a mental rule to do so? If we use a mental rule to apply a verbal rule, how do we apply the mental rule? As Chomsky says, if this objection were sound, it would seem to apply quite generally. Hence it would be a threat to the postulation of any mental entities to explain intentional behavior, including speech. Now the Wittgensteinian argument regards the mental entities as themselves language-like—that is how the "regress" is effected. Chomsky's internal rules and representations, as I understand them, are not language-like at all, and so the regress is blocked. The flesh-and-blood rules can be described in language (e.g., by a grammarian) just as the brass-and-steel settings on the difference machine can be shown on a blueprint. But the blueprint is not what causes the machine to work, and the grammarian's description of the rules and representations is not what we use, either consciously or unconsciously, in producing sentences. The grammarian's description is part of an account of a flesh-and-blood module in the brain that we do use.

The Chomsky program is easily misunderstood on this point because at a quite different level we also use rules of grammar to regiment our children and to make sense out of long-winded authors who need to be parsed in order to be understood. It cannot be too much emphasized that

Chomsky's rules and representations are not tools for pedants but descriptions of the brain. Would Wittgenstein be happy with this gloss? No, for he says, sometimes, that we should not aim at explanation at all, and in particular, our communication could have the character it does regardless of how the brain worked. And perhaps there is still a regress lurking around the corner—how do I know what I want the grammatical module to allow me to say, right now, with *this* sentence? Well, that will be a matter of interacting with other modules. There seems to be some nagging ill-formulated question that would arise even if we knew about all the modules—a question about which we may learn more from reading Wittgenstein than Chomsky.

Chomsky's psychological realism in any case has had plenty of critics, for he cannot point to any modules in the brain. He defends it as good methodology. It is the standard method of science, the "Galilean style," which has been the only show in town for the last three and a half centuries. Frame powerful hypotheses rich in explanatory power and try to work them out in detail. All hypotheses are tentative. Some will be refuted and all will be revised. A hypothesis made in this spirit takes for granted that what it is talking about is real. Certainly, grants Chomsky, there are philosophical questions about the "reality" of theoretical entities, but these are questions about physics just as much as psychology. By all means ask whether atoms and electrons are real, but don't think there is some special question about psychological realism.

Historians will have qualms about this simplified history of scientific method since Galileo, but certainly the method of hypothesis is respectable right now. We should distinguish two kinds of things: (1) a picture of what reality might be like and (2) a hypothesis which has some immediate experimental hookup with some observable consequences. Democritus and Lucretius told a story about atoms, saying, that is what the world is like, "atoms and the void." Powerful as this picture was, it had no observable consequence. Even the seventeenth-century atomists whose culmination was Newton chiefly advocated a picture of a world composed of little bouncy balls, with precious few observational consequences.

Only at the beginning of the nineteenth century did the atomist picture start to interlock with observational data, and only at the beginning of our century did the majority of physicists become convinced atomists. We might say that the picture guided the minds of men, but did not do any work. A hypothesis does work when it has specific observational consequences; such a hypothesis, when it involves theoretical entities, certainly takes for granted the reality of its entities. The critics of Chomsky's psychological realism may be thinking that he is offering only a picture, and then trying to pass that off as a hypothesis that does some work. To see if that is correct we should distinguish some parts of the doctrine.

There are four main ideas in Chomsky's work:

1) Transformational grammar: a conjectured and constantly revised set of rules and representations for some parts of English.

2) Universal grammar: the claim that all human languages share a common grammatical core.

3) Psychological realism: the grammar of a language is incarnate in the flesh and blood of its speakers.

4) Genetic grammar: a central part of everyone's grammar is inherited in his genes.

Genetic grammar commits you to universal grammar and psychological realism, but otherwise these four are pretty independent. The best transformational grammar may come from the pen of someone who hotly denies 2, 3, and 4. A psychological realist could reject universal and genetic grammar, holding that each language has its own psychological reality. A universal grammarian can reject inheritance—that seems to be Piaget's position during his debate with Chomsky.

A conjectured transformational grammar for English is of course a hypothesis that, in the terms I have been using here, does some work. One tests it against the phenomena of English sentences. What about the claim for universal grammar? That does work exactly once in these two books, rather late in the *Debate.* Chomsky examines relative and restrictive clauses. ("The man who came to dinner was ill" has the clause "who came to dinner" that restricts the subject. "The man, who came to dinner, was ill" contains a relative clause that says something about the man already singled out.) The kinds of clause behave differently. Chomsky offers a rule to explain the difference. But it does not apply in Japanese; indeed that language does not have a clear distinction between the two kinds of clause. So, we are told, something must be wrong with the rule. But we are given no rule that holds in Anglo-Japanese. This is a case in which the idea of universal grammar is doing some work. Several writers have tried to carry on discussions of it in this way, but there is no evidence in the books under review of much success. Only when we are getting somewhere with universal grammar will its critics think this is a working hypothesis and not a mere picture.

A picture of what the world might be like is very often vastly more important—and more long-lived—than any hypothesis. Atomism has endured forever. It was first propounded to explain some puzzles about motion and solidity that we have not quite forgotten. It is worth recalling the facts which Chomsky thinks are most surprising, and most worthy of understanding. There are two.

1) The fact that children come to talk grammatically at quite an early age. In general children are not taught to speak, and the words they overhear are insufficient to fix the grammar which, in fact, they acquire when quite young.

2) The fact that there is a *sensation* of grammar. We can tell almost at once which short sentences are grammatical. Chomsky drew our attention to a special case of this. Some sentences are ambiguous simply in virtue of their grammar; while very similar sentences are not; how come we so instantly tell the two kinds apart?

Chomsky has always found these two facts dramatic, demanding an explanation as profound as genetic universal grammar. This is not a hypothesis that explains the facts in any detail, but a picture of what the world might be like, and a proposal of where to look for detailed hypotheses. If one does not like the picture one has an obligation to produce another one (possibly playing down Chomsky's facts and emphasizing others). Hence the debate with Jean Piaget was a good idea, for here is another school of cognitive psychology that might give us another picture of the grammatical child.

Piaget has long studied the ways in which children mature in their abilities. His work has the greatest interest for our conceptions of space and time, topics which, for him, have a Kantian motivation. He is skeptical of standard evolutionary theory, for he thinks there is still some room for Lamarck-like adaptation of successive generations of a kind of organism to its environment. He thinks that a child, as it matures, repeats some of the stages in the intellectual development of mankind, so that the emergence of its reasoning skills resembles the history of mathematics itself. He claims to have found sharp discontinuities in the development of a child's abilities, discontinuities that correspond to differences in logical structure. He thinks human minds are born pretty empty but form successive spatial structures in the course of interacting with the world; the final product is "our" spatial world. Before that there are other spaces that the child inhabits, preconditions for the final spatialization that derives from the way in which the child comes to handle objects. If we transform this to the grammatical sphere, there would be no grammar carried in the genes. Just as there is a sequence of spatial structures that are "constructed" by the child in interaction with its environment, so we might by analogy expect a sequence of grammars, of which the end product is a grammar of English. The intervening grammars would apply to various levels of childish talk, and we might look for sharp differences between them. We would expect each successive child-grammar to be the product of the child's interaction with the people that talk to it, and its own attempts to communicate. Moreover, we could suppose that each child-grammar must be constructed before the child can pass on to the next more complex grammar, leading in due course to the steady state of adult English.

The *Debate* had promise but was a failure. Piaget is conciliatory, Chomsky firm. Piaget and his associates do not really attend to what I call the "sensation" of grammar. The format for the *Debate* was a French conference to which a small number of distinguished scientists and philosophers were invited. Interesting things were said and this book is a good bedside dipper. It is fun to read about

David Premack teaching plastic "words" to his chimpanzees. The implied argument is that the animals acquire a syntax too, so grammar can't be as specific to humans as Chomsky contends. I was glad to find Jean-Pierre Changeux complaining that linguists and the like keep on treating the brain and genetics as a "black box" when a lot is known. He speculates on the amount of information that can be genetically carried, notes that it is too little for something like grammar, but then makes a fairly standard remark of importance. If the genetic material is deployed in a hierarchical way, the possibilities of inheritance are immensely increased along with possibilities for minor deviations. As he says, this could be made to fit with Piaget's picture. But no one has yet made Piaget's picture mesh with the facts of grammar that Chomsky thinks are important. The conversations recorded in the *Debate* are about learning. They are quite idle until one thinks about the "sensation" of grammar. Hence the two sides in the debate simply don't speak to each other.

Is there any picture of grammar that can rival Chomsky's? There is a naïve picture. A child overhears lots of sentences and has a marvelous memory. Maybe we should not say "memory" but invent a world like the "cognize" that Chomsky substitutes for "know." Anyway the child files away lots of sentences, and constructs others by ringing a few changes on these. Most children do a lot of rehearsing in their cribs, and that, says the naïve picture, is a matter of storing sentences in the head, as well as hoping for some parental correction.

How does the naïve view differ from Chomsky's? It can have psychological realism. What a child learns is encoded at a physiological level. It can have universal grammar, but only on the side. It assumes all sorts of innate abilities, like the ability to imitate sounds. It might even use early work by Chomsky and Miller on the relation between short term and long term memory.

The naïve view can make no sense of deep structure, so the development of Chomsky's ideas away from deep structure lessens the contrast between these two pictures. The echo of a transformation that was used to prevent "want to" from turning into "wanna" is just what the naïve theorist would expect. There might be a big file of sentences encoded in the brain and the child hears "echoes" of these and so says "want to." Could trace theory be the theory that brings Chomsky back to naïve reflections on language?

The answer is a resounding NO but only because we come back, as always, to where Chomsky started. His first philosophy teacher was Nelson Goodman, who was Chomsky's sponsor when he was a Junior Fellow at Harvard, but who has no truck with innatism. Goodman showed in a vivid way that past experience is an inadequate guide to future experience. In Chomsky's terms, the past experience of a child is an inadequate guide to the grammar it so firmly masters. One step in Chomsky's argument has convinced almost every one of his readers: it is now a

commonplace. But if we are to reconsider the naïve theory for a moment, nothing should be commonplace. He says the child learns an infinite language on the basis of finite input. To which the naïve theorist can say Yes and No. Yes, for on the basis of the "sensation" of grammar, the child can then go to school and learn some rules, devised long ago by Latin teachers, or nowadays by mathematicians, on the basis of which it can both parse long obscure sentences and see how to generate indefinitely long sentences ("He swam" add "and" add "He swam" add "and" add etc.). But this reasoning surely uses a different module from the ones connected with the "sensation" of grammar which it was our task to explain? The class of sentences for which we have a "sensation" of grammar—and which gets the whole program going—does seem large but finite.

Is the grammar that the child acquires too "large" to be based on what it overhears? That is where we come down to details. In both books under review Chomsky cites some curious distinctions in our usage of reciprocal phrases such as "each other." He says all children make the distinctions but these cannot have been based on what they overheard. If you doubt this, he says in the course of the *Debate,* do an experiment. It would be some crazy experiment based on videotapes of twelve years of the lives of lots of children, but, says Chomsky, we'd learn little relevant from that. The naïve theorist will agree, but say that is because we have no idea what questions to ask from such an impossible videotape. What we need is a better theory of what the child remembers, when, and how it echoes its memories through trace theory.

When we have some such picture we can start to ask Piaget-like questions, Piaget found that there are sharp discontinuities between the ages at which children perform only slightly different spatial tasks. It would be an achievement to find similar discontinuities in the "sensation" of grammar. That would prove nothing about Piaget's picture, Chomsky would say we had only discovered facts about the triggering of grammatical modules. But one such single discovery would move two competing pictures a little closer to the point at which they would become working hypotheses. That, as always, is the way that speculation gets turned into knowledge.

Note

1. He died as this issue was going to press.

Ken Richardson (review date 2 January 1981)

SOURCE: "Aboard Noam's Ark," in *New Statesman,* January 2, 1981, p. 68.

[*In the following review, Richardson discusses Chomsky's elaboration of his linguistic concepts in* Rules and Representations *and the publication of two critical commentaries related to Chomsky's work.*]

Even the proverbial person-in-the-street must be aware that something exciting is going on in the scientific investigation of language. For the academic, however, the subject is boiling and the name of the prime instigator of all the excitement, Noam Chomsky, looms very large. Indeed his name is very rarely absent from *any* philosophical debate today, and probably comes top of a 20th-century citations league table in the human sciences.

The term revolution is regularly used to describe Chomsky's achievements in linguistics. On the other hand there is a barrage of criticism testifying to the fact that it's a very odd revolution indeed. What is strange about it is the way in which the dazzling new insights articulated by Chomsky about the nature of language have been framed in some astonishingly antiquated psychological lumber, in particular the theory stemming from Descartes and traceable to Plato that the essential qualities of language are genetically preprogrammed or 'inborn' like the sneeze, suckling and swallowing reflexes.

The theory is consistent with some of the most striking peculiarities of language: for instance, the presence in all languages of certain common features, or 'linguistic universals', such as the subject and predicate categories; the effortlessness and rapidity with which infants learn their language seemingly without overt instruction; and the fact that they do so in the face of only very imperfect or 'degenerate' language samples. It's the alarming implications of the theory for the whole nature of the human mind that cause all the trouble.

For instance the theory forces us into the belief that, since genetically preprogrammed, language must exist as a distinct 'faculty' of the mind alongside other, similarly preprogrammed, faculties such as numeracy (historians may here be reminded of the 18th- and 19th-century faculty psychologists who assessed people's characters by measuring the bumps on their heads); that experience serves merely as a triggering or priming function to the development of abilities which aren't learned but just 'grow' (we don't 'learn' to develop arms instead of wings, says Chomsky); and, most alarming of all, that what humans can ever know has already been laid down in our genetic endowments, other things (the understanding of human behaviour, perhaps) being 'beyond our cognitive reach', i.e. unknowable.

Because of the issues thus raised in psychology, the brain sciences and philosophy, as well as linguistics, there is little doubt that the whole event will be recorded as one of the outstanding debates of the 20th century. The present three books deal with most of these issues in different ways. Smith and Wilson provide a lucid account of 'Chomsky's theory' and of the most important criticisms of it. *Modern Linguistics* is especially instructive on the most original aspects of the theory—the nature of the so-called deep-structures, transformational rules, and so on—and provides abundant illustrations and a useful glossary. Even the naive reader will get something from it although the effort required will probably be more than the authors envisage.

In his most recent book, ***Rules and Representations***— another series of lectures involving a great deal of repetition—Chomsky does not attempt to write anything new so much as extend and clarify things that he has written before. It summarises his own views (in parts much revised over the years) of his theory today and of at least some of his critics. Unfortunately it also reveals still further the tendency often to be found in 'authorities', of writing with increasingly dogmatic tones. Here the theory is put more stridently and confidently than ever but too often in the form of assertions that are not backed up. This makes Chomsky appear very slippery at times. For instance, in support of his theory of innate language programming, he has often claimed that the language which infants actually hear is so imperfect as to make it unlikely that they could learn anything from it, except with great difficulty (listen to the umms and aahs, hesitations, false starts, grammatical errors, and so on, in an average conversation between adults and you'll know what he means). But this turns out not to be so for the special case of adults' talk to infants. Taped samples of such speech have shown it to consist of short, well-formed, simply-constructed utterances as if to deliberately provide the ideal stimulus for language learning (again the reader can make a rough check with some careful observation). Chomsky's response to this research tends to be dismissive—either not to discuss it, as in the present book, or, elsewhere, to state that it's of little relevance to the veracity of his theory anyway.

This is not to suggest that Chomsky *is* dogmatic: he can be eminently reasonable. What does come across from this and other recent works is his growing impatience with a refractory opposition, which, while remaining unconverted, has only puny alternatives to offer. 'Present me with a better theory and I'll start listening', is what Chomsky seems to be saying.

In *Making Sense,* Geoffrey Sampson attempts something along those lines by attacking the 'limited mind' view of the Chomsky school and replacing it with the 'creative mind' view based on the philosophy of science of Sir Karl Popper. The book is written in a lively style and the view he attacks most clearly portrayed, but his reply is often philosophical, often technical and often extremely thin. For instance, one of the corollaries of Chomsky's theory of genetic programming is that we are all born with the same potential for linguistic attainment. Unfortunately such is the complexity of language in use that no-one has yet seriously suggested how we might test this corollary. Sampson, however, finds it so distasteful as to put forward as 'evidence' his own 'strong impression that there are particular syntactic constructions . . . which are mastered only by the more competent speakers of a language'.

Chomsky has a right to expect more than this. But few critics are capable of grappling with the *totality* of the brilliant linguistic insights in their archaic psychological shell. The problem seems to be that the *description* of language, always the most impressive dimension of human behaviour, has far outstripped the *psychological* theory that can cope with it. This is a common phenomenon in science and the solution may just be a matter of time: present research in the so-called 'pragmatics' of communication, involving more complex presuppositions about the social context of language functions, is already throwing up new conceptions of language learning. But the anachronisms of modern linguistics are likely to persist until we are presented with entirely new theories of the whole nature of the human mind, which is what is really at issue in the Chomsky debate.

Walter Laqueur (review date 24 March 1982)

SOURCE: "The Politics of Adolescence," in *The New Republic,* Vol. 186, No. 12, March 24, 1982, pp. 37-9.

[*In the following review of* Towards the New Cold War, *Laqueur finds serious flaws in Chomsky's factual distortions and political idealism, despite crediting Chomsky as an interesting and impassioned intellectual.*]

There are, roughly speaking, two ways to review Mr. Chomsky's book [*Towards the New Cold War*]. One is to look for a particularly absurd statement or factual mistake (not necessarily of great relevance) early on in the book—for instance, the bomb explosion at the Munich October-fest in 1980, to which the author refers more than once. According to him, this was the second largest terrorist incident in Europe, killing fifty-three people. However, the number killed was in fact thirteen (even on the rare occasions when Mr. Chomsky is dealing with facts and not with fantasies, he exaggerates by a factor of, plus or minus, four or five). A few more minutes could then be spent in search of some glaring distortions—say on the origins of the cold war, or the militarism of the Kennedy Administration, or again on any number of factual points. Such an undertaking is not very arduous, for Chomsky transforms a well known Israeli writer into a general (Aluf Hareven), confuses a real general with a noted Russian novelist (Laskov), and mixes up a third general with Mussolini (Peled). A review of this kind would go on to point out that not much can be expected from a writer incapable of even spelling correctly the name of a well-known Harvard professor (Stanley Hoffmann), a writer for whom Jack Anderson and Israel Shahak are reliable witnesses for affairs of state, a writer who has tried to whitewash the mass murders in Cambodia, and collaborated with notorious French anti-Semites and neo-fascists in the denial of the Holocaust. Such a review would end with some suitable reflections about the kind of society in which such a squalid tract, such a clumsy piece of propaganda, such a ludicrous fabrication, intellectually worthless and morally grotesque, a parody of scholarship that reminds me of the worst excesses of Hitlerism and Stalinism, can be put out by a distinguished publishing house.

Le style c'est l'homme même, a distinguished Frenchman once said, but I am not sure whether he was altogether

right. Even if he was, there are of course other ways to review books. But the problem of style apart, there still remains the question of whether one should take Mr. Chomsky seriously. Einstein played the violin, Freud played cards, Marx used to take walks in Hampstead Heath, but we do not look to them for guidance on these activities. Should Mr. Chomsky command respect as a writer on politics because he has made a name for himself in linguistics? I think he should; he has had a wide audience, even though the number of his admirers has shrunk as world events have lately failed to bear out his predictions. But he still manages to provoke and anger quite a few people.

My own feelings have been different. While I cannot honestly describe myself as an admirer of Mr. Chomsky's writings, I have found them of interest. And I believe that he has fulfilled a useful function for a variety of reasons, some positive, others negative, and yet others neutral. In an age of academic insipidity and pussyfooting, shrillness has a certain entertainment value. Chomsky presents a fascinating psychological case and an invaluable educational example. He genuinely believes that he has never been wrong. And since there is a bit of a Chomsky in most of us, we ought to be grateful, from time to time, to be reminded that there, but for the grace of God. . . .

In defense of Chomsky, it must be said that his bark is sometimes worse than his bite. His new book starts with a long and acrimonious attack on Mrs. Claire Sterling and her book, *The Terror Network;* "absurd" is one of the least offensive epithets he applies to the work. In the end the reader is bound to reach the conclusion that Mrs. Sterling has invented all her stories, that there are no international links between terrorist groups and are no big powers supporting them. But whoever bothers to read Mr. Chomsky's fine print will find to his surprise that "it would be remarkable indeed if the Soviet Union were not engaged in international terrorism." Far from rejecting Mrs. Sterling's main argument, Chomsky actually accepts it. It should be noted in passing that although Mrs. Sterling was not able to substantiate some of her allegations in her book, a fact that was pointed out at the time by various reviewers (including the present writer), more evidence for linking the Red Brigades and other terrorists with Eastern Europe via Qaddafi and the PLO has since come to light, and not from American sources. Yet, to the best of my knowledge, no apologies have been extended to Mrs. Sterling by her critics.

If Mr. Chomsky is not always right, he is not always wrong. He may mix up the Israeli generals and his comments are curiously restrained when he deals with the Arab Begins. But this does not invalidate his criticisms of the disturbing developments in Israel. Coming from him, spiced with exaggerations, derived partly from doubtful sources, and altogether one-sided, these criticisms will have no impact whatever on those they should reach. They will be read with sympathetic interest in the offices of the oil companies and the international banks, in the Secretariat of the United Nations and the foreign ministries of many countries which, quite independently of Mr. Chomsky and for different reasons, have reached the conclusion that Israel is a nuisance and should be abolished. Once upon a time it was perhaps a little unpopular to criticize Israel's domestic and foreign policies in the American media. Now there is a global consensus against Israel, extending from the far right to the extreme left, and including the CIA and the Pentagon. Chomsky, the erstwhile outsider, has become a mainstream spokesman; if he feels a little uncomfortable in this company, he certainly does not show it.

But these are relatively minor issues. What makes the Chomsky phenomenon so interesting is rooted in a deeper level: time for him stood still in 1947 or thereabouts. True, the action may have moved to different countries since the early postwar years; but the basic issues have remained the same and so have his instincts, those of an eighteen-year-old product of the radical Zionist-socialist youth movement who has read Marx and, being a little precocious, has already proceeded to Rosa Luxemburg and Anton Pannekoek, whose visions of unconditional internationalism he fully shares. He is possessed by a surfeit of idealism, a burning wish to change the world, to search for total freedom and absolute social justice; an abhorrence of war and chauvinism; a contempt for those willing to compromise with the world as it is and who end up as traitors to the cause. From the perspective of an eighteen-year-old, the history of mankind is just beginning and everything is possible—provided only that there is the unconditional will to fight for the great revolution which will solve all problems, which will make Palestine a binational state and transform the Arab countries, Iran, and the third world in general, into genuine democratic societies, free from nationalist and racist prejudices and imbued with the spirit of humanism, tolerance, and nonviolence. This is the revolution that will destroy American imperialism, while the Soviet bureaucratic distortion of real socialism will wither away, no longer menaced by external enemies, or simply be swept away by the people. From afar a mighty chorus is already heard, "*C'est la lutte finale, groupons-nous, et demain / l'Internationale sera le genre humain.*"

This, then, is the vision, and I restate it here not in a spirit of ridicule. For it is in many ways a very attractive vision in its idealism, its refusal to be discouraged by the bitter experience of the past, when revolutions failed and brought worse tyranny. Without idealism and optimism there is not much hope for mankind, and Martin Buber was of course right when he wrote about adolescence as the eternal chance (*Glückschance*) of mankind. (I, however, am no longer certain that Buber had politics in mind when he wrote those lines, except perhaps in the vaguest way.)

But how is the vision to be realized? College freshmen reading the classics of political science will learn that politics as a vocation means compromise with realities; means giving a finger (and, on occasion, the whole hand) to the devil; means that there is no freedom, equality, and democracy even in revolutionary movements; means that the ethics of politics are not those of the prophet Isaiah and the Sermon on the Mount; means that post-revolutionary regimes are not markedly less oppressive and intolerant than their predecessors. The young Chomskys, needless to say, will reject such defeatist talk. But in the long run they cannot fail to notice that most of their contemporaries do not share their values and visions, be they of libertarian socialism or a binational state in Palestine; and that this rejection is not just limited to a few monopoly capitalists, their servants, and the fools brainwashed by the media into a false consciousness. Perhaps they need a little coercion for their own good?

The case of the binational state is a perfect illustration of Chomskyan politics. There is no denying that in a sensible world this would have been the ideal solution for both Jews and Arabs. Unfortunately, binationalism has not worked in India any better than in Cyprus or Lebanon. It does not function well even in such highly civilized countries as Canada or Belgium. It never had a chance in Palestine. Quoting a friendly witness, Mr. Chomsky puts the blame on the "Europe-oriented Israeli leadership afraid of the Levantinization of their society." But in fact almost all advocates of Arab-Jewish rapprochement came from these European-oriented circles, whereas Jews of Middle Eastern background (from whom Mr. Begin derives the majority of his votes) were always far more suspicious and hostile toward the Arabs. As for the Arabs, they regarded binationalism as a joke and not a very good one at that.

Mr. Chomsky presents essays "on the current crisis and how we got there." Let us assume for argument's sake that his descriptions and analyses are correct. Let us then imagine him a senior decision maker in Washington or Jerusalem and ask how would he lead us out of the crisis. The concerned reader will look in vain for answers—except perhaps such obvious advice as to engage in unilateral disarmament, to dismantle the industrial-military complex, to refrain from interventionism, to share our wealth with the third world, and to read Marx, Bakunin, and Pannekoek. Mr. Chomsky must know that if all these demands were fulfilled, even if America disappeared from the map altogether, the world would still not be a more peaceful place, nor would there be less oppression and injustice. He would probably argue that it is not the task of the intellectual to provide alternative strategies but to be critical, to negate. The only strategies he develops are for the use of sectarian groups, and they have the immense advantage that they need not bear any relation to realities: any statement, any promise can be made and any problem can be solved on the level of abstraction. For there is not the slightest danger that the ideological platform will ever be put to a test, that it will have any effect on the course of events, except perhaps in a negative way.

Thus we are back to the politics of adolescence and the youth movement of ideological purity, of unlimited idealism and of irresponsibility as a way of life. The idealism has meanwhile turned into almost pathological aggression; Saint-Just is now in his fifties. The growing divorce from reality makes it impossible to refute Mr. Chomsky, but it also makes rational discourse well-nigh impossible. Mr. Marcus Raskin in a blurb on the cover of the book says that Mr. Chomsky's essays are a strong blend of reason and passion. He forgot to add that the ratio of passion to reason is about ten to one, and that it is the kind of passion about which the poet wrote that "it left the ground to lose itself in the sky."

William Steif (review date June 1984)

SOURCE: "Impasse in the Middle East," in *The Progressive*, Vol. 48, No. 6, June, 1984, pp. 40-1.

[*In the following review, Steif offers positive evaluation of* The Fateful Triangle, *which he praises as "a powerful and thoroughly documented tract."*]

Each day's news brings fresh evidence of the disastrous policies the United States and its surrogate, Israel, pursue in the Middle East. The development of those policies over the past half-century, and their role in the continuing victimization of the Palestinian people, is the theme of Noam Chomsky's **The Fateful Triangle.**

Many American liberals will hate this book. People like Arthur Goldberg, Irving Howe, and *The New Republic*'s Martin Peretz (whom Chomsky singles out for special shellacking) will condemn or dismiss it. So will many sectors of the American media that have been taken into camp by the Washington-Tel Aviv axis. Chomsky will be accused of anti-Zionism, anti-Semitism, anti-Americanism, and that worst sin of any American Jew, "self-hate."

But **The Fateful Triangle** is a powerful and thoroughly documented tract. It demonstrates the increasing brutality of Israel and its sponsor, the United States, in the Middle East. In Chomsky's book, the chief victims appear to be Palestinians, but today he could also include the Lebanese, both Moslem and Christian.

After brief introductory remarks, Chomsky devotes more than 460 pages to just six chapters, each looking at an aspect of policy development:

The Fateful Triangle begins by discussing the origin of the "special relationship" between the United States and Israel, focusing on American pressure groups, American liberal and ideological support for Israel, and the concept of Israel as a "strategic asset," which translates as "client state."

In an analysis of "rejectionism" Chomsky turns that idea on its head. He notes that most Americans believe the Arab states (except for Egypt since 1977) and the Palestinian Liberation Organization have steadfastly rejected recognition of Israel. Actually, he shows, there have been Arab-PLO overtures toward a Middle Eastern settlement, including recognition of Israel, since well before the 1973 Yom Kippur War. He demonstrates that it is the Israelis who have rejected all Arab overtures because they were intent on creating a Greater Israel, encompassing the West Bank, Gaza Strip, Golan Heights, and possibly even the "North Bank" to the Litani or Awali Rivers in Lebanon. In this, says Chomsky, both major Israeli political groupings, Labor and the Likud, have been backed by the United States, which is eager to maintain its "strategic asset"—now the world's fourth-strongest military power—as a Middle East bulwark against the Soviet Union.

Chomsky's summary of the history of Palestine and Israel, from the British Mandate and the early Zionists to the present, stresses the Israeli rationalization for what he calls "the use of terror" against Arab civilian targets. He dredges up the terrorist backgrounds of Menachem Begin, Ariel Sharon, and Yitzhak Shamir, noting that "the PLO has the same sort of legitimacy that the Zionist movement had in the pre-state period." That fact, he says, is "recognized at some level within Israel and, I think, accounts for the bitter hatred of the PLO which, rational people must concede, has been recognized by Palestinians as 'their sole representative' whenever they have had a chance to express themselves."

In a 148-page chapter entitled "Peace for Galilee," the invading Israelis' slogan in June 1982, Chomsky recounts the awful massacres Lebanese Phalangists and Palestinians visited on one another in the 1970s, the cease-fire that preceded the Israeli invasion, and the Israeli pretext for the invasion. The author offers a cogent critique of the American media, the Syrian role, and the Israeli Defense Force's "humanitarianism," which wasn't humanitarian at all.

A chapter entitled "Aftermath" gives a blow-by-blow account of the Israeli invasion of Beirut, the Sabra-Shatila massacre, the Reagan "peace" plan, and the results of "Peace for Galilee." Chomsky reports on opposition within Israel to the Begin-Sharon-Shamir policies, and quotes Hebrew University Professor Yeshayahu Leibovitz, editor of *Encyclopedia Hebraica,* on the Sabra-Shatila atrocity: "The massacre was done by us. The Phalangists are mercenaries, exactly as the Ukrainians and the Croatians and the Slovakians were the mercenaries of Hitler, who organized them as soldiers to do the work for him. Even so have we organized the assassins in Lebanon in order to murder the Palestinians."

Chomsky concludes with a short chapter, "The Road to Armageddon," in which he addresses the threat that Israel might use nuclear warheads at some future point. He tags this the "Samson complex"—Samson's revenge on the Philistines, in which the strong man brought the Temple to ruins and "killed more Philistines than he had in a lifetime"—and argues that this is "not something to be taken lightly." It could be "a final solution from which few will escape."

Chomsky is often heavy-handed; the reader can do without obvious ironies that simply slow up his narrative. And he is by no means a master of the incisive word or the deft phrase; rather, he writes like what he is—an angry academic. But it is also his academic quality—his scholarly eagerness to nail down every point—that gives *The Fateful Triangle* its punch. The book contains 956 numbered footnotes, plus dozens of asterisked notes, and sometimes these are more interesting than the main text. I found citations of many friends and acquaintances in both the American and Israeli press, and saw only one obvious error—the misspelling of a reporter's name.

Another quibble: Chomsky doesn't tell us enough about himself or how he came to his intense interest in the Middle East. He relies heavily on Israel's lively and outspoken press, but does he read Hebrew? Did he do his own translating?

I also miss a sense of time and place. I have no idea, after reading Chomsky's book, whether he has ever been on the main street of Sidon, or in the rubble-strewn remnants of Palestinian refugee camps—like Ain el-Hilweh or Rashidieh. The reader needs occasional mental pictures of places like Galerie Semaan, a crossing point between East and West Beirut, as well as at least a glimpse of the studied elegance of former Lebanese Prime Minister Saeb Salam's house in West Beirut.

But Chomsky's analysis is on target. *The Fateful Triangle* should cause a profound reassessment of American policy. It should, but I doubt that it will.

Alan Tonelson (review date 13 April 1986)

SOURCE: "Institutional Structure Blues," in *New York Times Book Review*, April 13, 1986, p. 28.

[*In the following review, Tonelson offers unfavorable assessment of* Turning the Tide, *citing flaws in Chomsky's polemical tone and unwillingness to propose viable alternatives to the contemporary foreign policy he condemns.*]

Today, in the flush of the Reagan era, it is easy to forget America's debt to the New Left scholars and writers who have explored the dark side of American history, politics and foreign policy. This loosely knit band of thinkers has been much less successful, however, at turning its findings into a convincing wholesale indictment of current American public policies, much less a sound program for the future. The strengths and weaknesses of the New Left's approach are all showcased in *Turning the Tide,* a broadside against the United States record in Central America and around the world written by the Massachusetts Institute of Technology linguist and New Left stalwart Noam Chomsky.

Mr. Chomsky's thesis is simple—which, much contemporary foreign policy wisdom notwithstanding, is not necessarily a bad thing. He argues that "much of what U.S. governments do in the world" stems from the determination of American leaders to secure and preserve what he calls a "Fifth Freedom" utterly unlike Franklin Roosevelt's first Four: "the freedom to rob and to exploit" around the world. Worse, this drive is "rooted in the unchanging institutional structure" of "military-based state capitalism" that dominates American society. In its quest for tight control of foreign markets and resources, he argues, United States policy has "sought to destroy human rights, to lower living standards, and to prevent democratization, often with considerable passion and violence."

No one should dismiss Mr. Chomsky's arguments as perverse, 60's-era America-bashing without finishing his first and third chapters, which detail the horrifying atrocities committed in this century against Central American populations by local forces with which Washington worked closely, then and now. Like most of the book, these sections are "clip jobs" drawn from secondary source histories, from news articles and from reports by the usual assortment of liberal and left-leaning Latin America and human-rights groups.

But as the debate over United States involvement in Central America intensifies, it becomes doubly important to recognize how much high-quality evidence challenges the Administration's claims that in El Salvador decent civilians are firmly in control and the guerrillas are practically defeated, or that the Sandinistas are so repressive and so dangerous to the hemisphere that America simply has to do something. Indeed, the degree to which Mr. Chomsky can not only challenge but also persuasively reverse such claims about those forces responsible for the worst repression and aggression in Central America should jolt any fair-minded person who still buys the Administration's moral case for current United States policy. In addition, Mr. Chomsky amply documents his charge that even the country's best news organizations have too often swallowed the essentials of the Reagan Administration line in this conflict; he should only train his sights on some Congressional Democrats next.

Yet *Turning the Tide*—much of it turgidly written—is profoundly flawed. Mr. Chomsky should not have to call Jeane Kirkpatrick the Administration's "chief sadist-in-residence"; any record that is truly atrocious should speak for itself. Further, the author doesn't seem to know the difference between attributed and unattributed quotes, frequently treating the statements of nameless "U.S. officials" and "informed sources" who agree with him as revealed truth. Like most participants in the Central American controversy, Mr. Chomsky is often highly selective in his use of evidence. And it would be much harder to label him reflexively anti-Israel if, just once in his harsh description of the Jewish state as the handmaiden to American oppressors in Central America and a brutal colonizer at home, he mentioned that most of Israel's neighbors do not recognize the country's right to exist and remain officially at war with it.

Big theoretical problems abound too. A compelling one-dimensional interpretation of American foreign policy is not inconceivable, but Mr. Chomsky's version—"The guiding concern of U.S. foreign policy is the climate for U.S. business operations"—ignores too much of what the postwar world's Western creators not only said, but did. A corporate oppressor state that built up industrial centers in Western Europe and Japan in the stated hope that they would soon rival the United States is behaving in too peculiar a manner to warrant that title. And a system of domination that, for all the misery it may have helped to create, has not only brought record prosperity to the people of the industrialized world, but to South Korea, Taiwan and others in the third world as well—and permitted all of these populations to exercise unprecedented control over their destinies—cannot be explained by blanket condemnation.

Mr. Chomsky's analysis shows that his neglect of these points stems neither, from the polemicist's need to deceive, as his critics usually charge, nor from a sense of guilt run wild. Rather, it reflects a failure to think of United States national interests in a Hobbesian world in which tragic choices are sometimes unavoidable. Nowhere in **Turning the Tide** is there a serious discussion of what America needs to do in the world to provide for its security or prosperity. The author simply heaps scorn on the notion that America confronts forces that would be hostile no matter how benign Washington's international actions. And he tends to discuss America's material well-being as a right that is or is not due us—as though the international system we are stuck with for the foreseeable future permits us to deal with such matters primarily in legal or moral terms.

The choices made by America leaders might have been hideously or pathetically wrong. But they are most accurately seen as choices made to preserve specific interests (even if they have not honestly been presented as such) and best criticized as counterproductive, dangerous and or unnecessary. Otherwise one is reduced, like Mr. Chomsky, to debating points that are factually valid but useless as guides to American policy.

Because Mr. Chomsky provides rhetorical ammunition from a too-often-ignored and maligned perspective, he enlarges the bounds of today's foreign policy debate. But the terms of the debate remain largely sterile. How politically and militarily active does America need to be in this hemisphere to preserve its interests? How active does it need to be in the world? What roles, if any, can moralistic and legalistic concerns play in safeguarding American interests in today's state system? Merely posing these questions—and suggesting that not all worthy foreign policy goals are mutually re-enforcing—are acts of thinking far more radical than anything in **Turning the Tide.**

Noam Chomsky with Jim Peck (interview date July 1987)

SOURCE: "Noam Chomsky: An American Dissident," in *The Progressive*, Vol. 51, No. 7, July, 1987, pp. 22-5.

[*In the following interview, Chomsky discusses his political views, objection to the Vietnam War, alternatives to Western capitalist society, and the problem of public ignorance concerning politics and international affairs.*]

Noam Chomsky, Ferrari P. Ward Professor of Linguistics at the Massachusetts Institute of Technology, is widely regarded as the world's foremost authority in the field of structural linguistics. Since the mid-1960s, he has also been one of America's leading political dissidents, particularly in his outspoken criticism of U.S. policy toward the Third World.

Chomsky's **Pirates and Emperors: International Terrorism in the Real World** *was published last year by Claremont Research and Publications. Other recent books include* **Turning the Tide: U.S. Intervention in Central America and the Struggle for Peace** *(South End Press, 1985), and* **The Fateful Triangle: The United States, Israel, and the Palestinians** *(South End Press, 1983).*

Rejecting the clichés and easy assumptions of both Left and Right, Chomsky calls himself a libertarian and anarchist. "Ever since I've had any political awareness," he says. "I've felt either alone or part of a tiny minority."

[Peck]: *How many of the books you wrote over the years have been reviewed in the major professional journals?*

[Chomsky]: Well, in this country I don't recall offhand any case, ever. I suppose the reason is largely that this work is critical not only of the United States and U.S. policy but more crucially of the role of intellectuals in the United States. As a result, it's just beyond the pale. And when there are references, I think they are notable for their almost total lack of even a pretense of rational argument or concern for evidence.

The same is true pretty much of the media. My books on contemporary issues are generally reviewed quite widely in Canada, England, Australia, and elsewhere, but only sporadically here. I also find easy access to national TV and radio outside the United States, as well as journals. Though I've been highly critical of Israeli policy, I've been asked to write in the mainstream Israeli press. That is virtually unthinkable here.

Apart from the Soviet bloc, where I am under a total ban (including even linguistics), the United States is probably the country where I have least access to the media or journals of opinion. My experience in this respect is not at all unique; the same is true commonly for critics of U.S. policy and ideology.

When there is some reference to what I or other critics have said, it often seems that the commentators are barely aware of what the argument is, or what position is actually being formulated. I have found all sorts of strange illusions about what, say, my attitude was toward the Vietnam war, because elite intellectuals often simply cannot perceive that one could have the opinions that I do hold.

My attitude toward the American war in Vietnam was based on the principle that aggression is wrong, including the aggression of the United States against South Vietnam. There's only a small number of people in American academic circles who could even hear those words. They wouldn't know what I'm referring to when I talk about American aggression in South Vietnam. There is no such event in official history, though there clearly was in the real world. It seems difficult for elite intellectuals to believe that my opposition to the American attack against South Vietnam was based on the same principle that led me to oppose the Russian invasions of Czechoslovakia or Afghanistan.

There was a hope, at least in the 1960s, that people in the capitalist world could learn something from the Third World. Do you think that is so today?

I never thought the Third World liberation movements of the 1960s were likely to provide any useful lessons for Western socialists. They were confronted with all kinds of problems that we do not face, even apart from the problems of foreign attack and domestic national consolidation. We do not confront the problem of developing an industrial society under the onerous conditions that hold throughout most of the Third World. Honest libertarians should recognize these facts.

Take the Vietnam war. It was clear by the end of the 1960s that the United States had achieved its primary objectives. It had effectively destroyed the National Liberation Front of South Vietnam and the Pathet Lao in Laos, ensuring that only the harshest and most authoritarian elements in Indochina would survive, if any would. This was a major victory for U.S. aggression. Principled opponents of the U.S. war were therefore in the position of, in effect, helping to defend the only surviving resistance in Vietnam, which happened to be highly authoritarian state-socialist groups.

Now, I don't think that was a reason for not opposing the American war in Vietnam, but it was a reason why many anarchists could not throw themselves into that struggle with the energy and sympathy that they might have. Some did, but others were reluctant because they were highly critical of the regime that was to emerge, as I was. Within peace-movement groups, I tried to dissociate opposition to the American war from support for state socialism in Vietnam, but it was not easy to undertake serious opposition to imperial aggression, with the very real personal cost that this entailed, on such a basis.

In fact, the American movement tended to become quite pro-North Vietnamese—segments of it, at least. They felt they were not simply opposing the American war but defending the North Vietnamese vision of a future society.

I think there was the wish on the part of some to see a genuinely humane alternative society.

Yes. And many felt that this is what the North Vietnamese, the state-socialist bureaucrats, would create, which was highly unlikely, particularly as the war progressed with mounting terror and destruction.

The United States has never terminated its effort to win the war in Vietnam. It's still trying to win it, and in many ways it is winning. One of the ways it's winning is by imposing conditions which will bring out the repressive elements that were present in the Vietnamese communist movement.

American dissidents have to face the fact that they are living in a state with enormous power, used for murderous and destructive ends. What we do, the very acts we perform, will be exploited where possible for those ends. Honest people will have to fact the fact that they are morally responsible for the predictable human consequences of their acts. One of these acts is accurate criticism, accurate critical analysis of authoritarian state socialism in North Vietnam or in Cuba or in other countries that the United States is trying to undermine and subvert. The consequence of accurate critical analysis will be to buttress these efforts, contributing to suffering and oppression.

These dilemmas are hard to deal with. They are not unique to the United States. Should an honest Russian dissident, for example, publicly denounce the atrocities and oppressive character of the Afghan resistance, knowing that such accurate criticism will be exploited in support of Soviet aggression?

Suppose we could somehow manage to conduct this inquiry and discussion without contributing to the designs of imperialist power. For example, it's cheap and easy to say that these are repressive state-socialist societies. That's true. But then serious questions arise as to what one can do, say, in Indochina, in a society that has been so severely, almost lethally, damaged by destructive war and by a legacy of colonialism with horrifying effects, virtually unknown in the West.

Even apart from such colossal man-made disasters, what really are the prospects for development in Third World societies that are at a lower level of development today than were the industrializing societies of Europe and the United States in the Eighteenth Century? The industrializing societies of Europe and the United States were not faced with a hostile environment in which the major resources had already been preempted. These are really important things to think about. They raise the question whether development is even possible in the Third World.

You once wrote that if by some quirk of history the advanced Western powers should actually decide to genuinely give assistance to Third World countries, it wouldn't be all that easy to know what should be done or how to do it.

That's correct. These countries could become subsidiaries of Western capitalism. We have a good deal of experience with the consequences of that option. What other models of development are there? There's the authoritarian state-capitalist model of South Korea, or the authoritarian state-socialist model. Not very pretty, in many respects. But is there really a libertarian model of development that's meaningful? Maybe there is, but it requires some real work and thought to show that. It's not enough just to mouth slogans.

Intellectuals are often deeply involved with "traditions"— the "Marxist tradition." the "Freudian tradition." Is one of the aspects of the anarchist an uneasiness with any doctrine?

Well, anarchism isn't a doctrine. It's at most a historical tendency, a tendency of thought and action which has many different ways of developing and progressing and which, I would think, will continue as a permanent strand of human history.

Take the most optimistic assumptions: What we can expect is that in some new and better form of society in which certain oppressive structures have been overcome, we will simply discover new problems that haven't been obvious before. And the anarchists will then be revolutionaries trying to overcome these new kinds of oppression and unfairness and constraint that we weren't aware of before. Looking back over the past, that's pretty much what has happened.

Just take our own lifetimes: sexism, for example. Twenty years ago, it was not in the consciousness of most people as a form of oppression. Now it is a live issue which has reached a general level of consciousness and concern. The problems are still there, but at least they are on the agenda. And other will enter our awareness if the ones we now face are addressed.

What do you think of speaking in terms of a Marxist or Freudian tradition?

I think it's a bad idea. The whole concept of Marxist or Freudian or anything like that is very odd. These concepts belong to the history of organized religion. Any living person, no matter how gifted, will make some contributions intermingled with error and partial understanding. We try to understand and improve on their contributions and eliminate the errors. But how can you identify yourself as a Marxist, or a Freudian, or an X-ist, whoever X may be? That would be to treat the person as a God to be revered, not a human being whose contributions are to be assimilated and transcended. It's a crazy idea, a kind of idolatry.

And yet one to which many intellectuals have been drawn.

Well, because in subjects that really don't have a great deal of intellectual depth, that are not living intellectual disciplines that confront problems and try to overcome them, what you can do is accept the faith and repeat it.

I don't mean to suggest that this is a fair characterization of the work of those individuals who call themselves "Marxists" or "Freudians." But the fact that such concepts persist and are taken seriously is a sign of the intellectual inadequacy of the traditions, and probably hampers their further development. We should not be worshiping at shrines, but learning what we can from people who had something serious to say, or who did something valuable in their lives, while trying to overcome the inevitable errors and flaws.

Are there any particular movements toward building alternative structures today within Western capitalist societies that you find hopeful?

It's a complicated matter. Take the moves toward workers' self-management that you can detect with a sufficiently powerful microscope in Europe, and sometimes here. On the one hand, these integrate the work force into the system. They might lead to class harmony, suppression of industrial strife, acceptance of lower wages and higher profits. In this sense, they serve as a device for socializing the work force within the existing system of oppression.

On the other hand, they also have the possibility of developing the awareness and understanding that it is perfectly possible for workers to manage without authoritarian structures; that bosses are not needed; that there's no God-given necessity to have hierarchical structure of authority in the work place of a kind that we would call fascist in the political domain. It can lead to that.

The question is, how do these tendencies play themselves out? From the point of view of the capitalists themselves or the managerial elite or the state management, of course, any such forms of worker participation would be used to the extent possible as a technique of subordinating the work force. And the question is, to what extent can self-conscious working-class groups struggle against this and try to turn these efforts into something else?

You have spoken—in some places you call it a "Cartesian common sense"—of the common-sense capacities of the people. What do you mean by common sense? What does it mean in a society like ours?

Well, let me give an example. When I'm driving, I sometimes turn on the radio and I find very often that what I'm listening to is a discussion of sports. These are telephone conversations. People call in and have long and intricate discussions, and it's plain that quite a high degree of thought and analysis is going into that. People know a tremendous amount. They know all sorts of complicated details and enter into far-reaching discussion about whether the coach made the right decision yesterday, and so on.

These are ordinary people, not professionals, who are applying their intelligence and analytic skills in these areas and accumulating quite a lot of knowledge and, for all I know, understanding. On the other hand, when I hear people talk about, say, international affairs or domestic problems, it's at a level of superficiality which is beyond belief.

I think this concentration on such topics as sports makes a certain degree of sense. The way the system is set up, there is virtually nothing people can do anyway, without a degree of organization that's far beyond anything that exists now, to influence the real world. They might as well live in a fantasy world, and that's in fact what they do. I'm sure they are using their common sense and intellectual skills, but in an area which has no meaning and probably thrives because it has no meaning, as a displacement from the serious problems which one cannot influence and affect because the power happens to lie elsewhere.

Now it seems to me that some intellectual skill and capacity for understanding and for accumulating evidence and gaining information and thinking through problems could be used—would be used—under different systems of governance which involve popular participation in important decision-making, in areas that really matter to human life. There are areas where you need specialized knowledge; I'm not suggesting a kind of anti-intellectualism. But many things can be understood quite well without a very far-reaching, specialized knowledge. And, in fact, even a specialized knowledge in these areas is not beyond the reach of people who happen to be interested.

To take apart the system of illusions and deception which functions to prevent understanding of contemporary reality—that's not a task that requires extraordinary skill or understanding. It requires the kind of normal skepticism and willingness to apply one's analytical skills that almost all normal people have and can exercise. It just happens that they exercise them in analyzing what the New England Patriots ought to do next Sunday instead of questions that really matter for human life, their own included.

Are experts and intellectuals afraid of people who could apply the intelligence of sport to their own areas of competency in foreign affairs, social sciences, and so on?

I suspect this is rather common. Those areas of inquiry that have to do with problems of immediate human concern do not happen to be particularly profound or inaccessible to the ordinary person lacking any special training who takes the trouble to learn something about them. Commentary on public affairs in the mainstream literature is often shallow and uninformed. Everyone who writes or speaks about these matters knows how much you can get away with as long as you keep close to received doctrine.

I'm sure just about everyone exploits these privileges. I know I do. When I refer to Nazi crimes or Soviet atrocities, for example, I know that I will not be called upon to back up what I say, but a detailed scholarly apparatus is necessary if I say anything critical of one of the Holy States—the United States or Israel. This freedom from the requirements of evidence or even rationality is quite a convenience, as any informed reader of the media and journals of opinion, or even much of the scholarly literature, will quickly discover. It makes life easy, and permits expression of a good deal of nonsense or ignorant bias with impunity, also sheer slander. Evidence is unnecessary, argument beside the point.

Thus, a standard charge against American dissidents or even American liberals is that they claim that the United States is the sole source of evil in the world, or other similar idiocies. The convention is that such charges are entirely legitimate when the target is someone who does not march in the appropriate parades, and they are therefore produced without even a pretense of evidence. Adherence to the party line confers the right to act in ways that would properly be regarded as scandalous on the part of any critic of received orthodoxies. Too much public awareness might lead to a demand that standards of integrity should be met, which would certainly save a lot of forests from destruction, and would send many a reputation tumbling.

The right to lie in the service of power is guarded with considerable vigor and passion. This becomes evident whenever anyone takes the trouble to demonstrate that charges against some official enemy are inaccurate or, sometimes, pure invention. Anyone who points out that some charge against Cuba, Nicaragua, Vietnam, or some other official enemy is dubious or false will immediately be labeled an apologist for real or alleged crimes, a useful technique to ensure that rational standards will not be imposed.

The critic typically has little access to the media, and the personal consequences for the critic are sufficiently annoying to deter many from taking this course, particularly because some journals—*The New Republic,* for example—sink to the ultimate level of dishonesty and cowardice, regularly refusing even the right of response to slanders they publish. Hence the sacred right to lie is likely to be preserved without too serious a threat.

You have said that most intellectuals end up obfuscating reality. Do they understand the reality they are obfuscating? Do they understand the social processes they mystify?

Most people are not liars. They can't tolerate too much cognitive dissonance. I don't want to deny that there are outright liars, just brazen propagandists; you can find them in journalism and in the academic professions as well. But I don't think that's the norm. The norm is obedience, adoption of uncritical attitudes, taking the easy path of self-deception.

I think there's also a selective process in the academic professions and journalism—that is, people who are independent-minded and cannot be trusted to be obedient don't make it, by and large. They're often filtered out along the way.

You've written that Henry Kissinger's memoirs "give the impression of a middle-level manager who has learned to conceal vacuity with pretentious verbiage." You doubt that he has any subtle "conceptual framework" or global design. Why do such individuals gain such extraordinary reputations, given what you say about his actual abilities? What does this say about how our society operates?

Our society is not really based on public participation in decision-making in any significant sense. Rather, it is a system of elite decision and periodic public ratification. Certainly people would like to think there's somebody up there who knows what he's doing. Since we don't participate, we don't control, and we don't even think about questions of crucial importance, we hope somebody who has some competence is paying attention. Let's hope the ship has a captain, in other words. I think that's a factor.

But also, it is an important feature of the ideological system to impose on people the feeling that they really are incompetent to deal with these complex and important issues: They'd better leave it to the captain. One device is to develop a star system, an array of figures who are often media creations or creations of the academic propaganda establishment, whose deep insights we are supposed to admire and to whom we must happily and confidently assign the right to control our lives and control international affairs.

In fact, power is very highly concentrated in small interpenetrating elites, ultimately based on ownership of the private economy in large measure, but also on related ideological and political and managerial elites. This means that you have to establish the pretense that the participants of that elite know what they are doing and have the kind of understanding and access to information that is denied the rest of us, so that we poor slobs ought to just watch, not interfere.

It's in this context that we can understand the Kissinger phenomenon. His ignorance and foolishness really are a phenomenon, but he did have a marvelous talent, namely of playing the role of the philosopher who understands profound things in ways that are beyond the capacity of the ordinary person. He played that role quite elegantly. That's one reason why I think he was so attractive to the people who actually have power. That's just the kind of person they need.

Peter Osborne (review date 11 March 1988)

SOURCE: "Don't Look Away," in *New Statesman*, March 11, 1988, p. 33.

[*In the following review, Osborne discusses Chomsky's political activities and offers positive assessment of* The Chomsky Reader *and* The Culture of Terror.]

There was much concern among American political scientists in the late 1970s about the spread of something they called "Vietnam Syndrome". This was not, as might be supposed, anything to do with the US government's apparently incurable tendency to intervene militarily in the internal affairs of foreign states. Rather, it was a condition taken to be affecting the American people themselves: a morbid aversion to the consequences of just such interventions.

If, despite the tactical adjustment represented by the use of proxies in Central America, this syndrome remains at all widespread (and there is evidence to suggest that it does), it is largely thanks to Noam Chomsky and those like him, who have devoted their time and energy to publicising and documenting the human rights abuses which are so integral a part of US foreign policy. More than anyone else, perhaps, Chomsky has acted as the moral conscience of the American people; holding up a mirror to the acts of government in order to show just what it means to the people of Third World countries for their governments to become the recipients of "humanitarian aid" from the USA.

Chomsky is probably best known in Britain for his work in linguistics. Yet, as the lengthy interview about his intellectual development which prefaces *The Chomsky Reader* reveals, politics and its morality (or, more generally, its lack of it) has always been his main concern. Brought up in the cauldron of Jewish radicalism amongst the East coast immigrant communities of the United States before the war, Chomsky's political roots lie deep in the European anarchist and syndicalist traditions of the 1930s. And it is anarchist themes which continue to dominate his work: the critique of the state and of the complicity of intellectuals in justifying and sustaining its abuses of power; the violence and hypocrisy which underlie the liberal-democratic "consensus"; and, perhaps most important of all, an emphasis on the role of popular-democratic movements in the maintenance and extension of political freedoms.

The pieces collected together to form *The Chomsky Reader* range across the spectrum of Chomsky's political writings: from his essays on the responsibilities of intellectuals from the mid-'60s to excerpts and articles from the '80s on the New Cold War, the Middle East and Central America. A number of things stand out. One is the sheer geographical range of his interests, as he records the grim consequences of America's global role. Another, the thematic unity which nonetheless underlies and structures his depiction of that role. A third is the single-mindedness and moral seriousness with which he pursues his theme: the steady accumulation of evidence, the clarity and directness of the narrative line, the incisive use of historical and cross-cultural comparisons.

The argument—that economic self-interest, pursued by violence abroad and secrecy and deceit at home, lies at the core of American history—is a familiar one. It is in the detail of the demonstration and the disgust at its consequences (exemplified once more in his two recent pieces in the *New Statesman*) that the power of Chomsky's writing lies. Roosevelt's Four Freedoms (freedom of speech, freedom of worship, freedom from want, and freedom from fear), he argues, have in practice always been subordinated to a Fifth: "the freedom to rob, to exploit and dominate, to undertake any course of action to ensure that existing privilege is protected and advanced". It is through a deepening of his sense of the complexity of the processes through which this "Fifth Freedom" is exercised that Chomsky's writings have grown in strength over the years.

The renewed vigour which this gradual deepening of political perspective has imparted to Chomsky's work is displayed at full strength in *The Culture of Terrorism,* the latest in a series of analyses of the current operational state of US policy. The book began life as a postscript to certain foreign editions of *Turning the Tide* (1985). This was subsequently expanded and appears now as what is effectively a companion volume to Chomsky's recent Managua lectures, published in the USA in 1987 as *On Power and Ideology.* Its topic is the twists and turns of policy which have followed the Iran-contra scandal since the autumn of 1986; its theme: the light which this episode throws upon the basic character of American political culture, and upon the possible constraints which may nonetheless be imposed upon the exercise of power within this culture, however indirectly, by popular protest.

In particular, Chomsky is concerned to stress the "not insubstantial achievement" of popular oppositional movements in forcing US state terror underground in the late 1970s. For, he argues, this created the conditions for the foreign policy scandals of the mid-1980s. These have, if only temporarily, both weakened the government's position and given a fresh impulse to the opposition. This, in turn, has created a small "window of opportunity" for regional attempts to secure an alternative basis for the resolution of current conflicts. And what Chomsky maintains is that the "passive compliance" of those who fail actively to oppose the existing system is at base no different, morally, from that of those who chose "to look the other way" during the persecution of Jews in Germany in the '30s.

One may have reservations about the way in which, in certain of his more theoretical pieces, Chomsky seems to over-generalise his critique of American political science to throw doubt upon the usefulness of *any* social scientific approach to human behaviour; or harbour doubts about the moral simplicity of his populism. Yet it is precisely in this simplicity that the distinctiveness of Chomsky's contribution to the political thought of the time lies.

Brian Morton (review date 7 May 1988)

SOURCE: "Chomsky Then and Now," in *The Nation,* May 7, 1988, pp. 646-52.

[*In the following review of* The Chomsky Reader *and* The Culture of Terrorism, *Morton provides an overview of Chomsky's controversial political writings and activities and his largely unfavorable critical reception.*]

If only for the role he played during the Vietnam War, Noam Chomsky should be honored as a national hero. His later work requires delicate assessment . . . but let's begin at the beginning.

The antiwar movement was composed of several different strands. Many young people romanticized the National Liberation Front, cherishing visions of the gentle land Vietnam would become if the United States withdrew. Chomsky gave due weight to the fact that the N.L.F. and not the Saigon government represented Vietnamese nationalism, but he was never its partisan; he stressed that U.S. intervention in Vietnam was wrong in itself. "Just what might emerge from the shattered debris of South Vietnamese society, no one can predict with any confidence," he wrote in 1968. "It is clear, however, that under the American occupation there can be only unending tragedy."

When Chomsky looks back on the 1960s, his main concern is to defend the student movement, and so he speaks of the "notable improvement in the moral and intellectual climate" that it brought about. I think this is the right emphasis, but in putting it this way Chomsky doesn't quite do himself justice: it's easy to forget that he was often a sympathetic critic of the New Left. "We must guard against the kind of revolutionary rhetoric that would have had Karl Marx burn down the British Museum because it was merely part of a repressive society," he wrote in *American Power and the New Mandarins* (1967). "One who pays some attention to history will not be surprised if those who cry most loudly that we must smash and destroy are later found among the administrators of some new system of repression." He listened to the students, learned from them, argued with them.

Another strand of the antiwar movement was composed of the "pragmatic" or "responsible" critics: those who believed that the war was a misguided expression of our country's good intentions, and who turned against it only when they saw that we couldn't win it, or couldn't win it at an acceptable "cost." It was this strand that Chomsky criticized most searchingly, laying bare its misunderstandings with a sober passion. The war owed nothing to benevolent intentions: "As in the Philippines and Latin America, our efforts are directed to organizing . . . the society so as to ensure the domination of those elements that will enter into partnership with us." Nor was the cost of the war an admirable reason to oppose it: Chomsky urged a "recognition that what we have done in Vietnam is wrong, a criminal act." His critique of the war was clearly and unapologetically a moral critique.

Today, despite the best efforts of Ronald Reagan and an army of ideologists, the United States refuses to be cured of the Vietnam syndrome: we've prevented Reagan from savaging Nicaragua as earlier Presidents savaged Vietnam. In part this resistance is "pragmatic": not many objected to the quick and conclusive invasion of Grenada. But in part it's moral: Americans are no longer convinced that our government has the right to destroy any country it wants to. And to the extent that this is true, Chomsky, along with others like him, deserves much of the credit. He did his job well.

In case we were in danger of forgetting any of this, we now have **The Chomsky Reader** to remind us. A sampler of his political writings, the collection vividly illustrates the remarkable moral and intellectual consistency that he's maintained for more than twenty years.

Chomsky has often said that his political writings could have been done by anyone. In a sense this is true. There was nothing exotic about his critique of the U.S. role in Vietnam: He attempted no analysis of arcane economic or political structures. All he did was evaluate our government's actions by the same standards that we apply when we evaluate the actions of other governments.

Chomsky's accomplishment was to disenthrall himself from the delusions of nationalism. This is not to say that he tried to launch his critiques from somewhere in outer space: among the writers he drew on in his protest were Thoreau, Dwight Macdonald and Randolph Bourne. But he began from the premise that the United States "is no more engaged in programs of international good will than any other state has been." A simple enough idea, but one that most of the war's liberal critics could never bring themselves to accept.

Many writers slough off the nationalism they were born into; but most of them smuggle in a different nationalism through the back door. Part of Chomsky's moral authority derives from the fact that he's never done this. When he criticizes the United States for violating international law, we know that he would criticize any country that did the same thing.

I say "we," but this is just to be polite. Some of Chomsky's critics, with a comical inability to understand his point, have assumed that since he's such a severe critic of the United States, he must be some sort of Soviet apologist. This delusion won't survive the briefest glance at his writings.

An essay in **The Chomsky Reader** titled **"Afghanistan and South Vietnam"** makes this clear enough. Chomsky condemns the Soviet war against Afghanistan without reservation, and in exactly the same terms in which he'd condemned the U.S. war against Vietnam. He approvingly quotes from an editorial in *The Economist:* "An invader is an invader unless invited in by a government with a claim to legitimacy." He adds that "the government installed by the USSR to invite them in can hardly make such a claim, outside of the world of Orwellian Newspeak."

From his earliest political writings, Chomsky has been against both sides in the cold war. He views the cold war as an arrangement from which both superpowers benefit. The United States and the Soviet Union, he believes, are united in suppressing any strivings toward independence in less powerful nations. In the case of Nicaragua, for instance, Chomsky believes that the Reagan Administration has pursued a dual strategy. Its maximal goal has been to regain the kind of domination it enjoyed during the Somoza era. Its minimal goal has been to drive Nicaragua into the Soviet camp—to turn the country into the repressive Soviet satellite that Reagan claimed it already was.

There's some evidence for this picture of the cold war. In Seymour Hersh's *The Price of Power,* for instance, a former aide to Henry Kissinger is quoted as saying that Kissinger "saw Allende as being a far more serious threat than Castro. If Latin America ever became unraveled, it would never happen with a Castro. Allende was a living example of democratic social reform."

I do think Chomsky often draws this picture too neatly. Reagan and his men may simply be too stupid to have entertained a strategy as sophisticated as this. E. P. Thompson's view of the cold war is close to Chomsky's, but less mechanical: Thompson has more sense of the strains within and between the blocs. He too says that the superpowers are playing a game that suits them both; but he has more feeling for the danger that at any moment one of the players might sweep away the cards, knock over the table, and lunge for the other's throat.

As Chomsky makes clear in an interview that serves as a sort of introduction to **The Chomsky Reader,** he's been strongly influenced by anarchist thought, and accordingly maintains a healthy disrespect for all nation-states. The only trace of nationalism I can find in his writings is a negative one: He maintains that, as a U.S. citizen, he has a special responsibility to protest the crimes of the United States. He explained his view of the cold war, and of his own responsibilities, in **On Power and Ideology** (South End Press), a collection of lectures he gave in Nicaragua. After one talk, a member of the audience was disturbed that he had referred to Soviet "imperialism." Chomsky commented:

> There are two superpowers, one a huge power which happens to have its boot on your neck, another, a smaller power which happens to have its boot on other people's necks. In fact these two superpowers have a form of tacit cooperation in controlling much of the world.
>
> My own concern is primarily the terror and violence carried out by my own state, for two reasons. For one thing, because it happens to be the larger component of international violence. But also for a much more important reason than that; namely, I can do something about it. So even if the U.S. was responsible for 2 percent of the violence in the world . . . it would be that 2 percent I would be primarily responsible for.
>
> But I am also involved in protesting Soviet imperialism. . . . And I think that anyone in the Third World

would be making a grave error if they succumbed to illusions about these matters.

Chomsky's brand of libertarian socialism has few friends today. But this doesn't explain why he elicits such violent reactions. It's strange, isn't it, that he's never invited to write for *The New York Times* Op-Ed page or its *Book Review,* or for *Harper's,* or *The Atlantic,* or *The Village Voice.* Why is he so isolated?

In the Autumn 1985 issue of *Grand Street,* Christopher Hitchens examined the standard cases against Chomsky. It may be worthwhile to go over them again, both because many people never saw the article and because Hitchens, at some points, was too intent on acting as a counsel for the defense. He would have shown Chomsky more respect by arguing with him more.

One charge can be disposed of quickly. We sometimes hear that Chomsky was an apologist for the Khmer Rouge. His great offense, as it turns out, was to analyze critically the U.S. media's treatment of Cambodia. He never denied that terrible things were happening there: In *The Political Economy of Human Rights,* written with Edward S. Herman, he said that "the record of atrocities in Cambodia is substantial and often gruesome," that the Cambodian revolution was "one of the bloodiest" of the twentieth century, and that "when the facts are in, it may turn out that the more extreme condemnations were in fact correct." But he objected to the way in which ideologists here seized upon the most extreme claims, with no attempt to evaluate them, as a retrospective justification for the Vietnam War.

As Chomsky pointed out, massacres of similar scale were being committed at the same time by Indonesia in its invasion of East Timor. The United States could have used its considerable influence with Indonesia to stop these massacres. But the same editorialists who drew so much attention to Cambodia said almost nothing about East Timor. Cambodia was ideologically serviceable; East Timor was not.

Chomsky's attacks on Western ideologists did have a certain jeering tone, which, given the gravity of the subject, was out of place. *The Chomsky Reader* includes a more recent essay on Cambodia that is free of this tone.

The second complaint against Chomsky is that he defended the "right to lie" of Robert Faurisson, the French Holocaust revisionist. Faurisson, a professor of literature, had come out with an article denying the existence of the gas chambers. He was suspended from his classes—supposedly for his own protection, after he was assaulted by students—and was brought to trial for "falsification of history." Chomsky was asked to sign a petition that called on university and government officials to "ensure [Faurisson's] safety and free exercise of his legal rights," and he did so. The petition contained no endorsement of Faurisson's views. When Chomsky was assailed for having signed the petition, he wrote a short statement, **"Some**

Elementary Comments on the Right of Freedom of Expression," to clarify his reasons. Without Chomsky's consent, the essay was used as a preface for a book Faurisson wrote. Ever since then, Chomsky has been dogged by the charge that he endorsed the ideas of a neo-Nazi.

Chomsky wrote several things during this episode that should make even his admirers uncomfortable. By this I mean that he wrote several things that make *me* uncomfortable. We'll get to them later. The important point is that he's never written anything that can be taken as an endorsement of Faurisson's claims. Never.

His **"Elementary Comments"** essay was a straightforward defense of freedom of speech. Chomsky argued that "it is precisely in the case of horrendous ideas that the right of free expression must be most vigorously defended"—otherwise the right will not survive. In other statements on this question he repeated what he'd written years before: that the Holocaust was "the most fantastic outburst of collective insanity in human history." In an interview with the French newspaper *Lib ration* he clarified his position further, saying that "it is not by silencing [Faurisson] that you prove that his theses are ill-founded. It is by using all the documents, all the testimony of witnesses now at our disposal—and God knows that they are not lacking—in order to produce an irrefutable denial." Clear enough?

Chomsky is immensely productive: I'm reviewing two of his books because he came out with a second one before I could finish writing about the first. I can think of fifteen books he's published on political subjects, and I'm probably forgetting a few. If he did harbor any sneaking agnosticism about the existence of the Holocaust, it would have leaked out somewhere in his work.

No one who has attacked Chomsky on the Faurisson issue has ever tried to support the case with evidence from his other writings. There's a good reason for that—the evidence all goes the other way. Chomsky refers to Nazism often, and he always has; but never in the style of an agnostic. He's always given keen attention to the way governments do violence to language when they seek to mask the violence they do in the world. And when he wants us to see the wickedness of some apparently neutral phrase, he asks us to imagine it in the mouth of a Stalin or a Hitler. This is his standard method. From his earliest writings to his latest, Nazism has served him as a benchmark of pure and unquestionable evil.

Chomsky is a conscientious civil libertarian: He always signs petitions, in support of everybody's right to speak. If he had made an exception of Faurisson, *that* would have been odd. Some people have said that the revival of anti-Semitism in France makes this a special case. Chomsky's reply is that he doesn't think we should fight racism by denying racists their legal civil liberties.

It makes me angry that the ignorant and malicious picture of Chomsky as "soft on Nazism" is so widely believed. It makes me angry that I feel obliged to waste so many words going over it all again. If people want to argue with him, let them argue honestly; I want to argue with him too. But to harp on Faurisson is nothing but a way of avoiding real argument. And, sad to say, it's worked. Chomsky has become one of those people you don't have to read anymore. When his name comes up, sophisticated people smile. Chomsky . . . we all know where *he* ended up, don't we?

If some people cling to a distorted interpretation of the Faurisson affair, this may be because it helps them shrug off Chomsky's views about the Middle East.

"Surely it is obvious," Chomsky once wrote, "that a critical analysis of Israel institutions and practices does not in itself imply antagonism to the people of Israel, denial of the national rights of the Jews in Israel, or lack of concern for their just aspirations and needs. The demand for equal rights for Palestinians does not imply a demand for Arab dominance in the former Palestine, or a denial of Jewish national rights." If he believed this was obvious, he was optimistic. Fifteen years of wild responses to his writings on the Middle East have proved that it isn't obvious at all.

If Chomsky has acquired the reputation of being America's most prominent self-hating Jew, this is because, in the United States, discussion about the Middle East has until recently taken place within very narrow bounds. As Chomsky has often pointed out, many views that are considered at least worthy of discussion in Israel are considered unspeakably extreme here.

The many people who "know" what Chomsky thinks about the Middle East without having read his books might be surprised to learn that he views the conflict between Israel and the Palestinians as a conflict of "right against right"; that he calls for a two-state solution; and that he's repeatedly condemned the violence of the Palestine Liberation Organization as well as that of Israel.

Those who have read Chomsky's books on the Middle East and who thought them too critical of Israel might be surprised if they took another look at them now—now that the Palestinian uprising and the policy of "force, might, beatings" have made the ugliness of the occupation impossible to ignore. What struck some readers as inflamed hyperbole a few years ago seems common sense today.

On an issue as delicate as this, it's better to quote than to paraphrase. This is what he was writing in 1969:

> It is natural to think that security can be achieved only through strength and through the use of force against a threatening opponent. Perhaps so. But those who adopt this course must at least be clear about the likely dynamics of the process to which they are contributing: occupation, resistance, repression, more resistance, more repression, erosion of democracy, internal quandaries and demoralization, further polarization and extremism on both sides, and ultimately—one shrinks

> from the obvious conclusions. It is not evident that security is to be achieved through the use of force.

> Terroristic attacks on civilians simply consolidate Israeli opinion and drive the population into the hands of those who advocate the reliance on force. If this process does succeed in destroying Israeli democracy and turning Israel into a police state, the Palestinian Arabs will have gained very little thereby. Similarly, collective punishment, razing of houses and villages, detention, and exile, surely have the effect of strengthening the hands of those in the Palestinian Arab movement who see the physical destruction of Israeli society as the only solution.

Shocking? Extreme? What's shocking is that this was once considered extreme. Chomsky's great crime was to look at the realities of the occupation when most Americans preferred not to. He once wrote that American "supporters of Israel"—those who believe their support precludes criticism—might better be described as supporters of the moral degeneration of Israel. Was he wrong?

Chomsky has written two books about the Middle East. In *Peace in the Middle East?,* published in 1974, he urged a reconsideration of the old Socialist-Zionist dream of a binational state. By 1983, when he published *The Fateful Triangle,* he was no longer writing of such prospects. Most of the book is about the brutality of Israel's treatment of the Palestinians and the hypocrisy of most U.S. commentary on the Middle East. He criticizes Israel's refusal to negotiate with the P.L.O., which clearly represents the Palestinian people; he contrasts the "halting and sometimes ambiguous steps" that the mainstream of the P.L.O. has taken toward the acceptance of a two-state settlement with Israel's unwavering refusal to consider it; and he gives a long account of Operation Peace for Galilee—the 1982 invasion of Lebanon.

These are both extraordinary books. But if we put them side by side, we begin to sense a change in Chomsky's work, and not a pleasing change. You might say that Chomsky's political writings thus far can be divided into two periods, or two manners, with the break occurring somewhere in the late 1970s. The change is evident in all his writings; but since he's written only two books about the Middle East, one in each of what I call his two periods, the change is easy to spot when we compare them.

The shift I think I sense is that, in Chomsky's later work, we hear less of a humane, less of a human voice. Take a look at chapter one of *Peace in the Middle East?* Chomsky begins by thanking his Arab and Israeli students for their helpful criticisms, adding that "from many conversations with them, I feel that they are much closer to one another, in their fundamental aspirations, than they sometimes realize." Before discussing the problems of the Middle East in general, he talks about his personal reasons for caring about the subject:

> I grew up with a deep interest in the revival of Hebrew culture associated with the settlement of Palestine. I found myself . . . enormously attracted, emotionally and intellectually, by what I saw as a dramatic effort to

create, out of the wreckage of European civilization, some form of libertarian socialism in the Middle East. My sympathies were with those opposed to a Jewish state and concerned with Arab-Jewish cooperation, those who saw the primary issue not as a conflict of Arab and Jewish rights, but in very different terms: as a conflict between a potentially free, collective form of social organization as embodied in the Kibbutz and other socialist institutions on the one hand, and, on the other, the autocratic forms of modern social organization, either capitalist or state capitalist, or state socialist on the Soviet model. . . . I mention all of this to make clear that I inevitably view the continuing conflict from a very specific point of view. . . . Perhaps this personal history distorts my perspective. In any event, it should be understood by the reader.

Disavowing any claims to expertise, Chomsky also disavows any belief that Americans can solve the problems of the Middle East. But he says that "it is conceivable that Americans might make some contribution to the passive search for peace, by providing channels of communication, by broadening the scope of discussion and exploring basic issues in ways that are not easily open to those who see their lives as immediately threatened."

I find these passages beautiful. This earlier book, and his early work in general, seems the work of a man deeply patient, deeply reasonable, deeply humane. It's suffused with a luminous moral intelligence.

By the time he wrote *The Fateful Triangle,* his way of expressing himself had coarsened. This is from the second page of that book:

> Clearly, as long as the United States provides the wherewithal, Israel will use it for its purposes. These purposes are clear enough today, and have been clear to those who chose to understand for many years: to integrate the bulk of the occupied territories within Israel in some fashion while finding a way to reduce the Arab population; to disperse the scattered refugees and crush any manifestation of Palestinian nationalism or Palestinian culture; to gain control over southern Lebanon. Since these goals have long been obvious and have been shared in fundamental respects by the two major political groupings in Israel, there is little basis for condemning Israel when it exploits the position of regional power afforded it by the phenomenal quantities of U.S. aid in exactly the ways that would be anticipated by any person whose head is not buried in the sand.

The dominant feeling of the later book, as I read it, is anger. It's an admirable anger—he's angry about militarism and racism cloaking themselves in high morality—but I miss the gentleness that once accompanied the anger. Chomsky continues to say that the struggle between Israelis and Palestinians is a struggle of right against right: that hasn't changed. But the music is different. In his early work he wrote understandingly of the fears that keep each side from seeing the justice of the other's claims. He tried to be a peacemaker. He isn't trying to be that anymore.

In *Peace in the Middle East?* he writes that the Jewish "policy of *Havlagah*—restraint—in the late 1930s was not

only a moral achievement of the highest order, but was also, it seems, reasonably effective as a tactic. There were groups in the Jewish settlement that did believe in the resort to terror. . . . [but] tensions between these groups and the Socialist-Zionist settlers 'erupted in a miniature Jewish civil war early in the 1940s.'" In *The Fateful Triangle* he writes of the history and prehistory of the Jewish state almost as if it consisted of nothing *but* terror. He wrote the book just after the invasion of Lebanon, and he was exasperated by the widely held fiction (held less widely now) that Israel is uniquely gentle, even in war. He tells an important part of the story—the part that's traditionally been neglected or suppressed. But he tells it as if that's all there is to the story.

In Chomsky's early work, he was often careful to stress that he was offering opinions on subjects about which reasonable people might differ. The best example is **"Objectivity and Liberal Scholarship,"** a 1968 essay included in *The Chomsky Reader.* Here he subjects the work of the historian Gabriel Jackson to a stringent critique, but keeps reminding the reader that Jackson's work is "outstanding," "of very high caliber." I can find no comparable example of charity toward an intellectual opponent in his later work. He now seems to believe that the people he criticizes fall into one of two classes: liars or dupes. He's grown fond of phrases like "no rational person would deny," "no sane person could fail to see"—there are one or two of them in the passage I quoted from *The Fateful Triangle.* Even when he uses such phrases to introduce a claim that no rational person *would* deny, I still find it chilling. His fondness for such phrases sits uneasily with his libertarianism—there's a whiff of authoritarianism about them. I don't say that Chomsky has abandoned his libertarian beliefs; only that they're no longer so fully evident. They were once present even in his style. I don't think this is so anymore.

Chomsky's prose style was once measured, calm: it was a style that evidenced a faith in reason. From his current style, I get the impression that he continues to expose the reigning lies only because it's the moral thing to do, not because he expects to accomplish anything. Chomsky wouldn't *say* he believes this, for he always reminds his readers of the power of popular resistance. And yet his style exudes despair. In the old work as in the new, he criticizes the conformity of U.S. intellectuals. But look at his early essay **"The Responsibility of Intellectuals,"** and then look through *The Culture of Terrorism.* In the early piece, he refers to "a real or feigned naiveté with regard to American actions," to a "failure of skepticism," to "the intellectual attitudes that lie in the background of the latest savagery." He criticizes the intellectuals as a class, yes, but it's clear that the class is composed of human beings: The phrases I've quoted imply a world of human agency, a world in which people can sometimes be persuaded by reasonable arguments. When he speaks about conformity in his recent work, it's in a different voice. The Iran/*contra* scandal "imposed new demands for the ideological system, which must control the domestic damage and ensure that it is confined within narrow and politically meaningless bounds"; "furthermore, similar situations are bound to arise in the future, and historical engineering must ensure, without delay, that the proper arsenal of lessons will be available, to be deployed when needed." It's no longer human beings who put forth misleading ideas: it's "the ideological system," the "doctrinal system" or "historical engineering." Chomsky has become more structuralist. His later tone is that of a man who doesn't expect anything to change.

When I think of Chomsky's recent work, I think of Yeats's lines about Jonathan Swift: "Savage indignation . . . lacerate[s] his breast." Chomsky is savagely indignant because the values he cherishes are being strangled. But increasingly, the reasons for his indignation—the values he cherishes—are hard to see in his work. Only the indignation is clear.

One reason the Faurisson business has continued to dog him is that his exasperation led him to express himself in a way that invited misunderstandings. In the last paragraph of the **"Elementary Comments,"** he abruptly swerves away from the narrow and admirable defense of free speech to which he'd devoted the rest of the essay. "Putting this central issue aside," he writes, "is it true that Faurisson is an anti-Semite or a neo-Nazi? As noted earlier, I do not know his work very well. But from what I have read—largely as a result of the nature of the attacks on him—I find no evidence to support either conclusion. . . . As far as I can determine, he is a relatively apolitical liberal of some sort."

This is strange. How can he absolve Faurisson of the charge of anti-Semitism if he doesn't know his work very well? And even if he knew Faurisson's work by heart, wouldn't he have to be morally tone-deaf to brush aside the question of anti-Semitism so brusquely? Responding to critics on this point, Chomsky has explained that Faurisson has said that those who resisted the Nazis fought in the "right cause." It's conceivable, perhaps, that one can deny the existence of the gas chambers without being an anti-Semite. But if Chomsky thought this a point worth making, he should have argued it through, sensitively and patiently and clearly. Instead, he made a high-handed assertion, and left it at that.

Earlier in the **"Elementary Comments"** he refers to a critic's remark that the original petition supporting Faurisson's right to expression was "scandalous." Chomsky writes that this critic evidently misunderstood the petition's reference to Faurisson's "findings": "It is, of course, obvious that if I say that someone presented his 'findings' I imply nothing whatsoever about their character or validity; the statement is perfectly neutral in this respect." But in fact, the word is ambiguous: It can mean opinions, or it can mean discoveries. Chomsky must know this: I take it that the author of **The Logical Structure of Linguistic Theory** has a dictionary. Why couldn't he have acknowledged that the word is ambiguous? What would it have

cost him to acknowledge that the petition should have been worded more precisely? The basic issue remains the same: Chomsky can be justly proud of his support for free expression. But why can't he admit that, about this one word, he was really, just a little bit, *wrong?*

Replying to another critic, Chomsky said that he had often spoken "in support of the right of people I regard as war criminals to teach or even to conduct counterinsurgency research, at a time when it was being used to murder and destroy." This is true: Anyone who looks at David Caute's new book on 1968, *The Year of the Barricades,* will see that Chomsky consistently defended the rights of men he must have hated. He adds, "Since these stands evoked no protest, it follows that the uproar over my defense of Faurisson's rights is an exercise in hypocrisy, pure and simple."

Well, no. It *would* follow, if people were moved solely by logic. But they aren't; and it doesn't follow at all. I have no doubt that many people keep this thing alive dishonestly, because it delights them to discredit Chomsky in any cheap way they can. But there are many people who don't have the time to sift through every exchange between Chomsky and his critics, and who, reading phrases from him like "apolitical liberal," have thought the case closed. They judge too quickly, but it's easy to understand why they do. A fair-minded person who studied the matter would conclude that Chomsky is innocent of having endorsed Faurisson's views. But I suspect this person would conclude that Chomsky was innocent of sensitivity as well.

In the 1960s, Chomsky was widely respected. His articles on the war appeared in *The New York Review of Books;* Norman Mailer referred to the "tightly packed conceptual coils of Chomsky's intellections"; "his name," as Hitchens puts it, "had a kind of cachet." Around the mid-1970s this changed. *The New York Review* quietly dropped him; other liberal magazines followed suit. Perhaps his radicalism no longer appealed to them after the end of the war; perhaps they objected to his views on the Middle East, Cambodia and Faurisson gave the final turn to the screw. Chomsky is now treated with a weird mixture of neglect and abuse. His books are seldom even reviewed—he's not important enough for that, you see—but just about every journal in the country finds space to drop snide misrepresentations of what he's written about Cambodia, the Holocaust, Israel or anything else.

It's this, I think, that's put the bile in his voice. As he's been forced to the margins, he's become strident, rigid. But even if this does account for the change in his manner, it doesn't justify it.

The problems of Chomsky's later work are similar to the problems of the later work of Karl Marx—a writer whom Chomsky resembles a bit, in his searing logical rigor and his surgical sarcasm. Ignorant critics of Marx like to argue that his thought led in a straight line to Stalinism. It's a stupid idea, but I've often wished it were more *obviously* stupid.

After his beautiful philosophical work of the 1840s, Marx turned away from the language of morality. He grew so disgusted with the hypocrisies of bourgeois morality that he began to style himself an antimoralist, delighting in reductive demonstrations that moral claims were nothing more than masks for economic interests. Bending to a Darwinist age, he began to write as if socialism were an inevitability rather than a future that men and women might choose. He began to write in a less human voice. If you want to spend a month or so in the library you can come up with a strong case that Marx remained a humanist, remained an advocate of freedom to the end. But I've often wished that his voice were so humane, so generous, that this would be obvious to anyone who glanced at his work.

I wish the same of Chomsky. He's taken on too much of the harshness of the world he struggles against. I'd like to see him bring back into his work some of the gentleness, the generosity, of the world he envisions.

I look over what I've written, and I think it's right. But I'm hesitant about it all the same. I don't like the thought that my criticisms might be read with satisfaction by the people who enjoy misrepresenting Chomsky. So perhaps I should say explicitly that I take the trouble to argue with him only because I think he's the most valuable critic of American power that we have.

In *American Power and the New Mandarins,* Chomsky's first book of political essays, he gave us his responses to an unusual display in Chicago's Museum of Science and Industry. "What can one say about a country where a museum of science in a great city can feature an exhibit in which people fire machine guns from a helicopter at Vietnamese huts, with a light flashing when a hit is scored? What can one say about a country where such an idea can even be considered? You have to weep for this country."

From his earliest writings to his latest, Chomsky has looked with astonishment at what the powerful do to the powerless. He has never let his sense of outrage become dulled. If his voice has grown hoarse over twenty years, who can blame him? And who can feel superior? No one has given himself more deeply to the struggle against the horrors of our time. His hoarseness is a better thing than our suavity. I think again of Yeats's lines on Swift: "Imitate him if you dare . . . he / Served human liberty."

Edward P. Stabler, Jr. (review date September 1989)

SOURCE: A review of *Knowledge of Language* and *Language and Problems of Knowledge,* in *Philosophy of Science,* Vol. 56, No. 3, September, 1989, pp. 533-36.

[*In the following review, Stabler provides favorable assessment and summary of Chomsky's* Knowledge of Language *and* Language and Problems of Knowledge.]

Noam Chomsky has recently produced two more books about language for a general audience. (Earlier works of a similar character include *Cartesian Linguistics* (1966); *Language and Mind* (1968); *Problems of Knowledge and Freedom* (1971); *Reflections on Language* (1975); *Language and Responsibility* (1977); and *Rules and Representations* (1980).) They are both informal explorations of a wide range of issues relating to language and knowledge, refreshingly free of the academic parochialism that results from disciplinary inbreeding. Each covers new empirical ground, offering suggestions about how this material ought to be incorporated into the growing tradition of theoretical linguistics, and each offers some commentary on recent psychological and philosophical debates. Though the overarching perspectives of the two books are of course similar, they cover different material, and at different levels of sophistication—*Knowledge of Language* is the more demanding of the two. Either book could serve well as a language-oriented introduction to what is now called "cognitive science". And although Chomsky's general orientation is familiar to those who know his earlier works, new empirical observations and stimulating new suggestions make each of these new works pleasant and valuable reading. Since this review is to be brief, I will just outline some of the main points discussed in each book, attempting to note especially the new and most significant material.

Knowledge of Language begins with an informal characterization of "Plato's problem": "the problem of explaining how we can know so much given so little evidence". The problem is illustrated with a variety of examples of what a competent speaker of English must know. The examples are motivated by current work in theoretical linguistics, but the discussion (with the exception of a technical section mentioned below) is readily intelligible to the general reader. The general conclusions about what a learner must bring to the learning situation, presumably on the basis of an innate endowment, are surprising enough to inspire in a novice an interest in getting a more sophisticated grasp of the theoretical background. This is exactly the effect that a good introduction should have!

In the second chapter of *Knowledge of Language.* Chomsky describes a shift in perspective on linguistic theory. Whereas it has sometimes been regarded as the abstract study of the sets of grammatical strings of a language, an "external" language or "E-language", Chomsky urges persuasively that it is better regarded as the study of a speaker's "internal" knowledge of language, of "I-language". It is interesting to note in this context that Chomsky's recent technical work, such as *Barriers* (Cambridge, Massachusetts: MIT Press, 1986), relies primarily on *relative* grammaticality judgments rather than on simple yes or no judgments about whether a sentence is well-formed. And he has explicitly defined principles, such as "*n*-subjacency", which admit of more and less serious violations (in this case, depending on the value of *n* and certain other factors). So, for example, we have in the following three sentences one that is perfectly grammatical, one that is not good, and one that is very much worse:

What do you wonder about?

*What do you wonder how John fixed?

* Who do you wonder how fixed the car?

The severe ungrammaticality of the last example is explained by showing that it violates a certain principle of grammar, a principle that is not violated by the second example, which has only a weak I-subjacency violation. The first example violates no principles. So, from this perspective, the knowledge of language can be regarded as providing principles that indicate the level of grammaticality of a structure, and the idea that linguists study only a fixed and determinate set of perfectly grammatical strings is obviously inappropriate. In any case, on the view that linguists should be seen as studying I-language, linguistics is clearly a subdiscipline of psychology, and so it is appropriate for Chomsky to consider the psychological question of how a speaker's knowledge of language could be acquired, as well as such things as the relation of these matters to neurophysiology, as he does here.

A substantial shift in the approach of recent linguistic theory is described in some detail in the third chapter of **Knowledge of Language:** the shift from rule systems to principles. This important development has altered quite radically the character of linguistic theory. Chomsky here explains how the shift can be seen as a step towards a solution of the language acquisition problem, allowing us to identify specific parameters of variation in a much larger set of universal principles that apply to all possible human languages. Parts of this chapter will be difficult for the general reader, but these parts contain a number of points of interest for the linguist. Among other things, it is proposed that a constituent is "visible" to receive a theta-role only if it has case; that all theta-governed positions that receive theta-roles are filled at D-structure; that case is transferred to all elements of a chain and also by expletive-argument relations; and that structural case (nominative, objective) is assigned at S-structure, while inherent case (oblique, genitive) is realized at D-structure. Chomsky has not presented these views elsewhere, though some of them foreshadow the work in **Barriers.**

Chomsky devotes the fourth chapter of **Knowledge of Language** to critiques of alternative views. He considers at some length Saul Kripke's suggestion that the proposed conception of "knowledge of language" is undermined by Wittgensteinian considerations. Kripke argues that "If one person is considered in isolation, the notion of a rule as guiding a person can have *no* substantive content" (Saul Kripke, *Wittgenstein on Rules and Private Language.* Oxford: Basil Blackwell, 1983, p. 89). One of the ways Kripke defends this point is to claim that, apart from the intentions of the designer, there is no fact of the matter about what program a computing machine is following, because there could be no basis for distinguishing certain behaviour as a "malfunction". Chomsky responds by arguing that this distinction can be drawn by "a more general account of the properties of the mind/brain, an account

that defines 'malfunction' and 'intrusion of extraneous factors,' and is answerable to a wide range of empirical evidence" (p. 238). Unfortunately, he does not explain what sort of evidence could justify any particular definition of "malfunction", and so some doubts may yet lurk in the philosophical reader.

Chomsky considers other critics of his approach more briefly. He agrees with Dennett that rule systems might be only "tacitly represented", as the rules of addition are in a hand-calculator, but suggests that the best theories do not have this character: "Such possibilities cannot be ruled out *a priori*. The question is one of the best theory . . . objections of this nature . . . are beside the point" (p. 245). Chomsky rejects Quine's view that extensionally equivalent grammars cannot be empirically distinguished as representations of human linguistic competence unless they can be associated with distinct behavioural dispositions. He finds similar doubts about the legitimacy of attributing knowledge of language in Davidson, Dummett, and Searle. He says:

> The argument at issue has two steps: The first step involves the tentative conclusion that the statements of the best theory of the language are true; the second, that the elements (rules, etc.) invoked to explain . . . behavior in the best theory we can construct in fact guide . . . behavior. (p. 249)

Chomsky argues that the first step by its very nature involves distinguishing "extensionally equivalent" rule systems. The second step should be a trivial matter: "I cannot see that anything is involved in attributing causal efficacy to rules beyond the claim that these rules are constituent elements of the states postulated in an explanatory theory of behavior and enter into our best account of this behavior" (p. 253). At this point, though, Chomsky does not consider the structure of the linguistic theory that explains our behavior in any detail. It is instructive to recall that earlier in the book he notes that the theory of how knowledge of language is put to use "breaks into two parts: a 'perception problem' and a 'production problem'" (p. 25). He says, "The perception problem would be dealt with by construction of a parser that incorporates the rules of the I-language along with other elements: a certain organization of memory and access (perhaps a deterministic pushdown structure with a buffer of a certain size: see Marcus, 1980), certain heuristics, and so forth" (p. 25). If Marcus's work is to be taken as an example of the "incorporation" of the grammar that Chomsky envisions, then the relation between the grammar and the theories of linguistic performance will be quite remote—nearly as remote as the relation between rules for addition and the performance of the hand calculator. This is a familiar point, one that is surely familiar to Chomsky, so it is surprising that it is neglected here. The other aspect of language use, the production of linguistic behavior, is, Chomsky says, "considerably more obscure" (p. 25).

The fifth and final chapter of **Knowledge of Language** briefly notes that there seem to be domains unlike language in which knowledge acquisition seems to be a very difficult and precarious matter. Chomsky calls this "Orwell's problem," and uses political and historical knowledge as his example.

The second book under review here, *Language and Problems of Knowledge,* is based on lectures given in Managua, Nicaragua in 1986. It provides a more basic and informal introduction to Chomsky's views on language than *Knowledge of Language.* Again, Plato's problem is introduced, but this time it is illustrated with examples from Spanish, and considerable attention is devoted to differences between Spanish and English and other languages. In this light, Chomsky is able to show rather clearly how the different aspects of the languages are sorted into those that must be learned and those that speakers do not learn but must bring to the learning environment. He uses examples from sound structure and semantics to illustrate that the presumption of an extensive unlearned competence is not peculiar to syntax, but seems to be essential in every case where we have very much evidence about uniformities in the acquisition of a body of knowledge. He uses the relation between declarative sentences and corresponding interrogatives to illustrate the surprising structure-dependence of linguistic principles, and uses this, in turn, to illustrate the importance of Plato's problem. He then considers "Descartes' problem": "the problem of how language is used in the normal creative fashion" (p. 138). Here Chomsky takes the rather surprising line that the normal use of language is essentially non-deterministic. In other words, Descartes was right in thinking that we must be fundamentally different from, for example, computers that mimic human language performance, because a machine's performance is deterministic, compelled by its internal state and environment, whereas, in our language use, it is obvious that we are only "incited or inclined" by our state and environment. Chomsky says:

> The human may often, or even always, do what it is inclined to do, but each of us knows from introspection that we have a choice in the matter over a large range. And we can determine by experiment that this is true of other humans as well. (p. 139)

Chomsky does not say what experiments would demonstrate the freedom of human action in a universe where the gross behavior of other large objects (like computers) is determined, and one might well wonder what he has in mind here. Chomsky goes on to consider the Cartesian proposal that the mind must be distinct from any physical object, but argues that we no longer have a coherent notion of physical object that allows us to formulate such a view, or any other interesting "mind/body" thesis. He suggests that Descartes' problem may simply be beyond the range of human intellectual capacities.

A good deal of *Language and Problems of Knowledge* is devoted to developing the basics of Spanish grammar in Chomsky's framework. Chomsky presents an argument for the view that simple Spanish sentences, like sentences of English and every other language, have (at some level of representation) an Aristotelian subject-predicate structure. The predicate contains the object in such a structure, so there is a subject-object asymmetry unlike, for example, the symmetry in binary atomic predications of standard first-order logics. A number of other universals are introduced informally and illustrated: binding principles, X-bar principles, the option of movement, the projection principle, and case theory. The treatment of the Spanish clitics in this framework is of particular interest. Examples of specific parameters of linguistic variation are also presented: the null subject parameter which distinguishes, for example, most Romance languages like Spanish and Italian from French; and the head-first paramater which distinguishes, for example, Spanish and Miskito.

Noam Chomsky with Rick Szykowny (interview date November-December 1990)

SOURCE: "Bewildering the Herd," in *The Humanist,* Vol. 50, No. 6, November-December, 1990, pp. 8-17.

[*In the following interview, Chomsky discusses contemporary world affairs, including U.S.-Iraq tensions shortly before the Gulf War, and the negative influence of the American mass media as a force of institutional propaganda and political misrepresentation.*]

Reading the mainstream media, you'd never know that, for over 20 years, Noam Chomsky has been considered by many to be the most important political thinker in the United States. He is the author of *American Power and the New Mandarins, Towards a New Cold War, On Power and Ideology, The Culture of Terrorism,* and *Necessary Illusions,* to name but a few, and coauthor (with Edward S. Herman) of *The Political Economy of Human Rights* and *Manufacturing Consent.* Taken together, these works present an extraordinary critique of state and corporate power in the United States—particularly its influence on the media and American foreign policy. For his troubles, Chomsky has been virtually exiled from the media mainstream, as well as repeatedly vilified.

In 1939, while attending an experimental Deweyite school in his hometown of Philadelphia, Noam Chomsky published his first article: an editorial in the student newspaper on the fall of Barcelona during the Spanish Civil War. It was a few weeks after his tenth birthday.

By the time he was 30, Chomsky had already revolutionized the fields of linguistics and cognitive science with his theories of "transformational" or "generative" grammar and language acquisition. By the time he was 40, he had become one of this nation's most forceful and articulate opponents of the Vietnam War, which in turn led to his decades-long commitment to political and social activism. It was around this time that Chomsky published his celebrated essay, **"The Responsibility of Intellectuals,"** in the *New York Review of Books,* which read in part:

It is the responsibility of intellectuals to speak the truth and expose lies. Intellectuals are in a position to expose the lies of government, to analyze actions according to their causes and motives and often hidden intentions. In the Western world at least, they have the power that comes from political liberty, from access to information, and from freedom of expression. For a privileged minority, Western democracy provides the leisure, the facilities, and the training to seek the truth lying hidden behind the veil of distortion and misrepresentation, ideology, and class interest through which the events of current history are presented to us.

In 1988, just short of his sixtieth birthday, the Inamori Foundation announced that Chomsky had won the Kyoto Prize (often called the Japanese version of the Nobel Prize) in the basic sciences. *The Humanist* talked to Noam Chomsky on September 7, 1990.

[The Humanist:]: You take the average American who gets his or her information on the world at large from, say, the network news, from wire service reports in the daily newspaper, and maybe—if he or she is feeling especially dutiful—from CNN or "Nightline." How good a picture do they actually have of what's really happening in the world?

[Chomsky]: They get a good picture of how the state-corporate nexus in the United States would like to *depict* the things that are happening in the world . . . and occasionally more than that.

Occasionally more than that?

Yeah. But not most of the time. Most of the time the press is very disciplined.

Well, in short, what I'm asking is how well served are Americans by the mainstream media?

If you follow the mainstream media with great care and skepticism and approach it with the right understanding of how propaganda works, then you can learn a lot. The normal viewer or reader gets fed a propaganda line.

You've frequently stated that the Western media constitute the most awesome propaganda system that has ever existed in world history. But at the same time, the press tries to cultivate a mythology or popular image of itself as tireless, fearless seekers after the truth. You have them taking on the politicians, such as Dan Rather challenging George Bush on the air, or even toppling them from office, as Woodward and Bernstein allegedly did with Nixon. That's the public image of the media, and I think many people are going to be surprised to hear that they are being fed a line of propaganda.

Well, I doubt that many people would. Most polls indicate that the majority of the population regards the media as too subservient to power. But it's quite true that for educated people it would come as a surprise. And that's because they are the ones most subject to propaganda. They also participate in the indoctrination, so therefore they're the most committed to the system. You mentioned

that the media cultivate an image of a tribune of the people fighting power. Well, that's natural. How would a reasonable propaganda institution depict itself? But in order to determine the truth of the matter, you have to look at the particular cases. I think it is one of the best established conclusions in the social sciences that the media serve what we may call a propaganda function—that is, that they shape perceptions, select the events, offer interpretations, and so on, in conformity with the needs of the power centers in society, which are basically the state and the corporate world.

So, in other words, an adversarial press doesn't really exist in this country.

It exists out on the margins, and *occasionally* you'll find something in the mainstream. I mean, for example, there are cases where the press has stood up against a segment of power. In fact, the one you mentioned—Woodward and Bernstein helped topple a president—is the example that the media and everyone else constantly uses to show that the press is adversarial.

But there are very serious problems with that case that have been pointed out over and over again. In fact, what the example actually shows is the subordination of the media to power. And you can see that very clearly as soon as you take a look at the Watergate affair. What was the charge against Richard Nixon, after all? The charge against Nixon was that he attacked people with power—he sent a gang of petty criminals for some still unknown purpose to burglarize the Democratic party headquarters. Well, you know, the Democratic party represents essentially half of the corporate system. It's one of the two factions of the business party which runs the country. And that is real power. You don't attack real power, because people in power can defend themselves. We can easily demonstrate that that's exactly what was involved; in fact, history was kind enough to set up a controlled experiment for us. At the very moment of the Watergate exposures, there was also another set of exposures: namely, the FBI COINTELPRO operations which were exposed using the Freedom of Information Act right at the same time. Those were infinitely more serious than the Watergate caper. Those were actions not by a group of crooks mobilized by the president or a presidential committee but by the *national political police*. And it was not just Richard Nixon; it ran over a series of administrations. The exposures began with the Kennedy administration—in fact earlier, but primarily with the Kennedy administration—and ran right through the Nixon administration. What was exposed was extremely serious—far worse than anything in Watergate. For example, it included political assassination, instigation of ghetto riots, a long series of burglaries and harassment against a legal political party—namely, the Socialist Workers Party, which, unlike the Democratic party, is not powerful and did not have the capacity to defend itself. That aspect of COINTELPRO alone, which is just a tiny footnote to its operations, is far more important than Watergate.

So what we can look at is how the media responded to these two exposures: one, the relatively minor crookedness of the Watergate caper; and, two, a major government program of harassment, violence, assassination, attacks on legal political parties, and efforts to undermine popular organizations over a long period. The Watergate affair became a major issue, shaking the foundations of the republic. The COINTELPRO exposures are known only to a handful of people; the press wasn't interested in it. And that tells you exactly what was involved in Watergate: people with power can defend themselves, and the media will support people with power. Nothing else is involved.

Well, that's interesting, because you have the media reinforcing a false picture of what was going on then. I mean, they did not—

What I just said is virtually a truism. Here is something close to a controlled experiment. Two exposures at exactly the same time: one, an exposure of a very minor attack on people with power; the other, the exposure of a very major attack over a long period of time—with all sorts of ramifications—against a large part of the population, including political parties, without power. And how did the media respond to these two cases? Well, basically, they cared nothing about the major attack on the people without power, and they made a huge fuss about the minor attack on the people with power. So, what does a rational person conclude from this? Well, a rational person concludes from this example—which illustrates it rather dramatically—that the media serve power.

Well, I think it's especially pernicious, since Watergate was then touted as an example of the system working.

That shows how beautifully the propaganda system operates. It takes an example which proves its subordination to power and turns it into a demonstration of its adversarial role. That's brilliant.

You've made the continual argument that the function of the media is actually to obscure *what's happening in the world.*

To obscure . . . it's more complex than that. I mean, the media, after all, have a complex role. In fact, you can't put the media into a single category. First of all, let's make a rough distinction. On the one hand, there are the mass popular media—that includes everything from sports and sitcoms to network news and so forth—and their task is basically to divert the population, to make sure they don't get any funny ideas in their heads about participating in the shaping of public policy. On the other hand, there are the "elite" media, which are directed to what is sometimes called the "political class": the more educated, wealthy, articulate part of the population, the "managers"—cultural managers, political managers, economic managers. I'm talking here about the *New York Times* and the *Washington Post*—at least their front sections. Now, those media have a somewhat more complicated task. They

have to instill proper attitudes that serve as a mechanism of indoctrination in the interests of power. But they also have to present a *tolerably* realistic picture of the world, since, after all, their targets are the people actually making decisions, and those people better have a grasp of reality if the role they play is actually going to benefit those who wield power.

But you mean a specific *kind of reality—*

Well, you have to have some grasp of the real world, otherwise you get into trouble. So, take an investment banker or a state manager—someone involved in government—if those people don't have some grasp of reality, they're going to make moves which will be very harmful to the people who really pull the levers. So, therefore, they better have some grasp of reality. But that has to be shaped in the interests of power, and that's a delicate task. Universities have the same problem.

These are all the things you refer to as the ideological professions. *But their version of reality is not necessarily my or your version of reality.*

No, in fact, it's often quite different. And that's what you find in any system of power—the totalitarian state, the democratic state, and so on. In fact, it's just entirely natural that, where you have institutions with a degree of centralized power, they're going to use that power in their own interests. I don't think there's an exception to that in history. Now, we happen to live in a system with a very high degree of centralized power—primarily in the corporate world, which has enormous influences over all other institutions, including government and obviously the media; in fact, the media are major corporations. They have a point of view and shared interests and concerns—of course, there's some diversity within them—and naturally they are going to try to ensure that everything in their political, cultural, and ideological realm is going to be influenced to satisfy their needs. It would be astonishing if that were not true, and the evidence is overwhelming that it is true.

There have been a number of people, such as W. Lance Bennett in his book News: The Politics of Illusion, *who have argued that the American people were somewhat better served by the media in the early days of the republic, when the press consisted of numerous small journals and newspapers, all with what would today be considered their own bias or partisan position or political axe to grind. What do you make of the deification or cult of objectivity that characterizes mainstream news reporting today?*

Well, first of all, I think you want to be very careful about comparing different historical eras; it's a tricky question. It's certainly true that there was a lot more diversity in earlier years; you don't have to go back very far to find a lot of diversity.

On the other hand, it was also highly skewed toward power. For example, let's take the American Revolution.

The position of noted American libertarians, such as Thomas Jefferson and the founding fathers, was that there should be no tolerance at all for positions antagonistic to their own. The range of debate and discussion that was permitted in Nicaragua in the last 10 years while the country was under foreign attack was incomparably greater than anything Jefferson would have allowed—or that the United States has allowed under far less threatening circumstances.

As for the cult of objectivity, here, too, we have to be careful. Surely the media describe themselves as deeply committed to objectivity, but what propaganda institution would not make that claim? A serious person would want to ask if that were true. And the answer is that it's not true—it's very far from true.

A related question then is why do the media continually concentrate on the individual personalities involved in the issues rather than the institutional actors, which is something you yourself scrupulously avoid. For example, in the Iran-contra scandal, the media pretty willingly acquiesced to Reagan's efforts to make Oliver North and John Poindexter the fall guys.

Well, they also concentrated on Reagan himself. Remember, the big question was: did Reagan know—or did he remember—what the policies of his administration were? The reason the media concentrate on these matters is that they're irrelevant. And insignificant. What they obscure is the institutional factors that, in fact, determine policy. And in the Iran-contra affair, it was rather striking to see the way major issues were almost completely obscured. So, let's just take one of the obvious questions: you asked why they do that. Well, that's just in the service of their propaganda function. One of the main purposes of any ideological system is to divert attention away from the actual workings of power and to focus on marginal phenomena. Individuals can be replaced, and then these institutions can continue to function as they do. So, if you take a look at the Iran-contra thing, once again there are perfectly obvious questions that were never asked, which takes remarkable discipline.

For example, the Iran-contra affair focused on what had happened since the mid-1980s—from 1985, 1986 on—with regard to the U.S. sale of arms to Iran. Well, an obvious question arises: namely, what was going on before 1985? And there's an answer to this. Before 1985, the United States was authorizing the sale of arms to Iran via Israel—exactly as it was doing *after* 1985. Now at that time, remember, there were no hostages. So what's going on? If the whole operation was supposed to be an arms-for-hostages deal, how come we were doing exactly the same thing before there were any hostages?

Well, that's another obvious question, and there's an answer to that one, too. It's not a secret; for example, I was writing about it in 1982 and 1983. And the answer is that the United States was authorizing arms sales to Iran

via Israel in an effort to find elements within the Iranian military with whom they could establish contacts and who might be able to carry out a military coup to overthrow Khomeini. That was frankly, openly, and publicly admitted by top Israeli officials, including people high in the Mossad and others. And all the people who were later exposed in the Iran-contra affair were speaking quite publicly about this in the early 1980s. One of them, Uri Lubrani, said that, if we can find somebody in the military who is willing and able to shoot down 10,000 people in the street, we'll be able to restore the kind of regime we want, basically meaning the Shah. That's standard policy whenever there's hostility to some government: cut off aid to that government but arm the military in the hopes that elements within the military will carry out a coup. That was done in Chile, Indonesia—in fact, that's just normal. And it was being done in Iran in the early 1980s.

So, was there any discussion of this in the Iran-contra hearings? No, because, even though the question "What was happening *before* 1985?" was so obvious that it could hardly fail to come to the mind of anybody looking at the issues, the trouble is, if you ask it, you get the wrong answers. Better not to ask it. Therefore, this became one of many aspects of the Iran-contra affair that were effaced in what was, in fact, a coverup operation by Congress and the media.

I think it's kind of interesting to note in your discussions of American government that when you do refer to the government you almost invariably mean the executive. Do you consider Congress a confederacy of political eunuchs?

Well, I do discuss Congress to some extent, but it doesn't vary very much. I mean, there's a little diversity in Congress. If you get down to the House of Representatives, you'll find a scattering of people who will raise hard questions, such as Henry Gonzalez of Texas or Ted Weiss of New York or Ron Dellums and various people in the Black Caucus. I mean, there's a scattering of people who raise questions that barely make it to the media. But, by and large, Congress is very much constrained within the same very narrow elite consensus.

Well, do you feel also . . . I mean, I know that you have advanced these arguments and a number of other people have also advanced these arguments—they are there to be found by anyone who wants to seek them out. . . . But at the same time, I think there's a great effort in the mainstream media to write these arguments off as conspiracy theory.

That's one of the devices by which power defends itself—by calling any critical analysis of institutions a conspiracy theory. If you call it by that name, then somehow you don't have to pay attention to it. Edward Herman and I, in our recent book, ***Manufacturing Consent,*** go into this ploy. What we discuss in that book is simply the institutional factors that essentially set parameters for reporting and interpretation in the ideological institutions. Now, to call that a conspiracy theory is a little bit like saying that, when General Motors tries to increase its market share, it's engaged in a conspiracy. It's not. I mean, part of the structure of corporate capitalism is that the players in the game try to increase profits and market shares; in fact, if they didn't, they would no longer be players in the game. Any economist knows this. And it's not conspiracy theory to point that out; it's just taken for granted. If someone were to say, "Oh, no, that's a conspiracy," people would laugh.

Well, exactly the same is true when you discuss the more complex array of institutional factors that determine such things as what happens in the media. It's precisely the opposite of conspiracy theory. In fact, as you mentioned before, I generally tend to downplay the role of individuals—they're replaceable pieces. So, it's exactly the opposite of conspiracy theory. It's normal institutional analysis—the kind of analysis you do automatically when you're trying to understand how the world works. And to call it conspiracy theory is simply part of the effort to prevent an understanding of how the world works.

Well, I think also the term has been assigned a different meaning. If you look at the root of the term itself— conspire, to breathe together, breathe the same air—I mean, it seems to suggest a kind of shared interest on the part of the people "breathing together." It just seems that the word has been coopted for a different use now.

Well, certainly, it's supposed to have some sort of sinister meaning; it's a bunch of people getting together in back rooms deciding what appears in all the newspapers in this country. And sometimes that *does* happen; but, by and large, that's not the way it works. The way it works is the way we described in **Manufacturing Consent**. In fact, the model that we used—what we called the *propaganda model*—is essentially an uncontroversial guided free-market model.

An uncontroversial—

Guided free-market model—the kind that's *virtually* uncontroversial.

Hmmm. Well, can you say what issues the media reliably don't *cover? I mean, are there a series of issues that—*

Well, take some of the issues that we've mentioned. Any issue—anything that's going on—the media will shape and modify so that it serves the interests of established power. Now, established power may have several components, and these components may even be in conflict in some way, so you will get a diversity of tactical judgments.

Let's take, for example, the *major* foreign policy issue of the 1980s: Nicaragua. There was an elite consensus that we had to overthrow the Sandinistas and that we had to support murder and terror in El Salvador and Guatemala—

that was a given. But within that consensus, there were some tactical variations. For example, how do you overthrow the Sandinistas? Do you do it by terror and violence, the way the Reaganites wanted? Or do you do it by economic strangulation and a lower level of terror and other sorts of pressures, the way the "doves" wanted? That was the debate. That was the *only* debate. And the media kept to that line. In fact, I've done a rather detailed analysis of this. The fact is that in news reporting, in editorials, and even in opinion columns—which are supposed to reflect a diversity of opinion—the commitment to this position approached 100 percent. So, if you take a look at, say, the opinion columns in the *New York Times* and the *Washington Post,* as I did during the peak periods of debate, you'll find close to 100 percent support for the position that the Sandinistas have to be over-thrown and a debate over how it should be done. Now, that's the kind of uniformity you find in a totalitarian state, and it's the same with all the other issues that I've looked at. Ed Herman and I and others have looked at a very wide range of cases, and that's what you find throughout.

You speak of the media engaging in a practice that you call feigning dissent. *Is this an example of it?*

Yes. For example, let's take the question of how to overthrow the Sandinistas. In 1986, a poll revealed that about 80 percent of the people called "leaders"—which includes corporate executives and so on—were opposed to the contra option and thought that other means should be used to destroy the Sandinistas and restore the rulers of their choice. Other forceful and illegal measures—but not contras. The reason was simply cost effectiveness. They recognized that the contras are—as the liberals put it—an "imperfect instrument" to achieve our goals. Now, if the media were simply reflecting corporate interests, then about 80 percent of the commentary would have opposed the contras. Actually, it was about 50 percent, which means that the media were more supportive of the government's position than a propaganda model would predict. So, if you want, there *was* a defect in our model—namely, that we *underestimated* the degree of subordination of the media to the government. But that's about it.

Do you think right now that the media are helping to lead us into war in the Persian Gulf?

Definitely. It's a complicated story, but the options are basically either war or a negotiated settlement. Now, what are the opportunities for a negotiated settlement? Well, there have been opportunities which have not been explored. And it's very interesting to watch the way the media treated them. For example, on August 12, Iraq apparently offered to withdraw from Kuwait as part of a general withdrawal from occupied Arab lands. That would mean, with the withdrawal of Syrian troops from Lebanon, the withdrawal of Israeli troops from Lebanon, and the withdrawal of Israeli forces from the occupied territories, they would give up Kuwait. Well, that's not an entirely unreasonable proposal; you can imagine a basis for discussion. *It was dismissed.* It was dismissed in the *New York Times* in one sentence—in the course of a news article on another topic. TV news just laughed about it.

On August 19, Saddam Hussein suggested a general settlement treating the problem of Kuwait as an Arab problem to be settled by the Arab states in the manner of Syria in Lebanon and Morocco in the western Sahara. Well, that, too, was rejected at once—this time on the very plausible grounds that, in that arena, Iraq could have prevailed because it's the most powerful force in that part of the world. Well, that's correct, but there's a small point we're missing here: namely, that Saddam Hussein was just stealing a leaf from our book. Every time a U.S. intervention takes place in the Western hemisphere, we immediately warn the world to keep away, even vetoing U.N. Security Council resolutions condemning U.S. aggression on the grounds that it's a hemispheric issue and others should not be allowed to interfere. Well, sure, it's a hemispheric issue because, in the hemisphere, we are so powerful compared to anyone else that we expect to prevail. If it's wrong for Saddam Hussein—as it is—then it's wrong for us.

Take a more striking case: on August 23, an offer was transmitted to Washington from Iraq by a former high U.S. official with Middle East connections. That offer was an interesting one. According to memoranda and the testimony of the people involved, which was basically recognized as accurate by the administration, the offer included complete withdrawal from Kuwait, Iraqi control of the Rumailah oil field, which is almost entirely in Iraq except for a small corner in Kuwait—Iraq claims, maybe rightly, that Kuwait has been draining its resources, so they want a settlement which would guarantee them control over that oil field—general negotiations over security issues, and so on. They didn't even mention U.S. withdrawal from Saudi Arabia. Well, that's an interesting offer. What was the reaction to it? Well, first of all, it wasn't published. Six days later, *Newsday*—which is not the national press—published it very prominently as the cover story and gave all the details. The next day, the *New York Times*—the newspaper of record—mentioned it in a small paragraph on the continuation page of a story on another topic. The *Times* opened by quoting the government as saying that the offer is baloney. Then, after having framed the issue properly—in other words, that the offer is baloney—it went on to concede quietly that the *Newsday* story was accurate and that the *Times* had had the same information a week earlier but hadn't published it. And that was the end of *that* story.

This reveals some things about the media. First of all, it shows that, outside the national press, you occasionally do get deviations. So, for example, the *Newsday* report was an exposure of information not wanted by those people in power who are trying to avoid negotiations. So, these deviations can happen, and, when they do, you move to the phase of damage control. The way you deal with this information is by marginalizing it. First you present it as baloney; then you quietly concede it's true and that you knew it all along but were suppressing it. And that's the end of the story.

Well, what does that tell you? The choice again is a negotiated settlement or war. And we see the way the possibilities for a negotiated settlement are being dealt with. Well, that happens to be Washington's priority at the moment, so therefore it's the media's priority.

Washington's priority is war?

Washington's priority is not war but, rather, to achieve our ends by the threat or use of force.

That brings up another question: how much of a crisis is there really in the Persian Gulf?

If it did explode into war, the consequences could be catastrophic.

I don't mean after Bush inserted the troops into Saudi Arabia; I mean before.

Even then it was serious; Iraq's invasion of Kuwait was a very serious matter, and everything should be done to get them out of there. I mean, on grounds of principle and international law, it's not fundamentally different from the U.S. invasion of Panama or the Israeli invasion of Lebanon or a dozen other cases we can think of where we didn't care or we supported the aggression. But on the grounds of, say, human rights, it doesn't begin to compare with the Indonesian invasion of Timor, which led to near genocide and which we tacitly supported. So, the only "principle" involved here is that might does not make right unless we want it to, and in the other cases we wanted it to. But this is significant because it involves energy. The Arabian peninsula is the major energy reserve of the world, and it's been a major commitment of the United States since World War II that we or our clients control that source of energy and that no independent indigenous force is allowed to have a significant influence. Actually, years ago, at the time of the first oil crisis, I referred to this as "axiom one" of international affairs. These resources are controlled by the United States, U.S. corporations, and U.S. clients like Saudi Arabia, and we're not going to tolerate any indigenous threat to that control. A large part of our foreign policy turns around that issue. And there's absolutely no doubt whatsoever that Saddam Hussein is a monster and a gangster. But, of course, Hussein was just as much a monster and a gangster six weeks ago when he was a favored client of the United States—in fact, the United States was his largest trading partner, and the Bush administration had gone out of its way to offer him loans, credits, and so on. All of this was suppressed—virtually suppressed—by the media for a long time. He was just as much of a monster then. He's still a monster. Now, however, his monstrous acts happen to be harming U.S. interests, so therefore he's *portrayed* as a monster in the media.

I have a feeling that so much of the country has been conditioned now by this demonization in the press of Sad-

dam Hussein that they would say, "Why should we even take these proposals seriously?"

We should take them seriously because he's frightened. The demonization for once happens to be accurate; he is a demonic character, just as he was when the press was looking the other way. But the fact of the matter is that he got in over his head and he now realizes it, apparently. We don't know, incidentally, if these offers are genuine; there's only one way to find out—and that's to pursue them. And that's what Washington does not want to do. You can't miss the fact that the United States is isolated on this issue. Who else has troops in the region?

Well, it looks like the United States is bribing Egypt to put some troops in.

We're trying to turn the screws on other countries to get them to participate, which in itself is very striking. Right now, as you and I are talking, the U.S. government—Nicholas Brady and James Baker—are flying around the world trying very hard to get people to contribute. What does this mean that we're trying to *get* them to contribute? So far, they've refused, but, if we have to *make* them contribute, that shows our isolation. Yesterday [September 6], Germany announced that they would not pay anything for the American forces in Saudi Arabia—that this was a bilateral arrangement between the United States and Saudi Arabia and had nothing to do with Germany. Japan, the other major economic force in the world, has been saying that maybe they'll give some financial support to the countries that are being harmed by the embargo, or, you know, maybe they'll send a couple of jeeps. Egypt, which is a big, populous country with a very large army—a third of a million men—has sent 2,000 men armed with light weapons and jeeps. Hell, I can round up more than that from the people I know. As for Saudi Arabia, there were big headlines in this morning's paper saying that Saudi Arabia agrees to share the costs for the American soldiers. How very exciting. I mean, here are American soldiers sent to preserve the Saudi Arabian monarchy, and the Saudis are willing to pay some of the costs. Boy, that's really impressive.

Well, the United States wants to forgive Egypt its $7 billion debt and also make the Soviet Union a most-favored trading partner if they play along.

Play along just means give us a diplomatic cover—that's what it amounts to. Why is the United States so desperate for a diplomatic cover? In fact, why is everyone else in the world backing off from armed confrontation? These are things that a really objective media would want to be exploring. And again you find no discussion of it. And then you find an outraged editorial in the *New York Times* saying, "How come the world is playing the part of the bad guy?" But try to find some analyses of why that's true. Well, there are reasons; the reasons are pretty obvious. You know, the United States for a long period was the dominant force in the world—both economically and

militarily. It was agreed on all sides that, when the United States was intervening in the Third World, it was "politically weak" but economically and militarily strong. And you tend to lead with your strength. We had military and economic strength. Now, we are only one out of three. It's a tripolar world from an economic point of view. But the United States is still unique in military force. Nobody comes close; we are *the* military power. And with the withdrawal of the Soviet Union from world affairs, we're freer to use military force than before, because the Soviet deterrent has disappeared. And there's a natural temptation to lead with your strength, which in our case happens to be military. Germany and Japan have different interests, and the resolution of the issue by the exercise of force is not in those interests.

Do you think that there was any good reason for Bush to put all those ground troops into Saudi Arabia?

Not really, no. I mean, I think there were reasons for the world community to make it clear that it would not tolerate Iraqi aggression, it would not tolerate the takeover of Kuwait, and it would certainly not tolerate any threat to Saudi Arabia. I think to make that clear and explicit was absolutely valid and right, and I think that Bush really knows there's agreement about that in the world. The question is where do you go from there?

But my question is was there any real need for those troops to be committed? And didn't that dangerously raise the stakes?

We could argue that; I'm not completely convinced that there was. But you could argue that a military presence was necessary. It would have been far preferable to do it under the U.N.'s auspices. That also was not pursued. Or, rather, it was pursued, but the U.N. would not go along; in fact, the other world powers still have not really agreed to enforce the embargo. After a lot of arm-twisting, we finally got a U.N. Security Council resolution, but it was a very cautious one: it refused to authorize even the minimal use of force. Again, the United States is relatively isolated.

I think it's interesting that in the media you see a different sort of picture. For example, you were talking earlier about how weak and frightened Hussein actually is at this point—or at least frightened.

Well, he looks it. But again, you don't know whether this is bluster and posing—just an effort to get what he can—or if he really is frightened. And, as I said, there's only one way to find that out—and that's to pursue a negotiated settlement.

So, do you think Hussein is militarily as powerful as the media have presented him?

On this issue, I think the media are pretty accurate. If you look closely at the military analysis, you'll see that his military power is partly papier-mache. The army has poor morale, a limited capacity . . . but it depends by what standards you're judging. By Middle Eastern standards, it's a very powerful army. But if there's a war with the United States, Iraq will lose. If we wanted, we could blow the country out of the universe.

And what about the media's newfound appreciation of the United Nations now that it's allegedly voting on our side?

Well, that's an interesting story. The U.N. has come in for some quite unaccustomed praise. There's been article after article about how, with the end of the Cold War, and with the Russians no longer dragging their feet, the U.N. can finally function in the way it was originally designed to function. There's one slight problem, though. Certainly for the last 20 years, the U.N. has not been able to function because the United States has blocked it. We're far in the lead—far, far in the lead—in terms of Security Council vetos. On a whole range of issues—including the Middle East, the observance of international law, disarmament, the environment, you name it—the United States has vetoed Security Council resolutions repeatedly and has voted alone, or along with one or two client states, in the General Assembly. That's happened over and over again.

So, what does that tell you? Well, if you look at the attitude toward the U.N. in the United States, you find that, in the late 1940s, the U.N. was regarded quite favorably. At that time, after World War II, the United States was overwhelmingly dominant in the world and the U.N. could be counted on to follow U.S. orders on virtually everything. So, at that time, the U.N. was a fine thing, and the Russians—who were being outvoted because we were using the U.N. as an instrument against them—were the bad guys. Then the U.N. gradually fell out of favor, as U.S. dominance in the world declined. And as Third World countries gained independence and were able to join, the U.N. fell under what we call the "tyranny of the majority"—otherwise known as democracy—because it was no longer following U.S. orders. So, slowly, over the years, we lost interest in the U.N. By about 1970, the situation had gotten to the point where the United States was becoming increasingly isolated. And, by that time, the U.N. was just bad news; it was full of irrational anti-Americanism and so forth.

It's interesting to see how the discussion changed over those years. In the 1950s, the debate was why are the Russians so awful? By 1985, the debate was why is the world so awful? You had stories in the *New York Times Magazine* by their U.N. correspondent asking how come the whole world seems to be out of step. I mean, they're voting against us on everything; so, what's the matter with the world? And there were a number of thoughtful ruminations on *that* topic. Now, in this one instance, the U.N. is more or less acting in accordance with U.S. wishes—more or less. So, all of a sudden, the U.N. is a wonderful institution.

Well, anybody looking at this record would regard it as a comedy. Any sane person would. The U.N. is considered favorably to the extent that it follows U.S. orders; to the extent that it doesn't, it is looked upon unfavorably. Furthermore, for the past 20 years, the Soviet Union has, by and large—in fact, overwhelmingly—voted with the majority, the large majority. Those are the facts of the matter. Try to find a report in the press that even comes close to describing that. Well, that again shows you what a remarkable institution of distortion and deception the media are.

Not only that but . . . I don't know if you've been watching "Nightline" recently?

I don't watch it.

Well, Barbara Walters was on hectoring a German journalist and a Japanese trade ministry representative about whether or not they were going to contribute money. There was Barbara Walters, you know, speaking almost on behalf of the American people, asking them where's their damn money.

Well, an obvious question arises; namely, why . . . let's say she's the voice of the American government, not the American people . . . *why* does she have to hector representatives of Germany and Japan about giving us money? Why do we have to twist their arms to get them to pay for this? After all, they're more reliant on Middle East oil than we are. So, what's the matter? Well, maybe this says something about us. The possibility that there's something wrong with our policy, our commitment . . . that's something that can't be raised. I mean, it's just a law of logic that we're right in whatever we do. And even if the whole world disagrees with us—not just on this but on many other issues—the world is wrong. The world is not on the "team," you know, if it doesn't go along with us. We just take that for granted.

I brought that up because it wasn't as if this journalist had the keys to the German treasury. It wasn't news; it wasn't analysis. It just seemed to be a lot of posturing. Actually, this leads me to my next question. You concentrate mainly on the print media; is there any reason for that?

Yeah, I don't have the resources to cover television. Don't forget that, on this side of the fence, we don't have many resources. Everything I do is on my own time, mostly with my own money. On the other side of the fence, you have ample resources. And if you really want to cover television seriously, you have to go through the transcripts, which really takes time. Furthermore, to the extent that there have been studies of television—there have been some by others—it's almost invariably the case that the framing of the news on television is largely within the bounds set by the national print media. You can pretty well predict what's going to be on network television on any given evening by looking at the front page of the *New York Times* or the *Washington Post*.

Sure, even people within television freely admit that. Do you think there's any difference in terms of the effectiveness of indoctrination between broadcast media and the print media?

Yeah, for most of the population, television news' framing of the issues is probably much more influential.

Gore Vidal, among others, has suggested that people who are inundated by television news are easier to manipulate. Do you buy that?

Well, I think we again ought to make the distinction between the political class—those who are more active in political, economic, and cultural management, a minority of some 20 percent—and the rest of the population whose function is to be passive observers. For the large mass of the population, I suspect that the main impact of television comes not through the news but through mechanisms to divert their attention. That means network programming—everything from sports to sitcoms to fanciful pictures of the way life is "supposed" to be. Anything that has the effect of isolating people—keeping them separated from one another and focused on the tube—will make people passive observers.

Remember, after all, that this is basic liberal democratic theory—I'm not making it up. If you read, say, Walter Lippmann, the dean of American journalism, who is also considered a leading progressive, democratic theorist, his argument is that, for a democracy to function properly, there are two different roles that have to be played: one is the role of what he called the *specialized class*—the responsible men, a small minority—and the other is the role of the public, who he described as a "bewildered herd." The role of the public, then, is to be spectators, not participants; their role is just to watch and occasionally to ratify. The decision-making has to be in the hands of the elite. That's democracy.

And that was to be consciously directed?

Oh, well, I'm quoting Lippmann and he means it to be completely conscious. You can trace this to the founding fathers: the public are to be observers. The country was founded on the idea that . . . Well, John Jay [the president of the Constitutional Convention and the first chief justice of the Supreme Court] put it very concisely: "Those who own the country ought to govern it." That's the way the country was established, and that's the way it's been run.

Do you think things are getting better or worse in terms of the people's access to alternative news sources?

Oh, I think it's better.

Better?

For one thing, I think the media are better than they were 20, 25 years ago, and more open. I've been talking about how narrow they are, but it's a lot better than it was 25 to 30 years ago.

Why did this change occur?

Mainly because of the way everything changes—social change. Why do we have free speech? Not because anybody wrote it down on paper but because of centuries of struggle—popular struggle. Every social change comes about through a long-term process of struggle—whether it be the peace movement, the civil rights movement, the women's movement, or whatever.

And in the 1960s, there was a substantial popular awakening, which improved enormously the cultural and intellectual level of a large part of the population. And that's had an effect. There's been a tremendous effort to stamp it out, but I don't think it's working. It's had its effect on popular dissidence during the 1980s, which was greater than it has been in our recent history. And it's had an effect on the media and Congress. Many people have filtered into the system who came through that experience—and that's had an effect. So, now you have people in the media whose formative influences were in the 1960s' ferment—and sometimes you can see their effect. And the same thing holds true with Congress. Take the congressional human rights campaign, which is mistakenly attributed to the Carter administration; a lot of the initiative for it came from young people and grew out of the 1960s experience.

So, you think that people are getting—

I think it's marginally better in the mainstream institutions. Also, there are lots of alternatives. Take something like community-based radio, which is pretty widespread over the country—well, that really offers an alternative. Communities that have a community-based radio station are significantly different from others in terms of the liveliness and openness and vitality of the political discussion. I travel around the country a lot, and for me the difference is palpable.

So, you think that people are getting less *manipulable then?*

Yeah, I think so. You could see it in the 1980s. For example, when the Reagan administration came in, they expected to be able to carry out worldwide interventions the way the Kennedy administration did; Kennedy was their model. And the Kennedy administration was quite brazen about it; some of what they did was clandestine, but most of it was quite open. When they started bombing South Vietnam, it was on the front pages. When they sent troops to Vietnam, it was overt. The Reagan administration couldn't do that; they had to move at once to clandestine warfare—in fact, they mounted the largest campaign of clandestine terror in modern history, probably. Well, the scale of clandestine operations is a good measure of popular dissidence. Clandestine operations aren't secret from anybody except the domestic population. And they're inefficient. Any state will use overt violence if it can get away with it; it'll turn to covert violence when it can't get away with it.

Do you have any advice on how to escape this pervasive and continual indoctrination offered by the media?

People have to understand that it's necessary to undertake what you might call a course in intellectual self-defense.

You have to understand the nature of the material that is being imposed upon you and its institutional sources. When you do that, you can make corrections. It's very hard to do that as an isolated individual. But in solidarity with others, in communication with others, it can be done. It was done, for example, by the Central American solidarity movement, which was a very effective movement in the 1980s, and also by the anti-apartheid network, by the "green" movement, and by the women's movement. That's the way you combat it. An isolated individual—unless he or she is really heroic—can't prevail.

Phil Edwards (review date 5 July 1991)

SOURCE: "The Lone Arranger," in *New Statesman and Society,* July 5, 1991, p. 35.

[*In the following review, Edwards offers positive assessment of* Deterring Democracy, *though finds fault in Chomsky's "browbeating style."*]

The late Napoleon Duarte, president of El Salvador, was a right-wing Christian Democrat—demonstrably so after 1980, when a quarter of his party left and joined the guerrillas. At the time of the mid-1980s election in which Duarte lost power, the BBC news characterised him as "left of centre". Given that the only candidate to Duarte's right was a neo-fascist, this is a bit like calling Harvey Proctor a Red. A veil of normality had to be thrown over the facts, though: the elections were being held with US (and British) government approval.

There are many stories here as unpleasantly revealing as this one: this is a good book, but not entirely a good read. Part of the problem is the browbeating style in which much of it is written, by turns belligerently partisan and heavily ironic. Above all, Chomsky is that rare beast, a consistent anti-imperialist. This gives him a gift for drawing unpalatable but entirely logical conclusions that his more liberal rivals cannot match. I finished this book feeling weary and bruised, but with a deepened understanding of the dynamics of global politics before, during and after the cold war.

"Before, during and after"; this, in a nutshell, is Chomsky's main argument. So far from confining the superpowers to arm-wrestling across the Berlin Wall, the cold war saw the US wage war, directly and by proxy, against the threat of political and economic independence in countries around the world. The USSR, meanwhile, did little more than assist ex-colonial states that preferred Soviet patronage to US control. As the cold war ends, a major constraint on US imperialism vanishes, and the remaining superpower has the world to itself. The results, from Kurdistan to Kampuchea, are not going to be pretty.

To understand this development, we do not need to ascribe sadistic tendencies to national security advisors and directors of the CIA (though some of the historical evidence on this point is equivocal). Despite some gloomy remarks about the "national psychosis" of the US, Chomsky recognises the economic roots of imperialism. At home, business needs stability and guaranteed investment; business therefore gets a choice of two pro-business parties and a system of military Keynesianism. (The free market is fine for other countries: it makes it that much easier for the US to win.)

Abroad, business needs materials and markets; business gets them, regardless of the human costs. Any nation where US interests set the limits of the possible is therefore a "democratic" nation led by "moderates" (which, Chomsky helpfully informs us, was how the State Department regarded Mussolini in the 1930s). The US élites both shape the world and define the terms in which we know it. Only one real challenge to their global dominance is presented here: the economic power of the rival élites of Germany and Japan.

The only significant flaw in this compendious and thought-provoking work stems from Chomsky's conception of the élite, which is at once his favourite theme and his blind spot. Considering the industrial democracies, he argues that in some countries élite power is imposed by consensual means and has no need of cruder methods of enforcement; he then gives a brisk rundown of occasions on which precisely those methods were used (half a page on the Italian conspirators of P2, seven lines on the Gehlen organisation).

Chomsky is uninterested in the crucial question of how these two faces of politics fit together: whether by running a secret army staffed by ex-Nazis or by cutting income tax, the élites always win. Beside them, moreover, stands the "secular priesthood" of intellectuals, dedicated to "serving the owners of the state capitalist systems" when they cannot take power in their own right ("in the Leninist model").

So élite power rests on a *trahison des clercs:* an assumption that clarifies Chomsky's expressed contempt for Vaclav Havel as well as his general tendency to bellicose sarcasm. Looking outside the ranks of the élite, Chomsky gestures towards the "historic mission" of "people who regard themselves as moral agents", but his own mission is plainly that of the lone incorruptible within the élite world-machine. It is a position in which some uncomfortable truths can be told, but that holds out very little hope of anything actually changing.

Matthew Rothschild (review date October 1991)

SOURCE: "Impassioned Advocate," in *The Progressive,* Vol. 55, No. 10, October, 1991, pp. 39-43.

[*In the following review, Rothschild offers positive evaluation of* Deterring Democracy, *though he cites weaknesses in Chomsky's tendency toward conspiracy theory and contradictory portrayal of the American public's relation-ship to the media.*]

Noam Chomsky is the leading dissident in the United States. For twenty years, he has provided the most coherent left-wing analysis of U.S. foreign policy and the most trenchant critique of the mainstream media.

Though Chomsky has become almost a cult figure on campuses and in many progressive circles, he is a serious scholar and an impassioned advocate of human rights and genuine democracy. He's no sham artist: he's the genuine article—a person morally outraged at the cruel policies and blatant hypocrisies of his native land.

Chomsky's latest work, **Deterring Democracy,** is a fine introduction to his theories. The essays in this book, mostly taken from his contributions to *Z* magazine over the last two years, are written in plain English; even the uninitiated can understand his points. If you're looking for one book to show a friend or relative who expresses an interest in left-wing political analysis, this is it.

The book needs to be taken as a whole, for Chomsky's main arguments run in and out of every essay. He often picks up a thread from a previous essay, so the reader needs to refer back and forth to grab the nuances of his case. His arguments fall into two categories: a devastating indictment of U.S. foreign policy in the Third World, and a scorching condemnation of the way the mainstream media serve as apologists for that cruel policy.

As a primer on the moral bankruptcy of U.S. foreign policy, Chomsky's book is indispensable. But his theory is not without its weaknesses, especially in its media criticism. At times, Chomsky's theory borders on conspiracy, seeming to require that thousands of policymakers and media personnel have taken secret oaths to dupe the American public.

Chomsky's view of the American public also seems faulty. On the one hand, he suggests that media indoctrination is so powerful that it not only shields U.S. policy from criticism but also allows little room for anyone to dissent. On the other, he acknowledges the failure of the media to persuade the American public to go along with every noxious policy. Yet he never allows in his theory for the varying successes and failures of the propaganda system.

However, these weaknesses do not invalidate Chomsky's main contention. He demonstrates, through an impressive arrangement of undeniable facts, that U.S. foreign policy has wreaked enormous damage on the peoples of the Third World. And he shows, through innumerable telling examples, how the media time and again not only fail to hold U.S. policy up to scrutiny but eagerly sell that policy to the American people.

Chomsky's indignation can border on the lurid, as when he notes "how easily we refrain from seeing piles of bones and rivers of blood when we are the agents of misery and despair." But the central issue he grapples with—the suffering caused by U.S. policy, and why the American people allow it to go on—is crucial for all those who wish to understand and change our country's actions in the rest of the world.

Though he touches on earlier periods of U.S. history, Chomsky devotes most of his attention to the Cold War and post-Cold War era.

While conventional historians contend that the Cold War pitted the United States against the Soviet Union, Chomsky takes a different view. "For the U.S.S.R., the Cold War has been primarily a war against its satellites," he writes, "and for the U.S., a war against the Third World."

This war against the Third World will continue, Chomsky says. Expect "the post-Cold War era to be much like the past as far as relations between the United States and the Third World are concerned," he says, warning of "persistent support for human-rights violations, the general hostility to social reform, and the principled antagonism to democracy."

Since World War II, the United States has sought "to impose or maintain a global system that will serve state power and the closely linked interests of the masters of the private economy," Chomsky argues. In this scheme, the Third World supplies the raw materials for U.S. corporations. Chomsky quotes George Kennan explicitly consigning the Third World to such a role.

The insistence on controlling Third World resources has motivated U.S. interventions for the past forty-five years, Chomsky says. The U.S. Government has repeatedly used its full weight to crush any Third World "nationalist force that might try to use its own resources in conflict with U.S. interests." The overthrow of the Guatemalan government in 1954, the Indonesian government in 1965, the Chilean government in 1973, and the sabotaging of the Sandinista revolution in the 1980s all substantiate the argument.

The post-Cold War period is no different, though the rhetoric has changed because the Soviet Union is no longer a credible threat. This has created "the problem of the disappearing pretext," Chomsky says. "The Evil Empire has been invoked when needed for domestic economic management and for controlling the world system. A replacement will not be easy to find." Drug traffickers will not suffice, he says, for "the Third World itself is the real enemy."

The first two interventions that inaugurated George Bush's New World Order demonstrate the "continuity" in U.S. policy, Chomsky says, and he discusses in detail the invasion of Panama and the war against Iraq.

"The invasion of Panama is so familiar an exercise of U.S. power as to be no more than a footnote to history," he says. "Rhetoric aside, it remains a high priority to block independent nationalism."

Manuel Noriega's thuggery had nothing to do with the invasion, except as pretext. "Noriega was known to be a thug when he was a U.S. ally," says Chomsky, "and remained so with no relevant change as the Government (hence the media) turned against him."

Similarly, Saddam Hussein's "villainy is not the reason for his assumption of the role of Great Satan in August 1990," he argues. "It was apparent long before, and did not impede Washington's efforts to lend him aid and support. . . . Hussein became a demon in the usual fashion: when it was finally understood, beyond any doubt, that his independent nationalism threatened U.S. interests."

Chomsky holds no brief for Saddam: "By any standards, Saddam Hussein is a monstrous figure," he notes. But, says Chomsky, the only reason the United States turned against him was because he threatened U.S. control of oil.

Nor does Chomsky buy the argument that Saddam's weapons of mass destruction justified the war. "It is not the threat of mass destruction and the capacity to coerce that disturbs us," he notes. "Rather, it is important that it be wielded by the proper hands: ours or our client's."

The brutal U.S. policy in Central America in the 1980s outrages Chomsky perhaps more than any other. "Ten years ago, there were signs of hope for an end to the dark areas of terror and misery," he writes. But no longer. "The United States and its local allies could claim substantial success. The challenge to the traditional order was effectively contained. . . . Some 200,000 people had been killed. Countless others were maimed, tortured, 'disappeared,' driven from their homes. The people, the communities, the environment were devastated, possibly beyond repair. It was truly a grand victory."

The magnitude of the human suffering appalls Chomsky, as does the self-congratulation of U.S. policymakers and the media, who crow about the spread of democracy throughout Central America. As Chomsky devastatingly points out, behind the "façade of democratic forms . . . the power of the military and the privileged sectors was enhanced."

While U.S. policy aided and applauded the governments in El Salvador and Guatemala—two of the worst human-rights violators in the world—during the 1980s, it waged war against the Sandinista government in Nicaragua, which was trying to improve the lives of its citizens. "Hypocrisy is the name of the game," Chomsky says, and he proves the point with a damning indictment of the double standards the U.S. Government and the media imposed on Daniel Ortega.

Chomsky's reach is wide. He surveys not only the U.S. military interventions, but also the record of American economic interventions in the Third World. He cites the growing poverty, gross inequalities, and political repression in Brazil, Argentina, Chile, and the Philippines, as well as the mass starvation in Africa.

"The record shows," he says, "that the policies that are advocated or enforced by the Western powers, and the confident rhetoric that accompanies them, are guided by the self-interest of those who hold the reins, not by any solid understanding of the economics of development or any serious concern for the human impact of these decisions. Benefits that may accrue to others are largely incidental, as are the catastrophes that commonly ensue."

These days, Chomsky is most widely known not for his radical critique of U.S. foreign, which he shares with many on the Left. What distinguishes him above all is his media criticism.

Chomsky argues that the U.S. Government and the media operate a highly organized and efficient "indoctrination system" to "eliminate public meddling in policy formation." This postulate is the hinge between the two halves of Chomsky's theory, for it enables him to explain why the U.S. Government can get away with such an immoral foreign policy: The people have been duped.

"If ordinary folk are free to reflect on the causes of human misery," he writes sardonically, "they may well draw all the wrong conclusions. Therefore, they must be indoctrinated or diverted, a task that requires unremitting efforts."

Chomsky argues that since the United States is so free, the elite who run the country must depend on an elaborate propaganda system to serve their interests. Ruling elites in undemocratic governments can and do rely on force, he argues. But elites in formally democratic countries cannot rely so blatantly on force: instead, they must turn to controlling the thoughts of their citizens. "Control of thought is *more* important for governments that are free and popular than for despotic and military states."

In significant ways, the United States is more free than other societies. Chomsky acknowledges. Hence, the elite in the United States needs a more sophisticated propaganda system. "The techniques of manufacture of consent are most finely honed in the United States," he says.

What are these techniques? While Chomsky does not list them in any single place, he identifies several in the course of these essays. The first is diversion—with TV as the prime suspect.

"One fundamental goal of any well-crafted indoctrination program is to direct attention elsewhere, away from effective power, its roots, and the disguises it assumes," he writes. The people must be "diverted with emotionally potent over-simplifications, marginalized, and isolated. Ideally, each person should be alone in front of the television screen watching sports, soap operas, or comedies."

This isolation is crucial, as it deprives citizens of the ability to think and organize together. "As long as each individual is facing the television alone, formal freedom poses no threat to privilege."

But the dispensers of TV images are the least of Chomsky's culprits. His indictment is much more sweeping. He talks of a "hoax perpetrated by the media and intellectual community" to keep the public in the dark.

Their "task" or "assignment," says Chomsky, is "to shape the perceived historical record and the picture of the contemporary world in the interest of the powerful, thus ensuring that the public, properly bewildered, keeps to its place and function."

The media go about this task in several ways, he writes. They glorify the President, they "transmit" Washington's rhetoric, they insist on imputing the most benevolent motives to U.S. policy, they feast on fear, they ignore not only countervailing opinions but also countervailing facts, they apply double standards with impunity, and they constrict public debate so tightly that the views of fundamental critics are rarely, if ever, aired. Instead, they treat the public to a false debate between "hawks" and "doves," who only disagree over tactics, not fundamental policy.

Unfortunately, Chomsky does not delineate these various techniques in a methodical manner. But he does provide ample evidence to buttress his contention that the media are "the loyal servants" of the elite.

For instance, he offers *The New York Times* diplomatic correspondent, Neil Lewis, who wrote: "The yearning to see American-style democracy duplicated throughout the world has been a persistent theme in American foreign policy." Chomsky responds: "Even a cursory inspection of the historical record reveals that a persistent theme in American foreign policy has been the subversion and overthrow of parliamentary regimes, and the resort to violence to destroy popular organizations that might offer the majority of the population an opportunity to enter the political arena."

To illustrate bias in the way news is selected, Chomsky cites among other instances the way the media depict the United Nations. They routinely disregard the organization when it denounces the United States for opposing a comprehensive test ban or when it condemns Israeli policy in the West Bank and Gaza. "None of this was reported in the Free Press, the 'community of nations' being irrelevant when it fails to perceive the Truth." But when the United Nations goes along with the U.S. policy, the world body becomes legitimate. During the days leading up to the Iraq war, John Goshko of *The Washington Post* wrote that the United Nations "is suddenly working the way it was designed to," Chomsky notes. He concludes that "the U.N. is 'functional' today because it is (more or less) doing what Washington wants."

The media's use of double standards is most obvious in the case of Central America, Chomsky says. The media constantly ridiculed the Nicaraguan government under Daniel Ortega for using military measures to put down the contras, trained and financed by the CIA. One TV reporter called Ortega "the skunk at a picnic," referring to a summit meeting of Central American leaders. But "one will search in vain for a suggestion that El Salvador—or Guatemala, where the situation is even worse—should rein in its military," he writes. "Their leadership are not skunks at picnics, but estimable (if somewhat ineffectual) democrats, and the military rulers are 'reforming' and overcoming past harsh practices under benign U.S. influence—a permanent process, untroubled by annoying fact."

The media's treatment of the Sandinistas was "in the style of a totalitarian state," Chomsky writes. They greeted the defeat of the Sandinistas with "extraordinary uniformity," Chomsky writes, and he backs up his claim with numerous examples. By contrast, the Latin American press had a much more balanced interpretation of the Sandinista defeat, placing strong emphasis on the destabilizing role the United States played, Chomsky notes.

The media also act as though left-wing activists or critics in the United States don't exist. After Ortega lost, Elaine Sciolino of *The New York Times* wrote an article headed, AMERICANS UNITED IN JOY, BUT DIVIDED OVER POLICY. This is just too much for Chomsky. "Such phrases as 'United in Joy' are not entirely unknown," he writes. "One might find them, perhaps, in the North Korean or Albanian press."

Chomsky devotes an entire chapter to "The Agenda of the Doves," but by "doves" he means not genuinely radical critics but the liberals in the media and Congress who represent the furthest left-wing point on the continuum of *acceptable* debate.

Chomsky heaps scorn on these so-called doves for not disputing the underlying rationale of U.S. policy, for squabbling only over tactics. In this category, he places the commentators Hendrik Hertzberg, Michael Kinsley, Jefferson Morley, Stanley Hoffman, Mary McGrory, Tom Wicker, and Daniel Schorr. And he denounces such Democratic politicians as John Kerry, Patrick Leahy, Paul Tsongas, and Christopher Dodd.

"To understand our own cultural world, we must recognize that advocacy of terror is clear, explicit, and principled, across the political spectrum," he says. "It is superfluous to invoke the thoughts of Jeane Kirkpatrick, George Will, and the like." Instead, he cites the liberal doves.

"Consider political commentator Michael Kinsley, who represents 'the Left' in mainstream commentary and television debate," Chomsky writes. "When the State Department publicly confirmed U.S. support for terrorist attacks on agricultural cooperatives in Nicaragua, Kinsley wrote that we should not be too quick to condemn this official policy. Such international terrorist operations doubtless cause 'vast civilian suffering,' he conceded. But if they manage 'to undermine morale and confidence in the government,' then they may be 'perfectly legitimate.'"

When the media confine the "Left-Right" debate to such a narrow spectrum, they affect "the structuring of values and operative choices," Chomsky says. Since the public is not exposed to alternative views, it can only choose from those the media present. And when the media present only views that accommodate the power elite, they succeed in keeping "the giddy multitude in a state of implicit submission."

The difficulty I have with Chomsky's theory is not with his claim that the media serve the elite. By and large, they do. But he overstates the case; not every member of the mainstream media—and not every one of his excoriated doves—writes columns every time that support U.S. policy. Michael Kinsley opposed the Iraq war; Mary McGrory has denounced U.S. policy in El Salvador and Cambodia.

And his theory about why the media act so slavishly is inadequate. He implies—with such terms as "assignment," and "task," and "hoax"—that some kind of grand conspiracy exists to mislead the American people.

He is content to describe the media's functioning; he has little time for explaining it. He only adduces one argument for the media's behavior—that the media are themselves corporate giants that benefit from U.S. policy. "Articulate expression is shaped by the same private powers that control the economy," he says. "It is largely dominated by major corporations that sell audiences to advertisers and naturally reflect the interests of the owners and their market."

Certainly, this is part of the story. But there are other reasons for the media's behavior. For one thing, reporters and commentators are lazy and find it easier simply to transcribe the words of the policymakers than to dig for the truth. For another, they routinely censor themselves by cozying up to their sources in Washington. And finally—and here the argument turns viciously circular—the owners of the media are cowards when it comes to controversy, since they worry about alienating readers and viewers.

Chomsky disdains any inquiry into the media's—and the politicians'—conscious intentions. "In so far as one chooses to dwell on these insignificant questions, answers are highly uncertain," he says. "While such matters may be of interest to those entranced by the personalities of leaders, for people concerned to understand the world, and perhaps to change it, they are of marginal concern at best . . . matters of tenth-order significance."

But these questions aren't "insignificant." Chomsky posits a conspiracy to mislead without proving an intention to mislead. That the public is misled there can be no doubt. Yet Chomsky does not spell out how the collaboration occurs.

Most of the time he argues that the politicians and the media consciously participate in the hoax. "Throughout, we find that more intelligent elements are aware of the fraud used to beguile others and to defend oneself from unpleasant reality," he says. But then he hedges. It's not necessary to "assume conscious deceit," he says. "Rather, it is necessary only to recall the ease with which people can come to believe whatever is convenient to believe, however ludicrous it may be, and the filtering process that excludes those lacking these talents from positions of state and cultural management."

I also find Chomsky's discussion of the American public to be inadequate and contradictory. The thrust of his theory is to demonstrate the omnipotence of the media's propaganda system. Yet he shows repeatedly that "dissidence, activism, turbulence, and informal politics have been on the rise and impose constraints on state violence that are by no means negligible."

But his theories in this book do not allow for such dissidence and activism. He fails to explain how individuals or whole sectors of the society manage to elude the thought control of the media. This weakness is common to cultural-hegemony theorists from György Lukács to Herbert Marcuse. Somehow, the theorists need to provide enough room to allow themselves and other dissidents to transcend the thought control that afflicts the rest of society.

Finally, his theory tends to overemphasize the role of the media—as separate from other cultural agencies—in filling American citizens with opinions, attitudes, values, and perceptions. Chomsky implies that if only the media's daily lies and distortions can be penetrated or discarded, progressive politics will make a great advance.

But Chomsky disregards the thick residue of reaction that lines the culture in less direct ways—through the schools, religion, family, and the myriad of other institutions that transmit values and attitudes predisposing people against progressive politics.

Despite the profoundly depressing situation he describes, Chomsky maintains hope for "libertarian socialist and radical democratic ideas." He rests this hope on three assumptions.

The first is his claim that "the general public seems more opposed to violent intervention than before and—I hope, though I do not know—more committed to blocking it." While this claim might have been valid as it pertained to U.S. intervention in Central America during the 1980s, it was disproved during the Iraq war earlier this year, which won 90 per cent approval ratings in the public opinion polls.

The second is more metaphysical. Chomsky suggests there is a "natural belief" in justice and freedom. This belief is "confirmed by the fact that despite all efforts to contain them, the rabble continue to fight for their fundamental rights."

And third, buttressing this inherent inclination to fight for freedom, is the legacy of "Enlightenment thought on political and intellectual freedom," Chomsky says. "These ideas and values retain their power and their pertinence, though they are very remote from realization, anywhere."

Chomsky does not despair. He urges all of us to stand up against the immoral foreign policy of the U.S. Government and to foster the radically democratic values of the Enlightenment. Ending this powerful work, Chomsky offers the following admonition—and hope: "By denying the instinct for freedom, we will only prove that humans are a lethal mutation, an evolutionary dead end; by nurturing it, if it is real, we may find ways to deal with dreadful human tragedies and problems that are awesome in scale."

Noam Chomsky with Charles M. Young (interview date 28 May 1992)

SOURCE: "Noam Chomsky: Anarchy in the U.S.A.," in *Rolling Stone,* May 28, 1992, pp. 42, 45-7, 70-3.

[*In the following interview, preceded by an overview of Chomsky's career, Chomsky discusses his political and social views, his objection to media control and ideology, and his book* Deterring Democracy.]

When Michael Albert went to Poland in 1980, he discovered that the Poles assumed there were two Noam Chomskys. "In linguistics, he's the Freud," says Albert, Chomsky's editor at *Z Magazine* and a friend since the Sixties, when Albert, then a physics student, was organizing antiwar protests at MIT. "All the branches of modern linguistics stem from his work. And for over a quarter century his political analysis has inspired the peace movement. The Poles had no idea that one person could do all that."

Maintaining two full-time careers has required sacrifice, of course. On a recent *Saturday Night Live,* as an obvious plug, one of the actors carried a copy of **The Chomsky Reader** throughout a skit. Albert telephoned Chomsky to say, "Hey, you're on television!" and found himself having to explain what *Saturday Night Live* is. So Chomsky doesn't know a lot about popular culture. He doesn't watch TV. Despite his status as a hero in the anarchist wing of punk, he doesn't listen much to rock & roll. He rarely goes to movies. He has little time for a private life.

What Noam Chomsky does know about is how the human brain creates language. Consider for a moment that you are now reading and understanding a sentence that you have never read or understood before. Consider that you do this hundreds of times a day in exchanges of information vastly more complicated than the last sentence. How can such a high level of intelligence and creativity—fully in possession of the average person—be explained? "There's only one answer to that," says Chomsky. "It's built in. We're born with it. If a smart Martian came to

Earth, he would see that. He would see that all human languages are the same. The trick is to find the fundamental rules of all languages—a formidable but reachable goal."

Chomsky has spent his academic career doing highly technical research (anyone for finite automata theory?) in an effort to find those rules, called fixed universals. He theorizes that what we are born with is, roughly, a box of switches in the brain. The culture a child is born into determines how those switches are set. In one pattern the switches become Hungarian. In another, Urdu. In all cultures, the switches start clicking around the age of two, and the child will start producing original sentences much as he or she will start producing secondary sexual characteristics at eleven. A description of that box of switches will tell us a lot about how the brain thinks, which has hitherto been almost a complete mystery.

One of the implications of Chomsky's work (it isn't proved yet) is that human language and most behavior are "appropriate but uncaused," a highly heretical notion in the behaviorist wing of psychology. In other words, we are born with an enormous, unpredictable capacity for creativity, an "instinct for freedom." This concept places Chomsky at the frontier of psychology, philosophy and linguistics and square in the eighteenth-century tradition of the Enlightenment and radical libertarian philosophy.

Believing that the best way to maximize our genetically endowed freedom is through anarchism, which he defines as "libertarian socialism," Chomsky has been unrelenting in his attacks on the American hierarchy and the nation-state in general. This has made him a prophet dishonored in his own land. One of the most respected and influential intellectuals in the world outside the United States, he is barely known to the average American. His books are rarely reviewed in the major media or standard academic journals. His essays appear only in small left-wing magazines like *Z.* Network TV ignores him in favor of the General Electric-approved weenies who appear on Sunday-morning talk shows. When he is mentioned at all, he is usually smeared as a "self-hating Jew" for his devastating criticism of Israel's treatment of the Palestinians. He has left the *New York Times* in an especially vulnerable spot: How to explain that one of the smartest people on earth thinks the newspaper of record is a reeking pile of lies about U.S. war crimes? Even worse, he proves it on a regular basis. With footnotes. Well, there's just no explanation for such a thing, so the paper ignores him.

Noam Chomsky was born December 7th, 1928, in Philadelphia. His father, William, a Hebrew scholar, had emigrated from a small village in the Ukraine to avoid the draft. His mother, Elsie, was also a Hebrew scholar and a writer of children's books. By all accounts, young Noam was highly precocious, and his parents had the foresight to enroll him at an experimental progressive school. By the age of ten he was writing editorials defending the anarchists in the Spanish civil war. As a teenager he often took the train to New York to hang out at his uncle's newsstand, where working-class Jewish radicals would gather to discuss politics and literature. He got his Ph.D. in linguistics from the University of Pennsylvania and since 1955 has taught at MIT, where he has revolutionized his field several times. By the early Sixties, Chomsky had a very pleasant life carved out for himself: a house in the 'burbs, a young family he loved and fulfilling scientific work. Then he noticed the Vietnam War and began speaking against it long before it was physically safe to do so. He refused to pay his taxes (a protest he continued until the mid-Seventies) and helped to organize Resist, which counseled young men against the draft. When Dr. Benjamin Spock was put on trial for just that, Chomsky was an unindicted coconspirator. In 1967 he shared a jail cell with Norman Mailer after a demonstration at the Pentagon. In *The Armies of the Night,* Mailer noted that Chomsky, "although barely thirty, was considered a genius at MIT." Mailer saw him then as "a slim sharp-featured man with an ascetic expression, and an air of gentle but absolute moral integrity." The description remains apt.

Now sixty-three, Chomsky maintains a grueling schedule. By day he does his teaching and research. Several nights a week, in church basements around the nation, he gives lectures on the evils of U.S. foreign policy. In the isolated subculture of the genuine left, a Chomsky lecture will galvanize the atomized and leave a residue of moral energy for months. And he writes books faster than most of us read them. A good place to start is **The Chomsky Reader** (Pantheon), a collection of biting and often hilarious essays. His latest book is **Deterring Democracy** (Verso), a stunning evisceration of U.S. policy toward the Third World. If you prefer TV, you might try **Manufacturing Consent: Noam Chomsky and the Media,** an excellent two-part video biography. And many of his lectures are available on audiocassette (contact David Barsamian, P.O. Box 551, Boulder, CO 80306).

Oddly, he does not consider himself a writer. "I don't practice any craft," he insists. He says he hasn't even read his essay **"The Responsibility of Intellectuals,"** published in *The New York Review of Books* (which won't touch him now) in 1967. It was transcribed by a student from one of his off-the-cuff talks. Yet it defined the peace movement as much as any document and pushed the name Chomsky up there with Thoreau and Emerson in the literature of resistance. What is the responsibility of intellectuals? "To speak the truth and expose lies."

[Young]: Let's start with the title of your latest book, **Deterring Democracy.** *What do you mean by 'democracy,' what do our rulers mean by 'democracy,' and why are they deterring what you mean by 'democracy'?*

[Chomsky]: Well, like most terms of political discourse, *democracy* has two quite different meanings. There's the dictionary meaning, and then there's the meaning that is used for purposes of power and profit. According to the dictionary, you can say a system is democratic to the extent that citizens have ways to participate in some meaningful

fashion in decisions about public affairs. That's not a yes or a no matter. You have a lot of different dimensions in different societies. In the ideological sense of democracy—the Orwellian sense, in which the word is actually used—a society is democratic if it's run by business sectors that are subordinated to the business sectors that run the United States. If it has that property, it's a democracy. If it doesn't, then it's not.

So, for example, Guatemala in the early Fifties was a capitalist democracy in the dictionary sense of the word. In fact, it was one of the most democratic governments in the Third World anywhere. It had lots of popular support, there's no doubt about that. Read the CIA analyses. One of the things they were worried about was that the government had so much support. But Guatemala was following policies of which the United States did not approve: independent nationalism, domestic development, land reform and so on. This was harming the interests of the elements that the United States regards as the natural rulers—they being the business classes that are linked to U.S. corporations and the military, insofar as they follow U.S. orders. Therefore the United States had to overthrow that government in 1954 to safeguard what we call democracy.

Or Nicaragua in the Eighties, to take a more recent case. An election occurred there in 1984, in fact, but not according to U.S. ideology. In newspapers, in journals of opinion, there wasn't an election. The first election was in 1990, In historical reality, there was one in 1984. There has probably never been an election in history so closely investigated. The Latin American Studies Association, the professional association of Latin American scholars, did its first detailed analysis of any Latin American election. The Dutch government, which is very reactionary and pro-American, sent a delegation. The Irish parliament sent a delegation. Masses of observers. And the general conclusion, even by the most reactionary of them, was that this was a pretty effective election.

I recall reading arguments in Z Magazine *that there was more democracy in Nicaragua than there is in the United States during most presidential elections.*

In the dictionary sense, that is certainly arguable. In the formal sense—did the voting machines work and so on—it doesn't compare with the U.S. It's a Third World country. But it is quite common in Third World countries for there to be a broader range of choice than in the United States. That's because we have a democracy in the Orwellian sense. The government doesn't come in and stop candidates, but the breadth of choice is very narrow. Which is what we call an efficient democracy.

Anyhow, that election in 1984 did not take place, because it did not satisfy the condition that the U.S. could determine the outcome. In fact, the U.S. tried to disrupt the election in every possible way. The *contras,* who were just a terrorist force run by the U.S., did what they could to disrupt it. And did. They attacked polling booths and so forth. There was a U.S. candidate, a banker who had spent most of his life in the U.S. According to the press here, he was the popular candidate. There was no evidence for that. When it was clear he wasn't going to win, he was induced to withdraw. He was on the CIA payroll, it later turned out. And then the press here says, "Oh, there was no election, the major candidate withdrew." It was pooh-poohed as not a real election, which made it legitimate to go on attacking Nicaragua. Somoza didn't bother us, but this bothered us.

Then when the 1990 election came along, the country had already been driven into total misery. It had been virtually ruined by the combination of *contra* attacks and economic warfare that was probably even more lethal. When Nicaragua announced the election, the White House announced pretty clearly that a vote for the U.S. candidate would mean an end to economic strangulation.

Meanwhile, in violation of the agreement of Central American presidents that the U.S. terrorist forces should be disbanded, we continued to maintain the *contras*. This was called "humanitarian aid," which the World Court had already ruled was military aid. But that was only the World Court. And again we have the Orwellian question of what is law and what isn't. So we made it clear that the *contras* would continue their terrorist attacks unless the population voted our way. And then under conditions of terrorist attack and economic strangulation, an election took place. They voted George Bush's way, so that was an election. You can argue about why they did it. But the White House made it clear: "If you vote our way, you'll survive. If you vote the other way, Ethiopia will look good in comparison." Therefore, that was a free election. And the first one, which the U.S. could not control, wasn't a free election. Incidentally, there was something like unanimous agreement on this in the United States across the articulate spectrum.

Everyone from Michael Kinsley to Patrick Buchanan, the full range of opinion, from left to right.

Anthony Lewis. Everybody was just euphoric about the outcome of this democratic election. The *New York Times* was particularly funny. They had a headline saying, AMERICANS UNITED IN JOY—the kind of headline you'd see in some weird, exotic, totalitarian state, like Albania. Maybe. Another headline said, VICTORY FOR U.S. FAIR PLAY, meaning, "Vote our way or you die."

So you take your choice. Which language are you going to talk—English or Orwell? Orwell himself didn't have the imagination to think of these things.

Well, Nineteen Eighty-four *was as much about the United States and England as it was about Stalinist Russia.*

He may have meant it that way, but the only reason he became admired was that you could interpret both *Nineteen Eighty-four* and *Animal Farm* as being just about the Soviet Union. That made him acceptable.

Do you get sick when some far-night ideologue like Norman Podhoretz cites himself as being in Orwell's tradition of standing up to power and seeing through propaganda?

Given the part of Orwell that Podhoretz is talking about, he isn't being completely unrealistic. He's interested in the part of Orwell that was condemning the official enemy. But you might just as well say that Podhoretz is in the tradition of every Soviet commissar. Any Soviet commissar would condemn U.S. crimes. In fact, you could read *Pravda* and have tears rolling down your cheeks at the terrible treatment of blacks in the American South or American crimes in Indochina. They're just terribly emotional about U.S. crimes. Just as Norman Podhoretz is terribly emotional about *their* crimes.

But honest people, whether in the Soviet Union or here, will care about the crimes of the state that they are a part of and for which they bear some responsibility. We understand this when we talk about the Russians. We don't honor Russian party hacks who condemn American crimes. We honor Soviet dissidents who condemn Soviet crimes. Except we don't apply that same logic at home. That would be inconceivable. That would be rational. And honest. And if you're rational and honest, you're pretty much excluded from the educated classes, from the privileged classes. Those are properties that are very dangerous.

If you read the standard conservative columnists, they're very consistent about taking anything that connotes good and attributing it to power and anything that connotes bad and attributing it to the poor or some other scapegoat.

Yes, it's very consistent. And it's the exact analogue of what you find in *Pravda* in the days of Stalin. But in the Soviet Union under Stalin, you could sort of understand why somebody would be a party hack or else shut up. It was just too dangerous. Try to be an honest person, you end up in the gulag. Try to be an honest person in the United States, nothing much will happen to you.

Here, they make you poor.

And they can vilify you. There's a penalty involved. But it's nothing like being tortured or murdered. Here, it's a lot easier. That means the people who don't do it here, particularly the privileged ones, are at a much lower moral level than the worst commissars under Stalin.

Why is there less murder and torture here? If you look at Central America, our leaders are plainly capable of it. My interpretation of the Sixties—events like Kent State, the assassination of Fred Hampton of the Black Panthers, the framing of Geronimo Pratt—is that those events were meant to send the message that the death squads can operate here, too.

You have to understand the nature of American society. There was assassination of Black Panthers. The worst case I know of was the assassination of Fred Hampton. It's striking that they would pick him. The Panthers, like a lot of groups that come out of the ghetto, were a very mixed group. They ranged from ordinary thugs to serious organizers who were regarded as a real threat. Fred Hampton was an effective organizer in the Chicago ghetto. He was one of the main targets of the FBI terror campaign, and they ended up killing him with the cooperation of the Chicago police department after an FBI setup. But you'll notice nobody cared about that.

For example, that didn't come up in the Watergate hearings. Nobody said to Richard Nixon, "Wait a minute, you organized the Gestapo-style assassination of an organizer in the ghetto." What they said in the Watergate hearings was: "You called a powerful guy a bad name. The Constitution is collapsing."

So Fred Hampton could be assassinated. But privileged whites did not get assassinated, even ones who were very outspoken. That reflects the nature of American society. It is not a totalitarian state. It is a very free society that is off toward the capitalist end of the spectrum. It's not pure capitalist society, of course. Such a society couldn't exist for a week.

Don't you think that if the left ever gets its act together in the Nineties, we'll see more of that sort of government activity?

No, I don't think so.

Not like COINTELPRO?

Well, COINTELPRO, yeah. COINTELPRO was differentiated. COINTELPRO directed against blacks was murder. Against whites it was disruption, defamation, circulating stories about sexual conduct, things like that. That was a big difference, and the difference had to do with who is privileged and who is not privileged. In our society, people with power and wealth are relatively free. Freedom is a commodity, like anything else in capitalist society. You have as much of it as you can buy. And if you're wealthy and the right color, you can buy a lot. The privileged people who actually run the country, they don't want the state to have power to go after people like them. So they'll actually protect the civil rights of people they hate if they come from the right class.

Do you ever wonder about the psychology of these American commissars? You've written about the filtering process by which the obedient rise to the top and the disobedient end up elsewhere, but I wonder what goes on in their heads.

I don't think it's that hard to figure out. All the people I've ever met, including me, have done bad things in their lives, things that they know they shouldn't have done. There are few people who say, "I really did something rotten." What people usually do is make up a way of explaining why that was the right thing to do. That's pretty much the way belief formation works in general. You have some interest, something you want, and then you make up a belief system which makes that look right and just. And then you believe the belief system. It's a very common human failing.

Some people are better at it than others. The people who are best at it become commissars. It's always best to have columnists who believe what they're saying. Cynics tend to leave clues because they're always trying to get around the lying. So people who are capable of believing what is supportive of power and privilege—but coming at it, in their view, independently—those are the best.

The norm is that if you subordinate yourself to the interests of the powerful, whether it's parent or teacher or anybody else, and if you do it politely and willingly, you'll get ahead. Let's say you're a student in school and the teacher says something about American history and it's so absurd you feel like laughing. I remember this as a child. If you get up and say: "That's really foolish. Nobody could believe that. The facts are the other way around," you're going to get in trouble.

Do you remember the fact you came up with?

Well, this happened so often. I got thrown out of classes . . . not a lot. . . . I don't want to suggest it was any real . . . there are people who did it constantly, and they end up as behavior problems. You raise too many questions, you ask for reasons instead of just following orders, they put you in certain categories: hyperactive. Undisciplined. Overemotional. It goes all through your education and professional life. A journalist who starts picking on the wrong stories will be called in by the editor and told: "You're losing your objectivity. You're getting a little too emotionally involved in your stories. Why don't you work in the police court until you get it right?"

That does start in childhood. If you quietly accept and go along no matter what your feelings are, ultimately you internalize what you're saying, because it's too hard to believe one thing and say another. I can see it very strikingly in my own background. Go to any elite university and you are usually speaking to very disciplined people, people who have been selected for obedience. And that makes sense. If you're resisted the temptation to tell the teacher, "You're an asshole," which maybe he or she is, and if you don't say, "That's idiotic," when you get a stupid assignment, you will gradually pass through the required filters. You will end up at a good college and eventually with a good job.

To me the question is, Why is that one kid more resistant to lying to get ahead? There is such a thing as moral courage. Some people have it and some don't.

There are individual differences which we don't understand. Just like we don't understand why some people like math and some people like rock & roll. Fortunately for the human race, people are very different from one another. If we were all alike, life wouldn't be worth living. Probably a lot of the differences are genetically determined. Some of them have to do with the effect of early training on your genetic endowment. There are all kinds of reasons. Nobody understands a word of this, so you can speculate or have any intuition you like.

On the other hand, there are some things that if we're honest, I think we'll recognize. One of them is the capacity to form beliefs that are self-serving and then to believe those beliefs. If that's a major feature of your intellectual makeup, chances are you'll go far.

Take that issue of the *New York Times Book Review* [October 20th, 1991] and look at the review of the James Reston memoir. It says this was a man that everybody admired, had an independent eye, hated the Vietnam War and so on and so forth. The fact of the matter is, James Reston made a career out of having lunch with Dean Acheson and writing a column the next day from what Dean Acheson told him to say. And that was called an "insider's scoop." Very profound. As for hating the Vietnam War—he loved it. He was writing articles about how we were defining the principle that no people should be subjugated to anyone else. And our Creator endowed us with that destiny. The most embarrassing trash. But it doesn't matter. I'm sure whoever the reviewer was believes everything he was saying. And if he didn't believe it, he wouldn't be the reviewer.

It was Fred Barnes of The New Republic.

I don't know him. Maybe he thought he was telling the truth. Maybe he didn't. Maybe he's laughing.

You've never watched him on the Sunday talk shows?

No, I'm afraid I can't tolerate that. I wouldn't know him from Adam. Without knowing him, I suspect he believes it. My point is, the only people who make it to where they will be allowed to express themselves in that august medium are the ones who have already demonstrated their own subordination to power.

There are some journalists, I should tell you, who are very well aware of this and are trying to work within a system of power and authority that they understand very well. You know people like that. And I know people like that. I think it's very honorable to see what can be done within the institutions, despite their hierarchical, authoritarian structure.

During every election you read these heart-rending editorials about why it's so important to vote for whatever office happens to be on the ballot. Yet no one ever asks the question of why, if it's such a great idea to vote for your senator, it would not be an even greater idea to vote for your boss.

No, that's out. A crucial part of the ideology is that you're allowed to criticize Congress, the president, local politicians. You're allowed to say they're all crooks. But you're not allowed to say that the corporate system is at the heart of it all. In fact, you're not even allowed to see that. No, the idea of voting for your boss is just off the agenda.

But if you really believed in eighteenth-century libertarian doctrine, the doctrine of the Founding Fathers, that's just what you'd be asking. They were not just opposed to a powerful state. They were opposed to concentrations of power. It happened back in their day that the concentrations of power that were visible were the state and the feudal system and the church, so that's what they were against.

In the nineteenth century a new concentration of power came along that they hadn't paid a lot of attention to, namely corporate power; that had a degree of influence and domination over our lives well beyond what the Founding Fathers could have foreseen. Yet their principles would lead you to ask exactly that question: Why should we be subordinated to the boss? Why should investment decisions be in private hands? Why should private power determine what is produced and what is consumed and what are working conditions? Why should you follow orders? Why shouldn't everybody participate democratically and decide what is to be done?

Whenever the Times *or any other newspaper writes about the destruction of the ozone layer, they present it as this unavoidable tragedy, like an earthquake or a hurricane. Yet the chemistry of what chlorofluorocarbons do to ozone molecules has been known since 1973. Du Pont and our political rulers have been stonewalling, and now we're in a situation where hundreds of thousands of people are going to die of skin cancer and get cataracts. If these chemicals had been manufactured in Eastern Europe, we'd surely be blaming communism. But the idea that capitalism did this to us . . .*

Did this in its natural workings. Not out of corruption. It did it because what drives the system, and what's supposed to drive the system, is tomorrow's profit. People who think about long-term effects are out of the system, by its very nature. And that's supposed to be a good thing. In the economics literature, future lung cancers are called an "externality." It doesn't show up in the market system. When you're selling chemicals, you're supposed to be maximizing profit for the stockholders. And if you're not doing that, it's immoral. You don't maximize profit by worrying about people getting cancer in twenty years. If you do worry about that, you won't be chairman of the board very long. That's the way the system is built, and it's admired because of that property. Ask Milton Friedman. If Du Pont had started to worry about the ozone layer and had shifted their resources to deal with it, somebody else could well have driven them out of business. That's the nature of the system.

This is not a very profound comment. A twelve-year-old can understand it. But they better not. Just like they better not understand that there's a question about why you shouldn't be allowed to vote for your boss. Why have a boss at all? Why not have collective decision making? Nobody's shown that it can't work. Take any successful scientific enterprise—and MIT is one—people work *together*. I taught a class yesterday, and I was standing up front and the students were down there, but they were telling me things as much as I was telling them things. And they come in afterwards and tell me that I'm wrong. And then we try to figure it out. That's the way that you make progress. It's just taken for granted. If we had a system in which I was telling them what to think and they were not allowed to tell me when they thought I was off the wall, we would have nonsense.

What is the practical difference between an anarchist and a Marxist? The wisdom of having a vanguard party?

I'm completely opposed to that. First of all, Marxism, in my view, belongs in the history of organized religion. In fact, as a rule of thumb, any concept with a person's name on it belongs to religion, not rational discourse. There aren't any physicists who call themselves Einsteinians. And the same would be true of anybody crazy enough to call themselves Chomskian. In the real world you have individuals who were in the right place at the right time, or maybe they got a good brain wave or something, and they did something interesting. But I never heard of anyone who didn't make mistakes and whose work wasn't quickly improved on by others. That means if you identify yourself as a Marxist or a Freudian or anything else, you're worshiping at someone's shrine.

If the field of social and historical and economic analysis was so trivial that what somebody wrote a hundred years ago could still be authoritative, you might as well talk about some other topic. But as I understand Marx, he constructed a somewhat interesting theory of a rather abstract model of nineteenth-century capitalism. He did good journalism. And he had interesting ideas about history. He probably had about five sentences in his entire body of work about what a postcapitalist society is supposed to look like. Insofar as he has a legacy of actual policy and organizing, that's Leninist, which is probably the most reactionary wing of Marxism. Lenin was a pretty orthodox Marxist and, as I read him, never really believed that socialism was possible in Russia. The iron laws of history mandated that it come about in the advanced industrial societies. In fact, he and Trotsky moved very quickly to squash and destroy the socialist tendencies in the Russian Revolution: factory councils, anarchist worker organizations.

Lenin's idea was that you have a group of revolutionary intellectuals, who are the smart guys, and they're to drive the society to a better future, which the slobs are too dumb to understand. That's basically the idea, which is not all that different from the ideology of capitalist democracy. You can almost interchange them. If that's Marxism, we ought to be very much opposed to it. In my view, social-

ism was dealt an enormous blow in Russia in 1917, from which it has yet to recover.

You once pointed out how it was in the interest of both the United States and the Soviet Union to claim that what was going on there was socialism.

Oh, yeah. Very much in their interest. For the U.S. it had the obvious purpose of defaming alternatives to capitalist autocracy. And for the Soviet Union it had the benefit of giving the moral appeal of socialism, which was enormous. So for both power systems it was very utilitarian to propagate this outlandish lie that the Bolshevik revolution was socialist. If socialism means anything, it means worker control over the means of production and decision making, That's the minimum.

Have you ever thought about giving up? A lot of my friends have concluded that people are just sheep. I say that if that's so, we might as well join the Republicans, steal as much money as possible and live comfortably.

If there's nothing to be done. Well, we don't know if there's anything to be done or there isn't. Outside of science, nobody knows a lot about anything. Especially when it comes to human beings, we know almost nothing except what you feel intuitively or what your experience tells you. But if you look over history, you can see definite improvement in the past twenty or thirty years. I think there's been a cultural revolution in this country, and people in power are scared to death of it.

That's why there's all this comical stuff about political correctness. It's a kind of joke; it's so silly. Here are people who have run the ideological system with an iron hand, and then in some literature department somewhere, somebody says something that isn't orthodox, and they go crazy. I must have read 200 articles about this new orthodoxy taking over the universities, destroying the golden age of absolute freedom of speech. I haven't read one article defending it. If this is an orthodoxy that has taken over everything, how come *everybody* is attacking it? To the simple mentality of a commissar, this idea won't occur.

This stuff about the quincentennial is interesting in this respect. There's a big fuss now about the "left fascists," who are dumping on Columbus and denying all the wonderful things Columbus brought. What they're saying is, for 500 years we went along, denying two of the worst acts of genocide in human history, maybe *the* worst act—the destruction of the Native Americans, which was tens of millions of people—and the destruction of large numbers of Africans through the slave trade, both of which got their start through Columbus. We've been celebrating genocide for 500 years, and that's not a problem. The problem is that the left fascists are now reversing it.

Anyone with a gray cell ought to be saying. "Thank God the left fascists are taking over and trying to get this straight." Virtually no one is saying that, of course. Our more educated circles are as retrograde as they ever were. That the controversy is taking place now is a reflection of a very substantial improvement in the cultural climate.

Is that the true legacy of the Sixties?

The Sixties left an enormous legacy. Do you think there would have been a word of protest about the quincentennial if it hadn't been for the Sixties? Would there have been one person who stood up for Anita Hill and said, "This is a form of sexual harassment"? That's why everyone hates the Sixties. It might lead to real democracy. There was a phrase for it in the Seventies. It was called "the crisis of democracy." The crisis was that people weren't apathetic and passive anymore. They'd become organized and were trying to do something. This was the liberals, incidentally, who wrote the book *The Crisis of Democracy,* the people around Jimmy Carter, the Trilateral Commission.

The important aspect of the Sixties to understand is that the heroes were mostly people you never heard of: the Freedom Riders, the SNCC workers, the guys who were down there week after week getting their heads bashed in for organizing. In the Vietnam movement there was never any illusion about leadership. The leadership was whoever showed up. We're not allowed to understand that now. We are meant to think of popular movements as things that grow out of individual leadership and individual charisma. The reason we are meant to think that is that it disempowers people. It makes them think they can't do anything for themselves.

I'd like to ask you about another of your detractors. When Bill Moyers interviewed Tom Wolfe on PBS, Wolfe accused you of subscribing to the "cabal" theory of capitalism. In **Deterring Democracy** *you refer disparagingly to his description of the Reagan era as "one of the great golden moments that humanity has ever experienced."*

For people at his income level, that's quite true. In my view, it was crucially responsible for—not 100 percent—the catastrophe of capitalism that just devastated the Third World in the Eighties. It was what they call the "lost decade" in the Third World. Tens of millions of people suffering and dying. In just the years 1980 to '88, South African terror around its borders, supported by the United States, was responsible for about a million and a half people killed. If you count up the children who died of malnutrition as income levels dropped, you get a real monstrous toll. It's bad enough what happened in the United States, if you look at any group other than the privileged. If you add all that up, it's been a very ugly period. A person who could call that one of the golden moments in history . . . well, take Germany in 1939. A person who could call that one of the golden moments in history, we'd know what to think of him.

Did you read Paul Johnson's book Intellectuals?

It was quite comical. He concludes there that my opposition to the Vietnam War was deduced from syntax. He

literally says that. You have to be technically insane to be able to say a phrase like that.

I'd like you to respond to one quote from it: "Throughout the 1960s, intellectuals in the West . . . became increasingly agitated by American policy in Vietnam, and by the growing level of violence with which it was executed. Now therein lay a paradox. How came it that, at a time when intellectuals were increasingly willing to accept the use of violence in the pursuit of racial equality, or colonial liberation, or even by millenarian terrorist groups, they found it so repugnant when practised by a Western democratic government to protect three small territories from occupation by a totalitarian regime?"

Who were we saving it from? *We* attacked South Vietnam. There were no Russians, no Chinese, weren't even any North Vietnamese in the beginning. *We* attacked South Vietnam. That's saving? *We* brought Cambodia into the war by attacking it. *We* attacked Laos. For the sake of argument, let's forget that North Vietnam is Vietnam. Let's even forget that the government he says we were defending, Saigon, claimed that Vietnam was one indivisible country—that was article I of the constitution that the United States wrote for them. Let's forget all that stuff, and let's pretend that North Vietnam was the most monstrous society in history. We were attacking *South* Vietnam. As a commissar and party hack, Paul Johnson can't see that. He's not alone. Nobody can see it. The fact that the United States attacked South Vietnam, though trivially true, is just not a part of consciousness.

I remember a couple of weeks ago in the *New York Times Book Review,* there was a review of a book by Zalin Grant, a book about a Vietnamese collaborator. It was very laudatory about this man. He had collaborated with the French. Then he collaborated with the Americans. According to the book, around 1961 or 1962 he devised a technique by which the United States client regime sent out death squads to murder political organizers for the Viet Cong. These were called "counterterror teams." Talk of the level of perversity here. We invade another country. We set up a puppet government which everyone admits had no popular support. We send out death squads to kill their political organizers in their country, and our death squads are called counterterrorists. That appears in the *New York Times,* and nobody bats an eyelash. That says a lot about our intellectual culture. Against this background, Paul Johnson can write such perfect nonsense, mirroring his models in Stalinist Russia and Nazi Germany. And Norman Podhoretz will think it's fine.

Do you vote?

I tend to vote down at the lower levels, local officials, state representatives. Occasionally, I vote for president. I did vote against Ronald Reagan.

You voted for Walter Mondale?

I voted for whoever was running against Reagan. The Democrats could have nominated Charlie McCarthy, and I would have voted for him over Ronald Reagan and George Bush, because they're dangerous people. Well, not so much they themselves. Ronald Reagan wasn't president. It was a dirty secret that the reporters kept for eight years. During the Iran-*contra* hearings the Democrats were kind of surprised to discover that the president lied and nobody cared. That's because the population is sane. What difference does it make if this pathetic clown was told, or remembered, what the policy was. He wasn't supposed to know what was going on. He was supposed to show up now and then and read his lines. Maybe they told him, maybe they didn't. There could hardly be an issue of less significance.

But the point is, the people around him were extremely dangerous. They call themselves conservatives, which is nonsense. They're radical statists. They believe in a very powerful and violent and obtrusive state.

Do you have any wisdom on the current election campaign?

It's like one of the worst Third World elections. Take Honduras. Literally. They always have two rich guys with the same program, and the campaign consists of insults and comedy and circuses. There isn't any pretense of public involvement.

The only thing I like about Clinton is that he evaded the draft, and they're using that to nail him.

The one sensible thing that Clinton did in his entire life, and he's unwilling to stand up for it. It reminds me of Dukakis and the ACLU. The most shameful PR initiative in '88 was that line about Dukakis being a "card-carrying member of the ACLU," which implies that if you're in favor of the Constitution, you're a Communist. And Dukakis wouldn't say that. All he would say is: "No, I'm not really a member of the ACLU. I don't really believe in the Constitution." That was his only response, and that's what this thing is like. I have a feeling that the Democrats can't compete on this one. They're both business parties, but the Republicans make no claim of being anything else. The Democrats have all these pretenses about being the party of the people, and that keeps them so confused that they can't win these propaganda wars.

Will you bother to vote in November?

There is an issue that would make me vote—the prospect of another four years of court packing with ultraright jurists who hate civil rights. The court system has collapsed. The ACLU will simply not take cases to the federal courts anymore. Another four years of this will institute—I'm not joking—a fascist-style legal system in which civil rights just don't exist. If there's another issue, I can't find it.

The other night I was watching TV and a commercial came on for shock absorbers. The slogan was "It's not just your car, it's your freedom." I thought of you and your theory that people have an "instinct for freedom." Madison Avenue and our politicians must believe the same thing, because whenever they want to sell you shock absorbers or beer or a war, they try to associate it with freedom.

Sure. They know that's what people want. Like everything about human nature, you can't prove it. But in my experience and intuition, that's correct. People want to be free, independent, not oppressive, don't want to rob other people. I think most Americans would be horrified if they knew what they were doing in the world. And I think that's the reason for this whole edifice of lies.

It's an obvious question: Why don't our leaders tell the people the truth? When they're going to destroy Iraq, say, why don't they announce: "Look, we want to control the international oil system. We want to establish the principle that the world is ruled by force, because that's the only thing that we're good at. We want to prevent any independent nationalism. We've got nothing against Saddam Hussein. He's a friend of ours. He's tortured and gassed people. That was fine. But then he disobeyed orders. Therefore, he must be destroyed as a lesson to other people: Don't disobey orders."

Why don't they just say that? It has the advantage of being true. It's much easier to tell the truth than to concoct all sorts of crazy lies. Much less work. Why don't they say that? Because they know that's the only reason for all the fabrication. Our leaders believe that people are decent and that there is hope. And I think they're right. In fact, the more distortion and lies and deceit you hear, the more you know that people have an instinct for freedom.

Ron Grossman (essay date 1 January 1993)

SOURCE: "Strong Words," in *The Chicago Tribune,* January 1, 1993, p. 1.

[*In the following essay, Grossman provides an overview of Chomsky's career, achievements in the field of linguistics, and controversy surrounding his political views and activities.*]

Somehow, Noam Chomsky has managed to make himself both the Pied Piper and the odd man out of the ivory tower.

His fellow professors of linguistics divide history into two ages, B.C. and A.D.: Before Chomsky and After his Discoveries. In 1987, he won Japan's prestigious academic prize, the $285,000 Kyoto Award, for the revolutionary theory of language with which he essentially created modern linguistics.

There is scarcely a university post in the field that isn't held by a student of his, a student of a student of his, or someone who has peppered their own scholarly papers with abundant references to Chomsky.

He is, in fact, the king of the footnotes, and not just in his own rather arcane field. Linguistics isn't one of the sexier disciplines, even on heady campuses like the Massachusetts Institute of Technology, Chomsky's longtime home base, or nearby Harvard University. Airport newsstands don't stock linguistics textbooks.

But a survey of a standard reference work, the Arts & Humanities Citation Index, found that over the last dozen years Chomsky was the most often cited living author. Among intellectual luminaries of all eras, Chomsky placed eighth, just behind Plato and Sigmund Freud.

Getting that many people to read your books is no mean trick if your literary style favors phrases such as "generative transformational grammar"—and Chomsky's does.

Like an opera star, his personal appearances are booked a year or two in advance, both for scientific lectures and political speeches.

Since serving as professorial point-man for the campus opposition to the Vietnam War 25 years ago, Chomsky has continuously toured America's universities preaching the cause of radical dissent.

His audiences remain SRO. But each year, the number of Chomsky's political friends diminishes, even on the Left in whose ideological ranks he has marched since adolescence.

The New York Review of Books, house organ of the Eastern intellectual set, has closed its pages to Chomsky, a former contributor. Martin Peretz, editor of the New Republic, proclaims Chomsky's political writings "outside the pale of intellectual responsibility."

Writing in the leftish Nation magazine, one critic observed that Chomsky has "acquired the reputation as America's most prominent self-hating Jew."

Presumably he won that title by his fervent opposition to Israeli policies in the West Bank and Gaza. But Chomsky also has a knack for getting under the skin of those whose causes he champions. Speaking to a gathering of Palestinian intellectuals in Jerusalem, Chomsky proclaimed the PLO a "terrorist organization."

"I don't want any followers," the 64-year-old Chomsky explained, sitting in his MIT office. "My message, especially to students, is that they shouldn't be following anyone."

Chomsky is equally self-effacing about his scholarly accomplishments. Linguistics, he says, is still in the "pre-Galilean age," a reference to the period before the 17th Century when physics was less science than superstition. But his peers consider Chomsky not just their discipline's Galileo, but its Newton and Einstein, as well.

That's not bad billing, considering that when Chomsky was a student many of his professors thought there was little more to be learned about how humans use language.

While working on his Ph.D. in the 1950s, Chomsky was asked to give a talk at the University of Chicago. Such invitations are the academic world's way of scouting new talent for future job openings. To be polite, Chomsky asked his host, a senior professor of linguistics, what his own research field was.

"The fellow said: 'I'm not working on anything,'" Chomsky recalled. "He was convinced that linguistics was a completed science with nothing left to be discovered."

It is not surprising Chomsky wasn't offered an instructorship: The premise of his talk was that much of what linguists thought they knew wasn't true.

Beginning in the 19th Century, a series of pioneering linguists developed ever more sophisticated analyses of the world's languages. Chomsky's father, William Chomsky, made a significant contribution to that effort with studies of the Hebrew language.

ASKING THE QUESTION

By the middle years of the 20th Century, linguistics textbooks were thick with the myriad rules, plus a legion of exceptions to those rules, by which humans use language. As an undergraduate at the University of Pennsylvania, Chomsky took a look at that body of scholarship and asked himself a simple question. Asking the question proved to be the equivalent of the fabled apple that whizzed by Newton's head. "Discovery," Chomsky said, with 40 years worth of hindsight, "is the ability to be puzzled by simple things."

The question asked by undergraduate Chomsky: How do children learn to talk?

Chomsky noted that long before a child goes to school, he already knows a lot of language rules professional linguists took decades to discover. He doesn't know them by name as professors do. But in speaking, he knows to follow them.

In the 1950s, scholars assumed that children learn to speak by listening to their parents. Chomsky objected, noting that, if imitation is the route to speech, it should take children much longer to perfect their use of language. We should hear them struggling with one grammatical rule before trying another one. But children move from simple babbling to near mastery of their native tongue.

"Even as adults we're constantly producing sentences we've never heard before," Chomsky said.

PROGRAMMED TO LEARN

Such data only makes sense, Chomsky reasoned, if we assume the human brain is pre-wired, so to speak, for language. As part of its genetic inheritance, a child has a mental apparatus in which the rules of language are already present before he starts listening to the adults around him.

He doesn't store their speech patterns for future use, as Chomsky's professors thought. Rather, the child's "language motor" is triggered into action by what he hears. That is why a little bit of experience quickly gives him a sophisticated grasp of grammar and syntax.

While only dimly realizing it, Chomsky had recreated a fundamental philosophical position. Known as rationalism, its origins run back through the 17th Century French philosopher Rene Descartes to the ancient Greek sage Plato. They taught that humans are born with a set of ideas implanted in their brains.

In recent times that concept had been out of favor, especially in American university circles, for seeming too mystical. Modern psychologists assumed the brain is a blank slate at birth, and that our ideas are formed on the basis of our experiences.

Running against the prevailing intellectual grain, Chomsky had a difficult time getting his academic career started.

After college, he moved to Israel and lived on a kibbutz. As an adolescent, he had been a Zionist, though belonging to a left-wing movement that hoped to create a bi-national Jewish and Palestinian state.

Until landing a job at MIT in 1955, Chomsky thought he'd be confined to the sidelines of the intellectual life, like his father, who spent years as a Hebrew schoolteacher.

No sooner did he get a foot in the academic door than Chomsky challenged a superstar, B. F. Skinner, the high priest of behaviorism.

Making the breakthrough

A Harvard professor, Skinner preached that it is useless to speculate about mental processes because they can't be scientifically measured. So Skinner had invented his famous Skinner Box, a neutral environment where psychologists observe a subject's response to various stimuli.

"It was a perfect experimental method," Chomsky said. "The only problem with behaviorist psychology is it never discovered anything."

To understand his verdict, Chomsky suggested the following arm-chair experiment. Pick up a good novel and read a bit. Do the same with a psychology textbook, then ask yourself: Which author has more insight into what makes humans tick?

In his earliest essays, Chomsky argued that Skinner's behaviorism had reduced psychology to a vapid discipline that could do little more than restate the obvious in scientific jargon. By now, Chomsky virtually has won the argument: Behaviorism no longer dominates the social sciences, and a newer generation of cognitive psychologists follows Chomsky's lead in investigating the structure of the mind.

Chomsky's methods have also influenced a wide variety of other disciplines from literary criticism to child development—whence came all those citations and quotes that make him the footnote king.

"The breakthrough was there," Chomsky modestly said, "waiting to be made in the 1950s by anyone who knew something about computer theory, learned a little higher math and read a bit of European philosophy."

Toss in a working knowledge of Old Left political thought, and you pretty much have Chomsky's intellectual biography. As a teenager, he gravitated toward an uncle who ran a New York City newspaper stand that was a rendezvous for political dissidents.

"First he was a follower of Trotsky, then an anti-Trotskyite," Chomsky said. "He also taught himself so much of Freud he wound up as a lay psychoanalyst with a penthouse apartment."

His uncle passed on to the teenage Chomsky a profound suspicion of all forms of government. Today, Chomsky calls himself an anarchist-socialist.

His left-wing connections also provided him a mentor when he most needed one. In college, Chomsky recalled, he was bored with each subject as soon as he took a course in it. Then someone put him in touch with Zelig Harris, a left-leaning faculty member.

Because Harris was a linguist, Chomsky took a few classes in that subject. But Harris also steered Chomsky to the free-ranging course of studies that subsequently gave him the broad intellectual base for his ground-breaking work in linguistics.

For many years, Chomsky was politically inactive, his energies being taken up by his research. But in 1964, he decided he could no longer keep still on the issue of Vietnam. So, too, did other professors, most of whom went back to the classroom when that conflict ended.

"But I had a feeling that if I put a foot into the political water, it would be an endless sea of causes," Chomsky said. "Once the war was over, I knew I'd always find another issue I had to speak out on."

That insight proved prophetic, and Chomsky has been on the stump ever since. His critics chiefly recall his attacks on American policies, which have been both frequent and shrill.

But during the Cold War, Chomsky dished out the vitriol to both sides, avoiding the Old Left's tendency to overlook the Soviet Union's failings and the New Left's idealization of Castro.

"There was a lot of irrationality among campus radicals," Chomsky said. "It was easier for me to avoid that, since I started out as an anti-communist Leftist. I don't think that any state, whatever it calls itself, has any moral power over the individual."

A few years ago, that conviction inspired Chomsky to come to the defense of a right-wing French professor, an episode that cost Chomsky a lot of old friends.

FREE SPEECH IS THE ISSUE

Robert Faurisson, a teacher of literature at the University of Lyons, had been fired for contending there were no Nazi death camps during World War II. Chomsky signed a petition protesting Faurisson's dismissal. He also sent the Frenchman a note that, unknown to Chomsky, became part of a forward to a book in which Faurisson set out his ideas.

Chomsky says he himself has not the slightest doubt that millions of Jews died in the gas chambers. But if freedom of expression and inquiry mean anything, Chomsky argues, it is that a professor shouldn't be fired for his views, no matter how distasteful. He says he's never even bothered to read Faurisson's book.

"I didn't read Salman Rushdie's book either, but I signed a petition for him," Chomsky said.

And if Northwestern University ever tried to fire engineering professor Arthur Butz, who denies the existence of Holocaust death camps, "you can bet I'll campaign for his right of free speech too."

Being cited in an academic journal is one approximation of intellectual influence. Here are the top 10 most-cited sources in arts and humanities academic journals over a seven-year period inspected by the Institute for Scientific Information, publisher of the Arts & Humanities Index:

1) Karl Marx

2) Vladimir Lenin

3) William Shakespeare

4) Aristotle

5) Bible

6) Plato

7) Sigmund Freud

8) Noam Chomsky

9) Georg Hegel

10) Cicero

Richard Wolin (review date Summer 1995)

SOURCE: "Noam on the Range," in *Dissent,* Vol. 42, No. 3, Summer, 1995, pp. 419-23.

[*In the following review of* World Orders, Old and New, *Wolin finds fault in Chomsky's biased portrayal of the American government as a wholly negative, "monolithic" power structure.*]

Toward the third hour of the hagiographic documentary about Noam Chomsky, *Manufacturing Consent,* a moment of truth emerges. Chomsky is lecturing at the University of Wyoming. He has just finished his familiar stump speech: fifty reasons why we live in a totalitarian society. Striving to revive the old thesis about American society as a form of "soft totalitarianism," Chomsky argues that in the totalitarian societies of old, the state routinely used force to keep the public in line. In so-called democratic societies, he says, gentler techniques must be used to preserve order—thereby implying that though the means differ, the end results are more or less the same. During the ensuing question session an agitated undergraduate type steps to the microphone and has this to say:

> For the last hour and forty-one minutes you've been whining about the elite and how the government has been using thought control to keep people like yourself out of the public limelight. Now I don't see any CIA men waiting to drag you off. You were in the paper; that's where everyone here heard you were coming from, and I'm sure they're going to publish your comments in the paper. In a lot of countries you would have been shot for what you've done today. So what are you whining about? We are allowing you to speak. I don't see any thought control.

In response, Chomsky says something about its not being a question of individuals: "It has to do with marginalizing the public and ensuring that they don't get in the way of elites who are supposed to run things without interference." But his cover has been blown. The real difference between a genuine totalitarian society and our own— despite its manifest injustices and inequities—has suddenly been laid bare. In a real totalitarian society, someone like Chomsky would not be allowed to speak, let alone publish books (at an astronomical rate, one might add) that are widely discussed and reviewed. Why then does it take a twenty-year-old college student from Laramie, Wyoming, to point out the obvious?

What Chomsky seeks to show in *World Orders, Old and New* is that talk of a "new world order" is so much deceitful verbiage. Instead of a newfound international harmony, what we have now that communism has been expelled from the world stage is an unfettered opportunity for rapacious first world nations to exploit less fortunate inhabitants in other parts of the world. He begins with a review of U.S. foreign policy during the cold war, which he defines as a mechanism of "population control": a pretext for creating a security state that was as much concerned with domestic repression as with expanding U.S. influence abroad. Along the way Chomsky serves up a number of timeworn left-wing platitudes. Readers of his earlier books will be readily familiar with the arguments. They are not wrong, but the picture they paint is extremely partial.

In Chomsky's view the first and last word on world orders, old and new, was set forth by Winston Churchill following World War II: "The government of the world must be entrusted to satisfied nations, who wished nothing more for themselves than what they had. If the world-government were in the hands of hungry nations, there would always be danger. . . . Our power placed us above the rest. We were like rich men dwelling at peace within their habitations." Churchill's words become the book's leitmotif. As Chomsky glosses them: "To rule is the right and duty of rich men dwelling in deserved peace." World order, past and present, boils down to a type of "codified international piracy."

At several points in *World Orders* Chomsky describes contemporary American society as totalitarian in a non-metaphorical sense. His only hesitancy concerns whether the United States is "totalitarian" or "fascist." Often enough, he inclines toward the latter characterization. Journalistic support for the Gulf War amounted to an "exultant display of fascist values." The hidden agenda of the recent Middle East peace agreement permits "the United States and Israel [to move] towards more rational forms of imperial control [of the Occupied Territories]," such as those used by "the Soviet Union in Eastern Europe [and] Nazi Germany in occupied France." Concerning the chorus of media approval that greeted the Clinton administration's 1993 raid on Baghdad (in retaliation for Iraq's alleged plans to assassinate President Bush on a 1992 visit to Kuwait), Chomsky remarks: "The rulers of any totalitarian state would be impressed." Selected quotations, however, fail to do justice to the Orwellian vision of American political life on almost every page of this heavy-handed, fact-filled, citation-laden jeremiad.

It is fairly easy to identify what is amiss with Chomsky's views. Much less easy is the intricate task of sorting out what may be of value in Chomsky's hyperbolic saga of American totalitarianism at home and abroad. To paraphrase Delmore Schwartz: "Just because I am paranoid doesn't mean there aren't people who are really out to get me."

What is wrong with Chomsky's account is that it is too seamless, too monolithic. State Department strategists would, I'm sure, be extremely gratified if American "total world domination" functioned in reality as smoothly as Chomsky claims. For Chomsky's unilateralist model proceeds according to the assumption that U.S. policymakers themselves are free of competing factions or interests; that, likewise, U.S. allies always stand in agreement with American goals and intentions; that foreign policy is wholly insulated from popular domestic pressures and influences; and that the wishes and actions of the third world nations we are trying to rule present no obstacle to the realization of our aims.

At times, however, Chomsky tries to have it both ways. Thus, in a previous book, *Manufacturing Consent,* written with Edward Herman, he admits that tensions and divisions among ruling elites indeed exist. In the end, though, he concludes that such differences of opinion do not really matter—they are merely pseudo-differences. According to his "propaganda model" of opinion formation, dissent always takes place within well-defined limits. Any views that threaten to overstep these boundaries automatically fail to register. Upon closer inspection, these superficial differences of opinion are actually more insidious, argues Chomsky, inasmuch as they perpetuate the delusory image of a free society.

Chomsky is far from wrong in emphasizing the structural limits to opinion formation in an era in which corporate-owned mass media play such a disproportionate role in shaping public perceptions. The problem with the "propaganda model," however, is that it is only capable of providing a series of self-fulfilling prophecies. Since, according to this model, all differences of opinion are a priori "pseudo-differences," "authentic differences" by definition fail to register. One might ask Chomsky if, when, circa 1968, Walter Cronkite wondered aloud on the *CBS Evening News* what the hell we were doing in Vietnam—this was merely another instance of "pseudo-difference"? If so, what would a genuinely dissident opinion look like? In the end one gets the feeling that it is Chomsky himself who needs this monolithic image of opinion formation for the sake of confirming his own status as a maligned and misunderstood radical intellectual.

Let me try to expose some of the shortfalls of Chomsky's reasoning by way of an anecdote. I'll call it the "Andy fallacy." In the early 1980s I had a radical-activist friend from Berkeley named Andy. Andy loved to tell stories of how close we had come in the waning days of the Nixon administration to either a coup d' état, nuclear war, or (preferably) both. In the months preceding Reagan's reelection in 1984, Andy chose a different hobby horse to ride. He was convinced that as soon as Reagan was reelected, American troops would pour into Nicaragua to overthrow the Sandinistas.

Now I'll concede the point that if Reagan had been allowed to act in accordance with his preferences U.S. troops would have intervened. But the interesting thing is that this did not happen. And the reason for this is simple. In the aftermath of the Vietnam War a cultural consensus had developed about acceptable thresholds of American military intervention abroad—a consensus that considerably raised the domestic political stakes of any such move. As we now know, Reagan and his accomplices were instead forced to resort to a series of embarrassing illegalities—Iran-contra—which, when unmasked in 1986, paralyzed his ability to govern and permanently tarnished the image of his administration. In earlier works Chomsky has acknowledged the importance of an oppositional political consensus in deterring heightened levels of U.S. intervention in Central America (see, for example, *Turn-*

ing the Tide). But in *World Orders* such balanced insights are virtually nonexistent.

Chomsky views any expression of U.S. foreign-policy altruism—that is, claims to the effect that we are interested in promoting democracy and human rights in addition to the creation of "markets"—as so much ideological pap. In his view, our international policies and interventions are purely interest-driven, and the interests are of the basest sort. But the realities of global politics are more complex than he will allow. On this complicated terrain motives and interests are far from one-dimensional. They are economic, strategic, and—though Chomsky would be loath to admit it—at times ethical. Contra Chomsky, McDonald's and General Motors do not control the State Department—or at least not yet. Our interest in seeing democracy prosper in Eastern Europe, South Africa, and in South America is neither purely economic nor purely strategic—though only a naif would deny that such motives play a large role. There is also a moral-ideal component that derives from our own democratic traditions, according to which the principles of national self-determination and freedom count.

In a world where economic, military, and geopolitical competition is rife, questions of principle, unfortunately, rarely come first. But that is not to say à la Chomsky that they are nonexistent. At one or more levels they inevitably underlie foreign policy considerations. In ways that are often imperceptible, they set implicit limits to what we as a nation consider acceptable. Even the case of the Gulf War—the new world order litmus test, which, in Chomsky's eyes, we flunked spectacularly—involved a tissue of motivations and goals that are far from easy to sort out. Undeniably, national self-interest was prominent. But also at stake were solidarity with traditional allies (Israel as well as moderate Arab regimes), as well as the need to stand up to a regional tyrant. In fact, one of the main problems of Chomsky's approach is that it seems incapable of even acknowledging the concept of justifiable or legitimate strategic interests. Only if he were to acknowledge this concept would his criticisms of U.S. foreign policy take on a less monolithic cast and begin to make sense. For only then could one begin to distinguish between naked self-interest and a more principled and fair-minded orientation toward world affairs. As it is, Chomsky's leftism implicitly sanctions a neo-isolationism that, at the moment (and far from coincidentally), is also quite popular with the far right. Despite the failures of U.S. foreign policy past and present, the concept of moral leadership in the sphere of world politics remains a valuable aspiration.

Admittedly, postwar American foreign policy in Latin and Central America, Southeast Asia, and Iran (where in 1953 the United States helped to overthrow the Mossadegh regime in favor of the shah) has been a series of disasters predicated upon an imperious conception of national self-interest. This politics of cynicism and exploitation reached new heights with the Reagan administration's immoral

(and, as it turned out, erroneous) distinction between totalitarian regimes, said to be unreformable from within, and authoritarian dictatorships, with whom one could safely climb into bed without losing one's virtue. At issue are policies that wreaked untold misery on innocent third world peoples, policies that were motivated by an exaggerated fear of communism and a puritanical self-righteousness. In the words of the historian Louis Hartz, these actions were spurred by an ideology of "Americanism," which hypocritically proceeded to negate at will the rights to national self-determination of peoples around the globe. The final bill for such policies and practices, moreover, has yet to be paid in full.

This is the story that Chomsky tries to tell, but it has been told before and better by others. His critical flaw is to present a portrait of U.S. power at home and abroad so monolithic and impregnable that despair or inaction become the only possible responses. He thereby abets the process of depoliticization and left-wing marginalization he seeks to contest.

The last chapter of *World Orders* consists of a lengthy indictment of the recent Palestinian-Israeli peace accords. The accords were far from perfect, and there remains a long and difficult path ahead. But they should be acknowledged for what they were: a precarious yet historic first step. For the first time, the two protagonists are officially on speaking terms, and a negotiated settlement to the dispute, rather than a new Arab-Israeli war, is a tenuous possibility.

Chomsky, however, relentlessly indicts the opportunism of Arafat and the PLO for having signed the accords. He views the entire peace process as little more than a plot to preserve U.S.-Israeli political hegemony in the region. To be sure, the agreement came at a time when the PLO's popularity among Palestinians had waned considerably. With Hamas, a new uncompromising militancy has emerged on the scene, causing Israel to finally treat the PLO as a desirable partner in peace. In an imperfect international political scene, the Middle East is one of the least perfect regions. But at a time when one would do well to fan the precarious embers of hope, Chomsky heaps nothing but bile on those who seek compromise.

To psychologize Chomsky's long-standing contempt for Israel as a stereotypical instance of Jewish self-hatred would be simplistic. But even before his ignominious involvement in the Faurisson affair (for the relevant details, see Anson Rabinbach's article, "Memories of Assassins, Assassins of Memory," *Dissent,* Spring 1994), his views on Middle Eastern affairs had become suspect. In truth, Chomsky is grinding an all-too-familiar axe. The PLO, we are told, has displayed a willingness for peace for some time. There is nothing "mutual" about the conflict; instead, Israel alone, a proxy of U.S. imperialism, is at fault.

Almost lost amid Chomsky's rhetorical excesses in *World Orders, Old and New* is a timely (yet all too brief) discussion of economic "internationalization"—the 1980s buzz word for the growing world dominance of transnational corporations (TNCs), as supported by U.S.-dominated financial institutions such as the International Monetary Fund and the World Bank. Along with the nations of G-7 and the General Agreement on Tariffs and Trade, these corporations and organizations play an increasing role in determining the state of the world economy as well as the distribution of wealth among rich and poor nations. Yet, because they are multinational, they are less and less subject to controls. The conditions for debt repayment they have imposed on third world nations in South America and Africa have been notoriously draconian. Often, their harsh stipulations threaten to destabilize democratically elected regimes.

In Chomsky's words, the TNCs are "totalitarian in internal structure, quite unaccountable, absolutist in character, and immense in power." They herald the birth of a new world economic situation in which capital has become ruthless and, unlike labor, highly mobile. Unlike the corporations of old, today's TNCs are devoid of regional loyalties or a sense of an ethical obligation to their employees. According to one report, at present they control as much as one-third of the world's private-sector productive assets. As a result, in recent years corporate profits have risen dramatically while wages measured in real terms continue to sink. The current world economic order has practically nothing to do with free enterprise. Instead, it may more accurately be described as the type of "corporate mercantilism" whereby

> governance is increasingly in the hands of huge private institutions and their representatives. The institutions are totalitarian in character: in a corporation, power flows from top down, with the outside public excluded. . . . National governments, which in varying ways involve some measure of public participation, are constrained by such external factors to serve the interests of the rich and powerful even more than in the past.

But even such promising analyses risk becoming muddled. For one cannot claim at the same time that both U.S. interests (which are eminently national) and those of the TNCs (whose boundaries transcend the nation-state) predominate, when, in crucial respects, they operate at cross-purposes. Here, too, Chomsky's ideological obsessions stand in the way of the type of nuanced and responsible social analysis that is so desperately needed by the left today.

Robert F. Barsky (essay date 1997)

SOURCE: "Conclusion," in *Noam Chomsky: A Life of Dissent*, MIT Press, 1997, pp. 201-17.

[*In the following essay, Barsky provides an overview of Chomsky's linguistic studies, political engagement, and critical reception since the 1980s.*]

In the early 1980s, Chomsky made important progress in his linguistic work, which led him to embark upon what has been described as a "new program." The products of this are recorded in *Lectures on Government and Binding: The Pisa Lectures* (1981), *Knowledge of Language: Its Nature, Origin, and Use* (1986), *Barriers* (1986), and, finally, in a more accessible form, in *Language and Problems of Knowledge: The Managua Lectures* (1988), which also includes some political discussion arising out of questions posed by the Managua audience. *The Minimalist Program,* although not published until 1995, took shape around questions that came into focus in 1980 with the principles-and-parameters model.

These texts emerge from the postulate that languages have no language-particular rules or grammatical constructions of the traditional sort, but rather universal principles and a finite array of options for application. They represent significant advances in the field. In 1988, Chomsky stated that contemporary insights into "empty categories and the principles that govern them and that determine the nature of mental representations and computations in general," "the principles of phrase structure, binding theory, and other subsystems of universal grammar," are allowing us "to see into the hidden nature of the mind . . . really for the first time in history." These discoveries were, he insisted, comparable "with the discovery of waves, particles, genes and so on and the principles that hold of them, in the physical sciences"; furthermore, "we are approaching a situation that is comparable with the physical sciences in the seventeenth-century, when the great scientific revolution took place . . ." (*Language and Problems* 91-92). And, in the introduction to *The Minimalist Program,* he continued along this trajectory, claiming that "it is, I think, of considerable importance that we can at least formulate such questions today, and even approach them in some areas with a degree of success. If recent thinking along these lines is anywhere near accurate, a rich and exciting future lies ahead for the study of language and related disciplines" (9).

Chomsky's political work continued to evolve. While he consistently maintained the principles he had adopted so many years before, he now broadened his scope to address a larger number of issues. He delved deeper into media research (*Manufacturing Consent: The Political Economy of the Mass Media* [1988], with Edward S. Herman; *Necessary Illusions* [1989]), and explored other areas, such as Cold War, post-Cold War, and terrorist-style politics (*Towards a New Cold War: Essays on the Current Crisis and How We Got There* [1982]; *Pirates and Emperors: International Terrorism and the Real World* [1986]; *The Culture of Terrorism* [1988]; *Terrorizing the Neighbourhood: American Foreign Policy in the Post-Cold War Era* [1991]; *World Orders, Old and New* [1994]; *Powers and Prospects* [1996]), Israel (*The Fateful Triangle: The United States, Israel and the Palestinians* [1983]), Latin America (*Turning the Tide: U.S. Intervention in Central America and the Struggle for Peace* [1985]), Vietnam (*Rethinking Camelot: JFK, the Vietnam*

War, and U.S. Political Culture [1993]), and imperialism (*Deterring Democracy* [1991]; *Year 501: The Conquest Continues* [1993]). Two of the best anthologies of his work were also published during this period, *Language and Politics* (1988) and *The Chomsky Reader* (1987); two excellent introductions to his work were written by Carlos Otero (*Radical Priorities* [1981] and *Language and Politics* [1988]); and collections of interviews such as *Chronicles of Dissent* (1992) and *Keeping the Rabble in Line: Interviews with David Barsamian* (1994) gave the reader access to interviews on wide-ranging subjects.

Scanning this incomplete list of publications—produced during an era dominated by a virtual president named Ronald Reagan, an absurd arms race, the decline and dismantling of the Soviet Union, and superpower engagements with such world-menacing despots as Noriega, Hussein, Khaddafi, and Castro, as well as threats to the stability of the free world from Grenada, Nicaragua, and East Timor—it becomes evident that a synopsis of Chomsky's output over even a relatively short period would only amount to a scratch on the surface of an enormous body of work.

A better way to determine where Chomsky is standing at the present juncture, to communicate a sense of his current milieu, is to look at three issues in which he has become implicated. First, Chomsky has in recent times observed a growing cynicism in the American people, a conviction that the political system is manifestly biased against them and that real political power has eluded their grasp. Out of this cynicism they have, for example, voted against their own best interests (Chomsky cites a poll in which people were asked if they voted for Reagan; the majority responded "Yes," but when asked if they thought Reagan's policies would be beneficial to them they replied "No"). Second, Chomsky has noticed a related increase in the distance between the rulers and the ruled. This is the result of both the increased accumulation of power within a shrinking segment of the population, and the widely heralded "world market economy" (frequently described by Chomsky as a fraudulent label employed by the elite), which has been expanded thanks to the European Union, the North American Free Trade Agreement, and a new General Agreement on Tariffs and Trade treaty. Third, Chomsky has begun, in his political writings, to cite primary sources and media reports rather than the influential figures to whom he had once regularly turned. This phenomenon reflects the growth of popular movements and Chomsky's involvement in them. Also, Chomsky admits, "virtually no one shared my interest in anarchism (and Spanish anarchism) . . . and the deepening of my own understanding of the (left) libertarian tradition back to the Enlightenment and before was completely isolated from anyone I knew or know of" (31 Mar. 1995).

PUSHING THE LIMITS OF UNDERSTANDING

Despite the fact that he has been so often mired in controversy, Chomsky continues to receive respect and admiration from his peers. They have rewarded him for his many accomplishments with such honors as: the Distinguished Scientific Contribution Award, American Psychological Association (1984); the Kyoto Prize in Basic Science, Inamori Foundation (1988); and the Orwell Award, National Council of Teachers of English (1987 and 1989). He was also made an honorary member, Ges. Für Sprachwissenschaft, Germany in 1990, and, in the same year, became a William James fellow, American Psychological Association.

Incredible advancements, beginning in the early 1980s, have transformed the field of linguistics. Chomsky has been at the forefront of this activity, but credit is also due to scholars outside the United States and to those linguists who have conducted empirical studies of a vast range of typologically different languages. In a very general sense, Chomsky's linguistic work to date falls into three areas of research. These take the form of questions:

> 1. What do we know when we are able to speak and understand a language?
>
> 2. How is this language acquired?
>
> 3. How do we use this knowledge?
>
> (*Language and Problems* 133)

To question one, the answer is descriptive, so to pursue it we must "attempt to construct a grammar, a theory of a particular language that describes how this language assigns specific mental representations to each linguistic expression, determine its form and meaning." Next, we have to explain it by constructing "a theory of universal grammar, a theory of the fixed and invariant principles that constitute the human language faculty and the parameters of variation associated with them" (*Language and Problems* 133). If we are able to construct a universal grammar, we can then approach the second question, because "language learning . . . is the process of determining the values of the parameters left unspecified by universal grammar, of setting the switches that make the network function. . . ." The third question involves the study of "how people who have acquired a language put their knowledge to use in understanding what they hear and in expressing their thoughts" (*Language and Problems* 134). What remains for the future is a fourth question: "What are the physical mechanisms involved in the representation, acquisition, and the use of this knowledge?" (*Language and Problems* 133).

This question concerns the limits of human understanding. Even as he is making breakthroughs in his field, Chomsky is also becoming more and more concerned with the biological limits of the human being as they pertain to the fundamental questions of existence. Although the physical sciences have afforded us great insight into the workings of matter, studies of the mind have not yielded anywhere near as much useful and scientifically proven information about the basics of human nature. Questions posed by the Greeks, and repeated with variations by generation upon generation of thinkers ever since, remain unanswered.

Humankind will perhaps never be able to unravel these mysteries, but this does not mean that they cannot motivate research or generate other questions that might bring researchers closer to their goals.

In pursuit of answers to the overarching fourth question, Chomsky has asked, in the lectures he has given at MIT since the late 1980s:

> (1) What are the general conditions that the human language faculty should be expected to satisfy? (2) to what extent is the language faculty determined by these conditions, without special structure that lies beyond them? The first question in turn has two aspects: what conditions are imposed on the language faculty by virtue of (A) its place within the array of cognitive systems of the mind/brain, and (B) general considerations of conceptual naturalness that have some independent plausibility, namely: simplicity, economy, symmetry, non-redundancy, and the like? (***The Minimalist Program*** 1).

He has proceeded along these lines with apparent success, but notes that "what looks reasonable today is likely to take a different form tomorrow" (***The Minimalist Program*** 10). Though we have moved closer to uncovering some secrets that were previously thought to be impenetrable, there is, of course, no way of knowing where the limits to human knowledge lie.

Chomsky's own scientific work is dependent upon new empirical and theoretical ideas; the minimalist program, for example, owes its successes to the bold speculation that characterized the principles-and-parameters approach coupled with massive empirical data. This is not to say that Chomsky's most recent linguistic efforts represent a total break from his earlier work. Indeed, "the minimalist program shares several underlying factual assumptions with its predecessors back to the early 1950s, though these have taken somewhat different forms as inquiry has proceeded," and it borrows "from earlier work the assumption that the cognitive system interacts with the performance systems by means of levels of linguistic representation, in the technical sense of this notion" (***The Minimalist Program*** 2).

ART AND LITERATURE: AN UNDEFINABLE INFLUENCE

On occasion, Chomsky has suggested that the mysterious aspects of human existence and the limits of our knowledge are, in some ways, best explored in works of art. But he does not, like Adorno, Benjamin, Greenberg, or Hauser, seek within the domain of music, visual art, sculpture, or photography visions that offer, for example, alternatives to our present society:

> I seem to have a tin ear for atonal music, I'm afraid: past some Berg I mostly listen out of a sense of duty (I have some friends who are well-known composers, and I go to their concerts, for example). As for abstract art, my tastes also tend to fade out after cubism, mainly. Do I find "motivation, inspiration or philosophical truths" in any of this? As for motivation and inspira-

tion, who knows, maybe unconsciously. As for philosophical truths, not as I understand the term at least (in fact, I'm not convinced that the category exists—maybe my Wittgensteinian youth [is] showing). (8 Aug. 1994)

There are, however, frequent references to literature in Chomsky's writings, and several intersections exist between his work and literary texts. First, Chomsky-inspired linguistics has been employed by some critics in formulating their approaches to literary texts, particularly in areas such as semiotics, structuralism, and narratology. Second, Chomsky's philosophical work on creativity and performance has been used to enhance or critique theoretical treatments of literary texts. Third, the popularity of particular authors or literary texts, and the degree of ease or difficulty with which an author publishes a particular work in a particular place and time, are taken by Chomsky as gauges of the control exerted over public expression and the institutions that channel it. Chomsky's many remarks on Orwell bear upon this issue. For example:

> If Orwell, instead of writing *1984*—which was actually, in my opinion, his worst book, a kind of trivial caricature of the most totalitarian society in the world, which made him famous and everybody loved him, because it was the official enemy—if instead of doing that easy and relatively unimportant thing, he had done the hard and important thing, namely talk about Orwell's problem . . . [how is it that we know so little given the amount of evidence we have], he would not be famous and honored: he would be hated and reviled and marginalized. ("Creation")

Finally, Chomsky has suggested that literature can offer a far deeper insight into the whole human person than any mode of scientific inquiry. This notion is an interesting anomaly, given his fundamental belief in the power and value of pure sciences over social sciences. He nevertheless remains reticent about drawing "tight connections" between literature and knowledge because he can't really say whether literature has ever "changed [his] attitudes and understanding in any striking or crucial way":

> [I]f I want to understand, let's say, the nature of China and its revolution, I ought to be cautious about literary renditions. Look, there's no question that as a child, when I read about China, this influenced my attitudes—*Rickshaw Boy*, for example. That had a powerful effect when I read it. It was so long ago I don't remember a thing about it, except the impact. . . . Literature can heighten your imagination and insight and understanding, but it surely doesn't provide the evidence that you need to draw conclusions and substantiate conclusions. (***Chomsky Reader*** 4)

Literature from this standpoint is a means through which experiences can be reread and, potentially, reviewed. It would be difficult to determine whether certain attitudes precede someone's reading of literary texts (thus allowing certain ideas to resonate), or whether the literary texts themselves help form the attitudes (as Chomsky implies in his discussion of the role that these texts played for him as a child). But the actual relationship between literary knowledge and empirical fact is clearly problematic for Chomsky, to the point where he consciously blocks out any effects that literary texts might have for his analysis of particular situations. Nevertheless, Chomsky was, and continues to be, "powerfully influenced" by his broad readings of literary texts (8 Aug. 1994), although the nature of this influence is undefinable: "We learn from literature as we learn from life; no one knows how, but it surely happens. In fact, most of what we know about things that matter comes from such sources, surely not from considered rational inquiry (science), which sometimes reaches unparalleled depths of profundity, but has a rather narrow scope—a product, I assume, of special properties of human cognitive structure" (15 Dec. 1992). These "properties," like the physical mechanisms involved in the representation, acquisition, and the use of knowledge, are some of the areas of human nature that have always been virtually impenetrable. But, as his research and his remarks about literature imply, Chomsky considers that human nature may someday be describable, and aspects of it may even be understood—a possibility that many of his contemporaries don't admit, because they refuse to recognize that a human nature exists. To Chomsky, this kind of thinking is absurd: "Yes, I speak of human nature, but not for complicated reasons. I do so because I am not an imbecile, and do not believe that others should fall into culturally imposed imbecility. Thus, I do not want to cater to imbecility. Is my granddaughter different from a rock? From a bird? From a gorilla? If so, then there is such a thing as human nature. That's the end of the discussion: we then turn to asking what human nature is" (15 Dec. 1992). He goes on to speculate about the source of the denials of human nature:

> For intellectuals—that is, social, cultural, economic and political managers—it is very convenient to believe that people have "no nature," that they are completely malleable. That eliminates any moral barrier to manipulation and control, an attractive idea for those who expect to conduct the manipulation, and to gain power, prestige and wealth thereby. The doctrine is so utterly foolish that one has to seek an explanation. This is the one that intellectual and social history seem to me to suggest. (15 Dec. 1992)

There is, in the attitude expressed here, some indication of Chomsky's linguistic theory (all people have a characteristic creative capacity and share particular innate abilities), his opinion of most intellectuals (he uses the term "managers" in the same sense that Bakunin and Pannekoek did), his thoughts concerning appropriate environments for human development (beyond control and manipulation), and his suspicions about a collusion between elite powers and those who promote certain doctrines. Also evident in his commentary is the characteristic goad—the quality that nudges his readers to evaluate and reevaluate their basic assumptions in the name of both common sense (the granddaughter-rock comparison) and social autonomy (preaching "no nature" paves the way for social control à la, for example, Skinner). Chomsky the worker never lets up—his long product list testifies to this—and Chomsky the thinker doesn't let things pass without scrutiny, because to do so would be to risk falling into some carefully designed trap, the type of pitfall that left libertarians have long been at pains to expose.

FIGHTING FOR CONTROL

So what remains to be done? Struggle. Struggle in the face of biases that dog research of all types, of accepted dogma, of manipulation and propaganda; struggle to promote human freedom. Although the obstacles seem great, there are enough success stories from which to draw strength:

> We don't live under slavery because of popular struggles. We have freedom of speech because of popular struggles. It is never a gift from above. James Madison, one of the founding fathers, put it very clearly. He said a parchment barrier will never protect against tyranny. . . . nor are you ever going to get any gifts from above. Protection against tyranny comes from struggle, and it doesn't matter what kind of tyranny it is. And if that is carried out, it can achieve many gains. There has been a considerable expansion of the sphere of freedom over the centuries, and it has a long way to go. ("Creation")

But while Chomsky has made progress in recent years on the linguistics front, he cannot rest on his political-activist laurels. He is compelled to point continuously to the ways in which oppressive structures such as fascism and totalitarianism (which we like to believe have been dismantled, at least within our own society), as well as concentration camps, torture chambers, and "ethnic-cleansing" campaigns, still exist. Certainly anyone willing to take the time to examine the nature of governments, corporations—even leisure activities—knows this to be true: "Take professional sports. . . . It is hard to imagine anything that contributes more fundamentally to authoritarian attitudes. In professional sports you are a spectator, and there is a bunch of gladiators beating each other up, or something. And you are supposed to cheer for your gladiators. That is something you are taught from childhood" ("Creation").

Unfortunately, the task of publicly identifying such structures is arduous and time-consuming. Those who undertake it are also, in Chomsky's opinion, likely to be thwarted by a coerced and manipulative media, by government, and by corporate interests bent on obscuring pertinent information. While government may seem the most obvious culprit in such attempts at suppression, Chomsky stresses that the impression is purposefully constructed:

> The problem isn't "governments," at least in the West. They are not much involved in doctrinal management (though there are exceptions, like Woodrow Wilson and the Reaganites, both of whom ran huge state propaganda systems—illegal in the latter case; there were no relevant laws in the Wilson era). Doctrinal management is overwhelmingly the task of corporate propaganda, which is extraordinary in scale and very significant in impact; and [it is also] the task of the general intellectual community, including the acceptable dissidents (Irving Howe, founder of *Dissent,* etc.) who perform a very important service by setting the bounds of discussion and thus entrenching the unspoken presuppositions of the doctrinal system, a matter again that I've discussed at length. Anyway, governments are marginal, outside of totalitarian states, though attention is always

focused on them, to direct it away from what matters. (31 Mar. 1995)

Extra-governmental organizations—the IMF, the World Bank, the GATT council, and the G-7 executive—are also implicated in the campaign to exclude what Chomsky refers to as the "rabble" from the process of making the decisions and creating the policies that directly concern them:

> [A] technique of control which is actually being sort of pioneered in the contemporary period, both in the United States and Europe, is raising the level of decisions to be so remote from people's knowledge and understanding that they don't even know what is going on. They can't find out what is happening, and certainly can't influence it even if they do. That is part of the meaning of the "*de facto* world government" [a citation from the *Financial Times* that refers to a new set of emerging institutions outside of the national state] that is developing. ("Creation")

This kind of argument has familiar echoes, at least in terms of the values that underwrite it. It is, in spirit, the argument that Chomsky has always put forward, and it exists, in embryonic form, in the work of those who populate the milieu from which he emerged.

There is a sense that Chomsky's political work is, in its stubborn reiteration of fact and its insistence upon the absolute relevance of particular events, somehow untheoretical. In light of his previous commentary on intellectual obfuscation, the trivial observations that pass for political science, and unnecessarily complex language, his reply to such a charge is perhaps predictable:

> If someone can come up with a nontrivial theory that has some bearing on matters of human concern, with conclusions of any credibility that would alter the ways in which I or others view these matters without access to the "theory," I'd be the first to immerse myself in it, with delight. What I find, however, is intellectuals posturing before one another. Maybe that's my inability to discern important things, but if so, it should be possible to explain this to me. Many people in the academic and intellectual left complain at length about my "non-theoretical" stance, as do those elsewhere. But so far, no one has even tried to respond to this very simple challenge that any sane person would make, as far as I can see. What am I to conclude from that? (31 Mar. 1995)

And so, Chomsky continues to publish political works that are as powerful and consistent as ever. In all of these, right up to the recent ***World Orders, Old and New*** (1994), may be found resonances of fundamentally left-libertarian values. As ever, though, there are those who object violently to Chomsky's offerings. Ken Jowitt, for example, who reviewed ***World Orders*** for the 10 February 1995 edition of the *Times Literary Supplement,* declared that the book is an expression of its author's "unrelenting anger"; it also communicates his belief in a transnational corporate conspiracy, his dismissal of ideology as anything more than a "disguise" to be "unmasked," his prophetlike scorn for intellectual pharisees, his ahistorical view of history, and his "one-dimensional conception of power as vio-

lence." But this work, like Chomsky's other recent political publications, is better understood as speaking to libertarian anarchist groups, popular organizations, inchoate movements, as well as concerned and even desperate people; indeed, writes Chomsky, "that's the milieu I want to be a part of." These groups, unlike the narrower one composed mainly of intellectuals to which he spoke earlier in his career, are less thoroughly indoctrinated by systems of power, including corporations and institutions of higher learning, and more willing to think things through. To speak to these people is, for Chomsky, "an intellectual and emotional release, and I do, I'm sure, write and speak differently from 30 years ago, probably on all topics. But that's a step towards—not away from—the radical intellectual milieu that I've felt myself part of since adolescence" (31 Mar. 1995).

In electing to involve himself even more deeply in popular struggles, Chomsky has significantly accelerated his already hectic schedule. The range and pace of activities he records here (rather breathlessly) is typical:

> I recently spent a week in Australia, at the invitation of East Timorese refugees who wanted to focus attention on Australia's (horrible) policies of support for the Indonesian invasion and rip-off of East Timor's petroleum resources (I also gave talks there at universities, and on every other imaginable topic, but the focus was this, including a nationally televised talk at the National Press Club critically analyzing Australia's foreign policy and the self-serving lies with which it is concealed—this is Australia, not the U.S., a far more ideological society, where nothing of this sort would ever be allowed). Before that I spent a week in California, at the invitation of the Berkeley philosophy department for several lectures and the Stanford University program on ethics and public policy, but with most of my time devoted to talks in Oakland organized by Catholic Worker (which works in the slums, mainly with illegal refugees), another organized by Timorese students, a third for the biggest and oldest peace and justice group around (Palo Alto), another for the Middle East Children's Alliance, etc. All of these were benefits— that's a major way for such groups to raise money and increase public outreach, since the audiences are usually huge, with people who are interested. (31 Mar. 1995)

This is where Chomsky chooses to be; in both word and action, he has embraced activism more closely than ever before, and has turned his back, for the most part, on discussions of social theory. But while his heart is with those who share in the struggle, he continues in his academic work. Yet another glimpse at his full-tilt itinerary serves to demonstrate the way Chomsky prioritizes the two worlds within which he operates and how he manages to strike an at times delicate balance between them:

> The last time I was in Europe, a few months ago, was at the invitation of the U. of London for philosophy lectures, but that was combined with talks for popular audiences and activist groups at a town hall and downtown theatre, a visit to Portugal at the invitation of the Socialist Party, and a talk at Geneva organized by Women's International League for Peace and Freedom, mainly third world women and activist NGOS [non-governmental organizations]. (31 Mar. 1995)

Chomsky also gave the keynote address at a conference that he otherwise did not attend.

A LAST LOOK

So, as he works on the minimalist program—conducting linguistic research that could lead us to a better understanding of the mind/brain—Chomsky is also participating in activist initiatives around the world that call into question the tyrannical and oppressive structures that limit individual freedom and creativity. All this is bolstered by fifty years of commitment to ideas that in both the linguistic and political domains have stood the test of time by remaining topical and applicable. Generations of scholars have been trained by Chomsky. The Chomskys' lives today are simple, comfortable, and filled with the rewards of passionate teaching and research, and of dedication to a consistent set of values.

I would like to leave the reader with one last picture of Noam Chomsky. It is 1990, and he sits in a pub in Govan (a suburb of Glasgow), surrounded by the participants of a Self-Determination and Power Event. These include social workers; literati ("Bohemian writers," Chomsky says, "mostly outcasts," the most famous of whom is Jim Kelman [31 Mar. 1995]); educationists ("radical critics of the educational system, like Derek Rodgers"); anarchists and libertarian socialists; and people variously describing themselves as "feminist therapist," "systems analyst," "anti-poll-tax activist," "mother/student," "prison governor," "retail manager," and "boatbuilder/writer." The event, accompanied by a wonderful pub photo, is covered by the *Times Higher Education Supplement* of 26 January 1990 under the headline: "Pubs, Power and the Scottish Psyche: Olga Wojtas Reports from Govan on a Conference on Self-Determination." The 330 participants of the event (many of whom [are] "unemployed working class, activists of one or another sort, those considered to be 'riff-raff'"—"the kind of people," Chomsky says, that "I like and take seriously" [31 Mar. 1995]), which has been organized by the magazines *Scottish Child* and *Edinburgh Review* and the Free University of Glasgow (not a university in the accepted sense of the term), are interested in self-determination and a guru named Noam Chomsky, self-described "scourge of United States policies and champion of the ordinary person." Chomsky gives keynote speeches on both days of the event. The fact that he has decided to attend at all mystifies both the press and the establishment.

> Thus when an announcement came that I was going to be in Glasgow, I got a letter on very fancy letterhead from something called "the Scottish Foundation" inviting me to give a talk for them on Nicaragua. I of course agreed. Shortly after, I got another letter saying they'd just learned that I'd also be giving a talk organized by the free university, Kelman, and other scum, and they insisted that I cancel that invitation because they wouldn't tolerate the guilt by association. I don't recall whether I even bothered answering. (31 Mar. 1995)

In his talks, Chomsky disparages nationalism, the exercise of political power by leaders who do not answer to citizens, instruments of social control and isolationism such as television, and the collusion of media in the process of oppression and the spreading of lies. There remains, at the end of the event, the problem of "how to take on the bastards," as well as "an imbalance in that people seemed to feel they had to stay on an intellectual plane." Said one participant, "If I sound a bit frustrated, it's because I'm a bit frustrated" (Wojtas). But Chomsky is not there to lead.

He's sitting in the Govan pub, and, as always, he's insisting that the participants consider their own situation as clearheadedly as possible, and that they make their own decisions. The *Times Higher Education Supplement* has reported: "Professor Chomsky continued to duck the role of oracle, denying the need for oracles at all. There had been a sense, he recognized, that there was something deeply unsatisfying about general and abstract discussion which did not direct itself to concrete discussion of oppression and justice." Somebody recalls Vaclav Havel's dictum that "truth and love will triumph over hatred and lies." Chomsky's response? "It's a nice thought." Yes, but is it true or false? "Neither. It could become true, to the extent that people struggle to make it come true." Noam Chomsky, sixty-eight years old, Institute Professor, linguist, philosopher, grandfather, champion of ordinary people.

Neve Gordon (review date 14 June 1999)

SOURCE: "Neoliberals' Paleomarkets," in *The Nation*, June 14, 1999, pp. 34, 36.

[*In the following review, Gordon offers positive evaluation of* Profit Over People, *though notes contradictions concerning the incompatibility of social justice and free trade.*]

In a book of interviews published a few years ago, **Chronicles of Dissent,** Noam Chomsky recounted a childhood incident that shaped his life. One day during first grade, a group began taunting a fat boy from his class. Chomsky wanted to defend him but fled instead. Following the event he was totally ashamed, and he determined never again to run away. "That's the feeling that stuck with me," he says. "You should stick with the underdog." Sixty-five years have passed, and Chomsky remains faithful to that commitment, as evidenced by **Profit Over People,** his new book.

Since the demise of the cold war, received wisdom suggests that we are witnessing a rapid growth in democratization. Yet, if democracy is not merely a term attributed to a set of political procedures but also involves concrete "opportunities for people to manage their own collective and individual affairs," then democracy, according to Chomsky, is actually under attack.

Chomsky argues that there is an ongoing conversion of people from participants to spectators, maintaining that this trend is also found in Western industrialized countries. In the United States people have fewer opportunities to influence policies because of what Chomsky calls the "corporatization of America." By reducing "big government," decisions are transferred from the one form of power that happens to be somewhat accountable to the public into the hands of corporations, whose CEOs are, politically speaking, like tyrants, having little if any respect for the American public.

The ironic twist about this trend is that corporations have not acquired their power through fair play in the free market but rather as a result of government assistance. By making this claim Chomsky goes beyond Susan Strange's important book *The Retreat of the State: The Diffusion of Power in the World Economy* (1996). Strange depicts international political economy as a confrontation between big business, international bureaucrats and insurers on the one side, and state sovereignty on the other. She argues that economic actors have in many ways managed to usurp the power that had previously been in the hands of political actors. Chomsky's nuanced analysis of current political trends discloses a slightly different picture. He suggests that there is an alliance between the state and economic players. Although corporations support minimizing government, they want governments to maintain a degree of power since government intervention and not the rules of the free market insure a corporation's dominance.

Thus, contrary to the dominant neoliberal doctrine, which suggests that economic globalization points to the demise of the nation-state and to the free market's success, Chomsky shows that globalization is the result of ongoing government interference and precipitates poverty and ecological destruction. By disclosing the overarching patterns of neoliberalism, ***Profit Over People*** complements a number of studies—for instance, Thomas Klak's *Globalization and Neoliberalism: The Caribbean Context* (1997) and Gerardo Otero's *Neoliberalism Revisited: Economic Restructuring and Mexico's Political Future* (1996)—that have examined neoliberalism's effect on specific areas.

Chomsky's book comprises a series of articles that analyze some of the mechanisms that make the global economy tick, while underscoring the alarming consequences of globalization. The pages are packed with data and case studies—some not yet published in mainstream media—that are used to debunk prevailing myths.

While explicating the general trends underlying neoliberalism, Chomsky also pays special attention to the United States, analyzing its hegemonic role in world politics. As University of Illinois communications professor Robert McChesney points out in the book's introduction, the US government pushes "trade deals and other accords down the throats of the world's people to make it easier for corporations and the wealthy to dominate the economies of nations around the world without having obligations to the peoples of those nations."

For example, USAID and the World Bank intervened in Haiti's economy, replacing subsistence farming with agro-exports. Chomsky points out that "before the 'reforms' were instituted, local rice production supplied virtually all domestic needs," but "thanks to one-sided 'liberalization,' it now provides only 50 percent. . . . By such methods, the most impoverished country in the hemisphere has been turned into a leading purchaser of U.S.-produced rice, enriching publicly subsidized U.S. enterprises." The consequences, Chomsky concludes, "were the usual ones: profits for U.S. manufacturers and the Haitian super-rich, and a decline of 56 percent in Haitian wages" due to massive unemployment.

The market serves those with money, neglecting those trapped in poverty; and increased poverty, Chomsky points out, has a direct impact on the quality of democratic life. People living under dire conditions—the UN estimates that the disparity between the richest and poorest 20 percent of the world population increased by more than 50 percent from 1960 to 1989—have fewer opportunities for communal and personal development. And freedom without opportunities is like "a devil's gift."

While the connection Chomsky draws between the global economic order and the decline in democratic practices is insightful, I have one major reservation. If social justice is the objective, then trade will always need to be constrained, because the market does not have the capacity to make political distinctions, and it invariably treats everyone and everything as a commodity to be exchanged. In this age the state is the only force that can stand up to the market and check it. Chomsky intimates this on a few occasions, but downplays it, because, as a libertarian, he holds that only a minimal state—limited to extremely narrow functions—can be justified. His reticence about what the state's role should be within the context of a neoliberal world lays bare the tension, if not the contradiction, between his socialist and libertarian leanings.

In one of the rare passages in which he endorses government interference, Chomsky approvingly quotes Adam Smith's claim that the destructive force of the "invisible hand" must be constrained by the state. By endorsing Smith's rationale Chomsky also endorses liberalism's basic premise that the so-called invisible hand is not a product of government regulation—a claim that sits well with a libertarian worldview but appears antithetical to a socialist analysis. Perhaps this explains why Chomsky neglects to note—in this and other books—that on a metalevel laissez-faire is engendered by government intervention. Following Antonio Gramsci, I think it best to see free trade as a form of state regulation, introduced and maintained by legislative and coercive means.

In another sense, however, Chomsky parallels Gramsci, exemplifying the latter's motto "pessimism of the intellect, optimism of the will." Chomsky's analysis of current events does not shy away from the injustice he encounters, but he does not capitulate to a paralyzing despair. The tragedy, he notes, is that if we leave matters to the neoliberal global market, then every two hours "1,000 children will die from easily preventable disease, and almost twice that many women will die or suffer serious disabilities in pregnancy or childbirth for lack of simple remedies and care." Yet, as Chomsky points out, the market's oppressive manifestations cannot erase the rich record of popular struggles led by people committed to principles of justice and freedom, achievements that provide hope for a better future.

Noam Chomsky with David Barsamian (interview date September 1999)

SOURCE: "Noam Chomsky," in *The Progressive,* Vol. 63, No. 9, September, 1999, pp. 33-7.

[*In the following interview, Chomsky discusses critical disapproval of his views, media manipulation, Gulf War propaganda, inconsistent and hypocritical condemnations of international human rights offenders, and American politics.*]

Noam Chomsky, longtime political activist, writer, and professor of linguistics at MIT, is the author of numerous books and articles on U.S. foreign policy, international affairs, human rights, and the media. His works include *Manufacturing Consent,* with Ed Herman (Pantheon, 1988), *Deterring Democracy* (Verso, 1991), *World Orders, Old and New* (Columbia University, 1994), *Profit Over People* (Seven Stories, 1999), and *Fateful Triangle* (South End, revised edition, 1999). His latest book is *The New Military Humanism* (Common Courage, 1999).

I first wrote to Chomsky around 1980. Much to my surprise, he responded. We did our first interview four years later. We've done scores since then, resulting in a series of books as well as radio programs. The interview collections have sold in the hundreds of thousands, which is remarkable since they have had virtually no promotion and have not been reviewed even in left journals.

In working with Chomsky over the years, I've been struck with his consistency, patience, and equanimity. There are no power plays or superior airs. In terms of his intellectual chops, he is awesome in his ability to take a wide and disparate amount of information and cobble it into a coherent analysis.

Chomsky, now seventy, is indefatigable. In addition to producing a steady stream of articles and books on politics and linguistics, he maintains a heavy speaking schedule: He is in enormous demand and is often booked years in advance. He draws huge audiences wherever he goes, though not because of a flashy speaking style. As he once told me, "I'm not a charismatic speaker, and if I had the capacity to do so, I wouldn't do it. I'm really not interested in persuading people. What I like to do is help people persuade themselves." And this he has done probably with more diligence over a longer period of time than any other intellectual.

The *New Statesman* calls him "the conscience of the American people." To cite just one example of his solidarity, last year I asked him to come to Boulder to speak at KGNU community radio's twentieth anniversary. Notwithstanding being fatigued from recent surgery, he not only came but waived his fee.

Often Chomsky is introduced as someone who exemplifies the Quaker adage of speaking truth to power. He takes exception to that. He says the powerful already know what's going on. It is the people who need to hear the truth.

As a kid growing up in Philadelphia, when he wasn't writing articles in the school newspaper on the Spanish Civil War, he was a long-suffering Athletics baseball fan. In those days, he recalls, the A's were always getting creamed by the Yankees. "For children of first-generation Jewish immigrants, it was considered part of your Americanization to know more about baseball than anybody else," he says. Today, after years of not paying attention to sports, Chomsky takes his grandchildren to games. Nevertheless, his trenchant critique remains. "Sports," he says, "plays a societal role in engendering jingoist and chauvinist attitudes. They're designed to organize a community to be committed to their gladiators." If you are playing on a team, according to Chomsky, it's not much better. "They build up irrational attitudes of submission to authority."

I can see it now. Chomsky at the plate. Barsamian on the mound. The count is three and two, bottom of the ninth. His team is, of course, losing. Here's the pitch. And Chomsky swings, there's a long drive to deep left, and that ball is . . .

This interview is culled from four hours we did early in February in Lexington and Cambridge, Massachusetts.

[*Barsamian*]: *Our interviews are a kind of roulette. You really don't know where the questions are coming from or what kind of detail you'll need. How do you feel about that?*

[Chomsky]: You've got the upper hand. I'm just your servant. So I have the easy job. I just follow where you lead.

OK, you've said many times that you're not Amnesty International. What determines your involvement in an issue?

If you can't do anything about some problem, it doesn't help a lot to make big statements about it. We could all get together and say, "Condemn Genghis Khan," but there's no moral value. So the first question is, to what extent can we influence things? To the extent that U.S. power is directly involved, we can influence it more than if it's not directly involved, for example.

If it's a very popular issue, I don't feel that there's much advantage in my talking about it. Take South Africa. I said very little about apartheid, although I think overcoming it was an extremely important thing. It didn't seem like a useful contribution of my time to say "I agree," which I often did. I'd rather take issues that are being kept out of the public sphere and on which we can really do a lot and that are intrinsically important.

There are other things that are just personal. Ever since childhood, I happen to have been concerned with Israel, or what was Palestine. I grew up in that environment. I've lived there, read the Hebrew newspapers, have a lot of friends there—so naturally I'm involved in that.

The last time you were on National Public Radio's All Things Considered *was during the Gulf War in February 1991. Your commentary had to do with countries violating Security Council resolutions. You were imagining a U.S. bombing attack on Tel Aviv, Ankara, and Jakarta.*

If you look at the list of leading recipients of U.S. aid, virtually every one of them is a major human rights violator. In the Western Hemisphere, the leading recipient of military aid through the 1990s has been mostly Colombia, which also has the worst human rights record. That was the point of that comment. Of course, you don't have to bomb these countries. If you want to stop the terror and atrocities that they're carrying out, just stop supporting them.

Your two minute and thirty second commentary was surrounded by a virtual cacophony of Gulf War propaganda.

Recall the comment of Jeff Greenfield, who used to be on *Nightline*. He explained why they wouldn't have me on. He said there were two reasons. First of all, I'm from Neptune. Secondly, I lack concision. I agree with him.

On both counts? Neptune also?

In my two minutes and thirty seconds, I must have sounded to a reasonable listener as if I were from Neptune. There was no context, no background, no evidence, and it was completely different from everything they were hearing. The rational response is, "This guy must be from Neptune." That's correct.

It leaves you with very simple choices: Either you repeat the same conventional doctrines everybody else is spouting, or else you say something true, and it will sound like it's from Neptune. Concision requires that there be no evidence. The flood of unanimous doctrine ensures that it will sound as if it's off the wall.

I came across this quote from George Orwell. He says, "Circus dogs jump when the trainer cracks his whip. But the really well-trained dog is the one that turns his somersault when there's no whip."

I suspect he was talking about intellectuals. The intellectual class is supposed to be so well trained and so well indoctrinated that they don't need a whip. They just react spontaneously in the ways that will serve external power interests, without awareness, thinking they're doing honest, dedicated work. That's a real trained dog.

What kind of suggestions would you make to people who are trying to decode the news?

The first thing is to be very skeptical. Begin by asking, "How is power distributed in society? Who decides what's going to be produced, consumed, and distributed?" You can figure that out in most places pretty easily. Then you should ask whether policies and the shaping of information reflect the distribution of power. You typically find you can explain quite a lot that way.

Take Iraq. One question is, "Why are the U.S. and Britain bombing Iraq and insisting on maintaining sanctions?" If you look, you find answers that are given with near 100 percent agreement. You hear it from Tony Blair, Madeleine Albright, newspaper editors, and commentators. That answer is, "Saddam Hussein is a complete monster. He even committed the ultimate horror—namely, he gassed his own people. We can't let a creature like that survive."

As soon as anything's given with near unanimity, it should be a signal. Nothing is that clear. There happens to be an easy way to test it in this case: How did the U.S. and Britain react when Saddam Hussein committed the ultimate horror? It's on the record. This was in April 1988, the gassing of the Kurdish town of Halabja. The second major gassing occurs in August, five days after the cease-fire when Iran basically capitulated. The U.S. and Britain reacted by continuing—and, in fact, accelerating—their strong support for Saddam Hussein.

That tells you something right away: The gassing of his own people cannot possibly be the reason why the U.S. and Britain are now trying to destroy him. He's a monster, he committed one of the ultimate horrors, and the U.S. and Britain thought it was fine.

Elementary rationality just is not permitted. If anyone wants to test this, they can investigate how often that statement, "We have to bomb Saddam Hussein because he committed the ultimate horror," is followed by the three crucial words: "with our support."

When we look further, we find that a major and, indeed, conscious goal of those concerned with shaping thoughts and attitudes—the advertising and public relations industries and the responsible intellectuals who talk about how to run the world—is to regiment the minds of men as fully as the army regiments the body.

Secretary of Defense William Cohen kept his promise that he made in early 1998 after the public relations disaster at Ohio State: There will be no town meetings the next time we want to bomb Iraq.

They made a serious error that last time. In the buildup to the bombing of Iraq, they had arranged a very carefully planned town meeting, which looked very safe. It was in Columbus, Ohio. The questioners were selected in advance. They picked people they thought would be controlled. It looked like a nicely orchestrated propaganda exercise. But there was organizing in the background. Some of these polite people turned out to have some real questions. They asked them quietly and politely, but as soon as the first word of dissent broke through the uniformity, Cohen, Albright, and [National Security Adviser Sandy] Berger collapsed into gibberish. They couldn't respond. The audience reacted because the dissidence was right below the surface. It totally blew up. That was the context of Cohen's comment.

The bombing of Iraq last December was particularly striking. It was in flat violation of international law. The reason that the United States didn't go to the U.N. Security Council is perfectly obvious. It would not have permitted the bombing. So therefore the Security Council is another "hostile forum," and it's irrelevant. If the U.S. and Britain want to use force, they will. Furthermore, they did it in as brazen a way as possible to demonstrate their contempt for the U.N. and international law. The timing was picked just when the Security Council was meeting in an emergency session dealing with this crisis. Other council members had not been informed. That's a way of saying as clearly as possible, "You're irrelevant. International law is irrelevant. We are rogue states. We will use force and violence as we choose."

That's a big change from, say, 1947, when the contempt for international law was hidden in secret documents, which would be released forty years later. Now it is clear and out in the open. It receives . . . you can't even say the "approval" of intellectual opinion, because it's so deeply taken for granted it's not even noticed. It's just like the air you breathe.

We're a violent, terrorist state. We have a big flag saying: INTERNATIONAL LAW AND THE U.N. CHARTER ARE INAPPROPRIATE FOR US BECAUSE WE HAVE THE GUNS AND WE'RE GOING TO USE THEM. PERIOD.

Incidentally, it's not reported here, but the world does notice. In India, for example, the Indian Council of Jurists is actually bringing a case to the World Court charging the U.S. and Britain with war crimes. The Vatican called the bombing of Iraq "aggression." That got a little mention at the bottom of a page here and there. In the Arab world, it was widely condemned as aggression. In England, it was not as uniform as here. *The Observer* had a lead editorial condemning it as aggression.

One of the advantages of leaving the United States is to be exposed to different media. I was in Thailand in early January. The Nation is one of their two English-language newspapers. There was a very critical article entitled, "Containing America in the Post-Cold War Era." It was by Suravit Jayanama, who wrote, "While Washington talks about containing Saddam Hussein, what about the need to contain a superpower that zealously acts to protect its own interests?"

That's the attitude in much of the world, and with justice. When the world's only superpower, which has essentially a monopoly of force, announces openly, "We will use force and violence as we choose and if you don't like it, get out of the way," there's a reason why that should frighten people.

What about the legacies of this violence?

Look at Laos. It was saturated with probably hundreds of millions of pieces of ordnance. The U.S. government conceded that most of this bombing had nothing to do with the war in Vietnam. At that time, it was the most intensive bombing in history, aimed at a completely defenseless peasant society. I know something about this. I was there and was able to interview some of the refugees—there were tens of thousands—who had just been driven off the Plain of Jars.

The most lethal bombardment was what they called Bombies, little colorful things. They were designed to maim and kill people—that was their only purpose. This region is just littered with maybe hundreds of millions—nobody knows how much—unexploded ordnance. The victims are mainly children and farmers. In fact, the one careful province survey that was done found that 55 percent of the victims were children. Kids are playing. They see these colorful things and pick them up, and they and anyone else around are dead. Farmers hit them if they're trying to clear the ground. That's going on right now. We're not talking about ancient history.

The first group to try to do something about it was the Mennonites. The central Mennonite Committee has had volunteers working there since 1977, and they've been trying to publicize it and get people interested in it. They're trying to give people shovels. No high-tech equipment. There is a British volunteer group, a mine-detection group, professionals, but not the British government. And as the British press puts it, the Americans are notable by their absence.

According to the rightwing British press, the *Sunday Telegraph,* the British mine clearance group claims that the Pentagon will not even give them technical information that would allow them to defuse the bombs. So the British mine clearers themselves are at risk because this is secret information. The U.S. is now, after a lot of pressure, training some Laotians. There was a very proud article in *The Christian Science Monitor* about how the U.S. is such a humane society because we're training Laotians to clear away mines which somehow got there.

Those mines didn't come from Neptune, where I came from. We know where they came from, and we know who's not there getting rid of them.

You, Edward Said, Howard Zinn, and Ed Herman recently issued a statement on Iraq, saying, "The time has come for a call to action to people of conscience. We must organize and make this issue a priority, just as Americans organized to stop the war in Vietnam. We need a national campaign to lift the sanctions." I know you're not against sanctions in all instances, for example, you cite South Africa as quite a separate case.

For clarity, the four of us signed that statement. But it was written, organized, and publicized by Robert Jensen at the University of Texas. That illustrates something that we know is true all the time: The people who really do the work are rarely known. What is known is somebody who stood up and said something or signed a petition.

The burden of proof is always on any imposition of sanctions. Can that burden of proof be overcome? Sometimes. Take South Africa. Two comments about that. One is that sanctions were supported by the overwhelming majority of the population, as far as anybody could determine. If the population is in favor of them, that's an argument, not a proof, that maybe they're a good idea. Two, it would have been a good idea if the U.S. had observed the sanctions. The U.S. undermined them, U.S. trade and interactions with South Africa continued and I believe may have increased.

There was an A.P. report in mid-January 1999 about Israel. In response to criticism that Israeli security services use torture and excessive force when interrogating Palestinians, the government attorney, Yehuda Schaeffer, said, "In this, as in other matters, we are still a light unto the nations," referring to the century-old utopian Zionist slogan.

This has been a scandal even inside Israel. In fact, Israel does use torture, according to international standards. They're constantly condemned for this by human rights groups. Furthermore, they use it consistently. Arab prisoners who are often kept in administrative detention without charge are routinely tortured under interrogation. About ten years ago, this issue broke through to the public. A Druze military officer had been convicted for some crime. It turned out that he was innocent of the crime, and he had confessed to it. Immediately someone asked, "How come he confessed?" It turned out he had been tortured, and that became public.

For years, Palestinian prisoners when they came to court claimed that their confessions had been obtained under torture. The courts uniformly rejected that, all the way up to the High Court. They just dismissed that as false. After this Druze case, they had to recognize that, at least in this one instance, the confession was obtained under torture. Then came an inquiry. It turned out that they had been using torture routinely to interrogate. That was considered a huge scandal, not so much because they had used torture, but because the intelligence services hadn't told the Court. It was kind of like Watergate. It was not bombing Cambodia that was a crime, but not telling Congress about it that's the real crime. Here, too, the High Court condemned the fact that the intelligence services were misleading them, which was a joke. Everybody outside, except for the justices of the High Court, knew that the confessions were being obtained under torture. Moshe Etzioni, one of the High Court justices, was in London in 1977 or so. He had an interview with Amnesty International, which asked why they were getting such a tremendously high rate of confessions. Everybody knows what that means. He said, Arabs tend to confess; it's part of their nature. Amnesty published it without comment.

There was no doubt that Israel was using torture, but the courts, including the High Court, decided to believe the intelligence services. So their claim that they had been misled is a little misleading. They chose to be misled. At that point, the Landau Commission was formed, which had secret meetings and came out with partially public but partially secret recommendations about the use of . . . they didn't call it "torture," but force or pressure or some euphemism. The Landau Commission said no, you shouldn't use this except . . . and then came up with a secret protocol. Nobody knows what's in it. It describes the methods you're allowed to use. You can tell what those methods are by what has happened to prisoners.

There are good ways of studying this. You can take independent testimony from prisoners who don't know each other but have been in the same place, and see if they describe exactly the same thing. The human rights groups have been doing this for years. Probably Israeli torture has been more systematically and carefully investigated than any other. The reason is, you have to have higher standards in the investigation. If you discuss torture in Pakistan, you don't need very high standards. Some prisoner tells you he was tortured—OK, headline. You say the same thing about Israel, you've got to meet the standards of physics. So when the Swiss League of Human Rights or Amnesty International or the London Insight team for the *Sunday Times* or some major newspaper did studies of torture in Israel, they were extremely careful. Still they couldn't get them reported here.

What do you say to those who hear your critique of Israel and its use of torture and ask, "Well, what about Syria? Why aren't you talking about Libya or Iraq? Aren't things much worse there?"

Sure, I mentioned Pakistan. Those countries are much worse. I would agree. I'm not really making a critique. I'm just quoting Human Rights Watch and Amnesty International. These are very conservative comments. I would take the same point of view they do, that we should keep to explicit U.S. law, which bars aid to countries which systematically use torture. So I don't think we should be sending aid to Iraq. In fact, I protested strongly when we were doing exactly that in the 1980s. Of course, it's academic in the case of Iraq and Syria. But if you look at the leading recipients of U.S. aid like Israel, Egypt, Turkey, Pakistan, and Colombia, they use torture. All that aid's illegal.

What's your understanding of the ongoing crisis in global capitalism?

We should begin by recognizing that for a good part of the population of the world, and probably the vast majority, it's been a crisis for a long time. It's now called one because it's starting to affect the interests of rich and powerful people. Up until then it was just starving people.

What has happened, point number one is: Nobody really understands. The Bank for International Settlements—the central bank of central bankers, it's sometimes called, the most conservative, respectable institution in the universe—produces an annual report. The last one stated: We have to approach these questions with humility, because nobody has a clue as to what's going on. In fact, every international economist who is semi-honest tells you, "We don't really understand what's going on. But we have some ideas." So anything that's said, certainly anything that I say, you want to add many grains of salt to, because nobody really understands.

However, some things are moderately clear and there's a fair consensus. Through the Bretton Woods era, that's roughly the Second World War up to the early 1970s, exchange rates were pretty close to fixed, and capital was more or less controlled. So there wasn't extreme capital flow. That was changed in the early 1970s by decision. Capital flow was liberalized.

The international economic system is patched together with scotch tape. There was a study by the IMF. It has about 180 members. From 1980 to 1995, it found that something like a quarter of the members had serious banking crises, sometimes several, and two-thirds had one or another financial crisis. That's a lot. There's debate about this, but it seems that since the liberalization of financial markets, they have been extremely volatile, unpredictable, irrational, lots of crises. Nobody knows when they're going to blow up.

You can say, "Well, we can handle it." Maybe. One of the leading international economists. Paul Krugman, has an article in *Foreign Affairs* called something like "Depression-Era Economics," in which he basically says, "We don't understand what's happening. It's like the Depression. Maybe it'll be somehow patched together, but nobody can say. And nobody knows what to do."

There's one possibility that he rules out, and that is capital controls. He rules it out on theoretical grounds. He says capital controls lead to inefficient use of resources, and we can't have that. That's certainly true in a certain abstract model of the economy, the neoclassical model. Whether that model has anything to do with the real world is another question. The evidence doesn't seem to support it. Also one has to ask the question, "What is meant by 'efficient use of resources'?" That sounds like a nice, technical notion, but it's not. When you unpack it, it's a highly ideological notion. So you can efficiently use resources if

it increases gross national product. But increasing gross national product may harm everybody. That's efficient by some ideological measure, but not by other measures.

Let me just give you one example to illustrate. The Department of Transportation did a study one or two years ago. It tried to estimate the effect of the decline of spending on maintaining highways. There's been a considerable decline since the Reagan era, so a certain amount of money has been saved by not repairing highways. They tried to estimate the cost. I forget the exact number, but the cost was considerably higher than the savings. However, the cost is cost to individuals. If your car hits a pothole, it's a cost to you. To the economy, it's a gain. That improves the efficiency of the economy. Because if your car hits a pothole, you go to the garage and you pay a guy to fix it, or maybe you buy a new car—something more produced. It makes the economy more efficient in two ways. You've cut down the size of government, and everybody knows that government drags down the economy, so you've improved it that way. And you've increased profits and employment and production. Of course, for you as a person, there was a loss. But for the economy, there was a gain by the highly ideological way efficiency is measured. This is a tiny case. It extends across the board. So when one hears words like "efficiency" used, reach for your gray cells. Ask, "What exactly does that mean?"

Is Social Security broken? Does it need to be fixed?

Even before getting to that, how come people are talking about it? Just a few years ago, this was called the third rail of American politics. You couldn't touch it. Now the question is, "How do you save it?" That's quite an achievement for propaganda.

If indeed the economy is going to undergo a historically unprecedented slowdown as far into the future as we can see, then the stock market is going to undergo a sharp slowdown, too. You can't have it both ways. This is not a particularly radical criticism. You can read it in *Business Week*.

The Social Security Act said, "We care if some other elderly person starves. We don't want that to happen." The idea of putting it in the stock market, though it's framed in all sorts of fraudulent gobbledygook, is to break down that sense of social solidarity and say, "You care only about yourself. If that guy down the street when he gets to be seventy starves to death, that's not your problem. It's his problem. He invested badly, or he had bad luck." That's very good for rich people. But for everyone else, it depends on how you evaluate the risk. Social Security's been very effective in that respect. Starvation among the elderly has dropped considerably.

Has the same kind of propaganda campaign been conducted on public education?

Very much so. There's a campaign under way to essentially destroy the public education system along with every aspect of human life and attitudes and thought that involve social solidarity. It's being done in all sorts of ways. One is simply by underfunding. So if you can make the public schools really rotten, people will look for an alternative. Any service that's going to be privatized, the first thing you do is make it malfunction so people can say. "We want to get rid of it. It's not running. Let's give it to Lockheed."

What about privatizing Medicare?

A private institution has one goal: maximize profit, minimize human conditions. That means you try to attract the patients who are least risky and are not going to cost you much, and you get rid of the rest.

Do you think that domestic issues like Social Security, public education, Medicare, and health care could be lightning rods to organize around and create popular movements?

If these issues are brought to the forefront and are discussed honestly, there could be a lot of problems. It's the reason NAFTA was grossly distorted in the media coverage. After the fast-track fiasco a little over a year ago, *The Wall Street Journal* had an interesting article. They said that although it's a "no-brainer" that trade deals should be made by the President without any Congressional input, nevertheless the opposition has what they called an "ultimate weapon": The population is against it, and it's really hard to keep the population out.

For organizers, it should be a bonanza. I remember at the time of the 200th anniversary of the signing of the Declaration of Independence, in one amusing poll, they gave people slogans of various sorts and asked them to say whether those statements were in the Constitution or not. One of the statements was, "From each according to his ability, to each according to his needs." About half the population thought that was in the Constitution. Speak of an organizer's paradise! If those sentiments aren't developed and used, then organizers are failing.

With the constant and ever-increasing demands on your time, how do you keep up with everything?

Badly. There's no way to do it. There are physical limitations. The day is twenty-four hours long. If you do one thing, you're not doing something else. You cannot overcome the fact that time is finite. So you make your choices. Maybe badly, maybe well, but there's no algorithm, no procedure to give you the right answer.

Do you have a time that you particularly like to work?

Virtually all the time.

You've been disdainful of spectator sports, arguing that they distract people from paying attention to politics. But

last January, you knew not only which teams were in the Super Bowl, but also the outcome. Are you losing your grip?

I always read the front page at least of *The New York Times*. It said who won and what the score was. But it's even worse than that. I have a jock grandson who's finally helping me fulfill a secret dream to have an excuse to go to a professional basketball game. I don't know if I should admit it, but I'm actually going to my first game in around fifty years.

FURTHER READING

Biography

Barsky, Robert F. *Noam Chomsky: A Life of Dissent.* Cambridge: MIT Press, 1997.
    An intellectual biography of Chomsky.

Criticism

Cockburn, Alexander. "Models, Nature, and Language." *Grand Street* 13, No. 2 (Fall 1994): 170-6.
    Chomsky discusses scientific method, linguistic systems and cognition, and the concept of evolution.

Criticism

D'Agostino, Fred. *Chomsky's System of Ideas.* Oxford: Clarendon Press, 1986.
    A book-length study of Chomsky's linguistic theories, philosophical perspective, and political theory.

Fallows, James. "Double Moral Standards." *The Atlantic* 249, No. 2 (February 1982): 82-6.
    An unfavorable review of *Towards a New Cold War.* Fallows finds fault in Chomsky's argumentative style and strict moral dichotomies regarding American foreign policy.

Lyons, John. *Chomsky.* Hassocks, Sussex: The Harvester Press, 1977.
    A book-length study of Chomsky's linguistic theories and philosophical perspective.

McChesney, Robert W. "Noam Chomsky and the Struggle Against Neoliberalism." *Monthly Review* 50, No. 11 (April 1999): 40-7.
    McChesney outlines the development of neoliberalism in the West and the significance of Chomsky's resistance to its political and economic ideology and structures.

Modgil, Sohan, and Celia Modgil, eds. *Noam Chomsky: Consensus and Controversy.* New York: Falmer Press, 1987.

A collection of critical essays offering analysis of Chomsky's linguistic theories and their implications for the study of linguistics, psychology, philosophy, and politics.

Additional coverage of Chomsky's life and career is contained in the following sources published by the Gale Group: *Contemporary Authors,* **Vols. 17-20R;** *Contemporary Authors New Revision Series,* **Vols. 28, 62;** *DISCovering Authors 3.0,* **and** *Major 20th-Century Writers,* **Editions 1–2.**

Terry Eagleton
1943-

(Full name Terrence Francis Eagleton) English critic, novelist, essayist, nonfiction writer, screenwriter, and playwright.

The following entry presents an overview of Eagleton's career through 1999. For further information on his life and works, see *CLC*, Volume 63.

INTRODUCTION

An erudite scholar and influential cultural theorist, Terry Eagleton is widely regarded as the one of the foremost Marxist literary critics on the contemporary academic scene. With the publication of *Marxism and Literary Criticism* (1976) and *Literary Theory* (1983), a popular college text, Eagleton won recognition for producing highly informed though accessible works of literary criticism that explore the relationship between literature, history, and society. While Eagleton's Marxist perspective is clearly apparent in his writings, his work also demonstrates a regard for other theoretical approaches such as feminism and psychoanalysis. English by education as well as birth, Eagleton displays a notable concern for the history, politics, and culture of Ireland. By urging critics to move out of the isolation that academia tends to foster, he manifests a desire that criticism be used to promote a more equitable society.

BIOGRAPHICAL INFORMATION

Eagleton was born in Salford, England, where his father worked as an engineer. He attended local schools before studying at Cambridge University, where he received his B.A. in 1964. He earned his Ph.D. at Cambridge in 1968. While at Cambridge, he worked with the critic Raymond Williams, under whose influence he rejected the orthodoxies of New Criticism, a critical approach that treats the literary text as autonomous and unconnected to moral, historical, or political realities. Eagleton served as a fellow in English at Cambridge from 1964 to 1969 until moving to Oxford University. He was married from 1966 to 1976. At Oxford, he became a fellow and tutor in Poetry, a position that he held until 1989, when he became a lecturer in Critical Theory. Eagleton continues to work at Oxford, holding the post of Thomas Warton professor of English and Literature, which he received in 1992.

MAJOR WORKS

Eagleton's writings reflect his interest in examining ideologies as they are expressed in literature. The tool with which he prefers to explore ideologies is Marxist literary theory, which takes into account—unlike New Criticism—the relationships that historical, political, and social conditions have to works of literature. Eagleton's theoretical stance, while it has not remained static during his career, is apparent in his first book, *The New Left Church* (1966). In this work he combines literary criticism, Marxist political analysis, and Catholic theology in an attempt to reconcile Roman Catholicism with socialist humanism. With *Shakespeare and Society* (1967), he released his first book of criticism on a traditional literary topic. Demonstrating his rejection of New Criticism, Eagleton refuses to regard Shakespeare's work as an autonomous entity; instead, he treats his writings as inseparable from Elizabethan social issues. Investigating the conflict between individualism and social responsibility in Shakespeare's later plays, Eagleton argues that while Shakespeare was actually a political conservative who had an interest in maintaining the contemporary social order, his presentation of individualism and sexual desire undermines the conventional structures of law and marriage. Eagleton revisited this subject in *William Shakespeare* (1986).

In *The Body as Language* (1970), Eagleton confronts the human alienation that capitalism creates by advocating cooperation between Christianity and revolutionary socialism. Following this book, the author was not to return to Christian doctrine as a major topic in his writings. Instead, for his next two books Eagleton trained his Marxist theory on specific literary figures. *Exiles and Emigrés* (1970) examines why so much important twentieth-century English literature has been written by non-English authors such as Joseph Conrad, T. S. Eliot, Henry James, and James Joyce. *Myths of Power* (1975) looks at the work of the Brontë sisters in light of the emerging industrial class of their time. Eagleton's next work, *Marxism and Literary Criticism,* exerted a significant impact on the practice of literary criticism. Here Eagleton argues that the artist does not "create" something from nothing, but instead "produces" a work that is determined by historical and ideological conditions. In addition to presenting the concept of the author as producer, Eagleton also considers the relationships between form and content and that of the writer and social commitment. Asserting in *Criticism and Ideology* (1976) that Marxism is the only methodology free of the ideological bias that other analytical approaches entail, Eagleton maintains that the goal of criticism is to reveal the ideological forces that make up a text. In *Walter Benjamin* (1981), Eagleton argues that Benjamin's revolutionary criticism has not been given proper attention. He also displays in this work an interest in feminism. In *The Rape of Clarissa* (1982) Eagleton applied a feminist approach, in addition to Marxist and psychoanalytic theories, to his interpretation of the eighteenth-century novel *Clarissa* by Samuel Richardson.

Eagleton is perhaps best known for *Literary Theory,* which has become a popular instructional text among academics. In this work, Eagleton not only surveys such major literary theories as structuralism, semiotics, and phenomenology, but also discusses the historical and ideological conditions behind each theory to demonstrate its limitations as well as its significance. Eagleton also contends that students would benefit from a study of rhetoric, as was practiced from antiquity to the eighteenth century. He also favors a cultural discourse that would eradicate the distinctions between literature and non-literature. In *The Function of Criticism* (1984), which offers a polemical history of the critical establishment from the eighteenth century to the present, Eagleton attempts to sway criticism away from its preoccupation with literary texts and estrangement from society in the interest of returning it to its traditional involvement in cultural politics. In *Saints and Scholars* (1987), his only novel to date, Eagleton satirically explores the beginnings of modern European thought. Set in Ireland in 1916, the novel involves Irish revolutionary James Connolly, who has escaped his real-life execution, and his encounters with philosophers Ludwig Wittgenstein and Bertrand Russell; Leopold Bloom, the protagonist of James Joyce's *Ulysses;* and Mikhail Bakhtin's brother, Marxist literary critic Nikolai. Besides showing how religious, economic, and political forces affected society in the early twentieth century, their conversations serve as a debate of the theoretical and practical limitations of thought and social action.

Eagleton returned to criticism with *The Ideology of the Aesthetic* (1990), in which he illustrates how social and political forces influence a society's aesthetic conceptualizations. His analysis considers the work of Benjamin, Theodor Adorno, G. W. F. Hegel, Martin Heidegger, Immanuel Kant, and Friedrich Nietzsche to examine how these forces affect the formation of aesthetic thought. In *Ideology* (1991), Eagleton scrutinizes the concept of ideology itself and its various manifestations, again providing a survey of major theoretical positions and their proponents in the process. In *Heathcliff and the Great Hunger* (1995), Eagleton proposes that Heathcliff in Emily Brontë's *Wuthering Heights* was actually a refugee from the great Irish potato famine. In this series of essays, Eagleton confronts what he considers to be a revisionist view of Irish history, one that seeks to diminish the impact of the potato famine and nineteenth-century English politics on the period's writers. Eagleton also addressed issues concerning Irish culture in the essay collection *Crazy John and the Bishop* (1999). In *The Illusions of Postmodernism* (1996), Eagleton defends the relevance of Marxist theory against the current preference among critics for postmodernism. He argues that postmodernism, with its view of the world as fragmented and truth as indeterminate, is an inadequate successor to Marxism, which in its critique of capitalism can offer a more concrete moral vision for society.

CRITICAL RECEPTION

Even those colleagues who disagree with Eagleton's Marxist position and interpretation of ideology tend to commend his passionate writing. Eagleton has been praised for his humor and wit as well as for demonstrating a graceful style. In his first major work, *Marxism and Literary Criticism,* Eagleton was hailed not only for his writing technique but for his concise explication of the obtuse theories of European Marxist critics and his provoking treatment of the author as "producer." He was criticized, however, for a lack of textual examples and for being too self-referential. His second major work, *Literary Theory,* was similarly lauded by critics for serving as an accessible, comprehensible introduction to its subject. The book was also praised for its consideration of the relationship between literary theories and the ideological conditions in which they arise. On the other hand, many critics rejected his suggestion that literature and literary theory are illusions and that the study of literature be replaced with the study of rhetoric. *The Ideology of the Aesthetic* and *Ideology* also elicited considerable critical response, with many commending Eagleton's impressive range and insight into their subjects, and others finding his arguments flawed and merely polemical. His critics notwithstanding, Eagleton remains a prominent literary theorist, one who, having reexamined the tradition of criticism and the role of the critic, has greatly influenced both students and professional academics.

PRINCIPAL WORKS

The New Left Church (essays) 1966

Shakespeare and Society: Critical Studies in Shakespearean Drama (criticism) 1967

The Body as Language: Outline of a "New Left" Theology (nonfiction) 1970

Exiles and Emigrés: Studies in Modern Literature (criticism) 1970

Myths of Power: A Marxist Study of the Brontës (criticism) 1975

Criticism and Ideology: A Study of Marxist Literary Theory (criticism) 1976

Marxism and Literary Criticism (criticism) 1976

Walter Benjamin; or, Towards a Revolutionary Criticism (criticism) 1981

The Rape of Clarissa: Writing, Sexuality, and Class Struggle in Samuel Richardson (criticism) 1982

Literary Theory: An Introduction (criticism) 1983

The Function of Criticism: From the Spectator to Post-Structuralism (criticism) 1984

Against the Grain: Selected Essays, 1975-1985 (essays) 1986

William Shakespeare (criticism) 1986

Saints and Scholars (novel) 1987

The Ideology of the Aesthetic (criticism) 1990

CRITICISM

Geoffrey Thurley (review date 24 September 1982)

SOURCE: "Phallic Woman," in *New Statesman,* September 24, 1982, p. 28.

[*In the following review of* The Rape of Clarissa, *Thurley concludes that the work is "a vigorous and sometimes brilliant book" marred by Eagleton's "dogmatic intensity."*]

We can read *Clarissa* again, says Terry Eagleton, thanks to feminism and post-structuralism. It is now relevant, he argues [in **The Rape of Clarissa**], because it dramatises the scandal of rape in patriarchal society and opens up the possibility of a fully feminised social order. Eagleton assumes fixed meanings for masculine and feminine throughout. Women are tender, gentle and considerate (though also narcissistic in a way he approves of); men are brutal, rapacious and domineering.

Aristocracy is treated as historically masculine in contrast to the (feminine) bourgeoisie: bourgeois inwardness and kindness replaced aristocratic militancy in the 18th century. Lovelace is therefore an outdated Restoration rake, brutal and cynical yet also pathetic—an infantile sadist expressing his misogyny 'in the virulently anti-sexual act of rape'. Real sexuality involves 'adult relationship' not only beyond the rapist but quite simply impossible in the patriarchy in which Clarissa and Lovelace live.

Having disposed of all sexual relationships before the age of feminisation (which still hasn't quite arrived), Eagleton provides a hilarious account of Lovelace's inadequate 'love' in terms that are mainly Freudian, though also Lacanian. Clarissa is the 'phallic woman', maddeningly complete, the repository of the lost phallus; the boy's fear of castration is assuaged in the penis-lack of the mother, but he must constantly assure himself of his wholeness by robbing as many women as possible of theirs: 'With this phallus I thee castrate'. Richardson's novel vanishes from this part of Eagleton's book, becoming merely an instance of a general thesis. But Clarissa, it seems, is not only the phallus (the 'transcendental signifier'), she is also the letter, the body, the non-body, and a hole—nothing and everything. (You can get 'a whole' and 'a whore' from 'Harlowe', he smartly observes.) This ontological nuttiness derives in large measure from the linguistic inadequacy of post-structuralism.

Eagleton also makes Clarissa stand for an empiricist language-theory, taking the purpose of writing to be the representation of the real by unambiguous terms. This is what Derrida calls 'closure', and what he imagines empiricism to be about. Lovelace, on the other hand, is a 'post-structuralist precursor' and represents *jouissance*—language as play, disruptive and unpredictable. The novel thus enacts an ideological dilemma: proponent of the new bourgeois moralism (Clarissa's 'closure', the world of firm values), Richardson is yet outside this ideology by being able to imagine Lovelace's vicious if playful fantasising (the brutal world of aristocratic insouciance and power).

Paradoxically, the brutally masculine aristocrat now emerges as a representative of the feminine, since playfulness is feminine. If Eagleton doesn't seem aware of this confusion it is, I suspect, because his own puritan partisanship leads him to simplify the novel's (and life's) complexities. He won't let us say that Clarissa wants to be raped (rightly, of course: it's an outrageous assumption), but his prejudice about sexuality, allowing no virtue to men and nothing but virtue to women, blinds him to the element of genuine dalliance in the novel. If Clarissa isn't the sly whore of 'cavalier' criticism, she isn't Eagleton's saint either.

He speaks, finally, of *Clarissa* as providing 'damning documentary evidence against a society where the rape of a Clarissa is possible'. But in what society will rape not be possible? The only kind of society he seems able to imagine for women is the kind of all-female friendship prefigured by Clarissa's friend Anna Howe. Eagleton speaks of 'sisterly solidarity'. Elsewhere he speaks of 'human solidarity'; but his book is partisan and divisive.

Men just don't fit the Eagletonian scheme of things. Unfortunately they exist, with their troublesomely moveable parts, creating that 'insurmountable sexual difference' he wearily acknowledges. Rape is monstrous and tragic; but it is not all there is, or all there has been, to relations between men and women, even in patriarchal societies. This is a vigorous and sometimes brilliant book, but the underlying problems it attacks require to be inspected without the sort of dogmatic intensity Dr Eagleton brings to them.

Terence Hawkes (review date 3 June 1983)

SOURCE: "Skull Caps," in *New Statesman,* June 3, 1983, pp. 24-5.

[In the following review, Hawkes offers positive assessment of Literary Theory.]

As much goad as guide, Terry Eagleton's spirited introduction to literary theory [**Literary Theory**] has the sharp bite that only a trenchant and tough-minded argument can give. It puts an incisive and persuasive case: that in our society the discourses of literary criticism and of politics share a deep mutual involvement, so that to place something as ideologically sensitive as 'English' at the centre of a system of mass education implies and invokes relationships of real social power. Hence the urgency, the bitterness and the public interest in recent clashes over 'structuralism', 'deconstruction' and the like. At stake is not merely 'English', but the mysterious quality of *Englishness:* civilisation as we know it.

Eagleton puts his own cards firmly on the table and deals innocence out of the game. If criticism involves the continuation of politics by other means, there can be no criticism 'itself'. The even-handedness and neutrality beloved of examination boards exists only as a series of contrived stances or tricks of style masking a variety of prejudices. The most fundamental of these naturally sees theory as a foreign, intrusive body sullying the pure encounter between reader and text. But that pristine confrontation never really takes place. Some theory or other has us permanently in its anaesthetic grip and without it we would be unable to recognise a work of literature in the first place. Theory is the skull beneath criticism's skin.

As a result, Eagleton's insistently overt statement of his case functions as part of his argument as well as an effective stratagem in its deployment. The charge of partiality will of course always arise in a society reassured by the bellowing of academics in purple-faced pursuit of cool 'balance' and measured 'objectivity'. But the book preempts such blustering with its demonstration that terms of that sort constitute in themselves occasions of the political struggle on which it focuses. This in turn lends potency to its interrogation of the many similarly loaded concepts, such as 'tradition', 'taste', 'culture' and 'morality' in which much of our criticism still flagrantly traffics.

Rarely has a gaff been so productively blown. And the purchase on theory thus afforded is mercilessly seized. From a withering account of the needs and presuppositions which led to the invention of an entity called 'literature', Eagleton goes on to show how a ruthlessly narrowed canon of texts became, for ideological reasons, the lynch-pin of the education system. After a series of shocks and challenges to an inherited sense of settled Englishness—they include the Dublin rising, the First World War, industrial unrest, major police strikes and the impact of the Bolshevik revolution—it is hardly surprising that the Newbolt Report of 1921 offered 'English' as a kind of field-dressing to bind the wounds.

Eagleton's brisk, sceptical survey of the whole subsequent spectrum of literary theory moves nimbly, using an admirably straightforward style. It is a brilliant, agile performance: urgent and racy, witty and combative, lucid and compelling. The complexity of William Empson's position has never been more subtly mapped, and it would be hard to find a clearer account of Husserl and Heidegger or a defter unpicking of the implications of empiricism—to cite only three areas where explication at this level tends to get bogged down in complexities and evasions. The larger issues, Phenomenology, Hermeneutics, Reception Theory, Structuralism, Semiotics and Poststructuralism undergo a no less stringent sifting.

The book concludes with a resolute, hardheaded application of its own logic to itself. Readers expecting a final commitment to a radical Marxist or feminist criticism will find themselves facing instead a kind of auto-destruction. Eagleton ends by calling for the dissolution of literary criticism altogether and its replacement by what might be termed the study of discourse or, to revive an older term, rhetoric. For if literature has no claim to an objective, unproblematic standing, how can literary theory survive? If 'English' is a non-subject, then its practitioners, wholly compromised by the social context in which they operate, function less as purveyors of knowledge than as custodians of a particular discourse. And that suggests that a far more profitable area of study lies in what Foucault has called 'discursive practice': the analysis of the way specific discourses are constituted and the manner in which they compete in the construction of cultural meaning. It is a struggle whose outcome determines the central priorities—in effect, the realities—of our way of life.

The issue raised by this final position is ultimately a tactical one. For whatever its logical justification, it involves the effective abandonment of what history has made into the high ground of the battlefield. It hands 'literature' and thus 'English' back to those who, rejecting the logic, will not hesitate to claim victory in the struggle. Eagleton's argument begins with the audacious insertion of the study of literature into history. The revelation (as it will seem to some) that the subject not only *has* a history, but is irrevocably part of the historical process, forges a weapon of immense, bracing power. But history also determines the ground on which that weapon can best be used. The battle remains to be fought.

Lennard J. Davis (review date 21 January 1984)

SOURCE: "Does Literature Exist?," in *Nation*, January 21, 1984, pp. 59-60.

[In the following review, Davis offers positive evaluation of Literary Theory, *though is skeptical of Eagleton's Marxist ideology and devaluation of literature in favor of other mediums of representation.]*

Terry Eagleton's new book is a concise guide to the most interesting and mystifying trends in the study of literature over the last fifty years. Judging from **Literary Theory**'s positive reception in Britain and now America, it answers a need—and answers it well. But as I read along, I kept imagining a TV ad: "Can't decide between hermeneutical and structural approaches to literature? Embarrassed at parties by your faulty knowledge of deconstructionist or Marxist criticism? Let Terry Eagleton help you through with his handy patent-pending guide to the wonderful world of literary criticism." It is a strange moment in late capitalism when a Marxist guide to literary criticism seems as necessary to middle-class life as a Sony Walkman and an I.B.M. personal computer.

One might point out as a caveat to the general public that Eagleton's history of literary theory is not a disinterested one. As a Marxist, he has axes to grind along with the wares he displays. Rather than presenting a traditional literary history, he begins with the striking and contestable notion that there is no such thing as literature. Rather, he claims, literature and the cult of the literary are ideologies that exalt high cultural artifacts like novels, poems and plays over other forms of writing and representation.

An opening chapter explains that in the nineteenth century, English (as opposed to classical) literature served as a pedagogical tool to civilize and pacify marginal political groups, particularly women and the lower classes. Witness a statement by an early professor of English literature at Oxford:

> England is sick, and . . . English literature must save it. The Churches . . . having failed, and social remedies being slow, English literature has now a triple function: still, I suppose, to delight and instruct us, but also, and above all, to save our souls and heal the State.

Matthew Arnold, among other critics, fostered the idea that literature would civilize the lower classes, particularly since the middle classes "with their narrow, harsh, unintelligent, and unattractive spirit and culture, will almost certainly fail to mould or assimilate the masses below them." State schools teaching English literature would have to do the trick, since, as Eagleton puts it, "English was literally the poor man's Classics." Or, as one Royal Commission report recommended, English was suitable for civilizing "women . . . and the second- and third-rate men who . . . become schoolmasters." As English replaced religion and traditional morality as a means of social control, it became an ideology in itself.

To debunk the myth that literature is an overarching civilizing influence, Eagleton marshalls contemporary critical theories that have focused on the "literariness" of literary works. In explaining those, Eagleton works at a high level of generalization and superficiality—as indeed he must if he is to present all the acts in this circus. The Big Top includes formalism, English and American criticism (Arnold, Leavis and the New Critics), phenomenology, hermeneutics, reception and reader response theory, structuralism, semiotics, post-structuralism and deconstructionism, feminist and psychoanalytic criticism and, of course, Marxist literary theory. We get roughly ten pages of text for each theory, an overview that cannot hope to produce instant enlightenment in all cases. But on the whole, Eagleton is clear and cogent, and the general reader will certainly get some sense of the variety of critical approaches. Short bibliographies provide directions for further study of each theoretical school.

Still, he does present a stacked deck. Each of the methodologies is criticized for the same deficiency—for lacking the historical and materialist approach of Marxist criticism. But for Eagleton, even Marxist theory as it has been practiced is suspect because *all* literary criticism assumes that there is such a thing as literature. But if you recognize that literature is an illusion, as Eagleton suggests, since it is just "a name which people give from time to time for different reasons to certain kinds of writing within a whole field of what Michel Foucault has called 'discursive practices,'" then literary theory must also be an illusion. Consequently, Eagleton suggests that leftists and others should study all types of writing and representation—films, advertisements, textbooks, legal briefs, product warranties and the thousand other natural shocks the signifying system of a culture is heir to.

While Eagleton's proposal cannot be simply dismissed, it is difficult to imagine that the academic study of all those cultural discourses would result in something more inherently radical than the academic study of literature alone. Under Eagleton's guidance, literature would not have a privileged position, but scholarship still would. Unlike the British, Americans have been studying popular culture for some time without earthshaking results. The Center for the Study of Popular Culture in Bowling Green, Ohio, is a worthy institution, but hardly a storm center of revolution.

Nevertheless, **Literary Theory** can be read without its polemical side as a Cook's tour to the murky underworld of literary criticism. As such, it is as good a guide as Virgil was to Dante. But having gotten into the inferno of theoretical methods, the reader, like Dante, needs something akin to divine intervention to find the right road out.

Steven G. Kellman (review date Summer 1984)

SOURCE: "Miscellaneous," in *Modern Fiction Studies*, Vol. 30, No. 2, Summer, 1984, pp. 399-403.

[*In the following excerpted review essay, Kellman offers tempered assessment of* Literary Theory, *concluding that it should be read with a "blend of enthusiasm and wariness."*]

Although it mentions neither Wellek nor Warren, **Literary Theory: An Introduction** seems to aspire to be the *Theory of Literature* for a poststructuralist world, a more overtly partisan examination of the most influential schools of literary theory in recent decades. A Marxist with wit, Terry Eagleton is magisterial in his deployment of a wide range of ideas, but rarely dispassionate. However, after patient scrutiny of the writings of numerous contemporary critics, Eagleton confesses that he has not come to praise theory but to bury it. He rejects the claim that literary theory is a coherent discipline:

> It is an illusion first in the sense that literary theory, as I hope to have shown, is really no more than a branch of social ideologies, utterly without any unity or identity which would adequately distinguish it from philosophy, linguistics, psychology, cultural and sociological thought; and secondly in the sense that the one hope it has of distinguishing itself—clinging to an object named literature—is misplaced.

Literary study becomes a question not of any single unified subject but rather of a critical discourse that is culturally determined and tyrannically intolerant. After considering the possibilities for a theory of literature, Eagleton concludes by repudiating his subtitle; his book is "less an introduction than an obituary."

But it is a spirited elegy. Unlike too many other theorists, Marxist or otherwise, Eagleton writes with grace, clarity, and force. He succeeds in assimilating a motley crowd of structuralists, feminists, semioticians, hermeneuticians, psychoanalysts, and deconstructionists to his argument that there are no innocent readings, that every literary experience is shaped by ideology. Despite, and because of, its brevity, *Literary Theory: An Introduction* makes a compelling brief for a Marxist reading. Yet surely names such as Wayne Booth, Frank Kermode, Marshall McLuhan, Walter J. Ong, and Lionel Trilling are significant omissions from a work that purports to introduce us to recent Anglo-American theory. Others are dismissed with a rhetorical sneer: "Northrop Frye and the New Critics thought that they had pulled off a synthesis of the two [formalism and structuralism], but how many students of literature today read them?" Eagleton's case at this point seems built so tenuously on a mere question mark that it would be invalidated by the admission that one did indeed still read Frye and Ransom.

There is an occasional blooper ("The Prague Linguistic Circle was founded in 1926, and survived until the outbreak of the First World War"). But Eagleton proceeds through a series of remarkably penetrating and sympathetic accounts of the principles and practices of prominent theorists. His concern is not so much to refute them as to divulge their inadequacies. Yet he is emphatically not a pluralist, and his concluding chapter calls for a return to the methods of rhetoric, offering "political criticism" as a way to subsume everything that has gone before.

Literary Theory: An Introduction is designed sequentially to demonstrate the hegemony of political analysis. However, this is a game of categorical leapfrog, and it is quite possible to imagine the chapters of Eagleton's book reshuffled, with the resulting progression every bit as persuasive as the one in the published version. Political criticism, Eagleton argues eloquently, is not just another contending faction but rather, implicitly or explicitly, both

the foundation and the culmination of any discourse. As much can be, and is, claimed for psychoanalysis, semiotics, structuralism, and deconstruction.

In the clamorous quarrels between the moderns and the moderns, rival theorists do not seek annihilation so much as, like the Wife of Bath, sovereignty. In the definitive introduction to literary theory that is being written collectively, each would want control of the ultimate chapter. Ultimately, Terry Eagleton offers us a primer devoid of innocence, even of its own innocence. It is an introduction to a new stage in an ancient controversy. *Literary Theory: An Introduction* ought to be read with the same blend of enthusiasm and wariness with which it was written, but it ought to be read by anyone concerned with contemporary theory.

David Montrose (review date 5 October 1984)

SOURCE: A review of *The Function of Criticism,* in *New Statesman,* October 5, 1984, p. 33.

[*In the following review, Montrose offers positive assessment of* The Function of Criticism, *though notes its similarity to his earlier work on Walter Benjamin.*]

Terry Eagleton's essay [*The Function of Criticism*] seeks to 'recall criticism to its traditional role'—engagement in cultural politics—from what he considers a position of crisis, where it is narrowly preoccupied with literary texts and estranged from social life through confinement to Academe and 'the literary industry' (public relations branch). Central to his argument is Jürgen Habermas's notion of 'the public sphere': an arena which facilitates free and equal discourse, among individuals, on cultural questions. Eagleton's starting-point is early 18th-century England, where the coffee houses and clubs and such periodicals as Steele's *Tatler* and Addison's *Spectator* comprised a 'bourgeois public sphere' which sustained cultural consensus. That sphere's gradual disintegration by economic and political factors is subsequently charted in a brief (and confessedly selective) history of criticism in England.

The Victorian 'academicization of criticism' marked its demise as 'a socially active force'. Later, *Scrutiny* represented an attempt to reinvent the classic public sphere: an attempt doomed from the outset given the conditions of late capitalist society. Arriving at the present, Eagleton savages structuralism and deconstruction before promoting the 'revolutionary criticism' originally advanced in *Walter Benjamin* (1981)—wherein he parted company with his earlier work—as the only productive course that an enervated discipline can take as an alternative to withering away. Designed to assist 'the cultural emancipation of the masses', such criticism ideally requires (and currently lacks) a 'counterpublic sphere' based on institutions of popular culture and popular education. Feminism, though, provides a shining model: criticism that takes its impulse from a political movement.

As always, it is not necessary to agree with Eagleton's dark view of today's criticism, or his prescription for a better tomorrow's, to find him a splendid polemicist. Inevitably, though, the fact that *The Function of Criticism*—like its predecessor, *Literary Theory*—largely reproduces the message of **Walter Benjamin** does lead to its final impact being rather muffled.

Andrew Rissik (review date 21 March 1986)

SOURCE: "Having Their Way with Will," in *New Statesman,* March 21, 1986, pp. 26-7.

[*In the following review, Rissik offers negative assessment of* William Shakespeare.]

In her slim critical book [*Shakespeare*], Germaine Greer writes, 'The public duty of the playwright was to bring the caviare of his angelic intellectual exercise within the grasp of those savage hordes, who were quite capable of disrupting performances they could not follow.' In his study [***William Shakespeare***], Terry Eagleton, who is Tutor and Fellow in English at Wadham College, Oxford, tells us that 'it is difficult to read Shakespeare without feeling that he was almost certainly familiar with the writing of Hegel, Marx, Nietzsche, Freud, Wittgenstein and Derrida.'

Such fatuous tributes as these are, of course, only the most recent manifestations of a prevailing critical tendency to regard Shakespeare not as mere poet or dramatist but as God: all-knowing, all-wise and all-embracing. According to the unstoppable supply of critical books which pour yearly from the presses, Shakespeare had Christ's ability to read the human heart, Walt Disney's enchanting verve as a popular entertainer and Aristotle's pre-occupying High Seriousness. Although specific minor critics have specific minor criticisms, in each case the burden of the argument is the same. Shakespeare outdistanced and out-achieved everyone who had come before him and, in some way or other, his work anticipates everything that we have seen since. He is attended, centuries after his death, by the kind of elaborate rhetorical hyperbole which only a lunatic like Nero can have enjoyed during his own lifetime. In the Middle Ages, scholars laboured with indefatigable zeal to swell the vast edifice of Biblical criticism. Today we pay that compliment to Shakespeare, an innocent and unassuming dramatist who would have been appalled at such madness. One looks in vain, in the index of both books, for any reference to comparable dramatists such as Aeschylus, Sophocles or Chekhov, although, predictably, Brecht and Yeats turn up in both. Criticism of this kind regards Shakespeare's plays not as drama, not as enacted narrative and psychology, but as scripture. These texts are Holy Books.

Of the two, Terry Eagleton's is much the saner and more perceptive. It's a brief but knottily detailed account of the canon whose thesis is that Shakespeare's achievement is built on a number of philosophical paradoxes and antagonisms. The imaginative freedom of language contradicts and transcends the material intractability of the body; the anarchic, irrational impulse of sexuality runs counter to social custom, moral law and inherited political orthodoxy; the hierarchical, conservative Shakespeare who wrote the plays—the mercantile adventurer who retired to Stratford and lived as a country gentleman—is the mere outward identity of a far more radical and dangerous literary intelligence. This is the Shakespeare who had an intuitive knowledge of Marx and Nietzsche, whose work explodes the false, sentimentalising definitions imposed on it by Late Victorian critics, and Eagleton's book is most revealing when it is at its most caustically specific. I want to cheer him on when he says things like, 'The Senate, however, are not impressed, and Alcibiades is banished for his pains, if not for his atrocious verse' and '*King Lear* opens with a bout of severe linguistic inflation' or when he describes Cleopatra as 'less a rounded "character" than a complex flow of impulse'.

But there are other, deader, more constipated passages, rich in crypto-analytical bullshit. 'Desire in Shakespeare is often a kind of obsession, a well-nigh monomaniacal fixation on another which tends to paralyse the self to a rigid posture. In this sense, it has something of the density and inertia of the body itself.' This is academic psycho-babble, and one wants to answer it by yelling, McEnroe-like, 'You-Can*not*-Be-Serious!' Tautological and platitudinous, its own 'linguistic inflation' denies it precise meaning. Later, when he tells us that, in Shakespeare, desire is a cause of instability, one wants to reply that the same goes for almost every writer since Aeschylus. This isn't a critical insight. It's a commonplace of human nature. In the end, Eagleton's verbose textual ingenuity wrecks the book. When he announces, 'The name of Prospero's language is Ariel, who symbolises his word in action, the precise, fluent fulfilment of his desires,' the temptation to write in terms of symbolism and metaphor—to doodle with the freedom of language—has usurped the critic's responsibility to the complexity of his source. These grand, clever-sounding statements are simply a new form of old-fashioned pedagogic dogmatism. You teach Shakespeare by turning the relationships in his plays into a kind of rigid literary algebra.

The tragedy of so much contemporary Shakespearean criticism is that the people who write it want, more than anything, to be creative, and their 'creativity' shows. Terry Eagleton's ***William Shakespeare*** is an extraordinarily elaborate piece of work whose preoccupations and theories are so intense and fervid that they betray a fundamental indifference to the nominal subject. I can recall a deliriously serious, insanely well-footnoted essay by Parker Tyler, in which he argued that *The Great Escape* was a protracted metaphor for buggery. The film wasn't half as much fun as what Tyler said about it, but the fact that, after a fashion, Tyler's daft theory held up, didn't make it any less daft. Critics aren't jazz pianists, artists valued for their improvising bravura and, too often, they are no more intelligent or commonsensical than Shakespeare's Don Armado, that fantastic, flatulent Spaniard who travestied the impregnable conceit of Sir Walter Raleigh. . . .

The hardback editions of both books are expensively priced, but we should see them on the remainder shelves before too long.

Jean E. Howard (review date Spring 1987)

SOURCE: "Recent Studies in Elizabethan and Jacobean Drama," in *Studies in English Literature, 1500-1900,* Vol. 27, No. 2, Spring, 1987, pp. 321-79.

[In the following excerpted review essay, Howard offers unfavorable assessment of William Shakespeare, *which, she concludes, "is a book that overreaches itself."]*

The crassly pragmatic purpose of an *SEL* review is—ugly phrase—"information management." Publication proceeds at such a pace that no one can possibly absorb even a fraction of what is printed on Renaissance drama in a given year. An omnibus review such as this, published soon after the books themselves are published, supposedly gives overextended scholars some basis for deciding which of these scholarly and critical texts they will actually read. Consequently, I have in part proceeded as if I were simply composing an annotated bibliography, and to some extent that seems not a misrecognition of the nature of the task. On the other hand, description is not enough, and reading all these texts ideally puts one in the position to make larger statements about the state of criticism and scholarship in the field of Renaissance drama and to identify and evaluate those books that emerge from the pack as unusually provocative, ambitious, or significant. I have tried to do as much evaluating and sense-making as I could, though I am very aware of how little of that I have been able to do and of how few of these books have received anything like a comprehensive and careful "review" in this essay. Inevitably, I have devoted the most time to—and have been most critical of—books which interested me the most. I have said nothing about periodicals, books on medieval drama, or books in which only a single chapter was devoted to Renaissance plays.

A final word—all reviewers write from positions and not from a space of Olympian neutrality. As will be clear from what follows, I see literary studies to be in a state of turmoil and controversy inviting a scrutiny of critical practices that perhaps even a decade ago would have been unnecessary. Books which are self-conscious about their own modes of proceeding thus seem, at this moment, of particular value, especially as *they argue for,* rather than *assume,* the political and intellectual validity and urgency of what they undertake. I find valuable, as well, books which engage, rather than ignore, the challenges to traditional critical practice posed by contemporary critiques

of the concept of literary autonomy, by feminism, and by a range of other discourses loosely lumped under the category of "theory." These are not the only kinds of valuable books, as I also hope the review will make clear, but they often have seemed to me the ones where learning, risk, and commitment have most profitably intermingled. They acknowledge that scholarship and criticism are not self-evident and unchanging activities, but historically specific and contestatory practices through which, in part, a culture determines what *kinds* of knowledge at any given time will be deemed legitimate and important, and surely those determinations matter. . . .

The next three books [Eagleton's *William Shakespeare,* Terence Hawke's *That Shakespeherian Rag,* and Simon Shepherd's *Marlowe and the Politics of the Elizabethan Theatre*] are by British academics of the left (Malcolm Evans's book [*Signifying Nothing: Truth's True Contents in Shakespeare's Texts*] could be included here, too), and I group them together to call attention to the fact that these writers take up questions most American critics eschew, such as the political ramification of various appropriations of Shakespeare, including his use in the educational apparatus. These critics see texts as sites of social struggle and their own critical task as the creation of a politically and intellectually progressive approach to Renaissance plays. In foregrounding what is often suppressed in American criticism—i.e., the politics of reading and staging and "using" Shakespeare—their work is important.

The first of these books, Terry Eagleton's *William Shakespeare,* appears in the Rereading Literature series being published by Basil Blackwell with Eagleton as general editor. The series aims to reread the major works of the major authors of the British literary tradition in light of contemporary theoretical discourses such as semiotics, feminism, and Marxism, and thus to liberate the texts from more conservative and apolitical reading practices. Just how strongly and convincingly does Eagleton "reread" Shakespeare? It depends on where you start as a reader. The book is a kind of forced march through the canon (no play gets more than about five pages of analysis) with Marx, Lacan, and contemporary feminism guiding the way. For those familiar with contemporary theory, the conclusions Eagleton reaches probably won't be revolutionary. For those unfamiliar with these discourses, the book may be merely provoking, since it is written in a kind of shorthand which assumes prior acquaintance with the language of the poststructuralist moment.

Eagleton's basic argument is that Shakespeare is a political conservative with a strong investment in upholding a traditional feudal social order but articulating, as well, the transgressive power of sexual desire, linguistic excess, and bourgeois individualism as each fragments or disrupts the containing structures of marriage, law, and social hierarchy. Eagleton's strongest move is—however sketchily—to remind us of the historical specificity of Renaissance dramatic writing: its emergence at the moment when a nascent capitalism and a residual feudalism coincided, producing plays deeply fissured by ideological contradictions: and he works hard to expose the ways in which Shakespeare's devices of closure and containment are insufficient to control the forces threatening all structures of stability. Perhaps inevitably, Eagleton seems to privilege Shakespeare's tragedies because, for him, they most fully acknowledge the disruptive force of excessive desire: sexual, commercial, and linguistic. Macbeth, for example, becomes a figure whose aggressive bourgeois individualism breaks apart the unified self made possible—at least in theory—by accepting a socially defined role in a feudal social order. Eagleton is at his most iconoclastic when he scathingly reads Shakespeare's romances as powerful mystifications of a patriarchal social order in which inequalities of rank, gender, and property are represented as "natural" and in which the disruptive power of sexual desire is sidestepped by transposing wives into daughters and sentimentalizing, without disturbing, patriarchal authority. While there are strong and provocative moments in this book, it also seems thin and rushed, more given to strong local assertions than to sustained argument, and the threads by which Eagleton links these plays to their historical context are often very frail. It is a book that overreaches itself.

Michael Sprinker (review date Winter 1991)

SOURCE: "After the Revolution: Eagleton on Aesthetics," in *Contemporary Literature,* Vol. XXXII, No. 4, Winter, 1991, pp. 573-79.

[*In the following review of* The Ideology of the Aesthetic, *Sprinker discusses Eagleton's aesthetic perspective in light of Hegelian philosophy, and finds contradictions in the political aspects of Eagleton's conclusions.*]

Having been a reasonably diligent observer of Terry Eagleton's career since the mid 1970s, I remain of two minds about the body of work that has poured forth since *Criticism and Ideology*—in my view, his most original and significant contribution to literary theory. On the one hand, I greatly admire (perhaps even envy a bit) his facility as a writer—not merely the speed with which he is able to compose provocative and important studies as various and wide-ranging as his books on Walter Benjamin, the history of English criticism, and Samuel Richardson's *Clarissa;* his still-unsurpassed introduction to contemporary literary theory; and now his long meditation on the history of European aesthetics, but also the clarity he achieves in commenting on and (often enough) taking to task both Marxist and bourgeois theories. Eagleton is, in fine, a superior stylist and a gifted expositor of complex texts. On the other hand, I have consistently been suspicious of the very elegance and cleverness of his books, their literary grace setting off alarms in my mind's more finicky, scholarly recesses. Too frequently in his writing a fine rhetorical flourish is used to mask a logical equivocation or finesse a theoretical difficulty. *The Ideology of the*

Aesthetic possesses all the virtues and all the vices to which one has become accustomed in Eagleton's work. It is a monumental achievement that leaves one vaguely dissatisfied in the end, wishing for a less virtuoso performance and more hardheaded, systematic engagement with the argumentative structures of the texts discussed. In addition, there are political difficulties with the position he reaches; I shall deal with these at the end of this review.

No one should be overly critical of Eagleton's choice of authors and problems; he is comprehensive without being tediously enumerative. Perhaps Georg Lukács might have merited more attention, but I for one have no regrets that old warhorses from previous histories of aesthetics like Benedetto Croce or Roman Ingarden have been unceremoniously dropped to make room for figures hitherto treated marginally, Edmund Burke and Freud most prominently. At the same time, one might legitimately quarrel with the comparatively short shrift given Hegel, whose *Vorlesungen über die Aesthetik* remains the single most important text in the history of European aesthetics, not least because it poses (and virtually for the first time) the central problem for any comprehensive theory of art: to wit, the necessity to think of art as at once historically determinate and yet possessed of properties that give it universal, theoretical significance. Such was certainly Marx's difficulty in treating art, nor has it been transcended in the various attempts to produce an authentically materialist aesthetics this century, from Lukács to Benjamin and Theodor Adorno and beyond. We are all Hegelians, and generally orthodox ones at that, Paul de Man once opined, and I see no reason to revise that judgment on the evidence of Eagleton's new book. Let me illustrate what I mean by examining the very Hegelian premises that, more or less covertly, control the argument in *The Ideology of the Aesthetic.*

The book's fundamental claim is stated succinctly at the outset:

> The construction of the modern notion of the aesthetic artefact is thus inseparable from the construction of the dominant ideological forms of modern class-society, and indeed from a whole new form of human subjectivity appropriate to that social order. . . . But my argument is also that the aesthetic, understood in a certain sense, provides an unusually powerful challenge and alternative to these dominant ideological forms, and is in this sense an eminently contradictory phenomenon. (3)

Eagleton goes on to chart the itinerary of the aesthetic in a series of essays on, among others, A. G. Baumgarten, the Earl of Shaftesbury, Burke, Schiller, Benjamin, and Adorno. Inaugurated as "a discourse of the body" (13) in the mid eighteenth century, aesthetics has experienced numerous vicissitudes in its long march into the postmodern present, but from first to last it stands in a critical relation to the increasing alienation and commodification of social life that capitalism continuously imposes. The aesthetic is in effect the efficient means by which bourgeois society produces its own theoretical gravedigger.

Hegel had a name for this concept of the aesthetic: he called it romantic, designating thereby all art after Greek antiquity and characterizing it thus:

> Abandoning this [classical] principle, the romantic form of art cancels the undivided unity of classical art because it has won a content which goes beyond and above the classical form of art and its mode of expression. . . . In this way romantic art is the self-transcendence of art but within its own sphere and in the form of art itself.[1]

But as Eagleton observes, following the standard tradition of commentary, art itself is an inadequate form of understanding in Hegel's view. Full comprehension of the world comes only when the nonrepresentational mode of philosophical speculation appears on the scene.

Earlier in the *Aesthetics,* Hegel has this to say about the relationship between philosophy (meaning his own) and art:

> Philosophy has to consider an object in its necessity, not merely according to subjective necessity or external ordering, classification, etc.; it has to unfold and prove the object according to the necessity of its own inner nature. It is only this unfolding which constitutes the scientific element in the treatment of a subject. But in so far as the objective necessity of an object lies essentially in its logical and metaphysical nature, the treatment of art in isolation may, and indeed must, be exempt from absolute scientific rigour; art has so many preconditions both in respect of its content and in respect of its material and its medium, whereby it always simultaneously touches on the accidental; and so it is only in relation to the essential inner progress of its content and means of expression that we may refer to its *necessary* formation.[2]

Despite Hegel's notorious incapacity to appreciate the art of his contemporaries (Goethe was a notable exception), despite the unalloyed classicism of his definition of the aesthetic ("the sensory manifestation of the idea"), and despite the conventional view that insists on his philosophy's pan-logicism, the narrative of human history presented in the *Aesthetics* is romantic through and through. For what is romantic art, in Hegel's account, if not this recognition of the inadequacy of sensuous forms to represent the idea, the discovery that only thought itself can express the manifold of the real world, that truth lies not in the harmonious unity of beautiful appearance but in the diremption between intuition and concept that Hegel here names "science"? Romantic art is not, properly speaking, aesthetic at all; it is, rather, the disaggregation of thought from sensory experience, the final liberation from intuitionism that had dominated Western philosophy from Descartes down to Kant and leads a ghostly afterlife in contemporary philosophy of science from Popper to post-Husserlian phenomenology. *Pace* Eagleton, Hegel's philosophy of fine art stands decisively, perhaps uniquely, outside the ideology of the aesthetic.

But if art, as Hegel famously opined, is now "a thing of the past," what point can there be in studying, much less producing, it at all? Why would Hegel waste so much time

lecturing on a phenomenon that he believed to have been definitively transcended in his own philosophy? Hegel's answer is straightforward, and it is not all that different from what a Marxist would (or should) say in reply to the same question: "In works of art, the nations have deposited their richest inner intuitions and ideas, and art is often the key, and in many nations the sole key, to understanding their philosophy and religion." Or, as he goes on to say:

> Neither can the representation of art be called a deceptive appearance in comparison with the truer representations of historiography. For the latter has not even immediate existence but only the spiritual pure appearance thereof as the element of its portrayals, and its content remains burdened with the entire contingency of ordinary life and its events, complications, and individualities, whereas the work of art brings before us the eternal powers that govern history without this appendage of the immediate sensuous present and its unstable appearance.[3]

Hegel proves his own point by reading back from the artifacts of past social formations to the nature of those societies, discerning in the formal configurations of artworks the symptoms of those societies' underlying structures. We may at virtually every point wish to dispute the particular conclusions Hegel draws concerning Egypt, the Hellenic world, or the Christian Middle Ages. And yet the method of inquiry he follows remains the basis for any materialism worthy of the name.

Eagleton's own work returns again and again to the social conditions that caused specific aesthetic discourses to appear: nascent capitalism in Kierkegaard's Denmark; the historical struggle between bourgeois and Junker in Nietzsche's Germany; rapid German industrialization in Heidegger's lifetime; the rise of fascism upon which Adorno and Benjamin never ceased to meditate. Indeed, the very premise of Eagleton's study, we have remarked, is the manifest complicity, however complexly determined, between the discipline of aesthetics and the long social transformation from precapitalist to bourgeois society, a premise evident in the examples just cited. If the aesthetic is one of the pre-eminent ideologies by which the bourgeois attempts to secure its class rule, then it, too, like works of art in Hegel, reveals the material conditions characteristic of bourgeois society at various moments in its history. Philosophical or aesthetic ideologies are, in this construal, just bad (that is, imperspicuous) theories, raw materials for a properly scientific inquiry.

Many readers will recognize that I have ventriloquized an earlier Terry Eagleton here, the one who could write in ***Criticism and Ideology*** about the relationship between science (in that text, the science of criticism) and ideology as entailing the former's exteriority to the latter. As I have argued here, this is an eminently Hegelian notion of science. Nor has Eagleton left this view entirely behind. In his chapter on Marx, we find the following exemplary formulation:

> That final aestheticization of human existence which we call communism cannot be prematurely anticipated

by a reason which surrenders itself wholly to the ludic and poetic, to image and intuition. Instead, a rigorously analytical rationality is needed, to help unlock the contradictions which prevent us from attaining the condition in which instrumentalism may lose its unwelcome dominance. (227)

The science of art is a necessary condition for bringing into existence a world where art will have replaced science, where, to recall a famous passage in *The German Ideology,* we may all hunt in the morning, fish in the afternoon, and criticize after dinner.

This utopian projection of a postrevolutionary society motivates the final pages of *The Ideology of the Aesthetic,* where Eagleton offers his ultimate judgment on the meaning of aesthetic discourse. Without wishing to condemn altogether the utopian dimensions of Marxist thought, I must confess that this moment in Eagleton's text strikes me as utterly divorced from that "rigorously analytical rationality" he rightly deems essential to social transformation, a complete abandonment of historical materialist principles, at least insofar as I understand them. Eagleton writes:

> The fullest instance of free, reciprocal self-fulfillment is traditionally known as love; and there are many individuals who, as far as the personal life goes, have no doubt that this way of life represents the highest human value. . . . Radical politics addresses the question of what this love would mean at the level of a whole society. (413)

This concept of love is glossed earlier in a critique of Freud's "negatively, drastically impoverished view of human society," which finds nothing positive in "the Christian commandment to love all of one's neighbours":

> The Christian commandment to love others has little to do with libidinal cathexis, with the warm glow or the song of the heart. To love the Soviets, for example, means refusing even to consider incinerating them, even if the consequence of this is being incinerated by them ourselves. Simply to contemplate such a course of action, let alone energetically prepare for it, is morally wicked, a form of behaviour incompatible with love. It is absolutely wrong to prepare to commit genocide, the term "absolute" here meaning wrong irrespective of any concrete historical circumstances which could be stipulated as a justificatory context for such an action. (283)

Given this example, who outside the Pentagon and the Hoover Institute could dissent? But not all choices in politics involve the decision to commit genocide or not, though killing and severely punishing are often enough necessities in revolutionary struggle. If certain strands of liberation theology can make their accommodation with guerilla warriors in Central America, I see no reason why more hard-edged materialists can't say with perfect moral justification that ruling-class violence will have to be met with equal violence. Anything less is a recipe for passivity, hence defeat.

This is not to say that Eagleton's recommendation of love as a regulative ideal for a postrevolutionary future is

without merit. It is, however, to recognize that it amounts to little more than a recovery of the Kantian categorical imperative for Left purposes. Nowhere is this more apparent than in the penultimate paragraph of *The Ideology of the Aesthetic,* where Eagleton takes to task certain recent political trends that go under the label of "militant particularism":

> The privilege of the oppressor is his privilege to decide what he shall be; it is this right which the oppressed must demand too, which must be universalized. The universal, then, is not some realm of abstract duty set sternly against the particular; it is just every individual's equal right to have his or her difference respected, and to participate in the common process whereby that can be achieved. Identity is to this extent in the service of non-identity; but without such identity, no real non-identity can be attained. To acknowledge someone as a subject is at once to grant them the same status as oneself, and to recognize their otherness and autonomy. (414-15)

A society composed of individuals who live by this basic rule would be precisely what Schiller envisaged as "the aesthetic state," in the full political sense of the term that Schiller certainly intended.

As Eagleton himself knows—and expresses well throughout this book—such an ideal can only be realized in a postrevolutionary, that is, postclass, postgender, postethnic, postracial society. No such polity currently exists anywhere on earth, nor is one on the immediate horizon. For that reason alone, Eagleton's earlier judgment on the question of the aesthetic retains all its force today:

> Yet if Marxism has maintained a certain silence about aesthetic value, it may well be because the material conditions which would make such discourse fully possible do not as yet exist. The same holds for "morality." . . . It is, perhaps, in the provisional, strategic silence of those who refuse to speak "morally" and "aesthetically" that something of the true meaning of both terms is articulated.[4]

After the revolution, there will be time enough to think about a potentially nonideological concept of the aesthetic. As Louis Althusser was fond of observing, the future lasts a long time.

Notes

1. G. W. F. Hegel, *Aesthetics: Lectures on Fine Art,* trans. T. M. Knox (Oxford: Clarendon, 1975) 79-80.

2. Hegel 11-12.

3. Hegel 7, 9.

4. Terry Eagleton, *Criticism and Ideology* (London: NLB, 1976) 187.

Colin Lyas (review date April 1991)

SOURCE: A review of *The Ideology of the Aesthetic,* in *British Journal of Aesthetics,* Vol. 31, No. 2, April, 1991, pp. 169-71.

[*In the following review, Lyas offers positive evaluation of* The Ideology of the Aesthetic, *though finds fault in its omission of several key philosophers and Eagleton's conclusion.*]

[*The Ideology of the Aesthetic*], despite qualifications to which I will come, is one of the best *reads* in philosophy that I have had for many a long year. I turned to it, somewhat co-incidentally, after yet another of my periodic grazings in the fertile meadows of two works which illuminate many of the issues discussed by Eagleton, Bernard Williams's *Ethics and the Limits of Philosophy* and Roy Edgley's *Reason in Theory and Practice*. The effect was not unlike turning from *The Golden Bowl* to *The Old Curiosity Shop*. For this is a rumbustious, heart-in-the-right-place, cascade of a book. Read with due tolerance, a comment to which I shall return, it has the power to give pleasure and instruction, even if, in the end, one discovers the journey to have been more exciting than the destination.

Comparisons with fiction are not entirely unapt. On p. 196 the writer begins a chapter: 'The narrative so far . . .'. I do not think that Eagleton wishes to use the term 'narrative' in the sense in which it is used by many theorists who claim that all narratives are 'fictive', imposing, as they do, an arbitrary order on an intrinsically unstructured reality. That apart, the term 'narrative' is wholly in order for this work. For it tells a *story* the picaresque story of the search for a key that would unlock a philosophical problem and the story of the historically ordered succession of heroic and not so heroic figures who wrongly thought that they had found it where their predecessors had failed.

The key to the narrative is the philosophical problem whose history it traces. As Eagleton tells it, the traditional concern of philosophy is *thought,* theoretical reasoning, the conceptual, which 'conducts some shadowy existence in the recesses of the mind'. (13) Suddenly in the eighteenth century: 'It is as though philosophy suddenly wakes up to the fact that there is dense, swarming territory beyond its own mental enclave which threatens to fall utterly outside its sway. That territory is nothing less than the whole of our sensate life together—the business of affections and aversions, of how the world strikes the body on its sensory surfaces, of what takes root in the gaze and the guts.'

Once philosophy has woken up to that, the question is, What is to be done with that sensate life? Is it 'opaque to reason' (14)? If so, 'How can the absolute monarch of Reason retain its legitimacy, if what Kant called the "rabble" of the senses remains forever beyond its ken?' In response to this the eighteenth century saw the emergence of the category of the Aesthetic, which, initially with Baumgarten, becomes a faculty, somewhat inferior to logic, by which the domain of sensation is ordered into clear representations, a view which lived on, in amended forms, at least as long as Croce.

Baumgarten is the protagonist of Chapter One of Eagleton's history of the Aesthetic. The interest of that history for readers of this Journal will be apparent when I report that the subsequent chapters deal with Shaftesbury, Hume, Burke, Kant, Schiller, Fichte, Schelling, Hegel, Schopenhauer, Kierkegaard, Marx, Nietzsche, Freud, Heidegger, Benjamin, Adorno, Foucault and Lyotard. The narrative seeks to do various things. First, it seeks to show how each of the figures discussed tried to deal with the problem of the place to be assigned to the aesthetic, conceived as 'the whole region of human perception and sensation' (13), in the economy of human life. Second, it seeks to relate the twists and turns of this story to economic history, to connect, for example, the recognition of the 'gross and palpable dimension of the human' in the eighteenth century, with the need of absolutist powers to take cognizance of the claims of a rising bourgeois. The absolutist state confronted with its rising bourgeois is the correlative, writ large, of sovereign reason confronted with the 'long inarticulate rebellion' (13) of the body. Third, this is a critical history, so that at every juncture we are offered powerful criticisms of this or that answer to the problem with which Eagleton is concerned.

The book teems with ideas, asides, allusions, provocations and passions and calls for comments that far exceed any short review. Here I offer four brief observations.

First, I said earlier that the book should be read with tolerance. I say this because I can imagine experts on the various thinkers who are discussed feeling that those discussions are too sketchy to do justice to whoever is being dealt with. Eagleton does indeed go for the broad sweep but this is compensated for by the illumination that comes from placing this or that particular figure in terms of his contribution to an unfolding debate about a single problem. Here the discussion of Heidegger, to take but one example, seemed to me to be exemplary. I simply understand him and his place in the history of philosophy better as a result of reading this book.

Second, it seems to me that the correlation between, on the one hand, the grapplings of reason with the body and, on the other, the history of the modern state, for all that it is occasionally buttressed by some facts from economic history, is more provocatively suggested than demonstrated. But, again, if this encourages someone to attempt to fill in the appropriate demonstration, or even to think how, if at all, this could be done, Eagleton's suggestions will have done their job. Moreover, those who find this aspect of the book implausible or under-argued will find that the narrative history of the aesthetic as a philosophical notion does not depend for its power on speculations about the connection between that history and the history of the political economy of Europe.

Third, many of the criticisms offered of this or that thinker are of great power and interest. Here I draw attention to the unsparing comments on the unfortunate implications of things said by Nietzsche ('the annihilation of the decaying races' (quoted 245)), and Heidegger. Lyotard, not to mention Foucault, also seem to me to come in for long overdue critical scrutiny. That said, however, the book is very much about the shortcomings of others. When I said, at the outset, that the journey might be more interesting than the arrival, I had in mind the fact that at the end it was still unclear what we ought to give as an answer to the problem whose history is discussed in this book. I suggest later why this might be so.

Fourth, for all its undoubted learning and critical acumen, there were times when this book seemed to me philosophically dubious. (Eagleton disarmingly says 'I am not a professional philosopher' (12) (whatever that is), but the book *is* intended as a philosophical work.) One brief comment must suffice. We are told that the aesthetic arises when, in a post-Cartesian eighteenth century, theoretical reason needs to find some response to the body's revolt against its tyranny. Now it would be convenient if this *were* an eighteenth-century problem, for then it could be linked, as Eagleton links it, to eighteenth-century political conditions. But for all the attempt to invoke the influence of Descartes, the problem whose narrative Eagleton undertakes to relate is much older. It is in Plato that we find the clearest and most categorical recognition of the demands of the body and the appropriate response of reason to it, namely that reason shall subjugate the passions. And it is (as Williams suggests in the work to which I referred above) Aristotle, a philosopher who nowhere appears in Eagleton's narrative, who suggests that a reconciliation might be achieved by treating reason more as practical and collaborative with our wants than as tyrannical over them. I do not, moreover, think that Descartes 'overlooked' 'sensate life', 'affection and aversion' (13). Descartes did indeed initiate a philosophical narrative. For he separated mind and matter. It was this dualism of man and nature, with the consequent alienation of man and his environment, that Kant and Hegel sought to overcome: and it was Hegel's proposed solution that was to set the programme for so much subsequent philosophy. But the narrative of the uneasy history of the relation between reason and the passions is Platonic in its origins. Moreover to deal with it we need, as Roy Edgley's work suggests, the most careful and discriminating discussion of the nature of theoretical and practical reason. That this is no part of the purpose of Eagleton's book may explain why no real progress is made towards a positive solution to the problem that he raises.

I could imagine some who would be impatient with this book. I found it, as I have said, a thought-provoking and even, at times, a riveting read. I suspect those who are complete novices to these matters would find it hard going, and there are passages with the sense of which I still wrestle. These, however, are matched by passages which seemed to me very powerful and often moving pieces of writing.

Eric Griffiths (review date 28 June 1991)

SOURCE: "Dialectic Without Detail," in *Times Literary Supplement,* June 28, 1991, pp. 6-7.

[*In the following review, Griffiths offers unfavorable assessment of* Ideology.]

Though generally admiring William Empson's work, Terry Eagleton regretted that "it lacks . . . almost any concept of ideology". This is not strictly true: a formulation such as "language is essentially a social product, and much concerned with social relations, but we tend to hide this in our forms of speech so as to appear to utter impersonal truths" (*The Structure of Complex Words*) states clearly one classic account of ideological function. But you see what Professor-Elect Eagleton means: Empson makes his point unsystematically, as a general observation about human behaviour rather than as something determined by particular sociopolitical circumstance. When Empson says of the early eighteenth century in England, "There was the feeling that the unity of society had become somehow fishy", he sounds more jokey than a Marxist would allow himself to be about the matter, though his claim is one which a Marxist too might wish to make. The question, then, is whether, lacking a concept of ideology, Empson lacks anything worth regretting. What does "ideology" help us understand which would otherwise baffle us?

Eagleton has been devoted to the word for a good fifteen years, since *Criticism and Ideology* (1976). In his new book, *Ideology: An Introduction,* he explains his fidelity as follows: "The force of the term ideology lies in its capacity to discriminate between those power struggles which are somehow central to a whole form of social life, and those which are not." This cannot be true, and nor does Eagleton believe it. He criticizes those who extend the concept so broadly that it becomes "politically toothless", and the fact that it can be so extended shows that it does not of itself have a "capacity to discriminate" between those struggles which matter and those which don't. It is utterances and utterers that have power: not terms, whatever a peddler of talismans might have us believe. Empson's "somehow fishy" clearly lacks a rigour Eagleton thinks desirable, but it is not clear that his own "somehow central" manages any better. Whether anybody has been helped by "ideology" to manage any better is the subject of the central portion of Eagleton's new book, which is constructed as a sandwich, potted histories of ideologists between two slabs of contemporary skirmish. The historical portion is snappily done; many are the predecessors he reveres and dispatches—Marx, Lukács, Adorno. Fans of his style will recognize the method of earlier works, not quite *Bluffer's Guide* but *Struggler's Guide.* Strugglers would be better guided if Plato's basic account of forming the mind of a state in the *Republic* had been mentioned, or Machiavelli touched on, or Hegelian concepts such as *Wirklichkeit* and mutually recognitive self-consciousness received, if not a hearing, then an airing.

Destutt de Tracy, who started ideology off, hoped to be "a Newton of the science of thought", but nobody has yet produced a relevantly precise and explanatory law of ideological motion. Not Eagleton, anyway, whose bets are so thickly hedged that the reader wanders through his writings as through a maze. For example: ". . . ideology is a function of the relation of an utterance to its social context". But what is "the" relation of an utterance to its social context? There is no such single relation. There are many functions of the many relations of utterances to their contexts, so nothing which distinguishes the ideological from the non-ideological has been said, though Eagleton rightly believes that unless such a distinction can be made the concept of ideology is empty. That the concept might indeed be empty is a dread thought he courageously entertains: "If the concept is not to be entirely vacuous it must have rather more specific connotations of power-struggle and legitimation." Yet "connotations", however unspecifiedly specific, could never be enough to add substance to a theory.

He is committed to "a general materialist thesis that ideas and material activity are inseparably bound up together", though when he expounds that thesis on the next page as entailing that "for an action to be a human practice, it must incarnate meaning", his position is in no important sense "materialist". "Incarnate", after all, has specific connotations which have little to do with historical materialism sternly conceived; an arch-idealist could agree that "ideas and material activity are inseparably bound up together". Rogue Riderhood and Bradley Headstone drowned "inseparably bound up together", but this does not imply that one of them "determined" the other, and nothing less than that will do for a "materialist thesis", unless the word figures here only as one of those "modish, purely gestural uses of that most euphoric of radical buzz-words, materialist", as Eagleton bitingly puts it. A definite concept of causality, which is what ideology needs if it is to have explanatory power, is unavailable to Marxist thought, because it is impossible to experiment with history to test out the causally significant from the causally insignificant variables in the process of time. No doubt Marxist dialectic thinks itself above the crudities of "cause", as that notion was employed by the founders of the modern physical sciences, but it is to such a sense of "cause" that a Marxist account of culture must appeal if it is to have intellectual content or political portent.

Eagleton often has recourse to fuzzy metaphors of bondage, as when, discussing optatives like "May Margaret Thatcher reign for another thousand years!", he comments, "each of these speech acts is bound up with thoroughly questionable assumptions [such as] that another thousand years of Thatcher would have been a deeply desirable state of affairs . . .". It may have seemed like a thousand years to Terry Eagleton, but Mrs. Thatcher was not actually with us that long. That slip does not suggest a firm grip on political realities, but matters less than the theoretical nullity of "bound up with"; does he mean that sincerely saying "May Margaret Thatcher . . ." entails that the speaker believes her continued dominance would be a good thing, or entails the truth of that belief? Who can

say? Not the reader of this book, for Eagleton's phrasing is imprecise, as are most of his forays into the philosophy of language, where he flounders about, asserting that utterances are performatives when they are not, or that "I'm British and proud of it" "implies that being British is a virtue in itself, which is false". The proposition as stated has no such implication, nor would an utterance of the proposition necessarily imply it, because one good reason for adding "and proud of it" is that it strikes the speaker as possible to be British without being proud of it, which could not happen if the words implied what Eagleton says they do.

A man who lay under a tree for fifteen years, noting that apples fell and asserting that their fall was somehow bound up with something else, we would not call a physicist. Nor should we call Eagleton a theorist, literary or otherwise. It is true that the relations of social being and consciousness which an account of ideology must try to theorize are extremely various, to put it mildly, and perhaps have no specifiable regularity. That is why we need not regret anybody's lack of a concept of ideology, for this pseudo-notion serves only to foster an illusion of analysis which is intellectually unsupported and without political consequence. There is a pleasure to be gained from making pronouncements such as "ideological discourse typically displays a certain ratio between empirical propositions and what we might roughly term a world view", but really the "ratio" is *un*certain, and the use of a cold technicality such as "ratio" does no more than provide the user with a feeling of tough-mindedness. "What is most difficult here", as Wittgenstein said, "is to put this indefiniteness, correctly and unfalsified, into words"—the indefiniteness, in this case, of how the world bears upon thought, and vice versa. But there is all the difference in the world between the intellectual asceticism necessary correctly and without falsification to express the indefinite and a slurry such as the conclusion to ***Ideology: An introduction:*** "Ideology is a matter of . . . certain concrete discursive effects. . . . It represents the points where power impacts upon certain utterances. . . . the concept of ideology aims to disclose something of the relation between an utterance and its material conditions of possibility, when those conditions of possibility are viewed in the light of certain power-struggles. . . ."

Spattered with "certain"-ties though Eagleton's prose is, he is against being specific. He does not tell us which "concrete discursive effects", which "utterances", which "power-struggles" he is on about. Similarly, his concern "to bring about the kind of social conditions in which all men and women could genuinely participate in the formulation of meanings and values, without exclusion or domination" does not stretch to mentioning which kind of conditions these might be, or hinting how they might be brought about. In ***The Ideology of the Aesthetic,*** he is scornful of requests for detailed examples: "Those trained in literary critical habits of thought are usually enamoured of 'concrete illustration': but since I reject the idea that 'theory' is acceptable if and only if it performs the role of humble handmaiden to the aesthetic work, I have tried to frustrate this expectation as far as possible by remaining for the most part resolutely silent about particular artefacts." This is a procession of canards flying up Eagleton's intellectual stonewalling: to "reject an idea" is a lesser thing than to give arguments as to why it should be rejected; not only those caricatured as wishing to keep theory as a "humble handmaiden" like to see a bit of evidence once in a while: and "remaining . . . resolutely silent" is a gentle way of describing having absolutely nothing to say.

This derider of the concrete is the same Eagleton who urges attention to "the specificity of Marxism" and knows that "if a 'socialist common sense' is to be constructed, Gramsci's thesis will need to be carried into specific analyses". Not that he has ever bothered to do any of the historical work which he lavishly and on principle recommends. For a Marxist, he is very shy of labour. He is sure that "to analyse the ideological force of an utterance is, inseparably, to interpret its precise rhythm, inflection, intonality, and to refer it to its determining social context", but he confines his analyses to vague, coarse throw-aways, such as forgiving Raymond Williams for misunderstanding pastoral "understandably enough, for one from the rural proletariat", or retailing Fredric Jameson's view that "high modernism . . . was born at a stroke with mass commodity culture". Even works of art, those lamentable fetishes of the bourgeoisie, still show signs of having once been just that, *works:* not to attend to the particularity of their formation, as Eagleton determinedly does not attend, consigns you to the mystified realm of alienated labour or, to speak more simply, chatting about price-tags. It is not, for example, an escape from the gossip of salons to write about Shakespeare at length without considering which text of the plays you are reading, but merely a shift of salon.

His political judgment is displayed in his belief that Althusserian anti-humanism was "politically timely" (1986) but also that it completely failed to understand the events of 1968 in France (1991). The trenchancy of his theoretical critique amounts to no more than muttering "this is surely too economistic", "this case is . . . surely too one-sided", or "that there is something in this position is surely clear", like one of his own detested amateurish Oxford dons regretting that the young have surely gone a bit too far, though they may have a point. A Marxist could not but be ashamed of Eagleton's productions—their disgraceful sloppiness in formulation, the abeyance in them of any sense of history more detailed than that of a "quality" colour magazine, their self-publicizing, opportunism and political futility. A non-Marxist will find them just sadly unpersuasive, while also feeling indignation and dismay that an intellectual tradition as tireless, fervent and dogmatic as Marxism, a politics as laborious as socialism, should have as their figurehead of articulation in this country only Terry Eagleton.

Richard Schusterman (review date Summer 1991)

SOURCE: A review of *The Ideology of the Aesthetic,* in *Journal of Aesthetics and Art Criticism,* Vol. 49, No. 3, Summer, 1991, pp. 259-61.

[*In the following review of* The Ideology of the Aesthetic, *Schusterman praises Eagleton's insight and rhetorical turns, though finds shortcomings in the book's omissions and contradictory assertions.*]

The past decade of Anglo-American intellectual history has witnessed literary theory's undeniable emergence as the most influential, ambitious, and institutionally powerful genre of theoretical discourse in the humanities. The fact that it now prefers to call itself simply "theory," as if to encompass and exhaust the entire theoretical realm, is testimony to its ambition. But it also testifies, I believe, to a covert but nagging discomfort with its narrowly literary past, its institutional provenance in the Anglo-American world as a theoretical practice based in departments of English and foreign literature, dominated (if not originally formulated) by "language teachers" rather than so-called professional philosophers, who have traditionally held the honor of being Western culture's grand theorists. In its attempt both to escape its literary past and to avoid and outflank its closest neighbor and rival in Anglo-American philosophy departments, literary theory took care to distinguish itself sharply from the field of aesthetics, aligning itself instead with structuralist and then poststructuralist textual analysis and with general hermeneutics. Another good reason for ignoring philosophical aesthetics was that this discipline was dominated by a rigorous but excessively restrictive analytic paradigm which tended to dismiss as hopelessly confused and partisan any imaginative, revisionary, and politically committed aesthetics, whether continental or homegrown (as with Dewey).

In any case, Anglo-American literary theory has too long ignored the tradition of philosophical aesthetics from which it ultimately derives and to which it belongs. With its hard won confidence as a philosophical equal and its arsenal of textual and rhetorical strategies, literary theory can now confront and enrich this tradition. Terry Eagleton's new book is a bold and admirable attempt to do this by a critical reading of the modern history of philosophical aesthetics from Baumgarten to postmodernism. Though the project is dauntingly impressive, it is one well-suited to Eagleton's masterful talents of condensation and narration. The result is both very rewarding and frustratingly disappointing. Let me commend its rewards before registering my disappointments.

Written with engagingly impassioned commitment and keen wit, the book contains too many insights to list, let alone summarize. But there are three major (and somewhat interrelated) themes where Eagleton's contribution is particularly welcome and therapeutic. The first is his insistence on recognizing aesthetics "as a discourse of the body" (p. 14), in salubratory contrast to the dominant philosophical tendency since Kant and Hegel to disembody the aesthetic through over intellectualizing and spiritualizing it, as idealist philosophy would naturally tend to do. Eagleton makes his case for the sensual, bodily dimension of aesthetics partly by tracing its importance in Baumgarten's original aesthetic project of a science of sensation and in the empiricist theorists of taste, partly by exposing the difficulties and contradictions engendered through its attempted suppression in the spiritualizing tendencies of German idealism. But more importantly and fruitfully, he enlists the aid of more modern and materialist thinkers who emphasize the lived, desiring body—its formative senses, productive and libidinal energies, and satisfactions—as an indispensable locus of the aesthetic and a source of its great power, which renders the aesthetic pervasively potent beyond the compartmental limits of art, imploding into the very fabric of our ethical, social, and political life. Nietzsche along with Marx and Freud are great allies here, indeed "the three greatest aestheticians of the modern period . . . Marx with the laboring body, Nietzsche with the body as power, Freud with the body as desire" (p. 197). All, nonetheless, come in for criticism. Nietzsche is censured for his antisocial aestheticizing justification of the most rapacious values of the bourgeois market place "domination, aggression, exploitation, and appropriation" (p. 351). Freud is faulted for being "a pessimistic conservative authoritarian," failing to temper his penetrating exposure of human frailty and corruption with a "revolutionary commitment" and a more Christian or Marxist sense of love and brotherhood (p. 283). Even Marx is taken to task for an overly one-sided and insufficiently discriminating aesthetic ideal of human self-realization through the powers of production (pp. 220-225).

Obviously, Eagleton is using the term "aesthetic" more widely than is customary in recent philosophical aesthetics. That is precisely his point, and heralds the two other themes where his critical history makes a valuable contribution. The first of these might be called the complex functionality and ramified importance of the aesthetic. Rather than accept modernity's sharp distinction between the cognitive, ethico-political, and aesthetic spheres, together with the Kantian rider that the aesthetic sphere is one of free, disinterested purposelessness, Eagleton insists on the deep political dimension of the aesthetic. One of his major theses (which is already fairly familiar) is that the aesthetic and its discourse served a crucial project of politico-cultural hegemony, through which the order and consensus of a ruling ideology were not to be coerced on our senses and desires from without by external law or concept but rather introjected into the heart of our subjectivity and "natural" affections through the unforced force of aesthetic pleasure. Kant's notion of the aesthetic judgement, which though conceptless and subjective makes a claim to universal consensus, and which results from imagination's "free conformity to law," clearly evokes this political agenda. Similarly, the idea of aesthetic unity, which presents a concrete totality where material particulars are given independent expression while held together in an ordered unity through nonrepressive form, presents both a consoling comfort and a revolutionary ideal for society which is riven by class division or suffocated by conformist administrative formalisms. Moreover, so Eagleton argues, the aesthetic ideal of the unity of form and content lies at the motivating core of Marx's economic theory. Eagleton is surely right to insist on the political role and liberational potential of the aesthetic, even if one balks at his judging particular aesthetic theories by their value as "a basis on which to found a politics" (p. 370). Finally, with Nietzsche and Adorno in particular, the aesthetic is shown to have an essential cognitive role, he it shaping the facts of the world through motivated interpretation or providing a refuge for truth in a reality which is brutally false.

But in finding so many different uses and manifestations of the aesthetic, is not Eagleton just flouting and corrupting its true, established (and essentially Kantian) meaning as something characteristically formal, functionless, and fundamentally contrasted to the cognitive and practical? Again, raising this question of the univocity of the aesthetic is part of Eagleton's point and contribution. Looking at the long and tortured history of the concept, unblinkered by the professional philosopher's canonical reading of this history as the prelude and continuing postscript to aesthetic Kantianism, Eagleton can see more clearly the wealth of different and often contradictory meanings the term "aesthetic" has been able to carry. It designates (e.g., in Kierkegaard) the direct immediacy of sensuous perception and pleasure, as much as connoting contemplative distance and reflection. It reflects bodily interest and desire (e.g., in Marx, Nietzsche, and Freud) as well as signifying disinterested and will-less intellectual pleasure. It represents material and concrete particularity as well as the formal principle; the richly sensory and satisfying dimension of daily full-bodied living as well as a specially privileged and spiritualized domain set apart and above the quotidian. Recognizing this history of polysemy and variable application is very important for reminding us that the aesthetic is not a fixed, univocal notion but rather an essentially contested concept, and that there is thus no compelling reason for narrowly identifying its "proper use" or conception with the long dominant and increasingly conservative philosophical aesthetic tradition. If the meaning of the aesthetic is contestable, its value for culture legitimation and liberation makes it well worth contesting.

To recognize and affirm polysemy is not necessarily to pursue it till the term "aesthetic" comes close to mean everything and thus nothing. Unfortunately, Eagleton is not always careful of this distinction. Rather than helpfully trying to establish some classificatory analysis of classificatory ordering of the most important meaning or dimensions of the aesthetic, he simply takes advantage of whatever variant meaning happens to suit the vector of argumentation in which he is for the moment engaged. The result is a rhetorical *tour de force,* but also too often, a rather disappointing muddle. By a free-wheeling metonymic logic which is sure to exasperate many philosophers. Eagleton tends to reduce almost everything to the aesthetic by employing the following fallacious form of argument: if something is characterizable by a feature which characterizes the aesthetic (in any of the various uses thereof), it therefore represents the aesthetic. Thus, for Eagleton, whatever is conceived as autotelic or self-generating (like morality, God, or Being) or as disinterested (like justice or knowledge) is seen to be fundamentally aesthetic, since these properties have fundamentally defined the aesthetic in certain conceptions of this concept. His disarming introductory confession to not being a professional philosopher hardly seems to justify such logic, though it may exonerate him from minor philosophical errors (like conflating referential with cognitively objective discourse [p. 93]) which occasionally blemish a generally very accomplished text. Some philosophers, however, may also be ruffled by contradictions which seem to result less from the conflictual character of the aesthetic than from Eagleton's flamboyantly suasive rhetoric which throws cautious qualification to the wind: so that Schiller's aesthetic is conflictingly described as "socially useless" and "an active social force" (pp. 110, 117), while Nietzsche's aesthetic principle is defined as "the formless productive energies of life" and in the very next breath as "the stamping of form" on this "flux" (pp. 252-253).

Even if Eagleton's narrative makes no claim to completeness, there are some strikingly regrettable omissions. Given his emphasis on the bodily aesthetic, one should expect some sustained discussion of Merleau-Ponty. Moreover, his total neglect of twentieth-century Anglo-American aesthetics (even for the polemical purposes of refuting its theories or demonstrating their poverty) weakens his case for the central status of the aesthetic throughout Western culture. It also represents a lost opportunity to confront a politically conservative aesthetic tradition which menaces the revolutionary aesthetic Eagleton would urge, as it earlier stifled that of John Dewey. Eagleton could well have used Dewey as an ally, not only for advocating a global, embodied aesthetic deeply aware of art's socio-political dimension and liberational potential, and deeply critical of its compartmentalized and elitist distortions in capitalist society; but also for relieving a conceptual cramp between the aesthetic and the instrumental which sometimes seems to trouble Eagleton.

The mixture of pleasurable reward and disappointment is finally present in the book's style, which is worth mentioning not only because it is scintillatingly salient but because it intriguingly exemplifies one of the book's major themes. If the aesthetic aimed to make the hierarchical weight of a dominant ideology more pleasurable and appealing, so Eagleton seems desperately trying to liven up aesthetic theory's ponderous and often dreary history by a self-consciously entertaining style where jokes are so abundant and important that one wonders whether the motivating end of the paragraph is a warranted conclusion or simply a winning punch line. One is reluctant to fault Eagleton here, because so many works of aesthetics are aesthetically unreadable and excruciatingly boring. Eagleton's is blissfully not. Still, the extent of his efforts at philosophical music hall distract from the urgent seriousness of his arguments; and four hundred pages of his light-spirited and deliciously ornamented prose can give habitual readers of philosophy the uneasy feeling of having dined on a five pound box of chocolates.

Elizabeth Wright (review date July 1991)

SOURCE: A review of *The Ideology of the Aesthetic*, in *Modern Language Review*, Vol. 86, Pt. 3, July, 1991, pp. 653-54.

[*In the following review, Wright offers positive assessment of* The Ideology of the Aesthetic.]

What R. H. Tawney did for religion, Arnold Hauser for art history, Adorno for music, and Raymond Williams for literature, Terry Eagleton has done for aesthetics: namely, to uncover the ideological motivation that ideology itself exists to conceal. In spite of a modest disavowal he comes challengingly close to doing the same for philosophy. In the favoured definitions, self-confirming premises, chosen controversies, chosen opponents, bland ignorances, and shared assumptions of what is to be banally true, he charts a new map for aesthetic theory from Baumgarten to the postmoderns. It is part of Professor Eagleton's originality to realize that this is a demystification that has been imperative for some time. As one reads it, one has the refreshing feeling of at last having an illusion exorcised. In rending the ideological fabric, he brings into salience philosophical questions of the place of the aesthetic in the bases of culture and society, indeed, showing it to be essentially imbricated in knowledge and language, and, moreover, in ideology itself. Answering these questions is not part of his brief, but it is evidence of radical success that such questions have to be put.

Professor Eagleton does not claim to provide a history of ideology in aesthetics, but has rather taken certain key figures, mostly German, and analysed their basic positions in the light of the dominance of bourgeois individualism. The theories themselves are the historically concrete illustrations: the more he lays bare the individualist partiality that shapes and maintains the arguments under examination, the more evidence he is amassing in support of his thesis. It is a case of the scope of a theory being an element in its plausibility. When the problem of reconciling freedom and necessity is invested with the bourgeois fantasy of a sovereign self, then Kant's attempt to found a secure moral freedom outside determinism can be understood as a defensive idealization. Similarly, Schiller's *On the Aesthetic Education of Man* tries to effect the same reconciliation between the freedom of the 'sense-drive' and the necessity of the 'form-drive' via a 'play-drive' that would optimistically harness the dynamism of the former to duty in the latter. Professor Eagleton cannot help but see this as a hegemonic move to keep the suspicious world of the senses within the law without having recourse to the compulsion of the law. He avoids the cynicism to which such analyses might lead, for he sees Kant as still holding to the democratic notion of a 'kingdom of ends' (albeit of abstractly equal and indistinguishable citizens) and Schiller as sensitive to the stunting of capacities that a greedy civil society can bring about.

It is perhaps in his treatment of Jean-Francois Lyotard that Professor Eagleton shows a certain partiality, in that he accuses Lyotard of moral subjectivism in a theory that places undecidability as a stubborn aspect of the aesthetic and yet he praises Benjamin and Adorno for retaining a place for the sensory. Professor Eagleton approves of Benjamin's saying that 'there is no better starting point for thought than laughter' (p. 337), and yet he is suspicious of post-modernists who 'urge us to abandon truth for dance and laughter' (p. 227). It is precisely in the shifting about of Benjamin's 'constellations' on the stars of the sensory that those ironic transformations are made that might be said to be at the core of the aesthetic. In *Le Différend* Lyotard has addressed himself to the very questions Professor Eagleton has raised, namely, how 'given' truths and facts are established and transformed. It is in Lyotard's 'unpresentable' and Adorno's 'riddle-figures of empirical existence' that the Body, which Professor Eagleton professes to favour as a concept, shows its presence.

Terry Eagleton's book [*The Ideology of the Aesthetic*] is distinguished throughout by clarity of exegesis coupled with his usual lively wit and inventiveness. Thus, he ends his account of the dire relationships of the Lacanian family trio driven into misrecognition of desire, with the lapidary comment: 'None of these individuals desire each other in the least; it's nothing personal.'

David Lloyd (review date December 1991)

SOURCE: "In the Defiles of Analogy," in *Art History,* Vol. 14, No. 4, December, 1991, pp. 620-24.

[*In the following review, Lloyd offers unfavorable evaluation of* The Ideology of the Aesthetic, *though credits Eagleton's elucidation of the work of other major theorists.*]

At the time of writing, it is already clear enough to casual observation that Eagleton's *Ideology of the Aesthetic* has become something of an academic best seller. Accordingly, the usual concerns of an advance review give way here in this rather belated account to an assessment of the work's achievement, made all the more demanding by virtue of the book's wide circulation and probable influence. Fredric Jameson's comment on the cover, 'That contemporary theory would eventually turn back to consider its origins in the contradictions of philosophical

aesthetics was predictable', is certainly true, and marks the necessity of such a project. It must be said, of course, that such a project has been undertaken over a long period already in Germany, in the wake of both the Frankfurt School and Habermas, and in the work of the Budapest School, though Eagleton makes no acknowledgement of either corpus.[1] Nonetheless, the appearance of such work in English is much to be desired, especially at a moment when, in the face of cultural studies and multi-cultural transformations of curricula and institutions, the Right is busily trying to reclaim its rights over aesthetic culture. For two reasons, then, the intrinsic and strategic importance of the project and the wide circulation of the product, one wishes that Eagleton had done a better job on a work which, if only because it rushes in to fill a vacuum, is rapidly becoming 'indispensable'.

There are, indeed, many very valuable things in this work. It provides in many respects an excellent map of some of the most important thinkers in the rather undulating tradition (principally Anglo-German) of aesthetic thought, covering in addition to the predictable figures from Burke, Kant, Schiller and Hegel down to Lukacs and the Frankfurt School, a number of less evident ones, such as Kierkegaard and Schopenhauer. Eagleton rightly disclaims any systematic historical approach, casting the book rather as 'an attempt to find in the category of the aesthetic a way of gaining access to certain central questions of modern European thought—to light up, from that particular angle, a range of wider social, political and ethical issues'. Given the mediating position for Kant of aesthetic judgment between the practical and theoretical, or its politically formative function for Schiller, to take only two examples, the articulation of the aesthetic with 'wider issues' is entirely justified, indeed requisite, and Eagleton is right to insist throughout on its relation to the political and ethical. Each reader may regret that the book's scope omits or under-represents one or other significant writer (Gramsci and Arnold are my personal candidates for more extensive discussion), but such omissions are legitimate consequences of selection. What results are often excellent accounts of constellations such as the British Enlightenment or of individual figures (the chapter on Schiller being perhaps the best) which often produce pithy and portable aphorisms, such as 'If the aesthetic is to realize itself it must pass over into the political, which is what it secretly already was' or, in his valuable discussion of the relationship between ideological propositions and aesthetic analogical predication, 'ideological utterances conceal an essentially emotive content within a referential form, characterizing the lived relation of a speaker to the world in the act of appearing to characterize the world'. This familiar Wildean capacity in Eagleton leads one indeed to forgive the more excessive Celtic fantasies that are the residue of a larger project on Ireland and aesthetics from which the present work is a fortunate distillation—the best of these is the characterization of Irish colonial or Scots Lowland figures like Hutcheson, Hume, Smith and Ferguson as 'speaking up from the Gaelic [sic] margins . . . [to] denounce possessive individualism and bourgeois utility', though a close second comes the wildly un-grounded comment on Burke's 'anti-social' sublime: 'These, it may be noted, are the political thoughts of a man who as a child attended a hedge school in County Cork'.

A little ludicrous in their abstracted presentation, such remarks point towards a larger failure of the work exactly because, with a little more painstaking elaboration histori-cally and theoretically, they can be made to make a certain nuanced sense. Eagleton's sporadic aphoristic condensa-tions bespeak the influence of two masters of the style whom he discusses, Benjamin and Adorno. Unlike them, however, he rarely succeeds in sustaining the relentlessly dialectical movement of the aphoristic. The same could be said for the larger critical project of this work. Despite the appeals for dialectical method which virtually commence and conclude the book, Eagleton's method by and large falls short of that which he espouses. It is easy to agree with his concluding comment that 'The aesthetic is . . . a markedly contradictory concept, to which only a dialecti-cal thought can do sufficient justice. One of the most debilitating effects of much cultural theory at the present time has been the loss or rejection of that dialectical habit, which can now be safely consigned to the metaphysical ashcan'. Unfortunately, ***The Ideology of the Aesthetic*** is itself no outstanding example of dialectical method and, for all its valuable insights, it tends to hit its targets with the fortuitousness of Scud missiles, by multiplicity rather than by design.

Dialectical method certainly involves, but is by no means exhausted by the identification and immanent elaboration of contradictions within social or intellectual formations. It proceeds, as any critical philosophy, from a question as to the conditions of possibility of a given phenomenon, whether the commodity form or a cultural formation, and must therefore grasp its objects in their structural and historical differentiation as well as in their articulation. This implies, not the reification of social practices, as with exchange in bourgeois political economy or aesthetic experience even in Marx himself, but a painstaking and critical analysis of their differential relation to other spheres of practice which grasps both the historical condi-tions for their emergence and the structural conditions for their articulation with other spheres. The necessity for such a method is peculiarly evident in the analysis of the aesthetic sphere, which is nowhere more political and interested than in its claim to be free of political interest. Eagleton rightly identifies the persistent relationship between aesthetic culture and hegemony, but that relation-ship is posited throughout either analogically or in terms of direct identification, falling short throughout of an adequate account of the rationale for their articulation.

The borderline between analogy and immediacy of identification is always slender, but both constitute failures of dialectical method. ***The Ideology of the Aesthetic*** is full of both, and the methodological inadequacy is of real import, given the significance of the issues Eagleton broaches. We do need an adequate account of the relation-ship between aesthetics and hegemony precisely because the problem the materialist faces lies not so much in identifying all the theoretical fissures and contradictions of bourgeois ideology but in establishing why, to so disturb-ing an extent, it has proven so successful hegemonically. What can be seen in Eagleton's work as a constant recourse to analogical procedures is not simply the index of too hasty thinking but forecloses a fuller understanding of the transforming function of aesthetic culture in the maintenance of hegemony. (It is also, incidentally, a repeti-tion of the privileged, problematic, but enabling trope of aesthetics itself, as a careful reading of Kant would show.)[2] Any reader will be struck by the frequency of this analyti-cal shortcut, which is, it must be stressed, a common recourse of contemporary cultural studies and all the more to be resisted. The following examples will have to suffice.

One of the constant analogies posed by Eagleton in the course of his analysis of the aesthetic is one between the form of the subject and the form of the artwork and between both and the State. The perception of the likeness is valuable and just in most cases, but the simple expres-sion of it is not only inadequate but often inexact. Thus in the chapter 'Free Particulars', which deals principally with Rousseau and Kant, Eagleton makes the following series of remarks:

> This 'lawfulness without a law' signifies a deft compromise between mere subjectivism on the one hand, and an excessively abstract reason on the other. There is indeed for Kant a kind of 'law' at work in aesthetic judgment, but one which seems inseparable from the very particularity of the artefact. As such, Kant's 'lawfulness without a law' offers a parallel to that 'authority which is not an authority' (*The Social Contract*) which Rousseau finds in the structure of the ideal political state. In both cases, a universal law of a kind lives wholly in its free, individual incarnations, whether these are political subjects or the elements of the aesthetic artefact. The law simply is an assembly of autonomous, self-governing particulars working in spontaneous reciprocal harmony . . .

> Like the work of art as defined by the discourse of aesthetics, the bourgeois subject is autonomous and self-determining, acknowledges no merely extrinsic law but instead, in some mysterious fashion, gives the law to itself.

As this concatenation of 'seems', 'parallels', 'kind of', 'in some mysterious fashion' might suggest, this analysis is full of partially grasped truths and insufficiently deduced relationships. To indicate just a few: Kant's 'lawfulness without a law' is absolutely not a quality of the object of judgement (let alone of the artefact, about which Kant, who is principally concerned with beauty in nature has remarkably little to say), but, as he is at pains to point out, a *subjective* harmonizing of imagination and understand-ing ('lawfulness' can in any case be translated as 'lawlikeness' or 'conformity to law' [*Gesetzmaessigkeit*], which makes Kant's point clearer); accordingly, the talk of 'subjectivism' is profoundly confusing, since it implies a direct relation between the Kantian subject of judgement and a loosely conceived 'subjectivism', implying self-interest: in turn, it has to be said that the law does not inhabit individual incarnations, though they may conform to it. At a larger level of analysis, the analogy between Rousseau's social contract and the quality of 'lawfulness without a law' that defines a relation of the faculties in the Third Critique is inaccurate, since, as Kant moves from the discussion of the judgment to that of taste, it becomes apparent that he is concerned to relocate the notion of a 'social contract' in the form of common sense rather than in a quasi-historical moment of origin, thus pushing the kind of analysis that Rousseau conducts into a crucially more formal terrain. As for the 'work of art as defined by bourgeois aesthetics', it has to be said, if it is not too literal-minded, that it depends on which aesthetic, since it is by no means the case in Kant that the *work of art* gives a law to itself nor even that any subject does so that is not that rare thing, a genius. It is, perhaps, and in some versions of aesthetics, the case that the subject can be compared to the artwork, but by and large it is in the *relation* to the artwork, not by analogy with it, that the subject appears as self-determining. Nor is there anything 'mysterious' about it within the terms of aesthetic discourses themselves, since it derives from a quite coherent analysis of the subject.

Pedantic as these criticisms may seem, they are of real importance both to understanding the terms of given aesthetic discourses and to that of their gradual transformation. If we wish to understand the political effectiveness of an aesthetic discourse that seeks to distantiate itself from the political precisely in order to give the possibility of the political, then we must also be very clear concerning the distinction made within its tradition between the subject and the individual, and the distinction between that subject and the subject of psychoanalysis or that of political theory. Not that there are no lines of mediation to be drawn between these different theoretical usages, but in Eagleton's work there is a constant collapsing of these terms rather than an articulation of them. Thus, for example, where Eagleton claims that the concept of 'aesthetic disinterestedness involves a radical decentering of the subject', his invocation of a Lacanian vocabulary is desperately confusing, since the effects of decentring (or preferably, subordination) of the sensuous or empirical individual by the aesthetic subject of judgement have little or nothing to do, in any direct sense, with the displacement of the psychoanalytical subject by the real or the signifying chain. Consequently, some of the most irritating moments of this book are its recurrent 'subversions' of the aesthetic by appeal to surprisingly crude and reductive psychoanalytic 'readings'. At times, this is no more than a donnish pinning of the phallic tail to a philosophical ass, as when Heidegger's Being is made to reveal its tumescent form: 'Being is a kind of "jutting forth", and this uprightness or "erect standing there" is a permanent one, an unfolding which will never fall down. It would seem that this oldest of stand-bys is indeed always ready-to-hand.' Since this is the conclusion of the chapter, one is tempted to say, so what? It is scarcely surprising to find

that Heidegger's discourse is phallocentric, and surely there are more important things to be said about it. At other points, however, where a more extensive theoretical articulation of psychoanalysis with aesthetics is attempted, the results are far more deleterious to any proper understanding of the relationship between the psychoanalytical and the aesthetic subject, as in this comparison of Kant's subject of judgment to the Lacanian ego of the mirror stage:

> In both cases, an imaginary misrecognition takes place, although with a certain reversal of subject and object from the mirror of Lacan to the mirror of Kant. The Kantian subject of aesthetic judgement, who misperceives as a quality of the object what is in fact a pleasurable coordination of its own powers, and who constitutes in a mechanistic world a figure of idealized unity, resembles the infantile narcissist of the Lacanian mirror stage, whose misperceptions Louis Althusser has taught us to regard as an indispensable structure of all ideology.

If these relationships had been thought through instead of merely posited as resemblances, 'with a certain reversal', Eagleton might have come to the point of recognizing the crucial distinction between the Kantian subject and the Lacanian 'je'. 'The mirror stage is formative of the *I*' and not of the Subject, which, and Lacan is quite explicit about it, prefigures but does not yet constitute the Subject, which is formed in relation to the Symbolic dimension of the other, not in the Imaginary register of the relation to the ego-ideal?. He falls here, it must be said, into a crucial error that his teacher Althusser had already made in confusing the ego and the Subject, but a more considerate reading of Kant or Lacan or both might have helped. That in turn would have demanded a far less cavalier approach to psychoanalysis in its therapeutic dimension than we get in Eagleton's personifications of the super-ego: 'Such treatment must try to make the super-ego more tolerant and rational, to deflate its false idealism and undermine its Pharasaical pretensions.' Crucial to any understanding of psychoanalytic procedure, let alone its relation to aesthetic discourse, is an approach to the complex phenomenon of transference, which is, in Eagleton's account, entirely elided, with the result that the dialectic of the Subject in its relation to the Other cannot be worked through.[3]

Instances of what is in effect sloppy thinking, muddled through by the aid of the half-truths of striking analogies, are rife in *The Ideology of the Aesthetic* (a title which, though regrettably catchy, is in fact vertiginously incoherent once the attempt is made to analyse its meaning). It is hard to know to what to ascribe this lapsing on the part of a critic whose *Function of Criticism,* despite its slimness, actually provides a far more coherent account of the ideological workings of culture. The work as a whole is peculiarly individualistic in its account of the aesthetic, in the sense that it lacks any account of the institutional mediations which even so relentlessly critical a discourse as Kant's is forced towards and which aesthetic discourse after Schiller continually demands. Instead we get a work remarkably reminiscent of bourgeois histories of ideas, in which one individual figure follows another in loosely interconnected succession. This is not to demand of the book that it fulfil either the task of writing an institutional history of cultural or aesthetic education (though this would be valuable), nor that it attempt the task of producing a systematic history of influences and transformations within aesthetic philosophy. There is, indeed, a moment of truth in De Man's late problematization of any history of the aesthetic, problematic since history is a category questioned by aesthetic discourse.[4] From its founding texts, aesthetics tropes 'the civilizing process' (with which it must not be confused) into a uniform developmental history of humanity of which pedagogy is an inseparable correlative. The history of its developments is that of a transformation always registered within the terms that the aestheticization of history itself prescribes—where, that is, post-enlightenment historiography becomes a history of probability rather than possibilities.

This implies a double task for the materialist historian of aesthetics (since the only properly materialist aesthetics is the history of aesthetics). One element is a rigorously formal analysis of a discourse for which the formality of its definition of the human is indispensable and from whose formality alone can be explained its remarkable capacity to transfer geographically and historically the same regulative forms for human identity. This would amount to an analysis of the aesthetic as giving the forms for bourgeois ideology at both theoretical and practical/institutional levels and demands, above all, that one respect, in a way analogical thinking cannot, the distinction of spheres through which bourgeois social practice represents itself. The second element would be a history of counter-possibilities, of truncated or defeated conceptions of social organization or of community, whose realization has at one or other moment been prevented by the hegemony of an aesthetic discourse that sets the institutional terms for participation in the public sphere. In some respects a practical task of immense difficulty, this 'history of possibilities' is nonetheless a crucial undertaking. It is the task that two of the thinkers that Eagleton regards as being among the 'most creative, original cultural theorists Marxism has yet produced', Benjamin and Bakhtin, direct us. Eagleton's own undertaking of an indispensable project and the quasi-encyclopaedic volume of its product command respect. But the recognition of the importance of the project obliges equally the judgement that its execution is not adequate to the kind of thoroughgoing analysis of culture and hegemony that an increasingly embattled Marxism certainly requires.

Notes

1. See especially the work of Peter Bürger, Christa Bürger and Jochen Schulte-Sasse, as for example their collection *Zur Dichotomisierung von hoher und niederer Literatur* (Frankfurt-am-Main: Suhrkamp, 1982) and other collections by the same editors. For the Budapest School, see the excellent collection, *Reconstructing Aesthetics: Writings of the Budapest School,* Ferenc Feher and Agnes Heller, eds, Oxford, 1986.

2. On this topic, see David Lloyd, 'Analogies of the Aesthetic: The Politics of Culture and the Limits of Critique', *New Formations,* Spring 1990.

3. On transference, see especially Jacques Lacan, *The Four Fundamental Concepts of Psychoanalysis,* ed. Jacques-Alain Miller, trans. Alan Sheridan, Harmondsworth. 1977, chs. 17-19.

4. See especially his 'Aesthetic Formalization in Kleist's *Ueber das Marionettentheater*' in *The Rhetoric of Romanticism,* New York. 1984. pp. 263-6.

Greig Henderson (review date Winter 1991-92)

SOURCE: "Eagleton on Ideology: Six Types of Ambiguity," in *University of Toronto Quarterly,* Vol. 61, No. 2, Winter, 1991-92, pp. 280-88.

[*In the following review of* Ideology, *Henderson offers analysis of Eagleton's philosophical perspective and critical approach to the delineation of ideology. While citing many shortcomings and contradictions in the work, Henderson writes, "Eagleton's negotiation of this dense and difficult terrain is masterful."*]

'Ideology' is such a charged and vexed term that many people, taking in hand a volume about this topic, might well be tempted to follow Hume's famous advice. '*Does it contain any abstract reasoning concerning fact or number? Does it contain experimental reasoning concerning matter of fact and existence?* No. Commit it then to the flames: for it can contain but sophistry and illusion.' Nevertheless, pronouncements about the end of ideology are surely premature, and however enticing the prospects of committing it to the flames might be, this richly ambiguous term can still do useful conceptual work, as Eagleton's thought-provoking book [*Ideology*] amply and cogently demonstrates. Moreover, in this post-Nietzschean world, experimental reasoning concerning matter of fact and existence is itself likely to be labelled sophistry and illusion, matters of fact being, as everyone knows, matters of interpretation. Indeed, the place where a system of interested interpretations masquerades as a system of disinterested facts, where nature and universal essence are invoked and history and social existence obscured, where ideas are detached from the material conditions that enable them—this is the place where ideology lives, and this place no doubt is any society. But if ideology is such an all-pervasive phenomenon, and if would-be demystifiers are positioned within the social totality, how can they ever become fully conscious of their own ideological conditioning, how can they find some uncontaminated free space that escapes ideology's operations, how can they transcend the situatedness of their own discourse? Clearly, they cannot. And this is the uncomfortable consequence of embracing post-modern dogmas concerning, among other things, antifoundationalism (the belief that there are no empirical facts or rationalist ideas upon which knowledge is grounded), coherentism (the belief that propositions about the world can only achieve the truth of internal coherence and do not correspond to any external frame of reference), and relativism (the belief that everything is relative to the vocabulary and perspective of the observer whose own situatedness makes objectivity impossible). Although in practice we are remarkably adept at distinguishing our reasons from their rationalizations, and our ideas from their ideology, we know that such manoeuvrings are instances of self-deception and double-dealing. Here is the double bind that words ineluctably get us into; there are metalanguages, but no metalanguage. Yet if we truly believed what we mechanically utter, then how could we presume to write about, say, ideology? What status could ideological statements about ideology possibly enjoy? How could they avoid their own self-dismantling and self-devouring logic? Do the Nietzschean interpretations that demystify positivist and empiricist science and philosophy have any factual basis or metalinguistic authority? These are familiar questions, and we already know the turning and turning of the widening gyre, we already know that the logocentre cannot hold, that meaning is indeterminate, that the free play of signifiers is endless, that rhetoric subverts reference, that mere anarchy is loosed upon the wor(l)d. That these ideas spew forth so effortlessly—along with others about hegemony, discourse, legitimation, power, race, gender, sexual orientation, etc—indicates their ideological status. They are what Barthes calls the goes-without-saying, and for all of the routine self-reflexiveness that attends their articulation, they are almost a kind of theoretical unconscious. But that does not mean, as Eagleton points out, that this theoretical unconscious is necessarily false. Ideology, in the Althusserian sense of the term, embraces the ways we live our relations to society as a whole. It is thus a habitual style of perception that has affective and unconscious components as well as cognitive and conscious ones. It is one thing to expose the contradictions between what a text says and what a text does, and quite another to recognize our own inurement to contradictions between what we say and what we do. The contradictions we expose in no way eradicate the contradictions we live.

Eagleton's project hinges on a stipulated distinction between criticism and critique. The former presupposes some transcendental vantage-point; the latter recognizes the situatedness of one's own discourse, but nevertheless tries to get inside the discourse of the other. Any ideology is inconsistent enough to be turned against itself, and the analyst who deploys immanent critique rather than transcendental criticism can aid and abet an ideology's self-deconstruction and thus transvaluate its symbols of authority. The result may be to bring about social change; immanent critique may lead to emancipatory critique. Here as elsewhere, Eagleton is refreshingly commonsensical. 'The critique of ideology,' he writes, 'presumes that nobody is ever *wholly* mystified—that those subject to oppression experience *even now* hopes and desires which could only be realistically fulfilled by a transformation of their material conditions.' For 'however widespread "false consciousness" may be in social life, it can nevertheless be

claimed that most of what people say most of the time about the world must be true.' As Kenneth Burke puts it, 'if a people believe a belief and live, the fact of their survival tends to prove the adequacy of their belief.' And this, I think, is what Eagleton means by 'the moderate rationality of human beings in general.' 'To deny that ideology is fundamentally an affair of reason,' he writes, 'is not to conclude that it is immune to rationalist considerations altogether.' There would be little point in providing a critique of ideology if people were so ensnared in illusion, distortion, and mystification as to be incapable of change. Ideology, therefore, is not simply epistemological fraud. Nor is it simply 'the function of ideas within social life,' for this is to reduce it to the realm of sociological description. The point being not only to understand the world but also to change it, Eagleton must navigate between the Scylla of ideology as epistemological fraud and the Charybdis of ideology as sociological description. The former is too negative, whereas the latter is too neutral. To be fully grasped, ideology must be understood in its positive, negative, and neutral senses. But if ideology is understood in this wide-ranging way, it runs the risk of offering an embarrassment of polysemantic riches and of condemning its defenders to a great deal of dialectical shiftiness and hermeneutical wriggling. One might say that Eagleton's dilemma centres on his wanting to make ideological analysis part of both a positive and a negative hermeneutics.

In drawing his famous distinction between positive and negative hermeneutics, between a hermeneutics of restoration and a hermeneutics of suspicion, Ricoeur points to the essential duplicity of the hermeneutical motive itself. 'At one pole, hermeneutics is understood as the manifestation and restoration of a meaning addressed to me in the manner of a message, a proclamation . . . according to the other, it is understood as a demystification, as a reduction of illusion. . . . Hermeneutics seems . . . to be animated by this double motivation: willingness to suspect, willingness to listen; vow of rigor, vow of obedience.'

This double motivation is evident in Marxist thinking. On the one hand, dialectical materialism is a positive hermeneutics that sometimes advertises itself as a science of history, a science which reduces cultural phenomena in the ideological superstructure to modes of economic production in the material infrastructure. Yet, as Kenneth Burke points out, even the most unemotional scientific nomenclature is unavoidably suasive. The necessitarian underpinnings of Marx's economic causation theory notwithstanding, the utopianism implicit in his scientific understanding of history furnishes a potent image for action, and the notion of historical inevitability with its built-in teleology of proletarian victory is rhetorically appealing to the last who shall be first. As a positive hermeneutics, Marxism promises a restoration of plenitude, a life of unalienated labour and leisure, of psychological and social integration. This retrieval of meaning gives to human history a rationally coherent and causally intelligible sense of beginning, middle, and end. It offers nothing less than a totalizing master narrative that travels from genesis to apocalypse and culminates in the triumphant success of the human struggle to wrest a realm of freedom out of a realm of necessity. This master narrative is all the more compelling because it is assumed to be scientifically predestined. Nevertheless, as Burke points out, 'whatever may be the claims of Marxism as a "science," its terminology is not a neutral "preparation for action" but "inducement to action." In this sense, it is unsleepingly rhetorical,' its aim being, as we have noted, to change the world as well as to understand it.

On the other hand, dialectical materialism is a negative hermeneutics that demystifies bourgeois discourse by showing how such discourse transforms historically produced socioeconomic conditions into universal essences. Empires striving for world markets, Burke notes, become the ways of universal spirit. 'As a critique of capitalist rhetoric,' Burke writes, ideological analysis 'is designed to disclose (unmask) sinister *factional* interests concealed in the bourgeois terms for benign *universal* interests.' We are thus admonished to look for mystification at any point where the social divisiveness caused by property and the division of labour is obscured by unitary terms that conceal factional interests, making them seem natural and universal rather than historical and specific. Capitalist rhetoric, Burke suggests, gives us 'a fog of merger terms where the clarity of division terms is needed.' Yet however much Marxism contributes to the critique of ideology and to the demystification of political rhetoric, it remains itself both an ideology and a rhetoric.

Ricoeur's distinction and Burke's observations bring Eagleton's dilemma into focus. To surrender scientism and the utopianism it buttresses is to sacrifice a rhetorically inspiring narrative vision of considerable beauty and power. Yet Eagleton is far too epistemologically sophisticated to accept the base/superstructure model of so-called vulgar Marxism and the causal reductiveness it entails. Likewise, he is far too dialectically canny to embrace antifoundationalism, coherentism, or relativism as an alternative. He knows where these ideas lead. Marxism, for him, is not just another rhetorical voice in the foundationless conversation of history. Nevertheless, he wants to insist in a non-scientistic and non-reductivist way that matter rather than ideation is the motive force of history and that social being determines consciousness and not the other way around. Even if its truth is not grounded in historical or economic necessity, Marxism offers a positive vision of a better life that men and women could enjoy were they able to alter the material determinants of their social existence. Therefore, it does not suffice to view Marxism purely as a negative hermeneutics. This is one horn of the dilemma. Though Eagleton sometimes speaks of 'socialist ideology,' the words stick in his craw, the spectre of false consciousness looming uneasily in the background. However much he does not want to claim that ideology is mere illusion, distortion, or mystification, he also wants to exploit the genius of hermeneutical suspiciousness, carefully distinguishing socialist ideas from bourgeois ideology. This self-conscious equivocation, however, is the strength of Eagleton's approach. Without letting ideology drift off into the outer space of endless signification, Eagleton preserves the rich history and polysemy of the term by tracing the genesis of its multiple meanings and by showing how those meanings can serve the ends of practical analysis and application, his book being a rhetoric of social change as well as an analysis of ideological thinking.

Because ideology has to do not only with belief systems but also with questions of power, on one of its levels it involves '*legitimating* the power of a dominant social group or class.' According to Eagleton, this process of legitimation comprises promoting the beliefs and values of that group or class, naturalizing and universalizing those beliefs and values (i.e. making them seem natural rather than historical, universal rather than contingent), denigrating and excluding rival beliefs and values, and obscuring the class structure of society. But this ideology as legitimation thesis, useful as it is to negative hermeneutics, confines the term 'ideology' to dominant forms of thought, relies too heavily on the notion of false consciousness, and assumes that ideologies are homogeneous and monolithic. Though generally the ideology of an individual is a slight variant of the ideology distinguishing the class among which he or she arose, there is no neat one-to-one correspondence between classes and ideologies, and even 'the dominant ideology in advanced capitalist societies is internally fissured and contradictory,' every social formation being, as Raymond Williams points out, a complex amalgam of dominant, residual, and emergent forms of consciousness. For Eagleton, then, ideology as the legitimation of a dominant group or class is but one of six ways one might preliminarily define the term.

'We can mean by it, first,' he writes, 'the general material process of production of ideas, beliefs, and values in social life. Such a definition is both politically and epistemologically neutral, and is close to the broader meaning of the term "culture."' It denotes 'the whole complex of signifying practices and symbolic processes in a particular society.' Though this definition assumes the social determination of thought, it operates more in the realm of sociological description than in the realm of socialist theory.

Eagleton's second, slightly less general meaning of ideology 'turns on ideas and beliefs (whether true or false) which symbolize the conditions and experiences of a specific, socially significant group or class.' Here the term is akin to 'world view' without necessarily having the same philosophical seriousness. Using the term this way, one could, for instance, speak of yuppie ideology.

The third definition turns on the relations and conflicts between social groups or classes as they attempt to promote and legitimate their interests in the face of opposing interests. 'Ideology appears here as a suasive or rhetorical rather than a veridical kind of speech, concerned less with the situation "as it is" than with the production of certain useful effects for political purposes.'

According to Eagleton, a fourth meaning of ideology would retain this emphasis on the promotion and legitimation of sectoral interests, but confine it to the activities of a dominant social power. 'But this term,' he goes on to say, 'is still epistemologically neutral and can thus be refined into a fifth definition, in which ideology signifies ideas and beliefs which help to legitimate the interests of a ruling group or class specifically by distortion and dissimulation.' Yet he is honest enough to admit that 'on this last definition it is hard to know what to call a politically oppositional discourse which promotes and seeks to legitimate the interests of a subordinate group or class by such devices as the "naturalizing," universalizing, and cloaking of its real interests.'

Finally, for Eagleton, there is 'the possibility of a sixth meaning of ideology, which retains an emphasis on false or deceptive beliefs but regards such beliefs as arising not from the interests of a dominant class but from the material structure of society as a whole.' Marx's theory of the fetishism of commodities would be an instance of this, for if social phenomena cease to be recognizable as products of human activity, then it is easy for people to reify them, to perceive them as material things and thus to accept their existence as natural and inevitable. Consequently, Eagleton argues, 'the actual social relations between human beings are governed by the apparently autonomous interactions of the commodities they produce. . . . Men and women fashion products which then come to escape their control and determine the conditions of their existence. . . . Society is no longer perceptible as a human construct.' 'In capitalist society the commodity form permeates every aspect of social life, taking the shape of a pervasive mechanization, quantification, and dehumanization of human experience. The "wholeness" of society is broken up into so many discrete, specialized, technical operations, each of which comes to assume a semi-autonomous life of its own and to dominate human existence as a quasi-natural force.' Ideological mystification thus arises from the material structure of society as whole; it is built into the system, commodities exercising a tyrannical sway over social relations in general.

According to Eagleton's six provisional definitions, then, the term 'ideology' comprehends 1/ the complex of socially determined ideas, beliefs, and values that constitute a particular culture; 2/ the 'world view' of a socially significant group or class within that culture; 3/ the promotion and legitimation of that world view; 4/ the promotion and legitimation of the world view of the dominant group or class; 5/ the promotion and legitimation of this dominant world view by distortion or dissimulation; and 6/ ideas, beliefs, and values that arise from the material structure of society, from commodity fetishism and reification. These provisional definitions complicate the agenda considerably. Only 4, 5, and 6 are specifically Marxist, and only 5 and 6 foreground the idea of false consciousness.

It would seem, therefore, that ambiguity and ideology go hand in hand. As Eagleton points out, even *The German Ideology* 'hesitates significantly between a political and an epistemological definition of ideology.' Politically, it defines ideology as the ruling ideas of the ruling class. Epistemologically, it defines ideology as an illusory realm of consolation and coherence that offers an imaginary resolution of real contradictions and that blinds people to the harsh actuality of their social conditions. In the early Marx and Engels, then, ideology denotes illusory or socially disconnected beliefs, embracing both the notion of false consciousness and the notion of false causality that often goes with it, namely, the notion that ideas rather than material conditions are the motive force of history. But it can also 'signify those ideas which directly express the material interests of the dominant social class, and which are useful in promoting its rule.' Moreover, it can be further stretched to encompass 'all of the conceptual forms in which the class struggle as a whole is fought, which would presumably include the valid consciousness of politically revolutionary forces.' The end result is confusing at best, inconsistent at worst. Definitions 1 through 5 are mixed and blurred.

In its famous chapter on the fetishism of commodities, *Capital* introduces definition 6. If *The German Ideology* ascribes too much unreality to ideology, Eagleton argues, *Capital* ascribes too much reality. 'For *The German Ideology,* the opposite of ideology would seem to be seeing reality as it actually is; for *Capital* things are not so simple, since that reality, as we have seen, is now intrinsically treacherous, and there is thus the need for a special discourse known as science to penetrate its phenomenal forms and lay bare its essences.' Reification pervades social existence in its entirety. To counter the dominant ideology and its mystifications with the *science* of historical materialism, however, is fraught with difficulties; the positivist/empiricist model is precisely that which socialism attacks and scientism valorizes. The scientific option is a non-starter. In the same way that Enlightenment rationalism undoes itself, so too does Marxism as a science of history. Eagleton makes this point incisively:

> If all thought is socially determined, then so too must be Marxism, in which case what becomes of its claims to scientific objectivity? Yet if these claims are simply dropped, how are we to adjudicate between the truth of Marxism and the truth of the belief systems it opposes? Would not the opposite of the ruling ideology then be simply an alternative ideology, and on what rational grounds would we choose between them? We are sliding, in short, into the mire of historical relativism; but the only alternative to that would appear to be some form of positivism or scientific rationalism which repressed its own enabling historical conditions, and so was ideological in all the worst ways outlined by *The German Ideology.*

This is as honest a statement of the problem as one could imagine. No Marxist detractor could express it more forcibly. Marxism survives as a rhetoric of social change, its ideas being part of the active struggle to establish proletarian class consciousness, but its materialist analysis of sociohistorical formations loses its scientific status, and the terms 'proletarian class consciousness' and 'socialist ideology' become synonymous.

Ideological analysis survives mainly as a rhetoric of de-mystification and a negative hermeneutics, a means of exposing how discourses, mostly but not exclusively dominant ones, promote and legitimate themselves by naturalizing, universalizing, dissimulating, distorting, re-ifying, persuading (coercively or consensually), etc. But ideology is also positive to the extent to which one can use the same rhetorical tactics to promote and legitimate one's own vision of social change. So whereas Eagleton begins by rejecting the ideology as legitimation thesis, he ultimately ends up accepting something very much like it.

The strategic innovation of the primarily twentieth-century critics of ideology Eagleton discusses in the remainder of his book is to construe ideology as predominantly a function of discourse rather than consciousness. As he observes, 'it is with Gramsci that the crucial transition is effected from ideology as "systems of ideas" to ideology as lived, habitual social practice—which must then presumably encompass the unconscious, inarticulate dimensions of social experience as well as the workings of formal institutions.' This is a significant and productive transition; Freud joins hands with Marx.

Eagleton's negotiation of this dense and difficult terrain is masterful. He excels at both exposition and critique. For example, he carefully explains how Adorno sees the mechanism of exchange as the secret of ideology. Ideol-ogy, Adorno argues, is identity thinking; it pits an intel-ligible and familiar self against an unintelligible and alien other. Ideology homogenizes the world, whereas art, which values the sensuous particular over the seamless totality, makes room for difference. Adorno's ideal of 'togetherness in diversity' moves Eagleton to eloquence. 'The aim of socialism is to liberate the rich diversity of sensuous use—value from the metaphysical prison-house of exchange-value—to emancipate history from the specious equiva-lences imposed upon it by ideology and commodity production.' Nevertheless, Eagleton poses the key ques-tion: 'Does *all* ideology work by the identity principle, ruthlessly expunging whatever is heterogeneous to it?' The real ideological conditions of Western capitalist societies, he answers, are more various and pluralistic. Modern capitalism is not 'a seamless, pacified, self-regulating system.' The fetishism of commodities thrives on differ-ence, however spurious and however much a function of the fluctuation of fashion rather than the recognition of otherness such difference may be. One might even argue that the tolerance of pluralistic oppositional discourses is a means of attenuating and defusing them. The genius of the marketplace of ideas may reside in its lack of discrimina-tion; heterogeneity itself may contribute to capitalist hegemony.

Eagleton's discussion of Habermas is cogent and insight-ful. Enough of a closet 'rationalist' to resist making the term entirely pejorative, Eagleton appreciates the virtues of Habermas's view of ideology as 'a deformed discursive system,' 'a form of communication systematically distorted by power.' Even though Habermas contends that this distortion is systematic, he does not see ideology as an all-powerful and all-absorbent totalitarian system, and he posits communicative rationality as an alternative to ideological distortion. As Eagleton notes, Habermas seeks 'to extract from our linguistic practices the structure of some underlying "communicative rationality"—some "ideal speech situation" which glimmers faintly through our actual debased discourses.' Eagleton's subsequent discussion and extension of the parallels Habermas draws between psychoanalysis and the critique of ideology is incisive. As his earlier works also attest, Eagleton is sensitively attuned to the similarities and differences between Marx, Freud, and their disciples and commenta-tors.

Borrowing from Lacan, Althusser also links psychoanalysis and ideology. 'In the ideological sphere . . . the human subject transcends its true state of diffuseness or decentre-ment and finds a consolingly coherent image of itself reflected back in the "mirror" of a dominant discourse.' Ideology 'is not just a distortion or false reflection, a screen which intervenes between ourselves and reality or an automatic effect of commodity production. It is an indispensable medium for the production of human subjects.' Since ideology is largely habitual behaviour and unconscious thought, it is 'eternal' and will exist even in a socialist society. Ideology alone 'lends the human subject enough illusory, provisional coherence for it to become a practical social agent.' Ideology alone provides the subject a symbolic map of society, an imaginary model of the whole. The unified subject and the social whole may be fictions, but they are probably necessary fictions for the promotion and production of individual and social action, radical or otherwise. Ideology in this sense is an integral part of the psychopathology of everyday life. Not all closure, then, is invidiously totalitarian, for 'a certain provisional stability of identity is essential not only for psychical well-being but for revolutionary political agency. . . . Textuality, ambiguity, indeterminacy lie often enough on the side of dominant ideological discourses themselves.'

Many other interesting and illuminating things in this book remain unexplored—the witty skewering of Fish, Rorty, and their versions of neo-pragmatism, among others. Though Eagleton is passionately committed to a particular vision of social change, he is generally fair-minded in his expositions and critiques. I am ignoring his predictable sneers at such intellectual heavyweights as Thatcher, Re-agan, and Bush, his occasional reifying and fetishizing of late consumer capitalism as if it were some sort of ubiquitous monolith to be invoked rather than explained, and his choice not to consider conservative assessments of ideology; in these areas, perhaps, lies his own goes-without-saying. Nevertheless, Eagleton concludes, sensibly enough, that while ideology embraces reification, it is itself reification, the term being 'just a convenient way of categorizing under a single heading a whole lot of differ-ent things we do with signs.' There may be family resemblances between ideologies, but ideology has no es-sence. It is 'less . . . a particular set of discourses, than

. . . a particular set of effects *within* discourses.' As Voloshinov observes, 'without signs there is no ideology,' for the struggle of antagonistic social interests takes place at the level of the sign. 'Ideological power, as John B. Thompson puts it, is not just a matter of meaning, but of making a meaning *stick.*'

Eagleton's study demonstrates that 'the term ideology has a wide range of historical meanings, all the way from the unworkably broad sense of the social determination of thought to the suspiciously narrow idea of the deployment of false ideas in the direct interest of a ruling class.' He recognizes the necessity of seeing ideology as a function of discourse but is wary of inflating discourse to

> the point where it imperializes the whole world, eliding the distinction between thought and material reality. The effect of this is to undercut the critique of ideology—for if ideas and material reality are given indissolubly together, there can be no question of asking where social ideas actually hail from. The new "transcendental" hero is discourse itself, which is apparently prior to everything else. It is surely a little immodest of academics, professionally concerned with discourse as they are, to project their own preoccupations onto the whole world, in that ideology known as (post-) structuralism.

It may be immodest but it is not inconsistent, whereas Eagleton's wanting to preserve a categorical distinction between thought and material reality is both inconsistent and undialectical given his rejection of scientism and the base/superstructure model that undergirds it, and given his sense of the limitations of the false consciousness thesis. But, as the Emersonian saying goes, a foolish consistency is the hobgoblin of little minds. Somehow I prefer Eagleton's inconsistency to their immodesty. With ideology, it would seem, authors and critics alike are condemned to some measure of double-dealing; it goes with the territory.

Kate Soper (review date March-April 1992)

SOURCE: "The Ideology of the Aesthetic," in *New Left Review,* No. 192, March-April, 1992, pp. 120-32.

[*In the following review, Soper examines the development of Eagleton's theoretical analysis and socialist perspective in* The Ideology of the Aesthetic, *drawing attention to the "tensions, ambivalences, irresolutions, in Eagleton's book."*]

In Ingmar Bergman's film of *The Magic Flute,* the camera, throughout the overture, traverses the faces of an audience divided by age, sex, ethnicity and style, but united in its common rapture. It is a compelling image of the power of the 'aesthetic' to realize—despite everything that tends to human dispersion—an instance of humanist fusion; an instance, moreover, that seems all the more exalted because it depends on nothing but mutual inspiration, and all the more precious because of its fragile spontaneity. This audience, in its wordless communion, surely captures some-

thing of what Kant had in mind when he presented the aesthetic as the site of a reciprocity of feeling and intersubjectivity denied us in our rational or moral or purely sensual dealings with others. Yet it may also, one feels, capture rather more than Kant intended. For, separated though it may be in terms of years or nationality or personal comportment, there is one aspect in which this audience appears more homogeneous: it is undoubtedly essentially bourgeois. Perhaps we should say, then, that wittingly or unwittingly, Bergman has also registered something of the ideology of the aesthetic; something, that is, of what the bourgeoisie had wished the aesthetic to be, namely, an image of the achievement in reality not only of the consolidation of its own class, but of that promised society of freedom and equality through which it sought to legitimate its rule. For the aesthetic has figured in bourgeois thought both as a symbol of its aspired-to syntheses of mind and body, of the cognitive and sensual, of individual freedom and social harmony, and as a kind of bad faith, a way of refusing to come to terms with the fact that the material divisions of society cannot be miraculously rendered into a tensionless whole by purely artistic or spiritual means. There is, as it were, a whole part of society missing from the 'Kantian' audience.

It is this intricate double story of the aesthetic as sincere ideal of unity and as false universality that Terry Eagleton has undertaken to trace in his most wide-ranging and philosophically ambitious work to date. *The Ideology of the Aesthetic*[1] excites and pleases, not only because of the suppleness of its prose and the extent to which it is lit up by the pleasure Eagleton himself has had in its making, but because of its encyclopaedic grasp of ideas and the relative ease with which it guides us through the convolutions of a concept which, perhaps more than any other employed in philosophical discrimination, is the most volatile and difficult to fix. It is no easy task to determine the respective terrains of the rational or the ethical, or to say exactly where cognition gives way to some more intuitive or sensual mode of apprehension. It is even more difficult to specify the area of aesthetic understanding, which figures in modern European philosophy both as a mediator of ideality and materiality, and as something distinct from either. In its mediating function, the aesthetic sits uneasily between the mental and bodily poles that it sets out to synthesize; as the achievement of their unity, it appears as a mode of experience-cum-understanding that is transcendent to either, and entirely sui generis.

Such remarks may seem unduly abstract to anyone for whom 'aesthetics' has to do essentially with the appraisal of works of art, and refers to that branch of philosophy concerned with the value discriminations we bring to bear on the concrete artefacts of cultural production. But Eagleton has not written a history of aesthetics in this sense; nor is there any but passing reference to particular works of art in his book. Rather, taking his cue from the elaboration within the German philosophical tradition of the aesthetic as dealing in a kind of truth attainable neither in pure nor practical reason, he offers a cultural politics of this idea of truth from the mid eighteenth century to our own times—a history, that is, of the political role it has played within a philosophy that is itself a political response to its times, a product and maker of its ideological circumstances.

AN AMALGAM OF REACTIONARY AND UTOPIAN IMPULSES

Eagleton presents the aesthetic as a 'discourse of the body'[2] that enters German thought at the point of transition from feudal absolutism to modern bourgeois society. Though its tempering of the too abstract and overtly coercive claims of rationality may have served initially to shore up the old order, the emergence of the aesthetic is really a symptom of the moribund nature of that form of political authority, and comes as a response to the requirement of Enlightenment for a new kind of human subject ('one which, like the work of art itself, discovers the law in the depth of its own free identity, rather than in some oppressive external power' [p. 19]). In this, the aesthetic serves as a means of safe passage, whereby feudal hierarchy and patronage can yield to bourgeois individualism and the free anonymity of market relations, without risk of collapse into outright anarchy or overt rebellion against the imposition of any new form of order. Bourgeois society is to be rendered into an organic whole—but it is to be organic in a new way, a product of the heart's consent. If it knows a law, it is one that individuals have discovered within themselves and freely subscribed to; and the aesthetic is its reflection.

In its upward trajectory—from Kant to Hegel—this aesthetic thus registers an optimistic faith in the conformity of bourgeois society to reason and the natural ordering of things. The claims of the sensual can be respected, and all due weight given to lived experience and its particularity, without finally transgressing the preserve of rational and moral law, or threatening the privileged position of humanity within the universe of nature at large. But not only will this aestheticism in the end prove incapable of the political task it has set itself, that of compensating or substituting for the absence in reality of the harmonious society of self-regulating subjects it ideally projects; it also cannot, even in the phase of its consolidation as ideology, accomplish the philosophical task of reconciliation—or at least not without considerable stress and strain, a continual turning back on its own discourse in order to check the subsumption of the aesthetic within one or other of the domains it would mediate between. Thus Schiller attempts a corrective to the overly ascetic bias of Kantian theory, but only at the cost of revealing the aesthetic ideal as potential source of a Romantic critique of bourgeois industrialism. Hegel thereupon figures as a magnificent, if rather last-ditch, effort to overcome these tensions by projecting Kant's aesthetic function into the structure of reality itself: if Kant had left us deprived of any full-blown possession of the objective world, Hegel restores it to us as our rightful home.[3] But his recovery of the object from the limbo of unknowing to which Kant had consigned it (and also from its too overweening repossession in the subjective intuitionism of Fichte and Schelling) is also not without its flaw, since it is accomplished only by means of a theoretical edifice of such awesome complexity that it forfeits all ideological accessibility. Generated as it is entirely out of abstract reason and puritanically opposed to all 'graven images' and representations of the sensuous, the Hegelian system proves too incapable of engaging with common experience to serve as political legitimation. There are, moreover, Eagleton suggests, comparable tensions afflicting the 'aestheticization' of reason represented in the turn to empiricism within English philosophy (though this receives a relatively cursory treatment[4]). For here, too, the aesthetic comes forward as a political instrument, to be turned, on the one hand, as a progressive power against ruling-class rationalism, and, on the other hand, lending itself to a conservative—and even potentially fascistic—celebration of the natural, spontaneous organicism of the nation-state.

In a general sense, then, the aesthetic is revealed as an amalgam of reactionary and utopian impulses. In so far as its transfigurative vision is belied by the power relations and degenerate egoism of bourgeois society, it can act as a veil drawn over its ugliness; but in that same process it necessarily begins life as an immanent critique of the gap between this actuality and its sublime ideals, and thus of its own hypocrisies. The tension of the aesthetic within German idealism, as both legitimation of Enlightenment and rejection of its instrumental rationality, is therefore mirrored in the very differing uses to which it will be put in the hands of figures like Blake or Morris on the one hand, and Burke, Arnold, Carlisle, Ruskin and T. S. Eliot on the other.[5] Moreover, in so far as the philosophy of the aesthetic offers itself as an account of the source of values, there is a further schism between the more Kantian, autotelic approach, which views aesthetic values as somehow quite autonomous and self-derivative, and an approach that seeks to root these values more directly in the body and its affections.

If the ideological manoeuvrings of the bourgeois aesthetic in its more self-confident and positive trajectory can be seen as centred around an autotelic conception of value, its post-Hegelian and more subversive career (from Schopenhauer through Kierkegaard, Marx, Nietzsche and Freud) represents a de-spiritualization of the aesthetic, a turning back to the body and desire. The image of the aesthetic as 'lawfulness without law' and as sublime disinterest is thereby profoundly undermined in a shift toward that realm of instinct, will and full-blooded sensuality that it was supposed to keep in touch with, but only by purging it of its more carnal, ribald and excessive qualities. The elevation of will and instinct in the philosophies of Schopenhauer and Nietzsche thus pits the aesthetic against the pieties of bourgeois idealism; but at the same time, by virtue of its naturalization of greed, power lust and human hypocrisy, it becomes a more negative discourse altogether, appearing to remove all hope of any more exalted alternative. Schopenhauer's 'carnival of gloom and risible monomanic despondency'; Kierkegaard's denial of any originary innocence, and pre-emptive strike against the hollowness of bourgeois 'individuality'; Nietzsche's aesthetic as 'applied psychology' and disdain for all sentimentalism, and his contempt—shared by Kierkegaard and Heidegger—for 'mass man' and the philistine complacencies of 'average' living: all this is profoundly unsettling of the erstwhile faith in the aesthetic as promise of concord and equilibrium. But it is also the eruption of nihilism, elitism and irrationalism. The aesthetic is turned much more sharply in criticism of the self-deceptive aspirations of the existing order; but in the process it also becomes the vehicle of a self-punitive irony, a manic laughter at the follies of humankind, a morbid pleasure in the sheer incapacity of human beings to be even half-way decent, let alone to relish the sublime.

A DOUBLE NARRATIVE

The remaining four thinkers treated at length in this book—Marx, Freud, Benjamin and Adorno—fit less readily into this schema of the inflation and the self-deflation of the bourgeois aesthetic, though in their relations to each other they might be said to reproduce some of its counterpoint.

Marx, not surprisingly, figures as a point of renewal: as a dialectician of the senses who, in revealing that these acquire their form through material practice, and thus possess both objective and subjective dimensions of existence, blows wide open all pretensions to reconcile sense and spirit within an alienated social order. But, suggests Eagleton, Marx is Kantian enough in his early aspiration to overcome the antinomy of Nature and Humanity through the realization of 'species-being'; and even when he has put such idealism behind him, he retains something of that aesthetic in his projection of communism as a kind of unrepresentable sublime of indefinite abundance. What is different about Marx's 'utopian' aesthetics, however, is that it goes together with very stern insistence on the need for rational analysis of the present (with particular attention paid to the 'bad sides' by which history always proceeds), since this is the sole resource and condition of any possible good that may come in the future.

Yet, almost as soon as Marx has been congratulated on this realism, Eagleton is reminding us of the various notes of caution that Freud sounded against a belief in any too straightforwardly rational route to emancipation. For not only has Freud's recognition of the intimate relation between desire and submission to authority rendered obsolete any simplistic expression/repression model of power, Marx's included,[6] it has also poured cold water on any project aimed at the comfortable reinsertion of the body in the discourse of rationality. For Freud's message (at least in Eagleton's Lacanian reading of him), is that the body will never be quite at home in language. Law and the symbolic—in short, culture—is gained only at the cost of plenitude: of the desire not to desire.

It is true that this Freudian wet blanket is revealed to contain a number of dryer linings. If the law, for example,

is exposed as less transcendental to our caprices than it would purport to be, this is both the opportunity for changing its harsher dictates, as well as an obstacle to freeing us from our uncritical obedience to it; and if we cannot finally 'slay the father', that may be all to the good in breeding a certain scepticism, even humour, about the more exorbitant and absurd exactions of superego. Moreover, this recourse to comedy is not entirely foreign, claims Eagleton, even to Benjamin, who, despite his austerity in other respects, follows Bakhtin in referring us to the liberating resources of laughter.[7] But such optimism as this reveals is again reversed when we come to Adorno, who offers us a discourse of the body, but only, post-Auschwitz, of the body as site of suffering, and who therefore turns away from any affirmative aesthetic of the senses, however ironically handled. With Adorno, the problem of redemption, if it is possible at all, becomes the problem of how to aspire to any future happiness while still keeping faith with the pain of the past. 'Only by remaining faithful to the past can we prise loose its terrifying grip, and this fidelity is forever likely to paralyse us . . . If Adorno plies the steel, he does so as wounded surgeon, patient and physician together . . .' (p. 362).

There are clearly two schemas of understanding at work in this overall narrative of the aesthetic. One is that of the 'discourse of the body', or treatment of the aesthetic in terms of the mind-body polarity developed within bourgeois philosophy; the other is the Marxist perspective brought to philosophy itself. If the first is that through which we are invited to grasp what is specific to the aesthetic, the second is that which invites us to appreciate its status as 'ideology'. However, for a variety of reasons, the juxtaposition of these frameworks is not without its tensions. At the most general level there exists the problem that Eagleton is putting to use, and at times treating as a comprehensive and 'neutral' discourse; the same bourgeois philosophy that he is also, in some sense, denouncing as partial and prejudicial. I suggested earlier that Eagleton is offering a double narrative: of bourgeois philosophy as progressive and self-critical register of liberal-Enlightenment ideas, and as self-deluding grandiosity. And it is this doubleness that is responsible in no small part for the fertility of his book, and its lack of dogmatism. But such an exercize is bound to create a certain irresolution between the narrative that invites us to view philosophy as speaking only to the interests and tastes of the sherry-drinking classes, and the narrative that invites us to view this same philosophy as if it were a trustworthy guide to the nature and collective interests of bourgeois society at large—between the text that catches philosophy in its hegemonic purposes, and the text written under the influence of its success.

The general problem here has its more particular reflection in the instability of both the key concepts at work in the text: that of the 'body', and of 'ideology'. As far as the 'body' is concerned, the difficulty is that Eagleton invokes this notion as a general classifying system for all the thinkers under review, even though, as his own exposition makes clear, they diverge so considerably in the conception they bring to mind-body relations that it is unclear whether one can impute any commonly agreed object to their collective discourse at all. The problem is at its most acute in respect of those—Marx, Nietzsche, Freud—whom Eagleton precisely applauds for their project of reworking the aesthetic beginning from bodily foundations (Marx for the labouring body, Nietzsche for the body as power, Freud for the body as desire). This is for two related reasons: one, because what is arguably distinctive to this project is its exposure of the 'ideological' status of traditional philosophical thinking about mind and body, and two, because (at least in the case of Marx and Freud) this exposure involves a rejection of any biologically reductive account of ourselves as needing, desiring and sensual creatures. What is innovatory in Marx's approach is the emphasis placed on the mediation of biology by the social, on the historically developed quality of needs and wants, and on the degree to which even our senses are as much constituted by, as pre-given to, our particular environment and life experience. Freud, likewise, particularly if one follows Lacan in viewing the 'authentic' Freud as the anti-biologistic Freud, is precisely to be read as resisting any reduction of the cultural, and the desires it engenders, to the promptings of some natural reservoir of instinctual feelings: what is significant is not bodily functions or libidinal urges in themselves, but the interpretations brought to them in consequence of a culturally orchestrated intersubjective context.

In so far, then, as these 'great aestheticians of the body' subvert the very terms of the mind-body problem, there is something a little awkward about the use of that framework to represent their contribution (and this applies, by extension, to the Marxist aesthetic theory of Benjamin and Adorno as well). These points might be restated in terms of the overly metaphoric status of the concept of the 'body' in the text, given the range of more literal constructions that it is possible to place upon it: is it referring us to unmediated corporeality, or functioning as a synonym of the 'sensual'? Is this the 'body' as conceptualized within the empiricist-rationalist tradition of philosophy, or as conceived from the standpoint of those theories which challenge that tradition? Perhaps this ambiguity would not matter greatly were it not that it generates uncertainty about how far those forms of sensuality which are distinctive to aesthetic experience, and which relate to, but clearly do not reduce to, bodily sensations, are being respected. One can agree that there is something too puritanically abstracted from corporeal responses in the Kantian theory of the 'indifference' of a truly aesthetic contemplation, but in whatever ways the 'body' does enter into the experience it could not be adequately accounted for in purely physicalistic terms.[8]

An associated difficulty is that Eagleton constantly deploys the standard genderization of the mind-body divide as a means to explore philosophical antitheses. (Thus, the aesthetic is the 'feminization' of 'phallic' conscience, and associated with everything traditionally coded 'female'—

nature, taste, immanence, sentiment and, of course, 'body'—as opposed to the 'masculinity' of law, the symbolic, abstraction, transcendence, and so forth.) This is quite justified in so far as Eagleton is here registering philosophy's own sexual typology'; but there is something more problematic about his tendency to present this as having nothing but positive import for feminism, since that would seem to imply an overall acceptance of its gender essentialism. On the other hand, it may be a little unfair to quarrel with a gender subtext while laughing at the excellent jokes it affords (as, for example, in the case of Eagleton's deftness with Heidegger's 'readiness-to-hand'); and, besides, in mitigation, it has also to be said that Eagleton displays a rather endearing confusion around sexual identity. (Thus, Hegel's virilely penetrative *Geist* turns out to be endowed with womb-like properties, and the 'castrating feminine assault' of Nietzsche's truth suddenly finds itself in the camp of that 'patriarchal metaphysics' which is reeling from the female attack.)

IDEOLOGY AND THE SUBJECT

At a more fundamental level, however, these issues raise questions about the 'ideological' status of philosophy in Eagleton's account—specifically concerning its truth value and the extent of the influence it is seen to have upon society at large. In other words, are we dealing here with philosophy-as-ideology in the more conventional Marxist sense, that is, as one of those partial, inverted and abstract forms of 'pure' thought whereby the bourgeoisie, in blindness to the conditions of its thinking and hence of its rather parochial reach, presents its own interests as if they were valid for humanity in general? Or are we dealing with philosophy as the very terrain on which the respective claims of mind and body, materialism and idealism, are being arbitrated in a permanent process of revision and adjustment, and which is therefore to be viewed as a site of ideological conflicts generated within society as a whole? How far, to put the point crudely, does Marx contribute to, and how far does he explode, the 'ideology' of the aesthetic? And the same question arises with respect to many of the other thinkers treated in the book: how far are they part of philosophy's endless struggles with the errors of its ways, and how far a challenge to its pretensions to knowledge? In short, what is meant by 'ideology' here?

This question has obviously been of no small concern to Eagleton himself, given that his most recent book is devoted to a clarification of the confusions surrounding the concept. What is interesting about the book on ***Ideology,*** however, is that it does not tidy up the conceptual unclarities by offering us the essential 'true' theory of ideology. On the contrary, the pertinence of the concept is defended on Wittgensteinian lines: it is doubtful, says Eagleton, 'that one can ascribe to ideology any *invariable* characteristics at all. We are dealing less with some essence of ideology than with an overlapping network of "family resemblances".'[9] This precisely does *not* mean that 'ideology' can be assimilated to 'discourse' and absorbed within its concept. It means, rather, that only those discourses are ideological which have the 'family resemblance' of relating in a fairly direct way to the power struggles central to the reproduction of a given form of social life. For the most part, then, 'ideology' refers pejoratively to those 'signs, meanings and values which help to reproduce a dominant social power'; but it can also refer, in more neutral fashion, to 'any significant conjuncture between discourse and political interests'.[10]

If we now map this account of ideology back onto *The Ideology of the Aesthetic,* it arguably resolves some of the tensions I have been focusing on, for it could then be said that the book documents the 'ideology' of the aesthetic in both the more pejorative and the more neutral sense of the term—in other words, it offers a history of all the ways in which aesthetic discourse is in significant collusion or dissent from dominant political interests over a particular period of time. Some might question whether this *is* a resolution, as opposed to an acknowledgement, of such tensions, but I think Eagleton may be right that this is the best we can do with the concept.

All the same, one aspect of the argument of *The Ideology of the Aesthetic* remains unclear to me, and is arguably not quite in line with the approach adopted in *Ideology.* This concerns the role that Eagleton wants to accord ideology in the constitution of the subject. In *Ideology,* Eagleton is critical of Althusserian theory for presenting the autonomy of the subject as merely illusory,[11] and he also argues against viewing ideology as possessing a 'discursive omnipotence' to legislate social interests into being.[12] Ideology, he contends, may 'actively constitute subjects', but these same subjects are also 'always conflictively, precariously constituted', and in this sense are viewed as retaining some active centre of resistance to its 'constituting' work.[13]

Now, there is much in *The Ideology of the Aesthetic* that conforms to this argument. For, although the book contains a number of formulations referring us to what 'power' or the 'law' or 'commodity relations' need in the way of subjects, such antihumanist talk is continually off-set by appeals to the needs and capacities of human beings themselves. At various points, in fact, Eagleton offers a quite explicitly dialectical approach both to ideology and to those it interpellates. He tells us, for example, that

> There is a world of political difference between a law which the subject really does give to itself, in radical democratic style, and a decree which still descends from on high but which the subject now 'authenticates'. Free consent may thus be the antithesis of oppressive power, or a seductive form of collusion with it. To view the emergent middle-class order from either standpoint alone is surely too undialectical an approach. In one sense, the bourgeois subject is indeed mystified into mistaking necessity for freedom and oppression for autonomy. For power to be individually authenticated, there must be constructed within the subject a new form of inwardness which will do the unpalatable work of the law for it, and all the more effectively since that law has now apparently evaporated. In another sense, this policing belongs with the historic

victory of bourgeois liberty and democracy over a barbarously repressive state. As such, it contains within itself a genuinely utopian glimpse of a free, equal community of independent subjects. (p. 27)

Here, then, Eagleton appears to draw a definite, if fine, distinction between a genuinely autonomous moment of subjectivity and the 'autonomous subject' as a deluded construct of ideology. But this *is* a precarious dialectic, and it is not always clear how far Eagleton is committed to sustaining it. At times, in fact, one senses in his argument that, despite a reluctance to return to the Althusserian habits of the past, he still finds these more compelling than either of the other apparent options: the heresy of an explicitly 'humanist' subject, on the one hand, or the discourse of 'discourse' and deconstruction, on the other.

For example, in his concluding chapter on postmodernism Eagleton offers (rightly in my opinion) a general overview of this as a contradictory development that one can applaud as a radical politics at the service of authentic local and popular needs, but that one must denounce in so far as it reflects the logic of capitalist development. 'Much postmodernist culture,' he argues, 'is both radical and conservative, iconoclastic and incorporated' (p. 273). It is thus as ambivalent in its message about art and culture as it is in its attitude to history and truth. It demotically confounds hierarchies, but also follows the commodity itself in its erasure of truth, meaning and subjectivity.

Since capitalism is of its very nature transgressive of all boundaries between high and low, esoteric and demotic, the seemingly radical postmodernist attack on a sequestered art runs the risk of reproducing the very logic it opposes. Likewise, in its treatment of history and truth, postmodernism shows itself to be as much a disciple of the Fordist 'history is bunk' school of thought, and of Whitehall ways with truth, as of any more subversive doctrines.

Yet, even as Eagleton approves the genuinely subversive element in postmodernist critiques while reproving them for their denial of subjectivity and suppression of potentially radical meanings and values, he invites us to view the issues at stake in terms of a conflict in the ideological needs of the system. Thus, he writes, 'the mandarin culture of the high bourgeois epoch is progressively called into question by the later evolution of that very social system, but remains at certain ideological levels indispensable . . . partly because the subject as unique, autonomous, self-identical and self-determining remains a political and ideological requirement of the system, but partly because the commodity is incapable of generating a sufficiently legitimating ideology of its own' (pp. 374-5); or again, that 'the autonomous human subject is no clapped out metaphysical fantasy, to be dispersed at a touch of deconstruction, but a continuing ideological necessity constantly outstripped and decentred by the system itself' (p. 377).

So, it seems, then, that the hidden hand of ideology had been pulling the strings all the time, and it was only one of its more cunning ruses to have flashed us a glimpse of an autonomous subject whose autonomy appeared not to have been constructed by the system.[14]

Whatever the difficulties attaching to Eagleton's own argument, however, he is right to present postmodernism as deeply ambivalent in its approach to questions of cultural value and subjectivity—at least to the extent that it offers its own brand of populism as some kind of left-wing cultural positioning. In one sense, as Fredric Jameson has suggested, this populism can be viewed as a continuation or completion of the arguments developed by the New Left in opposition to the earlier Frankfurt School stress on the manipulations of the Culture Industry. In other words, it can be seen as continuing the shift away from a more elitist and negative appraisal of popular culture towards the view that some sort of radical potential is discernible within commodification itself, in so far as the consumerist desires it generates become the source of some deeper dissatisfaction with the system. On the other hand, the postmodernist twist that 'completes' this argument is extremely problematic, since instead of focusing on the 'dissatisfactions' bred by consumerism, it tends rather to congratulate mass tastes for their ever more refined appreciation of technical sophistication. What has therefore been eroded by this postmodernist radical populism is the very distinction between art and entertainment, 'high' and 'low', that sustained the critical edge of left-wing cultural theory. What has disappeared, as Jameson points out, is the standpoint of any 'genuinely aesthetic experience' of the kind formerly used to unmask the structures of commercial art.[15]

However, as Jameson also points out, this does not mean that the old problem of 'true' and 'false' happiness is not still with us: that is, whether 'watching thirty-five hours a week of technically expert and elegant television can be argued to be more deeply gratifying than watching thirty-five hours a week of 1950s "Culture Industry" programming'.[16] Moreover, since the postmodernist position relies on the assumption that the viewers of this non-manipulative high-tech chain of signifying images are themselves unconscious of the utopian wisdom of their so doing, it is unclear how any political messages can be adduced from it. Jameson himself concludes, therefore, that 'perhaps today, where the triumph of more utopian theories of mass culture seems complete and virtually hegemonic, we need the corrective of some new theory of manipulation, and of a properly postmodern commodification.'[17]

One can agree with this, and so presumably can Eagleton, given that it seems implied by his own portrayal of postmodernist 'radicalism' as altogether too collusive with the current dynamic of capitalism. But quite what form this theory could take remains obscure. Or, rather, it remains as difficult to supply such a theory as it is easy to state the fundamental problem to which it would provide the solution: how to give all due weight and respect to the mass tastes which must provide the springboard of any transformative politics, while in some sense also denouncing them as 'false'. The problem, of course, is not a new one for the Left, but lies at the heart of its entire 'democratic socialist' project. For, to put it simply, the sensibilities which both Eagleton and Jameson bring to their discussions of postmodernism speak to their continued conviction of the need to provide a 'democratic socialist' perspective within cultural studies, but also to a very keen awareness of the difficulties of sustaining such a project within the present climate.

This, in turn, raises the issue of how far one can continue to pose the question of its viability in terms of the need for the Left to provide an improved or more updated theory. It is certainly true that this wing of Marxism has always had a hard time engineering even a purely theoretical reconciliation between its democratic open speech ('trust to the people, for only they are in a position to speak to the authenticity of their desires') with its socialist aside ('the ventriloquists of capitalism do not know what they are missing'). And in this sense, one can understand the inclination to cast around for newer, and yet more sophisticated, theoretical resources to bring to the seemingly uncrackable nut. (Thus, Jameson thinks Adorno might just pull it off, with a little corrective from Williams; Eagleton, less confident of anyone in particular, agrees about Adorno and Williams, but believes Habermas has got some interesting ideas too, and then there's Benjamin, and Bakhtin, Freud possibly, not to mention some earlier voices . . .)

Yet, one might argue that the question of viability cannot be thought purely in terms of theoretical resources, in which the Left is not, in fact, so ill-equipped (with no mean contributions from Eagleton and Jameson themselves). The problem, arguably, is less one of finding the right voice than of finding enough of an audience, outside of the academy, that is responsive to it. And this raises the further question of how the Left should respond to the lack of popular interest in its own objectives. For, it can treat this as further proof of the powers of commodity society to manipulate happiness only at the cost of putting a question mark over its own political pertinence and popular engagement. This is not, by any means, to suggest that we should shut up, but only that we may be waiting for something more than can be provided by further refinements in our theoretical offerings. That said, I shall now make an obvious point (though it is also Adorno's, and he is never very obvious[18]): there are still people who are starving. In other words, one also has to say to the Left: 'Thou art to continue'—which is a point echoed in a more sombre clip from Shakespeare, by Eagleton himself, when, in approval of the idea that we should never allow despair finally to silence us, he quotes Edgar in *King Lear* to the effect that the worst is not upon us, so long as we can say 'this is the worst'.

It would be a touch melodramatic, not to say misleading, to suggest that it is only despair that fuels the continuing production of socialist theory. The point is, rather, that so long as there are so many being brought to the unspoken extreme, it seems important, however unpropitious the climate for its reception, to continue to provide a compelling voice of criticism. This applies, moreover, even to those areas of concern, such as the 'utopian' implications of First World cultural consumption, that may seem rather remote from the gnawings of the belly elsewhere. For the lines of connection here are not as tenuous as we are led to believe by those who have no patience with the furtherance of this exercise. And in any case, what we are talking about here has to do very directly with the formation and quality of our own culture, too.

I have made note of tensions, ambivalences, irresolutions in Eagleton's book. But had he written a work from which they were absent, it would be far less pertinent to our times. For anyone who remains intellectually interested in continuing the socialist dialogue around art and culture, and morally convinced that it should continue, his book provides both the substance of the ideas to do the thinking, and the wit and inspiration that stimulates the will for it.

Notes

1. Terry Eagleton, *The Ideology of the Aesthetic,* Blackwell, Oxford 1990. All unattributed page references in the text are to this work.

2. Ibid., p. 13. This follows Alexander Baumgarten's formulation, and is in line with the original Greek understanding of *aisthesis* as referring us to the domain of perception and sensation, in contrast to pure cognition.

3. By rejecting Kant's 'thing-in-itself,' and allowing the objective world to be fully knowable, Hegel denies to Nature its powers of estrangement, presenting it as essentially congenial to human purposes.

4. On the grounds that this topic has been covered fully enough elsewhere, and that the Anglophone tradition is in any case derivative of German philosophy. See ibid., p. II.

5. In a struggle around the 'aesthetic', which issues, by and large, in its capturing by the Right—an outcome that Eagleton describes as a 'devastating loss for the political left' (ibid., p. 60).

6. 'If the law and desire are born at a stroke, then there can be no question of positing an intrinsically creative desire which is merely stifled in its expressiveness by a recalcitrant power' (ibid., p. 274).

7. 'For both Bakhtin and Benjamin, laughter is the very type of expressive somatic utterance, which springs straight from the body's libidinal depths and so for Benjamin carries a resonance of the endangered symbolic or mimetic dimension of language' (ibid., p. 338).

8. What is peculiar to sensual experience, one might say, is that it is not reducible to the having of sensations, but involves a certain reflexivity, or cognitive savouring of their quality. The psychic and the sensory seem so intimately bound up in any distinctively sensual response that it seems impossible to do justice even to the more immediately sensual work of art of literature in purely bodily terms.

9. *Ideology: An Introduction,* Verso, London 1991, p. 222.

10. Ibid., p. 221.

11. Ibid., pp. 142-6, 152-3.

12. Ibid., p. 223.

13. Ibid., pp. 222-3.

14. And this is a position that is reflected in difficulties attaching to some of Eagleton's more specific arguments. Thus, bourgeois meaning is, as we have seen, in some sense to be preserved from the profanities of postmodernist eclecticism; but at the same time Joyce's *Ulysses* is congratulated for 'pulverizing' the 'bourgeois myth of immanent meaning' because it erodes the distinction between 'high and low, holy and profane, past and present, authenticity and derivativeness, and does so with all the vulgarity of the commodity itself'. Joyce's texts in general, in fact, 'turn the economic logic of capitalist life against its hallowed cultural forms, fastening tenaciously upon a contradiction within late bourgeois society between the realm of meaning—the symbolic order in which difference, uniqueness and privilege are the order of the day—and the sphere of production, which that symbolic order ironically helps to sustain' (*The Ideology of the Aesthetic,* pp. 375-6). The problem here, however, is not only that this is a defence of Joyce somewhat at odds with the terms of the polemic against postmodernism, but that it leaves it ambiguous whether we are to view Joyce as a self-consciously anticapitalistic writer or as the ideological reflector of its commodifying logic (and neither of these approaches, in fact, seems adequate). It also arguably evades the question of the rather 'high and holy' difficulties which the texts themselves present to the average 'lay' reader.

15. Fredric Jameson, *Late Marxism: Adorno, or the Persistence of the Dialectic,* London 1990, pp. 141-3.

16. Ibid., pp. 142-3.

17. Ibid., p. 143.

18. I refer here to Adorno's insistence 'that no one shall go hungry any more' (*Minima Moralia,* London 1974, p. 156) as a kind of material precondition or essential preliminary, whose necessity must be set against the 'luxury' of more metaphysical speculations on the difficulties, and possibly

ever-receding 'utopia', of final gratification. See Jameson's discussion, *Late Marxism,* pp. 114-15.

John McGowan (review date Spring 1993)

SOURCE: A review of *Ideology,* in *Southern Humanities Review,* Vol. XXVII, No. 2, Spring, 1993, pp. 166-69.

[*In the following review, McGowan offers positive evaluation of* Ideology, *though notes that some of Eagleton's arguments are undermined by equivocation.*]

Terry Eagleton has written a remarkable book. To enter the swamps of theorizing about ideology and to shed light invariably on every dense obscurity examined is work that calls to mind the lonely and noble labors of Spenserian and Tennysonian knights. No doubt we view such knightly endeavors with suspicion today, sensitive not only to the quixotic nature of quests for lucidity, but also to the self-aggrandizement and incipient elitism of those aiming to assume the mantle of heroic virtue. Eagleton's book is alternately embarrassed by and defiant about its determination to bring light to the benighted, but let me describe what he does before I ponder the puzzles of the tone in which he does it.

Eagleton begins by asserting that the notion of ideology is in crisis. He even claims that the dominant trend is to jettison the term altogether. Here he is mistaken. If anything, the concept of ideology is more prevalent than ever as the left's attention in recent years has swung almost entirely to issues of culture and social reproduction from earlier emphases on economic inequalities and matters of political organization. But just what ideology might mean has fallen victim to the general epistemological muddle in which the human sciences currently find themselves. The old simple alignment of ideology with false consciousness, with a specious rationalization or legitimation of the untraceable bald fact of exploitation, has gone by the boards since we can no longer locate the place from which one could differentiate the ideological (false) version of social facts from the scientific (true) version. Instead, contemporary discussions of ideology usually proclaim that all versions are interpretations and all are equally ideological. While making a few small concessions to this view, Eagleton's basic goal in this book is to avoid the insistence that all discourses have the same epistemological or ethical status. This knight insists that we can and must tell the good guys from the bad guys.

His strategy for reaching the dark tower of truth is to take us through an historical survey of some twenty-odd theorists—Marx, Gramsci, Althusser, Adorno, Habermas, and Freud among them. He presents each writer's thought, offers a few cogent criticisms, and suggests what elements of the thought he wants to salvage for his own purposes. These sections of the book are superb. Miraculously concise and astoundingly faithful to the complexity of the

originals, their sum effect is to bolster Eagleton's case that discourse does a lot of different things in a lot of different ways and that the continuing temptation of theory has been to take one form of discourse as the type of all discourse. Thus, he can argue that current theory's predilection to make all discourse one and to call that one *ideology* is only a most egregious case of theory missing the actual complexity of practice. And he can highlight how our contemporary emphasis on difference is almost always coupled with a levelling hostility toward any attempt to differentiate theoretically among various discourses or categories of action.

Not surprisingly, Eagleton's desire to save a notion of non-ideological discourse puts him more fully at odds with poststructuralist and postmodern theory than he has ever been before. Of course, the tension between Eagleton's Marxism and contemporary theory has surfaced before, especially in his repeated attacks on Paul de Man's work, but Eagleton was also a leading member of the generation of English leftists who slew their fathers—E. P. Thompson and Raymond Williams—by choosing French stepfathers (Althusser, Macherey, the poststructuralists) in their stead. In *Ideology,* however, the polemical skills Eagleton once deployed against Williams are directed at Althusser, Foucault, and, most fully, at the British Marxists still holding the French line: Paul Hirst, Barry Hindress, Ernesto Laclau and Chantal Mouffe.

What does Eagleton have to offer us as the means to distinguish among discourses that French theory would insist are all of a muchness? *Ideology* hints at two answers with a rather surprising diffidence while attempting more straightforwardly—and unsuccessfully, I'm afraid—to convince us of a third. Eagleton suggests that there are three ways we might evaluate discourses: by considering their effects in terms of ethical criteria, by examining their relation to reason, or by assessing their truth value. When pursuing the question of ethical evaluation, Eagleton appears ready to insist that there simply are unavoidable ethical imperatives. Some things are just wrong and we all know it. But just when it looks as if he is going to denounce ethical relativism, he loses his nerve. He switches from first to third person and tells us that the alternative to relativism is for "one" to accept the tenets of "moral realism," leaving unclear his own relation to this (to me) rather implausible position.

Eagleton performs a similar fade out when the criterion of "reason" is invoked. His first chapter ends with these words: "To deny that ideology is fundamentally an affair of reason is not to conclude that it is immune to rational considerations altogether. And 'reason' here would mean something like: the kind of discourse that would result from as many people as possible actively participating in a discussion of these matters in conditions as free as possible from domination." Such a position is clearly derived from Habermas, and the possibility of an appeal to reason is discussed again only in the book's section on Habermas (the clearest and least tendentious short summary of Habermas' work that I have ever read). Significantly, the Habermas section is the only discussion of another theorist that has no critique attached to it; yet Eagleton also never explicitly endorses Habermas' view either. He just presents that view and it remains curiously unconnected to everything else in the book.

On the question of truth value Eagleton does speak out. Although sensitive to the difficulties and embarrassments to which the notion of "false consciousness" (with its overtones of condescension, elitism, and outright tyranny) can lead, he finally insists that we cannot do without the concept. There are "objective interests," he argues, and a discourse that obscures those interests for the social agent is a discourse that offers a false image of a real social situation. As in the case of ethics, Eagleton takes the path here of insisting that we have a stark choice between relativism and objectivism. He does not deny discourse's power to foster illusion, only the notion that we cannot, finally, distinguish nonillusion from illusion.

Alas, his arguments for realism are no better and no more convincing than such arguments usually are. Eagleton covers much the same ground and with much the same arguments found in Gerald Graff's *Literature Against Itself.* And Eagleton displays much the same exasperated tone of common sense that characterizes the work of Graff, Searle, and other champions of plain fact. In stark contrast to his diffidence about moral realism, Eagleton is haughty, sarcastic, amused, and incredulous by turns in his descriptions of the absurd things the anti-realists claim to believe. Seemingly aware that he is actually unlikely to convince anyone in this long-running academic stand-off, all too often he strikes attitudes instead of offering arguments. His one full-length defense of "objective interests" uses a galley slave as its example, thus begging all the interesting and important questions raised by the more difficult cases of the working class or of women in a less than fully tyrannical society. Since various members of these groups evaluate their options and their interests differently, at stake is how we could judge one articulation of those interests as more adequate to their real situation than another. And behind this epistemological issue lurks the different issue of political prescription. Eagleton appears ready to insist that only a very narrow range of responses by a particular group can be "right." As he makes clear several times, he has little patience for the liberal value of "pluralism" or its radical cousin, "difference."

In trying to force us to choose between realism and relativism, Eagleton seems to believe that the destruction of their positions will mean that they must embrace his: "Relativism is no more than a will o' wisp: nobody in fact believes in it for a moment, as an hour's casual observation of their behavior will readily attest." But Eagleton misses his target here. The convincing part of the anti-realist case is not some claim that individuals do not live according to some very settled beliefs about reality but the claim that all such beliefs are contestable between individuals and appeals to reality often fail to settle those contests. What exasperates

Eagleton is the endlessness of debate about a matter he wants to declare absolutely settled.

Eagleton's epistemological and ethical positions are vitiated by his exclusion of the middles between the extremes of relativism and realism. A good case could be made that the notion of ideology is necessary precisely because that notion strives to articulate a middle position that takes into account, among other complexities, the influence on beliefs of power; social organization; social position; cultural traditions, images, and artifacts; and history. Such a position has to acknowledge the reality of these entities (power, history, and the rest) while also recognizing that the effects of these realities are mediated by the discursive forms by which they enter daily practice. The complexities involved here are so intricate and the debates over various formulations so continuous that the temptation to embrace a simple relativism or a simple realism is quite understandable. At its best, which is almost on every page, Eagleton's book keeps in front of us the full complexities of the issues that make a theory of ideology both necessary and frustrating. The result, often enough, is a splitting headache as every certainty dissolves before our eyes, but it is hardly the oddest consequence of our current historical straits (when the breathtaking pace of events in the rest of the world only serves to make the United States seem more nightmarishly glacial than ever) that we must thank Eagleton fervently for the headache and chastise him (gently, but firmly) when he tries, prematurely, to relieve the pain.

Michael Levenson (essay date Winter 1994)

SOURCE: "The Critic as Novelist," in *Wilson Quarterly,* Vol. XVIII, No. 1, Winter, 1994, pp. 116-24.

[*In the following excerpt, Levenson examines the motivation among literary theorists, including Eagleton, to write fiction and offers discussion of Eagleton's novel* Saints and Scholars.]

Misleading to call it a movement, and still worse to think of it as a program, but we now have seen enough minor literary eruptions to suspect that it is a cultural symptom that bears some reflection: this burst of novel-writing from people who have lived the conceptual life, the life of method and argument, who often carry leather cases, or who give public lectures and contribute essays to learned journals. In the past five years, some of the world's leading literary critics have turned novelists, and at the same time turned from the coterie audience gathered in the universities to the wider public made up of anyone who wants to read. Why do they do it? What do they want? Are they merely slumming in the bad streets of the imagination? Or are these just new cases of a few gifted people who always hoped to grow up to be novelists and decided to act before it was too late?

Literary critics are not alone in suddenly feeling the charm of novel-writing; it happens to historians and journalists, among others. But I intend to give reasons for taking the literary academic drift of the tide with special seriousness. I'll start by proposing a story of this century, inevitably a story with many chapters left out. It begins with the old provocations of modernism, especially those forbidding experiments of the third decade—Joyce's *Ulysses,* Woolf's *The Waves,* Eliot's *The Waste Land,* Pound's *Cantos*— works more than willing (in T. S. Eliot's phrase) to disturb and alarm the public. This they did.

One slowly building consequence of those literary agitations was the creation of criticism, criticism as we know it now—professional, sophisticated, ambitious. In significant respects, the modern professoriate within the humanities is one of the lasting (though inadvertent) achievements of the avant-garde. It is scarcely an accident that this century has seen the emergence of these rival siblings: a revolutionary avant-garde intent on speaking a new word, and an academic establishment that has perfected the skills of interpretation. Indeed, the academic standpoint must often be seen as a defense against the aggressions of modernism.

With the great postwar expansion of the university and with the exciting lure of interdisciplinary collaboration, the critical project took on ever more heady ambitions. Hopes of a grand synthesis—among, say, Marx and Freud and existentialism—led to the vision of a Total Theory, an exhaustive method that would take into account all relevant details on the way to its definitive interpretations. Jean-Paul Sartre gave one version of this comprehensive system of explanation, Herbert Marcuse another, and Northrop Frye a rival third. Theirs was a great dream of the 1950s and early '60s, when it seemed possible that many disciplines would meet in a grand methodological union.

But the theory project has fallen into a crisis. The dream of a Total Theory is no longer able to soothe any deep academic sleep. It just hasn't worked out: There were too many fissures in the great globe of perfect understanding. Total Theory has itself become a primary target of theoretical attack; the very idea of a seamless explanation that would find a home for every detail of a life, a text, an epoch now seems charmingly quaint.

With the fading of the missionary goal there has emerged a conspicuous revival of individualism in academic life. Of course, academics have never been free from the taint of self-interest. But now that it's so hard to believe that particular essays and books are part of some unfolding collective structure, everywhere you look you see eye-catching individual display. The dazzling feat of interpretive ingenuity, the bravura reading of a well-worn text, the memorably witty lecture, even the rhetorically bold introduction to the witty lecture, now comprise the intellectual currency of academic life: the public working of the quick mind as high theater.

No longer convinced that their academic labor is leading anywhere in particular, scholars give themselves to self-contained gestures of critical power. So, with the consummate dexterity of a practiced performer, new historicist Stephen Greenblatt (University of California, Berkeley) takes his audiences from the trial of a hermaphrodite to the green woods of Shakespearean comedy. And with a keen sense for the intellectual funny bone, Sandra Gilbert (Princeton) and Susan Gubar (University of California, Davis) leaven their feminist historical revisionism with the hilarity of a stand-up comedy duet. To perform an act of criticism at full mental stretch, to do so before the appreciative glances of one's well-trained colleagues, to provide through the course of an evening one full measure of conceptual edification—this now often seems sufficient, the best that can be hoped for. Indeed, there seems to be a general acceptance of the fact that as fast as it may be moving, literary criticism isn't headed anywhere in particular.

Tongues needn't cluck at this development; it's no worse than many others. Moreover, it has freed intellectuals for more daring swoops of thought, more adventurous tones of voice. You hear in the popular press the horror stories of violent rumbles between strong and weak political correctness factions, and you cringe. We all cringe. But this is what happens when the cauldron bubbles—it spatters the walls.

With the vogue of criticism as performance, with the shattered confidence in Total Theory, with the admiration accorded to individual virtuosity at the expense of common enterprise, the idea of criticism as a science (vintage 1966) seems a picturesque relic of a simpler time. Many now have unlearned the compulsions of Total Theory, and some have come to yearn for pleasure that *no* theory can give. Who can be surprised if the writing of novels suddenly seems an irresistible lure to these restless academics? . . .

In 1987 Terry Eagleton, well established as an internationally prominent Marxist critic, published a novel called **Saints and Scholars.** It takes the Irish uprising of 1916 as its pressing historical context and then imagines a set of improbable circumstances. What if the wounded revolutionary James Connolly, on the run from the British, hides in a cottage that had been rented by Ludwig Wittgenstein, still a young philosopher genius? What if Wittgenstein has been traveling with Nikolai Bakhtin, the boisterous brother of the Russian literary theorist Mikhail Bakhtin? And what if in the midst of this improbable encounter Leopold Bloom steps out of the pages of Joyce's *Ulysses* and stumbles into the panic?

In a prefatory note to the book, Eagleton points out that "this novel is not entirely fantasy." Wittgenstein and Nikolai Bakhtin were indeed friends; Wittgenstein did spend time in a cottage on the west coast of Ireland, "although at a later time than suggested here." Eagleton ends his note by observing that "most of the rest is invented."

But "invented" is too weak. What gives the novel its comedy and its charm is not merely that it spins out new fancies but that it so cheerfully refuses claims of historical fact. In its opening pages, which describe James Connolly on the point of execution by firing squad, *Saints and Scholars* looks to be a conventionally scrupulous historical fiction of the Irish revolt. But it is exactly scrupulous history that the book explodes. Faced with the awkwardness of "facts," it invents new ones.

At the center of the book is a debate between Connolly and Wittgenstein, the one upholding the imperative of revolution as the only response to crushing Irish misery, the other insisting that revolution is just another dangerous dream of purity. The dialogue between them is the best thing in the book. An exhausted Connolly, badly suffering from his wounds, holds on to revolutionary speech, even as his conviction weakens. The excitable Wittgenstein finds himself deeply moved by that speech and begins to try on Connolly's revolutionary truth: "What if he is right that crisis is common?" This is the Wittgenstein who had told Bakhtin earlier in the book that "out there in Europe the most dreadful war in history is now being waged. I came to this place because I couldn't stand it any longer. So I'm on the run—in hiding from history."

The Wittgenstein we know from the biographical record was scarcely on the run from history in 1916. On the contrary. He had left the security of Cambridge in order to join the Austrian army, in which he served at great personal peril; an artillery officer, he was taken prisoner of war by the Italian army. This was anything but a flight from history. Better to call it a determined press into the midst of history's most dangerous confusion. For Eagleton's purposes, though, Wittgenstein must be cast as a philosophical purist who has fled the impure swamp of social life.

It must have been very shortly before he sat down to compose his novel that Eagleton wrote a rather traditional essay called **"Wittgenstein's Friends."** It usefully places Wittgenstein in relation to recent poststructuralist theory, showing, for instance, the common ground between Wittgenstein and Derrida. From Eagleton's standpoint, both the school of Wittgenstein and the school of Derrida make telling critiques of metaphysics, with its longing for impeccably secure foundations and systematic truth, but both schools fail to engage the reality of politics. At this moment of impasse, the essay invokes a third figure to split the difference, Russian theorist Mikhail Bakhtin. For Eagleton, Bakhtin shows how it is possible to make a strong philosophical criticism of metaphysical abstraction from the standpoint of social engagement. The key thought is that the metaphysics of the philosophers and the tyranny of the politicians are in a fearful partnership that can be opposed only by a subversive energy. "Carnival" is Bakhtin's answer to oppression, where carnival implies a lusty release of the wild body, free to laugh, to mock, to enjoy.

In the fictional world of *Saints and Scholars,* Nikolai Bakhtin stands in for his brother's theory of carnival. Off in their Irish retreat, Wittgenstein becomes appalled by Nikolai's taste for food and wine; he calls Bakhtin a "disgusting walrus," at which point,

> Bakhtin begins to croon a Russian folk song inaccurately to himself. Then he breaks off and remarks, "Somebody is slaughtering somebody else." He licks his lips contentedly. "I think it's you, Ludwig, who's killing us all with your ridiculous purity."

> Wittgenstein leans swiftly across and grabs a half-empty bottle of wine from Bakhtin's cabinet. He says lightly: "I think you should drown in this." Bakhtin gives no response. "Do you hear me, Nikolai? I said I think you should drown in your own disgusting mess."

> Bakhtin opens his eyes for a moment and twists his lips upward in the shape of a slobbery kiss.

So why does Eagleton do it? Why does he play out in fiction what he had soberly enacted in his criticism? And why does he extravagantly "reinvent" a history that he knows so well?

The beginning of an answer is that Eagleton, like many others, must feel the desire to break free of the usual academic constraints—historical exactitude, intellectual precision, sound evidence. This must always be a temptation in academic life: to be done with its cautions and respectabilities. What makes it more urgent in Eagleton's case is that his career as a critic has been devoted to a vision of history—a revolutionary vision of social liberation—that has come under such tremendous stress. He has not blinked in the face of the oppositions, internal and external, within the Marxist tradition he has sought to extend. Competing methodologies, as well as sharp turns in political history, have brought large and difficult changes in Eagleton's life as a political critic.

Of all these changes, perhaps the most interesting has been Eagleton's recognition that pleasure—immediate delight, as in the love of a single line of poetry—can no longer be neglected by even the most committed criticism. We live at a moment, he writes, when "the relation between the kind of pleasure people take in art, and the pleasure they derive from striving to realize their political needs, has become extremely obscure." Our age has "a *political* problem about pleasure."

Saints and Scholars is a fantasy of historical coherence, a fantasy of our century's forces and powers brought into consoling relation. What Eagleton struggles toward in his theory, he brightly paints in his novel: a universe where pleasure and politics can meet and where the significance of our historical struggle has reassuringly distinct outlines. The comedy of Leopold Bloom set free from *Ulysses* to enter into drunken dialogue with Wittgenstein, Bakhtin, and Connolly is ticklishly sharp. But transcending the comedy of the image is its sheer romance, which reassuringly lets us feel that our modernity is not an ugly chaos but that it might have a tidy plot of its own. If we feel let down by history, implies Eagleton, then it's for us to reimagine the historical legacy, to revive ourselves with a daydream, a fully conscious daydream that admits its own need to find a refuge. . . .

None of these figures denies or repudiates his or her theoretical past, but each uses the past sometimes in a mood of nostalgia, sometimes in mockery, sometimes in cool detachment—in ways that would certainly have surprised their former selves. Kristeva's roman á clef only makes explicit what all of them have done: They have passed beyond their old austerity and have learned the joys of bringing intellectual life down into the muddy, uproarious world.

The pleasures in Umberto Eco's work are the pleasures of deep release, a full-souled indifference to the proprieties of critical discourse. When *The Name of the Rose* (and less frequently *Foucault's Pendulum*) succeeds, it is because Eco has allowed himself to forget the obligations of the perspicuous axiom and the clinching argument. If, in *The Samurai,* the pleasure is rarer and weaker, this is largely because as a novelist Kristeva is all the time remembering her other, older incarnation as a glistening intellectual, and because as she writes of that time she tastes bitter ashes.

But it may be the mixed satisfactions of Sontag and Eagleton that are most revealing. In *The Volcano Lover* and **Saints and Scholars** you find a giddy delight in sinuous plot, in its romance or its comedy, alongside a rueful, tacit awareness that such writing is not what was dreamed of one, two, and three decades ago. This double consciousness captures some of the unsettling complexity of the current cultural moment. A new sensibility (Sontag) and a new society (Eagleton) are what they pursued with daunting vigor, but nowadays it takes no special skeptical turn to see that sensibility and society are nothing so simple as "new." Their careers, their lives, and their writing provide sobering tokens of a milieu (ours) in which a (literary) opportunity seized coincides with a (critical) ideal abandoned.

What is likely to happen to this current of writing? Impossible to say. Still, it only takes a slightly generous view to see it as a sparkling tributary into the pool of culture. Whether it will yield work of lasting quality is unclear. But while we wait to find out, we can enjoy the fresh stirring of the old waters. That academic intellectuals should suddenly feel bouncy and vigorous at the thought of writing fiction—this may be a harbinger of the kind of hybrid we could sorely use, a hybrid that overcomes the division between those who imagine and those who ratiocinate, those who create and those who review their books. It's no ultimate synthesis, but it makes a colorful little picture within our larger gray: the sight of these self-reinventing theorists, these feeling intellectuals and pleasure-seeking rationalists, these academics laughing and weeping.

Patrick Colm Hogan (review date March 1994)

SOURCE: "The Persistence of Idealism," in *Philosophy of the Social Sciences,* Vol. 24, No. 1, March, 1994, pp. 84-92.

[*In the following review, Hogan offer positive evaluation of* Ideology, *though cites shortcomings in Eagleton's "idealist epistemology."*]

Ideology: An Introduction presents a conceptual and historical overview of the notion of ideology from the Enlightenment through "post-Marxism." It is lucid, informative, engaging, and well-argued. Although aimed at non-expert readers broadly familiar with debates in critical theory, it may be read productively by anyone from an advanced undergraduate to a specialist in political criticism. It works particularly well in a graduate Introduction to Literary Theory seminar, as I know from just having used it. Eagleton's discussions of such writers as Habermas, Gramsci, and Bourdieu help students to think about ideology more deeply and articulately, while his criticisms of current poststructural views encourage students to evaluate theories of ideology more critically and more practically.

The first two chapters present a clear statement of the nature and varieties of ideology. These chapters are particularly valuable because they situate the problem of ideology squarely within the realm of real politics. When confronted with a fashionable philosophical claim about politics, Eagleton asks, what does this mean in the real world, for real people, those who are suffering the real effects of oppression? He continually recurs to "that basic realism and intelligence of popular life which is so unpalatable to the elitist" (p. 14).

For this reason, Eagleton often finds poststructural and post-Marxist views wanting. In relation to these, he points out that, despite claims to the contrary,

> political radicals are quite as dedicated to the concept of privilege as their opponents: they believe, for example, that the level of food supplies in Mozambique is a weightier issue than the love life of Mickey Mouse. The claim that one kind of conflict is more important than another involves, of course, *arguing* for this priority and being open to disproval; but nobody actually believes that 'power is everywhere' in the sense that any manifestation of it is as significant as any other. On this issue, as perhaps on all others, nobody is in fact a relativist, whatever they may rhetorically assert. (pp. 8-9)

Similarly, he stresses that "ideology is less a matter of the inherent linguistic properties of a pronouncement than a question of who is saying what to whom for what purposes" (p. 9). It is a sad comment on the current state of political criticism that such statements need to be made at all. The same holds for Eagleton's unfashionable arguments that universalization is not necessarily pernicious, that such universals as freedom, justice, and equality are not wholly execrable (see p. 57), and that it is reasonable to accept that many things are part of human nature (pp. 59-60). In this and other ways, Eagleton's book is a welcome antidote to the pseudo-political posturing of much recent critical theory.

But, like any book, this one is not perfect. There are sections that seem slapdash, the analysis conceptually fuzzy or not well thought through (e.g., the isolation of six arbitrary and overlapping strategies for the legitimation of power, pp. 5-6). And at times the explications are superficial or misleading (e.g., the odd treatment of the Lacanian mirror stage). However, the most pervasive problem with the book derives from Eagleton's un-self-conscious adherence to an idealist epistemology. Many anomalies and confusions in Eagleton's argument are traceable to his implicit conception of knowledge. What makes this interesting and important is that Eagleton is not alone in adopting an idealist view; almost all literary theorists operate on precisely the same presuppositions. However, like Eagleton, they may not recognize this explicitly. Idealism provides a conception of knowledge that guides the way many theorists formulate arguments, isolate problems, construct models, and so forth—even many theorists who, if asked, would reject this conception of knowledge. In Eagleton's case, this is made all the more fascinating by the fact that he appears to be striving for another sort of epistemology. He repeatedly makes claims that are non- or anti-idealist. But he fails adequately to explicate and defend those claims because they are incoherent with his epistemological presuppositions.

In the remainder of this review, I focus on this epistemological issue, for it is of crucial importance not only to Eagleton's book but to all of contemporary literary theory. Specifically, I outline the idealist view of knowledge and what we might call the "inferentialist" or "propositional" alternative, examine some of the ways in which the former view underlies certain problems in Eagleton's argument, and finally, discuss how these problems dissolve when considered in inferential/propositional terms.

Idealist epistemology defines truth in terms of knowledge rather than the reverse.[1] In other words, in this view "The workers are oppressed" is true if and only if we know or might know that the workers are oppressed. The question then is what defines such knowledge and how do we achieve it? The idealist answer is coincidence between the knowing subject and the object known. This coincidence is achieved through unbiased experience. For example, I know that my desk is brown because I experience it directly and have no bias that would distort this experience. In other words, I am "objective." If I am not objective, if I do not distance myself from my own interests, then my cognition of a given object may be faulty and thus I may fail to conform my thought to reality. If I am objective, however, I (regularly) succeed in rendering my thought congruent with things.

This sort of epistemology underlies a range of seemingly disparate views, including versions of both the "correspondence" and "consensus" views of truth. Specifically, the correspondence view includes any version of idealist epistemology that stresses the possibility of cognitive coincidence between subject and object—for example, by way of representational identity between an idea and a thing.[2] The consensus view is perhaps the more common idealist view today. It includes any version of idealist epistemology that explicitly or implicitly stresses the problem of individual idiosyncrasy. Specifically, if truth is

cognitive identity with the object, but this identity is uncertain because of the possibility of distortion through personal interest or other biasing factors, then the best guarantee of such identity would seem to be consensus.

Yet even consensus might be biased—witness the many varieties of racist consensus. Among political writers, Habermas is perhaps the most prominent example of a consensus theorist who has taken up this problem. His solution, which has greatly influenced Eagleton, is to qualify consensus as "consensus in a nonoppressive society." Racist views arise due to the distorted interests, and pseudo-interests, inevitable in an oppressive society. In a nonoppressive society, these interests would not intervene, systematically perverting people's cognition; and thus consensus would be reliable. In Habermas, then, it seems clear that a consensus view of truth is a version of idealism. In effect, Habermas says that consensus does not provide grounds for judging thought/thing identity unless it is consensus of objective thinkers, and thinkers can be objective (in politically relevant matters) only in a nonoppressive society.

Skeptics of various sorts also hold to this idealist view. Indeed, it is common for literary thinkers to assume that cognition/object coincidence defines truth but to despair of such coincidence and thus to despair of truth. This is the sort of reasoning that Eagleton seeks to discredit. Eagleton wishes to hold onto the notion of truth. He views skepticism as both intellectually misguided and politically harmful, quite rightly I think. However, the skeptical criticisms of idealist epistemology are powerful, perhaps definitive. It is not at all clear that one can adopt idealist premises and rationally avoid skeptical conclusions. In other words, it is not clear that a view such as that of Habermas or Eagleton is intellectually viable. Eagleton may be defending valid conclusions on impossible grounds. And that is the central dilemma of the book.

At the outset, Eagleton explains that there are "three key doctrines of postmodernist thought" which "have conspired to discredit the classical concept of ideology" (p. xi). All three are derivative of idealist epistemology. The first is the "rejection of the notion of representation," which is to say the rejection of any mental entity that could define mind/object identity. The second is "epistemological skepticism," in effect the view that there is no way in which experience might yield direct cognition of an object. The third is the "reformulation of the relations between rationality, interests and power," which entails that there is never any such thing as objectivity (pp. xi-xii). In large measure, Eagleton's purpose is to respond to these doctrines and to reaffirm the classical concept of ideology. However, once again, Eagleton presupposes the idealist epistemology from which these doctrines derive, and skeptical conclusions may very well be entailed by such an epistemology.

But what is the alternative? What is an inferentialist or propositional epistemology? First of all, in this view, knowledge is derivative of truth, not vice versa. Propositions are true or false, and knowledge is belief in true propositions—or, rather, the acceptance of true propositions for reasons that are both rationally plausible and themselves true. (The reasons for this convoluted definition have to do with the resolution of philosophical paradoxes, which do not bear on our present concerns; I also leave aside the issue of whether we should speak more properly of propositions or theories and other issues internal to inferentialism.)

Specifically, a proposition asserts that certain objects or sets of objects have certain properties or stand in certain relations. These objects, properties, and relations may be fixed as we like; an inferentialist epistemology does not presuppose any preset division of the world. In other words, we may define "red" as "any surface which reflects white light of between 630 and 770 nanometers wavelength" or "between 620 and 700 nanometers" or "between 650 and 720 nanometers" and so on. This view does not require that there be essences that fix the meanings of words, determining, for example, that 630-770 nanometers is "naturally" one color and must be named as such. (Of course, someone may wish to add essences to this view, and many prominent theorists have—unfortunately, in my opinion; the point here is merely that the inferentialist view in no way presupposes essences.) On the other hand, once we have defined any given set of terms, then statements employing these terms are either true or false if the objects in question have the stipulated properties or stand in the stipulated relations. Thus once we have meanings for "desk," "red," and so forth, then "This desk is red" is either true or false of a given object, independent of cognitive issues.[3]

As to knowledge, we can never arrive at absolute certainty concerning the truth or falsity of a given empirical proposition, but we can infer tentatively that a given proposition is true or false through hypothesization based on observation along with general principles of logic, statistical significance, simplicity, and so forth. Note that in the inferentialist view, objectivity is a nonissue. There is the issue of whether one has examined alternative hypotheses—including the hypothesis of mistaken observation; the issue of whether one has accurately ranked alternatives for simplicity and explanatory capacity; the issue of whether one's logical inferences are valid. And in any given case, we may wish to explain an error—in, for example, logical inference—by reference to personal or collective bias. But in this view, it is the validity of the inference that is important. "Objectivity" is only of psychological or sociological interest once we have isolated or hypothesized an error.

Beyond the purely epistemological issues, there is an important political difference between idealist and inferentialist epistemologies, one critical to an understanding of both Eagleton and his opponents. Specifically, idealist epistemology tends to value the personal experiences of oppressed people; inferentialist epistemology tends to value systematic observation of the conditions of oppressed people—including, of course, self-observation, but self-observation qualified by statistical considerations, issues surrounding the validity of inferences concealed in self-observation, and so forth. Thus an inferentialist critique of ideology will be based on wide-ranging empirical study, relatively independent of individual experience, whereas an idealist critique will focus on precisely that individual experience, for, despite problems of "objectivity," it alone allows the possibility of mind/object identity.

In keeping with this, Eagleton begins his discussion of ideology, and his response to postmodernism, by insisting that ideological critique "seeks to inhabit the experience of the subject from the inside, in order to elicit those 'valid' features of that experience" (p. xiv). In other words, ideology is an obfuscation of one's genuine experience. It is, in the classic term, "false consciousness." If the distorting lens of ideology is removed, oppressed people will be able to experience their situation objectively and thus know it as it is. Indeed, the very possibility of critique is based on the presumption that oppressed people already have knowledge-yielding experience: "The critique of ideology, then, presumes that nobody is ever *wholly* mystified" (p. xiv). Later, following Gramsci—another idealist in epistemology—Eagleton stresses that critique must be based on the "discrepancy between official and practical consciousness—between those notions that the oppressed classes derive from their superiors and those that arise from their 'life situations'" (p. 50). "For Gramsci," he explains, "the consciousness of subordinated groups in society is typically fissured and uneven. Two conflicting conceptions of the world usually exist in such ideologies, the one drawn from the 'official' notions of the rulers, the other derived from an oppressed people's practical experience of social reality" (p. 118).

There are, however, serious problems with this approach. From inferentialist presuppositions, an individual's experiences are simply not generalizable or even explicable in isolation. If I am treated badly in a given job, I cannot conclude that Irish people or literary theorists or anarchists are typically treated badly. Similarly, a woman who is swiftly promoted, easily successful, and so forth cannot conclude that this is generally true for women. Personal experience may provide an orientation for research, but in and of itself it does not provide evidence for any generalization. Moreover, such generalization is problematic even from the perspective of idealism, for from idealist presuppositions, there is a problem, not of statistical significance but of whether or not objectivity is attainable.

Eagleton addresses this second, idealist problem—although not the first, inferential problem. The very possibility of ideology, he tells us, indicates that "all viewpoints are socially determined" (p. 51). But "if all thought is socially determined, then so too must be Marxism, in which case what becomes of its claims to scientific objectivity?" (p. 91), a scientific objectivity that presumptively operates to adjudicate between the true and false consciousness of the oppressed. Eagleton follows Lukacs in responding that to claim that all knowledge springs from a specific social standpoint is not to imply that any old social standpoint is as valuable for these purposes as any other. If what one is looking for is some understanding of the workings of imperialism as a whole, then one would be singularly ill-advised to consult the Governor General or the *Daily Telegraph*'s Africa correspondent, who will almost certainly deny its existence. (p. 97)

But this does not solve the problem. We have in effect asserted that the Governor General and the correspondent are not "objective" and thus that their claims will not be expressions of adequate cognition, but, as Eagleton asks, "from what viewpoint is *this* judgement made?" (p. 97). Or, further along, "The problem . . . is that any criticism of another's views as ideological is always susceptible to a swift *tu quoque*" (p. 108).

Note once again that these are problems only for the idealist view that critique must be based on the subject's experience. In inferentialist terms, there is no question of a tu quoque response, no issue of our viewpoint when we judge the claims of the Governor General. Rather, there are only the issues of evidence, alternative hypotheses, simplicity, and so forth. When, say, Noam Chomsky (an inferentialist) argues that the war in Vietnam was an imperialist war of aggression by the United States against the people of Vietnam, he argues this on inferential grounds. When Susan Faludi (an inferentialist) argues that women still suffer massive discrimination, she does not base this conclusion on the life experience or practical consciousness of the oppressed. Claims about Chomsky's or Faludi's biases are irrelevant to these arguments. Again, if someone shows that Chomsky or Faludi has skewed the evidence, failed to consider plausible alternative hypotheses, and so forth, then claims about biases may be of psychological interest in explaining this. However, it is the inferential objections alone that bear on the validity of their conclusions.

Unfortunately, Eagleton does not even conceive of an inferentialist alternative to idealism. Nor, for the most part, do other humanists, although inferentialism is standard in the physical sciences (if, for the most part, un-self-consciously). Indeed, Eagleton, like most humanists, misunderstands scientific epistemology as a naive assertion of absolute and unquestionable objectivity. Thus he urges us against "trusting to a scientific rationalism which float[s] disinterestedly above history" (p. 91). And he ridicules the idea that "the truth or falsity of statements is sublimely untainted by their social genesis" (p. 10). There is certainly an important issue here—the politics and ethics of particular scientific pursuits. Eagleton is right to imply that we should not remove science, or anything else, from social concerns. But this is a separate issue from that of epistemology in the natural sciences. The former bears on the practical goals of research, funding allocations, and so forth (e.g., war vs. health); the latter bears on general methods of investigation and the nature of descriptive claims and explanatory hypotheses. Eagleton's implicit conflation of these issues perverts his representation of the standard epistemology of natural science.

Given his distorted conception of the alternatives, Eagleton has no way of resolving the *tu quoque* dilemma other than steering a middle path between naive scientism and skeptical poststructuralism. Consequently, he maintains that "those who imagine that if truth is not absolute then there is no truth at all are simply closet transcendentalists, helplessly in thrall to the very case they reject" (p. 169). And "Marxism regards rationality neither as some ahistorical absolute, nor as the mere reflex of current powers and desires" (p. 171); "the last thing Marxism has ever credited is the fantasy that truth is somehow unhistorical" (p. 172). But these statements make sense only within an idealist epistemology. After all, the very notion of absolute truth is an idealist notion. Absolute truth is perfect cognition of the whole—the final stage of Spirit, in Hegel's Absolute Idealism. It is a notion that has no meaning in inferentialist terms. More important, Eagleton's statements are less a response to the skeptical dilemma than a restatement of it. They do not even point toward a solution of the problem that "to know what is rationally the case, I must . . . remove myself and my prejudices from the scene of inquiry, behave as though I were not there; but such a project can clearly never get off the ground" (p. 160). Again, within an idealist epistemology, it is not clear that there is any alternative to absolute knowledge other than relativism. Perhaps there is. But merely asserting a middle path is no argument for this. And that is all Eagleton does.

Eagleton makes a final stab at saving nonabsolute knowledge in his discussion of Hindess and Hirst. But this only provides one more reason why the idealist epistemology of the humanities should be abandoned and an inferentialist epistemology established in its place. Specifically, Eagleton takes up the challenge to essentialism posed by Hindess and Hirst and tries to save (Marxist) causal explanation from this challenge. "It is a rationalist fallacy, so Hindess and Hirst argue, to hold that what enables us to know is the fact that the world takes the shape of a concept—that it is somehow conveniently pre-structured to fit our cognition of it" (p. 203):

> Hindess and Hirst's "anti-epistemological" thesis is intended among other things to undermine the Marxist doctrine that a social formation is composed of different "levels", some of which exert more significant determinacy than others. For them, this is merely another instance of the rationalist illusion, which would view society as somehow already internally structured along the lines of the concepts by which we appropriate it in thought. (p. 204)

This too is a problem only within an idealist framework. If knowledge is the perfect coincidence of mind and object, and if the object is not formed by a separate essence but by our concepts, then our cognition of that object is nothing other than a cognition of our concepts; thus it cannot claim validity. This is merely the old objectivity problem in a new, linguistic guise.

On an inferentialist model, in contrast, this is no problem at all. Hindess and Hirst may well be correct that the world is not preformed by essences—I think they are (although for different reasons). But they are wrong that this in any way affects causal analysis. Once we have divided up the world, we will find causal patterns of some sort for our chosen objects, properties, and relations. On the other hand, not every division of the world yields equally fine-grained and equally powerful causal laws. That is the point of altering our divisions and positing new entities—in physics, for example. But there is nothing in an antiessentialist argument that contradicts this. Indeed, it is only under an antiessentialist view that such ongoing conceptual revision makes sense. Had Eagleton adopted an inferentialist view, he could have accepted Hindess and Hirst's antiessentialist premises but rejected their critique of causal determination, which is precisely what he finds problematic.

Unfortunately, Eagleton maintains his tacit idealism and keeps to his "middle path" view: the world is not entirely preformed, but it is not entirely created by our concepts either. However, this is far from cogent. For one thing, it is very hard to say what it means, or how it could occur, that the world is partially preformed and partially structured by our concepts. More important, there is no clear way of distinguishing between our formations and the preformed world and thus no way of avoiding the relativism eschewed by Eagleton. The problems faced by Hindess and Hirst do not indicate that the world is (partially) preformed (e.g., that light between 630 and 770 nanometers is one color in and of itself while that between 640 and 720 is not) but, rather, that truth should not be understood as a function of a subject's cognitive unity with an object and the resultant linking of truth with essentialism.

I have dwelt at length on the differences between an idealist and an inferentialist epistemology and on the problems with the former because the implicit reliance on an idealist epistemology is so widespread in the humanities, especially in literary theory. Eagleton's ***Ideology: An Introduction*** is a fine addition to the literature on ideology, a welcome complement to such books as Raymond Geuss's *The Idea of a Critical Theory*. It is a politically serious work by an independent thinker. What is unfortunate is that even at this far outpost of critical theory, even at the unfashionable margin of humanistic thinking on ideology, idealist epistemology still holds sway, and such irrelevant notions as objectivity—sometimes denied, sometimes affirmed—are still central to the debate.

Notes

1. By "epistemology" I mean the operative assumptions about knowledge that guide a thinker's research and argument. These assumptions may or may not be formulated in an explicit theory. Moreover, a writer's explicit theory of knowledge may or may not coincide with his or her tacit operative assumptions. The idealist view, as noted here, is founded on the notion that truth is a function of knowledge, with knowledge understood as subject/object coincidence. It was most fully developed as an explicit theory by German idealist writers such as Hegel. What I am calling "inferentialist" or "propositional" epistemology is based, in contrast, on the notion that knowledge is a function of truth, with truth understood as propositional or theoretical accuracy or adequacy. This has been the standard view in Anglo-American philosophy since the turn of the century. Although it has not been widely defended or even thematized, it is a view presupposed in writings by a range of logical empiricists, falsificationists, neo-Baconian verificationists, possible worlds theorists, and others. Perhaps more important, it is the operative epistemology of virtually all scientific research, from physics to linguistics (although idealist views do occasionally crop up in explicit theories—in theoretical physics most particularly). In the following pages, I do not wish to advocate any current theory based on inferential/propositional epistemology. Indeed, I find most of these to be mistaken (as I must, for they are mutually exclusive). I do wish to argue that an adequate epistemology must be inferential/propositional, not idealist, and that even such radical literary theorists as Eagleton are so thoroughly imbued with idealism that they cannot conceive of an inferential/propositional alternative.

2. Of course, the "correspondence" category also includes Tarski-type inferential/propositional views of truth. This is one reason why the term is too broad to be useful and why it and related categories should be replaced by the distinction between inferential/propositional and idealist epistemologies.

3. Idealist epistemology is frequently associated with an autonomistic conception of language, such as that put forth by Jacques Derrida. In this view—rejected by most contemporary linguists—language is independent of idiolect and thus semantic stipulation is not a real possibility. Discussion of this issue would take us far away from Eagleton's book, on which it bears only indirectly. For a criticism of deconstruction and essentialist autonomisms, see Patrick Colm Hogan, *The Politics of Interpretation: Ideology Professionalism, and the Study of Literature* (New York: Oxford University Press, 1990), 50-81, and "The Limits of Semiotics," *diacritics* (Spring 1992); for a discussion of essentialist autonomism in Hegelian thought, perhaps the paradigm case of idealism, see "Meaning and Hegel," *Southern Journal of Philosophy* 36, no. 1 (Spring 1980): 32-44. For the current linguistic view, see Noam Chomsky, *Knowledge of Language: Its Nature, Origin, and Use* (New York: Praeger, 1986), 19ff.

Christopher Norris (review date Fall 1994)

SOURCE: A review of *Ideology,* in *Comparative Literature,* Vol. 46, No. 4, Fall, 1994, pp. 390-93.

[In the following review, Norris offers positive evaluation of Ideology.*]*

This book finds Eagleton returning once again to a topic that has often preoccupied his thinking, from the high Althusserian rigor of *Criticism and Ideology* (1976) to his recent major work on the history of aesthetics as a surrogate form of ideological discourse. Not that he is merely recycling old ideas in a different polemical context. On the contrary, Eagleton's analysis has deepened and evolved over the years through exposure to the various contending schools of post-Althusserian theory. Some of these arguments he has taken on board, albeit with a growing measure of critical reserve. Others he has berated—not without reason—as philosophically incoherent, politically bankrupt, or irrelevant to the practical Marxist interest in grasping and transforming our conditions of life in the late twentieth-century Western liberal pseudo-democracies. Certainly Eagleton has taken full stock of those challenges to the Althusserian paradigm that have come from so many quarters of late (poststructuralist, postmodernist, neopragmatist, anti-foundationalist, etc.), and whose effect has been to generate a widespread suspicion of any such "discourse" ultimately wedded to the concepts and categories of Marxist *Ideologiekritik*. In a series of skirmishing polemical rejoinders he has managed to appropriate some elements of this current linguistic turn without giving way on the basic point, i.e. the primacy of real-world socio-economic conditions and the role of ideology as in some sense an alibi. a realm of false appearances or illusory knowledge-effects.

To the obvious question—in *what* sense, precisely?—his books have returned quite a range of differing answers, from the scientistic truth-claims of that early Althusserian phase to the mixture of activist rhetoric and "post-theoretical" skepticism that marked the concluding chapter of *Literary Theory* (1986). In fact one could chart the various visions and revisions of Eagleton's intellectual trajectory to date by tracing the way ideology has figured from one book to the next, not least in those periods when his writing registered a sense of unease with any too-confident beating of the bounds between theory (or Marxist "theoretical practice") and ideology as the realm of false consciousness or imaginary misrecognition. But he has never gone along with any version of that facile postmodernist wisdom which holds such talk to be hopelessly *passé,* just a product of the old "Enlightenment" ethos whose appeal to various categorical distinctions—truth falsehood, knowledge/belief, theory/ideology, etc.—has now been revealed as nothing more than a piece of self-serving bogus rhetoric. The upshot of this and previous variations on the end-of-ideology theme has always been to undermine any kind of argued oppositional critique by making out that consensus ideas and values go all the way down; that there is no getting outside the goldfish bowl (or "hermeneutic circle") of received opinion; and hence that we might as well give up on the effort—especially the self-deluding Marxist effort—to attain some critical perspective beyond what is currently and contingently "good in the way of belief."

Postmodernism is simply the latest name for this line of all-purpose conformist ideology whose uses have tended to become most apparent at times of widespread political retreat among thinkers of an erstwhile left or left-liberal persuasion. And nowhere are the signs more plainly to be read than in the current "post-Marxist" revisionist trend, which claims to have thought its way through and beyond all the categories of old-style *Ideologiekritik*. The result, as Eagleton wryly observes, is an odd situation where "radical" theorists are scrambling to vacate the moral and epistemological high ground, while on every hand we witness a spectacular resurgence of ideologies ranging from Christian and Islamic fundamentalism to George Bush's vaunted "New World Order," the rise of various nationalist or militant separatist movements, and, nearer home, "the most ideologically aggressive and explicit regime of living political memory, in a society which traditionally prefers its ruling values to remain implicit and oblique." When things have reached this point, he suggests, it is time to revisit some of the old arguments and see what is at stake in the postmodern turn against theory and all its works.

In this latest book Eagleton has two main purposes in view. One is to clear away some longstanding sources of confusion by examining the various senses that have attached to the term "ideology," from its Enlightenment origins to its complicated history in the recent (post-Althusserian) context of debate. The other—following directly from this—is to show how postmodernists, neopragmatists, and others have exploited those same confusions so as to make it appear that any talk of "ideology" is hooked on a hopelessly naive set of doctrines about knowledge, reality, and truth. This two-pronged approach enables him to cut through swathes of fashionable nonsense, from the notion (as propounded way back by Hindess and Hirst) that the real is entirely a product of this or that discourse, language-game, or "signifying practice," to the antics of a postmodern guru like Baudrillard, one for whom truth-talk is the merest of illusions since we now inhabit a world of free-floating signifiers, simulacra, or signs without referents, where "reality" is whatever we make of it according to the latest (no matter how distorted) consensus view. Then again, there is the line of supposedly knock-down neopragmatist argument—"travelling anti-theory" as it might be called—espoused by philosophers like Richard Rorty and a whole current school of literary critics, most prominent among them Stanley Fish. These thinkers claim to demonstrate the sheer *impossibility* of advancing any truth-claims save those that make sense by the lights of some existing "interpretive community," some in-place set of conventional beliefs impervious to any form of reasoned or principled critique.

To all of which Eagleton responds with a mixture of strong counter-argument on philosophic grounds and straightforward appeal to the social and political realities postmodernism so blithely brushes aside. Thus: "the thesis that objects are entirely internal to the discourses which constitute them raises the thorny problem of how we could ever judge that a discourse had constructed its object validly . . . How can anyone, on this theory, ever be wrong?" And with reference to later, more *à la mode* versions of the same ultra-relativist creed: "no individual life, not even Jean Baudrillard's, can survive entirely bereft of meaning, and any society which took this nihilistic road would be nurturing massive social disruption." What Eagleton's book brings out with particular force is the extent to which postmodernism and kindred discourse-oriented doctrines trade on a drastically simplified conception of language, one that takes over Saussure's synchronic-descriptive methodology—including its indifference to the referential aspect of the sign—but which raises that purely heuristic precept into a high point of anti-realist dogma with dire theoretical and political consequences. Along with this goes a widespread confusion—as remarked by realist opponents like Roy Bhaskar—between ontological and epistemological issues. Hence the patently absurd idea that since reality is always construed under a certain description, that is to say, in accordance with some pre-given set of linguistic or intra-discursive categories, *therefore* we might as well junk the belief in a real world of material objects, processes, and events that exist quite apart from our current (wholly "arbitrary") modes of conceptualization. And from here it is a short enough step to that point of extreme cognitive skepticism whose upshot—as with Baudrillard—is an attitude of last-ditch moral and political retreat.

Eagleton makes short work of such claims, together with the end-of-ideology thesis that they are commonly assumed to entail. For they will only seem convincing if one takes it as read that reality just is what we are given to make of it according to the dominant consensus view, or—in Rorty's neopragmatist parlance—what is currently and contingently "good in the way of belief." Otherwise this whole line of argument will appear nothing more than a handy escape route, a means of embracing conformist ideas and values while neatly avoiding such old-fashioned topics as the "political responsibility of the intellectuals." It is not only postmodernists who are travelling this road, as Eagleton reminds us in some sharply diagnostic pages devoted to those *soi-disant* "post-Marxist" thinkers (Laclau and Mouffe among them) who have set about recasting the political agenda through a process that reduces everything to the level of "discourses," "subject-positions," "enunciative modalities" and so forth. The obvious rejoinder, Eagleton writes,

> is that a practice may well be organized like a discourse, but as a matter of fact it is a practice rather than a discourse. It is needlessly obfuscating and homogenizing to subsume such things as preaching a sermon and dislodging a pebble from one's left ear under the same rubric. A way of *understanding* an object is simply projected into the object itself, in a familiar idealist move. The contemplative analysis of a practice suddenly reappears as its very essence . . . The category of discourse is inflated to the point where it imperializes the whole world, eliding the distinction between thought and material reality.

One should not be misled by the joky analogies and the throwaway turns of phrase into thinking that this is just a piece of interventionist polemics that sidesteps all the deeper theoretical problems. On the contrary, Eagleton displays a firm grasp of topics outside the charmed circle of postmodernist debate—among them, issues in epistemology, philosophy of language, historiography, sociology of knowledge, etc.—which are pretty much ignored by the end-of-ideology ideologues. Nothing could be further from the narrow-minded orthodoxy that begins with a handful of Saussurian slogans wrenched out of context and ends up endorsing a crudely literalized version of Derrida's cryptic statement, "there is nothing outside the text." Small wonder that Eagleton's writing should often take on a polemical tone, especially when engaging with thinkers like Baudrillard who push these confusions to the point of a full-scale exercise in political and intellectual bad faith.

That his book has received such a barrage of abuse from right-wing reviewers in the daily and weekly press is one sure sign that it raises questions conveniently shelved by other, more accommodating styles of thought. "If a theory of ideology has any use at all," he concludes, "it is in helping to illuminate the processes by which liberation from death-dealing beliefs may be practically effected." Postmodernism requires that we treat such claims as just another showing of the chronic old realist illusion, coupled with a species of quaint left moralism which rests on those same (non-existent) foundations of reality, truth, and critique. Anyone tempted to adopt this line might do well to consider Baudrillard's latest, sublimely fatuous pronouncements on the Gulf War as an instance of postmodern "hyperreality," a war that perhaps never occurred—for all that we can know—since it only took place in the fantasy realm of simulated images, war-game scenarios, hi-tech "saturation" coverage and so forth. One could hardly wish for a clearer illustration of the common postmodernist fallacy, the habit of jumping from a valid *diagnosis* of contemporary social ills to a set of half-baked antirealist doctrines—a wholesale negative ontology—which would treat that condition as a simply *inescapable* aspect of the way we live now. It is among the great merits of Eagleton's book that it yields no ground to these modish variations on a well-worn sophistical theme.

Patricia Craig (review date 27 May 1995)

SOURCE: "The Eternal Rocks Beneath," in *Spectator,* May 27, 1995, pp. 43-4.

[*In the following review, Craig offers positive evaluation of* Heathcliff and the Great Hunger.]

Terry Eagleton's cast of mind is erudite and ingenious, and his ingenuity is nowhere more in evidence than in the opening essay of this collection. *Heathcliff and the Great Hunger* superimposes an allegory of Irishness, in the person of Heathcliff himself, over the narrative of *Wuthering Heights:* this intractable Brontë character, Eagleton says, 'starts out as an image of the famished Irish immigrant, becomes a landless labourer set to work in the Heights, and ends up as a symbol of the constitutional nationalism of the Irish Parliamentary Party'. Before the audacity of this pronouncement can take our breath away—so that's what Emily Brontë had in mind, and we never knew—he goes on to make out quite a good case for this eccentric reading ('The hunger in *Wuthering Heights* is called Heathcliff . . .').

Where the facts don't fit the hypothesis, he simply acknowledges the discrepancy and carries on regardless; pointing it out himself before someone else can do so. For example, he mentions Branwell Brontë's visit to Liverpool in 1845, and surmises that he might have encountered an Irish urchin there and passed on the information to his sister. But Eagleton is making a point about the famine exodus out of Ireland—and as he says himself, the dates don't quite fit. The earliest famine refugees would have arrived in Liverpool in the autumn of that year, about the time when Emily Brontë was beginning her novel. Never mind—the infant Heathcliff is dirty and ragged, and speaks 'a kind of gibberish' which might well be identified as the Irish language. And his relations with the Lintons—if you want to pursue the allegory as far as it will go—could be said to show certain similarities to those of Ireland and England. (Oddly enough, Terry Eagleton makes nothing at all of the Brontës'—or Bruntys'—actual Co. Down origins.)

This is an expanded version of an essay which first appeared in the *Irish Review* in 1992; the additions mostly concern questions of land, politics, the catastrophic famine itself and its benumbing effect on the imagination (to which the dearth of actual famine literature testifies). All these matters are taken up in subsequent chapters of *Heathcliff and the Great Hunger,* ascendancy and hegemony, the difference between the two and the failure of the latter; the Anglo-Irish novel and all its implications; the entanglement of culture and politics and the reasons for their inseparability. It's a practice of Terry Eagleton's to advance his arguments by means of contradiction, paradox, or deadlocked assertion: opposites yoked together for maximum poignancy or ironic effect. Hence we get, 'the difference which props up his [i.e. the colonialist's] power is also what threatens to undo it'; 'the distance which enables true cognition is also what obstructs it' (*pace* Maria Edgeworth); 'Few pursuits were more native to the country than getting out of it.' It's one way to approach the complexities in Irish history (turning schisms into aphorisms), and also to enliven the academic study of literature, which can benefit from the odd touch of bravado. (Not, however, if it entails equating the Anglo-Irish gentry with Count Dracula: this is going too far, even if it's read as a follow-up to the Heathcliff/Ireland fusion.)

Terry Eagleton has engaged in an energetic reading programme—as his footnotes indicate—and much of what he has to say is of absorbing interest. (The odd inaccuracy aside—he doesn't seem to realise, for instance, that the 'Gaelic ballad' is as rare as a Garus turf-cutter on a social visit to the Big House. Gaelic literature comes in many forms, but not often in that particular one.)

One essay pays due—indeed, overdue—homage to the 17th-century philosopher Francis Hutcheson; while another (the one entitled **'The Archaic Avant-Garde'**, in a further instance of illuminating oxymoron) considers—among other things—the activities of feminist-republicans in the early part of the 20th century.

It's not Terry Eagleton's fault if the facts about these which seem most intriguing are also those most suggestive of out-and-out dottiness: Maud Gonne getting Yeats to put his ear to the Donegal ground in search of fairy music, Charlotte Despard opening a teetotal pub called the Despard Arms. He mentions Margaret Cousins, a suffragette of high courage and intelligence—but not her exorbitant aversion to sexual intercourse, which led her to comment, in the autobiography she wrote jointly with her husband, that she could never see a child in the street without being reminded of the 'shocking circumstance' which had brought it into existence. This tells us something about Irish puritanism, which could bear examination along with culture and conflict.

Never mind: there is plenty here to provoke both argument and assent. Eagleton is far from being a revisionist but he does at one point run through a selection of Irish revolutionaries, pointing out an illiberal aspect of each ('Charles Kickham [the Fenian novelist] . . . denounced the Land League as communistic . . . Arthur Griffith was a monarchical anti-Semite . . .'). Still, these are then excused as blind spots in an otherwise more-or-less enlightened agitators' agenda in the run-up to 1916: by no means 'a record to be scorned'.

Such anomalies of outlook, views you don't expect the holder to hold, can actually help to identify the ramifying strands in Irish nationalism, which has nearly as many forms of expression as there is ornamentation in the *Book of Kells*. Eagleton gets to grips with a good many of them, and with Irish literature and its limitations up until about 1920. With his eye ever alert for an unexpected item, he lets us know that Synge's elemental Aran Islands 'had a fishing industry directly linked by large trawlers to the London market' (but he doesn't indicate how much the playwright's narcotic quaintness owes to literal—not just vividly approximate but absolutely literal—translation from the Irish).

Heathcliff and the Great Hunger is resourceful and densely written; so densely, indeed, that the author has found it necessary at intervals to bring in something quirky, a joke or oddity among the historical data, to lighten the tone. Not that the latter is always attuned to merriment. Eagleton at one point reports the view of certain English officials, during the famine, to the effect that it served the Irish right for relying on such an uncouth form of nourishment. A more refined diet might produce more civilised behaviour.

Austen Morgan (review date 16 June 1995)

SOURCE: "Spud Bashing," in *New Statesman and Society,* June 16, 1995, pp. 37, 39.

[*In the following review, Morgan offers unfavorable assessment of* Heathcliff and the Great Hunger.]

Terry Eagleton is a professor of English at Oxford; Roy Foster the professor of Irish history there. Last year, Eagleton launched a violent attack on his colleague, accusing Foster, and Irish historians, of revisionism. There was also a pre-emptive strike against Foster's current project, the biography of W. B. Yeats. Eagleton accused him of raiding literature in a "reductive" manner, "paying only passing attention to the politics and poetics of form".

Now, with *Heathcliff and the Great Hunger,* Eagleton has continued the offensive with his great coat-trailing work on Irish history. At once the application of cultural theory to Ireland, and the insertion of Irish history into literary criticism, this set of essays intersperses slabs of impressionistic analysis of Victorian Ireland with studies of particular writers. The lead chapter, ripped from any context to catch the 150th anniversary of the famine ("a low-level nuclear attack"), is typical Eagletonism.

Heathcliff, he reveals, was an Irish famine victim—ever if Earnshaw's discovery in Liverpool might have been a gypsy or a Creole or something else, and Emily Brontë began *Wuthering Heights* before the potato blight impacted. There is one brief reference to the Brontë family's Irish (not Ulster) origins, and no investigation worth the name.

Some years ago, Eagleton seemed to apologise for all that Marxist cultural theory when he descended to writing literature himself. It could have been a response to 1989. But it's now clear that this was a retreat into identity politics, which has produced the absurdity of a postmodernist at war with himself. In the foreword to his play, *Saint Oscar,* he came out as "one of Irish working-class provenance . . . teaching in the very belly of the beast". Nice work, if you can get it.

In this book, he is an "Irish Catholic". Although he admits to being a "semi-outsider", he bristles at Irish scholars weary of the indulgent posturing of Irish men (and women) abroad. And he can't resist a cheap jibe at Irish historians. While he is still formally at war with postmodernism, he reveals complicity in its social-intellectual base. Every time he has to justify his apologia for violent Irish nationalism, he makes the analogy with women and blacks. Liberalism and pluralism are dispatched, and the historical necessity of fundamentalism espoused.

Revisionism is surely the *essence* of historical endeavour, a sign of intellectual life. A national school of academic history developed in Ireland from the 1930s. By the mid-1960s, it was well on its way to achieving hegemony over the "1916 and all that" Sinn Fein version. Its key text—based on a series of television programmes—is T. W. Moody and F. X. Martin's *Course of Irish History* (1967). During the northern troubles, revisionism came to be pressed as a charge by the likes of Desmond Fennell, Eamon de Valera's representative on earth.

But it took the Field Day company—founded in the hunger strikes of 1980-81 as the cultural wing of the SDLP, while some of its prominent associates were consorting with Sinn Fein—to create the bogey of revisionism. The cultural proponents of nationality imagined an explanation for their political failure: it was all the fault of the historians. Finally, a Savonarola emerged in 1989, in the form of the Cambridge Irish cleric, Brendan Bradshaw. This heresy hunter was determined to re-evangelise Ireland. Irish historians, he warned, were out to deny the famine, Bradshaw being apparently oblivious to F. S. L. Lyons' popular textbook—*Ireland since the Famine* (1971).

This is the moment of Eagleton the oppressed Irish Catholic, packing them in among the dreaming spires. *Heathcliff and the Great Hunger* has been written with Lacan, Althusser and Derrida on the one side, a pile of mainly 19th-century Irish novels on the other, and secondary works of Irish history on the floor. If things were bad when Eagleton knew no Irish history, they are much worse after he has consulted the academic literature.

There are passages where Eagleton, having done no primary research himself, has to accept the conclusion of a community of scholars. But these are overwhelmed by a flood of generalisations, based upon the Manichean opposition of "Ireland" and "Britain"—the idea of burning everything from Britain but her coal. Its likely source is the British left's post-1968 championing of Irish republicanism. The tragic irony of this book, which berates postmodernism for its failure to deploy the concept of class, is Eagleton's failure to get a handle on Irish economic and political development.

It is a truism that cultural theorists do not address culture, but Eagleton does not even survey the literary culture of a given time and place. The Ulster-born Francis Hutcheson—a colonialist if ever there was one!—is approved for his "moral sense" philosophy, and credited with being "a remote precursor of Romantic nationalism". Eagleton then gets into the canon, with Maria Edgeworth and Lady Morgan. There follow Irish Gothic, then Yeats and Joyce. He finishes off with Wilde and Shaw. His insights into these writers, with occasional pointed anecdotes, are lost by the overall thrust of the book: to present Ireland as a unique nation where culture was preeminent, then subject to the horrors of colonialism, to be followed inevitably by the shaking-off of the yoke.

It becomes virtuoso word-play, with ideas continually rubbed together, leaving the impression that Eagleton is unable to deal with unmediated reality. With the collapse of Marxism, irrationalism has taken over. While he gets drawn deeper into the Irish cultural revival (an experience that awaits an historical assessment, despite the worldwide interest in its writers), he moves further away from the reality of 19th-century sectarian division. Self-government was the product of Irish Catholic achievement and the need for separation, but it has been over-shadowed by the failure of nationalism, particularly its violent variety. Separatism as a viable strategy came to an end in the 1960s; the IRA of the past 25 years has no political achievement to its credit.

It is a historical question whether Years should have worried, in "Easter 1916", about whether that play of his (*Cathleen Ni Houlihan*) sent out "certain men the English shot". It was, until recently, a political question whether eminent figures on the British left shared in the moral responsibility for Ulster violence. My interim view is that a Brit-hating IRA did not need metropolitan apologists and that identity merchants like Eagleton—more Irish than the Irish—are symptomatic of a dissonance, but also a tolerance, in English cultural life.

He dedicates his book—a homage to Lady Morgan—to "the wild Irish girl". Whoever this is (and it certainly isn't Mary Robinson), it says a great deal about the man. Gerry Adams likes to have analogies drawn between himself and Nelson Mandela: this is, of course, preposterous. Eagleton, one must assume, is an admirer of that great man as Mandela tries to construct a non-racial South Africa. But, on a reading of *Heathcliff and the Great Hunger,* I can only conclude that his preference—given his enthusiasm for Romanticism—would be for Winnie.

Denis Donoghue (review date 21-28 August 1995)

SOURCE: "I Am Not Heathcliff," in *New Republic,* August 21-28, 1995, pp. 42-5.

[*In the following review, Donoghue provides summary and tempered analysis of* Heathcliff and the Great Hunger.]

"The British don't believe Ireland is real; they just drop their fantasies here." In a wild romance called *Saints and Scholars,* which appeared in 1987, Terry Eagleton ascribed that assertion to James Connolly, one of the leaders of the Easter Rising, 1916. It is also the main idea of Eagleton's new book.

In his very professorial novel, Eagleton developed the conceit that Connolly, Commandant-General of the Irish Volunteers and the Irish Citizen Army, was not executed on May 12, 1916 for his part in the Easter Rising. Instead, he escaped from Dublin and lit out for Connemara. There he took refuge in a cottage which happened to be occupied by the philosopher Wittgenstein and his friend Nikolai Bakhtin, brother of the literary scholar Mikhail Bakhtin. Waiting for reinforcements, Connolly diverted himself from the pain of a gunshot wound by engaging these foreign gentlemen in high discussion of war, symbolism, language, martyrdom and the rhetorical success of failure.

Bakhtin, sodden with drink, says of the soldiers killing one another in France: "If there are bodies in torment there are bodies in ecstasy." Wittgenstein, having remarkably little to say for himself, quotes Walter Benjamin without acknowledgement to the effect that there is no document of civilization that is not at the same time a document of barbarism. More succinctly: "For every cathedral a pit of bones: for every masterpiece, misery." Ireland being Ireland, reinforcements fail to arrive, but a man named Leopold Bloom turns up, freed of his domestic duties in Dublin by the elopement of his wife, Molly, with an aspiring writer named Stephen Dedalus. When a squad of British soldiers descends on the cottage to arrest Connolly. Bloom exhibits his love of humanity by shooting one of them. Chapman by name, in the back. Natives and émigrés are then conveyed to Galway by car. Wittgenstein passes the motoring time, which would have passed anyway, by admonishing himself with some well-chosen sentences deflected from Samuel Beckett: "You must go on. I can't go on, I'll go on." What more is there to say in a country, as Eagleton describes it, driven mad with alien fantasy?

Some passages from *Saints and Scholars,* and also from Eagleton's *The Ideology of the Aesthetic,* turn up again in *Heathcliff and the Great Hunger,* but the context of their appearance is now a more sober discourse. Eagleton has gathered into his new book a number of his essays on Irish literature and society from the eighteenth century to the early twentieth century: roughly, from Swift to Yeats and Joyce. His main themes are: why the Anglo-Irish or Protestant Ascendancy failed to achieve hegemony and settled for the rough stuff of coercion; the moral philosophy of Francis Hutcheson (1694-1746); the relations, such as they have been, between Britain and Ireland; Anglo-Irish fiction; culture and politics from Davis to Joyce; nationalism; and Ireland since the Famine.

But the main point of the book is to claim that James Connolly, a true socialist, knew what the British have been up to all these centuries in Ireland: not grabbing land, guarding their western flank, or making more Empire, but discarding their fantasies. This notion is developed in the book's title and in its first essay. In the fourth chapter of *Wuthering Heights,* old Earnshaw sets off to walk from the Heights to Liverpool. On his return a few days later, he brings back a foundling he has come upon in the city, "a dirty, ragged, black-haired child; big enough both to walk and talk . . . yet, when it was set on its feet, it only stared round, and repeated over and over again some gibberish that nobody could understand." The child is soon called Heathcliff. Eagleton plays with the fancy—it is no more than that, and the chronology is a poor fit, as he acknowledges—that Heathcliff is the abandoned child of an Irish emigrant family, a ferocious waif of Nature who talks the gibberish of the Irish language and grows up to be a nuisance in the Heights and a menace to Thrushcross Grange.

Heathcliff is a force of Nature which the civil society of the Grange can't accommodate and so must try to destroy.

For Eagleton, he becomes an emblem of Ireland, the vehicle and the victim of England's bad dreams:

> Ireland, in this as in other ways, then comes to figure as the monstrous unconscious of the metropolitan society, the secret materialist history of endemically idealist England. It incarnates, for Carlyle, Froude and others, the Tennysonian nightmare of a Nature red in tooth and claw, obdurately resistant to refinement. When the child Heathcliff trespasses on the Grange, the neurasthenically cultivated Lintons set the dogs on him, forced for a moment to expose the veiled violence which helps to prop them up.

I think I know what "materialist" and "idealist" are doing in that remarkably polemical first sentence. Let us suppose that England dumps its fantasies on Ireland so that it can proceed unburdened on its empiricist, imperial way. Eagleton thinks, presumably, that British culture is idealist to the extent that it validates its practices by submitting them to the rule of consciousness. And whatever it cannot convert to consciousness must be nasty matter, to be disposed of in waste ground. Such matter, like the force attributed to the witches in *Macbeth,* cannot be contained within the official rhetoric of British culture. Ireland and *Wuthering Heights,* Eagleton says, are therefore names for the "sickening precariousness" of that formation.

Heathcliff is "a fragment of the Famine," and the later chapters of *Wuthering Heights* show what happened to the survivors of the Great Hunger of 1845-1851:

> Heathcliff . . . is a notoriously split subject: if he goes through the motions of undermining the ruling order from within, his soul remains arrested and fixated in the imaginary relation with Catherine. Indeed he engages in the former kind of activity precisely to avenge himself for the unavailability of the latter. Heathcliff starts out as an image of the famished Irish immigrant, becomes a landless laborer set to work in the Heights, and ends up as a symbol of the constitutional nationalism of the Irish parliamentary party.

No writer is on oath in driving a conceit, but Eagleton should have let this one rest long before coming to the Irish Parliamentary Party. He has evidently forgotten that the Party, torn by the defeat of Parnell, was brushed aside by a new generation of nationalists, and that the new forms of energy culminated, by intent or not, in the Easter Rising and the founding of the Irish Free State. And a good thing, too, in my opinion.

As an allegory of the relation between Ireland and England, the story of Heathcliff and Catherine is interesting to begin with, but daft in the end. Heathcliff is real to himself, but it is the gist of Eagleton's argument that modern Ireland is not real to itself because England, needing Ireland as a place of fantasy, hasn't allowed it to be real. Ireland is fixated, therefore, in an imaginary relation with England: *this* is the source of all our woes and follies. Pursuing this chimera, Eagleton has sustained himself on Fredric Jameson's *The Political Unconscious.* He interprets Jameson's book rather freely, in these terms:

> To grasp the notion of a political unconscious, one would need to imagine that our everyday social practices and relations, with all their implicit violence, longing and anxiety, were all the time weaving a kind of fantastic subtext to themselves in some entirely imaginary place, a kind of invisible verso to the recto of our waking life, as intimate and alien to it as id to ego, in which those familiar social processes are refigured in the light of all that they have abruptly repressed, and so as monstrously distorted images through which the shape of everyday political society is nonetheless dimly discernible.

Not the liveliest of Eagleton's sentences, but the argument is clear enough. Like Jameson, Eagleton thinks he knows what reality is, and also that he can separate it cleanly from fantasy. As a positivist and a Marxist, he defines reality as "our everyday social practices and relations." These do not include myths, religious beliefs and practices, or those acts of imagination which are not socially embedded. Eagleton calls such acts fantasies and throws them into Jameson's trash can. Jameson's argument, too, depends upon an arbitrary distinction between socially authenticated motives and the rest; and this notion is never far from Eagleton's thoughts. He reverts to it when his argument is otherwise idling, or (with more hope of success) when he tries to explain a number of Irish fictions which are commonly known as Protestant Gothic, including Charles Maturin's *Melmoth the Wanderer* (1820), Sheridan Le Fanu's *Uncle Silas* (1864) and Bram Stoker's *Dracula* (1897). They are romances of ruined families, suicides, vampires, decayed houses, graveyards, tales from beyond the tomb. "Protestant Gothic," as Eagleton says, "might be dubbed the political unconscious of Anglo-Irish society, the place where its fears and fantasies most definitively emerge."

Eagleton's understanding of Ireland is a familiar one. Everybody agrees that Ireland is a rural, pre-industrial society that has developed quite differently from Britain. Having little or no natural resources, Ireland has been unable to move into heavy industry. It has not had an Industrial Revolution, apart from a small area surrounding Belfast and the Lagan Valley. As a direct result, according to Eagleton, "Ireland was in general a profoundly conservative society, with only a weak ideology of modernization."

It is a further consequence that Ireland "lacks a mainstream liberal tradition." Liberalism has not flourished there, apparently, because the few cities and large towns in Ireland failed to produce a strong middle class when such a thing was needed and might have worked for a progressive cause. In the eighteenth century, Ireland's Catholic peasants were governed—no, dominated—by a junta of Protestant burghers and landlords who eventually called themselves the Ascendancy. When it appeared, at the end of the century, that Catholics would have to be allowed to vote, their masters banded together in the Protestant interest. A few members of the Ascendancy were decent enough fellows, no doubt, but most of their colleagues were louts on horseback. Edmund Burke denounced the Protestant Ascendancy, in his *Letter to Richard Burke* and *Letter to Sir Hercules Langrishe,* both written in 1792, as a group determined "to keep a dominion over the rest by reducing them to absolute slavery under a military power."

That pleasure didn't end in 1800 when Pitt, the British Prime Minister, bribed the Ascendancy to abolish the short-lived Irish Parliament—Grattan's Parliament, 1782-1800—and enter upon a so-called Union of Great Britain and Ireland. No one could have predicted that British governments in the nineteenth century would gradually undermine the Ascendancy that enforced British interests in Ireland. British administrations started giving some measure of justice to the peasants.

Reluctantly, indeed. When a fungus struck the potato crop in August 1845, the government of Sir Robert Peel did the poor best it could to forestall starvation, but Lord John Russell, Peel's successor, soon gave up the effort as a bad job. Besides, there were influential people in Westminster who thought the Famine a benign act of God to reduce the crazy, fast-breeding Irish to a manageable number. After the Famine, the chastened survivors might be drawn into the secular decorum of Britain. In the later years of the nineteenth century the Ascendancy began to lose its power, not because its members saw the injustice of coercing the Catholics, but because the big landlords and burghers were too feeble to hold on to the dominion they enjoyed. It took many years of famine, emigration, broken promises, and the gradual transfer of land from landlord to tenant, however, before the Ascendancy became the merely picturesque remnant that it is now. A wise mind could have written the script of that decline in advance. The rest is contemporary history.

Eagleton's first concern is the relation, as he divines it, between these social and political conditions and the literature that arose from them. He is a Marxist, and so he thinks of modern literature mainly as the novel, which rather straitens his view of Irish literature. And, as a Marxist, he assumes that the vocation of fiction is to be realistic. He also seems to agree with V. S. Pritchett that the English tradition of fiction "is hardheaded, moralistic, and sociable, vegetating in good sense and a general experience of the world." The realistic novel is possible, according to Eagleton, only when the society to which it refers is settled and relations among the social classes can be understood within a vision of society as a whole. He concedes that realism is often found in collusion with powerful men, but at least it intuits a structure of worldly relations complete enough to constitute a culture.

No such felicity has obtained in Ireland. "Culture demands a material base," Eagleton says, "and a society as impoverished as Ireland was hardly in a position to provide one." As a result, Irish literature features "a gap between consciousness and action," a discrepancy "between rhetoric and reality," "a hiatus between the experience it has to record and the conventions available for articulating it." Realism "aspires to a unity of subject and object, of the psychological and the social, but these in Ireland tend to split into separate genres." Eagleton takes from Benjamin

a reference to the "sickness of tradition," a condition in which "truth and wisdom have decayed but the forms of their transmissibility are preserved." Surprisingly, Eagleton finds this sickness in Joyce's *Dubliners,* "a work which preserves the forms of storytelling but empties them remorselessly of their content." More pervasively in Irish fiction, according to Eagleton, it is a mark of this disjunction that the language used lives at a remove from the world to which it ostensibly refers. Such language brings things into existence, or into a fantasy of existence; it doesn't find stability by referring to a world that it claims already to know and to understand. Hence the desperate eloquence of Irish writing.

This reading of Irish fiction is not entirely new. We find the gist of it in several studies which suppose that the artistic forms used by a client nation imitate those of its master. As in W. J. McCormack's *Ascendancy and Tradition* (1985), which speaks of Irish fiction in the Benjaminian terms of discrepancy and allegory:

> The priority of meaning over experience for Irish writing is one way of observing a tendency towards allegory in certain large areas of nineteenth-century fiction. The same proposition might be stated conversely as the tendency towards abstract experience in this colonial fiction, a tendency we shall trace in some work by Maria Edgeworth, Sheridan Le Fanu, and Charles Lever.

Eagleton's book examines this discrepancy, if that is what it must be called, over a wide range of Irish fiction. Nearly every modern novelist of any significance is brought under the sway of Eagleton's dominant idea: Edgeworth, Lady Morgan, Maturin, Le Fanu, John and Michael Banim, Gerald Griffin, William Carleton, Lever, Somerville and Ross, Stoker, George Moore and James Stephens. Moore is particularly interesting to Eagleton, since he was an absentee landlord with his eye on London and Paris. He was in Paris when he learned that his tenants in the West of Ireland were striking for a reduction of their rents. The only thing to do was to settle in London and live by his pen; but he kept up an aesthetic relation to an Ireland already being "performed," in Yeats's aesthetic terms. Eagleton's pages on Moore are provocative, but he should have given him credit as one of Joyce's precursors in the short story. There is also a long essay on Wilde as thinker, but Wilde without the plays is not of much interest. Eagleton's references to Shaw, Joyce and Yeats are perfunctory, a serious limitation in the study of Irish literature; but by then the book is coming to an end.

The most arguable part of the book depends on Eagleton's assumptions about realism and the novel. I don't understand why he ignores the fact, which Northrop Frye clarified many years ago, that there are at least four forms of prose fiction. Frye called them novel, romance, confession and anatomy. Each of these is animated by a different sense of life and a corresponding relation to language. *Wuthering Heights,* as a case in point, is a romance, not a novel. Frye wrote of it:

> The conventions of *Wuthering Heights* are linked rather with the tale and the ballad. They seem to have more

affinity with tragedy, and the tragic emotions of passion and fury, which would shatter the balance of tone in Jane Austen, can be safely accommodated here.

English fiction, which includes Jane Austen and George Eliot among its novelists, has Emily Brontë, Scott, and Morris among its romancers. Unwilling to treat the four forms of fiction on equal terms and to cope with their different epistemological and social axioms, Eagleton is forced to keep asking the same question: why does Irish fiction in the nineteenth century feature an equivocal relation to the realism dominant in England and France? He doesn't consider the possibility that Irish fictions might be fulfilling other observances of genre, like the fictions of Swift, Peacock, Hawthorne, Poe, and Melville, which give little credence to realism.

Not that Eagleton blames Irish writers for failing to write *Pride and Prejudice.*

> That the Anglo-Irish novel is only ambiguously realist is no more a failure on its part than the fact that Jacobean tragedy is not Arnold Bennett. A literary tradition which includes such largely non-realist works as Swift's *Gulliver's Travels,* Edgeworth's *Castle Rackrent,* Maturin's *Melmoth the Wanderer,* Sheridan Le Fanu's *Uncle Silas,* Stoker's *Dracula,* and Joyce's *Ulysses* need not be rebuked for lapsing from some Platonic norm of mimesis. On the contrary, it is in its refusal to conform to that paradigm, or its apparent unconsciousness of it, that much of its fascination lies.

But suppose it were not a matter of refusal or of unconsciousness. Suppose it were a matter of choice. Then a different set of questions would arise. Eagleton can't get out of the fixation of thinking that, because Ireland was and still partly is a colony of Britain, its writers live in the predicament of every subaltern literature and are doomed to be victims. He never considers the possibility that Irish writers write as they do because they choose to employ diverse forms of fiction rather than because they are reacting to a realist norm prescribed for them by Britain. Eagleton presents even the most powerful of Irish writers, Swift, Yeats and Joyce, as victims, determined by the colonial mess in which they found themselves entangled.

His comments on Swift are acute, up to the point of their reference to *Gulliver's Travels:*

> Swift reviles the British for reducing the Irish to slaves, then condemns the Irish for internalizing this slavery, which is at once more and less reason for excoriating the British, and excellent reason for loathing oneself. The Gulliver who is caught on the hop between conflicting cultural norms, whose whole existence is a barely tolerable in-betweenness, is then an appropriate figure for an Ascendancy which was both colonized and colonialist.

This is lively stuff, but it denotes a bizarre reading of *Gulliver's Travels,* a book that seems to me to have far more to do with Hobbes and Locke than with the Ascendancy.

Even Yeats is construed as a writer desperately writing himself out of a predicament enforced by Britain:

Yeats fashions his images and then claims to have stumbled across them in the immanent structure of the real. He is forever conjuring from the world with one hand what he has just slipped into it with the other, to the point where in "The Fisherman" he can address an entire poem to one of his own images, treating the mind-created as an autonomous object. The faith that reality is a construct of the mind, which allows a sinking Ascendancy to assert a last edge over a history which flouts them, is not entirely at one with the equally ideological enterprise of giving authority to your myths by projecting them into the world. It is the difference between subjective and objective idealism, and Yeats draws on either epistemological strategy as it suits him.

Yeats's fisherman is not an autonomous object. He is a type of person, persuasively drawn into place and time by Yeats's references to "grey Connemara cloth," local landscape and the accoutrements of rod and line. Yeats does not suppose, in this poem, that reality is a construct of the mind. On the larger issue, it is quite wrong to think that Yeats identified himself so completely with the Ascendancy that its decline and fall compelled his styles.

And Joyce, too, is presented as a victim of British culture:

> The wealth of his language is an implicit satire of the seedy world it records; but it also graces and dignifies that world, in democratic defiance of the Coole Park idealism which would belittle it. Joyce thus buys his opposition to that idealism at the price of a naturalism which implies that no radical change is really possible, that everything is a recycled, intertextual version of something else, and so undercuts Yeatsian apocalypse and the fantasies of the radical right at the risk of a serene celebration of the given or a mild Bloomian reformism. The limits of his textual politics are thus the limits of a naturalistic aesthetics.

Really? When I read *The Dead,* the trip to Cork and the Christmas dinner scenes in *A Portrait of the Artist as a Young Man,* and the scene of Paddy Dignam's funeral in *Ulysses,* I find it hard to worry about the limits of Joyce's textual politics.

I am becoming quarrelsome, as if Eagleton's book were only an application of standard Marxism to Irish fiction. Every now and again Eagleton breaks out in a rash of such tendentiousness, but more often in this book he takes his Marxism lightly. There are the usual quotations from Gramsci, Benjamin and Raymond Williams, but Eagleton isn't singing the same old song. This is not altogether surprising. It would be hard to bring a strict Marxist analysis to bear on Irish culture, a formation in most respects archaic, deliberately unmodern, rural at heart as well as on principle. No mines, no factories, no proletariat to which a revolutionary role could plausibly be assigned.

If Benjamin is right in saying that history is always recited in favor of the people who have won and that there has never been a history of the defeated, the winners in the long run of Irish history are the latecomers, middle-class Catholics who aspired to jobs in an Irish Civil Service and Irish professions. No wonder Marxism has always been a bit of a sport in Ireland. The working man's hero Jim Larkin had his day in the Dublin strike of 1913, but when that ended the initiative passed to Padraic Pearse, Catholic teacher and poet, not to Eagleton's beloved socialist Connolly. The Easter Rising was a Catholic, middle-class affair. Pearse, according to Yeats, summoned the mythical Cuchulain to his side in the General Post Office. Maybe he did; but he also saw himself on a cross beside Christ.

For a secular Englishman of positivist bias, Eagleton is remarkably well-disposed to Ireland. He thinks the Irish Free State turned out to be a poor, conservative thing, but he speaks warmly of the nationalism that brought it about. Nationalism, he says with still another glance at Benjamin, "is a politics of the aura in an age of mechanical reproduction." Eagleton's sympathetic commentary on Ireland and on Irish nationalism is, to begin with, a family sentiment. His grandparents emigrated from Ireland to Britain and his mother was born in the Irish community of Bacup, a small mill-town in Lancashire. But his attitude to modern Ireland is also explained by his contempt for the Protestant Ascendancy and the successive British governments its members claimed to support. He notes that "Irish nationalism has been on the whole more remarkable for its ecumenism than its sectarian zeal:"

> From Tone's "common name of Irishman" to early Sinn Fein's Davisite notion of a comprehensive nation, most nationalist trends, including the Irish Republican Brotherhood, were at pains to rally to their banners the non-Catholic and non-Gael, however notionally or perfunctorily . . . Padraic Pearse saw fit to rebuke the Ancient Order of Hibernians for excluding Protestants from their ranks.

It is good to have this on record.

Heathcliff and the Great Hunger is in the nationalist tradition of Irish writing. It indicts Britain for centuries of neglect, condescension, and folly. Nothing new in that: we have been hearing such charges since John Mitchel's *History of Ireland* appeared in 1869. But Eagleton's book raises these issues at an awkward time, when many commentators on Irish history and culture are settling for a spiritless form of revisionism. It is understandable that, after twenty-seven years of violence in Northern Ireland, many historians wish to be released from the whole story of Irish nationalism, Fenianism, Catholic-and-Protestant, and drums under the window. But it is a vain endeavor. I wish the present "peace process" every success, but in the meantime I continue to think that the partition of Ireland was wretched in principle and abominable in its practice. I don't regard the cause of Irish unity as worth a drop of anyone's blood, so I deplore the military and paramilitary actions which have taken place in Northern Ireland. I have little hope of seeing Ireland united in peace, but I dearly wish I might, and I would pray for it if I thought prayer would help.

Nicholas Daly (review date Winter 1996)

SOURCE: "Reading Irish Culture," in *Novel: A Forum on Fiction*, Vol. 29, No. 2, Winter, 1996, pp. 248-49.

[*In the following review, Daly offers positive assessment of* Heathcliff and the Great Hunger.]

In his "Introduction" to *The Ideology of the Aesthetic* (1990), Terry Eagleton mentions that he had originally conceived of that work "as a kind of doubled text, in which an account of European aesthetic theory would be coupled at every point to a consideration of the literary culture of Ireland." The daunting potential size of such a work led to his decision to "reserve [it] either for a patented board game, in which players would be awarded points for producing the most fanciful possible connections between European philosophers and Irish writers, or for some future study." Regretfully, the board game has never appeared, but *Heathcliff and the Great Hunger* would appear to be that "future study." The essays range from the title piece, an interesting attempt to read *Wuthering Heights* in the context of the Irish famine of the 1840s, to an appreciation of the 18th-century Irish philosopher, Francis Hutcheson, to a discussion of the traces of Lamarckian thought in the writings of Oscar Wilde and G. B. Shaw. The vestiges of the earlier work are visible in the recurrent attempts to trace the peculiar modalities that the aesthetics of politics and the politics of the aesthetic assume in a colonial culture, though these essays are as much concerned with cultural history as with the history of ideas.

Singer Tom Waits remarks somewhere that "Jesus is always going for the big picture, but he's always there to help us out with the little jams too," and one might say the same about Eagleton's ambitious efforts to provide a sort of map of Irish cultural history from the end of the seventeenth century to the early twentieth century, while also trying to present more detailed accounts of particular figures and particular texts. The comparatively loose structure of the book, both in terms of the way the chapters fit together and the way individual chapters are assembled, turns out to be one of its strengths in this respect. Thus in one of the longer chapters, "Ascendancy and Hegemony," Eagleton provides an excellent account of the difficulties the Anglo-Irish faced in securing hegemony in a country where the spheres of religion and primary education were largely outside their influence, but he also finds time for a more theoretical meditation on the instability of the opposition consent/coercion, a discussion of the cultural significance of the Anglo-Irish Big House, and some astute comments on agrarian secret societies. Similarly, the longest chapter of the book, on the Anglo-Irish novel, couples a meditation on the failure of Ireland to produce a realist novel tradition with a series of extended readings of novels by Maria Edgeworth, Lady Morgan, William Carleton, J. S. Le Fanu and many others; the individual readings sometimes support, sometimes undermine, the more abstract account of the fate of realism in colonial Ireland. At other times, though, this compendiousness can appear clumsy, and even eccentric. For example, chapter 7, "The Archaic Avant-Garde," utilizes Perry Anderson's theory of the roots of modernism to good effect, showing how Ireland's "combined and uneven development" influences the distinctive modernist production of Yeats, Synge and the other revivalists, as well as Irish nationalist discourse. But in the same chapter, Eagleton also finds time to tell us that Charlotte Despard, one of the many women who played an important (and sadly often forgotten) role in the movement for Irish independence, at one point "threw in her lot with the Irish Vegetarian Society, whose president was Mrs. Ham and whose vice-presidents were Mrs. Joynt and Mrs. Hogg" (296). This is funny—very funny, even—but it might have been better to make it an amusing footnote rather than an amusing digression.

This is not to say that humor is a merely decorative feature of Eagleton's work. While the early ***Criticism and Ideology*** (1976) was written with all the high scientific seriousness of structuralism, in recent years, he has made the abrupt transition from theoretical discourse to colloquial humor one of the most engaging traits of his writing. In this respect, Eagleton's prose remains worlds away from the austere and elegant periods of Fredric Jameson, arguably Eagleton's only rival for the title of the Greatest Living Marxist Literary Critic. Where Jameson's long, accumulative sentences demonstrate *in parvo* his desire to totalize, Eagleton uses the short ironic sentence and the farcical example to reveal the contradictions and fissures of ideology. His essay on Francis Hutcheson, for example, is perhaps the most determinedly theoretical of the essays, and would not have been out of place as an extra chapter of ***The Ideology of the Aesthetic,*** but even there Eagleton can bring a light touch to critique. Glossing Hutcheson's equation of moderation with virtue, he comments "vice, then, is immoderacy, and a temperate desire to torture is presumably harmless" (113). At other times, the humor is broader but no less effective. Thus in his reading of Brontë's Heathcliff as a paradoxical figure, both archaic and modern "like the Irish revolution itself" (21), I think we really do see that archaicness the more clearly for being told that "it is hard to imagine Heathcliff doing the dishes or wheeling the pram" (21). Elsewhere, seemingly throwaway comparisons convey real insights, as when he remarks that Wilde "is in all kinds of ways the Irish Roland Barthes" (329).

If Eagleton's prose has little in common with Jameson's, there are nonetheless points of comparison. One of the leitmotifs of ***Heathcliff and the Great Hunger*** is the contention that culture retained a certain autonomy in British culture with respect to the political, allowing for the Arnoldian resolution of political contradictions at another level, but that no such separation existed in colonial Ireland, where all cultural production immediately entered the force-field of the political, and where the apparatus of colonial repression remained too obvious to allow for any ruling class hegemony to take hold properly. This is not in the end so very different from what Jameson says about Ireland in his essay, "Modernism and Imperialism" (1988), where he counterposes the fictional worlds of E. M. Forster and James Joyce, arguing that the development of an imperial global economy shuts the metropolitan Forster off from the possibility of a totalizing vision that remains available to the colonial Joyce. Eagleton in fact cites this

essay, while questioning its findings, but he himself follows a similar binary logic by representing Ireland as a place where the Real (whether as famine, or colonial oppression) intrudes too dramatically for the imaginary solutions of culture to work. One feels at times that Eagleton needs Ireland to appear as the socially transparent double to a putatively opaque England.

For the most part though, ***Heathcliff and the Great Hunger***'s attention to the local and the particular, and its assumption that "paradox, metonymy and oxymoron" are the tropes that link imperial Britain and colonial Ireland help to avoid such over-schematic oppositions. These essays represent an impressive attempt to use Marxist theory to explore cultural production in a specific colonial situation. They are packed with insights: local and historical insights as well as more broadly theoretical ones. One feels almost fully compensated for the loss of that board game.

Andrew R. Cooper (review date March 1996)

SOURCE: A review of *Ideology,* in *Notes and Queries,* Vol. 43, No. 1, March, 1996, pp. 119-21.

[*In the following excerpted review, Cooper offers tempered analysis of* Ideology, *which he contrasts with Leonard Jackson's* The Dematerialisation of Karl Marx.]

Eagleton and [Leonard] Jackson have produced two books that it is tempting to read as symptomatic of the state of Marxist literary theory in the 1990s at a time when 'world Communism has collapsed', (Jackson). Eagleton's anthology of extracts from eighteen writers [***Ideology***] takes its title from the claim that *ideology* is indeed the major concern of twentieth-century Marxist and Post-Marxist theory; for Jackson, on the other hand, Eagleton is classed as a bogeyman of English departments for precisely the reason that he and other 'Althusserians' have shifted attention away from the economic materialism of Marx's original writings, and have thereby 'dematerialised' not only Marx and Engels but the whole study of literature. The prospect of a lively debate between these two antithetical positions is rather dampened by the sense that both representatives have somehow lost their way. It is hard not to read Eagleton's selection of theorists as a mirror of his own development in the last two decades—perhaps an unfair assumption, but one which nevertheless underlines the reader's feeling that the penultimate section of his book [entitled] 'Althusser and After' should have a large question mark. Jackson is clearly concerned to go back to a pre-Althusser period in order to rediscover what Marxism can offer the study of literature; unfortunately, the desire to revitalize the 'pre-cultural materialist' writings of Christopher Caudwell holds the concomitant implication that we need not concern ourselves with works beyond the 'modern' period as defined by *Ulysses*.

To take ***Ideology*** first is immediately to run the risk of positioning oneself in the territory defined by Jackson as the 'discursive idealism' of 'Western Marxism'. It would certainly be true to say that the 'Introduction' to this book gives us Eagleton at his eloquent, mellifluous best. We are gifted twenty pages of highly persuasive monologue, the principal purpose of which is to convince that ideology is 'a matter of *discourse*—of practical communication between historically situated subjects—rather than just of *language*'. In its entirety, this section is an intoxicating brew of the rhetoric and user-friendly phrasing found in Eagleton's work from *Literary Theory: An Introduction* to *The Ideology of the Aesthetic.* The contrast between those texts and the sometimes stolid, sometimes abstruse, accounts of ideology which form the body of this book only serves to emphasize the double-edged nature of Eagleton's status among the undergraduate population of this country's universities as one of the foremost Marxist theorists. Despite his claims that ideology is a neutral term, there is an exclusive emphasis upon the Marxist tradition with no mention at all of how those concerned with race, gender, right-wing politics, or even religious fundamentalism, have approached the subject.

What does become clear from reading these extracts is that any threads or continuities in the early texts (duly stressed by cross-referencing within and between the pieces chosen), begin to become far less certain in the Post-Althusserian period. For instance, the 'science' versus 'ideology' debate is neatly and economically played out for the reader, as are the questions over what constitutes class and consciousness. The extensive use of Lukács fits comfortably into the broaching of questions over legitimation and relativism. Although sometimes overlong, excerpts from Mannheim (providing the historical contextualization required by the absence of a commentary or annotations from Eagleton). Goldmann, Althusser, Hirst, Poulantzas, Rancière, and Barthes (*sic*) provide an insightful and largely accurate representation of the history of the concept of ideology for Marxist thinkers. Any such connections are harder to discern in the collection of extracts found in the final section, 'Modern Debates'. Of course, this is an indication of the diversity of approaches put forward under the umbrella of Marxism by writers such as Williams, Habermas, and Frow. There are, however, some oddities. Whilst Geertz, Mepham, and Gouldner contribute and problematize the use of language-based models, Elster and Geuss serve to do little more here than accentuate the post-Modernist/post-Marxist (post-*The Ideology of the Aesthetic?*) dependency upon psychoanalytical theory to buttress the claims of more recent Marxist commentators.

In *theory,* one should be able to turn to Jackson's book [*The Dematerialisation of Karl Marx*] for an explication of the significance of some, if not all, of the writers chosen by Eagleton. Indeed, the subtitle 'Literature and Marxist Theory' promises much more than this. However, despite the apparent motivation to outline the contribution of Marxist theorists to the interpretation of literary texts, Jackson's book fails to deliver either a coherent and incisive overview, or an alternative approach. . . .

However, neither quips nor the ultimate conclusion that literature is simply 'worth anthropological study', promise much for the student who, party to the confusion over what Marxism can offer in the 1990s, turns to Eagleton or Jackson for advice.

Katie Trumpener (review date March 1997)

SOURCE: A review of *Heathcliff and the Great Hunger,* in *Modern Language Quarterly,* Vol. 58, No. 1, March, 1997, pp. 114-18.

[*In the following review, Trumpener offers positive assessment of* Heathcliff and the Great Hunger *and comments on the book's critical reception.*]

Over the last twenty years groundbreaking books by British, Irish, and American academics have shaped a new field of Irish literary and cultural studies. A series of monographic studies in the tradition of Daniel Corkery's *Synge and Anglo Irish Literature* (1931) have used the oeuvres and careers of particular authors to show how Ireland's social conditions and political tensions molded Anglo-Irish consciousness and literature, from Swift's counter-Augustan aesthetic to a peculiarly Anglo-Irish mode of gothic.[1] And a series of ambitious historical overviews, essay collections, and anthologies have explored the status of Ireland as an exemplary or prototypical British colony, the continuities and discontinuities of Anglo-Irish culture, and the shifting relationship between English-language and Gaelic literatures.[2] Terry Eagleton's latest book builds on this stimulating body of work and moves the discussion to a new level of analytic sophistication.

In overlapping essays on Irish political, cultural, and literary history, *Heathcliff and the Great Hunger* ranges from the Irish subtext of Emily Brontë's *Wuthering Heights,* radical Enlightenment philosopher Francis Hutcheson, the developmental history of the nineteenth-century Anglo-Irish novel, and the contrasts offered by the careers of Oscar Wilde and George Bernard Shaw to the more general problem of hegemony, the ideology of "ascendancy" in the colonial situation of Ireland, and the peculiar development of an avant-garde aesthetic under "archaic" social and political conditions. Eagleton moves, then, between exemplary readings of individual figures, works, genres, and broad historical or theoretical issues, between the illumination of specific formal structures, specific historical phenomena, and a speculative attempt to develop new models of domination and cultural self-understanding out of the particularities of the Irish case. The alternation produces a book of peculiarly uneven texture, which serves, in part, to illustrate one of Eagleton's principal themes, the unsettling effects of uneven development on literary form, as on political consciousness and culture. While the argument is by now familiar (at least in its broad contours).[3] Eagleton mounts a detailed and compelling account of its local consequences and suggestively sketches its broadest theoretical implications.

He is largely successful in sidestepping the main danger of this kind of argument, that by emphasizing the uneven and contradictory development of Ireland, the Irish novel, and the Irish avant-garde, one reinforces the notion of an (unproblematic) English or British standard from which Ireland, as ever, deviates. Instead, Eagleton conveys both the rich vitality and the troubled dividedness of Irish cultural forms, showing us why these apparently opposed characteristics are functions of one another. In his magisterial chapter on the Irish novel, in "Ascendancy and Hegemony," and in "Culture and Politics," in particular, the discrete pieces of the argument are brought together in a dialectical dance, evoking the dynamic Eagleton ascribes to (Anglo-) Irish culture as a whole. He narrates the history of the Irish novel, for instance, both by drawing a series of sketches (invariably deft, evocative, and illuminating) of individual novelists, their oeuvres, and their careers and by drawing attention to the larger patterns of continuity, alternation, and contradiction that this series, *as* a series, makes visible; one of the finest (and most comprehensive) overviews of the Irish novel to date, the chapter has the explanatory power of Lukács's best work. The essay on hegemony and Irish history has an even more obvious dialectical structure, as it moves from the attempt to describe the structure of hegemony in the abstract (drawing equally on Freudian and Lacanian psychoanalysis and on Gramscian and Althusserian theories of ideology) to examine the emergence and recurrent contradictions of ascendancy ideology over the course of postconquest history and finally, in an apparent about-face, to tackle the problem all over again from the other side, by examining the history of nationalist resistance. "Culture and Politics" returns to the coherence and contradictions of Irish nationalist movements, describing the history of a particular political struggle in relationship to larger questions of *mentalité,* cultural practices, and artistic forms; the piece is at once historical meditation and theoretical meditation on the reconcilability of psychoanalysis, ethnography, historiography, and literary scholarship as modes of cultural description.

Heathcliff and the Great Hunger's own integration of political, economic, and literary history is exemplary. Nonetheless, the book may well not attract the number or kinds of readers it deserves. Like Eagleton's previous books, it seems addressed to the intelligent novice, yet it presupposes considerable background knowledge. Some readers, furthermore, will be disoriented by its odd mixture of dense local argumentation and loose overall structure; several chapters, including the title essay, suffer from argumentative drift. (It might have been a better, or at least a more accessible, book at half the length, if the individual case studies had been integrated into the more comprehensive chapters or left out altogether.) Although some readers may be stimulated by Eagleton's attempts to translate between Irish and other European cultural histories or theoretical vernaculars, some will be seriously

irritated, with partial justification. When Eagleton provocatively presents the Irish bard as a "cultural *Gauleiter*" (230), Daniel Corkery as "the Irish Zhdanov" (231), or Oscar Wilde as "the Irish Roland Barthes" (329), just what is he trying to accomplish, and who, exactly, will such acts of translation help? At moments Eagleton seems to address an audience, educated solely under the poststructuralist dispensation and now trying to move from "theory" into historicism, for whom Barthes and Lacan are fixed points of reference but Wilde and Shaw are not. Such readers may well be part of Eagleton's usual audience, but with so few preexisting historical coordinates, how are they to process so detailed and dense a historical analysis?

Eagleton has long been Britain's most visible (and most controversial) Marxist literary and cultural critic and, for a generation of Anglo-American students of literature, one of the primary defenders, purveyors, and explicators of literary and social theory: his previous books include synthetic introductions to Walter Benjamin, to early-twentieth-century central European Marxist aesthetic debates, to theories of ideology and the public sphere from Althusser and to Habermas, to "literary theory" as an emerging academic field, and most recently to German idealist philosophy. These books often draw on works from the canon of English literature (the Brontës, George Eliot, Hardy) or describe turning points in the history of English literary culture (the coffeehouse culture that grew up around the *Spectator;* the advent of novelistic realism) to illustrate their theoretical arguments and to exemplify the possibilities (and difficulties) of reading literature as a social force. Yet such analysis has never been very sustained. In its extensive attention to the literary and cultural history of Ireland, then, *Heathcliff and the Great Hunger* represents a departure for Eagleton, in most respects a highly successful one; it may be his best book to date. Characteristically, however, it too seems to have grown out of a study whose real emphasis was theoretical. As Eagleton writes in the introduction to his last book, *The Ideology of the Aesthetic,* he originally intended to illustrate his account of the history of German philosophy with selected excursuses about Irish literature, only to realize that the "doubled text" would be too complicated and confusing for most readers; the Irish material deserved a venue of its own.[4] *Heathcliff and the Great Hunger* does present Eagleton's arguments about Ireland in more organic form, yet the traces of its piecemeal composition remain, and the reader may still be perplexed.

The uncomprehending reviews of this book in the mainstream press, and the reviewers' often nasty attacks on Eagleton's Marxism and on his advocacy of high theory, however, have a different animus: anger over a view of Irish history that deviates from that of the British government (indeed, as Eagleton himself stresses, from revisionist and relativizing tendencies in recent Irish historiography) and over the growing influence of the colonialism model in discussions of Ireland. Denis Donoghue, writing in the *New Republic,* accuses Eagleton of stressing the social embedding of culture at the expense of "myths, religious beliefs and practices," all simply thrown into "Jameson's trash can."[5] Yet Eagleton's "Culture and Politics" carefully unpacks the theoretical problems involved in calibrating a lived culture and its records, developing a Bakhtinian account precisely of the way myths, beliefs, and practices, along with social pressures and contradictions, are transmuted into literary form. The *Economist,* reviewing the book under the caption "Irish History: Academic Blarney," not only denounces Eagleton's view of Irish history but criticizes his use of jargon and impugns his scholarship: his "show of erudition is sustained by confidence that the reader cannot possibly have read, or dream of reading, everything the writer writes about."[6] In fact, Eagleton's genuinely erudite book demonstrates an unusually thorough and nuanced grasp of Ireland's literary, cultural, and political history and explicates key problems in Irish cultural historiography with remarkable lucidity. ***Heathcliff and the Great Hunger*** should be of real interest to all scholars of Ireland and of post-Enlightenment Britain, indeed to anyone interested in the conjunctions of history, ideology, and culture. If Eagleton's book has occasioned public polemics against the recent direction of Irish studies, it also conveys the forcefulness and importance of this new work.

Notes

1. Corkery, *Synge and Anglo-Irish Literature* (1931; rpt. New York: Russell and Russell, 1965). See W. J. McCormack, *Sheridan LeFanu and Victorian Ireland* (Oxford: Clarendon, 1980); Carole Fabricant, *Swift's Landscape* (Baltimore, Md.: Johns Hopkins University Press, 1982); and David Lloyd, *Nationalism and Minor Literature: James Clarence Mangan and the Emergence of Irish Cultural Nationalism* (Berkeley: University of California Press, 1987).

2. See, for instance, John Hutchison, *The Dynamics of Cultural Nationalism: The Gaelic Revival and the Creation of the Irish Nation State* (London: Allen and Unwin, 1987); David Cairns and Shaun Richards, *Writing Ireland: Colonialism, Nationalism, and Culture* (Manchester: Manchester University Press, 1988); David Lloyd, *Anomalous States: Irish Writing and the Post-Colonial Moment* (Durham, N.G.: Duke University Press, 1993); Brendan Bradshaw, Andrew Hadfield, and Willy Maley, eds., *Representing Ireland: Literature and the Origins of Conflict, 1534-1660* (Cambridge: Cambridge University Press, 1993); Christopher Morash, *Writing the Irish Famine* (Oxford: Clarendon, 1995); W. J. McCormack, *Ascendancy and Tradition in Anglo-Irish Literary History from 1789 to 1939* (Oxford: Clarendon, 1985); Norman Vance, *Irish Literature: A Social History: Tradition, Identity, and Difference* (Oxford: Basil Blackwell, 1990); Seamus Deane, *A Short History of Irish Literature* (London: Hutchinson, 1986); Michelle O'Riordan, *The Gaelic Mind and the Collapse of the Gaelic World* (Cork: Cork University Press, 1990), a return to the issues raised by Daniel Corkery's pioneering *Hidden Ireland: A Study of Gaelic Munster in the Eighteenth Century* (Dublin: Gill, 1925); Thomas Kinsella, trans. and ed., *An Duanaire, 1600-1900: Poems of the Dispossessed* (Mountrath: Dolman, 1981); and Seamus Deane et al., *The Field Day Anthology of Irish Writing,* 3 vols. (Lawrence Hill, Derry: Field Day, 1991).

3. See, for instance, Michael Hechter, *Internal Colonialism: The Celtic Fringe in British National Development, 1536-1966* (Berkeley: University of California Press, 1975); Tom Nairn, *The Break-up of Britain: Crisis and Neo-Nationalism* (London: New Left Books, 1977); and Lloyd, *Anomalous States.*

4. Eagleton, *The Ideology of the Aesthetic* (Oxford: Basil Blackwell, 1990), 11.

5. Donoghue, "I Am Not Heathcliff," *New Republic,* 21-28 August 1995, 42-5.

6. "Irish History: Academic Blarney," *Economist,* 24 June 1995, 83.

Ian Pindar (review date 28 March 1997)

SOURCE: "Tickling the Starving," in *Times Literary Supplement,* March 28, 1997, p. 25.

[*In the following review, Pindar offers unfavorable assessment of* The Illusions of Postmodernism.]

"Speaking as a hierarchical, essentialistic, teleological, metahistorical, universalist humanist, I imagine I have some explaining to do." Terry Eagleton begins and ends his latest book, ***The Illusions of Postmodernism,*** at a disadvantage to which he readily admits. Put at its crudest, postmodernism is in, hip, trendy, sexy. Marxism—or what he now prefers to call socialism—is not.

If his broad-brush approach to one of the most elusive movements of modern times appears unsatisfactory it is as well to remember that his target is not postmodernism proper but "what a particular kind of student today is likely to believe". His own students—"too young to recall a mass radical politics"—have unthinkingly succumbed to a fashionable postmodern "sensibility". It is understandable that a vigorous thinker who has spent most of his career espousing the cause of radical Marxism should feel that it is the time, rather than himself, that is out of joint. This book is less a critique than an exercise in retaliatory caricature. In Eagleton's hands, though, this is a strength, not a weakness, and ***The Illusions of Postmodernism*** makes entertaining reading.

The story goes that postmodernism is the direct result of the Left's "failure of nerve" in 1968. It is odd that a thinker so concerned at his students' "post-political apathy" should also be so scathing about *les événements.* According to Eagleton, 1968 is the precise point in history when the

Left went soft and—to borrow a phrase from his ***Literary Theory***—"the student movement was flushed off the streets and driven underground into discourse". It is all downhill from here. The only moment in recent history when students actively engaged with the State in the name of the working class is vilified as the dawn of a "politically disorientated age". For a writer so enamoured of contradiction, there is a paradox here which seems to have passed him by. The postmodern apoliticism he detests appears to be a direct result of the sort of student radicalism he complains is lacking in the present generation. If you're a young person, you just can't win.

Hovering over his pages is some as yet unrealized "ambitious political project", but he won't tell us what it is. Sometimes he slips into praising the "precious symbolic resources" of "pre-modern" societies, but most of the time he wisely keeps it vague. Like most thinkers on the Left in the present climate, he is keen to start the ball rolling, but anxious not to score own goals. He is reduced to speaking only of "a kind of absolute moral value . . . a telos of a kind", because he knows he is treading on eggshells. Nevertheless, he rarely misses an opportunity to hark back to some ill-defined, bygone "age of political militancy", of "self-risking and extravagant expenditure"; and yet it is arguable that the intellectuals who gave their support to *les événements* were far more "self-risking" than Eagleton has ever been at Oxford. In contrast with a "newfangled postmodernist" like Foucault, for instance, who braved tear-gas and batons on behalf of students, prisoners and immigrants (incurring a fractured rib in the process), the Thomas Warton Professor of English appears to be a rather cuddly, desk-bound radical. This is because the more militant postmodernists were not constrained by a disdainful, quasi-mystical sense that the time is not propitious. By positing some fast-receding future of socialist renewal for which everyone is not quite ready, Eagleton can confidently sit this one out, armed with all the inexorable logic of a Railtrack official that the revolution won't run on time today, due to the wrong sort of *Geist*.

At times, one has the lingering feeling that he has chosen to square up to the wrong adversary. We might agree that "talk of whether the signifier produces the signified or vice versa . . . is not quite what stormed the Winter Palace or brought down the Heath government", but I don't recall Derrida ever claiming that it would. Postmodernism stands accused of subverting everything and transforming nothing. But philosophical inquiry has always had more to do with solipsism than socialism. Philosophers are taking all the flak for the failure of politics itself, and there can be few who seriously believe that this is because our politicians have read too much Baudrillard. Eagleton is shooting the messenger.

One of the pleasures of the book is fitting the names to the parodies. By not naming names, Eagleton can have it all his own way; after all, he is dealing with "the general tenor of postmodern culture . . . in its less astute, more 'popular' form". He can set up an anonymous cultural

relativist and then knock him down by arguing that "it is hard to imagine a situation in which tickling the starving would be preferable to feeding them". This sounds persuasive, but, to my knowledge, there is not a paper in the postmodern canon entitled "Why We Should Tickle the Starving". Nevertheless he should be listened to when he asks what postmodernism has to say about suffering, for instance, or economic exploitation. Eagleton adamantly refuses to "go relativist", and he is rightly concerned that young intellectuals are colluding with "the civilized face of a barbarously uncaring order". He is also right to remind us that some hierarchical notions (that equality is better than inequality, for instance) cannot be blithely deconstructed without complicity. "Perhaps", he suggests provocatively and only half in jest, "Pontius Pilate was the first postmodernist."

He ends on a warning note that a precious postmodernist would not be much use against a fascist invasion; but one would not instinctively knock on Eagleton's door for assistance either. He appears to overlook an important, antifascist strand of postmodernism, which argues for revolution in the interstices, as it were; something akin to Auden's unimportant clerk, who "Writes I DO NOT LIKE MY WORK / On a pink official form". The grand narratives are blind to this private, Kafkaesque resistance to what is offered us, and Eagleton feels he can afford to be snooty about micropolitics because it leaves no record of itself in the history books. It might not storm the Winter Palace, but this is because underlying much postmodernism is the belief that power corrupts. Eagleton does not subscribe to this view, and the sooner the working classes can "usurp the power of capital" the better.

It is to be hoped that Eagleton will not spend the remainder of his days being a thorn in postmodernism's side. As ironic testament to the movement's all-pervading power, he has written a book about postmodernism, not about socialism. His avowed intention in this book is to "embarrass" postmodernists, but how do you embarrass those who have already resolved to live in contradiction without shame?

Colin Mooers (review date October 1997)

SOURCE: "The Illusions of Postmodernism," in *Monthly Review,* Vol. 49, No. 5, October, 1997, pp. 58-61.

[*In the following review, Mooers offers positive assessment of* The Illusions of Postmodernism.]

A grammatically-correct friend explained to me recently that when terms like "Post-Modernism" are written as "Postmodernism" it represents the linguistic equivalent of coming of age. Which, like so many apparently momentous passages in life, may be full of sound and fury, but in the end signify very little. Nevertheless, as Terry Eagleton points out in the preface to this very clever and readable book, "Part of the power of postmodernism is that it exists, whereas how true this is of socialism these days is rather more debateable. *Pace* Hegel, it would seem at present that what is real is irrational, and what is rational is unreal."

The Illusions of Postmodernism sets out to challenge not so much the heavy hitters of the postmodernist canon but the "sensibility of postmodernism" which has seeped down to become part of the intellectual "common sense" of many young (and not-so-young) people, especially if they have come within a stones throw of a university classroom in the past ten years. As Eagleton explains, "Postmodernism is a style of thought which is suspicious of classical notions of truth, reason, identity, and objectivity, of the idea of universal progress or emancipation, of single frameworks, grand narratives or ultimate grounds of explanation. Against these Enlightenment norms, it sees the world as contingent, ungrounded, diverse, unstable, indeterminate, a set of disunified cultures or interpretations which breed a degree of skepticism about the objectivity of truth, history, and norms, the giveness of natures and the coherence of identities."

For the not-so-young adherents of postmodernism, the appeal of this way of viewing things has much to do with the fact that the world has not turned out quite as expected. For many, the youthful political optimism that the world could be set to rights which inspired a generation of radicals thirty years ago, has given way to a kind of "libertarian pessimism," a belief that not much change is possible (or perhaps even desirable) and maybe capitalism isn't so bad after all, especially in its more exotic consumer forms. "Radicals, like everyone else," Eagleton reminds us, "can come to hug their chains, decorate their prison cells, rearrange the deck chairs on the *Titanic* and discover true freedom in dire necessity."

In a satirical first chapter (which first appeared in *MR* July-August 1995 and subsequently in the *MRP* collection *In Defence of History*), Eagleton invites us, using a rhetorical device dear to postmodernists, to imagine a world in which the Left had suffered a crippling political defeat. In such a world one would expect that big ideas like "social totality," "class system," and "mode of production" would become suspect, in part because the only kind of political activity around would seem to be restricted to the cracks and crevices of the system. The grand political projects of yesterday would have given way to an apparently more feasible and sensible "micropolitics." One could visualize a new politics celebrating the fragmentary and the ephemeral aspects of life emerging, or perhaps "a new somatics" in which the body (but definitely not labouring ones) would be seen as the primary site of struggle and resistance. In the realm of knowledge one could imagine the belief taking hold that not much of anything could really be known for sure about the world—which raises the sticky question of how one would know that such a belief was true in the first place. If all scientific and other forms of knowledge had been levelled to the common denomina-

tor of "culture," with no culturally produced "discourse" any better than another, one could equally conceive of many well-intentioned people at a loss to justify why democracy might be preferable, to say, fascism. When political horizons shrink, "rigorous, determinate knowledge is rather less in demand when there seems no question of full-blooded political transformation."

Like all good political satire, Eagleton's actual message isn't very funny at all. The world he depicts is, of course, not fictional but entirely real. It is the depressingly familiar intellectual and political landscape inhabited by much of what is left of the Left. But, as Eagleton is well aware, his thought-experiment raises an important question. For younger adherents of postmodernism, the experience of political defeat has been largely absent: "If postmodernism were nothing but the backwash of political debacle, it would be hard, impressionistically speaking, to account for its often exuberant tone, and impossible to account for any of its positive attributes." Among postmodernism's positive achievements has been to highlight issues of gender, race and ethnicity as well as placing questions of sexuality, desire and identity firmly on the political agenda. Marxism has dealt tolerably well with the first set of issues but less well with the latter. Postmodernism can at least be credited with "an immeasurable deepening of the fleshless, anaemic, tight-lipped politics of an earlier era."

The problem is that it has done so in a haphazard, one-sided and frequently censorious manner. For all its emphasis on the "cultural" and the "material," postmodernism has a skewed conception of both. "One may, by and large, speak of human culture but not human nature, gender but not class, the body but not biology, *jouissance* but not justice, post-colonialism but not the petty bourgeoisie." For example, class is reduced in laundry-list fashion to "classism" alongside racism and sexism, as if it were the result of discriminatory practices directed against people from certain social backgrounds. This confused form of culturalism, as Eagleton observes, "is bound to miss what is peculiar about those forms of oppression which move at the interface of Nature and Culture." Women's oppression and racism have social roots as does class exploitation. But women and people of colour are oppressed as *women* and *people of colour*. In a liberated world there will still be women and people of colour but not proletarians.

Postmodernism's aversion to anything that smacks of "grand narratives" or teleology also prevents it from grasping just how mired we still are in what Eagleton calls "the impossibilities of modernity." Put simply, for well over two hundred years liberal capitalism has been promising "liberty, equality and fraternity" for all but has instead delivered a world in which these ideals are systematically subverted by its own operations. The "liberty" of capitalists to accumulate wealth undermines the freedom of just about everyone else; political equality is subdued and restricted by the overarching powers of capital. It has been the task of socialism to point out these contradictions and to offer a way of overcoming them. It is no excuse for letting capitalism off the hook if what has gone by the name of socialism for most of this century has failed to achieve these ends.

One of the odd things about postmodernism is its remarkable lack of self-awareness about its own place in history. Just when capitalism has entered perhaps its most "totalizing" phase, "history" and "totality" have fallen out of fashion. But, as Eagleton points out, "though we may forget about totality, we may be sure that it will not forget about us." In the current period postmodernism plays a contradictory role, at once aggressively exposing and uncritically celebrating, aspects of capitalism. It is, Eagleton suggests, radical and conservative at the same time, which is true of capitalism too. The logic of the capitalist market is disruptive, wildly transgressive and saturated with desire. Consequently, it is always in danger of dissolving its own moral and ideological foundations. At the same time, it retains a resolute commitment to its own values, ensuring that those who "transgress," for example, rights to property, are duly punished. That is why capitalists are, in one sense, "spontaneous postmodernists"; ideological guardians of the system cannot afford to be. Postmodernism may be compatible with certain aspects of capitalism's current *zeitgeist,* especially its rampant consumerism. But it is hardly a suitable ideology for a system which still depends so deeply on the moral and physical discipline of those whose labour it exploits.

There is one sense, though, in which postmodernism and Marxism share a common set of goals. Both wish for a world in which plurality and difference are respected, in which people are able to choose whatever identity suits them, and where human desires and their gratification can be savoured to the full. The problem is that some postmodernists think that we are already there. Radical postmodernists think it still lies somewhere in the future but have very little to say about how we might get there. This is where "grand narratives" like Marxism come in handy. Marxism may not have a lot to crow about these days, but its method of understanding the world and its moral vision of the kind of society needed to replace the present system, still remains superior to anything on offer from postmodernism. This superb book goes a great distance toward explaining why.

Brenda Maddox (review date 23 July 1999)

SOURCE: "Bogged Down," in *Times Literary Supplement,* July 23, 1999, p. 30.

[*In the following review, Maddox offers unfavorable assessment of* Crazy John and the Bishop.]

This combative book [*Crazy John and the Bishop*] is aimed at unnamed foes. In the small world of Irish Studies, they presumably know who they are. The innocent reader can only guess.

What the enemies are guilty of is less obscure. Terry Eagleton, Warton Professor of English Literature at Oxford, dislikes postmodernism and revisionism applied to Irish culture. He wants the philosophy, poetry and prose written on what he calls "the wrong side of St George's Channel" to be read in the social and historical context of Ireland's religion and education, not in terms of signifiers and postcolonial utterance.

He despises the tweezering out of the great names, such as Joyce, Yeats and Beckett, for world literature, as if the lesser lights of Irish writing were not as important to the national tradition as they are to England's. And he has no patience with the brisk, revisionist, or cock-up, school of historians of Ireland who argue that the Great Famine and the Easter Rising have been romanticized and overwritten. Holding up examples of caring landlords and inefficient revolutionaries is an attempt, he argues, to deprive these events of their symbolic importance in the Irish drive for self-government.

So far, so good. Eagleton directs his gaze at the neglected, the hidden, the underrated or forgotten among Irish writers. He rescues, for example, William Dunkin, the neoclassical Dublin poet and friend of Swift, whom he praises for elegance and wit. Dunkin's "The Art of Gate-Passing or the Murphaeid", written in 1729 as a tribute to the under-porter of Trinity College, exhibits the Irish flair for blending high style and low subject-matter that Eagleton calls a consistent motif from Sterne through Joyce to Flann O'Brien.

In the title essay, he contrasts John Toland (1670-1722), an Irish-speaking shepherd turned European rationalist intellectual, with Bishop William Berkeley, to highlight the Irish conflict between the seen and the unseen. In "Christianity not Mysterious", the free-thinking Toland attacked the language of miracle; he believed that religion must explain itself in clear language; otherwise, it was a tool for manipulating the masses for political ends. The idealist Berkeley, in contrast, defended divine mystery and semantic ambiguity—not because, as Eagleton points out, the Bishop believed that natural objects exist only in the human mind, but rather because the language that describes nature is unreal. Therefore, as Berkeley told his commonplace book, "we Irish men are apt to think something & nothing near neighbours".

In the struggle between the two ways of thought in Ireland, Eagleton declares Berkeley the winner. With a few exceptions like Toland, he maintains, rationalism, in the manner of Descartes and Spinoza, never took root in "this intensely religious, custom-bound society". Irish culture, therefore, entered the nineteenth century with a high regard for feeling, or sensibility, and a great tolerance of a blurred distinction between body and mind.

Eagleton, in one of his many cracks at the postmodernists, mocks their politically correct insistence that assigning similar psychological traits to people who have been shaped by similar conditions of culture and geography is racial stereotyping. He is wise to do so, for where would Irish Studies be without its generalizations on Irish character? Eagleton, for his part, confidently pronounces the Irish, if not more genial than the English, more *congenial*. The social pressures in a rural agrarian society to associate, in pubs, at fairs, markets and wakes create a solidarity, he argues, that led to nationalism. The fellowship of public places also offered a relief from the tyranny of the father. In few societies have the personal and the political been more entwined than in Ireland.

Eagleton's case would be better served if he wrote better himself. Much of his prose is impenetrable; some paragraphs run on for a page and a half, while the antecedents for many "it's" and "this's" can be hard to find. The book will disappoint the audience with a hunger for more in the vein of his essay **Heathcliff and the Great Hunger,** an accessible, informative thesis on the Irish paradox: that the same culture which yielded masterpieces of modernism also produced (until recently) a censorious sectarian nation. But this book of essays gives every sign of not being written for the general reader.

FURTHER READING

Criticism

Alter, Robert. "The Decline and Fall of Literary Criticism." *Commentary* 77, No. 3 (March 1984): 50-6.

> A negative review of *Literary Theory,* which Alter cites as an example of the wayward and irrelevant critical concerns of poststructuralist and Marxist literary theorists.

Lord, Timothy C. "A Paradigm Case of Polemical History: Terry Eagleton's *The Ideology of the Aesthetic.*" *Clio: A Journal of Literature, History, and the Philosophy of History* 22, No. 4 (Summer 1993): 337-56.

> Delineates and analyzes the characteristics of "polemical history" through the example of Eagleton's *The Ideology of the Aesthetic.*

William H. Gass
1924-

(Full name William Howard Gass) American novelist, short story writer, essayist, and critic.

The following entry presents an overview of Gass's career through 1998. For further information on his life and works, see *CLC,* Volumes 1, 2, 8, 11, 15, and 39.

INTRODUCTION

A precise and highly regarded literary stylist, William H. Gass prefers to be known as a "writer of prose" rather than a novelist, short story writer, postmodern theorist, or essayist, as his body of work attests to. Gass is distinguished for his preoccupation with the literary and the philosophical facets of language, particularly his view that a writer should not attempt to represent the world through mimesis, the imitation of nature, but should instead use language to create his or her own imaginary world. For his emphatic insistence on the purely aesthetic significance of the written text, Gass has become known as a literary figure who defies the restrictions of genre. His innovative works, including the novels *Omensetter's Luck* (1966) and *The Tunnel,* (1994), the novella *Willie Masters' Lonesome Wife,* (1971), and several volumes of critical essays, have earned Gass a reputation as a brilliant and imaginative literary experimenter.

BIOGRAPHICAL INFORMATION

Born in Fargo, North Dakota, early on Gass moved with his family to Warren, Ohio. His Depression-era childhood was complicated by his mother's alcoholism and his father's crippling arthritis. Gass's inability to deal with his family's problems influenced his decision during college to adopt a formalist aesthetic, which afforded him emotional detachment in his writing. Gass studied for a year at Kenyon College in Ohio, then spent a brief period at Ohio Wesleyan University. He entered World War II service in 1943. After the war, Gass returned to Kenyon, where he majored in philosophy and audited classes given by poet John Crowe Ransom. After graduating from Kenyon, Gass entered Cornell University, where he continued his study of philosophy. A lack of courses on aesthetic theory impelled him to study the philosophy of language. Having studied the theory of metaphor under Max Black, Gass produced a dissertation entitled "A Philosophical Investigation of Metaphor." While at Cornell, Gass was influenced by the philosophy of Ludwig Wittgenstein, particularly his investigations into the language-mind-reality relationship and his conception of philosophy as an activity done for its own sake, divorced from content. Gass was also inspired by the work of Gertrude Stein and began experimenting with the sentence as the basic unit of writing. Gass joined the faculty of the College of Wooster in Ohio in 1950 as an instructor of philosophy and was awarded his Ph.D. from Cornell in 1954. After leaving Wooster, Gass taught at Purdue University until 1969. In 1958 Gass had several stories published by the magazine *Accent,* which also published sections from the novel *Omensetter's Luck.* Gass spent a dozen years writing this novel; at one point the only manuscript copy was stolen, hampering his progress. Though *Omensetter's Luck* was rejected by several publishers, it was eventually printed and established Gass as a significant American literary figure. His next book, *In the Heart of the Heart of the Country* (1968), a collection of five stories, solidified his popularity among critics and academics. In 1969 Gass began teaching at Washington University in St. Louis, where, since 1979, he has held the position of David May Distinguished University Professor in the Humanities. Gass subsequently published several books, including *Fiction and the Figures of Life* (1970), *Willie Masters' Lonesome Wife,* and *On Being Blue* (1975), before finishing his magnum opus, *The Tunnel* in 1994. Known as a slow, careful writer, Gass began *The Tunnel* nearly thirty years before its publication, in the meantime releasing portions in literary journals. *The Tunnel* won both the PEN/Faulkner Award for Fiction and the American Book Award in 1996. Two of his essay collections, *The Habitations of the Word* (1984) and *Finding a Form* (1996), have won the National Book Critics Circle award for criticism. Gass won the National Institute for Arts and Letters prize for literature in 1975.

MAJOR WORKS

In both his experimental fiction and critical essays, Gass evinces his preoccupation with the importance of the word over content and form over plot. The novel *Omensetter's Luck,* for example, is divided into different sections and incorporates several narrative styles and the use of experimental techniques to subvert the conventions of realism. The protagonist, Brackett Omensetter, displays, like Adam before the Fall, a naturalness and lack of self-consciousness. Arriving with his family in a small Ohio town in the 1890s, Omensetter stands in direct contrast with the town's preacher, Jethro Furber, who is obsessed with death and sex. Furber, believing that Man's Fall necessitates a separation from nature, views Omensetter's lack of a sense of guilt as a personal threat. Isolated from other individuals, Furber attempts to find refuge in the rhetoric offered by his own mind. Despite the book's emphasis on language over narrative conventions, however, a dramatic conflict does exist between Omensetter and Furber, demonstrating a tension that exists in Gass's work between the use of language as an end in itself and language as a means to an end. Similar to the depiction of Furber in *Omensetter's Luck,* the story collection *In the Heart of the Heart of the Country* focuses on lonely individuals. These characters retreat into fantasy and reveal their inner selves only through their patterned use of language. The title story considers an isolated narrator who attempts to create an aesthetic unity around his life by organizing descriptions of his town into blocks of prose poems, a process that only isolates him further.

Gass's own aesthetic principles are put forth in *Fiction and the Figures of Life.* Collecting together essays by the author on language, philosophy, and literature, the work argues for the virtues of art. Gass maintains that, as opposed to the functional use of words as signs in everyday language, words in novels are aesthetic signs that serve only an aesthetic design. The novelist, in turn, should not be concerned primarily with providing an accurate portrayal of the world; instead, according to Gass, the novelist should create his own aesthetic world based on language. In *Willie Masters' Lonesome Wife,* Gass illustrated his belief that words in literature are not just vehicles with which to view the world, but are aesthetic

objects in themselves. This "essay-novella," as Gass termed it, calls attention to the physical aspects of language through its use of variously colored and textured paper, photographs, and its experiments with typefaces. The virtually plotless book presents sections that correspond to the stages of sexual intercourse that the narrator, Baby Babs Masters, is having with her lover. In so doing, the book invites readers to respond to the sensuousness of language. The extended essay *On Being Blue* continues Gass's exploration of the complex manner in which words relate to the world. Gass looks at the many meanings of the word "blue" and the attributes of "blueness." While the essay collection *The Habitations of the Word* further delineates Gass's defense of art as a state not governed by moral conventions, a more personal argument for the autonomy of language in fiction is presented in *Finding a Form. The Tunnel*, Gass's long-awaited masterwork, eschews morality for the sake of art in unusually discomfiting terms. The novel centers upon the reprehensible narrator William Kohler, a history professor who has almost completed his own magnum opus, called *Guilt and Innocence in Hitler's Germany,* a sympathetic treatment of the Third Reich. Instead of writing the remaining introduction, Kohler begins to dig a tunnel out of his basement, the act of digging carrying him further from finishing his book. Gass's insistence on the insignificance of plot in fiction finds its representation in Kohler's futile tunnel project. Much of the novel involves Kohler's reminiscences about his family, his Nazi sympathizing former professor in Germany, Kohler's debates with department colleagues, and his perceptions of his personal life. As *The Tunnel*'s narrator makes correlations between his domestic life and the Holocaust, an event normally viewed as having such extreme moral implications that it prohibits comparisons to other circumstances, the novel reiterates Gass's stance that words in fiction are removed from moral responsibility.

CRITICAL RECEPTION

Critics and scholars have praised Gass for his technical accomplishments, his discerning insight into how words are used and perceived, and his deft handling of words to create a remarkable array of inventive metaphors. Upon its publication, *Omensetter's Luck* was recognized as a startling achievement for its combination of trenchant thought and physical language. The work prompted comparisons with literary formalists James Joyce and William Faulkner, and the Symbolists in light of Gass's pursuit of technique for its own sake. However, for his relentless efforts to discredit and break free from conventional narrative forms, Gass is often referred to as a postmodern writer and grouped with contemporaries Donald Barthelme, Robert Coover, John Barth, and Thomas Pynchon. Gass's critical essays on the primacy of language and the written word, particularly in *The Habitations of the Word* and *Finding a Form,* are highly regarded. Commentators note that in *On Being Blue* Gass effectively combines philosophy and imaginative speculation to create a text that blurs the definition of the discursive essay. Critics immediately hailed *The Tunnel* as an important accomplishment, though many reviewers acknowledged that additional time would be required to study and adequately assess the complicated work's significance. While Gass's rejection of such conventions as character, plot, and realism has been seen as a desire to separate the novel from a smothering emphasis on moralizing, some critics have expressed impatience with his writing. Noting that not everyone is as dissatisfied as Gass with fiction's attempts at realism, such critics contend that Gass's word associations do not compensate for the elimination of conventional structure and that he has substituted literary gimmicks for characters. Nevertheless, Gass's imaginative and indefatigable defense of the aesthetic value of language within fiction has accorded him a unique status and critical renown among twentieth-century American writers.

PRINCIPAL WORKS

Omensetter's Luck (novel) 1966
In the Heart of the Heart of the Country (short stories) 1968
Fiction and the Figures of Life (essays) 1970
Willie Masters' Lonesome Wife (novella) 1971
On Being Blue (essay) 1975
The World Within the Word (essays) 1978
The First Winter of My Married Life (short story) 1979
The Habitations of the Word: Essays (essays) 1984
Words about the Nature of Things (nonfiction) 1985
A Temple of Texts (nonfiction) 1990
The Tunnel (novel) 1994
Finding a Form (essays) 1996
Cartesian Sonata and Other Novellas (novellas) 1998
Reading Rilke: Reflections on the Problems of Translation (criticism) 1999

*First published in *TriQuarterly* magazine, 1968.

CRITICISM

Richard J. Schneider (review date Winter 1979-1980)

SOURCE: A review of *The World Within the Word*, in *Modern Fiction Studies*, Vol. 25, No. 4, Winter, 1979-1980, pp. 757-58.

[*In the following favorable review of* The World Within the Word, *Schneider discusses Gass's critical views on literature.*]

Following close on the heels of John Gardner's *On Moral Fiction*, William Gass's second collection of essays seems almost a counter-attack. To Gardner's call for fiction of moral concern, Gass replies that "Poetry [which for Gass usually includes fiction and essays] is not a kind of communication, but a construction in consciousness." On the thread of this premise, Gass strings essays about an impressively eclectic range of topics, including suicide, psychology, philosophy, mathematics, and linguistics as well as literature.

Gass begins by stripping the reader of two widespread misconceptions about what "poetry" is. In several essays on death and suicide, Gass reminds us that literature is not the cathartic escape from life, either for the writer or the reader, that most readers take it to be. Using Hart Crane, Malcolm Lowry, and his own mother as examples, he insists that although suicide may be an escape from life, literature certainly is not. Though an artist may refuse to face the challenge of his own life, he cannot refuse the challenge of his art's form: "Poetry is cathartic only for the unserious, for in front of the rush of expressive need stands the barrier of form." Writing is harder than living: "Writing. Not writing. Twin terrors. Putting one's mother into words. . . . It may have been easier to put her in her grave." The second misconception Gass attempts to destroy is that literature imitates life. For him life and art are irreconcilably separate. In discussions of Faulkner, Stein, Colette, Proust, Valéry, Sartre, Nabokov, Freud, and Henry Miller, he emphasizes that all of these writers forged in their writing the order they failed to find in their lives. "Faulkner's life," for instance, "was nothing until it found its way into Faulkner's language. Faulkner's language was largely unintrigued by Faulkner's life." Such writers write not to communicate ideas to their readers but to create themselves and their worlds through language.

Having attacked at length these misconceptions about the writer and his art, Gass concludes with three essays which explain his own concept of the function of language in literature. In the best of the three, **"Carrots, Noses, Snow, Rose, Roses,"** he theorizes about language while making a case for short fiction as the most significant genre in contemporary literature. Novelists, he complains, no longer recognize "the vast difference between the literary use of language and any other," and our poets "have embraced carelessness like a cocotte." He likes essayists who, like him, "experiment with the interplay of genres," but he admires most such writers of short fiction as Nabokov, Borges, Beckett, and Barth for "their esthetic exploitation of language, . . . their depth of commitment, to their medium, . . . their range of conceptual understanding, . . . [and] the purity of their closed forms." For these writers, as for Gass himself, a word is like the carrot we use to make a snowman's nose: "the carrot does not simply stand for or resemble a nose, *it literally is a nose now*" (Gass's emphases). Words are things in themselves, not merely imitations of things. They create a world which need not be related to the moral systems of our own world.

Poetry is not communication? Art is harder than life? Words create their own worlds? Though not new, these continue to be difficult ideas to swallow for those who view literature as a moral vehicle. Of course, probably neither Gardner's moral view nor Gass's formalist view of literature is wholly right. Just as Gardner's fiction reveals his love for the texture of words, Gass's own beautifully crafted sentences in his essays and fiction are often filled with deep moral concern about the unfulfilled potential of our lives. Gass's ideas are becoming increasingly convincing and increasingly important, however, in light of our society's increasing carelessness about language. Whether or not we agree with his premises, we must thank him for patiently insisting that we re-examine the potential of language and literature in the hope of reducing "the number of dunderheads reading Balzac the way they would skim *Business Week.*"

Charles Caramello (essay date 1983)

SOURCE: "Fleshing Out *Willie Masters' Lonesome Wife,*" in *Silverless Mirrors: Book, Self, and Postmodern American Fiction,* Tallahassee, FL: University Presses of Florida, 1983, pp. 97-111.

[*In the following essay, Caramello examines Gass's postmodern ambivalence toward authority, textuality, and the deconstruction of reality in* Willie Masters' Lonesome Wife.]

> If dreams are made of imagination, I'm not afraid of my own creation.
>
> Rodgers and Hart, "Isn't It Romantic?"
>
> But though he had breathed heavily, groaned as if ecstatic, what he'd really felt throughout was an odd detachment, as though someone else were Master.
>
> John Barth, "Lost in the Funhouse"

William H. Gass calls a brief encounter with Wittgenstein "the most important intellectual experience of my life";[1] he is acidic on the topic of Sartrean *engagement* in literature;[2] he describes himself as "very much a Valérian";[3] and he consistently argues that art "teaches nothing. It simply shows us what beauty, perfection, sensuality, and meaning are" (*Fiction and the Figures of Life,* 274). The title of his collection of stories, *In the Heart of the Heart of the Country,* implies a position: there is no heart at the center of fiction; there is only language, the phrase "the heart." The title of his second collection of essays, *The World Within the Word,* neatly encoding both an aesthetics and a metaphysics, expresses a position: language contains a world, language seeks to contain the world that contains it.

The epistemic shift that Derrida associates with "the end of the book and the beginning of writing" and that Roland Barthes designates as that "from work to text"—the shift we have considered at length—bears directly on the issues raised by Gass's fiction. Derrida, we recall, speaks of the cultural categories of "a good and a bad writing: the good and natural is the divine inscription in the heart and the soul; the perverse and artful is technique, exiled in the ex-teriority of the body." Predicated on a metaphysics of presence and authority—on the idea of the Book—the dichotomy collapses once one acknowledges the decentered play of "writing."[4] William Gass would seem to have acknowledged this play. But if we can consider Barthes's "work" and "Text" as analogous to Derrida's "book" and "writing"—recalling Barthes's use of "work" to refer to the concept of literature as that which is produced by a discrete authorial presence and "Text" to refer to the concept of literature as that which is produced largely in its reception, that which is cut loose in the intertext, that which participates in the phenomenon that he describes as "the death of the author," that in which there is "no other origin than language itself, language which ceaselessly calls into question all origins"[5]—then we might have to place Gass on the side of book, work, and authority.

Indeed, Gass's work reveals a deep ambivalence on this matter of textuality and authority, the ambivalence that obtains throughout postmodern American fiction. His brief novella, *Willie Masters' Lonesome Wife,* published over a decade ago, both represents and manifests this ambivalence.[6]

I

It is appropriate that the first line of the preface to Gass's first collection of essays, *Fiction and the Figures of Life,* refers to Valéry, for Gass avows himself among the most formalistic of contemporary American writers.[7] We might note, very briefly, that for Valéry poetry is to prose as dancing is to walking;[8] that poetry "stimulates us to reconstruct it identically" (72); that a poem should reveal "an intimate union between the word and the mind" (74); that "a poem is really a kind of machine for producing the poetic state of mind by means of words" (79). While ordinary spoken language is transparent and autodestructive—"*Its task is fulfilled when each sentence has been completely abolished, annulled, and replaced by the meaning*"—"poetic language must preserve itself, through itself, and remain the same, *not to be altered by the act of intelligence that finds or gives it a meaning*" (171). The poet himself "is no longer the disheveled madman," but "a cool scientist, almost an algebraist, in the service of a subtle dreamer" (315). The poet must dream, that is, but he must also transform this dream into "an artificial and ideal order by means of a material of vulgar origin" (192): common language. The poet must, moreover, be as precise as possible, for the inherent multivalence of poetic language predisposes it to violation, allows the reader to "corrupt" or "disfigure" its meaning (204). The extreme of interpretation—to reduce a poem to its prose statement, "*to make of a poem a matter for instruction or examinations*"—is "no slight matter of heresy," but "a real perversion" (98).

Gass, too, has been a consistent defender of poetry as a special discourse; he argues that words undergo "ontological transformations" when shifted from common language to contextualized poetic forms.[9] He feels likewise, however, about prose literature; he argues that "there are no descriptions in fiction, there are only constructions"; that "the lines of the novelist . . . are not likely interpretations of anything, but are the thing itself"; that "there are no events but words in fiction" (*Fiction and the Figures of Life,* 17, 18, 30). He maintains that "the novelist, if he is any good, will keep us kindly imprisoned in his language" (*Fiction and the Figures of Life,* 8) and that the reader should "feel the way he feels when he listens to music—when he listens properly, that is."[10] Although Gass wants the reader's "effort of understanding a work," he does not want his or her "creative co-operation" ("P-V," 133). "Anything that the reader is creatively going to be asked to put in," he says, "I'll put in. I don't want him meddling around with my stuff" ("P-V," 147).[11] He opposes "pretentious claims for literature as a source of knowledge" (GI, 33) and believes, generally, that the work is a closed spatial construction with, at best, an indirect relationship to the world. One of Gass's preferred metaphors for fiction is sculpture. Fiction, he writes, is like a statue pointing with "outstretched arm and finger": "Though pointing, the finger bids us stay instead, and we journey slowly back along the tension of the arm. In our hearts we know what actually surrounds the statue. The same surrounds every other work of art: empty space and silence" (*Fiction and the Figures of Life,* 49).

The interior monologue of a woman named Babs, the narrative of *Willie Masters' Lonesome Wife* is printed with widely varied typefaces on pages of varied colors and textures—pages enclosed within front and back cover photographs of a nude female torso. The book presents itself as the sculptured body of a woman, self-contained and self-generated. At the same time, however, this book as woman is obsessed with sexual penetration and claims to want to remain open to it. On the one hand, we have Gass, coupling with his own imagination, creating an interior monologue seamless with its physical vehicle—a perfect union, it would seem, of mind and word, of intelligence and body. From this perspective, Gass remains in control—orchestrating language and graphics—of a purely formalistic fiction. On the other hand, we have the reader faced with a highly discontinuous text, a fiction he or she cannot fulfill, a fiction whose varied designs, colors, and textures, whose metaphoric flights and narrative dislocations, whose elaborate fabric of reference (in just sixty pages: Homer, Dante, Shakespeare, Dryden, Goethe, Tolstoy, Gogol, Lawrence, Hardy, James, Flaubert, Baudelaire, Apollinaire, Stein, Joyce, Beckett, and many others), all resist reading as anything less than writing. From this perspective, author relinquishes his control to the fortuities of the intertext. On the one hand, we have a voyeur's art; on the other hand, we have an appeal for book and reader to couple and to come together. And between clashing conceptions of the writer as master and the reader as lover stands this ambiguous literary text itself: a book as woman that seems to dissociate itself from both Molly Bloom and Anna Livia Plurabelle while clearly dependent on their priority;[12] an erotic text that oscillates between, in Roland Barthes's terms, *plaisir* and *jouissance.*

Willie Masters' Lonesome Wife exemplifies the problematics of the book in postmodernism for two reasons. First, Gass has exploited the physics of the book to flesh out fiction, to make the book a body, to render concrete his aesthetics of an opaque, palpable language. Second, his metaphysics and his erotics of the Book reveal an ambivalence—concentrated in this virtuosic performance—with respect to the positions of author and reader in relation to the literary text. Although the metaphor of sculpture does describe, almost literally, this book that presents itself as the body of a woman, metaphors of performance, which also recur in it, may be, finally, more appropriate. Gass, that is, makes the book perform in the play of textuality, but he also remains authoritarian about the status of the performing selves associated with that play. If we consider the problematics of writer, reader, and book separately, we will see how ambivalent Gass's position is.

The novelist, Gass has written, wants language to be "an utterly receptive woman" (*Fiction and the Figures of Life,* 13); his business is not "to render the world," but "to *make* one, and to make one from the only medium of which he is a master—language" (*Fiction and the Figures of Life,* 24). In *Willie Masters' Lonesome Wife* we read that the penis is "the very instrument and emblem of the imagination" (49), and someone in this theater of voices adds: "Yet I have put my hand upon this body, here, as no man ever has, and I have even felt my pencil stir, grow great with blood. But never has it swollen up in love. It moves in anger, always, against its paper" (51). We also read that the "man of imagination"

> experiences his speech as he does himself when he's most fit, when he is *One*—and moving smoothly as a stream. Imagination is, as Sam [a voice in the text] said, the unifying power, and the acts of the imagination are our most free and natural; they represent us at our best. (51)

The elements of this phallo- and logocentric vision culminate in the work's final lines:

> It's not the languid pissing prose we've got, we need; but poetry, the human muse, full up, erect and on the charge, impetuous and hot and loud and wild like Messalina going to the stews, or those damn rockets streaming headstrong into the stars. (60)

In sum, we find an attitude that Charles Rosen has characterized well with reference, appropriately, to Liszt's *Grande Fantaisie* on themes from Mozart's *Don Giovanni:* "the virtuosity of Liszt's fantasy," Rosen notes, "acts as a symbol of virility and dominance, a displacement of erotic mastery."[13] Gass, in fact, points to such a displacement himself in his titular wordplay: Will he master his lonesome wife?

The title, however, alludes not only to the romantic impulse (Goethe's *Wilheim Meister*) and, perhaps, to an opposed idea of the pure poem (Mallarmé as *le Matre*), but, more important, to Shakespeare.[14] With reference to the Sonnets, Northrop Frye has articulated a crucial element of sexual-textual mastery:

The true father or shaping spirit of the poem is the form of the poem itself, and this form is a manifestation of the universal spirit of poetry, the "onlie begetter" of Shakespeare's sonnets who was not Shakespeare himself, much less that depressing ghost Mr. W. H., but Shakespeare's subject, the master-mistress of his passion. When a poet speaks of the *internal* spirit which shapes the poem, he is apt to drop the traditional appeal to female Muses and think of himself as in a feminine, or at least receptive, relation to some god or lord, whether Apollo, Dionysus, Eros, Christ, or (as in Milton) the Holy Spirit.[15]

The poet, that is, can invert his masculine posture and claim to be mastered by all of poetry as a context and by the things of the world. Gass refers to such an inversion when he writes of D. H. Lawrence: "Yet when Lawrence felt he *could* go unprotected, when he allowed things, landscapes, people, to enter *him* . . . then there was no greater sensualist, no more vital, free, and complete a man, no more loyal and tender a lover" (*Fiction and the Figures of Life*, 220). He also affects its practice in *Willie Masters' Lonesome Wife.* We should recall that a central theme of the book is that the wife's lovers "protect" themselves with condoms; that as she strives for "completion," she complains of her having to "complete" her lovers ("I dream like Madame Bovary. Only I don't die during endings. I never die. They fall asleep on me and shrivel up. I write the *finis* for them, close the covers, shelf the book" [7]); that her principal objection is that her lovers lack "tenderness." The ambiguity with regard to the question of mastery as it pertains to the master-writer, then, also informs the question of completion as it pertains to the lover-reader. As complement to the wordplay on the husband's name (Will he master his lonesome wife?), Gass has a tacit and less subtle wordplay based on the lover's name, Phil Gelvin: Will Phil fulfill her by filling her with Phil?

When Larry McCaffery—in a fine essay called "The Art of Metafiction: William Gass's *Willie Masters' Lonesome Wife*"—identifies "the central metaphor of the whole work: that a parallel exists—or should exist—between a woman and her lover, between the work of art and the artist, between a book and its reader,"[16] he identifies the problem correctly. But in his determination to interpret this work as a "remarkably pure" metafiction, McCaffery effects a reduction of its ambiguity that, in my opinion, causes him to misformulate important implications of this metaphor.

I do not believe that *Willie Masters' Lonesome Wife* finally coincides with McCaffery's reading of it:

> Gass, thus, invites one to enter his work of art—a woman made of words and paper—with the same sort of excitement, participation, and creative energy as one would enter a woman's body in sexual intercourse. . . . Unfortunately, as we discover from Babs, all too frequently those who enter her do so without enthusiasm, often seemingly unaware that she is there at all. ("AM," 25)

McCaffery's reading fails to account for a fundamental ambiguity in this work *as a book*: it is *here*, as a physical object, but, as Gass has elsewhere argued, a book is also *not here;* it is a Platonic idea, separate from its physical manifestation and from its reader who, when similarly abstracted, "is just as far away and metaphysical as the book" (see "P-V," 141-44).

The identity of the wife-book, then, is also internally ambiguous, not only because she-it is "created" by an author and a reader whose statuses are ambiguous, but because her-its status as self-creator is ambiguous. The wife-book appears to be autotelic:

> Departure is my name. I travel, dream. I feel sometimes as if I *were* imagination (that spider goddess and thread-spinning muse)—imagination imagining itself imagine. Then I *am* as it *is,* reflecting on my own revolving, as though a record might take down its turning and in that self-responsive way comprise a song which sings its singing back upon its notes as purely as a mirror, and like a mirror endlessly unimages itself, yet is none the less an image (just as much a woman, gauzy muse and hot-pants goddess quite the same), for all that generosity—for all that giving of itself and flowing constantly away. (7)

(The passage, printed on a page whose opposite mirrors it, is rife with images of reflexivity, mirroring, and turning.) Rendering visually Gass's fiction-as-sculpture metaphor, a photograph of a woman's arm emerges from the binding on the first page after the cover and points to the title *Willie Masters' Lonesome Wife.* This is not Michelangelo's finger of God instilling vitality in Adam— which it visually echoes and which would be consistent with the idea of the author as master—but the finger of the wife creating herself as a self-inspired Eve. She is imagination imagining herself imagine in a masturbatory play that, as Gass has her say, does not require cheap and mimetic pornography or fetish objects to produce pleasure:

> when I am masturbating I—by Christ—call, witch up, conjure images and pictures, visions, fancies, wishes . . . wishes! They're obedient to no one. I have faeries straddle me, and angels, demons, stallions, dogs, as well as women. I will translate, just as Bottom was, my poor homeless lonely finger into anything. (45)

As desiring machine, the wife Gass creates is actually less desirous of her reader, despite her protests, than she is of herself.

And who is this wife, this imagination imagining herself imagine, if not the book as a textual performance? McCaffery goes wrong, I believe, when he identifies her only as "lady language." That identification results from a misreading of this important sentence: "I am that lady language chose to make her playhouse of" (59). The "lady" is not "language"; "language" is also feminine ("her"), but it is not the predicate noun of the "I" of the sentence. "I" and "lady" refer to something *of which* language makes a playhouse: that something appears to be imagination performing itself in a book *as* a "writerly" text. The book is the playhouse of imagination in both senses of the word "playhouse." It is a place for games: a place where the play of language plays (with) itself; and it is a theater: a performance space for the *presumably* interacting performances of writer, book, and reader.

We should recall that Babs, the wife, is not only a "whore" (8, 11, 54), but that she was a stripper (9, 23). She also says, however: "Until my flesh began to lose its grip, I danced in the blue light with the best, and then I married Willie so I could dance the same dance still, the dance I'm dancing now, and not feel lonely" (9). She remains a performer, performing the stripper's dance in language, the dance of the tease, which she must also perform as a sexual performance that defers orgasm. It is not the case, unfortunately, that "in performance, all difficulties disappear" (29). If I can do so with good humor, I would say that McCaffery—as the book shouts at its reader—has "BEEN HAD . . . FROM START TO FINISH" (53). As Willie (the whore) Master, Gass no more invites the reader to enter this woman than she herself extends such an invitation. To her, legitimately, the reader is a "sad sour stew-faced sonofabitch" (53) for whom she has considerable contempt. *Willie Masters' Lonesome Wife* is stripper's art, but what disturbs is not simply its deferral of orgasm; it is that the deferral, the dance, also seems to lack an affirmative joy.

II

In *The Pleasure of the Text,* Roland Barthes writes:

> The pleasure of the text is not the pleasure of the corporeal striptease or of narrative suspense. In these cases [texts of pleasure], there is no tear, no edges: a gradual unveiling: the entire excitation takes refuge in the *hope* of seeing the sexual organ (schoolboy's dream) or in knowing the end of the story (novelistic satisfaction). Paradoxically (since it is mass-consumed), this is a far more intellectual pleasure than the other: [it is] an Oedipal pleasure (to denude, to know, to learn the origin and the end), if it is true that every narrative (every unveiling of the truth) is a staging of the (absent, hidden, or hypostatized) father—which would explain the solidarity of narrative forms, of family structures, and of prohibitions of nudity, all collected in our culture in the myth of Noah's sons covering his nakedness.[17]

What disturbs about *Willie Masters' Lonesome Wife* is that it appears to be striptease within a striptease, revealing the apparatus of revealing—"the staging of an appearance-as-disappearance" (*PT,* 10)—but that it does not, finally, effect this apparent unmaking. For crucial to Barthes's idea of the text as tissue is that it does not veil a truth; it is, rather, a "perpetual interweaving; lost in this tissue—this texture—the subject unmakes himself, like a spider dissolving in the constructive secretions of its web" (*PT,* 64).

The wife as subject is certainly made to unmake herself ("a mirror endlessly unimag[ing] itself") in this fashion, as, more important, *Willie Masters' Lonesome Wife* appears to unmake the reader as subject in terms that Barthes uses to describe the *plaisir-jouissance* overlap:

> Text of pleasure [*plaisir*] the text that contents, fills, grants euphoria; the text that comes from culture and does not break with it, is linked to a *comfortable* practice of reading. Text of bliss [*jouissance*]: the text that imposes a state of loss, the text that discomforts . . . , unsettles the reader's historical, cultural, psychological assumptions, the consistency of his tastes, values, memories, brings to a crisis his relation with language. (*PT,* 14)

Gass's book guarantees such a loss for the reader, who must chase asterisked footnotes several pages ahead of the narrative's body, who must balance multiple narrations on the same page, who is accused of being a foot fetishist for reading the footnotes, and who is told in one particularly nasty note that he (the implied reader of this work is clearly male, a Baudelairean double: "dear brother, lover, fellow reader") is a "bastard" hated with "a niggerish hate," an "ass-plugger" trapped "deep inside me like they say in the songs, fast as a ship in antarctic ice" (19-20).[18] Even the reader who has played the game, who has not been "a literalist at loving," is told "YOU'VE BEEN HAD . . . FROM START TO FINISH" (53). *Willie Masters' Lonesome Wife,* moreover, *sounds* like the "writing aloud" (*l'écriture . . . haute voix*) that Barthes identifies with textual *jouissance:* "we can hear the grain of the throat, the patina of consonants, the voluptuousness of vowels, a whole carnal stereophony: the articulation of the body, of the tongue, not that of meaning, of language" (*PT,* 66-67).

What disturbs is that Gass does not unmake himself as master, does not subvert his own authority (although he does render it ambiguous), and does not disrupt our cultural or sexual assumptions. Without shame, that is, Gass exposes the nudity of the *wife* (on the cover), and he forces *her* to strip beyond her legitimate attack on the male reader to this capitulation: "But let's not quarrel. Though you'll [Phil Gelvin] not be back, your brother will. Tell him he is responsible for me, and that I give as good as I receive. If he will be attentive, thoughtful, warm and kind, I shall be passionate and beautiful" (59). Gass, in short, must force her to capitulate to the male reader's fantasy because that reader, Gass knows from Baudelaire, is *his,* the writer's, double. Even more, Gass forces her to mouth the phallic plea for metaphor at the book's end. Gass does not stage his unveiling as a master, or father, in the text or—since his formalist aesthetics precludes it—through the "Text." He does not reveal Noah's nakedness, allowing the reader the gratifying but traumatic glimpses that Joyce does in the closure-disclosure apparatus of *Finnegans Wake.* But neither does he quite stage an appearance-as-disappearance. He displaces erotic mastery as virtuosity; he makes the woman speak his voice, the voice of the male. What disturbs in this book is its sexual encroachment, its hegemony of the female voice towards ends not altogether pleasant. Chronologically following *Ulysses* and *Finnegans Wake,* Gass's book seems ideologically to lag behind them.

What Gass, again, does not unmake is himself as master: as authority. Important to Barthes's theory of textual-sexual play is his perception of the text as a dismembered body: "the text itself, a diagrammatic and not an imitative structure, can reveal itself in the form of a body, split into fetish objects, into erotic sites" (*PT,* 56). Gass dismembers the wife in this way, but a writer who says in an interview:

> Whenever I find myself working at white heat, I stop until I cool off. I write very slowly, laboriously, without exhilaration, without pleasure, though with a great deal of tension and exasperation. . . .

and who adds:

> I am . . . a Protestant, wholly inner-directed, and concerned only too exclusively with *my* salvation, *my* relation to the beautiful, *my* state of mind, body, soul. . . . The interactions which interest me tend to be interactions between parts of my own being. . . . (GI, 38, 40)

does not seem to have similarly dismembered or dispersed himself.

This protection would be consistent with Gass's aesthetics. He argues that "where language is used as an art it is no longer used merely to communicate. It demands to be treated as a thing, inert and voiceless" (*Fiction and the Figures of Life,* 93); that the writer is the "maker" of a totally self-contained verbal world beyond which "there is literally nothing" (*Fiction and the Figures of Life,* 48); that language is "opaque" (*Fiction and the Figures of Life,* 48); that theories "which think of fiction as a mirror or a window onto life" are "absurd" (*Fiction and the Figures of Life,* 38); that "Relevance is meaningless to [art]. A work of art is made to last as a valuable being in the world. As such it may develop, over time, useful relations to the world; but just as human beings ultimately must find their value in themselves, so works of art must *be relevant by being*" (GI, 40); that, finally, "books are more real than the world, . . . they're more high-powered ontologically" ("P-V," 143). Gass essentially divorces from history both the production and the reception of the text. Although Barthes, for example, explores the disruption of narrative structure and of the physical book in personal and erotic terms, he has also argued that this disruption is politically significant. In an early essay, "Literature and Discontinuity," he writes (with reference to Michel Butor) that "*the Book-as-Object is materially identified with the Book-as-Idea,* the technique of printing with the literary institution, so that to attack the material regularity of the work is to attack the very idea of literature."[19] It is to reject the metaphysics of the Book and its sacrosanct Author, and it is to subvert, in some indirect way, the social institutions that depend upon that metaphysics for their legitimacy. Although Gass clearly practices such disruption, he seems not to obviate but to continue to imbue authority with mystery.

The mystification is linked by Gass and by Barthes, albeit differently, to an erotics of literature. Gass writes, for example:

> The purpose of a literary work is the capture of consciousness, and the consequent creation, in you, of an imagined sensibility, so that while you read you are

that patient pool or cataract of concepts which the author has constructed; and though at first it might seem as if the richness of life had been replaced by something less so—senseless noises, abstract meanings, mere shadows of worldly employment—yet the new self with which fine fiction and good poetry should provide you is as wide as the mind is, and musicked deep with feeling. . . . Because a consciousness electrified by beauty—is that not the aim and emblem and the ending of all finely made love?

Are you afraid?

(*Fiction and the Figures of Life,* 33)

Consciousness as the end of love: we read in *Willie Masters' Lonesome Wife* that "there's no woman who's not, deep inside her, theoretical" (8); and later: "how close, in the end, is a cunt to a concept—we enter both with joy" (59). The most curious and troubling ambiguity of *Willie Masters' Lonesome Wife* is that it embodies woman as book only then to disembody both as pure consciousness. This is the consciousness of Willie Master(bator): ceaseless reverberations between Narcissus and Echo. We can begin to see why Gass also wants to warn of mistaking the word for flesh, of living in fiction "when on our own we scarcely breathe" (*Fiction and the Figures of Life,* 37); why he criticizes Gertrude Stein's work as revealing a "desire to gain by artifice a safety from the world—to find a way of thinking without the risks of feeling" (*Fiction and the Figures of Life,* 89); why he "see[s] no reason to regard literature as a superior source of truth, or even as a reliable source of truth at all" (GI, 33); and why the final injunction of *Willie Masters' Lonesome Wife* is: "YOU HAVE FALLEN INTO ART—RETURN TO LIFE" (60).

Freed from the tics of his nervous prose and the archness of his critical prescriptions—concentrated in this book— Gass's ambivalence compels attention. He seems as reluctant, finally, to accept a metonymical textual play of language that fragments the body into erotic sites as he is to accept a metaphorical presence of language that, as in Norman O. Brown, unifies the mind and body as a sensual whole: "Everything is only a metaphor; there is only poetry."[20] For Gass, the bottom line remains separation: fiction as the vehicle of a metaphor whose subject is the world of the reader (see "P-V," 133).[21] The imagining that is the wife, as McCaffery's reading suggests, seems to be *here,* in the language and in the book:

> No one can imagine—simply—merely; one must imagine within words or paint or metal, communicating genes or multiplying numbers. Imagination is its medium realized. You are your body . . . and the poet is his language (35);

> I'm only a string of noises, after all—nothing more really—an arrangement, a column of air moving up and down (36);

> The usual view is that you see through me, through what I am really—significant sound (48);

> This moon, then, is something like me. For one thing, I'm an image. (56)

This wife, to import a phrase of Susanne Langer with which Gass might agree, is "significant form," a complete image in herself, and separate from the world: the split between "you, the world; and I, the language" (58) continues to gape. "I can't complain," she says. "You're supposed to be lonely—getting fucked" (7).

But complain of separation she constantly must: her lover "even carried his sperm away in a little rubber sack" (54); "he put his penis in a plastic bag" (55); "Thus we never touched, nor would have, though he feared me greatly, when we fucked. Afterward, he carried his seed off safely in a sack" (55-56). Separation is absolute between writer and reader:

> The muddy circle you see just before you and below you represents the ring left on a leaf of the manuscript by my coffee cup. Represents, I say, because, as you must surely realize, this book is many removes from anything I've set pen, hand, or cup to. . . . All contact—merest contact—any contact—is impossible, logically impossible (there's not even a crack between us) (39);

between reader and book:

> As you see, its center's empty [the same circular stain, now inscribed "This is the moon of daylight"], no glow there. And I am lonely. This stupid creature who just now has left me . . . did not, in his address, at any time, construct me. He made nothing, I swear—nothing. Empty I began, and empty I remained (55);

between writer and book:

> When a letter comes, if you will follow me, there is no author fastened to it like the stamp; the words which speak, they are the body of the speaker. It's just the same with me. These words are all I am. Believe me. Pity me. Not even the Dane is any more than that. (58)

When this letter—this woman as letter, as "I"—comes, she must come alone. The four sections of the book may represent stages of sexual excitation, as McCaffery suggests, but these are not stages of intercourse. This is soft-core porn. Unfulfilled by Phil, from whom she is always separated, Babs is left with her own finger—the finger of the statue, of the masturbator—a finger that Gass has allowed her: "But can you imagine any woman thinking: I've Phyllis folded up in my in-between? It's not such a bad idea, though" (13).[22] This is the finger as the penis as the pencil, "moving in anger, always, against its paper."

Melville's "dead letters," separated from origin and end, would seem to have reappeared in American fiction, this time as "French letters," for the brown circular stains in *Willie Masters' Lonesome Wife* are also condom stains.[23] The final one encircles the navel of the (photograph of the) woman's body—a woman who is neither, finally, the navel-less Eve associated with Molly Bloom, nor the omphalos of Anna Livia Plurabelle: a phallic OM as the originary Word made feminine and entered into history. But neither is she their joyful decentering. She is the book that we can open but cannot penetrate (the navel as false vagina): the physical book as the metaphysical Book that we, in fact, cannot enter with joy.

III

The Gass of whom I have been speaking is, in a real sense, as much a persona as a person, as much a construction of quotations as a living writer. And the position of even this "textual" Gass is difficult to state with certainty, for the disposition of voices in *Willie Masters' Lonesome Wife* is complex. Gass speaks as Babs, as Willie's wife, "in a feminine, or at least receptive, relation to some god or lord." But he may also speak "silently," in the composition itself, as Willie. Willie is his double, just as Phil Gelvin is Willie's double, just as the reader is Phil Gelvin's double. "Responsible" for the wife's creation, Gass may be implying through this chain of substitutions that he is also as "responsible" for her loneliness as the reader is.

Gass has criticized Nabokov's novels as being "attacks upon their readers, though not like . . . Baudelaire's, who called his *lecteur* a hypocrite, because he also called him his double, his *frère*" (*Fiction and the Figures of Life,* 116). He has also written that Nabokov's "novels are frequently formless, or when form presides it's mechanical, lacking instinct, desire, feeling, life (nostalgia is the honest bloodstream of his books, their skin his witty and wonderful eye)" (*Fiction and the Figures of Life,* 117). What Gass seems not to admire in Nabokov is the gamesmanship, especially when it is pedantic and when it does not sever itself from a conception of author as Master so much as refract this mastery in elaborate mirrorings. "Even a sentence which fails the demands of the body," Gass writes,

> which calls upon only the deductive faculty, which does not fuse the total self in a single act of sense and thought and feeling, is artistically incomplete, for when the great dancer leaps, he leaves nothing of himself behind, he leaps with, and *into,* all he is, and never merely climbs the air with his feet. Nabokov's novels often . . . seem like those Renaissance designs of flying machines—dreams enclosed in finely drawn lines—which are intended to intrigue, to dazzle, but not to fly.

> Form makes a body of a book, puts all its parts in a system of internal relations so severe, uncompromising, and complete that changes in them anywhere alter everything; it also unties the work from its author and the world, establishing, with them, only external relations, and never borrowing its being from things outside itself. A still umbilicaled book is no more formed than a fetus.

(*Fiction and the Figures of Life,* 118-19)

In his quest for "significant form"—for a self-contained book-body, for an *un*-umbilicaled "wife"—Gass creates a work that is intended to intrigue, to dazzle, *perhaps* to couple and to come with its reader, but *not* to conceive a perpetually open textuality. We might wish to say of Gass what one character in John Rechy's *City of Night* says of another: "And where his heart should be, there is a novel."[24] Nostalgia, however, may also be the honest bloodstream of Gass's book.

Gass's ironic comments on what Derrida might term the cultural rejection of writing as primary often take a curious expression:

> That novels should be made of words, and merely words, is shocking, really. It's as though you had discovered that your wife were made of rubber: the bliss of all those years, the fears . . . from sponge. . . . For the novelist to be at all, in any way, like a mathematician is shocking. It's worse than discovering your privates are plastic.
>
> (*Fiction and the Figures of Life,* 27-28)

We should recall how often penises and breasts appear as balloons in *Willie Masters' Lonesome Wife,* how pivotal the image of the "plastic sack" is, and how Babs positions herself as imagination imagining itself imagine against men who no longer can imagine without outside stimuli: "and so they need some flesh-like copy, some sexy pix and rubber lover, a substitute in plasti-goop or blanket-cloth to keep them safe, to keep them clean of fact and fancy" (7). It is impossible to tell, finally, whether Gass champions textuality as sexuality or whether he seeks the metaphoric speech of love's body: an honest nostalgia.

It is very likely, however, that this dichotomy does not apply; that this nostalgia is the sentimental underbelly of a brilliant but brittle aesthetic surface; that Gass sustains a modernist dream of form, a dream that his ambivalence operates within, disrupts, and begins to subvert. Gass wants to leap, unified, into the dance of art, "leaving nothing of himself behind"; but he also wants to stage himself as a master, as a performing self, in a stripper's dance. The two desires may be incompatible. Gass, as he says of Nabokov, does not so much disappear as withdraw behind multiple refractions.[25] In this, he may participate in what Herbert Blau views, negatively, as a postmodern solipsism:

> The solipsistic self is a tautology—all assertions curving back upon themselves in a kind of metaphysical redundancy. If the self is neither body nor soul but only self, not anything else in the world, it is only a metaphysical subject—it vanishes behind the mirror of thought. . . . It would seem as if in this mirror there is only one future, and that is the future of an illusion.[26]

I would say that in *Willie Masters' Lonesome Wife,* Gass is at the extreme verge of modernist authority as it enters a postmodern funhouse of mirrors—a funhouse from which it may yet emerge in another transformation.

Notes

1. William H. Gass, *Fiction and the Figures of Life* (New York: Random House/Vintage, 1958-71), 248.

2. See, for example, "Theatrical Sartre," *New York Review of Books,* 14 October 1976, 16-24; reprinted as "Sartre on Theater" in *The World Within the Word* (Boston: Nonpareil, 1979), 177-202. In "A Memory of a Master," Gass writes, with reference to Wittgenstein: "How pale seems Sartre's *engagement* against the deep and fiery colors of that purely saintly involvement" (*Fiction and the Figures of Life,* 250).

3. "Pole-Vaulting in Top Hats: A Public Conversation with John Barth, William Gass, and Ishmael Reed,"

introduced by James McKenzie, *Modern Fiction Studies* 22 (1976): 147. Hereafter cited in text as "P-V."

4. See Jacques Derrida, *Of Grammatology,* trans. Gayatri Chakravorty Spivak (Baltimore: Johns Hopkins University Press, 1976), 6-26. The quotation is from p. 17.

5. See Roland Barthes, "From Work to Text" and "The Death of the Author," in *Image-Music-Text,* essays by Barthes selected and trans. by Stephen Heath (New York: Hill and Wang, 1977), 155-64, 142-48. The quotation is from p. 142.

6. *Willie Masters' Lonesome Wife* was originally published as *TriQuarterly* Supplement Number Two (1968) and was reissued in hardcover by Alfred A. Knopf in 1971. Although the reissue does not contain the same front and back cover photographs or the same variations in paginal colors and textures, the graphics and text are identical to those of the original. Both issues give design credit to Lawrence Levy and photography credit to Burton L. Rudman. Both are unpaginated.

References to *Willie Masters' Lonesome Wife* are cited in the text. For the reader's convenience, I am supplying pagination.

7. My remark needs some qualification. In an interview conducted by Thomas LeClair and published in the *Paris Review,* no. 70 (1977): 61-94, Gass says that he had once been a "formalist" but had eventually emerged from his "formal phase": "So now I try to manage two horses: there is one called Valéry and another called Rilke. . . . Intellectually, Valéry is still the person I admire most among artists I admire most; but when it comes to the fashioning of my own work now, I am aiming at a Rilkean kind of celebrational object, thing, *Dinge*" (63). I, too, see the Gass of *Willie Masters' Lonesome Wife* as a Valérian formalist aiming elsewhere, though not necessarily towards Rilke.

8. Paul Valéry, *The Art of Poetry,* trans. Denise Folliot, vol. 7 of the Collected Works of Paul Valéry, Bollingen Series 45 (New York: Pantheon, 1958), 70. Subsequent references cited in text.

9. See, for example, William H. Gass, "Carrots, Noses, Snow, Rose, Roses," *Journal of Philosophy* 73 (1976): 725-39, followed by two replies to Gass, 739-43. See, also, Gass, "The Ontology of the Sentence, or How to Make a World of Words." Both essays appear in *The World Within the Word,* 280-307, 308-338.

10. William Gass, interviewed by Carole Spearin McCauley, in *The New Fiction: Interviews with Innovative American Writers,* ed. Joe David Bellamy (Urbana: University of Illinois Press, 1974), 34-35. Hereafter cited in text as GI.

11. Gass is specifically repudiating Robbe-Grillet's pronouncement: "For, far from neglecting him, the

author today proclaims his absolute need of the reader's cooperation, an active, conscious, *creative* assistance. What he asks of him is no longer to receive ready-made a world completed, full, closed upon itself, but on the contrary to participate in a creation, to invent in his turn the work—and the world—and thus to learn to invent his own life" (*For a New Novel,* trans. Richard Howard [New York: Grove Press, 1965], 156).

12. Echoing Joyce's beautiful closing of the *Wake*'s ALP section, Gass's "wife" says: "You don't go hithering and thithering, do you?" (4). When she says, later, "Screw—they say, screw—what an ideal did any of them ever? It's the lady who wooves and woggles, Nail—bang!—sure—nail is nearer theirs" (10), she may have in mind Joyce's comment that "*Penelope is the clou* of [*Ulysses*]," and the well-known passage describing *Penelope*'s "four cardinal points" that follows (see James Joyce, *Letters,* vol. 1, ed. Stuart Gilbert [New York: Viking, 1957], 170). The photograph that opens *Willie Masters'* text—a woman about to eat an alphabet-block of the letter "S"—visually echoes the stately "S" that opens *Ulysses* and carries the same suggestion of textual circularity.

13. Charles Rosen, "Romantic Documents," *New York Review of Books,* 15 May 1975, 17.

14. In the McCauley interview, Gass says: "The jokes are there—in Goethe, in Shakespeare, etc." (38).

15. Northrop Frye, *Anatomy of Criticism* (New York: Atheneum, 1967), 98. That Gass as metafictionist seems to have focused on the Shakespeare of the Sonnets may be doubly allusive, given Oscar Wilde's superb metafiction, "The Portrait of Mr. W. H."

16. Larry McCaffery, "The Art of Metafiction: William Gass's *Willie Masters' Lonesome Wife,*" *Critique* 18 (1976): 24-25. Hereafter cited in text as "AM."

17. Roland Barthes, *The Pleasure of the Text,* trans. Richard Miller (New York: Hill and Wang, 1975), 10. Hereafter cited in text as *PT.*

18. Cf. Gass's comment in "The Concept of Character in Fiction" that "the writer must not let the reader out; the sculptor must not let the eye fall from the end of his statue's finger; the musician must not let the listener dream. Of course, he will; but let the blame be on himself" (*Fiction and the Figures of Life,* 54). Babs seems to have in mind Cole Porter's "I've Got You Under My Skin."

19. Roland Barthes, "Literature and Discontinuity," in *Critical Essays,* trans. Richard Howard (Evanston: Northwestern University Press, 1972), 173.

20. Norman O. Brown, *Love's Body* (New York: Random House/Vintage, 1966), 266.

21. Gass's theory of metaphor is obviously more complex than this remark suggests. For a recent and fully developed statement of that theory, see his "Representation and The War For Reality," *Salmagundi,* no. 55 (1982): 61-102, followed by two responses to Gass, pp. 103-18.

22. Babs is pondering various names given parts of the body, especially those—Lawrence's "John Thomas," for example—men give their penises. "They ought to name their noses like they named their pricks" (3), she says earlier, introducing the Gogol allusion on which the second part of the novella is centered. Here, clitoral "Phyllis" replaces phallic "Phil."

23. My thanks to Professor Iwao Iwamoto for pointing this out to me.

24. John Rechy, *City of Night* (New York: Grove Press, 1963), 73.

25. Gass speaks of Nabokov as a "godlike contriver" (*Fiction and the Figures of Life,* 116), and writes elsewhere that "if the aesthetic aim of any fiction is the creation of a world, then the writer is creator—he is god—and the relation of the writer to his work represents in ideal form the relation of the fabled Creator to His creation" (*Fiction and the Figures of Life,* 18). To the extent that this god is, for Gass, a disappearing god (see *Fiction and the Figures of Life,* 18-23), Gass shifts toward the position—expressed by John Barth in "Life-Story," another metafictional tale of wives and lovers—that "the old analogy between Author and God, novel and world, can no longer be employed unless deliberately as a false analogy" (*Lost in the Funhouse* [Garden City: Doubleday, 1968], 128).

26. Herbert Blau, *Take Up the Bodies: Theater at the Vanishing Point* (Urbana: University of Illinois Press, 1982), 265.

Charlotte Byrd Hadella (essay date Fall 1988)

SOURCE: "The Winter Wasteland of William Gass's 'In the Heart of the Heart of the Country,'" in *Critique: Studies in Contemporary Fiction,* Vol. XXX, No. 1, Fall, 1988, pp. 49-58.

[*In the following essay, Hadella examines Gass's theoretical perspective, literary allusion, and narrative authority in "In the Heart of the Heart of the Country." According to Hadella, the narrator's "attempt to control his world through language fails because he lacks love, the vital ingredient needed to transform language into art."*]

"Models interfere with the imagination," William Gass insists in response to a question about how or where he gets the material for his fiction.[1] In this same interview, however, Gass confesses: "The only time I ever used a 'model' in writing was when, as a formal device, and to amuse myself, I chose to get the facts about 'B' in **'In the Heart of the Heart of the Country'** exactly right."[2] An important connection exists, I believe, between Gass's theory about the stifling effect of models on the imagination and the fact that he uses a model to create "B" in **"In the Heart of the Heart of the Country."** The narrator in that story, a "teacher, poet, folded lover," constantly seeks models for his work and his life, and these models certainly interfere with his imagination.[3] He shuns human connections and seeks literary ones; he hides behind an image of himself that he has fabricated from literary models: he is W. B. Yeats's aging artist and the etherized patient from T. S. Eliot's "Prufrock"; at various times throughout the narrative, he is Whitman's oratorical singer or Rilke's "poet of the spiritual" (202). Yet this narrator/poet is miserable, lonely, and lost in a fragmented world, much like the world of Eliot's *The Waste Land,* because he fails to participate fully in either art or life.

The reference to Yeats's Byzantium in the opening lines of the story signals that the narrator has left one world and entered another—the world of his own imagination.[4] This first segment of **"In the Heart"** is titled "A Place," and it characterizes the world of the story, "B," as a place that is stagnant and decaying behind a veneer of progress and pleasantness. "B" is "fastened to a field in Indiana," and it "always puts its best side to the highway"; for instance, on one lawn stands a "wood or plastic iron deer," a mock representative of the artifice of Yeats's Byzantium—a substitute for the natural, sensual world that is subject to decay (172). Also in "B", according to the narrator, the lawns are green in spring; but a careful reader will realize that spring never arrives in the story. As Gass leads us into his story, we move away from the best side of town and into an unmistakable wasteland where "gravel dust rises like breath behind the wagons" (173). "A Place" concludes with the narrator's announcement that he is "in retirement from love," an indication that we are, indeed, in an emotional wasteland **"In the Heart of the Heart of the Country"** (173).

With the fragmented structure of his story, Gass conveys a subliminal message of the isolation, loneliness, and departmentalized perception of his narrator. The thirty-six segments offer descriptions of, and/or observations about such varied topics as weather, church, politics, education, business, people, and wires, indicating that the narrator is somehow trying to "measure the whole" in his book of critical essays, *The World Within the Word.* After defining words as "deposits of meaning made almost glacially over ages . . . names for thoughts and things acts and other energies which only passion has command of," Gass refers to T. S. Eliot's coffee spoon metaphor in "The Love Song of J. Alfred Prufrock" to illustrate his definition:

> Prufrock did not measure out his life One/Two, One/Two, but carefully, in coffee spoons, from which the sugar slid, no doubt, like snow, and the beverage circled to their stir as soundlessly as a rolled eye. Morning, noon, evenings, afternoons. There was the polite chink as they came to rest in the saucers—chink chink chink . . . a complete world unfolds from the phrase like an auto map reveals its roads. In metaphor, meanings model one another, wear their clothes. What the poet tries to measure is the whole.[5]

However, Gass's narrator, more like Prufrock the character than Eliot the poet, slips into pools of words that drown his "measurements" in solipsistic emotional paralysis. Because Gass's poet has retired from love, he lacks the passion to command language and his stifling self-consciousness renders him unable to maintain a metaphorical vision.

In the first "Weather" section, Gass introduces the information that the narrator is a writer and that he blames the weather for his mood. Thus, the narrator reports that "it is a rare day, a day to remark on, when the sky lifts and allows the heart up. I am keeping count, and as I write this page, it is eleven days since I have seen the sun" (173). Bruce Bassoff aptly observes in "The Sacrificial World of William Gass," "that the climate of **"In the Heart"** is an objective correlative for the inner state of the narrator."[6] That this inner state is winter, the season of stasis, of withdrawal from life, is in keeping with the wasteland imagery that opens the story of a place whose inhabitants are "lonely and empty" and "barren and loveless" (180). The next "Weather" section (segment 15) emphasizes the ubiquitous grayness of winter—even "speech is gray" (180). This segment also includes a hellish description of summer:

> The heat is pure distraction. Steeped in our fluids, miserable in the folds of our bodies, we can scarcely think of anything but our sticky parts. Hot cyclonic winds and storms of dust criscross the country. . . . (180-81)

Through the narrator's obsessive attention to weather, Gass emphasizes a controlling irony in the story: though the narrator complains about the weather, he is the one who is responsible for the world in which he lives. His complaints suggest that he does not accept this responsibility.

Frederick Busch argues that in **"In the Heart of the Heart of the Country,"** the narrator's world is "the refuge or prison he creates for himself. So we have a man who has fled the world of nature, who has somehow fallen, and who is now trapped (or hiding, or both) in his imagination. This little story is a saga of the mind."[7] Therefore, the present-tense season for "B" is always winter because the narrator's mood is a perpetual winter. The poet/narrator avoids thinking of spring as the season of rebirth and renewal. Thus, even when he does mention spring rain, the rain mentioned is only a memory, and it is not associated with desire or awakening to life; instead, he insists that "in the spring it rains as well, and trees fill with ice" (181).

By the time he narrates the final "Weather" section of the story, Gass's poet has begun to realize the fallacy of blaming the weather for his barren, loveless predicament. He claims: "I would rather it were the weather that was to blame for what I am and what my friends and neighbors are—we who live here in the heart of the country"; but he equivocates in the next sentence with "better the weather, the wind, the pale dying snow . . . the snow—why not the snow?" (191). In the following paragraph, however, the poet again attempts to accept responsibility for his world by stating, "a cold fall rain is blackening the trees or the air is like lilac and full of parachuting seeds. Who cares to live in any season but his own?" (192). But he backs away immediately from the frightful prospect that he has created his own sickness and answers himself; "Still I suspect the secret's in this snow, the secret of our sickness, if we could only diagnose it, for we are all dying like the elms in Urbana" (192). Thus, we are back to winter again in the heart of the country of this story.

Gass's poet, finding himself in a dormant winter state, attempts to gain a new perspective in the section titled "My House" (segment 3) by climbing the high stumps of the headless maple trees behind his house "like a boy to watch the country sail away . . ." (173). Here he has the revelation that "I think then I know why I've come here: to see, and so to go out against new things" (173). But his resolution lasts only as long as he is perched upon his tree stump. By the next "house" section (segment 7), the poet has retreated from his perch; he has moved inside where he faces his inability to create; he seems to have abandoned his resolution to "go out against new things." Here we find that "leaves move in the windows," and the narrator cannot tell us "how beautiful it is, what it means" (175). The next "house" section, "My House, This Place and Body" (segment 13), illustrates the narrator's final retreat from his previous resolution. Here, he explains: "I've fallen as fast as the poet, to the sixth sort of body, this house in B, in Indiana, with its blue gray bewitching windows, holy magical insides. Great thick evergreens protect its entry. And I live *in*" (179). Following this announcement of total withdrawal, Gass reasserts his narrator's connection to the land with "this country takes me over in the way I occupy myself when I am well" (179). But the poet is not well; he has not been able to re-create the "ecstasy on a tree stump," which originally inspired him to "go out against new things" (173).

In fact, he has achieved the reverse of meaningful interaction with humanity or movement toward new knowledge: he now "lives in" and his thoughts are dominated by his past, and particularly his failed love affair. But in spite of his self pity and narrow perception, the poet continues to make metaphors. He calls his love a fiction, "a figure out of Twain" (179); and later, as Busch notes, "the beloved is on a raft with the poet and is simultaneously the river on which they drift. She becomes a metaphor for the Finn-like journey from the real and noxious world."[8] Gass's achievement in this metaphor is twofold: he demonstrates that his narrator still has creative powers, the recuperative powers necessary to deliver himself from his living hell; however, the narrator's creative production is clearly limited by his solipsism, and thus incapable of becoming something new, something separate from its maker: a work of art.[9]

The section that follows "My House, This Place and Body" consists of one paragraph titled "The Same Person"

(segment 14) that intensifies the theme that the narrator's ability to make metaphors cannot save him as long as he lacks love and flees from commitment to his community. In this passage, the narrator encounters Billy Holsclaw at the post office. The details of the segment contribute to Gass's portrait of his narrator as a person who deliberately cuts himself off from humanity. The setting is ironic since the post office itself represents connections with the world outside of the character's immediate sphere—communications, messages sent forth, messages received. And here Billy Holsclaw talks "greedily" to his neighbor "about the weather" (179). The narrator observes: "His [Billy's] head bobs on a wild flood of words, and I take the violence to be a measure of his eagerness for speech" (179-80). But instead of responding to Billy's need for fellowship, the narrator retreats: "I leave him . . . and our encounter drives me sadly home to poetry—where there's no answer" (180).

The two remaining sections that deal specifically with Billy, "That Same Person" (segment 23) and "The First Person" (segment 33) support the interpretation that Gass employs "fluid identifications" for his narrator, and that Billy is one of these identifications.[10] The narrator, therefore, expresses his own desire for stasis when he says about Billy, "Quite selfishly I want him to remain the way he is—counting his sticks and logs, sitting on his sill in the soft early sun—though I'm not sure what his presence means to me . . . or to anyone" (190). Immediately following this passage, the poet reasserts that "Byzantium" desire to become a work of art and thus remove himself from the world of senses and decay. He speculates, "whether, given time, I might someday find a figure in our language which would serve him [Billy] faithfully, and furnish his poverty and loneliness richly out" (190). Here he projects onto Billy that which he desires for himself—immortality through art.

That Gass's narrator shuns Billy because he shuns the natural forces of life is expressed most clearly in "The First Person." The poet confesses that by severing himself from humanity, "I did not restore my house to its youth, but to its age" (202). Though Billy is old, tattered, and almost blind, the narrator says, "I'm inclined to say you [Billy] aren't half the cripple I am, for there is nothing left of me but mouth" (202). But he retracts this metaphor as just "another lie of poetry" before finally declaring: "My organs are all there, though it's there where I fail—at the roots of my experience" (202). Here the poet recognizes that he has the equipment to be human (bodily organs), but that he has cut himself off from the community of human experience, the roots of humanity. Thus Gass articulates in **"In the Heart"** perhaps the most important theme from Eliot, the central question in *The Waste Land:* "What are the roots that clutch?"[11] Eliot suggests that the roots, which keep modern man alive, are the roots of myth, of death, and of rebirth. Christ's sacrifice is part of this continuum, and Christ's message merges in *The Waste Land* with the Vedic order: "Give. Sympathize. Control." When Gass's narrator says that he has failed at the roots of his experience, he is recognizing that his experience has not been human: his love has been a fiction (179), his childhood a lie of poetry (205), and his present existence is a retirement from love (173).

Admittedly unsuccessful at both art and life, the poet/narrator of **"In the Heart"** cannot see that his failure results from his unwillingness to give to either of these processes the central ingredient of both—love. He tries, instead, to substitute order. Beginning the first of three "Politics" sections (segment 8) with the half sentence "for all those not in love," the poet signals that he is actually addressing himself. He proceeds, then, with a brief paragraph about two political figures, Batista and Castro, who have been engaged in a power struggle for control of Cuba. Perhaps because he identifies with Batista, a man who has lost his power, the poet's commentary in "Politics" degenerates into egocentric metaphor with "A squad of Pershing Rifles at the moment, I make myself Right Face: Legislation packs the screw of my intestines. Well, king of the classroom's king of the hill. You used to waddle when you walked because my sperm between your legs was draining to a towel" (175).

Finally, this section turns into a Whitman parody with "I chant, I beg, I command, I sing—" (175). Alluding to the conclusions of the first and second sections of *The Waste Land,* Gass's poet sings:

> Good-bye . . . Good-bye . . . Oh, I shall always wait
> You, Larry, traveler—
> stranger,
> son,
> —my friend—
> my little girl, my poem, my heart, my self, my child-hood. (175-76)

This conflation of the conclusions to "The Burial of the Dead" and "A Game of Chess" suggests that the poet of **"In the Heart"** is trying desperately to unify his own experiences through another writer's consciousness.

But none of his literary models can contain the material that Gass's narrator would like to pour into them, and the attempt at narrative control in "Politics" fails by breaking into a lamentation of personal bewilderment and ineffectiveness. Interrupting the political discussion, and introducing the Whitman parody and the Eliot allusion, the poet whimpers: "I cannot write the poetry of such proposals, the poetry of politics, though sometimes—often—always now—I am in an uneasy place of equal powers which makes a state" (175). The "uneasy place" for the narrator is a zone of his own invention. Caught between the equal powers of life and death, he finds himself in a state of living death. Escape requires change, and change is what this character fears the most. Therefore, instead of venturing forth into the unknown, making new relationships, Gass's narrator tries to enter the world of literature and thus escapes death.

In "Politics" and similar sections containing spliced allusions and frustrated rantings, Gass demonstrates the futil-ity of his character's attempt to find a formula for his feelings or a system of values through literature. As Charles Newman explains Gass's theory of fiction, "it [fiction] is a process of signification which does not unify experiences but is its own experience."[12] According to Gass, truths exist within the world of a piece of fiction that apply to that fiction. When we sever these truths from their fictional universe, we inevitably distort what we have extracted by trying to fit that fragment of fiction into our lives in any meaningful way. The work itself is truth, complete and whole, and the process of reading it is the process of discovering the world of truths within the words. Gass will allow that good works of literature deal with ambiguities that "can be made into an orderly revelation of meaning"; but readers are to measure their lives against that meaning, not extract that meaning to live by.[13] Thus, the poet/narrator of **"In the Heart of the Heart of the Country"** fails to find meaning in his life because he refuses to participate in the process of living.

At times, however, the poet of this story appears to be committed to his quest for physical, spiritual, and emotional restoration. In the fourth "house" section, "My House, My Cat, My Company" (segment 18), he declares resolutely, "I must organize myself," (182) which reveals that he is attempting to exert some kind of control over his life. This control is manifest through language as the poet divides his existence into titled sections that vary in content, structure, and point of view. But his search is characterized generally by directionless commentary that invariably slips away from objective observations or rational discourse into narcissistic whining. As he casts about for topics of discussion, the "folded lover" admits his lack of control:

> My will is like the rosy dustlike light in this room: soft, diffuse, and generally comforting. It lets me do . . . anything . . . nothing. My ears hear what they happen to; I eat what's put before me, my eyes see what blunders into them; my thoughts are not thoughts, they are dreams. I'm empty or I'm full . . . depending; and I cannot choose. (182)

Here, the narrative voice of control discloses itself as a mere pose, the echo of modern consciousness.[14]

When Gass's narrator announces in "My House, My Cat, My Company" (segment 18) that "I am learning to restore myself, my house, my body, by paying court to gardens, cats and running water, and with neighbors keeping company," he seems to have reached beyond himself to make a meaningful human connection (183). He refers to his eighty-five year old neighbor, Mrs. Desmond, as his "right-hand friend" and describes her obsession with loss and death (183). In the next paragraph of this segment, however, the poet reveals that he and Mrs. Desmond do not really communicate, that there is no real relationship between them: "We do not converse. She visits me to talk. My task to murmur. . . . Her talk's a fence—a shade drawn, window fastened, door that's locked. . . ." (184). Thus, in his "listening posture," the narrator retreats to his past, remembers listening to his grandfather talk, compares himself to "badly stacked cards," and recalls his lost love affair in terms of a card game (184). This scene underscores the fact that the only character with whom the narrator even pretends to keep company is a character who, like himself, uses language as a protective fence to bar any real contact with others.[15]

Gass describes his poet as "one person who's having a lot of problems looking at certain things in the town in a certain way"; he adds that his poet, in fact, "is suffering from a lack of perception of the world."[16] Everywhere the narrator looks in "B," he sees himself, his own inadequacies, metaphors for blindness and failure. One of three "Business" sections (segment 22), for instance, focuses on failed enterprises. A particularly vivid image in the section is a torn campaign poster that blocks the windows of a watch repair shop and urges viewers "to vote for half an orange beblazoned man who as a whole one failed two years ago to win at his election" (189). Significantly, this poster blocks the narrator's view of a watch repair shop, a place where broken timing mechanisms can be restored. This image draws attention to the fact that the poet is stuck in time, suffering from a perpetual winter, fearing both life and death.[17]

The very next passage articulates explicitly the narrator's fear of the unknown:

> What do the sightless windows see, I wonder, when the sun throws a passerby against them? Here a stair unfolds toward the street—dark, rickety, and treacherous—and I always feel, as I pass it, that if I just went carefully up and turned the corner at the landing, I would find myself out of the world. But I've never had the courage. (189-90),

The poet himself is the half man on the poster who "failed two years ago to win at his election" (189). Instead of going on with his life, "going out against new things," he clings to his past failures and shuns pathways that lead to unknown experience. In this passage, Gass's poet echoes Prufrock's question: "Do I dare / Disturb the universe?"

By beginning the story with words lifted from Yeats, then relying upon images, patterns, and themes from Eliot, Rilke, Whitman, and others, Gass underlines an important impulse of his narrator's character: he approaches art, as well as life, selfishly, with a limited consciousness that attempts to appropriate words, experiences, and emotions from other sources because his own creative and procreative faculties are paralyzed. In **The World Within the Word,** Gass exhorts readers to "watch out for images which are merely telephonic sums, for explanations which aren't really meant but are, like plastic bosoms and paste gems, only designed to dazzle. We confine ourselves to too few models, and sometimes live in them as if they were, themselves, the world."[18] In the narrator of **"In the Heart,"** Gass creates a character who dramatically cripples himself with explanations only designed to dazzle, a character who confines himself to too few models and lives in those models as if they were the world. His attempt to find his

own poetic voice is obstructed by the clutter of poetic images, phrases, and postures that he borrows from the world of literature and tries to piece together to make his own statement.

That the narrator's own words out of which he models his wasteland world are barriers to his renewal is most evident in the final "house" section, "House, My Breath and Window" (segment 28). In this segment, consisting of one long single paragraph, the narrator explains that his window "is a grave, and all that lies within it's dead" (195). What lies within this death frame is not only the view of the world outside, but also the narrator's reflection that merges with the outside setting by the end of the paragraph. The poet's breath becomes visible on the glass, he says, to "befog its country and bespill myself" (195). In this scene, Gass dramatizes how his narrator's words blur the outside world and drive him in upon himself. The poet speaks to his own reflection here; he becomes his own audience: "Ah, my friend, your face is pale, the weather cloudy: a street has been felled through your chin, bare trees do nothing, houses take root in their rectangles, a steeple stands up in your head. You speak of loving; then give me a kiss. The pane is cold" (196).

The narrator's narcissistic gesture epitomizes the personal limitations that trap him in his cold, static world. The poet cannot find his way out of this wasteland because his vision encompasses only himself. He grasps only a fragment of Eliot's climactic message at the end of *The Waste Land.* He gives to no one; he sympathizes only with himself; and his attempt to control his world through language fails because he lacks love, the vital ingredient needed to transform language into art. At the end of the story, Gass's poet/narrator remains, still, in the wasteland winter of his own imagination.

Notes

1. Joe David Bellamy, *The New Fiction: Interviews With Innovative American Writers* (Chicago: U of P, 1974) 36.

2. Bellamy 36. Surprisingly few critics have tried to explicate the story or to come to a satisfactory understanding of the narrator's character. The most comprehensive study of "In the Heart" is Frederick Busch's article, "But This Is What It Is Like To Live in Hell: William H. Gass's 'In the Heart of the Heart of the Country,'" *Modern Fiction Studies,* 19.1 (Spring 1973) 97-108. Also, Bruce Bassoff includes a brief discussion of the story as part of his article, "The Sacrificial World of William Gass: *In the Heart of the Heart of the Country,"* Critique: Studies in Modern Fiction,* 18.1 (Fall 1976) 36-58.

3. William H. Gass, "In the Heart of the Heart of the Country," *In the Heart of the Heart of the Country and Other Stories* (New York: Harper and Row Publishers, 1968) 175. Subsequent references to the story are cited from this edition and noted by page number in the text of the essay. To distinguish

between sections of the story that have identical titles, and to assist the reader in making sequential connections between story segments, I have numbered the segments of the story and make a note of the number whenever I refer to a section not previously mentioned.

4. Both Busch and Bassoff discuss the implications of Gass's allusions to Yeats's poem.

5. William H. Gass, *The World Within the Word* (New York: Alfred A. Knopf, 1978) 275.

6. Bassoff 47.

7. Busch 100.

8. Busch 102.

9. William Gass, *Fiction and the Figures of Life* (New York: Alfred A. Knopf) 284-85.

10. Bassoff 38.

11. All references to T. S Eliot's poem, *The Waste Land,* are cited from *The Norton Anthology of Modern Poetry,* ed. Richard Ellman and Robert O'Clair (New York: W.W. Norton and Company, 1973) 459-71.

12. Charles Newman, *The Post-Modern Aura: The Act of Fiction in an Age of Inflation* (Evanston: Northwestern UP, 1985) 63-64.

13. "A Colloquy with William H. Gass," *Modern Fiction Studies,* 29.4 (Winter 1983) 608. See also Ned French, "Against the Grain: Theory and Practice in the Work of William H. Gass," *Iowa Review,* 7.1 (Spring 1976) 102.

14. Bassoff introduces his discussion of "In the Heart" by calling the story "a fiction about the relation between poetry and false consciousness."

15. Bassoff 49.

16. "A Colloquy With William H. Gass," 607.

17. Busch 106.

18. *The World Within the Word,* 274.

Kevin J. H. Dettmar (essay date Fall 1991)

SOURCE: "'Yung and Easily Freudened':[1] William Gass's 'The Pedersen Kid,'" in *Review of Contemporary Fiction,* Vol. 11, No. 3, Fall, 1991, pp. 88-101.

[*In the following essay, Dettmar provides analysis of initiation themes, postmodern literary techniques, and psychoanalytic associations in Gass's story "The Pedersen Kid." Dettmar concludes, "Jorge is not just another 'little Oedipus'—rather he's a little Freud, both author and subject of his own case history."*]

> *Hans:* "What I've told you isn't the least true."
>
> *Father:* "How much of it's true?"
>
> "None of it's true; I only told you for fun. . . ."[2]

William Gass's first story, **"The Pedersen Kid,"** is a weird and unsettling piece; but in spite of the menacing atmosphere it evokes, its stylistic daring has to date not been sufficiently appreciated by critics. Larry McCaffery, for instance, contrasts "the early, somewhat realistic methods of **'The Pedersen Kid'**" to the "highly experimental, plotless arrangements of **'In the Heart of the Heart of the Country.'**"[3] **"The Pedersen Kid,"** after all, manipulates a fairly common plot device—McCaffery calls it "an almost classically rendered initiation formula."[4]

While clearly a story of initiation, it is an initiation with a particularly overt Freudian bent—a *Bildungsroman,* or better a *Künstlerroman,* written by a man who knows his Freud.[5] **"The Pedersen Kid"** narrates the coming of age of a young boy—the overcoming of the obstacles to freedom, the creation of a free identity, free from parental determination. Freud famously dubbed this struggle the "family romance"; and the day narrated in **"The Pedersen Kid"** marks the culmination of the Segren/Esbyorn family romance, a day after which nothing will ever be the same for Jorge—and he knows it. "I was on the edge of something wonderful," he writes; "I felt it trembling in me strangely. . . ."[6]

The story opens with a disguised birth scene. The corn crib has spawned a pretender, and the Kid, a changeling, is adopted, carried into Jorge's house, and nursed back to life. An intruder has insinuated himself into the Segren family romance, and Jorge's role has been usurped; as Arthur Saltzman remarks, "the appearance of the Pedersen kid emphasizes for Jorge his peripheral position."[7] The result of this disruption in family dynamics, Freud claims, is always resentment: "The elder child expresses unconcealed hostility towards his rival, which finds vent in unfriendly criticisms of it, in wishes that 'the stork should take it away again,' and occasionally even in small attacks upon the creature lying helpless in the cradle."[8]

A timeless battle is being reenacted, a battle as old as Cain and Abel. When the Kid appears, diverting his Ma's attention, Jorge declares: "I decided I hated the Pedersen kid too, dying in our kitchen while I was away where I couldn't watch, dying just to pleasure Hans" (3). Saltzman comments that "Jorge's immediate reaction to the arrival of the helpless Pedersen kid is one of resentment, for the frozen child commands center stage in a way Jorge, who regularly dodges physical abuse, never has";[9] and the culmination of Jorge's jealousy is his declaration that the Kid is dead. At this critical moment, Jorge creates a fiction to make sense for himself of the scene in the kitchen:

> He was cold all right, and wet. I had my arm behind his back. He sure felt dead. . . .
>
> He felt cold and slimy. He sure was dead. We had a dead body in our kitchen. All the time he'd been dead. When Hans had brought him in, he'd been dead. I couldn't see him breathing. He was awful skinny, sunk between the ribs. We were getting him ready to bake.

Hans was basting him. I had my arm around him, holding him up. He was dead and I had hold of him. (10)

Jorge creates a narrative by which to understand the presence of the cold and slimy body in his arms. His decision that the Kid is dead leads him to assert that "all the time he'd been dead"; not wanting the Kid to have died in his kitchen, or to be linked himself to the Kid's death, Jorge "rewrites" the Kid's demise, displacing the guilt safely outside the Segren house. "He sure *felt* dead. . . . He sure *was* dead"; spurred on by wish fulfillment, Jorge commits an imaginary, daydream homicide, nearly fratricide. Braced by his story, Jorge doggedly asserts the Kid's death to both Big Hans and his Ma, emphatically repeating "He *is* dead. He *is*" (10).

This is an important step for Jorge. To make sense for himself of the disturbing events in the kitchen is of course important, but Jorge will not assume his rightful position in the Segren household until he can articulate himself to those around him. Saltzman writes that in confronting the naked boy on the kitchen table, "Gass's characters are essentially faced with a malleable text, and they all take advantage of their opportunities to exercise subjective interests so as to develop a private understanding. Big Hans, Pa, and Jorge may be viewed at this point as fiction-makers, not just as an audience for the Pedersen kid."[10] A fierce struggle for power is going on through words, battles to recapture and rewrite the past and take control of the present through storytelling, reminiscent of the skirmishes between Spooner and Hirst in Pinter's *No Man's Land*.

A second narrative convention Gass employs in this coming-of-age tale is the story of youth recollected and written in the tranquility of later years. The artistry with which the narrative unfolds is finally Jorge's strongest claim to fame; R. E. Johnson observes that by the time we reach the end of **"The Pedersen Kid,"** we realize that "the 'story' has been Jorge's generation of himself by fits and starts, by cutting himself off from everything else in the world at the same time he gave meaning to it in the telling. . . . In Part I it is Pa's action that is determinative of where the story will go in Part II; in Part II it is Hans' action; in Part III it is Jorge's action which is determinative of where the story will go in Parts I and II and III."[11] Jorge is the smallest, weakest male in a contentious household; it comes as no surprise, then, that he chooses the familiar Joycean weapons—silence, exile, and cunning. Masculine strife is not new to this house; compared to Big Hans and his Pa, the Kid is a relatively impotent adversary for Jorge, and as the Kid lies unconscious on the kitchen table, Jorge vanquishes him with a glance: "By now the kid was naked. I was satisfied mine was bigger" (2). As the story progresses, however, we are increasingly aware that Jorge's real battle is not with the Kid; in these early pages, Jorge uses the Kid as a proxy for getting at a more menacing opponent—Big Hans—who himself is but a surrogate for Jorge's Pa.

At the story's abrupt opening, Big Han(d)s stand(s) strong—big hands of the obstetrician attending at the Kid's birth. We watch the power struggle between Hans and Jorge take shape immediately, Hans giving the directions ("Get some snow and call your pa") and Jorge doing his best to look like he's not following them ("I tried not to hurry"). Big Hans controls discourse as a part of his overall command of the situation; it is after all Big Hans's voice that initiates the story. In this battle of rivals, Big Hans is both obstetrician (Latin *obstare,* "to stand near") and obstacle (*obstare,* "to stand in the way"). Like the Father, he helps bring new life into the world; but, also like the Father, he must at some point be got past if the son himself is to establish for himself a separate and unique identity.

Big Hans—Hans Esbyorn, not Segren: not brother Hans, but hired Hans, a pair of hired hands, an unwelcome intruder in the family setting. In his early notes toward **"The Pedersen Kid,"** Gass declared to himself that "the problem is to present evil as a visitation—sudden, mysterious, violent, inexplicable" (xxvi); the finished story presents us with at least three sudden visitations. The first, in the story's first paragraph, is the appearance of the Kid. The resurrected Kid, in turn, brings news of the story's principal evil visitant, Yellow Gloves, and the remainder of the story moves toward Jorge's encounter with him. But near the close of the story, Jorge thinks back to a third visitation—the one which had brought Big Hans to the Segren place years before:

> Pa had taken the wagon to town. The sun was shining. Pa had gone to meet Big Hans at the station. There was snow around but mud was flowing and the fields had green in them again. Mud rode up on the wagon wheels. There was sweet air sometimes and the creek had water with the winter going. Through a crack in the privy door I saw him take the wagon to the train. . . . Big Hans was stronger than Simon, I thought. He let me help him with his chores, and we talked, and later he showed me some of the pictures in his magazines. See anything like that around here? he'd say, shaking his head. Only teats like that round here is on a cow. And he would tease, laughing while he spun the pages, giving me only a glimpse. Or he would come up and spank me on the rump. (69-70)

Jorge has come to view Big Hans as an adopted sibling and a rival; but when he first arrived on the scene, Jorge saw in him a virile surrogate for the Father Jorge had begun to hate. Big Hans, for instance, is "stronger than Simon," Jorge thinks—and throughout the story Horse Simon is linked to Jorge's Pa. Big Hans, in his vulgar way, initiates Jorge into the mysteries of sex, allowing Jorge an occasional peek at his pornographic magazines; but that gift turns out to be a mixed blessing, Hans toying with Jorge's burgeoning sexual feelings, feelings Jorge does not yet fully understand.

Rather than a hostile gesture toward his father, however, Jorge's adoption of Big Hans as a foster father can be understood as a desperate attempt to restore the lost Father of his youth. Freud analyzes the motive behind this wish to replace one's father as "only an expression of the child's longing for the happy, vanished days when his father seemed to him the noblest and strongest of men and his mother the dearest and loveliest of women. He is turning away from the father whom he knows to-day to the father in whom he believed in the earlier years of his childhood; and his phantasy is no more than the expression of a regret that those happy days have gone."[12] The Father whom Jorge knows today, as we deduce quite quickly, is a monster on the order of Huck Finn's Pap;[13] yet like Huck, Jorge cannot separate his horror at what his Pa has become from his deep attachment to what he used to be. The usurping rival against whom Saint Jorge battles[14] is finally neither the Pedersen Kid nor Big Hans, but behind them both, above them both, casting his long shadow over them both, Jorge's Pa. "I looked past Hans and Pa was watching from the doorway" (24).

Under the cover of dream symbolism and condensation, what Gass in the preface calls "a frost of epistemological doubt" (xxvii), an ageless scene is reenacted—perhaps one of the oldest scenes, the originary narratives of Western tradition. Certainly Freud thought so; in *The Psychopathology of Everyday Life,* he speaks of "the universal human application of the Oedipus myth,"[15] one of the fundamental meaning-making structures of the human mind—those structures that Jung would later call "archetypal." Gass himself speaks of the social function of such stories: "After those stories which we once employed to hold the ears of children came those calculated to suspend—not just you or me, but everyone—our souls like white rags in a line of wash; and these were written to manipulate a kind of universal mechanism in our psyches" (xxii-xxiii). Were it simply structured by the myth of Oedipus, **"The Pedersen Kid"** would bear the same relation to Sophocles' *Oedipus Rex* that Eliot believed Joyce's *Ulysses* bore to the *Odyssey.* This would make **"The Pedersen Kid"** a quintessentially *modernist* fiction, manipulating, as Eliot says of *Ulysses,* "a continuous parallel between contemporaneity and antiquity."[16]

But Gass's method is far more cunning. Jorge is not simply another in a long series of little Oedipuses; he is, more specifically, *Freud*'s little Oedipus, from the famous case history of "little Hans," itself a stylistically daring initiation story. The proper analogue for **"The Pedersen Kid"**'s "mythical method" is therefore not Joyce (at least as he was read by Eliot),[17] but D. M. Thomas, whose *The White Hotel* is constructed around an imaginative reinhabitation of Freud's case histories of Anna O. and "Dora." Gass's writing is often referred to as "metafiction," and **"The Pedersen Kid"** employs what we might call the "metamythical method"—using not ancient myth, but modern reappropriation of ancient myth, as a vehicle for its fictional structure and play.

Section 3 of *The White Hotel* is a pastiche of the Freudian case history. In his note to the novel, Thomas explains the relationship between original and copy this way: "Freud becomes one of the dramatis personae, in fact, as discoverer of the great and beautiful modern myth of psychoanalysis. By myth, I mean a poetic, dramatic expression of a hidden truth; and in placing this emphasis, I do not intend to put into question the scientific validity of psychoanalysis."[18] Thomas has said in an interview that his interest in Freud grew out of "reading Freud for pleasure, more as a storyteller, as a myth maker, than as a scientist or an ideologist of the mind."[19] Gass's interest in Freud is quite similar; he was struck, he says in **"The Anatomy of Mind,"** with the way Freud "saw everything as if it were taking place in a book."[20]

"The Pedersen Kid" contains its share of shadowy figures, characters who are named, spoken of by Jorge, Big Hans, Pa and Ma, but who never appear; among them is a "Little Hans," mentioned three times on one page, then never spoken of again. The existence of a "Little" Hans (Pedersen) explains why the Segrens' Hans is "Big" Hans; but the introduction of this Little Hans is in all other respects gratuitous. Why is he mentioned at all? The name may be meant to tip us off that **"The Pedersen Kid"** can be read as a version of Freud's "Analysis of a Phobia in a Five-Year-Old Boy" (1909); that case history, the story of "Little Hans," is Freud's most compelling illustration of the reenactment of the Oedipal situation in the life of a young boy. Freud calls Hans "a little Oedipus";[21] Gass's Jorge boasts that Hans's meanness toward him is nothing more than "a blister on my heel" (20), making Jorge too an Oedipus, "swollen-footed." Other more significant similarities emerge as we gaze longer at Gass's complex weave; but merely to suggest Gass's familiarity with Freud's Little Hans, surely one of Freud's most celebrated case histories, would be of little value here. If **"The Pedersen Kid"** is a rewriting of Freud's "Little Hans,"[22] well, little Hans's early childhood was itself a "rewriting" of Sophocles' drama, which is in turn but the oldest extant version of one of western civilization's oldest stories.

Discovering the Freudian pattern in **"The Pedersen Kid"** does not require an extraordinarily ingenious reader; the story is built up of some of the most self-conscious, even gratuitous, Freudian symbolism in all of contemporary fiction. Gass wears his Freud on his sleeve, and wears it proudly. Some years ago Bruce Bassoff noted in passing that the story is amenable to a Freudian reading; he briefly invokes Freud's name, but to no real analytical purpose.[23] Bassoff's hesitancy is quite understandable; for how can one proceed with a Freudian reading of a text that flaunts its Freud—one that is so "easily freudened"? For every "decoding" we propose, every dream interpretation we wish to make, every unconscious motivation we wish to lay bare, we have the uncanny sense that Gass has beat us to it—and Freudian criticism cannot be effectively used to master an unruly text if that text anticipates all its "insights."

Gass has often expressed his desire that his work be read on its own terms; in *Fiction and the Figures of Life* he puts it this way: "It seems like a country-headed thing to say: that literature is language; that stories and the places and people in them are merely made of words."[24] And what better way to head off an unwanted reading than for the writer to plant it himself? Gass told an interviewer that "What you want to do is to create a work that can be read non referentially. . . . Fiction, god damn it, is fiction."[25] An orthodox Freudian reading only works insofar as it uncovers signs that point to a hidden order, hidden even from the writer; but in **"The Pedersen Kid"** Gass has made that order and its concomitant signs—Freudian symbols—flagrant, loud, *audacious*. Such is the fate of the modernists' "mythical method" in the hands of the post-modernists.

Jorge, like his pre-Christian forebear Oedipus, must kill his father; this murder is at the very core of Freud's Oedipus complex. Jorge's Pa is Magnus, "mighty one"; as such he is emblematic of all fathers, and the young son's feelings toward his father, as Freud notes, cannot but be ambivalent: "Organic necessity introduces into a man's relation to his father an emotional ambivalence which we have found most strikingly expressed in the Greek myth of King Oedipus. . . . The hatred of his father that arises in a boy from rivalry for his mother is not able to achieve uninhibited sway over his mind; it has to contend against his old-established affection and admiration for the very same person."[26] Neither pure hatred nor pure love, but a bewildering, paralyzing mixture. Jorge's ambivalent feelings toward his father have strong parallels in the case history of Little Hans, whose patricidal impulses first came to light through his irrational fear of horses. "We have learned the immediate precipitating cause after which his phobia broke out," Freud tells us: "This was when the boy saw a big heavy horse fall down; and one at least of the interpretations of this impression seems to be that emphasized by his father, namely, that Hans at that moment perceived a wish that his father might fall down in the same way—and be dead."[27] When Little Hans tells his father of his fear—his disguised desire—he distances himself from his wish for his father's death: his fear is not that he will kill his father, but simply that his father will die:

> "The horses are so proud," he said, "that I'm afraid they'll fall down". . . .
>
> *Father:* "So you want me to fall down?"
>
> *Hans:* "Yes. You've got to be naked [meaning "bare-foot"] . . . and knock up against a stone and bleed, and then I'll be able to be alone with Mummy for a little bit at all events. When you come up into our flat I'll be able to run away quick so that you don't see."[28]

Little Hans's violent impulses are thus doubly displaced. It is horses, not his father, who are in danger; furthermore, he does not threaten the horses himself—he is merely afraid for them.

The most famous chapter of Faulkner's *As I Lay Dying* is quite short: "My mother is a fish." The corresponding chapters of both "Little Hans" and **"The Pedersen Kid"** would read "My father is a horse." When Pa makes his entrance in I.iii, his first reported words, appropriately enough, are "Ever think of a horse?" (24); one of Jorge's earliest descriptions of his father, after he has been struck

while trying to wake him, is that "he was like a mean horse to come at from the rear" (4). Time and again throughout the story Pa is associated with horses, either the Segrens' horse Simon, the Pedersens' horse, or the horse that the three "magi" find dead in the snow. As Jorge has not failed to notice, Pa is far more intimate and gentle with horses than he is with any of the story's humans. After we've seen him cruelly strike his son, Jorge's Pa shows great concern for his horse; with the Pedersens' mare, Pa's manner is even more seductive: "Pedersen's horse was in the barn. Pa kept her quiet. He rubbed his hand along her flank. He laid his head upon her neck and whispered in her ear. She shook herself and nickered" (59). Since Pa is so closely associated with horses, since he *is* a horse in Jorge's imagination, it is perhaps not surprising that the dead horse Jorge finds in the snow anticipates the death of his father by just a few minutes: "the legs that lay in front of me weren't mine. I'd gone out in the blazing air. It was queer. Out of the snow I'd kicked away with my foot stuck a horse's hoof and I didn't feel the least terror or surprise" (48).

Even more frequently than he is associated with horses, Pa is associated with excrement—with shit. Jorge's first description of his Pa makes this connection explicit: Pa is described as lying in his bed "lumped under the covers at the end like dung covered with snow" (3). When Jorge persists in trying to wake Pa, he is threatened with an allusion to one of the most potent communal memories of the Segren clan:

> Out. You want me to drop my pot?
>
> He was about to get up so I got out, slamming the door. He was beginning to see he was too mad to sleep. Then he threw things. Once he went after Hans and dumped his pot over the banister. Pa'd been shit-sick in that pot. Hans got an ax. He didn't even bother to wipe himself off and he chopped part of Pa's door down before he stopped. (5)

To be splattered with the Father's "shit" is the very image of death. As crazy as it may seem, Jorge does love his Pa; at the same time, his Pa is fatally linked with excrement, decay—with shit. Filial love is erected on paternal decay; the young son, knowing nothing firsthand of decay and death, sees in the decline of his father the awful specter of his own mortality. Little Hans, like Jorge, was obsessed with excrement; interestingly enough, he often confused the German words *schiessen* and *scheissen*—"shooting" and "shitting." Both boys associate "shitting" with killing; seen in this light the Oedipal murder comes to seem a misguided form of self-defense—the son kills the father in order not to be implicated in the cycle of life, decay, and death.

This murder is, of course, no ordinary homicide; it is the murder of the physically mature, sexually dominant father by the sexually immature son. It comes as no surprise, then, that this murder is carried out as a symbolic castration of the father. The archetypal, perhaps mythical, phallic murderer of **"The Pedersen Kid"** is the absent killer

Yellow Gloves. In restaging the murder at the Pedersens' place, Big Hans's description of Yellow Gloves's gun sounds suspiciously like the killer's penis, or, more to the point, Hans's own penis: "He's got me and your ma and your pa lined up with our hands here back of our necks, and he's got a rifle in between them yellow gloves and he's waving the point of it up and down in front of your ma's face real slow and quiet" (19). Of course, rifles, pistols, and revolvers are but the best known of the symbols of male genitalia;[29] for Yellow Gloves to wave the point of his "rifle" up and down in Mrs. Segren's face, or most especially for Big Hans to reenact that scene here in the Segrens' kitchen with the neck of a whiskey bottle, is a symbolic rape of Jorge's Ma. For all the indifference, even annoyance, that he shows toward her during the story, Jorge certainly will not allow an outsider, either Yellow Gloves or Big Hans, to possess his mother in this way.

Jorge is poignantly aware of his lesser genital gifts. In his imagination he figures himself in terms that connote sexual immaturity—"I'd just been given a pistol that shot BBs" (49). Jorge's pistol is a weapon of sorts, but nothing in comparison to Yellow Gloves's rifle, Pa's shotgun, or even Big Hans's forty-five. When the three set out to find Yellow Gloves, Big Hans subjects Jorge to ritual humiliation: "Hans had his shotgun and the forty-five he'd stolen from the Navy. He made me load it and when I'd stuck it in my belt he'd said it'd likely go off and keep me from ever getting out to stud" (34). When Jorge turned his pistol on Pa and Big Hans in the snow, "Pa took the gun away, putting it in his pocket. He had his shotgun hanging easy over his left arm but he slapped me and I bit my tongue" (52).

Although he is keenly aware of his inferior endowment, Jorge does his best to keep up his morale. Even when he stands to suffer by comparison, Jorge is constantly pitting his phallus against those of others. Freud's Little Hans shared Jorge's predilection; as Freud informs us, Little Hans "repeatedly expressed both to his father and his mother his regret that he had never yet seen their widdlers; and it was probably the need *for making a comparison* which impelled him to do this. The ego is always the standard by which one measures the external world; one learns to understand it by means of a constant comparison with oneself."[30] Little Hans and Jorge clearly share this penchant for genital comparison. When the Kid is naked on the kitchen table, Jorge takes a peek and is satisfied that "his" is bigger. And Hans's, we learn, is bigger than Jorge's: "Even if his cock was thicker . . . I was here and he was in the snow. I was satisfied" (72).

As the search party approaches the Pedersen place, Jorge can see "the chimney very black in the sun stick up from the steep bright pitch like a dead cigar rough-ashed with snow" (45). The empty Pedersen house, with its great phallus of a chimney standing up like a beacon, comes to represent a "Promised Land" to Jorge; and in order to gain the house, he believes, and take possession of it, he must overcome his companions. Jorge tells his dying Pa "I was cold in your house always" (74); and Jorge's victory over

his Pa coincides with his taking possession of a new home. Jorge's account of his winning of the Pedersen house is figured as a sexual conquest: "I crawled to the south side of the house and broke a casement window with the gun I had forgot I had and climbed down into the basement ripping my jacket on the glass" (62). Again, the Freudian symbolism is not particularly subtle, but it does find confirmation in the story of Little Hans:

> *Hans:* "I say, I thought something this morning again."
>
> *Father:* "What?"
>
> *Hans:* "I went with you in the train, and we smashed a window and the policeman took us off with him."[31]

In his daydream, Little Hans and his father smashed a window while in a train, an appropriately phallic penetration; in **"The Pedersen Kid,"** Jorge gains access by using the gun he had forgot he had. Freud analyzed Little Hans's fantasy this way: "He had a suspicion that to take possession of his mother was forbidden; he had come up against the barrier against incest. . . . His father, he thought, also did that enigmatic forbidden something with his mother which he replaced by an act of violence such as smashing a window-pane or forcing a way into an enclosed space. . . . We can only say that they were symbolic phantasies of intercourse."[32]

The establishment of the son's own home is concomitant with the death of the Father. To mature is to leave the Father's house; and in this new place, Jorge will be his own master: "In the spring I'd shit with the door open, watching the blackbirds" (51). This self-imposed exile is a step in the resolution of the Oedipus complex. "Exile," however, is the adult label for it; from the son's point of view this leave-taking is experienced as banishment. An author's life is often a story of banishment and/or exile; it is the story of a number of the authors Gass himself names in the preface: Franz Kafka, James Joyce, Joseph Conrad. . . . According to Kristeva, it is only on the death of the Father that the son can become aware of his vocation as author: "without banishment, there is no possible release from the grip of paternal Death. This act of loving and its incumbent writing spring from the Death of the Father—from the Death of the third person. . . . Assumption of self through the dead father turns the banished writer into a father in spite of himself."[33]

The Pedersen house appears to the three "wise men" traveling through the snow to be a sanctuary in the midst of a vast waste. That waste of snow is especially troubling to Jorge; the immense expanse of snow seems to bear an almost metaphysical import for him:

> The snow dazzle struck me and the pain of the space around us. . . . It was frightening—the endless white space. I'd have to keep my head down. . . . I stood as still as I could in the tubes of my clothes, the snow shifting strangely in my eyes, alone, frightened by the space that was bowling up inside me, a white blank glittering waste like the waste outside, coldly burning, roughed with waves, and I wanted to curl up, face to

my thighs, but I knew my tears would freeze my lashes together. (35, 39, 45)

There's something peculiar about Jorge's fear of the snow, "the endless white space." He associates it with his father: "I hated him. Jesus, how I did. But no more like a father. Like the burning space" (47). And for Jorge the budding author, the blank space is also the terrifying empty page, the page on which he is compelled to write the story of the Father. Jorge must overcome the blank page as he does the Father if he is to slough off the Oedipal burden and bring his own authority to his writing.

Once inside the Pedersen place, however, Jorge is no longer talking about the burning space; instead, his energy is directed toward what he calls his "new blank land": "The Pedersen kid—maybe he'd been a message of some sort. No, I liked better the idea that we'd been prisoners exchanged. I was back in my own country. No, it was more like I'd been given a country. A new blank land. More and more, while we'd been coming, I'd been slipping out of myself, pushed out by the cold maybe" (62-63). Jorge is finally in the house; the story opened with Big Hans "in the house with what he had" before Jorge "reached the steps" (1), but that usurpation has been righted here. Righted and *written;* for it is when Jorge takes possession of this new blank land, free of the burden of birth and filiation, that he truly begins to write. In the end, Jorge turns out to be the author of his own case history; Saltzman writes that Jorge "manages to create and interpret the plot that contains him; that is the nature of his heroism. He seizes destiny imaginatively, and that is the wellspring of power. . . . By preferring the realm of metaphor over physical environment, Jorge creates a surrogate world, in which his own aspirations can be attained and are the dominant, actual ones."[34] Consider, as an example, his description of his posture in the basement:

> Distantly I felt the soft points of my shoulders in my jacket, the heavy line of my cap around my forehead, and on the hard floor my harder feet, and to my chest my hugged-tight knees. I felt them but I felt them differently . . . like the pressure of a bolt through steel or the cinch of leather harness or the squeeze of wood by wood in floors . . . like the twist and pinch, the painful yield of tender tight together wheels, and swollen bars, and in deep winter springs. (63-64)

This passage is remarkable in part for the awareness Jorge shows of his body; up to this point in the story Jorge has seemed rather a stranger in his own body, while here he is clearly very much at home. But even more remarkable, surely, is the limpid prose in which Jorge renders his sense perceptions; this is the self-conscious craftsmanship of a poet, and no longer the workmanlike reportage of the dutiful son who, in I.ii., had written: "I heard the dripping clearly, and I heard Hans swallow. I heard the water and the whiskey fall. I heard the frost on the window melt to the sill and drop into the sink" (23).

In his new home, Jorge evokes another moment of heightened perception as he reaches the main floor: "There was light in the kitchen. It came through the crack I'd left in the closet door to comfort me. But the light was fading. Through the crack I could see the sink, now milky. Flakes began to slide out of the sky and rub their corners off on the pane before they were caught by the wind again and blown away. In the gray I couldn't see them. Then they would come—suddenly—from it, like chaff from grain, and brush the window while the wind eddied" (68). Jorge's first important act, on taking possession of the house, is to *write* it, for it is only through writing that it becomes fully his. Through the power of writing, even the snow outside his window comes under his control: "The snow was coming. It was coming almost even with the ground, *my* snow" (68, emphasis added).

The absolute freedom that Jorge enjoys in the Pedersen house is at the same time a terrible freedom; without guidelines, Jorge has become a law unto himself. His is a new blank land, and this new land will be precisely what Jorge chooses to make of it. Not surprisingly, one of his first reactions to this complete freedom is to fall back on the model of the father: "I knew I was all muddled up and scared and crazy and I tried to think god damn over and over or what the hell or jesus christ, instead, but it didn't work. All that could happen was alone with me and I was alone with it" (75). "God damn," "what the hell," "jesus christ": these are the words of the father. Upon gaining his own land, the son's first response is to reinstate the law of the father. It is an old pattern; as a young nation, we tried to make George Washington king.

The failure of his father, however, has given Jorge the courage to go it alone. Jorge's new house, and his virgin snow-covered territory, is distinguished by its lack of landmarks; the old roadmaps are no longer of any use. The blankness, the whiteness is terrifying; but for the young writer, it is also exhilarating: "The road was gone. Fences, bushes, old machinery: what there might be in any yard was all gone under snow. . . . The path I'd taken from the barn to the house was filled and the sun was burning brightly on it" (77-78). Saltzman remarks that "what had earlier been the white of bleakness and despair is transformed into the white of unbridled possibility—the artist's open canvas awaiting his unique imprint."[35] Alone in his own house, all his kin "dead," Jorge is faced with the opportunity that other authors—including Gass himself—only dream of: the chance to create himself anew. In the preface Gass confesses that "Even as a grown man I was still desperately boasting that I'd choose another cunt to come from. Well, Balzac wanted his *de,* and I wanted my anonymity" (xvii). When he later returns to the same issue, Gass declares "if someone were to ask me once again of the circumstances of my birth, I think I should answer finally that I was born somewhere in the middle of my first book" (xliv). The ultimate irony, of course, is that the death of the father has freed Jorge to write; and yet Jorge's assumption of authorship, of *authority,* has surreptitiously made a father of Jorge himself, "a father in spite of himself, a father under protest, a false father who doesn't want to be a father, but nonetheless believes in being one."[36]

Kristeva's remarks on Beckett's *First Love* are strangely appropriate to Gass's text; she writes of the writer-to-be's banishment as

> above/beyond a life of love. A life always off to one side, at an impassable distance, mourning a love. A fragile, uncertain life, where, without spending the saved-up paternal capital in one's pockets, he discovers the price of warmth (of a hothouse, of a room, of a turd) and the boredom of those humans who provide it—but who waste it, too. It is a life apart from the paternal country where nonetheless lies the obsessed self's unshakable quiet, frozen forever, bored but solid.[37]

In spite of everything, Jorge has implicated himself once again in the cycle of filiation, of fathering, of authoring. Gass has written that "Freud had the hero's need to be self-made to such an extraordinary degree he replaced his father first with Fliess and finally with himself";[38] the same can of course be said for Jorge, who attempted to replace his aging father with the young and virile Big Hans, only to kill them both off and fill that role himself. Jorge has triumphed in his Oedipal drama, killing off his rivals through words, imaginatively spoken and poetically inscribed; but the battle is not over, for, as Gass says, "To be born unencumbered is not the complete advantage one might immediately imagine. Although the struggle to free one's youthful self of religion, relatives, and region is thereby greatly simplified, since there are no complicated cuffs to be unclasped, no subtle knots to be untied, the self in question is as vague and vaguely messy as a smudged line" (xv-xvi). As **"The Pedersen Kid"** ends, Jorge has been reborn theoretically unencumbered of kin, but he is as yet only "as vague and vaguely messy as a smudged line"; it remains to be seen whether he will have the strength of character to shake off completely the sins of the Father, lest they be visited on him and his even to the seventh generation. But Jorge has created for himself a new blank land of his own to work. *The world,* it would seem, *is all before him;* for as **"The Pedersen Kid"** closes, Jorge is not just another "little Oedipus"—rather he's a little Freud, both author and subject of his own case history. And that's certainly the best seat in the house.

Notes

1. James Joyce, *Finnegans Wake* (New York: Viking, 1939), 115.

2. Sigmund Freud, *The Standard Edition of the Complete Psychological Works of Sigmund Freud,* trans., ed. James Strachey and Anna Freud, 24 vols. (London: Hogarth, 1966-74), 10:80, 84.

3. Larry McCaffery, *The Metafictional Muse: The Works of Robert Coover, Donald Barthelme, and William H. Gass* (Pittsburgh: Univ. of Pittsburgh Press, 1982), 183.

4. McCaffery, 185.

5. Gass's three-part review essay on Freud, "The Anatomy of Mind," makes quite clear the depth of his knowledge of Freud; it is collected in Gass's *World Within the Word* (New York: Knopf, 1978), 208-52.

6. William H. Gass, *In the Heart of the Heart of the Country and Other Stories* (Boston: Godine, 1981), 65. Subsequent references to this work will be cited parenthetically in the text.

7. Arthur M. Saltzman, *The Fiction of William Gass: The Consolation of Language* (Carbondale: Southern Illinois Univ. Press, 1986), 62.

8. Freud, 9:212.

9. Saltzman, 61.

10. Saltzman, 62.

11. R. E. Johnson, "Structuralism and Contemporary Fiction," *Soundings* 63.2 (Summer 1975): 290.

12. Freud, 9:241.

13. Patricia Kane points out the similarity between the two characters, remarking that Jorge's life "suggests what Huck Finn's might have been if Pap and his mother had settled down on a Dakota farm" ("The Sun Burned on the Snow: Gass's 'The Pedersen Kid,'" *Critique* 14.2 [1972]: 89).

14. The chivalric image is Jorge's: "It was like I was setting out to do something special and big—like a knight setting out—worth remembering" (32-33).

15. Freud, 6:178.

16. T. S. Eliot, *The Selected Prose of T. S. Eliot,* ed. Frank Kermode (New York: Harcourt, Brace, Jovanovich/Farrar, Straus, Giroux, 1975), 177.

17. It has often been remarked that Eliot's description of Joyce's "mythical method" is far more accurate as a description of Eliot's own poetics than of Joyce's. In fact, I believe Joyce's appropriation of Homer to be much more complex than Eliot would allow—in fact, much more in line with the procedures of Gass and Thomas than space here allows me to develop.

18. D. M. Thomas, *The White Hotel* (New York: Pocket Books, 1981), n.p.

19. *Contemporary Authors,* ed. Linda Metzger and Deborah A. Straub, New Revision Series (Detroit: Gale, 1986), 17:446.

20. Gass, *The World Within the Word,* 212.

21. Freud, 10:111.

22. Which Freud, early on, would not take credit for having written; on first publication "Little Hans" "was described not as 'by' Freud, but only as 'communicated by' him" (Freud, 10:4).

23. Bruce Bassoff, "The Sacrificial World of William Gass: *In the Heart of the Heart of the Country,*" *Critique* 18.1 (1976): 36-58.

24. William H. Gass, *Fiction and the Figures of Life* (Boston: Godine, 1979), 27.

25. Thomas LeClair, "A Conversation with William Gass," *Chicago Review* 30.2 (1978): 97.

26. Freud, 13:243, 129.

27. Freud, 10:51-52.

28. Freud, 10:82.

29. Freud, 15:154.

30. Freud, 10:107.

31. Freud, 10:41.

32. Freud, 10:41, 123.

33. Julia Kristeva, *Desire in Language: A Semiotic Approach to Literature and Art*, ed. Leon S. Roudiez, trans. Thomas Gora, Alice Jardine, and Leon S. Roudiez (New York: Columbia Univ. Press, 1980), 150-51.

34. Saltzman, 70.

35. Saltzman, 67-68.

36. Kristeva, 151.

37. Kristeva, 150.

38. Gass, *The World Within the Word*, 211. Indeed, the history of the psychoanalytic movement could itself be written as a family romance, Freud replacing his own father with Breuer and Fliess, and later being betrayed by his own "son," the "little Oedipus" Carl Jung.

Reginald Dyck (essay date Fall 1991)

SOURCE: "William Gass: A 'Purified Modernist' in a Postmodern World," in *Review of Contemporary Fiction*, Vol. 11, No. 3, Fall, 1991, pp. 124-30.

[*In the following essay, Dyck examines underlying modernist aspects of Gass's postmodern literary and theoretical perspective, including comparative analysis of Gass's story "Icicles" and Wright Morris's novel* Ceremony in Lone Tree. *"Although modernist in its formal aesthetics," Dyck writes, "Gass's world of words reflects a postmodern perspective on contemporary culture."*]

> I don't regard myself as a postmodernist. . . . I prefer to think of myself as a purified modernist. In architecture that would mean modernism without social content: Corbusier not building for society.
>
> —William Gass[1]

When William Gass claims, "I think that literature is not a form of communication,"[2] he seems to preclude a social interpretation of his work. "Serious writing must nowadays be written for the sake of the art,"[3] he asserts. Baudelaire made this claim in the context of his resistance to the commodification of art; Gass in his formalist rhetoric is resisting the traditional ways of reading fostered by the fiction of realism.[4] Yet while his critical writing works to convince his readers to resist the old ways, it also acknowledges that his fiction has a significant relationship to the social world.

Most people, Gass states, read fiction as history without graphs or dates, an approach that falsifies by creating expectations fiction does not intend to fulfill.[5] "I object to so-called extraliterary qualities because they get confused with the merit of the book" ("Colloquy" 589). The word *because* is important; Gass's point is not that extraliterary qualities do not exist, but that they are too easily misread. The danger is that literature "provides a sense of verification (a feeling) without the fact of verification (the validating process)."[6] For example, although Gass did careful research for **"In the Heart of the Heart of the Country,"** the story should not be read simply as an exposé of rural Midwestern towns or American society as a whole. Gass explains that "the story is not an accurate picture: it's an accurate construction. Not even 'accurate': just a construction of one person's way of looking at things" ("Colloquy" 607). Rather than an objective report, the story presents the consciousness of a particular type of character in a particular type of place.

Another way that readers misread is by emphasizing plot as the central quality of fiction. The well-constructed plot as a moral equation has been for novelists a way of making sense of the chaos of life, and readers have accepted that construction as the import of the novel. Consequently, the novelist as artist is slighted in favor of the novelist as philosopher or sociologist. Gass has been challenged most vigorously by John Gardner, who argues for the inescapably moral nature of literature: "In literature, structure is the evolving sequence of dramatized events tending toward understanding and assertion; that is, toward some meticulously qualified belief."[7] It is not that Gass is unaware of the moral views fiction presents, but that his interest is in the dramatic tensions those views create rather than their correctness. Nabokov's *Lolita* is to be read in this way as well. Both authors want readers to look at their fiction as objects of art, not as moral treatises.

Therefore Gass calls himself a "purified modernist." In an essay subtitled "Demystifying the Ideology of Modernism," Fredric Jameson asks "what kind of society it can be in which works of art have become autonomous to this degree, in which the older social and cultic functions of literature have become so unfamiliar as to have made us forgetful . . . of the power and influence which a socially living art can exercise?"[8] Sociologist Todd Gitlin, in describing the helplessness reflected in post-1960s culture, provides an answer: "Self-regarding irony and blankness are a way of staving off anxieties, rages, terrors and hungers that have been kicked up but cannot find resolution."[9] When Gass began to publish his short stories in the midfifties, the modernist belief in the autonomous power of imagination, part of the Romantic view of the artist, had turned to doubt. Yet even if the imagination is understood as inevitably shaped by its social milieu, how can an artist fulfill the traditional bardic function of making sense of the world in a seemingly meaningless, mass society that does not take artists seriously?

Postmodern art has responded to this loss of meaning in two ways: with a sense of liberation or with a sense of isolation and betrayal.[10] Although Gass's criticism celebrates the first, his fictional characters experience the second. The celebration stems from his claim to have separated beauty from truth, or fiction from society. However, Gass's escape into the artistry of language is not complete, nor does he intend it to be.

To the extent that novels are forms of communication, Gass explains, they work not as direct descriptions but as constructed metaphors for our world (58). Metaphors are models of reality that posit conceptual connections among data. As much as novelists might strive for concreteness, they can only use words, which can never directly describe but must interpret. Thus, "The purpose of a literary work is the capture of consciousness, and the consequent creation, in you, of an imagined sensibility, so that while you read you are that patient pool or cataract of concepts which the author has constructed" (33).

The opening of **"In the Heart of the Heart of the Country"** emphasizes the idea of the story as a model of consciousness. Echoing Yeats's "Sailing to Byzantium," the poet/narrator states, "So I have sailed the seas and come . . . to B . . ." (172). Gass plays on "to B" not only as an ironic reference to Yeats's Byzantium as an "artifice of reality," but also as a verb of being which alerts the reader that what follows is not literal description of a particular rural town but the creation of a fictional character's consciousness. The reader is presented with a model of what it would be like to be a poet "in retirement from love" and living in "a small town fastened to a field in Indiana." However, this does not preclude a social reading of the story; B is in the state of Indiana, and we do recognize the poet as our contemporary. The models Gass creates are as embedded in culture as their creator's imagination inevitably is.

Metafiction, such as Gass writes, openly exposes itself as a constructed model by showing us characters in the process of creating "a system of meaning which will help to supply their lives with hope, order, possibly even some measure of beauty."[11] These metafictional models-within-models offer more than just aesthetic pleasures to the characters that create them. For example, at the end of **"The Pedersen Kid,"** we see Jorge creating a world of the imagination as an alternative to the mean, narrow one in which he lives with his parents and the hired man. In reading we are moved not only by Gass's display of craftsmanship but also by his presentation of the pain that drives his young character into this imaginary world. Through the story, we also understand something about the motivations and methods for the model-building process. In a sense Jorge confirms Gitlin's analysis of postmodern culture. Jorge's helplessness as a young boy in a violent, uncaring world motivates him to imagine a world of snow, the Pedersen kid, himself, and no adults. Patricia Waugh gives this explanation of metafictional model-building:

> Metafiction, then, does not abandon "the real world" for the narcissistic pleasures of the imagination. What

it does is to re-examine the conventions of realism in order to discover—through its own self-reflection—a fictional form that is culturally relevant and comprehensible to contemporary readers. In showing us how literary fiction creates its imaginary worlds, metafiction helps us to understand how the reality we live day by day is similarly constructed, similarly "written."[12]

Gass explains that the point for the reader is not to assess the accuracy of the model that either a character or the story as a whole creates. "I think of the text you are reading as the metaphorical model that reassesses yours, rather than the other way around" ("Colloquy" 592). In claiming this privileged position for art, Gass shows his modernist affinities. He also guardedly claims fiction as an agent for change. The novel both displays and argues (63), and thus challenges our own conceptions of the world. But Gass gives a continual warning, "Still for us it is only 'as if'" (71). The novel remains a world of words.

Although modernist in its formalist aesthetic, Gass's world of words reflects a postmodern perspective on contemporary culture. A comparison of Wright Morris's *Ceremony in Lone Tree,* a late-modern novel, with Gass's story **"Icicles"** makes this clear. Both writers wrote these works at about the same time, experimented with nontraditional forms and understand fiction as a model of consciousness. Yet the model Morris creates in *Ceremony,* published in 1960, and Gass's in **"Icicles,"** which first appeared in 1963, suggest significantly different worlds. The central characters, Boyd in *Ceremony* and Fender in **"Icicles,"** best exemplify this difference.

The modernist revolt against tradition deeply marks Boyd's outrageous actions; he wants to shock others out of the "hereditary sleeping sickness"[13] of their middle-class lives. If the modernist faith in the artist's ability to change society has been depleted—Boyd's self-exile in Mexico suggests this—his return to Nebraska indicates his continuing stake in it. His bringing along a young friend whom he calls Daughter, a gesture he seems to have borrowed from *Lolita,* is one attempt to shock his friends' sense of propriety, and thus awaken them to the emptiness of their unreflected lives.

In "The Culture of Modernism," Irving Howe describes modernist writers as "an avant-garde marked by aggressive defensiveness, extreme self-consciousness, prophetic inclination, and the stigmata of alienation."[14] Although true of Boyd, none of this characterizes Gass's Fender. Because he cannot believe that his actions matter, he is not one of those who "chose and oppose." Instead, he is a "confused self," "a diffuse, unfocused protean self which cannot define issues in any determinate way." As a postmodern character, Fender is not oppressed by tradition as Boyd is, but by the "meaninglessness and triviality of freedom itself, which is unable to locate any bearings amid the incoherent and apparently aimless massiveness of society."[15]

Because Fender's world seems to have experienced the effects of cultural entropy longer than Boyd's, Fender no longer has the energy for rebellious, audacious acts. Even if Boyd's idealism is largely exhausted, his rebellion keeps him in a dynamic relationship with society. Whereas Boyd brazenly attempts to walk on water and then creates a public account of his failure, Fender counts the contents of his pot pie but only thinks about writing a letter of complaint. Boyd has the energy of restlessness; Fender has the lethargy of listlessness.

Because Boyd's energy pushes him outward and Fender's lethargy focuses inward, they turn to aesthetics with different intentions. Boyd transforms his water-walking failure into a play and a novel; his inner struggle directs him toward an audience. Fender develops a private aesthetic of icicles which estranges him from others because it allows him to escape from the public world. Coming home from a humiliating real-estate job, Fender becomes fascinated by the icicles that block part of his picture window. At first he reacts professionally, considering them a nuisance and a sales problem. Then he creates images out of them: parsnips, the insides of caves, sets of teeth. Although he is surprised and embarrassed at his new interest, he soon becomes protective of it. Finally he does not care that his appreciation is not socially acceptable: "Only the icicles mattered." He wants to bring their beauty inside himself. The icicles stand in opposition to the social world where, because "Everything is property," Fender comes to see himself as a decrepit piece of real estate (159). Although the outside world still threatens to intrude, he retreats as much as he can into a private, aesthetic world of icicles. As he does, a sense of comfort displaces his listlessness.

This retreat is made easier by Fender's lack of personal history. He jokes at a party, truthfully he realizes afterward, that "he couldn't tell the story of his life because he couldn't in the least remember it" (139). Although this frees him from Boyd's struggle to extricate himself from the restraints of his past, Fender also lacks history's consolations. The present must carry the whole weight of his existence, and when it fails to support him, Fender can only escape into a world of imagination: "There's no one to help you, Fender, you have no history, remember?" (152).

Analogously, Fender is more disconnected from society than Boyd in spite of leading a more conventional life. Boyd may drop out of society, but his need to shock his childhood friends reveals his contradictory desire to belong while asserting his difference from their deadening middle-class lives. Fender has the trappings of that middle-class world, a job and a house, but neither provides him with social relationships. His dinner, here an ironic symbol of disconnectedness, illustrates his passive isolation. Rather than enjoying conversation and friendship, he eats in silence without even a television to bring in the outside world. The pot pie establishes only a pathetic commercial connection.

Because of his helplessness, Fender finally stops struggling with society, leaves his job, and retreats into a self-contained world of icicles and language. Boyd also retreats into language, but he uses it as a defensive weapon, not as a blanket in which to hide himself as Fender does. In not taking an antagonistic stance against society, Fender moves beyond alienation. Instead of the heroic alienation and anxiety of modernism, he lives with the fragmentation and decentering of postmodernism. Thus he goes gently into that good night of death-in-language while Boyd rages against the dying of the light by setting off fireworks with his wit in order to expose his society's emptiness.

Boyd chooses to stand outside of society; Fender finds himself invisible within it. The census did not miss Fender because he refused to be counted: he was bitter that he had to call attention to his own existence (147). His escape into imagination is by default and provides him little comfort because the social world continues to impinge. The values of real estate insinuate themselves so that he comes to think, "I do not even occupy myself." Rather than having escaped, he discovers that "his inner exclamations were like advertising signs." Therefore he wants to "drive himself into wordlessness" (157-58).

As a result, Fender, like Jacob Horner in Barth's *End of the Road*, becomes paralyzed. At the end of the story he protects himself by turning the children playing outside into a field of colors, yet his world of icicles is still vulnerable to their attack as "they [come] down the hill like a snowfall of rocks" (162). **"Icicles"** ends with Fender's aesthetic world threatened by the world that surrounds him. Caught between these worlds, Fender can do nothing to save himself. This conclusion contrasts with the ending of *Ceremony*: rather than paralysis there is a sudden awakening as Boyd's audacity has its effect. Following his example of doing "something crazy" as "the only way to leave an impression" (167), Lois shoots a pistol—symbol of violence and sexuality—and startles the others out of their habitual responses. Even if Morris does not imply that the changes are permanent, he does suggest that the paralysis of his characters' cliché-filled lives is not inevitable. A sense of powerlessness and inevitability does mark **"Icicles,"** thus placing it beyond the modernist energy of resistance.

Like his characters, Gass also stands between two worlds. While working within the modern aesthetic of a unique and personal style, his fiction engages a world that offers little opportunity for individualism. The "bourgeois ego," if liberated from the anxiety that drives Boyd to audacity, is also "liberated from every other kind of feeling as well, since there is no longer a self present to do the feeling" but instead only "'intensities' . . . free-floating and impersonal."[16] That is Fender's dilemma.

Rather than as a purified modernist, "Corbusier not building for society," Gass can better be understood as a modernist engaging a postmodern, mass society that does little to encourage artists, or any individuals, to think that they can affect their world. His fiction does celebrate the artistic possibilities of language, but just as Yeats's poet sails for Byzantium as a paltry old man who can no longer find a place in his native country, Gass's characters— Fender, Jorge, the poet in B, Rev. Furber—escape into an imaginary world as a retirement from love and a retreat from a world that is too much mere real estate.

Denis Donoghue claims that in Gass's fiction "the sentences make an arbitrary festival, a circus of pleasures, satisfactions corresponding to the smile with which desperate remedies, duly considered, are set aside."[17] I read that smile as a wince and find the festival less arbitrary, the pleasures more troubling, and the desperate remedies still being desperately held to.

Notes

1. Brooke K. Horvath, et al., "A Colloquy with William H. Gass," *Modern Fiction Studies* 29 (Winter 1983): 597; hereafter cited in the text as "Colloquy."

2. Jeffrey L. Duncan, "A Conversation with Stanley Elkin and William H. Gass," *Iowa Review* 7 (Spring 1971): 49.

3. William H. Gass, Preface, *In the Heart of the Heart of the Country and Other Stories* (Boston: Godine, 1981), xviii.

4. Ned French makes the connection between Gass and Baudelaire in "Against the Grain: Theory and Practice in the Work of William H. Gass," *Iowa Review* 7 (Spring 1971): 100-101.

5. William H. Gass, *Fiction and the Figures of Life* (Boston: Godine, 1979), 30; references to Gass's critical writing will be from this work and will be cited by page number in the text. References to his fiction will be from *In the Heart of the Heart of the Country* (n. 3 above).

6. Carole Spearin McCauley, "William H. Gass," in *The New Fiction: Interviews with Innovative American Writers,* ed. Joe David Bellamy (Urbana: Univ. of Illinois Press, 1974), 33.

7. John Gardner, *On Moral Fiction* (New York: Basic Books, 1977), 65.

8. Fredric R. Jameson, "Beyond the Cave: Demystifying the Ideology of Modernism," *Bulletin of the Midwest Modern Language Association* (Spring 1975): 3.

9. Todd Gitlin, "Hip-Deep in Postmodernism." *New York Times Book Review,* 6 November 1988, 36.

10. Gerald Graff, "The Myth of the Postmodern Breakthrough," *TriQuarterly* 26 (Winter 1973): 391.

11. Larry McCaffery, *The Metafictional Muse: The Works of Robert Coover, Donald Barthelme, and William H. Gass* (Pittsburgh: Univ. of Pittsburgh Press, 1982), 4.

12. Patricia Waugh, *Metafiction: The Theory and Practice of Self-Conscious Fiction* (London and New York: Methuen, 1984), 18.

13. Eugene Zamiain, "On Literature, Revolution and Entropy," quoted in Irving Howe, "The Culture of Modernism" in *Decline of the New* (New York: Harcourt Brace Jovanovich, 1970), 11.

14. Howe, "Culture of Modernism," 5.

15. Gerald Graff, "Babbitt at the Abyss: the Social Context of Postmodern American Fiction," *TriQuarterly* 33 (1975): 61.

16. Fredric Jameson, "Postmodernism: Or, the Cultural Logic of Late Capitalism," *New Left Review* 146 (1984): 62. Jameson makes an insightful comparison of the modern and postmodern sense of self, in part through a comparison of Edvard Munch's *The Scream* and Andy Warhol's depictions of Marilyn Monroe, 61-64.

17. Denis Donoghue, *Ferocious Alphabets* (Boston: Little, Brown, 1981), 89.

Arthur M. Saltzman (essay date Fall 1991)

SOURCE: "Where Words Dwell Adored: An Introduction to William Gass," in *Review of Contemporary Fiction,* Vol. 11, No. 3, Fall, 1991, pp. 7-14.

[*In the following essay, Saltzman provides an overview of Gass's postmodern linguistic techniques and theoretical perspective.*]

William Gass builds sentences, sentences that are their own best excuse for being, sentences that seduce, like a bold, new Annunciation, through the ear. They can be as delicately suspended as a bridge of web spun by the spider that serves as metaphor for the artist in *Omensetter's Luck;* or they can be arches of triumph, solid and lasting and right as pillars set in concrete; or they can lie quietly, feeding and fattening on our attention before we notice that we are noticing their tug at the imagination.

Marooned in their own minds, Gass's protagonists find in sentences their only reliable company, and the sentences they discover are sensitive to their environments: they stagger along with Jorge Seagren through the implacable winter landscape of **"The Pedersen Kid"**; or they endlessly worm through the internal sermons and seethings of the Reverend Jethro Furber in *Omensetter's Luck;* or they imitate the ubiquitous collapse, in stages, of the nameless narrator of **"In the Heart of the Heart of the Country,"** as seen in the bitter litany that opens the section entitled "Weather":

> The sides of the buildings, the roofs, the limbs of the trees are gray. Streets, sidewalks, faces, feelings—they are gray. Speech is gray, and the grass where it shows. Every flank and front, each top is gray. Everything is gray: hair, eyes, window glass, the hawkers' bills and touters' posters, lips, teeth, poles and metal signs— they're gray, quite gray, Cars are gray, Boots, shoes, suits, hats, gloves are gray. Horses, sheep, and cows, cats killed in the road, squirrels in the same way, spar-

rows, doves, and pigeons, all are gray, everything is gray, and everyone is out of luck who lives here.[1]

Characters in their slow death throes find that their sentences are all that is beautiful about them anymore.

For most of us, every other thought is a casualty of distraction, lost in the reckless stammer of the day's other matters; circumstances forever direct us elsewhere, and our "noises . . . simply leak from us like a washerless tap."[2] For Gass, each sentence has its essence, its soul, which is the best exemplification of our own: "If we think it odd the gods should always choose a voice so full and gloriously throated, when they could presumably toot through any instrument," he declares in **"The Soul Inside the Sentence,"** "we should remember that it is their choice of such a golden throat, each time, that makes them gods."[3] Language is more than personal expression, it is spiritual investment. If it is not, he admonishes, our utterances are forever flaccid and phatic—"the tongue is like a stale bun in the mouth."[4] The unarticulated life is not worth living: "So walk around unrewritten, if you like. Live on broken phrases and syllable gristle, telegraphese and film reviews. No one will suspect . . . until you speak, and your soul falls out of your mouth like a can of corn from the shelf."[5]

In fact, Gass argues, we would do well to imitate the rigor of the finest rhetoric, for "Consciousness is all the holiness we have,"[6] and its quality is wholly dependent upon its vehicle. Let the minimalists make all of their linguistic moves with pawns! Gass everywhere demonstrates that the habitations of the word are commodious, luxurious accommodations. Only when the page is exploited "as a field for the voice,"[7] only when we work to muster or to accommodate sentences that deliver "a self which is so certain of its spirit and so insistent on its presence that it puts itself in its syllables like Mr. Gorgeous in his shimmering gown"[8] do we come to understand what inveterate bottom-liners never will: the process is the payoff. So whereas John Gardner, Gass's most notorious opponent on the subject of moral fiction, accused him of perpetrating "mere language," Gass maintains by argument and example that there is nothing "mere" about it. Words are the crux of our concepts, belief's bearings.

That many of Gass's protagonists are themselves verbal artists is a commonplace of Gass criticism, and Gass himself has acknowledged that his heroes are those to whom he has vouchsafed the greatest capacity for articulation. (A careful reading of the theoretical pieces makes it clear that Gass does not believe that the concept of character is obsolete; on the contrary, it must be expanded to admit any and all linguistic "nodes" in a text where language functions self-evidently and with symbolic impact.) Hence, it is the Reverend Jethro Furber, for all his perversion and duplicity, who takes center stage in *Omensetter's Luck,* whereas the prelapsarian, preconscious Brackett Omensetter is but a hollow, a seductive, impossible dream. So, too, are that same novel's decrepit custodian of the past, Israbestis Tott, the abused Jorge Sea-

gren in **"The Pedersen Kid,"** Willie Masters' incorrigibly playful and demanding wife, the nameless narrator who "lives *in*" in **"In the Heart of the Heart of the Country,"** and most recently, William Frederick Kohler, the obsessive historian of *The Tunnel*—all are extolled for their aesthetic achievements despite their various personal failings in other respects. It is important, however, not to minimize this contradiction; to be sure, what enables a Jethro Furber to reside exclusively behind his beautiful barriers of abstraction without regard to the human consequences of his actions is the kind of tyranny that claims eloquence to be not only his edge but his sole ethic. How to grapple with the contention that consciousness is all the holiness we have when such an ugly consciousness prevails is one of the central problems in Gass's fiction.

A second prominent issue that arises when we read Gass is the uneasy relationship between his antimimetic principles and the realistic (meaning both representational and practical) compromises that are everywhere apparent in his pages. Gass is perhaps most often associated with the position that the medium of fiction barges in on its components: characters are confessed as bodies of words, settings as limiting linguistic conveniences, plots as generic enchantments. Everywhere in Gass, whether in the form of outright disclaimers in essays like **"The Concept of Character in Fiction," "The Medium of Fiction," "In Terms of the Toenail,"** or **"Carrots, Noses, Snow, Rose, Roses"** (all from his inaugural volume of nonfiction, *Fiction and the Figures of Life*), or in the form of the preening sentences themselves, lie cautions against suspending disbelief. On the other hand, what better catalog of small-town Midwestern activities and attitudes will we find than **"In the Heart of the Heart of the Country"**? (And how many readers have written Gass to congratulate him on getting their Iowas, their Indianas, right?) What rendition of the frozen Dakota landscape supersedes the descriptions in **"The Pedersen Kid"**? For a matchless study of stalled prospects, read **"Icicles"**; for displaced sensuality, there is no substitute for **"Mrs. Mean"**; for an understanding of parochial fears, the people of Gilean, Ohio, in *Omensetter's Luck* are a case study. And most solemn of all are the murderous echoes of Nazi crimes that haunt the lyrical "flights" of Kohler, whose tunnel is simultaneously an escape route into rhetoric and a self-interment in the intractable data of the death camps. Thus, for all his pronouncements to the contrary, Gass traffics in disciplines, dialects, and private demons like an insider.

Gass's sentences are models of supremely elongated attention. They coil patiently around their subject, frequently nosing it with metaphor or assailing it with alliteration. Whether occasioned by the presence of a likeminded writer (Stein, Colette, Valéry, Emerson, Plato, and Faulkner among them, to give a sample of the range of his company) or by such intricate philosophical surgery as his rumination on the word *and*, Gass writes the way a jazz musician jams—to show us, and to show off. Consider this passage on the being of "blue":

> The word itself has another color. It's not a word with any resonance, although the *e* was once pronounced.

There is only the bump now between *b* and *l,* the relief at the end, the whew. It hasn't the sly turn which crimson takes halfway through, yellow's deceptive jelly, or the rolled-down sound in brown. It hasn't violet's rapid sexual shudder, or like a rough road the irregularity of ultramarine, the low puddle in mauve like a pancake covered with cream, the disapproving purse to pink, the assertive brevity of red, the whine of green. What did Rimbaud know about the vowels we cannot also find outside the lines in which the poet takes an angry piss at heaven? The blue perhaps of the aster or the iris or the air a fist has bruised?[9]

At the risk of diminishing the visceral pleasures of this paragraph, excavation yields a good deal about Gass's method. For example, Gass is often quite deliberate about wedding sentence form with content. In detailing the way the word *blue* emerges from the mouth, he imitates both the "bump" at the beginning of the word (in the opening clause of the sentence, which similarly employs the soft stops in "bump," "between," and "b") and "the relief at the end" with the "whew" that quietly exhausts our breath, which has been sapped by the three sentence sections and the long *es* of "between" and "relief"—like "blue," the sentence relieves us and itself. Gass effects a similar sensation with a previous sentence in *On Being Blue,* in which he is incriminating the slovenliness of sexual detailing in some erotic literature: "Without plan or purpose we slide from substance to sensation, fact to feeling, all *out* becomes *in,* and we hear only exclamations of suspicious satisfaction: the ums, the ohs, the ahs."[10] Greasing the skids of the sentence with all of those *ss,* tumbling out the breath from comma to comma, he ends with the last gasps which, to be sure, have lost their sexual impact and instead are nothing more than the only sounds we can muster.

Then, of course, there are the other attendant colors that swell the cast of characters, whose brief entrances and exits belie the cleverness of their captions. (Surely, each teases us with the possibility that it might serve as effectively as blue as the "star" of the inquiry—as no less profitable a mantra.) The descriptive bits about each color clearly mimic the sound and effect of the color itself; or better, they subsequently determine the quality of each color as though they were character notes at the opening of a play. Hence, because we are alerted to the "turn" in the word *crimson,* we are apt to accept its slyness on the word of the author who has disarmed us with the revelation that, yes, here is another word that suddenly wears its strangeness like a sheen. (In writing of Gass, one is moved to try to write *like* him, and to founder in the fun of trying to.) *Yellow* is "deceptive" in part because *deceptive* smuggles the same subtle sound in its middle, and because jelly, which continues the bridge of soft *es* and thereby seems related to its precedents in the sentence, is itself a sort of uneasy solid. Meter also carries the argument along: the blunt accents of "the rolled-down sound in brown," the curious approach-avoidance of trochees in "hasn't violet's rapid sexual shudder," and the equation of rhythm and meaning in "irregularity" and "ultramarine" have all been tested for sound and sense alike. Each of the colors Gass includes here are comparably disclosed, and none earns

the trust or carries the imaginative weight Gass desires—none but blue. He sets us up for leaps of faith like that, the way he does again at the end of the paragraph by gathering asters and irises in preparation for the bruising of the air, which has unaccountably grown flesh much as colors have assumed character traits.

In honoring one of Gass's protracted sentences from **"The Ontology of the Sentence, or How to Make A World of Words,"** Paul West notes that Gass "reaches a point of voluptuous crisis, at which there is nothing that doesn't belong in the next sentence."[11] Voluptuousness is precisely the point behind Gass's penchant for catalogs, which are as much celebrations of verbal abundance as they are accumulations of evidence to prop up a thesis. "Lists are finally for those who love language," Gass declares, "the vowel-swollen cheek, the lilting, dancing tongue, because lists are fields full of words, and roving bands of 'and.'"[12] Consider the opening pages of *On Being Blue:* the incantatory excess, the generous sweep. Clearly we have been delivered into the hands of the perfect host—erudite, hospitable, a connoisseur of many concerns:

> Blue pencils, blue noses, blue movies, laws, blue legs and stockings, the language of birds, bees, and flowers as sung by longshoremen, that lead-like look the skin has when affected by cold, contusion, sickness, fear; the rotten rum or gin they call blue ruin and the blue devils of its delirium; Russian cats and oysters, a withheld or imprisoned breath, the blue they say that diamonds have, deep holes in the ocean and the blazers English athletes earn that gentlemen may wear; afflictions of the spirit—dumps, mopes, Mondays—all that's dismal—low-down gloomy music, Nova Scotians, cyanosis, hair rinse, bluing bleach; the rare blue dahlia like that blue moon shrewd things happen only once in, or the call for trumps in whist (but who remembers whist or what the death of unplayed games is like?), and correspondingly the flag, Blue Peter, which is our signal for getting under way; a swift pitch, Confederate money, the shaded slopes of clouds and mountains, and so the constantly increasing absentness of Heaven . . . [13]

The remarkable democracy of this catalog, drawing as it does the mundane and the esoteric, the rude and the ethereal alike into its compass, seems to allow us to witness the writing in the act. As the nouns jostle one another in their unaccustomed context, as ideas marinate in associations taken from all manner of learning, unexpected energies are released. Words, concepts, images—these are the featured players in the story of the sentence in the making.

Notice how Gass plays out a sentence the way a surfer might squeeze out all the performance he can from his wave; or, just as an expert fisherman reels in and eases off on his catch, Gass patiently works his topic into his grasp. This particular offering is an homage to the word *hillious* in the course of Gass's exploration of **"Representation and the War for Reality":**

> Yet this being which began with a frail umbilical to its referent—a mother who will not remain to sustain it

but comes into view on occasion the way a busy parent sees its children—this being that began so slimly soon has grown a core, a center, and although it is only a crossing of contexts, a corner, a relation between relations, it is a city of sorts, and has its own life in it, its own character, it has a nature—a 'hilliousness' like San Francisco's; so that now our word, a vacant universal when its meanings were not yet its own, but assigned it like busywork for the otherwise unemployed, is a complete, complex, and quite singular creature, conscious of its rights, its past, its rich roundabouts of reference and suggestion, definition, its variety and ambiguity of use, its layered ironies and opposing inclinations, its elegance, status, social tone, its fully formed though frazzled and untidy self; and it is in this refulgent condition that the word presents itself to the artist: as a silted-up symbol for his ardent declaiming, signs inside the sign of itself the way feelings mingle with other feelings when lips meet—when the history of earlier encounters, kisses, eye-closing contacts, modify one another amid all that moisture which has not yet turned to spit—and consequently is now a sign which is prepared to establish the most profound relations with others of its sort to shape—what?—a simple sentence like a single berry plucked from its bush to melt in a cautious music in the mouth.[14]

This is delicate engineering done with jeweler's tools. On the one hand, Gass draws out sentence segments and fastens their ligatures with surgical concentration upon the shape, heft, and specific density of their elements; on the other hand, Gass trusts the unpremeditated tumble of thoughts into other thoughts, the way images of birth beget kisses, spit, berries, and music in the shifting, looping itinerary of this exemplary sentence, whose "episodic" structure connotes hierarchies, way stations, and tributaries that highlight the process of thought. The resulting combination is a kind of measured rapture, at once fastidious and freewheeling. Like e. e. Cummings and Wallace Stevens (to invoke two otherwise vastly different poets), Gass is quite the exhibitionist when it comes to the pleasure he takes in words for their own splendid sake; like William Faulkner and Stanley Elkin (to select a precursor and a peer who share his passion for sentences), Gass makes it clear that wealth and wisdom are in the writing itself—in the negotiations and adhesions that occur among concepts, allusions, and details borne along by the rhythmic pulse of the line. We recall Faulkner's wish "to say it all . . . between one Cap and one period."[15] In defiance of silence, these authors show how sentences, for all their delicacy, can be superstructures on which to found all manner of possibility.

Style, then, is the issue that permeates assessments of William Gass, and it is prominently featured in the discussions to follow. At the root of each scrimmage between aesthetic and moral responsibilities, and between textual and extratextual realities, are the sentences that compel attention in the first place—"sentences, by the hundreds," says Ihab Hassan, "that would tempt Torquemada to forgive for each word a heretic at the stake."[16] A kind of fundamentalist regard for his craft pervades the fiction and the essays alike. Time and again, Gass enjoins us to marshal the scrupulousness, patience, and luxurious appreciation necessary to unlock the sensuous potential of

words—"love lavished on words" is the phrase he uses in *On Being Blue,* and in *Willie Masters' Lonesome Wife* he demonstrates how the same qualities are shared by good lovers and good readers. But what we might emphasize by way of completing this introduction is the question of whether a commitment to art for art's sake is politically evasive or ethically indefensible, as some detractors have suggested. Alvin H. Rosenfeld, for instance, is troubled by the very satisfactions Gass's talents afford because they may represent a kind of subterfuge whereby virtuosity supplants or pretends to compensate for virtue. Responding to *The Tunnel,* the massive novel still in-progress after more than twenty years, Rosenfeld worries that "the Orphic way out of or around the holocaust" may be meretricious or, worse, a betrayal of conscience:

> Pondering Hitler's murderous deed doubtless is one of the imperative tasks of our time, and one would not want to prevent fiction from taking part in it, but a fiction that would celebrate or seek pleasure in transmutations of the monstrous crime yields not so much aesthetic order as aesthetic alibis—beautifully textured, elaborate lies, but lies all the same.[17]

Is it irresponsible—is it hedonistic—to offer the rigor of sentences while millions suffer real death sentences? Is lyricism truly instructive or valorous under such conditions?

Gass responds by insisting that a revolution of consciousness inevitably includes political and ethical components; furthermore, as embodiments of our best selves, as it were, our most stalwart sentences serve as models of moral behavior. As he claims in **"Culture, Self, and Style,"** "The cultures I should like to count as highest, then, are those which enable the people . . . to become as individual, as conscious, as critical, as whole in themselves, as a good sentence."[18] Thus, Gass's defense goes beyond the contention that the writer's top priority and essential litmus test is that he write well. It argues that encouraging our ability to appreciate good writing is ultimately the best protection the author can provide us against bad writing, be it merely inept or downright manipulative. A reading diet rich in challenging metaphor and risky alliteration does not corrupt but engages the proper habits of critical thought, without which readers could be recipients of philosophical considerations but never their arbiters. Or, as Gass makes the case for commitment as an aesthetic principle,

> To seek the truth (which requires method), to endeavor to be just (which depends on process), to create and serve beauty (which is the formal object of style), these old "ha-has," like peace and freedom and respect for persons, are seldom aims or states of the world these days, but only words most likely found in Sunday schools, or adrift like booze on the breath of cheapjacks, preachers, politicians, teachers, popes; nevertheless, they can still be sweet on the right tongue, and name our ends and our most honorable dreams.[19]

This is what it means to argue that Gass's prose—soaring, supple, startling—asks us to live up to it. And if, as contemporary linguists assert, reality is as much constituted as evoked by language, we must be scrupulous indeed about how we word our world, for each phrase fates us.

The suggestion that the price of love well-made on the page is a compromise of sensitivity to life misses what makes prose vital and memorable, which is not, or at least, not first, the lesson but the language. It is this assumption that unites all of Gass's verbal enterprises, and that undergirds each of the essays presented here, whether its principal scrutiny be cast upon the fiction or the nonfiction. Words are not only the vehicle of thought and feeling, they are their source, and Gass makes it his business to return us from distraction. Tony Tanner explains, "You can find a person's politics, as you can find his ethics, in his sentences."[20] William Gass discovers "the soul inside the sentence" as well.

Notes

1. William H. Gass, "In the Heart of the Heart of the Country," *In the Heart of the Heart of the Country and Other Stories* (New York: Harper & Row, 1968), 180.

2. William H. Gass, "The Soul Inside the Sentence," *Habitations of the Word: Essays* (New York: Simon and Schuster, 1985), 122.

3. "The Soul Inside the Sentence," 117.

4. William H. Gass, "On Talking to Oneself," *Habitations of the Word,* 211.

5. "On Talking to Oneself," 213.

6. William H. Gass, "Culture, Self, and Style," *Habitations of the Word,* 202.

7. William H. Gass, "The Habitations of the Word," *Habitations of the Word,* 264.

8. William H. Gass, "The Death of the Author," *Habitations of the Word,* 287.

9. William H. Gass, *On Being Blue: A Philosophical Inquiry* (Boston: David R. Godine, 1976), 34.

10. *On Being Blue,* 17.

11. Paul West, "The World within the Word" (review), *Sheer Fiction* (New Paltz, NY: McPherson, 1987), 206.

12. William H. Gass, "And," *Habitations of the Word,* 178.

13. *On Being Blue,* 3.

14. William H. Gass, "Representation and the War for Reality," *Habitations of the Word,* 96.

15. Quoted in Donald M. Kartiganer, "William Faulkner," *Columbia Literary History of the United States,* ed. Emory Elliott et al. (New York: Columbia Univ. Press, 1988), 887.

16. Ihab Hassan, "Wars of Desire, Politics of the Word," *Salmagundi* 55 (Winter 1982): 118.

17. Alvin H. Rosenfeld, "The Virtuoso and the Gravity of History," *Salmagundi* 55 (Winter 1982): 109, 108.

18. "Culture, Self, and Style," 203.

19. "Culture, Self, and Style," 203.

20. Tony Tanner, "Frames and Sentences," in *Representation and Performance in Postmodern Fiction,* ed. Maurice Couturier (Delta, 1982), 29.

Philip Stevick (essay date Fall 1991)

SOURCE: "William Gass and the Real World," in *Review of Contemporary Fiction,* Vol. 11, No. 3, Fall, 1991, pp. 71-7.

[*In the following essay, Stevick examines the significance of Gass's comments on his own work in light of his problematic insistence on the nonreferentiality of his texts. Stevick draws attention to paradoxical distinctions between Gass's authorial persona and his actual existence as creator and critic of his own writing.*]

Not very many writers refuse to talk about their work these days. A writer has to be resolutely reclusive to do so, or perhaps supremely rude. People do ask. It is probably attractive for most writers to respond, partly because the questions in most interviews are thoughtful, incisive, and not self-promotive, partly because it is surely good for the ego, creating a secondary level of discourse in which one comments on one's own work, Narcissus as Narcissus, in Tate's classic phrase. Once done, those commentaries can have every possible result and readers will use them as they wish, regarding them as essential keys to the work, like Hopkins talking about sprung rhythm, regarding them as one reader's opinion, no more privileged than any other merely because the reader happens to be the writer, or regarding them as harmless obbligatos, virtuoso exercises in which we are permitted to hear the writer's voice in what seems a more informal setting than the primary works themselves.

The interchanges involving writers as auto-commentators would make an attractive history, especially in the past thirty years. One thinks of that splendidly resonant sentence "Fragments are the only forms I trust," spoken by the narrator of "See the Moon," and Barthelme's attempts ever since to disavow the sentence as his personal credo. Or one thinks of Hawkes, protesting to bemused audiences over the years that his fictions have nothing to do with his inner life. Or one thinks of Barth explaining and explaining that neither his fiction nor his criticism is intended to express a situation in which the possibilities of narration are "exhausted."

William Gass's statements on his own work carry more authority than any of the other members of that rich and fascinating group we have come to think of as the prominent postmodernists or postrealists or metafictionists. It is not primarily because he has spoken and written quite a lot and obviously has a fondness for critical commentary with a polemical edge, although that is true. It is not because everything he says is stylish and witty, although it is. It is that he has spent a lifetime perfecting his skills as a disputant, a professional philosopher, and even before his opponent has opened his mouth, Gass has reduced him to idiocy. It is hard to find people who cherish Gass's opinions. But it is harder to find people who argue them away.

In 1976, *Shenandoah* published a symposium with Gass, Walker Percy, Grace Paley, and Donald Barthelme as participants.[1] It makes as good an example as any of Gass in action. The participants are very different from each other, strenuous, witty, passionate. But soon into the symposium, there is a choosing up of sides and it is Gass against the others. It is Grace Paley who is the most irritated: clearly, she believes that any given story of hers discovers modes of feeling, say, between parent and child, explores what things cost, how much things hurt. Gass's position is clearly universalizing: it is not simply his own fiction he describes but fiction qua fiction, all fiction. That global intent, plus more than a touch of a lecture style, puts him in the position not only of describing to Paley (and Percy and Barthelme) what they do; he condescends to them for imagining that they do otherwise. So caught up is he in the energy of the symposium that Gass creates moments of fiction. Imagining direct quotations, supplying a suggestive detail or two, he presents for our amused delectation the image of himself, after a public reading, listening, yet again, with scorn, to the person who wants to tell him how evocative his fiction is of small-town life in the Midwest. Or we see him opening his fan mail, painfully reading how some bumpkin reader thinks he has got the experience in question "right."

What the position is that so engages the voice and self of Gass is, of course, the rigorous insistence on the artifice of fiction, its status as a verbal construct, a made thing, in which its excellence resides in the coherence, the intricacy, the style of its construction. It is a position that dismisses the truth claims of fiction, dismisses its referential value, its capacity to stand in some relation, however oblique, to "experience." To ask of fiction that it convey the look and feel of the phenomenal world, the inner lives of human figures, an ordering of the raw materials that add up to the way we live now is not only, for Gass, to beg every relevant philosophical question; it is also to violate the nature of fiction, which has, as its only subject, the language of which it is made.

The best way of interrogating such a position is surely not to ask whether it is right or wrong but whether it is useful or illuminating, whether it bears some discernible relation to the art we recognize as fiction, as practiced in various times and places, and, for that matter, as practiced by Gass himself. And the way to test it is not to measure it against standards of philosophical rigor but to measure it against

fiction in general and Gass's fiction in particular. I quote from a representative passage from Gass's best-known fiction, **"In the Heart of the Heart of the Country."**

> Buses like great orange animals move through the early light to school. There the children will be taught to read and warned against Communism. By Miss Janet Jakes. That's not her name. Her name is Helen something—Scott or James. A teacher twenty years. She's now worn smooth, and has a face, Wilfred says, like a mail-order ax.[2]

It is a passage that has been read, by now, by thousands of people, in different ways. But it is surely not presumptuous to imagine certain common patterns of reading that would tend to unite that disparate audience and that would demonstrate, in some sense, what Gass makes when he writes fiction.

The buses move. The reader is reminded that large vehicles, traveling slowly, seem self-propelled, detached from human agency. Imagining the buses as animals suggests the vision of the child, the ease with which we may all, up to a certain age, see headlights as eyes, the grill as nose and mouth, the vehicle as body; but it may also suggest the haunting animism of the opening pages of *Bleak House;* it may, God help us, remind us of all those advertisers who have sought to persuade us that a car is like a shark or a tiger. They move through the early light. Nothing is said of roads and stop signs, waiting children, other vehicles. The buses move through light, as if Monet, taking a break from the water lilies, had decided to paint a schoolbus. And the bus moves in a village setting so small and so quiet that nothing else competes with it.

Surely no reader responds to that sentence as a small miracle of language. As language, there is nothing remarkable about it. The sentence surely seeks to evoke a recognition and to render the thing recalled in a slightly unusual way. "Defamiliarization," the Russian formalists called it. Tolstoy and Chekhov would have understood what is being attempted. "Defamiliarization," of course, is pointless unless a writer can assume a reader who is "familiar" in the first place with the thing described. There are such things as schoolbuses, as every reader of Gass knows and as Gass knows they know, and we all know what they look like.

"Taught to read and warned against Communism": not a zeugma, not quite a syllepsis, that coordinate linkage is meant to jar, nonetheless, with two such disparate subjects yoked together with an "and," as if equal. It is a hit, of course, at a mindless nativism, jingoism; and it is meant to register the state of mind of a particular historical moment, the post-McCarthy, Manichean, Cold War paranoia of the late fifties. To readers who were alive then and found that whole gestalt not to their taste, that single phrase, that mere half sentence, will act like a semiological cue, activating John Foster Dulles, Cardinal Spellman, editorials in the *Chicago Tribune,* John Wayne. Readers who were not alive then will need some help. Janet Jakes does not now rail against communism in the town of B—. That cultural moment is long past. But whether a reader approaches it out of his own vital memory or as a bit of document, evoking something out of recent history, there is no doubt that a reader, any reader, will understand that phrase to refer to aspects of American experience in, say, 1958.

"Janet Jakes," the narrator calls her, playfully, maliciously. And some readers will understand that it is not simply a ludic alliteration that the narrator has bestowed on her but that giving her the surname Jakes suggests the excremental, the anal retentive, playing upon poor Helen Scott a primitive joke in which her last name is equated with shit. A teacher worn smooth. It is not a phrase that seems at all likely for someone of another profession, a lawyer, an accountant. There is a special hostility carried by the phrase, the hostility of the verbal and sensitive for the custodians of words in our youth who fulfilled their function with such a weary lack of wit. One assumes a kinship between Gass and the narrator; and both of them reach out to readers now. We all had a lot of bad teachers back then and they were all named Janet Jakes.

A face like a mail-order ax. The ax one understands well enough. It is a face hard and angular, so little animated as to suggest the metallic, like a tool for attacking trees, or, occasionally, people. But why a mail-order ax? It is a phrase as amusingly hostile as it is, surely in part because it defies explanation. It is Wilfred's phrase and is obviously meant to tap into the resources of folk invective. Containing Wilfred's phrase, the paragraph, and the fiction from which it comes, aims to render a voice, knowing, observant, too clever to be vulnerable yet vulnerable all the same, in touch with the nuances of high art and the directness of the folk, searching in all of the manifestations of small-town narrowness for images that can seem to stand for the personal hurt that the voice projects.

I do not mean primarily to offer guidance in the way in which that little paragraph should be read, although I seem to do so. I mean only to suggest certain essential moves which a reader must be prepared to make. A reader from a part of the world that lacks schoolbuses and is unaware of their conventional coloration will be puzzled by the description, assuming perhaps that orange (or yellow) buses are an inscrutable feature of the town of B—. Or a reader unaware of the simple-minded geometries of the Cold War will assume that reading and the evils of communism are subjects of equal import in American education and that the speaker of the fiction approves.

All fiction (excepting such wonderful exercises in the autotelic as Walter Abish's *Alphabetical Africa*) depends upon a community of information and value among readers. **"In the Heart of the Heart of the Country"** depends upon such a community rather more than most fiction. There is scarcely a sentence in the entire story that does not depend upon a bond or pact with the reader, the writer understanding that the reader will recall schoolbuses, the Cold War, and bad teachers *in a particular way.* It is surely

one of the most rhetorical pieces of fiction written in the last thirty years, endlessly nudging, cajoling, manipulating. Anyone who has tried to teach the story to eighteen-year-olds will know how disappointingly flat the story seems to them: the reading of it depends upon a vital engagement with a culture they do not know and an enthusiastic assent to a large range of judgments of that culture which they could not possibly make. All of this seems so obvious that one may wonder why I have gone to such labor to make the point. The reason takes us to the place where I began. Gass has gone to considerable pains to undermine or deny the point I am seeking to make.

Let us assume that I have tilted things a bit: Gass's position is less unaccountable as a description of certain other works of his, *Willie Masters' Lonesome Wife* for example, which is not about Willie Masters, or his wife, or about schoolbuses, or the United States in the fifties. It is, indisputably, "about" signs and symbols, language, point of view, printed marks on a page, coherence and congruence, fiction, art. Still, the paragraph I quote is *there;* I did not make it up; it really is by Gass; and it is, indisputably, about something besides itself.

How to reconcile the polemical position with the authorial is less difficult than it would seem. For a long time now we have known better than to confuse an author's voices, in print, with what we imagine as his authentic self. If, in Conrad's work, Marlow speaks to us, we attribute his opinions to Marlow, not Conrad. If, on the other hand, somebody speaks to us out of Conrad's fiction who is not Marlow but seemingly Conrad himself, it is not, we know, Conrad but "Conrad," a specialized author-voice. If we read a letter by Conrad, the author may be Conrad, or "Conrad," or ((Conrad)), or (Conrad). Perhaps if we had been in his presence, he would have spoken in a voice as authentic as anybody's ever is. But every utterance that survives his personal presence is a fiction and a tactic, one of several possible voices devised for the occasion.

We are comfortable, as readers and critics, with a writer's versions of his own voice and the multiple ironies that play across his presentation of self—if the writer in question is of an earlier period. When we confront our contemporaries, that ease seems to leave us and a numbing innocence sets in. The Gass whose words are recorded in the transcript of a panel discussion in the pages of *Shenandoah* is not Gass; it is "Gass," an ingenious and fascinating variation of an authentic Gass whom we can never know, a character, as contrived and as fictive as Raskolnikov, a second self (or a third or a fourth self), a wizard, a rhetor, a humbug, an imposter pretending to be Gass. The odd success of that voice is that it has succeeded in persuading us that it speaks with authority on the fiction of Gass.

Three things need to be said about that voice and posture. The first is that it is not very good philosophy. In the last few years a number of books have appeared treating questions of truth, fictionality, artifice, and belief. I think, for example, of Thomas Pavel's *Fictional Worlds* (1986) and Michael Riffaterre's *Fictional Truth* (1990), each quite different from the other but both supple, complex, and sophisticated. Both books are more recent than the major statements of Gass on the question. But neither they nor other comparable works have sprung, in the last decade, from nothing, rather from a long debate on questions of the relation between fiction and world. Gass's statements really do not stand in any relation to that ongoing debate.

The second thing about those statements is that they are, in a sense, quite true. I mean not only that they are true in the sense in which *some* of Gass's fiction does try to cut loose from referentiality. Rather, I mean that insofar as the Gass who participates in panels and writes essays on fiction is, indeed, a fiction himself, then the images of his writing have no bearing on his experience because he, "Gass," not Gass, has no experience. This is, I think, no idle paradox. No one knows the motives of Gass, but it is not difficult to imagine a kind of willed and happy split between the Gass who drinks his coffee and reads his paper in the city of St. Louis and the "Gass" who drinks nothing, reads nothing, and has never lived in "B—. . . a small town fastened to a field in Indiana."

The third thing that needs to be said is that Gass has, by accident or design, created a literary experience that is new and altogether startling. Other contemporary writers ask to be read by the book, occasionally by the period or stage of a career. It is Gass, more than any other American writer now alive, who asks to be read by the oeuvre. There is a sense, a little like Sterne, a little like Whitman, that his work is all one work, still evolving. It is difficult to read middle Gass without wondering about, and seeking out, early Gass, impossible to read middle Gass without musing on the fate of **The Tunnel.** The body of work seems so whole and continuous partly because the nonfiction and the fiction overlap so easily that a distinction between them seems artificial.

Other bodies of work contain a canonical area of autocommentary: James's New York Edition with its prefaces comes to mind. With James, it is an expository mode commenting on a fictive mode. In the case of Gass, not only is the critical prose continuous with the lyrical, nonfictional prose; both of them are continuous with the fiction, and all of them are continuous with the interviews, the panel presentations, the off-the-cuff remarks. Far from the bimodal arrangement of the New York Edition, Gass's oeuvre is pan-modal and everything comments on everything else.

There is something definitive about James's bimodal method. There are the early works, in all of their splendid integrity, and there are the prefaces, in all of their late-James authority, and one measures the distance between, understands, mediates, works it out. Gass is more complicated, or more devious. Everything is an *essai*, the fiction, the "criticism," the remarks, the panel pronouncements. All of these are equal to all of the others and they all work against each other, so that what one is left with is a bundle of tensions and contradictions, which may or may not be what Gass intended. For all of the energy and ingenuity of reader-response criticism in the last thirty years, no one has commented on what happens when a reader does not trust what a writer says about his own work.

What happens, at least in Gass, is a fabric in which every strand pulls against every other and the result, contemplating the whole of the oeuvre, is a tension and unease unprecedented in American writing and in no way allayed by the cool elegance of the prose. So it is that for Gass to be elegantly and ingeniously wrong about himself is to sustain a project in which the inner contractions are precisely the point.

Notes

1. "A Symposium on Fiction," *Shenandoah* 27 (Winter 1976): 3-31.

2. William H. Gass, *In the Heart of The Heart of The Country* (New York: Harper & Row, 1968), 187.

Robert Kelly (review date 26 February 1995)

SOURCE: "A Repulsively Lonely Man," in *New York Times Book Review,* February 26, 1995, pp. 1, 17-8.

[*In the following review, Kelly provides summary analysis of* The Tunnel, *which he describes as "an infuriating and offensive masterpiece."*]

If you want to go down into the self, you'd better go armed to the teeth. Paul Valéry says that somewhere, and it was what came to mind as I began reading **The Tunnel,** this huge and long-awaited novel by William H. Gass, the masterpiece, one must presume, of this 70-year-old American master.

A middle-aged professor of history at a Midwestern university takes to going down into the cellar of his big middle-class house, away from his unloved, undesired, unloving wife. He starts tunneling down through the floor and out beyond the foundations, lying on his fat belly and squirming past trowelfuls of clay and dirt and dust on his way out. He is escaping from his life.

That is the operative metaphor of this 652-page book, yet in only a few of its many chapters is the actual tunneling presented in ordinary narrative space as ordinary narrated event. Mostly the book is remembrance, invective and expostulation, along with lewd instances and merry excuses, and the tunnel remains just a motif, a poetic image occasionally stumbled into in the midst of other things. All the things, in fact, that Mr. Gass has provided his professor with in the way of the arms and weapons he will need to dig out of his life. As we know, and not just from Freud and other psychoenterologists, the only way to dig out of your life is to dig through it. So the professor talks from the middle of his life, backward, forward, remembering a furtive love life that is mostly skin and spurt, the nasty trivial obsessions of academic life, his horrible home.

The Tunnel is maddening, enthralling, appalling, coarse, romantic, sprawling, bawling. It is driven by language and all the gloriously phony precisions the dictionary makes available. It is not a nice book. It will have enemies, and I am not sure after one reading (forgive me, it's a big book) that I am not one of them. Let me tell you what I can.

There was a little boy, an only child, raised in a bleak Midwestern town by an alcoholic mother and a verbally brutal father. It would not take a Dickens to borrow the reader's sympathy and show us the little boy's suffering, his slow escape from that abusive milieu, and to delicately sketch the paths of liberty the boy might find, or the hopeless mire into which he might, reader signing, fall back.

But that is not William Gass's way. Instead, he leaps ahead half a century and gives us the sex-besotted, verbally brutal professor the boy becomes, a gross character with fascist views and a taste for sly affairs with his students. He gives us the thick of the man, the dirt to tunnel through. To get, if we get, at last to the truth of him. In fact, it is not till more than 600 pages into the book that we learn anything like the full particulars of the boy's youth. And when we get there, it is only to doubt that history is any more meaningful when it reveals origins than when it displays the blood and ordure of results.

Our professor of history is William Kohler (the name reminds us of plumbing fixtures), who occupies a wooden chair once held by his teacher, a German scholar named Tabor, who introduced him to the dangerous paths of history-by-paradox, to the historian as the creator of history. A loud know-it-all, Kohler began his academic career with a treatise that seemed to deny the probity and necessity of the Nuremberg Trials. Kohler has now crowned his work with a massive study called "Guilt and Innocence in Hitler's Germany," among the typescript pages of which he interleaves the pages he is writing, the ones we seem to be reading. The novel is then to be understood as the hidden, personal expression of that mind that publicly announces itself in a strange study of the range of German innocence.

Once I tried to write a novel in the voice of someone I detested, while still engaging the reader's fellow feeling. Alas, it was all too easy. And the reader found it all too easy to accept my monster as a hero. There is a *trohison des clercs* not confined to historians and political analysts. Novelists and poets too can commit the treason of the intellectuals. Kohler's whole existence, his operatic self-pity, the very articulateness of his self-justifications, affront our sense of right and of intellectual responsibility. Yet this is where the satiric novelist works best, exploring this plausible monster, our shadow man.

In creating such a character, Mr. Gass avails himself of classic arms of modernism: allusion, puzzle, style as flesh,

language as fable. In those particulars he will not at all disappoint the readers who were so excited by his stories (**"In the Heart of the Heart of the Country"**) a quarter-century ago, his novel *Omensetter's Luck,* the enthralling essays of *On Being Blue,* and, closest in many ways to the book at hand, that nonpareil shimmer of text and image in the novella *Willie Masters' Lonesome Wife,* a foretaste of what we find in *The Tunnel.*

But here the typographical games seem (unlike those in the novella) playful rather than evocative. And while Mr. Gass uses some devices Georges Perec or Harry Mathews might wield as strategies of composition, or grids of meaning, here the devices seem decorative, not so much claims on the reader's puzzle-solving faculties as rewards to the writer for going on, allowing himself some smutty doggerel after a night's hard noveling.

The real structure of the novel seems episodic, spasmodic, and thus apt enough for tunneling and boweling along. The first 50 pages or so are hard going, a Wagnerian wash of false starts, motifs, recollections, anticipations. Music helps; the rhythmic pressure of his language is seductive and bears along ever-interesting images and ideas. So much stuff in this novel! Old High Overdo is spoken here, burgessing and rabelaising; a favorite trick for a Gassian paragraph is to be a list of items rhythmically, sometimes even rhymingly, thrown together.

We first strike steady narrative with a splendid bravura chapter on the childhood town. We follow page after page of nostalgic detail through beautifully circumstanced streets, until slowly we realize that in all this Joycean summoning there is no one present except a plump little lonely boy, all alone in an unpeopled town. And that sets the measure of the book. This is a book about a monstrously lonely man, and how he makes himself so.

For the first few hundred pages not one of the few characters says anything at all except about the narrator. They have no selves except what they say about Willie young or old. The narrator has engulfed their reality, made their words his own.

Martha, his wife; Tabor, his teacher; his oddly-named colleagues in the Nabokovian history department; the imaginal (and maybe imaginary) Susu, with whom he has erotic escapades: lost Lou; fresh little Ru—all the u-girls of his life. We learn about these people, but few of them ever take on any kind of dimensionality, they are voices prodding, blaming, pleasing, leaving Willie.

All except Tabor. He's real enough. (He's usually called Mad Meg, after Bruegel's painting of the madwoman.) Kohler's mother is Margaret too, also a Meg, so the novel has two Mad Megs. Kohler winds up his youth by putting her into a madhouse. It's Tabor who sets Kohler off on his path of study—the darkest business of this novel—Hitler and the Holocaust.

In one of the strongest chapters in the book, Kohler goes through his own memories of researching Kristallnacht, the terrible first act in the war against the Jews, purportedly unleashed in response to the assassination in Paris of a German diplomat by an enraged Jew. Mr. Gass interweaves Kohler's studies of himself and his own reactions (of course) and his debunking guesses about the unethical motives of the assassin, with paragraphs ostensibly recording the memories of someone who actually took part in attacking the Jews.

The horror here and throughout *The Tunnel* is the way history is personalized, the plight of any individual equated with the plight of nations. The theory of Kohler's treatise seems to be something like this: Hitler was a wimp and couldn't have done a thing by himself; it was the massive resentment of the German people that did his work. So the German people are guilty, and the Nazis curiously innocent—dreamers who chanced to dream out loud and cause a 12-year riot of destruction.

What Kohler makes of this is a Party of Disappointed People, a PdP to match Hitler's NSDAP (the Nazi Party). All through *The Tunnel* we find cartoons, jokes, party platform planks, regalia, for this party of the resentful, the envious, the spiteful, the bigoted. (There is even a long chapter in defense of bigotry.) But like the central metaphor of the tunnel itself, the PdP never gets anywhere. It is never narrated, just thought about, played with. Its flags are funny, its party fez is a treat. But its implications are horrendous. Hitler was just a joke; it's the people who did it.

I can't imagine William Gass believing this, any more than I can believe that the Vorticist novelist and painter Wyndham Lewis (whom Mr. Gass often interestingly resembles in daring and despondency) really doubted that the Jews were human. The risk is the representation. One offers a character, and the character is taken as a man, then as a hero. When Kohler, speaking of his own resentment, remarks about Hitler, "I would have followed him just to get even," one senses maybe a comic exaggeration and tries to keep going. But when in the course of his endless bitter reflections on his failed marriage, Kohler exclaims "I've been in bedrooms as bad as Belsen," we recognize only iniquitous nonsense. There is no bedroom as bad as Belsen, and to say so is to signal that you do not know what Belsen is.

In whose hands are we as we read? Much of the time, we revel in the sheer glory of Mr. Gass's phenomenal prose style, his unflagging energy, in a prose that seems to embrace and swallow everything and make all things alive with interest. He can touch the secret waters of childhood, and spell out (in a beautiful chapter called "Do Rivers") the delicate silence of the body after love. But in the same invented character we keep coming up against raw bitterness, bigotries no fresher than Archie Bunker, intolerably lighthearted deployment of Nazi vileness.

While it is impressive that a novelist can pull off the tricks of creating such a sexist, bigoted, hate-filled character and

of making the reader accept his vision of the real, there is a risk, one that every satirist takes. The risk is being believed, taken literally. To this day, we tend to think Jonathan Swift loathed humankind on the strength of Gulliver's aversion. William Gass takes the risk, and it is no small achievement to make us take our bearings from Swift and Wyndham Lewis and those magniloquent sourpusses Louis-Ferdinand Celine and Samuel Beckett, ghosts who seem to hover, as James Joyce does too, over this novel. But it is not much comfort to lay aside this infuriating and offensive masterpiece and call it a satire, as if a genre could heal the wounds it so delights to display. It will be years before we know what to make of it.

Merle Rubin (review date 6 March 1995)

SOURCE: "Notes From a Postmodern 'Underground Man,'" in *The Christian Science Monitor,* March 6, 1995, p. 13.

[*In the following review, Rubin offers unfavorable assessment of* The Tunnel.]

William H. Gass's first novel, **Omensetter's Luck,** was published in 1966. **The Tunnel,** his second full-length novel, has been more than 30 years in the works, we are told, which would place its beginnings at least three years before the publication of his first book.

In the interim, Gass has produced a modest yet considerable body of short fiction and essays that have established him as one of the more innovative and intellectually challenging writers of this era. His essays approach a variety of subjects—the art of fiction to the emotions evoked by the color blue—from expected angles, while his fiction—always experimental—bears the stamp of a serious mind at play.

The narrator and hero of **The Tunnel** is William Frederick Kohler, a fifty-ish professor of history at a Midwestern university. He is not only distinctly unheroic, but he also is not really a narrator. Instead of telling a story, he ruminates and fulminates in circles, like a caged animal. Kohler, it might be said, is a caged mind, a prisoner of a painful self-knowledge that has turned into self-disgust.

As the novel opens, Kohler has just completed his *magnum opus:* a vast, carefully argued tome entitled "Guilt and Innocence in Hitler's Germany." Although the book does not, apparently, absolve the Nazis of guilt, it does challenge some generally accepted interpretations of German war crimes. (What it would seem to resemble—not so much in content as in the kind of controversy aroused—is not the recent spate of fraudulent pseudo-histories that deny the existence of the death camps, but rather, something more akin to Hannah Arendt's 1963 "Eichmann in Jerusalem: A Report on the Banality of Evil.")

As Kohler starts to write the introduction to his otherwise completed work, he finds himself writing something else entirely: a wildly subjective, disorganized, undignified screed of self-revelation that is in every way the opposite of his serenely objective historical study. Turning his own life inside out, Kohler discloses a crazy quilt of memories from an ordinary yet unhappy childhood, lamentations for a lost love affair, complaints against his hapless wife and children, snide comments on his colleagues, and bitter outbursts of resentment and misanthropy, punctuated by a steady stream of obscene limericks.

At the same time he is writing this private "history," Kohler is also secretly digging a tunnel out from the basement of his house. His motive, it would seem, is not escape—unless escape means getting away from other people by burrowing relentlessly into oneself. (His motive, more likely, is providing his author with a metaphor!)

Kohler has led a very ordinary life. An American of German extraction, he grew up on a Midwestern farm, served in World War II, married a woman of similar background, fathered two sons, and rose up the academic ladder. Kohler's one taste of true love was an adulterous affair with a sweet-natured younger woman who eventually left him because of what she termed his "loathsome mind."

His formative intellectual experience was falling under the spell of a crazy, charismatic German historian, Magus Tabor, a Nazi sympathizer who preached that historians must shape history rather than just record it.

Tunneling pointlessly beneath his house, wallowing in self-pity, and ruthlessly exposing his bottomless sense of disappointment, Kohler is a latter-day version of Dostoyevsky's "underground man." But Gass's postmodern nihilist is more interested in revenge than freedom. With bitter irony, he dreams of a Party of the Disappointed People, untold hordes who are filled with envy, resentment, and other "passive emotions," smoldering inwardly, waiting only for another *Führer* to give them the chance to vent their grievances on another set of victims.

Why should Kohler—who has a home, a family, a job with tenure—feel such disappointment? Because, this novel suggests, disappointment is a phenomenon more pervasive than hunger, poverty, or homelessness, affecting all levels of society. The potential fascist, Gass (and Kohler) warn, can be found anywhere people feel they have been cheated of what was rightfully theirs to expect.

Unfortunately, Gass's exhaustive exploration of the fascist state of soul is far more meandering and repetitive than Dostoyevsky's "Notes from the Underground." Although parts of *The Tunnel* are strongly conceived and powerfully written, Gass has not quite solved the artistic problem of how to write an energizing book about a dispiriting subject.

Michael Dirda (review date 12 March 1995)

SOURCE: "In the Dark Chambers of the Soul," in *Washington Post Book World,* March 12, 1995, pp. 1, 10.

[*In the following review, Dirda offers positive assessment of* The Tunnel.]

Long awaited. Eagerly anticipated. Thirty years in the making. Such siren calls have sounded before—most recently luring us to Harold Brodkey's *Runaway Soul* and Norman Mailer's *Harlot's Ghost.* Each time we wonder, could this be it? Our age's *Ulysses?* Our *Magic Mountain?* So we plunk down our cash, lug our shiny purchase home, swiftly read up to page 47 or 99—and then sigh. The great book, the masterpiece is, well, okay. No great shakes. Not bad really. But hardly the work of a god.

Doubtless we'd be less disillusioned if we didn't keep getting our hopes up so high. Because William H. Gass has been working on *The Tunnel* nearly half his life, I wanted the novel to be a transfiguring experience, the kind of book that blows readers away, creates acolytes and strolls into the canon like a boulevardier into a cafe.

Sometimes, it would seem, hopes are fulfilled instead of dashed.

The Tunnel strikes me as an extraordinary achievement, a literary treat with more than a few shocking tricks inside it. For 650 pages one of the consummate magicians of English prose pulls rabbits out of sentences and creates shimmering metaphors before your very eyes. He dazzles and amazes. But be warned: He does so on his own terms and some readers may be confused, bored or repulsed.

First some background.

William H. Gass began work on *The Tunnel* back in 1966. He once told an interviewer: "Who knows, perhaps it will be such a good book no one will want to publish it. I live on that hope." Over the years a dozen sections of the novel appeared in little, arty or even glossy magazines. During the same time, Gass established himself as a major essayist (the racy *On Being Blue,* 1976), a playful experimentalist (the even racier *Willie Master's Lonesome Wife,* 1968), and a leading philosopher of fiction (three collections, most recently *Habitations of the Word,* 1985). All these built upon the reputation of a legendary debut novel, *Omensetter's Luck* (1966), and a collection of short stories with a catchy title that has passed into the language: *In the Heart of the Heart of the Country* (1968). In his spare time Gass taught, mainly at Washington University in St. Louis, and read as intently as a Cistercian: He carefully parsed the prose of Gertrude Stein, aspired to the easy philosophical address of Paul Valéry, worshipped before the achievement and example of Rilke.

And took his sweet time with *The Tunnel:* "I hope that it will be really original in form and effect, although mere originality is not what I'm after." No speedy Updike he. "I write slowly." he once confessed, "because I write badly. I have to rewrite everything many many times just to achieve mediocrity." Yet in his essays and fiction, Gass's patient effort never shows, only a stylish perfection of tone and rhythm, along with a steady rain of unexpected simile. A meek professor's voice is "soft, soothing yet sugarless, deferential, low without sounding sexy, clear through, crisp enough, unaccented, unaffected, proper without being prim—in short, ideal if it were a telephone operator's, or if you wished to speak to the dying." Gass's prose doesn't need to aspire to the condition of music, it is music, meant to be sung, performed, listened to. The text itself becomes a score, the means to elicit hitherto unheard yet heavenly verbal melodies.

Not everyone, of course, cares for such *bel canto* splendor. A few pages into some of Gass's essay-arias readers have been known to scream, "What's the point? Get on with it already." The late John "Moral Fiction" Gardner (who as an editor published Gass's first story) frequently debated his old friend, insisting that writing was more than rococo decoration. But Gass never wavered: Words alone are certain good. Or even beyond good and evil. The description of a girl being viciously beaten (from John Hawkes's *The Lime Twig*) is "impossible to overpraise . . . An example of total control." In *Under the Volcano*, Gass insisted, Malcolm Lowry is "constructing a place, not describing one; he is making a Mexico for the mind, where, strictly speaking, there are no menacing volcanoes, only menacing phrases." The folks who go to books for lifelike characters or plots "are really not interested in literature. They are interested in folks."

Given all this—the novel's abnormally long gestation, its author's Pateresque ideals, a high butter-fat prose—given all this, one might expect to find **The Tunnel** nothing less than a mining disaster. The sort of thing to inspire a folksong. Big Bad Bill. Instead the genial and ingenious Gass has created a cave of wonders. Barring a few deliberately dense, semi-philosophical sections, **The Tunnel** is by turns funny, lyrically beautiful, disturbing, pathetic and perplexing enough to keep scholars busy for decades. Several of its characters—Uncle Balt, for instance, and Culp, who is writing a limerickal history of the world—are pretty clearly imaginary, projections of the narrator-hero's unhinged psyche. Throughout, Gass carefully smudges the line where the narrator's rhetorical exaggeration leaves off and a kind of real madness sets in. No doubt future graduate students will clarify these and other matters. For today's readers it is enough to pause, again and again, at such quietly perfect sentences as "I do the dishes in this house and so I care about the cleanliness of tines" or "A shoe is a poor swatter; it has no holes and advertises its coming."

Gass's prose invites admiration. Not so his hero, the historian William Frederick Kohler. A bigot and a Nazi sympathizer, this fat professor sexually exploits his students, mocks his colleagues, scorns his wife and ignores his children. Kohler (miner in German) is the kind of guy who casually sets fire to insects and somehow manages to strangle a pet cat. As a boy he swipes pennies and bicycles, as a student in 1930s Germany he lobs a brick through a Jewish storewindow on *Kristallnacht*. He also serves up four-letter words with five-star mastery; few of his opinions even gesture toward the politically correct. Now middle-aged at the end of the '60s, he feels washed up, despondent, self-pitying and bitter. His sole interests have devolved to digging a tunnel in his basement and composing a preface to "Guilt and Innocence in Hitler's Germany," his "courageous revamp of the Third Reich and what it was." Unable to focus on his preface, he writes instead about himself and his unhappy, frustrating past.

What are we to make of Kohler? There lies the nub, the mystery of Gass's novel. At times Kohler enchants with his memories of boyhood reading, then repels us with what his lost mistress, Lou—her name a tribute, I suspect, to Rilke's beloved Lou Andreas Salome—once called his "loathesome" mind: He may casually refer to "jewspapers" or defend his father's hatred for Asiatic neighbors whose main crime lies in their not being the right kind of people. Then again Kohler can be heartbreaking as he depicts his sorrowful childhood—alcoholic mother, crippled Dad, obsessive aunt. He can make us see and smell those old corner candy stores, ride along on a Sunday drive in the country, feel the anguish of a birthday party to which no one comes, taste the breakfast he makes for himself. For all his sheer awfulness it's hard to determine whether he is finally a man more sinned against than sinning. "My face simply serves as a place to put my palms."

Kohler, I think, represents that insulted and injured party that resides deep, sometimes not so deep, inside all of us. As he himself writes "if we spoke emotion's language openly . . . then the child whose doll is broken would demand destruction for the world." He dubs this sentiment the "fascism of the heart." A bigot, Kohler says elsewhere, "is a person who has suffered an unmerited injustice, one which hasn't been put right, and woe to others if he ever has a chance to get his own back." Even in his work on the Third Reich, the historian wants, as he notes with sickly humor, to put himself "in the villain's place, to imagine the unimaginable." Which, of course, is just what William Gass is triumphantly doing. In several senses, Kohler almost certainly descends from Dostoevsky's bitter, self-contradictory Underground Man.

Kohler's character will provoke debate. Gass's trickiness—is our "hero" actually constructing a tunnel or is he only digging into his past and self through his writing?—will keep one balanced between uncertainties. In what ways does it matter that Kohler's parents seem to mirror Gass's own? How many different kinds of tunnel—womb, tomb, excretory tract, closet, trunk, even the name Gass (alley in German)—can one spot in these 650 often close and claustrophobic pages? There seem to be various chronological disparities—for instance, on one page Kohler's kids appear to be driving off to college, at others they seem to be youngsters still living at home. What about those curious repetitions, e.g., we are told twice about how Kohler's mother apparently lost her rings, and he himself presents slightly differing accounts of what he was doing on the day his bed-ridden father was taken to the hospital. Is there artistry here? Or editorial oversight, the result of cobbling together a novel from many short sections? Do we really need the book's occasional typographical tricks and illustrations? All interesting questions—for another day.

For now, let us rejoice in Gass's plenty—his language on the page. Here, duly labeled, are some characteristic examples, though Gass's most delicious effects arise in paragraphs and longer passages. As in a proper epic, Kohler opens by asking for divine help: "Flounce from your stew, you sluttish Muse, and bring me a pleasant subject." There are sly self-references: "Martha hates it when I shape my sentences. She says it doesn't sound sincere." Wit: One of Kohler's colleagues "is invariably prepared to grant you your point . . . after he has blunted it." Capsule descriptions: "a smug moral look to him as if he'd eaten oatmeal for breakfast." Sick humor: "my Brown Shirt rig (what an unhappy Halloween that was)." Neat paradoxes: "You only hate what's going on in the world because it interferes with your indifference." Memorable comparisons: "as useful as a jackknife in the hands of an Eagle Scout." Rhetorical tricks: "Our party"—Kohler's imagined Party of Disappointed People—"shall have planks, by god, planks we shall walk our enemies out on." Definitions: Causes, we learn, are "lies that advertise, lies that have fan clubs." Occasional buried allusions: "it drizzles in my heart as it drizzles on the town." Short stories in a sentence: "Culp . . . claimed he went to work solely to summon the strength, simply to find the courage (he said), only to gain time (he would insist) to close the clasp on his briefcase and go home."

At one point, Kohler remarks that "the secret of life is paying absolute attention to what is going on." This is certainly how *The Tunnel* deserves to be read. It contains great beauty, as well as perversity and ugliness, much rage and a terrible sadness. "Never look beneath the surface of life," writes Kohler, "beneath the surface of life is the pit, the abyss, the awful truth." Perhaps Gass has managed, after all, to join his aestheticism to a moral fiction. By the end Kohler comes to seem a kind of fractured Everyman, broken by his past, his prejudices, his unfulfilled dreams. "I cannot complain," he says for all of us. "Yet I do. I do."

Michael Silverblatt (review date 19 March 1995)

SOURCE: "A Small Apartment in Hell," in *Los Angeles Times Book Review*, March 19, 1995, pp. 1, 12-3.

[*In the following review, Silverblatt offers high praise for* The Tunnel.]

The Tunnel is the most beautiful, most complex, most disturbing novel to be published in my lifetime. It took nearly 30 years to write, including long periods of silence and the author's repeated decisions to abandon the work; but some of us have been peeping over William Gass' shoulder, reading sections as they appeared in literary magazines beginning in 1969 when a chapter called "We Have Not Lived the Right Life" appeared in the New American Review.

That piece took my breath away. The narrator, William Kohler, a professor of modern German history and specialist in the Third Reich, told us about the Midwestern town where he was born, called Grand ("simply Grand"). The beleaguered town is visited by dust storms and swarms of grasshoppers, tornadoes and blizzards, no plague more devastating than the invasion of relatives come to celebrate a cousin's wedding:

> Ponderous aunts and uncles, uncles lean as withered beans, aunts pale as piecrust, grandmapas with rheum and gout, cousins shrill as sirens, sounding themselves through the house like warnings of death from the air (later in London, I heard them often), cousins who scratched you under the table, all agloat cousins who told on other cousins, cousins who scooped up fistfuls of mashed potato and let it slime over their wrists; aunts who wore hats in the house, aunts who starched and ironed linens, aunts who stirred pots, flagellated rugs, opened doors for dogs, swatted flies, and reminisced fondly of death and diseases as if they were high school dances, former flames; uncles and great-uncles who, like the hoppers, spat long brown jets of chewing tobacco across the railings while they rocked; nieces and nephews, a few of those too, who peed in their pants, threw up, bawled, and beat you on the shins and ankles with alphabet blocks; relatives at every conceivable remove, but not removed, each noisily present. . . .

The sentence swelled and flooded over three pages, a vast paragraph wave of nausea written so beautifully, so lovingly that it reads like a celebration, sweeping to such a crescendo that I couldn't stop to savor its phrase-by-phrase marvels of sound, of metaphor, of placement, of compact description. I read it aloud to friends, to teachers, to whoever would listen. Its rhythms entered my conversational speech. As the years passed and *The Tunnel* continued to appear in the literary magazines, I came to recognize that the material was dark and difficult and that the prose was designed to render the intractability of the themes at their different levels of difficulty.

Now at last we have *The Tunnel.* For months I have been digging through it. A bleak, black book, it engenders awe and despair. I have read it in its entirely 4 1/2; times, each time finding its resonance and beauty so great as to demand another reading. As I read, I found myself devastated by the thoroughness of the book's annihilating sensibility and revived by the beauty of its language, the complexity of its design, the melancholy, horror and stoic sympathy in its rendering of what we used to call the human condition.

For here you will see the seasons change, and when winter thaws, you will see and hear prose melt. You will sit in weeds by the banks of the Wabash and you will draw rivers in loving strokes down the body of a lost love and witness a prose that can caress as it touches the page. You will be abraded by the harshness of the narrator's rejection of humanity and you will be drawn, miserably, into the contemplation of a consciousness that has seen the nightmares and aberrations of history not as exceptions to the human but as the ultimate expression of the human.

What is *The Tunnel* about? Where are we when we start? For convenience, I will quote from William Gass' own description of his book. William Frederick Kohler "teaches history at a major mid-western university. He has studied in Germany during the thirties, returned with the 1st Army during the invasion as a debriefer, then as a consultant during the Nuremberg Trials. Writes a book called Nuremburg Notes. Its softness earns him some suspicion. He has been working for many years on his magnum opus: 'Guilt and Innocence in Hitler's Germany.' As the novel begins, he has just concluded this book and has begun a self-congratulatory preface when he finds himself blocked and unable to continue. He finds himself writing these pages instead. Since they are exceedingly personal, and he doesn't want his wife to see them, he hides them between the pages of 'Guilt and Innocence,' since he knows she will never read them."

For 30 years, Gass has been living inside Kohler; it must have been like inhabiting a small apartment in hell. At one point Gass wanted the book jacket designed without any author's name. What you were to be holding in your hands was, presumably, the tunnel itself, a burrowing into blackness. Physically, Kohler is fat, as big as Hermann Goering, big as his book, big as the tunnel he is digging under his house to escape his life. The tunnel is Kohler-shaped, an emptiness stretched to re-womb and/or bury him. Kohler presents himself as spiteful and abusive, vicious and bigoted (he's being euphemistic: I'd say genocidal).

Why should we want to spend time in such a frightening, awful presence?

Come on, you're kidding. Does this question need to be answered? At this hour of the world? Have you read Dostoevsky? Shakespeare? Actually, though, the question is interesting, because unlike the great monsters of literature—Garcia Marquez's dictators. Rabelais' giants—Kohler is powerless, pathetic and pitiable. Our terror in reading is at finding how many places he seems to be like us. Toward the end of the novel, when you read Kohler's lecture, "Being a Bigot," you'll feel, at first, an easy superiority. You snicker with condescension. Then you hear Kohler saying things that people around you say every day—when their cars are broken into, when a proselytizer rings the doorbell with some pamphlets. The problem with the character is not that he is a monster; the problem is that the monster has taken recognizable human form. Ordinary people feel their disappointments with burning resentment everyday. Ordinary people think of hitting their children; some ordinary people do. The monstrous is all around us. We feel comfortable blaming a Hitler, but in this book Hitler is just a spark that sets resentment ablaze.

The ancestor authors for this book are Flaubert, Rilke and Joyce. Flaubert because he describes with loving, careful relish the bourgeois life which, as we know from his letters, he ardently deplored. Rilke because of the ambience of pure loss in his poetry and prose, and because of his decision to find a way to praise poverty and desolation, a level of praise that turns his writing into a spiritual project. Joyce because of his systems and his archeology of minutiae—newspapers and garbage floating in the Liffey, making complete itineraries that Joyce chooses to keep track of—and, most crucially, his aesthetic decision to leave the author out of the novel, lounging indifferently above, paring his fingernails. These three are the most passionately human writers of modern literature, but they have come to suspect that something is encroaching on, is infecting, what was previously considered human. In *The Tunnel* that infection has become an epidemic.

So, instead of writing his preface, Kohler begins to dream and doodle. He writes about his childhood, his years as a student in Germany, his time in the army, his marriage, his most memorable infidelity, his greatest love, his uncircumcised and small penis, his love of sweets. He writes about his alcoholic mother: his demanding, unsatisfiable, bigoted father; his passionate, word-drunk teacher-mentor in Germany: his pack-rat maiden aunt under whose bed he remembers finding dozens of empty boxes nesting inside one another, box upon box.

Itemizations, listings of all kinds are clearly essential to the book. Because Kohler studies genocide, he knows that anything not individualized becomes a part of the mass—and masses are murdered or forgotten. History is, to certain eyes, the story of mass uprisings; to other eyes it is the story of the doings of the great. His obsession to list innumerable details is linked with a desire to rescue the individual from the giant mouth of the great death pit, symbolized by the mass burials in the camps over the Polish border.

When Kohler left Grand, he fled from family, "nervous; bent; randy and dissatisfied; vexed; so much so I removed my person from my cousin's wedding celebration (for which I'd bought a new blue suit), and amid hostile uncomprehending faces, angry arguments and explanations, coupled myself to one of those trains like a car crammed with refugees, and had myself drawn away toward history and other desperations." He flees to Germany, where he studies history.

Upon his return, he settles, with a degree, a teaching appointment and a wife, into his "life in a chair" (we are made to remember that the French word *chair* means *flesh*). He has two children, one of whom he can't bring himself to call by name (the careful reader will intuit that this child bears the name Adolf), a no longer desirable wife, unbearable colleagues and affairs real, imagined and remembered with girls whose names all rhyme: Lou, Rue and Susu. (The still more careful reader will come to be aware that when he hears that "ooh" sound, there is some unsatisfying sexual spending going on in the vicinity, as in that "new blue suit" above.)

Kohler writes about his colleagues in the history department, four ludicrous professors, none more or less ludicrous and pathetic than Kohler is himself. We hear their insane quarrels about the nature of history, and as their views of history begin to coincide with their family situations we discover the next link in the long chain of substitution that binds this book: Kohler sees in his family and its quarrels and secrecies the needs of a secretly rising party—the Party of the disappointed People.

For it is "the fascism of the heart" that is the subject of this book. The Third Reich is seen as the active uprising of the passive attitudes and emotions. What are they? Envy, Spite, Secretiveness, Resentment, Bigotry, Long-suffering, Frigidity, Niggardliness, Malice, Sullenness, Churlishness, Hypocrisy, Self-pity, Vindictiveness, Pettiness, Procrastination, Sloth and Jealousy. They are immortalized right in the front of the book, on multicolored pennants (penance?), seen as soon as the title page is flipped. These are the repressed and emerging emotions of the Party of the disappointed People (PdP), Gass' vision of a new Nazi Party in the process of coalescing, until, one day, led by a Führer, the disappointed people will rise. (We are told that America will not have a Führer. The first dictator of America will be called Coach.)

Resentment brings the party into being: "Bad luck alone does not embitter us that badly . . . nor does the feeling that our affairs might have been better managed move us out of range of ordinary disappointment; it is when we recognize that the loss has been caused in great part by others; that it needn't have happened; that there is an enemy out there who has stolen our leaf, soured our wine, infected our book of splendid verse with filthy rhymes; then we are filled with resentment and would hang the villains from that bough we would have lounged in liquorous love beneath had the tree not been cut down by greedy and dim-witted loggers in the pay of the lumber interests. Watch out, then, watch out for us, be on your guard, look sharp, both ways, when we learn—we, in any numbers—when we find who is forcing us—wife, children, Commies, fat cats, Jews—to give up life in order to survive. It is this condition in men that makes them ideal candidates for the Party of the disappointed People."

The tunnel begins to form itself inside Kohler. His past—down to the nonexistence of Santy Claus, down to a disappointing birthday party, an unhappy fumble with a cousin in a car—his past is an assemblage of rejections, betrayals and unpleasant surprises that reflect an inability to accept the nature of life itself. Life is an aggregate of unkept promises, but in his obsession with everyday disappointments, Kohler hollows out the core of life, tunneling deeper and evacuating the content. The book likens his process to a difficult bowel movement.

Kohler imagines himself the possible leader of the potential PdP, and his manuscript is strewn with sample slogans, proclamations and doodles, designs for banners and uniforms, terrifying swastika-like symbols. As he emp-ties himself of his life, he digs (in fact? in metaphor?) a tunnel through the cellar floor, an escape route, whose entrance he hides beneath an abandoned furnace. He hides the dirt from his dig in the drawers of his wife's cumbersome Victorian dressers and armoires. ("I don't want your dirt in my drawers, any more than I want your ideas in my head," says his wife with apparent calm.)

If you sit down to read *The Tunnel,* really read it, you can not help but come away altered. Not because the world it describes is imaginary, but rather because in *The Tunnel* states of reality are multiple and simultaneous. How literature does this is a question of style. Imagine meeting yourself as a fatso in a Dickens novel, now you are abject in a Raymond Carver story, now obsessed and lurid in a case study by Freud, and now, barely there, you're abstracted by Plato. Do you still know who you are? William Gass can give us a Raymond Carver character as analyzed by Freud blown up into a balloon by Dickens' caricaturing style—and give us a Platonic theory of identity as an encore. Can Gass still be himself? I would recognize a page of William Gass anywhere.

There is another, related, paradox: What is outside us as reality and what is inside us as perception do not match. In Gass' novel, the world is observed, internalized as thought and then externalized as language. This amounts to three worlds simultaneously rendered: the world as it would exist if it could exist without us, the world as taken into the mind's convoluted darkness, and then the world blended with our thoughts about it and alchemized in language. The book consists of worded thoughts, the silent mind given language and exteriorized on the page—exteriorized interiority.

Gass describes reality as being like a fly that is caught in three different webs at the same time. Kohler has evacuated himself in word, thought and deed. He has performed the most rigorously fearless moral inventory in all of literature. This is the ennobling or elevating aspect of this tunnel to hell. At the end of the book, Kohler's manuscript lies on his desk, covered with earth and dirt, and he is ready to die, or abide, or mourn: "Meanwhile carry on without complaining. No arm with armband raised on high. No more booming bands, no searchlit skies. Or shall I, like the rivers, rise? Ah. Well. Is rising wise? Revolver like the Führer near an ear. Or lay my mind down by sorrow's side."

This masterpiece, which begins with the information that "the descent to hell is the same from every place," ends elsewhere. Kohler, brutally honest, cannot say where he is now, but I am reminded of the great final paragraph of Italo Calvino's "Invisible Cities":

> The Inferno of the living is not something that will be, if there is one, it is what is already here, the inferno where we live every day, that we form by being together. There are two ways to escape suffering it. The first is easy for many, accept the inferno and become such a part of it that you can no longer see it. The

second is risky and demands constant vigilance and apprehension, seek and learn to recognize who and what, in the midst of hell, are not hell, then make them endure, give them space.

John Leonard (review date 20 March 1995)

SOURCE: "Splendor in the Gass,?" in *The Nation,* March 20, 1995, pp. 388, 390.

[*In the following review, Leonard offers favorable evaluation of* The Tunnel, *concluding that is "a splendid, daunting, loathsome novel."*]

Your wife is fat. Your penis is tiny. Your children are sallow-faced louts. Your mistress dumped you because you have "a loathsome mind." Your colleagues in the history department at a Midwestern university are charlatans and poltroons. Your "post-Bomb pre-Boom" students on the banks of the Wabash are either boring pests or sexual prey. The preface you are writing to your magnum opus, *Guilt and Innocence in Hitler's Germany*—"This is to introduce a work on death by one who's spent his life in a chair"—has turned into a night-shriek. And you are also digging a tunnel in your cellar. To escape from what? From marriage, mind and matter, as if they were concentration camps: "There is no final safety from oneself. It is something we often say, but only the mad believe it, the consequences are so awesome, and so infinite. In that sense Hitler's been the only God. But must I always live in Germany?"

In the noisome 1960s, contemplating "first love, first nights, last stands," at age 50 and the end of his rope, William Frederick Kohler bares his teeth to tear at everything that tethers him: childhood, ego, landscape, language, narratology, Western Civ. It goes without saying that he is also trapped in this panopticon of a postmodern novel that William Gass has been torturing for three decades, as Giacometti tortured metals. Alice down a rabbit hole, Dostoyevsky underground, Orpheus descending: "I am distance itself," says K. "I stand alone on an empty page like a period put down in a snowfall." As his introduction turns into a howl (Henry Adams does *Mein Kampf*), a dozen fonts change points and riot in bolds and italics, outlines and shadows, sub- and super-scripts. Type shifts shape to form cellar steps, male genitalia, a Star of David. The book tunnels itself, "as long as a chimney," carting up dirt, wading through bile, digging out from under cave-ins, excavating emptiness: *Holes, Wombs. Archeologies.* For such a transgressive text, there are also a surprising number of limericks, many about nuns, most obscene. Not that we can trust a word of it, but this is what we're told. . . .

About K's childhood: Silence, exile, punning. He was born in Iowa and raised in Ohio. His arthritic father, a failed architect (Albert Speer? Ayn Rand?), hated him. His alcoholic mother, who forgot to invite any of his friends to his birthday party, went mad in a cyclone and died in an asylum, smelling of juniper like a shrub, combing glass out of her hair. Besides cyclones and a plague of locusts, there was also "The Sunday Drive" into the Heart of the Heart of the Country, achingly evoked in a brilliant chapter as long as a novella, only then to be despoiled, as if, with "a little Führer" at the steering wheel, internal combustion can only produce more poison Gass. "My father taught me how to be a failure. He taught me bigotry and bitterness. I never acquired his courage, because I caught a case of cowardice from my mother—soft as cotton—and I was born with her desperate orality, her slow insistent cruelty—like quicksand—her engulfing love." No wonder he will beat up on his own infant son.

About K's marriage: It's hateful. "Once upon a time, Martha and I slept naked, and we were all the flannel one another needed. Now she goes about layered in ghost garb like a contemporary text." She also collects heavy antique furniture with a view to opening a shop. Into these bureau drawers K will empty his dug-up dirt. "I think what bothers me most about you," she tells him, "is that you're not ashamed of what you are." Worse than her calumnies on his character are her criticisms of his prose: "Martha hates it when I shape my sentences. She says it doesn't sound sincere. . . . She says it falsifies feeling." What sincerity? What feeling? "What does my work do but simply remove some of the armor, the glamour, of Evil. It small-*e*'s it. It shakes a little sugar on the shit. It dares to see a bit of the okay in our great bugaboche. Inexcusable. Slander our saints if you will, but please leave our Satan undefiled by any virtue, his successes inexplicable by any standard." No wonder he will pounce on corn-fed coeds.

About K's education: He grew up mapping emotional climates, and longed to be a poet. Rilke is all over these pages; Homer and Virgil; Dante, Shakespeare, Goethe and Blake; Baudelaire and Hölderlin; adumbrations of Yeats ("old clothes hangered in a closet"), T. S. Eliot (a party of Prufrocks) and Ezra Pound (whom he most resembles). But he abandons poetry, to get at the uglier truths. As a graduate student in prewar Germany, where on Kristallnacht he may have hurled a stone himself, K trifles with the Gypsy Susu, who will pay with her head for violating the Nazi dietary laws by eating the roasted thumbs of Jews; and finds his mentor in Magus Tabor, "Mad Meg"—author of *The Eternal Significance of the Caesar, The Death of Destiny* and *The Failure of the Future,* an amalgam of all that's monstrous in Nietzsche, Spengler and Heidegger, who deplores the Greeks because "the German mind has been so sodomized by these splendid pederasts, we don't know which of our holes is for what"; who preaches that history is half provocation and half revenge, and either American or Mongol, liking "both size and winning"; who believes that "anything of which you could form a passionate conception automatically *was,* because the pure purpose of things lay in their most powerful description." K laps it up, including the swastika: "Has ever a company contrived a better logo? Perhaps Mercedes-Benz." No wonder that Indiana will seem so disappointing upon his return to the States: "I suspect that the first dictator of this country will be called Coach."

About K's career: He got tenure early on, when it was easy, on the basis of his first book, *Nuremberg Notes*, which ridiculed war-crimes trials. Said a reviewer: "Professor Kohler has given to the German mind a public place in nature." Yes, he thinks: "Men may walk about it now like someone waiting for a bus, and feed the birds." What he has done since is "inhale hate like hemp." It's O.K. to be anti-Semitic, if you despise everybody else *too*. He encourages his own doctoral candidates to cobble up theses on fascist symps like D'Annunzio. On a pane of window, a white of page, a black of board, he spies "the utter absence of significance; it is the world as unread and unreadable." Under the sun porch he has stored his trunk of Nazi memorabilia: armband, swagger stick, schnapps flask, silver braid, black boots. He dreams of, and designs, similar insignia for an imaginary Party of the Disappointed People (PdP), every resentful manjackboot of them a Prufrock: "My god, to be a man as I am—smothered with women and children like a duck with onions." But: "History startled me. Melting one small Jew to keep the ovens cool. And then another . . . Schopenhauer, you old fool, this world was never my Idea." K will never be a Coach.

There is no light at the end of this *Tunnel,* not even a whimper, merely a pun, like a shaggy God story, except that God is dead and so are Author Gods. As if he were Isaiah Berlin's evil twin, Gass kills off everybody who was anybody in the Western intellectual tradition—from Plato to Wittgenstein, Pythagoras to Spinoza, Democritus to Durkheim, Aquinas to Unamuno, Tacitus to Gibbon, Parmenides to Hume. Off with their chockablock heads: "Hegel, Bergson, Toynbee, Marx, Buber, Sartre, Niebuhr, and other dead-again Christians." Poets like Pindar and Milton and Wordsworth and Cavafy. And novelists too: Cervantes, de Sade, Pavese, Céline (of course!) and Nabokov. In the service of what? In the service of Kohler's disillusionment. In this most savage of academic novels (by comparison, Mary McCarthy is Mary Poppins), K's a Nabokovian himself, more like a Kinbote than a Pnin, but witless from his blind misreading of the black and white squares. He has come to the conclusion that all history— kings, princes, classes, clans, causes, gods, heroes, coincidences, conspiracies, cabals; Chinese stages and Russian periods and Soviet steps and forward leaps and new world orders; the study of language, the science of men in time or the process by which consciousness seeks to contain its sievelike self—is a cover-up for what any one man, tribe, culture or nation-state will do to any other if it ever gets the power and the chance. "Who of us has not destroyed our enemies in our heads. Suppose but a whisper of our wishes leaked out and half a continent was ready to rise and do our bidding?" We've been at it since Carthage: "Nature punishes gluttony, not avarice or hate. To Nature it's most important that you get a good night's sleep." Who, knowing that we are born stupid and die dumb and leave behind our little lumps of language like a turd, wouldn't become a "friend of Fascist thought"?

No wonder Primo Levi threw himself down a Turin stairwell.

To empty this Kohler out on us, gravedigger Gass has composed a kind of anticanticle, an aria of obloquy. Each paragraph, each sentence, every clause, every phrase, has been burnished breathless, willfully wrought, stippled stark, with an obsessiveness bordering on Brodkey baroque. Not a lyric, but it's laced with acid. Not a whale tooth, but it's scrimshawed. The eye can't rest, nor the mind mist. But isn't this the whole idea? "Syllables catch fire, General. Towns do. Concepts are pulled apart like the joints of a chicken. Substance. Listen to the mind munch. Consonants, General, explode like grenades. Vowels rot in some soft southern mouth, and meaning escapes from those ooooos as from an ass." So much for high culture. Consciousness is noise: Bach and Buchenwald. One thinks of Ezra Pound, that "broken bundle of mirrors" by the waters of Rapallo, wandering Lear-like into his Waste Land madness, a flotsam of Homer and Confucius, of Li Po and Eliot, troubadours and Rosicrucians, Mussolini and Social Credit; that godfather of Modernism, who was ignorant of Marx and uncomprehending of Freud; that critic of literature who'd never read the Russians; that critic of art who'd missed Picasso's point; a tone-deaf composer of tuneless operas with his Brain Sperm and Funny Money theories, and a hatred of "the democratic virus." "Pull down thy vanity!" the old goat cried, and his vanity pulled him so far down that he was vile. Now meet K, for whom history is "horse drop, cow plop, nose snot, rope knot, flesh rot, ink blot, blood clot, street shout," whacking away on his little weenie, a one-man marching band of the banality of evil. Gass has written a splendid, daunting, loathsome novel.

Steven Moore (review date Spring 1995)

SOURCE: A review of *The Tunnel,* in *Review of Contemporary Fiction,* Vol. 15, No. 1, Spring, 1995, pp. 159-60.

[*In the following review, Moore offers high praise for* The Tunnel.]

I'm grateful that I lived long enough to see this. For nearly thirty years Gass has been publishing sections of *The Tunnel* in literary journals (including this one) and as fine press books, and as I devoured these I wondered, as many did, when and if the finished book would appear and whether the whole would be greater than its parts. That question has now been answered beyond my wildest expectations; *The Tunnel* is a stupendous achievement and obviously one of the greatest novels of the century, a novel to set beside the masterpieces of Proust, Joyce, and Musil as well as those of Gass's illustrious contemporaries. Although he has been grouped over the years with such novelists as Pynchon, Gaddis, Coover, Barth, and Elkin, he didn't have a novel in the same league as *Gravity's Rainbow, J R, The Public Burning, LETTERS,* or *George*

Mills. His first two books of fiction, **Omensetter's Luck** and **In the Heart of the Heart of the Country,** are exquisite achievements, but more along the lines of *V.* and *Pricksongs and Descants,* respectively. **Willie Masters' Lonesome Wife** is a brilliant tour de force, but at 64 pages hardly qualifies as a novel. But now with **The Tunnel** Gass has a novel that rivals, perhaps even surpasses those meganovels of his colleagues; it was never a competition, but Gass is now unquestionably in the heavyweight division.

At this early date, and within this limited space, only a bird's-eye view can be given of such a complex novel. So: it's 1967 and a Midwestern history professor has finally finished writing his magnum opus, *Guilt and Innocence in Hitler's Germany.* All that remains is to write the introduction, but instead he begins to write about his own life, which becomes the first-person novel we're reading. Fat and fifty-something, William Frederick Kohler is a bitter man, but a literate one, and as he pours out his litany of complaint and disappointment he erects a great cathedral of rhetoric, "*un livre intérieur,* as Proust puts it," as Kohler puts it. A professional lifetime spent studying Nazism—in a rash moment while studying in Germany in the 1930s, Kohler even participated in *Kristallnacht*—has led him to brood on "the fascism of the heart," both his own and his family's. Such brooding hovers over his childhood in Iowa, his student years in Germany, and his married and professional life in Indiana. It's a novel about history, about hatred, about unhappiness.

But above all it's a novel about language, about a life in language. At an early age Kohler gave up poetry for history, but poetry marked him for her own and dictates every word he utters. Kohler's powerful, polyphonic prose interrogates and illuminates every aspect of his miserable life, and in this regard **The Tunnel** resembles other huge, word-mad novels (*Under the Volcano, Visions of Cody, Miss MacIntosh, My Darling, Mulligan Stew, Darconville's Cat*) where rhetorical energy and excess redeem personal failure and emptiness. The sheer beauty and bravura of Gass's sentences are overwhelming, breathtaking; the novel is a pharaoh's tomb of linguistic treasures. At one point Kohler's wife Martha demands: "tell it straight—the way it is, not what it's like." Kohler wants to tell what it has been *like* to live his life, hence his impassioned use of metaphors, symbols, tropes, allusions. As a result, language is not merely foregrounded here but given a life of its own: "My father is dressed in a thick green woodman's plaid wool shirt, so heavy with adjectives he can hardly lift his arms." Like **Willie Masters,** the pages are adorned with typographical devices, illustrations, different fonts, and special effects. Readers who, like the wife, prefer their prose straight are advised to look elsewhere.

It will takes years of study to excavate fully the artistry of **The Tunnel,** and I can't think of another novel of recent years more deserving of such attention. This is truly one of the great books of our time.

Gary Percesepe (review date Summer 1995)

SOURCE: A review of *The Tunnel,* in *Antioch Review,* Vol. 53, No. 3, Summer, 1995, pp. 380-1.

[*In the following review, Percesepe provides a summary of* The Tunnel *and comments on its critical controversy.*]

Having completed his magnum opus, *Guilt & Innocence in Hitler's Germany,* William Frederick Kohler, distinguished professor of history at a distinguished Indiana University, sits in his chair, intending to write an introduction. Blocked, he writes instead a history of history, or better a history of the historian-as-liar, lout, and loser. Fearing his wife will discover it, he hides the new manuscript by slipping it into the pages of his book. Meanwhile, he begins digging a tunnel out from the basement of his house.

He is *not* a nice man, this Kohler. He speaks with the volume turned up. He lies like a rug and his sins are not small. He gives new meaning to the phrase "unreliable narrator." Kohler's excavations replace the objective with the subjective, the public with the private, the innocent with the guilty, the carefully reasoned causes of history with the shape-shifting meanderings of his burrowing into self, into women, with the Holocaust as host and every man a meanie, Fascists of the heart.

Gass's book [**The Tunnel**] will be hated, which is a lot to say for a book these days. There will be the usual grumbling about morality in fiction. John Gardner started this line with Gass, and his surrogates will surely queue up in reviewing stands and dissertation lines to castigate Gass for the crimes of this novel—already the *New York Times* reviewer cannot forgive him for writing of "bedrooms as bad as Belsen"—but Gass hasn't changed his mind for over thirty years. *He's mad in the mouth and he can write.* He's been digging this tunnel in all possible ways since his first published story, **"The Pedersen Kid"** (published by Gardner, ironically). His credo is that there is freedom and safety in sentences, and language replaces the life. He's playing the one note he knows. If you don't like it, I suppose he'd say, fine. Go dig your own tunnel.

Louis Menand (review date 13 July 1995)

SOURCE: "Journey into the Dark," in *New York Review of Books,* July 13, 1995, pp. 8-10.

[*In the following review, Menand provides a summary of* The Tunnel *and discusses the novel's problematic espousal of bigotry, hate, and amorality. According to Menand, the many biographic parallels between author and protagonist, as well as Gass's resistance to conventional forms of fictional distancing, make it difficult to separate Gass's own ideas from those of his reprehensible character, Kohler.*]

The Tunnel is about a man who undertakes to establish an identity between the frustrations and disappointments of ordinary domestic life and the Holocaust. The man is a professor of history at a university in the American Midwest. The frustrations and disappointments are his own—*The Tunnel* is, in effect, his memoir—and they are of a fairly mundane sort: an alcoholic mother, a sexually stagnant marriage, a failed love affair, uninteresting children, dim students, bickering colleagues, and a general sense of lost entitlement. He has just completed a scholarly study, *Guilt and Innocence in Hitler's Germany,* intended to subvert conventional notions about the morality of the Holocaust. He now writes *The Tunnel* as a kind of companion volume—so that his wife will not know what he's up to, he interleaves the sheets of the two manuscripts on his desk—in which he gives vent to his many resentments, bigotries, and fantasies of revenge, and in which he identifies himself regularly and admiringly with the Nazis.

William Gass is said to have spent thirty years writing this book. It is his second novel. His first, *Omensetter's Luck,* appeared in 1966; he is also, of course, the author of a number of volumes of essays and short fiction. In trying to make sense of a project to which so much time has been dedicated, readers will naturally look for a way to distinguish Gass himself from the petty, self-absorbed, and deeply unpleasant narrator he has created. They will not want to imagine that the narrator's sour nihilism is also Gass's, or that these indecent and seemingly interminable confessions are only displaced autobiography; and they will therefore make every interpretative effort to peel Gass away, so to speak, from the text he has produced. They will find this extremely difficult to do.

The narrator's name is also William, and he has been given a last name, Kohler, that, like Gass, is an easy occasion for schoolyard humor. (Kohler is the brand name of a toilet maker.) Kohler tells us he was born in Iowa; Gass was born in North Dakota. Kohler's father becomes crippled by arthritis, and his mother is an alcoholic who finally has to be institutionalized; these seem to be copies of Gass's own parents, as he has described them in his nonfictional writing. Kohler eventually attends Harvard (Gass went to Cornell); after duty in the Second World War (in which Gass also served), he marries a woman named Martha, with whom he has two children (as does Gass), and he returns to the Midwest to a career (like Gass's) as a professor. Kohler makes frequent reference to his rotundity, which photographs and personal observation confirm to be a feature of the Gass physique, and to his unusually small penis, for which the evidence needed to establish a correspondence is happily lacking. Kohler is a few years older than Gass (who was born in 1924); but this is to make it possible for him to visit Nazi Germany in the late Thirties, and to be middle-aged, the time of reflection and regret, in the late Sixties, which is the period in which the book is set.

Kohler is also (again, like his creator) something of a philosopher. His interpretation of the Holocaust is based on a theory about the nature of history, which he explains as follows: "Neither guilt nor innocence are ontological elements in history; they are merely ideological factors to which a skillful propaganda can seem to lend a causal force, and in that fashion furnish others. . . . If there is a truly diabolical ingredient to events . . . it lies in the nature of History itself, for *it is the chronicle of the cause which causes, not the cause.*" The syntax of the last sentence might be a little clearer: what is meant is that people are incited to act not by past events, but by representations of past events ("it is the *chronicle . . . which causes*"), and those representations reflect the selfish interests of the people who do the representing. There is no past; there are only texts.

Kohler's initiation into this line of thinking comes, as he tells us, during a student visit to Germany in 1938. There he sits at the feet of a professor named Magus Tabor (or "Mad Meg," as Kohler affectionately calls him), whose histrionic lectures on the uses of history take up many pages of *The Tunnel.* These are mostly Nietzschean deconstructions with a Nazi twist—such as, "There is no Nature which we are compelled to obey, only a Culture which various interests conspire to place on its empty throne," and "It's a war of lie against lie in this world where we are," and "Myths are history, and myths are made, preserved, and propagated in some language. Now then, my pure, young, decent countrymen: whose tongue shall be the one to wag?"

Kohler discovers in these exhortations an appealing philosophy of life, for they justify his sense that the will makes its own truth, and they permit him to understand Nazism as a splendid casting off of self-deception, a bold acknowledgment that morality is simply the mask that disguises the real motive for human action, which is the desire to be the dog on top. He declares to Tabor his admiration for the "New Germany"; he participates in the rioting on *Kristallnacht;* he returns to America. The details of his subsequent military service are sketchy, but he is evidently present at the Nuremberg trials, which he pronounces a "charade," on grounds that if there is guilt in merely wishing the extermination of the Jews, no one is innocent. "Who of us has not destroyed our enemies in our heads," as he puts it. "Suppose but a whisper of our wishes leaked out and half a continent was ready to rise and do your bidding?" He publishes these observations in a book called *Nuremberg Notes,* which is roundly attacked, but which launches his academic career.

About half of *The Tunnel* is taken up with reflections, in this vein, on the nature of history and our knowledge of the past, presented in the form of Tabor's monologues, office debates among Kohler's history-department colleagues, and the musings of Kohler himself. The remainder consists of Kohler's recollections of various aspects of his private life—his parents and relations, his childhood terrors and ecstasies, the early years of his marriage, his love affair with a local salesgirl, his daily routine, and his tunnel. The latter is a harebrained attempt to construct an escape tunnel in the basement of his own house, an undertaking involving complicated schemes of concealment which are minutely described and which include breaking the neck of his wife's cat and disposing of the corpse.

The personal stories are interwoven with the reflections on history, and the strands are matched in two ways. There is, first, a continual figuring of domestic events in the language of the Third Reich. "A little Führer's been my father," Kohler says; or, "I've been in bedrooms as bad as Belsen"; or (about his tunnel), "I am running away from home . . . I am escaping the camp." An abusive tirade by his father is compared with a Nazi murdering Jews. A marital quarrel in which dishes are broken is made to recall *Kristallnacht*. Kohler's banishment from his wife's bed evokes Germany's disgrace following the Treaty of Versailles. He catches the spirit of his married life at middle age in the phrase "as we auschwitz along on our merry way."

Kohler's ambition for this "domestic epic," as he terms it, is to achieve for personal life what he imagines Hitler has achieved for political life: to unmask its brutality, to expose "the fascism of the heart." Underwriting this enterprise is a theory of personal relations which is isomorphic, as he tells us, with Tabor's theory of history. "I can tell myself the truth, too," he says, "as Magus Tabor taught me, because ordinary life is supported by lies, made endurable through self-deception." Underneath the smiling fakery, underneath the cosmetic surface of daily existence, there is only "the pit, the abyss, the awful truth, a truth that cannot be lived with, that cannot be abided: human worthlessness, our worthlessness, yours and mine." Domestic life and Nazism are thus related thematically as well as metaphorically, and Kohler is given an extended fantasy about organizing a political party for the scorned and the embittered, those who feel defeated by life, shut out of the banquet. He proposes to name this "the Party of the Disappointed People." Various banners and insignia, the latter looking somehow like biologized swastikas, are designed and are illustrated in the text, and a manifesto is drafted. Bigots, it is explained, will form "the backbone of the Party," along with "all who are downwardly destined." There are dreams of future triumph:

> The Nazi movement was a pinnacle, but it peaked only for a moment. Its remnants may hope for more lasting luck next time, but I am confident that my group, the PdP, already huge, although a sleeping giant, will wake, will rise, will thrive.

The tunnel itself, at one point, is represented as a kind of monument to the movement. "Trajan's column is a solid tunnel turning through the sky," Kohler explains, "while my pillar will be made of air and go the other way; it will celebrate defeat, not victory."

But the tunnel as a symbol is clearly intended to ramify in other directions as well. It is, for one thing, a substitute vagina: "I have my own hole now," says Kohler, with his wife in mind, "your cunt is not the only cave." But it also links up with a series of images, arising repeatedly in a variety of contexts, of circular shapes—not only "cunts" (a favorite subject of reflection throughout), but wedding bands, cyclones, coffee-cup rings, mouths, the letter *O*, and so on. A tunnel is a nothing enclosed by something not itself, and we are expected to see that this might be a fair description of Being, of life in the body: "a tall dark column of damp air," as Kohler describes one character, "hole going nowhere—yes—wind across the mouth of a bottle." Existence is a noise produced out of a hollowness. There is nothing within; there is only the form and the sounds it makes. The essence is empty.

This is, as it happens, exactly the theme of Gass's most famous work of fiction, the short story **"In the Heart of the Heart of the Country"** (1968). And the dismissal of content as anything other than an effect of the manipulation of form, as something "deeper" than the aesthetic surface, has been the constant argument of his criticism.[1] It is alarming to discover these thoughts among the musings of a bigot, and this is therefore the place where most readers will wish that the point of distinction between the two Williams were a little more obvious.

But Kohler turns out to share not only Gass's conception of Being but most of Gass's literary tastes as well. He describes himself (in much the same terms that Gass has) as an addictive reader in his childhood; literature was his escape tunnel from his loveless life. In *The Tunnel* Kohler imitates Sterne and Joyce: he alludes to Flaubert ("I carry on the spirit of Flaubert," he says), to Proust, and to Plato. He reveals himself to be (again like Gass) a particular devotee of Rilke. The final pages of the text are given over in part to translations and variations on a number of Rilke's poems, and Kohler refers several times, with particular insistence, to Rilke's great poem "The Panther," a work from which many of the *The Tunnel*'s motifs—the prisonhouse of signs, the nothingness of the world, the compulsive circling, the paralyzed will, the abysmal heart—might be said to have been directly culled. What possessed Gass to force, from the most intimate material of his own life, the perverse growth of William Kohler? Why this particular *fleur du mal?*

Writers double themselves all the time in their fictions, of course. That's one of the reasons for writing them: to clone yourself and set yourself out on a different path, or to reconfigure yourself as a marginal observer of your own childhood, as Lawrence does with Rupert Birkin in *Women in Love,* and as Woolf does with Lily Briscoe in *To the Lighthouse;* or to split yourself in two and reimagine one side of yourself through the eyes of the other, as Joyce does in *Ulysses,* and as Nabokov does in *Pale Fire.* The remarkable thing about fictional narratives is that readers have so little trouble dissociating the author from the double. Even three-year-olds know that Dr. Seuss is not the Cat in the Hat; and I suspect that if they could articulate the sense they have of the text, they could also explain precisely the way in which Dr. Seuss is *not* not the

Cat in the Hat, as well. The reason for this is that making copies of ourselves and setting them in motion in imaginary space is built in to the way minds work. We do it all the time—when we plan for a future event, when we relive the past, when we daydream.

The Tunnel is extremely resistant to this ordinary readerly operation of dissociation. The resistance gives the book a certain power and even fascination; but it is hard, in the end, to feel that the resulting indeterminacy is intentional. Part of the problem is structural. There is, to begin with, trouble in deciding the book's genre, and where the genre is undecidable, one of the techniques of reading, which is to make sense of texts against their conventions, is blocked. *The Tunnel* is not a novel. Apart from the narrator, it has no characters (though it has some extended descriptions of characters) and it has no plot. Everything is recollected; nothing is dramatized. It makes some claims, in the early going, to be a kind of inverted epic, and Kohler composes an appropriate invocation of the muses ("Sing of disappointments more repeated than the batter of the sea, of lives embittered by resentments so ubiquitous the ocean's salt seems thinly shaken," and so forth). But apart from its scale, there is nothing generically epic about the book. It begins and ends in essentially the same place. As a piece of writing it is, like its protagonist, singularly inert. It performs very large circles around a stasis.

There are also, simply on the level of storytelling, a number of puzzling inconsistencies. Kohler tells us, for example, that he was married in 1940, and makes an elaborate point about the significance of the date; some 200 pages later, he informs us that he married after the war. A long episode in which Kohler's mother misplaces her wedding ring is given, with (apparently) only minor differences, twice in the book. Kohler seems to claim, in the process of making a difficult metaphysical point, that the brick he threw on *Kristallnacht* sailed through an open window and never broke glass; in the actual *Kristallnacht* episode, he throws two bricks, and both are described as breaking glass. If the discrepancies are deliberate, no means are provided for grasping the significance they are intended to have.

And there is, finally, the problem of tone. In his most experimental work of fiction, *Willie Masters' Lonesome Wife* (1968), Gass argued that the times demand "a diction which contains the quaint, the rare, the technical, the obsolete, the old, the lent, the nonce, the local slang and argot of the street, in neighborly confinement," and *The Tunnel* enacts this democracy of diction, this radical mingling of discourses, to an ostentatious degree. There is a lot of Rilke, and there are many limericks. Passages of refined lyricism give way to excited excurses on farting. There are long, memoiristic set pieces, delicately turned and philosophically shaded; and there is this:

> In my trunk I have a cartoon—the newspaper brittle and yellow now—of the scurrilous anti-Semitic sort I so love to collect. The upper legs and lower belly of a prone and naked male are shown. There, a thick and circumcised cock rises out of an ugly crosshatch of hair. Around the cock, however, is wrapped a fist, thrust—one feels forcefully—from the sleeve of a uniformed arm coming toward one like a blow in the shadowy background. Although the fat fingers of the fist cover most of the cock, its Semitic circumcision and glistening head are clearly shown, if rather crudely drawn. Adorning a middle finger of the fist is a large ring with a round face on which a swastika has been boldly incised in heavy ink. The original was in simple black and white, of course. I colored the cock's head red with a crayon later, and made the ring yellow as a winter squash. It is an arresting image.

And this:

> *They discovered in one of the camps*
> how to make Jews into lamps;
> but whenever they skinned them,
> the dirty kikes bit them
> so, their jaws held by wires,
> with a fine pair of pliers,
> they extracted their teeth in advance.

And this:

> I want you to see a Jew's cock—hatless, raw-headed, red as an alcoholic's nose—rise. Any Jew's will do. They are famously the same. Call one up. You get the joke? Well, laugh then, so I'll know. Consider the wrinkled daddy-dinkums that you've made. Feeling qualmish? I want you to watch it while it slowly swells, twitches throughout its formerly flaccid length as though a little link of sausage were alive. I want you to watch closely while it shivers from a hairy thigh and lifts, enlarging as it goes, straightening, becoming stiff as a pole for the German flag, but bearing another banner, oh yes . . . and so . . .
>
> sickening the swollen veins, the kosher crown, the sticky bead like sweat that rises to its top like bullet grease to lubricate the dome . . .
>
> ah, is it not—this image—hideous and tummy turning?
>
> . . . oh yes, but why?
>
> *. . . because it means more Jews.*

The obvious prima facie difference between Gass and Kohler is that Gass is a professor of English and Kohler is professor of history. "I gave up poetry for history in my youth." Kohler tells us, more than once, and this suggests the place where the character is meant to be split off from the author. Kohler is a Gass who took another path, a Gass who has abandoned the consolations of aesthetic form. More encouragingly: literature is what saved Gass from becoming Kohler. But there are two ways to take this. One is to understand Gass to be suggesting that literature survives the abyss as history cannot, because literature has not (as Kohler says history has) been "buggered by ideology." And Kohler is given a little speech, near the close of his text, in praise of poetry, which he makes in pretty much those terms:

> I was slow to realize how poetry created a permanent and universal present like a frieze of stone, and was therefore what any one of us might see and feel who followed its lines and felt its forms: it was the oil of all

ills, didn't the poets claim? the salt of sadness in every tear, artful fence for the stolen kiss. Poetry was not merely what stood in front of your eye like a palace guard (for poetry believes in nothing but the reenactment of its rituals), it *was* those eyes, their pupil'd core, the scene itself.

(The last sentence is essentially a redaction of "The Panther.")

But it is also possible to read **The Tunnel** as a work of self-criticism. Because he emerged on the literary scene in the Sixties, at the same moment as Thomas Pynchon, John Barth, and Donald Barthelme, Gass is commonly classified as a postmodernist, with the implication that he regards "the aesthetic" as just one more ideology of the modern age, another discourse to be parodied, pilloried, and debunked. Hence the mix of high and low diction, the generic indeterminacy, the typographical avant-gardism, the self-conscious punning and wordplay are commonly interpreted as assaults on the purity of form. But the implication is entirely mistaken. Gass is a literary formalist, an aesthete straight out of the nineteenth-century tradition; and his nihilism is entirely consistent with the nihilism of Flaubert, Pater, Joyce, and Stevens.

"My eyes are tired," wrote Joyce near the end of his life. "For over half a century they have gazed into nullity, where they have found a lovely nothing." The eyes that have gazed into the life represented in **The Tunnel,** though, have found an unlovely nothing, and it may be that the purpose of the book is to demonstrate the exhaustion of the modern faith in aesthetic form. Gass may have asked himself not "What would have happened to me if I had had to give up poetry?" but "What would someone like me, whose belief in poetry is founded on a conviction about the nothingness of the world against the power of the word, say if he were asked to make moral sense of an event like the Holocaust?" It may be that **The Tunnel** is an excavation of Gass's own assumptions, and that the book announces not the triumph of formalism, but its defeat. It is impossible to know.

Genre, linear narrative, and diction are props, of course; they are conventions, mere artifices of sense-making. But they are part of the language, too, just as much as words are. One sometimes feels with Gass that he has respect for no unit of language greater than the word, and that he believes that words will carry him through, will create their own pattern of association, their own form, so long as he doesn't submit them to the coercions of conventional structure and selection. If you collapse conventional structure, though, you need some other, unconventional, structure to take its place. Otherwise, all you can make is a pile of words.

Note

1. Much of it is collected in *Fiction and the Figures of Life* (1970), *The World Within the Word* (1978), and *On Being Blue* (1976), all published by Godine.

Jim Lewis (review date February 1997)

SOURCE: A review of *Finding a Form,* in *Artforum,* February, 1997, Vol. 35, No. 6, pp. 19-20.

[*In the following review, Lewis comments on Gass's literary aesthetic and offers positive evaluation of* Finding a Form.]

I happened to be passing through St. Louis one summer weekend in 1989 and, having a day to kill, I took a chance and telephoned William Gass in his offices at the philosophy department at Washington University. Ordinarily I would have hesitated before trying to contact a writer whom I admired; but Gass, as a philosopher, essayist, and novelist, was more important to me than most, and as luck would have it, he was in and invited me over. I remember that the campus was lovely; I remember that Gass was gray-haired and gracious. I remember very little of the conversation itself, except for our closing exchange. At the time I was in my mid '20s, and Angry; Gass was in his mid '60s, and Even Angrier; he'd once invented a character who said, "I want to rise so high . . . that when I shit I won't miss anybody." It was a line I found hard to imagine coming from the generous, seemingly benign man before me; nevertheless, I asked him how he managed his own well-documented rage, expecting, I suppose, some sagacious words on self-possession, a la Montaigne or Emerson. "Oh," he said cheerfully, "I go into the kitchen and break dishes."

If **Finding a Form** is any evidence, there's less intact crockery than ever in Gass' home, but his cupboard's loss is our gain. This is his fourth collection of essays on literature and philosophy, and it comes, surprisingly quickly, on the heels of the publication of **The Tunnel,** an enormous novel that occupied its author for several decades. The newer book gathers together nineteen pieces, on Robert Walser, Ezra Pound, and Ford Madox Ford; on Nietzsche and Wittgenstein; on avant-gardism and formalism; on the mediocrity of the Pulitzer Prize and the pitfalls of writing fiction in the present tense. It is a beautiful book, a dignified and deeply ambitious book, a dazzling book, and in many regards a troubling book.

Gass is an aesthete: the sort of writer, uncommon these days, who believes that art occupies a realm of its own, that its central qualities have no counterpart in the world outside—no counterpart, and indeed no equal. He loves literature, philosophy, and the essay, and his erudition is spectacular, as is his capacity to be moved; he does not like contemporary culture—movies and television, music, advertising—not because of prudery or puritanism (he is, in fact, an epicurean of sorts; certainly few authors in English write more strikingly about sex), but because he finds their pleasures faint, degraded, and corrupt. In an age when the banalities of cultural studies have become an inescapable presence in every academic journal and college curriculum, it's exhilarating to experience the withering blasts of Gass' ire, and listen to him as he enlarges upon them by citing passages of poetry or prose that he particularly admires, wrapping the whole in an ornate latticework of example, exhortation, supposition, cross-reference, and caustic aside. One can, of course, disagree with his tastes and beliefs, in whole or in part, but it's difficult not to admire the force and frankness with which he writes. Thus:

> I do happen to feel, with Theodor Adorno, that writing a book is a very important ethical act, consuming so much of one's life; and that, in these disgusting times, a writer who does not pursue an alienating formalism (but rather tries to buck us up and tell us not to spit in the face of the present, instead of continuing to serve this corrupt and debauched society although it shits on every walk and befouls every free breath), is, if not a pawn of the system (a lackey, we used to say), then probably a liar and a hypocrite.

There is not a word wasted in that passage, not a punch pulled, but reading Gass hasn't always been such an unmixed pleasure. I've always suspected that he was an inherently mediocre writer who, by dint of enormous intelligence and unceasing effort, was slowly making himself into a master. In the past, even in the midst of such marvels as **"On Being Blue,"** an extended essay on the erotic arts, one could occasionally see him straining for effect. He is now seventy-two, and at the top of his form: gone are the forced-sounding metaphors that sometimes marred his earlier prose, gone the sporadic, ill-managed, and sarcastic lapses into vernacular, the typographical games, the mere misanthropy and bursts of petulance. Where once one might have found oneself lost in a swamp of prose, within which the author himself seemed to have abandoned his theme, now the paragraphs are modulated with utter confidence, and if the argument sometimes wanders, we know nonetheless that Gass is leading us someplace. *Finding a Form* is a grand peroration, from a man who has thought and studied and written with extraordinary diligence and love of his chosen art.

For those readers not specifically concerned with literature, the essays on themes derived from the book's title will probably be the most generative. And I believe that every art-school student in the country should be presented with **"The Vicissitudes of the Avant-Garde,"** an essay that begins with the poet Pierre de Ronsard, to whom the term was first applied, and traces the subsequent structure and fate of the phenomenon with a brutally honest hand; he compares Le Corbusier's program of civic self-betterment to that of a Rotarian, for example; and he points out the existence of a "conservative avant-garde" (among whose members he includes Pound and Eliot, Lawrence, and Celine) with an unhappy tendency to fall into racism and fascism.

Still, a potential problem begins to appear with Gass' argument here. Writing against Pound et al., he says, "Art, the honest article, lives (with other realities) only in an active present." So it does: but he condemns the present, too, in the passage I copied out above, and others like it throughout the book. So an obsession with the past is culpable, and a capitulation to the present is worse—and for the record, Gass dismisses Futurism, too. What then remains? An art, he argues, that is permanently original, permanently present, and he provides a list of those works that he believes belong in such a category (Bach is on it, and so is Schoenberg, Henry James and Gertrude Stein, Duchamp and Rothko).

I suspect that Gass is indulging in a certain degree of hand waving here; his point depends more on rhetoric than on argument. But it would be a mistake to accuse him, therefore, of succumbing to conservative canon mongering. In fact, one of the most agreeable of Gass' traits is the deftness with which he sidesteps the common political categories of contemporary thought— radical, liberal, reactionary. I sometimes think he would say almost anything, if he felt he could say it well. Caveat lector: No real criticism occurs in *Finding a Form,* and no real theory emerges from it. It is more the record of one man's reading, with all its crankiness and inconsistency left intact and uncorrected, and worth attending to as such—not because Gass is entirely original, still less because he's obviously right, but because the evidence he marshals for his archaic cause is so lovingly assembled, and exquisitely expressed, that the whole book bids to illustrate the thesis it expresses: for it is itself so well made as to be inherently valuable, and I am glad it exists.

As I've said, it is a furious piece of work. But it ends with a spectacular, art-affirming passage, a single paragraph, composed of a single sentence several hundred words long. I can't quote it all here, but it ends with "joy," and the word is fully justified. It serves, moreover, as a kind of kaleidoscope lens through which one can look back on the book, indeed the career, that precedes it. Of course, it is joy he's been after all along, and joy that he provides. As a promoter of difficult pleasures, more precious for being hard won, Gass has no contemporary equal.

Maureen Howard (review date 9 March 1997)

SOURCE: "In the Heart of the Heart of the Text," in *New York Times Book Review,* March 9, 1997, p. 6.

[*In the following review, Howard offers positive evaluation of* Finding a Form.]

William H. Gass is embattled. It's awful out there where the stale sweets of commerce are served up as art, laced with dope for the dopes, violence injected for the numb. As a gentleman trained in philosophy, a writer of distinguished fiction, an honored academic, Mr. Gass has his rights, if not every right, to remain sore. And in *Finding a Form* he confronts the conundrum of the writer that he has faced in previous essays: the word is sacred, though there are no longer sacred texts; "writing puts the writer in illusory command of the world, empowers someone otherwise powerless, but with a power no more pointed than a pencil."

Yes, the old genetics: in the beginning was the word, but once made flesh the word was heir to ills as well as miracles. Words, sentences, the form that the writer must find for them in a work that may be called art, are real; possessed of their own reality, they need not reflect any social or moral reality the work is responsible only to its own perfection. These are the tenets of Gassian belief that underscore this collection of occasional pieces, reviews and contemplations. I have no argument with the Grecian urn on its pedestal, no aim to so contextualize a Shakespeare sonnet that I no longer hear the pure beauty of a rhyme. However, I will take Mr. Gass at his word about the will to belief on the part of the artist: "Disbelief is healthier, is a better exercise for the mind, and I admire it even when I see someone's disbelief busy disbelieving me." My position as a reader of these essays is much like my standing as a lapsed Roman Catholic. I am not sufficiently fallen away. So we are both hedging our bets, writer and reader, though Mr. Gass, for one aphoristic moment, lets me off the hook: "The reader's freedom is a holy thing."

Yet how dominant his voice. There is no American writer who so wants to hold me in his sway. He is an illusionist in command of his performance when he celebrates, less so when he scolds. His reviews of Robert Walser, the Swiss fabulator of the ordinary, and of the dream fiction of Danilo Kis, in which, "sentence by sentence, the song is built and immeasurable meanings meant," are mighty appreciations. With generosity he gives way to a like, yet other, sensibility and to another's informing mind. He is equally giving in **"A Fiesta for the Form,"** his praise song to the exotic birds of metafiction—Gabriel García Márquez, Jorge Luis Borges, Julio Cortázar—who invented forms beyond the 19th-century novel's mimetic trappings. They are his sort of folk, while Ford Madox Ford is not, for Ford's impressionism, like Impressionism itself, is seen as "the last bow" to "the old order." Ford fails as a modern, and therefore fails.

But are we not all trapped in our time, though many artists strain against it? The American metafictionists of the 1960's—John Barth, Donald Barthelme, Robert Coover, William Gass—made the radical break from high modern as well as from the paraphernalia of character and plot in the bourgeois novel in their particular time, an era of post-postwar fiction's first romance with the academy. I suppose there is no line drawn in the sands of time between defending one's artistic beliefs and becoming somewhat cranky and defensive about them.

But then, Mr. Gass likes a good scramble. In reviewing biographies of Nietzsche and Wittgenstein, he gets in the ring with these sadly human supermen. Sentence by sparring sentence he's up for it: Nietzsche, he says, "habitually confuses psychology and logic; he has a smeary mind." Wittgenstein "rarely troubled to hide the fact that what was most important to him was the course and quality of his own mind. It was, after all, his art." That might be said of Mr. Gass; in fact, he says it of himself by his display of

mind on the page, especially in the essay **"The Book as a Container of Consciousness."** Here he writes, "How bodylike the book is, how mindlike the text." The Cartesian split is mended by a transcendence in which he, as reader of true art, becomes one with the words, the page. For him, it is a communion of self with text devoutly to be wished.

I beg to ask a question or two, but the man at the podium has long been entitled to his captive audience. What's more, my questions are crude, tired classroom jargon: What of "the other"? Is it such a descent from grace just to listen to others? What the grown man sitting next to me on the subway, slowly drawing a finger under the simple words in his adult-literacy text, might say to me (his words will not be written)—must it be of no interest, his esthetic of no worth? How philistine my questions, shameful the tatty petticoat of my liberal "constructs," and I leave the class in disgrace to ask myself: Why rail at popular culture, as Mr. Gass often does, when it's been with us so long? Mummery, bearbaiting, Vauxhall, the lady-book telling the language of flowers. Yes, the wonders of technology have proliferated trash at an unimagined rate, but if the outrage of a brilliant man sounds curmudgeonly, his grumbling will come off as merely personal and pre-empt any serious discussion of culture.

It may not be fair to say that as a philosopher William Gass is a writer of fiction; yet I do think it can be said that he is no longer doing philosophy in *Finding a Form,* no longer engaging in its discourse. In cavalier fashion, he works the room solo: "My stories are malevolently anti-narrative, and my essays are maliciously anti-expository, but the ideology of my opposition arrived long after my antagonism had become a trait of character." If I take "expository" to be an elucidation of argument or intent, I am freed to follow the play of the writer's mind, to bend to his will to take me where he wills. Reading these essays is like watching a glass blower at work over the flame, seeing his forms emerge—at times amusing trinkets, at times vessels of beauty and purpose. To me the trinkets are those occasional pieces in which attitude interferes with reason: scoring off the irritating inequities of literary prizes, expressing dismay at the glut of ill-conceived autobiographies—sensational or dull—and slamming yet another nail in the coffin of the avant-garde. The vases of Mr. Gass's making (something like extruded golden bowls with nearly undetectable flaws) would be in such a thoughtful essay as **"The Story of the State of Nature,"** in which he mounts, in clear expository fashion, an entire history of narrative, from our simple linear game of reading for the end to the complexities and accumulations of reading the lifelike whole.

A striking theme in *Finding a Form* is that of exile, the garden lost to our first parents, lost to us: "To be a preacher is to bring your sense of sin to the front of the church, but to be an artist is to give to every mean and ardent, petty and profound, feature of the soul a glorious, godlike shape." I feel that Mr. Gass is the preacher, and that his belief in the artist is a flamboyant transgression, yet a belief as solid as the chair he sat in for 26 years writing his massive novel ***The Tunnel.*** I do not confuse Mr. Gass with his professorial antihero, Kohler, a dislikable chap excavating the past, though the novelist speaks of listening to his own words as if in Kohler-like confinement.

To search out the right word and claim it, to spin or etch or agonize over the trajectory of each sentence, demands an enormous investment of mind and body. No one in the world can possibly care as much as the inmate, the self-enchanter. It has always been so, but seems more so now that words themselves are marginalized, devalued as subtitles for the picture show. I admire Mr. Gass's play of mind and serious meditations, even his will, though often I disbelieve him. Stanley Cavell, the philosopher who gave us our Thoreau, tells us in "The Senses of Walden": "Writing—heroic writing, the writing of a nation's scripture—must assume the conditions of language as such; re-experience, as it, were, the fact that there is such a thing as language at all and assume responsibility for it—find a way to acknowledge it—until the nation is capable of serious speech again." Against the odds, William Gass, a tortured man in the attic, has empowered himself to write scripture in an unredemptive time.

John O'Brien (review date Spring 1997)

SOURCE: A review of *Finding a Form,* in *Review of Contemporary Fiction,* Vol. 17, No. 1, Spring, 1997, pp. 170-1.

[*In the following review, O'Brien offers praise for* Finding a Form.]

Gass is a writer who has always believed in public discourse, that the act of the critic and scholar is to engage as wide an audience as possible in matters of serious intent (that is, that these things matter or at least have consequences for the body politic) and that, therefore, the form of the discourse must itself be engaging, resonate, enlivening, and at times, vituperative. The present collection hits the mark in every way, though one may mourn that there are not more critics who see their function as this, as opposed to the academic specialist who, if he speaks to anyone more than himself, speaks only to other, specialists in deadening prose. One might especially wish that other novelists might so speak more often, though of course one knows that many of them have little critical ability and can speak, quite poorly and unintelligently, only about themselves. Gass is this rare figure whose critical abilities go hand-in-hand with his fictional ones.

Appropriately enough, this volume opens with a biting attack on award giving, starting with the Pulitzer for fiction, which has a remarkable history of recognizing the bad and the forgettable, and moving on to many others that champion the mediocre and fashionable in the name of literary quality. This essay is followed by one given to the subject of the use of the present tense in fiction, a practice Gass generally abhors but one which is perfectly suited to readers raised on television and those writers who have their fingers on the pulse of their generation (the minimalists, of course, come in for the most severe tongue lashings here).

In another essay, one that begins with rather painful descriptions of his childhood and therefore partial explanation for his having become a writer rather than a car salesman or a contented businessman, Gass lays down his aesthetic, which has always been his aesthetic, old-fashioned (Aristotle, Aquinas, Gilson) and therefore radical for our times: "I believe that the artist's fundamental loyalty must be to form, and his energy employed in the activity of making. . . . The poet, every artist, is a maker whose aim is to make something supremely worthwhile, to make something inherently valuable in itself." All of this is opposed to such perennially acclaimed aims as understanding the world, understanding ourselves or those near and dear to us, reflecting or mirroring one thing or another, making the world a better place, societal improvement, the betterment of one group or another (women, blacks, gays, the aristocracy, whatever), or the ever-favorite replication of reality in a kind of condensed version that makes reality even more real.

Other chapters are given to Wittgenstein, Nietzsche, Robert Walser, Gass's beloved Spanish (well, at least one, Juan Goytisolo) and Latin Americans (Fuentes, Lezama Lema, Cabrera Infante, Cortazar, Vargas Llosa, though one glaring omission here is Fernando del Paso, an omission I am sure Mr. Gass will rectify in any future edition), Danilo Kis, Ford Madox Ford, and of course Gertrude Stein roams the pages freely. And there is, towards the end, a particularly interesting chapter entitled **"The Music of Prose."** The temptation here, which I will resist, is to quote endlessly from Gass. Better just to go read the book, but rather than reading it cover to cover, one should more profitably read a chapter a day—there is too much in each of them to move swiftly on. Or one may be better advised to stop and reread the works he has reference to (I do not remember my Walser the way that Gass remembers his).

The book is an utter pleasure and is itself a working demonstration of the author's recurring theme: the celebration of language and the power of prose to create and re-create the world. I will not bother to say that it should be the winner of one of those prizes that Gass scorns, nor do I think he need worry about this happening; his politics, aesthetics, and intelligence are wrong for the committees.

Marcus Klein (essay date Summer 1997)

SOURCE: "Postmodernizing the Holocaust: William Gass in *The Tunnel*," in *New England Review,* Vol. 18, No. 3, Summer, 1997, pp. 79-87.

[*In the following essay, Klein examines Gass's postmodern conflation of personal and national history, morality, and guilt associated with the horrors of Nazi Germany as presented through the protagonist, Kohler, in* The Tunnel. *"Given the perspective to which we are invited," Klein concludes, "Kohler's evil amounts to an irrelevant tawdriness."*]

The subject is the Shoah, the Catastrophe, and how to account for it—a subject in history, to say the least, to which Gass as novelist and as theorist of fiction brings a presumption of the uncertainty of narrative and of the autonomy of language. This of course is nothing like Holocaust-denial. To the contrary, it is engagement of any sort that is thrown into doubt, in the postmodern way. "Postmodernism" no doubt is showing its age and has become distended and shapeless, applied to anything seeming a little bit impertinent, but the epistemological skepticism (sometimes despairing when rendered, often joking) remains basic. And in the case of this very long, perplexed, extravagant, antic novel, some twenty-six years in the making (so it is said) because the stakes are high while the gestures of demonstration are virtually unbounded . . . for such reasons this has the look of a serious inquiry. Not that something of the same has not been tried before: among prime instances, Thomas Pynchon variously; Robert Coover's *The Public Burning* (Nixon and the Rosenbergs); John Barth's *Giles Goat-Boy* (the Cold War). But here now is postmodern idea and practice brought to bear on the worst that modern history has known, offering occasion for contemplation as to just how serious such an enterprise as this actually is or is not or might be. What consequences are here for the learning, so one might ask, and to what end, and with what implication for what, for some approximately twenty-six years, has been a dominating if not quite a prevailing mode of perception.

The story goes this way: William Kohler, a professor of history at a Midwestern university, having finished the main text of his study entitled *Guilt and Innocence in Hitler's Germany,* is now ready to write the introduction to it, and that preparation constitutes the occasion of **The Tunnel.** Contemplation of his introduction leads him to consideration of the past and present of his own life along with questions of guilt and innocence of the personal sort (and, for reasons which remain obscure, also leads him to the digging of a tunnel in the basement of his home). In the 1930s, as a young man, Kohler had studied history and philosophy at a German university with a famous professor who had become a Nazi apologist—Heidegger, of course, here named "Magus Tabor"—and Kohler had been present in Germany at the beginnings of the Nazi era. He now thinks about his German experience, about his childhood, about his wife and his children, his love affairs, and his colleagues and his relations with them. He is a lonely man, and disappointed. He thinks that he might form a new political party, the "Party of Disappointed People." At the beginning of his 652 oversized pages of monologue he says, "Endings possess me." At the end, page 652, he invokes sorrow. Shall I, he says, "lay my mind down by

sorrow's side." While in between the pages wander and lurch, interrupted by splotches in various colors here and there, shifts in typefaces, smudges, numerologies, and numerous other challenges to syntax.

I. INNOCENCE

Kohler wishes to write such an introduction to his book on the Germans, so he says, as might raise an "arch of triumph" for himself, or might constitute the placing of a wreath upon his own brow. At the end, however, his monologue modulates into retreat. He contemplates burial of his work, will settle for decency, dignity, and forethoughtfulness: "Make my wrong right," he says. "Take one day like a pill to prevent the illness of another." And that this constitutes dramatic and necessary realization rather than, perhaps, weary wisdom, is to be understood by negative reference on the one hand to a Leni Riefenstahl idea of German joy ("No arm with armband raised on high. No more booming bands, no searchlit skies") and on the other hand to Kohler's own history of passions often perverse, always promising a vitality, but, in the end, either lost or unachieved. That tunnel, which in fact serves as only an occasional trope in **The Tunnel,** at this ending would seem to figure for the birth which is a fall: "Or shall I, like the rivers, rise? Ah. Well. Is rising wise? Revolver like the Führer near an ear. Or lay my mind down by sorrow's side."

Nor is this movement only, opportunistically, voluptuous. (As in: "Come then, Sorrow! / Sweetest Sorrow! / Like an own babe I nurse thee on my breast. . . . I thought to leave thee / And deceive thee, / But now of all the world I love thee best.") Nor is it admonitory. (One thinks of Dr. Tamkin's advice to another Wilhelm, in Bellow's *Seize the Day:* "I want to tell you, don't marry suffering. Some people do. They get married to it, and sleep and eat together, just as husband and wife. If they go with joy they think it's adultery.")

On the other hand, and to look back, there is something surprising about this result following upon all of that presumption of a tortured mind which for many years has been at the work of personal confrontation of great evil. After the Holocaust . . . only "sorrow"? And not even quite that, but rather a resolve of dedication as to a lady.

But then again that surprise is there only after the looking back, for something has happened in the meantime, inevitably no doubt as the novel has more and more converted history to a matter of personal perception, so that Kohler's own resolution, in its pitch and its modulation, is after all apt termination of what the novel has come to be.

It is a different novel in approximately its second half. For one thing, there is occasional evidence of some simple authorial forgetfulness, no doubt consequent upon that twenty-six years of labor which went into it. Louis Menand in the review in *New York Review of Books* points to discrepancies in the account of Kohler's participation in the events of November 9, 1938, Kristallnacht—did Kohler break glass or not? Gass has him saying both that he did not and that he did, and there is no indication that we are to understand that Kohler is a man who has imperfect recollection of factually discrete events. Again: On page one there are a William (seeming to be other than the narrator), an Olive, a Reynolds, a Rosie, and an Alice who commits her Tampax to the trash. And that is the last of William, Olive, Reynolds, Rosie, and this Alice. On page two we learn that Kohler had served as some kind of consultant (on "'dirty Fascist things'") at the Nuremberg Trials—an important datum, one would think, which is briefly recalled on page 368, and then again forgotten. Kohler is a boy in North Dakota *circa* page 100, and is growing up in Ohio pages 475ff.

More largely, many of what are Gass's various extravagances of the first half, of syntax and pictoriograph composition and other, have tended to dwindle away in the second, giving way to fairly straightforward accounts of present adventure and, especially, recollections of family history. And that latter content indeed virtually displaces what initially had been proposed as the rationale for the whole, namely Kohler's attempt to account for "Guilt and Innocence in Hitler's Germany" with emphasis in all perversity on the innocence.

Perhaps all of this above had led to a cul-de-sac somewhere around year thirteen, a cul-de-sac arrived at through both the disruptions of narrative and the attempt to confront the Holocaust in terms other than moral and with response other than horror. There would seem to be an unmarked crisis *circa* page 417, when Kohler asserts the "relative resilience to tampering, to falsification" of historical fact, thereby importantly appearing to reject the teachings of Magus Tabor—but for no reason that this text in itself has provided. Kohler will go on to speculate on the nature of "fact," but the significant thing is that the tale in itself has not demanded such speculation, except insofar as that the idea that historical fact is malleable in the hands of the historian has finally in itself not led anywhere in novelistic terms.

In any event, the novel's large, specifically stated thesis, that "Fascism" is in "the heart"—to quote the flap copy, which no doubt Gass approved and which perhaps he wrote—would seem not only to have provided the basis for the historian William Kohler's ruminations on his own history but also, it would seem, to have provided the route by which William Gass was able to amble back into quite familiar territory: that of his first novel, *Omensetter's Luck,* and the tales collected in *In the Heart of the Heart of the Country,* and then *Willie Master's Lonesome Wife.* The home place in all of these is the place of middling grotesque lives, sometimes comically grotesque and sometimes only radiant, which are unexpected because hidden within the ordinary. The great revelation of *Omensetter's Luck,* it is to be recalled, is that the central character, Brackett Omensetter, is a perfectly ordinary

man. And as for geography, appropriately the home place is the Middle West, which is Gass country certainly much more emphatically than ever is Germany, whether Hitler's or Herder's. ("There is nothing genuinely German about me," says Kohler several times, and he is right—discounting only the German origins of somber postmodernist jesting.) Sherwood Anderson comes to mind—unto the faith, indeed, in the awful mystery of the words, the cunning little words, although here bolstered by language theory, and with the sometimes consequent feeling that nothing will stop the flow of them. Or perhaps Ed Howe or Edward Eggleston, those earlier exploiters of the drear country of passions imprisoned and lives ending in, exactly, disappointment.

When Kohler invents his "Party of Disappointed People," that after all is something quite considerably less dire than National Socialism. The invention is witty and plaintive, and is mordant-comical to the degree that it at once appeals to universality and announces inadequacy. Everyone is "disappointed"—excepting of course those persons for whom catastrophe has changed everything. A low-grade chronic resentment is plausibly The Human Condition, virtually in a medical sense. Your wife is fat. Your children are no great shakes—are irritating, to tell the truth. Your mother was an embarrassment. You can't stand the furniture. Your desk is a mess. Your colleagues are getting ahead of you. Lovers have left you. You make filth in mind and body. The message is: Sound familiar? The lurking, infusing irony of the "Party of Disappointed People" is in the fact that "Disappointment" is the common condition which pretty much ends in itself, and to make the joke that there might be a "Party" of the disappointed is to see at once that the universal condition is not a public condition. The Disenfranchised might make a clamor. The Discriminated-Against, surely. Perhaps the Disenchanted. But Disappointment, like Sorrow, is a material for an ode or a roundelay, not for an assault on public history.

Much of *The Tunnel,* especially in the second half, is in fact William Kohler's song of sorrows and of disappointments suffered, or not even that necessarily, but his recollection of losses, and much of that, presented in relatively discrete straightforward segments, and taken for itself, is sad and lovely—indicating probably that Gass is so good a novelist that after all he will not be thesis-driven.

There is a tale about Kohler's "Uncle Balt," which in fact occurs rather early on. It begins: "Yet why should I remember Uncle Balt," and in truth there is little of a thematic necessity despite the presuming title of the section: "Uncle Balt and the Nature of Being." Uncle Balt is a loner out there (and back there) in the loneliness of an American Midwestern farm. "Tall, thin, slightly cadaverous," it is said: "Uncle Balt's voice issued from his body as from a length of pipe." When he does speak, as recollection would have it, his speech is the gnomic, ironic, ritualized language of a folkish American Midwest. Uncle Balt is a joshing misogynist. He talks—or, better, utters—in an idiom which by convention announces stubbornness and self-doubt both at once. He says of women: "NO KNITTIN, JUST NATTERIN. . . . CHITCHAT IN A HAT. . . . THEY'LL HOPPER A MAN IN HALF, GRAZE YOU TO THE GROUND," as a man might say who has known grasshoppers. Of work and the young boy William Kohler's not doing it: "WHAT HAPPENED TODAY? NO HOEIN, NO ROWIN, NO PLANTIN, NO WEEDIN OR PINCHIN BACK, I BET." Uncle Balt works from dawn to dark and dies alone in his fields—in order to affirm a region.

And quite despite that attributed "fascism of the heart" and despite the sometime grotesqueness of the materials, there is much yearning in Kohler's recollections, especially in his recollections of family, approaching but then easing away from larger implication.

Father was a bigot, so Kohler says. "He taught me bigotry and bitterness." And that certainly might look forward to the fascism of the heart, but it is said also that Father held two jobs during the Depression, working long heartless hours, took the family on memorable Sunday drives ending at the ice cream store, hung around the garage (explicitly not the saloon nor the pool hall), and suffered an alcoholic wife, not to speak of the son, Kohler himself, who was a bookish lad, and inept, and a masturbator. As for the bigotry, the total evidence is Father's outrage directed against the next-door neighbors, Asians of some kind seemingly, who in fact, as reported, are difficult neighbors. They do strange things with chickens. They dry their underclothes on bushes. They parade around their lot, tootling, as it is said, like crazy.

And there was a maiden aunt who moved in and was a compulsive gift-giver. No fascist she, of course. Her name is "Auntie," signifying something at once generic and somewhat comic. For years she had been nursing a vengeance directed against a former employer for whom she had been a stenographer and accountant and whom she had served loyally, and who had fired her. To what narrative end does any of this lead, one may ask, and the answer is that she is there either because she was there (Did the boy William Gass back in North Dakota have an Auntie? Not unlikely), or because the maiden aunt is another confirmation of the region of the disappointments. Indeed, she is a better emblem of the place than some others, with the frustration of her loyalties and her inapt, self-defeating attempts to compel love and family.

Much of this novel about the Holocaust is given to memories of Kohler's boozy, vague, sloppy, mortifying mother. She bleeds on the carpet during her menstrual periods. She bestows her unlikely sexual favors on the bakery delivery man, who brings her gin. There is one strikingly wrought episode in which Mother prepares a birthday party for the twelve-year-old boy. Generally she is too drunk even to attend parties, but she bakes a cake, a three-layer chocolate cake, the middle layer surrounded with a kind of chocolate pudding, the top covered with Hershey's kisses, frosting dripping along the sides, which

sinks and resolves into glop . . . and the half-blown balloons are allowed to drift around the yard, but no matter because Mother in her vagueness had forgotten to mail the invitations—to the boyhood chums who in any event were not such because the kid didn't have any friends. At age fifteen the boy takes Mother off to be institutionalized, and she will die.

Given the specificity it is difficult to think that all of this is simply wild invention on the part of the author (Gass, not Kohler), but then it happens in any event that Gass retrieves Mother from simple grotesqueness while providing Kohler with an understanding the only appropriate synonym for which is love:

> Why [he wonders], when my mother found the envelopes in the utensil drawer, and knew, then, that she had forgotten to mail the invitations, let alone collect regrets, did she go ahead and bake such an ambitious cake, the recipe for which would make even an accomplished cook a little nervous, even if her anxieties might have been relieved by knowing no one was coming; although she would have to expect her husband's exasperation, and believe in my disappointment at not being surprised? Go figure. Maybe she felt from the first she had to do the right thing by me, and throw a party for my birthday, and make me a cake as it was customary for mothers to do, and carry on, in spite of every obstacle, perhaps with the help of a swallow or two of gin [and so on].

In one of the loveliest paragraphs of this long novel Kohler imagines a reverie for Mother:

> . . . afraid to sleep because when you slept you were no longer alone; and knowing loneliness like a spouse, as if it were simply the only condition of life, however unfriendly, however ugly and hard; hating loneliness, yet fearful of anything else but loneliness; having been disappointed—the word is too weak—at every social turn: no longer going out, attending church, having dinner parties, playing bridge with friends; . . . well, you have a little nip now and then, what harm? it's small expense, you've saved a bit on duds since you don't have any need or interest in pretty clothes, no one looks at you with desire, or touches you with pleasure, or talks to you as if you might be amusing, or finds it fun to be in your presence, or delights in your appearance, or compliments you on your looks, or wit, or skill with food or figures, facts or fucking, so you have a pick-me-up now and then, just to jolt the spirits, merely to erase a little melancholy when it comes on in the middle of a morning . . . there's no friend to phone, so why bother to watch your weight or wash or read books or plan the future, the future is your enemy, only the past can be stood, because the past is thank god dead, perhaps a little toast to that, all those increasingly gloriously golden days, when your breasts were young, and you thought, I can do that. . . .

That there is considerable investment of self in this reverie on the part at least of the narrator, maybe of the author, is obvious, and on the part of the narrator, in any event, that investment is made explicit. This middling, personal, abiding, heartbreaking, humdrum of disappointment . . . Too weak a term? Not really. That's what the mass of human beings really lead lives of. This commonplace of disappointment, come to the point of crisis, is Kohler's quite genuine eloquence.

But on the other hand . . .

II. Look Who Thinks He's Guilty

There is good reason to pluck these sentences from both the sheer inordinateness of *The Tunnel* and Gass's deliberate strategies for undermining narrative. Already in the stories in *In the Heart of the Heart of the Country* Gass had pretty much abandoned linear plot. Already in *Willie Master's Lonesome Wife* he had begun to play with graphics and colors upon the page, in place of narrative. In *The Tunnel* there are places where the first-person narration (and there is no other) goes on and on so endlessly circumstantially in a process of associative increments as in effect not merely to interrogate but to cancel narration, and these places are not few. It takes Kohler twelve oversized pages (437-449) to get up in the morning—to turn off the alarm, go to the toilet, brush his teeth, gargle, put on his pants, and so on, in a way calculated, so it must be, to make the reader doze—and that Gass is constantly aware of a reader reading is beyond doubt. The trickster-ism with graphics is here in *The Tunnel* carried to the point where pages of prose are made to be entirely illeg-ible—pages are smeared, as with dirty carbon paper or printer cartridge; words are placed in non-linear order; sentences from here and there are interleaved, not with any perceptible intent to create fugues of meaning. Page numbers are dropped. Pagination from author's proofs is inserted. There are drawings which look like—take your pick—illustrations by Jean Arp for the poems of Tristan Tzara, or amoebae.

The purpose of all of this is clear enough, deriving as it does from a postmodernist orthodoxy already waning by the time of the 1995 publication of *The Tunnel.* Narration, once again, is suspect. Language itself is always (already) arbitrary. Does the Word encompass the world outside of the word? Gass clearly began there, although, once again, his novel clearly pulled elsewhere.

No doubt that these ideas promised relevance to a reflec-tion on the Holocaust. Kohler's intellectual father, Magus Tabor, is the principal elaborator of the idea that language creates historical fact, and, as the novel makes him to be, Magus Tabor is at once intellectually powerful, hence seductive, and repulsive, and he is a Nazi, all, again, with clear reference to Heidegger. And the novel itself, in its strategies of composition, would seem to want to exploit the same ambiguities. It springs from ideas which once and not long ago seduced a great many people (people with advanced degrees in philosophy and literature), ideas which are at the same time repellant, virtually in a physi-cal sense. *The Tunnel* is a novel which you are invited to read and which often enough shuts the door in your face, declaring itself to be unreadable.

Nonetheless, and despite deliberated equivocations and contrarinesses, the novel does begin with and takes its

basic subject matter from that one enormous, imperious historical fact, which it does moralize. How to explain the Holocaust? The novel is pinned to that subject and to that question, which indeed it answers. Kohler has written his book on "Guilt and Innocence in Hitler's Germany." We don't know much about that book, but Gass does give us the first sentence: "Time cannot do to ordinary things what we timelessly do to one another." And that might be just Kohler's idea except that, for all of the somewhat tangle of the syntax, it amounts to the same thing as to speak of "the fascism of the heart"—the phrase which is used to advertise *The Tunnel,* and which occurs at least a couple of times within the text itself. Fascism, that is to say, and quite simply, is not an event but is regarded as the same thing as "evil"—lower-case *e,* as Kohler elsewhere insists—and it is the human thing.

And to say that is to say that we are all fascists albeit in our littler ways, and then to say that is to say in turn that we are all guilty, Jews quite specifically included ("now you wish to hang Herr Goering. . . . well, I tell you, give a Jew a hammer and he'll break your head, the teeth of every tiger are alike, it's in the species, it's deep in our dirty genes").

That we are all guilty is everywhere a perversely generous (Christian) platitude requiring some detail of demonstra-tion, and in this case Kohler's 652-page confessional memoir is all that we can have because narrative and language dogmatically back off from matter outside the skull. This acutely lonely man reflects on his life and is spiteful. He might be Dostoyevsky's Underground Man—surely that is one of the allusions suggested by his tunnel-ing in the basement—except indeed that the scene of the life is not nineteenth-century Russia but is close to hand, perhaps in his hand. In truth he is much closer to being a figure drawn from that other Midwesterner James Thurber. He is victimized by domestic life, his own particular one but entirely recognizable. He is beset and imprisoned—by a fat and flaccid wife, by children whom he doesn't like (he seems to know the name of only one of his two sons) and who don't like him, and by a house and furniture and the problems of career, and so forth. And *therefore* we are to know that Kohler understands how a people might let loose . . . and kill Jews.

Gass's Kohler is emphatically not Gass himself. It is neces-sary to say that because some of the reviewers of the novel have wanted to note the parallels between the two—both are in fact Midwesterners, both are professors, both are Americans with German antecedents, they have the same first name, and other things. The interviewer for *The New York Times Book Review* thought it right to ask Gass how deeply he identified with his protagonist—an odd ques-tion, one would think, given this Kohler. (Gass said that he has experienced loneliness, like everyone else, but that was the extent of the identification.)

On the other hand it is humanly difficult to think that this 652-page monologue is entirely made up, that there is no author within the prose, or that Kohler is entirely an "unreliable narrator" kept devilishly just beyond the reader's reach.

And more to the point, Gass certainly is deeply implicated in the moralizing which the novel itself does accomplish, to the extent that it is he after all who has invented this adventure in the imagination of evil.

One would ask finally, of just what and to what degree is Kohler guilty? The limitations of a prescriptively Midwestern sort perhaps prevent extravagances, but in any event Kohler's individual acts of trespass are not many and altogether are small potatoes, as we Midwesterners say, and besides that, are pretty much forgiven by act of the novel. Kohler has a lousy attitude toward his wife, but she has her own peculiarities. There is a section called "Child Abuse" which might be promising, but in fact is recollection merely of a time when Kohler as a young father was briefly left alone with an infant son who wouldn't stop crying and Kohler had yelled at him to SHUT UP! That's all. No real harm done, despite the insertion into this recollection of reminders of the voice of the Führer. Kohler has pawed at some of his female students, but his marriage is depicted as a sexless one. He has had one extended affair with a girl named Lou, but he had really been in love with her. And, besides, she had left him, and so the adultery, if it amounted to so much as that, is embalmed in melancholy. The man is to be pitied.

None of this is necessarily negligible, except that this novel of reflection on the Holocaust (which did happen, quite outside of this novel) wants to make it all seem to be tremendously more.

The novel brings to bear all kinds of exorbitances. There is the sheer length of it. There is the well-advertised fact that it took so long to write. There is the usualness of a prose which advances on a principle of discontinuousness, so that there is almost constant implication that there is more meaning there than the prose can encompass. Hence, again, the drawings and the colors and the typographical antics. The implication is of overload. Beyond these stratagems, moreover, there is much talk of cocks and cunts, being a repeated effort toward rhetorical shock. And many another thing. Lou, when discovered, had worked in the jewelry store of a five-and-dime (like Hart Crane's Woolworth madonna), which is probably to suggest something like a folk motif. The fact that there are points of identity between Kohler and his author might well suggest an additional burden of authority—after all, it could well be that it is not a fictional character talking, but the author. Again, Kohler as writer invokes the Muses, all of them and several of his own invention, and the spirits, as well, of Homer, Virgil, Dante, and Milton, and given the gigantism of Gass's novel, it might well be Gass who is doing the invoking. This middling man Kohler, like middling, domestic Leopold Bloom before him, is to be epical, if not on the basis of his own plain story then by other means.

Joyce's invoked history was after all mostly a literary one. Maybe that is the difference. To be invited by this novel to contemplate the Holocaust and then to be introduced to the sins of William Kohler is to discover some considerable pretension at work, if not indeed a prescription for moral blindness. Given the perspective to which we are invited, Kohler's evil amounts to an irrelevant tawdriness. Or should amount to such; there is some discrepancy of magnitude here. While to say that deep in his heart this tawdry Kohler is a Fascist, maybe even just potentially—like all of us—and is a vessel for the kind of guilt that made the Holocaust, is to put another construction upon "banality of evil" (and there are numerous indications in the novel that Gass has taken license from Hannah Arendt). It is to reduce the horror itself to a banality, and thereby to dismiss it. Concerned as he is with his penis and his fat wife and lost Lou, and the rest, William Kohler cannot have the faintest idea of the event of the slaughter of the six million.

Some such smallness might well result when, in the postmodern way, history becomes no more than the record of the historian's altogether commonplace anxieties. He has met the enemy. . . .

Kenneth Haynes (review date Fall 1997)

SOURCE: A review of *The Tunnel*, in *Sewanee Review*, Vol. CV, No. 4, Fall, 1997, pp. cxx-cxxii.

[*In the following review, Haynes offers positive assessment of* The Tunnel.]

To **The Tunnel** William H. Gass has brought Flaubert's ambition to write a book with no subject, a book that would be held together by the strength of its style alone, to creating a book on the Holocaust. Or rather a book on a book on the Holocaust: the protagonist William Kohler, a middle-aged professor of history in a midwestern university, has just finished a large work on Hitler's Germany. Surreptitiously he now writes these pages, a mixture of embittered personal history and of angry and ironic philosophic reflection. We learn about his childhood humiliations under a bullying father and self-destructive mother, his infatuation with an aesthetic philosophy of history while a student in Weimar Germany, the erosions and degradations of his marriage, various petty and sterile quarrels with colleagues, and other disappointments. His spirits rise when he decides to dig a tunnel under the house. While writing these private pages, he shrinks the Holocaust in a series of limericks, freely appeals to it in metaphors and similes of his own trivial disappointments, and indulges in anti-Semitism when it serves his embittered stance.

For instance he brings a pseudological rigor to his misanthropy when he remarks that the murdered Jews include "thousands of thieves, murderers, shylocks, con men, homos, hoboes, wastrels, peevish clerks, shysters, drunkards, hopheads, Don Juans, pipsqueaks, debtors, premature ejaculators, epileptics, fibbers, frigid females, faddists, nags, nailbiters and bedwetters, frumps, fanatics, friggers, bullies, cripples, fancy ladies." The monologue of this hateful man is coercive and all-encompassing: there is never an opportunity to stand back from it, and we may even lose the obvious perspective that the Nazi terror was infinitely worse than the "mean and silly carking" of any part of humanity. Gass's ability to create a totality in which Kohler's easy cynicism seems to be a hard-won realism, where his petty and insignificant frustrations seem to be genuine indications that the world is evil, and where his self-pity feels attractive and justified, is a technical accomplishment, at least, of enormous difficulty.

Almost every page of the book is intolerable. Limericks, self-conscious and self-regarding phrases, fantastic similes, graphic and typographic tricks, and unrelenting alliteration fill the pages, all of which insist continually on the arbitrary nature of the language, the emptiness of its conceits, its forged pretensions. Kohler issues more fiats to symbols than W. B. Yeats ever did; a blackboard and a window become donnish excursus into philosophy. The discussions of philosophy are as empty as the symbols, and they make clear the egotistical, self-deluding, and destructive impulses behind argument and belief.

"How hollow heart and full of filth thou art," as Samuel Beckett turned La Rochefoucauld's phrase, compacts the two themes of the book, hollowness and filth. The tunnel Kohler digs, his cesspool heart, his conceited language, and his brutish history are empty; the excavated filth is hidden away. We listen with horrified and temporary sympathy to a base mind believing its excuses, palliating its faults, and discharging its venom.

But why should we listen? Besides the fact that such a monologue can be done, and done excruciatingly well, why do it? In one sense it is an improper question: an artist can choose his or her subject. The subject is not simply indifferent, however, because the Holocaust is not simply a subject. One way to begin to see the relation of ethics and aesthetics in the book is to note that Kristallnacht is at the center. Kohler, a student in Germany, throws a rock through both a Jewish and a non-Jewish shop window, and with that action the terrible convergence of the petty with the tragic becomes evident. The descent from thoughtlessness and passive self-absorption to public atrocity takes an instant. Gass's aesthetic makes a self-sustained world out of such self-absorption. The book is meant to collide constantly with the reader's knowledge of the murderous consequences.

Though a monologue, the novel nonetheless must let the other characters enter somehow. The recollections from childhood of his mother and father and of his Uncle Balt are among the most vivid. The section "Fugue," for instance, is a tour de force but not only that; the device of counterpoint permits the tracing of the child's mind in its

humiliation and disappointment as it is forced to go over and over the same ground ("My dad wouldn't let me have a dog. A dog? A dog we don't need").

The absence of direct dialogue also means that there is no point of reference outside his ravings, his unreliable memory, and his dissembled honesty. We have only these pages offered as his transcribed consciousness, and so some questions for the work are psychological. What motivates him to dig the tunnel, or what does the digging express about him? Is the tunnel more than a conceit? Can we recognize Kohler as human?

A lovingly rendered assault on the ear, on goodness, and on reason, *The Tunnel* has not yet found its readers. The outlines of its structure, the dilations and contractions of its chronology, and its aesthetic remain to be elucidated. But its picture of the subterranean fury of disappointed people has no equal. It is horrible to admit that it may be prophetic. Books have their fates.

Arthur Saltzman (review date Fall 1998)

SOURCE: A review of *Cartesian Sonata and Other Novellas,* in *Review of Contemporary Fiction,* Vol. 18, No. 3, Fall, 1998, p. 232.

[*In the following review, Saltzman offers positive assessment of* Cartesian Sonata and Other Novellas.]

William Gass regularly demonstrates how the artist's devotion is best measured by his concern for the language he cultivates; his scruple and injunction is that beauty, vision, and morality require the precision and ingenuity of sentences lovingly constructed. Indeed, the dry prairie solitudes that dominate these four novellas prove to be rich soil for linguistic enterprises. Disappointments and hatreds still sparkle with imagery and inspire alliterative runs that belie the conditions of the characters, whose funks and futilities recall those of Gass's previous Midwestern populations in *Omensetter's Luck* and *In the Heart of the Heart of the Country*.

The title novella features a poisonous marriage reminiscent of the Kohlers in *The Tunnel*. It pits airy, clairvoyant Ella Bend Hess against her abusive Caliban of a husband, Edgar—mind and matter, recoiling from one another, yet inevitably knotted together in mutual complaint. Gass again makes exquisite rhetorical capital out of such unsentimental motives as blame, anger, misogyny, guilt, and disaffection. Thus, even as "Cartesian Sonata" steeps the human spirit in a muddle of primal urges, it strives to redeem our creatureliness through style.

While *Cartesian Sonata* reworks writings going back over thirty years, the other three novellas are of recent vintage. Gass's consistency of theme and method over that period suggests that his fictions elaborate the artistic philosophy of his renowned essays. Walt Riff, an itinerant accountant and cooker of books, finds religion in the abundant, meticulously cared-for kitsch at a rural **"Bed and Breakfast."** Pinched, despairing, and Emma Bishop beats a retreat into an obsession with poetry in **"Emma Enters a Sentence of Elizabeth Bishop's."** And Luther Penner, **"The Master of Secret Revenges,"** refines an aesthetic of retribution in the fevered tradition of Jethro Furber, to name another of Gass's prominent fascists of the heart.

A lavish imagination is all that is lovely about any of Gass's isolated minds. In each novella, meanness or poverty sets us up for ambushes by lines too marvelous to miss.

James Wood (review date 1 November 1998)

SOURCE: "Wrestling with God," in *New York Times Book Review,* November 1, 1998, p. 9.

[*In the following review, Wood offers positive evaluation of* Cartesian Sonata and Other Novellas, *though notes contradictions and shortcomings in the work.*]

William Gass is the philosopher-novelist who wants to scramble our p's and q's. For many years, in both essays and novels, he has fought what he sees as the unthinking realism of American fiction. Instead of the blank essences of traditional fiction, he wants the subtle absences of the *nouveau roman*: instead of characters, he organizes his fictions around "symbolic centers"; instead of the architecture of plot, he attends to the fabric of form; instead of the management of reality, he prefers to liberate the sentence. The writer's task is not to make the reader believe in a world: Gass has argued that "one of the most petty of human desires is the desire to be believed, on the one hand, and the will to belief, on the other." The writer's task, as he sees it, is to stimulate disbelief, to tickle the reader's alienation.

Yet the contradictions and difficulties of being an avant-garde novelist—and, in particular, a novelist who is philosophically skeptical—are everywhere apparent in Gass's two most recent works, a collection of essays, *Finding a Form* (1996), and now *Cartesian Sonata,* a gathering of four novellas. The awkward truth is that fiction, because it is the most illusionistic of arts, is the least amenable to the kind of skepticism Gass professes. Fiction, though it may play with disbelief, labors on behalf of belief. As soon as fiction creates a human being, it signs a contract with reality, however unfair or fraudulent that contract may be; and fiction, unlike poetry, has a primary involvement with the human.

Gass is rather squeezed by this challenge. He caricatures realism as a Victorian invention, and makes it seem much less flexible than it actually is; he has sarcastically dismissed the "clear-cut characters," the "unambiguous values" and "sweet sentimentality" of the 19th-century novel, as if George Eliot, Gogol and Flaubert had never

existed. Yet at the same time he appears to want the effects, if not the burdens, of the fictive illusion. For instance, his fiction wants, and needs, human beings, and therefore characters. Indeed, he has written that "if I alter my reader's consciousness, it will be because I have constructed a consciousness of which others may wish to become aware, or even, for a short time, share," which might as well be a minimal description of Thackeray as of Gass.

His disdain for contemporary American realism is invigorating and extremely intelligent, but his own solution does not seem to be a genuinely new fiction. It is rather the enactment, in fiction, of precisely an invigorating and intelligent disdain for realism. Thus each of the novellas in *Cartesian Sonata* is about a character with a name and a history and an inner life. In **"Bed and Breakfast,"** a traveling salesman named Walter Riff becomes so enamored of one of the inns he stays at that he decides never to leave it; in **"Emma Enters a Sentence of Elizabeth Bishop's,"** a touching story, an unhappy spinster named Emma Bishop sits in an Iowa farmhouse and ponders the similarities between herself and two poets, Marianne Moore and Elizabeth Bishop; and in the title novella, Gass tells the tale of Ella Bend Hess, whose wild clairvoyance and offbeat mysticism—she hears inaudible sounds and feels impalpable textures—causes a rift with her lumberingly conventional husband.

But because Gass feels that he, and we, must not be allowed to "believe" in characters, he fiddles with their unreality. Posing as God, Gass tells us that he originally made Ella Hess rather differently: "I'd given her a long nose, I remember—no good reason why. Now her nose is middling." Likewise, Emma Bishop thinks to herself, most unconvincingly, that she is really a fictional character, not an actual human, rather like Emma Woodhouse and Emma Bovary: "Like those Emmas before me. I read of love in the light of a half-life." Yet a writer's deconstructions of reality need to be as convincing as his constructions, and Gass's apologies for his own realism seem a little halfhearted. Beckett often informs us of the arbitrariness of his people, placements and furniture, but his scrupulousness is in the service of a larger, and tormented, metaphysical uncertainty. Gass's reminders may be skeptical, but they are in the service of a philosophical complacency.

Gass's more systematic approach to the awkward reality of his own characters is to write over them, to soap them so nicely in words that they are washed away. He has a formidable lyrical power—dainty, rich, elastic—and he uses it to create streams of consciousness that move between third-person narration and interior soliloquy. All the novellas but the last one allow their characters to speak directly to the reader, by way of broken monologues. This technique, developed by Jane Austen and refined by James Joyce and Virginia Woolf, exists for the revelation of character; it is the soul's stutter. ("Ulysses," so often recently derided as an impossibly radical text, is actually the very summation of the traditional novelistic devotion to human beings.) Novelists who use stream of consciousness must calibrate their language so that it seems the plausible emanation of the character's consciousness.

Gass, typically torn, uses this mode, yet powerfully scrawls his signature all over it. Thus Emma Bishop likens herself to Emma Bovary simply because Gass thinks she should. This same woman, supposedly an unfulfilled spinster, speaks a writer's toughened vernacular: "I learned to read on the sly. I failed my grades, though in this dinky town you were advanced so your puberty would not contaminate the kiddies. . . . I read on the sly the way some kids smoked or stroked one another through their clothes." Absurdly, Ella Hess's doltish husband thinks to himself that his wife "hasn't enough blood in the narrow channels of her flesh to pink a tear, while mine is like sand in a sand clock, almost wholly in my head—thick, moist, flushed, hot." Too often, Gass's stream of consciousness seems only a vessel for his own wordy authority.

In fact, to write over one's characters, to give them thoughts and verbal powers only a writer could have, is to turn those people into writers. So Ella Hess's clairvoyance is not really affecting or convincing and seems only a way for Gass to create a character who apprehends the world with sensuous attention, as a Gass-like writer would. Walter Riff, the traveling salesman, falls in love with the objects in the bedroom of his chosen inn, and this allows Gass to use him as a writer, as a seeing eye: "His appetite," Gass writes, "was in his eyes." But Walter Riff rather disappears as a result. And Emma Bishop is every writer's dream, someone literate enough to read modern poetry. Only in the book's last novella does Gass create a life with a moving otherness. In **"The Master of Secret Revenges,"** he tells the story of Luther Penner, a brilliant but unstable child who, for no reason, decides that the principle by which he will live is revenge. Some mysterious fire burns in Luther's heart, and so in the heart of this beautiful story, Luther is a character who flies out of Gass's over-anxious grasp.

In a strange way, Gass is as involved with character as are the realists he so thoughtfully deposes. If they rather idly clothe their fictional creations, Gass rather neurotically unclothes his. But he cannot avoid the human, and he cannot avoid illusion, and his fiction describes a strange crescent around the unavoidable. His recoil is more respectable than most writer's embraces; but it is still a recoil, for all that.

FURTHER READING

Criticism

Charyn, Jerome. "Three Critical Notes." *Review of Contemporary Fiction* 12, No. 2 (Summer 1992): 120-3.
  Charyn reflects on his initial reading of "The Pedersen Kid" and the story's significance in contemporary American literature.

Feld, Ross. "Timing and Spacing the As If: Poetic Prose and Prosaic Poetry." *Parnassus* 20, Nos. 1 and 2 (January 1995): 11-31.
  Feld comments on the function of poetry and prose and offers unfavorable evaluation of *The Tunnel*.

Kaufmann, Michael. "The Textual Body: William Gass's *Willie Masters' Lonesome Wife*." *Critique: Studies in Contemporary Fiction* XXXV, No. 1 (Fall 1993): 27-42.
  Examines the interrelationship between author, reader, text, and reality as reflected in the linguistic construction of Gass's fictional wife in *Willie Masters' Lonesome Wife*.

LaHood, Marvin J. Review of *Cartesian Sonata and Other Novellas,* by William H. Gass. *World Literature Today* 73, No. 2 (Spring 1999): 333-4.
  Offers a summary and equivocal judgement of *Cartesian Sonata and Other Novellas.*

McCourt, James. "Fiction in Review." *Yale Review* 83, No. 3 (July 1995): 159-69.
  Examines the psychological, literary, and mythological themes of *The Tunnel,* drawing parallels to the dilemmas of Hamlet and Daedelus.

Stewart, Susan. "An American Faust." *American Literature* 69, No. 2 (June 1997): 399-416.
  Provides an overview of the central themes, structure, and literary allusions of *The Tunnel,* drawing attention to the novel's associations with the Faust stories of Johann Wolfgang von Goethe and Thomas Mann.

Varsava, Jerry A. "Mimesis and the Reader: A Reading." In *Contingent Meanings: Postmodern Fiction, Mimesis, and the Reader,* pp. 2-40. Tallahassee, FL: Florida State University Press, 1990.
  Includes discussion of Gass's postmodern literary and theoretical principles.

Additional coverage of Gass's life and career is contained in the following sources published by the Gale Group: *Contemporary Authors,* **Vols. 17-20R;** *Contemporary Authors New Revision Series,* **Vols. 30, 71;** *Dictionary of Literary Biography,* **Vol. 2;** *Major 20th-Century Writers* **Vols. 1, 2; and** *Short Story Criticism,* **Vol. 12.**

Robert Kroetsch
1927-

Canadian novelist, poet, critic, editor, and travel writer.

The following entry provides an overview of Kroetsch's career through 1998. For further information on his life and works, see *CLC,* Volumes 5, 23, and 57.

INTRODUCTION

Kroetsch is considered one of Canada's foremost practitioners and theoreticians of postmodern literature. Like many experimental writers, Kroetsch subverts such literary conventions as plot and character development and writes in a playful, ironic, and self-reflexive style. Central to Kroetsch's fiction is the importance of place and its impact on the psyche. He is particularly admired for his depictions of the Canadian prairie landscape.

BIOGRAPHICAL INFORMATION

Kroetsch was born in Heisler, Alberta, Canada, and raised on his family's farm. His childhood in rural Alberta, where most of his fiction is set, informs both his fiction and his poetry. His family's penchant for storytelling imbued Kroetsch with a deep appreciation for oral narrative, which often emerges in his writing in the form of tall tales and ribald humor. After graduating from the University of Alberta in 1948, Kroetsch worked for six years in the Canadian North. His initial jobs on riverboats on the Mackenzie River led to the conception of his first and most conventional novel, *But We Are Exiles* (1966). In 1961 Kroetsch received his Ph.D. from the University of Iowa, and he worked as a professor at the State University of New York at Binghamton from 1961 to 1978. In 1978 Kroetsch accepted a professorship at the University of Manitoba, Winnipeg. He has won several awards for his fiction and was co-founder and editor of the postmodern literary journal *Boundary 2.*

MAJOR WORKS

Kroetsch's novels *The Words of My Roaring* (1966), *The Studhorse Man* (1970), and *Gone Indian* (1973) comprise what he calls the "Out West" triptych. In these works, Kroetsch explores the myths surrounding the Canadian prairie while also incorporating Greek and Roman mythic structures and recording momentous social changes from the 1930s to the 1970s. *The Words of My Roaring* also chronicles political upheavals in Depression-era Alberta. Kroetsch's next novel, *Badlands* (1975), revolves around a

1916 paleontological expedition in Alberta led by William Dawes, who is obsessed with finding large dinosaur fossils in hopes of achieving renown in the science world. In *What the Crow Said* (1978) Kroetsch uses magical realism to explore gender differences in Big Indian, Alberta. *Alibi* (1983) reiterates his interest in the quest myth and the rejuvenating power of water. William Dorfendorf, who procures objects for a mysterious oilman and collector, is sent on a worldwide search for the "perfect spa." Through his quest, Dorfendorf comes to understand the fundamental dichotomies of body and soul, sex and death, and art and life. *The Puppeteer* (1995) is a postmodern detective story in which Kroetsch almost entirely abandons conventional storytelling techniques, settling instead on an experimental form in which he lifts and rearranges scenes and characters from previous works. In 1998 Kroetsch published *The Man from the Creeks,* a novel about the gold rush in the American and Canadian West in the 1890s. Several themes in Kroetsch's fiction recur throughout his poetry. In his early verse, collected in *The Stone Hammer Poems* (1975), Kroetsch depicts prairie life in an imagistic, unaffected manner. Much of his subsequent poetry displays an irreverence toward language in order to expand its limits. Since 1975, Kroetsch has been composing an extended long poem-in-progress entitled "Field Notes." A collage of memories, anecdotes, documents, and tall tales reflecting his preoccupation with the difficulties of literary expression, persona, and the burden of traditional poetic forms, "Field Notes" has been published in partial form in the volumes *Seed Catalogue: Poems* (1978), *The Ledger* (1979), *The Sad Phoenician* (1979), and *Advice to My Friends* (1985). In 1989 the volume was published as *The Complete Field Notes.* Kroetsch is also highly regarded as a literary theorist, and his criticism is considered a major informative factor in all of his writings. *The Lovely Treachery of Words* (1989) exemplifies his thoughts on literature, writing, and language. In 1995 Kroetsch added to his writings about language by publishing *A Likely Story*, a memoir and explanation of his life as a writer.

CRITICAL RECEPTION

Kroetsch is considered one of the most imaginative and important writers of the postmodern movement. Highly influenced by theorists such as Ferdinand de Saussure and Jacques Derrida, his fiction and poetry as well as his criticism are deeply entrenched in deconstructionism's focus on relativity and absence of definite meaning. While this quality has drawn much praise from some commentators, others have found his works oblique and at times overbearing with literary jargon and trends. Nonetheless, Kroetsch is admired for experimenting with literary forms and for his role in bringing contemporary Canadian writing to the forefront of the world literary scene.

PRINCIPAL WORKS

But We Are Exiles (novel) 1966
The Words of My Roaring (novel) 1966
The Studhorse Man (novel) 1970
Gone Indian (novel) 1973
Badlands (novel) 1975
The Stone Hammer Poems: 1960-1975 (poetry) 1975
Seed Catalogue: Poems (poetry) 1978
What the Crow Said (novel) 1978
The Ledger (poetry) 1979
The Sad Phoenician (poetry) 1979
The Crow Journals (nonfiction) 1980
Field Notes (poetry) 1981
Alibi (novel) 1983
Advice to My Friends: A Continuing Poem (poetry) 1985
Gaining Ground: European Critics on Canadian Literature [editor; with Reingard M. Nischik] (essays) 1985
The Complete Field Notes: The Long Poems of Robert Kroetsch (poetry) 1989
The Lovely Treachery of Words: Essays Selected and New (essays) 1989
A Likely Story: The Writing Life (nonfiction) 1995
The Puppeteer (novel) 1995
The Man from the Creeks (novel) 1998

CRITICISM

Geert Lernout (review date March 1986)

SOURCE: A review of *Gaining Ground: European Critics on Canadian Literature,* in *Canadian Forum,* Vol. LXV, No. 755, March, 1986, p. 38.

[*In the following review, Lernout praises the essays in* Gaining Ground.]

As the title of this book indicates, Canadian literature is slowly becoming recognized in Europe. But one of the editors, Reingard Nischik, warns against a too facile optimism. In her article on the history of European interest in CanLit, Nischik quite rightly points out that Canadians seem to lack a clear picture of what is really going on in Europe. In less than 30 pages she gives an account of the CanLit scene in 18 European countries and adds an admirably complete bibliography of European studies on Canadian Literature.

What emerges first in the article is that there has been European interest in Canada for only the past 10 years. This is hardly surprising. Ten years ago, when I was a sophomore in Antwerp, I was told that because America does not have a history it cannot have a literature. The people in power—European universities used to be a lot less democratic than North-American ones—stuck to Shakespeare, Milton and (maybe) a few romantics. Modern British literature is written by civilized Englishmen (preferably Oxbridge graduates) about civilized Englishmen. Usually only one person, a specialist in Shakespeare's minor contemporaries who speaks an almost obsolete English, decides what will be taught, on what his students will write their dissertations and who will get the tenure-track jobs. It does not pay to specialize in Canadian literature, especially not if you're interested in both Canadian literatures. That this situation is slowly changing is a result of the decentralization of the '70s, which saw the emergence of new and experimental universities and effective cultural policies on the part of Canadian embassies.

The critical essays in this volume testify to the seriousness of European critics. All of these essays could have been published in the best Canadian journals; they are all very well researched, take into account the latest criticism and show an acute awareness of critical theory that is sometimes lacking in similar Canadian work. Simone Vauthier's essay on *The Wars* refers to Genette's work on narratology. Pierre Spriet's to Ruwet, Riffaterre and Chatman and there is even an essay by one of the foremost European narratologists, Franz K. Stanzel.

Only two essays discuss *Québecois* writers, an emphasis that partly reflects the marginal situation of minor francophone literatures in Europe but is surely aggravated by the fact that the vast majority of these critics comes from Austria, Switzerland and Germany. Another striking emphasis in this volume is the result of the relative novelty of CanLit in Europe: all but three essays discuss works of writers who are still active today and more than half deal with post-modern novels. There could be various reasons for this. Maybe the post-modernists travel to Europe more often (the idea for the book came to Kroetsch and Nischik over a *Kölsch* in the shadow of the Cologne cathedral); maybe Walter Pache is right when he states in his essay that whereas Canadian modernists anticipated a national identity by defining national themes, Canadian postmodernists "adopt themes freely from international sources and adapt them to domestic uses." Today, the creative act itself becomes a productive force in the creation of a national identity. If this were true, Europeans would be more interested in the "domestic use" of international themes than in Canadian themes. I don't think we are; the attraction of Kroetsch's prairie novels, of Hodgins's Vancouver Island stories and of Rudy Wiebe's work lies in the themes and in the settings, in the wildness and wonder of people and landscape.

In the most interesting essay in this collection, Eva-Marie Kröller writes a fascinating account of 19th-century

Canadians visiting the Rhine valley. This is not just literary criticism, it is much more: Kröller moves from comparisons between the Drachenfels and Cape Diamond to Canadian reactions to the Franco-Prussian war, the influence of the Nazarene concept of art on *Québecois* frescoes and finally to the ironic treatment of German romanticism in Gallant's *The Peignitz Junction*, Laurence's *The Stone Angel* and Paul Hiebert's *Sarah Binks*.

What I missed in *Gaining Ground* is a discussion of works by and about Canada's immigrants, who are of course also emigrants from somewhere. Such a project could not be confined to high literary texts; it would have to include "pulp," oral tales, diaries and travel literature, not necessarily in English or French. German, Portuguese, Dutch and Italian stories of emigration are as much a part of the Canadian heritage as West-Indian, Chinese and Japanese ones. It is here that European critics could make a worthwhile contribution. But this is merely an idea for a second volume, not a critique of this excellent collection of essays.

Sylvia Söderlind (review date Winter 1987)

SOURCE: "Views from Afar," in *Essays on Canadian Writing*, No. 35, Winter, 1987, pp. 111-16.

[*In the following review, Söderlind praises* Gaining Ground *for its successful attempt to begin a dialogue between the literatures of Canada and Europe.*]

In case anyone still doubted it, this collection confirms what has been rumoured for some time: Canadian literature is gaining ground in the universities of Europe. With few exceptions the seventeen essays included in the volume indicate that a good number of critics have spent considerable time and effort in getting to know our literature and our history. The authors represent a wide geographical, as well as critical, spectrum. The main centres for Canadian studies in Europe are found in West Germany, Italy, and France; and places like Kiel, Bologna, and Bordeaux have come to be synonymous with Canadian studies. The growing interest in the field is also illustrated in the seven associations devoted to Canadian studies that have sprung up all over the continent in the last decade. The most recent ones are found in the Netherlands and Scandinavia; a Swedish journal has dedicated a recent issue exclusively to Canadian arts, music, and literature. Reingard M. Nischik's informative survey of the status of Canadian studies in the various countries shows that Canlit entered the European academic establishment by way of Commonwealth studies, a fact that may account for the rather poor representation of French-Canadian literature in the collection: only two essays deal with Québécois writers. The vigorous European branch of ACLALS (The Association for Commonwealth Literature and Language Studies), which has been very active in promoting Canadian literature, is usually located in the English departments and tends to be geared towards the anglophone parts of the Commonwealth. The efforts of the Canadian government to sell the country abroad can also be discerned, for instance, in the choice of writers discussed in the various essays. Many of them have toured Europe at the expense of External Affairs. Besides giving a good picture of the history and the present status of Canadian studies in Europe, Nischik provides useful biographical information about the contributors, as well as an impressive bibliography of publications in the field from different countries. One aspect excluded from Nischik's discussion is the question of translations. It would have been interesting to know what writers have been made available to a wider public in other languages, and to get an idea of how far Canadian literature has reached beyond the academic community.

The Commonwealth context gives a slant to the study of Canada's literature different from the often deplored parochialism that has so long prevailed among the country's own critics. The Canadian works are often seen in a context of other new literatures in English, or in a general framework of post-colonialism. Nischik, who teaches at the University of Cologne, sees the difference in perspective between European and Canadian critics as a result of the distance between them, which makes it possible for the European to apply a more rigorous critical methodology based on formal and generic features rather than on exclusively thematic ones. This does not mean that thematic studies are excluded from the collection; there are in fact several. Nevertheless, the essays represent a wider variety of critical approaches than is usually seen in Canadian criticism. This gives them an added interest: they reveal what particular types of criticism are popular in Europe at the moment. Psychoanalysis and deconstruction are rather conspicuously (some may say refreshingly) absent, and narratology and feminism seem to be more dominant. Cedric May's study of Alain Grandbois' poetry can be qualified as high structuralism, while Pierre Spriet's analysis of Rudy Wiebe borrows heavily from Riffaterrean semiotics. Rather different from the other essays, Eva-Marie Kröller's "Nineteenth-Century Canadians and the Rhine Valley," which appropriately closes the volume, provides a much broader context and is one of the few that deal with a comparison between a Canadian and a European aesthetics. Rudolf Bader, in a discussion of Grove's particular brand of naturalism, does touch on his roots in a European tradition, and Franz K. Stanzel talks about Eli Mandel and John Robert Colombo in the same breath as Peter Handke; but rather than a comparative study, these critics offer a more general generic discussion. European critics would seem to be ideally placed to provide this kind of juxtaposition of writers and literatures from the old and new countries, and its absence is a bit disappointing. Such comparisons would be particularly interesting in light of Canada's frequent status as a mythical territory for European writers. (One only has to consult a major influence like Michel Tournier to stumble on this.) Indeed, much of the fascination Canada holds for Europeans seems to stem from its transformation from a mythic ground into a real place. The preoccupation with place in

Canadian fiction has, of course, become a bit of a cliché, but it definitely comes through as the common denominator in the essays. Borges' apocryphal remark about Canada being so far away that it hardly exists, which is quoted in one of the papers, could almost function as an epigraph for the whole volume: it is the becoming real of this faraway country that preoccupies the European critics.

With few exceptions the essays deal with contemporary writers and are placed loosely in a framework of postmodernism and, more implicitly, feminism. Three of them are devoted, wholly or in part, to Rudy Wiebe, a frequent visitor to Europe, two to Robert Kroetsch, and two to Margaret Atwood. Other writers discussed are Timothy Findley, Alice Munro, Aritha van Herk, Mavis Gallant, George Bowering, and Jack Hodgins. The short story has often been considered as the Canadian genre par excellence, and generically the "short story ensemble" (171) is the most dominant subject. Thus, for instance, Margaret Laurence is represented by *A Bird in the House*, Hodgins by *Spit Delaney's Island*, Munro by *Lives of Girls and Women* and *Who Do You Think You Are?*, Gallant by "Orphans' Progress"; and Karla El-Hassan includes Leacock's *Sunshine Sketches of a Little Town* in the same category. Only two essays discuss poetry: May's analysis of Alain Grandbois' *Les iles de la nuit* and Franz K. Stanzel's study of the found poem. Stanzel's discussion is perhaps the least interesting from a Canadian point of view. Rather than defining the typically Canadian characteristics of the poetry, Stanzel proposes a general typology of the genre, using Canadian examples merely as illustrations. A similar generic perspective is exemplified in Paul Goetsch's discussion of Atwood's *Life Before Man* as a novel of manners, in the tradition of Austen, Trollope, and James. Simone Vauthier, in one of the strongest contributions, sees Findley's *The Wars* in the context of war fiction. Clearly influenced by narratological theories, Vauthier's essay focuses on such aspects as focalization, space, and time, and elucidates the dichotomies between scriptor and implied author, and between novel and narration. A related approach is found in Nischik's discussion of the novels of van Herk, a writer popular in Europe.

Another successful discussion in terms of generic convention is Coral Ann Howells' "Worlds Alongside: Contradictory Discourses in the Fiction of Alice Munro and Margaret Atwood." Howells analyzes their different treatment of the conflict between reality and fantasy and argues that, while in Atwood's work the two are mutually exclusive, they coexist in a state of "mutual contrariety" in Munro's (122). With its feminist slant and its insightful textual analyses, Howells' essay is an example of the balance between methodological rigour and respect for the text, which is characteristic of good criticism. Rather than being imposed from a preconceived model, the dichotomy she discovers stems from the texts themselves. The same can be said about Giovanna Capone's discussion of *A Bird in the House*, which approaches, from a more thematic angle, a motif similar to the dichotomy studied by Howells. Capone sees Laurence's short-story ensemble as ordered by the opposition, or the distance, between the real and the imaginary, a familiar tension in Canadian fiction, and one that is also in the background of Wolfgang Kloos's reading of Rudy Wiebe's *The Scorched-Wood People*.

Wiebe is also the subject of Pierre Spriet's essay on the thematics of failure, which demonstrates a familiar problem for many critics. Spriet concentrates on Wiebe's latest novel, *My Lovely Enemy*, which he tries to make fit into a pattern already established for the author's other works. Instead of questioning the validity of the thematics he has established as fundamental to Wiebe, Spriet insists on making the new text fit into it, and the result is not quite convincing. The essay also contains an unfortunate racial generalization in the opening paragraph, where Spriet lists among the protagonists of the "lunatic fringe" peopling Wiebe's novels, "dreamers, dissenters, Indians, outlaws" (53).

The Commonwealth and post-colonial connection is particularly visible in Jürgen Schäfer's discussion of the changing image of the Indian, by way of a comparison between Wiebe's *The Temptations of Big Bear* and Kroetsch's *Gone Indian*. Schäfer draws several parallels between Wiebe's masterpiece and Chinua Achebe's *Things Fall Apart*, and he sees colonization in a wide sense as a metaphor for modern alienation. The Nigerian novel is arguably the best-known depiction of a post-colonial culture in disintegration, but the similarities pointed out between the two novels at times seem a bit strained. (It could probably be argued that *Gone Indian* is equally related to Achebe's novel by way of their shared intertextual parentage in Yeats's "The Second Coming," but that is another issue.)

Schäfer's discussion of *Gone Indian* can be juxtaposed with that of Walter Pache in "The Fiction Makes Us Real: Aspects of Postmodernism in Canada," which is more generic than thematic in its approach, as the title indicates. Pache, who clearly possesses a good knowledge of the history of Canadian literature, places Kroetsch, together with George Bowering, in the general framework of postmodernism, a concept which underlies many of the studies in the collection. Kroetsch is seen as the father of Canadian postmodernism, and **The Studhorse Man** and **Gone Indian** as "paradigmatic examples of postmodern narrative in Canada" (70). Pache, the driving force behind Canadian literary studies at Trier, West Germany, draws some interesting conclusions concerning the particularly Canadian brand of postmodernism. Although Kroetsch, like most of his colleagues, opposes the traditional imposition of order on the text, he is, says Pache, Canadian insofar as he does not go to extremes but rather strives for a balance between "structural artifact and unstructured fabulation" (71). It is thus caution, or at least moderation, that characterizes Canada's variant of the genre. Pache's emphasis on this want of extremism, however, may be due to his focusing on the latter aspect, the fabulation, rather than on the often ingenious formalism that characterizes Kroetsch's novels. The structural intricacies of the two texts remain subservient to the story in a hierarchy that has been put into question recently. Kroetsch's own contention that Canada never had a modernist period comes to mind when Pache claims that postmodernism and postcolonialism go hand in hand. It was not until American literature reached a point of exhaustion and lost its dominance that Canadian literature really came into its own.

Postmodernism is also the focus of Rosmarin Heidenreich's study of Hubert Aquin's novel *Trou de mémoire*. Like Pache's and Spriet's essays, it focuses on aspects of undecidability and openness, features that are generally seen as defining the genre. The choice of writers like Aquin and Kroetsch to illustrate the typical open work is, however, rather problematic and will only work if the emphasis is put on the fabulation that Pache underlines. Narrative, or diegetic, openness does not necessarily exclude or contradict a certain formal hermeticism. It could indeed be argued that some of the tensions often felt in what is generally called postmodern works stem from the simultaneous presence of the two opposite movements, as Pache implies, although his analysis does not quite bear it out. Heidenreich's study of Holbein's anamorphic painting "The Ambassadors," which provides the central formal metaphor of Aquin's text, would in fact seem to contradict the novel's claim to openness. The painting is a rather strictly hermetic mannerist portrait, in which two images, one overt and one covert, stand in a clear relation of opposition. If, as Heidenreich claims, there is an obvious isomorphism between painting and novel, the latter's claim to openness is illusory. There are no signs of the recent controversy surrounding the term "postmodernism" in any of the essays.

The shortest essay in the book, Waldemar Zacharasiewicz's "The Invention of a Region: The Art of Fiction in Jack Hodgins' Stories," suggests a potentially fruitful direction for comparative studies. The author, who teaches in Vienna, juxtaposes Hodgins with writers of the American South, notably Faulkner and Flannery O'Connor. The Gothic of the South is more commonly associated with the literature of Quebec or of rural Ontario, as in Howells' discussion of Munro and Atwood. Although Zacharasiewicz's comparison, which is based on both thematic and stylistic features, quite convincingly shows a number of similarities, particularly between Hodgins' and O'Connor's stories, his conclusion is questionable. He contends that Hodgins is more of a modernist than a postmodernist, a claim that would reveal the writer as something of an anomaly in Canada. It is the limitation of the comparison to *Spit Delaney's Island* that permits this contention. Hodgins' later stories would, no doubt, reveal a similar affinity with the South, but it is unlikely that the same thing could be said about his novels.

We can only be grateful for the enthusiasm shared by Kroetsch and Nischik over a beer in Munich that eventually led to the publication of this book. It is to be hoped that it will encourage further transatlantic dialogue.

George Bowery (review date April 1989)

SOURCE: A review of *The Lovely Treachery of Words,* in *Books in Canada*, Vol. 18, No. 3, April, 1989, p. 22.

[*In the following review, Bowery praises Kroetsch's literary criticism in* The Lovely Treachery of Words.]

In Canada we often write "poet-novelist" before a writer's name. We have to do this more than most countries do. Of course most of these poet-novelists toss off an essay from time to time. But we seldom feel that it would be sensible to write "poet-novelist-critic."

Margaret Atwood writes reviews and makes the odd address to a group of elected representatives. A long time ago Michael Ondaatje wrote a little chapbook on Leonard Cohen; bp Nichol wrote in all three forms, but you had to take his word about which was which.

Robert Kroetsch was successful first as a novelist. Then he became the first novelist to influence the poets as a poet. Next to Atwood he is the most often interviewed writer in the country. All along he has been not only writing the literary essay, but also reinventing it. He has not just written the requisite papers of a writer who works at universities; he has produced *famous* essays. They have introduced famous phrases into the literature.

Some of those famous essays, such as **"Unhiding the Hidden"** and **"An Erotics of Space,"** reappear in this collection.

When I go to conferences on Canadian literature in New Zealand and Australia and Italy and Germany, it is Kroetsch I hear those foreigners writing about. Maybe this is because he practises literary theory. In so doing he breaks an old Anglo-Canadian proscription against thinking about what you are doing in the making of literature.

There are 17 essays in this collection. Some of them appeared in an earlier collection of Kroetsch's essays, edited by bp Nichol and Frank Davey, and published as an issue of their journal, *Open Letter* in 1983. (It has been for five years a much-annotated college textbook.) The rest are treatments of narrative in Canadian fiction. In fact only one of the essays is in total about verse, the much-presented **"For Play and Entrance; the Contemporary Canadian Long Poem."**

Kroetsch performs what seems to be a paradox (and he will not be unhappy to see that word). He casts his eye and nets wide over Canadian narrative, from Haliburton to Buckler, Ross, Laurence, and Audrey Thomas. He is all-embracing, too widely encouraging, according to some of his readers. He finds valuable stuff practically anywhere in our letters. Yet he is the most *readable* critic, and I think that is so because he treats his criticism as part of a multilogue with our other writers. In a book-length interview he once said, "I think criticism is really a version of story . . . the story of our search for story."

That word "our" appears often in Kroetsch's writing. His subject is sometimes the ways in which we can make ourselves Canadians. That is likely part of the reason that so many of these essays were begun as papers at international conferences. But Kroetsch connects finding ourselves with finding a way to speak. He takes chances, foolish ones sometimes, and that promotes our faith. He takes plunges, sees something delicious in the new European theory deli and gobbles it down without sitting at their table.

Narrative strategies are his preoccupation. Northrop Frye, he says here, is our epic poet. Christopher Columbus is the mythic hero. Christopher Columbus was an Orpheus. America was not his Hades but his Eurydice.

Kroetsch finds Orpheus all over Canadian literature, in which the wounded artist is so often the central figure, in which we find so many idyllic and doomed couples, in which our citizens are under the ground, at the bottom of a lake, buried by snow or earth or trees. Here we see the way that Orpheus haunts Malcolm Lowry's fiction. Howard O'Hagan's Tay John is "an inverse Orpheus figure. He has come up from under the ground, not with speech or poetry, but with silence."

What I like about things such as Kroetsch's discovery of Orpheus among us supposedly placid Canadians is the excitement in the finding. Kroetsch does not present the waxed and polished fruits of his research. We see always the autobiographical, the search. We get a man standing by his words, not behind them. He is writing his reading. Thus we are invited to do and offer our own.

A bonus in this volume is an irregular piece called **"Towards an Essay: My Upstate New York Journals."** This resembles *The Crow Journals*, and dates from 1970 to 1974. The last entry we get is another of Kroetsch's demonstrations against closure: "I said to Jane, what is the subject of a love poem? She said, There can only be one subject of a love poem. What? I asked her." Orpheus, we reflect, went to Hell to try to erase closure.

"To reveal all is to end the story," Kroetsch says to begin one essay. So he tells us what he prizes among the deferred, the hidden, the secret, including silence as a narrative strategy. He loves those secretive writers: Grove, Lowry, O'Hagan, Sheila Watson. His famous "unnaming" and "uncreating" are actions taken against enclosing history. They are meant to return us to origins, where myth can precede factism, to "avoid both meaning and conclusiveness," he once said.

So one might anticipate, while enjoying these essays, that there is more to come, more beginnings. Even though these essays are pressed between boards made by the Oxford University Press, Orpheus's head will continue to sing along its river path to the never reachable sea.

John Clement Ball (essay date Fall 1989)

SOURCE: "The Carnival of Babel: The Construction of

Voice in Robert Kroetsch's 'Out West' Triptych," in *Essays on Canadian Writing,* No. 39, Fall, 1989, pp. 1-22.

[*In the following essay, Ball examines the place and meaning of silence and voice in Kroetsch's 'Out West' series of novels.*]

From one so concerned with the multiplicitous nature of voice and the elusiveness of meaning, Robert Kroetsch's work has displayed a remarkable cohesiveness. As a writer whose many voices include those of poet, novelist, postmodern theorist, and intensely nationalistic critic of Canadian literature, he is also his own best explicator. A Kroetsch essay about an Atwood or Ross novel works equally well as commentary about the author's own fiction, because of the way ideas echo back and forth. Likewise, his fiction can help unravel his often puzzling theoretical statements.

Kroetsch began his writing career as a novelist, and his most clearly formative period comprised the years 1966 to 1973, when the three novels of his "Out West" triptych— *The Words of My Roaring*, *The Studhorse Man*, and *Gone Indian*—were published. Most of his critical writings and interviews have been produced since then, and almost without exception their themes and assumptions can be traced back to problems tackled by Kroetsch in those three books. The "working-out" process so evident in the triptych is what allows Kroetsch the sure-footedness of the stances that he takes as a critic.

One of the many refrains that echoes through the text of *The Words of My Roaring* concerns what the novel's narrator, Johnnie Backstrom, calls "the old dualities" (94). "We confuse beginnings, endings," he says. "They are so alike so often" (7). The opposition, or duality, of beginnings and endings frustrates Johnnie, as do other dualities. He says to the disembodied voice of Applecart on the radio: "Always the old dualities. When you're in a tight fix: mind and body, right and wrong. Fill the old grab bag with something for everybody. When you're cornered: good and evil, black and white, up and down, damnation—" (94). Kroetsch as a critic often expresses concepts in terms of dualities. The two most important of these are founded on the opposition of horse and house, and of Coyote and God. In describing the two pairs, Kroetsch implies that the two sides are necessarily always separate and distinct; the very nature of the oppositions they embody demands it.

The horse-house duality is described in Kroetsch's essay, **"The Fear of Women in Prairie Fiction"**,:

> The basic grammatical pair in the story-line (the energy-line) of prairie fiction is house: horse. To be *on* a horse is to move: motion into distance. To be *in* a house is to be fixed: a centering unto stasis. Horse is masculine. House is feminine. Horse: house. Masculine: feminine. On: in. Motion: stasis. A woman ain't supposed to move. Pleasure: duty.

(76)

As a metaphor for oppositions or dualities that occur at the level of plot and characters—that is, on the level of story—horse-house can be called the duality of story.

Kroetsch's other duality, Coyote-God, can be called the duality of writing, or the duality of book, because it is a metaphor for two different approaches to the creation of a work of art, to the writing down of story. In **"Death Is a Happy Ending: A Dialogue in Thirteen Parts (with Diane Bessai),"** he proclaims:

> the artist him/her self:
>
> in the long run, given the choice of being God or Coyote, will, most mornings, choose to be Coyote:
>
> he lets in the irrational along with the rational, the pre-moral along with the moral. He is a shape-shifter, at least in the limited way of old lady Potter. He is the charlatan-healer, like Felix Prosper, the low-down Buddha-bellied fiddler midwife (him/her) rather than Joyce's high priest of art.
>
>   (209)

Coyote, by letting everything into his art—that is by making it inclusive rather than exclusive, unpredictable rather than familiar, an embodiment of chaos more than order—allows his text to exist "not as artifact but as enabling act" and permit "not meaning but the possibility of meanings" (208). Kroetsch puts the Coyote-God duality into the context of other, specifically Canadian dualities, later in the Bessai dialogue:

> The double hook. The total ambiguity that is so essentially Canadian: be it in terms of two solitudes, the bush garden, Jungian opposites, or the raw and cooked binary structures of Levi-Strauss. Behind the multiplying theories of Canadian literature is always the pattern of equally matched opposites.
>
>   Coyote : God
>   Self : Community
>   Energy : Stasis
>
>   (215)

Coyote's artistic stance becomes one of personal vision (self) as opposed to group vision (community), of energy over stasis. This final pair is significant in its similarity to the motion-stasis element of the horse-house duality. There appears to be some connection between the duality of story and the duality of book.

The most important duality to the story of **The Words of My Roaring** is established in the opening scene, where Johnnie is set in opposition (both on a real political level, and on a number of symbolic levels) to Doc. The two figures are contrasted through a number of details of appearance and behaviour:

>   Johnnie : Doc
>   holes in sleeves : "looks like a million"
>   parched throat : more water than he needs
>   perfect teeth : gold teeth
>   son (first-born) : father
>   death-manager (endings) : birth-manager (beginnings)

>   clown : hero
>   butt of jokes : maker of jokes
>   big : small
> destroyer (Jonah, later) : healer
>   heavy drinker : light drinker
>   no money : lots of money
> not talking (speechless) : talking

The last of these oppositions, the fact that throughout most of the chapter Doc is talking and Johnnie is silent, is notable in that it introduces Johnnie as a character whose natural state is speechlessness. There are dozens of occasions throughout the novel on which Johnnie is either "struck dumb," "silent," or "speechless." As an undertaker, he says, "Silence is my business, I deal in silence" (23). At one of the many points that he is rendered silent by the presence of Doc's daughter, Helen, he philosophises, "Speechless we come into this world; speechless we go out. What a hell of a state, to be speechless in between" (56).

However, although Johnnie can be seen as a character whose essential mode is one of speechlessness, he is also a character who grows into speech. When he finally does speak in the opening scene, he promises that it will rain. He has spoken where previously he was silent, given himself a platform where he had none before. He has by these few spontaneous words—and this is borne out by the events of the novel—turned himself from a nobody into a somebody. Throughout the story he is variously struck dumb by large crowds, Helen, Jonah's death, people's expectations of him; nevertheless, he also makes several significant speeches to large crowds, at least one to Helen, and manages to speak volumes by silently nodding at the auction for the Model-A. When the prophet speaks and commands a crowd just prior to that auction, Johnnie participates, heckling and asking him to elaborate, speaking quite comfortably instead of awkwardly remaining silent, as he did in the first scene until Doc put him on the spot. Likewise, a comparison of the first of Applecart's radio speeches, at which Johnnie is the silent link between Applecart's disembodied voice and the ears of the community, with the second of these, at which Johnnie's own words are so filled with antagonistic energy that he smashes the radio, cuts off Applecart's words, and replaces them with his own, reveals Johnnie as a character becoming increasingly less speechless. If he is speaking against the words of others much of the time, he is also speaking against his own silence.

If this is what Johnnie the character is doing on the level of story, it is also what Johnnie the storyteller is doing on the level of book. On this level he is not speechless at all: he speaks the entire book. The style of prose and the rhythms of the language that Johnnie uses to tell his story are those of oral speech. He repeats things, especially descriptions of himself, over and over. A passage like "I've got these huge hands. Huge. Positively huge" (162), especially when it comes after countless other passages about the size of his hands, feet, nose, chin, and so on, owes its origin to an oral model of storytelling. Recurring connectives such as "let me tell you" and "I must confess" also encourage the reader to hear Johnnie's voice as an aural voice. The book can be read as a spoken confession, and as with any confession, the telling of story is as important as the content of the story itself.

In a 1972 interview with Donald Cameron, Kroetsch speaks of "the oral tradition which is the stuff of literature." This oral tradition, which in Canada often emerges as a regional voice, is "where writers find liberation. What we have to do in Canada is concentrate on hearing this voice that is within us, and trusting it" (85). In *Labyrinths of Voice: Conversations with Robert Kroetsch*, he tells how his bilingual parents stopped speaking German the day he was born so he would "be assimilated and totally English-speaking." As a result, "there's a sense of guilt in me about that silence that my birth occasioned" (141). When asked in what way language is an *ongoing* problem for him, Kroetsch says:

> I started out with an interest in what I suppose we'd call *voice*—though it's a hell of a difficult word to define—*voice* as a grounding in a speech model as opposed to what I learned to do as a *writer* of language. . . . I was very quick at learning this writing-it-down, and again I felt almost guilty at my ability to write out my own speech patterns or voice.
>
> (141–42)

Further in that conversation, Kroetsch returns to the subject:

> I have a particular faith, still, in the occasion of speaking, and I have, maybe, more trust of that occasion than the writing I engage in. And, yet, I go on writing, so why? . . . I suppose I write against systems. . . . And I write against silence too.
>
> (160)

If writing against silence is what Kroetsch the author is doing, speaking against silence is what his hero, Johnnie Backstrom, is doing, narrating and confessing his story in place of the silence that would be there if he had not done so. On the level of book—the level of telling of story—speaking or writing *in place of* silence is the same as speaking or writing *against* silence, since silence is destroyed by that act. That act is also a creation of the self *out of* silence, which is the same creative act that Johnnie the character performs on the level of story. He creates himself in relation to his community by the act of speaking, beginning with the words, "Mister, how would you like some rain?" (8). There is an unusual correspondence, then, between the level of story and the level of book. On both levels the main event is a voice speaking against silence and creating a self.

This does not mean that the I-creator (Johnnie as narrator) and the I-created (Johnnie as character) have for the first time in the history of first-person narrative become identical. Not only is this theoretically impossible, but Johnnie is not even a particularly reliable narrator. He creates an exaggerated, larger-than-life version of himself, and there are some obvious dislocations between what he tells of himself and what his self-described actions show us, as when he describes himself as "seldom speechless" (73). However, there is an association of the two I's in the same way that there is an association of the levels of story and its telling: on both levels, and for both creator and created, the same essential process is described by this book. *Words* is in fact *about* this very kind of unity—the bringing together of normally separate things, the resolution of dichotomies or dualities—and in doing this Kroetsch has undone his own interpretation of prairie mythology.

In **"The Fear of Women in Prairie Fiction,"** Kroetsch uses horse-house as a metaphor for a duality at the cornerstone of prairie writing. The separateness of horse and house is nothing short of the difference between man and woman—between the male's typical role of orphan, cowboy, and outlaw, and the female qualities of domesticity, stability, and nurturing. This pairing is never satisfactorily resolved in a way that does not make the man "the diminished hero" and the woman "the more-than-life figure" (80, 81). Two metaphors are used in prairie fiction to represent the failure of male-female unity: the failure of sex and the failure of the dance.

> The failure of the male protagonists, at the centre of each book, to enter into the dance, is symptomatic of what is wrong. The women can dance. Their appropriate partners cannot. The harmony suggested by dance—implications of sex, of marriage, of art, of a unified world—all are lost because of the male characters. The males are obedient to versions of self that keep them at a distance—the male as orphan, as cowboy, as outlaw.
>
> (79)

The masculine-feminine (horse-house) duality has another important aspect in Kroetsch's essay:

> We conceive of external space as male, internal space as female. More precisely, the penis: external, expandable, expendable; the vagina: internal, eternal. The maleness verges on mere absence. The femaleness verges on mystery; it is a space that is not a space. External space is the silence that needs to speak, or that needs to be spoken. It is male. The having spoken is the book. It is female. It is closed.
>
> (73–74)

Words breaks down the dualities in a number of ways. Johnnie comes together with Helen through the dance and through sex. As a dancer he is one of the best and most popular in town; and the sex takes place every night for a week in a beautiful, Eden-like garden. Moreover, Johnnie does not need a corresponding female character to speak his silence; he does it himself. In this context he is an embodiment of both male "silence" and of female "having spoken" and "book." In these various ways Kroetsch is bringing horse and house, male and female, together, and in ways that do not diminish the man's heroic stature or threaten the integrity of his role as cowboy, orphan, and outlaw. By unifying elements that he has said are not unified in prairie fiction, Kroetsch is writing against the prairie mythology (the "systems") that he himself has identified.

This is a suitable project for the author, according to Kroetsch in *Labyrinths of Voice*:

> *Neuman*: The telling of a particular myth in a Kroetsch novel then must be analogous to the act of deconstructing myth itself. It would not be unlike the turning of a particular myth, say the quest myth, into the activity of the writer. . . .
>
> *Kroetsch*: That's right. You tell your way out of the story, in a sense. I think what it really comes down to is that we are entrapped in those mythic stories; we can surrender to them or we can tell our way out. . . .
>
> (96)

Kroetsch's purpose in *Words* can be seen as the deconstruction of the systems that have defined prairie literature, through the integration of dualities that have always defined a separateness. The horse-house duality of story breaks down when we have a male character achieving union with the feminine world through dance, sex (albeit on an illicit level) and, most importantly, by speaking his own silence. This process of constructing a voice out of silence is accomplished by Johnnie as a character (on the level of story) and as a narrator (telling his story on the level of book); form and content are thus neatly aligned. What about the duality of book? Kroetsch presents Coyote-God as a metaphor for two choices, two different artistic stances, but a degree of integration occurs here as well. Johnnie, by the end of the novel, has found a way to integrate the anarchy of self with the order of community. Remaining himself, he has moved from the periphery to the centre, from outlaw to hero. As teller of his own story, he is both the trickster as author and the author as high priest (in the sense of proclaimer). And by turning the rhythms of oral storytelling into words on a page, Kroetsch and Johnnie have both integrated the ephemeral, spontaneous spoken word with the permanent, ordered written word.

As for Johnnie's favourite duality of beginnings and endings, at the end of the book (which is also the end of his existence on the level of book), he is at the beginning of a speech. That closing speech begins where his opening speech ended, with the word "Rain" (211). On the level of story, Johnnie is, at this point, at the true beginning of speech—full, confident, resolved speech (even if the speech he is making is still in his head, and is therefore silent). On the level of book, the end is the first time since the beginning that Johnnie has stopped talking and become silent. The end is thus both the beginning of speech and the beginning of silence.

There is a neatness to *Words*, an order brought on by this knitting together of dualities, that Kroetsch undoes in the second and third novels of his "Out West" triptych. Writing and speaking, protagonist and narrative voice: these pairs of ingredients are as likely to form a violent concoction as a smooth and tasteful blend in *The Studhorse Man* and *Gone Indian*. In **"The Exploding Porcupine: Violence of Form in English-Canadian Fiction,"** a 1980 essay that can be read as a postmodern manifesto, Kroetsch writes:

> The theory of answers, for us, is a dangerous one. We must resist endings, violently. And so we turn from content to the container; we turn from the tale to the telling. It is form itself, traditional form, that forces resolution. In our most ambitious writing, we do violence by doing violence to form.
>
> (191)

If *Words* is the closest the triptych comes to "traditional form," and Johnnie's beginning-into-speech an ambiguous but nevertheless definite "resolution," a comparison of Kroetsch's treatments of two parallel incidents in *Words* and *Gone Indian* suggests what he might mean by more "ambitious" writing.

A tragic accident occurs in the first novel when the rodeo clown mistimes his jump away from a charging bull, gets caught, is severely mangled, and dies. In *Gone Indian* a similarly carnivalesque occasion (the ice festival) is the site of the cowboy's ski-jumping accident; he lands on his head, but all we are told of his fate is three rumours: he's dead, he's in hospital and "silly in the rafters" (78), or he's fine but being paid to keep a low profile. Kroetsch gives the clown scene in *Words* a definite resolution, the ultimate closure of death. He also gives it meaning: it becomes the motivation for Johnnie's "first major speech" and the first time he shows himself "a leader" (108). In *Gone Indian*, however, the cowboy's accident is both unresolved and without a clear significance: we are not told its outcome, and the sum total of its related effect on Jeremy is that he is "left alone again" (77). It happens, and then is over, forgotten, because something else is happening. It becomes just another incident, no more or less meaningful than any other. We ask, "What happened?" but where we look for resolution, Kroetsch has given us silence; where we look for a single voice, a single answer, he has given us several. "The ultimate violence that might to done to story is silence" (192), Kroetsch says in **"The Exploding Porcupine."** The cowboy's ending has not been, and never will be, spoken in terms of traditional narrative. Jeremy's fate at the end of the novel is likewise unresolved.

Using Kroetsch's ideas and language, this resistance to closure might be called the silence of the ending that is not spoken. But this would assume that a definitive ending does exist, and has simply not been put into words. Alternatively, the endings that *are* put into words—the three rumours about the cowboy and Madham's speculations regarding Jeremy's disappearance—can be considered to be all that really exists. This is to accept the primacy of text and the inseparability of story from its manifestation *as* text. Kroetsch often refers to Babel in critical writings and conversations; a world whose language has been confounded into languages he sees as a desirable dwelling place for a Canadian writer.[1] In *Labyrinths of Voice* he calls the Babel myth "a great thing, one of the greatest things that has happened to mankind. From the Tower of Babel all of a sudden, we gain all the languages we have" (116). Further on he says:

> I have learned a little more clearly that to go from metaphor to metonymy is to go from the temptation of

the single to the allure of multiplicity. Instead of the temptations of "origin" we have genealogies that multiply our connections into the past, into the world.

(117)

In the context of Babel, Kroetsch's multiple-choice endings are a natural response to a chaotic world whose meaning is not reducible to single answers, to simple resolutions. There are too many voices to be heard. Where **Words** presents a single voice, a single character, in a process of becoming that can be traced back to a single origin ("Mister, how would you like some rain?"), the older Kroetsch of **The Studhorse Man** and **Gone Indian** does real violence to traditional form not so much through silence as through an increased willingness to let loose the voices of Babel.

These voices creep in innocuously enough in **The Studhorse Man**. The novel's opening reads like third-person narration focusing on a protagonist, but in the fourth paragraph the voice is revealed as an I-narrator. At this point the reader's incipient sense of story is displaced; by definition this will be more than just Hazard's story. And while this I-narrator, later identified as Demeter Proudfoot, self-appointed biographer of Hazard Lepage, remains the voice that speaks to the reader directly, this apparent singularity is deceiving. For unlike the simplicity of Johnnie Backstrom telling his own story with his own voice, Demeter is a man of many voices, and the story he tells is both his own and that of an other.

Demeter has a strong voice but not a consistent one. As a biographer he simultaneously believes himself to be presenting an "extremely objective account of the life of one good man" (145) and, now and then, "straying from the mere facts" (12), allowing himself, "of necessity, [to] be interpretive upon occasion" (18). He prides himself on research that enables him to list every object on Hazard's bookshelves (9–10) and finds him measuring railway ties at a railway station (24); yet he admits, at one crucial point, that "I have not the foggiest notion how the two men got out of their fix" (99), and at another that he must infer material at a point "where I neglected to make notes, having somehow lost my pencil" (113). Such apparently contradictory approaches to his biographical "obligation" (61) highlight both Demeter's own deficiencies as narrator, and the impossibility of any biographer presenting a complete, truthful, and "objective" account of someone's life. The difference between Demeter and most biographers is that Demeter speaks not only in the voice of storyteller but also as commentator on the necessarily creative act of storytelling that biography is.

A number of other people's voices speak through Demeter's unifying voice. On the level of story, just as Doc Murdoch, Helen, and others speak through Johnnie's narrative in **Words**, Hazard, Utter, and Martha are voices speaking through Demeter's narrative. But while, on the level of book, or telling of story, Johnnie's only research is his own experience, Demeter's research is eclectic, and is affected by a number of voices both inside and outside the story of Hazard's life. Demeter's primary research appears to be several conversations he had with Hazard on the Eshpeter Ranch, most of which are preserved in note form. Other voices that inform Demeter's narrative are those of Lady Eshpeter (who, being blind, describes scenes based on what she remembers overhearing), Martha, and of course Demeter's own voice describing his experiences in the sections where his life overlaps with Hazard's. Even the doctor who steals the chapters on Demeter's theory of nakedness (98) is a voice: while only present as an absence, his is a censoring voice that nevertheless affects the way story becomes book.

Demeter's narrative style also reflects a multiplicity that Johnnie's, rooted as it is in oral confession, does not. Demeter's voice is flexible, allowing him to sound on one page like a dreamy philosopher ("Is the truth of the beast in the flesh and confusion or in the few skillfully arranged lines?" [134]), and on another like a precision-minded scientist ("The space between must be filled with water that has been heated to a temperature of not less than 105°F. and not more than 115°F." [137]). When describing Martha's naked moonlit body his writing is so full of stock phrases ("the round perfection of her belly," "her long and creamy thighs," "my hard longing," "my savage pleasure" [65]) that Demeter seems, for a page or two, to have co-opted an entire language, one drawn from an established subliterary tradition. Likewise a chase scene is described by Demeter (who was not there) with all the hilarious detail of a comic Keystone Cops-style film, blatantly copying that story model with all of its usual conventions fully intact:

> The chase was on. Hazard galloped his horses through the city streets, yelled at, pursued, condemned, the milkwagon jumping over sidewalks and streetcar tracks, the load of milk bottles spilling out to become white telltale blotches on the snow. Policemen appeared from nowhere, a pair at this corner, a pair in that doorway. Streets became blind alleys. A track through the snow became a snowbank. "Stop! Stop him! Stop!" people yelled, standing motionless in swirls of powdered snow. "Stop that man!" a policeman ordered to a poor chap who had just driven his car into a lamppost. "Stop him!" two women pleaded when he galloped over their grocery cart behind a Safeway store. But, luckily, Hazard ran into a troop movement. The column of marching soldiers came between him and two dozen pursuers, and the soldiers, lacking a command, would not break rank. They would not stop.

(43–44)

Typically, Demeter drops this borrowed voice after the one paragraph, but not before the reader has been shown that his narrative owes as much to a fictional storytelling tradition as to a biographical one.

Other voices used in the text include the archaic and intrusive "Dear reader" addresses, the hockey-announcer voice that Demeter briefly tries on (122–23), and the voice of a biblical genealogical tradition that informs the history of the Lepage stallion (71–72). This jumble of languages and voice that Demeter employs, and that speaks through him and his research, is revealed gradually throughout the novel. The reader begins with no awareness that there is a narrator; once he makes himself known, the narrator is assumed to be reliable. Even his early discussions of the necessity to combine recording of facts with interpretation sound innocent enough. But as the elements of memory, on-the-spot research, note-taking, interviews with different participants, censorship, interpretation, guesswork, omissions, borrowed languages, and personal theorizing become apparent, the reader is forced to recognize contradictions. As the central figure and primary source of research, Hazard, next to Demeter, has the most prominent voice in the book, yet when Hazard's memory of P. Cockburn differs from what Demeter's study turns up (31), the reader must confront the unreliability of memory, and therefore of many of the "facts" in the book. Hazard, who tells his story to Demeter, is an unreliable narrator: his memory is inaccurate, and occasionally during their sessions he is so unwell that he can only "grunt and shake his head" (108–09). Demeter, who tells the story to us, is unreliable by definition if Hazard is, but he is also writing the story with incomplete and eclectic research, some twenty years after the events it describes, and from a madhouse.

Kroetsch, in a *Canadian Fiction Magazine* interview (1977), was asked if he liked unreliable narrators:

> I might take the extreme position that there are no "correct" accounts. My narrators are simply like people in life—each one is of necessity an unreliable narrator. I—and the reader—have to hear something of the nature of that unreliability.
>
> (44)

For the reader of **The Studhorse Man**, hearing that unreliability involves more than just accepting that the traditional unity of narrative has been undermined by a proliferation of voices. The reader must also witness the complete subversion of biographical form. The first major passage in which the rules of biography are broken occurs when Demeter abruptly shifts from Hazard's story back some years to the erotic description of his own personal experience of spying on a naked Martha. This scene has nothing to do with Hazard, but has profound significance for Demeter himself. It is an event that, at the time, made him speechless: "I could find no voice to answer with. My very wanting had choked me into silence" (65). Like Johnnie in **Words**, however, Demeter is here giving voice to his own silence, speaking his own speechlessness. Significantly, this is the point in the novel at which he first tells the reader his name. As such it is a turning point: throughout the rest of the novel Demeter increasingly brings himself into the story, and describes from his own perspective incidents involving both himself and Hazard, to a point where, as Kroetsch puts it, "He starts to see himself as the hero as he sits in the bathtub writing the book" ("Interview" 39).

Demeter writes against the silence that his relatives, by institutionalizing him, have imposed. By turning the story

of another man's life into the story of his own, he defines himself, not just as a being, but as a kind of coyote trickster figure who achieves a peculiar version of integration completely different from Johnnie Backstrom's speaking himself into union with his community. Demeter, alone in his bathtub, is both the epitome of house (stasis) as opposed to horse (motion), and of self (nonconformity, isolation) as opposed to community (integration). The old dualities have remained separate; yet, as Kroetsch explains, "Demeter literally gets himself together by putting those two figures—Hazard and himself—together" (*Labyrinths* 173). By speaking himself into existence as "D. Proudfoot, Studhorse Man" (156), he achieves a personal integration that is completely self-contained, and he does it through nothing more or less than an act of narrative.

Kroetsch has said one of his interests in writing the "Out West" triptych was the "questioning of narrative itself" ("Interview" 44). Narrative in **The Studhorse Man** turns out to be a slippery, often deceptive thing: omnipresent, its origins and purposes are not always apparent, and as a tool its powers can be employed towards virtually anyone's personal agenda. While Demeter's manipulation of narrative is both more obvious and more benign than Madham's in **Gone Indian**, the fact that he usurps the hero's role and deconstructs the reader's expectations of the biographical form makes his use of narrative powerfully disarming. As an inheritor of the post-Babel world, the reader must recognize the multiplicity of voices and languages that may speak through a single voice, and the fuzziness of the boundaries between fictional and factual storytelling. When Kroetsch, through Demeter, says that Hazard is "terrified of history" (33), the reader may be tempted by the *double entendre* of history: his story. When story and history blur together and narrative forces an "objective account of the life of one good man" off the rails, the discomfited reader may indeed find the process terrifying.

For Kroetsch, this is the challenge that he sets the reader, the challenge of participation:

> I'm interested in sharing with the reader the fact that I'm making a fiction. One of the assumptions of the old style realism is that the novel isn't a fiction. Verisimilitude, the text-books demand. And I'm no longer interested in that. I want the reader to be engaged with me in fiction making. I work a reader pretty hard, I guess, in that I want him to enter into the process with me.
>
> ("Interview" 42)

The reader in effect becomes another voice informing the narrative, which is an appropriate role given Kroetsch's belief in the ubiquitousness of the storytelling impulse:

> Go to any kitchen table at which there are more than three people assembled—People tell stories and in that sense use narrative to construct a reality. . . . Of course, they work in a very short form. The oral storyteller probably has less impulse to "deconstruct" his inherited conventions. . . . I think some of the conventions of fiction control too much our way of seeing the

world. It starts to get interesting when you take those conventions and both use them and work against them.

("Interview" 39)

Kroetsch's development of this deconstructive approach through the "Out West" trilogy can be examined in the context of the relationship between oral and written story-telling. In *Words*, there is a direct correspondence between Johnnie's spoken confession and the words on the page; there is one narrative and one voice. In *The Studhorse Man*, Demeter uses oral accounts of Hazard's life provided by several people as part of his research, but these reminiscences often prove incomplete or inaccurate. Ultimately all such material must be filtered through the writer's memory, his ability to take notes, his tendency to pursue tangents, and his personal reasons for writing the story in the first place. For this reason, the oral raw material and the "portentous volume" (175) that results from it may in some places directly correspond and in others deviate wildly, but with only one source of information (i.e., Demeter), and a fictional one at that, the reader cannot investigate the "truth" of such matters. In *Gone Indian* the oral raw material is presented directly, in the form of transcriptions. However, the primacy of Jeremy's version of events is undercut in a number of ways. He takes the tape recorder on his journey not to fulfill a storytelling impulse—after all, he is talking to a machine, and therefore more to himself than to his absent audience of one—but rather acting on "instructions" from Madham and as a substitute for writing, because of "his inability to get things down on paper" (1). Upon transcription his oral account—his voice—is edited, commented upon, criticized, speculated upon, and roughly half of it is completely rewritten. Madham, who admits from the outset that he feels "under no obligation to explain anything" (1), takes possession of Jeremy's story and uses it as a vehicle to construct, or at least reinforce, his own reality. By abandoning even the illusion of a single voice, Kroetsch takes his deconstruction of the conventional novel even further than he did in *The Studhorse Man*.

The purpose of this deconstructive approach is not, however, to do violence to form for its own sake. For Kroetsch it is part of a grander scheme in which the artist in a new country must, as he has most recently expressed it, "relate that newly evolving identity to its inherited or 'given' names" by holding "those names in suspension, to let identity speak itself out of a willed namelessness" (**"Canadian Writing"** 127). The concept of unnaming in order to name, first articulated by Kroetsch in his 1974 essay, **"Unhiding the Hidden: Recent Canadian Fiction,"** is necessitated by the absence in Canada of an indigenous literary tradition:

> The Canadian writer's particular predicament is that he works with a language, within a literature, that appears to be authentically his own, and not a borrowing. But just as there was in the Latin word a concealed Greek experience, so there is in the Canadian word a concealed other experience, sometimes British, sometimes American.

(43)

If our language is inherited from elsewhere, then so must be the forms in which our language is ordered, expressed. Establishing a new literature requires not only finding a new language but new forms and structures to house it. The first step, however, for the writer setting out to "uninvent the world" (**"Unhiding"** 43) is to represent it symbolically through some form of unnaming engaged in by a character. In the three novels examined in **"Unhiding the Hidden,"** Atwood's *Surfacing*, Davies's *The Manticore*, and Wiebe's *The Temptations of Big Bear*, the process is represented in story as, respectively, a stripping away of the earthly artifacts (including clothes) that contain the past, a retreat into a cave, and the victimization of a native tribe. On the level of book, Kroetsch as storyteller increasingly deconstructs traditional (and therefore inherited) novelistic forms in the three "Out West" novels. On the level of story he demonstrates the complete cycle of unnaming and renaming only in the final book of the triptych, *Gone Indian*.

Unlike the initially silent Johnnie Backstrom who creates himself out of nothing by telling his own story, and unlike Demeter who creates himself out of someone else's story, Jeremy Sadness must go through an unnaming—a loss of a previous identity—before he can be renamed. He begins his journey (paradoxically) as an American graduate student, with a name, an identity, and a two-part mission: to attend a job interview in Alberta, and to follow an innate impulse toward the frontier. Immediately upon arrival in Edmonton he loses his suitcase, a physical loss of identity that is also psychological: "Just for a moment, Professor, I couldn't remember my name. For a fatal moment my stumbling, ossified, PhD-seeking mind was a clean sheet" (7). The sheet-cleaning process continues as Jeremy accepts the new identity thrust on him, misses his job interview, and buys a new set of clothes even after he has found his own suitcase. But the renaming that goes on initially—Jeremy as Roger Dorck, Jeremy as Winter King—only creates interim identities, as Jeremy becomes even further removed from his former self. The final abandonment—the final unnaming—occurs during the snowshoe race, and is symbolized by Jeremy's discarding his jacket (and his keys). Just prior to this he has begun renaming his environment to suit the new identity he is preparing to take on, unhiding hidden things that he wants to see:

> I dodged around a crater in the snow; a dip, I decided, that must conceal a buffalo wallow. A lone tree in the distance was a rubbing tree. I decided that too. Buffalo trails, deep ruts in the hidden earth, came down through the coulees, down to the slow river and the salt licks and the water. I swear I could smell the blood of a buffalo jump: right there in those hills the Cree and Blackfoot drove the unknown herds to a fatal leap.

(85)

At the end of the race Jeremy is mistaken for an Indian, and cannot identify himself otherwise because "I would not speak. For if I had tried, it would have been a tongue I did not understand" (93). Having unnamed himself, he has lost language; at this point in the cycle all of the languages of Babel are possible, but none has been claimed. Jeremy then meets Daniel Beaver and his wife, who assist him in his transformation into Indian (he already has braids at this point) by supplying moccasins and a leather jacket with fringes. In a dream Jeremy sees himself as an Indian warrior, and undergoes a renaming by Poundmaker, from "Antelope Standing Still" to "Has-Two-Chances." In another dream he becomes a buffalo. So obsessed is he with his new identities that when called upon to fulfill a previously named role, that of beauty contest judge, he deconstructs the entire ritual by naming Jill, instead of one of the contestants, as Winter Queen.

The renaming of Jeremy Sadness into a multitude of identities—Roger Dorck, Has-Two-Chances, Buffalo, Grey Owl, and even vestiges of the former self that he never completely leaves behind—suggests that the uninvention of the world can open up a number of possibilities. Madham defines this as a "consequence of the northern prairies" and calls it "the diffusion of personality into a complex of possibilities rather than a concluded self" (152). In terms of Canadian literature, this means that a writer who peels away the layers of inherited languages and literary traditions to get to the silence of an unnamed world can build in a number of directions of top of that foundation. The languages that emerge may be as multiplicitous as those of Babel, but they will be the writer's own. In **"Canadian Writing: No Name Is My Name,"** a recent essay that continues the work of **"Unhiding the Hidden,"** Kroetsch says:

> It may well be that the villain (namelessness) turns out to be the hero in the story of the Canadian story. The nameless figure who seems to threaten us may in fact be leading us to high ground. To avoid a name does not . . . deprive one of an identity; indeed, it may offer a plurality of identities.
>
> (128)

To what does this world of multiple possibilities lead? In general, it leads to an avoidance of simple answers or conclusions, to an approach to writing that "resist[s] endings, violently" (**"Exploding"** 191). In *Gone Indian* specifically, it means resistance to closure, resistance to an ending that would force more precise definition. Jeremy's trip to Notikeewin does not so much end as become displaced from the present into the past, into history. Jeremy, in all of his various identities, moves from being a voice (or voices) present on the open prairie to being a silent absence. The writing down of a world of possibilities involves the recognition and expression of chaos, resisting the usual tendency of narrative to act as an ordering mechanism upon the chaos that is out there in the world of experience. When narrative itself evokes chaos, a number of changes must be made to the traditional roles of reader, writer, and text. What a world of multiple possibilities leads to, then, on the level of book, is a breaking down of established orders, of traditional roles and hierarchies. On the level of story Kroetsch has a metaphor for this: the carnival.

In a 1982 essay entitled **"Carnival and Violence: A Meditation,"** Kroetsch takes his interpretation of the carnival from the Russian critic, Mikhail Bakhtin:

> "One might say that carnival celebrated liberation from the prevailing truth and from the established order; it marked the suspension of all hierarchical rank, privileges, norms, and prohibitions. Carnival was the true feast of time, the feast of becoming, change, and renewal. It was hostile to all that was immortalized and completed."
>
> (111)

In the world of carnival, the division between performer and spectator breaks down, and without the distancing properties of established order, a kind of chaos reigns. The carnival is a communal, participatory event, allowing "'the *free, familiar contact among people*'" (114). Without hierarchies, identities are lost; the participants are temporarily unnamed and may create whatever identity they like and wear it as a mask. For Kroetsch,

> carnival rejoices not in our completeness but in our incompleteness; the mask allows us to partake of several possibilities; we are allowed to cross boundaries; we can at once be serious and mocking, be ourselves and caricature other, be others and criticize ourselves.
>
> (**"Carnival"** 116)

In all three "Out West" novels a version of carnival serves as a focal event, and as a turning point in the progress of the central character. In *Words* Johnnie moves from confused speechlessness during the search for Jonah's body, even though "A compulsion to talk was storming inside me," (75), to the confidence of his first big speech where "I didn't so much speak as roar" (108), by finding himself at the centre of attention at two successive carnivals. The auction, where he heckles the prophet's speech but does nothing more constructive than bid $128 that he does not have for the Model-A, is a kind of prelude to the next day's rodeo. (Later that day he talks back to Applecart on the radio, and makes brief stabs at speeches, but to an audience of none.) The second and more important carnival-like event is the rodeo, at which the clown's accidental death motivates Johnnie's highly successful "hind-tit speech" (114). Johnnie, who has recently been saying "Sometimes it seems that chaos is the only order" (101), uses the bewildered chaos of the crowd after the accident as an opportunity: he orders the crowd behind him with a spontaneous speech that will unify them, and him with them. He creates his own role, and fulfills it, undergoing a kind of renewal in this carnivalesque environment.

In *The Studhorse Man* the wedding is the carnival. Traditionally a symbol of unity, order, and renewal, the wedding in this case is also Demeter's first appearance in the main plot (i.e., the story of Hazard), and the first time Hazard and Demeter have come together in the same place. Apart from the one earlier diversion where he describes his peeping-tom experience with Martha, this is the first extended scene in which the story is told from Demeter's perspective. It is, therefore, the beginning of Demeter's transition from biographer to subject, and of the transition in narrative method from a researched story to a lived one. The further integration of Hazard and Demeter that has occurred by the end of the novel is begun here; this is where Demeter really starts to wear the mask he has been playing with off and on.

The carnival as event and metaphor is most prominent in *Gone Indian*. It is during the winter festival that Jeremy discards his jacket and keys, symbolically reducing his identity to a void from which he can recreate himself freely. Identities that are imposed on him, especially the identity of Dorck and the consequent role of beauty contest judge, he now has the ability to reject: given a choice of three identical possibilities he steps outside and makes up his own rules, thereby reinventing the roles of Winter King and Winter Queen. The identities that he embraces are those he chooses, and in a carnival world he not only can do that, he can get away with it.

While rodeos, weddings, and festivals are the most likely sources of the carnivalesque spirit, the environment of liberation from order and rebirth into multiple possibilities is itself situated within a larger place. In **"Carnival and Violence: A Meditation,"** Kroetsch says: "I grew up in a rural part of Western Canada, where a trace of carnival, if not the carnivalization of literature, was vital and alive. We measured time by wedding dances and sports days and rodeos" (120). The prairie, as the setting for the "Out West" novels, is the home of their carnivals. Kroetsch comes close to identifying the carnivalesque with the prairie itself when he quotes Frederick Jackson Turner's "The significance of the Frontier in American History" as the epigraph to *Gone Indian*: "For a moment, at the frontier, the bonds of custom are broken and unrestraint is triumphant." If the prairie as frontier—as new place, as the boundary between known and unknown—is a natural location for the becoming world of carnival, it also is a natural metaphor for the larger place of which it is a part: the new, becoming country of Canada with its new, becoming literature.

In the essay, **"On Being an Alberta Writer,"** Kroetsch discusses his disillusionment when, as a young boy, his father told him that the place he was playing in was a buffalo wallow:

> What buffalo? I asked. . . . When? From where? . . . Even at that young age I was secure in the illusion that the land my parents and grandparents homesteaded had had no prior occupants, animal or human. Ours was the ultimate tabula rasa. We were the truly innocent.
>
> (218)

This experience, Kroetsch says, was "how I first began to be skeptical of the writing that I read" (218). That writing, suddenly, was rendered less pure when the land was revealed as being contaminated by previous users. Neither the place called home nor the writing that came from it

had been formed from first principles. This early realization indicates two important assumptions of Kroetsch's own writing. First, writing springs from a sense of place: the writing that comes *from* a place (such as the prairies) will be the writing *of* that place. Second, a tabula rasa, or blank slate, is a solid and desirable place to begin putting something—a home, an identity, a literature. These assumptions form the intuitive foundation upon which Kroetsch as critic and novelist derives many of his concepts: Jeremy's need to strip off old identities before taking on new ones, the notion of unnaming in order to name, the attraction of carnival with its promise of renewal through the abandoning of structures. But perhaps most important, the reality of the prairie and the attraction of the blank slate that he thought he knew taught Kroetsch about the significance of silence, a silence that, he says, is most noticeable when it stems from an absence, an abandonment: "I responded to those discoveries of absence, to that invisibility, to that silence, by knowing I had to make up a story. *Our* story" (**"On Being"** 219).

Note

1. For example, see the last paragraph of Kroetsch's "Beyond Nationalism: A Prologue."

Works Cited

Kroetsch, Robert. "Beyond Nationalism: A Prologue." *The Canadian Literary Scene in Global Perspective*. Spec. issue of *Mosaic* 14.2 (1981): v-xi. (Rpt. in *Essays* 83–89.)

⸺. "Canadian Writing: No Name Is My Name." *The Forty-Ninth and Other Parallels: Contemporary Canadian Perspectives*. Ed. David Staines, Amherst: U of Massachusetts P, 1986. 116–28.

⸺. "Carnival and Violence: A Meditation." *Essays* 111–22.

⸺, and Diane Bessai. "Death Is a Happy Ending: A Dialogue in Thirteen Parts." *Figures in a Ground: Canadian Essays on Modern Literature Collected in Honor of Sheila Watson*. Ed. Diane Bessai and David Jackel. Saskatoon: Western Producer Prairie, 1978. 206–15.

⸺. "The Exploding Porcupine: Violence of Form in English-Canadian Fiction." *Violence in the Canadian Novel Since 1960*. Ed. Terry Goldie and Virginia Harger-Grinling. St. John's: Memorial U of Newfoundland, 1980. 191–99. (Rpt. in *Essays* 57–64.)

⸺. "The Fear of Women in Prairie Fiction: An Erotics of Space." *Crossing Frontiers: Papers in American and Canadian Western Literature*. Ed. Dick Harrison, Edmonton: U of Alberta P, 1978. 73–83. (Rpt. in *Essays* 47–55.)

⸺. *Gone Indian*, Toronto: new, 1973.

⸺. "An Interview with Robert Kroetsch." With Geoff Hancock. *Canadian Fiction Magazine* 24–25 (1977): 33–52.

⸺. "On Being an Alberta Writer: Or, I Wanted to Tell Our Story." *The New Provinces: Alberta and*

Saskatchewan, 1905–1980. Ed. Howard Palmer and Donald Smith. Vancouver: Tantalus, 1980. 217–27. (Rpt. in *Essays* 69–80.)

———. "Robert Kroetsch: The American Experience and the Canadian Voice." *Conversations with Canadian Novelists*. Vol. 1. With Donald Cameron. Toronto: Macmillan, 1973. 81–95. 2 vols.

———. *Robert Kroetsch: Essays*. Ed. Frank Davey and bp Nichol. Spec. issue of *Open Letter* 5th ser. 4 (1983).

———. *The Studhorse Man*. Toronto: Macmillan, 1969.

———. "Unhiding the Hidden: Recent Canadian Fiction." *Journal of Canadian Fiction* 3.3 (1974): 43–45. (Rpt. in *Essays* 17–21.)

———. *The Words of My Roaring*. Toronto: Macmillan, 1966.

Neuman, Shirley, and Robert Wilson. *Labyrinths of Voice: Conversations with Robert Kroetsch*. Western Canadian Literary Documents Series 3. Edmonton: NeWest, 1982.

John Thieme (essay date 29 November-1 December 1989)

SOURCE: "There's No Business Like Snow Business: Narrative Voice in Robert Kroetsch's *Gone Indian*," in *Multiple Voices: Recent Canadian Fiction,* edited by Jeanne Delbaere, November 29-December 1, 1989, pp. 202-16.

[*In the following essay, Thieme discusses* Gone Indian *as a post-modernist retelling of the frontier story.*]

In *Gone Indian* (1973), the second novel in Robert Kroetsch's 'Out West' triptych, an American graduate student, Jeremy Sadness, journeys to Edmonton for an interview for an academic post, which he never attends. On arrival at Edmonton Airport he is immediately confronted by a notion of alternative identity and what is referred to as 'the possibility of transformation',[1] when he finds that the suitcase he has claimed is not his own, but that of one Roger Dorck, a barrister and solicitor resident in a town called Notikeewin. Strip-searched along with a character he initially labels 'the world's most beautiful blonde' (p. 8), but who proves to be a transvestite, Jeremy quickly concludes 'This is a peculiar land. . . . Illusion is rife' (p. 8) and this episode proves to be a pattern for his numerous subsequent encounters with fluid or overlapping identities. The switching of suitcases suggests that Roger Dorck may be an *alter ego* for Jeremy, but this is only one of a number of possible alternative roles available to him. Accepting a lift to Notikeewin from a returning rodeo-circuit rider, Jeremy is struck by the white emptiness of the terrain through which he is driven and it seems that the signifying systems of his eastern academic upbringing are being confounded by the mirage-like quality of the prairie winter landscape. On arrival in Notikeewin his habitual modes of perception are further dislocated as he is plunged into the carnivalesque world of the town's an-nual winter festival, at which Dorck (the name is slang for 'phallus',[2] suggesting a Rabelaisian carnivalesque subversion[3]), who has suffered a snowmobile accident and is now comatose in the local hospital, was to preside as king.

Jeremy speculates that Notikeewin may be a Cree or Blackfoot word (p. 12) and in fact the name derives from the Cree '*nolnigiwin-sipi*' which means 'fighting river'.[4] This is highly appropriate as the setting for a text which not only accords the mock-epic games of the winter festival (a kind of northwestern equivalent of Homeric or Virgilian games) a central role,[5] but one which locates itself at the site of conflicting discourses. Jeremy is himself torn between different discursive systems: he is a product of his scholarly training, in which myth criticism appears to have played an important part, but frequently rebels against academe, opposing its language with a youthful, phallogocentric discourse; and he has 'dreamed northwest' (p. 6), availed himself of a particular version of the Frontier myth centred on the figure of the Englishman Archie Belaney who reinvented himself as 'the truest Indian of them all' (p. 80), Grey Owl.[6] Inherent in Belaney's transformation of self is the notion of the journey west as a journey to new beginnings[7] and it is no coincidence that some of Jeremy's abortive attempts at writing his doctoral dissertation have begun with a focus on the archetypal westward journey to the Americas, that undertaken by Columbus himself. The myth of western freedom and renewal is further underscored by *Gone Indian*'s epigraph, 'For a moment, at the frontier, the bonds of custom are broken and unrestraint is triumphant' (p. [vii]), which is taken from *the* classic American text in the formulation of the myth of the Frontier, Frederick Jackson Turner's 'The Significance of the Frontier in American History'.[8] Within the novel a Tristan and Iseult parallel—Jeremy is sent to Edmonton by his supervisor, Professor *Mark* Madham, just as Tristan is sent to Ireland by King Mark[9]—provides another variation on the pattern of westward journeying.

However, in this latter-day version of the Columbus quest, Canada has become the Promised Land, has taken over the role of the place of potential renewal and references to western mythologies are compounded with allusions to *polar* exploration: at various points Jeremy's journey is likened to those of Scott (p. 40), Ross in search of the lost Franklin (p. 57) and a member of Shackleton's expedition (p. 124). The Canadian northwest is envisaged as the contemporary Frontier, the place where 'the bonds of custom are broken and unrestraint is triumphant' and Edmonton is referred to as 'that last city on the far, last edge of our civilization' (p. 6). Such a conception is, of course, like all versions of place, no more than a mental construct, but it is not one which is peculiar to the text. It can be related to a contemporary collective perception of the city, which is most evident in the coming together of those two quintessential latter-day expressions of the American Dream, the shopping mall and the theme park, in the form of West Edmonton Mall, reputedly the world's largest shopping centre and a place of northwestern pilgrimage on the Canadian 'far, last edge' which even includes a replica of Columbus's ship the Santa Maria as one of its central exhibits.

Gone Indian is, however, concerned with far more than a simple cultural re-reading of the myth of the Frontier in which the Canadian northwest has become the borderline place where new beginnings are possible. It is, even more obviously than the two previous volumes in the 'Out West' triptych, *The Words of My Roaring* (1966) and *The Studhorse Man* (1969), a postmodernist work which foregrounds signifying practices and constructs the Frontier as much as a site of liberation from prevalent discursive systems, among which academic analysis and legal and quasi-legal judgement are particularly prominent, as an actual geographical locus at which some kind of physical emancipation occurs. In Aritha van Herk's words, *Gone Indian* is 'a novel about the transformation of the novel, what happens to the old (academic) order when the post-modern writer attacks it'.[10] Jeremy Sadness's journey into the Alberta park lands becomes an initiation into a blank *tabula rasa*-like world, in which language breaks down and the text repeatedly associates the snow-shrouded landscape with death and silence, with a pre- (or post-?) linguistic world in which the distinctions of language that create the sense of discrete identity, whether for people, objects or concepts, dissolve into an undifferentiated primeval (or apocalyptic?) mass. As in other Kroetsch novels',[11] this world is associated with animal identity—particularly with the buffalo, but also with several other Canadian animals such as the beaver, bear, rabbit and owl; it is associated with Plains Indian identity, with a pure, Edenic-like lovemaking[12] and, most prominently of all in *Gone Indian*, with the all-enveloping snow in which Jeremy repeatedly finds himself immersed.

'Snow' is a signifier that particularly characterizes the northern, Canadian world, and comments in two other Canadian novels of the 1970s provide an interesting context for the way in which it is used in *Gone Indian*. Both Margaret Atwood's *Surfacing* (1972) and Margaret Laurence's *The Diviners* (1974) stress the importance of words for 'snow' in Inuit culture. In *Surfacing* the un-named narrator/protagonist bemoans the inadequacy of the English word 'love' for describing the complex range of emotions evoked by it and reflects that 'the Eskimoes had fifty-two names for snow',[13] which has a similar, central importance in their culture. *The Diviners* echoes this, putting the count of 'eskimo' words for 'snow' at a more modest twenty-five and attributing this number to the Inuit need to be able to distinguish between different varieties of the substance in order to survive.[14] One *might* argue that even in the English-Canadian context there is a need for a range of signifiers to provide some kind of account of the multiplicity of forms that the element can take: the blanket term 'snow' offers no opportunities for making distinctions amid this plurality. On one level, then, 'snow' provides an index of a complex, polymorphous phenomenon being strait-jacketed within a single, monolithic pattern of signification; 'snow' reduces multi-voiced disparate

identity into univocal simplism. On another level *Gone Indian* suggests that this abnegation of differentiation offers liberation from 'the old (academic) order'. Jeremy Sadness's entry into the snow carnival world can be read as involving a loss of identity, a symbolic death, but such a death simultaneously offers the possibility of rebirth into a new identity—comparable with Archie Belaney's metamorphosis into Grey Owl—*and* an alternative universe of discourse, which is associated with a Plains Indian sensibility. A comment by Kroetsch in *Labyrinths of Voice*, his book-length, deconstructed interview with Shirley Neuman and Robert Wilson, elaborates on this:

> *To go Indian*: an ambiguous phrase: to become released or wild in the carnival sense. And I was playing that off against the professor (Madham) and graduate student (Sadness)—people who are into the whole notion of control . . . ordering, explaining. It is their extreme movement from the professorial stance into carnival that interested me. Sadness arrives in a carnival: he is both released and realized by that: he is completed by that, even by the loss of identity and the shift into a new identity by accident, by the mixing of life and death that takes place, the kind of phallic connection. So the carnivalization is what? It's happening to the characters and it's happening to the novel. It's double.[15]

According to *one* possible version of Jeremy's eventual fate, offered in the closing pages of the text, he actually succeeds in finally realizing his Grey Owl fantasy. This account is disputed, but even the main alternative possibility has him dying/disappearing into a new identity as he leaps from a high-level railway bridge in the middle of a *snow*storm.[16]

So 'snow' functions in *Gone Indian* both as the prime element of the winter festival world and as an index of the process of carnivalization which the novel itself is undergoing, the process in which the ostensible plot, a comic reworking of the 'monomyth' quest paradigm, outlined by Joseph Campbell[17] and others, is being subverted. But 'snow' is also important in another sense: *the narrative is a protracted snow-job*, a labyrinth of suspect, if not downright unreliable traces, among which Professor Madham's frame-narrative is the most elaborate piece of sleight-of-hand, and it is this aspect of the text, the playful, postmodernist use of narrative voice, which I wish to concentrate on as the main focus for the rest of this paper.

In *Labyrinths of Voice* a passage from Julia Kristeva, quoted immediately after the Kroetsch comment just cited as one of the many intertextual traces that productively disrupt the narrative flow of the three-way interview, draws attention to the unstable focalization of carnival discourse: 'The scene of the carnival introduces the split speech act: the *actor* and the *crowd* are each in turn simultaneously subject and addressee of discourse.'[18] *Gone Indian* works in just this way with first-person narrators also occupying the role of second-person narratees—thus Madham both receives Jeremy's tapes and mediates them by offering his own account of what happened to his protégé—to a point where *authority* is completely undermined, and with readers finding themselves in analogous situation to Jeremy Sadness as they are forced to cross a frontier of signification beyond which conventional conceptions of narrative coherence and unitary signification no longer obtain. Even the notion of stable, autonomous character collapses: towards the end of the novel Madham comments that the northern prairies frustrate normal 'human definition', because they make for 'the diffusion of personality into a complex of possibilities rather than a concluded self' (p. 152) and elsewhere Kroetsch himself has referred to the reader as:

> a character out of one of the novels the novelist is deconstructing. He expects certain consolations: of plot, of motivation, of characterization, of conclusion. . . . And he, the old reader, must slowly unlearn concepts of character. Of motivation. Of plot and ending. He must, to sum it up in one expression, acquire Negative Capability. He has entered a world where possibilities not only co-exist but contradict.[19]

So the act of consuming the text propels its readers into the position of having to author their own versions from the incomplete clues that are on offer. As one critic has put it, *Gone Indian* 'could be read as a detective novel where the intrigue takes place on the level of language, the suspects are words and the victim is identity'.[20] In such a scheme the reader is consigned to playing the part of detective and, while this may always be true of the reading experience, it is a role which assumes a particular urgency in the consumption of a postmodernist prairie text.

The process of detection has to come to terms with the novel's puzzling use of a polyphonic narrative method. Superficially there are only two narrative voices: those of Professor Madham and Jeremy Sadness. Madham is the main frame-narrator and he purports to offer an edited version—an edited version which suggests a kind of academic hatchet-job—of the audio-tapes Jeremy has been making during his time in Alberta. Sometimes Madham *appears* to be giving a verbatim transcription of the tapes—such is the level of narrative uncertainty associated with his voice that one hesitates to say categorically that these are Jeremy's utterances; at other times he provides his own summary of Jeremy's oral reports, freely admitting that he is only 'transcribing a few passages' (p. 1) and has 'had to select from the tapes, in spite of Jeremy's instructions to the contrary: the mere onslaught of detail merely overwhelms. We grasp at something else' (p. 13). His account is, then, a doctored version and the particular nature of this doctoring is fairly clearly associated with the 'old (academic) order'—on one occasion he even offers an academic footnote (p. 144)![21]

So, on the surface, the text offers its readers a dialogue between *two* voices: between professor and student, between scribal and oral discourse, between academic control and youthful iconoclasm, between a westerner come east (Madham confesses his origins were in Alberta) and an easterner gone west, gone Indian. However, the element of split-speech does not stop here. Both voices

exhibit tensions and inconsistencies which are centred on the dialogic aspects inherent within them: Jeremy makes his tapes for Madham and Madham's narrative is similarly informed by the prominent presence of an addressee—he writes to Jill Sunderman, a young woman with whom Jeremy has become involved in Alberta.

Jeremy's oral account is mainly narrated in the genre of confession. Chapter 16 of the text, in which he visits a priest and confesses his inability to be *un*chaste ('Father, listen . . . I can't get a hard-on in bed', p. 35) is a clear parody of this mode of utterance, and more generally his monologues are a form of confession to Madham, against whose authority he frequently rebels. All Kroetsch's earlier fiction, from **But We Are Exiles** (1965) onwards, is founded on a struggle between a patriarch and a young pretender who would usurp this older man's power, and **Gone Indian** continues this pattern. Jeremy's narrative, despite supposed censoring from Madham, is liberally dotted with undeleted expletives, many of which are directed against his mentor. So, although the version of his tapes that Madham offers shows him on one level to be a product of his eastern, academic upbringing, an element of western, carnivalesque subversion looms larger. Jeremy's narration can be seen as representative of a new generation's attempt to rid itself of the language of the Father,[22] the old (academic) order', but significantly Madham remains a necessary addressee for him until he chooses silence at the end of the novel. There is no overt Oedipal attempt, on his part, to dislodge the Father, though one could argue that the procedures of the text, which are themselves carnivalesque, involve just such a patricide.

While it is clear that Jeremy's tapes exhibit the interplay of conflicting discursive codes, it is perhaps less obviously so where Madham's narration is concerned. Madham may appear to write in a unitary unfragmented, academic mode, to act as a mediating voice for what he refers to as 'the inconsistencies and contradictions' (p. 5) of Jeremy's recordings. Such a reading is, however, I would suggest, untenable. It is within Madham's account that the real fragmentation, ironies and discontinuities of the text reside. He is both the ultimate puppet-master who pulls all the narrative strings and a chameleon-like trickster whose every word involves a kind of double-speak.

Gone Indian opens with a letter written by Madham to Jill Sunderman from an address in Binghamton, New York, which is the same as that at which Robert Kroetsch was living at the time of writing **Gone Indian**[23] (another level of postmodernist play is at work here). Although Jill remains the addressee of all his subsequent utterances, the epistolary form is only used in this initial section. Its effect is to foreground her second-person presence as the recipient of his narrative. While Jeremy confesses to Madham, *he* is in a sense confessing to Jill Sunderman. Since the account he provides for her frequently records events in which she has been directly involved, some readers of the novel have objected to this method on the grounds of implausibility. Why should he be telling Jill what she already knows?[24] There are, however, various possible justifications for such apparent recapitulation. Throughout Madham speaks in the avuncular tones of a professor who is used to having the last word. He is the possessor of the tapes and, within the dialogic structure of the novel, has the last word since he is able to comment on Jeremy's account, a process which, needless to say, does not operate in reverse. His Christian name, Mark, suggests one of the most important ways in which academic authority is exercised and, from this first letter, which concludes with his assertion that he is 'unfallen' (p. 3), onwards, he displays little modesty or sense of self-doubt. Jeremy, in contrast, is constantly forced to come to terms with fallen identity—a *fall* into carnivalesque chaos is a major motif of **Gone Indian** on both thematic and discursive levels[25]—and finally he appears to find freedom through a fortunate fall into darkness, a void of signification.[26]

Madham's relating to Jill what she may already reasonably be expected to know can also be justified in other ways. On one occasion he tells her that she may wish to square Jeremy's account with her own recollection (p. 38), thus explicitly casting doubt on the reliability of the supposedly definitive narrative he is retelling. Most significantly of all, though, Madham's own identity is *not* unitary. His name, like all the names in **Gone Indian**,[27] is richly suggestive and among the possibilities it evokes are those of crazed professor (mad-ham); first man (Adam), fallen or unfallen; and gender bender (madam). Even more markedly than Jeremy, Madham is a split subject and his claim to perfection, enacted on a formal level by his attempt to encase Jeremy's diffuse outpourings within the framework of his bland, superficially monolithic academic voice, can be read as the ultimate snow-job of the text.

While Jeremy has gone west, Madham has, many years before, come east, transforming himself from an Albertan frontiersman into a professor. So a role reversal is clearly implied, with Jeremy and Madham as obviously foils to one another as any pair of Conradian or Dostoyevskyan doubles. However, again more is involved than just this and the most satisfactory explanation of why Madham tells Jill what she already presumably knows is that he is, unbeknown to her, her father, and is consequently engaged in another kind of confessional discourse, albeit a veiled one. The evidence for such a reading is extensive, if not *completely* conclusive[28]—the open-ended nature of the novel's postmodernist practice allows nothing to be finalized. After Jill's father, Robert Sunderman, died/disappeared, he phoned his wife Bea, with whom Jeremy also becomes involved and with whom *he* ultimately dies/disappears, and so appears to have faked his death by drowning. Madham's narrative offers several clues that he may be the former Robert Sunderman,[29] among them a reference to his having been a hockey-player in his youth (p. 37), his remark that he has 'come to love [Bea Sunderman's]' old house as well as if it were [his] own' (p. 154) and, most suggestive of all, an apparent slip of the tongue close to the end of the novel when, speaking of

Robert Sunderman's disappearance, he says 'I shall never forget it' (p. 155). So the burden of evidence points towards a solution of the mystery in which Sunderman is seen as having killed off his old identity by *sundering*[30] himself from his prairie roots and reinventing himself as Madham. Yet in important respects his past remains with him and this helps to explain inconsistencies which are prominent in his own behaviour. Although he criticizes Jeremy for his phallic obsessions, he is usurping *his* role by sleeping with his wife, Carol. Although he has repudiated the West by coming east and donning the mantle of a professor, he nonetheless engages in animal-like lovemaking with Carol beside the buffalo enclosure of a zoo on a hillside near Binghamton (p. 3).

So the role-exchange pattern cuts both ways, with neither character fully possessed of the identity to which he aspires. However, whereas Jeremy's voice—as reported by Madham—moves away from a fixed position and finally at the end of his last tape surrenders itself to silence, as he lies in bed with Bea Sunderman vowing never to get up until, in a new ice age, he is enveloped by a glacier, 'the primal stuff in primal motion' (p. 150), Madham's academic pontifications attempt to impose an enclosing univocalism, which is only transcended in the last moment of his account, when he envisages Jeremy and Bea leaping into nothingness from the railway bridge. The freeze-frame quality of this ending leaves the narrative open, with the kinetic lovers immortalized, but not finalized, in a moment of stasis reminiscent of those on Keats's Grecian Urn.

The confusion and transformations of identity within the text are multiple: the transvestite youth Jeremy encounters at Edmonton Airport thinks he is a buffalo, as does Jeremy himself later on; Jeremy's wife Carol is compared with Jill Sunderman; Madham is very probably Robert Sunderman. Jeremy, who throughout the action of the novel has been unable to make love while lying down (a curious example of vertical man unable to function in a horizontal world—to borrow Laurie Ricou's terminology[31]) finally achieves regeneration in Robert Sunderman's bed, as Bea sleeps with him, thinking he is her lost, young husband returned. And Jeremy's identity is blurred not only with Sunderman/Madham's, but also with that of the comatose Dorck. In a dream in which the Plains Indians repossess what is now the city of Edmonton, Jeremy is renamed 'Has-Two-Chances' (p. 106) and at the end of the novel may have fulfilled his Grey Owl fantasy. In short, **Gone Indian** is saturated with references to possible transformations of identity to a point where the very notion of discrete, separate selfhood withers away.

A central scene—it is anticipated more than once before it actually occurs—takes place when Jeremy is drafted into judging a beauty contest to find a queen for the annual Notikeewin festival. This reads like a bizarre parody of the Judgement of Paris, since there are three contestants who are identical in every respect, another instance of the winter carnival world's confounding the academic urge to differentiate. Again the suggestion is that the northern plains render such activity meaningless and finally the text subsides into the silence of the snow-covered world, as Jeremy stops talking and Madham imagines him jumping into emptiness.

At the beginning of **Gone Indian** Madham presents his narrative as a response to Jill Sunderman's request that he "'explain everything'", but says he feels 'under no obligation to explain anything' (p. 1). Despite his unreliability as a narrator, this comment can be seen to foreground the novel's procedures: as a postmodernist text it resists transparent reading and notions of unitary and completed signification. However, the collapse of discrete identity and sharply individualized narrative voices in a world where snow is the Great Leveller is not simply a process of negation; it opens up multiple possibilities for transforming personality and cultural and discursive codes.

Gone Indian occupies a unique place among the cluster of revisionist texts that reshaped attitudes towards North American Indians in the late 1960s and early 1970s.[32] Unlike such works as Thomas Berger's *Little Big Man* (1964) and Dee Brown's *Bury My Heart at Wounded Knee: An Indian History of the American West* (1971), it is only incidentally involved in promulgating a new Indian historiography. It is less concerned with celebrating the return of the vanishing American than with the potential Plains Indian culture offers for WASP self-renewal. Its Indian characters, Daniel Beaver and his wife, function primarily as the repository of an alternative mode of discourse—one which is associated with silence and a lack of competitiveness that is the antithesis of the American Dream. The Cree Daniel Beaver emerges as an archetypal Canadian beautiful loser, when he subverts the heroic ideal of the quasi-epic winter games in which he is competing by throwing a dog-sleigh race he has virtually won just before the finishing line (p. 79). Jeremy's abandonment of his academic career and his tape recorder, his descent into silence, exile and cunning, involves a similar abnegation of language and the success ethic, and completes the process of surrendering autonomous selfhood in which he has been engaged from the moment of his arrival amid the snow of the winter carnival world. The text's subversive use of narrative voice and carnivalization of the form of the novel involves a parallel movement away from definitive, unitary signification. Both character and novel have gone Indian.

Notes

1. *Gone Indian* (1973; Nanaimo: Theytus, 1981), p. 7. Subsequent references are to this edition and are included in the text.

2. Robert Kroetsch, letter to Jim Bacque, 28 November 1972, University of Calgary MsC 27.1.13.33.

3. Kroetsch discusses carnivalization, with reference to the work of Mikhail Bakhtin and Julia Kristeva, in 'Carnival and Violence: A Meditation', *Robert Kroetsch: Essays*, eds. Frank Davey and bpNichol, *Open Letter*, 5, 4 (Spring 1983), pp. 111–22. See also *Labyrinths of Voice: Conversations with Robert Kroetsch*, eds. Shirley Neuman and Robert Wilson (Edmonton: NeWest Press, 1982), pp. 35–7.

4. Hugh A. Dempsey, *Indian Names for Albertan Communities* (Calgary: Glenbow Museum, revised edn., 1987), p. 15, gives this as the derivation of the name of the village of Notikewin, which is further north in Alberta. The Battle River, the area in which the 'Out West' triptych is set, was once known as the Notikeewin. I am indebted to Robert Kroetsch for this information.

5. *Funeral Games* was a working-title for the novel: an alternative title for an early draft entitled *Buffalo Woman*, University of Calgary MsC 27.12.1–3; and the first of eight possible titles which appear on the title-page of a second draft, University of Calgary MsC 27.12.4–6.

6. Belaney was born in Hastings, England in 1888 and went to Canada in 1906. There he associated with the Ojibwa, married an Iroquois wife and, claiming in the first of his books, *The Men of the Last Frontier* (1931), that he was the son of a Scot and an Apache, began calling himself Grey Owl. In 1931 he began to lecture on conservation. In the same year he went to live in Western Canada where he wrote three very popular books, *Pilgrims of the Wild* (1934), *Sajo and the Beaver People* (1935) and *Tales of an Empty Cabin* (1936). His true identity was only discovered after his death in 1938.

7. Kroetsch stresses the importance of the western quest for new beginnings in his review of Dick Harrison's *Unnamed Country*, 'The Disappearing Father and Harrison's Born-Again and Again and Again West', *Essays on Canadian Writing*, 11 (Summer 1978), pp. 7–9.

8. Turner's thesis was first delivered as an address to the American Historical Association in 1893. It is included in his *The Frontier in American History* (1920).

9. Cf. Robert Kroetsch, letter to Ingrid Cook, New Press, Toronto, 17 November 1972, '. . . from Tristan to Columbus to Trudeau, men have gone west in search of new loves, new worlds, new identities', University of Calgary MsC 27.1.13.32d; and letter to Patricia Knox, New Press, Toronto, 13 April 1973, describing *Gone Indian* as 'a novel about going west; not just my going, no, the going of Columbus from the Old World in search of the New, the going of Tristan in search of a new lay for the old king, the going out of and into that produced Canada, the Canadians, the change, the metamorphosis, ideally represented by and in the transubstantiation of the body and dreams of the English boy, Archie Belaney (fatherless, and seeking a father) into the Great Canadian Indian, Grey Owl . . .', University of Calgary MsC 27.1.13.40c.

10. *The Robert Kroetsch Papers First Accession: An Inventory of the Archive*, eds. Jean F. Tener and

Apollonia Steele (Calgary: University of Calgary Press, 1986), p. xxvi.

11. Particularly *Badlands* (1975). See my discussion of this aspect of the novel in 'Beyond History: Margaret Atwood's *Surfacing* and Robert Kroetsch's *Badlands*', in *Re-visions of Canadian Literature*, ed. Shirley Chew (Leeds: University of Leeds, 1985), pp. 71–87.

12. See particularly p. 147.

13. *Surfacing* (1972; London: Virago, 1979), p. 106.

14. *The Diviners* (1974; Bantam-Seal: New York and Toronto, 1975), p. 407.

15. *Labyrinths of Voice*, pp. 36–7.

16. Earlier in the novel a high level bridge has been associated with the possibility of a fall from language and fixed identity, when Jeremy makes love to Jill Sunderman in a cloud of *snow* on the High Level Bridge across the North Saskatchewan River in Edmonton, p. 59. Jeremy's first encounter with Plains Indian identity, in the form of Daniel Beaver, a 'Pied Piper' or spirit-guide in the process of his initiation into an alternative mode of discourse, also takes place on this bridge, p. 63.

17. In *The Hero with a Thousand Faces* (Cleveland: Meridian Books, 1956), p. 30, Campbell identifies the 'formula represented in the rites of passage: *separation—initiation—return*' as the 'nuclear unit of the monomyth'. Jeremy's journey frustrates completion of this 'formula', when his initiation leads not to return but disappearance. *Gone Indian* also employs the pattern of shamanistic descent outlined by Campbell, op. cit., pp. 98–101, an aspect of the novel which is discussed by Peter Thomas, *Robert Kroetsch*, (Vancouver: Douglas and McIntyre, 1980), Ch. 4.

18. 'The Bounded Text', *Desire in Language: A Semiotic Approach to Literature and Art*, ed. Leon S. Roudiez, trans. Thomas Gora, Alice Jardine and Leon S. Roudiez (New York: Columbia University Press, 1980), p. 46. Quoted in *Labyrinths of Voice*, p. 37.

19. *Labyrinths of Voice*, pp. 176–7.

20. Sylvia Söderlind, 'Identity and Metamorphosis in Canadian Fiction since the Sixties' in *A Sense of Place: Essays in Post-Colonial Literatures*, ed. Britta Olinder (Gothenburg: University of Gothenburg, 1984), p. 82.

21. In an earlier draft of the novel Madham's comments appear as footnotes, University of Calgary MsC 27.12.1–3.

22. Kroetsch discusses paternalistic models of influence in *Labyrinths of Voice*—see particularly, pp. 19–24.

23. 48 Lathrop Avenue, Binghamton, New York 13905.

24. See Robert Kroetsch, letter to Jim Bacque, 28 November 1972, University of Calgary MsC 27.1.13.33.

25. The text uses the fall metaphor to suggest an attempted escape from the anxiety of influence. Cf. *Labyrinths of Voice*, pp. 25–6.

26. Again an archetypal American theme, that of the *felix culpa* (see R. W. B. Lewis's *The American Adam*, Chicago: University of Chicago Press, 1956), is displaced from a modernist, mythic reading to a postmodernist reading which foregrounds signifying practices.

27. Jeremy has been named after Jeremy Bentham, by a lost father who wants him 'to grow up . . . to be a professor' (p. 52); he blames much of his 'irrational need to seek out the wilderness . . . on the accident of his name: that one portion of identity which is at once so totally invented and so totally real' (p. 51). The names in Kroetsch's novels up to *Badlands* are discussed in W. F. H. Nicolaisen, 'Ordering the Chaos: Name Strategies in Robert Kroetsch's novels', *Essays on Canadian Writing*, 11 (Summer 1978), pp. 55–65.

28. In an earlier draft of the novel, it *is* conclusive: after visiting the comatose Dorck in hospital, Jeremy sees Madham walk by and realizes that he is the 'dead and gone Robert Sunderman', University of Calgary MsC 27.12.1–3.249.

29. See Arnold E. Davidson, 'Will the Real Mark Madham Please Stand Up: A Note on Robert Kroetsch's *Gone Indian*', *Studies in Canadian Literature*, 6, 1 (1981), pp. 135–9.

30. Linda Hutcheon, *The Canadian Postmodern* (Toronto: OUP, 1988), p. 171 considers the implication of the name Sunderman in relation to Jill and Bea and suggests that 'while there are indeed images connecting women to enclosure in Kroetsch's novels . . . the notion of "sundering man" may well be a positive, in the sense of both a breaking-up of male hegemony and a contesting of the notion of single, coherent subjectivity'.

31. Laurence Ricou, *Vertical Man/Horizontal World: Man and Landscape in Canadian Prairie Fiction* (Vancouver: University of British Columbia Press, 1973).

32. The novel's title can, of course, also be taken to refer to the contemporary situation of the Indian.

David Creelman (essay date 1991)

SOURCE: "Robert Kroetsch: Criticism in the Middle Ground," in *Studies in Canadian Literature,* Vol. 16, No. 1, 1991, pp. 63-81.

[*In the following essay, Creelman examines Kroetsch's "critical plurality."*]

I

One of the things we seek, I think, is freedom from definition, because definition is as restrictive as cosmology.

(*Labyrinths of Voice* 7)

Robert Kroetsch's career as a writer has been marked throughout by his attempts to "kick free" from the many literary traditions and models that threaten to confine his texts. In his novels, Kroetsch has disrupted the conventions of characterization and plot structure in an effort to make the reader a more active participant in the signifying process. In his long poems he has broken down distinctions of genre by mixing lyrical meditations and prosaic reflections, and has erased the distinctions between literary and non-literary discourses by filling his texts with passages from newspapers, seed catalogues, and farmer's diaries. In his essays and interviews—our main source of information about his theoretical positions—Kroetsch makes similar moves to free himself from the logocentric and positivistic impulses of thematic criticism and New criticism, by searching out positions that proclaim a faith in process and multiplicity. His rebellion from the traditional critical stances of Eliot, Leavis, Brooks, and Richards is complete and certain; but Kroetsch is not always as clear about what positions he is rebelling towards. Having passed through stages in which he aligned himself with structuralist and phenomenological schools, Kroetsch has, in the last ten years, drawn closer to post-structuralist theories; though his relationship with those discourses are troubled at best. Robert Lecker has called his methods deconstructionist, and Donna Bennett has linked him with Foucault, Derrida, Kristeva, and Barthes, but when we carefully examine the oppositions which structure his texts, and excavate the assumptions behind them, we discover that Kroetsch's "kicking free" from logocentrism does not entail a complete acceptance of post-structuralist thought.[1]

Kroetsch's search for critical plurality has drawn him towards a playful mix of epistemologies: at times he privileges concepts of presence; more frequently he is drawn towards theories of absence. Indeed, some commentators have characterized Kroetsch's theoretical positions and critical practices through the use of a border metaphor: "If Kroetsch is a borderman it is because he chooses to live in two worlds, both of which he rejects."[2] For Robert Lecker and Linda Hutcheon, Kroetsch's decision to promote multiplicity while recognizing his involvement with logocentrism becomes the essential and defining feature of his criticism:

> Kroetsch's poetic is about the paradox of creative choice, it is about the contradictions in the reading/writing process. If we ignore those contradictions, if we forget Kroetsch's fertile border, we run the risk of naming an author who, like his tricksters, remains powerfully unnamed.[3]

> This double seduction is never resolved in any ecstatic union of poles, however. The tensions remain unresolved.[4]

Both critics develop an image of an ever restless Kroetsch who tirelessly subverts "the one" while never stopping long enough to set down permanent roots of his own:

> Any attempts at totalizing systems of thought or expression are subverted, even at the moment of their installation. The tension between use and abuse is critical: there is no resolution in either direction.[5]

As we shall see, this border metaphor is problematic, but at least it provides an accurate introduction to Kroetsch's habit of structuring his world in dualities: his habit of fostering pluralities and chaos while still being marginally involved in the positivistic structures.

The benefits of tentatively linking Kroetsch to the border metaphor becomes clear as we investigate his interviews and essays and discover that he repeatedly develops his ideas through a series of comparisons and contrasts. As a result his texts are filled with oppositions, in which a first term concerned with a static vision of the world is rejected in favour of a second more radical term which focuses on process and activity. This movement from stasis to animation is at the base of Kroetsch's desire to replace centrality with chaos, God with Coyote, myth with oral anecdote, metaphor with metonymy, and traditional reading styles with archaeological models. This shift also grounds his vision of critical writing as the continuation of story.

Fundamental to Kroetsch's critical vision is a deep distrust of unitary and singular interpretations of the world. While he recognizes that "the temptation of meaning is upon us all the time" (**Labyrinths of Voice** 15),[6] Kroetsch fears monolithic interpretations of the world because they destroy the diversity essential to life: "We don't want that center which encompasses, which entraps. . . . One version of entrapment is simply being dead center, being caught in any dead center" (*LV* 130). Given his recognition that "making historical, cultural, or linguistic diversity into one is a present danger" (*LV* 118), it is not surprising that Kroetsch rejects the primary symbols of unity in Western culture: the Garden of Eden, and the Christian/Hebraic God. In opposition to logocentric visions of the world, Kroetsch endorses a decentering of unity through a recognition of the "total ambiguity" that lies behind language, society, and culture (*LV* 124). Within multiplicity Kroetsch finds the freedom to confront the chaos of experience and in that confrontation discovers the vitality of life. The new emblems of Kroetsch's chaos become the tower of Babel and the trickster Coyote, both of which represent the confusion of a world freed from oppressive cosmologies:

> I now happen to think that it was a great thing, one of the greatest things that has happened to mankind. From the tower of Babel all of a sudden, we gain all the languages we have.
>
> (*LV* 116)

> The trickster's a mythic figure that really speaks to me. Partly this is because a trickster breaks down systems. There is no logic to his behaviour, or only an anti-logic. . . . He's energy independent of moral structure and moral interpretation. He's very subversive, very carnivalesque.
>
> (*LV* 99–100)

The tyranny of system is also challenged structurally in Kroetsch's essays as he refuses to develop logical arguments, preferring instead to follow the Coyote's anti-logic by assembling papers from series of loosely connected fragments. By rejecting logical structures, Kroetsch frees his readers into a field of language from which they are able to construct their own significance. In the same way, Kroetsch endorses the forms of parody and satire for they speak by repeating a recognizable form or model while at the same time inserting a critical difference which reminds the reader that "you can't believe that there is only one assertible meaning in that story" (*LV* 89).

In his fictions and in *Labyrinths of Voice*, one of the totalizing forces which Kroetsch works hardest to decenter is the power of myth. As a collection of narratives that has descended through the ages and accumulated a stable set of meanings, Western myth is something Kroetsch finds "frightening because it is entrapping" (*LV* 96). With its predetermined set of meanings and interpretations, myth, especially as it is used by the Moderns, removes the reader's freedom to construct her own meanings and inscribes her within an already defined system. Kroetsch's solution to the totalizing power of myth is not simply to abandon mythic structures and allusions, but rather to break them down by retelling them in a new context. The regeneration of myth through recontextualization is the focus of Kroetsch's concept of the anecdote. As a fresh story which is grounded in a specific local context, and does not yet carry an inherited set of meanings, the patterns of anecdote provide an effective means of retelling/ replacing monolithic myths: it "touches upon larger patterns without involving itself with them. . . . Anecdote stays looser than myth because it hasn't compromised itself for a larger pattern. . . . Anecdote frees up the grammar of narrative" (*LV* 115).

Just as Kroetsch uses anecdote to disrupt myth, so he celebrates oral speech as a means of resisting the canons of literature. It is important to note from the beginning that Kroetsch's privileging of the oral over the literary is in no way a rejection of, or even a resistance to, Derrida's assertions that speech is a form of writing. In *Of Grammatology*, his seminal critique of Saussure and Rousseau, Derrida confronts western philosophy's long tradition of viewing speech as a natural, direct communication, and "writing as an oblique representation of representation." The privileging of speech represses certain features of language such as *différance*, which, if recognized, would undermine the metaphysics of presence that have characterized Western thought since the days of Plato.[7] Through his work with the logic of the supplement, Derrida reverses this hierarchy of speech/writing, repositions speech under the broader category of "*archi-écriture*," and thus demonstrates that all language, be it speech or writing, is part of a nonrepresentational, arbitrary, differential system of signifiers and signifieds.

Kroetsch's celebration of the oral is not a return to a metaphysics of presence in speech; rather he sees, in the oral traditions of the "chant, song, ballad, [and] tall tale" (*LV* 39), and in the "art speech" of such artists as Wiebe and Laurence, a fluidity and transience that foregrounds the deeper absence of all languages.[8] Oppressed by the canon of English literature, with its pressures to maintain a certain body of traditions which he finds "over-whelming" (*LV* 3), Kroetsch turns to the informalities and incompletion of the spoken word to decenter the conventional body of works. The literary / oral binary is an opportunity to violate the canon, to reopen the borders of literature and deny its totalizing impulses: "I keep thinking of Artaud: 'Literature is bullshit.' He didn't say writing was bullshit, he said literature is bullshit, because to make it into literature is to systematize" (*LV* 160). As we shall see, Kroetsch eventually pulls back from the full implications of deconstruction, but at least he agrees with one of Derrida's fundamental deductions: though one can be used to rejuvenate the other, "there is no difference finally between written text and spoken text" (*LV* 39).

At a more concrete level Kroetsch privileges a series of literary techniques which help texts—both critical and fictional—break from the confining practices of the past. For example, rather than encouraging the use of such figures as similes and metaphors—devices which create closed systems by replacing one term with another—Kroetsch stresses the importance of metonymy and synecdoche, figures which move the reader from a part to a whole, initiating him into a chain of signifiers which highlights the material and differential nature of language. Metonymy becomes a means of reminding the reader that reading a text is only a matter of following/choosing a series of traces: thus, instead of the "temptations of 'origins'" inherent in figures of replacement, "we have genealogies that multiply our connections into the past, into the world" (*LV* 117).

As a writer, Kroetsch attempts to foster multiplicity and process by stressing metonymy, anti-logical structures, anecdote, and oral stories. On the other side of the page, he continues to encourage plurality by proposing that readers abandon traditional practises of interpretation, and adopt an archaeological model of reading which focuses on the fragmented nature of the text.

Though Kroetsch refers to the writings of Michel Foucault as he develops his model of archaeological reading, there is actually very little similarity between the two authors' practises. For Foucault, "archaeology" is a powerful term referring to the process of unlayering the many ideologies and struggles which are imprinted in the text by the social and political powers of their day. Foucault rejects any possibility that language can be separated from the use of power, and thus his textual excavations are primarily concerned with the ideologies at work in the structures.[9] Kroetsch, on the other hand, is not interested in the power structures embedded in texts; indeed, he claims "I'm quite aware of being without ideology" (*LV* 33). Thus archaeological reading practises become a way, not to a deeper understanding of western society, but to empower the reader and make her a more active participant in the signifying process.

In Kroetsch's world all texts, be they postmodern or classic realism, are artifacts of language that are inherently self contradictory and fragmented. While traditional interpretive reading strategies encourage the reader to ignore the seams in a text, Kroetsch encourages us to focus on the textual breaks and the reader, "like the writer, becomes archaeologist, seeking the grammar of the fragments."[10] Like the realm of the oral for the writer, "archaeology, of necessity, involves violence" (EP 111), but out of this violation of unity comes a new freedom: "Archaeology allows [for] the fragmentary nature of the story, against the coercive unity of traditional history. Archaeology allows for discontinuity. It allows the layering. It allows for imaginative speculation." (BAW 76). Kroetsch's archaeological model for reading forces the reader to take control and construct his/her own sets of meanings in much the same way that Roland Barthes encourages the reader to read in a writerly way, to uncover and recover the playfulness of language which rests in every text. The activity of "uncovering," "uncreating," and "unnaming" a text encourages the reader to fully recognize and accept the *jouissance* inherent in the world of differential language. The reader, like the writer, is given greater freedom if he/she accept the second terms of Kroetsch's dualities.

As Robert Kroetsch proselytizes for multiplicity, plurality, process, and chaos, he is well aware that he himself is caught in a contradiction. Each stage of rebellion against the unifying forces, each attempt to critique the logocentric, involves a certain level of complicity with the very forces that are being attacked. In order to encourage the absence and silence of meaning beneath language, Kroetsch must write and speak—involving himself in the traditions of Western discourse. To encourage anti-logic, chaos, and confusion, Kroetsch must, even in his most story-like criticism, retain some semblance of logic order and coherence in order for his message to be effective. The paradox that critique necessarily includes complicity is recognized by Kroetsch as he admits:

> One can't escape by discontinuity itself—it contains the word continuity doesn't it? It says dis/continuity. I am totally involved in a sense of the tradition, but I relate to it by discontinuity. Not to have that is to be just absorbed into tradition or erased by it.
>
> (*LV* 26)

As Kroetsch strengthens his vision of multiplicity, many of the traditional boundaries between genres begin to dissolve. Oral speech becomes a model for written text, prose is blended with poetry, and criticism is merged with the larger field of writing. Roland Barthes, in *SZ*, was one of the first post-structuralist critics to envision criticism, not as a metalinguistic supplement hovering over the text, but rather as a creative—even primary—extension of the initial text. Kroetsch echoes these sentiments when he claims:

> I think criticism is really a version of story you see; I think we are telling the story to each other of how we get a story. It is the story of our search for story. That's why criticism is so exciting. Not because it provides answers, but because it is a version of story.
>
> (*LV* 30)

Kroetsch himself is aware that not all of his essays live up to these intentions to continue the story without providing answers and conclusions, and in many cases, as Barbara Godard has pointed out, "the deconstructive influence remains essentially a stylistic one."[11] For example, though the nine fragments of "Effing the Ineffable" disrupt the structural logic of an essay, in the last two sections Kroetsch suggests that writers can reach a state of wholeness called "Voice," and then reaffirms this allusion to presence by poetically linking a series of writers with totalizing images which capture their characters: "Chuff Chuff says Lorna Uher, I am the Great Beetle of Love . . . Chuff Chuff says Robert Kroetsch, I am the Red-Winged Blackbird."[12] Nor, as shall be seen, is this essay alone in its return to rather structuralist and positivistic visions of the world. In a few cases, however, Kroetsch's form and content come together to create a strong story / criticism that resists closure and unified meanings. Kroetsch is often able to walk the border in his essays without stumbling.

Kroetsch's analysis of novels by Sinclair Ross and Willa Cather—**"The Fear of Women in Prairie Fiction"**—was written in 1978, shortly before Kroetsch's interviews showed the marks of his full initiation into deconstructive criticism; but nonetheless this essay does attempt to map out the gender concerns of the novel without providing a solid conclusion. As Jeanette Seim points out, Kroetsch's subversion of the horse/house binary, and his portrayal of women as the controlling figures while men become the characters of compromise, shows a deconstructionist desire to rewrite the primary novels without proclaiming a single interpretation.[13] Similarly, in **"Beyond Nationalism: A Prologue"** Kroetsch proposes that Canadians attempt to locate their literature though a genealogical model that affirms rather than represses the wide diversity of Canada's many texts. Though the essay is limited by Kroetsch's decision to trace the thematic rather than the formal multiplicities, the analysis does effectively resist any attempts to hierarchize the many novels under consideration, and suggests instead that we view the wide variety of fictions ranging from Ross to Hodgins as part of the "nightmare and welcome dream of Babel."[14] Perhaps the best example of criticism as story would be **"For Play and Entrance: the Contemporary Canadian Long Poem,"** a fragmented and wandering essay which grafts observations about the importance of beginnings, language, delay, and absence in the long poem, with many passages from the texts of contemporary artists. In the end, **"For Play and Entrance"** functions as much as a creative collage and long poem, as it does as a critical commentary.

Using the metaphor that Kroetsch continually balances and unbalances himself along an epistemological border is very useful in understanding the dualities which obsess him, the writing and reading practices that interest him, and the attempts he has made to produce a new type of response to Canadian texts. However, the border metaphor does have some disadvantages in that it veils those occasions in Kroetsch's interviews and essays when he attempts to establish himself in a single, stable philosophic space.

II

> I guess I have the absurd hope that if I provide twenty names, then somewhere I will reach a point where they all connect and become more realized or identifiable.
>
> (*LV* 93)

As the many oppositions of his interviews and essays demonstrate, Kroetsch has attempted to kick free from the defining, oppressing power of logocentrism. But, while Kroetsch has fled away from the spectres of presence and unity, he is not always clear about what he is heading towards: his relationship with post-structuralist discourses—currently the dominant ideological alternative for those critics interested in overturning logocentric discourses—is troubled and uncertain. In such essays as **"The Fear of Prairie Women," "Beyond Nationalism," "For Play and Entrance,"** and most recently ***"Hear Us O Lord and the Orpheus Occasion,"*** he has ventured productively near post-structuralism, but throughout the rest of his work there are recurring hesitations that complicate the suggestions that Kroetsch happily flits between presence and absence along a borderline. Kroetsch's frequent reservations about the full critical implications of post-Saussurian thought, his attraction to such traditional concepts as mimesis, and his underpinning need to preserve some elements of order, all indicate that Kroetsch has turned the supposed middle border he continually transgresses into a solid middle ground of his own—a position which rejects logocentrism while still resisting the full implications of post structuralism. There is, in Kroetsch's criticism, as Barbara Godard has pointed out, "a metaphysical presence in the valorization of absence," and this presence/position becomes clearer as we push into Kroetsch's hesitations about contemporary criticism, and examine the apriorias of his thought.[15]

The foundation stone of post-structuralist discourse is located in Saussure's discovery that the sign not only consists of a signifier and a signified that are related deferentially and arbitrarily, but that language is completely non-referential, having absolutely no contact with the continuum of reality. At first Kroetsch appears to accept this definition of the sign as we can see in this exchange with Shirley Neuman:

> *Kroetsch*: I don't think I understood at first how language is separate from what it signifies. I was interested in language as signifying things that were not allowed, were taboo . . . it's only recently that I came to see that what language signified was language.
>
> *Neuman*: In linguistic terms, every sign refers to another sign. So that in effect, the temptation of meaning . . . means resisting the linguistic convention of the unity of signifier and signified in the sign.
>
> *Kroetsch*: Yes I think there's a real danger in our society of a simple belief in that conclusion . . . Rudy [Wiebe] has a much stronger belief in that connection that I have for example.
>
> (*LV* 143)

As language becomes nonreferential, as signifiers trace only to the next signifier, never fixing on the signified, the possibility of mimesis in literature disappears. Instead of writing so as to capture reality and communicate it to the reader, the "serious writer," in Kroetsch's mind, must now inject a "kind of mockery into our sense of security in the mimetic" (*LV* 200), in order to remind the reader that language can never capture the Truth.

Yet even as Kroetsch appears to endorse the basic tenets of post-structuralism, he sounds notes of resistance—sometimes simply expressed as a sense of unease that the sign is being too quickly divorced from its referent:

> They made a simple equation between literature and reality. I argued for game theory in order to correct that oversimplification. Yet at this point I am somewhat worried about my own sense of divorce from the equation, from mimesis. One is always moving back and forth between positions.
>
> (*LV* 73)

> I'm uneasy about my own interest, really troubled. In fact I am uneasy about the whole South American school of magic realism. But I am totally seduced by it . . . that allowing into language of every story possibility, and thus the whole world . . . I'm very uneasy about my own fascination with language as that which is signified.
>
> (*LV* 159)

This note of resistance sounds throughout Kroetsch's interviews and finally near the end of ***Labyrinth of Voice*** he retracts his support for the differential arbitrary sign by regrounding language, tentatively, in experience. Although the exchange is lengthy it is worth reviewing in its entirety.

> *Kroetsch*: But I think there is also another grounding and for me it's very important to go back and test what I really call ground, using that word deliberately. Ground as something that precedes interpretation or categorization—or what I'm calling meaning. Realizing of course that the act of naming was already an alteration of sorts. . . . I do get satisfaction out of many kinds of accuracy. I go check things compulsively. But I don't return to experience under the illusion that I'm going to write it down as it is. I mean, I'll even go look at the color of the sky when I'm writing.
>
> *Neuman*: Would it be correct to say then that your obsessive checking of things is an activity you know to be fundamentally meaningless since the language you use has to do with language, not with whatever is out the window.
>
> *Kroetsch*: Well there's another possibility that for me is very generative: I like the feeling of the physical world; it turns me on to look at a street or to think what does a hand look like? I find energy in the dialectic of language and ground.
>
> (*LV* 200–202)

At the end of the exchange Kroetsch has clearly appeared in a newly constructed middle position. While agreeing that language cannot capture experience as it is, he pointedly refuses to endorse Neuman's challenge that language is solely self-referential, insisting instead that some dialectic is possible between the sign and the preinterpretive ground of experience. Such a linkage of language and experience is radically different from such theorists as Barthes, Derrida, and Kristeva, and helps us understand how, in such essays as his 1985 **"The Grammar of Silence,"** Kroetsch can suggest that writers can discover a new native voice by "bringing the signifier and signified back into conjunction through a change in story model," or that a new life is possible when the signified is "joined again with its signifier, and name and object come together."[16] The careful reader of *Labyrinths of Voice* cannot help but notice that while interviewers Shirley Neuman and Robert Wilson are deeply grounded in the current French theorists (indeed they are the ones who compiled the many quotes which flood the book), Kroetsch is more reticent about the abysses in post-structuralist epistomologies.

In order to resist the full impact of post-structuralist discourse, while still rejecting the overt logocentrism and unifying power of traditional criticism, Kroetsch constructs a linguistic middle position. Nor are Kroetsch's comments on language the only places where we can see the crystallization of this middle ground. Rather than viewing Kroetsch as treading the border between a series of binaries, it becomes much more productive to look for incidences of triads—textual moments when Kroetsch considers the contrasting ideas of new criticism and deconstruction and responds by constructing his own solid mediating voice.

In the first section of *Labyrinths of Voice*, Robert Kroetsch launches a brief attack against confining interpretative strategies by opposing logocentrism with the concept of game: "The difference between game and cosmology is an important one. Cosmologies invite closure. Game insists on its own fictionality" (*LV* 27). While such critical schools as the Leavisites insist that art represents life, reflecting its real emotions and problems (a position which forces the reader to draw moralistic conclusions about texts), Kroetsch proposes that literature should be approached as a game—a playful make believe world—separated from reality and the necessity of finding clear, firm answers. Initially, Kroetsch goes so far as to connect this playful criticism with the non-representational theory of language he later rejects:

> I play on the edge of convention; I suppose that's one place where I bend the rules. I think I also take the risk of falling right into language: the danger of language taking over. There is an anxiety about language being separate from reality or being its own reality. I think that a kind of erasure of self goes on in fiction making. It's interesting that we play the game isn't it? . . . The two words contradict each other in a significant way. Play resists the necessary rules of game.
>
> (*LV* 50)

As a model of criticism that urges readers and writers to throw themselves into the differential fabric of language, the game model draws Kroetsch nearer to his anxiety about nonreferential signifying systems. Yet even as Kroetsch approaches the void here and elsewhere he defends himself, unconsciously, by situating the potential anarchy of play under or within the safer structure of game. For

example, at one point Wilson criticizes Leavisite and psychoanalytic criticism which are bound by inflexible rules, and praises deconstruction for being "an informal game, such as children play on playgrounds where they simply kick the ball this way and that, without any anticipated goal" (*LV* 63–64). Kroetsch attempts to recuperate a sense of order not by contradicting Wilson, but by drawing an analogy. He proposes that "Surrealist literature is also a kind of informal play," in which rules "do not seem to be operating," however, "Surrealism, like all writing is true playing. By the time you write the work, you have a game plan" (*LV* 64). The potential purposelessness of surreal play is confined by Kroetsch within the structures of planned rules.

As the violence of play is contained Kroetsch begins to see, within the theory of games, the possibility of resurrecting the concept of mimesis. Just as he reconnected language to experience through the positing of a preinterpretive ground, so he suggests that game, while unable to represent the true substance of the real, may imitate the processes of the real. Literature as game cannot reflect real emotions, but may be able to enact the anxiety of people caught in the games of their lives:

> First of all, game is seen as a preparation for life. If we look at children playing, or at animals playing, there is a kind of mimetic function at a further remove. It is almost a structuralist parallel, isn't it?
>
> (*LV* 64)

> This must be one of the functions of art: to put us into situations where we apprehend the rules only up to a point. This is where art, by the paradox of its differences from life, again becomes mimetic. We are all in games where we can't quite perceive the rules.
>
> (*LV* 68)

By situating "games" within a framework of mimesis, Kroetsch displays a positivistic impulse which arises again at the end of *Labyrinths of Voice* and in the essay **"Carnival and Violence: A Meditation,"** when he endorses the theories of Bakhtin.

For a critic like Kroetsch, who is looking for the middle ground between logocentrism and *différance*, Bakhtin's notion of the carnival is a very attractive option. In his work on nineteenth century novelists, Bakhtin develops the theory that fiction grew, not out of the romance patterns of the middle ages (a theory that suggests the novel is an essentially closed genre), but rather from the prose satires and parodies of the seventeenth century (a position that views the novel as inherently disruptive and ideologically challenging form). While shying away from Bakhtin's Marxist ideology, Kroetsch cleaves to the concept of "the carnivalesque" in which texts, their readers, and even the whole society, sanction a temporary release from the repressive systems of society and indulge in a wild process of celebration and festival. For a critic who has already privileged multiplicity, Babel, Coyote, and anti-logic, the carnival's emphasis on "becoming, change, and renewal," through a "liberation from the prevailing truth and the established order," and through a "suspension of all hierarchical rank, privileges, norms, and prohibitions," would be enormously attractive.[17] One aspect of carnival that Kroetsch especially supports is the fact that though social structures are threatened they are never in danger of disappearing. As the carnival spreads through language, texts, and society, conventional structures are either: "temporarily collapsed" only to reemerge later when the festival ends (CV 101), "turned upside down and inside out" in the creation of a new society which is then the mirror reflection of its predecessor (CV 99), or in the most violent of occurrences the "carnivalesque is a process of renewal by destruction" (CV 104). The carnivalesque contains a revolutionary impulse in its vision of language as a disruptive force, but in the end Kroetsch ensures that some form of order will be maintained or rebuilt: "We are carnivalized into the possibility of our own being."[18] Neil Randall has pointed out that in his fiction Kroetsch uses the idea of carnival to attack the center, but in his criticism and theory, the carnival is used to retain that center.[19] The logocentric, conventional world can be rejected, but that rejection through carnival need not include support for the opposite extreme of complete chaos and confusion.

Kroetsch's rebellion against centered, monolithic systems is clearly more complex than the border metaphor or his interest in oppositions would initially lead us to believe. His rejection of confining and defining structures is complete, but his revolution does not go as far as the theorists who draw from the writings of Derrida and Foucault. Kroetsch insists on violence in language and through that violence the destruction of modernism, but once a new space is cleared Kroetsch is equally determined to rebuild and retell: "A loose generalization would have it that creation and destruction go hand in hand. But my destruction would have it take the form of trying to make an old story work, for instance having to almost destroy the old story to tell it anew."[20] Once again Kroetsch invokes the conditional 'almost' in order to halt the process of violence and restart the reconstruction. Robert Kroetsch has made productive use of such language-oriented terms as freeplay, violence, destruction, and decentering, but significantly missing from his critical lexicon is the verb dismantle. Unlike Edward Said who draws from Foucault in order to dismantle hierarchies rather than simply reversing them, Kroetsch insists on decentering only until he has created a space for his own voice, after which the revolutionary fervour subsides. Unlike the American deconstructionists who are distinguished from the New Critics, by Barbara Johnson, by their refusal to reassemble the discovered textual disorder, Kroetsch is tentatively willing to embark on rebuilding projects.[21]

Certainly there is an emerging "metaphysics of presence" in Kroetsch's "valorization of absence," or more precisely a negative hermeneutics, which arises as silence, absence, violence, and chaos all become conditions of the texts rather than processes in the text. The metaphysics of presence are further strengthened as Kroetsch shifts to more positivistic theories such as language's dialectic with

ground, game's linkage with mimesis, and carnival's retention of structure. Robert Kroetsch simply refuses to use the *différance* of language to deconstruct texts and leave them unassembled: he must begin his own theoretical and fictional reconstructions.

The theoretical impulse to secure a middle ground inevitably makes its mark on Kroetsch's critical articles. His intentions as stated in *Labyrinths of Voice*, to make criticism into a version of story which provides no answers, begins to change as he attends to his negative hierarchies and his positivistic conceptions of language and game. The Kroetsch who speaks from his middle positions continues to speak against centering critical practises, but instead of using criticism to engage in creative play, he begins to evaluate themes and build structures, a process that involves a level of value judgement as well as a separation of criticism from the art it studies.

An example of Kroetsch's tendency to move from playful criticism towards hierarchical criticism can be seen in his essay **"Contemporary Standards in the Canadian Novel,"** an essay written in 1978 two years before the marks of deconstruction really began to appear in his work. In this article—which reasserts the importance of Richardson, Ross, Buckler, Laurence, Davies, Ondaatje, Lowry, etc., as essential Canadian novelists—Kroetsch struggles with the issue of developing canons before establishing his own. Though he is "tempted to agree that the only way we can avoid dodging [new literary voices] . . . is by accepting everything," he ultimately concludes that "one of the ways in which we build a culture is by selecting and elaborating a few texts."[22]

Even after deconstructive terms appear in **"The Exploding Porcupine: Violence of Form in English Canadian Fiction,"** Kroetsch continues to treat criticism as a secondary, metalinguistic activity, by establishing a hierarchy of violence in Canadian fictions. Rather than playfully extending the texts in question, Kroetsch's paper evaluates them and constructs three categories: he labels Watson and Ross novelists of disbelief; Wiebe and Hodgins are termed writers of the apocalypse; and finally Ondaatje and Thomas, the most disruptive of the set, are named violent "Gangsters of Love." Kroetsch has succeeded in his rebellion against system and is now able to detail the formal and thematic value of violence in Canadian fiction, but his use of hierarchy signals a conventional vision of criticism underpinning his work.

Similarly, Kroetsch's studies of Moodie, Haliburton, and Carrier, in his essay **"Carnival and Violence,"** show a continuing trend towards using and recuperating the concept of carnival by using it as a thematic guide rather than as a textual practice. By using Bakhtin's theory of carnival as a touchstone, Kroetsch condemns Moodie's conservative outlook, admires Haliburton's ability to reverse orders, and praises Carrier's violence in *La Guerre, Yes Sir*, but fails to disrupt the whole idea of value judgements. The same tame use of criticism can be seen in

Kroetsch's analysis of Grove in **"The Grammar of Silence: Narrative Pattern in Ethic Writing,"** an essay which details Grove's logocentric visions of the world but does not attempt to challenge or dismantle the assumptions of the realistic texts.

Robert Kroetsch's ability to form a mediating ground between the confining practices of traditional criticism and the dismantling practises of post-structuralism have given him a unique position in Canadian letters. As a writer of novels and poems, Kroetsch has made the most of his rebellion from unity, and has created a series of texts which force the reader to participate in the signifying process. As a writer of articles and a participant in interviews, Kroetsch may, at times, fall short of his own goal to erase the boundaries between commentary and art, but he has nonetheless articulated an innovative position from which he has made these major contributions to our understanding of contemporary Canadian fiction and poetry. Robert Kroetsch has resisted the full impact of post-structuralism, but he has constructed a very strong postmodern position from which he will continue to decenter and disrupt Canadian traditions.

Notes

1. Robert Lecker, "Bordering On: Robert Kroetsch's Aesthetic," *Journal of Canadian Studies* 17.3 (Fall 1982): 132.

   Donna Bennett, "Weathercock: The Directions of Report," *Essays on Robert Kroetsch, Open Letter* 5th ser. 8–9 (Summer/Fall 1984): 138–139.

2. Lecker, 127.

3. Lecker, 133.

4. Linda Hutcheon, "Seeing Double: Concluding with Kroetsch," *The Canadian Postmodern* (Toronto: Oxford UP, 1988) 163.

5. Hutcheon, 183.

6. Robert Kroetsch, *Labyrinths of Voice*, eds. Shirley Neuman and Robert Wilson (Edmonton: NeWest Press, 1982). Hereafter referred to as *LV*.

7. Jacques Derrida, *Of Grammatology*, trans. G. C. Spivak (Baltimore: Johns Hopkins, 1974). For a very brief but clear introduction to Derrida's thoughts see: Jonathan Culler, "Jacques Derrida," *Structuralism and Since*, ed. John Sturrock (New York: Oxford UP, 1979).

8. Robert Kroetsch, "On Being an Alberta Writer," orig. pub. 1980, rpt. in "Essays," *Open Letter*, eds. Frank Davey and b.p. Nichol, 5th ser. 4 (Spring 1983): 75. Hereafter referred to as BAW.

9. Michel Foucault, *The Archaeology of Knowledge*, trans. A.M. Sheridan Smith (New York: Pantheon Books, 1971).

10. Robert Kroetsch, "The Exploding Porcupine: Violence of Form in English Canadian Fiction," orig. pub. 1980. rpt. in *The Lovely Treachery of Words* (Toronto: Oxford UP, 1989) 112. Hereafter referred to as EP.

11. Barbara Godard, "Other Fictions: Robert Kroetsch's Criticism," *Essays on Robert Kroetsch, Open Letter* 5th ser. 8–9, (Summer/Fall 1984): 18.

12. Robert Kroetsch, "Effing the Ineffable," orig. pub. in 1976, rpt. in "Essays," *Open Letter*, eds. Frank Davey and b.p. Nichol, 5th ser. 4 (Spring 1983): 24. Hereafter referred to as EI.

13. Jeanette Seim, "Horses and Houses," *Essays on Robert Kroetsch, Open Letter*, 5th Ser. 8–9 (Summer/Fall 1984).

14. Robert Kroetsch, "Beyond Nationalism: A Prologue," orig. pub. in 1981, rpt. in *The Lovely Treachery of Words* (Toronto: Oxford UP, 1989) 71. Hereafter referred to as BN.

15. Godard, 17.

16. Robert Kroetsch, "The Grammar of Silence: Narrative Pattern in Ethnic Writing," *Canadian Literature* 106 (Fall 1985): 71, 74. Hereafter referred to as GS.

17. Robert Kroetsch, "Carnival and Violence: A Meditation," orig. pub. in 1982, rpt. in *The Lovely Treachery of Words* (Toronto: Oxford UP, 1989) 96. Hereafter referred to as CV.

18. Robert Kroetsch, "Learning the Hero from Northrop Frye," *The Lovely Treachery of Words* (Toronto: Oxford UP, 1989) 160.

19. Neil Randall, "Carnival and Intertext: Humour in *What the Crow Said* and *The Studhorse Man*," *Studies in Canadian Literature* 14. 1 (1989).

20. Robert Kroetsch, "Uncovering our Dream World: An Interview with Robert Kroetsch," eds. Robert Enright and Dennis Cooley, *Essays in Canadian Writing* 18–19 (Summer/Fall 1980): 28.

21. Godard, 17.

22. Robert Kroetsch, "Contemporary Standards in the Canadian Novel," orig. pub. in 1978, rpt. in "Essays," *Open Letter*, eds. Frank Davey and b.p. Nichol, 5th ser. 4 (Spring 1983): 39–40.

Works Cited

Bennett, Donna. "Weathercock: The Directions of Report." *Essays on Robert Kroetsch, Open Letter* 5th ser. 8–9, (Summer/Fall 1984): 116–145.

Culler, Jonathan, "Jacques Derrida." *Structuralism and Since*. Ed. John Sturrock. New York: Oxford UP, 1979.

Derrida, Jacques. *Of Grammatology*. Trans. G. C. Spivak. Baltimore: Johns Hopkins, 1974.

Godard, Barbara. "Other Fictions: Robert Kroetsch's Criticism." *Essays on Robert Kroetsch, Open Letter* 5th ser. 8–9, (Summer/Fall 1984): 5–21.

Hutcheon, Linda. "Seeing Double: Concluding with Kroetsch." *The Canadian Postmodern*. Toronto: Oxford UP, 1988.

Kroetsch, Robert. "Essays." *Open Letter* 5th ser. 4 (Spring 1983).

———. "The Grammar of Silence: Narrative Pattern in Ethnic Writing." *Canadian Literature* 106 (Fall 1985): 65–74.

———. *Labyrinths of Voice.* Eds. Shirley Neuman and Robert Wilson. Edmonton: NeWest Press, 1982.

———. *The Lovely Treachery of Words.* Toronto: Oxford UP, 1989.

———. "Uncovering our Dream World: An Interview with Robert Kroetsch." Eds. Robert Enright and Dennis Cooley. *Essays on Canadian Writing* 18–19 (Summer/Fall 1980): 21–32.

Lecker, Robert. "Bordering On: Robert Kroetsch's Aesthetic." *Journal of Canadian Studies* 17.3 (Fall 1982): 124–133.

Randall, Neil. "Carnival and Intertext: Humour in *What the Crow Said* and *The Studhorse Man.*" *Studies in Canadian Literature* 14.1 (1989): 85–98.

Seim, Jeanette. "Horses and Houses." *Essays on Robert Kroetsch, Open Letter* 5th Ser. 8–9 (Summer/Fall 1984): 99–115.

Dorothy Seaton (essay date Spring 1991)

SOURCE: "The Post-Colonial as Deconstruction: Land and Language in Kroetsch"s *Badlands*," in *Canadian Literature,* No. 128, Spring, 1991, pp. 77-89.

[*In the following essay, Seaton argues that Kroetsch deconstructs the myths of land and language in* Badlands.]

It is commonly argued that early imperial discourses of the New World inscribe an effort to make strange new lands familiar to Eurocentric systems of meaning and understanding.[1] However, conceptualised from the start as the site of the strange, the new lands continued to resist European epistemological appropriation and whatever the imperial's claims to control and knowledge, the sign of the land continued to enter the discourse as a site of the unknown and the resistant.[2] Now, current criticism often characterises post-colonial writing as constructing *counter-discourses* to the once-dominant imperial discourse, writing against the imperial's inappropriately Eurocentric systems of understanding, and instead writing the land as an element within *local* constructs of meaning and value. But the counter-discursive strategy still shares with the imperial certain basic assumptions about the relations among humans, discourse, and land: both discursive strategies still inscribe a belief that the land, though conceptualised initially as a site of the strange and the resistant, can somehow be controlled and familiarised by discourse, contained within the epistemological system of one discourse or another.[3]

However, a second, far more radically subversive possibility is available to the post-colonial effort of re-writing the strange land: that of the *deconstructive.* Unlike the counter-discursive, the deconstructive entirely rejects the possibility of achieving a "correct" or "appropriate" rendering of the land in *any* discourse, whether imperial or post-colonial, and it embraces instead the endless strangeness of both land and discourse, interrogating the very capacity of discourse to constitute the land. The sign of the land is conceptualised from the start as the site of resistance to discursive containment, this resistance understood within a larger system by which discourse in general, like the specific discourse of the land, depends upon an initial, irrevocable, and all-affecting assumption of difference, deferral, resistance. Any of the systems of understanding and containing the land, whether in the dominant discourse of the imperial, or in the post-colonial's newer, presumably more appropriate counter-discourses of the land, are based upon an initial experience of displacement and otherness, and it is this radical strangeness that such contemporary novels as Robert Kroetsch's *Badlands* seem to address in the writing of New World lands. Land and discourse are by definition signs ultimately of strangeness, of the undecidable and the resistant.[4]

In *Badlands,* the dominant image by which this deconstructive impulse works, in connection with the land, is that of *archaeology.* The image works to site the deconstruction of language in the land itself, in that the practice of archaeological excavation, entering the ground, deconstructs the New World myths of identity which have thus far created meaning in the intertextual tradition of post-colonial writing. Because of the nature of this breakdown of myth, language itself comes under scrutiny. Individual myths, along with the larger mythological systems of nation and identity, are broken down so that they can no longer express their appropriate values, even within the limits which they themselves set. The binary oppositions which the myths propose, in order to define their own values, are subverted.[5] Archaeology, then—the act of entering the land—becomes the practice both by which myths are proposed, and by which these myths are subverted. The archaeological expedition as the reconstruction and retrieval of history, as an act of male heroic self-construction, as a journey in search of sources and origins (and so on), is also a journey of the loss and deconstruction of history, of the subversion of such male heroic myths as Dawe is entered upon, and of a movement away from sources. The land becomes the place where such oppositions, rather than being arranged hierarchically in order to structure meaning and value, are instead brought together and made at once to interact endlessly and undecidably, and eventually to collapse entirely into one another.

What is finally deconstructed are not only the myths of the land, but also the myth, perhaps, of language itself: if the basic structure of binary oppositions—in terms of which the elements of language are defined in relation to each other—are subverted, language itself becomes a problematic medium and practice. The land, as the object of archaeological examination, is written as itself a text, so that its treatment can be read as a discussion about the nature of language and discourse in general. This ground-work of language—groundwork for all the other discourses the novel examines—is itself the site being investigated, excavated, and contaminated.[6] The archaeological expedition, then, becomes at once a search for and the loss of language. Discourse itself, in spite of all the words of the novel, begins to break down; and within this breakdown, the discursive constructs of land and language must become equally unstable—at the same time as they perform within the discourse as the agent and site of such a breakdown of the Western systems of meaning which they construct.

The archaeological expedition, of course, takes the form of a river trip, flowing downstream on the Red Deer, through the layers of time deposited over millennia of the land's changes. The notion of the river trip as a journey of discovery is a familiar mythological construction in Canadian self-definition: as told in the proto-texts of Canadian history and identity, the exploration and fur trade narratives, it is largely through river voyages, of course, that Canada was explored, named, and defined. Dawe's journey draws upon the ideologies inherent in these earlier journeys of national self-definition, in this case the defining given the particular form of the search for history and origins. Here, however, such a quest involves the search for dinosaur bones, the remains of dead and extinct creatures: the search for origins, on the basis of which to define the young nation, is the search for the bones of death. The binary oppositions of birth and death, of origins and endings, begin already to be brought into disrupting interaction, so that origins are to be discovered in death, and beginnings are positioned in relation to endings: the myth, for example, whereby national identity was seen to begin with river journeys of exploration, is rewritten as a journey as much into death as into birth.

Yet the paradoxes of the search for "bones" do not end with this scrambling of the basic life/death opposition. Web participates, however reluctantly, in Dawe's search for dinosaur bones, but his real interest in bones is in the "bone-ons" he is perpetually developing throughout the novel, whether when contemplating Anna Yellowbird's uncertain presence somewhere along the shore they are journeying past,[7] or discussing the finer points of relationships between humans and snakes (16) or bears (155) or gopher holes (204). His "bone" is generally a central figure, one way or another, in his wild tales of physical and sexual prowess: the *"western yarn[s],"* the exaggerated stories of strength and achievement, which are another element of Western Canadian myth-making (45, Kroetsch's italics). The stories deny in their simple volubility and vigour the death which the dinosaur bones suggests: speaking of his hypothetical death and the coffin he would be buried in, Web protests, "'Bone-on I'm developing now, it'll take them a week to get the lid down'" (16).

Web's exaggerated and endlessly voluble discourse of the "bones" of masculine self-definition—and by connection, of Western Canadian self-definition—opposes Dawe's

alternative text of self-definition, of the dinosaur bone-beds, as is most graphically evoked in Tune's dying in the effort to recover the bones of history. Though Tune has thus far not entered fully into the realms of masculine discourse which Web exemplifies, having failed to lose his virginity in the Drumheller whorehouse, his simultaneous admiration for and skepticism about Web's tall tales (his tall tales about tail), suggest that he is coming to understand and appreciate the discourse. As the summer progresses, he is losing his boyish fat and growing into his adult body, in preparation for heading off to that other testing ground for discourses of male self-definition: war. But not having had a chance to experience fully the pleasures of Web's discourse of "bones," he is subsumed by Dawe's alternative discourse of bones, sacrificed to Dawe's fanatical desire for fame and fortune as a paleontologist:

> From seventy million years deep in the black matrix of the past, the bones must leap to light. Must loose themselves from the bentonite. Must make their finders rich and famous. The bones that must satisfy their finders.
>
> (31)

However, Dawe's quest for self-definition, through the search for origins in the bones of dead dinosaurs, is not so different from Web's constant self-definition through his repeated, endlessly elaborated adventures with his "bones"—as the reference to satisfaction suggests, in the above quotation. Both searches demand that the bones—the discourses—satisfy their readers'/writer's needs.[8] And both quests take size as the measure of their achievement: the bigger the bone the better—the bigger and more ambitious the myth-making, the more totalising the discursive system, the better. The final, largest dinosaur, *Daweosaurus*, is found when Web falls out of the sky while having sex with Anna Yellowbird in the middle of a twister, landing so that he straddles the fossil, "bone" and bone meeting painfully for Web, but fruitfully for Dawe (207).

But if this meeting of bones here favours Dawe's notion of self-definition through the recovery of the text of the land's past, equally strong is Web's opposing view of self-construction through the rejection of the past, endlessly starting anew. Web has burnt down his father's house, and possibly his father with it, before departing on the life that leads him, ironically, to Dawe's expedition in search of the past (4). But though he participates, however reluctantly, in the river journey of Dawe's effort to construct meaning from the text of the past, Web's fear of water continues to signal his fear and rejection of this past. The muddy water of the river, perhaps even more than the bones of the dinosaurs, comes to suggest the connection between the past, as inscribed in the text of the land, and the men currently excavating that past—a connection particularly suggested in the events following McBride's falling overboard. McBride finally reappears miles downriver, paddling his pig trough shaped like a coffin, and landing on the farmer's shore, his emergence from the water becomes the emergence of the first land creature from the depths:

> the . . . woman [the farmer's wife] . . . saw . . . the man caked in mud from his feet to his hair, his body

like an alligator's; she saw him step from his trough and into the willows. And it was not the smell that came with him that made her hesitate; she knew the smell of skunk. It was the man himself, coming formless out of the mud. Onto the land. The mud, the grey mud, cold, reptilian, come sliding into the yellow-green flame of the shore's willows.

(42–43)

McBride is the one man on the expedition who has "*the ability to become a hero*," but "*the wisdom not to*" (45, Kroetsch's italics): he is the one man who might actually live the heroism of Dawe's and Web's mythologising discourses, but he rejects such discourse entirely and abandons Dawe's expedition into death, in favour of his life on the land with his family. Similarly, he is the one who lives the past, slathering himself with the mud from which he came, and emerging into human life, moving away from the bone-signs of the deadly discourses.

Web's fear of this seminal water, contrarily, and his simultaneous self-creation through his myth-making, reiterate his fear of the past. But his fear, perhaps precisely because it is still accompanied by his own discourses of self-construction, does not allow him to escape the past—the river—as seen when he follows McBride to the ferry crossing. McBride's escape from the journey into death and discourse takes the form of this ferry trip across the river, the irony being that the trip is precisely not the journey across the Styx into Hades, under the guidance of the other-worldly ferryman. Rather, as above, it is the journey of his return to life—a journey which the ferryman, associating Web with the expedition in search of bones, will not allow Web to make. "'Dead is dead,'" the ferryman shouts at Web. "'We don't need none of you damned graverobbers down here'" (54). Web's active rejection of the past—of the dinosaur bones of self-constructing discourse—nevertheless implies a continued connection with the past, as it allows or prevents self-constitution in discourse.

Dawe's construction of the myth of the land's history, then, is one way of defining self and nation, perhaps a notably staid and stodgy method associated with the established practices of the East—Dawe, after all, is only plundering the bone beds in Western Canada in order to take the bones back East and there to catalogue them into the accepted discourses of history and nation. Web's myth-construction, on the other hand, enters as an alternative possible way of defining nation, as frontier, as the locus of heroic acts of self-definition, as the land of tall tales—a Western construction depending upon the myth that constructs the West as the place to start again, to escape the bonds of the past. Web's tall tales are set against the long tails of the dinosaurs Dawe is excavating—against the never-recovered long tail of the *Daweosaurus* which was the intended object of the dynamite that instead killed Tune.

Both Web's and Dawe's discourses fail to fulfill their mythical agenda, however, of the construction of self and nation. Dawe's exercise of recovering history is at best only fragmentary:[9] the fossil of his *Daweosaurus*, as above, is missing its tail, which he must construct by guess-work in a museum back East. And his general practice, of searching only for the largest bones, blinds him to many of the other elements of the text deposited by time: he misses all the smaller and less spectacular signs of the land's past. While Dawe is in Drumheller, for example, down in the coal mine searching for someone to replace McBride on the expedition, he is suddenly struck with

the truth of what he already knew: here, once, there were green branches of fig trees. Sycamores. Magnolias. A delta and a swamp. On this spot: *Ornithomimus* snapping fruit from the high branches, digging for the eggs of other dinosaurs. Carnivorous *Tyrannosaurus rex* stalking *Saurolophus*; dinosaur stalking dinosaur; the quiet, day-long hunt, the sudden murderous lunge, the huge and bone-cracking jaws finding at last the solid-crested skull, the long tails flailing the water a frothed red.

(81)

Yet he will still not stop more than momentarily to examine the leaf patterns in the piece of coal Grimlich shows him—the smaller signs in time's text—and he heads immediately for the bonebeds again, the moment a new crew member has been recruited. The past he is constructing for Eastern notions of national identity is in fact only bits and pieces of the past, parts of it based upon the specimens found in the Badlands—specimens which are themselves already mineral substitutes for the actual dinosaur bones (56)—parts of it sheer guesswork, and much of it just plain absent.

Web's alternative constructions, which speak of a more Western Canadian construction of identity, also fail actually to define such identity, in that they work far more to deconstruct the concept of nation than to define it. His stories invariably suggest a barely contained chaos of radical, directionless energy, far from the value-laden order and encompassing system which usually characterise national myths. Lies, he discovers, are far more interesting than the ostensible truth, in any case: speaking of his effort to trace the departed McBride and bring him back to the boat, he protests untruthfully that he saw neither

"Hide nor hair," . . . elaborating his lie, delighting in the ambiguity of his discovery, the skeleton that was not the beast, not even the bones of the sought beast but the chemical replacement of what had been the bones: "Didn't find hide nor hair—"

(56)

Neither his discourse of "bones," nor Dawe's dinosaur-bone discourse, answers the desire for wholeness and satisfaction that both discourses create,[10] and the closest they come to constructing such individual or national identity as the myth-making might aim at, is through the ambiguous practice of lies—of endless substitution. The signs never speak directly of the reality or the truth, but only make gestures at it, offering uncertain dis-/replacements which connect only with other such implacements. Thus, whether constructing or deconstructing ideas of nationality and identity, both of the discourses, as discourses, result in the same failure of language. In the much-quoted words of Anna Dawe, "*there are no truths, only correspondences*" (45, Kroetsch's italics).

There *is* one moment of satisfaction for both Web's and Dawe's discourses—the one orgasm that Web actually has in the entire novel, while having sex with Anna Yellowbird in the storm—the incident ending when Web lands crotch first on the *Daweosaurus*. But the moment of satisfaction, as we have seen already, is the moment of reconnection with the dead, with Dawe's dinosaur bones, which, bearing Dawe's name, will be shipped back East to be incorporated into its stultifying systems of decided meaning. Web's own description of his encounter with Anna Yellowbird—particularly, of course, the moment of orgasm—is couched in terms of destruction and death:

> "we were locked together up there like two howling dogs. . . . And just goddamned then the lightning struck us. . . . the bolt came streaking straight at us, the ball of fire came WHAM—and sweet mother of Christ the blue flames shot out of our ears, off our fingertips, our glowing hair stood on end, my prick was like an exploding torpedo. . . ." Web trying to capture his spouting words. "And the crack of thunder deafened us. The inverted universe and undescended testicles of the divine, the refucking-union with the dead—"
>
> (206–7)

The lightning storm might replicate the first galvanising lightning that is theorised to have catalysed life from the mud on the edge of the primeval water, but in Web's use of it in his discourse of self-creation, it also links him back with the death of history. Web may try to escape the past by burning down his father's hut with his father still inside, but as long as he is controlled by his "spouting" discourse, constructing himself through the endless substitutions of language, he can never escape the death and the bones of the past. As Anna Dawe comments of Web:

> *Total and absurd male that he was, he assumed, like a male author, an omniscience that was not ever his, a scheme that was not ever there. Holding the past in contempt, he dared foretell for himself not so much a future as an orgasm. But we women take our time.*
>
> (76, Kroetsch's italics)

Web foretells the orgasm, which reconnects him with the death of the past, the death of discourse.

But as the last words of the quotation suggest, outside the oppositions which establish the differences—and ultimate similarities—between the male discourses, is a third possibility entirely: the female and the a-discursive: silence. Breaking into the interplay of life and death in the male discourses, then, is a radically alternative possibility, which, because it has thus far been so completely proscribed from the myth-making discourses of men—myths that construct meaning through the establishment and stabilising of such oppositions—breaks entirely away

from all such oppositions, and heads into undefinable, unidentifiable, realms outside language. Archaeology in the novel has worked to excavate the various discourses of the land, whether the text of the land itself in its layers of time's inscription, Dawe's discourse of Eastern ideas of national and individual male identity, or Web's "yarns" constructing a Western identity of wild action and superhuman performance. At the same time as the act of excavation reveals and orders the signs of such discourses, it demonstrates the incompleteness of discourses—of such falsely totalising systems of substitution—and thereby problematises the very notion of language itself. Having reached such a point, then, it is possible to speculate—only speculate, of course, in an area by definition of radical uncertainty and strangeness—about what might lie outside of the endlessly self-constituting, endlessly unravelling construct of language.

As I begin to suggest already, this speculation takes place in the novel principally under the sign of the women (and the native), especially of Anna Dawe and her namesake, Anna Yellowbird. Within the main discourse of the novel—that describing the actual archaeological expedition of 1916, interspersed with Dawe's field notes—Anna Yellowbird represents one possible way of constructing the a-discursivity that surrounds the field of language. This is perhaps seen most clearly in the description of Dawe's having sex with her, where Dawe tries repeatedly to construct her as the sign against which he is defining himself in his male myth of his self, but where she repeatedly fades away from his discursive grasp, always evading definition or focus:

> at that split second of penetration he must, he would, raise up with him into that underworld of his rampaging need the knowledge of all his life: into that sought darkness, that exquisite inundation, he would carry in his mind, in his head, the memory of wife and home, his driving ambitions that had swept him into this canyon, the furious desire and dream that had brought him here to these badlands, to these burnt prairies and scalded buttes; conquer, he told himself, conquer; and out of that blasting sun, into the darkness of her body he must, rising, plunge:
>
> and found instead that at each moment of entry into the dark, wet heat of her body the outside world was lost, and he, in a new paroxysm that erased the past, spent each night's accumulated recollection in that little time of going in; the motion that erased the ticking clock, the wide earth:
>
> . . . Until he began to believe that only his humped back might save him from some absolute surrender. . . . Dawe, not moving at first, wanting not to move, yielding to her passion, her violence, her tenderness; his male sense of surrender surprised and violated and fulfilled:
>
> She made him lose the past. He began to hate her for that.
>
> (195–96)

Dawe, trying to use Anna Yellowbird as the vessel, female and Indian, in which he can construct and thereby contain his personal history—his identity—finds in the moment of fulfillment that his discourse has failed, and that he has not made a monument of his history, but has lost it entirely. Her yielding to him becomes a kind of endless yielding of the discourse which he has tried to embody in her, with the result that the discourse falls apart entirely.

The land has appeared in the novel as the site and agent of the various discourses' fragmentation—the storm rejoining Web to "the inverted universe and undescended testicles of the divine, the refucking-union with the dead" (207), and depositing him on the dead bones of Dawe's satisfaction. Parallel to and extension upon this fragmentation is the female (and/or native) realm, not just of fragmented discourse, but also of complete departure from it. In the darkness of the coal mine, Dawe is presented, in the fossilised leaf, with evidence of the incompleteness of his falsely totalising discourse; in the darkness of Anna Yellowbird's body, his discourse is completely subsumed, and during the time of his relations with her, he becomes vague and indifferent, and has great difficulty keeping up the field notes in which, thus far, he has been recording his journey to fame as a paleontologist.

An alternative approach to speculation about the a-discursive in the novel occurs in the use of the second level of narrative, of Anna Dawe's framing narrative. At its simplest, the construct works to place a female voice outside of and surrounding the male discourses which appear in the framed narrative of the expedition. Then, the action which Anna Dawe's narrative tells is precisely that of reading the male discourses and of destroying them. The reading she performs on the discourses is what is written in the first level of narrative: the level I have principally been examining. This reading is precisely one that deconstructs the discourses and that problematises the entire concept of discourse. Her framing narrative supports this process of deconstruction partly in the continuing comment on the specific incidents of the first narrative— such as those in italics—which encourage a reading of the first text involving the sort of discourse analysis I have attempted above.[11]

The texts of male discourse are thus subsumed by the discourse of a narrative which, at the same time as constructing them, has deconstructed them. Then, in the concluding pages of the novel, the destruction of the actual artifacts of Dawe's discourse—his field notes—can take place. Significantly, this act of destruction takes the form of an alternative journey which writes over the older journey, reversing its direction, and heading for different sources, different points of beginning again, than Web's or Dawe's journeys did. Anna Dawe collects an aged Anna Yellowbird from the bar of a prairie hotel and heads West, back up the Red Deer river into the mountains—and towards the river's source in a glacial lake. The journey is Westward, away from the suffocation of Eastern Canadian constructs of meaning; it is a journey to purge Anna Dawe of her father's words: his dead dinosaur bones, his dead bones at the bottom of Lake Superior, his death-bringing "bone" that penetrated Anna Yellowbird and that fathered Anna Dawe. Unlike Dawe's search for origins in the dead layers of history, the Annas' quest for origins takes them to the brand new waters of the lake, untouched by history, untouched by discourse.

By the lake, laughing at the ridiculous figure of the male grizzly, his balls hanging from the net, they are at last freed from the weight of all the discourse they have been fleeing, and throw the photographs and field notes into the lake to drown as Dawe himself did.[12] Leaving the lake under the light of the stars, in Anna Dawe's description, they

> *looked at those billions of years of light, and Anna [Yellowbird] looked at the stars, and Anna looked at the stars and then at me, and she did not mention dinosaurs or men or their discipline or their courage or their goddamned honour or their goddamned fucking fame or their goddamned fucking death-fucking death. . . . And we did not once look back, not once, ever.*

(270, Kroetsch's italics)

The lake absorbs the deadly discourse, the death inscribed in constructions of history and identity, and the sight of the stars, while their very light refers to ages gone past, also suggests the possibility of endless renewal. While the land can be seen, as in the layers of the badlands, to be itself a text, a language, it also represents that which might be beyond the constructions and constraints of language.

In the imposition of their desires on the land—in their discourses—the men create the land as a linguistic construct, contained within and controlled by the encompassing effort of their discourses. But the very fact of the land's being created as a language means that it must also cause the subversion and eventual deconstruction of the very constructs which rendered it as such a language in the first place. Then, the notion of language thus so radically destabilised, the land can be reintroduced as possible site of that which is outside of language entirely. The inescapable irony, that such speculation must take place within the very medium which it works to deconstruct— that Anna Dawe's position as a possible representative of the a-discursive must be communicated by her in discourse—does not negate the deconstruction of history, identity and discourse that has been performed. Rather, it represents an opening into the endlessly circling argument that is language itself, in which the effort to define land and language—even to define them as sites of the radical undecidability and resistance to definition that characterises language—must precisely occur within this ceaselessly shifting and deferring medium of language itself. Anna Dawe's discourse becomes an opening into a sort of impossible Möbius strip,[13] that turns again and again back on itself at the same time as it twists to a new level of speculation and thought. Such an opening, by virtue of being an opening, also suggests the possibility of escape, at the same time as it implies here the entrance into an endlessly deferring, endlessly deferred en/closure. The land as discourse becomes such a Möbius strip, referring always to language at the same time as it perpetually suggests an alternative possibility of that which is never touched by language.

The result, then, is a post-colonial discourse that engages very clearly with all the activities of myth-making and history-writing that have been used to construct post-colonial belonging and identity here in these lands. The novel helps to inscribe the land, both as sign and as actual physical territory, as the authorising site of the values and meanings upon which the post-colonial counter-discourse bases its subversion of the once-dominant imperial discourses. But at the same time, the land, precisely because it is the object of this discursive and territorial contention between the imperial and the local, ultimately enters the discourse as the site of the radical uncertainty which suffuses all the junctures between the signs of a discourse: the land, as the endlessly unsatisfactory and fragmented object of Dawe's discourses about meaning and identity, comes to represent precisely the fragmentations, replacements, and substitutions which characterise discourse in general, whether dominant imperial or post-colonial counter-discourse. This deconstructive post-colonial discourse, rather than merely replacing one system of meaning with another, instead destabilises the notion of any meaning, and locates the source of this instability in that very object which, in both imperial and counter-discursive epistemologies, has been constructed as *the* most stable and unchanging of ideologically-loaded signs: the sign of the land. In the deconstructive enterprise, the new land, like language itself, is still used to construct meaning; but at the same time, it must re-enter the discourse as precisely that which, endlessly and inevitably, *subverts* meaning, again and again.

Notes

1. See, for example, Kateryna Arthur. "Pioneering Perceptions: Australia and Canada," in *Regionalism and National Identity: Essays on Canadian, Australian and New Zealand Topics*, ed. James Acheson and Reginald Berry (Christchurch: Association of Canadian Studies in Australia and New Zealand, 1985), 202; I. S. MacLaren, "The Aesthetic Map of the North, 1845–1859," *Arctic*, 38 (1985), 89; MacLaren, "Retaining Captaincy of the Soul: Response to Nature in the First Franklin Expedition," *Essays on Canadian Writing*, 28 (1984), 57–58; D. E. S. Maxwell, "Landscape and Theme," in *Commonwealth Literature: Unity and Diversity in a Common Culture* (London: Heinemann, 1965), 83–84.

2. See, for example, my argument in "Colonising Discourses: The Land in Australian and Western Canadian Exploration Narratives," *Australian-Canadian Studies*, forthcoming 1989. Arthur develops a similar notion, in her use of the image of *ostraneniye* to discuss early discursive responses to Australian and Canadian landscapes. The aesthetic strategy of *ostraneniye* (making strange), translated here into the aesthetic dilemma

of artists and writers encountering an already-strange landscape, "[impedes] habitual reception, interferes with transmission, and so enforces a dynamic, constructive (or deconstructive) vision of the object [of the strange landscape]" (207). "Visions of the two countries are constantly altered. . . . Pioneering in the realm of perception is not just a thing of the past" (209). See also MacLaren, "The Aesthetic Map of the North," 101–2; and MacLaren, "'. . . where nothing moves and nothing changes': The Second Arctic Expedition of John Ross (1829–1833)," *Dalhousie Review*, 62 (1982), 485–94.

3. Helen Tiffin argues the correlation of the post-colonial with the counter-discursive in her "Post-Colonial Literatures and Counter-Discourses" (*Kunapipi*, 9·3 [1987], 17–34), drawing upon Richard Terdiman's discussion of "the potential and limitations of counter-discursive literary revolution within a dominant discourse" (Tiffin, n. 3, p. 33), in his *Discourse/Counter-discourse: The Theory and Practice of Symbolic Resistance in Nineteenth-Century France* (Ithaca and London: Cornell UP, 1985). Terdiman notes that counter-discourses "implicitly evoke a principle of order just as systematic as that which sustains the discourses they seek to subvert. Ultimately, in the image of the counterhegemonic . . . the counter-discourse always projects, just over its own horizon, the dream of victoriously replacing its antagonist" (56–57). In the context of post-colonial counter-discursive contention, Tiffin similarly quotes J. M. Coetzee's expression of discomfort with a subversive, relativising reading he performs on several novels, when he says that "it is a mode of reading which, subverting the dominant, is in peril, like all triumphant subversion, of becoming the dominant in turn" (Tiffin, 32). The post-colonial counter-discourse of the land, then, may subvert the once-dominant imperial discourse, but it also inscribes an equally tyrannic version of writing the land, as part of local, post-colonial identity and meaning. There's still a sense of a need to "get it right," to see and thereby to write the land as it "really is," rather than a movement, such as Homi K. Bhabha discusses, to go beyond the imperialism of this European-grown notion of an (ideal) unmediated text evoking a transcendental reality ("Representation and the Colonial Text: A Critical Exploration of Some Forms of Mimeticism," in *The Theory of Reading*, Frank Gloversmith, ed. [Brighton: Harvester, 1984], 96–99).

4. Finally, however, it ought to be noted that my distinction between counter-discursive and deconstructive efforts is somewhat artificial, each movement sharing strategies and effects with the other. Many of the subversive strategies to be found in Kroetsch's novel could be shown to work within either general strategy of subversion. I note that

Tiffin's article suggests a different way of viewing the post-colonial's subversive strategies, in that a division between counter-discursive and deconstructive practices and effects is not made at all. She says that the danger that the counter-discursive might become dominant in turn is not a problem in "post-colonial inversions of imperial formations," because in the post-colonial context, these subversions are "deliberately provisional; they do not overturn or invert the dominant in order to become dominant in their turn, but to question the foundations of the ontologies and epistemological systems which would see such binary structures as inescapable" (32). However, this latter description seems to me to be a workable definition precisely of how the more generally subversive strategy of deconstruction differs from the counter-discursive as Terdiman describes it. In the context of my discussion, some distinction can be made, I think, between whether a novel works to replace the imperialist formulations of the land, which it works to subvert, with some other system by which to organize understanding of the land; or whether it seems to aim at a more general subversion of Western thought and of the constructs which constitute the thought, thus preventing the proposal of any alternate systems. As my argument runs, I see *Badlands* as primarily performing the latter action.

5. Stephen Slemon similarly discusses the (eventual) breakdown of binary oppositions in another of Kroetsch's novels, *What the Crow Said*, as a movement towards—or gesture at—a post-colonial discourse "beyond binary constriction." ("Magic Realism as Post-Colonial Discourse," *Canadian Literature*, 116 [1988], 15.)

6. Shirley Neuman and Robert Wilson, *Labyrinths of Voice: Conversations with Robert Kroetsch* (Edmonton: NeWest, 1982), 14–15. The discussion here of contamination of the archaeological site is in reference to a model of the text as object of *intertextual* excavation, tracing the influences, repetitions and subversions of precedent works; but I think the image can be applied to discourse in the way I attempt above, given the ubiquity of the structure, and the resulting multiplicity of its possible applications, in *Badlands*. (See also Brian Edwards, "Alberta and the Bush: The Deconstruction of National Identity in Post-modernist Canadian and Australian Fiction," *World Literature Written in English*, 25 [1985], 164.) In the context of my argument, the site of discourse, in a sense, is contaminated by discourse itself—by the desire which informs its very existence.

7. Robert Kroetsch, *Badlands* (Toronto: General, 1982), 16. Further references are to this edition.

8. Neuman and Wilson, pp. 19–21ff.; Brian Edwards, "Textual Erotics, the Meta-Perspective and Reading Instruction in Robert Kroetsch's Later Fiction," *Australian-Canadian Studies* 5.2 (1987), 69–72.

9. Neuman and Wilson, 9–11.

10. Homi K. Bhabha, "The Other Question: Difference, Discrimination and the Discourse of Colonialism," in *Literature, Politics and Theory* (London and New York: Methuen, 1986), 151.

11. Note particularly the passage I have quoted, writing Web as a male author arrogating total omniscience to himself (*Badlands*, 76).

12. Paul Duthie, "New Land—Old Culture," Unpublished essay, 1987, 37; Edwards, "Textual Erotics, the Meta-Perspective and Reading Instruction in Robert Kroetsch's Later Fiction," 165.

13. "A continuous one-sided surface, as formed by half-twisting a strip, as of paper or cloth, and joining the ends" (*The Macquarie Dictionary*, 2nd ed.). The effect is a figure which, as one follows the surface through its turn, brings one both through a twist and thus apparently to a new surface, at the same time as it circles unavoidably back to its starting point. It both changes and doesn't change.

Kathleen Wall (essay date Spring 1991)

SOURCE: "What Kroetsch Said: The Problem of Meaning and Language in *What the Crow Said*," in *Canadian Literature*, No. 128, Spring, 1991, pp. 90-105.

[*In the following essay, Wall examines the meaning of Kroetsch's apparently chaotic approach to criticism in* What the Crow Said.]

> I think criticism is really a version of story, you see; I think we are telling the story to each other of how we get at story. It is the story of our search for story. That's why criticism is so exciting. Not because it provides answers, but because it is a version of story.
>
> (**LV** 30) [1]

Were it not for Robert Kroetsch's generous attitude toward the critic's role, it would seem an act of hubris to attempt to interpret **What the Crow Said**, the novel that he wrote as his "own personal struggle with the temptation of meaning." I think the critic can, however, delineate the parameters and expression of that temptation without ignoring his injunction that the temptation to impose meaning "is the reader's struggle too" (**LV** 15). In this novel, the tendency to impose meaning not only creates a dilemma for the writer and the reader: it is a central issue for the characters as well.

The world of **What the Crow Said** is a world without order—as we conventionally expect it: time warps frequently, and the laws of probable cause and effect do not seem to operate in Big Indian. Winter comes after spring and lasts an entire year, Liebhaber remembers the future, Vera Lang is impregnated by bees, a man missing one leg and his genitals impregnates Rose Lang, a child who sings in the womb is born into silence. The improbabilities in Kroetsch's text go on and on.[2] The community's response to this chaos is to assign meaning and causality willy-nilly: in fact the book opens with just such an attempt to explain life in Big Indian:

> People, years later, blamed everything on the bees; it was the bees, they said, seducing Vera Lang, that started everything. How the town came to prosper, and then to decline, and how the road never got built, the highway that would have joined the town and the municipality to the world beyond, and how the sky itself, finally, took umbrage: it was because one afternoon in April the swarming bees found Vera Lang asleep, there in a patch of wild flowers on the edge of the valley.
>
> (7)

Nearly everyone partakes of this strategy: when Skandl loses Martin Lang's body, he blames it on the comatose Liebhaber. Liebhaber's four minutes of coherence in the Lang Household are attributed to Tiddy's statement: "It's snowing" (39). People believe that the first hand of schmier dealt at the Church of the Final Virgin was brought about by Eli Wurtz's comment, "*Du* son of a gun" upon seeing the unwell, diminished Liebhaber. Blame for the "war with the sky" is variously attributed: some "blamed recent developments on the moment when the ice began to form on the wings of the Piper Cub in which John Skandl was flying home to Big Indian" (146). Others believe that Vera's boy is somehow to blame. When the plague of salamanders arrives, "Someone blamed the wind. Someone said it was the departure of the black crow that did it" (150). Vera's decision to take a husband is said to be caused by the cry of Joe Lightning as he falls out of the sky. People also respond to the uncontrollable chaos by trying to assert that they might have or can have some control over events. When, in August, it continues to snow, men aver that things might be different if they found Lang's corpse: "If they had found the corpse, the few men who went on seeking it, then something might have changed. The digging of a grave, attendance at a wake, the ceremony of burial, any one of those events might have made things normal again. The bees were to blame" (44). These myriad efforts to attribute cause and lay blame are a desperate attempt to assert that some kind of order, some kind of definable causality, regardless of how bizarre, operates in Big Indian.

It is appropriately difficult, given Kroetsch's preoccupation with the "temptation of meaning" to decide which causes actually operate meaningfully in Kroetsch's border cosmos, and which are asserted by the inhabitants of Big Indian in an effort to impose a perceived, explicable order on a world that seems to defy one's logical or experiential expectations. This difficulty is attributable to Kroetsch's use of a communal third person narrator, one who has entered the world of Big Indian with the inhabitants, and refrains from making judgements about the characters' behavior. Complicating matters even more is our own distinct sense that Big Indian does indeed have its own

laws that do not necessarily have a direct referent in our world.[3] It is only with respect to "what the crow said" that we begin to suspect that the attribution of meaning and causality is a desperate and foolish effort. Thus the work deconstructs itself for us, leaving us uncertain about which attributed causes are operative and which are wishful thinking.

It is initially the year-long winter that unhinges the characters' sense that the world they inhabit is predictable and orderly. Certainly, Martin Lang's death illustrates the fate of those who, either on the prairies or in Big Indian, expect to "believe June was June" (18). John Skandl's response is another kind of folly: in opposition to the temporal and spatial blankness of an unending winter, he decides to construct a tower made from the very materials that winter provides. Needing to fix himself in a now unreliable, floating universe, Skandl will construct "a beacon, a fixed point in the endless winter" (33). His tower will assert meaning in the face of unmeaning (blank) winter, will function as "a center. A beacon. A guide. A warning sign" (41). Pre-deconstructionist man, he believes his phallic signifier is transparent, its meaning utterly clear. As a tower of babble (49), it demonstrates both man's foolish impertinence in believing he can control and manipulate his world, and the "danger of making everything into one" (L 118), echoing the structuralist belief that language is a transparent medium with a single dimension, a single meaning.

In spite of Robert Lecker's assertion (99) that the old binaries, which typically cause an interesting tension in Kroetsch's work, are not present in **What the Crow Said**, I find them functioning in a very lively way. The most common (culturally imposed) binary opposition between men and women becomes obvious in the scene where members of the community evaluate and comment upon Skandl's tower. It is the "*men* who would dream it in that snow-buried town" (41, emphasis mine). The women, on the other hand, argue against the ice (49). Tiddy Lang, in particular, is concerned about the implications of the tower: "Tiddy now recognized that the men, in their desperate confusion, were trying to get to heaven. They must be stopped. She was trying to find words. Tiddy, who did not argue at all. She was trying to imagine words" (50).

The men have, through their construction of the tower, been attempting to impose order, meaning, even purpose on the year-long (now seemingly endless) winter; in building the tower and in turning ice to profit they are asserting the primacy of culture over nature, and attempting, in Simone de Beauvoir's words, to "transcend" the limitations or circumstances imposed by nature.[4] Tiddy's sense that they are attempting to get to heaven and Skandl's assertion that they must continue to build the tower higher and higher are both images of transcendence. It is a sterile proceeding, however, this icy preoccupation, one that the earth eventually defies by sending spring thaw.

The women's general opposition to the tower makes us aware that their response to the untimely and protracted winter has been of an entirely different order than that of the men. As Lecker (98) and Thomas (102) have both pointed out, Kroetsch has gone out of his way to emphasize the chthonic qualities of the Lang women, both through oblique—and often subverted—references to myth and through evocative, concrete details of their involvement in the earthly cycles and farm matters. Vera, Tiddy, and Old Lady Lang are indeed virgin, earth mother, and wise old crone. Vera's mating of the bees recalls Danae (Lecker 98), who is also the north European triple goddess, Danae (Walker 206–7); floating down the river in the granary, her hand on her pubis, she recalls both Botticelli's Birth of Venus, and Ceres, goddess of grain. Tiddy, with her perfect breasts, recalls the earth mother, Cybele the many-breasted. When she turns her mourning for Martin to an effort to heal Liebhaber, she recalls Demeter, who in her grief for Persephone became nursemaid to Demophon and nearly conferred immortality upon the child. This proliferation of goddess imagery allows Kroetsch to avoid being "entrapped in those mythic stories" (L 96), entrapment that might occur if he were to fall into repeating the myths in which the figures play a major part. Instead, the many oblong, oblique references invite the unfolding of many layers which evoke, but do not necessarily *mean* a whole range of feminine archetypes.

One of Kroetsch's first entries concerning **What the Crow Said in his Crow Journals** concerns his wish to make not only the tall tale and the mythological part of his book, but to maintain at the same time "always the hard core of detail" (**CJ** 11). This endeavor on Kroetsch's part has been questioned by Lecker (99), who obviously ignored the rich, evocative detail of daily domestic life on the Lang farm. Perhaps the hard core of detail of women's lives is invisible in more ways than one; however, the descriptions of the women's routines illustrate that while the men have been building a tower, the women have gone on with their chores and their lives, not particularly disturbed by the strange weather, except insofar as it is an inconvenience. Vera, for example, knows that spring is inevitable. And descriptions of Tiddy evoke a woman comfortable in time, in life, and in nature:

> Sometimes the cows mooed. Sometimes they didn't. Sometimes the chickens laid. Sometimes they needed oyster shells. Sometimes the thistles or the pigweeds grew faster than the wheat. Sometimes hail fell instead of rain. Sometimes the dust blew through closed windows. Tiddy, with her hardheaded radiance, held together the past and the future. Her daughters went on maturing. Her mother grew older, more wrinkled, forever clutching her ball of sorrow in a pocket of her apron. JG was more work than all the others, all the conundrums of the world, put together. He grew larger. He said nothing. Tiddy accepted his existence as she accepted the stinkweeds, the grasshoppers, the green grass in the spring, the sun.
>
> (68–9)

The scene at the tower, the men approving the endeavour, the women opposing it, crystallizes the binary opposition of man and women, culture and nature, the transcendence and entrapment, except that in Kroetsch's cosmogony, the last element is reversed. By attempting to control and utilize the weather or give a meaningful centre to the blank landscape, the men entrap themselves in their preoccupation. It is the women who transcend by continuing their chthonic life, accepting of the weather and unconcerned about its implications. Vera, knowing spring will inevitably arrive, calmly plans and waits, learning about bees.

Liebhaber, however, doesn't quite fit in the male category, largely I suspect because his relationship to language and order (the phallic signifier of the tower of babble)—to meaning—is more problematic. While Tiddy is marrying, Liebhaber is fighting with the double bind of language. On the one hand, words, despite their arbitrariness, remain fixed: no matter how or where he distributes the letters, "out" remains "out." This culturally-defined fixedness that he recognizes he cannot transcend seems to bind him to death with its over-determinacy. In an attempt to foil the over-determinacy of the letters O U T, Liebhaber attempts "a sequence of illogical sentences; he printed across the linoleum of his living room floor: I'M NOT ALONE. REALLY. He ran out of punctuation. He found his apostrophes and periods, what few he had, in a shoe box under his bed. He concluded his trilogy of sentences with I'M NOT" (55). The problem with Liebhaber's three sentences is not that they are illogical, but that they have too many meanings. Our immediate reaction is to "naturalize" those three statements,[5] so that they "mean" something, so that they assert that Liebhaber strongly believes that he is not alone; we see them as a psychological protestation against his loneliness as Tiddy marries. Doing so, we discover another property of language, its ability to express false statements; for Liebhaber, at the moment of Tiddy's marriage, likely feels more alone than ever. Yet the sentence, "I'm not," which we take as a reiteration of "I'm not alone," might also refer to Liebhaber's ontological status as a character in a book who both exists, as a linguistic phenomenon, and does not exist. These and other possible meanings make us aware that language is not an unbiased medium; it can be used to lie. Nor is it transparent and entirely clear, for it conveys the meaning (or illogical non-meaning) that we expect it to convey.

Liebhaber's ambivalent relationship to language recognizes the problem of meaning, just as Liebhaber recognizes the ridiculousness of Skandl's tower. If Skandl is pre-deconstructionist man, innocently able to assert his ability to create a transparent, meaningful, directive phallic signifier (which Tiddy finds attractive, as do some of the French theorists find Lacan's notion of the phallic signifier), Liebhaber is on the way to becoming a post-structuralist, uneasily aware of language's problems, in spite of the fact that, like the post-modern writer, he makes his living/meaning through language.

Also like the post-modern writer, Liebhaber believes uneasily in the ability of language to create an ontology. During the dedication of the tower, Liebhaber at first attempts to undermine Skandl's ascendency/transcendence by lying about the signs of spring: "I heard a flight of geese heading north"; "'Cowpie,' Liebhaber shouted. 'I found a soft cowpie. Somewhere the grass is green'" (48–9). Part of this strikes us as sheer bravado; part strikes us as truth: for indeed, *somewhere* the grass is green; part strikes us as prophecy. We finally must acknowledge the creative element of language when the narrator comments that "Liebhaber, recklessly, in an endless winter, invented a spring" (49). Even Liebhaber's use of language to evoke, lie about, create a spring, bespeaks of language's multiplicity, its multiple uses.

In spite of Liebhaber's more realistic attitude toward meaning, he nevertheless succumbs to a desire to control, to order the world around him. Because he's relatively useless around the farm, Liebhaber helps Tiddy choose a hired hand: Liebhaber's candidate is Mick O'Halloran, who is missing one leg and his genitals, "and while his disability limited his usefulness on the farm, Liebhaber felt it was more than compensated for by the security he provided in a household made up of a grass widow and six unmarried young women" (66). Yet Liebhaber's judgment proves to be wrong when Mick, against all probability and reason, impregnates Rose.

His second lapse in judgment occurs when he helps Tiddy with cow breeding and ends up perfecting the three-titted cow (70); again a pregnancy results, this time the relationship is between Nick Droniuk, who helps with the artificial insemination, and Anna Marie. Finally, Liebhaber agrees to referee the hockey games, a role in which he exults: "Liebhaber, as referee, removed yet always there, watched the disputes, the hard checking, the high sticking, the errors, the affections and dissatisfactions of the swarming, eager players. The rougher the game became, the clearer his vision. He was some kind of arbitrator, the civilizing man: at the center, and yet uninvolved. The dispassionate man at the passionate core, witnessing both jealousy and desire, separate from either" (72). As referee, Liebhaber is the representative of civilization, culture, order, a patriarch who takes pride in his ability, "single-handedly, to restore order" (73).

But this effort of control, belief in order, patriarchal absolutism, also collapses when we find that Gladys was impregnated on the ice by "everybody"—and perhaps it was even her presence on the ice that limited the dispute. In spite of his judicial pretensions, Liebhaber finds he cannot control the fertility of Tiddy's daughters, as if the female and natural world remains uncontrollably outside his dominion. It is his inability to control, grasp this unfolding, fecund world, as well as his inability to see the world truly, or to see the same truth that others see, or to live in a world where one can identify absolute truth—that accounts for the protracted game of schmier. For in yet another of those questionable attributions of cause, we are told "That was the cause of the schmier game—the inadequacy of truth" (76).

I was interested in the literal use of game in daily life. In a small town, in a rural area where card playing especially is very central, I was influenced by the old women in the community who would read cards. I had two aunts who on occasion would read cards and read them with an ambiguous sense that it was just playing but at the same time that it was serious. That ambiguity intrigued me no end. I think that even in the most elaborate games, like religion, there is that double sense. The notion of necessary fiction really relates to that, doesn't it?

(**LV** 49)

Thomas has complained of the sheer volume of human excrement in Kroetsch's novel (115), yet the unappetizing conditions of the schmier game aptly illustrate the lengths to which Liebhaber and his crew will go in order to confine themselves to a microcosm that has definable rules. In both **The Crow Journals** and **Labyrinths of Voice**, Kroetsch discusses his view of the world: that we exist within the godgame. That is, we know some, but by no means all, of life's rules. Games seemingly exist as antidotes to or relief from the godgame. Huizinga, whose book, *Homo Ludens*, influenced Kroetsch, describes those parameters of game that make it a free space, in some way unhampered by the unknown or partly known rules of the godgame: "Here, then, we have the first main characteristic of play: that it is free, is in fact freedom. A second characteristic is closely connected with this, namely, that play is not 'ordinary' or 'real' life. It is rather a stepping out of 'real' life into a temporary sphere of activity with a disposition all of its own" (quoted in **LV** 66). Playing schmier, the men separate themselves from the world they cannot control, placing themselves in a microcosm where they are capable of "ignoring the weather, ignoring time, family, duty, season; ignoring everything but their one passion" (90). Moreover, the rules of the game structure their lives in a way the rules of the godgame, with its year-long winters and genital-less men who impregnate girls, cannot. In **Labyrinths of Voice** Kroetsch comments: "I take a card game very seriously. For me, a card game is a model of life. . . . Card games are interesting because, on the one hand, there are absolute rules and, on the other, inside those rules there is absolute chance, or at least an indefinite mathematically large number of chances that even to deal yourself the same hand would be a grotesque unlikelihood. There are absolute rules and there is chance" (**LV** 64–5).

The second use of cards intrudes for a moment as Old Lady Lang "reads" the players' hands. When Old Lady Lang predicts Liebhaber's future, to die, of love, in the Lang house, Liebhaber plays even more ferociously: "That was the first time, really, that he recognized the seriousness of their game" (93). At this point in the novel, the deck of cards has two orders of meaning, one as a referent to the lives of the players, one as the symbols in the abstract order of the game. Although the men give some credence to her interpretation, having "never seen their cards in quite that way before" they would seem, ultimately, to reject the referential possibilities of the deck, concluding that "there was no meaning anywhere in the world" (94).

When they finally move their game from the Lang household to Isadore Heck's shack, they attempt to escape the world of meaning, to leave Old Lady Lang, who believes the cards can have a divinatory function, to move into the shack of Heck, who disbelieves in everything. Only the possibility of love calls them away to the wedding ceremony at the Church of the Final Virgin, though here Eli Wurtz's chance comment, *"du son of a gun"*—so unfit do they look for real life—"causes" them to deal another hand. It is in the basement of the Church that the game is invested with a referential significance by the entry of Marvin Straw.

The desire, first of Liebhaber, then of the whole crew, to save Jerry Lapanne's life invests the game with a purpose it has previously lacked, changing the rules, making them unusually flexible and fluid, even imposing different rules on different players. It would almost seem that this flexibility, the cracks in the otherwise rigid society, allows the entry of Martin Lang's ghost into their midst, as if to say 'This is what happens when you relax the rules a little: the unpredictable bursts in on you,' leaving the players "totally without hope" (113), except in their belief that Skandl will return. When they are told by Vera that Skandl has disappeared, we see the extent that they have created an isolated world for themselves. Liebhaber does not want to believe in Skandl's death because it will force him to "surrender . . . the world" (123). The creation of insular cosmos of the schmier game has allowed them to ignore what they previously could not control. Playing schmier, their lives structured by other rules and other kinds of chance, they have avoided the unpredictable, natural world, refusing "to give any credence to the weather, especially to the idea of seasons" (123).

The schmier players have, in a parodic way, created a culture, an organization of human beings governed by shared values and established rules. It is a culture designed to insulate them from the unpredictability of the natural world and the domestic hegemony of women.[6] Their culture, however, in its exclusivity and insularity is not, in the long run, "civilized." Ignoring the needs of their bodies and the impact of the weather upon their health, developing a "technology" solely devoted to making moonshine and eating without being involved in the production of their food, ceasing to use tools altogether, their lives are a parody of civilization. When Tiddy comes to seduce them with food, we find Liebhaber "ahead in the game, about to win a few nails and some pieces of broken glass and a pile of round stones they'd dug up from the frozen riverbed with their bare hands" (126). Even the medium of exchange, while still governing their insular culture, has no intrinsic value.

Yet the offerings made by Tiddy suggest that, unpredictable as nature is, it has continued: she has butter, jam, preserves, honey in the comb. It is the women who, as a productive, patient part of the natural world, have transcended, the men who have remained static, imprisoned within the card game that provided the structure of their microcosm.

The schmier game intensifies the binary polarization. At first, it is a time that is pleasant; the women in the kitchen watch over sleeping babies, talk of gardening and sewing, enjoy having the "men in the dining room, out of the way, playing cards" (81). By doing the men's chores, the women allow the players to remain apart from the more demanding "real world"; they allow the separateness of the world of the schmier game and the world of the godgame. Eventually, Tiddy realizes the benefits of the system: "the women were running the world better than had the men; she was content to let them go on with their game of schmier" (85). That the schmier game is meant partly to protect the men from the women is revealed when the men discuss whether or not to attend the wedding of Cathy and Joe Lightning; they consider not going because it will mean "surrendering to the women" (101). Unlike Lecker (104), who believes that the female characters are parodies, I am inclined to see the male characters as parodic. Obviously Kroetsch is "questioning precisely those binary male/female divisions" (Lecker 104), but while the women may seem almost static in their chthonic associations and habits, at least they persist, without damage to themselves or to others; nor do we see their sensuous persistence as quite so ridiculous as the frantic efforts of men to escape what they cannot control or control what they cannot escape. At times I am inclined to see one tension of the novel in terms of two distinct plot types: the plot of the male quest to tame the universe vs the plot of the chthonic woman who is content to "ing." Perhaps Lecker's (male) reading which views the women as "a joke" and my (female) reading which views the men's various ferocious struggles as ridiculous illustrate how the tension of two different types of possible plots deconstruct the novel.

> *Back last night from Castlegar, B.C. Flew in there from Calgary. The plane goes down a river valley, with mountains on both sides, makes a sharp left turn around a jump, a shoulder of mountain, a cliff. We turned. A small plane crossed the landing field when we were almost down. Great surge of engine power. Great surge of adrenaline. Got down next try, and I lectured myself on loving the earth, not the sky. Came time to drive to Fred Wah's mountainside house—a mud slide had closed the road. Had to drive 65 miles to go 15. On the mountain roads. Next day I lectured myself on loving the sky.*
>
> **(CJ** 53)

This conflict between male and female, between quest and persistence, between transcendence and immanence is continued in the war with the sky, which Thomas views as a "parodied 'metaphysical' version of [the] conflict of purpose" between the men who are trying to get to heaven and the "closure of female locus" the men are attempting to escape (Thomas III). But the men's battle is more than an escape from female closure, it is a war fought against time and death and nature, those laws outside our province but which "culture" seeks nevertheless to control with technology. In this war, the sky, the very symbol of transcendence, turns against them as if to indicate the folly of the undertaking.

The death of Skandl is the first symptom of the war between the earth and the sky, Skandl's death in the piper cub mocking his effort at transcendence. The natural world similarly mocks the predictions, already difficult to interpret, of Vera's boy. J. G.'s death indicates the folly of any search for eternity/infinity (symbolized by his figure eights and his agelessness) and escape from time: indeed, J. G.'s seeming physical escape from the kind of time that ages results in the innocent stupidity that allows him to believe he can fly.

The first battle actively fought arises as a result of the men's decision to go hunting rather than to clean up after the salamanders, which they regard as women's work. Yet later they admit that they wanted to avoid, could not face, "the stink of death." In this novel, women deal with death while men attempt to ignore it. Going hunting involves them in another exclusively male society, and another "game," but here nature plays a part and adversely changes the rules: the wind is so high and fierce that the ducks can't get down to the earth, and the ammunition the hunters fire turns on them.

While having a referential tie to the climate of the prairies, the war with the sky illustrates the male characters' second response to the world they cannot control. No war seems to exist as long as the predictions of Vera's boy are accurate, and the farmers believe in a friendly, predictable universe. Once the salamanders remind them of death, as part of the natural cycle of things, once the plague reminds them that nature's overwhelming force is outside the province of their control or prediction, their only response is an aggressive one.

Joe Lightning is one of the few male characters whose attitude toward the war seems sensible: "being the descendent of warriors, he knew when not to fight" (154). Playing, perhaps, with the stereotype of the native as "natural man," Kroetsch creates a character who believes "in the union of elements," and who, rather than antagonistically battling with the sky, seeks to learn its secrets. As a shuffleboard champion, Joe is invested with the obsessive horizontality of the prairie dweller, though unlike the other characters, he brings some skill and purpose to his obsession. His flight with the eagle is all the more heroic because he allows the new, vertical perspective to challenge his expectations and perspectives: "He was surprised at how small the town looked, the once immense town where he'd been ignored, insulted; perhaps the recognition occasioned his first laugh" (157). His fall has the character of ecstasy about it. Although he does not master the sky, he learns something of the truth that Heck glimpsed from his canon, something of the perspective and awe that generates "a version of a prayer, a kind of holy laugh" (159). As one of the first people, it is ironically appropriate that he experiences the Adamic fall into the church outhouse hole. His adventure in the sky does not kill him, however: he is one of the few who takes on the sky without dying—because he does so in a non-adversarial frame of mind. What does kill him is society's unwillingness to rescue him lest they get shit on their Sunday clothes: implying that those who do not war with the sky are outside community, outside society, outside the false "transcendence" of the male characters in the book.

In contrast, Nick Droniuk's accidental death is caused by his raging at the sky for not conforming to Vera's boy's predictions; Eli Wurtz is killed by a train while he hopes the thundershowers predicted by Vera's boy have finally arrived. The train arrives instead. Mick O'Halloran dies of a loss of faith when he finds his oil well is dry: he puts his weight on his missing leg and it fails to support him. Such deaths are caused, however, not so much by the sky's determination to do battle, to be hostile, as by the victims' foolish beliefs that nature is predictable. Their folly is highlighted by their choice of oracles. Nick and Eli, along with the rest of the community, place great faith in the predictions of Vera's boy, in spite of the fact that the narrator makes a point to remark on the unintelligibility of his pronouncements: "The only minor difficulty was that he spoke, always, a language that no one quite understood" (139). One is tempted to recall the Oracle at Delphi, which required expert (and even suspect) interpreters. Even his last "prediction," "The ercilessmay unsay shall urnbay us," (144), is a description only of the present, not of the future. It is, in short, the community's need to believe that the natural world is predictable, thereby giving them some mode of control or controlled response, that causes the deaths attributed to the sky. Meanwhile, the prairies are simply going on as the prairies, predictable only in their unpredictability and their harshness.

Their other oracle, the crow, is no more reliable. Our narrative experience of the crow is of a rather filthy-mouthed bird whose most common oracular pronouncement is "total asshole." He does, indeed, curse the people with abnormal deaths—which come true (with the notable exception of Liebhaber). He understands Vera Lang's relationship to the natural world; when Liebhaber does not, the crow suggests that Liebhaber kill himself. In short, the crow curses and belittles: he is not oracular. Yet in the midst of the first battle with the sky, "the black crow was first quoted as an authority. Men asked each other, what did the crow say about the flight of birds in a high wind? What did it say about salamanders? They wished the crow hadn't left them; they wanted to ask all the questions they'd neglected to ask while the crow was in their midst. And even while the crow had been talking, meditative and wise, they'd neglected to listen, they realized. Now and then someone claimed to quote the black crow on the subject of women or guns" (152).

In short, is it the same quest for meaning, known causality, predictability—for truth—that catapulted them into the schmier game that now launches the battle with the sky. If manly separation into a more predictable, ordered world of cards and drink is no longer possible, then aggression, downright war is a second-best alternative. They want the world to have a coherent meaning, and in typical patriarchal fashion think of beating it into submission.

Liebhaber's quest for immortality, which he believes capturing the truth will bestow on him, is present at the outset. It hinges upon his ability to fix truth with a certainty that he attributes to Heck toward the novel's close, when Heck so officiously proclaims that someone left his canon out in the rain, ruining it: "Liebhaber was indignant: no man could be certain of anything on this lunatic, spun and dying planet. Heck was unyielding; he had guessed the way to heaven" (206–7). For Liebhaber, language is one of the possible vehicles of truth: in an earlier endeavor he had tried to reach truth by composing "absolutely true accounts of events; he would print only one copy before distributing the eight-point type back to its comforting chaos" (67–8). For some reason, this habit of Liebhaber's makes me recall the old "if a tree falls in a forest and no one hears it" question. Certainly, this approach to truth does not satisfy Liebhaber, for it is made in isolation from community; he is soon back on Tiddy's farm, perfecting the three-titted cow. Yet while language is here presented as an agency of truth, and hence immortality, Liebhaber also views it as part of what binds him to death (54); Kroetsch's text suggests, however, that Liebhaber comes closer to the truth when he claims that Gutenberg is the evil agent of language's death-like grasp.

Print fixes: by recording a symbolic representation of the past, it makes memory irrelevant (116); it organizes, through the alphabet, much of our life, subjecting us to the "tyranny of rote" (68). Once again, the male/female binary is evoked with respect to this ambivalent fascination with print: "It is his *men* who are print-oriented, who are therefore maimed and destroyed by their need to imprint themselves in a visual manner on their place and time. His women, earthy and fecund, exist in another world, one closer to the natural yet ritualized continuity of folk traditions" (Hutcheon 54). For the female characters, language has a fluidity, a flexibility that it does not possess for men, indicated by their use of the expression "It's snowing." These words have a metonymic as well as literal meaning, given that they signalled Tiddy's first moments of desire after her husband's death, and her subsequent impregnation by Skandl/Liebhaber. Thereafter, they indicate her daughter's pregnancies.

Only fear of death frees Liebhaber from Gutenberg's curse, without which "he would have lived another life" (163). Yet, under his boat, believing that he is about to drown, believing that he's free of Gutenberg and movable (or immovable?) type, he makes an effort to "write his own story, at last. He tried again, working with furious intent: *Enough would be enough.* He liked that. He could account for events, announce the presence of design, under the apparent chaos. *Enough.* That one, sufficient word, so neatly balanced against itself. He had no idea how long he'd been under the hull. Perhaps it was night now. Surely someone would miss him. All night he would type; everything set, everything forgotten. But now he had escaped; he had recovered the night, a dream, and memory. He would compose a novel one sentence long, a novel anyone could memorize. *You in my arms.* Yes, that would do it. He tested for revision, recited the four words . . ." (163–4).

The scene strongly suggests that it is not language that is problematic, for it is to language, to story, that Liebhaber turns in the moment he believes to be a prelude to his death. What he is free of is not language, but the tyranny of convention, here symbolized by the fixedness of type and its immutable record of the "past," and overcome by Liebhaber's evocative, suggestive texts that swell with but do not limit meaning. At the outset of the novel, he remembers the future, and he could then and there have typeset Martin Lang's death, except that he feels the possibilities to snatch Lang out of his own story seem lessened if the record already exists. Yet the experiences of Lang and Lapanne suggest that people cannot be snatched from their stories; that their life-narrative continues regardless of Liebhaber's attempt to avert Lang's freezing and Lapanne's hanging. Like the post-modern writer, Liebhaber is trapped by the self-generated direction of narration, in spite of his efforts either to subvert or follow the conventions.

Liebhaber's ambivalent approach to linguistic meaning echoes or influences (one is not sure of the causal relationship here) his approach to the war with the sky, which expresses love as well as war. The canon used to shoot the fertilising bees is certainly as phallic as it is martial. The rain-coated and hail-encased bees suggest a kind of literal "seeding" of the clouds that gives the water vapor a centre to cluster around until it becomes heavy enough to produce rain. On a second level, however, the canonade of bees is symbolic of the sexual act, almost partaking of the conventional in its symbolism. It is the expression of paradoxical war and truce, rage and love. By articulating the paradox of Liebhaber's response to nature, the canonade symbolizes acceptance of nature's own, indifferent, paradoxical role in life and death, in time and timelessness.

The acceptance of death at the novel's close frees Liebhaber from the tyrannies that have so preoccupied him: he admits that Gutenberg is only a scribe and that the agent of tyranny is not print or language, but the way they are inscribed, with believed absolutism, by humans. He cannot quite understand what the crow says (217), now not needing to attribute meaning wherever possible.

Emphasizing this acceptance, he lies in Tiddy's bed, contented, knowing "after all, he is only dying" (217)—evoking the Renaissance pun on dying—and thereby language's exuberant refusal to be fixed by Gutenberg or anyone else. Finally, time itself seems free from absolutes: Gladys's daughter bounces her ball off the housewall and Grandma Lang is breaking the sprouts off the potatoes, as she is at the novel's outset, evoking the cyclicality of time, its crafty ability to turn back on and repeat itself. At the same time, however, human memory allows for the collapse of time so that, lying in bed with Liebhaber, "Tiddy remembered everything. She could hardly tell her memory from the moment; all her life she'd meant to write something down" (214). But because she has not succumbed to the conventions of chronology by fixing her story, her experience is endowed with a spontaneous richness:

> Tiddy, then, taking every man who had ever loved her. It was dark outside. The tower of ice, in the depths of her present mind, flared a crystal white. The white tower was almost blue. He had been so huge, John Skandl; he smelled of horses. Her husband was plowing the snow. His arms upraised against the night, against the held and invisible horses, his hair alive in the combing wind. Those same men who had loved her. Liebhaber: 'Whoa.' . . . She is living for the moment. She kisses Liebhaber, hard. And hard. He, the having lover, thirty-three minutes in one best trial. Tiddy was proud of him. "Now," she said. "Now. No. Now. Child. Husband. Son. Brother. Old man. Friend. Helper. Enemy Lover.
>
> (215–6)
>
> *I deconstruct even after I've come to the end of deconstruction:*
>
> (**CJ** 67)

Kroetsch's text ultimately *means* not to expect/impose/attribute meaning (carelessly?). To do so is to trust unworthy oracles, to depend on the undependable, finally to be part of one's own wounding or demise in one's war with a world that does not operate according to "human" rules. To accept the ambiguities of life, to accept, for instance, that one is only dying, or to "live for the moment" frees one from the fruitless quest for meaning, locates one in a rich present that contains within itself the past and the future.

The novel does, as it were, deconstruct itself as the conclusions that we draw about the text—beware of expecting/imposing meaning—must ultimately be turned loose on the text itself. What the crow actually said was not particularly important or insightful: what about what Kroetsch said? The novel might indeed be said to express the post-modern angst of writing against the sense what one creates has no (fixed) meaning. It might equally well be said that the novel expresses the playfulness released when one is freed from the "temptation of meaning." Or, like Liebhaber's three "illogical" sentences composed as an attempt to escape the fixedness of print, **What the Crow Said** might also be said to express the exuberance of language, narrative, and myth that results not in meaninglessness, but in manymeaning. In his **Crow Journals**, Kroetsch writes "I am sick of the tyranny of narrative. And fascinated by the narrative that I'm creating. And that's the whole story" (67). In a very real way, that ambivalence is the whole story behind both the writing of **What the Crow Said** and Kroetsch's own struggle with his postmodern view.

Notes

1. Robert Kroetsch's non-fiction will be cited parenthetically in the text, using the following abbreviations: LV for *Labyrinths of Voice*, and CJ for *Crow Journals*. References to *What the Crow Said* will appear with page numbers alone.

2. I speak here of improbabilities in the logical sense, in the sense that in order to avoid committing the causal fallacy one must be able explain the way in which the cause produced the effect. We cannot, for example, determine how Eli Wurtz's comment *caused* the game of schmier. Yet within the context of the novel, the causal sequences do not always seem improbable.

3. Kroetsch has commented on the problematic relationship between art and world in *Labyrinths of Voice*: "Yet we do draw from the world: the great novels, in some way, are drawn from the world. Now *how* they are drawn from the world is the question? It isn't just a question of illusion or mimesis or anything like that. It *is* a question of axioms. . . . Finally, I don't believe that art is completely removed from nature, but I don't know what the hell nature becomes in art. . . . One thing that used to trouble me was the way in which so many readers and writers didn't see the game dimension at all. They made a simple equation between literature and reality. I argued for game theory in order to correct that over-simplification. Yet at this point I am somewhat worried about my own sense of divorce from that equation, from mimesis. One is always moving back and forth between positions." Kroetsch's final comment upon this dilemma is that "I would suggest that the fascinating place is right between the two"—between, that is, game and mimesis" (72–3).

4. The following passage from *The Second Sex* aptly describes the culturally determined roles of immanence and transcendence Simone de Beauvoir attributes to women and men, roles which are echoed in Kroetsch's novel: "[Woman's] role was only nourishing, never creative. In no domain did she create; she maintained the life of the tribe by giving it children and bread, nothing more. She remained doomed to immanence, incarnating only the static aspect of society, closed in upon itself. Whereas man went on monopolizing the functions which threw open that society toward nature and toward the rest of humanity. The only employments worthy of him were war, hunting, fishing; he made conquest of foreign booty and bestowed it on the tribe; war, hunting, and fishing represented an expansion of existence, its projection toward the world. The male remained alone the incarnation of transcendence. He did not as yet have the practical means for wholly dominating Woman-Earth; as yet he did not dare to stand up against her—but already he desired to break away from her." (83)

5. See the concept of naturalization in Jonathan Culler's *Structuralist Poetics*.

6. Kroetsch himself identifies the quest as a flight from women and from their social and erotic hegemony. See *The Crow Journals*, 20.

Works Cited

Culler, Jonathan. *Structuralist Poetics: Structuralism, Linguistics, and the Study of Literature*. London: Routledge & Kegan Paul, 1975.

Culler, Jonathan. *On Deconstruction: Theory and Criticism after Structuralism*. Ithaca, N.Y.: Cornell UP, 1982.

De Beauvoir, Simone. *The Second Sex*. New York: Vintage, 1974.

Hutcheon, Linda. *The Canadian Postmodern: A Study of Contemporary English-Canadian Fiction*. Toronto: Oxford, 1988.

Kroetsch, Robert. *The Crow Journals*. Edmonton: NeWest, 1980.

———. *What the Crow Said*. Toronto: General, 1978.

Lecker, Robert. *Robert Kroetsch*. Boston: Twayne, 1980.

Lernout, Geert. "Twenty-Five Years of Solitude." *Canadian Literature*, 104 (Spring 1985), 52–64.

Neuman, Shirley, and Robert Wilson. *Labyrinths of Voice: Conversations with Robert Kroetsch*. Edmonton: NeWest, 1982.

Thomas, Peter. *Robert Kroetsch*. Vancouver: Douglas & McIntyre, 1980.

Walker, Barbara. *The Woman's Encyclopedia of Myths and Secrets*. New York: Harper & Row, 1983.

Weedon, Chris. *Poststructuralist Theory and Feminist Practice*. Oxford: Basil Blackwell, 1987.

Manina Jones (essay date 1992)

SOURCE: "Rooting the Borrowed Word: Appropriation and Voice in Kroetsch's *Seed Catalogue*," in *Inside the Poem: Essays and Poems in Honour of Donald Stephens*, 1992, pp. 113-22.

[*In the following essay, Jones discusses the problem of finding an authentic Canadian voice in "Seed Catalogue."*]

> "Once upon a time he was a gardener of the possible fruition."
>
> (Kroetsch, *Completed Field Notes*, 255)

LYRE, LYRE, PANTS ON FIRE

Robert Kroetsch's essay **"Unhiding the Hidden"** begins with an expression of the desire for—and the impossibility of producing—genuinely "original" writing in Canada, that is, writing rooted entirely in its place of origin, writing that speaks with a singular Canadian voice. "The particular predicament" of the Canadian writer, as Kroetsch describes it, is that he[1] doesn't really live in a new world, but inherits a pre-existent linguistic and experiential grounding from elsewhere: "he works with a language, within a literature, that appears to be authentically his

own, and not a borrowing," but which, no matter how familiar it may initially seem, is in fact borrowed (17):

> The Roman writer borrowed a Greek word into a Latin context. The Canadian writer borrows an English word into an English-language context, a French word into a French-language context. The process of rooting that borrowed word, that totally exact homonym, in authentic experience, is then, must be, a radical one.
>
> (18)

Kroetsch reiterates the problem in his essay **"No Name Is My Name"**: "The Canadian writer in English must speak a new culture not with new names but with an abundance of names inherited from Britain and the United States. And that predicament is in turn doubled—by the writing done in the French language in Canada" (51). Despite the "Adamic impulse" Kroetsch sees as characteristic of the literature of a "new place" (**"No Name,"** 41), then, the Canadian writer is no Adam in a New World garden, speaking a pristine language and simply naming the world into existence; his predicament (the word is used in both essays) is that his language and his world are *prae-dicare*, already spoken forth.

Kroetsch's speculation on the problem of Canadian voice in both these essays fails to recognize a number of issues, not the least of which might include the different predicaments of Canadian writers whose first language is neither English nor French, or that of First Nations writers for whom the geography now designated as Canada is not a "new place" at all. What Kroetsch at least potentially does identify is a kind of postcolonial political struggle at the level of the sign. Even more generally, his essays skirt the possibility that the Canadian writer's predicament is a particular version of every language-user's struggle with what Mikhail Bakhtin describes as the always "'already bespoke quality of the world,'" which is tied up with "the 'already uttered' quality of language" itself (331):

> Language is not a neutral medium that passes freely and easily into the private property of the speaker's intentions; it is populated—overpopulated—with the intentions of others. Expropriating it, forcing it to submit to one's own intentions and accents, is a difficult and complicated process.
>
> (294)

This "dialogic inter-orientation with the alien word," Bakhtin notes, significantly, is a condition of speaking that could have been escaped only by "the mythical Adam, who approached a virginal and as yet verbally unqualified world with the first word" (279). Bakhtin condemns poetry—implicitly lyric poetry, which presumes to speak with an individual voice, for a unitary consciousness and single intention—as the form least capable of evoking the dialogic process. The language of the (lyric) poet, according to Bakhtin, aspires to be Adamic, appears to be his own: "he makes use of each form, each word, each expression according to its unmediated power to assign meaning (as it were, 'without quotation marks') that is, as a pure and direct expression of his own intention" (285).[2]

Kroetsch's **"Seed Catalogue"** is a poem that is self-conscious about putting quotation marks and their equivalents into poetry. Quotation marks and various inferential agents[3] indicate the appropriation of the words of others from elsewhere and their insertion into the poem, drawing attention to—and celebrating—the *mediated* assigning of meaning, the *im*pure, *in*direct nature of expression. Shirley Neuman has described the conspicuously intertextual result of this strategy in Kroetsch's poetry. The "intertext" (Kroetsch's term) is "the space shared by the relations between different poetic texts in the frame of a larger 'Collected Poem.' The 'poem' exists in the lacunae and intersections between the different texts it holds in its space" ("Allow self," 115). "Poetic text" is, in the case of **"Seed Catalogue,"** clearly a relative designation, since it encompasses much material that leads another life as discursive prose. **"Seed Catalogue"** is, in Neuman's term, a "collected poem," because it is a poem whose constituent elements are obviously collected from elsewhere.

Inorganic Gardening

Despite the garden imagery that permeates **"Seed Catalogue,"** then, it is a text that resists the myth of organic form, according to which a poem grows "naturally" and homogeneously from the innate properties of its material and the personality of the poet. **"Seed Catalogue"** begins, for example, by drawing attention to the fact that it has already begun. It opens, not with the words of the poet, but with a citation from a seed catalogue advertising "Copenhagen Market Cabbage" (32), whose name reinforces its status both as a vegetable strain "foreign" to Canadian soil, and as an instance of the "alien word," an imported textual product. While the poem begins, naturally enough, with the label "I," the citation itself is tagged "No. 176," emphasizing a slippage or discontinuity between "inside" and "outside" texts.

Each textual component of the poem is, to use a figure associated with gardening, "grafted" onto the larger body. The term "graft" is employed in Arturo Schwartz's description of what he terms (recalling Dadaist practice in the visual arts) the "printed ready-made," an extract of a printed text introduced by the poet into his composition: "Such intervention is of botanic nature: it has affinity with the grafting practised by the gardener to modify the flower or fruit of a plant" (29). This intervention may be of a botanic nature, but it is not, strictly speaking, organic. Indeed, the method is also a "graft" in the sense that the poet illicitly "plays dirty" with the poetic conventions of both lyric voice and organic form.

In **"Seed Catalogue,"** further, it is impossible to sustain an opposition between "rooted" and "grafted" texts. E. D. Blodgett identifies as dialogic—or what he terms "interdiscursive"—the effect of this strategy: "the various texts become commentaries for each other" (202). **"Seed Catalogue,"** then, is a choric locus, or what Kroetsch calls a "shared book" (**"Statement,"** 311), but not only because it is a communal document that incorporates other people's words. The individual word is opened up and multiplied, and lyric voice itself is exposed as a fiction. The poem thus provides a provocative response to the linguistic dilemma posed in the two Kroetsch essays cited at the beginning of this article: it is literally pro-vocative in its teasing out of a multiplicity of voices using the "inherited word." In **"Seed Catalogue,"** Kroetsch, significantly, *finds* (rather than originates) a response precisely by the repetition of inherited language, with a significant difference. Instead of attempting to replace the borrowed word—repeatability, as Derrida demonstrates, is a feature of writing (179–80), so that replacing "used" language is an impossibility—**"Seed Catalogue"** suggests a re-placing or resituating of it through citation. A citation is by definition a text that has precisely the same form as its historical antecedent; it is, in the words of **"Unhiding the Hidden,"** a "totally exact homonym" that "reroots" the word by excerpting and contextually rerouting it.

In **"The Moment of the Discovery of America Continues,"** Kroetsch describes the "translation" of the 1917 seed catalogue he found in the Glenbow archives in 1975 into the poem **"Seed Catalogue"** as one such rerouting/rerooting (11). This "idiomatic" movement, in which the poet is as much an interpreter of the given text as an originating speaker, is clearly one version of "homolinguistic translation," a poetic tactic Douglas Barbour identifies with the denial of the lyric impulse (58). In **"Seed Catalogue"** homolinguistic translation has the effect of producing a heterogeneous poetic voice which emanates, not from an "original" poetic speaker, but from within the already spoken or written local, communal language of the prairie town. **"Seed Catalogue"** repeatedly inquires into the origin and development of the poetic speaker—*How do you grow a poet?*" (41, 42, 43, 44)—but as Blodgett comments in his discussion of Kroetsch's **The Ledger**, the appropriation of "outside texts" into the poem prevents the poetic totalization of language, the exclusive valorizing of voice as monologic presence (200), because the "origin" of the "text" is another text. Indeed, to return to the Edenic scenario proposed earlier, **"Seed Catalogue"** not only parodies the myth of the Fall, as Smaro Kamboureli observes (112), but also parodies by textualizing the myth of an Edenic, "original" language. The poem is writing about writing about the desire for, the imagination of, as-yet-unrealized gardens: "Into the dark of January / the seed catalogue bloomed // a winter proposition, if / spring should come, then" (33).[4] It is the seed catalogue, and not a garden that blooms forth here. The implied duplication of the poem's title (**"Seed Catalogue"**/seed catalogue) is a reminder—indeed, an epitome—of the textual, citational nature of the poem's affiliation with the "outside" that it literally reproduces. The title's doubleness also signals the ambivalent relationship between prosaic and poetic texts that **"Seed Catalogue"** sustains.

One response **"Seed Catalogue"** provides to the question *How do you grow a poet?*" (42) consists of a list of prescriptions that again contradicts the idea of an original, Adamic lyric speaker. The list humorously indicates not only the obvious necessity that the poet's physical well-being be maintained, but also suggests the importance to the poet of an already written inheritance of language, and the pre-scripted nature of the linguistic utterance itself. **"Seed Catalogue"**'s prescriptions incorporate local wisdom about spiritual and physical health into the poem, re-reading and revaluing the "prosaic" regional idiom:

> For appetite: cod-liver
> oil.
> For bronchitis: mustard
> plasters.
> For pallor and failure to fill
> the woodbox: sulphur
> & molasses.
> For self-abuse: ten Our
> Fathers & ten Hail Marys.
> For regular bowels: Sunny Boy
> Cereal.
>
> (42)

The question *"How do you grow a gardener?"* doubles the query about growing a poet. The former question is followed earlier in the poem by a listing of seed-names (34), and the parallel implies a correspondence between poet and gardener, gardener's seeds and poet's prescriptions: words themselves. Indeed, the Derridean association between the Latin word for seed, *seme*, and the Greek for sign, *sema*, is persistently evoked in **"Seed Catalogue."** This is, significantly, a false etymology, an apparently original "root" connection that turns out to be a purely textual one.

When the question *"How do you grow a poet?"* is again posed, the response takes the form of another foregrounded prescription, the citation of a product testimonial from the seed catalogue: "'It's a pleasure to advise that I / won the First Prize at the Calgary / Horticultural Show . . . This is my / first attempt. I used your seeds'" (42). The seed catalogue is a publication that provides a kind of local forum—it places on display (in order to profit from) the statements of its community of correspondents. So too does the **"Seed Catalogue,"** but the poem encourages a generically (at least) double reading. The happy gardener of the prose citation is, in effect, already a poet and doesn't know it ("advise" and "Prize," for example, are rhymes)— **"Seed Catalogue"** shows it. The gardener's "first attempt" at horticulture is not primal ("I used your seeds"), and neither is the poet's citational gesture original. The writer of the testimonial letter in the seed catalogue and its re-writer, the poet of **"Seed Catalogue,"** achieve a "spectacular" success based, in effect, on the fruitfulness of someone else's prior seminal product . . .

Now, List-en Here

. . . And on their own ability to tend seeds and attend to words, respectively. The poet in this context must be an avid listener to language: "My mother said: / Did you wash your ears? / You could grow cabbages / in those ears" (32). It should be noted that these lines are themselves a citation, a linguistic inheritance from the poet's mother—they are juxtaposed with a quotation from the seed catalogue (another vernacular inheritance) that describes the Copenhagen Market Cabbage in terms of genealogy: "[it] is in every respect a *thoroughbred*, a *cabbage* of *highest pedigree*" (32). The poet, because he has attended to the metaphorical resonances of the language of the catalogue, has recognized its "poetic" potential, "transplanted" it into the poem, and allowed it to grow in significance.

This passage about the poet's ears might elicit recollections of the poet in William Carlos Williams' *Paterson*, a similarly fecund character whose voice is also both interrogated and interrogatory: "His ears are toadstools, his fingers have begun to sprout leaves (his voice is drowned under the falls)" (83). Williams' poem is a kind of pre-text for **"Seed Catalogue"** in its "listening" to and poetic recitation of the language of locality, its use of unassimilated citations to generate a localized voice and sense of place. *Paterson* cites Ezra Pound's comment on Williams' refusal of formal closure in his poems: "Your interest is in the bloody loam but what / I'm after is the finished product" (37). The poets of both *Paterson* and **"Seed Catalogue"** have what amounts to a "dirty mind": they provide a fertile matrix for the growth of given germs of meaning. **"Seed Catalogue"**'s interest in the "growth of the poet's mind," as Shirley Neuman perceives, places it in relation to Wordsworth's *The Prelude* as well ("Allow self," 121). The poet's mind in Kroetsch's text, however, is not presented as the source of an integral voice, but as a locus of textual intersection.[5]

What does remain of the lyric impulse in **"Seed Catalogue"** is an openness to, and foregrounding of, what Northrop Frye calls lyrical "babble" (275), in everyday speech, a playful affirmation of the singing voice of language, its musical possibilities that border on nonsense: "I don't give a damn if I do die do die do die do die do die / do die do die do die do die do die do die do / die do / die do die do die do die do die do die do die do / die do die / do" (40). The words of this silly—but memorable—little ditty are, ironically, about the defiance of death. Their musical sound functions typically as a mnemonic device, demonstrating the "death-defying" ability of language to survive over time through the significant poetic gesture of recitation. **"Seed Catalogue"** is not just a "collected poem," then; it is also a re-collected poem, in which recitation is a method of translating "then" to "now," of "seeding/time" (44), or growing a past: *"But how do you grow a poet?* // Start: with an invocation / invoke—// His muse is / his muse/if / memory is"* (41). The word itself is a kind of muse, and voicing it is in itself both an inspiration and a remembering. Implicit in the word "muse," for example, is a connection between inspiration, the musical, mnemonic elements of language, and the poet's meditative musings: "no memory then / no meditation / no song (shit / we're up against it)" (41).

An s-catalogue-ical Poetics

The last lines of this passage seem to emphasize the poet's limitations, which are elaborated at length in the list that catalogues "the absence of . . ." various commodities and qualities in the prairie milieu (39). **"Seed Catalogue,"** however, not only counteracts but subverts such limitations by producing what might be seen as a productively excremental vision (what more fertile place is there than up against shit?), in its poetically unconventional emphasis on the colloquial bawdy/body and its functions; in its formal recycling, via a citational strategy, of what might normally be considered a corpus of verbal refuse; and in its oral folk-tale or "bullshitting" impulse. Scatological imagery, for example, is used to describe the kind of record or trace that the poet leaves in his passage through the landscape:

> only a scarred
> page, a spoor of wording
> a reduction to mere black
>
> and white/a pile of rabbit
> turds that tells us
> all spring long
> where the track was.
>
> (43)

The poet of **"Seed Catalogue"** tracks down accounts of the past, leaving a literally documentary record that is the trace of a trace of a communal past: this is, notably, "a pile of rabbit / turds that *tells us*" (emphasis added). In a poem named for a seed catalogue, "spoor" inevitably resonates with the botanical "spore," and evokes the textual process of dissemination, a sowing/scattering-about of meaning, a planting that is limitlessly transplanted.

Early on in the poem, **"Seed Catalogue"** makes a connection between its scatological preoccupation, the notion of poetry as song, and the language of the seed catalogue:

> No. 25—*McKenzie's Improved Golden Wax Bean*:
> "THE MOST PRIZED OF ALL BEANS. *Virtue* is its own reward. We have had *many expressions* from *keen discriminating gardeners extolling our seed* and *this variety*."
>
> Beans, beans,
> the musical fruit;
> the more you eat,
> the more you virtue.
>
> (33)

Virtue, it would seem, is its own re-word. This popular children's rhyme about flatulence (which is, after all, like the folk tradition of the tall tale, an expulsion of "hot air") is (re)cited, and itself takes in the language of the seed catalogue, censoring the traditional last word of the verse in favour of the more decorous, but nonsensical "virtue." Few readers of the poem, however, would forget that the conventional last word is the musical word, the word that rhymes, "toot." Beans—and, by humourous extension, the

linguistic endowment of the poet's past—are both extolled and re-told/tolled (or resounded), with a difference.

What's New?

In a 1978 article on Kroetsch's poetry, Susan Wood expresses what is essentially a dissatisfaction with the unconventional nature of this strategy, or what she calls Kroetsch's "wavering" in **"Seed Catalogue"** between prose and poetry, as well as his unwillingness "to transcend the prairie town reality, which he records in its flat colloquial language. . . . We've 'heard it' before, so what's new?" (36). Wood, in effect, restates the problem of originality, and relates it to the poem's indeterminate genre. One effect of the generic instability Wood identifies is the possibility that the "flat colloquial language" used might be seen as a kind of prose poetry in its ability to voice a prairie colloquy. It is not, according to the logic of the poem, necessary to "transcend" prairie town reality in order to read it as "poetic." In fact, **"Seed Catalogue"** offers the possibility that it is necessary only to repeat that colloquial language in a new context, to (aesthetically) frame it with quotation marks, to (poetically) re-cite it.

The poem stresses its own reliance on the oral tradition of re-sounding old phrases and stories, a tradition in which the storyteller is not an "original," but remembers, elaborates on, and recontextualizes a legacy of stories: "—You ever hear the one about the woman who buried / her husband with his ass sticking out of the ground / so that every time she happened to walk by she could / give it a swift kick? //—Yeh, I heard it" (40). This "dirty" joke presents yet another twist on the botanical metaphor of "planting." Not only is the anecdote strategically "planted" in the poem by the canny poet, the joke is that finality is again spurned through an act of iteration, since the wife in the story always gets another kick at the can. As does the storyteller: the punchline of *his* joke is the listener's response, which draws attention to the context of reiterated telling. Or, to put it another way, response is, in this context, the "kicker."

Re-seeding Heir-lines

"Seed Catalogue" represents another incident in which the speaker's father tells and retells the story of his shooting at a badger, allowing the tale to conform, not simply to his original intention when he shot at the badger, but to his reconstruction of intention with each recontextualized telling. In the first version of the story, the poet's father shoots at the badger, but misses and mistakenly hits a magpie, "A week later," however, "my father told the story again. In that version he intended to hit the magpie. Magpies, he explained, are a nuisance" (35). In the context of the oral folk-tale, intention is not simply a prior design, a predetermined, immutable meaning; it is, *pace* Wordsworth, a postludic act, a playful reinterpretation of the given verbal text. In the interview ***Labyrinths of Voice***, Kroetsch points out both the importance of the linguistic inheritance of the past, and the danger of "the heirloom model for inherited stories," which suggests that the past is "a fixed thing": "I suppose that is one of the things print did to us: we suddenly have a fixed text. I'm still tempted by oral models where the story in the act of retelling is always responsive to individuals, to the place, to invention" (13). The re-telling of received stories in **"Seed Catalogue"** unfixes the given text, gesturing toward certain characteristics of the oral tradition, and placing the poet in what appears to be a long (story/genetic) line of prairie bullshitters. His recontextualized telling of the father's story allows yet another range of possible inflections, but it also allows the accents of his father's voice to remain: the badger "was digging holes in the potato patch, threatening man and beast with broken limbs (I *quote*)" (35, emphasis added).

Since "will" or intention is something shown to be less than final in the inheritance of the past, the inclusion in the poem of a "last will and testament" must be seen as ironic indeed. What is inherited in that will, however, is not simply the material objects that it represents—"*To my son Frederick my carpenter tools*" (47)—but also the language of the document that is simultaneously prosaically familiar and poetically defamiliarized. **"Seed Catalogue"** uses the materials at hand—the will, the seed catalogue, letters, and other inherited texts—in order to reconstruct and revalue the local past, a past on which the present community depends for its existence. It is significant, then, that when the question, "*How do you grow a prairie town?*" is posed, the response provided—"Rebuild the hotel when it burns down. Bigger. Fill it / full of a lot of A-1 Hard Northern Bullshitters" (40)—allies the notion of reconstruction with the exaggerating impulse of the tall tale as "bullshit." It also, significantly, names storytellers after a local variety of a seed ("A-1 Hard Northern").

The poet's father passes on the narrative tradition of the tall tale. It is his mother, however, who subtly alerts the poet—as well as the poem's reader—to the traces of semiotic multiplicity in the most mundane of expressions. The poet in/of **"Seed Catalogue"** listens carefully to the inherited words of the (m)other, the voice that is at once familiar and alien, and represents it: "Bring me the radish seeds, / my mother whispered" (33). "Radish" is a word whose root is "root," and "seeds" a word whose meaning is, at least in the false etymology already suggested, "meaning." **"Seed Catalogue"** represents a search for roots and meanings, and, inevitably, a search for roots *as* meanings. This "radical" approach means that the poem is not simply a nostalgic return to an original Garden, or even a garden, but rather, as the title of the larger work of which it is a part indicates, the prolific yield of a "field" of "notes."

Notes

0. I would like to thank Susan Rudy Dorscht for her valuable advice on this paper.

1. The gendered pronoun is Kroetsch's. I have maintained it for the sake of consistency.

2. For a discussion of the difficulties Bakhtin encounters in trying to maintain the ultimately untenable binary opposition novel/(lyric) poetry, particularly when his theories about the dialogized nature of consciousness and the internally dialogized quality of the word itself are taken into account, see Tzvetan Todorov's *Mikhail Bakhtin: The Dialogical Principle*.

3. Julia Kristeva calls "inferential agents" words that mediate between the author's enunciation and that of others, such as "if, *as* Vergil *says* . . ." "and *thereupon* Saint Jerome *says*," etc. (see pp. 45–6). As E. D. Blodgett implies, spatial arrangement in "Seed Catalogue" might be considered an inferential agent, since it too designates the enunciation of others (202).

4. All references to "Seed Catalogue" are in Kroetsch's *Completed Field Notes*.

5. For more on *Field Notes* and autobiography, see both Neuman articles listed in the Works Cited, and Susan Rudy Dorscht's "On Sending Yourself: Kroetsch and the New Autobiography."

Works Cited

Bakhtin, Mikhail. *The Dialogic Imagination: Four Essays*. Caryl Emerson and Michael Holquist, trans., Michael Holquist, ed. Austin: Univ. of Texas Press, 1981.

Barbour, Douglas. "Lyric/Anti-Lyric: Some Notes About a Concept." *Line*, 3 (Spring 1984): 45–63.

Blodgett, E. D. "The Book, Its Discourse, and the Lyric: Notes on Robert Kroetsch's *Field Notes*." *Open Letter*, 5th Series, 8–9 (Summer-Fall 1984): 195–205.

Derrida, Jacques. "Signature Event Context." Samuel Weber and Jeffrey Mehlman, trans. *Glyph I*. Baltimore: Johns Hopkins Univ. Press, 1977: 172–97.

Dorscht, Susan Rudy. "On Sending Yourself: Kroetsch and the New Autobiography." *Signature*, 2 (Winter 1989): 27–41.

Frye, Northrop. *Anatomy of Criticism: Four Essays*. Princeton: Princeton Univ. Press, 1957.

Kamboureli, Smaro. *On the Edge of Genre: The Contemporary Canadian Long Poem*. Toronto: Univ. of Toronto Press, 1991.

Kristeva, Julia. *Desire in Language: A Semiotic Approach to Literature and Art*. New York: Columbia Univ. Press, 1980.

Kroetsch, Robert. *Completed Field Notes: The Long Poems of Robert Kroetsch*. Toronto: McClelland and Stewart, 1989.

———. "The Moment of the Discovery of America Continues." *The Lovely Treachery of Words: Essays Selected and New*. Toronto: Oxford, 1989: 1–20.

———. "No Name Is My Name." *The Lovely Treachery of Words*, 41–52.

———. "Reciting the Emptiness." *The Lovely Treachery of Words*, 34–40.

———. "Statement by the Poet." *The Long Poem Anthology*. Michael Ondaatje, ed. Toronto: Coach House, 1979: 311–12.

———. "Unhiding the Hidden." *Open Letter*, 5th Series, 4 (Spring 1983): 17–22.

———. Shirley Neuman and Robert Wilson. *Labyrinths of Voice: Conversations with Robert Kroetsch*. Edmonton: NeWest, 1982.

Neuman, Shirley. "Allow self, portraying self: Autobiography in *Field Notes.*" *Line*, 1.2 (Fall 1983): 104–21.

———. "Figuring the Reader, Figuring the Self in *Field Notes*: Double or Noting." *Open Letter*, 5th Series, 8–9 (Summer-Fall 1984): 176–94.

Schwartz, Arturo. "Contributions to a Poetic of the Ready-made." John A. Stevens, trans. *Marcel Duchamp: Ready-mades, etc. (1918–1964)*. Paris: le Terrain Vague, 1964: 13–41.

Todorov, Tzvetan. *Mikhail Bakhtin: The Dialogical Principle*. Vlad Godzich, trans. Minneapolis: Univ. of Minnesota Press, 1984.

Williams, William Carlos. *Paterson*. New York: New Directions, 1963.

Wood, Susan. "Reinventing the Word: Kroetsch's Poetry." *Canadian Literature*, 77 (Summer 1978): 28–39.

Martin Kuester (essay date 1992)

SOURCE: "Kroetsch's Fragments: Approaching the Narrative Structure of His Novels," in *Postmodern Fiction in Canada*, 1992, pp. 137-60.

[*In the following essay, Kuester presents an overview of the narrative techniques used in Kroetsch's novels.*]

In this age of postmodernism, the belief in a coherent world governed by logically derived laws of causality has given way to a cosmology seeing man in a shattered world of fragments. In the late 1960s and 1970s, the concept of postmodernism stressing the disorientation of the individual (and the artist) in such a fragmented world, was applied to literature by American critics such as Leslie Fiedler and Richard Wasson. For Wasson, the postmodernists represent a new sensibility: whereas for some modernists, such as T. S. Eliot, Ezra Pound, and James Joyce, "experience was full of paradoxes and contingencies which the great poet ordered through metaphor," postmodern writers are no longer able or willing to create such all-encompassing metaphors. They rather "desire to get back to particulars, to restore literary language to its proper role which for them means revealing 'the raggedness, the incompleteness of it all'" (Wasson 462, 476).

Among those contemporary Canadian writers who have taken an active part in the theoretical discussions regarding postmodernism, Robert Kroetsch certainly holds the top position. As a professor of English who taught for over fifteen years in the United States, Kroetsch has always been in close touch with American theories of postmodernism, all the more because he was co-editor, with William Spanos, of the only journal completely devoted to the study of postmodernism, *Boundary 2*. His interviews and essays are among the most important statements of a postmodern Canadian position, so that it cannot come as a surprise that Canadian and European critics alike have referred to him as "Mr Canadian Postmodern" (Hutcheon, *The Canadian Postmodern* 160) or "Canada's postmodernist *extra-ordinaire*" (Lernout 137).

Much of Kroetsch's interest in his postmodern narratives centres on experiments with perspective and point of view and, above all, on mythological and archaeological patterns of postmodern writing. Frank Davey sums up Kroetsch's philosophical position as one implying "radical suspicion—ultimately denial—of the existence independent of temporal embodiment of idea, archetype, essence or Platonic form, and its rejection of traditional systematic philosophy in which all being is to be harmonized and explained" (Davey, 8). The word *deconstruction* becomes the key term in Kroetsch's aesthetics, describing his attitude towards all convention, tradition, or cosmology. It is based on his "deep suspicion of all referential frames, myth, fictions, the sensory world" (Thomas, *RK* 14–15). For example, Kroetsch is obsessed with one of the first conventions that human beings are confronted with: that of naming. He is all in favour of uninventing the word (and thus the world), of the un-naming of place before it can be re-named in a noncolonial, non-European, truly Canadian way: "The Canadian writer must uninvent the word. He must destroy the homonymous American and English languages that keep him from hearing his own tongue. But to uninvent the word, he knows, is to uninvent the world" ("A Canadian Issue" 39). However, he does not only apply the principle of deconstruction in a nationalistic and thematic way: "Kroetsch's compulsion to deconstruct is contained in this wish to strip down complex narrative forms to elemental story" (Thomas, *RK* 120). In the following pages, I want to have a closer look at the way in which the incoherent cosmology of postmodernism is reflected in Kroetsch's work, especially in the narrative structure of his novels. References to his theoretical statements, most of them collected in a special issue of the journal *Open Letter* or in his Selected Essays, *The Lovely Treachery of Words*, will be made in passing.

Kroetsch's first novel, *But We Are Exiles* (1965), is still in many regards a very conventional novel. Peter Guy, a young student, loses his girlfriend, Kettle Fraser, to Michael Hornyak, whom he had thought of as a friend. Smarting, he heads up north, away from civilization, and takes a job as a riverboat pilot on the Mackenzie River, but then his boat is ironically bought up by Hornyak. The latter dies in an accident that Peter might have prevented, and—like Coleridge's Ancient Mariner—Peter has to carry the burden of guilt until he replaces Hornyak's corpse in his canoe and/or coffin in a snowstorm on Great Slave Lake. Whereas the novel is, generally speaking, a third-person narrative told from Peter's perspective, there are also situations resembling that of the author lost in the postmodern world. Peter, the pilot, is the only person who can make any coherent sense out of an almost postmodern mass of details: "These were his secrets. . . . An order maintained as precariously as that maintained by the hands on the wheel. The chaos held in check . . ." (18–19). In this description of Peter Guy as the centre of the world that is "held in delicate and fluid balance by the pilot" (18), traditional narrative structure is 'exploded.' While at first, Guy's thoughts are still rendered through the voice of the narrator, soon his views are expressed in first-person narrative without any conventional notation of direct speech: "Here the pilot's eyes and hands were in isolated yet absolute command. Pure. He wanted to shout the word. This is mine. Storm, ice, wind, rock—those can challenge me" (19). In the end, he loses that challenge.

Morton Ross's criticism of *Exiles*, that "Kroetsch's choice of method leaves the more profound dimensions of his material in the realm of chaos—provocative, but in the last analysis unclear" (Ross 104), is looking for a certainty and clarity that Kroetsch is simply not willing to give him. But whereas the world described and its chaos have already postmodern overtones, the writing is still rather traditional. Postmodernism does not extend to the structure of his writing yet, and the same might also be said of Kroetsch's second novel, *The Words of My Roaring*. Published in 1966, it is the first of three novels set in a fictional part of rural Alberta. *Words* depicts the region of Notikeewin, Coulee Hill and Wildfire Lake in the 1930s, at the beginning of the era of the Social Credit movement, whereas the second part, *The Studhorse Man*, shows it towards the end of World War II, and the third, *Gone Indian*, is set in the author's present in the 1970s. One might say that the trilogy approaches the future constituency of John Backstrom MLA from three different narrative perspectives.

Backstrom, undertaker and candidate for public office, is the hero and first-person narrator of *The Words of My Roaring*. Highly aware of the implications of his use of different narrative structures and perspectives, Kroetsch explained his changing over from the third-person narrative in *Exiles* to first person in *Words* as "a change in our view of what we know and how we know it," because "we're reduced to private visions in our time—there's no longer a trust in the shared, the community vision" (Cameron 89). Nevertheless, this kind of community vision exists in Kroetsch's work, even in first-person narrative, when he falls back on the tall tale tradition of the prairies and its deconstruction of notions of realism: "The people in the beer-parlour, they both know that they're lying and that they're telling the truth. They know they've stretched it and it's fun to stretch it but they've also said something" (Neuman and Wilson 237). The voice of *Words* is clearly such an orally conceived one with overtones of the tall tale and carnivalistic exaggeration, of beer-parlour bragging and electoral campaigning: "Our endless talk is

the ultimate poem of the prairies," Kroetsch claims, "In a culture besieged by foreign television and paperbacks and movies, the oral tradition is the means of survival" ("One for the Road" 30). Backstrom introduces himself in this very style: "My name, let me say once and for all, is Johnnie Backstrom, and I am six-four in my stocking feet, or nearly so, a man consumed by high ambitions, pretty well hung, and famed as a heller with women" (4). His political leader, William Applecart, has a simple message for the drought-stricken farmers: "He just ripped loose about everything. It made us all feel a lot better, even me" (33). Whereas his rival Doc Murdoch stands for the old order, Backstrom's only true belief is in chaos: "Sometimes it seems that chaos is the only order. The only real order . . . I needed chaos, the old chaos . . ." (101). In the end, his prophetic election promise of rain comes true in the scorched region.

Peter Thomas calls Johnnie Backstrom's an "expansive, hyperbolic subjective voice which 'explodes' the fearful, repressed symmetries of Kroetsch's first novel." But he has to admit that, although "*The Words of My Roaring* is not a formally innovative novel, it opened the way to what was to come" (Thomas, *RK* 39, 50). So once more, as in *But We Are Exiles*, most of the postmodern aspects of the novel are to be found in its content—the apocalyptic vision of William Applecart and Johnnie Backstrom—rather than in its form, but Backstrom's kind of reasoning and of structuring his fragmentary thoughts by free association already points in a certain direction: Kroetsch has given up on the modernist's structuring metaphor which was all-encompassing and replaced it by a new way of reading the world that has strong affinities with the cosmology of the postmodern. This new way of reading the world finds its appropriate epistemology in the anarchistic randomness of knowledge envisaged by Paul Feyerabend, for whom knowledge has become "an ever increasing ocean of mutually incompatible (and perhaps even incommensurable) alternatives, each single theory, each fairy tale, each myth that is part of the collection forcing the others into a greater articulation and all of them contributing, via this process of completion, to the development of our consciousness" (Feyerabend 30). This kind of knowledge resembles in its structure the *bricolage* of Claude Lévi-Strauss's myths that often "look more or less like shreds and patches, if I may say so; disconnected stories are put one after the other without any clear relationship between them" (Lévi-Strauss 34). Just as, according to the above quotations, knowledge is randomly assembled, mythical thinking builds narrative that is loosely structured around the "odds and ends" of history.

The modernists had used ancient myths in order to give a formal structure to their narratives: T. S. Eliot saw the "mythical method" as "simply a way of controlling, of ordering, of giving a shape and a significance to the immense panorama of futility and anarchy which is contemporary history" (Eliot 188, 187). While thus at least in certain kinds of modern literature a definite mythical structure can be found, control and order are often the very notions rejected by the authors of postmodern literature: classical myths used in Joycean fashion cannot express the incoherence of the postmodern world. The myth of the *bricoleur* is a much better structuring device in postmodern works of literature. Kroetsch, who himself points to his indebtedness to Lévi-Strauss's theories (Neuman and Wilson 92), claims that "the Modernist was tempted by the cohesive dimension of mythology, while the Postmodernist is more tempted by those momentary insights that spring up here and there" (112). "We have sought out the decentering rather than the centering function of myth" (130), and here myths are no longer God-given but rather man-made, avoiding meaning as well as closure.

Even though *The Words of My Roaring* as a whole does not yet have this kind of *bricolage* mythical structure, it contains scenes in which Backstrom gets carried away in his anecdotes and approaches and becomes a *bricoleur* constructing new myths. Before the background of a (postmodern?) chaos of furniture and household goods, Backstrom encounters a prophet, a man for whom any causal relationship, any logical way of arguing is nonexistent. The prophet's car becomes an example of the creation of a tale, or a *bricolage*:

> Right before my eyes, people started making up stories about it, guessing where it came from, what kind of speed it was good for. "Doesn't run on gas," somebody said, "runs on water." "Where would you get the water?" somebody asked him. "That old coot is well over a hundred," somebody said. "Shouldn't be driving to begin with." Then an argument developed over the prophet's age; some people insisted, give him a bath and he'll look like a young man. "Give that car a good scrubbing," somebody said—he bent and spat on a fender and rubbed the dirt—"and it'll look like new."
>
> (85)

A similar *bricolage* structure also works in the second *Out West* novel, *The Studhorse Man*, even on the level of its contents: it depicts the victory of technology over nature, and its ending foreshadows one of the most revolutionary developments in human society, the invention of the birth control pill. As in a *bricolage*, relics from the past are here put to new use in the present: the horse—whose old function has become superfluous in the agricultural structure of the modern world—is now integrated into its pharmaceutical structure. But the first-person narrator in *The Studhorse Man*, Demeter Proudfoot, is certainly unaware of this structural peculiarity of this complex narrative in which he proves to be even less reliable than Backstrom was in his wildest election speeches. Demeter Proudfoot re-constructs the biography of Alberta's last studhorse man, Hazard Lepage. His reliability as a biographer is not necessarily enhanced by his being confined to a mental institution. He controls the narrative and can do as he likes, unhampered by any rational pattern. His metafictional remarks illustrate the reader's dependence upon him, even when unfortunately Demeter often finds himself "straying from the mere facts" (12). And he, the scribe "long[ing] for a whole image of the vanished past" (34), does not have anything

but fragments from which he reconstructs Hazard's odyssey. Working in his bathtub, he sorts his material on filing cards. Every now and then he feels the urge to restructure the past in order "to suggest an order that was not necessarily present in Hazard's rambling conversation" (40). His contemplations regarding the order of the world are relevant to a postmodern view: "I myself prefer an ordered world, even if I must order it through a posture of madness" (61).

Kroetsch has often used the image of the archaeologist for his technique of writing, and this is also the technique that Demeter uses: like an archaeologist, he relies on single specimens, found objects, "so called real situations" (Hancock 36) and real persons. These found objects are of course only fragments, in no order whatsoever, but as Kroetsch says, "I like the sense of fragment and what fragment does: the demands fragment makes on us for shaping, for telling, for imagining" (Neuman and Wilson 167). A good example of the construction of a whole story (and history) around a found object is the stone hammer in Kroetsch's ***Stone Hammer Poems***, in which the process of imagination starts from the position of the observer and leads to a "weblike" structure of association in which "each separate strand . . . is finally perceived to be part of a pattern" (Wood 30).

The shaping of a narrative out of fragments also involves the reader, since it is not only the author who is engaged in this process. Kroetsch knows, however, that sometimes readers are not willing or able to take part in the "archaeological act" (Kroetsch 1989, 69) of reestablishing the connections and missing links between the objects found on the site, because they are used to seeing them in "the museums where it's all carefully assembled and tagged and explained" (Neuman and Wilson 167): "Archaeology allows the fragmentary nature of the story, against the coerced unity of traditional history. Archaeology allows for discontinuity. It allows for imaginative speculations" (**"On Being an Alberta Writer"** 76).

In *The Studhorse Man*, Demeter's view of the world from the asylum, a peculiar perspective, is made possible through a special contraption enabling him "to see out of my window without leaving my bathtub. A mirror is so placed above my sink that I have been able to sit for hours, attempting to imagine what in fact did happen (allowing for the reversal of the image) exactly where I imagine it. It is the *time* that I must reconstruct, not space" (85). Unfortunately Demeter himself, whose credibility has been shown to be more than questionable, often does not trust Hazard's own account of his life. But if he has to admit to some weaknesses in his hero's character, he relativizes those by alluding to other historical figures: "It is not easy to admit of weaknesses in one's hero. Sir John A. Macdonald tippled, let his biographers quibble as they will. Hazard Lepage was a man of inordinate lust" (31).

Through Demeter's metafictional remarks, *The Studhorse Man* becomes of course more overtly postmodern than the earlier novels. Peter Thomas remarks for example that it "is Kroetsch's first novel where the self-conscious demonstration of narrative technique, the book's reflection upon its own process, is a predominant interest" (Thomas, *RK* 121). One may even, with Brian Ross, "find in Hazard Lepage's quest an allegory of the writer's search for the future of his art" (B. Ross 67). The novel's metafictionality and the problematization of its narratorial voice turn *The Studhorse Man* into the first of many texts that justify Linda Hutcheon's calling Kroetsch Mr. Canadian Postmodern.

Whereas in *The Studhorse Man* a biographer reconstructs another character's life, thoughts, and motivations, in *Gone Indian* the narrative structure is even more complicated: in this third novel of the *Out West* trilogy, we see a narrator editing another person's narrative. For the first time in Kroetsch's novels does the subject of a 'biography' have a chance to speak for himself. An eternal Ph.D. candidate in literature, Jeremy Sadness is sent from New York State to Edmonton by his thesis supervisor, Professor Mark R. Madham, who is from this very part of the world. Due to a sequence of chance events, Jeremy does not go to the University of Alberta for a job interview but rather ends up judging a beauty contest at the Notikeewin winter festival and disappears into the Albertan winter together with a woman who has long been waiting for her vanished husband. This husband in turn, as Arnold Davidson convincingly argues, has re-surfaced in the States as Madham, Jeremy's supervisor. Madham's explanation and interpretation of Jeremy's Albertan odyssey—a framed first-person narrative—is addressed to Jill Sunderman, the above-named lady's daughter, and it is based upon the thoughts and insights that the not very eloquent graduate student had to confide to a tape recorder because he cannot bring enough order into his thoughts to be able to write them down. Madham, the professorial narrator in the frame narrative, denies any responsibility for his story and feels "under no obligation to explain anything" (1). Far from trying to transcribe the tapes in a scholarly manner that aims at establishing the truth, he is guided by personal prejudice and sexual interest in Jeremy's wife, even if all this is disguised as belonging to the "professor's domain: the world of reflection, of understanding. The insight born of leisurely and loving meditation" (13). That is why he is "transcribing a few passages from those same tapes, simply that you might better appreciate the kind of rascal you found yourself involved with" (1–2). Madham's assertion that Jeremy's tapes "can be taken at face value" is undermined by Carol Sadness's assertion that her husband "was faking everything from the moment he spoke the first sentence into the recorder" (2).

Gone Indian is the first of Kroetsch's novels to overtly have two narrators. Both of them share the postmodern world-view, so that Madham should know better than to try and establish a coherent argument out of Jeremy's fragmentary tapes. Kroetsch himself claims that "Madham is a very devious character and I think he is also acting out the reading act, he is taking fragments . . . and he is imposing an order: that's what readers do" (Neuman and Wilson 176). Of course, Madham's point of view is far from impartial since he wants to establish Jeremy's death as a fact in order to legalize his affair with Jeremy's wife, Carol, but the last small fragment in his jigsaw puzzle is missing, and thus his universe does not cohere. While Demeter in *The Studhorse Man* said that "I myself prefer an ordered world, even if I must order it through an order of *madness* . . ." (61, emphasis added), the narratorial posture in *Gone Indian* is broken up into the two narrators *Mad*ham and Sad*ness*.

Many critics regard *Badlands* as Kroetsch's best novel. This judgment may also have to do with the fact that, at first sight, *Badlands* is less experimental than its predecessor and thus comes close to being a traditional novel in the realistic vein. Set in the Alberta badlands, it goes back to the time of the First World War, William Dawe's first archaeological expedition and the recovery of Albertan (pre-)history by—and on behalf of—(Eastern) Canada. What is clearer than in the other novels is the distinction between the two time-levels, that of the original Red Deer River expedition in 1916 and that of Dawe's daughter Anna coming to Alberta in 1972 in order to do research on the spot. This latter narrative is a first-person narrative, whereas the rest, the report of the original expedition, is a third-person narrative.

A 'chronology,' a list of events at the beginning, gives the novel a quasi-factual dimension as it seems to establish a verifiable and reliable structure underlying the narrative: among them most importantly Dawe's 1916 expedition and, in the summer of 1972, Anna's attempt at 'reconstructing' her father's history and at freeing herself from the grip that her father still has on her. Anna has only her father's field notes, the conversations before his death, and the memories of her native friend Anna Yellowbird, who had accompanied her father, to rely on when trying to form her own picture of the expedition. His field notes prove to be less than accurate and reliable sources for the expedition report that Anna pieces together. In Robert Wilson's words,

> The parasitical relationship to the story which shows up already in Demeter also shows up strongly in *Badlands* where Anna is parasitical upon a slender and stunted story of her father's but tells it and then comments upon it so that she *does* create herself through a parasitical relationship to the story which is both retelling and interpreting it.
>
> (Neuman and Wilson 175)

The difficulties that "a reader accustomed to the conventional, modernist handling of narrative angle" has in assessing the narrative structure of *Badlands* are summarized by Laurie Ricou, who claims that "*Badlands*, by having no explicit fiction about the narrative angle, expresses Kroetsch's own frustration with the demand for consistency" (Ricou 120).

Anna's introduction to the novel situates her as the narrator and archaeologist of her father's biography as well as of her own material. She had never received a personal letter from her father, only field notes: "God help us," she sighs, "we are a people raised not on love letters or lyric poems or even cries of rebellion or ecstasy or pain or regret, but rather on old hoards of field notes" (8). The field notes integrated into the novel are from the start commented on and criticized, and thus relativized, by the narrator:

> *Tuesday, June 27. Arrived Trail Creek shortly before noon. Climbed up out of the valley in order to find a farm or ranch, buy some fresh food, send off some letters.* And then, either to amplify his heroic endurance or to underline his disappointment, he added: *Encountered a pitiful young squaw who seemed to think*—He broke off the enlarging sentence, surprised at his own unscientific noting of the world. He scratched, righteously, pompously, in his cramped hand on the next line: *she would accompany my expedition.*
>
> (11)

Anna Dawe's report differs from her father's male narrative. She does not rely, like Demeter or Madham, on "the curious little narrative tricks of a mad adventure: the lies that enable the lovers to meet, the mystery of who did the killing, the suspense before victory." Men "have their open spaces, and translate them into a fabled hunting." Women, however, "have only time to survive in, time, without either lies or mystery or suspense; we live and then die in time" (27). Commenting on a tall tale, she dismisses its author as a "total and absurd male" assuming "an omniscience that was not ever his, a scheme that was not ever there" (76). Whereas male authors and narrators are striving to establish an order out of their fragments, however chaotic it may seem, Kroetsch's first female narrator, Anna Dawe, has finally developed the better strategy: she patiently awaits the further development of the story. This is what Anna Yellowbird, the incorporation of the old native as well as the postmodern spirit, has taught her: "the possibility of harmony, of accepting inconsistency and opposites. . . . one exchanges the comfort of absolutes or absolution, for life which is a mixture of darkness and glory that resists our attempts to order it" (Grace 33). And Anna Dawe, after reconstructing her father's story, but before having written anything down, arrives at a moment of release from the gathering of documents, from the (male) obsession to find an order, to "fill the gap." High up in the mountains, having read Dawe's rather pompous final entry—"I have come to the end of words" (269)—she "took that last field book with the last pompous sentence he ever wrote, the only poem he ever wrote, a love poem, to me, his only daughter, and I threw it into the lake where it too might drown" (270). She must, one is forced to conclude, have quoted the field book from memory in the version that she tells in *Badlands*. The loss proves to be no loss at all because it gives her the possibility to create "a woman's form for a woman's view of the west" (Ricou 120), and because "in the act of telling itself, she creates an unexpected empathy with her father writing which helps to proclaim her own identity, and even, perhaps, to bridge the great divide of death" (Williams 236).

What the Crow Said is Robert Kroetsch's flirt with magic realism, in which he leaves behind not only the demands of realism that he had seemingly come to accept in *Badlands*. Big Indian, a little town straddling the border of the provinces of Alberta and Saskatchewan, is confronted with fantastic events that take place during a time span of several years. Everything starts with the impregnation of the virgin Vera Lang by a swarm of bees, and the story culminates in a great flood. The events include a talking crow, prophecies correct and false, memories of things past and future, unbelievable success stories, and an apocalyptic war between earth and sky. The story is told by an omniscient narrator, a community voice, that can no longer rely on a more or less factual background or on "the hard core of detail." This and the laws of causality and realist fiction have been left far behind in the magically realistic realm of Big Indian. The hero of *Crow* is Gus Liebhaber, typesetter, printer, and sometimes editor of the *Big Indian Signal*, who—since Gutenberg's invention made remembering the past superfluous—has acquired the art of remembering the future. *What the Crow Said* has moved away from the dualism of narrative perspectives, which is often also the dualism of "creative characters" and "ordering interpreters" (Hutcheon, *The Canadian Postmodern* 160), that was dominant from *Exiles* (Michael Hornyak/Peter Guy) through *Words* (Backstrom/Murdoch), *The Studhorse Man* (Hazard/Demeter) and *Gone Indian* (Sadness/Madham) to *Badlands* (William Dawe/Anna Dawe). Liebhaber, though certainly an important figure who sometimes would like to become the scribe of his community, is only one among many characters. Although chronological, the plot of *Crow* is fragmented into many directions, so that it is difficult for a casual reader not to lose his orientation. Sam Solecki even had the impression, "erroneous probably—that Kroetsch wrote *What the Crow Said* simply by writing one extravagant episode after another until his creative energy and imagination gave out," and he finally calls it "an assembly of brilliant parts that fail to cohere into a significant whole" (Solecki 327). Equally disappointed, Peter Thomas states that "it would be unproductive to summarize the 'plot' of a novel which is clearly part of the war against plot (to adopt the title of one of Jeremy's abortive theses)" (Thomas, "RK and Silence" 38).

In spite of his knowledge of the future, Liebhaber is no longer able to compose a coherent story when he is confronted with "the heaped scrawls and scratches and guesses and advertisements" that his boss leaves to him with the instruction to compose a newspaper: "He couldn't finish the story; he couldn't complete the page and add the quoins, check the footstick, the sidestick, lock up the form . . ." (16). Chaos confronts him in the form of his collection of wood type, an "intricate knot of language that bound him to death" (54). He tries to 'deconstruct' language but is still confronted with the presence of letters that have a residual meaning. At one point, trapped under his boat, he seems to have worked out his philosophical problems and frees himself from Gutenberg's curse: "Yes, he was writing his own story, at last." He has found the key to chaos:

> He could account for event, announce the presence of design, under the apparent chaos. . . . [N]ow he had escaped, he had recovered the night, and dream, and memory. He would compose a novel one sentence long, a novel anyone could memorize. *You in my arms.*
>
> (163–64)

Consequently, Liebhaber knows now that "Gutenberg, too, was only a scribe" (216), and finds refuge with the women of the Lang family: "Liebhaber is happy. He cannot remember anything" (217).

What the Crow Said no longer can or even tries to establish its own reliability by means of reference to sources, fragments (or in Kroetsch's terms, excerpts) from the real world; its universe is isolated from any outside civilization. Here we have what Robert Wilson describes as the goal of many fabulists: "to replace reality, to find in the emergent literary alternative a self-contained and independent structure that cannot be judged by the actual world but may judge it" (Wilson 38). One may wonder, however, to what extent it is possible to judge the world from an independent structure that is totally cut off from the real world. Robert Lecker argues that whereas Kroetsch's earlier "mythological fictions" "blend larger-than-life meanings and relationships with a recognition of daily, local, ritualized occurrences" (Lecker, *RK* 99), such a recognition is no longer possible in *Crow*. Normally, although Kroetsch believes in the "uninvention of the world," the deconstructive activity is for him not purely destructive but rather "implies, for all its attraction to disorder, a recovery of order, control" (Kroetsch 1989: 109). Or, as David Creelman (77) has it, "unlike the American deconstructionists who are distinguished . . . by their refusal to reassemble the discovered textual disorder, Kroetsch is tentatively willing to embark on rebuilding projects." In Kroetsch's own words, "to go into pure chaos is to vanish" (Neuman and Wilson 25), and in order to keep himself from slipping into this chaos, he normally hangs on to some basic facts, some non-literary structuring devices around which he constructs his narrative: found objects, texts, a ledger, a seed catalogue, snapshots, lists, genealogies. In *Crow*, he leaves these behind, and challenges his readers to come to terms with a Kroetsch novel without a binary structure to fall back on.

In *Alibi*, his latest novel, Kroetsch returns to the binary structure of "creative characters" and "ordering interpreters." Still, it is his most experimental novelistic work in that he shows us a narrative in the process of being written and revised much in the way that an alibi sometimes tends to need revision. At the end of the novel, the alibi is still under revision: he leaves us alone with a series of notes. The dualistic structure between underlying notes and a parasitic new version produced on the basis of them provides us with a similar relationship as that between subtexts and supertexts in *Gone Indian* or *Badlands*. Here,

the underlying text is William William Dorfen's expedition report. Dorfen—or, for short, Dorf—works for the oil baron Jack Deemer, for whom he travels all over the world acquiring obscure collector's items. In *Alibi*, he searches England, Wales, Portugal, and Greece for a spa that he finally finds close to his home town of Calgary in the Rocky Mountains. While in Portugal, Dorf is suspected of having murdered Julie Magnuson, his own and his employer's mistress. He claims, however, that Julie must have stolen his car and driven, or have been driven, down a precipice. This version of events, Dorf's alibi, suggests that another one of Julie's lovers, dwarfish Dr. De Medeiros, might be responsible for her death (145).

Whereas the reader at first has the impression that he or she is reading Dorf's entries in a journal that his sometime companion Karen Strike had given him for his birthday, one realizes towards the end that the chapters composing the main part of the book are not Dorf's original entries but revisions. Only the appendix, "Dorfendorf's Journal," is the "true" underlying text, giving us entries that have not yet been transcribed and end abruptly on August 13. As these are the notes that Dorf took while transcribing the older entries, they are full of metafictional comments.

The very last entry describes an event which may explain the sudden end of the journal and novel: Dorf has retreated to a solitary cabin by a lake in order to finish his literary work in close contact with nature. Trying to keep the approaching De Medeiros from disturbing two newly hatched ospreys, he makes no effort at saving the doctor from the danger of drowning, so that his sudden disappearance is not surprising.

The "parasitical" commentary on the underlying text just summarized is given from Karen Strike's perspective. She is supposed to be finishing the process of editing that Dorf had started, of giving the text a presentable form: "Let Karen put in some headings, some chapter titles to trap the unwary eye and lure the customer; she with her gift for compromise" (231). That is what she has done: her headlines are partly synopses of the contents, partly cryptic allusions that can only be understood in a second reading, such as the mention of a "Journal that William William Dorfen Kept but Did not Keep" (168), and partly ironic devices by means of which the omniscient editor keeps her distance from Dorf's comparatively ignorant text.

At first sight, Karen's headlines seem to be the only editorial intervention in Dorf's expedition report and "unedited" notes. Considering Madham's manipulation in *Gone Indian* and Anna Dawe's in *Badlands*, however, one may doubt Karen's reticence: not only translators can be traitors—editors also have the opportunity to manipulate texts or to deconstruct them and use them parasitically to further their own purposes. Whereas Karen's visible influence seems to be limited to "some headings, some chapter titles," it may well reach much further than Stanley Fogel assumes when he comments upon the last, "autobiographical," entries in Dorf's journal: "He remains, after all, at the end of *Alibi*, writing his own alibi, the journal that is the sign of his continuing condition" (Fogel 92). Robert Lecker is fully aware of the novel's ambiguous narrative structure: "Although *Alibi* first appears to be a relatively conventional narrative presented by Dorf, it is in fact a highly contrived story presented via Karen, whose role as editor and editorializer is only revealed at the end of the book through what is presumably Dorf's 'authentic' journal" (Lecker, "Con/Texts of Desire" 92). Lecker's analysis does more justice to the complexity of *Alibi*, but Fogel's "continuing condition" is also an important element of the novel: writing as process. As in the case of *Badlands*, different interpretations are not only possible; they are even encouraged by the ambiguous narrative structure. Ambiguity is part of the novels themselves.

While Dawe's field notes in *Badlands*, the truthfulness of which was severely doubted by Anna, were notes written in the distant past, Dorf himself starts the process of writing and editing his own notes. The main part of the novel consists of his own revisions—or emendations, as he calls them—but the text underlying his revisions is the diary: "The original notes, Karen's birthday journal, to me are only the negatives which now I develop" (232). The text edited by Karen thus is not at all the original journal, the original event, and consequently the reader is one step further removed from the "truth."

On the other hand, Dorf's metafictional comments in the appendix afford an insight into the process of writing. This time the comments are not those of an editor who is removed in time and space, but those of the writer himself who—through the writing process—distances himself from the original events and consciously prohibits or impedes the suspension of this distance: "I transcribe the notes from my journal into a proper manuscript. I tear out the transcribed page from the journal" (229).

It is hardly surprising that Dorf, who is after all composing his alibi, destroys his original notes. Madham and Anna Dawe had done the same. The revised version replaces the underlying original text, and it is factually and temporally removed from the original situation. Writing is a process of re-telling by means of signs, a process that involves differences and manipulation. This mode of distancing is comparable with Derrida's principle of *différance*. In Derridean theory the text, which is composed of signs, is temporally and spatially different from the original event:

> . . . the substitution of the sign for the thing itself is both *secondary* and *provisional*: it is second in order after an original and lost presence, a presence from which the sign would be derived. It is provisional with respect to this final and missing presence, in view of which the sign would serve as a movement of mediation.
>
> (Derrida 138)

Derrida's concept of the *différant* text as a provisional arrangement is also applicable to *Alibi*, as the underlying

text was destroyed and one can no longer find out what (and if) anything was changed. The semiotic indeterminacy of the text is even more apparent in our case because the narrative point of view of the first-person narrator cannot be pinned down. The tense of his reports shifts between present and past, and sometimes words like *now* seem to refer to the time of the entry into the journal, whereas at other times they relate to the moment of transcription. When the remark "last Wednesday" (8) at one point seems to qualify him clearly as a narrator "in the midst of things," he also has information at hand that he can only have as a narrator reminiscing in hindsight. For example he concludes at one point, "In sum, I was a happy man. And I might have remained such, had Deemer not sent me that unfortunate message" (7).

Not only Karen Strike's commentary is parasitical in (probably) using Dorf's text in a way that differs from his original intention; Dorf's own text is also parasitical, as it re-interprets the situation depicted in the journal and integrates it into the new frame of an alibi. Karen is right when she points out to him that "You invent yourself, each time you sit down to make an entry . . ." (61), and "You do these real 'takes' on this Dorf guy that you're trying to put together" (62).

Dorf admits that the construction of his text has involved manipulations, when he insists on the reliability of one particular self-quotation: "I must let this entry stand as I originally wrote it, in the interest of making clear my own integrity; I have emended and summarized elsewhere only to establish a narrative account whose clarity matches my insight . . ." (100). At other instances, Dorf also refers to the important function of his own commentary, for example when he comments on the collections that he acquires for Deemer: "The collection itself only confirms the discontinuity of this scattered world; it's my talk that puts it together. I rave the world into coherence for Deemer" (195). But there is one collection of fragments that Dorf has to re-interpret and make coherent for himself: "I am trying to make sense of my journal, since I was sometimes remiss, sometimes left little gaps here and there. I make a correction, where necessary" (231). What makes up the special character of *Alibi* is that both processes of editing—Dorf's editing of his journal and Karen's comment upon his text—take place at the same time (even though one after the other) and that both have not come to a conclusion at the end of the book:

> Yes, today, even while I tear out sheets from the front of the journal, I write new notes on the sheets at the end. The journal itself was intended to cover a mere calendar year. Even with those first pages vanishing, a handful each day, I have too many blank sheets remaining.
>
> (230)

The transcription of the journal is thus an unfinished process: as Fogel put it, a "continuing condition."

In *Alibi*, Kroetsch has integrated the parodic process of self-editing into his novel. The reader realizes that Dorf's writing about himself and Karen's editing result in texts shaped and determined by certain purposes; even if Dorf pretends to have written them for nothing else than self-knowledge: "I will show my journal to no one . . ." (135). Both textual levels are "deconstructive" as they re-interpret old relationships and embed them in new contexts. Dorf correctly realizes that many events only make sense in hindsight, when they are embedded in new and all-embracing interpretations: "Yesterday made sense, I can see it all now, but today doesn't. Maybe that's what journals are about" (39). Past occurrences only make sense in the present context, new texts only in comparison with old ones. That is why diaries have to be rewritten. The revised texts are parasites feeding on the energy of the original text and redirect it by embedding it in a new context, whether it be by adding many lines (like Dorf) or by just inserting a few titles (like Karen). If this technique is reminiscent of the technique of parody mentioned at the beginning, that is no coincidence. Linda Hutcheon once remarked in an essay that "parodic art both deviates from a literary norm and includes that norm within itself as background material" (Hutcheon, "Parody without Ridicule" 204). In *Alibi*, the norms parodied are that of the diary (Dorf's birthday journal is parodied in his expedition report or alibi) and that of the expedition report itself, which is parodied by Karen's comments.

While a novel such as *The Words of My Roaring* displays this act of parody or—in Lévi-Strauss's terms—*bricolage* on the autobiographical level of Backstrom's reminiscing about his own life, and while *Badlands* is an example of the use of such techniques on the biographical level of Anna Dawe's reconstruction of her father's life, *Alibi* unites in itself the characteristics of both strategies. Dorf writes his version of the search for the lost spa as an autobiography dominated by his endeavour to construct an alibi. Karen, who had warned him that his alibi "had better be airtight" (219), adds a biographical level to Dorf's autobiographical one.

The alibi constructed by Dorf is double: *alibi* is defined by *Webster's* as "a plea of having been at the time of the commission of an act elsewhere than at the place of commission." This refers to Dorf's involvement in Julie Magnuson's mysterious death in Portugal. On the other hand, *alibi* can also mean "an excuse usually intended to avert blame or punishment (as for failure or negligence)," and if we understand the word in this sense, it would refer to Dorf's responsibility for Medeiros's death. Here, as well as concerning the narrative structure of his book, Kroetsch leaves us in doubt. The only thing we as readers can understand and 'trace' is the act of writing, not the events to which the text refers, an insight already won from historiographical metafiction. *Alibi* sketches what happens when we write alibis, and in a sense all human memory tends to be selective and becomes a kind of alibi, especially historical writing. There is always a difference between a written text and the truth, because the purpose for which a text was written frames its views and our views of it. The construction of alibis was already part of

Kroetsch's earlier novels, witness for example Demeter Proudfoot's version of Hazard Lepage's story, or Mark Madham's version of Jeremy Sadness's tape. In order to render past events plausible in hindsight, one has to go beyond pure description and documentation. Kroetsch's writers and editors all do what Dorf suggests to Karen when she starts to film a documentary: "Fake the real" (52).

Reading and tracing the narrative structures of Kroetsch's novels from the relatively simple third-person perspective of *Exiles* through the tall tales of Johnnie Backstrom, Demeter Proudfoot, and Mark Madham, through Anna Dawe's female version of her father's story, to the magically coherent incoherence of *What the Crow Said* and the Derridean trace of an alibi in *Alibi*, the reader participates in the endeavours of an author who again and again lives up to his claim that "I work a reader pretty hard, I guess, in that I want him to enter into the process [of fiction making] with me" (Hancock 42). Kroetsch's interest in and production of writerly structured narratives rather than traditionally formed ones shows that he, too, believes that traditional narrative is dead if we mean by that a narrative relying on "a social order of meaning, a political economy and collective psychology." The writer of a postmodern text can no longer rely on such a firmly established world-view, and this is Kroetsch's message to his readers. Thus—and more radically so than most of his Canadian colleagues—he does what Richard Harvey Brown defines as the task of the postmodern writer: he "tries to invent a new way of reading the world. Instead of reconstructing the world in terms of an earlier, conventional code, he deconstructs conventional experience through a new form of encoding" (R. H. Brown 545, 546).

Works Cited

Brown, Richard Harvey, "The Position of the Narrative in Contemporary Society." *New Literary History* 11,3 (1980): 545–550.

Brown, Russell M. "An Interview with Robert Kroetsch." *University of Windsor Review* 7, 2 (1972): 1–18.

Cameron, Donald. "Robert Kroetsch: The American Experience and the Canadian Voice." *Conversations with Canadian Novelists*. Vol. 1. Toronto: Macmillan, 1973. 81–95.

Creelman, David. "Robert Kroetsch: Criticism in the Middle Ground." *Studies in Canadian Literature/Études en littérature canadienne* 16,1 (1991): 63–81.

Davey, Frank. Introduction. *Open Letter* 5,4 (1983): 8.

Davidson, Arnold E. "Will the Real R. Mark Madham Please Stand Up: A Note on Robert Kroetsch's *Gone Indian*." *Studies in Canadian Literature* 6,1 (1981): 135–139.

Derrida, Jacques. "Différance." *Speech and Phenomena And Other Essays on Husserl's Theory of Signs*. Trans. David B. Allison. Evanston: Northwestern University Press, 1973. 129–160.

Eliot, T. S. 'Ulysses, Order, and Myth.' *Selected Prose of T. S. Eliot.* Ed. Frank Kermode. New York: Harcourt Brace Jovanovich/Farrar, Straus and Giroux, 1975. 175–178.

Feyerabend, Paul K. *Against Method: Outline of an Anarchistic Theory of Knowledge.* London: New Left Books, 1975.

Fogel, Stanley. *A Tale of Two Countries: Contemporary Fiction in Canada and the United States.* Toronto: ECW Press, 1984.

Grace, Sherrill. "Wastelands and Badlands: The Legacies of Pynchon and Kroetsch." *Mosaic* 14,2 (1981): 21–34.

Hancock, Geoff. "An Interview with Robert Kroetsch." *Canadian Fiction Magazine* 24–25 (1977): 32–52.

Hutcheon, Linda. *The Canadian Postmodern: A Study of Contemporary English-Canadian Fiction.* Toronto: Oxford University Press, 1988.

———. "Parody without Ridicule: Observations on Modern Literary Parody." *Canadian Review of Comparative Literature* 5,2 (1978): 201–211.

Kroetsch, Robert. *Alibi.* Toronto: Stoddart, 1983.

———. *Badlands.* 1975. Toronto: General Publishing, 1982.

———. *But We Are Exiles.* 1965. Laurentian Library. Toronto: Macmillan, 1977.

———. "A Canadian Issue." *Boundary 2* 3,1 (1974): 1–2.

———. *Gone Indian.* 1973. Nanaimo, B.C.: Theytus Books, 1981.

———. *The Lovely Treachery of Words: Essays Selected and New.* Toronto: Oxford University Press, 1989.

———. "On Being an Alberta Writer." *Open Letter* 5,4 (1983): 69–80.

———. "One for the Road." *Open Letter* 5,4 (1983): 30–31.

———. *Seed Catalogue.* Winnipeg: Turnstone, 1979.

———. *The Studhorse Man.* 1969. Markham, Ont.: PaperJacks, 1980.

———. *What the Crow Said.* 1978. Markham, Ont.: PaperJacks, 1979.

———. *The Words of My Roaring.* 1966. Markham, Ont.: PaperJacks, 1977.

Lecker, Robert. "Con/Texts of Desire: Robert K'oetsch's *Alibi.*" *Open Letter* 5,8–9 (1984): 83–98.

———. *Robert Kroetsch.* Boston: Twayne, 1986.

Lernout, Geert. "Postmodernist Fiction in Canada." *Postmodern Fiction in Europe and the Americas.* Ed. Theo D'haen and Hans Bertens. Amsterdam: Rodopi; Antwerpen: Restant, 1988. 127–141.

Lévi-Strauss, Claude. *Myth and Meaning.* New York: Schocken Books, 1979.

Neuman, Shirley and Robert Wilson. *Labyrinths of Voice: Conversations with Robert Kroetsch.* Edmonton: NeWest, 1982

Ricou, Laurence. "Field Notes and Notes in a Field: Forms of the West in Robert Kroetsch and Tom Robbins." *Journal of Canadian Fiction* 17,3 (1982): 117–123.

Ross, Brian L. "The Naked Narrator: *The Studhorse Man* and the Structuralist Imagination." *Canadian Literature* 104 (1985): 65–73.

Ross, Morton L. "Robert Kroetsch and His Novels." *Writers of the Prairies.* Ed. Donald G. Stephens. Vancouver: University of British Columbia Press, 1973. 101–114.

Solecki, Sam. "Letters in Canada: Fiction." *University of Toronto Quarterly* 48,4 (1978): 326–27.

Thomas, Peter. *Robert Kroetsch.* Vancouver: Douglas & McIntyre, 1980.

———. "Robert Kroetsch and Silence." *Essays on Canadian Writing* 18–19 (1980): 33–53.

Wasson, Richard. "Notes on a New Sensibility." *Partisan Review* 36,3 (1969): 460–477.

Wilson, Robert. "On the Boundary of The Magic and The Real: Notes on Inter-American Fiction." *The Compass: A Provincial Review* 6 (1979): 37–53.

Williams, David. *Confessional Fictions: A Portrait of the Artist in the Canadian Novel.* Toronto: University of Toronto Press, 1991.

Wood, Susan. "Reinventing the Word: Kroetsch's Poetry." *Canadian Literature* 77 (1978): 28–39.

Richard Lane (essay date 1993)

SOURCE: "The Double Guide: Through the Labyrinth with Robert Kroetsch," in *Journal of Commonwealth Literature,* Vol. XXVIII, No. 2, 1993, pp. 19-27.

[*In the following essay, Lane examines Kroetsch's novels and poetry in order to understand his literary theory, particularly in* Labyrinths of Voice.]

How do we find our way through a textual labyrinth? Already, in the etymology of its name, the notion of doubling forms part of a trace that leads us to the Minotaur and the Classical world. But readers of literary criticism know that the concept of a labyrinth can also lead into the contemporary postmodern world of uncertainty. Just over ten years ago, Robert Kroetsch published his **Labyrinths of Voice** (1982),[1] with which some critics believed the Canadian postmodern had arrived.[2] Douglas Barbour soon noted how the "questioning" of the three speakers in **Labyrinths** is a "quest/ioning". Barbour's word-play, or oscillation of meaning, brings us to another important postmodern concept: that of the unresolved quest (unresolved, since resolution would neatly unify or package postmodern fragmentation and uncertainty). As Barbour said, way back then:

Robert Kroetsch is one of the most self-consciously aware writers around today, fascinated by the theoretical roots of his art; in the theoretical routes of the labyrinth of the interview which is no longer simply interview, he and his co-speakers/seekers lead us into a series of open-ended speculations about contemporary writing and literature as a whole.[3]

The word "roots" switches to "routes", neither signification gaining priority. Both signifiers are part of the labyrinth metaphor; the search backwards to some kind of entry-point to the labyrinth can only take place through the process of speculation and writing, the route of *Labyrinths*. "Open-ended" speculation, because in the postmodern labyrinth, knowledge-structures contain their own aporetic fault-lines leading to self-deconstruction.

But where does this leave the reader, trying to find her or his way through *Labyrinths*, knowing that every argument is liable to fracture, to go off in a number of directions, or to disseminate itself across the text? Perhaps we should follow the common-sense advice of an early *Labyrinths* reviewer, who notes that "If you really want to understand Kroetsch better, re-read his novels and poems".[4] Ironically this advice, which suggests steering clear of too much theory, argues for a shift from the mainly spoken form of the pseudo-interview, to the written form of Kroetsch's fictional texts, a clue that behind the common-sense lurks Derrida, after all.

Open-ended speculation and "quest/ioning" are found, most obligingly, in Kroetsch's *Alibi* (1983).[5] Indeed, if *Alibi* is used as a guide through *Labyrinths*, we quickly find that the two texts share similar strategies, undermining the separation of "criticism" and "art". Thus both texts reveal the intersection of legacy (literary/critical heritage) and the creative or artistic "leg-work"[6] of Kroetsch's texts—in other words, a plexus composed of structural enclosures and the creative, internal critique (of such enclosures). As the narrator of **"Seed Catalogue"** says: "We give form to this land by running / a series of posts and three strands / of barbed wire around a quarter section".[7] The metaphoric logic of the enclosure in Kroetsch's texts works in much the same way, where the legacy is that structure "fenced in" which the deconstructor then interrogates from within: "Systems are open to adjustment, to change, to game, to our elaboration".[8] An oscillation continually takes place between the enclosure of influence and the labyrinthine reworking of given forms. However, it still might not be clear as to why the labyrinth should even be considered an enabling metaphor for postmodernism, since in spatial terms, the labyrinth could be regarded as an essentially closed or finite form that counter-acts the ethos of postmodernism, that is the labyrinth as having an absolute origin and centre. There are two ways of complicating such a static view. First is the concept of the labyrinth within a labyrinth, that is the pseudo-infinite regress of paths leading to themselves (an idea of great interest to Borges). Second is the notion that any fixed structure contains the possibility of its own transgression. That is to say, we are back to the aporetic fault-lines, but this time by suggesting that the limit is a symbiotic partner of transgression, where we understand the labyrinth as an

algorithm (a procedure, a method) rather than a static figure standing in for postmodernism in some limited way.

As signalled by the novel ***Badlands*** (1975),[9] the enclosure in Kroetsch's work (any static form), must be archaeologically uncovered, disturbed and disseminated across the land/text. The digging tool or writing implement is thus doubled, becoming simultaneously the "creating tool". Digging *and* creating equals the simultaneous action, or "hard graft" of the legacy/leg-work. This simultaneous action explains the continual critical reference to Kroetsch's need to create a paradoxical silence with words, new literary forms with the building blocks of the old. Sherrill Grace notes:

> Language for Kroetsch can be liberating. Paradoxically it can be used to suggest the silence of the uncreated because it is only with language that we can break free from, or decreate, the prisons of inherited words or stories in order to discover a fresh reality that expresses us better than the inherited one.[10]

Enclosure, legacy, inheritance: all suggest a classification of literary forms, a theory of the literary that belongs to a scientific desire to objectify the features of a text. The foregrounding in Kroetsch of the internal critique shifts the labyrinth structure from work of fiction to work of criticism and back again, a continual movement back and forth that resists the classificatory desire, forming a more flexible form of "literary critique".

"Literary critique" in its poststructuralist sense reads "literary gaming". As Edward Said notes in *Beginnings*, "Theory assumes the evident irregularity and discontinuity of knowledge—and hence its lack of a single central logos . . .".[11] Thus theory/gaming images the epistemology of its own production, yet, in producing meaning itself, multiplies meaning: "True theory, says Deleuze, does not totalize, it multiplies."[12] Said is concerned here with Vico (amongst others) in relation to literary and philosophical beginnings. Here is a way of recuperating the historical legacy, with this notion of beginnings, where "a beginning is at once never given and always indefinite."[13] The power of the legacy need not overwhelm the contemporary project of writing: "As Vico himself said, just because a belief is fantastic to us now does not mean that that belief did not serve some valid purpose for the mind that created it and held it: this is the most insistent lesson of his historiography."[14] History, become narrative, become game, rejects the closure of teleology; there is a switching here from the designs of nature, to the designs of the narrator, that representative of the effaced author whose signature constantly throws him or her back into view. When Kroetsch calls Roland Barthes a "creative writer",[15] he simultaneously signs himself as critic-creator.

The critic-creator performs a more complex writing task than the common-sense critic would perhaps envision. An example of this complexity can be discovered by regarding the "Banff Springs Hotel" scene in *Alibi* as a textual palimpsest, upon which the etymology of "legacy" is traced. Alan Bass, the translator of Derrida's *Postcard*, notes in his Glossary how "the original pronunciation [of "legs" = "legacy"] was the same as *lais*, from the verb *laisser*, to leave . . . *lais* was both the ancient form of legs and the term for a narrative or lyric poem."[16] The legacy is not just that which is left behind; it has a double sense in that it is also the process which must be worked out ("leg-work"), the process being the construction of signification operating with the simultaneous critique of the inheritance. Thus *Alibi* is the construction of a narrative inextricably linked with other generic forms. The "Banff Springs Hotel" foregrounds this interplay of signification: "I found a dark, stone stairway. I went down carefully, carefully I went down, the heavy stone steps. Into a darkness that was watery thick."[17] The genre of the detective story becomes mixed with that of the Gothic novel; the labyrinth metaphor enables the writer to cross generic forms, or, as at an intersection, quickly switch the text into other generic modes. As long as the labyrinth metaphor is the horizon of the text's own writing or creation, the narrative does not have to remain within any single system of closure. In other words, the metaphor initiates further textual production, further textual strategies to avoid/evade generic closure.

Back in the "Banff Springs Hotel", the floor of the room that Dorf enters is also made of the cold stone of the stairway in the labyrinthine entrance. The entrance to the labyrinth has, of course, led to more labyrinths where the reflections multiply "three recessed windows [which] imitated the squares in the rug" and "the panelled walls, dark, almost invisible, were a maze too . . .".[18] Dorf loses his sense of direction, but this is not surprising when out of the darkness he steps into doubling and reflection. The rug that is there to screen the cold stone floor is both a simulation of a fixed stylistic period, the twenties, and of "something infinitely old". The rug both recreates the signs of a historic period and sweeps them away in its obvious synthetic quality; it signals the genuine and the simulacrum. "Infinitely old" suggests a period without origin, a beginning that can be endlessly duplicated, at any time ("Fake the real" Dorf will say later on, but the "real" is already a simulacrum in this sense of beginnings, where authenticity as a concept is erased—thus "the real would suffice").[19]

The "game" section of *Labyrinths* gives the reader a clue as to how literature can be criticism, and vice-versa, in Kroetsch's work:

> It's interesting that we *play* the *game*, isn't it? There is a double thing that goes on even in the statement which is very fascinating to me. The two words contradict each other in a signifying way. *Play* resists the necessary rules of the *game*.[20]

At this point in *Labyrinths*, Wilson and Neuman are both concerned with the reification of game conventions. Two positions are offered: first, where the rules of the game (the strict boundaries regulating literary production) are regarded as being "more rigid than they actually are", and

second, where the rules of the game are incorporated into the text to undergo criticism, to enable the critical freedom of playing with these regulations. As Neuman notes, Sterne does both: "In the example of *Tristram Shandy* . . . Sterne can only play against the rules by first incorporating them into his text, but incorporating them in a more rigid form than they have taken in the novels against which he is reacting. He must pretend they are more rigid than they actually are."[21] I will argue that, in the postmodern text such as *Alibi*, the rules are not artificially inflated to be blown down or away, and that the notion of play (as part of the very productive structure of the text) does not mean that such texts cannot be read in a more conventional manner. For example, it is possible to take a conservative position where a narrative such as Pynchon's *The Crying of Lot 49* would be read as reinforcing the conventional quest motif, reinforcing a literary tradition rather than playing "against" that tradition. The "game of chess" is never really over in these literary terms, so long as the pieces remain in play. Somebody may say, as Wilson remarks, "'Well, that's not chess' and walk away",[22] but another person can just as easily decide otherwise: the game is now called postmodern chess, following an altered set of rules.

For Kroetsch "game" equals "literature", whereas "play" equals "writing". Writing is that which constantly escapes rigid formulation, escapes producing game-rules which cannot be broken. Another doubling occurs here; for the writer constantly to evade the formulation of rigid rules, he or she must perform a vigilant self-criticism. How does the critic respond though, if the criteria of evaluation are constantly undergoing transformation? How does the critic go beyond the catalogue, the list, the discussion of the markers of postmodern carnivalization?

Dorf's double in *Alibi* is Manny the spa-doctor, a dwarf involved in the rites (or rut) of carnival, the desire-process that overturns routine and an acceptance of things as they are in the world. A political reading of carnival (of which there are accounts *ad nauseam*) may suggest the revolutionary power inherent in such an activity and/or discourse, such as Kristeva's proposal "that the infraction of formal literary codes of language is identical to challenging official law.[23] This is analogous to the concept of disrupting the game:

> All play has its rules. They determine what "holds" in the temporary world circumscribed by play. The rules of a game are absolutely binding and allow no doubt as soon as the rules are transgressed the whole play-world collapses. The game is over.[24]

Huizinga suggests that the "spoil-sports" who ruin the game may sometimes create a new community of their own, with a new set of rules. What is suggested in his account of game/play, is that the game is in a sense perfect or ideal for it to be ruined in the first place. For the writer as player, this is not so, and thus the rules of the game must be constantly transgressed.

Another view of the play-activity "carnival" is that of a temporary, self-contained activity after which order will always be restored. This is where the carnivalesque inversion serves to magnify a structure that is already in place (in the game-rules), revealing the subjugated signifiers that the subject depends on. A place of legitimized carnival (although the players are supposed to be temporary residents) is the spa. The carnivalesque reveals that, with the activity towards cure, arises the production of "poison" (the pharmakon).[25] The spa town of Bath, for example, was described in the 1700's as "A valley of pleasure, yet a sink of iniquity . . . The plain fact was that for a gentleman to visit the place was as likely to bring on the pox as cure it."[26] Similarly, the mud bath at Laspi in *Alibi*, reveals the behind of society, that in which Dorf has trouble immersing himself: "I couldn't quite immerse myself in that stinking thick mud where all the sick and the maimed did their suffering and their hoping. And their pissing and their bleeding and their farting."[27] However, once he has entered the mud, a strange transformation takes place: "The others began to turn their heads into masks, into sculptures, into faces that were other than their own . . . I looked down at all those floating heads on the mud, and suddenly they were beautiful; those men were strong and powerful and handsome again."[28] The transformation from the grotesque body to the heroic masks and sculptures of a more classical representation entices Dorf to experience (once more) the pleasures of the body. For the duration of the game-space of the mud-bath, the sick and the maimed are restored to health and beauty; the mud which acts as a supplement or ornament, becomes in the suspended space of the game the "essence" (under erasure) of being, where sickness belongs to another world. But this carnivalesque inversion does not exclude the signs of the sick body, for a more accurate description of this process is that of "inmixing" the signifiers of the subject; the fat man "is" the smelly woman. As White and Stallybrass put it:

> Carnival gives symbolic and ritual play, and active display, to the inmixing of the subject, to the heterodox, messy, excessive and unfinished informalities of the body and social life. It attacks the authority of the ego (by rituals of degradation and by the use of masks and costume) and flaunts the material body as a pleasurable grotesquerie—protuberant, fat, disproportionate, open at the orifices.[29]

The emphasis in the quotation should be placed for our reading on the "unfinished informalities" not only of the body, but of the carnival structure itself. Kroetsch plays with the carnival as a way of dis-playing the fixed game rules of the literary legacy (doing the work of the normally "external" critic). The carnival is not a fixed structure (except in its abstract ideality); rather there is a collection of events, of discourses, that may be grouped in passing under the heading "carnival". The carnivalesque is a play concept that constantly undergoes self-transformation to escape the confines of a strictly rigid critical definition. As Stallybrass and White note, ". . . a convincing map of the transformation of carnival involves tracing migrations, concealment, metamorphoses, fragmentations, internalization and neurotic sublimations . . .".[30]

We have seen that the strategies of *Alibi* double those of *Labyrinths* (and vice-versa), the focus on Kroetsch's writing as a "play" structure showing one way in which rigid formulations are transgressed. In *Alibi*, the fictional narrator is the text's own literary critic who tears out the pages of the journal, transcribing the playful writing "into a proper manuscript", or that which, as De Man says, already deconstructs itself: "Literature—the only language that is already deconstructed, that manifests its own mediated, rhetorical, nonreferential status without any help from the critic."[31] The doubling of "journal" and "novel", with the various mediators, can be read as disrupting the relationship of legitimation between reader and text, where the reader claims a certain amount of stable knowledge (the stuff of which academic papers are normally written). In *Labyrinths*, Neuman makes a provocative statement concerning the need for "other disciplines" to account for knowledge, since the focus upon the signifier as that which disrupts the enclosures of knowledge (writing as signifier as play) would tend to weaken "the conviction that language is knowledge".[32] Thus, by systematically mapping out the game rules of deconstruction, postmodernism/structuralism, archaeology, etc, the critic can account for the literary text. As Dorf says: "I am trying to make sense of my journal, since I was sometimes remiss, sometimes left little gaps here and there. I make a correction, where necessary."[33]

The desire for knowledge from "other disciplines" suggests that the postmodernist focus upon language as writing (in the Derridean sense), destroys any notion of stability, which is a fallacy. Kroetsch notes: "I was interested in language as signifying things that were not allowed, were taboo . . .".[34] The most taboo signification of all may be that language may be viewed as a process which signifies only more or other language (and here we can opt for a Schopenhauerian pessimism[35] or a Nietzschean affirmation[36] in such an endless process). At the opening of *Alibi*, the effaced character "Jack Deemer" sends messages which must be acted upon, but which have no ground other than their performance, the use to which they are put:

> . . . he's a great one for sending messages. His minions live in a kind of dread of memos or post cards or, for that matter, scraps of toilet paper scrawled with instructions for which there is no explanation, no place to seek clarification.[37]

These messages are not to be explained in a conventional way at the end of the novel, for the end is unlocatable. Deemer's physical arrival (that hoped-for referent behind all those annoying signifiers) is endlessly replayed where "Karen must fake the end of her documentary. She has persuaded her little gang to restage the arrival."[38] What is left is the protagonist living with the violation of the darkened spa, yet still writing, through a process of transliteration and transcoding. The textual play of the signifier continues, both where Deemer's messages are acted upon as the incentive for further questing (the ever-expanding collection) and with the "faking of the real"—the simulation of the signifier.

Have I answered my opening question, or doubled it? Have I turned the question inwards, upon itself, in that process so annoying to those who seek a way through the postmodern labyrinth? The mirroring, or back and forth movement between **Labyrinths** and **Alibi**, has shown that the answers to questions of guidance lie "within" the texts; that the complicated aporetic structures that are a necessary condition for postmodern transgression also explain Kroetsch's use of a Derridean, playful writing. Those waiting for a transcendental signifier from Jack Deemer, or elsewhere, with which to *relève*[39] themselves up out of the labyrinth (that is, to revert to the metaphysical system of rigid significations which the postmodern process undermine) will be waiting a very long time indeed.

Notes

1. S. Neuman and R. Wilson, eds, *Labyrinths of Voice: Conversations with Robert Kroetsch*, Edmonton: NeWest Press, 1982.

2. J. Conklin, review of *Labyrinths of Voice, Quill & Quire*, April 1983, p. 31.

3. D. Barbour, review of *Labyrinths of Voice*, NeWest Review, 8, No. 9, Summer 1983, p. 16.

4. P. Precosky, review of *Labyrinths of Voice, Canadian Book Review Annual*, 1982, Toronto: Simon & Pierre, 1983, p. 233.

5. Robert Kroetsch, *Alibi*, Toronto: New Press, 1983.

6. Alan Bass, translator's note to Jacques Derrida, *The Postcard: From Socrates to Freud and Beyond*, Chicago: U of Chicago P, 1987, p. 292.

7. Robert Kroetsch, *Completed Field Notes: The Long Poems of Robert Kroetsch*, Toronto: McClelland & Stewart, 1989, p. 42.

8. *Labyrinths*, p. 28.

9. Robert Kroetsch, *Badlands*, Toronto: New Press, 1975.

10. Sherrill Grace, "Wastelands & Badlands: The Legacies of Pynchon and Kroetsch", *Mosaic*, 14, 2, Spring 1981, p. 23.

11. Edward Said, *Beginnings, Intentions & Method*, New York: Columbia UP, 1985, p. 378.

12. *ibid*.

13. *ibid*, p. 350.

14. *ibid*, p. 361.

15. *Labyrinths*, p. 41.

16. *Postcard*, p. xxiii.

17. *Alibi*, p. 47.

18. *ibid*, p. 48.

19. *ibid*, p. 52.

20. *Labyrinths*, p. 50.

21. *ibid*, p. 52.

22. *Labyrinths*, p. 52.

23. A. White & P. Stallybrass, *The Politics and Poetics of Transgression*, London: Methuen, 1986, p. 201.

24. J. Huizinga, *Homo Ludens: A Study of the Play Element in Culture*, London: Routledge, 1949, p. 11.

25. See Jacques Derrida's discussion of the pharmakon in his *Dissemination*, trans. Barbara Johnson, Chicago: U of Chicago P, 1981.

26. R. S. Neale, *Bath 1680–1850: A Social History or A Valley of Pleasure Yet A Sink of Iniquity*, London: Routledge, 1981, pp. 12–17.

27. *Alibi*, p. 165.

28. *ibid*, pp. 165–6.

29. *The Politics and Poetics of Transgression*, p. 183.

30. *ibid*, p. 180.

31. G. Ulmer, "Jacques Derrida and Paul De Man: On/In Rousseau's Faults", *The Eighteenth Century*, 20, 2, 1979, p. 174.

32. *Labyrinths*, p. 159.

33. *Alibi*, p. 231.

34. *Labyrinths*, p. 142.

35. See, for example, Georg Simmel's discussion of the "Metaphysics of the Will" in his *Schopenhauer and Nietzsche*, trans. Helmut Loiskandl, Deena Weinstein & Michael Weinstein, Urbana & Chicago: U of Illinois P, 1991.

36. See, for example, Jacques Derrida's "Structure, Sign and Play in the Discourse of the Human Sciences", especially pp. 292–3, in *Writing and Difference*, trans. Alan Bass, Chicago: U of Chicago P, 1978.

37. *Alibi*, p. 7.

38. *ibid*, p. 231.

39. See translator's note 23 in Jacques Derrida, *Margins of Philosophy*, trans. Alan Bass, Sussex: Harvester Press, 1982, for a discussion of Derrida's *relève*, a translation of Hegel's *Aufhebung* or sublation. *Aufhebung* literally means "lifting up"; but it also contains the double meaning of conservation and negation (p. 20).

J. R. Snyder (essay date 1993)

SOURCE: "A Map of Misreading: Gender, Identity, and Freedom in Robert Kroetsch's *Gone Indian*," in *Studies in Canadian Literature,* Vol. 18, No. 1, 1993, pp. 1-17.

[*In the following essay, Snyder examines the ways in which* Gone Indian *has been misunderstood and suggests ways to correct the misreadings.*]

M. E. Turner, among several others, has contended that the discussion of Robert Kroetsch's work is too often based upon the critical positions set out in Kroetsch's own theoretical work; Kroetsch's literary output has enjoyed a high level of acceptance because Kroetsch's criticism implicitly posits his own works as models for postmodern fiction and poetry. Although Turner's argument is over-stated, it is often difficult to separate Kroetsch's novels from his critical pronouncements. In at least one instructive case, though, this tendency results in fallacious conclusions, not because of the naive linking of an author's artistic and critical statements, but because of a fundamental misreading of both the critical and the literary texts.

"The Fear of Women in Prairie Fiction: An Erotics of Space" is Kroetsch's most frequently cited theoretical statement. *Gone Indian* is perhaps Kroetsch's most under-appreciated novel. Both works have been consistently misread on the basis of what critics have anticipated Kroetsch *ought* to be saying, what they were prepared to accept his saying. Recently, from the perspective of "third-wave feminism" (or "feminization of deconstruction"), Susan Rudy-Dorscht identifies the central misreading of Kroetsch's **"Erotics of Space"** (a misreading which is apparent even without that perspective). It has been read as being prescriptive of Kroetsch's conception of male-female relationships rather than descriptive of the relationships discerned in previous prairie fiction:

> Although Kroetsch recognizes that traditionally we have "conceived of external space as male, internal space as female. More precisely, the penis: external, expandable, expendable; the vagina: internal, eternal," his reading of the sexual/textual politics between male and female overturns these phallocentric assumptions.
>
> (*The Studhorse Man* 26)

Rudy-Dorscht seeks to replace both first-wave feminism—that which calls for "texts written by biological women . . . [to] be recognized, included, and valued within the canon"—and second-wave feminism—which "rests upon the notions of femininity as an essential difference and of female writing as a writing of the body" (26)—with third-wave feminism because the prior two positions perpetuate the reductive dualism of male-female. As she writes in *Telling the Difference: Rereading 'Woman,'* her doctoral thesis on Kroetsch's novels (but not, except glancingly, *Gone Indian*),

> The third attitude in feminist thinking undermines the hierarchy of the binary opposition which permits questions of equality to be asked and finds, with Barbara Johnson, that differences between seemingly stable categories are based on "a repression of differences within entities, ways in which an entity differs from itself."
>
> (7)

Critics of Kroetsch's fiction, and of *Gone Indian* in particular, similarly perpetuate the repressive binarism his characters seek to escape. His characters are typically plagued by a dichotomous view of existence, and critics tend to be entrapped by that view as well, seeing the resolution of each novel as an assertion of the primacy of the vital, active half of each binary opposition over the repressive, stultifying half. As David Creelman writes,

> his texts are filled with oppositions, in which a first term concerned with a static vision of the world is rejected in favour of a second more radical term which focuses on process and activity.
>
> (64–5)

Instead, though, the novels portray the struggle to escape the definition of identity in the restrictive binary form of "if I'm not that, then I must be this." Kroetsch's protagonists typically find—although usually not by seeking it—a way to define identity without resorting to that binarism, or evade defining it at all. Rudy-Dorscht's position, clearly, is applicable to the larger question of identity, whether its derivation is related to gender or not. If Jeremy Sadness, the central character in *Gone Indian*, defines himself as opposite to Professor Madham, or embraces Western Canada as opposed to Eastern Canada, or seeks to be Indian as opposed to White, or establishes his maleness in opposition to femaleness, or establishes any facet of his identity by differentiation on the basis of the many binary oppositions at play in the novel, his sense of identity is still constructed and constrained by the reductive, dualistic thinking which sponsors the binaries.

Jeremy Sadness has been saddled with a quest and an identity not his own. His struggle to earn a Ph.D. and become a professional academic derives from the wish of both parents that he should be unlike his seaman father, and from Professor Madham's example and advice as his thesis supervisor and surrogate parent. Jeremy's journey west in search of academic employment is also clearly not of his choosing. His precarious marital and financial situations seem similarly to have been imposed upon him. Evidently as a result of these burdens, Jeremy is burdened also with a handicap: he cannot achieve an erection lying down. To find a cure for his sexual dysfunction, Jeremy must cast off inherited and imposed restrictions on identity, not only his own but those of others. Jeremy's response is to embark on a quest westward in order to become Grey Owl. Transforming himself into Grey Owl—going Indian—is the active half of the binary: Jeremy opposes his dream of becoming Grey Owl to the dream his parents and Madham share of his becoming an academic: he will become Grey Owl instead of becoming Jeremy Bentham.

Professor Madham, responding to Jill Sunderman's appeal to "explain everything" (1) about the disappearance of Jeremy with her mother, Bea, constructs a narrative out of the cassette tapes he claims Jeremy filled while on his quest. The book's forty-six sections are narrated alternately by Madham and Sadness. The doubled narrative pattern suggests the binary opposition of Sadness and Madham: Jeremy feels himself to be antithetically opposed to Madham and what he represents, as many of the critics have noted. But, as Sadness is progressively affected by his experience in the Northwest, he feels less and less need to speak to his cassette recorder and to Madham—he removes himself from the dialogue. As Jeremy tends increasingly towards silence late in the book, Madham fills the silence for him, interjecting commentary into even those sections ostensibly narrated by Jeremy. The final chapter should be in Jeremy's voice, but since that voice has been silenced—at least in terms of this coercive, reductive narrative dichotomy—Madham has the last word.

Professor Madham clearly is, if not a madman, then a seriously unbalanced and unreliable narrator. Madham tells Jill that, while he has done some editing, most of the narrative is a direct transcription of Jeremy's tapes, but she and the reader have only Madham's assertion for this. We have no way of confirming the veracity of any of the information presented, so the game becomes to learn about the narrator and to try to piece together the story through his disorderings of it. The reader is forced to accept that there is no final solution, no single ending—"Endings be damned" (24). Like the prairies' promise of diffusion of identity rather than a concluded self, the book remains an open field, a wealth of possibilities offering a series of metamorphoses, rather than a single switch from one pole to its opposite.

One of the dangers for the reader playing this game is to fail to maintain adequate critical distance from the attitudes and assumptions of the characters, or mistakenly to identify them with Kroetsch's own. Peter Thomas, for example, simplifies the novel as being typical Kroetsch: "once more Kroetsch pairs a restrained central character with his unrestrained *doppelganger*" (69). To Robert Lecker the novel presents "a typical Kroetschian conflict between a father figure aligned with the East, the rooted past, narrative definition, and institutionalized learning, and a surrogate son whose dream is counter-East, who responds unpredictably to immediate circumstances, who thrives on inventing himself" (62). Arnold Davidson refers to the book in terms of the "hoary opposition of youth versus age. . . ." (136). Peter Sinnema concludes that Jeremy and Madham remain trapped in a dialectic opposition:

> Whereas Jeremy can see himself becoming Madham within the dialectic . . . he cannot go Indian. Braids versus brush-cut is a gap impossible to span, but the episteme of Binghamton . . . binds Jeremy into a system of knowledge enabling dialogue with Mark Madham. Overdetermined by the valorized ambiguity of ***Gone Indian*** which throws him into a dialectical contiguity with Madham, Jeremy cannot abandon notions of indigenous Otherness in the very moment he quests to go Indian.
>
> (94)

Jeremy's dream *is* "counter-East" and to "go Indian" initially, but by the end of the novel, he has dropped out of the dialogue that Sinnema cites: Jeremy no longer "quests to go Indian." Jeremy originally wants to become Grey Owl, who "killed" his former self as Archie Belaney to become reborn as an Indian naturalist and author. Stanley Fogel contends that Jeremy's dream "To become Grey Owl is to free himself from the welter of words that paralyses him . . ." (84). Most opinions of the novel similarly view the dream to become Grey Owl as freeing, but Jeremy's vague struggle to become Grey Owl actually paralyses him from taking action, leading him to reject actual possibilities for transformation. Jeremy's wilful at-

tempt to become Grey Owl is as wrong-headed as Madham's trying to turn Jeremy into a younger version of himself. When Daniel Beaver tells Jeremy that Grey Owl would be proud of the way Sadness handled himself in the fight after the snowshoe race, Jeremy's reaction makes clear that it is to a misty ideal of Grey Owl that he aspires:

> "He was a good fighter," Daniel explained. "He killed a man himself one time, in a fight."
>
> "He killed himself," I whispered. I didn't dare flex a muscle. "He killed Archie Belaney. Then he became Grey Owl."
>
> "I never heard of that," Daniel said. "But once he killed a man. Another man. He was quick with a knife, Grey Owl. He liked to drink. He liked women. . . ."
>
> "You didn't know him," I said aloud, defending Grey Owl. No one could say those things about my borderman. My pathfinder.
>
> (100–101)

The temptation to which Fogel and others appear to succumb is to see Madham as the negative role model and Grey Owl as the positive role model simply because Jeremy sees them that way. Surely Madham, rather than being merely emblematic of a "rooted past" and the repressive East, is as much a product of transformation as Grey Owl, even if we disallow the hinted possibility of his being the mature Robert Sunderman, Bea's absent husband. Madham grew up in the West and reinvented himself; he dreamed East and pursued a counter-quest to become an academic intellectual. And, just as surely, Grey Owl is as much a concluded self as Madham, his character set down, idealized, and reified in the books he published and the invented history he told—no refuge from a paralysing welter of words there.

Jeremy's first name was the dubious last gift of his father, who disappeared after naming him for Jeremy Bentham in the hope, Jeremy's mother tells him, that he would grow up to be a professor (52). Madham takes over as surrogate father, further encouraging academic discipline and rationality. Again the temptation is to label this inherited desire negative and Jeremy's desire for transformation positive, but the desire to become a professor would surely seem a dream of transformation for Jeremy's father, a rootless sailor, and for Madham as well, who has undergone such a metamorphosis, leaving behind in his boyhood the Northwest Jeremy seeks. And the dream of becoming Grey Owl is equally an inherited desire. The tailor across the hall from Sadness's childhood home, who also assumes the role of surrogate father, provides an alternative to the ambition Jeremy's real father held for him: "He *gave* me *his* dream of the European boy who became . . . pathfinder . . . borderman . . . the truest Indian of them all" (emphasis added) (94). The desire to become Grey Owl, however positive that ambition may seem when contrasted to the notion of emulating Jeremy Bentham, is nonetheless someone else's dream and a dream to adopt someone else's identity.

The misreading of the critical text and the novel are linked most clearly in the reactions of most critics to the role of female characters in *Gone Indian*; the critical responses tend similarly to simplify the complexity, ambiguity, and indeterminate nature of most of the characters in the book, male or female. Few characters in the novel are what or who they seem to be, and fewer still remain consistent throughout the narrative, so it is unlikely that a whole class of characters could be relegated to a single, unambiguous and unchanging role. Citing Thomas, though, Lecker notes a typical male-female opposition:

> . . . Jeremy must flee several constraints. One of these is Woman. Like Dorck, Jeremy persistently tries to escape from Bea and Jill Sunderman, both of whom threaten to sunder man in time. Conforming to Kroetsch's female stereotype, they are cast "as representatives of the female claim in time."
>
> (69)

Lecker, like Thomas and many others, fails to recognize that this "female stereotype" is being exploded in Kroetsch's work. Lecker confuses the stereotype of the entrapping, domesticating female Kroetsch perceives in earlier Prairie writing (and describes in **"The Fear of Women in Prairie Fiction"**) with the role of the female in Kroetsch's own fiction.

The role of Woman as Lecker and Thomas discuss it corresponds more with how the male characters and narrators perceive the female characters than with how the reader comes to understand them. Linda Hutcheon attributes at least some of this distortion to the gender-bias of male critics, but, regardless of its source, her description of its result is germane. She points out that there are varied images of the female in the novel, not just the entrapping Woman:

> . . . while there are indeed images connecting women to enclosure in Kroetsch's novels, these are often the images offered by a male narrator and reflect more upon his individual (limited) view of women than upon the text's view as a whole. Bea and Jill . . . may indeed be named the ominous "Sunderman," but . . . first of all, it is Bea's *husband's* name, and second, within a postmodern perspective, the notion of 'sundering man' may well be a positive. . . . Kroetsch has always . . . worked to show how male and female roles are fictions. . . .
>
> (171)

Madham's reaction to Carol Sadness's last statement in the book indicates the degree to which the reader's perception of the female characters is determined by their presentation by the male narrators. As he attempts to convince her that her husband must have died in the collision with the train or the fall from the bridge, Carol interrupts, "I would have gone with him." "It is that kind of silliness that intrudes upon reason" (153) is Madham's only comment, but the surprise the reader experiences at Carol's remark is due to the limited perspective both Madham and Jeremy—and so the reader—have of her. Neither can see her as anything but a single, stereotypical entity. To Jeremy, she is the demanding shrew of a wife he left behind; to Madham, she is the youthful, adoring sop for his ego.

Jeremy defines her as being like Madham; Madham defines her as opposed to Jeremy; neither sees her as herself, or guesses that she may share the desire for freedom that each imagines is a solely male quest.

Critical views of this book, then, tend to over-simplify the oppositions—East-West, male-female, stasis-flux, reason-intuition, and the rest—by not giving full weight to the shifting nature of the opposed pairs, and to what often turns out to be the near identity of apparent opposites. Kroetsch's position is not that we live in a dualistic, dichotomized world, but that the human mind seeks dualistic structures and easily assimilated binary oppositions. What he says of the doubled world of *The Double Hook* is clearly applicable to his own work: "should not the dichotomies themselves be dissolved?" ("Death" 210). In the same passage Kroetsch notes that James, the pivotal figure in Sheila Watson's novel, is "freed . . . from freedom," from the need to be the questing male, seeking invulnerablity in isolation. Kroetsch's novels similarly celebrate those characters who break out of the binary pattern, albeit often only briefly, not those who demonstrate the dominance of one aspect of a dualistic opposition, even if it is the "active" half. Jeremy is not celebrated for championing the West versus Madham's East, or for asserting male isolation over female domesticity, but because at the end, and briefly during the narrative, he is able to make his mind a virtual blank, to experience without interpreting, without reducing existence to a system of binary opposites. When he is with Bea in bed, for instance, he feels like the "free man freed from his freedom" (149), is "as blank as the darkness" (146), and considers writing a thesis entitled "The Quest Unquestioned" (149).

And although Sadness is thought to be in opposition to Madham, the two are more alike than not. Throughout the novel Jeremy is tormented by the notion that "There is always a loser. . . . There is always a winner" (120), a logical outcropping of the habit of binary thinking. He may disdain Madham's academicism, but he is possessed of it as well. When Jeremy is asked at the Winter Carnival to pick the Winter Queen, to distinguish again between the winner and the losers, he is unnerved by the silence of the virtually identical candidates. Despite his dream of returning to elemental silence in the indifferent North, the experience of actual silence engenders only confusion and anxiety and leaves him yearning for the comforting if illusory solidity of Madham's scholarly outlook:

> Not once did any one of the candidates speak a word. Not a human word. To me, a man forever attracted to the maelstrom. Something in me wanted to write in the margins of those lives: Awk. Frag. Emph. Cap. Fig. Instead I was offered silence. What in heaven was I supposed to judge?
>
> (114)

Sadness shares Madham's tendency to reduce the world to a comprehensible form, despite his attraction to the "maelstrom," and as the narrative unfolds it becomes increasingly apparent that Madham is also more like than unlike Sadness, taking over Jeremy's role as the mate of Carol, even imitating the lovemaking of the buffalo as Jeremy aspires to do. He shares, Jeremy says, Jeremy's impotence, and while Sadness has been stalled on his dissertation for nine years, Madham has been unable to finish his own masterwork for fifteen. Madham is not simply an Eastern, establishment academic who desires order for its own sake; he claims to have experienced at an early age the dissolution of identity and the fearsome indifference of the blank prairie that Sadness now faces, and he has asserted order in opposition to it. If anything, Madham is more aware than Jeremy of the opportunity afforded by the frontier for transformation, noting that Carol could not "grasp the consequences of the northern prairies to human definition: the diffusion of personality into a complex of possibilities rather than a concluded self" (152). Immediately after the passage above, he complains of being stifled by the Binghamton weather, one of the many signals that Madham is not the "concluded self" he believes himself to be.

The lack of solidity in the apparent opposition of Sadness and Madham is emblematic of the fluid state of identity in the novel from its beginning. Entering the carnivalistic world of the Northwest at Edmonton airport, Jeremy gets his first exposure to a land in which "Illusion is rife" (8). Having mistakenly picked up baggage belonging to Roger Dorck, he is detained in a holding cell with a young woman who turns out to be a young man, who claims further to have been a buffalo in a past life. Inspired by this vision of transformation, Jeremy determines to escape, "DISGUISED AS MYSELF" (11). That Jeremy considers his own public self a disguise underscores the distinction between perceived self and the unconcluded self or selves concealed by that pretense. This is one of the many transitory and unsatisfactory metamorphoses Jeremy will undergo. Although he already dresses and wears his hair like an Indian (albeit a stereotypical Indian—Daniel Beaver's children mock him for this [65]), he feels he has become even more an Indian when he receives Daniel's jacket (93). He has also become Roger Dorck, and so the carnival's Winter King and the judge of the Winter Queen contest. He becomes a mock prisoner, and, in his dream, a buffalo and Has-Two-Chances (106). He becomes a corpse in a coffin, and flirts with being Robert Sunderman. Significantly, though, it is when he is not consciously seeking to *become* someone, but merely thoughtlessly voids his own received identity, that he finds the freedom and peace he seeks. In Madham's words, as he allows Digger, a fellow reveler, to assume his identity, "The metamorphosis, one is tempted to say, was complete. Jeremy [was] no longer himself," having "unwittingly lent his precious self to that old gravedigger" (139).

Although Jeremy often yearns for the solidity of identity that Madham represents, he desires equally the release from fixed identity that Madham rejected when he fled the Northwest in his youth. Madham's escape is typical of the many responses by men to similar threats to their sense of an inviolate, unitary identity. The evasion of responsibility

and vulnerability is the quest for freedom for the novel's men, but Jeremy is "freed from his freedom," his need to pursue that quest further. Kroetsch's novels typically present an elemental opposition of earth and sky, of body and soul, represented in images of the spirit soaring and then being pulled to earth again by the weight of the body's demands. Also typical is the male characters' seeking freedom from domesticating women. The desire to fly, to escape the pull of the earth and of women becomes a central motif in this novel too. Sadness imagines Dorck's snowmobile accident as a beautiful moment: ". . . he leaped up and over; like a dream of himself he climbed, into the night air, free of the earth at last, his freed engine roaring" (26). The only drawback to this sort of flight, of course, is that it ends in a fall: it cannot be sustained. The liberation that Sadness finally arrives at by rejecting this opposition of earth/sky and man/woman can be sustained, perhaps, because it does not depend upon the continual escape from women. Rather than the flight from Woman ending in a paralysing fall back to earth, Jeremy soars with a woman and manages to stay aloft. Although this is only conjecture—the fate of Sadness and Bea is ambiguous—it is supported at least by Jeremy's choice of vehicle. Like Dorck before him, Jeremy's flight begins on a snowmobile, but rather than a Skidoo or Bombardier, Sadness identifies the make as a Sleipnir, which confuses Madham (somewhat improbably) (137). (The immediate source of Sleipnir is likely *As For Me and My House*—a central text for **"The Fear of Women in Prairie Fiction,"** too—in which the narrator, Mrs. Bentley, imagines that the men in her life would like to transform their horse into a "Sleipnir or Pegasus" to escape her [140].) The snowmobile is named for the legendary eight-legged steed of Odin, the Norse equivalent of Pegasus. Among other deeds, Odin rode Sleipnir into the land of the dead and returned again, and it is exactly that kind of experience that is suggested here, especially in that an undertaker supplied the vehicle and that Jeremy emerged from a coffin to begin his journey. The dissolution of Jeremy's identity, the breaking down of the schematized patterns of thought, is a kind of death, but, unlike the "deaths" of Sunderman and Dorck, it is not a descent into paralysis, into the closure of coma or the freezing waters (or the paralysis of a "concluded self" that Madham suffers). Rather, it is suggested, Jeremy *and* Bea leap into the abyss but are saved from their apparent fate by their choice of vehicle and, more importantly, the warmth of each other's body—everything else, all of the restrictive elements of identity, falls away. Again, it is not a matter of fleeing Woman—except as a constraining, falsifying conception—but of breaking out of the prison of perceived identity, being a man and a woman, not Man and Woman, which even Madham recognizes: "Perhaps what really matters is the warmth each finds in the other's body. Two bodies. Warm. The rest is fiction . . ." (157).

Before this end is reached, though, the journey on the snowmobile takes Sadness first to Sunderman's house, WORLDS END. During his first visit, he had seen it as a contrast to the images of flight and freedom. Jeremy likens it to Madham's house, its interior an "imprisoned garden"

(31), a world of plentitude and fertility encased, contained, controlled. The house is filled also with clocks—"Someone didn't trust the sun" (32)—which no longer tick. This house of clocks is the evidence claimed by most critics, Lecker, Thomas and Fogel among them, for labelling Bea and Jill as "representatives of the female claim in time" (Thomas 72), and Bea as "seeking to reduce the questing male to slippered pantaloon" (Thomas 79). Robert Lecker, citing both of the statements by Thomas above, insists that WORLDS END is "filled with artificial time. . . . dominated by time, days, dates, numbers, history, closure. . . . both Madham and Bea are interested in closed structures that leave no room for Jeremy's achronological quest" (70). But time is not an issue in Bea's house; the clocks do not tick and the plants do not depend upon seasons, so the interior of the house is "achronological" too. Also, Bea and her house are in a virtual state of suspended chronology because of her abandonment by her husband—and by Dorck, who had taken his place—so it does not seem fair or logical to associate that state with "Woman." As Hutcheon suggests, it is Robert Sunderman who does the sundering, not his wife and daughter, who have had that name and the state it suggests imposed upon them.

Lecker and Thomas and others talk in terms of Jeremy's escaping Madham, Jill, and Bea so that he can be freed into his quest, but in this novel, as in Kroetsch's others, freedom consists not of the liberty to pursue the quest but in being liberated *from* it. Although Sadness initially likens Bea to Madham because he believes that she, too, wants to fix his identity, to transform him into her errant husband, Jeremy comes to perceive in Bea an opportunity to avoid establishing a concrete, singular self. When he returns to WORLDS END on the Sleipnir, he finds not a trapped Eden but a pre-Edenic darkness, a blankness, in which he is able to escape the academic need to explain and to find "a suitable metaphor" for his experience (148). He sees himself as the "free man freed from his freedom" (149), freed from the demands of the imposed male quest story that drives most of Kroetsch's male characters.

Jeremy's flight is clearly not away from women or even Woman, especially in that his ability to gain an erection in bed with a woman is the barometer of his psychic well-being. It is when Jeremy's focus shifts from his desire to escape domestic entrapment and preserve his male solitude to a desire to interact openly and directly with a woman that that barometer begins to rise. At WORLDS END, Jeremy joins Bea in bed, and, finally, instead of envying and emulating the flight of Robert Sunderman and Roger Dorck, Sadness empathizes with the woman they have abandoned:

> All those years she had been waiting and now he had returned to the bed that was kept for him. . . . As if every woman kept a bed, not for a husband, not for her everyday lover, but for the mysterious youth who one night years ago walked into the darkness, vanished from the very surface of the earth. . . . And after all the waiting of all those women, one figure had finally returned. Finally. At last.

> And then I made a discovery.
> I was in bed. I had an erection.

> (148)

Clearly, then, it is not Bea, or Woman, or even WORLDS END itself that restrains Jeremy, since when he returns to all three with an altered inner vision he finds himself healed and liberated by them, not weakened and entrapped. It is worth noting, too, that the males in the story seem more desirous of stopping time than the females: not seeking to live outside time or with time, but selfishly to halt it, as it appears to be stopped in Bea's house. Madham suggests that it is Robert Sunderman who seeks to halt the flow of time, imagining the young Sunderman on the ice of the river: "his child-bride pregnant, the boy-husband alone, already regretting the boyhood he could not quite surrender . . ." (155). Dorck's flying and falling result in a similar halting of time: when he wakes, he remembers nothing from the moment of Sunderman's disappearance (155). Time is restarted for Bea and Jeremy at WORLDS END, not because Jeremy has completed his quest for a new identity, becoming Grey Owl, but because he has been freed from his male need to escape Woman and Time. WORLDS END, then, is not World's End with a missing apostrophe, not the trapped, entrapping Eden; it is instead a promise that worlds do end, that the "cosmologies of belief" (to use Kroetsch's phrase) can be escaped. Jeremy does not assume, so far as we can know, a new identity, but appears to allow the layers of identity to become diffuse and open. He is very nearly a blank, unthinking and nonverbal, by the narrative's close.

The depiction of the experience Sadness has on his journey to WORLDS END is typical of how Kroetsch images the fluidity of identity. In such cases, the character is exposed to some overwhelming elemental force: an overflowing river, a whirlwind, a swarm of bees, an avalanche, or the like. To reach Bea, Sadness must pass through a blinding blizzard. The elemental chaos of the swirling snow forces him to find his own way, to create a new path, just as he is seeking to find a native, fluid identity instead of appropriating another's. "I was in the trackless snow, making my own path" (144), no longer seeking to become Grey Owl, "my pathfinder" (101), nor even becoming his own pathfinder, but forging entirely new, untrodden paths. He puts his trust in "a homing instinct that resided as much in my hands as in my head" (144). Upon his arrival, he becomes aware that something different, something alive, has entered the house with him: "Of this I am certain, however: a clock that had not been ticking began to tick" (146). As in the blizzard when he found that his instinct and body were a better guide than his intellect, now, in bed with Bea, "All thinking had swooned from my mind. I was as blank as the darkness around me" (146). The cause of his previous impotency becomes clear when it recurs briefly: "Yes, I was thinking again. . . . I was paralysed into thought. I was once again a total stranger to my own prick. I was at a dead loss as to what I must do." (147). Fortunately, Bea possesses the solution. She, "That invisible woman," is suddenly an earth figure, bringing to the entire room, the "smell of earth":

. . . not of flowers only, but the dark breathing silence of ferns in crevices of rock. The lichens, orange and yellow, on a rotting limb. The green moss, cool to the sliding mouse. The smell of a northern forest, where the snow melts itself black into the last shade.

(147)

She facilitates the final step in the process of dissolution of Jeremy's identity, the confrontation with silence, at which Jeremy paled earlier. Bea does not represent the caretaker of imprisoned Edens, but:

The Columbus quest for the oldest New World. The darkest gold. The last first. I was lifting my hidden face. To the gateway beyond. To the place of difficult entrance. To the real gate to the dreamed cave. . . .

I had tongued the unspeakable silence.

(147)

Jeremy, by his physical union with Bea, has transcended language and his inherited voice to find the silence and fresh beginning he had sought. It is a perpetual return to the point of origin, of creation, always beginning again, never concluding. Their union is beyond words:

To speak would be to boast. And I was speechless. Perhaps I roared. I am not certain now. I did not moan. To say that we were joined, Bea and I, would be, once again, to underline the failure of language. We were wedded in the smithy of our mutual desire. Fused in the bellowed flame. Tonged and hammered. . . . No no no no no no. I have ransacked my twenty-five years of education for a suitable metaphor. I have done a quick review of logic, called upon the paradigms of literature and history. I have put to test the whole theory of a liberal education.

Nothing.

Absolutely nothing.

I only know that for a long, long time I had not heard the ticking clocks.

(148)

The clocks continue to tick—time is not stopped—but in his altered state, they are no longer a source of anxiety for Sadness. Unlike the other male characters in the story, rather than running away from Woman and Time, Sadness has come to terms with time and mortality by accepting and connecting with an individual woman, cutting through the layers of inherited and imposed identity which imprisoned both him and Bea. In terms Kroetsch has used often, Jeremy is freed from being questing Ulysses, Bea from being patient Penelope.

Again, then, according to most readings of the novel, the possibilities of transformation offered Sadness in **Gone Indian** are represented by Madham and Bentham on the one hand and Grey Owl on the other. Jeremy Bentham figures in the narration only in the image of his preserved body in a glass case in University College, but early in the novel the other two possibilities are opposed in Jeremy's mind. His discussion with his professor makes clear that he can become Madham *or* Grey Owl:

"Sadness . . . there's only one problem in this world that you take seriously. . . . Why did Archie Belaney become Grey Owl?"

"The story of a man," I agreed, "who died into a new life."

"He faked the death."

"But woke up free nevertheless."

"Be serious."

"One false move, Professor, and instead of addressing you, I'll be you. That's serious."

(62)

By the end of the novel, though, *all* of the models of identity are rejected. Jeremy Bentham is permanently fixed in his glass case, having "become his own icon" (51). Grey Owl's created self is permanently set in type. And Madham, who has similarly re-invented himself, strives mightily to maintain his concluded self and resist further transformation. Of all the characters in the novel, Jeremy ends up most like his real father, rather than any of the surrogates. His father's identity is an enigma, his only connection with the family since Jeremy's birth an unsigned postcard from Genoa—like Jeremy, he appears not to trust his own name. But unlike even that role model, and contrary to the claims of Lecker, Thomas, Fogel, and others, Sadness does not seek freedom by escaping Woman and Eastern intellectualism by dreaming West in order to become Grey Owl or anyone else. Instead, he discovers the fluidity of identity and recognizes that both he and Bea have been trapped by the restrictive conceptions they have of themselves and each other. In an interview with Alan Twigg, Kroetsch responds to the comment that women often escape traditional roles only to discover that there are no obvious alternative roles by agreeing, but saying also that the same is true for men. More importantly, though, Kroetsch views this lack of clear role models as a boon:

In order to go west, a man had to define himself as an orphan, as an outlaw, as a cowboy. With those definitions, how can you marry a woman? How can you enter the house again? You have to lose that self-definition. That's the problem for the male. He must break his self-inflicted definition of maleness.

(112)

Kroetsch's characters may experience an initial anxiety at this dissolution of identity, but this anxiety is typically followed by an acceptance of the continuing freedom that dissolution brings. Rather than escaping Woman, Jeremy finds a woman, recognizes the entrapping and isolating nature of the male quest he has followed, and achieves an authentic relationship with her on the basis of that recognition. He and she are not Man and Woman, but human, possessed of protean identities that continue to shift because they are not rigidly fixed in a repressive dichotomy of gender.

Works Cited

Creelman, David. "Robert Kroetsch: Criticism in the Middle Ground." *Studies in Canadian Literature* 16.1 (1991): 63–81.

Davidson, Arnold. "Will the Real R. Mark Madham Please Stand Up: A Note on Robert Kroetsch's *Gone Indian.*" *Studies in Canadian Literature* 5 (1980): 127–37.

Fogel, Stanley. *A Tale of Two Countries: Contemporary Fiction in Canada and the United States*, Toronto: ECW Press, 1984.

Hutcheon, Linda. *The Canadian Postmodern: A Study of Contemporary English-Canadian Fiction*, Toronto: Oxford UP, 1988.

Kroetsch, Robert. "The Fear of Women in Prairie Fiction: An Erotics of Space." *Open Letter* 5.4 (1983): 47–55.

———. *Gone Indian.* Toronto: new press, 1975.

———, and Diane Bessai. "Death is a Happy Ending: A Dialogue in Thirteen Parts." *Figures in a Ground.* Ed. Diane Bessai and David Jackel. Saskatoon: Western Producer Prairie Books, 1978. 206–215.

Lecker, Robert. *Robert Kroetsch.* Twayne's World Authors Series: Canadian Literature. Boston: Twayne, 1986.

Ross, Sinclair. *As For Me and My House.* Toronto: McClelland and Stewart, 1989.

Rudy-Dorscht, Susan. "How *The Studhorse Man Makes* Love: A Postfeminist Analysis." *Canadian Literature* 119 (1988): 25–31.

———. *Telling the Difference: Rereading 'Woman,' with Robert Kroetsch's Writing.* Ph.D. dissertation. York University. June 1988.

Sinnema, Peter W. "Quest(ion)ing *Gone Indian*'s Dialectic: Subversive Repetition and the Possibility of a "Centred" Indigene." *World Literature Written in English* 30.2 (1990): 85–95.

Thomas, Peter. *Robert Kroetsch.* Studies in Canadian Literature Series 13. Vancouver: Douglas & McIntyre, 1980.

Turner, M. E. "Canadian Literature and Robert Kroetsch: A Case of Canonization." *Dalhousie Review* 67.1 (1987): 56–72.

Twigg, Alan. "Male: Robert Kroetsch." *For Openers: Conversations with 24 Canadian Writers.* Alan Twigg. Madeira Park, B.C.: Harbour, 1981. 107–116.

Douglas Glover (review date February 1993)

SOURCE: A review of *The Puppeteer,* in *Books in Canada,* Vol. XXII, No. 1, February, 1993, pp. 40-41.

[*In the following review, Glover calls* The Puppeteer "*a literary confection of the first order," but concedes that it may not be for everyone.*]

I once knew a man in New York who worked as a buyer of rare works of art, which he collected worldwide, mostly as a tax dodge for wealthy clients who paid low prices and then donated the works to institutions at inflated paper values. One of his clients happened to be a Calgary oil baron who might have been a model for the mythically rich, half-blind transvestite millionaire named Jack Deemer who narrates Robert Kroetsch's clever new avant-garde novel **The Puppeteer**.

Jack Deemer is a collector extraordinaire—of people as well as *objects d'art*. He has warehouses full of the latter, but people he has found somewhat less tractable. His wife Julie, for example, is dead, killed in a mysterious car crash in Portugal four years before, after spending a vacation in bed with Billy Dorfendorf, Deemer's collecting agent, and a Portuguese dwarf named Dr. Manuel De Medeiros, who scouted spas for his wealthy but ailing master.

Dorfendorf subsequently murders Dr. De Medeiros in an undeveloped British Columbia spa called Deadman Spring, although no body is ever found. Hunted by both the police and Deemer, Dorfendorf has gone into hiding in Vancouver where he works nights as a, yes, social-worker-cum-pizza-delivery-man known as Papa B.

Enter a writer named Maggie Wilder, recently settled in Vancouver after abandoning her icon-collecting husband to his obsessions in Greece. Maggie plans to hole up in her cousin George's house (George is a botanist, a collector of rainforest plants that litter the house) and write a biography of her wedding dress, which she happens to be wearing the night she opens the door to take delivery of a pizza.

Maggie's wedding dress just happens to be the wedding dress Julie wore when she married Jack Deemer. It was hand-made by a woman named Josie Povich who just happens to work in the pizzeria for which Dorfendorf makes deliveries. Maggie bought the dress second-hand, after Deemer returned it to Josie the day after his wedding. The dress is the reason Maggie married her icon-collecting husband—the dress is a strange and magical object, the reason for everything and the object of everyone's desire.

It is not clear why Jack Deemer wants the wedding dress back, but he does. Nor is it absolutely clear why he returned it to Josie Povich after the wedding in the first place. But this is part of the structural charm of the avant-garde. Motivation, a stalwart crutch of verisimilitude, isn't important, whereas coincidence, repeating imagery, and repeated event are.

The Puppeteer is a whimsical tissue of coincidence and repeated pattern (embroidered on the wedding dress is a miniature copy of the wedding dress). At every point it intentionally disappoints conventional novelistic expectation. It leaves its tools in the wall, so to speak.

It plays with literary echoes—and is a sort of murder mystery (though it turns out there hasn't been a murder). The puppeteer motif brings to mind John Fowles's *The Magus.* Deemer is an ancient magician, an oil-patch Tiresias. And the unexpected shifts of point of view—the novel begins in the third person in Maggie's mind but intermittently slips into Jack Deemer's first person—look backward to Nabokov or Hubert Aquin.

The Puppeteer also relies heavily on set-piece riffs, heavy with implication and connected to the narrative proper by a network of analogies and repetitions. For example, there is a lovely sequence of scenes after Papa B. takes refuge in Maggie's attic. Papa B. turns the attic into a Greek shadow-puppet theatre, acting out his version of the novel (like the dress embroidered on the dress), mesmerizing Maggie, gradually winning her over and luring her into the (shadow) play.

This is all splendid fun, a literary confection of the first order that is still perhaps an acquired taste (some readers will balk at giving up their standard plots and emotional hooks). And it is not without meaning. Kroetsch deploys two of his own early literary hobby-horses—collecting and spas—as, one suspects, a half-mocking critique of white Western civilization. Are we not, he seems to say, dooming ourselves to pratfall and tragicomedy with our obsession about controlling material things and prolonging life?

But such thematic interpretation is peripheral to Kroetsch's main project, which is really a critique of conventional theories of meaning and the traditional novel. The book's final joke involves some Greek icons that Deemer is trying to collect (read, "steal") from Maggie's husband, one of which represents the face of God.

The substance of *The Puppeteer* keeps disappearing as the reader reads, and the ever-beckoning, ever-receding picture of God is like the meaning of the book, an emblem of all meaning—which is to say that the universe is a riddle, sure enough, and a bit of a tease.

Douglas Reimer (essay date Spring 1993)

SOURCE: "Heideggarian Elements in Robert Kroetsch's *Seed Catalogue*," in *Canadian Literature*, No. 136, Spring, 1993, pp. 115-28.

[*In the following essay, Reimer locates Heidegger's notions about authentic truth and being in Kroetsch's* Seed Catalogue.]

Robert Kroetsch's *Seed Catalogue* is neither phenomenological nor structuralist, to borrow a distinction made by David Carroll in *The Subject in Question* (15). That is, it is neither subject-centered nor language-centered, but belongs, instead, to a third, rare, more sylleptic mode of writing aware of and making use of the conventions of the other two. As David Arnason has shown in "Robert Kroetsch: The Deconstruction of the Metanarrative of the Cowboy," *Seed Catalogue* deconstructs ideologies which have become familiar to us concerning the Western hero and the purpose and function of the poem and the poet on the prairie, and is concerned with language and the way writing is a supplement to speech and experience.[1] Yet the poem seems to some extent at least to have retained the phenomenological subject, the philosophical subject. Furthermore, it appears to be deeply concerned with the

problem of truth and, in this light, practices a Heideggerian uninventing and unnaming. It uninvents spring, for instance: the spring season that opens the poem is not renamed but deconstructed much like the dismantling of storm windows (Brown 154) when the weather changes:

> We took the storm windows/off
> the south side of the house
> and put them on the hotbed.
> Then it was spring. Or, no
> then winter was ending.

> (*Seed Catalogue* 109)

For all its promised warmth and renewal, the spring retains winter and cold and death within it and this metaphor (with its negating "no") appears to reflect what Heidegger thinks about both truth and Being. *Dasein*, authentic Being, is fundamentally aware of its own dying, knows that death is its "ownmost" possibility. Authentic, moral living cannot come about without the newness and the extraordinariness which *angst* and the certainty of death, unmitigated by transcendentalism or spiritualism of any kind, give to *dasein*. Truth and untruth have a similar paradoxical relationship and neither *is* without the other, any more than Being *is* authentic without the knowledge of history (change) at its centre. The poet in *Seed Catalogue* is a Heideggerian poet who, through his consciousness of Being and his facing up to death, provides for his people and for his prairie community.

The philosophical subject is central to Heidegger, though as William Barrett notes, nowhere in his writings do you find references to either "man" or "consciousness" (218): the subject is too important a question to name and thus, like the existential humanists or the pre-Romantics (and to an extent the Romantics), to bind and imprison within one, permanent, unchanging and suffocating understanding of his Being—to take history "forever" out of the Being of being. The poet, who falls off his horse in the poem's opening lines, is never named either—he is just the nameless cowboy unhorsed,[2] yet he is also the conventional autobiographical subject, the poet writing a poem about becoming a poet. Not unlike the description of the will-less protagonist which opens Sinclair Ross's *As For Me and My House* (1941),[3] this first picture we have of the subject is self-deprecating:

> Winter was ending.
> This is what happened:
> we were harrowing the garden.
> You've got to understand this:
> I was sitting on the horse.
> The horse was standing still.
> I fell off.

> (110)

This subject is not the ordinary prairie farm boy who, if he ever fell off a horse, would fall off one that was galloping, or at least in motion. Eventually this incompetence makes sense. The subject is a budding poet—a "sissy" (Arnason 82), not quite a man, someone who, on the prairies, is looked upon with contempt and expected to "hang around the girlies." His father's prohibition against writing, and particularly against writing poetry, makes clear the extent to which the poet is alienated from the prairie community, to the point even of having his sonship implicitly questioned. The father attempts to drive the poetic spirit out of his son with hard work:

> First off I want you to take that
> crowbar and drive 1,156 holes
> in that gumbo.
> And the next time you want to
> write a poem
> we'll start the haying.

(119)

But the father doesn't succeed and the rest of the poem continues the fragmented story of the boy's growing consciousness of the world around him and of his development as a poet in the unlikely poetic soil of the Canadian prairies. His memories include the death of his mother, his father's unsuccessful attempts at shooting a badger on the farm and the myth he builds for himself about the event later, his various experiences with sex as a boy, drinking bouts with friends and their revelries, and his own perceptions of the role of the poet in the community.

You can't escape the fact of the phenomenological subject in *Seed Catalogue* which is a prairie *künstlerroman*; an autobiography; our prairie version of Wordsworth's *The Prelude*. The poem is not, however, at all self-conscious in the sense of Romantic (Hegelian, Kantian) self-consciousness, the sort which Geoffrey Hartman describes in his "Romanticism and 'anti-selfconsciousness'." In fact, its purpose is to re-write or unname exactly that sort of super self-consciousness which makes an idol of individual self-awareness. We do find out a little about the subject: the location of "the home place: N. E. 17–42–16-W 4th Meridian," the names of a few relatives, and the fact that he has certain writer friends such as Al Purdy and Rudy Wiebe. Because of the general sparseness of detail, however, and the unconvincing neglect to provide enough biographical information to help the reader locate the subject neatly in time and place, the poem is really not a traditional autobiography. The biographical specificity is more the identity of the home of all prairie small-town people than of the poet himself. *Seed Catalogue*'s self-less consciousness is the self under erasure.

If *Seed Catalogue* is erasing the self, finding only traces of the past of self whose Being is no longer recoverable, and who is always-already Being in a future time, then it is writing as supplement, writing that is aware of its own disjunctiveness and dissociation from the "reality" of the thing it has chosen to describe. The subject is "Pinch Me" (*Seed Catalogue* 131n) who is left at the end of the poem when Adam and Eve both "got drownded" (44). He is the "Pinch Me," of "pinch me to see if I am dreaming," and the ending (all endings which conventional poetry dramatizes are rewritten in this poem) is only the question

after which you hope to find an answer or at least a response—some sort of continuation.[4]

Heidegger's "The Origin of the Work of Art," is helpful here. In it, he establishes the "thingly character" (19) of works of art:

> Works of art are shipped like coal from the Ruhr and logs from the Black Forest. During the First World War Holderlin's hymns were packed in the soldier's knapsack together with cleaning gear. Beethoven's quartets lie in the storerooms of the publishing house like potatoes in a cellar.

(19)

"Thingness" is the essence of an entity before various traits have gathered around it: "Obviously, a thing is not merely an aggregate of traits, nor an accumulation of properties by which that aggregate arises. A thing, as everyone thinks he knows, is that around which the properties have assembled" (23). Things, for Heidegger, including works of art, are not simply constructs without a reference outside of the "mere" chain of signifiers which describe them. The early Greeks knew about this "rootedness" of things. Things had in them a thereness, a Being of beings: ("*hupokeimenon* . . . the core of the thing, something always already there" 23). Not so for the Western world and the interpretation of Being (presence) it standardized later. There was a rootlessness to its understanding of Being from the Romans on—an inauthenticity at the heart of all things that resulted from the falseness of their translation of Greek experience into their language: "Roman thought takes over the Greek words without a corresponding, equally authentic experience of what they say, without the Greek word. The rootlessness of Western thought begins with this translation" (23). There is for Heidegger an original, irreducible, essential quality in things; in this sense he is essentialist.[5]

This question of the thingness of the work of art is important for *Seed Catalogue*. Out of its thingness the work of art derives all its power for it is, like any other work, functional, and productive. It has "reliability" and it describes the reliability of the objects and experiences it focuses on, as, for instance, Van Gogh's painting of the peasant's pair of shoes tells all about the work they do (Shaver 244); about the industry of the one who used them, about the particular function they served for the user, as well as about something more original in which these shoes are rooted—a *truth* about shoes: "The art work let's us know what shoes are in truth" (35). So, the object of art is to get us in touch with the original Being of things. Art, itself an original thing before the concept of art, has incredible power to present Being which is by nature hidden from us. In this sense, in his discussion of what it means to be an artist on the prairie, the poet of *Seed Catalogue* is engaged in the question of the truth of his art. How does his work truly represent the prairies? How can a poet be made in an environment which is so unfriendly to poets? In a world in which no cultural things work on the imaginations of the inhabitants nor act out their equipmentness and their reliability, how can you hope to ever begin the poetic project? How can the truth of art and the truth of being a poet originate in a land where such Being has no visible being?

> This dilemma is the very heart of the list of absences
> in the poem:
> How do you grow a past/
> to live in
>
> the absence of silkworms
> the absence of clay and wattles (whatever the hell
> they are)
> the absence of Lord Nelson
> the absence of kings and queens
> the absence of a bottle opener, and me with a vicious
> attack of the 26-ounce flu
> the absence of both Sartre and Heidegger
>
> (29)

and so on. Are these merely absences, merely the presence of metaphysical trace as Barbara Godard suggests in "Other Fictions: Robert Kroetsch's Criticism" (17)? If they are presences, then what sort of presences are they and how is the poet making us aware of the presence rather than the absence of the thing he is attempting to "set forward"—the prairie and its concealed Being?

Heidegger says about things that we experience their presence by experiencing their absence. We cannot receive a strong impression of a thing's thingness without closing ourselves to its sensations: "In order to hear a *bare* sound we have to listen away from things, divert our ear from them, i.e., listen abstractly" (26). The thing which is the sound cannot be brought near without abstracting it and removing it from its context. The Parthenon, the Cathédrale de Chartres, Sartre and Heidegger become clear to us in the remove of the context of **Seed Catalogue**. We know them better and more fully here than they could be known in their own fully familiar and sensuously cultural homeland. They are objectified here. This is a duplicity which startles the prairie writer/reader who is accustomed to lamenting the absence of culture in his back yard. The thingness of Sartre is closer to us than to the French, thus, but the unknowable Being of Sartre's being is not. We have it more and in purer form than they over there, but the abstraction of Sartre and the other cultural icons onto Canadian soil makes the whole unpalatable and inordinately unlikely:

> In the thing-concept . . . there is not so much an assault upon the thing as rather an inordinate attempt to bring it into the greatest possible proximity to us. But a thing never reaches that position as long as we assign as its thingly feature what is perceived by the senses. Whereas the first interpretation keeps the thing at arm's length from us, as it were, and sets it too far off, the second makes it press too hard upon us. In both interpretations the thing vanishes.
>
> (26)

The insertion of the familiar in the midst of the unfamiliar does two things: it heightens our awareness of the thing-

ness (Being) of the prairie objects slipped into the list of cultural absences (a condom dispenser, Louis Riel, *The Western Producer*, the principal's new car, and so on) and it displaces the nearness of the European art/ifacts and either makes them less inordinate and out of context or makes them more "pressing" and so irrelevant to us. This is exactly the poet's role in the process of finding out truth. If this juxtaposition of prairie experience and European art/experience is serviceable to us as a "work" then **Seed Catalogue** is continuing to uncover the truth.

The question of truth in works of art leads to the question of the best truth-teller society can expect to find, and thus ultimately to the role of the poet in the community. Related to the way we try to experience things, as familiar and as unfamiliar, is a third possibility which is to leave the thing in its constancy. The latter is what the poet does best. Kroetsch, in the list of absences, is not analyzing the things themselves, but setting them in such a light, in such a state of *dasein* (startled and startling into sudden emergence into light), and in such a state of opposition that thinking occurs. Not inordinate "philosophical" thinking, and not the splitting of the object thought about from itself (the subject), but thinking which leaves the thing thought about whole: "We ought to turn toward the being, think about it in regard to its being, but by means of this thinking at the same time let it rest upon itself in its very own being" (31).

The truth of a thing, the Being of a being, is revealed by remaining unrevealed, though thought about. Truth is also untruth. Knowing is also not knowing. Inventing is uninventing:

> But it is not we who presuppose the unconcealedness of beings; rather, the unconcealedness of beings (Being) puts us into such a condition of being that in our representation we always remain installed within and in attendance upon unconcealedness.
>
> ("Origin" 52)

The subject of **Seed Catalogue**, the poet, is the thinker, and this is just as much a dichotomy as truth = non-truth, and being = non-being. How can the poet with his unsystematic methods and his dependence on and attendance on the emotional be a thinker in Heidegger's sense of a thoughtful mind which by mediation works at preventing the race of the rest of the world towards technological thoughtlessness?[6] Furthermore, how can a thinker be *grown* on the prairie? You can train and educate an analytic philosopher, the academy can build a scientist, but how can the small town (Heisler/Todtnau) *grow* a poet? How can it grow a poet as indigenous to its place and earth as carrots and turnips and radishes? The paradox of "how do you *grow* a poet?" is precisely, too, how do you grow a thinker? How do you grow a thinker about truth in a land and age (epoch) which resists poetry and thinking—where the best we can come up with is a digger of fenceposts, a writer of huge fiction and a galloper of caribou horses through restaurants?

The good poet is the best thinker, "the precursor of poets in a destitute time" (**"What Are Poets For?"** 142). He heralds in the future with his work. In fact, the future's presence would not be available to the world without the poet: "The precursor, however, does not go off into a future; rather, he arrives out of that future, in such a way that the future is present only in the arrival of his words" (142). The good poet is not just one manifestation of truth in the world but the very measure or gauge of present Being whose work is the place to look for evidence of the state Being is in, in the world. He has to, then, be more of a thinker, more willing to risk rejection, and more deeply involved in authentic living himself than the philosopher could be. The location of authenticity, *Seed Catalogue* tells us, is in the garden and not in the academy, in the clearing and not in the library. The title of the poem, the narrative voice which tells us that love "is a leaping up and down" (113), the colloquial and humorous voice of the seed catalogue persona imitating, poorly, what it thinks is a refined British voice, the voice with its cowboy concerns which informs the reluctant waitress that Pete Knight, the king of all cowboys is dead (123), all these are authentic, oral voices,[7] The voice of being is the voice of people who are kin to nature—the farmer and the poet familiar with the farm,[8] the poet-*manqué* in one sense, are the best gauges of authentic living.

The best gauge of Heidegger's thinking about the poet is his own poetry. In an appropriate selection called "The Thinker as Poet," Heidegger explains, in verse, the qualities which make the good poet. Good thinking is discursive thinking: "That is the proper hour of discourse. / Discourse cheers us to companionable / Reflection" (6). Prophetic vision, clear sight, "precursive" sight, is poetic sight: "Only image formed keeps the vision. Yet image formed rests in the poem" (6). Poetry is dangerous to thinking, but it is a "good" danger: "The good and thus wholesome / Danger is the nighness of the singing poet" (8); but "philosophizing" is a "bad" danger to thinking: "The bad and thus muddled danger / is philosophizing" (8). Good thinking is courageous, slow, patient, and possibly most of all, "playful." The way poetry "plays" with language, philosophy cannot:

> All our heart's courage is the
> echoing response to the
> first call of Being which
> gathers our thinking into the
> play of the world.
>
>   (9)

The central concern for both Heidegger and Kroetsch about thinking and Being and the event of things (lovers, towns, poets) is their growing: "But poetry that thinks is in truth / the topology of Being" and "Singing and thinking are the stems / neighbor to poetry. / They grow out of Being and reach into truth" (13). In the spirit of this assertion, Kroetsch asks, "how do you grow a poet?" (118). As a way of answering his own question, he dramatically, and intellectually, deconstructs the myth of the sterility of the prairie.[9] The winter of the stillness of poetic presence, the presence of thinking, on the prairie is over:

> The end of winter
> seeding/time.
>
> How do you grow
> a poet?
>
>   (36)

This poem is the beginning of seeding time—the poem about a seed catalogue is a planting in the "ground" of the "oral" prairies (the written word planted in the oral ground to gain or impart fertility), the non-intellectual prairies, the place of farmers, seeders, of poets of a new order (not of the sort Britain produced over the last 700 years, for instance), and the question about growing a poet *is* the seed in the ground of prairie stillness and the invisibility of prairie presence. The poem's question about the poet is the precursor of future prairie presence, prairie culture becoming, emerging into light. It is the poet nurturing "our" being, the "crackle" of "our" voices as Dennis Cooley says it is *The Vernacular Muse* (182), and in that sense it is a rescuing of prairie from its status as a marginalized and self-deprecating lower class which always already shuts up in the presence of high European culture.

The absences in *Seed Catalogue*, the absence of Aeneas and Heraclitus and the Parthenon are presences of a past which mean little for the present. Kroetsch thinks into being our "dwelling" (**"Being, Dwelling, Thinking"** *passim*). The absence of Aeneas is replaced by the presence of "the Strauss boy [who] . . . could piss higher on a barn than any of us" (29). The absence of kings and queens is replaced with a story of "bullshitters"[10] unreserved carnival celebration: "the absence of a bottle opener, and me with a vicious attack of the 26-ounce flu (29)." Notice how there is no desire in the imported absences mentioned while the "present" prairie absences are all about the juice and "fire" of living: "the absence of a condom dispenser in the Lethbridge Hotel," "the absence of the girl who said that if the Edmonton / Eskimos won the Grey Cup she'd let me kiss / her nipples in the foyer of the Palliser / Hotel," and being in "love" with "an old Blood whore" (29). Here there is "poetry" we understand.

Kroetsch is "setting back" *Seed Catalogue* into the earth of the prairie, of small town Alberta, in order to let that earth be earth: "That into which the work sets itself back and which it causes to come forth in this setting back of itself we called the earth. Earth is that which comes forth and shelters. . . . The work moves the earth itself into the Open of a world and keeps it there. *The work lets the earth be an earth*" ("Origin" 46). Part of the prairie earth is the indigenous, indestructible, eternal brome grass, for instance:

> *Brome Grass* (Bromus Inermis): No amount of cold will kill it. *It withstands* the summer suns. Water may stand on it for several weeks without apparent injury. The roots push through the soil, throwing up new plants continually. *It starts quicker* than other grasses in the spring. *Remains green* longer in the fall. *Flourishes under absolute neglect.*

Brome grass is hardy, of course, but so are prairie people. Another part of this prairie earth is the peculiar mixture of homegrown remedies for physical illness and spiritual "diseases":

> For appetite: cod-liver
> oil
> For bronchitis: mustard
> plasters
> For pallor and failure to fill
> the woodbox: sulphur
> & molasses.
> For self-abuse: ten Our
> Fathers and ten Hail Marys
> For regular bowels: Sunny Boy
> Cereal
>
> (119)

And there are also our particular prairie encumbrances to "romance": always a pair of skates in every story, always ice skating or hockey at the heart of every narrative:

> or that
> girl in the skating
> rink shack who had on
> so much underwear you
> didn't have enough
> prick to get past her/
> CCM skates
>
> (119)

The prairie world blossoms, grows, emerges in this poem, becomes unhidden and uninvented. This "new" world is, in *Seed Catalogue* and out of it, as particular and complex, as capable of being set forth and of sheltering, as there is will to think about it or time and space for the work to record it. The poet's work cares for this world in a way which does not analyse the earth out of its context and out of significance.

All the questions *Seed Catalogue*'s subject asks—"How do you grow a gardener?" (111), "How do you grow a past?" (116), "How do you grow a prairie town?" (117), "How do you grow a lover?" (115), "How do you grow a poet?" (119)—are dramatizations of methods of consciousness: the desire to know, the ache to separate things from their ground and to analyse them as distinct and unattached things, as objects outside of history. Such questioning is usually the mark of a Western philosophical, analytical inquiry. But these particular questions are somehow all wrong, too, for that analytic tradition. They are not questions about justice, Truth, God, Trees, the Sun, and so on, detached from human emotion. They are a poet's questions—a poet's consciousness which is, in this case, not logical but evocative. These questions never get answered; are dropped as soon as asked. The formula doesn't get completed. There are no certainties. The questions, no more than the imperative, finally, to the poet to "teach us to love our dying" (42), do not provide solutions but answer back with more poetry. In that way they partake of the Heideggerian principle that poetry with its natural

duplicity, its trait of being set back in the earth, is the thought of truth.

This last point about dying is, perhaps, the most Heideggerian aspect of *Seed Catalogue*. Here we have Heidegger's notion of the difference between the one undifferentiated, "pre-philosophical" self who has not yet encountered the terror of his own non-being and the self who has and whose struggle with angst will eventually lend dignity to existence. The poet of *Seed Catalogue* is an alone and "anxious" Self, speaking his way toward understanding in the Heideggerian non-abstract sense of "unconcealedness" and "un-hiddenness":

> In this world that lies before him, open beneath the light, things lie unconcealed (also concealed); but un-concealedness, or un-hiddenness, for Heidegger, is truth; and therefore so far as man exists, he exists 'in the truth.' Truth and Being are thus inseparable, given always together, in the simple sense that a world with things in it opens up around man the moment he exists. Most of the time, however, man does not let himself see what really happens in seeing.
>
> (Barrett 222)

In the realm of speech and language, death is best represented by silence. Tongue-tiedness. Wordlessness. A fighting for breath. The truth of death is silence, just as death finally leaves each of us speechless. Tongue-tied. Silence is language confronting the absence at the very heart of presence. That is, silence is courage. A standing at the edge of the abyss. A looking at the terror, a looking right at non-being. Silence is an awakening; a being born of understanding. Language without silence is simply chatter, just another one of the ways modern Being avoids facing the silence of its own non-Being.

When Being faces its own non-Being, all the everyday ordinariness of Being and Being's nothingness or nowhere-ness disappears: Being is brought face to face with death. Angst brings you to a place of something, a not-nothingness. In that sense, *Seed Catalogue* is, in aggregate, a gift to the people of the prairie, the poet's contribution to their survival and his part in "keeping the farmyard in shape." This is important for understanding the duplicity of the poem. That the question of dying is central to *Seed Catalogue* is made clear by the preponderance of deaths in it: the mother in her grave when the poem begins; the magpie and badger, one shot at and killed by the father (112); the husband who has been buried "with his ass sticking out of the ground" (117); the Crees "surprised . . . to death" (121) on the Oldman River by the Bloods; Pete Knight, "King / of *All* cowboys" (123—whose death by falling off a horse, implicates the poet, who also has fallen off his horse, in his own death);[11] Henry L. Kroetsch, patriarch, whose "last will and testament" (124) are recorded in the poem; Freddie Kroetsch, the best barn builder in the area, dead but "remembered" (124) by the poet; the poet's cousin Kenneth MacDonald whose bomber is shot down over Cologne in 1943 (126); and finally Adam and Eve themselves who we are told "got drownded" (127). The powerful request, "Poet, teach us to love our dying" (126) is a cry for help rising out of the community which has not allowed itself to recognize the neurosis which living and dying entail, made all the more unbearable by the suppression inherent in the various simplifying dualities by which people live and think. The poet knows, for instance, that religions tend to make us "love" our dying and to provide easy solutions for the fear of death by proclaiming everlasting and joyous living after this life. Such promises are placebos and solaces which keep life ordinary and "secure" and are illustrated by the priest's facile solution to the poet's and Germaine's expression of the great body and soul problem. The two young people have discovered the pleasure of each others' bodies and when the boy makes a confession, the priest shows no willingness to acknowledge the complexity of the conflict between culturally-determined codes of behaviour and raging natural desire. He simply calls it "playing dirty" (114) and admonishes him: "keep your peter in your pants for the next thirteen years" (114). Typical of the independent spirit of the poet, he can't and doesn't listen to advice, and he and Germaine choose, instead, to "die" once more: "we decided we could do it / just one more time" (115).[12] If the love in "love our dying" means "loving" private *angst*, having the conscience to experience it, and having good faith that drives one to look into the abyss of death and non-being, then such a "work" which can do this is, for the good poet, a worthwhile and moral work. If "love" on the other hand means skirting death and loving death falsely, loving what is really not death at all but an escape from it, then such a work would be unworthy of the good poet. In either case, the concern with the poet's role in 'teaching' the community (presenting Being for the community) and the climactic position of death at the centre of this autobiographical poem shows Heidegger's influence.

"The history of being (for the West), Heidegger says, begins with the fall of Being. Kroetsch's cowboy/poet falls into an originary site of Being—back into the garden. Paradise Regained. Eve is at the centre of this garden; but she is dead. She has experienced dying; knows it well. She whispers for the poet to bring her the radish seeds while the people about him call to him to be taught about death. She has already (always/already?) learned this and her whisper is seductive and oddly generative:

> This is what happened—at my mother's wake. This
> is a fact—the World Series was in progress. The
> Cincinnati Reds were playing the Detroit Tigers.
> It was raining. The road to the graveyard was barely
> passable. The horse was standing still. Bring me
> the radish seeds, my mother whispered

This poem is not authenticity all done, *fait accompli*, nor the utter relinquishment of power and will and a clear-eyed facing of death. The will to power is still there and it expresses itself in the fact of the poet's words, in his backward-lookingness, in his longing to superimpose the stories of his youth over the problems of today, and in his very love of life, which is a looking at the past. Heideggerian Being is historical, but it is forward-looking history

because the primary mood of Being is awareness of the future—of death. The poem ends with that realization and it plays out the sequence of obsession with the past, of the young life of the poet with his desires—for language, for the garden, for Germaine, for another.[13] But the questions, the "how do you"'s, point him always back to the future.

Seeing is not seeing. Answering is questioning. The clarity of Aristotle is blindness. The questions of the poet are answers. They are desiring sight without seeing. They are supplementing the presence which is all around them in science books, in seed catalogues, in the ir/replaceable objects of the sort Mary Hauck brings with her to Canada, to Alberta, and which burn to the ground in the Heisler Hotel fire. They are the real absences at the centre of *Seed Catalogue*. From expository discourse the poet returns to the interrogative. The interrogative is a paradox—it too has doubleness at its centre. Answered, the interrogative is all of Western philosophy in a nutshell—completion, ending, transcendence above the now of Being into the eternity of knowing, truth without history or change, the end of the matter. Unanswered, it is the orient. Unanswered, it is Openness, only a beginning, a failure in the best sense of the word. Unanswered, it is the failure of completion, the postponement of orgasm[14] and the death of desire. Unanswered, the interrogative is the *angst* of failure, and the call for more.

Notes

1. See the essay in general, and specially his discussion of Derrida's notion, in *Of Grammatology 141–57*, of the utter absence of signification outside the text.

2. See "The Fear of Women in Prairie Fiction." Kroetsch discusses here the tension between house and horse on the Canadian prairie and the perennial struggle for male independence (80).

3. Kroetsch has often said that Ross's *As For Me and My House* was the most important book in his development as a prairie writer proud of his heritage. See "The Moment of the Discovery of America Continues" 4.

4. *Seed Catalogue* is thus one side of a dialogue. In this sense, the poem is Derridean in its double, saying what it never yet has said, not answering its own questions, finding the aporias in the utopian text, laying traps for the logic of this text about Adam and Eve and the poet in the paradisal garden.

5. The idea of the essential, transcendental, and metaphysical quality of things is the core of Derrida's argument with Heidegger.

6. In *Discourse on Thinking*, Heidegger distinguishes between calculative thinking and meditative thinking and says that it is the second kind which the modern world needs more of. "[Meditative thinking] is thinking which contemplates the meaning which reigns in everything that is" (46).

7. For discussions of orality in *Seed Catalogue* see among others Arnason 84, Wood 84, Ricou 116, and Munton 91.

8. This recalls Wordsworth's famous injunction in the Preface to *The Lyrical Ballads* about rustics being the most fit subjects for poetry.

9. According to Laurie Ricou in "Prairie Poetry and Metaphors of Plain/s Space," *Seed Catalogue* and other Kroetsch long poems refuse the "abstractions" (112) and "disappearing landscapes" (115) typical of conventional prairie landscape poetry.

10. "Bullshit artists" are the best poets in an oral tradition according to Kroetsch. See his discussion of Glen Sorestad's poetry, "The Moment of the Discovery of America Continues" (17–18).

11. The poet's death is further suggested by the fact that he falls into a garden; no one is left in the garden at the end of the poem.

12. The connection between death and sex is made more explicitly in the "I don't give a damn if I do die do die do die" scene (117) which, as Arnason points out, involves a priest catching a boy in a graveyard in the act of masturbation and warning him that he will die if he carries on with his "self-abuse" (86).

13. He wishes to be a postman so he could "deliver real words / to real people" (117). The poem begins and ends in a garden, the home garden and the Garden of Eden; the last garden is lush and inviting, a place "where the brome grass was up to [Cindy's] hips" (127). The incident with Germaine is left unfinished and begging for completion or continuation; she seems to be there waiting for him, whispering to us. His mother's death, though mesmerizing as a voice speaking from the grave, is not lamented by the poet—even here there is incompletion and powerful, unfulfilled, interrupted desire.

14. Frank Davey's very important essay on the debate between "delay" and "prolongation" takes issue with Kroetsch's assertion that the long poem in Canada is essentially a story of neurotic compulsion and the failure to end the poem out of fear of climax and closure. What Kroetsch discusses as a fear of orgasm, Davey calls instead a celebration of prolonged, continual orgasm ("The Language of the Contemporary Canadian Long Poem" *passim*).

Works Cited

Arnason, David. "Robert Kroetsch's *Seed Catalogue*: The Deconstruction of the Meta-narrative of the Cowboy." *Contemporary Manitoba Writers New Critical Studies*. Ed. Kenneth James Hughes. Winnipeg: Turnstone, 1990. 79–92.

Barrett, William. *Irrational Man: A Study in Existential Philosophy*. New York: Doubleday, 1962.

Brown, Russell, "Seeds and Stones: Unhiding in Kroetsch's Poetry." *Open Letter* 5.8–9 (1984): 154–75.

Carroll, David. *The Subject in Question: The Languages of Theory and the Strategies of Fiction*. Chicago: U Chicago P, 1982.

Cooley, Dennis. "The Vernacular Muse in Prairie Poetry." *The Vernacular Muse: The Eye and Ear in Contemporary Literature*. Winnipeg: Turnstone Press, 1987. 171–83.

Davey, Frank. "The Language of the Contemporary Canadian Long Poem." *Surviving the Paraphrase: Eleven Essays on Canadian Literature*. Winnipeg: Turnstone, 1983. 184–93.

Derrida, Jacques. *Of Grammatology*. Baltimore: John Hopkins UP, 1974.

Godard, Barbara. "Other Fictions: Robert Kroetsch's Criticism." *Open Letter* 5.8–9 (1984): 5–21.

Hartman, Geoffrey II. "Romanticism and 'Anti-Self-Consciousness'." *Romanticism and Consciousness: Essays in Criticism*. Ed. Harold Bloom. New York: Norton; 1970. 46–56.

Heidegger, Martin. *Discourse on Thinking*. Trans. John M. Anderson and E. Hans Freund. New York: Harper and Row, 1966.

———. "The Origin of the Work of Art." *Poetry, Language, Thought*. Trans. Albert Hofstadter. New York: Harper Colophon Books, 1971. 15–88.

———. "The Thinker as Poet." *Poetry, Language, Thought*. Trans. Albert Hofstadter. New York: Harper Colophon Books, 1971. 1–14.

———. "What are Poets For?" *Poetry, Language, Thought*. Trans. Albert Hofstadter. New York: Harper Colophon Books, 1971. 89–142.

———. "Building Dwelling Thinking." *Poetry, Language, Thought*. Trans. Albert Hofstadter. New York: Harper Colophon Books, 1971. 143–62.

Kroetsch, Robert. *Seed Catalogue, a/long prairie lines*, Ed. Daniel S. Lenoski. Winnipeg: Turnstone, 1989. 109–32.

———. "The Moment of the Discovery of America Continues." *The Lovely Treachery of Words: Essays Selected and New*. Toronto: Oxford, 1989. 1–20.

———. "The Fear of Women in Prairie Fiction: An Erotics of Space." *The Lovely Treachery of Words: Essays Selected and New*. Toronto: Oxford, 1989. 73–83.

Munton, Ann. "The Structural Horizons of Prairie Poetics: The Long Poem, Eli Mandel, Andrew Suknaski, and Robert Kroetsch." *Dalhousie Review* 63.1 (1983): 69–97.

Ricou, Laurie. "Prairie Poetry and Metaphors of Plain/s Space." *Great Plains Quarterly* 3.2 (1983): 109–19.

Shaver, Gilbert J. "Martin Heidegger: *Poetry, Language, Thought*. *Boundary* 2 1.1 (1973): 742–49.

Wood, Susan. "Reinventing The Word: Kroetsch's Poetry." *Canadian Literature* 77 (1978): 28–41.

David Wylynko (review date July-August 1993)

SOURCE: "Pulling Strings," in *The Canadian Forum*, Vol. LXXII, No. 821, July-August, 1993, pp. 43-44.

[In the following review, Wylynko praises The Puppeteer *for Kroetsch's examination of the ephemeral and the permanent.]*

Like a pulp fiction murder mystery, Robert Kroetsch's **The Puppeteer** leads a host of bizarre characters through a fast-paced chase for icons, money and one another. But the plot line is merely a disguise for Kroetsch's mockery of this popular form, and a mockery of the human need for permanence that motivates these pursuits. As in all of Kroetsch's fiction, the novel's central task is to illustrate how sharply humanity's approach to life conflicts with the ways of nature.

In a universe whose only true constant is change, we tend to surround ourselves with things. We buy products, and their apparent permanence allows us to see life itself as a product, a stable entity. The reality we fear is that life is a process, one of birth, maturation, decay and death, with no preconceived universal meaning. Kroetsch ridicules this fear, and encourages the reader to embrace the beauty of life's cyclical quality.

The action is steered by the novel's narrator, Jack Deemer, a millionaire Calgary oilman who uses his wealth to collect a wide variety of items. Deemer fancies himself a descendant of history's great collectors—Hadrian, Phillip II, and of course, Columbus, who, in acquiring the so-called New World for Europe, was "perhaps the greatest collector of them all". As a puppeteer uses strings, Deemer uses money to manipulate the other characters in aid of his passion for collecting.

The novel is a sequel to *Alibi*, in which Deemer sends his agent, the despondent middle-aged William Dorfen, to search through Alberta and Europe for a spa, symbol of youth and regeneration. Along the way, Dorfen becomes implicated in the suspected deaths of Deemer's wife Julie Magnuson and her doctor/lover Manuel de Meirdos. The bodies are never found. When *The Puppeteer* begins, Dorfen, fearful of Deemer's vow to gain vengeance for Julie's death, has been hiding out in Vancouver for four years. Here he meets Maggie Wilder, a middle-aged writer who, having fled her husband, sits in the attic of a borrowed house in her wedding dress, typing.

Maggie's wedding dress is representative of the sense of permanence humans seek in material goods. A wedding dress is typically bought, worn and stored in the attic. On a much broader level, Deemer sets out to collect all the natural and man-made attributes of the world, until he has "four warehouses crammed with collections from around this spinning top we call a globe". The novel suggests that this is the human approach to all of nature, the planet having "become an attic" through which we "rummage".

Intrigued by Dorfen, Maggie journeys to Deadman Springs near Banff to uncover his past adventures. There she finds Karen Strike, a documentary journalist employed by Deemer to photograph, piece by piece, the entire lake where Dorfen presumably was involved in Dr. de Meirdos' death. Absurdly, he sends her back each season to photograph the lake all over again. The function of photography is central to the collection of products. In order to collect things and to assign them value, we must first delineate them from another. In taking pictures, we specify an object and separate it from the natural whole. This act facilitates the Cartesian subject-object dualism that is central to Western thought, the scientific classification and dissection that helps us to understand nature's components and at the same time lose sight of its essential unity. Framed, the photograph captures the object in a permanent time and place, allowing us to believe that permanence exists.

In the narrative structure, Kroetsch attempts to break down this sense of permanence by showing novel writing, like life, to be a process. When Maggie returns from the Spring, she finds that Dorfen has moved into her attic and is making puppets that mimic the novel's characters. Harrassed victim turned puppeteer, Dorfen's rendition of events reveals Deemer's version to be merely a contrivance, subject to the changing whims of the ultimate puppeteer, Kroetsch himself.

This brand of narrative trickery, common throughout his work, has claimed for Kroetsch the reputation of ultimate postmodern writer. Writing that acknowledges itself as contrived corresponds perfectly with Kroetsch's effort to illustrate the contrivances of all of humanity's constructs, and the impact these constructs have on nature. In the race to collect, to gather, to put under glass, we transform the natural community into something artificial, unnatural, a purely human playground.

Yet, as Kroetsch also realizes, words themselves function every bit as much as photography to delineate objects, give them a human meaning, and provide opportunity to foster the sense of permanence we crave. In the quest for icons that brings the novel to a tumultuous climax, tantamount to a cops and robbers television series with everyone rushing to get the money, Deemer sarcastically asserts that he would "put words themselves under lock and key" if he could, along with beaches, lakes and the very darkness he lives in. In like manner, the novel will be collected as a finished product and put on the shelf.

In *The Puppeteer*, Kroetsch the artist melds with the theorist to at once provide a brilliant depiction of the human need to make an ephemeral world permanent while acknowledging that his own written work will fall victim to this obsession. But for the same reason the collector collects, the artist must write. As Kroetsch notes in his essay, **"Beyond Nationalism: a Prologue"**, it is simply our nature that "(h)earing the silence of the world, the failure of the world to announce meaning, we tell stories. 'Once upon a time there was . . .'"

Liz Caile (review date September-October 1993)

SOURCE: A review of *Alberta,* in *Bloomsbury Review,* Vol. 13, No. 5, September-October, 1993, p. 15.

The Canadian province of Alberta corresponds to states to the south wherein plains and mountains meet. In *Alberta*, Robert Kroetsch describes the contrasting elements of splendid peaks and vast rolling plains, of wide rivers and parched homesteads, of coal mines, wheat and oil fields, of an Indian past and robust upstart cities.

Alberta's settlers have maintained their distinctive cultural groupings to a greater extent than in the United States, however. Its northern placement introduces muskeg and glaciers to the equation. Its people—in many ways the focus of the book—seem a thinner layer atop a larger land.

Robert Kroetsch gives us a writer's travel guide—a profile of a province, a portrait of the people who live on it. Names roll out from his account with their own poetry. He utters them with obvious relish, appreciating their intrinsic rhythms and imagery.

NeWest's *Alberta* is a second edition, coming 25 years after the original publication. It opens with a foreword, a 1990s writing-class road trip, and closes with remarks by novelist Rudy Wiebe. The several parts of the book fit together, yet easily break apart into separate sections.

The middle of the book, Kroetsch's original *Alberta*, is itself a pastiche of seasons and road trips, interviews and vignettes, camping and horse-pack adventures, shot through with history—like veins of cinnamon. The virtue of the book lies with Kroetsch's dry wit, his fascination with individual Albertans, and his poetic prose:

> In the south, the Oldman and the Bow flow together to become the South Saskatchewan, and all of them sprout tall cottonwoods in the shortgrass country of Blackfoot memories and cattle and wheat.

One of the most pleasing stories is of a trip he, his wife, and another couple made from Banff to Jasper, with time to marvel at the Athabasca glacier. The trip is quintessential car camping, before the sport had been attacked by a merchandising fervor.

Kroetsch does not theorize much, except perhaps on the attraction of Bible-belt religion to the people of the province where he was born. We are left to form our own opinions, trusting his telling of the story. He never over-reaches his experience as the descendant of European immigrants, though he shares respect and sorrow with the tribes of the province. Wiebe's afterword expresses a contemporary rage at the way the tribal past of the province has been discarded by other writers.

Reflecting on the simple entertainments of rural Alberta, Kroetsch remembers his time on the baseball diamond:

> Maybe that did it, I thought—maybe that was one of the things that turned me into a writer—my playing far out in the field. The playing, and the watching that went with it. The listening, out there. The wanting to enter the game while fearing that someone might hit the ball in my direction. The being isolated, out there in the prairie wind and the summer light; my striking up a conversation with a nearby gopher as I watched the pitched ball. . . . The caring so much, so enduringly, for the movements of small creatures, for the ongoing game, for all the shouting and the laughter that are some of the various names of love.

From left field, Kroetsch gives us Alberta. His perspective is enhanced by the photographs of Harry Savage—small reproductions, nicely composed, framing the colorful features of the land.

Robert Kroetsch with Lee Spinks (interview date 1994)

SOURCE: "Puppets and Puppeteers: Robert Kroetsch Interviewed by Lee Spinks," in *Journal of Commonwealth Literature*, Vol. XXIX, No. 2, 1994, pp. 13-22.

[In the following interview, Kroetsch discusses his fiction and poetry.]

The following conversation took place in Hull on 24 October 1993 over a period of two hours. Robert Kroetsch speaks slowly and deliberately, often pausing to revise a word or qualify a phrase or statement. His sentences are frequently punctuated by a staccato burst of laughter.

[Lee Spinks]: Perhaps we might begin, Bob, with your most recent novel. Why did you return in **The Puppeteer** *to the landscape and characters of* **Alibi**? *Was it from a sense of unfinished business, or did the earlier novel continue to nag away at your imagination?*

[Robert Kroetsch]: No, I had originally planned a much more ambitious story. I was going to look at this group of characters every ten years or so and see what happened to them, to treat them as human beings in a certain way. But after the second volume I think I've abandoned the idea. It was a wonderful idea [laughs]. But somehow it just isn't working for me.

So the characters were going to be periodically picked up, dusted down, and reintroduced into your fiction?

Well I was going to pick up different characters at different stages. In the next volume I had planned to pick up on that young woman Karen Strike and see how she looked at the story. That was my idea.

Is there any connection here with the cyclical narrative model of, say, Updike's Rabbit novels in which the repetition of a character becomes an index for the state of a nation?

Well I thought it would reflect that and also I thought it would reflect what I thought about the novel at the time from a stylistic point of view. I wanted to get a changing record of my different opinions about the novel's styles and possibilities. But that's off the agenda now. It was wearing me out.

*So **The Puppeteer** wasn't originally conceived simply as a sequel?*

Oh no! You see I had never really intended it as a sequel because you might be given a narrator in later novels who takes you back into earlier times. I had, in a certain way, thought of the novels as a diptych: the notion from art of two facing pictures. As my larger scheme collapsed, the notion of a diptych became more attractive.

The idea of a family of interconnected novels, with characters floating across different times, appeals to you, doesn't it?

Yes, that's right. I think that's because I write short novels—or shorter novels at any rate—but I'm always attracted to the idea of a larger novel and the idea of a group of stories was my way to get at it. I think in some literatures—I think Chinese is one—the shorter novel and the longer novel are different genres. The same distinction between forms holds for me: I think of the short story as a very different form from the short novel. I have very little understanding of the short story. I think that the short novel is my form in a way [laughs] . . . 230 pages or whatever.

*One interesting feature of **The Puppeteer** is your decision to introduce the narrative voice of Jack Deemer. What was the reason for this?*

I was interested in Jack Deemer's impulse to collect everything, to collect the world in a sense. This obsession of his had several consequences: one was that he would want to collect other peoples stories and, ultimately, other people. I had planned that in a vague way all along. But the dialogue he gets into with that third person came as a surprise.

The figure of the collector recurs frequently in your fiction: Demeter Proudfoot collects the smallest details of Hazard Lepage's life, William Dawe collects dinosaur bones, Jack Deemer collects unusual cultural icons. What attracts you to the type of the collector?

Well, first of all, I'm not a collector in any way myself. I'm fascinated by it though because collecting functions as a model for what culture is in a way, even in a basic activity like education. It's a very long story, I know, but even by the time you move from a culture of hunting and gathering to whatever comes after, collecting becomes possible and ultimately significant. And the idea of collecting as a metaphor for this kind of development is very interesting to me.

Is there a sense in which the collector functions as an encyclopedic realist novelist in contrast to the imperatives of our "postmodern" age?

Oh, I think so. I think he has a strong impulse to make the world cohere in any way possible. In a certain way, he's a modernist, I suppose, in my sense of what a modernist is. Collecting also throws up interesting interpretative problems because it insists upon taking things out of context. Nowadays we tend to believe that context is so important; but by taking things out of context and placing them in a museum, or whatever, it's possible to radically alter their meaning. And that makes us uneasy. Just look at our contemporary unease about past archaeological and anthropological studies. We live in an age of enormous doubt and the urge to collect is an interesting expression of this condition.

*There's contradiction in Deemer's position, though, isn't there? In **Alibi** he collects to escape time, but in **The Puppeteer** he collects versions of eschatological narratives, plural interpretations of the end of the world. Doesn't he seem to hesitate between univocity and polyvocality?*

Sure, although we shouldn't put the whole blame on Deemer; this is, after all, partly my fear of a single story [laughs]. There's an important point here though about the paradox of narrative: the storyteller, by writing the story down and arresting time and story makes it possible for interpretation to function. Deemer's different narratives or collections rely to some extent on the notion of a single narrative; but then the single story opens out into a number of different narratives. His activities as a collector, in a sense, almost violate the principle of story. And that's why he's positioned as both reader and writer in the text, looking over Maggie's shoulder as a reader but also intruding all the time to the point where he starts believing that it might be his story that he's writing down. And let's not forget: there's a question all the time about how well he can really see. He exploits the notion that he can't see and he exploits the notion that he can. Which is itself a version of an old, rather classical, conceit: the blind man seeing.

The Puppeteer, *it seems to me, is organized around two central images: Julie Magnusson's wedding dress and the figure of the puppeteer. What attracted you to these images?*

Well, in a way I began from the notion of icon; I was interested in discovering exactly what the contemporary icons are. That's why I got interested in pizza: it looks like an icon to me. I first got interested in the great Byzantine icons because of the traditions behind the painting. There's a certain kind of resistance to perspective that interested me; the trick of perspective that we get in the renaissance is, after all, a trick: you get tired of it after a while. And as a consequence of resisting the depth of perspective, the notion of surface gets to be so interesting. We have become so adept at seeing depth that we can hardly recognize surface anymore. We can hardly see a cup of coffee. I can't remember exactly how I got interested in the wedding dress, but once she put on that wedding dress I was away; it was a very important moment for me in the story. She put it on and it enabled her to talk. I have no idea where it came from. In some way, I suppose, it's elements of Magic Realism, especially since what's on the wedding dress keeps changing. The emergence of the puppeteer image is a little more defined. When I was over in Greece I became interested in the idea of the shadow puppets, who seemed to enjoy a certain advantage over our string puppets; the mechanics were different: you could use those lovely bright colours, and shadows, in a different way. And then I began to study the puppet figures that they were using, and Karaghiosi was a trickster-tricked figure and I'm always a sucker for that idea [laughs]. So I got, interested in that. And also the whole notion that the Greeks used these puppets as a rather subversive method of telling stories when they were occupied by the Turks; and then behind that the entire unravelling story that goes back to China and Indonesia or wherever the shadow puppets come from.

This seems to link up with those scenes in Maggie's attic where characters go to see a show but then become so implicated in or consumed by the events they witness that these stories take over their lives.

Absolutely. And this raises that whole question of how we enter the story. Instead of separating the characters from the action by the arch that you might find in some theatres, I was much more interested in the idea of carnival where you can be looking around, enjoying your distance, while being at the same time part of the spectacle. I was excited by the possibility that these characters could start off outside the story, almost in a critical position if you like, and then gradually become seduced into entering the story. And carnival also has those other aspects—the subversion of order and the overturning of hierarchies—that have always attracted me.

Both the image of the wedding dress and the puppeteer are bound up in some way with the endless reproducibility of story and the human need to keep shuffling between versions of identity. Might **The Puppeteer** *be described as a modern Shakespearean romance in which people have to adopt different disguises to become what they really are?*

Yes, I'm sure it could. Frye's book on Shakespeare was a very instructive book for me because he showed me what Shakespeare was up to. Insofar as I'm really far more attracted to a comic rather than a tragic vision, the comparison with romance is a fascinating one. I'm interested in doubles; and the book plays with the idea of moving between genders. It's a complicated question where I stand in relation to romance, but one connection is that I like the outrageousness of the storytelling. To tell a story is, after all, already a slightly preposterous thing to do: the world is already too jumbled to accept a single narrative structure. And that's also the idea in romance, that people need to accept disguises to discover more about their real self. That appeals to me: I'm totally opposed to the notion that underneath my mask there's a true self, because the masks are, in an important sense, what I really am. That idea that we're fooling anybody with our

disguises is to fool ourselves, especially since the masks we pick for ourselves are so revealing. I think the book says "The Pizza Man. That was her first name for him." So as she goes through names it's not a question of one being wrong and another being right; it's a far more complex problem. It's the idea that identity is actually found through narrative or story. And this is linked to a very contemporary resistance to the idea of a bounded self: the idea that this, here and now, is what I am and that I have to be consistent with it, when it's the gaps and contradictions that enable me to be alive in the world. There's an obvious connection here with the discontinuities of the postmodern novel and what I'm saying here about identity. But then I think that postmodernism, with its whole set of illogical responses and contradictions, is a much better guide to how we live than most.

The plots of both **Alibi** *and* **The Puppeteer** *oscillate between Canada and Europe, and between the Old and the New World. Are you conscious of this tension elsewhere in your work?*

Yes, although I was much more conscious of this binary when I was younger. I call it a binary, and it is, but it's much more than that: it gave me permission to write in an important sense. The whole experience of the new place demanded a new telling of the story. Mind you, my whole notion of story was different then. In later years I've become more and more intrigued by—this is probably not true [laughs]—the way the act of telling becomes part of the story. I always was though, wasn't I, from *The Studhorse Man* onwards or even before then? So I probably have to take that back [laughs].

Any discussion of the relationship between the Old and New World must include the various effects of linguistic and cultural colonialism. Do you consider yourself a post-colonial writer, and if so how has this perception influenced your work?

Well, first of all, let's remember that the phrase "post-colonial" wasn't around very much when I was a younger writer. I wish it had been, because I think it's a very useful phrase for me. I suppose at an early stage a lot of what's now called post-colonial thought was based upon the model of margin and centre. I think there's a danger in making that a very stable or static model because what, after all, is the "centre" or the "margin"? These things are very fluid and we need forms that are able to accommodate that fluidity.

You have written of the Canadian experience of inhabiting a "mandarin language" that doesn't have its roots in the New World landscape. Was this mis-match between the world you perceived around you and the codes available to represent it one reason for your abandonment of realism as a literary mode?

That's a good question. It touches on some issues that are really important to my conception of the act of writing but that I haven't really resolved. Perhaps I write because I haven't resolved them. Could you say some more? It really fascinates me, this question of the relationship between realism and a mandarin language.

Well, it could be said that one of the defining features of realism as a mode of address is that it eliminates the space between experience and representation in the name of discursive transparency. But this makes realism a problematic mode for the post-colonial subject which defines itself by the difference between the landscape it inhabits and the codes available to represent it.

Gee, that's great; I really like that. That really explains things for me. And this is exactly why I can't be a realist; it's all tied up with this notion of difference and language.

This ambivalence about realist fiction has always been present in your work, hasn't it? I'm thinking of even those early stories like **"That Yellow Prairie Sky"** *which juxtapose mimetic description with dislocated paragraphs of highly charged poetic discourse.*

That's right; God, it's weird to see these connections. But you're right. I remember the editor of the journal in which that particular story was placed was a little uneasy about it—that distance from or distrust of a realist frame. But it's certainly there: that desire to break down any semblance of a coherent discourse, even in that story, which was actually one of the first longer pieces I ever wrote. God, I'll have to think about this more; I had never fully made the connections in my mind.

This whole question is bound up, though, with the problem of writing a new country in an old language, isn't it?

Oh, yes, without doubt. I just today read an article in *The Times Higher Education Supplement* about Mark Twain and how apparently when he was working on *Huckleberry Finn* he had heard a young black boy speaking and he picked up some linguistic clues from there on how to tell a story by breaking up a certain conventional kind of realism. And this distrust of realism runs right through North American writing: they embrace it but they also buck against it.

Probing this question of writing in a mandarin language, one of the most remarkable features of your fiction is that each of your novels adopts a different style: one is written in a realist mode, another in a kind of postmodern pastiche, a third borrows from Magic Realism. What motivates your continual experimentation with literary form?

Well, I'm not sure that this should even be called experimentation; I think it's a manifestation in the writer of the things I'm talking about in the stories. One keeps changing, redefining oneself, and there isn't a secret centre, although this loss of a centre has its attendant freedoms. It enables you to say one thing, shift your voice

a little, and then you can say another thing. If you shift the story form you can always say something else and explore different angles. It also makes sense that given what I'm saying about narrative and identity in a single novel that I would begin to write a group of interrelated novels out of this method. This kind of constant metamorphosis is also a strategy for survival: if you think you're on the margin you keep shape-shifting; this stops you being caught or at least defined against your own wishes.

It's a very different idea of survival from the Atwood thematic, isn't it?

Oh, absolutely. And make no mistake: it's often very tough on the reader, because they have to keep entertaining new possibilities. An Atwood reader is offered a certain kind of security; at least they have a ground or footing that they can feel sure about. I've gone the other way; perhaps some of my readers have fallen off the edge [laughs]. I was talking to an agent in London a week or so ago, and he said I go too far in a certain way: you lose readers like this. I have to admit that's not just a possibility; it's probably a fact. On the other hand, one hopes that it's rewarding to the reader in the long run.

Do you see any similarities between the themes and concerns of Canadian writing and those of writers from the other former colonies: Australia, West Indies, India for example?

Sure, I'm fascinated by an Australian writer like Peter Carey, for example. His work is very instructive to me. This term "post-colonial" is necessarily very broad, though; I learned a lot from nineteenth-century American writing, where the American writer still felt that he or she was in what we would now call a post-colonial situation. So you get, as in Twain, their railing against Europe but their running off towards Europe, or Hawthorne literally going to live in Europe for a long time. Or even the heavy-duty argument you get running through the Modernist poets about what to do about Europe: Eliot and Pound going to Europe, and Williams and Stevens saying "That was fatal; you never should have done that". Australian writing interests me: *Illywhacker* is a form of Magic Realism, I suppose, which delights in this outrageous making of story out of this marginal world. I think that with the writers on the margins there's this sense that the hierarchy's broken down so you can use what you please; you don't have to say "This wouldn't be proper in a novel," or "This would violate the rules". It's all just material sitting out there. This happened more, I think, for the Australians than the Canadians because they're so far from the world, in a way, and we're always so close to America. So I feel a great sympathy with the Australian fiction writers, although I must say that their poetry often seems a little old-fashioned to me.

Moving on to your poetry, one of the things that interested me when I first read it was the phenomenological impulse to get back to the bedrock of place and identity before the land was written. Do you recognize this impulse in your work?

Oh yes. In fact I was very much taken by the concept of phenomenology earlier in my life—I'm thinking of **Stone Hammer Poem** in particular—and the challenge of making it an active, not a fixed concept. The challenge of getting back before the land was written by anything else, something that exists prior to language or writing. But at the same time feeling it slip away on you as you try to write it down. The same thing happened to me when I went to see the Rosetta Stone: the fact that here was a language that no one could read; it would just drive you mad to try. And so surface becomes engrossing once more.

The poetry that you wrote in the 1970's, though, seems to inhabit a deconstructive vocabulary. Were you consciously aware of this transition?

Very much so. Although I didn't read the notion of "deconstruction" and then systematically apply it to my work. I was *doing* it, getting it often from American poetry, I think. But deconstruction gave me a way to talk about the tensions and contradictions that I had already experienced. It also gave me a more solid theoretical base, I suppose. I was just ready for that theory to strike [laughs]. The whole notion of writing language against itself fascinates me. And there's a whole extended notion of the post-colonial there: what is the mandarin language concealing or not concealing? Which brings us back to how you write in the language that you were given. For me it was a matter of going to sub-literary sources: using the ledger, for example, which hadn't been thought of as a literary tool. Or the seed catalogue, which seemed totally unliterary and gave me a new way to go back to the language I had inherited.

Are the **Field Notes** *continuing or has* **The Puppeteer** *consumed all your time and energy?*

Well, I'm working on a novel right now which I think is independent of the **Field Notes**. It's a kind of anti-autobiography. Its anti-autobiographical in the sense that I think "autobiography" is a fairly fraudulent notion although a fascinating one: it trades on the belief that a statement must be true because the author said it, when the person least likely to tell the truth is the author. It trades on a fraudulent discourse of truth. The **Field Notes**, it seems to me, was a genuine attempt to write a long poem which I've now either finished or abandoned. This anti-autobiography that I'm working on now could conceivably have some poetry in it, but it's difficult to insert poetry into an autobiographical form. At the moment I've written four or five essays that may go into it. One of my strategies is to take a small event and read it very hard to see if it might have had consequences for my thinking, like my going up North, for example, which I've written an essay about: it's called **"Why I Went up North, and What I Found When He Got There."** So the genres will get a little bent once again. But it's probably bad luck to say too much about the new book. You'll have to wait and see.

John Clement Ball (essay date Summer 1994)

SOURCE: "Framing the American Abroad: A Comparative

Study of Robert Kroetsch's *Gone Indian* and Janet Frame's *The Carpathians,*" in *Canadian Literature,* No. 141, Summer 1994, pp. 38-49.

[In the following essay, Ball discusses similarities in the treatment of colonialism in Gone Indian *and Frame's* The Carpathians.]

> It is the paradox of Columbus' perceptual moment that it cannot end. The moment of the discovery of America continues. Its reenactment becomes our terrifying test of greatness; we demand to hear again and always the cry into mystery, into an opening. We demand, of the risking eye, new geographies. And the search that was once the test of sailor and horse and canoe is now the test of the poet.
>
> Kroetsch **"Moment,"** 25

When Christopher Columbus "discovered" America he was, like other explorers, acting as the agent of a higher authority that remained nominally in control from a relatively stationary position—at home on the throne, at the centre of imperial power. Once he set sail from that imperial centre, however, Columbus himself was the one really in charge: no higher human authority was present to direct or curtail his actions, or to prevent him from making one of the most significant and far-reaching errors in Western history. When Columbus began treating the Americas as Asia, he was unknowingly subverting the very project he had been authorized to undertake. His freedom to do so demonstrates an unpredictable dynamic that straddles the gaps of geography and power established by any act of imperial exploration. There is potentially a big discrepancy between the agent-explorer's actions faced with a concrete object of discovery and the authorizing mandate from home that frames his journey. As middle-man, the agent-explorer subdivides the familiar colonial gap—between imperial oppressor and the peoples and places over whom it exercises its self-appointed power—into two gaps. Versions of those two gaps—between the imperial project's two locuses of power, and between the agent-explorer and what he encounters—appear as textual dislocations and narrative gulfs in two quest novels from former settler colonies: Robert Kroetsch's **Gone Indian** (1973) and Janet Frame's *The Carpathians* (1988).

The Kroetsch novel has an explicit Columbus intertext. Its protagonist, Jeremy Sadness, is an American graduate student from Manhattan sent by his supervisor, Mark Madham, on a journey to fulfill his "deep American need to seek out the frontier" (5). Jeremy's thesis, which he is perpetually unable to begin, let alone finish, has, as one of its false starts, the following first sentence: "Christopher Columbus, not knowing that he had not come to the Indies, named the inhabitants of that new world—" (21). And there it ends—or doesn't. One of the titles he tries out is "The Columbus Quest: The Dream, the Journey, the Surprise" (62). Like Columbus, Jeremy has a dream—of the frontier of his imagination, and of himself as Grey Owl—he makes a journey—to the small Alberta town of Notikeewin—and is surprised—repeatedly. His quest is deconstructed in the surreal, carnivalesque world of the prairies during a winter festival, a world where social roles are exchanged and identities become so blurred that Jeremy can be unnamed—stripped of his previous identity—and renamed into a multiplicity of new identities that include buffalo, Roger Dorck the Winter King, and Indian. He can dream the dreams of a mute aboriginal woman. He can subvert his original mission, to attend a job interview arranged by his supervisor, simply by failing to show up for his appointment. Like Isabella and Ferdinand back in Spain, Madham is unable to control the activities of his agent-explorer. Or is he? Just as Columbus's voyage was framed by the imperial project of which it was a part, Jeremy's adventures as narrative are framed and ultimately controlled by Madham, who, from his fixed position in Binghamton, New York, is the stationary centre of power over this text. To Madham at the time of framing, as to us, Jeremy exists only as text, as narrative. Madham transcribes, edits and critiques the tapes on which Jeremy reports his experiences. As motivating cause of Jeremy's journey, and as intrusive framing narrator, Madham retains control over his apparently out-of-control agent by reconstituting Jeremy's actions as a U.S.-based narrative. In this late twentieth-century recasting of the Columbus quest, the neo-imperial centre of power has become what 500 years ago was the object of discovery: America.

The inclusion of a U.S.-based framing narrator is just one of many intriguing correspondences between *Gone Indian* and *The Carpathians*. Both novels follow the travels of a "child of Manhattan" (*Gone Indian*, 5) to a fictional town in, respectively, Alberta and New Zealand's North Island. The town's names, Notikeewin and Puamahara, suggest aboriginal languages, and both Kroetsch and Frame use aboriginal history and experience as touchstones for the local, and for their explorations of such themes as the reconstitution of language, the appropriation of narrative point of view, and the destabilization of the subject. But while both novels concern quests for knowledge of the other, the unknown, generically they are cast as very different kinds of story: *Gone Indian* as a parody of the picaresque western with the roaming cowboy hero, and *The Carpathians* as suburban anti-pastoral with a female protagonist and a domestic setting.

In Janet Frame's layered metafiction, narrative frames blur ontological boundaries both from inside and outside the story, multiplying narrative points of view even more than Kroetsch's book does. Frame's questing protagonist, Mattina Brecon, is manipulated *as* text first by Dinny Wheatstone, the "imposter novelist" of Kowhai Street, who provides a typescript for Mattina to read which describes, in the past tense, Mattina's actions over the next several weeks. Because the typescript substitutes for the events it describes—because, as Susan Ash explains, "It is Mattina's process of reading the typescript which makes these events actual or 'real'" (2)—the novel here places signifier and signified in an overlapping relation that renders them indistinguishable. Another character *in* the text, Mattina's

son John Henry, is revealed in opening and closing notes as the text's *Ur*-narrator, creator *of* "this, my second novel," in which "The characters and happenings . . . are all invented and bear no relation to actual persons living or dead" (7). Claiming at the end that his mother and father died when he was seven, John Henry the framer fractures the expected correspondence to himself as a character, Mattina's son John Henry who writes *his* second novel within the pages of the framer John Henry's fictional creation. And the concluding note's teasing remark that "perhaps the town of Puamahara, which I in my turn visited, never existed" (196) is simply the final spin on a destruction of "the painful opposites and contradictions of everyday life" (114) that is Frame's procedure and her theme. Frame conflates experience and imagination, text and event, envisaging a universe in which "it seemed that lost became found, death became life, all the anguished opposites reverted to their partner in peace yet did not vanish: one united with the other" (114). And while John Henry's concluding remarks may, as Suzette Henke points out, permit a reading of 'his' novel as "a psychic strategy for coping with . . . Oedipal loss" (36), the novel that Janet Frame has written challenges, through its narratorial free play, the reader's attempt to pin down an interpretation based on the apparent dictates of any one of its multiple frames. The narrative layering creates too many ambiguous ironies and deferrals of meaning. So even though John Henry, the text's apparent framer of last recourse, is set up like Mark Madham as a U.S.-based controlling voice, the model of neo-imperial invasion and exploration seems here to be built on too destabilized a foundation to embrace without more detailed comparison of the concerns and strategies of the two novels. Not least among the destabilizing factors is, of course, the irony that while both novels posit U.S.-based framers as the controllers of discourse, both are post-colonial fictions created and controlled by their real framers of last recourse, the Canadian Robert Kroetsch and the New Zealander Janet Frame.

Kroetsch's interest in Columbus revolves around "the perceptual moment" in which the explorer misrecognized and misnamed the "Indians" of the Americas. That moment of misnaming is paradigmatic of a process of imperial appropriation through textual authority that has become, for Kroetsch, the chief burden and challenge of the New World writer. In his essay, **"Unhiding the Hidden,"** he writes:

> At one time I considered it the task of the Canadian writer to give names to his experience, to be the namer. I now suspect that, on the contrary, it is his task to unname. . . . The Canadian writer's particular predicament is that he works with a language, within a literature, that appears to be authentically his own, and not a borrowing. But just as there was in the Latin word a concealed Greek experience, so there is in the Canadian word a concealed other experience, sometimes British, sometimes American.

> (43)

Gone Indian can be read as a fictional enactment of that process of unnaming. Jeremy's experience of the frontier turns him into the very opposite of the "integrated Being" that Madham struggles to remain: Jeremy's unnaming and renaming into multiple possibilities represents what Madham calls "the consequence of the northern prairies to human definition: the diffusion of personality into a complex of possibilities rather than a concluded self" (152). While the processes of unnaming and renaming occur throughout the novel, beginning from Jeremy's arrival at the airport, the central event is a literal stripping-down of identity symbolized by the discarding of his jacket and keys during the snowshoe race. At this point, language has also been discarded: misrecognized as an Indian after winning the race, Jeremy replies to questions and harassment with silence because "if I had tried [speaking], it would have been a tongue I did not understand" (93). And even though as Indian, Jeremy is restricted by definition to the inauthentic imposter-status of his model, Grey Owl, this new identity nevertheless becomes an ennabling condition of imagination, allowing him to enter the dreams of the silent Indian woman, Mrs. Beaver. And along with the other identities that he collects along the way, it allows him to escape quite literally from the fixity of lived experience to the realm of imagined, multiple possibilities. Defying the control of his American framing narrator, he frustrates closure by disappearing without a trace, leaving Madham to speculate on various imagined ends. As Peter Thomas explains, Jeremy uses "trickster cunning" to "escape into ficticity and story" (78). Kroetsch dramatizes the post-colonial problematic of cultural inheritance and independence by locating textual authority in the neo-imperial centre and then undercutting that authority through liberating gestures within the story.

Simon During describes the initial encounter between whites and Maoris in New Zealand as a site of misrecognition and misnaming. Like Columbus misnaming the Indians, the Pakeha invaders misrecognized the locals as "cannibals," "savages"; they in turn were misrecognized by the Maori as "gnomes," "whales," and "floating islands." The words of pre-colonial Maori language, adjusting to new social realities, "began to lose their meaning until no consensus remains as to what certain words 'mean'" (41). Janet Frame, not unlike Kroetsch, centres her novel on an event that enacts "the natural destruction of known language" (Frame, 119). Portrayed as a quasi-science-fictional, Kafkaesque nightmare of unexplained and unexplainable occurrences, Frame's apocalypse, with its alphabets raining down like nuclear fallout and its transformation of ordinary New Zealanders into non-verbal, primal-screaming victims, is a more ambiguous, far less hopeful event than Kroetsch's liberation into possibilities. As Susan Ash points out, *The Carpathians* narrates the collapse of language without attempting to symbolize its possible replacement" (1).

The differences between Kroetsch's and Frame's prospects for language are evident in their varying uses of the motif of writer's block to represent a failure of words. Kroetsch's Jeremy, despite years of unsuccessful attempts to write his thesis, never stops trying to begin, and his many aborted

titles and first sentences become at least a catalogue of the possible. Mattina's husband Jake, struggling for thirty years to write his second novel, appears no further ahead at the end than at the beginning; his excuses and earnest promises are the only verbal products related to his novel that we are shown. The fact that he has been writing journalism and essays seems almost unimportant to him, to his family and to Frame's novel in the mutual preoccupation with his failure to novelize—for in Frame's world imaginative fiction is a privileged discourse.

In the aftermath of the midnight rain and the collapse of language it brings about, the forces of destruction, silence and obliteration of memory appear to have triumphed. Frame evokes totalitarian paranoia in her descriptions of anonymous, androgynous figures dressed in white removing the residents of Kowhai Street in vans and putting their houses up for sale. The only voice available to speak for the new reality is the eerily evasive real estate agent Albion Cook, whose name combines Blake's England with Blake's contemporary and the Southern Hemisphere's nearest equivalent to Columbus, James Cook. Far from Kroetsch's themes of purgation and renewed authenticity, Frame appears to suggest a regression to a colonial state where tribal memory is under siege and "strangers" (as the Kowhai Street residents call themselves) become silenced victims scarcely remembered or mourned by their successors. The Gravity Star, Frame's astrophysical metaphor for perceptual sea-change, can become a liberating phenomenon only to those who are prepared to adapt to "the demolishing of logical thought, its replacement by new concepts starting at the root of thought" (119). For those wedded to the traditional binary oppositions of self and other, "here and there" (14), that supported the imperial projects, the failure to adjust to post-colonial necessities will have tragic consequences. It is one of Frame's bitter ironies that the motivation to "preserve the memory of Kowhai Street and its people" (165) comes not from New Zealanders, but from Mattina and her family, invaders from a neo-imperial power filling a perceived void with a necessary act of appropriation—appropriating story and point of view.

Nicholas Birns says that *The Carpathians*, "with its emphasis on time, loss, and continuity, is clearly Frame's most explicit effort at confronting New Zealand's cultural inheritance" (18). Recently New Zealand has made strides towards recuperation of the losses its aboriginals suffered in colonial history, but Mark Williams points out that this "understandable cultural wish" carries the risk of self-deception. If Maori culture is embraced by the Pakeha as no more than "a decorative sign of difference," its use as a sign of distinctiveness from European culture remains ironically structured on a European dualism that preserves "the separation of head and heart, reason and feeling" (18–19). In Puamahara, this reclamation takes place in both Pakeha and Maori communities, represented by a learning or relearning of Maori language that means different things in the two contexts. Madge McMurtrie's Pakeha grandniece Sharon, learning Maori at school, points to an absorption of the previously denied "other" into the dominant culture; this activity can be viewed either liberally as progress or territorially as appropriation. On the other hand Hene Hanuere, the Maori shopkeeper, tells Mattina wistfully that "it's not so easy" relearning Maori at her age because "it's been away so long":

> "We're all changing back now. It's strange, you know. Like someone you turned out of your house years ago, and now they've come home and you're shy, and ashamed of having turned them out and you have to get to know them all over again and you're scared in case you make a mistake in front of the young ones, for the youngest ones know it all. You know, it's been lonely without our language. People from overseas sometimes understand this more than those living here."
>
> (26)

The Maori children, who are further away temporally from the suppressed past, can get psychologically closer to it because their elders have "been brought up Pakeha" (26). This generation gap creates an uneasy sense of fracture and discontinuity between past reality and whatever form its present resurrection and transformation will take, casting a shadow over the good intentions of the recuperative project.

The aboriginal contexts provide both Frame and Kroetsch with tangible historical models for the post-colonial theme of the decimation of language and the systems of thought that rely on language. In the historical contexts of Cook and Columbus and their successors, that destruction was part of an incipient colonizing project of subjection and assimilation. In the contemporary context, a parallel process, whether it is called "unnaming" or "the natural destruction of known language," carries the potential of liberation from colonial mentalities. And in a social climate that stresses revaluation and recuperation of aboriginal cultural losses, these narratives of deferred, slippery referentiality and unrealistic events are able to sink strong roots into the ground of real political projects. In fact, Kroetsch's novel, if not exactly prophetic of the current Canadian climate of increased sympathy to aboriginal perspectives, certainly finds itself open to interpretations that foreground its conceptions of "Indian" and language now more clearly than might have been possible in 1973. Jeremy is mistaken for an Indian by his fellow whites and later finds his dreams infiltrated by a Blackfoot tribal memory. In one dream he becomes Poundmaker's warrior, an Indian subject, and absorbs the memory of the other into his own through an act of imagination. As Buffalo Man making love to Buffalo Woman, he gains a stake in the land as the Indians knew it—in the ecosystem that white intervention disrupted. And his role as "listener" is, for Mrs. Beaver, a victory; he is the white man empathizing with and taking responsibility for a past in which his racial forebears were the other, the enemy. By reclaiming her lost past through *his* imagination, she helps him internalize a new point of view and a new language, an act made possible by his willingness to "uninvent" himself—to enter other identities and reject the language that articulates "the systems that threaten to define [him]" (Kroetsch **"Unhiding,"** 43–44).

But if there are positive transformations possible in these encounters of white with aboriginal, both authors remain conscious of the delusions enabled by insincere or inauthentic appropriation. The failure of perception that causes Kowhai Street's tragedy is demonstrated in part by the residents' isolating attitudes and the provincialism that locates quality elsewhere—in the "centres" of Auckland, England, or America. But it is symbolized by the cynicism that surrounds the town's "rediscovery" of the Maori legend of the Memory Flower. Distracted by the perceived bright lights of other places or times, residents like the Shannons, Dorothy Townsend and Hercus Millow are inclined to view the Memory Flower as of no more significance than any other "tourist promotion" (21), a clever way to give visitors "a feeling that when they're in Puamahara they've arrived somewhere" (39). And perhaps no more serious attitude is deserved by the lonely, shabbily-maintained kitsch sculpture that represents the Memory Flower. Perhaps the local cynicism is simply a reflection of the attitude behind its government-sponsored rediscovery in the first place. It is only the outsider Mattina who takes the legend's ramifications seriously; for the locals it is a missed opportunity. As she says:

> "I thought . . . that I'd find the Memory Flower, the land memory growing in the air, so to speak, with everyone certain as could be of the knowledge of the programme of time, learning the language of the memory, like the computer language, to include the geography, history, creating the future. . . . It sounds crazy, I guess. It's the idea you get about other places. But I do feel that having the memory at hand, even if it is buried in legend, is having access to a rare treasure. Such memories are being lost rapidly and everywhere we are trying to find them, to revive them. Puamahara in the Maharawhenua could be the place for pilgrims (I guess I'm a pilgrim) to be healed of their separation from the Memory Flower."
>
> (60–1)

It is because of this failure that the destruction visited upon the Kowhai Street residents does not result in the kind of renewal that Kroetsch's novel imagines.

However, there are difficulties with Kroetsch's use of aboriginal materials, too. When Jeremy "dreamed always a far interior that he might in the flesh inhabit," his model was Grey Owl; he tells the Customs agent on arrival in Edmonton that he wants to "become" Grey Owl (5–6). As a white man perhaps his choice is unavoidable, but his desire to become an imitation of Indian rather than the thing itself becomes problematic when he later declares Grey Owl "the truest Indian of them all" (80) because he refused to kill animals. Here Jeremy seems to be using white stereotypes of Indian identity and philosophy—simplified notions based on the interconnectedness of human and animal realms—to render the inauthentic white version of Indian "truer" than the authentic Indian experience, which does involve killing. Clearly there are dangers of misrecognition and misnaming in the present-day encounter of aboriginals and whites as profound as those of Columbus and Cook. *Gone Indian* also undercuts its own optimistic themes by locating the desired unnaming and renewal in a farcical narrative acted out by an often passive, impressionable and erratic character, a renegade American trickster whose enactment of a necessary process takes place with a cavalier, self-centred individualism that uses but does not include the members of the Canadian community in which it takes place.

The duality of individual and community is one that Kroetsch has articulated in his criticism. Explaining that "Behind the multiplying theories of Canadian literature is always the pattern of equally matched opposites," he associates "Self: Community" with "Energy: Stasis" (Kroetsch and Bessai, 215). In another essay he establishes some related dualities:

> The basic grammatical pair in the story-line (the energy-line) of prairie fiction is house: horse. To be on a horse is to move: motion into distance. To be in a house is to be fixed: a centering unto stasis. Horse is masculine. House is feminine. Horse: house. Masculine: feminine. On: in. Motion: stasis.
>
> (**"Fear of Women,"** 76)

Kroetsch's paradigms are apt to a comparison of *Gone Indian* and *The Carpathians*. Where the Kroetsch novel privileges the "masculine" principles of motion, energy and the individual quest, including sexual *con*quest, Frame's Mattina pursues her antipodean quest through a largely static domesticity, rarely leaving Kowhai Street, undergoing even such dislocating experiences as the reading of Dinny's typescript and the trauma of the midnight rain within the walls of her temporary home. The people Mattina observes, the Kowhai Street residents sheltered in their homes, also seem static compared to the constant motion of Kroetsch's characters. The act of observation rarely transcends the fixed binaries of observer-observed, self-other, and it is tempting to interpret the failure that Frame's novel seems to imply as related to an absent element of the carnivalesque. In his essay **"Carnival and Violence,"** Kroetsch borrows Bakhtin's notion of the carnivalesque to describe a liberating state of being located on the frontier, one in which normally fixed identities and hierarchical social roles are in a fluid state of becoming, of mutation, transformation and exchange. While the spirit of the carnivalesque is productive in Kroetsch's novel, it is absent from Frame's more pessimistic vision.

And while Mattina's quest is an individual one, she is not the subject of *The Carpathians* in the way that Jeremy is of *Gone Indian*. The residents of Kowhai Street—a group that fails to achieve its potential as a community—are the narrative's main interest. Mattina is important primarily as a frame: as the observer and interpreter of the community, and as preserver of its story as memory. Ultimately, of course, even these framing roles are superceded by John Henry, the largest framer within the text, just as Jeremy as subject is controlled by Madham, and his subjectivity threatened by Madham's attempts to assert himself as subject.

It is more important to the post-colonial visions of both *Gone Indian* and *The Carpathians* that their superceding

narrative frame-narrators are American than it is that their central characters—the agent-explorers Jeremy and Mattina—are American. The explorers, despite their limitations, do strive for an open-minded and positive embracing of the requirements of place; they respond and adapt to their destinations rather than imposing themselves. Once the explorer has left the "centre" of neo-imperial power— New York—for the "margin"—Puamahara or Notikeewin—she or he becomes implicated in the place itself, in its stories and realities, just as Cook and Columbus did. But if the final mediating power—the framer, Madham or John Henry—remains located at the centre, in a place with expansive global "cultural authority" (Said, 291), a gap of narrative control will be constructed that sustains the colonial tensions of speaking versus being spoken for. As long as this gap exists, there will be competing claims on authorship and authority. What power the "margin" has to tell its own stories will be overshadowed by a stronger interpretive power located elsewhere, just as the political authorization for Columbus and Cook's journeys remained at the centre. Kroetsch, by making Madham such an articulate spokesman for his own egotism and delusions, offers more hope for dismissing the centre's claims for authority than Frame does; her John Henry as *Ur*-narrator is so minimally presented as to be almost invisible. An important but uncomfortable post-colonial problematic emerges from these two novels: they deliberately compromise their own status as locally framed and authorized texts by deferring narrative authority *in* the text to an "other" located at the centre of global cultural imperialism.

Works Cited

Ash, Susan. "The Narrative Frame: Unleashing (Im)possibilities." *Australian and New Zealand Studies in Canada* 5 (1991): 1–15.

Birns, Nicholas. "Gravity Star and Memory Flower: Space, Time and Language in *The Carpathians." Australian and New Zealand Studies in Canada* 5 (1991): 16–28.

During, Simon, "Waiting for the Post: Some Relations Between Modernity, Colonization, and Writing." *Ariel* 20.4 (1989): 31–61. Rpt. in *Past the Last Post: Theorizing Post-Colonialism and Post-Modernism.* Ed. Ian Adam and Helen Tiffin. Calgary: U of Calgary P, 1990. 23–45.

Frame, Janet. *The Carpathians.* 1988. London: Pandora, 1989.

Henke, Suzette. "The Postmodern Frame: Metalepsis and Discursive Fragmentation in Janet Frame's *The Carpathians." Australian and New Zealand Studies in Canada* 5 (1991): 29–38.

Kroetsch, Robert. "Carnival and Violence: A Meditation." *Essays* 111–22. Rpt. in *Lovely Treachery* 95–107.

———, and Diane Bessai. "Death is a Happy Ending: A Dialogue in Thirteen Parts." *Figures in a Ground: Canadian Essays on Modern Literature Collected in Honour of Sheila Watson.* Ed. Diane Bessai and David Jackel. Saskatoon: Western Producer Prairie, 1978. 206–15.

———. "The Fear of Women in Prairie Fiction: An Erotics of Space." *Crossing Frontiers: Papers in American and Canadian Western Literature*. Ed. Dick Harrison. Edmonton: U of Alberta P, 1979. 73–83. Rpt. in *Essays* 47–56. Rpt. in *Lovely Treachery* 73–83.

———. *Gone Indian*. 1973. Nanaimo, B.C.: Theytus, 1981.

———. *The Lovely Treachery of Words: Essays Selected and New*. Toronto: Oxford UP, 1989.

———. "The Moment of the Discovery of America Continues." *Essays* 25–32. Expanded and rpt. in *Lovely Treachery* 1–20.

———, *Robert Kroetsch: Essays*. Ed. Frank Davey and bp Nichol. Spec. issue of *Open Letter* 5th ser. 4 (1983).

———. "Unhiding the Hidden: Recent Canadian Fiction." *Journal of Canadian Fiction* 3.3 (1974). 43–45. Rpt. in *Essays* 17–21. Rpt. in *Lovely Treachery* 58–63.

Said, Edward. *Culture and Imperialism*. New York: Alfred A. Knopf, 1993.

Thomas, Peter. *Robert Kroetsch*. Vancouver: Douglas & McIntyre, 1980.

Williams, Mark. *Leaving the Highway: Six Contemporary New Zealand Novelists*. Auckland: Auckland UP, 1990.

Laurie Ricou (review date Autumn 1995)

SOURCE: A review of *The Puppeteer*, in *Canadian Literature*, No. 146, Autumn, 1995, pp. 140-41.

[*In the following review, Ricou praises Kroetsch's deft use of language in* The Puppeteer.]

Robert Kroetsch's novels always pause to make you think. They make you think about truth and desire, about who tells story and what language is worth. They often make you stop to marvel at how things happen or why some machine works the way it does. I especially like the way they often force you to re-think everyday things you had never thought deserved thinking about.

The Puppeteer made me pause to ponder pizza. Pizza, I thought, is closer to a truly multinational, multicultural food than the infamous Big Mac. It is predictably, unpredictable: it can have an infinite number of toppings mixed in an endless confusion. Except when it is rectangular, it is round—both a satisfying whole and without beginning or end. Pizza is food for puppeteers.

The Puppeteer makes you think about how pizza is like a novel: "The rubble and design of a pizza, its ordered blur of colours and textures and shapes, arouse in me the collector's will to win." The design is more dependent than any of the earlier novels (except *Alibi*, to which it is both sequel and, perhaps, the field notes) on that paradigm of postmodernism: the detective mystery.

Maggie Wilder is contemplating her own murder. Julie Magnuson's car went off a cliff. There is no body. Jack Deemer is the murderer or the narrator or the detective. Manuel De Medeiros, dwarf spa doctor, is suspected of the murder. Maggie, guided by the old buzzards Ida Babcock and Josie Pavich, sets off through the mazes of Italian streets and gardens in search of the murderer. Papa B, the pizza delivery man in the Greek cassock, retreats to Maggie's attic where he tries to find, in elaborate productions of shadow puppetry, the ultimate narrative variation which will solve every mystery. *Alibi*'s Billy Billy Dorfendorf, Deemer's agent, may be Papa B. There is a design here, and the suspense of a rainsoaked west coast mystery by Earl W. Emerson. But perhaps the suspense resides in the mystery of (the desire for) motive. You think you know what you're eating, but you keep being puzzled by this or that morsel under the mozzarella. The design of the pizza is discovered in accident and the ingredients to hand.

Many of the varieties listed on this menu will be familiar. An endlessly elusive intertext in **The Puppeteer** consists in Kroetsch's rewriting characters, motifs and incidents from his earlier work. Most of the cast of characters from **Alibi** find new alibis and aliases here; but in the blur of colours, we also readily detect the obsessive collector of **Badlands**, the out-West tall tales of **What the Crow Said**, Demeter Proudfoot's irony of biography, the puzzles of conjunction from the **The Sad Phoenician** and the garden mysteries of **Seed Catalogue**. Borrowings are overt yet puckish: in that wedge, I tasted Bowering; in other slices I found Ted Blodgett, Robert Harlow, bp nichol, and David Lodge.

The novel is a pizza of places. It evokes Vancouver's nights in dramatically rainy scenes. But it also has exquisite descriptions of the Tivoli Gardens, of the streetscapes of Sifnos, and of the piazzas of Rome. The novel cherishes cappucino, gelati and *obiter dicta*. And it delights in the writer as *compiler*, in the language of collection. It sustains the joy of **Alibi** in collecting collections. Any collection will do as long as it is already in the form of a collection: "one hundred and twenty-four weak excuses. Portions of a tongue. Eighty-two reasons why up and down are the same thing."

That's the pizza formula: put anything in you like, don't fret over the combination, cover it in cheese and bake in a very hot oven. Presto. A novel you can read with your fingers.

Of course, you can't review a pizza by listing its ingredients, however exotic or ordinary. The best way to convey the flavour is to share a slice or two. I have persuaded myself that I can recognize a Kroetschian sentence—I like to imagine that if I found a cold sentence in the refrigerator I would know if it had been baked by Kroetsch. Something like, "Maggie in that instant wanted to believe him" or "He was deaf, the man, to any kind of snooping." In the first example ambivalent love is puzzled by a prepositional phrase. Normative syntax would likely have "That instant Maggie wanted to believe him." Or, possibly, "*for* that instant." Kroetsch's sentence exaggerates the interruption between subject and predicate, between human being and desire, and the textures mixed by the drifting modifier 'in.' Kroetsch likes to focus on those nuances of connection that are prepositions. The second sentence also has a built-in hesitation, an unnecessary apposition, but also one removed from its antecedent. It offers precision and delivers confusion; it offers tentativeness and delivers wonder.

I began this review by celebrating Kroetsch's focus on the banal but beautiful detail. Imagine if one of the "poetic" and "idiosyncratic" essays in Roland Barthes' *Mythologies* had been devoted to pizza. Now expand that cynicism and delight in mass culture to novel length. *The Puppeteer* gives a comparable pleasure of style. So perhaps the best way to end a review is by chopping up some of the ingredients in Kroetsch's kitchen. Make mine a syntax special. A large please.

> Far above, something terrible was happening. Had happened. Would happen.

> They were in the belly of a great whale, and the whale was the shape of light, barely sustaining itself against the Pacific darkness.

> And if the two old women, a single moment earlier, had been little more than a pair of strangers, in the moment of Maggie's speaking they became her allies, friendly co-conspirators in a treacherous world.

> The floating words attached themselves to tongues.

> No, I am not a foreigner, but I am a foreigner, yes.

Papa B., the narrator muses, speaks pizza as if it were a language. And Robert K., I am persuaded, savours language as if it were a pizza.

Tim Bowling (essay review November 1995)

SOURCE: "A Somewhat Schizophrenic Package: Robert Kroetsch's Anti-Memoirs," in *Books in Canada,* Vol. 24, No. 8, November, 1995, p. 15.

[*In the following review, Bowling finds* A Likely Story *compelling but ultimately uneven because of Kroetsch's overbearing use of theory.*]

The most important point to make about *A Likely Story* is that it's not an autobiography, at least not in any conventional sense. In fact, the author himself claims that such a genre is impossible. As a result, the book is entirely free of literary gossip, contains only a minimal amount of personal information, and avoids the axe-grinding that often accompanies writers' explorations of their careers. Yes, this does sound dull, but Robert Kroetsch is one of Canada's liveliest and most original literary theorists, not to mention an accomplished poet and novelist, and what he has to say about writing makes for a compelling, though uneven, read.

The opening piece, **"Why I Went Up North and What I Found When He Got There"**, sets the tone for the whole book. Here, Kroetsch investigates his reasons for heading to the Northwest Territories as a young would-be-writer fresh out of university, and his recollections of that experience are vivid and enlightening. He writes of a dangerous journey on a riverboat and of losing his virginity, but these are only incidental stories: what matters most is how the North changed and shaped his attitudes towards identity, and informed his ideas about narrative, time, voice, all those ingredients essential to the storyteller's craft:

"Insofar as the North carnivalizes given Canadian assumptions—turning upside-down assumptions about time, about direction, about urban ambition, about America—it seemed an escape from the authority of tradition and hierarchy, an escape that would allow me to become a storyteller."

In the most general terms, Kroetsch is postmodernist. He approaches the art of writing with a questioning, probing, even suspicious mind, repeatedly asking himself and the reader, "What is the real story? Is there such a thing?" Whether he's discussing Margaret Laurence's *The Diviners* or the effect of the prairies on a writer's development, it's obvious that he feels passionately and thinks deeply about literature. His essay **"D-Day and After: Remembering a Scrapbook I Cannot Find"** is particularly interesting; its anecdotal style houses many subtle and intelligent statements on literary craft.

But halfway through, *A Likely Story* bogs down under the weight of so much theory, and what begins as a winning mixture of the personal and the academic becomes a private game designed for those with some specialized knowledge of current critical discourse. The long closing essay, **"The Poetics of Rita Kleinhart"**, is especially frustrating, as the author's attempt at a humorous mock-biography comes across as self-indulgently clever.

Ultimately, these seven essays and three poems form a schizophrenic package, one that is alternately fascinating and opaque. Readers looking for specific comments on Kroetsch's own poems and novels will be disappointed by his detached tone and refusal to engage in intimate revelation.

However, as an exploration of certain technical themes that haunt many contemporary writers, *A Likely Story* proves a useful and insightful reference.

Wanda Campbell (essay date 1996)

SOURCE: "Strange Plantings: Robert Kroetsch's *Seed Catalogue,*" in *Studies in Canadian Literature,* Vol. 21, No. 1, 1996, pp. 17-36.

[*In the following essay, Campbell argues that* Seed Catalogue *depends on an organic structure that evokes meaning from its content.*]

My poem *Seed Catalogue* is about a prairie garden. I actually used the McKenzie Seed Catalogue from McKenzie Seeds in Brandon. This was part of my effort to locate the poem in a particular place and then I expanded the poem outward to whatever other models I wanted—the garden of Eden or whatever—so that I could get all those garden echoes working together. We have an experience of particular garden here. There are certain kinds of things we can grow and certain things we can't grow. The garden gives us shape.

(Robert Kroetsch qtd. in MacKinnon 15)

It is my impression that *all* parts of speech suddenly, in composition by field, are fresh for both sound and percussive use, spring up like unknown, unnamed vegetables in the patch, when you work it, come spring.

(Charles Olson, "Projective Verse" 21)

Much has been made of Robert Kroetsch's use of an archaeological model derived from a variety of sources including Martin Heidegger, William Carlos Williams, Charles Olson, and Michel Foucault, but, in his long poem *Seed Catalogue* at least, Kroetsch makes use of what might be called a horticultural model. As Robert Lecker points out, Kroetsch "continues to wrestle with tradition and innovation" (123) in his poetry. The patterns that grow out of the poem are not merely accidental unearthings on the part of the reader, but the result of intentional plantings on the part of the writer. Influenced by Olson's emphasis on *process* and *kinetics*, Kroetsch seeks a form that emerges directly out of the content rather than one that is artificially imposed, and yet he manages to write "a long work that has some kind of (under erasure) unity," (**"For Play and Entrance,"** *LTW* 118). He does so by adopting as his central metaphor the seed, which signifies both intentionality and surprise, flight and ground.

As Kroetsch himself suggests, the central model for *Seed Catalogue* is the Garden of Eden, which informs the text from the opening descriptions of planting to the final riddle. The Garden for Kroetsch becomes a kind a sacred middle ground between the male field and the female house, the most fertile ground for the growth of the poet which is the central subject of the poem. The plantings are "strange" and the harvest unexpected, but there is no doubt that a gardener has been at work.

Despite his "distrust of system, of grid, of monisms, of cosmologies perhaps . . ." (**"For Play and Entrance"** *LTW* 118), Kroetsch writes that he was "much and directly influenced" by *The Secular Scripture* (**"Learning the Hero from Northrop Frye"** *LTW* 160). He also expresses enthusiasm for Carl Jung; "He is something of a goldmine, especially his works on alchemy" (*LV* 104). In *Psychology and Alchemy*, Jung summarizes the attractions of the horticultural model:

That we are bound to the earth does not mean that we cannot grow; on the contrary it is the *sine qua non* of growth. No noble, well-grown tree ever disowned its dark roots, for it grows not only upward but downward as well.

(110)

The energy of Kroetsch's long poem *Seed Catalogue* emerges from the tension between this downward and upward movement, between the seed full of explosive potential and the careful containment of the catalogue (Greek *kata* down + *legein* to select). The "notes" of Kroetsch's poem are not simply the jottings of the archaeologist, or "finding man," but those of a composition that is more carefully orchestrated than we have been led to believe.

The implications of the metaphor of the seed are manifold. By emphasizing "the kind of unwritten poem implicit in the seed" (Marshall 44), Kroetsch carries the image beyond the traditional associations, an enterprise for which he finds a model in the poetry of William Carlos Williams, who refers early in his long poem *Paterson* to "[t]he multiple seed, / packed tight with detail, soured, / . . . lost in the flux and the mind. . . ." (12). Kroetsch expands upon his understanding of Williams's use of the image of the seed:

Again it's so different from the metaphoric use of seed that we have, say, in the Bible. I think we are seeing the seed in quite a different way now as poets. Partly because we resist . . . we resist metaphor. Why the hell use it metaphorically when the-thing-itself is so interesting.

(Marshall 25)

The image of the seed is especially attractive to Kroetsch because of its dual potential for upward and downward movement, a "double vision" ingrained in Kroetsch's imagination during his childhood in Heisler which, as a farming and a mining community, provided both surface and underworld metaphors (MacKinnon 3–4).

Just as the structure of *The Ledger* was determined by an actual ledger kept by Kroetsch's grandfather and presented to him by his Aunt Mary O'Conner, the particular structure of *Seed Catalogue* was suggested by the document named in the title. Kroetsch reveals that the similarity between the two poems might well have been more pronounced had he not forgotten his notes in Winnipeg when he set about writing the poem (Cooley 25). Responding to a 1917 seed catalogue he found in the Glenbow archives, Kroetsch set about writing a poem that would bring together "the oral tradition and the myth of origins" (**"On Being An Alberta Writer"** 76), and provide a poetic equivalent to the 'speech' of a seed catalogue, which for Kroetsch was not just a random document: "When my mother died I became the family gardener. . . . When I found that seed catalogue my whole self was vulnerable and exposed" (Marshall 50). He reveals that self through a tale of origins expressed, not as chronological autobiography, but as synchronous garden.

Seed—The ovules of a plant when preserved for the purpose of propagating a new crop.

Seed Catalogue begins abruptly with a listing from the catalogue for "Copenhagen Market Cabbage" complete with catalogue number. Pamela Banting expresses regret that even those critics most sensitive to textual nuance tend to "privilege the Kroetsch-written sections" over the subtext (qtd. in Brown *Long-liners* 290). The passages from the catalogue merit careful attention, both for what they say and do not say. According to Russell Brown, the lesson implicit in the opening lines of **Seed Catalogue** is that "from the apparently innocent, 'documentary,' past we may inherit imported meaning and ways of seeing" (**"Seeds and Stones"** 158). A cabbage bearing the name of Denmark's capital is "introduced" into a prairie garden, bringing with it a history and a pedigree. Both the cabbage itself and the language that describes it are inherited stories, and throughout his writing, Kroetsch expresses a skepticism about history.

The fact that this peculiar landscape demands new ways of seeing is imaged in the storm windows which are removed from the house and placed on the hotbed. The same windows offer two ways to defeat the weather, keeping the "flurry" of snow out, and keeping the "flurry" of growth in. Like lenses, the windows provide the double vision necessary to cope with the prairie's unpredictable climate: the palimpsestic notion of "under erasure" to which Kroetsch refers in **"For Play and Entrance"** (*LTW* 118), also operates: spring is discarded but still faintly visible. In the original Turnstone edition of **Seed Catalogue**, the text of the poem is printed over a palimpsest of actual pages from a seed catalogue, an effect which visually reinforces Kroetsch's intertextual technique. Dominated by the extremes of "January snow" and "summer sun," prairie weather does not offer the temperate transition of spring that is so central to the poetic tradition elsewhere in the world. The absence of spring draws attention to the need for a new mythology to interpret a new landscape.

Following directly upon the heels of the poet's rearticulation of the climate is a letter of response to the producers of the seed catalogue. The inherited vocabulary and cheerful hyperbole of W. W. Lyon's letter resembles the text of the catalogue but stands in sharp contrast to the poet's efforts to be accurate about his environment. The literary formality of the letter, despite the demotic "Cabbage were dandy," also contrasts with the genuine orality of the mother's voice: "Did you wash your ears? / You could grow cabbages / in those ears" (I.17–19). Her assertion at first appears as exaggerated as those of Lyon, but as the poem develops it becomes clear that the young poet's ears are, after all, a garden in which language (both imported and indigenous) is taking root. Kroetsch often refers to his early initiation into the oral culture of the prairies through a multitude of voices ranging from relatives to hired men. He is able to distinguish between the various voices that enter his poem by using a flexible left-hand margin, a technique he learned from Williams and Stevens, and which, according to Kroetsch, reflects the space and silence of the prairies (Cooley 27).

The poet's fall from the horse in the opening section is central to the imagery of the poem in two major ways.

First, it establishes the position of the poet in relation to the dominant myths of prairie life and, second, it foreshadows a fall from innocence. The stage is set: "We were harrowing the garden" (I. 22). Harrowing, of course, means the ploughing or loosening of the ground with a farm implement equipped with discs or hooks, but it can also mean "to distress greatly" (*OED*). Since the previous passage establishes the poet's ears as a garden of sorts, the ridicule that follows his fall from the horse may well be a torment to him. According to Kroetsch, the horse in the prairie dialectic signifies the male myth, a designation that corresponds to the traditional associations of the mounted knight, a posture which he himself failed to achieve. So, the young poet falls from the male world of the horse into the ambiguous garden where his mother invites his participation in the acts of creation and naming. Kroetsch re-articulates the fall from grace into nature as a fall into language and "ground." As the hired man points out, "the horse was standing still" (I.32). For the poet, the horse is standing still—the romantic tradition of the male as hero has ground to a halt. But the horse is *still* standing; the male tradition and the tall tales which celebrate it are still available to the poet as fuel for his imagination. Unlike Pete Knight, "the Bronc-Busting Champion of the World," who falls off a horse into death, the young poet falls off a horse into life, to be rooted in the garden of new possibilities: "Cover him up and see what grows" (I.51).

Much as the mother's gentle whisper intersects the boisterous commentary of the hired man, the blooming of the seed catalogue intersects the winter in which it arrives. Remembering a future season through the magic of language, the catalogue is "a winter proposition" (I.35)—a scheme, an invitation, a truth to be demonstrated. The seed catalogue is itself a kind of tall tale, insisting that "McKenzie's Improved Golden Wax Bean" is "THE MOST PRIZED OF ALL BEANS" (I.38–39). Kroetsch works to undermine this hyperbole through a rhyme which substitutes "virtue" for "toot," thus suggesting that such a notion is the mere passing of wind.

The mother, meanwhile, is ordering her corner of the world with binder twine. Later, it is upon sacks in which binder twine is shipped that the poet and Germaine become "like / one" (III.39). The female presence is binding up the distances and binding up the wounds. In contrast, the father's tools for ordering his world are fenceposts and barbed wire, items to keep things in and out. He is confused by the gentle intimacy of the garden world," puzzled / by any garden that was smaller than a / quarter-section of wheat and summerfallow" (I.52–54). He commands a home place defined by the points of the compass and surveyor's math: "N.E. 17–42–16–w4th Meridian" (I.55), a place where both absence and presence are defined by extremes.

> No trees
> around the house.
> Only the wind.
> Only the January snow.
> Only the summer sun.

The home place:
a terrible symmetry.

(I.59–65)

However, even in this brief passage describing the prairie as a place of absence, we find allusions to two poetic models, one indigenous and one imported. "Only the wind" echoes the closing lines of Anne Marriott's *The Wind Our Enemy*, a poem about the prairies in which the appearance of absence is revealed to be a powerful source of presence. The phrase "a terrible symmetry" echoes Blake's (and Frye's) "fearful symmetry": the prairie landscape may appear always as "tyger" and never as "lamb," but even the tyger is a result of the creative act, the framing hand, the speaking word. Even absence provides a kind of symmetry. "Even abandonment gives us memory" (**"On Being An Alberta Writer"** 71). It is in this context that Kroetsch introduces the first of the questions about growth that echo through the poem as a kind of refrain: "How do you grow a gardener?" (I.66) The catalogue of garden varieties that follows reminds the reader that the poet is not only referring to the actual gardener, but also to the poet himself who, like Adam, was both gardener and namer. Listed without context, the names of the various vegetables take on a music of their own. According to Olson, from whom Kroetsch learned some of his poetic craft, "words juxtapose in beauty" through their syllables (17).

The "terrible symmetry" of the home place is mirrored by the terrible symmetry of life and death, garden and grave. The road between these extremes, though "barely / passable" (I.76–77), must be travelled by the poet. Even as the poet remembers the moment in which his mother is planted in the earth, he remembers her invitation to creativity through the newly planted seed: "Bring me / the radish seeds, my mother whispered" (I.77–78). As Kroetsch says elsewhere: "Endings have stems and blossoms" (***Completed Field Notes*** 231).

SEED—THE GERM OR LATENT BEGINNING OF SOME
GROWTH OR DEVELOPMENT.

Juxtaposed against the gentle simplicity of the mother's voice that closes Section One is the elaborate mythologizing of the story-telling father in Section Two. What appears to be a tall tale of the contest between man and badger can also be interpreted as an exploration of the confrontation between "talking father" and "writing son," the story teller and the poet. Just as the antics of the badger inspire the father's tale, the father's challenge inspires the badger to extravagant escapes, which parallel the son's literary endeavours. In Kroetsch's poem **"The Silent Poet Sequence,"** the poet describes his clandestine activity: "I go out at night, with my shovel, I dig deep holes / in the neighbours' lawns" (***Completed Field Notes*** 76). Later in *Seed Catalogue* the father offers labour as an alternative to an activity that he cannot understand: "And the next time you want to / write a poem / we'll start the haying" (VI.66–68). Similarly, the father cannot understand why "so fine a fellow" as the badger would choose to live under

ground. In the opening section, the young poet has fallen off a horse and into the earth: "just / about planted the little bugger" (I.50). The poet, too, looks "like a little man, come out / of the ground" (II.5–6). The poem, like the seed, becomes Kroetsch's record of his search for the ground from which he came. The poet, like the badger, is attracted by "the cool of roots," the solace of isolation, and the violence implicit in the act of unearthing. Though the father is puzzled by this downward desire because it contrasts with his own upward desire for building and flight, he cannot, of course, shoot the son. The son, likewise, can never fully escape the father: "They carried on like that all / summer" (II.11–12). The twine that binds the two together despite their differences is love. In love, the father threatens over and over. In love, the son repeatedly stands up to his challenge. In love, the son burrows into the ground that gives rise to the poet. In the end, the father tells a different story, in which a different nuisance (the magpie) is destroyed, while insisting that that was his original intention: "Just call me sure-shot, / my father added" (II.26–27). The story is not the story, Kroetsch reminds his readers, but the process of the story, not the harvest but the planting. There must always be enlargement, re-invention and change.

SEED—SEMEN, THE MALE FERTILIZING ELEMENT.

Love is first introduced as a binding element between man/father and badger/son, and in Section Three the notion of love is expanded to include Eros. This new direction is signalled by the sensual language of the catalogue entry for Hubbard Squash. To this point, the vegetables listed have promised pedigree and virtue, but the Hubbard squash rewards mankind's "particular fondness" with sensual delights. As the catalogue writer points out, where there is a need, nature provides. In this context, the *italicized* phrase: "*Love is a leaping up / and down*" (III.4–5) describes more than the action of the badger who refuses to get shot and refuses to dig his holes elsewhere. Similarly, "*Love / is a break in the warm flesh*" (III.6–7) signifies more than the penetration of the father's bullet into the feathers of the magpie. The growth of the sensual squash is described in the seed catalogue, but the young poet must discover the growth of Eros for himself. He must ask: "But how do you grow a lover?" (III.12).

The "winter proposition" offered (with illustrations) by the priest is not, like the seed catalogue, a promise (with illustrations) of coming fertility, but rather an insistence upon chastity and the fires of hell. The difference becomes painfully clear to the children on only the second day of catechism. Here Kroetsch provides an important clue to the structure of the poem as a whole. Catechism, a method of instruction which proceeds by question and answer, may well be the model for the series of questions that give *Seed Catalogue* its shape. Many manuals of catechism deal not only with questions of scripture and doctrine, but also with questions of behaviour and morality such as "How must we express our love to our fellow creatures?"

Against such a backdrop, the poet must consider his own question: "How do you grow a lover?" He had believed that it meant becoming "like/one" as Adam and Eve did in the garden, but he discovers, to his dismay, that Adam and Eve fell out of the garden into sin. Still innocent, and without a name for the union they have dreamed, Germaine and the poet climb into a granary and become "like/one" (III.39). Only after the priest calls it *playing dirty* is the thing they have discovered dis/covered into nakedness and shame. They fall from myth into language, and it is language that transforms a tale of sexual initiation into something more profound.

The fact that Germaine and the poet make love on "smooth sheets" of paper from the gunny sacks reinforces the parallel between the sexual act and the writing act, a connection Kroetsch often makes in essays and interviews. Germaine, "with her dress up and her *bloomers* down" (III.50), becomes a muse for the young poet. She, as her name suggests, is fertile ground in which he plants the seeds of his imagination. But the priest names their world "out of existence" (III.44). Language creates absence as well as trace. The lovers have fallen from the garden, the boy has fallen from the horse, and the poet's understanding of language has fallen from innocence. Now he must unname it back to the beginning.

In so doing, Kroetsch attempts one more retelling of the Genesis story, "one meta-narrative that has asserted itself persistently in the New World context" (**"Disunity as Unity"** *LTW* 31). Apparently, this dream of Eden first entered Kroetsch's psyche through the various tellings of his mother and father—his mother who lovingly learned the names of the flowers and birds of her native Alberta, and his father who "had for all his life an intense Edenic recollection of a lost home," the green pastures of Ontario (Thomas, *Robert Kroetsch* 11). Kroetsch is fascinated by the story of the Garden of Eden because it invites a variety of tellings that range from ancient myth to child's riddle. In *Seed Catalogue*, the riddle of "Adam and Eve and Pinch-Me" is given in answer to the poet's question "But how?" How does one become a lover when the priest insists upon abstinence? How does one become a poet when the land insists upon silence? These questions await answers, just as the riddle awaits a solution.

SEED—THE OVA OF THE SILKWORM.

The absences that define Heisler, beginning with the absence of silkworms, are cleverly catalogued in a list that interweaves the cultural and the historical, the public and the private. The wit, however, does not disguise the fact that the books and historical records which might provide models for the re-invention of the self are largely missing. Kroetsch describes the "three or four books" that were in his house while growing up: one about looking after horses, one on wild flowers, and one on threshing machines (Hancock 47). In the absence of the written word, the poet turns to the spoken word as a means of survival.

Mary Hauck arrives in Heisler on a January day, bringing her hope chest, which, like the seed catalogue itself, is full of imported elegance and dreams yet to be fulfilled. Only when the contents of her hope chest are destroyed by fire, and her European and Eastern Canadian inheritance is lost, can she find a place in this new world. The way is now clear for the growth of a prairie town. However, the gopher which provides the model for the prairie town's human structures (telephone pole / grain elevators / church steeple) and the human needs they represent (communication / physical / spiritual sustenance) is apt to vanish as suddenly as it appeared. In the process of learning how to grow a past, the prairie town is perpetually threatened by absence. Nonetheless, the "Bullshitters" confront the silence with talk that includes both the fanciful and the profane. Even the joke "about the woman who buried / her husband with his ass sticking out of the ground" (IV.62–63), maintains a continuity with the theme of planting that recurs throughout the poem.

SEED—IN GLASS-MAKING, A MINUTE BUBBLE
ARISING IN GLASS DURING FUSION.

The fusion between imported and indigenous that occurs in the heart of the fire completes the apprenticeship of the poet, which is as arduous as that of the gardener. Just as the gardener's first planting is devoured, his first efforts to "deliver real words / to real people" are ignored (V.5–6). His father wishes him to become a different kind of "postman," driving fenceposts with a crowbar. Meeting with no success or encouragement, the youth gives in to despair: "I don't give a damn if I do die do die . . ." (V.9), but even this apparent submission becomes a kind of song (in contrast to a story), echoing a line from Ervin Rouse's "Orange Blossom Special" popularized by Johnny Cash. In this echo of the rhythm of the train-track, the positive (do) struggles with the negative (die), but the final word of the incantation is "do," which prepares the way for the next question to be posed, "How *do* you grow a poet?" Out of the furnace, and out of the fusion, a seed is born.

CATECHISM—A SUMMARY OF THE PRINCIPLES OF A
CREED IN THE FORM OF QUESTIONS AND ANSWERS.

In Section Six, at the heart of the poem, Kroetsch lays bare his technique, and his *telos*. His seed catalogue is not just an enumeration, though it certainly incorporates lists of all kinds; it is a catechism designed to instruct and reveal through questions and answers. Having explored the beginnings of his personal apprenticeship, Kroetsch now outlines the struggle for poetry in a prairie literature dominated by fiction. The environment may be hostile, but Kroetsch, for one, is determined to develop a hybrid that is up to the challenge.

The seed catalogue offers information on how cauliflowers should be grown, but not on how poets should be grown. Where does one begin? There are, of course, the classical formulas, the first of which is the invocation of the muse. The young poet turns to the muses for inspiration, only to be reminded that they are the daughters of Mnemosyne, and on the prairies Memory has been undermined by fire, forgetfulness, and the fearful symmetry of an empty landscape. Instead of Calliope, or Erato, or Polyhymnia, the poet finds only the girls he has "felt up," "necked with" or fondled in the skating rink shack (VI.20–33). Perhaps the prairies offer no adequate muse. (Significantly, Kroetsch dedicates the **Completed Field Notes** to Ishtar, the Babylonian goddess of love and war he describes as "that undiscoverable and discovered reader towards whom one, always, writes," and to his daughters.) The tender portrait of the mother that appears in the poem's final pages suggests that she may well be his most enduring muse, but in this part of the poem she still represents an absence.

What then of the other opening formula, "Once upon a time . . ."? The poet attempts to apply it to the home place, only to be stopped by the realization that it is a fictional rather than a poetic device: "—Hey, wait a minute. / That's a story" (VI.35–36). In an attempt to explain his observation that "the prairies developed a tradition of fiction before developing a tradition of poetry," Kroetsch suggests that the realistic mode of fiction lent itself to the "harshness" of the prairie experience (**"On Being An Alberta Writer"** 74–75). Once again, he is faced with the fact that "story" intervenes with the growth of the poetic tradition.

His parents know the formulas for growing a healthy boy (with cod-liver oil and Sunny Boy Cereal) and a competent farmer (with hard labour and haying), but no one has yet devised a way to grow a prairie poet. The father gives form to the land with barbed wire, but clearly this is an inadequate model, as is the prairie road which merely marks "the shortest distance / between nowhere and nowhere" (VI.71–72). If this road is a poem, there is no sign of its maker:

> As for the poet himself
> we can find no record
> of his having traversed
> the land/in either direction.

(VI.78–81),

The creator has disappeared. He is lost. All that remains is "a scarred / page, a spoor of wording" (VI.83–84). However, like the poet's secret shining from the bottom of the sea in A. M. Klein's "Portrait of the Poet as Landscape," this humble trace of words, this mere "pile of rabbit turds," is enough to reveal "all spring long / where the track was" (VI.88–89). Spring on the prairies, we have been told, is a season that hardly exists. But for that briefest of moments, we can see the poet's path.

The phrase "poet . . . say uncle" (VI.90) is followed by the italicized question "How?" which both echoes the earlier questions and implies that the poet either does not know how or is unwilling to give up or admit defeat. Also, by making tongue-in-cheek reference to the greeting of the Hollywood Indian, Kroetsch prepares for the poet's real life encounter with the aboriginal, the truly indigenous, in his environment.

The novelist Rudy Wiebe is now introduced into the poem, insisting that the only way to conquer the vastness of the prairie landscape is to "lay great black steel lines of / fiction" (VI.92–93). In this, Wiebe echoes the desire of the poet's storytelling father who insists that the only way to give form to the land is "by running / a series of posts and three strands / of barbed wire around a quarter-section" (VI.60–62), and those who believed that the "great black steel lines" of the railway would allow the iron horse to conquer prairie distances. Despite his quarrel with Wiebe's insistence upon fiction as the preferred prairie genre, Kroetsch acknowledges the gifts Wiebe has bestowed upon his writing friends, including glimpses of indigenous history and inherited language. The word *Lebensglied* which Wiebe points out, appears only once in Rilke's poetry:

> Auf einmal fasst die Rosenpflückerin
> die volle Knospe seines Lebensgliedes,
> und an dem Schreck des Unterschiedes
> schwinden die [linden] Gärten in ihr hin
>
> All at once the girl gathering roses seizes
> the full bud of his lifelimb,
> and at the shock of the difference
> the [linden] gardens within her fade away[1]

One tribe of Indians is "surprised . . . to death" by another in the "coulee," a prairie word for a deep ravine or dry stream bed. Similarly, the rose gatherer of Rilke's poem takes hold of the "lifelimb" or "life's member" only to be overwhelmed by it. Every garden holds its surprises, and "the shock of the difference" is not to be underestimated. Perhaps the giant "geometry" of prairie geography and prairie fiction is an effort to fulfill humankind's "blessed rage for order." Yet, Kroetsch warns against a simple belief in the convention of the unity of signifier and signified, a temptation to meaning he suggests is attractive to Wiebe (*LV* 143). In the sections that follow, Kroetsch posits several alternatives. Kroetsch uses the form of the catechism to achieve a kind of unity, while resisting "the ferocious principles of closure" (**"For Play and Entrance,"** *LTW* 118) by providing many possible answers to each question.

Thus far, many possible models for the prairie poem have been implied, ranging from badger hole to rabbit turd, but the most developed and powerful image of the poet can be found in the description of Brome Grass that opens section seven. Though the passage resembles the previous quotations from the seed catalogue, there are several significant differences. The entry does not begin with the usual catalogue number, nor does it employ the high-flown and hyperbolic language of the earlier entries (with the possible exception of "Flourishes"). In addition, both the common and the Latin names are included, as if to acknowledge the dual heritage of the Canadian poet. Through a factual description which captures the vernacular simplicity of the spoken word, Kroetsch manages to foreground many of the qualities already highlighted as essential to the development of the poet. "No amount of cold will kill it. It / *withstands* the summer suns." The poet both withstands and stands with the terrible symmetry of his home place. "Water may stand on it for several / weeks without apparent injury." Though Adam and Eve are "drownded," the poet remains. "The roots push through the soil, / throwing up new plants continually." Delighting in the duality of the border-place, the poet moves downward into the earth and the buried past, and upward into the glory and grief of flight ". . . continually." The poet is forever involved in the process of story, of language, of strange plantings and unexpected harvests. "*Starts quicker* than other / grasses in the spring." Even before the snow has melted, the poet's track is visible. "*Remains green* longer in the fall." The poet's *fall* from the horse is a fall *into* the garden, not out of it; refusing to surrender to absence and death, the poet retains the desire for greenness and growth. "*Flourishes un- / der absolute neglect.*" Despite the *absence* of "Aeneas" and "clay and wattles" (as in Yeats's "Lake Isle of Innis-free"), and the *presence* of crowbars and mustard plasters, the poet endures his long apprenticeship. He survives the winter to arrive at last at "seeding / time" (VII.8), a phrase which implies both the time for cultivation and the cultivation of time. In explaining his dual allegiance to fiction and poetry, Kroetsch writes: "There's something you can do in a poem that you just can't do in a novel—concepts of time and of language" (Cooley 31). Freed from narrative chronology, the poet can allow all of the fragments he uncovers to "juxtapose in beauty," to use Olson's phrase.

For the last time Kroetsch asks the central question of *Seed Catalogue*, "How do you grow a poet?" and again, he provides, not one answer, but many. There is no right answer, no single version. "Even in the Genesis story," Kroetsch reminds us, "one discovers that there are three versions, one on top of the other" (*LV* 118). The palimpsest of prairie poetry implies a similar multiplicity. In Sections Seven through Ten, Kroetsch explores a variety of muses, models, and methods which add to his understanding of the poetic process and contribute to his apprenticeship as a prairie poet.

MUSES—NINE GODDESSES, THE OFFSPRING OF ZEUS AND MNEMOSYNE, WHO INSPIRE POETRY, ETC.

One of Kroetsch's guides in learning to respond to life as it is lived around him was Al Purdy. "In abandoning given verse forms for the colloquial, the prosaic, telling yarns in the oral tradition, Purdy was central" (Cooley 28). Purdy and Kroetsch reject the "still point of the turning world" offered by T. S. Eliot in *Burnt Norton*, in favour of the "turning centre in the still world" (VII.13). The power of poetry allows Purdy to gallop a Cariboo horse through an Edmonton restaurant, to transform a dinner party into a carnival, to surprise an ordered world through language. Through metaphor he becomes a new kind of cowboy, creating a new mythology.

The poet also finds muses among his own relatives, his own memories. The poet remembers the Last Will and Testament of his grandfather who gave "Uncle Freddie" his carpenter tools. This builder who mapped his world with perfect horse-barns endures even when the world has no more use for his artistry. Uncle Freddie refuses to say Uncle. He learns not only to make, but to make do. Although his craft appears to have outstripped its usefulness, its perfection endures. The craft of poetry may also be "archaic like the fletcher's" (Klein), but that does negate its worth or excuse the poet from bringing new forms to life. Uncle Freddie has been bequeathed carpenter tools, but he reminds his nephew that the greatest tool of all is the imagination. Although deeply impoverished, he maintains his rituals and his pride, replacing the coffee he cannot afford with hot water with cream and sugar in it. From him the poet learns how to honour the illusion, how to remember not to forget.

This lesson is reiterated by the cousin who drops bombs on the land of his ancestors. His fall from his plane, reminiscent of the cowboy's fall from his horse, signals a "fatal occasion" (IX.16). He forgets that the land upon which he brings destruction ("It was a strange / planting" [IX.11–12]) is the land where his family first took root. Forgetfulness is a dangerous muse, burying the past and devouring the future. She has "Blood / on her green thumb" (IX.35–36), resulting in a "terrible symmetry" from which escape is impossible.

The poet finally reveals his ultimate muse in the person of his mother, who is addressed in a passage preceded by the final entry from the seed catalogue. This listing for the *Spencer Sweet Pea* is a price list reminiscent of the passage in William's *Paterson* where the chattels of Cornelius Doremus are appraised (45–6). But Kroetsch's list reveals that the more you purchase the less it costs—the more you invest, the higher the yield. The sweet peas, like all the other plantings in the poem, are at once upward, "climbing the stretched / binder twine," and downward, rooted in a deep and familiar soil. The poet believed himself to be bereft of models in a world of absence, but he now remembers the simple lessons taught to him by his mother and her garden: the grace of living, the beauty of weariness, the strength of place.

MODEL—A PERSON, OR A WORK, THAT IS PROPOSED OR ADOPTED FOR IMITATION; AN EXEMPLAR.

The poet must be open to the experience of life as captured in literature and in art, though these must be defined in the widest possible sense. To illustrate how the seed catalogue is a document as revealing and as valid as any other, Kroetsch shows how the entry for the "Japanese Morning Glory" evokes a variety of possibilities for interpreting the home place. A harsh environment teaches the characters of Sheila Watson's novel a harsh lesson: to catch the glory is also to hook the mourning. "The double hook: / the home-place" (VII.36–37). In the particular Japanese print to which Kroetsch refers—Hiroshige's "Shono-Haku-u"—the surprise that upsets man's careful plans is also a confrontation with an unpredictable climate. The artist Hiroshige belonged to the Ukiyo-E school:

> "E" means picture in Japanese, and Ukiyo (literally "floating world") suggests the transitory, shifting, at times treacherous existence to which man is condemned. Ukiyo-e are the genre depiction of people who, although well aware of the snares and tricks in store for them, still do their best to snatch as much pleasure and enjoyment out of life as they can.
>
> (Suzuki 6)

The print entitled "Shono-Haku-u," which portrays "bare-assed travellers, caught in a sudden shower" (**Seed Catalogue** VII.31), perfectly captures the philosophy of the Ukiyo-E. Caught in a storm they could neither predict nor avoid, the men rush forward into the weather with heads bent. For them there is no shelter. Only the rain. Only the wind. A terrible symmetry. Always the double hook, the glory and the mourning, in Japan as on the prairies. The phrase "the stations of the way" (VII.38), which closes this description, refers to the title of the series of Japanese prints, "Fifty-Three Stations on the Tokaido." These depict many of the stations or post-towns on the Tokaido Highway, which stretched a distance of about 300 miles from Kyoto to present-day Tokyo. In the context of what follows, it may also be an allusion to the stations of the cross that lead to "the other garden," Gethsemane. (In a 1976 entry in **The Crow Journals**, Kroetsch's mention of "The Stations of the Cross" on a hill in Qu'Appelle Valley, Saskatchewan, is followed by an elaborate rejection of the tenets of Modernism [58]). For Kroetsch, as for the pioneers who preceded him, ordering an unfamiliar terrain with familiar forms is a double-hook experience. Eden and Gethsemane go hand in hand. Nonetheless, Kroetsch hopes to grow like the brome grass of the prairies, to flourish under neglect, to catch the glory as well as the mourning, to combine the imported and the indigenous into a hybrid that can survive.

"How do you grow a garden?" Mary, Mary, quite contrary, plants her garden with silver bells and cockle shells. Mary Hauck of Bruce County, Ontario plants hers with silver spoons and English china. But the prairie poet cannot afford to be contrary or ecologically ignorant regarding which hybrids will thrive in his home place. He must plant his garden with varieties as strong and sturdy as brome grass, plants that endure drowning and cold to grow as tall as a horse's hips. The intimate tone of the letter describing "the longest brome grass" in one individual's memory contrasts sharply with the distanced and artificial voice of Lyon, whose cabbages were "dandy." This letter, with its combination of the ordinary and the evocative, like the garden itself, suggests a pattern for the prairie poet. It is signed by "Amie," a real person perhaps, but certainly a friend.

> METHOD—A SPECIAL FORM OF PROCEDURE
> ESPECIALLY IN ANY BRANCH OF MENTAL ACTIVITY;
> A WAY OF DOING THINGS.

The prairie poet must discover new ways to "deliver the pain." When the Bronc-Busting Champion of the World

falls off his horse into death—his own death and the death of the male myth of the conquering hero—the way is cleared for a new hero. Both a real cowboy who achieved international success in rodeo between 1932 and 1936, and one of the last representatives of the chivalric order suggested by his name, Pete *Knight* finds his story coming to an abrupt and unceremonious end. The rock upon which the Western myth is built has eroded. The once epic hero has been diminished out of existence and his myth dismissed as madness ("You some kind of nut / or something?" [VII.20–21]), thus clearing the way for the poet. In his essay **"Learning the Hero from Northrop Frye,"** Kroetsch draws attention to the following passage from *The Secular Scripture*:

> The real hero becomes the poet, not the agent of force or cunning whom the poet may celebrate. In proportion as this happens, the inherently revolutionary quality in romance begins to emerge from all the nostalgia about a vanished past.
>
> (*LTW* 178)

The hero falls off his horse and dies, in contrast to the poet who, in the poem's opening section, falls off his horse and lives. "Cover him up, see what grows." The poet is, indeed, as the lady at the end of the bar would have it, "some kind of nut" from which new mythologies will sprout.

The "terrible symmetry" that haunts the entire poem is reflected typographically in the opening of the poem's final section, in which the double column format that Kroetsch had earlier used in **The Ledger** to "express a dual perception" (Thomas 29) is again in evidence. The use of the slash in the left hand column invites a further multiplicity of readings. In the line, "After the bomb / blossoms," the slash allows the word "blossoms" to be interpreted as either a verb or a noun, implying both endings and beginnings. Similarly, in "Poet, teach us / to love our dying," the phrase "our dying" can be interpreted as the process of mortality that we must embrace as a necessary half of the double hook. "Our dying" may also be interpreted as those among us (mother, father, cousins, uncles, great-grandmother . . .) who have succumbed to "the danger of merely living" (IX.1).

"West is a winter place" characterised on the surface by absence, death, the empty page. It is also a "palimpsest." Under the erasure, another text can be read. Under the snow, a seed is burrowing. Into the January darkness, the seed catalogue blooms. The harshness of winter may invite a flight, an escape and evasion, but the model of the garden offers a place to be rooted, and a place to grow.

Does the world of **Seed Catalogue** remain harsh to the end, as some critics have argued? The reprise of the passage in Section One that first established the land as absence appears to confirm that it does. However, the echo of Marriott, "only the wind," is now incorporated into a sentence, as if to suggest that the presence of the wind is sufficient to challenge the absence of trees, to inspire and to animate. The land may suggest absence, but the celebration of that absence results in a poem.

Seed Catalogue closes with one last "method" open to the poet, the riddle, an ironic extension of the catechism which reflects the postmodern resistance to closure and elitism. The riddle, according to Kroetsch, is more than just a "purely verbal game . . . You can start to read a riddle as a great insight into human uncertainty, self-deception and so forth" (*LV* 81–82). The riddle in *Seed Catalogue* that is begun in Section Three and continued in the final lines is only completed in the mind of the reader:

> Adam and Eve and Pinch-Me
> went down to the river to swim—
> Adam and Eve got drownded.
> Who was left?

The poem itself resists closure, but the answer of "Pinch-Me" that arises in the reader's mind establishes a connection of tremendous immediacy between the poet and his audience. For this kind of poem to succeed there must be complicity between actor and audience, poet and reader, a reaching across the spaces between people (as in a pinch). Adam and Eve (the original gardeners, namers, lovers) and the poet's parents may have vanished, but the poet and Pinch-Me remain. Kroetsch accomplishes what he set out to do. Throughout the poem and in its final lines he brings together the oral tradition and the myth of origins. Eden endures, though in accordance with the archeological model, as riddle and repository.

Note

1. I am indebted to Angela Esterhammer at the University of Western Ontario for her assistance with the translation of Rilke's poem. The German language allows for the invention of compounds such as *Lebensgliedes*. *Leben* can only mean "life" but *glied* has several implications: its primary meaning is "limb" (both botanical and anatomical), but it can also mean "member, part, organ," which can mean "penis" or "virile." Other less common meanings are "link" as in "the missing link" and the biblical idea of "generation" (*Langenscheidt's*). Such a multiplicity of meanings would certainly have been attractive to Kroetsch. The italicized definitions are from the *OED*.

Works Cited

Brown, Russell. "On Not Saying Uncle: Kroetsch and the Place of Place in the Long Poem." *Long-liners* Issue of *Open Letter* 6. 2–3 (Summer/ Fall 1985): 257–266.

———."Seeds and Stones: Unhiding in Kroetsch's Poetry." *Open Letter* 5.8–9 (1984): 154–75.

Cooley, Dennis, and Robert Enright. "Uncovering Our Dream World: An Interview with Robert Kroetsch. *RePlacing*. Downsview, ON: ECW, 1980. 21–32.

Hancock, Geoff. "An Interview with Robert Kroetsch." *Canadian Fiction Magazine* 24–25 (Spring/Summer 1977): 33–52.

Jung, Carl. *Psychology and Alchemy*. Trans. R. F. C. Hull. London: Routledge, 1953.

Klein, A. M. *The Collected Poems of A. M. Klein*. Toronto: McGraw-Hill, 1974.

Kroetsch, Robert. *Completed Field Notes: The Long Poems of Robert Kroetsch*. Toronto: McClelland, 1989.

———. *The Crow Journals*. Edmonton: NeWest, 1980.

———. *Labyrinths of Voice*. Eds. Shirley Neuman and Robert Wilson. Edmonton: NeWest, 1982.

———. *The Lovely Treachery of Words: Essays Selected and New*. Toronto: Oxford UP, 1989.

———. "On Being An Alberta Writer." *Robert Kroetsch: Essays* in *Open Letter* 5.4 (Spring 1983): 69–80.

Lecker, Robert. *Robert Kroetsch*. TWAS 768. Boston: Twayne, 1986.

Marshall, John. "From *The Remembrance Day Tapes*: Interviews with Robert Kroetsch." *Island 7* (1980): 35–50.

MacKinnon, Brian. "The Writer Has Got to Know where He Lives: An Interview with Robert Kroetsch." *Writers News Manitoba* 4.1 (1982): 3–18.

Suzuki, Takahashi. *Hiroshige*. London: Elek, 1958.

Thomas, Peter. *Robert Kroetsch*. Vancouver: Douglas, 1980.

Williams, William Carlos. *Paterson*. New York: New Classics, 1951.

David Williams (essay date Summer 1996)

SOURCE: "Cyberwriting and the Borders of Identity: 'What's in a Name' in Kroetsch's *The Puppeteer* and Mistry's *Such a Long Journey*?," in *Canadian Literature*, No. 149, Summer, 1996, pp. 55-71.

[*In the following essay, Williams discusses the notion of self in the post-modern world as it appears in* The Puppeteer *and Mistry's* Such a Long Journey.]

Borders are fast disappearing in the new Europe, along the information highway, and in the mega-channel universe. Hong Kong's Star Satellite, carrying five television channels to fifty-three countries, has already changed the face of Asia. In India, a new generation openly celebrates the country's "Californication," while their elders debate "The Challenge of the Open Skies" (Joseph) to a state broadcast monopoly. Given such a fundamental shift in the mode of information, we might ask whether the nation state, or local culture, or even the concept of a substantial self can survive the communications revolution?

Five hundred years ago, Gutenberg threatened speech communities in Europe with a similar loss of identity. With the benefit of hindsight, we can understand how the book redefined the human subject as being self-bounded and self-contained, much like the bound volume which came to occupy a reader's inmost consciousness. "I think; therefore I am," the philosopher established as the surest ground of metaphysics; but what made this idea thinkable was the very subjectivity engendered by the book. The new religion of the Book also brought about a revolution in church and state, undermining age-old hierarchies. Henceforth, the privileging of a sovereign consciousness, which demanded increasingly liberal values, would change all the old forms of social and state organization.

Now, in the midst of another communications revolution, the modern philosopher announces "The End of the Book and the Beginning of Writing." Though Jacques Derrida has had little to say about electronic writing per se, several comments suggest that he would locate us between the epoch of the book and that of the electronic mark. In *Of Grammatology* he argues that the artificial intelligence of the "cybernetic *program*" has tended "to oust all metaphysical concepts—including the concepts of soul, of life, of value, of choice, of memory—which until recently served to separate the machine from man" (9). In consequence, the very "constitution of subjectivity" (113) in technological societies has been altered, as Mark Poster claims in his study of "Derrida and Electronic Writing," by the immateriality of new forms of script: "The writer encounters his or her words in a form that is evanescent, [as] instantly transformable" as mental images, and so "the human being recognizes itself in the uncanny immateriality of the machine" (111–12).

This uncanny "mentality" of the machine underwrites the paradigm shift in recent theories of the humanities which have made language or culture, not nature, the final ground of interpretation. Forty years ago, Roland Barthes foresaw that, because "man in a bourgeois society is at every turn plunged into a false Nature" (156), the mythologist must decode the myth of a culture, to expose it as an alibi. Today, it remains the critic's task to expose the stubborn alibi that linguistic determinations and other forms of social construction are really facts of nature; questions of race and gender have also brought to light transcultural systems of domination which at every turn oppress women and non-Europeans. Again, it is Derrida who, as Gayatri Spivak says, "has most overtly investigated the possibilities of 'the name of woman' as a corollary to the project of charging 'the ends of man.' In *Of Grammatology* he relates the privileging of the sovereign subject not only with phonocentrism (primacy of voice-consciousness) and logocentrism (primacy of the word as law), but also with phallocentrism (primacy of the phallus as arbiter of [legal] identity)" (Spivak 144).

This large-scale critique of the metaphysics of identity no longer privileges the subject as a sovereign consciousness, nor gender and race as facts of nature. Even the nature of our sensory perceptions—our entire positivist epistemology—is called into question by computer-generated virtual realities. For the first time, those who make it down the on-ramp onto the information highway sense how their nerve-endings no longer stop with their fingertips, but reach around the globe. And so the "uncanny immateriality" of the machine raises new questions about the space of our communities and even the integrity of our bodies. Where should we re-draw the borders of an identity once based on the book?

A longtime spokesman for the critical avant-garde, Robert Kroetsch has been gradually reworking French anti-humanist assumptions into a recognizably Canadian context. In an essay entitled **"No Name is My Name,"** he argues that a "willed namelessness" has always been the cultural norm in Canadian writing, a norm that he values since it holds out at least a hope of "plural identities" (*Lovely* 51–2)—an obvious social good in a society made up of so many races, languages, and ethnic groups. But Kroetsch also confesses his scepticism about the "very notion of self" (47), such scepticism being perhaps "the most significant consequence of structuralism: its rejection of the notion of the 'subject'" (Culler 28).

By contrast, a writer of colour from a more traditional society, such as Rohinton Mistry, seems to take the old humanist assumptions as a given. *Such a Long Journey*, the first novel by an Indian immigrant to win the Governor General''s Award for Fiction (1991), sees the threat of ethnocentrism to personal identity, but takes refuge in a kind of universalism tied to English itself as the guarantor of identity. When a Parsi character bemoans the loss of his familiar world in the changed street names of Bombay, Mistry's protagonist asks, "What's in a name?" To which his friend Dinshawji replies:

> No, Gustad. . . . You are wrong. Names are so important. I grow up on Lamington Road. But it has disappeared, in its place is Dadasaheb Bhadkhamkar Marg. My school was on Carnac Road. Now suddenly it's on Lokmanya Tilak Marg. I live at Sleater Road. Soon that will also disappear. My whole life I have come to work at Flora Fountain. And one fine day the name changes. So what happens to the life I have lived? Was I living the wrong life, with all the wrong names? Will I get a second chance to live it all again, with these new names? Tell me what happens to my life. Rubbed out, just like that?
>
> (Mistry 74)

What Dinshawji laments in the loss of the old names is the loss of the old logocentric security, that metaphysical reassurance via language "of the meaning of being in general as presence" (Derrida 12). Though Dinshawji resists the loss of his social identity and even his personal history to the politics of "Maharashtra for Maharashtrians" (73), the erasure of the old names also eradicates his world, makes absent what should be "naturally" present. Ultimately, he experiences the rewriting of the map of his neighbourhood as an interruption in his self-presence. A life by any other name would not be the same life. But in terms of the old metaphysics of identity, his ultimate appeal is to the fixity of print.

Conversely, the characters in Kroetsch's latest novel, ***The Puppeteer*** (1992), are regularly "exchanged for each other, and again" (126); lovers engage in "Finding other names" (127); and the words of two narrators—one speaking and the other typing—blend on the page as their personal identities begin to merge. ***The Puppeteer*** marks something of a narratological departure, even for someone as experimental as Kroetsch. It should come as no surprise that this is his first novel composed on the computer. It seems to me, the effect of the new technology on the writer's process is decisive: "Writing at the border of subject and object" (Poster 111), the old Cartesian subject no longer stands "outside the world of objects in a position that enables certain knowledge of an opposing world of objects" (99). Instead, the experience of "computer writing resembles a borderline event, one where the two sides of the line lose their solidity and stability" (111).

The epochal difference between the typographic and the electronic mark may finally serve to determine "What's in a name?" for both Mistry and Kroetsch. But we would first need to locate the differences in writing between an electronic society (Canada in the 1990s) and a traditional one (India in the 1970s). What are the consequences in either case for the character of the book? Can Mistry, who has lived in Canada since 1975, possibly resist the effects of his new milieu? Or can the country he recalls in his writing ever escape the logic of technology?

In Jacques Derrida's critique of Western logocentrism, the breakdown of the classical logic of identity occurs in the shift from an epistemology based on speech and presence to one based on new forms of writing, belatedly exposing an absence at the heart of writing in general. But technological change only exposes what Derrida claims was repressed in the whole history of writing by a metaphysics of presence—that language itself is "always already a writing" (106). For alphabetic script reveals what was always intrinsic to the system of language, even as its phonetic character helped to maintain our illusion that what we read was "united to the voice and to breath," and so was "not grammatological but pneumatological" (17).

A computer monitor more obviously takes our breath away, dispersing the mind and its mental images in a mirror outside itself, even as it "depersonalizes the text, removes all traces of individuality from writing, de-individualizes the graphic mark" (Poster 113). Yet alphabetic writing always had the same hidden power to open "a fissure between the author and the idea" (Poster 125), to disperse the identity of a speaking subject still conceived in the instant of "hearing (understanding)-oneself-speak" (Derrida 7). The "electronic mark" only "radicalizes the anti-logocentric tendencies that deconstruction argues are inherent in all writing" (Poster 123), for it "puts into question the qualities of subjectivity . . . [vestigially] associated with writing and more generally with rationality" (112–13).

"The Battle of Proper Names" in *Of Grammatology* concludes that what's in a name is more likely the whole coercive network of relations bounding the subject. Only the phonocentric illusion of hearing/understanding oneself speak hides this coercion and helps to naturalize the whole system of differences. But what the "concealment of writing and the effacement and obliteration of the so-called proper name" can no longer hide is "the originary violence of language which consists in inscribing within a difference, in classifying . . . In effect, it reveals the first nomination which was already an expropriation" (*Grammatology* 112). To name is to mark off territory, to set social bounds or limits, to forcibly erect boundaries which seem natural, which are "*perceived* by the *social* and *moral consciousness* as the proper, the reassuring seal of self-identity."

Mistry's protagonist in *Such a Long Journey*, expressing an awareness that "the reassuring seal of self-identity" is a social and political fiction, says, "Why worry about it? I say, if it keeps the Marathas happy, give them a few roads to rename" (73). But the novel seems to foreclose on such political questions when Gustad's friend protests the violence done to his own identity, meanwhile ignoring the violence done by the British name-giver to Maratha identity, much less the "originary violence" of naming itself.

Resisting loss at every turn, the narrative structure of *Such a Long Journey* thus enacts what Derrida saw in Lévi-Strauss as "a sort of ethic of presence, an ethic of nostalgia for origins" (*Writing* 292), which sends Gustad Noble on his own long journey toward a recuperation of lost beginnings. The "original" loss in Gustad's life is the innocence of a happy childhood, when the Noble family could still afford a vacation with the luxury of mosquito nettings at a hill station: he likes to recall "That picture of my mother—locked away for ever in my mind: my mother through the white, diaphanous mosquito net, saying goodnight-Godblessyou, smiling, soft and evanescent, floating before my sleepy eyes, floating for ever with her eyes so gentle and kind" (242). Even a toy seen in the Chor Bazaar reminds Gustad of the thieving uncle who gambled away his father's bookstore: "And what had become of the Meccano set? Lost with everything else, no doubt, during the bankruptcy. The word had the sound of a deadly virus, the way it had ravaged the family" (101). Even the feel of a fountain pen between his fingers evokes a powerful nostalgia for the world of childhood: "This was the bloody problem with modern education. In the name of progress they discarded seemingly unimportant things, without knowing that what they were chucking out the window of modernity was tradition. And if tradition was lost, then the loss of respect for those who respected and loved tradition always followed" (61).

His son Sohrab's lack of respect for paternal authority threatens Gustad's traditional values with their inner contradiction: "He will have to come to me. When he learns respect. Till then, he is not my son. My son is dead" (52). Just as hard on his friends, Gustad will not forgive Major Jimmy Bilimoria for packing up and leaving their apartment building without a trace: "Without saying a word to us. That's friendship. Worthless and meaningless" (49). The xenophobic force of tradition even shows up in a symbol of seeming inclusiveness, a sort of ecumenical wall separating the apartment compound from the street. A refuge from the Hindu majority, the concrete wall is a border marked by the odour of a counter-territoriality. Each day at dawn, Gustad suffers both the stench of urine and the sting of mosquitoes as he performs his kusti prayers, sheltered all the while from the stares of passersby. He hires a pavement artist to draw pictures of the gods and goddesses and saints and mosques of all the world's religions. But the wall is neither as holy nor as ecumenical as it first appears, since its saintly face masks a more divisive purpose: to preserve the Parsi in his self-sameness and hierarchical privilege, and to protect him from the threat of difference, of Otherness itself.

Gustad also erects other walls to hedge him in from the world. To his wife's dismay, he will not take down the blackout paper tacked to the windows nine years earlier, during a devastating war with China when even Nehru broke under the treachery of his Chinese brother Chou En-lai. Gustad has learned too well the truth of brotherhood, as revealed in the biblical story about "Cain and Abel . . . Fairy tales, I used to think. But from the distance of years, how true. My own father's case. His drunken, gambling brother who destroyed him as surely as crushing his skull. And Jimmy, another kind of Cain. Killed trust, love, respect, everything" (178). All that saves Gustad from the fate of Abel is a few pieces of rescued "furniture from his childhood gathered comfortably about him. The pieces stood like parentheses around his entire life, the sentinels of his sanity" (6).

Neither is he alone in this novel in clinging to remnants of a happier past. Miss Kutpitia, a neighbour in Khodadad Building, appears to be an Indian Miss Havisham, a Dickensian woman who has stopped the clock in her apartment at a point thirty-five years ago when her motherless nephew—her sole reason for living—was killed in an auto crash. Tenants who come to use her telephone are kept at bay in a little vestibule, and are never permitted to see beyond the closed door into the inner apartment where, "Like *tohruns* and garlands of gloom, the cobwebs had spread their clinging arms and embraced the relics of Miss Kutpitia's grief-stricken past" (284).

Ultimately, so many images of loss remind us of the condition of the emigré author for whom Gustad's sentiments are quite natural: "How much of all this does Sohrab remember, he wondered. Very little, I think. For now. But one day he will remember every bit. As I do, about my father. Always begins after the loss is complete, the remembering" (210). The childhood home is not so easily foregone, it would seem; its loss looms large within and without the text, as does the nostalgic yearning to reconstitute that absence in language, in a logocentric guarantee of presence. No wonder, then, that the names

must not change, lest it should turn out, as Dinshawji says, that he was "living the wrong life, with all the wrong names" (74).

And yet, as Laurie Coutino tells Gustad in shame and terrible anguish, "Mr Dinshawji has ruined my own name for me" (176). For the incorrigible flirt and joker, playing on the Parsi word for the male member, has told her that he wants her "to meet his *lorri*. . . . 'You can play with my little *lorri*,' he said, 'such fun two of you will have together.'" In his thoughtless way, Dinshawji has named her his thing, has committed precisely the kind of linguistic violence that Derrida describes in "the first nomination which was already an expropriation" (112). For Dinshawji has literally made the woman's proper name improper, has turned "Laurie" into the metaphorical measure of his own narcissism by appropriating her identity to that of his "lorri."

A third story of naming is just as violent, and ultimately quite as disruptive of self-presence. The local physician, Dr Paymaster, had some fifty years ago purchased the closed-down dispensary of Dr R. C. Lord, MBBS, MD Estd 1892. Revered for a sense of humour which could make his patients laugh their sickness away, Dr Paymaster one day committed the terrible blunder of removing the old doctor's sign and putting up his own shingle. "The very next day, the dispensary was in turmoil. Patients were marching in and marching out, demanding to know who this Dr Paymaster was" (113). The only way the new doctor could recover his practice was to hang up the old sign with the former doctor's name on it, "and the confusion vanished overnight. And overnight, Dr Paymaster sorrowfully realized something they never taught in medical college: like any consumer product, a doctor's name was infinitely more important than his skills." But he has had to give up his proper name to practice those skills, has had to accept being renamed within the generalized writing of a community which resists real change. And so the loss of his proper name turns out to be no change at all; it is simply another means of conserving the past.

Even in its narrative form, there could be a parallel between the novel and what Mistry calls "a country stuck in the nineteenth century" (155). Technically, there are very few risks, and very few discoveries, in the use of a limited third-person narrator to present differing points of view at the level of alternating chapters, or scenes, or even paragraphs. Narrative omniscience, like the fixity of print in a sign that cannot be changed, becomes a larger mark of continuity with the past, of the reassuring sense of an author-God.

Kroetsch's *The Puppeteer*, on the other hand, demands to be read in the new social context of "the borderline event" of electronic writing. The borderline between the writing and reading subject immediately begins to blur as the apparent narrator, Jack Deemer, reads the typescript of its protagonist-author Maggie Wilder in the very process of its production. In Deemer's words, "Maggie Wilder is writing this. Reading over her left shoulder, I become a loving supporter, the champion of her need to get the story of her wedding dress down on paper. Now and then I say a few words, joining myself into her train of thought. Sometimes, perhaps just to tease me, she scrambles a few of my words in amongst her own" (17).

The "borderline" identity of the narrator is further complicated by questions arising out of various forms of theatrical performance in the narrative. At the heart of the story is a puppet show put on by Dorf, the narrator of a previous Kroetsch novel, *Alibi*, who is now hiding out in Maggie's attic from his old boss Jack Deemer. Maggie, in the early stages of a separation from her husband, has walled herself in from the world quite as much as Mistry's Gustad Noble with his blackout paper on all the windows, much less Billy Dorf disguised as a monk and hiding in her attic, calling himself Papa B. Yet Dorf, alias Papa B, who has also spent three years in hiding in a Greek monastery, tries to reach Maggie through "Karaghiosi, the most popular of all the Greek shadow puppets" (115). Within the frame of a simple set, screened by a white bed-sheet, the puppet comes knocking

> with his long, hinged right arm. "Are you locked in there, Maggie Wilder? Do you want out?"
>
> "I'm not at home to you," a voice answered. "Leave me alone."
>
> There was no figure to be seen inside the house, only a voice to be heard. Papa B was speaking both voices, but neither was his. The voice of the second and invisible speaker, Maggie recognized, was an imitation of her own.
>
> (116)

Wishing to unmask the pretender, Maggie wilfully violates the theatrical frame by speaking in her own person to the puppet, the stage persona of Papa B: "Karaghiosi, you are always pretending to be someone you aren't. I know that much about you. You're pretending to be Papa B" (117). Papa B, who is pretending to be Karaghiosi, is accused of pretending to be Papa B, of playing himself. Yet he is also pretending to be Maggie, using her voice to ask her to give up her own identity, to play their mutual friend Inez: "Maggie was shocked and yet excited too, by the name she was given. She had become part of the play. She liked that" (117). And so the audience of one surrenders her proper name to the play of signification, crossing the line into the space of performance. Like the users of electronic message services, she appears to embrace the circumstance that "Identity is fictionalized in the structure of the communication" (Poster 117).

Later, however, when Maggie is seated once again at her desk, another puppet dressed up as a monkish Papa B addresses her in her own person: "Tell [Karaghiosi] that you don't want to be alone" (121). The breaking of the frame from the other side of the stage now strangely unsettles Maggie: "She could not, that second night, bear the directness of the puppets' approach. One of the puppets was

asking her simply to play herself, and Maggie found the assignment impossible" (122). The borders of identity begin to blur as well for Papa B whom Maggie has forced to play himself: "The voice of the monk was almost but not quite that of Papa B. Papa B, trying to imitate his own voice, was hesitating" (121). The "real" voice of Papa B now belongs to Karaghiosi, as it were, while his imitation of himself sounds inauthentic—authenticity receding into infinity in all these deliberate confusions of identity. Now it is Jack Deemer, the narrator, who puts the problem most succinctly: "Who was the puppet, who the puppeteer?" (123).

Since it is Deemer who winds up with the girl at the end of the novel, his narrative substitution of himself for Papa B almost makes up for his impotence to change the past. Certainly, he would have us believe that the whole affair has been staged for his benefit: "Maggie, I suspect, felt that in telling me the story of her love affair with puppets was telling me back into my own desire" (119). Ultimately, then, Deemer calls for another ending to the whole performance:

> They were the puppets, Maggie and Dorf, not Karaghiosi. That ancient Greek shadow puppet became master. It was he who manipulated their desire. . . . Karaghiosi, that slave and fool, became master. . . . Maggie taking the pain of Karaghiosi's heave. They were exchanged for each other, and again. They were orphaned into rhapsodies of desire. . . . "Karaghiosi," she said, calling him back. She said the name, making a small experiment into the naming of a wish. The whispered name was a reassurance to her own wet tongue, and she wondered whose hair touched her small breasts. . . . They were a frenzy of silence. They laughed, then, after, finding shirts and socks, pyjama bottoms and the cold cups of brassieres, there in the rank dark. Finding other names.
>
> (126–7)

In the act of love, the lovers have been exchanged for one another, have for the moment become truly *Other*. Crossing borders of flesh, they have "traded places," to cite the title of Maggie's first published collection of short stories. And so have the puppets and puppeteer been exchanged for one another, even as the reader (Deemer) and the author (Maggie who types the text before our eyes) have also traded places.

The other site of borderline events in the novel is the elaborate wedding dress which Maggie wears to the typewriter because "she could hear the story she intended to tell" (2) whenever she puts it on. Maggie wants "to write the autobiography of a wedding dress" (15), partly out of the conceit, as she says, that "dresses could talk" (27), and partly out of a conviction, as another character says, that "Brides look alike—in the long run, it's the dresses that differ" (28). Now, even the boundaries of genre begin to blur as the speaking subject is displaced from person to thing, and history (or perhaps biography if the dress has a "life"), dissolves into *auto*-biography, the dress "writing" its own story as told to Maggie, just as Maggie writes her own story as told to Jack Deemer.

The dress, however, is not unique to Maggie; it has been worn before by Deemer's wife Julie Magnuson, and it seems, according to its maker, to have been "double digit bad luck" (52). As a signifier, it encodes a social practice whereby each bride who wears it is supposed to find a new name and a new social identity. Julie was supposed to become the wife of Fish, who had even "asked for one small detail to be included in the flow and drift of details on the dress" (58)—a rainbow trout. But the dress, which keeps its identity as a differential mark in a system of differences without positive terms, contains a myriad of signs, just as a bride like Julie who marries and remarries carries the potential of many new names. The sign of the fish cannot even save Fish from being waylayed en route to the altar, where the bride is claimed instead by Jack Deemer: "In the tumult of the dress we were the story," Deemer says, "that Josie Pavich had only guessed; we were the lovers in animal form that she had so carefully pictured, the man with the body of a fish, the horse-headed man, the woman with octopus arms" (137). The dress, in other words, is a sign of the whole underlying system of *metamorphoses* encoded in weddings; it speaks of the bride and groom as shape-changers, and of their shifting identities in marriage.

Even Jack Deemer, who dons the dress in disguise at the end of the novel, becomes other than he is, and henceforth speaks differently: "I put it on. And then something precious happened. Wearing the dress, I was no longer simply myself" (251). At first, the dress merely puts him in mind of the woman he once married: "Waiting there, sitting, pacing, I came to understand how Julie Magnuson must have felt on the morning of her delayed wedding" (252). And yet he continues to wear the dress after an accident at the Greek chapel where the "monk" Dorf falls over a cliff to his death. The ruthless old collector who had once sought Dorf's life is apparently changed enough by the dress to persuade Maggie to live with him and to work "on—dare we say?—a saint's life" (264). "Papa B is seen as something of a saint by the monks and priests of Mount Athos" (264), not least because his cassock has turned him into "the monk he had so long pretended to be" (250), the true performer of his part. So, too, Deemer is transformed by his performance as "Maggie puts a beach towel over the shoulders of my wedding dress and tells me to close my eyes, which is hardly necessary, and she shaves me and does my hair. "'You must look the part,' she tells me, often, while she is doing this" (266). Feminised by the dress-as-sign, this most manipulative of men winds up in the role of a bride.

Of all the borders which are crossed in *The Puppeteer*, this one—the subversion of gender identity—is the least "natural" or, in narrative terms, the most forced. For Jack Deemer is a man who is not above murder, a wealthy thug, by his own admission, whom "people mention with curiosity and disgust. You don't put together a collection of collections without first putting together a little heap of the stuff that buys collections. Once in a while I had to make the rules fit the occasion" (71). How, then, could

such a macho man be so easily taken over by his own disguise? Or how could a dress—even if it is a linguistic sign—gain total control over its speaking subject? Why, in a word, should we be willing to see an incorrigibly male identity erased at the touch of another signifying system?

In a postmodern society already beginning to ask whether gender is determined by anatomy or by culture, the wedding dress evokes the "genderless anonymity" (Poster 121) of electronic communications. For individuals linked through computers now converse, "often on an enduring basis, without considerations that derive from the presence to the partner of their body, their voice, their sex, many of the markings of their personal history. Conversationalists are in the position of fiction writers who compose themselves as characters in the process of writing, inventing themselves" (117). In the immaterial medium of the new writing, material differences such as gender no longer have to determine the old borders of identity.

Though a wedding dress is not a computer, it is clearly a form of address, serving as a medium of communication. "If dresses could talk" (27), Maggie says, then dons it to write "her autobiography of a dress" (23). Much like the "mirror effect of the computer" which "doubles the subject of writing" (Poster 112), the dress doubles Maggie's subjectivity. Her identity is thus dispersed as much as Deemer's in wearing this dress, much as any writing subject in computer communications is "dispersed in a postmodern semantic field of time/space, inner/outer, mind/matter" (Poster 115). Through the fluid medium of the gown, the writer is made an amanuensis for the object itself which turns into a speaking subject. So inner/outer, mind/matter, are also reversible semantic fields in the dress.

The indelible mark, however, of the new context of communications to which the dress belongs is a figure of itself. Almost at the outset of the story, Maggie notices "for the first time, in the intricate embroidery and beadwork on her lap, the outline in miniature of the dress she was wearing. The dressmaker who had filled the dress with detail had, with the same care, left blank an outline of the dress no larger than a postage stamp" (3–4). This self-reflexive sign of the sign—the so-called *mise en abyme*—puts into an abyss, or subverts the authority of, the real, as does a television monitor on the desk of the television announcer, receding into infinity. We are reminded that the world we "see" is mediated, or constructed by the medium which shapes our perception; it no longer has its "real" ground outside itself, and yet it has the power to change the way we see ourselves.

Take another look at *Such a Long Journey* and you will find, even in a supposedly traditional novel, the telltale mark of this same *mise en abyme*:

> Gustad looked closely at what seemed a very familiar place. "Looks like our wall," he said tentatively.
>
> "Absolutely correct. It's now a sacred place, is it not? So it rightfully deserves to be painted on a wall of holy men and holy places."

Gustad bent down to get a better look at the wall featuring a painting of the wall featuring a painting of the wall featuring a . . .

(288)

The infinite regress of a picture on the wall of Gustad's compound shows how Mistry's traditional world is no more immune than Kroetsch's postmodern world to the effects of modern technology. Here, however, we might read the sign of Mistry's postcolonial resistance to a form of realism which would naturalize the status quo, or legitimate the existing social order. For the self-reflexive picture displays a figure founded only on itself, a sign which is wholly arbitrary and conventional, and yet which has been allowed to stand, in the name of Dada Ormuzd and *kusti* prayers, as the ground of social division. In this space of the wall-within-a-wall can be seen another space in which the *post-* of postcolonialism, "like that of postmodernism," emerges as "a *post-* that challenges earlier legitimating narratives" (Appiah 353). Suddenly, the painter's *mise en abyme*, like the postrealist mark of cyberspace, puts into an abyss the social reality of a wall which on its painted side displays the face of universal brotherhood, but on its blank side reveals the face of social partition.

Finally, in this space, we ought to observe how the postrealist ideology of postcolonial writing can have a very different motivation from that of postmodern writing. As Kwame Appiah remarks of a postrealist impulse in African writing of the past two decades:

> Far from being a celebration of the nation, . . . the novels of the second, postcolonial, stage are novels of delegitimation: they reject not only the Western *imperium* but also the nationalist project of the postcolonial national bourgeoisie. And, so it seems to me, the basis for that project of delegitimation cannot be the postmodernist one: rather, it is grounded in an appeal to an ethical universal. Indeed it is based, as intellectual responses to oppression in Africa largely are based, in an appeal to a certain simple respect for human suffering, a fundamental revolt against the endless misery of the last thirty years.

(353)

Mistry's delegitimation of the nationalist project of the postcolonial bourgeoisie is nowhere more apparent than in the suffering of Gustad's long-lost "brother" at the hands of RAW and the Indian Congress Party. As Major Jimmy Bilimoria says on his deathbed, "Gustad, it is beyond the common man's imagination, the things being done by those in power" (280). This same subplot of embezzlement and atonement nearly defies belief, using wild gossip and innuendo to offer a postrealist critique of the elected oppressor. But Mistry's inclusion of pseudo-documents and digests from newspapers also delegitimates the "realism" of journalism itself as a tool of the national bourgeoisie who equate Mother India with Mother Indira: "the line between the two was fast being blurred by the Prime Minister's far-sighted propagandists who saw its value for future election campaigns" (298). In the concluding "*morcha*" of the people on their corrupt governors, the novel

ultimately appeals to an ethical universal which Dr Paymaster, its reluctant leader, can only trope in terms of suffering human flesh: "You see, the municipal corruption is merely the bad smell, which will disappear as soon as the gangrenous government at the centre is removed. True, they said, but we cannot hold our breath for ever, we have to do something about the stink" (313).

In the final analysis, doing "something about the stink" in this novel requires more than direct political action. The political and the aesthetic meet again in the figure of that wall which speaks of universal brotherhood and social partition. Since both meanings are imaginary constructs, not facts of nature, the sign itself is bound to change. In the end, Gustad has to accept the idea that the social wall must come down. "The pavement artist, awaiting his turn to speak, said despondently, "Please, sir, they are telling me I have to give up my wall." Gustad had gathered this from the new notice on the pillar, the cement-mixers, and the waiting lorries. For the briefest of moments he felt the impending loss cut deeply, through memory and time; the collapse of the wall would wreck the past and the future" (329). But in the battle of demonstrators to save the wall, it is the idiot Tehmul, the neighbourhood man-child who worships Gustad, who is killed. Tehmul, it seems, has been made a scapegoat by Gustad's wife Dilnavaz, by a mother who is willing to sacrifice one of the "children of God" for the sake of her own estranged son. For Dilnavaz employs a witch in the person of Miss Kutpitia to cast a spell on Tehmul in hope of purging the evil from Sohrab; coincidentally or not, the idiot dies because his life means less to her than her own child's life. Thus the wall of family continues to partition the world even behind the outer wall of Parsi identity.

Gustad, however, is surprised to find that the "wreck [of] the past and the future" which he had feared in the tumbling of the wall only makes him more open to past and future both. At the death of his mother thirty years before, he had been unable to shed a single tear: "Seeing his once invincible father behave in this broken manner" had made him swear silently "to himself, then and there, that he would never indulge in tears—not before anyone, nor in private, no matter what suffering or sorrow fell upon his shoulders; tears were useless, the weakness of women, and of men who allowed themselves to be broken" (101). But at the sight of the idiot child's broken skull, something finally breaks in him as well: "His voice was soft and steady, and his hand steady and light upon Tehmul's head, as the tears ran down his cheeks. He started another cycle [of prayers], and yet another, and he could not stop the tears . . . the salt water of his eyes as much for himself as for Tehmul. As much for Tehmul as for Jimmy. And for Dinshawji, for Pappa and Mamma, for Grandpa and Grandma, all who had had to wait for so long" (337). In weeping for his dead mother, Gustad cradles the head of the dead man-child in a way which makes him virtually a Parsi Pietà, as truly feminised as Kroetsch's Jack Deemer.

What Gustad has not yet seen, of course, is that he has already assumed the role of a father to poor Tehmul; every "child of God" is become as one of his own sons. But accepting the loss of this child finally opens his eyes, quite literally: "Gustad turned around. He saw his son standing in the doorway, and each held the other's eyes. Still he sat, gazing upon his son, and Sohrab waited motionless in the doorway, till at last Gustad got to his feet slowly. Then he went up and put his arms around him. "Yes," said Gustad, running his bloodstained fingers once through Sohrab's hair. "Yes," he said, "yes," and hugged him tightly once more" (337). The estranged son and the lost child Tehmul have also traded places.

Though the reader and narrator are not explicitly exchanged for one another in *Such a Long Journey*, the pavement artist is at least aware of such aesthetic economies: "In a world where roadside latrines become temples and shrines, and temples and shrines become dust and ruin, does it matter where [I go]?" (338). Not that he has entirely escaped the temptation himself of monumental art: "The agreeable neighbourhood and the solidity of the long, black wall were reawakening in him the usual sources of human sorrow: a yearning for permanence, for roots, for something he could call his own, something immutable" (184). He has even given up his coloured chalks not long before this and has begun to paint in oils, giving way to the aesthetic temptation to construct a wall against time itself. But in the best Hindu fashion, he learns that nothing is eternal, not even art. And so the aesthetic wall is breached anew, if in a different sense from the way in which Kroetsch's puppeteer "had gone through the frame" (153). For here, too, the reader finds that art cannot erect a boundary against life, though Mistry more modestly concedes the superior power to nature and to social forces which exceed his own technology.

Finally, it is the entirely natural force of decay—a sign written indelibly in human flesh—which marks a significant difference between the postcolonial and the postmodern novel. As Deemer relates the story of Dorf's death in **The Puppeteer**, he tells how the latter "had fallen straight down [the cliff] and landed on his head, somehow causing some of the bones of his neck to force his tongue out of his mouth" (257). But in bringing the body back up the cliff, "the sling either slipped or broke and poor Dorf was in for a second crash" (260). This comic treatment of a corpse points to what has been left out of cyberspace or the world of virtual reality: the body which suffers. But it also opens to question that founding absence in the "science" of grammatology: the breath of the body. For, as Derrida notes with astounding equanimity, "What writing itself, in its nonphonetic moment, betrays, is life. It menaces at once the breath, the spirit, and history as the spirit's relationship with itself" (*Of Grammatology* 25). That indifference to the presence of the body (of writer or of reader) and its material conditions exposes the continuing idealism of the postmodernist or the poststructuralist—

the material trace of writing somehow exceeding, or transcending, the material conditions of its own production.

By contrast, the scene of Dinshawji's funeral in *Such a Long Journey* conveys "a certain simple respect for human suffering" which is never far from view in the postcolonial novel; inevitably, it restores us to the terrible burden of human flesh and the limits of the mortal body. On the march up the hill to those hideous vultures waiting in the Tower of Silence, Gustad realizes how the solemn sound of feet on the gravel "was magnificent, awe-inspiring. Crunch, crunch, crunch. Grinding, grating, rasping. The millwheel of death. Grinding down the pieces of a life, to fit death's specifications" (253). Which is not to say that a Parsi can see no humour in death: in a repeated funeral scene the "vulture controversy" between orthodox and progressive Parsis turns as funny as any comic scene in Kroetsch.

But what lingers in this second funeral scene is the gratitude of the sole other mourner for Major Bilimoria, a Muslim comrade whose life he had saved on the battlefield in Kashmir in 1948: "Ghulam wiped his eyes with the back of his hand. He said, his voice steady now, 'Your Parsi priests don't allow outsiders like me to go inside'" (322). In the end Gustad's story takes down the wall between Parsi and non-Parsi alike. Now Mistry can take us up the hill with Gustad where not even the women are allowed to go, but where we—women and other outsiders—are permitted vicariously to pay our last respects to the dead. To return to one of the book's predominant visual figures, the blackout paper which the protagonist takes down in the end allows us to see in as much as it allows Gustad to see out. And what we find at last is that story does—has always done—what is not unique to the new technologies: it blurs the boundaries of subject-object division, does away with borders, displaces the binary of Self and Other. Finally, what the Anglo-Indian writer reminds us in the West is that Eastern identity has always been given to ceaseless change.

Works cited

Appiah, Kwame Anthony. "Is the Post- in Postmodernism the Post- in Postcolonial?" *Critical Inquiry* 17 (Winter 1991): 336–57.

Barthes, Roland. *Mythologies*. 1957. Trans. Annette Lavers. New York: Hill & Wang, 1972.

Culler, Jonathan. *Structuralist Poetics: Structuralism, Linguistics, and the Study of Literature*. Ithaca, N.Y.: Cornell UP, 1975.

Derrida, Jacques. *Of Grammatology*. Trans. Gayatri Chakravorty Spivak. Baltimore & London: The Johns Hopkins UP, 1976.

———. *Writing and Difference*. Trans. with introd. by Alan Bass. Chicago: U Chicago P, 1978.

Joseph, Abraham. "The Challenge of the Open Skies." Paper presented to the Xth International Conference of the Indian Association for Canadian Studies, Goa University, May 10–13, 1994.

Kroetsch, Robert. *The Lovely Treachery of Words: Essays Selected and New*. Toronto: Oxford UP, 1989.

———. *The Puppeteer*. Toronto: Random House, 1992.

Mistry, Rohinton. *Such a Long Journey*. Toronto: McClelland & Stewart, 1991.

Poster, Mark. *The Mode of Information: Poststructuralism and Social Context*. Chicago: U Chicago P, 1990.

Spivak, Gayatri Chakravorty. *In Other Worlds: Essays in Cultural Politics*. New York: Routledge, 1988.

David Creelman (review date Spring 1998)

SOURCE: A review of *A Likely Story: The Writing Life,* in *Canadian Literature,* No. 156, Spring, 1998, pp. 145-46.

[*In the following review, Creelman praises* A Likely Story, *although he admits the book contains little new material.*]

For decades post-structuralists and cultural historians have been reminding us that the subject/self is an unstable construct of an unstable language, and that the author—if alive at all—is a function of the culture and not an independent creative identity. Yet despite these admonitions, we are still tempted to explore the inner-workings and reflections of the besieged writer. A collection of essays by Robert Kroetsch and two volumes of interviews by Jean Royer and Eleanor Wachtel sharpen this sense of temptation as they promise to inform us about the writer's life.

Although promotional materials refer to the collection as "confessional," the acknowledgement page of Robert Kroetsch's *A Likely Story* distances the text from the problems associated with autobiography, noting that "these fugitive pieces . . . are concerned with the writing life, not with the personal life, of the writer." A well known star of Canadian literature, Kroetsch frequently addresses literary conferences, and this volume brings together some of the talks he has given since 1989. The pieces are designed for public presentation; they are witty, humorous, allusive to personal experience, and strongly oral in their style and tone. Kroetsch is a brilliant story-teller and these essays mix disarmingly casual narratives from childhood and early adulthood with incisive comments about literary texts. Arranged according to the dates when they were produced, the informal essays address some of Kroetsch's key concerns as a writer.

Beyond all else, Kroetsch is fascinated with the process of writing. Steeped in contemporary theory, he employs his poetic sensibility and develop metaphors, symbols, and simple narratives to examine the writing game without suggesting that the process can be stabilized or contained. Though he does not develop new or innovative critical positions, Kroetsch insists that writing is a mixture of desire and promise, trace and absence. Multiple analogies are suggested. Writing stories, he claims, is like venturing into the north to discover the "silence that would let me tell stories of my own." The writer then mutates into a wanderer like the mad trapper Albert Johnson who "wore the silence of the artist like a badge, an indication of his will toward self-destruction." Texts eventually function like scrapbooks which allow "us to bring into play whole areas of memory. And desire. And laughter." The collection reiterates the idea that literature is a form of play and is finally impossible to pin down.

At the same time as Kroetsch insists that writing constantly slips away from definitive interpretation, he also suggests that writers are deeply influenced by culture and geography: "the plains or the prairies enable us to recognize ourselves as writers." He claims that prairie writers have been educated in the assumptions of the European tradition, but they simultaneously recognize their existence on a geographic margin and thus must always reinscribe and resist the centrist discourse. For a writer who claims to suspect essentialist practices, Kroetsch comes close to reading geography as a transcendental signified, capable of defining all those who write within its bounds: "we who are twice marginalized cannot forget, dare not forget, the unspeakably empty page. The page that is our weather, our river, our rocks." But then Kroetsch has always loved to dance along the edge of deconstruction and essentialism and these essays provide entertaining examples of his skill on the tightrope.

Besides the talks which examine literary absence and regional presence, *A Likely Story* also includes some fine discussions of specific writers including Wallace Stegner, Rudy Wiebe, Rita Kleinhart, and Margaret Laurence and two lyrical poems which are anchored in family experiences. For Kroetsch scholars who have been mining *The Lovely Treachery of Words* for nearly a decade, patiently waiting for a collection to document Kroetsch's latest critical shifts and innovations, *A Likely Story: The Writing Life* offers little fresh material. But for readers who are looking for witty, challenging, and entertaining reflections on a writer's experiences, this is a fine, pleasurable text.

FURTHER READING

Criticism

Garrett-Petts, W. F. and Lawrence, Donald. "Thawing the Frozen Image/Word: Vernacular Postmodern Aesthetics." *Mosaic* 31, No. 1 (March 1998): 143–78.

Discusses Kroetsch's contribution to a postmodern aesthetic, one which consists of language's material presence, the frozen words trope, and how Kroet- sch—as contrasted with Canadian pictorial art— engages in a vernacular exploration of visual/verbal limitations.

Additional coverage of Kroetsch's life and career is contained in the following sources published by the Gale Group: *Contemporary Authors,* **Vols. 17-20R;** *Contemporary Authors New Revision Series,* **Vols. 8, 38;** *DISCovering Authors: Canadian; DISCovering Authors Modules: Poets; Dictionary of Literary Biography,* **Vol. 53; and** *Major 20th-Century Writers,* **Edition 1.**

Alicia Ostriker
1937-

(Full name Alicia Suskin Ostriker) American poet, critic, and editor.

The following entry provides an overview of Ostriker's career through 1998.

INTRODUCTION

An accomplished poet and literary critic, Ostriker has combined her passion for both poetry and criticism to create a body of work that primarily focuses on women's issues in American society, yet also embraces a universal feminism. Influenced by the visionary poetics of early nineteenth-century British poet and artist William Blake, much of Ostriker's poetry concerns the personal, domestic, and professional roles of women in the contemporary world and the ways these roles influence women's notions of self-identity. With frankness, clarity, and ethical insight equal to that evinced in her poetry, Ostriker has examined the relationship between gender and literature in her criticism, especially in the controversial study *Stealing the Language* (1986). Critics of Ostriker's writings generally have focused on her literary scholarship rather than her poetry.

BIOGRAPHICAL INFORMATION

Born in 1937 in Brooklyn, New York, Ostriker was raised in a Manhattan housing project by her college-educated parents, David and Beatrice Suskin. Her mother often read Shakespeare and Browning to Ostriker as a girl, which prompted her to begin writing her own poetry. Ostriker's first ambition, however, was to become an artist, and as an adolescent she showed an affinity for producing sketches and for studying art. In 1958 she married Jeremiah Ostriker, and one year later earned a bachelor's degree in English from Brandeis University. Ostriker pursued graduate studies at the University of Wisconsin, which granted her a Ph.D. in 1964, a year after the birth of her first child. Her dissertation on William Blake eventually became her first published work, *Vision and Verse in William Blake* (1965); she also edited a volume of his complete poetry in 1977. In 1965 Ostriker joined the English faculty at Rutgers University, where she has held a professorship since 1972. In 1969 she published her first book of poems, *Songs*, most of which she had written as a student. Ostriker worked to refine her poetic voice in subsequent volumes entitled *Once More Out of Darkness* (1971) and *A Dream of Springtime* (1979). By the early 1980s she had mastered her art form, producing *The Mother/Child Papers* (1980) and *A Woman Under the Surface* (1982). In 1983 she published her first book-length piece of feminist literary criticism, *Writing Like a Woman*. In 1986 *Stealing the Language* appeared, along with another poetry collection, *The Imaginary Lover,* which won the William Carlos Williams Prize from the Poetry Society of America. After the publication of *Green Age* (1989), Ostriker turned her attention toward her Jewish heritage and biblical scholarship by exploring the traditions of Judaism in the context of feminism in *Feminist Revision and the Bible* (1992) and *The Nakedness of the Fathers* (1994). Following her experiences with breast cancer in the mid-1990s, Ostriker published two more volumes of poetry: *The Crack in Everything* (1996), which includes a poetry sequence titled "The Mastectomy Poems"; and a collection of selected poems from throughout her career, titled *The Little Space* (1998).

MAJOR WORKS

Ostriker's first book of poems, *Songs,* assumes a rather conventional voice but exhibits formal versatility and socially conscientious themes. In the free-verse poetry of *Once More Out of Darkness* and *A Dream of Springtime* Ostriker's own voice becomes more evident. Such autobiographical themes as pregnancy, childbirth, and the poet's childhood, family relationships, and professional experiences dominate both collections, although the latter also addresses politics and history. In the experimental poems of *The Mother/Child Papers* the circumstances of Ostriker's life are set against events of the Vietnam War era. Divided into four sections, the verses draw parallels between her roles as wife, mother, and teacher, the inherent death and corruption of war, and the eternal life and beauty of art. *A Woman Under the Surface* increasingly focuses on explicitly feminist themes, refining the then-emergent identity of the female poet by referencing other women's poetry as well as revising conventional representations of women in art and myth. The poetry of *The Imaginary Lover* continues to voice feminist themes in the tradition of Adrienne Rich and H. D., delving into the sometimes painful relations between men and women, and between mothers and daughters. Regarded as one of Ostriker's most visionary collections, *Green Age* addresses the effects of the aging process and spiritual growth on the search for identity as woman and poet, frequently expressing anger at the limitations placed on women in patriarchal Jewish traditions and rituals. The themes of *The Crack in Everything* encompass the details of female life in the contemporary world, featuring diverse commentary on current events and concluding with a moving account of Ostriker's bout with breast cancer. Another significant part of Ostriker's literary career is her feminist literary criticism. *Writing Like a Woman* outlines the historical development of feminist writing by analyzing the rhetoric of such poets as Adrienne Rich, Anne Sexton, and Sylvia Plath. The thesis of *Stealing the Language* posits the existence of a feminist literary aesthetic by describing a fundamental difference between poetry written by men and that written by women, which, according to Ostriker, is based on experiences unique to each gender. Containing a thematic overview of the works of famous and lesser-known contemporary women poets, this study uses gender as the analytic criteria to assess the political and social concerns of poetry written by women.

CRITICAL RECEPTION

A good part of the critical response to Ostriker's writings has concentrated on her literary scholarship, particularly the thesis and methodology of *Stealing the Language,* which generated significant controversy. Ranging from hearty endorsement to harsh censure, criticism of Ostriker's views ignited a lively debate among feminist and traditional literary critics alike. Some commentators praised the insights of Ostriker's scholarship, applauding it as groundbreaking and calling the book a landmark study.

Other reviewers objected to Ostriker's failure to include experimental poets in her analysis of contemporary poetry as well as to her identification of women poets' primary motivations for writing, citing especially her emphasis on power and female self-definition. In comparison, Ostriker's poetry has received relatively little analysis, although reviewers often comment on the socially conscientious themes and lucid style of her verse as well as its intimate tone. Furthermore, many critics appreciate the psychological resonance of Ostriker's best poems. As Janet Ruth Heller explains, "Ostriker is urging us readers to take the risk of journeying through our own lives and to explore the meaning of our experiences. Only after psychological probing can we learn to sing our own songs and tell our own stories."

PRINCIPAL WORKS

Vision and Verse in William Blake (criticism) 1965
Songs (poetry) 1969
Once More Out of Darkness, and Other Poems (poetry) 1971
William Blake: Complete Poems [editor] (poetry) 1977
A Dream of Springtime (poetry) 1979
The Mother/Child Papers (poetry) 1980
A Woman Under the Surface: Poems and Prose Poems (poetry) 1982
Writing Like a Woman (criticism) 1983
The Imaginary Lover (poetry) 1986
Stealing the Language: The Emergence of Women's Poetry in America (criticism) 1986
Green Age (poetry) 1989
Feminist Revision and the Bible (criticism) 1992
The Nakedness of the Fathers: Biblical Visions and Revisions (criticism) 1994
The Crack in Everything (poetry) 1996
The Little Space: Poems Selected and New, 1968-1998 (poetry) 1998

CRITICISM

Martin K. Nurmi (review date July 1967)

SOURCE: A review of *Vision and Verse in William Blake,* in *Journal of English and Germanic Philology,* Vol. LXVI, July, 1967, pp. 461-63.

[*In the following review, Nurmi assesses the success of Ostriker's metrical analysis in* Vision and Verse in William Blake, *revealing the limitations of her technique.*]

The analyst of Blake's prosody, in dealing with almost any of his lyrics after *Poetical Sketches,* operates under more than the usual handicaps, because the sound of the poems can only with great difficulty be directly connected with the meaning. In a symbolic poem like "The Tyger" especially, the sound is hard to associate with anything but the surface meaning of the words, and the surface meaning is only the starting point. A subtle prosodic study of the poem could be conducted within the limits of what we are given in the text, to show us how the sound patterns help to create the powerful symbol of the ambiguously dread tiger. But Miss Ostriker in her prosodic analysis [*Vision and Verse in William Blake*] does not seem satisfied to do this, and we are told that in the first stanza "Almost every word is knit up through sound with every other word, and this in itself suggests the idea of the demiurge's infinitely painstaking design" (p. 86). This seems to me rather far-fetched and to claim much too much for what sound alone can tell us—even if one grants that the tiger *is* the creation of a demiurge.

Miss Ostriker, who writes poems herself, approaches Blake with something of the attitude of a fellow professional, interested in technique. There is perhaps nothing wrong with this in a book on his verse. But Miss Ostriker puts too much emphasis on technique. She would reduce the complexity of "The Fly," for instance, by saying it is "an excellent example of a poem which achieves its ends through surface manipulation" (p. 70). Her reading of it doesn't bear her out. And what seems like a technical point of view of the professional craftsman who artfully manipulates his matter as materials in a construction gets developed to an extreme when she says, "As he proceeded in his Prophetic Books, Blake pushed God, his idea of ultimate unity, ever further back from the fallen world, apparently the better to enjoy the reunion of God and Man when it came, as it does on the final plate of *Jerusalem*" (p. 121). If I don't misread this, she comes dangerously close to denying the poet-prophet his prophecy and making him into a mere craftsman instead.

Much of Miss Ostriker's prosodic analysis is sound, though severely limited by her decision to stick almost exclusively with two degrees of accent. It points out sound effects in somewhat the way the program notes for a symphony concert descriptively direct the listeners' attention to rhythmic motifs, thematic entries, and orchestration. But occasionally we find some serious lapses. "Spring," for instance, is said to "jingle" like "Jack and Jill." It seems to me almost impossible to read this poem aloud without feeling that the lines form pulses of a rhythmic phrase extending through to the last line of the stanza and producing something of the musical effect of a bourée: "Sound the Flute! / Now it's mute. / Birds delight / Day and Night / Nightingale / In the dale / Lark in Sky / Merrily / Merrily Merrily to welcome in the Year." Surely Blake, who earlier had sung his lyrics to tunes of his own composition that were good enough to be "noted down by musical professors" (see Symons, *William Blake*, p. 360), would have heard the lines of this song as impulses within the larger rhythmical unit of the stanza and not as discrete rhyming jingles. And one can't help but be puzzled, at

least, to be told that the following passage from *The Four Zoas* is an example of the "lyric" style from the prophecies used for matter that is "mild and gentle":

> In pits & dens & shades of death in shapes of torment & woe
> The plates the Screws and Racks & Saws & cords & fires & floods
> The cruel joy of Luvahs daughters lacerating with knives. . . .

> (p. 175)

Miss Ostriker's scheme for analysis, which is the conventional one of scanning lines and feet, works about as well as this kind of analysis can when Blake writes in conventional feet or modulates his rhythms in a way that allows noting inversions or substitutions of conventional feet. And she does a good job, especially with inversions and substitutions, in the *Songs*. But she becomes troubled by passages where ordinary scansion doesn't yield regular results, as in the opening of *The French Revolution*:

> The Dead brood over Europe, the cloud and vision descends over chearful France;
> O cloud well appointed! Sick, sick, the Prince on his couch, wreath'd in dim
> And appalling mist. . . .

She is bothered because Blake does not at once establish the anapests which will come later. In general, she finds *The French Revolution* to have "many smooth sections, but it also has many instances of rhythmical confusion" (p. 156). "Smoothness" seems a strange thing to require of a poem that shows the beginnings of apocalypse in revolution.

Miss Ostriker's discussion of the later prophecies makes a noble attempt to deal with the complex style of these works without forcing them either into prose or conventional verse. But she doesn't allow herself enough space to do much more than make a few general observations. She affirms but doesn't adequately illustrate the metrical richness of *The Four Zoas* and fails to note the dramatic character of this work, which has a great effect on its verse techniques.

Miss Ostriker seems to feel defeated by her task at the outset, remarking in the preface, "If you write about Blake, you cannot expect to please everyone," and "if you write about metrics, you cannot expect to please anyone." I don't think failure to please is quite so inevitable in a metrical study of Blake or anyone else. Miss Ostriker doesn't succeed as well as she might, it seems to me, because she limited the subtlety of her analysis by choosing tools that are not precise enough, because she sets too much store by technique in itself, and because she sometimes expects things of Blake's verse that he wasn't trying to supply.

Robert Joe Stout (review date Winter 1981)

SOURCE: "One of Each—with Echoes," in *Southwest Review*, Vol. 65, No. 1, Winter, 1981, pp. 110-14.

[In the following excerpt, Stout praises the syntactical clarity and emotional restraint of Ostriker's poetic vision in A Dream of Springtime.*]*

Words clash, streak the mind with sunbursts, ricochet and swoop into irony—ah! but Hopkins, Hopkins did it better! And Sexton, really tough, didn't lapse into cute words, or kitten's play. And Roethke, the academician, kept control, both of reader and himself: his meanings were graspable— and profound.

But that's the rub. To be different is not to be bad, or wrong, nor does it make the poems less important. One Hopkins, one Sexton, one Roethke were enough. These three contemporary poets [Francis Sullivan, Terry Kennedy, and Alicia Ostriker], put into circulation in attractive packages by The Smith in conjunction with Horizon Press, are vivaciously themselves, whatever echoes might infiltrate their lines and thoughts. . . .

Unlike Sullivan [in her *Spy Wednesday's Kind*], Alicia Ostriker is never abstruse; and unlike Kennedy [in his *durango*], she tempers even her most emotional passages with intellect [in *A Dream of Springtime*]. Yeats, Ecclesiastes, and Whitman mingle with current events to locate the poems in a university setting. Even when the poet is angry, or sarcastic, she is comfortable with classical references. **"The Clock above the Kitchen Door Says One"** concludes,

> . . . I want you to love me
> Here in the Corner Tavern, while I tell you
> About Poetry.—We wipe our mouths with paper napkins,
> We're spitting blood, we're coughing, we're killing time,
> We're eating lunch. Keats was dead when he was your age,
> When he was my age, Mozart.

And teaching poetry becomes the subject matter for writing poems, as in **"My Lecture to the Writing Students"**:

> . . . the poem
> Is insane, it wants
>
> To tie tin cans to its tail
> To fly away with General Motors under one arm
> The Sacred Heart under the other, it wants
>
> To express the fluid explosion in your mind
> The subjective,
> Transient, and not verbal
>
> (the smell like an orange
> how you feel about your father)
>
> In a form objective, permanent
> And verbal. . . .

Cezanne and Kierkegaard mingle with crepe paper and the *Daily News* to pull the reader into Ostriker's vision, seeing what she sees, reacting as she seems to react, ever the observer, ever aware that she is watching herself as well as others. As in the title poem, **"A Dream of Springtime"**:

> Somebody is very thoughtfully making love. That's all
> I can think of. The sheets are greyed and mussed,
> The blankets far gone. The room is immobile and nothing
> Much. They have a lot of cigarette butts in the glass
> Ashtray. It's like walking up a street
> Looking in the storewindows, something always
> Mysteriously profound looking back. . . .

A Dream of Springtime is a book worth many times its price.

Mary Lynn Broe (review date Spring 1984)

SOURCE: "An Aesthetic of Pain," in *Prairie Schooner*, Vol. 58, No. 1, Spring, 1984, pp. 82-84.

[In the following review, Broe highlights various thematic and formal concerns in A Woman Under the Surface *which, according to Broe, revise the relation between contemporary feminist artistic principles and female life.]*

Like Orpheus, Alicia Ostriker makes "that journey / Down from song, down to the impulse of singing" in her fifth volume of poems, *A Woman Under the Surface*. But unlike Orpheus, who "could not carry, haul, rob / His bride back," Ostriker makes us feel the unsentimental solid-iron aesthetic of pain, fear, and bitter beauty that undercuts her singing. In **"For the Daughters"** she announces:

> Song, as you gather it, is not desire,
> Not some requirement you may finally fill.
> Song is being. For the god, trivial.
> But when *are* we? And when does he deliver
>
> To our existence here the earth and stars?

Within the four sections, Ostriker reinvents the Eros/Psyche myth (women's curiosities are no longer punished), a host of family spirits and struggles, the political understatement of news events from National Public Radio. In deadpan narration, she exposes the gap between the bland public voice of a consumer society that tames violence and the real horror of death, maiming, and daily terror (**"The Demonstration," "This Dreamer Cometh,"** and **"Terrorist Trial and the Games"**). In rewriting the **"History of America,"** she deftly sets "a prior circle: a mouth" against "a linear projection: a route."

Most successful, perhaps, is her homage to various artists—Dante, Matisse, Van Gogh, Renoir, Rilke. Probing the relation of art to life, she finds that the source of creative power is often the source of one's crippling or destruction. We see Renoir "at the end painting with brushes strapped to his hand / Arthritic, crippled—his palette aroused 'to crepuscular / Pinks, oranges, reds, his nudes ever more voluptuous.'" All the while, the "plump, middle-class Parisiennes" continue their languid, post-war indulgences. In **"A Minor Van Gogh,"** "the strokes are pulses," an ironic counterpoint to the artist's end:

> . . . The strokes
> Rush forward, waving their hats, identical,
> All elements alike, all particles
> Of Christ's material dancing, even
> The shadowed furrow saying *I exist, I live!*

It is Claude Monet's life that raises the central question. At first a bourgeois "glutton of light," Monet lost his eyesight around 1922 and began to paint "red / Mud and whiplashes . . . the waterlilies bursting like painless bombs." And the poet asks, "Is it from him? or around him? His old man's forehead / Garlanded."

Open to the "virtue of the pure unknown," Ostriker never bends her knee to cliché, never makes ideological genuflections before the sentimental or the unrevised. Her verse gleams with the quicksilver of a blackbelt's revenge: a verse with registered iambs and feet, yet lulled by the rule of the contemplative like a mandolin concerto. She prefers the pure elevation of September ("definite as wood") to the celebrated lushness of April:

> . . . being keen
> To race through walls, to experience all
> Conceivable human passion,
> To be broken man, while still a girl?

Ostriker's imagination breaks forth like the rough hind leg of the centaur at the very moment when neat closure or appeal to the ordinary might slow the verse. In **"Anxiety About Dying,"** the poet waves goodbye to her teeth: "It seems they are leaving by train for a vacation / I'll meet them in the country when I can." She glories in contradictions, verifying Whitman's claim that "I am large, I contain multitudes." In the midst of lovemaking, a blackbird's serrated wing passes soundlessly between lovers, then lifts to a black dot in the sky. Ironic anthropomorphism surrounds the "geriatric" San Juan waterfront, a "relation between building / And vegetation, which the big hotels, lifting their knees, trample." In the words of pseudo-science she narrates a husband's betrayal: "When she returned home, conditions / Were such that she believed a betrayal of synchronicity / And a lapse of energy and love had occurred." A young girl kicks her father in the stomach for faking a heart attack, but the price of her new serenity ("light as a fleet of balloons") is imposed silence. A runner sees the "bright bone under brown landscape" and

> Begins to feel how fire invades a body
>
> From within, first the splinters
> And crumpled paper, then the middle wood
> And the great damp logs splendidly catching.

Evident in her clear ironies and luminous imagery is pure motion: the diver's body "saying a kind of prayer," words and language useless.

"Goddesses, mortal women, pigs and homecoming"—these are the ingredients of Ostriker's redefined mythmaking, the simple story that underlies everything. In the opening poem, women gathered in a beige, soundproofed waiting room fear betrayal of their bodies. They are divided from this awareness, however—as they are from each other—by rings, tweeds, social structures. Only a woman's piercing scream unites them in silent knowledge of the body's truth. In this post-Rich world, the shipwrecked self has learned not only what tools one can do without, learned the medium where women can escape, but also how to define "the living mind you fail to describe / In your dead language." Ostriker casts aside Adrienne Rich's androgyne and the wreck of historical consciousness for a new, utopian revenge. In **"The Exchange,"** a powerful new myth figure swimming below a nuclear family climbs into the boat, changes places with the speaker, and even strangles her children:

> Skin dripping, she will take my car, drive home.
>
> When my husband answers the doorbell and sees
> This magnificent naked woman, bits of sunlight
> Glittering on her pubic fur, her muscular
> Arm will surround his neck, once for each insult
>
> Endured. He will see the blackbird in her eye,
> Her dying mouth incapable of speech,
> And I, having exchanged with her, will swim
> Away, in the cool water, out of reach.

And in the final poems, tutored by such mistresses, woman yields to a new imperative: "Now you know how to sing / Now you have to make / Your own story." Practicing the very best principle of revisionism in her poetry, Ostriker can say with confidence of her own work:

> When she sings, when she dances, it is asking
> How to capture, how to keep, how to give back, unmasking
> Beauty, the seed to the sower, the gift to the giver—
>
> Go, book, and say this time she conquers.

Daisy Aldan (review date Spring 1987)

SOURCE: A review of *Stealing the Language*, in *World Literature Today*, Vol. 61, No. 2, Spring, 1987, pp. 291-92.

[*In the following review, Aldan disputes Ostriker's definitions of gynocentric poetics in* Stealing the Language.]

I was among those who believed that if a woman poet's work was outstanding, it would achieve its deserved recognition in spite of man's traditional attitude toward it. In [*Stealing the Language*,] her survey of American women's poetry from the time of Anne Bradstreet to the present, Alicia Ostriker presents ample convincing evidence to show that I was laboring under a delusion. Despite the fact that not too many of the women poets mentioned who wrote before and during the Victorian era (with a few exceptions) equaled the achievements of the best of the male poets during that time (for whatever reasons), denigration by male critics, even until recently, exceeded justification. The author maintains that the poets she deals with are challenging and transforming the history of poetry, and she attempts to understand "the powerful collective voice in which they participate." One of Ostriker's assumptions is that women's verse has a history, a terrain: "Many of its practitioners believe it has something like a language."

In her evaluation of the contemporary, Ostriker focuses on a number of well-known and a few not-so-well-known women poets and attempts to define and illustrate their concerns, patterns, and questionable innovations. Since her opening arguments are lucid and enlightening, one looks forward to the revelations one hopes to meet; one comes away disappointed, however, for Ostriker beats a particular drum and chooses examples to sustain her melody, even from among fine women authors whose concerns are largely other than those she emphasizes. Urging us to accept the fact that there is a category "as distinctly women's poetry" which indicates "forms and styles particular to and appropriate to" her exploration, she outlines the following motifs inherent within it: the quest for identity, the obstacle of the divided self, the centrality of the body, the release of forbidden anger, the imperative of intimacy. The quest for identity, she says, registers marginality, images of nonexistence, invisibility, petrification, blurredness, and deformity, which indicates a divided self. Women writers, she contends, have been imprisoned in an "oppressor's language" which denies them access to authoritative expression. Thus they give vent to their aggressive, hitherto thwarted impulses. However, "Magic shimmers about the best violence poems whether vengefully phallic, self punishing ultra feminine, or most angrily and helplessly both." Some women poets believe that "female creativity is and should be intrinsically carnal basing itself in women's unique maternal relation and in sexual sensation."

How can we not fail to be shocked by that last statement, for have not men since the beginning of patriarchal dominance used those very terms to relegate women to an inferior social position? If what the author says were indeed the case, we would have to be moved to tears and give up hope for humanity. Fortunately, it is only one facet of a more complex picture. As publisher of a small press for the past thirty years, editor of several literary magazines, teacher of poetry workshops, and a woman poet, my experience differs widely from Ostriker's. The many manuscripts of women's poetry which come into my hands each year and which are created in my workshops lead me to the conclusion that women are indeed "writing more boldly and with a greater freedom than ever before," but that there is a high artistry and concern as well as a deepening vision, which are the qualities that are achieving respect and recognition, rather than the examples presented in **Stealing the Language**. The majority of the

poems I see are not filled with hysterical rage, self-pity, explicit sexual depictions that are beyond imagination, or sterile complaints. It is a disservice to such outstanding poets as May Swenson, Muriel Rukeyser, Joyce Carol Oates, and Denise Levertov to imply that what they are concerned with are death wishes, rape, sex, and pathological states. These can hardly be said to be inherent in the larger portion of their creations, and we may be grateful indeed that this is the case.

Ostriker bewails the "culturally depleted present," but most of the works she quotes are depleting that present still further. Wit, grace, skill, eloquence, objectivity, lucidity, knowledge, the qualities which must invest all good art, are termed "male values" and are relegated to "academic modernism"; women poets must therefore evoke formlessness and vulgarity. Do we not demean women still further by such assumptions? Another assumption is that works by women poets express a "drive for power." Shall female dominance replace male dominance then? As for the search for identity, it has been a quest of both male and female poets since the dawn of the Age of Consciousness in the fifteenth century. Also, anger, violence, obscenities, and pathological states have been explored ad nauseam since the sixties by male poets and can hardly be said to indicate innovations in language or concern. At one point she quotes Coleridge: "The highest art is that which presses most matter and spirit into least space." However, with the exception of her discussion of the poems of that remarkable poet Hilda Doolittle (in a section toward the close of the book which seems totally divorced from the rest of the text), *spirit,* in the best sense of that word, is largely excluded. What readers of poetry wish to feel that they are "walking on broken glass," as Ostriker says one does when reading a work she greatly admires by Anne Sexton, "The Jesus Papers"?

Ostriker has not convinced me, nor will she convince any reader of taste, knowledge, and experience in life and art, that she has made a case for women's poetry as being distinct from male poetry, or that the poetic results which emerge—one relative to style, one to content—contribute to "what we must finally recognize as gynocentric poetics." Indeed, her point of view and her vision seem limited. A typical poem that she finds admirable is the following piece by June Jordan:

> Today is 2 weeks after the fact
> of that man straddling
> his knees either side of my chest
> his hairy arm and powerful left hand
> flat to the pillow while he rammed
> what he described as his quote big dick
> unquote into my mouth
> and shouted out: "D'ya want to swallow
> my big dick: Well, do ya?"
>
> He was being rhetorical.
> My silence was peculiar
> to the female.

It is not the subject matter I object to, but the absence of originality and skill in expressing it. Does placing the sentences into verse make it a poem? And how has the poet succeeded in expressing her experience better than is done in cheap pulp journalistic writing by men? Let the reader decide.

Rita Dove (review date Summer 1987)

SOURCE: A review of *Stealing the Language*, in *Phi Kappa Phi Journal*, Vol. 67, No. 3, pp. 45-6.

[*In the following review, Dove admires the contents and insights of* Stealing the Language.]

An impeccable piece of scholarship that's as exciting as a detective novel—impossible? Not as far as Alicia Ostriker is concerned. Her book ***Stealing the Language: The Emergence of Women's Poetry in America*** is much more than a portrait of this besieged literary landscape—hers is the clear-eyed commentary of an insider who nonetheless knows her trade. In the true mission of the literary mind, Ostriker offers not only analysis, but vision.

After a concise and comprehensive survey of American women's poetry from 1650–1960 (illustrated by a brilliant exegesis of Emily Dickinson's "I'm Nobody! Who Are You?"), Ostriker investigates the schizophrenic heritage of the woman artist who, possessed of creative energy but forbidden to use it lest she be accused of being "unwomanly," resorted to various strategies to circumvent exposure—double entendre, male personae, allegorical complaint when direct protest was unacceptable. Far too often silence was the only alternative.

Internal conflict and the consequent search for identity form the theoretical basis for discussion of work by Sylvia Plath, Denise Levertov, and Margaret Atwood in chapter two; chapter three probes attitudes toward and metaphors of the body. Chapter four discusses the anger in women's poetry (much of it internalized in revenge fantasies or images of victimization) as a reaction to a society which undervalues—even fears—emotion. Chapter five, titled "The Imperative for Intimacy," cites poets such as Maxine Kumin, Audre Lorde, and Judy Grahn who are challenging the existing patterns of polarity (male/female, mind/body) and dominance (mother/child, husband/wife, man/nature). Finally, chapter six considers various theories on patriarchal versus "feminine" language and offers Ostriker's suggestion for expanding the existing literary structures: revisionist mythmaking. Basing her argument on three long poetic works—H. D.'s *Helen in Egypt,* Susan Griffin's *Woman and Nature,*, and Anne Sexton's *Transformations,* Ostriker demonstrates how each poet, revising the "official versions," respectively, of Helen of Troy, Mother Nature, and Grimm's fairy tales, opens our eyes to the horrific imbalances championed in seemingly harmless folklore.

There are no easy solutions, and Ostriker is careful to foil those who would buy wholesale judgments. She acknowl-

edges that Sylvia Plath's anger resulted in self-destruction . . . but not before she avenged herself on paper, upstaging the men in her life—Herr God, Herr Lucifer, and Daddy—in her poems. Then there's Marianne Moore, carefully self-effacing in public yet angry enough in the poem "Marriage" to write: "men have power / and sometimes one is made to feel it." The relentlessly cerebral edge of her poems, plus the assortment of small armored creatures that populate her work, serve as acknowledgment of and protest against her powerlessness. Ostriker counters the patronizing praise accorded Elizabeth Bishop by demonstrating how two of her most famous poems—"In the Waiting Room" and "The Moose"—are characterized by a meandering thought-line and identification with the feminine (the naked breasts in the *National Geographic* magazine, the female moose whose appearance transforms a country bus trip).

Ostriker's language is neither condescending nor impenetrable; it is convincing without being de-emotionalized. She is equally skilled at providing a line-by-line analysis or limning the broader spectrum of events which helped shape literary consciousness. Third-world poets are richly represented; so are younger and more experimental ones.

The generous footnotes are nearly as fascinating as the book itself. I especially appreciated the bibliographical listings grouped according to themes, such as "poems on muteness" and "poems on the labors of beauty." Two substantial lists of myth–poems—the first pre-, the second post-1960—are included in the footnotes to chapter six.

It almost goes without saying that ***Stealing the Language*** is ideal for classroom use, and not only for women's studies; creative writing, literature, and literary criticism students would benefit as well. The book is informative and challenging, scholarly and personable.

Ellen Bryant Voigt (essay date Summer 1987)

SOURCE: "Poetry and Gender," in *The Kenyon Review*, Vol. 9, Summer, 1987, pp. 127-40.

[*In the following essay, Voigt addresses various implications of the female poetic aesthetic outlined in* Stealing the Language, *suggesting that differences in women's poetry, rather than similarities, would better illuminate female experience.*]

> The belief that true poetry is genderless—which is a disguised form of believing that true poetry is masculine—means that we have not learned to see women poets generically, to recognize the tradition they belong to, or discuss either the limitations or the strengths of that tradition. . . . [1]

> Undoubtedly gender does play an important part in the making of any art, but art is art and to separate writings, paintings, musical compositions, etc., into two sexes is to emphasize values in them that are *not* art. [2]

As to the poetical Character itself, . . . it is not itself—it has no self—it is every thing and nothing—It has no character—. . . . It is a wretched thing to confess; but is a very fact that not one word I ever utter can be taken for granted as an opinion growing out of my identical nature—how can it, when I have no nature?[3]

Although few poets may be left who endorse Keats's definition of "poetical Character," surprisingly many, some of them women, believe that the individual self of the artist—sexual, ethnic, historical, political and geographical—is subverted to the uses and priorities of his or her art. Among recent and widespread efforts to replace "individual" with "collective" in defining the self, such a belief is not merely unfashionable but politically retrograde, for it is with the fervor of revolution that much is being written about "women's literature."

The bias against women in publication history, corresponding easily to the cultural bias Mary Ellmann discusses thoroughly, and wittily, in *Thinking about Women*,[4] is well documented. In roughly eight hundred years of English literature, only the most recent one hundred have included substantial participation by women. In the past twenty-five years, however, that participation has increased astonishingly—an example of free enterprise Ronald Reagan might cherish, so rapidly did publishers respond to the demands of women as a book-buying constituency—and contemporary writers who so wish are now able to find models of their own gender in great variety.

Clearly, anthologies and journals devoted exclusively to work by women, as well as feminist criticism and the women's political movement, were primary factors in the reversal. But the establishment of a separate-but-equal category has led to a broader claim: that this literary work belongs to a distinct, parallel tradition with its own purpose, criteria, and aesthetic priorities. This view is often made imperative by the premise that women have been excluded from the canon not only because of sexist bias among individual critics and reviewers but because sexism has inhered within the very definitions of art, deposited there by its (primarily male) practitioners. Whether intended as adversarial or merely just, the us/them division long insured by *them,* and only briefly seen to diminish somewhat in bookstore and periodicals, has been restored by *us.*

The complexity of this issue is compounded by the breadth of the label in general use, "women writers." The coinage appears direct and uncomplicated, but the use of a noun as a modifier is never without some ambiguity: does the term indicate a woman who writes, or a writer who is a woman? That is, what is the relative importance of gender to an aesthetic? And although, as Jarrell pointed out, the pigs are seldom asked what they think about bacon, has there been another critical classification which conscripted so many writers a priori?

In *Stealing the Language*, Alicia Ostriker dismisses such concern:

. . . most critics and professors of literature, including modern literature, deny that "women's poetry," as distinct from poetry by individual women, exists. Some women writers agree. Some will not permit their work to appear in women's anthologies.

. . . Yet we do not hesitate to use the term "American poetry" (or "French poetry" or "Russian poetry") on the grounds that American (or French or Russian) poets are diverse. Should we call Whitman, Frost, and Stevens "poets" but not "American poets"?

(pp. 8-9)

At issue, of course, is the extent to which the label is meant to describe the work. Both Whitman and Frost were self-consciously "American," which is to say they saw such an affiliation as primary and strove to make poems from a local (rather than British) idiom. Thus, we can locate in their work characteristics which correspond to what we think of as American poetry, later revised and refined by Williams and others, particularly in regard to style and diction. With Stevens, the case is far more difficult and the term runs the risk of obscuring both his intentions and his achievement. With Stevens, we use the label for convenience (somewhat like putting the duckbill platypus in with the mammals), for the illumination of contrast, and for the chance to claim him.

Even so, the influence of Emerson, say, can be traced in Stevens, while a parallel importance of Bradstreet to Bishop or to Plath is harder to track. Ostriker invites the equation:

In what follows I therefore make the assumption that "women's poetry" exists in much the same sense that "American poetry" exists. It has a history. It has a terrain. Many of its practitioners believe it has something like a language.

(p. 9)

But she avoids the direct question of *literary* precursors, presenting virtually no evidence that women were heavily influenced by other women's work (as distinct from the example of their success) prior to the 1960s; instead, the "history" presented is largely the story of how literary work by women has been received—which in turn reflects the way women have been viewed in the culture.

A similar sociological focus pervades Sandra Gilbert and Susan Gubar's much heralded but controversial *Norton Anthology of Literature by Women*. In the introductory material to each section the editors locate individual women within the contours of the existing tradition (acknowledging that women "were influenced by [and influenced]" male writers) but they have supplanted the usual literary periods with others that correspond to significant changes in the cultural attitudes toward, and life patterns of, women. The structure of the book, then, groups writers according to similarities of circumstance in which they wrote; similarities within the work itself are left to brief introductory comment, proximity, and the shaping influence of the editors' choices. (That influence, of course, is pronounced—like Ostriker though less insistent, the editors prefer instances of women writing directly about distinctly female, rather than universal, experience. If the anthology is faulted on which writers, or which examples of their work, were thought representative, and faulted more vigorously than usual, it is because the category is so diverse and the lens so circumscribed: which animal, indeed, can represent the mammals?)

Ostriker, on the other hand, takes the similarity of circumstance to be equivalent to a similarity of aesthetic purpose, and works this assumption both vertically (Bradstreet to Grahn) and horizontally (as in the curious pairing of Bishop and Sexton). She says in her introduction that her subject is "the extraordinary tide of poetry by American women in our own time," an "increasing proportion" of which "is explicitly female in the sense that the writers have chosen to explore experiences central to their sex and to find forms and styles appropriate to their exploration," and she takes 1960 as an "approximate point of departure," listing "breakthrough and highly influential books" by poets whose publication dates coincide with the discovery of *The Second Sex* in this country (and incidentally the publication of Lowell's *Life Studies*) and the emerging women's political movement. Some of them defined their aesthetic with gender primary in the definition; some located precursors among women of earlier generations. The most influential figure among this number for Ostriker seems to be Adrienne Rich, who is listed with sixty-eight references in the Index (as compared to ten for Mona Van Duyn and eleven for Muriel Rukeyser, two other "breakthrough poets"); at least, the feminist agenda articulated by Rich in the 1970s seems to correspond to the "new thing" Ostriker applauds, which is "notoriously difficult to define precisely."

It may have been somewhat foggy in the minds of its practitioners at the time as well, insofar as Rich, Rukeyser, Plath, Sexton, Levertov *et al.* were working independently in the 1960s and not collectively as the Black Mountain or Transcendental writers may be said to have been. Nevertheless, Ostriker intends to locate the foundation of this "tide" or renascence in earlier writers, and depends on the consistent difficulty of the writer's (and woman's) position to make her case (many of the women cited are introduced with a succinct career summary). In doing so, she adds to Gilbert and Gubar's notion of "anxiety of literary authority" a close attention to various women's sense of audience and where it impinged on or enabled the poetry. (In fact, this might have provided a stable thesis for the entire book; certainly it makes germane her recurring reference to mistreatment and misreading by critics—those poets who wish[ed] to articulate an aesthetic of gender are the same group, essentially, who identify their readership, or constituency, as primarily women.) In particular, in discussions of Dickinson's "duplicity" and the hard style ("exoskeletal") of many contemporary women, both of which are viewed as responses to audience, the book comes closest to the kind of aesthetic similarities that might suggest literary affinity. But whereas with Bradstreet and Dickinson, who offer historically isolated oeuvres, Os-

triker considers individual pieces as poems as well as sociopolitical documents, after that she seems impatient with such detail; her primary purpose—to describe an exclusive aesthetic through survey—leads her to a focus on theme and a reliance on paraphrase that leave transitions from the sociological to the literary largely unsupported.

One way to secure a connection among women writing in different periods and with differing aesthetic priorities would be to work deductively from a comprehensive theory of feminine psychology. Ostriker presents no such theory on which to base her arguments, and in fact resists the method ("I attempt to read by the light that poems themselves emit, rather than by the fixed beam of one or another theory"); however, many of her generalizations, in their easy exchange of "woman" and "woman poet," imply that primary similarities exist within the psychology of all women and inexorably shape the literature women make, regardless of the conscious intentions of the makers.

Even when a rigorous and comprehensive theory of feminine psychology emerges, the literary question will, I think, continue to be muddied to the extent that poetry always confounds psychology: that is, the extent to which the disciplines of art transform or override the imperatives of the individuated ego. What continues to fascinate is what Ostriker promises to explore in her Introduction—the question of style, that is, the arrangement of aesthetic elements independent of subject matter. Ostriker chastises those reviewers and critics who condemned work because of its "feminine style" (for example, the elegance of Bogan) while supporting their basic premise—that style is identifiable as to gender—in her own practice (for example, the self-effacement of Bradstreet). Yet her stylistic examples almost always double as examples of theme or subject.

Ellmann's discussion of tone in *Thinking about Women* is to the point here. After analyzing prose passages which demonstrate in their diction and syntax the authoritative tone, Ellmann locates its rise (and its association with the masculine) in the nineteenth century, noting that earlier no distinction was fixed between the intellectual authority and intimate emotion in Donne's sermons:

> But such a distinction is endemic to the nineteenth century. It was then, when women first began to publish not only as novelists but as (what we call) intellectuals, that a method of male utterance codified itself; and, as a result, a genuine difference seemed discernible between the ways in which men think and write, and the ways in which women think and write. . . . So Dickens recorded his conviction that George Eliot's *Scenes from Clerical Life*, published anonymously, must be written by a woman. The dichotomy was established: the dominant and masculine mode possessing the properties of reason and knowledge, the subsidiary and feminine mode possessing feelings and intuitions. If this dichotomy was unreal, it was not less dedicated on the part, particularly, of the dominant mode.
>
> (p. 158)

That Ellmann does find it "unreal"—though she includes instances of women and men in this century perpetuating the dichotomy—is made definite in her disagreement with Virginia Woolf. Here is the citation from Woolf:

> She [Dorothy Richardson] has invented, or, if she has not invented, developed and applied to her own uses, a sentence which we might call the psychological sentence of the feminine gender. It is of a more elastic fibre than the old, capable of stretching to the extreme, of suspending the frailest particles, of enveloping the vaguest shapes. Other writers of the opposite sex have used sentences of this description and stretched them to the extreme. But there is a difference. Miss Richardson has fashioned her sentence consciously, in order that it may descend to the depths and investigate the crannies of Miriam Henderson's consciousness. It is a woman's sentence, but only in the sense that it is used to describe a woman's mind by a writer who is neither proud nor afraid of anything that she may discover in the psychology of her sex.

> (p. 172)

Then Ellmann's crisp reply:

> But, in fact, it seems impossible to determine a sexual sentence. As Virginia Woolf herself makes clear, the only certain femininity is in Dorothy Richardson's subject. Her sentence has more in common with Henry James' or Joyce's than with, say, George Eliot's.

> (pp. 172-173)

And a sentence of Richardson's promptly follows in support.

What Ellmann sets in contrast to the "now outmoded" tone of authority is the use of wit, defined as the "means of relinquishing authority." Ostriker makes a similar point but claims the tactic as feminine. Ellmann, acknowledging she has "perhaps not helped at all those obsessed readers like Dickens who are bent upon identifying the sex of writers," summarizes this way:

> As both simple authority and simple sensibility have become anachronistic, writers cohabit an area of prose in which sudden alternations of the reckless and the sly, the wildly voluble and the laconic, define only a mutual and refreshing disturbance of mind.

> (p. 170)

That sentence appeared in 1968, when Ostriker's "*quelque chose DE NOUVEAU*" was underway, and prefigures this passage from Carol Gilligan's *In a Different Language*, a study of psychological theory and women's development:

> The different voice I describe is characterized not by gender but theme. Its association with women is an empirical observation, and it is primarily through women's voices that I trace its development. But this association is not absolute, and the contrasts between male and female voices are presented here to highlight a distinction between two modes of thought and to focus a problem of interpretation rather than to represent a generalization about either sex. In tracing development, I point to the interplay of these voices within each sex and suggest that their convergence marks times of crisis and change.[5]

There is not a great deal of interplay in *Stealing the Language*. The book is structured chronologically with a specific look at Bradstreet and Dickinson, then an examination of later poems paired by theme, and finally a catalog of proliferating examples. While the method is inductive, however, the mind-set is deductive: that is, Ostriker leaves as assumptions—and reads by their light—the notions that gender is pronounced in poems and that a tradition of women's work exists and can be described. In addition, her preference for recent gender-specific poetry undermines her scholarship—the characteristics of individual poets' work are analyzed at the outset, when examples are few, but summarized and asserted at the very point of diversity where support for the argument is crucial. And finally, there is, overriding, the simultaneous wish, embodied in the label "women's poetry," for the inclusive (all women) and the exclusive (no men), by which *tradition* rather than *movement* might become the legitimate designation.

Impatience is often attendant on conviction. Since Ostriker is redressing imbalance, and says she is confined to "only a fraction of the poems . . . [she] would have enjoyed discussing," perhaps she assumed the established other would speak of itself/himself in the margins of her pages. Nevertheless, some comparison of Bradstreet to Edward Taylor's self-effacing, domestic imagery ("Make me, O Lord, Thy spinning wheel complete") is necessary to establish those qualities as unmistakably female. Likewise, the discussion of Plath's "feminine" treatment of the divided self is unconvincing without any mention of the idea of the double which already existed in literature (the subject of Plath's honors essay at Smith). Elizabeth Bishop's "In the Waiting Room" is clearly a great poem, but does Ostriker mean to suggest that "the quest for identity" was one of Bishop's primary themes, or that it occurs more in Bishop than in Lowell? Did contemporary women who "reverse man's division from nature" read Hopkins or Roethke, Whitman or Wright? This is not to say that Ostriker fails entirely to make direct comparisons with male writers, but that material is too often chosen to illuminate difference at the expense of similarity. If women writers are more playful than men, it should be demonstrated in light of Berryman, Patchen or Ashbury; if Plath's view of death as perfection in *Ariel* differs from that in the earlier "Sailing to Byzantium," such a case needs to be made.

Ostriker might address this criticism with numbers—might reply that more women share Plath's vision than do men, that the characteristics she enumerates occur repeatedly in the work of contemporary women but only rarely in the work of men. She suggests as much in her general method, in her reliance (in the second half of the book) on paraphrase and commentary rather than analysis of the poems, and in such considerations of style as do occur. However, to borrow a sentence from Ellmann:

> Quantity here [about the topic of femininity], as elsewhere, suggests the strength of the proleptic impulse: the desire to prove is abundant even when proof is not.

> (p. 59)

Consider the quantification, for instance, behind Ostriker's statement that "whether or not they deal directly with the self, or with sexuality as such, contemporary women poets employ anatomical imagery both more frequently and far more intimately than male poets" (p. 92). This would appear to address the heart of the issue: a repeating, perhaps unconscious stylistic attribute extraneous to subject. Yet, the footnote reveals that Ostriker's samples of one thousand lines each by male and female poets, on which the statement is predicated, were taken from, on the one hand, general anthologies of 1962 and 1969 (Berg and Mezey's *Naked Poetry*, and Donald Hall's *Contemporary Poetry*), and on the other, *Rising Tides*, a 1973 anthology dedicated to the presentation of an alternative, distinctly female, and previously neglected poetry: that is, a collection in which reference to the female self, thereby the body, was surely one criterion for inclusion.

At the end of the footnote, Ostriker makes the following comment:

> A different selection might of course have produced slightly different figures, but if the selection were made from poems published only in the 1970s, the gap between masculine reticence and feminine expressiveness about the body would appear even more pronounced.
>
> (p. 259)

Struck by such adamant speculation, I tried my own limited test. To avoid perpetuating the editorial preference unavoidable in anthologies, I went directly to the poets and chose the first three books on my shelf by women, then the first three by men, which were published in the 1970s, contained approximately fifty pages (of which only the first fifty were surveyed), and relied typically on a poetic line of roughly five to eight syllables (like Ostriker, I was too lazy to count words). Here are my findings, ordered by preponderance of references to the body (parts and functions—sweating, bleeding, giving birth, having sex):

> 204—Galway Kinnell, *The Book of Nightmares* (1971)
> 162—Phillip Levine, *The Names of the Lost* (1976)
> 118—Robert Haas, *Field Guide* (1973)
> 110—Tess Gallagher, *Introduction to the Double* (1976)
> 67—Sandra McPherson, *The Year of Our Birth* (1978)
> 40—Elizabeth Bishop, *Geography III* (1976)

Of course, books published in the 1970s could have collected work initially published earlier; perhaps, too, limiting review to the first fifty pages skewed the data—if anatomical reference is a bold and subversive act, one might well save it for the back of the book. So I extended my study to six more poets whose recent books were still stacked on my desk, this time disregarding line length and surveying all the pages of the book. Here are the additional findings, ranked according to average number of body references per page:

> 4.2—Stephen Dobyns, *Black Dog, Red Dog* (1984), 373 references in 89 pages

> 2.6—Gregory Orr, *We Must Make a Kingdom of It* (1986), 138 references in 54 pages
> 2.3—Lisel Mueller, *Second Language* (1986), 165 references in 72 pages
> 1.9—Thomas Lux, *Half-Promised Land* (1986), 136 references in 72 pages
> 1.5—Heather McHugh, *A World of Difference* (1981), 80 references in 52 pages
> 1.3—Mary Oliver, *Dream Work* (1986), 117 references in 89 pages.

As for qualitative difference claimed by Ostriker: Mueller (highest average among the women) used twenty-one references to eyes (including eyeholes and eyelash), sixteen to head and face, ten to arms, twenty to hands and twelve to skin; specific mention is made of fingernails, wrist and temples, but mainly there are teeth, bones, blood, heart and "body." The list does not differ significantly from that of Lux, most anatomically reticent among the men—skin, hair, fingers, head recur—except for his single-usage nouns: synapse, cranium, breasts, calf, jaw, rib, chin, ankles, skull, groin, heartbone, elbow, liver; spine appears twice, spit twice, lungs three times; no mention of voice (six times in Mueller).

Though my study is as statistically insignificant, and inconclusive, as Ostriker's it does suggest that we have not been reading the same poets—but Ostriker claims to describe my library as well as hers. Meanwhile, her zeal for keeping men out is matched by her eagerness to bring women in under the categorical umbrellas. And though I am glad to have an expanded reading list, she breezes past the actual poems so quickly no evidence arises for replacing Mary Oliver with Sharon Barba or Yosana Akiko as representative of women's attitudes toward nature; for the first of these two poets there is only this sample of her nature imagery—"that dark watery place"—and for the second, no quotation at all. When Ostriker does refer to familiar poems, the handling of them also relies predominantly on paraphrase, and on unfamiliar readings that go unsupported. There is only this about Louise Gluck's "Portrait," which Ostriker cites as an example of "women's invisibility poems" where "there is usually a sexual script" and "the poet is perhaps erotically dependent":

> Louise Gluck, a poet fascinated with border states between existence and nonexistence, in "Portrait" imagines herself a child drawing a figure that is only an outline, "white all through," until a lover draws the heart. . . .
>
> (p. 67)

Now the full text of Gluck's poem (not provided by Ostriker):

> A child draws the outline of a body.
> She draws what she can, but it is white all through,
> she cannot fill in what she knows is there.
> Within the unsupported line, she knows
> that life is missing; she has cut

one background from another. Like a child,
she turns to her mother.

And you draw the heart
against the emptiness she has created.[6]

"Portrait"

Why Ostriker ignores the immediate noun referent (mother) for the penultimate pronoun (you), in favor of the sudden appearance of a lover, is not revealed.

Hurrying to establish category and similarity, a common "terrain," Ostriker, herself a poet, too often fails to note difference, fails to bother with tone and nuance, with complexity—and what is poetry without these? Notably absent also in her book is discrimination. Sexton's small lyric, "Housewife," is simply not of sufficient heft to balance "at an opposite pole" from Bishop's "In the Waiting Room," yet the two poems are given equal treatment as examples of the quest for identity. Finally, "women writing strongly as women" are not always writing strongly as poets. While Ostriker summarizes far more than she quotes, when she does quote, the lines are often so flat, so devoid of interesting syntax, imagery, word choice and rhythm as to make one wonder on what grounds, beyond thematic example, Ostriker commends them to the reader. Since the quotations are usually brief it seems unfair to repeat them here, but surely Eloise Healy would not wish to be represented only by these lines:

Your god wears a mosaic suit
of hard mirrors and his clothes are too small.
They pinch him like metaphysics . . .

He has never perspired, has no handkerchief.
He is barely aware you worship him,
fretting as he does about his own existence.

(p. 138)

After the *Norton Anthology of Literature by Women* first appeared, a substantial amount of venom was exchanged in letters to the editor following Gail Godwin's negative but mild review in the *New York Times*. Part of the passion derives from the historical moment: given the long siege, the tacticians must have expected disagreements in the trenches to be set aside for a solid front against the enemy. (Perhaps this is why Ostriker treats the "strengths" of women's poetry and not the "limitations.")

But the divergence of opinion among women about what makes good art is at least as vigorous as that of the literary population at large, and it is naturally evidenced when books such as the *Norton Anthology of Literature by Women* or *Stealing the Language* appear, books which purport to describe the field but have in mind a particular battalion. Similar outbreaks attended the Berg and Mezey anthology mentioned earlier, *Naked Poetry,* as they will always greet examples of the time-honored tactic—asserting a minority position as the true and unsung majority view and/or the wave of the future. As with the Beat Movement, conviction intensifies around the question of

"women's literature" because it engages the nonliterary community as well: that is, the literary aspect arose in the wake of a political movement, and poems, which are also social documents, provide confirmation of the critique of culture going on elsewhere.

Another recognized tactic, which can sometimes rankle the troops, is for the oppressed to confirm the very qualities charged against them and convert condemnation into praise. It is hard to review Ostriker's list of feminine characteristics—intimacy, eroticism, anger, the divided self, nature as an extension of the female body—without recalling the stereotypes she rightly decries ("virgin or whore, angel or vixen, love-object, temptress or muse"). The relegation of women to feelings and intuition, as opposed to reason and knowledge, remains vigorous in a passage such as this:

As with women's erotic fantasies, the sensation of release rather than control is an aesthetic effect sought by women poets of all stripes. . . . [T]he imperative of intimacy often seems to shift the center of gravity in women's poems to a center of levity. . . . They joke, they play, they are silly, they are ludicrous—which is to say they are *ludic*: anti-Apollonian, Dionysiac, Carnavalesque. . . . there surfaces in women's poems a kind of giddy glee. . . . We may compare Fraser's dance metaphor [boogaloo of joy] with Yeats' ecstatic solemnity in the dance trope at the close of "Among School Children" or Eliot's liturgical tone describing the dance in "East Coker."

(pp. 200-201)

Compare that from Ostriker to this from Addison (quoted by Ellmann):

Women in their nature are much more gay and joyous than men; whether it be that their blood is more refined, their fibres more delicate, and their animal spirits more light; vivacity is the gift of women, gravity that of men.

(p. 66)

Whereas the one celebrates and the other patronizes, what has changed except the anatomical source of the characteristic?

Ostriker's anti-Apollonian, Dionysiac alignment for women is not made explicitly in connection with Bradstreet but appears soon thereafter. In the first chapter of *Stealing the Language*—which includes a review of the pressures exerted on American women to be modest and self-effacing—there is this conclusion:

These women [Reese, Guiney, Crapsey, Teasdale, Wylie, Millay, Taggard, Bogan] composed the first substantial body of lyric poetry which is worth anything in the United States . . . yet their collective impact is not acknowledged as a movement, nor has it had an impact on critical theory.

There are several reasons for this neglect, all perhaps subsumed in the observation that men, not women, have written most of the literary manifestos in the twentieth century. . . . [M]odernism took another direction, away from beauty as such, song as such. The great male moderns concern themselves with the decline of western values, the death of God, man's alienation from nature. If there is any single thing in common among Eliot, Pound, Frost, Stevens, and Williams, it is that these giant figures labor under a sense of devastating loss, which is seen as historical and social, and their work is a wrestling to erect some other saving structure. The women, however, tend to write like pagans, as if the death of God (and His civilization, and His culture, and His myths) were no loss to them. Indeed, it may have been a relief. A corollary difference is that the women write personally, whereas the reigning doctrine of modernism became impersonality: Yeats' "all that is merely personal soon rots," or the "extinction of personality" called for by Eliot.

(pp. 46-47)

It is difficult to untangle the various strands of assertion here, but the identification of women with the Natural Life Force, with Beauty and Song, with a personal rather than cultural focus, and away from the central ideas of the century, is self-evident, as is the linking of "personal" writing to what Bogan (who, like H. D., was about as personal and anti-intellectual in her poems as Eliot) called "the line of feeling." Even were her generalizations accurate, Ostriker is supporting a reductive—and limiting—equation between gender and form; if in fact she's right—if women's natural literary gift *is* exclusively lyric—then literary mastery is achieved only by exception, since great poetry from Donne to Dickinson has always encompassed both emotional intensity and intellectual rigor.

Again, however, Ostriker buries the literary question in political rhetoric: were it not for the winds of fashion, and the (male) modernist manifestos, one would see that Teasdale, Wylie, Reese, Crapsey *et al.* have produced a body of work as significant as that of (not E. A. Robinson or Robinson Jeffers, other poets swept out by the modernist broom, but) Eliot, Pound, Frost, Stevens and Williams.

At the Skidmore College Millay Conference in October, 1986—a celebration of the receipt of Millay's papers by the college—modernism was also the primary villain, diverting attention away from hard assessment. After Millay's biographer, Nancy Milford, provided an introduction to the figure; after the critics' panel recounted the sexist reviews and the reputation's decline (but quoted no actual lines by Millay); after three poets (Richard Eberhart, Katha Pollitt and myself) read from their own work and Eberhart delivered a gracious tribute, the two women on the poets' panel resurrected a question from the audience the night before: could it be that the talent was major but the work was not? that too much of it relied on a rigid and inauthentic persona, diction already archaic in the 1920s, and sentimentality? The author of *Zelda* had left early and could not comment, but the response of the invited feminist critics was immediate: we had been blinded to Millay's virtues by modernism. In fact, a novelist had suggested earlier, perhaps our standards were themselves suspect—what was so bad about sentimentality? Was it not the established male tradition that had decided, in recoil from the quintessentially female, it should be eschewed?

One's answers—that it was not modernism that happened but modern life; that sentimentality is reductive and

dangerous, whatever its source—are of course inadequate against the most persuasive tactic of all: discredit the victims' ability to recognize the extent to which they have been, to use the euphemism, *had*.

One practical virtue of anthologies is that they sometimes provide a larger, or different, taste of poets whose hash had been previously settled. Millay is represented in the standard *Norton Introduction to Literature* (fourth edition, 1986) only by two sonnets from 1923, "What Lips My Lips Have Kissed" and "I, Being Born a Woman and Distressed" (also reprinted in the Norton-distributed *American Tradition in Literature*, Vol. 2, fourth edition, Grosset & Dunlap, 1974). There is no entry at all in the revised edition of *The Norton Anthology of Poetry* (1975); the third edition (1983) allots two full pages—including the ubiquitous "I, Being Born a Woman," four entries from 1920 when Millay was twenty-eight, and three pieces from the 1930s. The *Norton Anthology of Literature by Women* repeats the aphoristic "First Fig" and "Second Fig," as well as the apparently irresistible "I, Being Born" and its contemporary "Oh, sleep forever in the Latmian cave," but supplements that selection with free verse and idiomatic pieces from the 1930s and 1950s as well as the full text of "Sonnets from an Ungrafted Tree," a sequence which rivals (but postdates) Frost's "Hill Wife" and "Home Burial" in its dramatic presentation of character.

The latter were not, of course, the poems that made her famous, and while it is salient to consider the sexism that no doubt cast its probing light on the more facile and melodramatic poems, one should likewise not forget that at midcareer, less than sixty years ago, Millay was writing lines such as:

> Gone in good sooth you are: not even in dream
> You come. As if the strictures of the light,
> Laid on our glances to their disesteem,
> Extended even to shadows and the night;[7]

and

> Ah, drink again
> This river that is the taker-away of pain,
> And the giver-back of beauty![8]

The failure may be as interesting as the success—one looks forward to Milford's biography to suggest why this talent needed the confirmation of compatible manifestos when Dickinson's did not, and whether feminine character is as susceptible as male to what is tediously called the "bitch goddess," and to what extent Millay might be a more helpful model to young women writing poems than Frost, another poet trapped in a persona. Eventually, in-depth studies of individual writers may allow some insight into that group of "feminine sonneteers" (Bogan's phrase) writing early in the century; after all, the real issue is the relationship of poetry not to gender but to character, of which gender is merely one part.

The recent Pound anniversary, with its flurry of reassessment, reminds us just how complicated that relationship is. As Ellmann notes,

[I]ndividual character is finally impenetrable, and the character, say, of an entire nation so obscure that to offer its definition is considered obscurantism, or worse. . . . But even those who despise the mode of thought cannot help but practice it. And a hope to repress sexual characterization, the most entrenched form of the general mode, would be . . . futile.

(p. 56)

"Gender-conditioning" is the term in general use in women's studies that addresses character and straddles the old "nature vs. nurture" debate. It suggests that although anatomy itself may no longer be destiny, the response to gender—expectations and strictures from the culture—is an equally determining force, imprinting the individual developing psyche. But even were this conditioning the same in every instance, surely the initial material was various, and poetry is at least as diverse as the population that produces it. When studying the poetry of a nation or a period, one must attend to the ways individual talents manifest different responses to similar circumstances. If female experience—whether deriving from inherent feminine nature or in response to cultural bias—is to be the primary given, then one will better understand the poetry it informs by examining the *differences* between Bogan and Millay, Bishop and Sexton, Gluck and Pastan. If truly little difference is to be found, if contemporary women's poems do sound alike, sharing the same themes and the same tone—as Ostriker's book, and many journals and anthologies devoted exclusively to women, would have us believe—then we must be writing very poorly indeed.

In a revolutionary time, every action, or action eschewed, is a political act. Some believe what's best for the Women's Movement (the ERA having been defeated in my state and others) is for women to write increasingly about themselves, write with anger and polemic, disregarding what chafes and restrains. But as Tom McGrath explains in the *North Dakota Quarterly* (Fall 1982):

There have been a lot of tactical poems directed to particular things, and those poems now are good in a certain sort of way, but the events they were about *have moved out from under them* [his italics]. Somebody asked Engels, "What happened to all the revolutionary poetry of 1848?" He replied: "It died with the political prejudices of the time."

To believe that sexism is a doomed prejudice may take greater idealism than one can muster, but what is best for poetry, including the poetry made by women, is fidelity to the most rigorous standards possible.

Recently a young poet in Ames, Iowa, confided that the *Norton Anthology of Literature by Women, No More Masks, Rising Tides* and other anthologies of women's work had given her, as a member of largely male writing classes, permission to write about her own life, from a feminine sensibility. The footnote I make to her expression of gratitude suggests an additional set of permissions: that she can also write about something else if she chooses, that she is free to embrace Bishop or Berryman, Donne or

Dickinson as legitimate precursors, or to differ from them all as far as discipline, courage and talent will support.

Notes

1. Alicia Suskin Ostriker, *Stealing The Language* (Boston: Beacon Press, 1986), p. 9.

2. Elizabeth Bishop, letter to Joan Keefe, reprinted from the *Norton Anthology of Literature by Women*, Sandra Gilbert and Susan Gubar, eds. (New York: W. W. Norton & Co., 1985), p. 1739.

3. John Keats, letter to Richard Woodhouse, *Criticism: Twenty Major Statements*, ed. Charles Kaplan (San Francisco: Chandler, 1985), p. 347.

4. Mary Ellmann, *Thinking about Women* (New York: Harcourt Brace Jovanovich, 1986).

5. Carol Gilligan, *In a Different Language* (Cambridge: Harvard University Press, 1982), p. 2.

6. Louise Gluck, *Descending Figure* (New York: Ecco, 1980), p. 21.

7. Edna St. Vincent Millay, *Collected Poems* (New York: Harper & Row, 1956), p. 650.

8. Ibid., p. 253.

Wendy Martin (review date October 1987)

SOURCE: A review of *Stealing the Language*, in *American Literature*, Vol. 59, No. 3, October, 1987, pp. 464-67.

[*In the following review, Martin discusses the main themes of* Stealing the Language, *commending its personal style and the inclusiveness of poets represented.*]

Beginning with Claudine Hermann's imperative that women writers must be "voleuses de langue"—thieves of language—Alicia Ostriker studies the American women poets who have claimed a poetic voice in spite of a tradition that too often ignores women's writing. ***Stealing the Language: The Emergence of Women's Poetry in America***, then, is an extended discussion of the tradition of women's artistic self-assertion that defies masculine cultural hegemony; in addition, this study provides an analysis of the challenge posed by the feminist aesthetic to the centrality of post-modernist style. Asserting that the feminist movement has served as a catalyst for innovative poetry that addresses itself to the particular concerns of women, Ostriker argues that this new poetry by women presents a radical alternative to traditional poetics: "We need to recognize that our customary literary language is systematically gendered in ways that influence what we approve and disapprove of, making it extremely difficult for us to acknowledge certain kinds of originality—of difference—in women poets" (pp. 2–3). Insisting that our aesthetic priorities are based on the valorization of the masculine, Ostriker attempts to map out a new territory of the experience and concerns shared by women. Here Ostriker is working in the tradition established by Sandra

Gilbert and Susan Gubar, Elaine Showalter, Cheryl Walker, myself and others who have observed that women writers often assume diminutive poses disguising their rebelliousness with a masque of pious obedience in order to escape the criticism of men. Thus, the truths of women's experience are often submerged; at the same time, these self-protective strategies are nevertheless subversive to masculine ideology.

Taking 1960 as an approximate point of departure, Ostriker makes it clear that she is not studying individual accomplishment but the collective achievement of a new generation of women poets. This generation can be characterized by a profound commitment to feminist-activist values (Adrienne Rich, Audre Lorde, Judy Grahn); or, at the very least, by feminist consciousness (Louise Glück, June Jordan, Diane Wakowski). In presenting an overview of contemporary women poets, Ostriker is vulnerable to the charge of inadequate aesthetic discrimination (for example, she implies that Adrienne Rich and Judy Grahn are of equal accomplishment). Nevertheless, the study does give us a useful overview of recent women poets in their ethnic, social, and sexual diversity. As Ostriker observes, the "vitality" of this new community of poets "derives from an explosive attempt to overcome [the] mental and moral confinement" of previous generations of women writers (p. 10). In contrast to their predecessors, many contemporary women writers celebrate aesthetic and cultural freedom, especially the freedom from the traditional constraint of having to please men in art and in life.

Chapter I is a brief survey of the colonial and Victorian American women poets that demonstrates the crippling effects of genteel femininity. The need for women to dissemble frailty in order to be protected, the model of powerlessness, and the confined physical and psychological space assigned to women were almost insurmountable obstacles to artistic achievement. Not until the flapper poets of the 1920s—Genevieve Taggard, Edna St. Vincent Millay, Muriel Rukeyser—was there a concerted effort to break out of the cage of domesticity. These modern women poets often rejected false modesty and wrote candidly about female sexuality as well as about their emotional and social priorities. This boldness of the women writers of the 20s made it possible for their disciples in the 60s and 70s to write openly of socio-economic injustice and racial intolerance as well as gender bias.

In Chapter II Ostriker explores the efforts of poets like Robin Morgan, Marge Piercy, and June Jordan to shatter the silence, and to destroy the bonds of invisibility and muteness that result in women's passivity, marginality, and self-hatred. Part of this process of consciousness raising and speaking out is the effort to give birth to a new self that is not characterized by ontological dualisms. Ostriker argues that in this attempt to transcend oppressive bifurcations, women's poetry strives for an aesthetics of process, or "jouissance," a phrase she borrows from Hélène Cixous.

Chapter III is an analysis of what Ostriker, along with many feminist critics, sees as a feminine aesthetic that is grounded in the body and in natural processes. This organic mode described by writers like Susan Griffin and Estella Lauter suggests a non-hierarchical relationship between mind and body or nature and culture. It is perhaps best exemplified in the work of Adrienne Rich, Maxine Kumin, and Audre Lorde. Chapter IV explores what happens when female anger is transmuted into liberating energy. Contrasting Rich with Plath and Sexton, Ostriker observes that through a feminist analysis of anger, Rich has managed to avoid the entropic effects of internalized rage which paralyzed and ultimately destroyed both Plath and Sexton.

Finally, in chapter V Ostriker defines and explains a "female erotics" which includes the new primacy of the experience of motherhood, the centrality of female biology, and the anarchistic implications of female sexuality. In this chapter, Ostriker also provides a summary of women poets who have not received attention from mainstream critics and readers but who nevertheless have achieved a grass-roots reputation for their candid explorations of female experience. Poets like Mona Van Duyn, Alta, Lucille Clifton, and Judy Grahn all have a large following, and Ostriker includes them in her discussion because so many readers respond to their work.

Stealing the Language is written in a lively, readable style, sometimes more personal than scholarly. The strength of this book lies in Ostriker's discussion of numerous poets who might not otherwise receive substantial recognition but whose work nevertheless forms the foundation for a female poetics. Ostriker's study would be considerably strengthened by more extensive historical analysis and by more elaborate discussion of stylistic characteristics of the poetry she cites. If this study runs the risk of being discursive and descriptive, it nevertheless breaks important new ground which others will cultivate for some time to come.

Bonnie Costello (review date Summer 1988)

SOURCE: "Writing Like a Woman," in *Contemporary Literature*, Vol. 29, No. 2, Summer, 1988, pp. 305-10.

[*In the following review, Costello exposes a number of pitfalls attending the theoretical orientation of* Stealing the Language.]

Alicia Ostriker's *Stealing the Language: The Emergence of Women's Poetry in America* is the latest in a rash of studies that have attempted to define poetry by women as generically distinct from the dominant male tradition. Suzanne Juhasz's *Naked and Fiery Forms*, Emily Stipes Watt's *The Poetry of American Women from 1632 to 1945*, and Margaret Homans's *Women Writers and Poetic Identity* are the book's major precursors, and it appears simultaneously with Paula Bennett's *My Life, a Loaded Gun*, a study of anger in women's poetry. The appearance of Gilbert and Gubar's *Norton Anthology of Women's Literature* crowned the notion of a female tradition and helped to complete a second stage of feminist criticism. No longer would the feminist critic's task be to liberate women writers from a gender-based system of exclusion; now gender difference would be highlighted and the literary canon forced open to admit that difference on equal terms. Ostriker's book contributes significantly to this enterprise, outlining a set of stances and preoccupations that have arisen in the development of women's poetry. But her book also shares the many pitfalls of this enterprise: a theme-bound reading of poetry, an inadvertent reinforcement of female stereotypes originating in the male mythology, a retention of female identity within a binary structure of relatedness to men, and a prescriptive rather than descriptive relationship to poetry by women.

The fundamental confusions of Ostriker's book (and others like it) are embedded in its title. Does "women's poetry" name all poetry by women or a special category of poetry by women that focuses on questions of female identity? Since the major task of the book is to define a genre, this is an important question. How broadly can we identify gender as the determining factor of authenticity and power in poetry? Ostriker's claims are very broad, but her examples derive from poetry that deals explicitly with the female self. She does not examine the validity of her generic argument in poems where the "woman question" is not at issue. Few would deny that a group of women writers since the sixties have taken up women's experience under patriarchy as their subject matter and have tended to echo the range of ideas raised by feminists throughout the culture. And few would deny that gender is a powerful determinant of vision. It is quite another thing to argue that gender identity is the inevitable subject of poetic vision. If many of our best women writers eschew that label, it is less because "woman writer" has meant "inferior writer" in our culture, or because they deny the importance of their female experience, than because their humanity takes precedence over gender. Ostriker is far readier than most writers are to see gender as absolute, to deny the possibility of the universal in art, to see the goal of poetry by women as an explicit, unified female subjectivity.

If there has been a double bind for the woman poet in patriarchal society (as Juhasz, Homans, Ostriker, and others have all argued), she is now threatened by a new one, created in the name of feminism:

> Insofar as women's poetry attempts timidly to adjust itself to literary standards which exclude the female, it dooms itself to insignificance. Where it speaks in its own voice, it enlarges literature. The belief that true poetry is genderless—which is a disguised form of believing that true poetry is masculine—means that we have not learned to see women poets generically, to recognize the tradition they belong to or to discuss either the limitations or the strengths of that tradition.
>
> (*Stealing the Language* 9)

Ostriker herself determines when a voice is authentically female and when it has adjusted itself to male standards.

Ironically, the true female self in Ostriker is predicated upon the patriarchy it seeks to upset. Ostriker's own strategies are defensive. We are told on page nine that "most critics and professors of literature, including modern literature, deny that 'women's' poetry, as distinct from poetry by individual women, exists." A quick glance at curricula across the country, or at the programs for MLA in the last decade, ought to dispel this suspicion. But certainly few would argue, as Ostriker does, that women writers must be seen in a women's tradition to be best understood: "Without a sense of the multiple and complex patterns of thought, feeling, verbal resonance, and even vocabulary shared by women writers, we cannot read any woman adequately" (9). On the contrary, in many cases such a generic frame distorts rather than illuminates the achievements of women poets. Thus the rich ambiguity, indirection, restraint, reticence, irony, abstraction of Dickinson, Moore, Bishop are reduced to defensive or at best subversive strategies directed at patriarchy. "The deepest feeling always shows itself in silence; / not in silence, but restraint," writes Marianne Moore.[1] Ostriker never entertains this notion. The metaphysical reach of many women poets is ignored in favor of their ideological status. Dickinson's ambivalence and ambiguity Ostriker names, pejoratively, "duplicity," apparently unaware that in doing so she participates in a traditional male stereotype of female behavior. She assumes that personal directness has more aesthetic as well as psychological integrity ("women write personally," she asserts). Doubleness is allowed as a self-transcending strategy for men and only a defensive or repressive one for women. Cerebration is masculine; women belong to the "line of feeling." Yeats is allowed to resolve his split ego in a very naive reading of "Sailing to Byzantium," but self-division in women's writing remains schizophrenic. Ostriker's most promising argument concerns the release of body language in women's poetry and the special position women take toward nature. But in celebrating this release she comes close at times to reducing mind to body rather than obliterating the Cartesian dualism. Also suggestive is her claim that women poets respond to an "imperative of intimacy" that challenges the logocentric/phallocentric conception of self. But she does not sufficiently distinguish this "weak ego boundary" from the "weak ego" that limits the value of earlier women poets. Nor does her argument confront the major critique of poetic subjectivity launched by contemporary theory.

Ostriker's title also suggests a historical argument, but she does little to gauge the relation of this genre's internal history to larger movements in literary history. The female "line of feeling" might easily be identified with late Victorian and Georgian poetry, the "exoskeleton style" with modernism. The more direct assertion of female experience coincides with the confessional movement which rejected modernism's impersonality. The dominant aesthetic has provided women poets with as many opportunities and discoveries as obstacles or diversions, and they are not readily alienated from it. Indeed, women have helped to shape the dominant tradition—a credit Ostriker is unable to allow them. The hard modernism of Stein,

Amy Lowell, Moore, and others might be considered original rather than male derivative. Certainly a number of male poets and critics—among them William Carlos Williams, William Gass, John Ashbery, and Brad Leithauser—have read these women as originals. More troubling than Ostriker's underestimation of the greats is her indifference to questions of quality in an argument that invites such questions. Men, she reminds us, have undervalued poetry by women. Yet she seems to judge this poetry by ideological rather than aesthetic standards. If this is a problematic distinction, it needs to be addressed as such. But to my ear much of the poetry Ostriker finds noteworthy is sentimental, crude, sensationalist, or hackneyed. She provides no defense of it as art, attending only to its attitudes toward femininity and patriarchy. And some of our best contemporary women poets—Jorie Graham, Ann Lauterbach, Pam Alexander, Heather McHugh—are not even mentioned.

This unwillingness to erect new aesthetic criteria in place of that rejected as male biased belies the title of the book. *Stealing the Language* really deals very little with language except as a byproduct of semantics. Ostriker's title is itself stolen from Claudine Herrmann's *Les Voleuses de langue* and thus invites comparison with work in French feminist theory and the concept of *écriture féminine*. Whatever one thinks of the conclusions drawn by this movement (which includes Julia Kristeva, Luce Irigaray, Hélène Cixous, and others), its ambition is to define within male-dominated discourse a distinctly female discourse with its own structure and diction, not necessarily about the female body and female experience as such, but about a consciousness emerging from these. Ostriker has not really met the challenge of *écriture féminine*, let alone addressed its critics (among them, French feminists such as Monique Wittig). Even her chapter "Thieves of Language," which mentions Herrmann, deals with mythology rather than language itself, thus remaining in the realm of images. This may be because the highly metaphoric tendency in *écriture féminine* is alien to Ostriker's empirical mind. Indeed, in this third phase of feminist criticism, the specificity of gender determination becomes suspect. In her essay "Mallarmé as Mother," for instance, Barbara Johnson, an unusually astute critic on most occasions, makes an oddly circular move in which she first identifies Mallarmé's linguistic structures as maternal and then argues that men have appropriated female power.[2] But such arguments at least acknowledge that a discourse originating in female experience can be shared. The closest Ostriker comes to a consideration of linguistic structures and lyric stances is in her discussion of the fluid ego membrane in women's writing. But she restricts this to the subject of maternal and sexual intimacy and does not extend it to consciousness generally. If she had, the polyphonous self in John Ashbery, the self of interpenetration in Gary Snyder, though not always thematized in terms of gender, might meet her criteria. Perhaps these structures are more prominent among women. By confining the forms of consciousness to their experiential sources she severely limits women's power to change the dominant tradition, to influence men.

Ostriker's book cannot fully accommodate those poems that present the experiential world as partial, poems of intellectual and metaphysical ambition, or poems that present any serious difficulty through their conceptual or figurative reach. Indeed, almost all of the poems Ostriker quotes take gendered experience as their subject and offer an uncomplicated view of it. But what about the many poems on other subjects? Do these belong to the "genre" of women's poetry? Jorie Graham's poetry is conspicuously absent from Ostriker's discussion, though the female body and female occupations and concerns often provide her image base. The question haunting all Graham's poems is the ancient, unresolved one, "in what manner the body is united with the soule." The female vantage point is for her the concrete from which the universal is projected. Of course that universal is altered by the perspective, but it is not bound by it. Because to Graham the soul is not defined by the body, or even by history, the question can be shared. Themes of sex, love, privacy in her poems appeal to a plural audience; indeed, a nongendered "we" or "us" often speaks in the presence of the female body, not to achieve a sexless objectivity but to unite readers before the shared mystery of embodiment. Graham's universal is not a disguised adherence to male or female bias. She deliberately mingles these points of view. Conventional roles and symbols are reversed and meshed. Thus in "San Sepolcro" she allows herself no special female privilege before the painted body of Mary in labor. She is one of "the living," Mary a symbol of the mind's power to conceive eternity—thus partaking of both male and female mythology. Male and female stereotypes are transcended in this poem. The self of the poet is a transparent vessel ("snow having made me / a world of bone / seen through to") but also active ("I can take you there").[3] This structure is repeated in the presentation of Mary, whose figure unites male mind and female body—or rather erases these gender associations without at all sterilizing the image. This body is laboring yet at the same time is penetrable, like the poet. One can argue that only a woman poet could so reconstruct Mariology, yet the aim of the poem is inclusive. This is not a personal poem, though it is certainly intimate, nor does Mary represent "woman." Yet to me it is more exquisite, and more expressive of my consciousness, than anything Ostriker quotes, except perhaps from Dickinson, Bishop, or Glück, Graham's major female precursors.

Of course female experience shapes the consciousness of women, though in what ways or how absolutely we still don't know with any precision. And of course women have increasingly allowed these shaping principles to inform their artistic vision. But many have resisted labeling this vision as female precisely because they wish to make it available to all readers, because female identity is their means (one among many), not their end, and because the urge to write is generated from very private and very universal longings. The "emergence" Ostriker writes of privileges polemical and theme-bound feminist poetry. This is a very narrow program for women poets.

Notes

1. Marianne Moore, "Silence," *The Complete Poems of Marianne Moore* (New York: Viking, 1981) 91.

2. Barbara Johnson, "Mallarmé as Mother: A Preliminary Sketch," *Denver Quarterly* 18.4 (1984): 77-83.

3. Jorie Graham, "San Sepolcro," *Erosion* (Princeton: Princeton UP, 1983) 2-3.

Bonnie Costello (essay date Fall 1989)

SOURCE: "Response to Alicia Ostriker," in *Contemporary Literature*, Vol. 30, No. 3, Fall, 1989, pp. 465-69.

[*In the following essay, Costello defends her opinion of* Stealing the Language, *reiterating that Ostriker's reasoning is flawed.*]

Alicia Ostriker and I disagree about the meaning and value of the category "women's poetry." I welcome this opportunity to further articulate my view on a widely debated topic. Ostriker protests that I have broadened her use of the phrase, but her own introduction [to ***Stealing the Language***] makes far-reaching claims. "My subject is the extraordinary tide of poetry by American women in our own time" (7). "The belief that true poetry is genderless— which is a disguised form of believing that true poetry is masculine—means that we have not learned to see women poets *generically,* to recognize the tradition they belong to. . . . Without a sense of the multiple and complex patterns of thought, feeling, verbal resonance, and even vocabulary shared by women writers, we cannot read any woman adequately" (9; italics mine). Such general statements in an introduction promise more than a book about a particular group since the sixties who take explicitly female experience as their subject. At the very least such statements create a context for the study of this "movement" which privileges its achievements over other poetic achievements by women. The language of this privileging is ambiguous: "Insofar as it [poetry by women] attempts timidly to adjust itself to literary standards which exclude the female, it dooms itself to insignificance" (9). But those "literary standards" are barely sketched and no timid adjustments are examined. Thus one might infer that any poetry which does not *include* the female as its orientation and focus is insignificant. This is a Catch-22 for women poets who, while they may still encounter some prejudice from men uncomfortable with women as writers, now meet rejection from feminists for not explicitly addressing their writing to the matter of womankind. Poets of a philosophical bent have particularly suffered under such standards.

Nowhere in my review do I argue that, in Ostriker's words, "whatever is explicitly identified in any way as female cannot exemplify 'humanity'" and so forth. Nor would I support such an argument; my example of Jorie Graham plainly contradicts it. Gender is an important component

of experience. But it is one among many and does not distinguish poetry from other forms of cultural behavior. My concern, rather, is that the category "woman" has become all too indeterminate. "Woman" now usurps other pressing claims of identity, narrowing the range of consciousness or associating all forms of consciousness with gender. None of the "motifs" or styles Ostriker lists originate in or are peculiar to contemporary women's poetry. The sense of marginality is central to romanticism. A great deal of literature is subversive in one way or another, but especially modern literature. Images of the body and a reunion of earth and spirit are characteristic of poetry from the sixties and seventies. Revisionist myth-making is the fuel of literary history. If certain poets have approached these "motifs" through a feminist lens this does not give them claim to discovery. Many lenses have been applied. Gender in itself cannot be proven a determinant of style. When questions of "female identity" take on "wider ramifications for poetry," the gender specificity of those ramifications becomes highly metaphoric.

The nature of female aesthetics has been hotly debated among French feminists. The work of Hélène Cixous is particularly relevant, but her positions are neither sufficiently understood nor tested. Cixous's *écriture féminine* sees feminine texts as those that "work on difference," challenge logocentric structures, and rejoice in the pleasures of open textuality. But this description fits many modern writers. Since Cixous rejects thematic and empiricist emphases (such as predominate in Ostriker and other American feminists), indeed any essentializing of the female, it is unclear on what basis this deconstructive view of textuality can be called "feminine" at all.

Ostriker presumes a great deal about my taste, converting my incidental list of a few first-rate female writers to a closed canon. I made no statement, positive or negative, about Plath, Rich, H. D., and others, about their particular qualities of joy, jive, and so forth, or about my taste in male poets. Yet I do believe in discriminations of aesthetic value, culturally and historically contingent as they may be. The terms which define what is poetry of a high order must and do constantly change. Judgments tend to be unconscious; overt principles of value are often too rigid to accommodate the rich possibilities of language. But evaluation is a necessary part of literary criticism and judgments must be defended, if only on an *ad hoc* basis. Ostriker's judgments, along with those of many feminist critics, are driven by thematically conceived questions of gender. They accommodate very little complexity, thematic or otherwise. Form becomes a mere device of statement. But in my opinion many of the poems Ostriker quotes lack both formal and thematic rigor. Susan Griffin's "I Like to Think of Harriet Tubman" is a bad poem, as the excerpt Ostriker quotes (185) suggests:

> The legal answer
> to the problem of feeding children
> is ten free lunches every month,
> being equal, in the child's real life,

to eating lunch every other day.
Monday but not Tuesday.

. . . . .

And when I think of the President
and the law, and the problem of
feeding children, I like to
think of Harriet Tubman
and her revolver.

The poem, writes Ostriker, illustrates "the intersection of the domestic sphere assigned to mothers and the wider world" and protests against "the president and other men who make and revere the law at the expense of starving children" (185). This pseudocausality she takes for granted. But the very terms in which this so-called "maternal thinking" are couched are crudely propagandistic (and a discredit to mothers). Surely it is one task of poetry to defend us against such crimes of language, not to perpetrate them. Harriet Tubman is a banner imported without reasoned or even deeply imagined connection to the issue at hand. The loaded opposition of "children" and "the President / and the law" is a similar abuse of language which allows the author an unearned righteousness. Many male writers have examined the intersection of the domestic and wider worlds more acutely. The poem lacks any interesting rhythm, any surprise or challenge, mental or emotional. Simple truths, the compression of broad considerations, the restraint against formulaic ideas are not the same as easy assertions, whether they be discursive, descriptive, or otherwise. I might almost agree with Ntozake Shange's message (quoted in Ostriker 207):

quite simply a poem shd fill you up with something /
cd make you swoon, stop in yr tracks, change yr mind,
or make it up, a poem shd happen to you like cold
water or a kiss.

But who can trust this voice which betrays its own imperative with clichés? It is not from "moral intensity," "spirituality," "cruel satire" that I shrink, but from flaccid, manipulative, muddled, or passive uses of the medium of language (rampant among the quotations in Ostriker's book).

Ostriker recognizes diversity among women poets primarily in social terms ("heterosexual and lesbian writers, women of color and white women . . ."). Such classifications may sometimes describe differences of subject, imagery, and even diction, but they should never be essentialized. Rita Dove (never mentioned in **Stealing the Language**) received the Pulitzer Prize recently because she is one of our best poets, not because she happens to be a black woman. Among her many virtues are a richly historical yet strongly lyric imagination, a stunning versatility and control of diction, syntax, rhetoric, and rhythm, a remarkable facility for metaphor, a capacity for visualizing through many perspectives and time frames, an intellectual depth and complexity. In these ways she has much in common with Keats and little with June Jordan. Has she timidly adjusted herself to male standards? Read "Dusting," the first poem in *Museum*, which describes the daydreams of a black maid. Dove's poetic strength derives

not from resisting white male discourse but from resisting all forms of complacency inherent in the medium and culture. The avant-garde Language poet Leslie Scalapino (another left unmentioned) explores questions of selfhood through radical permutations of pronominal phrases. Her talent far surpasses that of Alta, who is avant-garde in little more than the arbitrary breaking of compositional rules.

The issues raised in this debate certainly cannot be resolved here. They have to do with the influence of gender (or for that matter of any single social, historical, or biological aspect of identity) on the production of writing; with the question of universalism (can there be a "universal" value or quality which is not really an essentialized cultural bias?); with the nature of poetry itself and its role in culture. It is a flaw of Ostriker's book that it does not engage these questions more vigorously, more fully informed by the broad contemporary debate. And it is at least surprising that a poet-critic should be so indifferent to the unique characteristics of poetry, should be so ready to convert poetry to an index of feminist consciousness. To *risk* in poetry is to cast off quick-fix labels and social cant, not just of declared oppressors but of apparent defenders as well, and to face what Marianne Moore called "the warfare of imagination and medium."[1]

Note

1. Marianne Moore, "Comment," *The Complete Prose of Marianne Moore*, ed. Patricia C. Willis (New York: Viking, 1986) 177.

Anne Finch (review date Summer 1990)

SOURCE: "Poets of Our Time," in *Belle Lettres*, Summer, 1990, pp. 30-1.

[*In the following excerpt, Finch examines the "attitude" expressed in* Green Age.]

These three books of poetry [*Baptism of Desire* by Louise Erdrich, **Green Age** by Alicia Ostriker, and *Toluca Street* by Maxine Scates], written by three women coming from very different places as poets at the beginning of the end of our century, make a revealing cross-section. Louise Erdrich, a successful novelist who has written only one other book of poems, presumably uses poetry to write in ways not possible with the novel form. Alicia Suskin Ostriker, well-established as a poet, uses this volume to continue ideas developed in six other books of poems and three books of poetry criticism. Maxine Scates is new to the poetry scene; this first book of poems is published as the winner of an annual national poetry competition. . . .

If Erdrich arrives at ordinariness with relief after her book's wild journey, neither Ostriker nor Scates ever left it far behind to begin with. In spite of repeated small epiphanies and flights, both of their books rest firmly in the physically obvious world. Perhaps the maple tree in *Green Age*'s second poem **"A Young Woman, A Tree,"** is the best figure for the kind of movement that Ostriker explores:

> The secret leafless system
> That digs in dark
> Its thick intelligent arms
> And stubborn hands
> Under the shops, the streets,
> The subways, the granite,
> The sewage pipes'
> Cold slime,
> As deep as that

The world Ostriker presents is a sobering one, as real as that "cold slime"; her habitual act is one of disenchantment. Her poems derive much of their tension (and, hence, rhetorical power) from this often shocking act of disillusioning. In the suite of daughter poems, for instance, a family cat seems to be thinking of "German prison camps [and] South American torturers," while the daughter herself is compared to "an apple nobody wanted / or was ever going to want" (**"Bitterness"**). In poems with more public themes, such as **"A Meditation in Seven Days,"** the harshness is often not even the result of metaphor, but instead appears as unqualified fact:

> In filth, three timid children prod him
> While screwing their faces up from the stink
> That emanates from his mouth—
> He has beaten them black and blue . . .

Ostriker's process of disenchantment works best in this book when the graveness of her vision is lightened and complicated by a riveting, wry black humor. Frustrated with a depressed friend who says she hates the world, the speaker concludes:

> Do you know, to hate the world
> Makes you my enemy?
> *I love the world,* I reply
> Sticking the knife in.
> *I'm trying to help,* I mutter
> Twisting it.

In passages like this, the daring candor illuminates the world more brightly because the speaker has turned it first on herself. In **"Windshield,"** one of the most successful poems in the book, the speaker responds with an awesome and furious humor to the murder of a friend by urban would-be windshield cleaners:

> Up at the red light now, they are doing their crisp dance
> With their rags and squeegees
> Around a helpless Subaru.
> Watch it, mister—
> A warrior strut . . .

. . . Ostriker communicates an attitude. . . .

Judith Pierce Rosenberg (essay date Spring 1993)

SOURCE: "Profile: Alicia Suskin Ostriker," in *Belles Lettres*, Vol. 8, No. 3, Spring, 1993, pp. 26-9.

[*In the following essay, Rosenberg sketches Ostriker's life and career, incorporating the writer's own comments on her work as both poet and mother.*]

Alicia Suskin Ostriker, 55, was one of the first women in America to publish poems about her experience as a mother. She began composing the title poem of the chapbook, *Once More Out of Darkness*, during her second pregnancy in 1964-5. "I started writing about motherhood almost as soon as I was a mother. My first long poem about pregnancy and birth was put together from jottings I'd made during my first two pregnancies, which were 18 months apart. At that time, I was writing because writing was what I did. It didn't occur to me that I hadn't seen any poetry about pregnancy and childbirth until I was well along in shaping that poem [**"Once More Out of Darkness"**]. That was a radicalizing moment for me as a writer. So I started writing from a maternal perspective before getting to the point of feeling imprisoned by motherhood— that came much later."

Ostriker's first child was due in August 1963, in the same week she handed in her Ph.D. dissertation. Six months after her second daughter, Eve, was born in February 1965, Ostriker began teaching at Rutgers University, where she is a professor of English. Her son, Gabriel, was born in 1970. Three factors influenced Ostriker's decision to combine career and children in an era when few women did: ambition, a desire to organize her life differently from her mother's, and a husband who said he would divorce her if she ever turned into a housewife. Her husband of 34 years, Jeremiah P. Ostriker, is a professor of astrophysics at Princeton University; the couple lives in Princeton, New Jersey.

Ostriker is the author of seven books of poetry: *Songs* (1969), *Once More Out of Darkness and Other Poems* (1974), *A Dream of Springtime* (1979), *The Mother/Child Papers* (1980), *A Woman under the Surface: Poems and Prose Poems* (1982), *The Imaginary Lover* (1986), and *Green Age* (1989). She edited *William Blake: The Complete Poems* (1977) and has also written critical works on women's poetry such as *Writing Like a Woman* (1983) and *Stealing the Language: The Emergence of Women's Poetry in America* (1986). Her most recent book is *Feminist Revision and the Bible*, part of the Bucknell Series in Literary Theory, published in 1993.

When her children were small, she recalls, "It was pillar to post. I constantly felt guilty for not doing enough for my students, not doing enough for my children, not having time to write, and so on. This is a very familiar story: there were never enough minutes in the day, I was always exhausted. But I was keenly aware and proud that this was my choice. I didn't know anybody else who was trying to have babies and a career simultaneously. I did have the support of my husband, so the exhaustion and the craziness and the guilt were balanced by my strong sense of intentionality. This was a life I was choosing, and I didn't want to give up any piece of it."

Ostriker, who has a B.A. from Brandeis and an M.A. and Ph.D. from the University of Wisconsin, says, "Being a college teacher was something I'd wanted to do for years—that's why I went to graduate school. Writing my dissertation, on the other hand, was complete hell. I swore I would never write another critical book after that one. Later, I changed my mind on that score."

Ostriker's dissertation, *Vision and Verse in William Blake*, initiated her career as a Blake scholar. "One reason I worked on Blake, who was my guru and my main man for many years, is that his writing is so revolutionary. He was a proto-feminist; he explores the meaning of maternity and paternity in our culture more deeply than any previous poet; and he writes about the experience and the significance of sexuality more interestingly and more powerfully than any poet before D. H. Lawrence."

In the midst of her busy life as professor, wife, and mother, Ostriker continued to write poetry, as she had since childhood. She had neither a specific time nor a particular place set aside for that writing. "Poetry was always in the interstices of everything else, the nooks and crannies. It was always time stolen from other responsibilities. Everything else in my life was being done for someone or something else: someone needed me to do it or I was being paid to do it. Poetry was the one thing that I did for myself alone, with the sense that no one on earth except myself gave a damn whether I did it or not. In my early years, I didn't make other things move over very much for it; it was always on the run.

"Where did I write? Oh, I wrote everywhere. I wrote while I was driving. I wrote sitting on buses. I wrote on the living room sofa. I wrote in bed. I even used to share a desk in my husband's office at Princeton and work there. I never did much writing at Rutgers because if you kept a typewriter in an office there it would be stolen.

"For many years it was difficult for me to do any concentrated writing at home—not counting jots and scribbles. Scribbling something down in the first place can be done anywhere because it's done spontaneously—it just happens. But the work of revising needs peace and quiet. Concentration was difficult for me at home, because home was the place where I was responsible, where I was the mom, even when someone else was ostensibly taking care of the children. I just necessarily always had an ear to everything that was going on. We had *au pair* girls for 10 years, through the time my son was three and we started sending him to daycare. Having an *au pair* helped, but home was still the domestic space rather than the writing space."

When the family moved to its current residence in 1975, Ostriker gained a study, which doubles as a guest room; in the years since her youngest child entered high school, she has been able to do more concentrated writing at home. But even then, with more time and a room of her own, Ostriker's method of writing poetry has not changed. "For me, the initial writing of poetry is never place-dependent because it always interrupts something else that I'm doing. I never sit down and decide to write a poem."

Ostriker illustrated the covers of two of her early books of poetry with her own woodcuts. Although she was able to write poetry "on the run," she was not able to continue doing graphic art.

"That was the real trade-off," she says. "When I had children, I stopped putting time into art. I had taken courses in graphics and did etchings and woodcuts. That turned into annual Christmas card-making with the kids, which was the only kind of sustained visual project I ever did after they were born. I carry sketchbooks, and still enjoy drawing, but graphic art requires time and space." She has not gone back to graphic arts, "because the writing meanwhile expanded exponentially."

Her children have been a major theme in all of Ostriker's books after the first. *The Mother/Child Papers* places family life in the context of history. It was begun in 1970 when her son Gabriel was born, a few days after the United States invaded Cambodia and four student protesters were shot by members of the National Guard at Kent State University. The first section of the book includes poems that juxtapose the joy of giving birth with a mother's horror at the violence of war and her fears for her son's future. Ostriker writes,

> . . . *she has thrown a newspaper to the floor, her television is dark, her intention is to possess this baby, this piece of earth, not to surrender a boy to the ring of killers. They bring him, crying. Her throat leaps.*

Among her more recent works with a maternal theme are the sequence of poems to her older daughter in *The Imaginary Lover* and a suite of birthday poems to her younger daughter in *Green Age*.

Ostriker speaks in the measured tones of a professor; she is clearly accustomed to having her words copied down in the notebooks of her students. Asked to what extent motherhood influenced her imagery in general, she answers, "My guess is that the experience of maternity saturates every single thing I do. Maternity augments one's vision, one's sense of reality, one's sense of self. I believe that I'm maternally motivated toward the world and not just toward my children. Certainly I'm maternally motivated toward my students, who are a big part of my life. But in addition, my views of art, history, politics, all sorts of issues are in part determined by that double experience that motherhood brings of idealism and practicality. Children represent at once infinite hope and stony intractability—and the world is like that, too.

"I have found that the writing I've done about family, about my children, is often the work that audiences are most engaged with and most responsive to. When I read the mother-daughter poems from *The Imaginary Lover*, people will always come up from the audience and request copies for mothers or daughters. These are themes that speak universally to audiences and to readers. Although, when I and others first began writing about motherhood, the literary and critical response was, of course, this doesn't belong in poetry, this is trivial, it's not universal enough. One change in the literary scene since I started writing is that it has become quite normal rather than exceptional for women to write from the position of motherhood. It was almost unheard of when I started writing but it doesn't surprise anyone now."

Does that also mean that poems on a maternal theme are accepted now within the academic world and taught in university courses? "That, of course, moves more slowly, just as any avant-garde work exists before it's accepted. Canonization obviously takes longer than production. I would say the two most important poets getting into the classroom now who write as mothers are Anne Sexton and Sharon Olds. Maxine Kumin, too. Maxine is certainly accepted, canonized, was poetry consultant at the Library of Congress and is a Chancellor of the Academy of Poets. A great piece of her work is what she calls 'the tribal poems.'"

Another change Ostriker has seen is in the attitude her women students have toward motherhood. One class in the 1970s had such a negative reaction to the pregnancy/birth theme of her early poem, **"Once More Out of Darkness,"** that in response Ostriker wrote **"Propaganda Poem: Maybe for Some Young Mamas."** Her students today see maternity differently. "There is no longer a feminist party line opposing motherhood. That has fortunately faded away. Young women today, I believe, see motherhood as a personal rather than an ideological choice. What has not changed very much, although it has changed to a certain degree, is the extent to which fathers are prepared to invest their time and souls deeply in the nurturing and raising of their children. I know some couples in which the fathers take equal care, but they are exceptional." In her own case, although her husband has always been very supportive of her work, in terms of helping out with the children, Ostriker describes him as "more supportive theoretically than practically."

Asked what advice she would give to young women on combining creative work with child rearing, Ostriker notes, "The most important thing for a young mother to remember is that children and the experiences of maternity—ranging from ecstasy to hellish depression—are valid material for art. We require artists to explore and define the significance of all human experience, and the vision of motherhood that mothers will propose is obviously going to differ from the views of 'experts' such as male doctors, psychologists, and novelists. Mothers can use their lives as raw material for art just the same as Monet used landscape or Dante used Florentine politics. They can record everything.

"One of my great regrets is that I didn't write down more. You think you'll remember everything, and then you forget." The poet urges women to keep journals and use tape recorders, cameras, and video to capture those fleeting moments. "And don't be afraid to be honest," she adds. "Don't sanitize your feelings, don't be sentimental. The culture has plenty of sentimentalized versions of motherhood. What we need is reality—the whole array of realities that have never before gotten into books," including the realities of those who are not white and middle class.

In retrospect, Ostriker says of her own experience in combining writing and mothering, "I'm sure that many people will tell you this: taking care of children is a tremendous drain on your time, your spirit, your feelings, your self-image, and there's no way around that. The positive side is that having children keeps you real, keeps you open and on your toes, and is a continuing learning experience. It gives your mind and your passions a constant workout—which, if you want to keep them alive, is not a bad thing to have happen."

Now that her children are all in their twenties and living away from home, is she still able to give her passions a constant workout? "I worry about that a lot. I worry about cooling down and I try to find other ways of keeping hot. The question of what to replace motherhood with is a real question when you've defined yourself as a writer for many years through motherhood as I have. When that consuming and absorbing interest subsides, what can you find to replace it? I think I'm still in the process of discovering that."

Doris Earnshaw (review date Winter 1997)

SOURCE: A review of *The Crack in Everything*, in *World Literature Today*, Vol. 71, No. 1, Winter, 1997, pp. 156.

[*In the following review, Earnshaw applauds Ostriker's achievement in* The Crack in Everything.]

In her eighth volume of poems [*The Crack in Everything*], Alicia Suskin Ostriker puts no barriers of arcane language between herself and her reader. Her style combines acute observation in plain speech with halting rhythms of run-on lines as though she is thinking it out as she goes. Most poems begin with a setting: the beach, a bar, dance floor, classroom, hospital. The characters and story unwind, holding us charmed until the poem ends with a question, an ambiguity, an enlightenment. A mature American woman's voice speaks deliberately of her many concerns: her marriage, family relations, war horrors abroad, needy students, and, surprisingly, in a final series of poems, her mastectomy.

The forty-plus poems, most of them previously published, are in four sections. Units 1 and 3 divide the whole, and 2 and 4 are each a single long poem. Part 1 begins with character studies (people and animals) evoking the poet's empathy. A dog on the beach leaps for joy, a baby in

Somalia starves to death, Shostakovich writes music that defies the tyrant. I especially like **"Globule,"** dedicated to Elizabeth Bishop, which describes a jellyfish and ends, "Both a thing contained and container of mystery, / Smoothness inside of smoothness, cold in cold. // Wishing only to be as I am, transparent."

Section 2, "The Book of Life," is dedicated to Sheila Solomon, Ostriker's close friend in the years of being Jewish mothers of young children. Their frustration of no time to practice their arts as they care for babies and husband (the experience Adrienne Rich called "the trial by fire") makes them grapple for a toehold: "Certain women survive / Their erotic petals and pollen, grasp dirt, bite stone / Muttering I can't go on, I'll go on." Even more disheartening is their realization that their place as women in the Jewish orthodoxy cannot be accepted, although they are among the faithful.

Part 3 becomes more personal and interior. Philosophical meditation in **"The Nature of Beauty"** and **"The Glassblower's Breath"** and other poems is still tied to narrative experience, but the tone is softer, deeper. Dropping a former lover when he reappears in her life, however strong the attraction, might have been treated comically; instead, the poet recognizes "time's arrow . . . the least relenting thing / in the known universe." This section has two beautiful poems on marriage.

"The Mastectomy Poems" of part 4, a series of twelve poems, take us through the experience of breast cancer from the shock of announcement, to decision-making, through the hospital stay, to a return to "normal life" with adjustments to inner feelings and friends' responses. The series concludes with an ode to the absent breast and emotional recovery. The tone is sober and honest and will surely bring a varied response. After my initial surprise, I applaud the poem, thinking of the body violence in the literature of wars and of the millions of American women who need this experience to be voiced.

Although Ostriker writes in an accessible style, at times even prosy, her choices are backed up by a career as a prominent scholar and critic. She began publishing with studies of William Blake and English metrics. She has written a valuable history of American women poets, *Stealing the Language: The Emergence of Women's Poetry in America* (1986), and two books of Bible criticism: *Feminist Revision and the Bible* (1993) and *The Nakedness of the Fathers* (1994). Reading her whole work, we understand the poetry's place in her remarkably rich range of voice: delicious comedy in *The Nakedness of the Fathers* (the dialogue of King David and the Queen of Sheba should be on Broadway), argumentative brilliance in *Feminist Revision*, and, in the poetry, warmth of heart.

Allison Townsend (review date March 1997)

SOURCE: "No Pain, No Gain," in *Women's Review of Books*, Vol. XIV, No. 6, March, 1997, pp. 12-13.

[*In the following excerpt, Townsend highlights thematic concerns of* The Crack in Everything.]

In **"The Class,"** in Alicia Suskin Ostriker's eighth collection, **The Crack in Everything**, the speaker/teacher says her job is to give her students "permission / to gather pain into language," to make an art that is not "divisible from dirt, / from rotten life," because, she believes, "Against evidence . . . / Poetry heals or redeems suffering," even if it is "not the poet who is healed, / But someone else, years later." Ostriker examines subjects as diverse as "weightless / unstoppable neutrinos / leaving their silvery trace / in vacuum chambers," a Times Square bag lady in her "cape of rusty razor blades," three million dead "stacked . . . like sticks" in winter, or the "nectar / in the bottom of a cup / This blissfulness in which I strip and dive." This world is seen against the undercurrent of mortality that pulses beneath even the most optimistic poems.

Ostriker writes from a level of awareness that is both heartbreaking and healing, precisely because it encompasses so much loss. She searches for what, in the title of one poem, she calls **"The Vocabulary of Joy,"** noting how very difficult indeed it is to "define . . . happiness, / Though surely you know what I mean / In the late twentieth century // when I say this."

The book moves from examinations of contemporary events to meditations on art and artists, to musings about the meaning of existence, to the closing, more immediately personal poems on age, illness and healing. Part of Ostriker's search is the search for self in mid-life. *Don't I know you from somewhere?* the speaker asks in **"Neoplatonic Riff."** *Didn't I use to be you?* "Looking like a grownup, but still / Crayoning in the outlines, a good child, / A good committee member," she finds herself in her fifties, still trying to figure out who she is.

One of Ostriker's greatest strengths as poet has always been the lack of separation between self and world in her work. Immediate, passionate and direct, even the more public poems in this collection possess an intimacy that startles the reader. Capable of personifying subjects as diverse as a California surfer, a migrant, even a "globule" of transparent life, Ostriker also testifies to the horrors of our time. In poems like **"The Russian Army Goes Into Baku"** and **"The Eighth and the Thirteenth"** she looks at cruelty and violence with a fierce and unblinking eye.

In the splendid extended sequence "The Book of Life," she reflects on the strength of spirituality and the friendships of female creators. "To whom shall we say / *Inscribe me in the book of life*," she asks—

To whom if not each other
To whom if not our damaged children
To whom if not our piteous ancestors
To whom if not the lovely ugly forms
We have created,
The forms we wish to coax
From the clay of nonexistence—

However persistent the voice
That rasps hopeless, that claims
Your fault, your fault—
As if outside the synagogue we stood
On holier ground in a perennial garden
Jews like ourselves have just begun to plant.

(p. 45)

Here, in one seamless stanza, the speaker embraces self, family, friends, creative work and spirituality, making what must die away into life.

Like [poet Lucille] Clifton, Ostriker describes the experience of mastectomy, writing a path though the "riddle" of illness with clarity and grace. "You think it will never happen to you," she begins, whirling us into diagnosis, surgery and recovery with the peculiar intimacy of the second person. There is shock here. The post-op scar is a "skinny stripe / That won't come off with soap / A scarlet letter lacking a meaning . . . / It's nothing." There is grief: "Was I succulent? Was I juicy? / you sliced me like a green honeydew." There is rage. The poet is careful never to say "the thing that is forbidden to say," never invites her colleagues "to view it pickled in a Mason jar." There is healing: "Like one of those trees with a major limb lopped / I'm a shade more sublime today than yesterday." And finally, in the delightfully understated **"Epilogue: Nevertheless,"** there is recovery. "It actually takes me a while," she says, "To realize what they have in mind" when friends ask how she is feeling. Book-bag on her back, she is out the door, to whatever comes next. These strong, tough-minded, lyrical poems take us there too. . . .

Ostriker, though often tender, is overall witty and urbane, a poet of intellect whose voice is filtered through an actual social consciousness.

Marilyn Hacker (review date 12 May 1997)

SOURCE: "Tectonic Shifts," in *The Nation,* Vol. 264, No. 18, May 12, 1997, pp. 54-7.

[*In the following review, Hacker concentrates on the themes of* The Crack in Everything, *ranging from female artists, classroom experiences, and the physical and emotional scars of breast cancer.*]

Alicia Ostriker's work joins the humanitarian's unalienated will to ameliorate suffering and share what's of value (which energizes progressive political engagement) to the humanist's hunger to re-engage with and continually redefine intellectual (specifically literary, also spiritual) traditions: the pedagogical passion. She is a Blake scholar and a Bible scholar, a feminist critic whose work continues to germinate a wider-branching, inclusive literary purview, a Jew whose writings are informed by, while they interrogate, that heritage and history. She is a mother and a teacher. She is also an important American poet, whose writing is enriched, and enriches its readers, by all those sometimes conflicting identities.

The Crack in Everything is her eighth collection of poems (and her thirteenth book). Ostriker is not a "difficult" poet, demanding of the reader a primary concern with the construction (or deconstruction) of literary edifices: She is a Socratic poet, who engages the reader in complex examinations by means of simple questions, deceptively simple declarative sentences.

I picked the books to come along with me
On this retreat at the last moment
. . . . .
In Chicago, Petersburg, Tokyo, the dancers
Hit the floor running
. . . . .
We say things in this class. Like why it hurts.
. . . . .
I called him fool, she said
It just slipped out

A series of homages to other ordinary/extraordinary women frames the book's first half. Two dramatic monologues, spoken by a middle-class and a working-class woman, confronting the end (or not) of marriage, are followed, mirrored, by two magnificent portraits of known artists—the painter Alice Neel and the poet May Swenson—in which Ostriker meticulously details the way various ordinarinesses can coalesce into genius.

After a vivid introductory stanza in which all the senses are called to witness, in counterpoint with a litany of American brand names, Neel, quintessential urban American painter, speaks (through the poet) for herself:

You got to understand, this existence is it,
I blame nobody, I just paint, paint is thicker than water,
Blood, or dollars. My friends and neighbors are made
Of paint, would you believe it, paintslabs and brush-strokes
Right down to the kishkes, as my grandfather would say.
Like bandaged Andy, not smart enough to duck.

Palette knife jabs, carnation, ochre, viridian.

—and continues, relentlessly, to recount her descent into and emergence from mental illness.

Swenson's portrait is structured on word-and-eye-perfect observation: of a tortoise, which generates the image of the child-poet examining the animal, and the mature poet's own not untortoiselike, equally cannily observed physical presence. "Amphibian, crustacean?" Ostriker asks, to begin, and concludes, "It's friendly. Really a mammal." A modest inference to which Swenson would readily have assented, as she'd have been pleased to be glimpsed in her own naturalist's glass.

These strains meet in the book's long centerpiece, **"The Book of Life,"** addressed to sculptor Sheila Solomon, whose work readers won't know as they do Neel's and Swenson's. The theme of the poet's and sculptor's correspondences and their differences, as artists, as friends, as Jews, as parents, interweaves with descriptions of the sculptor's work and workplace, and with the story of a third friend, who died of cancer in early middle age:

> You started the eight-foot goddess
> The year Cynthia spent dying,
> The same year you were sculpting
> Her small bald head
> Fretting you couldn't get
> The form.

In five sections, seven dense pages, **"The Book of Life"** is more like the notebook (writers' "books of life") from which a complex poem might be drawn. "Figurative sculpture is dead," the sculptor is told, but persists in her own (figurative, majestic) vision. This poem, with its doubled or tripled levels of narration and description, left me wishing for what I equate with the figurative in poetry: the fixed structure of accentual-syllabic form to order its plunges and ascents through the sculptor's studio and garden, the friends' shared history. (Ostriker is, in general, a poet whose formal strategies inspire confidence, and seem the outer manifestation of the poem's intentions, whether in the Sapphic echoes of the triplet stanzas of the epithalamium **"Extraterrestrial,"** the clear-cut free-verse couplets of the May Swenson tribute or the Augustan rhymed pentameter, witty and elegiac, of **"After the Reunion."**)

Ostriker is a teacher by vocation, one feels, not just economic necessity: a poet/scholar who teaches not only "creative writing" but the creative *reading* that sustains the republic of letters. Many poets and novelists teach. Ostriker (along with Toi Derricotte and Marie Ponsot) is one of the few who has written about, recognized and re-created the pedagogic relationship as one of the quintessentially human connections, as fit a subject for poetry as erotic love or the changes spring rings on a meadow. Her students, as individuals or cohered into a class, are present in a group of these poems, where the dynamic that fuels a class's work together is examined—not a lecturer imprinting young minds blank as new tapes but a multivocal conversation, a collective expedition:

> All semester they brought it back
> A piece at a time, like the limbs of Osiris.

Generous as she is, Ostriker can permit herself the rueful professorial aside that the one student who "gets" Emily Dickinson, after the teacher's inspired cadenza on her poems, is "the boy / Who'd had four years of Latin / In high school and loved Virgil." And, activist as she has always been, Ostriker cannot view the university in a vacuum, peopled only by students and teachers. **"Lock-out,"** the poem that opens the university sequence, is spoken largely by a middle-aged Latino security guard, aware of how the imported hegemony of English has inflected his life and the lives of the continent's native peoples.

The contemplative poem **"After Illness"** makes graceful reference to gratuitous, inevitable bodily destiny, different but equally mortal for each individual:

> What is a dance without some mad randomness
> Making it up? Look, getting sick
> Was like being born,
>
> They singled you out from among the others
> With whom you were innocently twirling,
> Doing a samba across the cumulonimbus,
>
> They said *you*, they said *now*.

Three pages, two sections later, still in a cropped triplet stanza, the poet/speaker refers to "my mastectomy"—but in a subordinate clause of a sentence whose (conditional) object, and objective, is "mourning" and "feeling," counterbalanced by imagined indulgence of an improvident infatuation; the conclusion is that any consciously determined subject matter of meditation "By definition isn't it!" In this elegant philosophical play, mastectomy seems to enter almost offhandedly into the discourse, until the reader realizes how it informs the earlier stanzas about the dance of randomness, the falling into the body of illness as we've fallen into our bodies at birth. The balance between the raw, unresolved mourning for Cynthia in **"The Book of Life"** and this almost ludic intrusion of the harsh word "mastectomy" with its vulnerable "my" prepares the reader for the book's concluding and conclusive achievement, "The Mastectomy Poems," a twelve-poem sequence.

In the book's preceding sections, Ostriker has displayed a virtuoso register of styles, voices, forms: the dramatic monologue/word-portrait; the aphoristic or fable-like narrative in meter and rhyme; the pedagogical "I" addressing a plural "thou"; the quotidian anecdotal that shifts subtly into the meditative or the surreal. She deploys all of these in "The Mastectomy Poems" to create a mosaic of a woman's changing inner and outer life as she undergoes this ordeal (become so horrifyingly common as to resemble a rite of passage). All the while, given the book's structure, in the augmented formal echoes of its preceding themes, she reiterates as subtext that the breast cancer survivor is, chastened and changed, the same woman, the same artist and citizen, that she was before—she who praises other women (here, a breast surgeon) in the exercise of their vocations:

> I shook your hand before I went.
> Your nod was brief, your manner confident,
> A ship's captain, and there I lay, a chart
> Of the bay, no reefs, no shoals

a sensual/social woman:

> I told a man *I've resolved*
> *To be as sexy with one breast*
> *As other people are with two*
> And he looked away

a lyric economist of meter and rhyme:

> And now the anesthesiologist
> Tells something reassuring to my ear—
> And a red moon is stripping to her waist—
> *How good it is, not to be anywhere*

a teacher and member of the academic community:

> First classes, the sun is out, the darlings
> Troop in, my colleagues
> Tell me I look normal. I am normal.

Always, though, underneath the surface, under the "Black and red China silk jacket," is the shocked, transformed body, the "skinny stripe," "short piece of cosmic string" of the mastectomy scar, at once sign of escape and *memento mori.*

Omnipresent, too, the scar's double, is the lost breast, also with a double significance, first as instrument of pleasure, self-contained sustenance, bodily benignity, badge of responsible womanhood: "my right guess, my true information," transformed into a kind of time bomb, storehouse of explosives, inert but dangerous matter:

> Jug of star fluid, breakable cup—
> Someone shoveled your good and bad crumbs
> Together into a plastic container . . .
> For breast tissue is like silicon.

And the breast, or the ghost breast, marks mortality now even more than the scar:

> *Carry me mama.* Sweetheart,
> I hear you, I will come.

"The River" concludes: the generative constant rescue mission of maternity thus transformed into the poet's prescience of death.

Abruptly, the sequence's next, last poem begins and ends with the speaker back in the quotidian world of work and talk: "The bookbag on my back, I'm out the door"—a teacher again, with the vivacity and accoutrements of a young student in her self-description. "Winter turns to spring / The way it does," and she unthinkingly answers the anxious *"How are you feeling"* with anecdotes about family and work. The "woman under the surface" is back on the surface, in her disguise as an ordinary worker-bee, an ordinariness like that which camouflages the genius of Swenson and Neel in their poem-portraits. But this section is titled "Epilogue"—which gives us the double message that, despite the brisk exit-line, the poem's real conclusion is the haunted one of **"The River."**

One section of "The Mastectomy Poems" has an epigraph—referring to "an ordinary woman"—from a poem by Lucille Clifton. Clifton too was treated for breast cancer, a few years after Ostriker. Some, only some, of the contemporary American writers who are living with, or who have succumbed to, breast cancer are, in no particular order: Pat Parker, Audre Lorde, Susan Sontag, Maxine Kumin, Eve Kosofsky Sedgwick, Penelope Austin, Edith Konecky, Hilda Raz, Patricia Goedicke, June Jordan, myself; black, white, Jewish; fat, thin and middling; lesbian, straight (and middling); childless and multiparous "And"—to borrow the title of a poem by Melvin Dixon about friends lost to AIDS—"These Are Just a Few."

The Crack in Everything: Is it a shift in the earth's tectonic plates, the purposeful Zen flaw in a ceramic vase that individualizes its perfection, the long pink keloid ridge on a newly flat chest? All of the above. This is not a polemic, a book with an aim, a recovery manual. It reaffirms the poet's unique and contradictory role, at once storyteller and witness, s/he who makes of language not a prison but a prism, refracting and re-combining the spectrum of human possibilities.

John Taylor (review date June 1997)

SOURCE: A review of *The Crack in Everything,* in *Poetry,* Vol. CLXX, No. 3, June, 1997, pp. 174-77.

[*In the following review, Taylor considers the significance of and justification for widely mixed themes in* The Crack in Everything.]

Alicia Suskin Ostriker's new collection [*The Crack in Everything*] may at first surprise the reader with its multifarious subject matter (the "everything" referred to in the title), but this impression of heterogeneity takes on a compelling significance and justification by "The Mastectomy Poems," the fourth and last section. Here the disparate "cracks" that have been observed in others and in various societal phenomena fissure all the way back to the empathic observer, that is, brutally converge on the poet herself. "You never think it will happen to you," she avows in the first of twelve candid poems, "Then as you sit paging a magazine . . . / Waiting to be routinely waved good-bye / . . . the mammogram technician / Says *Sorry, we need to do this again.*" Ostriker describes her operation (a powerful poem is addressed to her doctor), meditates on **"What Was Lost,"** before investigating her feelings as she recovers. During her convalescence, for instance, she breaks off an icicle, declaring it to be "A brandished javelin / Made of sheer / Stolen light / To which the palm sticks / As the shock of cold / Instantly shoots through the arm / To the heart— / I need a language like that."

Ostriker indeed seeks a language capable of taking on "the extremes" (as she puts in **"Marie at Tea"**), which is to say that she strives to perceive the malefic, debilitating, or cancerous fractures beneath the smooth, deceiving surfaces of reality. This pursuit is admittedly arduous. "What the eye instantly consents to," she specifies in **"Still Life: A Glassful of Zinnias on my Daughter's Kitchen Table,"** "Language stumbles after / Like some rejected / Clumsy perpetual lover . . . / Encouraging himself: maybe this time / She'll go with me." Yet struggling with language is not the only difficulty. It is remarkable how often Ostriker mediates reality through the creativity of others. Poems here concern, allude to, or invoke Wittgenstein, Rothko, van Gogh, May Swenson, Elizabeth Bishop, Wallace Stevens, Shostakovich, Plato, Chekhov, Rumi, T. S. Eliot, Emily Dickinson, *et al.* Is their presence perhaps sometimes more self-hindering than enlightening? Even the last Mastectomy Poem concludes with Ostriker running off with a "bookbag on [her] back." Several *engagé* poems—memorably, those set in Somalia or at a rape trial where the victim is a retarded girl—likewise seem reactions, however justifiably indignant, not to what Ostriker has eye-witnessed (or experienced in her own body) but rather to what she has learned through the news media.

This is not to suggest that Ostriker's bookbag is overly burdensome; only that the problem of "paying attention"—not just to extraordinary events, but also to zinnias on a kitchen table—functions here as a sort of Achilles' heel for the poet. Her occasional under-estimations of the ordinary, as opposed to her eagerness to point up the dramatic, work like insidious cracks weakening or diverting the emotional intensity of some of these poems. Perhaps the poet relies, in places, not confidently enough on her own perceptive gifts, although her talent is evident in the arresting detail of **"Locker Room Conversation"** or in the delightful opening poem, which depicts dogs plunging "straight into / The foaming breakers // Like diving birds, letting the green turbulence / Toss them, until they snap and sink // Teeth into floating wood / Then bound back to their owners." This canine image of "passionate speed / For nothing, / For absolutely nothing but joy" is the touchstone—not yet marred by illness or moral iniquity—against which the reader will measure the destructive cracks in everything else. Interestingly, some longer poems begin as detailed, firmly-structured narratives, then conclude in fragments or with an oblique, even dissociated, twist—a sign, too, that a former wholeness has crumbled. This quality is particularly striking in a diary-like poem, **"Taylor Lake,"** where Ostriker first relates a family hike in the mountains, then abruptly records the tale of a man who has sat down with children in a sandbox.

Too many poems, however, include facile pronouncements. In **"The Vocabulary of Joy,"** for example, Ostriker exclaims her "happiness" while she watches a laughing, racially-mixed family—a sentiment that she cannot convey more graphically, however, for she adds only: "Though surely you know what I mean / In the late twentieth century // When I say this." It is a pity that Ostriker has not dissected her "happiness"; such remarks in any case dull the vibrancy of the present, which she had nevertheless evoked with gusto: "Father to shoulders hoists / Their slender redhead daughter, who // Laughs and shouts, pulling his hair, / *You're fun, Daddy.*" **"Lockout"** similarly perks our interest in a campus security guard who helps the poet unlock her office door; yet we never get to know this man, for the poem turns to the way he was treated at

school: "They hit my hands with rulers and made me eat soap / For speaking my own language, Spanish." We sympathize, but the poem goes no further than this revelation of organized brutality; the security guard is ultimately used as a mere political symbol.

This tendency to take stands crops up even in the complex, ambitious long-poem, **"The Book of Life,"** which is a challenging exploration of Judaism. A few cumbersome lines ("She used to describe the folk music scene in America / —*Before money made a hole in it* / *And the joy spilled out*") distract from the poignancy of a folksinger's death. "Her daughters assembled," writes Ostriker, "As she slept and woke, slept and moaned. / They made the decision to switch / To the intravenous." This simple, moving scene illustrates our (once again) late-twentieth-century manner of seeing off our parents and loved-ones. In contrast to allusions to ever-shifting socio-economic realities, do not these grave gestures and the random, telling remembrances that follow ("A pair of butter-soft, cherry-red / Italian gloves . . . / her tragicomic love affairs, / Her taste in flowers, Catalan cooking, / Shelves of tattered blues and flamenco records"), suffice in giving us the essential—a lasting, universal emotion?

Sharon Dolin (review date September-October 1997)

SOURCE: "How the Light Gets In," in *American Book Review*, Vol. 18, No. 6, September-October, 1997, pp. 23-4.

[*In the following excerpt, Dolin delineates the themes and style of* The Crack in Everything.]

The Crack in Everything, Alicia Ostriker's eighth volume of poetry, is a mature work, filled with wisdom about personal grief and the world. According to the Kabbala, upon the creation of the world, the vessels into which light was poured cracked, and now it is up to human beings to repair the world's brokenness. And though Ostriker knows that she can't fix most things, including herself, she uses her poems to teach us—and herself—that "a crack in everything" is, in words she borrows from Leonard Cohen, "how the light gets in." *Pears, Lake, Sun*, Sandy Solomon's first book of poems and the winner of the 1995 Agnes Lynch Starrett Award, also uses brokenness to illumine the harsh surfaces of the world. Both volumes seem centrally concerned with grief—Ostriker having survived breast cancer, Solomon having lost her lover to a muscular degenerative disease. In each case, the poet knows just how much language can and cannot accomplish and the poems become a study in compassion for the self and others.

Halfway through Ostriker's book she announces the themes of loss, illness, and mortality in a long meditative poem called **"The Book of Life,"** which is about what we do with our loved ones who begin losing their faculties and what we think we'll do with ourselves: "When we think, not of death / But of the decay before it—before us. . . ." Her friend, to whom the poem is addressed, finds the words that will carry: "*Whoever we are, we'll be to the end.*" Then Ostriker gives a narrative description in simple colloquial language, unadorned by metaphor, of another friend's decision to die in place of "more chemo":

> Lingering? Fuck that, she said.
> Morphine for the pain against the pain.
> That final day, her daughters assembled
> As she slept and woke, slept and moaned.
> They made the decision to switch
> To the intravenous. It was morphine all the way then.
> All night they waked and watched her sleep
> And said from time to time, as she almost surfaced,
> She'd sing a line from one of the folk songs
> On her Elektra records, that she recorded
> When they were kids
> And she was almost famous,
> As if to sing herself back to sleep,
> Then sank again, rose and sank.
>
> (from **"The Book of Life"**)

When Ostriker confronts her own illness, we are prepared for her bravery: "What I want / Is to listen, what I want / Is to follow instructions" (from **"After Illness"**). And for several poems, she does ask questions: of nature, of a campus security guard, even of her students. We encounter "The Mastectomy Poems," a sequence that deals with Ostriker's cancer directly, in the final section of the book. Breast cancer is one of those subjects you might feel you've read enough poems about. But these poems are so understated that they are as much about what can't be said—even about a reader's own resistance to reading about illness out of a talismanic fear that it might happen to you by coming into contact with it on the page. So the first poem opens aggressively, addressing that fear quite directly in the second person feminine singular:

> You never think it will happen to you,
> What happens every day to other women,
> Then as you sit paging a magazine,
> Its beauties lying idly in your lap,
> Waiting to be routinely waved good-bye
> Until next year, the mammogram technician
> Says *Sorry, we need to do this again.*
>
> (from **"1. The Bridge"**)

In this age of disease, Ostriker has figured out what poetry can say through negation. In **"Riddle: Post-Op,"** under "squares of gauze," the speaker exhibits the angry metaphoric profusions of Sylvia Plath's late poetry:

> I've got a secret, I've a riddle
> That's not a chestful of medals
> Or a jeweled lapel pin
> And not the trimly sewn
> Breast pocket of a tailored business suit
> It doesn't need a hanky
> It's not the friendly slit of a zipper
> Or a dolphin grin

> Or a kind word from the heart
> Not a twig from a dogwood tree
> Not really a worm . . .
>
> . . .
> A scarlet letter lacking a meaning
> Guess what it is
> It's nothing.

This anaphoric list offers a chilling display of the limits of metaphor. And this "nothing," this sense of **"What Was Lost,"** as she titles one poem in the series, is what each of us—in aging, illness, and death—has to confront. Yet though a contrived sense of normalcy returns—"The falsie on my left makes me / In a certain sense more perfectly normal" (from **"8. Normal"**)—and though the sequence and the volume ends with the poet declaring, "*I'm fine, I say I'm great, I'm clean* / The book bag on my back, I have to run" (from **"12. Epilogue: Nevertheless"**), the jarring, almost too-perfect iambic pentameter last line makes the voice feel forced, as though it were the words themselves that were steeling her against the fear of not being fine.

The Crack in Everything is about so much more than cancer and personal illness that I wished "The Mastectomy Poems" hadn't been placed at the end. Better to have opened out into the world of brokenness and mortality with this new vision and to encounter her poem about the black families whose homes were torched by Philadelphia's authorities: "The angel lifted a voice / Like a furious siren . . . And it sang through the desolate fumes . . ." (from **"Deaf Cities"**) or about **"The Boys, The Broom Handle, the Retarded Girl,"** "who was asking for it." The irony builds throughout the poem until it burns with its own embers of rage.

Ostriker exhibits enormous range; she can also speak in the voice of migrant workers who are fully imagined waking up to the beauty of California—

> Desire comes up in us
> Like the morning sun
> over the Great Central Valley

—before assuming the shackles of work, and the reader is caught by surprise, as are the men, from one stanza to the next. She can evoke the voice of a dying baby: "compared to being buried alive," "Death by starvation. Is very good, yes, good / As life can be" (from **"Somalia"**). Or Aphrodite in the form of a "[c]razy lady" living in the Port Authority Terminal in New York City. The most experimental are a group of ekphrastic poems. **"Nude Descending"** manages to evoke the confused cubist abstraction of Duchamp's famous painting as well as to wrest back from the male painter some of the woman's autonomy.

By far the most breathtaking poem in the entire collection is **"The Eighth and Thirteenth,"** a poem chosen by Adrienne Rich to appear in *The Best American Poetry: 1996.* If Adorno said one shouldn't write poetry after the Holocaust, then this poem proves that a poet of Ostriker's strengths can and should write poems *about* the Holocaust. Ostriker, caught by happenstance listening to Shostakovich's Eighth "on public radio," has written a poem that avalanches down the page:

> . . . An avalanche
> of iron violins. At Leningrad
> During the years of siege
> Between bombardment, hunger,
> And three subfreezing winters,
> Three million dead were born
> Out of Christ's bloody side. Like icy
> Fetuses. For months
> One could not bury them, the earth
> And they alike were adamant.
> You stacked the dead like sticks until May's mud,
> When, of course, there was pestilence.
> But the music continues. It has no other choice.

Then the poet moves on to deliberately play Shostakovich's "Thirteenth," a memorial to the massacre of Kiev's Jews. The poem weaves in narrative, Ostriker's commentary, passages from Shostakovich's notebooks, and Tsvetaeva's *"All poets are Jews."* Illness produces silence or a negation or profusion of metaphors in Ostriker's poetry, the Holocaust in memory produces a collage of voices in place of the silenced. The poem is a masterful crescendo—howbeit mid-volume—to a masterful book about what we can and cannot master, and to what we can at least bear witness. . . .

Diana Hume George (review date December 1998)

SOURCE: "Repairing the World," in *Women's Review of Books*, Vol. XVI, No. 3, December, 1998, pp. 10-11.

[*In the following review, George provides an overview of the principal themes of Ostriker's career within the context of the poetry in* Stealing the Language *and* Writing Like a Woman *and her two groundbreaking revisionist volumes on the Bible.*]

In a conversation many years ago about her own poetry and that of Anne Sexton and Alicia Ostriker, Maxine Kumin told me that she thought of all love poetry as elegiac. For three decades Alicia Suskin Ostriker has been writing an extended elegiac love poem, in the way of Emily Dickinson's letter to the world "that never wrote to me". She asks for an answer that she does not expect, because that answer would take the form of global transformation. No matter if she knows humanity isn't yet up to the task of loving-kindness toward itself; she writes the poems anyway.

Ostriker is among America's leading poet-critics, with eight books of poetry, critical studies including *Stealing in Language: The Emergence of Women's Poetry in America* (Beacon, 1986) and *Writing Like a Woman* (University of Michigan, 1983), and two groundbreaking

revisionist volumes on the Bible. An academic with a comprehensive command of the male canon, Ostriker challenged it early in her career, and whatever her misgivings about being labeled an intellectual, she is justifiably stuck with that title. It's not so terrible to be an intellectual if you're also a visionary, and now that Ginsberg is gone, Ostriker is contemporary poetry's most Blakean figure. Like Blake's, her vision of how things might be is grounded in anatomy of how things are. Ostriker is in love with a wounded world and wants us to heal it with the force of human imagination, compassion, and love. And she thinks we actually could. This is not a metaphor.

Themes Ostriker anatomized in other American women poets are exhibited amply in *The Little Space: Poems Selected and New, 1968-1998*: the natural world as a continuation of the body, anger juxtaposed with the imperative of intimacy, autonomy and self-definition emerging from cultural erasure. In the recent work, Ostriker grows toward what I'd call wisdom literature. *The Little Space* contains plenty of that, so my major complaint is simple: about two hundred pages seems, well, too little a space for a poet this large. Some of her finest poems are not here, such as **"Dreaming of Her," "As in a Gallery," "Downstairs," "Wanting All," "While Driving North."** I'd have horse-traded a few of her formally fine, judicious, tame poems about art for these wild-minded works, tonal balance be damned. That said, this is a wonderful book.

"Writing like a woman" for Ostriker originally meant meditating on motherhood as an act of love. Her thinking on maternity is central to her poetry, even to her poetics, in which death is countered by the genuine heroism of giving birth. When her son is born in 1970, the doctor remarks that he will make a good soldier. "The Guards kneeled" becomes a premonitory chant not only for Ostriker's early poems, but for her life's work:

> The Guards kneeled, they raised their weapons, they fired
> into the crowd to protect the peace.
> There was a sharp orange-red explosion, diminished
> by the great warm daylight, a match scratching,
> a whine, a tender thud, then the sweet tunnel, then nothing.
> Then the tunnel again, the immense difficulty, pressure, then the head
> finally is liberated, then they pull the body out.
>
> (**"Mother/Child,"** p. 26)

Far from holding only men responsible for war, Ostriker continuously acknowledges her own complicity in the design, even as she labors to imagine a way out. Her deterministic bent poises delicately against indomitable optimism. In the midst of a moment of pure laughter, her infant stares at her, "intense, impersonal, like icy dawn / like the son of beauty, the bow bent, and the arrows drawn." She cannot know whether his will be the arrows of desire or of destruction. "I want to tell you it is not your fault. / It is your fault." Their intimacy will remain with him, even after he has turned away from her in order "not to waste breath," to become a man.

You will never forget this,
will always seek, beyond every division,
a healing of division, renewed touch.

("Mother/Child: Coda," p. 37)

If the poet is afraid of loss, separation, betrayal, death, violence from without and within—and she is—she is fearless about her fear. The speaker of **"Message from the Sleeper at Hell's Mouth"** knows damnable things, but in this early foray into revisionist mythmaking (from *A Woman Under the Surface*, 1982), Ostriker offers a plural reading of the ur-texts of Western culture. Like Sexton's, her revisionist language and tone alternate between jazzy update and lyrical sway. At the end of this poem cycle, represented too slimly here, Psyche asks, "Anyway, what is the soul / But a dream of itself?"

The figure Ostriker calls "the imaginary lover," after whom she titles her 1986 collection, is another form of Psyche's wounded lover, Eros, and she pursues him throughout her work. And let there be no mistake about the scope of the quest, because Ostriker's poetry is about the soul's desire. The beloved Eros is not only a husband, a lover, a son and daughters, a dead father, a living mother; it is the human community itself, and the earth on which these many feet walk. In **"The Marriage Nocturne,"** Ostriker's speaker drives home to her husband "through this wounded / World that we cannot heal, that is our bride." This external world opens out to us from within the mind in "Letting the Doves Out," where the lover is described as a "form in the mind / On whom, as on a screen, I project designs, / Images, whose presence makes me dilate . . ."

The prophetic urge always drives Ostriker back from hell's or heaven's mouth to the ordinary world inhabited by women and men like herself, where the real work of survival happens, or does not. **"Surviving"** is about Paula Modersohn-Becker, Ostriker's mother, all women artists whose lives were cut short or unfulfilled. "How can the broken mothers teach us?" she asks. In **"The War of Men and Women,"** a companion lament (at least I read it as one) that is as fine as Rich's "Diving into the Wreck" poems, ours is the failure of the imagination to "join our life with the dangerous life of the other." That failure to reach out to each other over the chasm of difference—any kind of alienating difference—has cost us so much that "we would need an archaeology / Of pain to trace the course of this frozen river."

Any poet with an agenda so urgent might be expected to offer a grim vision, but this isn't true of Ostriker, whose laughter often echoes through even the earnest stuff. Most of her readers know this from **"Everywoman Her Own Theology"**:

My proposals, or should I say requirements,
Include at least one image of a god,
Virile, beard optional, one of a goddess
Nubile, breast size approximating mine,
One divine baby, one lion, one lamb,
All nude as figs, all dancing wildly. . . .

Ethically, I am looking for
An absolute endorsement of loving-kindness.

(p. 97)

That wish for unconditional kindness defines her spiritual quest poetry as she enters the 1990s. In the final section of *Green Age* (1989), she writes of the beloved Friend that Rumi called God. Finding the Friend in ordinary people, in children now grown, in students and strangers, she addresses a "you" on whom she confers multiple identities. **"The Death Ghazals"** challenges that other God, the Father God, whom she also addresses in *Feminist Revision and the Bible* and in *The Nakedness of the Fathers: Biblical Visions and Revisions*, books from which it is now difficult to separate her poetry: "Does your smeared forehead out-top the gracious mountains?" And in **"A Meditation in Seven Days,"** she forces entry, as female and as Jew, into the sacred patriarchal place. "Fearful, I see my hand is on the latch / I am the woman, and about to enter."

Kumin's sense of elegy certainly applies to Ostriker's recent work, where dirge is often joined to songs of joy. Loss upon loss stacks up over the years in the life of the poet, the country, the globe, and readers can see it in this volume as we move toward *The Crack in Everything* (1996). But it is not herself she mourns—as the title of this volume indicates, Ostriker prefers humility about one's own little space in the universe to the counter-stance of arrogance. Indeed, she thinks herself fortunate, for now she has faced down death. In the excerpts from **"The Mastectomy Poems,"** wit wins over despair, as in **"Mastectomy,"** where she asks her doctor, "Was I succulent? Was I juicy?"

I thought you sliced me like green honeydew
Or like a pomegranate full of seeds
Tart as Persephone's, those electric dots
That kept that girl in hell,
Those jelly pips that made her queen of death.

(p. 204)

The "Uncollected and New" section is disappointingly short, as is the custom in collections, with only nine pieces, nearly half poems inspired by works of art. This is one of Ostriker's career-long interests and she serves it well, in poems always accomplished, polished, far-reaching, formal—but it's simply not one of my favorite things to watch her do. Here, though, one is a stunner, up there with her lifelong best. **"From the Prado Rotunda: The Family of Charles IV, and Others"** is about Goya, about all of us:

If he is leading us by the hand like babes
To worship the abject monstrous because it exists, to sniff
Hysteria from within like an infection
Among the tambourines and the fans and the mantillas,
If Goya's lascivious Maja
Nude and clothed in the duplicity

Native to women
Makes your mouth water—
If her pale legs flow strangely together
As if glued to a board they cannot
bend at the knee,
As if returning to fishtails—

The painting is never what is *there,*
It throbs with the mystery
Of your own sick-to-death soul
Which demands, like everything alive,
Love.

(p. 221)

"Holocaust" is the inverse of the same human tendencies "in the fiery patriotic mind":

You as a child first feeling that excitement
At the cave mouth—
Sparks flying upward to emulate stars

You dancing to emulate the fierce commotion
Your mouth greasy after eating
Running with the dogs round the circle

The hiss, the crackle, the boom, the fragrance—
The sweet savor—

You draw close enough to set
Two hard fires ablaze in your two eyes
And they never go out—

(pp. 225-226)

It is no accident that the last poem here is **"About Time,"** the body's "loop from clay to clay / Interrupted. Wrestled, made to gleam." Ostriker follows her own advice: "Express your anger like a swan." That is what she has always done, in poems where language does not evade its own knowledge of how Yeats' "terrible beauty is born."

FURTHER READING

Criticism

Hampl, Patricia. "Surviving a Life in the Present." *New York Times Book Review* (20 July 1986): 15.
    Brief review of Ostriker's *The Imaginary Lover.*

Phillips, Robert. "Poems, Mostly Personal, Some Historical, Many Unnecessary." *Hudson Review* 49, No. 4 (Winter 1997): 659–68.
    Includes Ostriker in a discussion of contemporary poetry and its voluminous output.

Rosenberg, Liz. "The Power of Victims." *New York Times Book Review* (20 July 1986): 21.
    Reviews Ostriker's *Stealing the Language: The Emergence of Women's Poetry in America.*

Additional coverage of Ostriker's life and career is contained in the following sources published by the Gale Group: *Contemporary Authors Autobiography Series,* **Vol. 24;** *Contemporary Authors* **First Revision, Vols. 25-28;** *Contemporary Authors New Revision Series,* **Vols. 10, 30, 62; and** *Dictionary of Literary Biography,* **Vol. 120.**

D. M. Thomas
1935-

(Full name Donald Michael Thomas) English novelist, poet, dramatist, translator, biographer, and memoirist.

The following entry presents an overview of Thomas's career through 1998. For further information on his life and works, see *CLC,* Volumes 13, 22, and 31.

INTRODUCTION

English writer D. M. Thomas attracted a large audience and widespread acclaim on both sides of the Atlantic with the publication of his third novel, *The White Hotel* (1981). This unanticipated best-seller explores archetypal themes of sex and death in the graphic, and often shocking, context of Freudian psychoanalytic theory and the Holocaust. In this and other works, Thomas employs metafictional literary techniques, including hallucinatory temporal shifts and a combination of poetry, prose, and verbatim texts by other authors, to challenge conventional notions about genre and authorship. Thomas has also won distinction for his earlier poetry and subsequent "Russian Nights" series of novels, though he remains best known for *The White Hotel.*

BIOGRAPHICAL INFORMATION

The descendent of generations of Cornish tin miners, Thomas was born in the coastal village of Carnkie, England, in 1935. At age 14 Thomas moved with his parents to Australia, where his older sister had relocated upon her marriage. The family lived there for two years, after which they returned once again to England, where Thomas completed secondary school and then entered two years of compulsory national service. During this time he was assigned to an army intelligence section involved with producing Russian-speaking interrogators. While he scored poorly on his final examination, the experience sparked his interest in Russian literature and inspired his future translations of Russian works. He went on to study English at Oxford University, where he received a B.A. in 1958 and an M.A. in 1961. He taught at a grammar school in Devonshire from 1960 to 1964 before joining the Hereford College of Education as a lecturer in English. A large portion of Thomas's early poetry involved science-fiction themes and was published in related magazines. A sampling of the writer's poetry was published for the first time in a book in *Modern Poets 11* (1968). His first individual collection of poetry soon followed with the release of *Two Voices* (1968). While still at Hereford, Thomas published several more collections of poetry as well as his first translation, Anna Akhmatova's *Requiem and Poem without a Hero* (1976). There he also began the novel *Birthstone* (1980), but interrupted its progress to quickly complete *The Flute-Player,* (1978) for which he won a Gollancz fantasy-novel contest. Thomas was head of the English department at Hereford when the college was closed in 1978. Deciding to make writing a full-time career, Thomas returned to Oxford to write *The White Hotel.* Initially regarded with little enthusiasm in Britain, the novel proved a major critical and popular success in the United States. He was invited to lecture at American University in Washington, D.C., but, unwilling to be perceived as a "successful author," he returned after just a week to Cornwall, where his children and two former wives resided. Since his return, he has remained in Cornwall, continuing to compose poetry, translate Russian-language works, and write novels. He published a biography of Alexander Solzhenitsyn in 1998.

MAJOR WORKS

While Thomas is best known for his novel *The White Hotel,* he is also an accomplished poet. Following the publication of *Modern Poets 11,* the author quickly began to reject the conventions of science fiction to include images of contemporary life. The collection *Two Voices* includes the ten-poem sequence "Requiem for Aberfan," which tells of the deaths of more than one hundred children and adults in a landslide in the coal-mining village of Aberfan. The sequence juxtaposes Thomas's poems with actual prose accounts of the event, a technique he would also employ in later works. Thomas continued to experiment with literary styles and images in the poetry collection *Logan Stone* (1971), after the publication of which he began to move away from elaborate poetic constructions. *The Shaft* (1973), for instance, found its focusing image in the reopening of the Cornish tin mines. The volumes *Love and Other Deaths* (1975) and *The Honeymoon Voyage* (1978) explore the themes of death and sexual attraction. The poems of *Love and Other Deaths* range from "Lilith-prints," in which Lilith is Eve's apocryphal rival, to poems about his dying parents. The title poem of *The Honeymoon Voyage,* in turn, explores his mother's death through his newlywed parents' trip to California. The controlled form and simple images for which Thomas strove in his poetry is reflected in his appreciation for the works of the Russian poet Anna Akhmatova. He has translated several original volumes of her poetry, as well as her *Selected Poems* (1983). Akhmatova became the inspiration for the protagonist in Thomas's novel *The Flute-Player.* Elena is a beautiful young musician who helps a group of persecuted artists survive in a totalitarian state. Thomas's second novel, *Birthstone,* involves an American woman and her son who travel to Cornwall in search of their ancestry. Their guide is a Welsh woman with a split personality who moves between the past and present. His next novel, *The White Hotel,* is divided into six sections, preceded by a prologue involving a fictional correspondence between Freud and his colleagues about one of his female patients. The first section is comprised of a graphically sexual and violent poem in which the patient describes her fantasy of an affair with Freud's son at a white hotel, an image of both innocence and death. The following section is a prose version of the fantasy. The fourth section, a pastiche of actual Freud case histories, consists of Freud's analysis of his patient, who is revealed to be Lisa Erdman, a Russian-Jewish opera singer. The next sections depict Lisa, after her treatment by Freud, moving to Kiev with her Russian husband. Following her husband's disappearance in the Stalinist purges, she and her stepson are killed along with thousands of other Russian Jews in the massacre at Babi Yar. (Thomas inserts into this portion of the novel the testimony of the massacre's sole survivor, taken from Anatoli Kuznetsov's book *Babi Yar.*) The final, surreal section of the novel finds Lisa reunited with such figures as her mother and Freud in the new Jewish paradise of Palestine.

After *The White Hotel,* Thomas began what would become the "Russian Nights" quintet of novels. This series of books on storytelling begins with *Ararat* (1983), in which a Russian poet named Rozanov improvises a story about three writers who meet at a conference and agree to collaborate on their own improvisation. Among them is a poet named Surkov who invents alternative endings for an unfinished story, "Egyptian Nights," by the Russian writer Alexander Pushkin. (Thomas translated and inserted an actual fragment of Pushkin's "Egyptian Nights" in the novel.) The Pushkin story involves a poet named Charsky who befriends an Italian storyteller, who has his own tale to tell. The subsequent novels in the series—*Swallow* (1984), *Sphinx* (1986), and *Summit* (1987)—continue the trend of improvisations and stories within stories until concluding with *Lying Together* (1990), in which the earlier fictions are found to be the work of a British writer named Don Thomas and his Russian friends. Among Thomas's more recent novels is *Pictures at an Exhibition* (1993), a novel set during the Holocaust, in which, like *The White Hotel,* Thomas combines dreams and Freudian analysis, mass murder, and the textual use of historical documents. Thomas's other novels include: *Flying in to Love* (1992), which revolves around the assassination of President John F. Kennedy; *Eating Pavlova* (1994), an imaginative depiction of Freud in London shortly before his death; and *Lady with a Laptop* (1996), a satire on writing workshops and New Age therapy.

CRITICAL RECEPTION

Thomas was a little known poet and translator of Russian verse before writing *The White Hotel,* which remains the work for which he is most famous. Critical response to his writing reached its peak with that novel, and reviews of work subsequent to *The White Hotel* rarely, if ever, fail to mention his magnum opus. His pre-*White Hotel* poetry has been commended for bringing together different textures and texts, reflecting the author's fascination with eroticism, dreams, and death. These same observations were made regarding *The White Hotel.* The novel initially attracted little attention from local reviewers in Britain, but when it arrived in the United States it became a bestseller. American reviewers lauded it as a brilliant tour de force, praising its adroit series of narrative voices and thematic consideration of psychoanalysis, the Holocaust, and female sexuality. The frank depiction of sexuality seen in Thomas's earlier work received reactions ranging from "pornographic" (mainly from British reviewers) to "erotic" (mostly American). Thomas, however, received a significant amount of negative criticism for his use of outside texts in *The White Hotel,* including passages taken directly from Freud's writings and testimony taken from Kuznetsov's book on the massacre at Babi Yar. Thomas has received similar criticism for relying too heavily on previous translations for his own translation of Pushkin's *The Bronze Horseman* (1982), and for inappropriately incorporating Nazi documents into the narrative of *Pictures at an Exhibition.* Since *The White Hotel,* critical reaction to Thomas's novels has been more reserved. The "Russian Nights" quintet was praised for its intricate layering of stories within stories, but generally thought to lack substance. While his more recent work has failed to duplicate the success of his breakthrough novel, *The White Hotel* is still regarded as a remarkable accomplishment, and it continues to receive much critical interest and ongoing scholarly evaluation.

PRINCIPAL WORKS

Modern Poets 11 [with Peter Redgrove and D. M. Black] (poetry) 1968
Two Voices (poetry) 1968
Logan Stone (poetry) 1971
The Shaft (poetry) 1973
Love and Other Deaths (poetry) 1975
Requiem and Poem without a Hero [by Anna Akhmatova; translator] (poetry) 1976
The Flute-Player (novel) 1978
The Honeymoon Voyage (poetry) 1978
Way of All the Earth [by Anna Akhmatova; translator] (poetry) 1979
Birthstone (novel) 1980
Dreaming in Bronze (poetry) 1981
Invisible Threads [by Yevgeny Yevtushenko; translator] (poetry) 1981
The White Hotel (novel) 1981
The Bronze Horseman [by Alexander Pushkin; translator] (poetry) 1982
*Ararat (novel) 1983
A Dove in Santiago [by Yevgeny Yevtushenko; translator] (poetry) 1983
News from the Front [with Sylvia Kantaris] (poetry) 1983
Selected Poems [by Anna Akhmatova; translator] (poetry) 1983
*Swallow (novel) 1984
Boris Godunov [by Alexander Pushkin] (drama) 1985
You Will Hear Thunder [by Anna Akhmatova; translator] (poetry) 1985
*Sphinx (novel) 1986
*Summit (novel) 1987
Memories and Hallucinations: A Memoir (memoir) 1988
*Lying Together (novel) 1990
Flying in to Love (novel) 1992
The Puberty Tree: New and Selected Poems (poetry) 1992
Pictures at an Exhibition (novel) 1993
Eating Pavlova (novel) 1994
Lady with a Laptop (novel) 1996
Alexander Solzhenitsyn: A Century in His Life (biography) 1998

*All part of the "Russian Nights" series.

CRITICISM

Michele Slung (review date 28 March 1981)

SOURCE: "A Freudian Journey," in *New Republic*, March 28, 1981, pp. 35-37.

[*In the following review, Slung offers favorable evaluation of* The White Hotel.]

"The psyche of an hysteric is like a child who has a secret, which no one must know, but everyone must guess. And so he makes it easier by scattering clues."

In this beautifully imagined novel by British poet D. M. Thomas, Sigmund Freud is a character and utters the above words during the course of an analysis. The year is 1919, his patient a 29-year-old woman whom he calls, in customary fashion, by a false name in her case history. Thus the cellist "Frau Anna G." is actually one Elisabeth Erdman, an opera singer who has come to 19 Berggasse because she has been suffering from a variety of debilitating ailments believed by the doctor referring her to Freud to be psychogenic.

At this time the real Freud had published such works as *The Interpretation of Dreams, The Psychopathology of Everyday Life,* and *Totem and Taboo.* He had broken with Jung. His standing in the Viennese community, as well as in the international medical community, was assured, his years of "isolation" behind him. Freud's private practice, which had grown smaller during wartime, was again busy. The Freud Thomas gives us, viewed through the lens of fiction, does not seem to be different from the Freud of contemporary witnesses: he is kind, diplomatic, tolerant, insightful, self-assured.

Frau Anna, or Lisa, as she is known outside the pages of Freud's notes, is, on the other hand, a paradigm. Though the etiology of her case is Thomas's, there are components that derive from Freud's own work. For example, Lisa walks bent forward from the middle, as did one of Freud's classic studies, Fraulein Elisabeth von R. Her breast and ovarian neuralgia, her anorectic appearance and respiratory difficulties, her recurring hallucinations—all of Lisa's symptoms are taken from the literature of hysteria.

When she comes to consult Freud, Lisa professes to feel certain that he will diagnose her disturbances as organic. Freud, of course, intuits otherwise. His treatment of Lisa goes on for some months as he extracts her memories, dreams, and fantasies, all the while probing determinedly, like a psychic dentist, for the infected spot. In the later stages, however, she becomes resistant and Freud, exasperated, contemplates terminating her analysis.

Suddenly, to Freud's amazement, Lisa returns from a holiday at an Alpine spa, having gained weight and confidence. "Here in short," he comments, "was not the painfully thin, depressed invalid I expected, but an attractive, slightly coquettish young lady, bouncing with health and vigour." To a colleague he describes this startling transformation as "A *genuine* pseudocyesis!" for Lisa has delivered herself of a manuscript, a surreal portrait that is a sublimely erotic fantasy of her visit to Gastein, and Freud rightly believes that the key to her neurosis will be found in it.

The White Hotel is a novel in seven parts, including a prologue. Five of them are directly concerned with Lisa's psychoanalysis; two are not and take place a number of years later. Yet the interior landscape of Lisa's mind is the essence of the book; as Thomas's poetic transformations show us, it is both a personal and a collective phenomenon. The clues that Freud unravels, finding his way through the maze to Lisa's secret, lead him to both specific and general conclusions, the latter reinforcing his desire to complete a work he has been in doubt over, *Beyond the Pleasure Principle.*

Specifically, the "white hotel" is the stopping-off place for Lisa's imaginary journey. There, as in any dream world, the most disparate events are equalized. Disasters occur—a flood, a fire—but the survivors absorb the horrors and carry on as before. Repression does not exist in the environs of the white hotel, and Lisa's concupiscence, once freed from restraints, gains such momentum that her breasts, "so endlessly had they been sucked on," give out enough milk to fill wine glasses for others to drink.

Lisa's vision of the white hotel is seen by Freud and the reader in two versions. One recounts the fantasy in an almost rollicking near-rhyme, its sensuous lilt like water slapping on a dock. The second appears after Freud requests that she analyze her own material "in a restrained and sober manner." What he then receives is "an *inundation* of the irrational and libidinous," a magnificent primer of psychiatric symbolism, "thrown off with all the belle in-différence of an hysteric." From this, and his subsequent questioning of Lisa, Freud realizes that, though there is a "'good' side of the white hotel, its abundant hospitality. . . . the shadow of destructiveness cannot be ignored for a single moment, least of all in the times of greatest pleasure." He also sees

> the tragic paradox controlling Frau Anna's destiny. She possessed a craving to satisfy the demand of her libido; yet at the same time an imperious demand, on the part of some force I did not comprehend, to poison the well of her pleasure at its source. She had, by her own admission, an unusually strong maternal instinct; yet an absolute edict, imposed by some autocrat I could not name, against having children. She loved food; yet she would not eat.

Moreover, in his quest for synthesis, Freud begins to understand that Frau Anna/Lisa can shed light on his inchoate theory of the death instinct. He looks at the larger implications of Lisa's condition, "Eros in combat with Thanatos," and starts to regard her "not as a woman separated from the rest of us by her illness, but as someone in whom an hysteria exaggerated and highlighted a *universal* struggle between the life instinct and the death instinct."

At last Freud, telling Lisa he has cured her of "everything but life," brings their sessions to an end. The conflicts raging within her, which, in addition to sexual ones, include feelings about her half-Jewish parentage, cannot be totally extirpated by Freud. Transmuting Lisa's "hysterical misery into common unhappiness" is sufficient success, however, and nine years pass in the interlude before we see her again.

Now having attained some European reputation as a singer, Lisa is on her way to Milan to take up an engagement substituting for an injured Russian diva at La Scala. Since *The White Hotel* is a novel of journeys and destinations, of *process,* this is, in fact, a route that brings both life and death, for, in Italy, she meets the man who will eventually become her husband and make her a stepmother. He also, being a Russian Jew, is the instrument by which fate brings Lisa to join the 30,000 dead in the hellish ravine, Babi Yar.

Marriage and assumed maternity allow Lisa to release her long-banked-up store of nurture; heretofore unthinkable evil, which even fiction cannot disguise as a mere historical event, then rapes her evolved womanhood. Thomas's evocation of the horror of the mass slaughter ("No one could have imagined the scene, because it was happening.") is less than 20 pages long, yet it wipes from the reader's mind all that has gone before. It takes Thomas to draw us back, to remind us of the "white hotel" (the myriad interconnections of consciousness and the unconscious) that exists for every human being. Of the murdered masses, he says, for a moment assuming them able to speak about themselves, "If a Sigmund Freud had been listening and taking notes from the time of Adam, he would still not fully have explored even a single group, even a single person."

A coda brings Lisa to life again: she has traveled once more, this time arriving in a great, good place—Israel. She has previously had partial resurrections, by Freud, by her husband. This one is complete, and all the clues scattered earlier are woven together into a somehow reassuring unity, reassuring even in the aftermath of the agony.

The "compulsion to repetition" is one of the cornerstones of Freud's thought in *Beyond the Pleasure Principle.* And repetition, stunningly enacted in imagery that continually circles in on itself, is the method by which Thomas binds us to his prose. The white hotel is the leitmotif: it reminds us that Freud, in *The Interpretation of Dreams,* states that dream symbols "frequently have more than one or even several meanings, and, as with Chinese script, the correct interpretation can only be arrived at one each occasion from the context."

The white hotel is the place where we are not; it is also eternally somewhere inside us. It is pre-birth and yet it is after-life. Speaking vulgarly, it can be seen as the place we check in when we check out, in either sleep or death. If, as Freud surmises, the white hotel is one's mother's body ("the original white hotel—we have all stayed there—the mother's womb"), then we must not forget that Lisa's mother perished while in a hotel. And, of course, the very word "hysteria" derives from "suffering in the womb," and so. . . . each new idea carries us, swirling in ambiguity, further along.

In *The White Hotel,* Thomas once again reveals the obsessions with love and death, suffering and artistry that are to be found in his earlier work. (In his previous novel, *The Flute Player,* the heroine dreams of sexual exploration and writing verse, and she has premonitions of violent death; in his poem, **"Vienna. Zurich. Constance,"** Thomas shows his interest in Freud and Jung.) The richness of this book is reminiscent of a painstakingly woven tapestry; one can focus on the details but must be absorbed by the whole. Even the beginning of the world is here ("a very soft, sighing sound," not a Big Bang), as well as the birth of Christ. Thomas's admiration for Freud, now a mythic figure, is such that he makes this shadow that looms so large over 20th-century Western civilization into a human-scale, wise man. But more importantly, Thomas bares his own humanity, as he searches in the ashes of the Holocaust for the soul of man, that "far country which cannot be approached or explored."

Thomas Flanagan (review date 2 May 1981)

SOURCE: "To Babi Yar and Beyond," in *Nation,* May 2, 1981, pp. 537-39.

[*In the following review, Flanagan offers positive evaluation of* The White Hotel.]

This novel by the English poet D. M. Thomas is a book of extraordinary beauty, power and audacity—powerful and beautiful in its conception, audacious in its manner of execution. It is as stunning a work of fiction as has appeared in a long while. If it falls short of its ambitions, as I believe it does, this is because those ambitions are so large.

Its most obvious, although not its deepest, originality is one of form. The novel is an account of the life and death and the state of being after death of an opera singer named Lisa Erdman, but the account is not given in straightforward narrative. Thomas, however, is not one of those writers who, having been informed by the hum of the general culture that "narrative" has fallen from favor, has looked about for more modish equivalents. His form issues directly from his vision, is compelled by his vision, and has two distinct but closely joined consequences for the reader. It becomes literally impossible to respond to the novel without making crucial decisions as to the events and meanings of Lisa's life—without, that is, disentangling the submerged narrative from the manner of its telling, the shifting viewpoints and chronologies, the rich and shifting imagery.

Lisa Erdman's "biography," told as straightforward narrative, would read something like this: she is born in Russia of a Jewish father and a Polish Catholic mother, becomes a singer, has an affair with a young radical, moves to Vienna and marries. She separates from her husband at the time of World War I and comes to experience hysterical pains in breast and ovary so debilitating that she turns for relief to psychoanalysis, becoming one of Freud's patients.

The pains are in the left breast and the left ovary, which puzzles Freud, for he knows that "the unconscious is a precise and even pedantic symbolist." This puzzle aside, Thomas's imagined but authentic Freud explores Lisa's damaged psyche gently, resourcefully, peeling back layer after layer of screening memories and resistances, and bringing her at last to a childhood vision of mother, aunt and aunt's husband, locked in erotic union.

Freud obtains something like a partial remission of her symptoms, and she goes on to an undistinguished singing career, brightened by a solitary success at La Scala. Much later, the baritone with whom she had sung there in *Eugene Onegin* summons her back to Kiev, to marry him and to care for his young son, Kolya. He is swept away in one of Stalin's purges, and she endures in poverty. Then, in 1941, she and Kolya, with numberless thousands, are slaughtered by the Nazis in the dreadful ravine of Babi Yar. Her death is gruesome and obscene: an S.S. man crashes his jackboot into her left breast, and a Ukrainian guard ends matters by driving a bayonet into her womb in a travesty of intercourse. After that, though, she finds herself in a Palestine which is not quite the actual Palestine—peaceful and humdrum, despite olive trees and palms and oases, at once matter-of-fact and eerie—where she meets her dead mother and Kolya, and sees, at a distance, Freud himself.

But we experience the novel with the events ordered differently, and presented in a series of disparate textures. It opens with a series of letters by Freud and his younger colleagues, one written in 1909, others in 1920 after he has begun treatment of Lisa. One of these contains a kind of "journal" in verse, written by his patient after a brief holiday at the resort in Gastein, and set down between the staves of a score of *Don Giovanni*. It is accompanied by an "analysis" which he had urged her to write in "a restrained and sober manner," but which is in fact a wild, lyrical, irrational embroidery upon her original fantasy.

These two documents create with hallucinatory energy and vividness a white hotel, within which the writer experiences moments that fuse an intense eroticism and an equally intense violence. They remain in our mind throughout what follows, not only because of their overwhelming immediacy but because they articulate images—of breast, leaf, blood, fire, milk—that appear and reappear later, with shifting yet accumulating significances.

They are followed in the text by Freud's study of his patient, *Frau Anna G.,* which was to have been published in Frankfurt in 1932, to honor both Goethe's centenary and the fortieth anniversary of his own *Studies in Hysteria.* With the coming of the Nazis, however, the project was abandoned. A footnote reminds us that his works were burned on a bonfire in Berlin—one of the novel's many fires, some real and some hallucinated. The "study" is a model of affectionate impersonation, capturing both Freud's civilized, humane, even faintly philistine social attitudes and his daring, courageous understanding of the individual psyche. Within it, Lisa Erdman's fantasy of the white hotel, with its blissful images of oral gratification, its violently destructive counterimages, is artfully joined to her painfully remembered past. The white hotel unlocks for her what she perhaps remembers as happening long ago in a summer house in Odessa, and the "case" is "solved." The hotel, which "speaks in the language of flowers, scents, and tastes," is the place without sin, the body of the mother. From this study, the novel moves forward to a deceptively conventional third-person narrative that carries Lisa to Babi Yar and beyond.

By then, however, the reader has been made uneasily aware—by image, symbol, reference, by the novel's very structure—that far more has been at stake than Lisa Erdman's damaged psyche. The fate of our culture has been implied—a culture which has embraced a Mozart, a Goethe, a Pushkin, a Freud, but also a Hitler, a Stalin, the bayonet of a Ukrainian guard. Lisa has been presented as a woman of average impulses and affections—her history no more bizarre than the secret psychic history of any of us—and of only average, unreflecting intelligence. The history of our age has touched her life at each of its stages, indeed her life is destroyed by our history, but that history has not touched her conscious mind.

It has its image, however, within her unconscious, although, of course, neither Freud nor she herself is aware of this. The full weight of the novel rests upon this irony. Freud's insights, so the novel implies, can carry us to the very edge of what can be apprehended and conquered by the rational, humane intellect. But those very symbols that have yielded themselves to the rational intellect also bear meanings, significations, prophecies, which lie beyond the humane and must be called, for want of better words, spiritual, demonic, angelic. Neither Lisa Erdman nor her supremely rational physician can know that her breast and ovary ache not from a remembered sorrow but from a violation which lies waiting in her, and our, future. Still less can they know, or would they believe, that the mother's consoling breast, the white hotel, awaits her after death, by the waters of Jordan.

This expansion of imagery and structure from the fate of an individual to the fate of the culture itself is a dazzling accomplishment, but it has exacted a price. To persuade us of its authenticity, Thomas has gifted Lisa Erdman with what Freud calls telepathic powers. She herself calls it second sight—an ability to discern in others anxieties that lie below the level of consciousness, to foresee, without understanding, the future. By this device, Thomas hopes to validate the meanings of his symbols as not merely private but communal and, ultimately, apocalyptic. But the device remains a device, a willed literary artifice that demands, but cannot fully claim, our assent. And at the end we are left with a "solution" more esthetically satisfying, perhaps, than that of the rational psychologist, but just as arbitrary.

Thomas is no less imprisoned by the conditions of his art than was Freud by his. His deepest theme, the joined threads of desolation and joy, is communicable only through images that are mute save in their power and their beauty, his "explanation" imperils both of these qualities.

The White Hotel seeks to fuse the sufferings of an individual with the horrors of this unspeakable century, and to suggest, by radiance of image and form, that all of them can be confronted. It is an impossible ambition, or at least so it must seem to those who, like myself, cannot accept, even as metaphor, a River Jordan flowing somewhere, somehow, beyond the sandpits of Babi Yar. But D. M. Thomas has come wonderfully close.

John H. Barnsley (essay date Fall 1982)

SOURCE: "The White Hotel," in *Antioch Review,* Vol. 40, No. 4, Fall, 1982, pp. 448-60.

[*In the following essay, Barnsley comments on the popularity of* The White Hotel *and provides a summary of the novel's plot, characters, and central themes.*]

I must confess to being an avid, if often disillusioned, reader of bestsellers. Popularity does not imply merit, of course, and academics tend to assume it never does: the esoteric article in a limited-circulation, "prestige" journal is more their acme of success. But some recognized stylists achieve bestsellerdom—Updike, Bellow, Roth, Cheever, Murdoch, Burgess. Further, there are some books—we might cite Doctorow's *Ragtime* and even Blatty's *The Exorcist*—which, though obviously geared for the mass market, do achieve a certain populist craftsmanship that gives pleasure. True, there are some distinctly unimpressive bestsellers: anything by Harold Robbins, or a book like Mario Puzo's recent *Fools Die,* which is an obviously exploitative, prurient account of the Las Vegas demi-monde and from which one turns to a decent sociological account of the same subculture with some relief. In fact, over-all, the experience of reading bestsellers is akin to that of watching television: one must wade through vast wastelands of uninspired dross to get to something really interesting.

Yet such reading has interest and justification. In *La Nausée* Sartre has Roquentin argue that to present human life as a narrative is always to falsify it. To say the least, this is counter-intuitive. For in actual life narratability is an important aspect of the intelligibility of action and event, and we are our own novelists in a stronger sense than we are our own philosophers and sociologists. We constantly, to ourselves and others, tell our own story: we "make sense" of ourselves through narration. It is not surprising, therefore, that the central—most popular, most influential—narratives of a society are an important clue to its culture, just as the *Iliad* and *Odyssey* are, albeit *faute de mieux,* to the understanding of early Greece. Moreover, the modern popular novel has probably a particular appeal and relevance to modern man's "homeless mind" (as sociologist Peter Berger puts it), because the evolving narrative of the individual is characteristically a search for meaning. The modern hero is normally *en route,* from one situation to another—like, in a different *nomos,* the medieval quest. The airport is one characteristic locale of the modern hero or heroine.

Unsurprisingly, then, our impression is that modern best-sellers tend to reflect consensual values, if in a partial and selective way. Most adopt specifically contemporary locales, and those set in the past—like Erica Jong's recent *Fanny* and, again, E. L. Doctorow's *Ragtime*—tend to throw a distinctly contemporary light and evaluation on that past. Examples of such recurrent consensual values are materialism, "bourgeois" individualism, status, mobility (geographic and social), youthfulness, sexuality and sexual "frankness," and *machismo* for men, beauty for women. The novels also reflect conventional ambivalencies toward such matters as technology and deviance. They reflect too, by omission, those values that seem to be on the wane, particularly among the young, a central example being the Victorian value of hard work—though as a partial counter-example one might cite Jeffrey Archer's *Kane and Abel,* which is, in large part, a retelling of Horatio Alger's rags-to-riches stories in modern context. In this sense most popular novels are conservative: despite occasional cynicism (now almost *de rigueur* in the spy genre), they do not significantly unmask or disrupt the status quo and insofar as they offer criticisms of institutions these are usually generally recognized ones.

However, occasionally a bestseller arises that holds special interest for us because it raises issues of central concern. One such case is **The White Hotel** (Viking) by D. M. Thomas, a Cornishman born in 1935. This is a current bestseller on both sides of the Atlantic, and the film rights (a necessary rite of passage for full bestsellerdom) have been sold for a half-million dollars. The book has received a variety of plaudits: "a reminder that fiction can amaze" said *Time* magazine; "heart-stunning" said *The New York Times* and "Precise, troubling, brilliant" said the British *Observer.* The book is distinctive (like, say, the lightweight *Jonathan Livingston Seagull*) in not having been designed as a bestseller. Its author has rather been surprised and embarrassed by its success: he said in an interview that the book had for him "lost its virginity" as a commercial product and that it was now "The Off-White Hotel."

For a complex, literary work like this, which operates on several levels and embodies various ambiguities, it is difficult to give a brief, adequate summary. However, the main themes may be outlined before discussion.

The book begins with a number of letters, dated 1909, 1920, and 1931, some from Sigmund Freud to fellow analysts, in which we learn of patient's writings that are to be published. The writings concern a "white hotel" and Freud describes them as "obscene" but revealing and a

fellow-analyst depicts their content as "like Eden before the Fall." Our appetites thus whetted, we are introduced to the writings themselves—an erotic and imaginative poem and "The Gastein Journal," which spells out the theme of the poem. Briefly, the writings tell of a young woman who meets a soldier (and ex-prisoner of war) on a train. The soldier is Freud's son and the two begin an erotic relationship leading to a stay at an unspecified "white hotel" where much lovemaking occurs, some of it involving other guests—for instance, at one point the diners take it in turn to suckle the girl's lactating breasts. The "white hotel" is a hospitable place, with efficient staff and good food, and is set beside a lake in the mountains. But curious, apocalyptic events occur there: particular guests see lightning striking the lake, falling stars, red elm leaves, a school of whales; a Lutheran pastor witnesses a breast flying through the yew trees; another, a petrified embryo floating in the lake; another, a womb gliding across the lake. The lovers see an orange grove fall into the lake and there is a mysterious flood and fire in which several are killed and then an equally mysterious earthquake and avalanche buries the mourners. Later, snow falls to bury the hotel and a cable-car suddenly breaks, causing a number to fall to their death. No explanation for these events is given, though a nun comments cryptically, "Nothing is sinful here because of the Spring."

The book then turns to a case-history by Freud. His patient, "Frau Anna," the writer of the "white hotel" poem and journal, is, like the heroine of her writings, a twenty-nine-year-old opera singer separated from her husband. Her extended analysis begins in 1919 and her complaint is that she has suffered for four years with severe pains in her left breast and ovary, as well as having a chronic respiratory condition, anorexia nervosa, and visual hallucinations. Freud diagnoses her pains as psychosomatic products of sexual hysteria and explores her childhood in Russia (she moved to Vienna in her late teens). From this, Freud finds grounds for neurosis in the early loss of her mother (at age five) and her father's neglect, but is unsure of the "hidden factor" producing her hysteria. He comments apropos this: "What she had in her consciousness was only a secret and not a foreign body. She both knew and did not know. In a sense, too, her mind was attempting to tell us what was wrong; for the repressed idea creates its own apt symbol. The psyche of an hysteric is like a child who has a secret, which no one must know, but everyone must guess. And so he must make it easier by scattering clues. Clearly the child in Frau Anna's mind was telling us to look at her breast and her ovary: and precisely the left breast and ovary, for the unconscious is a precise and even pedantic symbolist."

Still, no progress is made for many weeks. "Anna" is reticent and evasive, though at one point she recalls a dream that Freud is able, to his own satisfaction, to interpret symbolically: a train journey and bridge are both symbols of dying, a drying-out umbrella in a hall is symbolic of a discharged penis (!), and so on. Freud says her dream "could not have been clearer"—it expresses her desire to be her brother. But then Freud's daughter dies, and "Anna" claims her dream was a premonition of this, being "cursed with what is called second sight." Freud replies that she must have discerned his subconscious anxieties about his daughter.

"Anna" then visits Gastein, an Austrian health resort and spa, and returns in a carefree mood. Freud suggests she write down her impressions of Gastein and this produces her "white hotel" writings. Freud sees the journal especially as an uncensored, "courageous" document, holding the key to her self and her maladies. Rejecting (unlike some of his followers) a rigid classification of the symbols, he remarks on "the over-all feeling of the white hotel, its wholehearted commitment to orality—sucking, biting, eating, gorging, taking in, with all the blissful narcissism of a baby at the breast. Here is the oceanic oneness of the child's first years, the auto-erotic paradise, the map of our first country of love—thrown off with all the *belle indifférence* of an hysteric." It enables Freud (and here fiction can exploit an autobiographical lacuna) to make a theoretical advance—to recognize Eros as in constant combat with Thanatos. As he comments: "The shadowy ideas of my half-completed essay, *Beyond the Pleasure Principle* [1920], began, almost imperceptibly, to take concrete shape, as I pondered the tragic paradox controlling Frau Anna's destiny. She possessed a craving to satisfy the demand of her libido; yet at the same time an imperious demand, on the part of some force I did not comprehend, to poison the well of her pleasure at its source. . . . I began to see Frau Anna, not as a woman separated from the rest of us by her illness, but as someone in whom an hysteria exaggerated and highlighted a *universal* struggle between the life instinct and the death instinct." Shortly thereafter, Freud "stumbles over" the clue to "Anna's" hysteria: in brief, her father's harshness led her to idealize her mother and, subsequently aided by mother figures, she developed a suppressed homosexuality. Hence her symptoms sprang from her "unconscious hatred of her distorted femininity." Freud is not sure why the pains occur specifically on the left side, but is able to judge that her journal is "really" about "Anna" and her mother and expresses a pre-Oedipal longing "to return to the haven of security, the original white hotel—we have all stayed there—the mother's womb." (A footnote, analyzing the analyst, suggests Freud's emphasis on the mother's role may be due to the recent death of his own mother, on 12 September 1930.) The role of the journal for Freud is thus therapeutic: it shows the unconscious preparing the psyche for the eventual release of repressed ideas into consciousness, so moving the patient ("with moderate help from the physician") toward psychological health, through acceptance of her mother's mysterious individuality (she had been traumatized by a childhood discovery of adultery between her mother and uncle).

The book then changes gear: from being a novel of ideas it becomes more a novel of events. We learn "Frau Anna" is Elisabeth Erdman—"Lisa"—and we follow her career as a "second-best" opera singer. She remarries, this time a widowed Russian opera singer, and acquires a stepson. Meanwhile her hallucinations, pains, and breathlessness recur—despite Freud's "cure"—in response to a variety of incidents—a friend expecting a baby, the same friend's death (of which she had a premonition), a lack of reply to a letter to Freud, a proposal of marriage. She also has an interesting correspondence with Freud, who writes for permission to publish her writings. In her reply she admits to having misled him on some incidents in her life ("you saw what I wanted you to see"). In particular, she retells, traumatically, her story of once being "captured" by sailors in Russia and taken to a ship where she thinks they are going to kill her (and where she saw a burning waterfront; hence, she says, the burning hotel in her writings). But instead the sailors abuse her and force her to commit fellatio as a "dirty Jewess." It was the first time she learnt there was anything *bad* about being Jewish (she is actually half-Jewish), though she now remembers that there was a lot of anti-Semitism in Russia at the time, as well as revolutionary feeling. Since that time, raised as a Catholic, she has hidden her Jewish blood—hence her evasiveness and lies to Freud, knowing him to be Jewish. She says her father was afterwards good to her but to blame, in her eyes, for being Jewish. Further, she blames the breakup of her first marriage on this issue—because of her husband's fierce anti-Semitism whilst unaware that she herself was Jewish—and not on sexual problems, as she had first led Freud to believe. She suggests her asthma was initially because of her fellatio with the sailors (an event she found in retrospect arousing) and so "hysterical," but regards her pains as organic and rejects Freud's theory of her homosexuality. Freud for his part continues to think her mother's situation is at the root of her troubles. But he accepts that she has had a correct premonition of his grandson's death and ascribes this to telepathy, a factor he says he would devote his life to investigating were he to live it over again.

The next and penultimate chapter finds Lisa and her stepson living in poverty in the Podol slum in Kiev, hoping to emigrate to Palestine. Her husband (also Jewish) has been interminably jailed for treason, though on trivial grounds. In 1941 the Germans enter the city and a week later a notice commands all "Yids"—the official term—to assemble near the cemetery. Once assembled, the Jews are assaulted, stripped, and then systematically shot in the ravine of Babi Yar. At first Lisa and her stepson escape by pretending not to be Jewish, but then the onlookers are ordered to be shot too. She jumps unharmed on to a pile of bodies but is found by an SS man, who kicks her in her left breast and pelvis. Earth is thrown over the bodies and there is a danger of being buried alive (claustrophobia was always one of her recurrent nightmares). Then she is found alive, raped and bayoneted in her vagina and left for dead. In all, a quarter of a million people are to die at Babi Yar.

The final chapter is mysterious—part life-after-death, part dream-of-Zion. It finds Lisa in Palestine with her stepson at an immigration camp. Freud, now infirm, is there too. She meets her mother, who "confesses" to her relationship with her uncle, and is eventually physically reunited with her by suckling at her breast.

This, in outline, is the story of **The White Hotel**. It is of course a tragedy: a melancholy, reflective, moving book that is well above average (not least in *profondeurs*) for a bestseller. Indeed, its bestseller status is something of a mystery: one doubts that it is solely a product of energetic marketing or the book's explicit sexual content, although these factors are no doubt part of the story. There are some flaws—for instance, Freud's case-history is rather "lighter" in style than the actual Freud's actual case-histories, and Lisa's imaginative writings seem rather too "professional" to be the convincing product of a neurotic opera singer—but the book "works" well because it raises questions both moral and interpretive.

The over-all "movement" of the book is from introspection to extrospection, from psychic realities to social ones, from, indeed, the province of depth psychology to that of social science. Thus, aside from the tragic ending, Lisa's revelation of her problems arising specifically from her status as a Jewess, with the anti-Semitic sailors (and so with her father) and with her first husband, suggest that *ethnic* factors, and not, as with Freud, purely sexual ones, enter into the etiology of her illness. (An implication might be that Freud too insufficiently recognized the relevance of his Jewish status and, further, of social variables generally.) In fact, on closer examination one finds that social realities do make brief entrances, in illuminating and usually ironic ways, in the earlier, introspective parts of the book. For instance, when Freud diagnoses anorexia nervosa from Lisa's meagre appearance, he has to add that few in Vienna at that time (1919) had enough to eat. Also, when able to make little progress in analysis with her, he has to note that "Partly the circumstances in which we worked were to blame; it was difficult to create an atmosphere of confidence, in an unheated room in winter, with patient and physician dressed in coats, mufflers and gloves." (A footnote informs us that fuel for heating and lighting was in desperately short supply after the war.) Further, speaking of her journal, Freud comments that "I was now dealing with an inflated imagination that knew no bounds, like the currency of those months—a suitcase of notes that would not buy a single loaf." Such incidental observations, of the world around patient and analyst, serve as a kind of ironic commentary on Freud's absorption with the psyche.

Secondly, we should note that, whatever her particularities, Lisa is a distinctly and recognizably *modern* character. Her life is like that of most modern heroes and heroines in fiction, and not least in best-sellers, in that it exhibits little *moral* unity, no over-all *telos* (as Marcuse says, an unfashionable but necessary concept), but is rather one of episodes and contingency and a prey to circumstance. In this it may well be true to much twentieth-century life as actually lived, and so she may be treated as a cultural type. She is a "homeless" heroine. Her constant train journeys, in reality and in dreams, serve as a metaphor of her rootlessness and she remarks at one point: "I'm not even sure where home is. I was born in the Ukraine but my mother was Polish. There's even a trace of Romany, I'm told! I've lived in Vienna for nearly twenty years. So you tell *me* what my homeland is."

She is essentially an unexceptional character, even if her end is exceptionally tragic (albeit shared eventually with six million others). Her only exceptionality is really her "hysteria" (and clairvoyance). Hence, although the horrors of Babi Yar enter as a savage climax, the main focus of the book is the mysterious "white hotel" manuscript and Freud's response to it and its author. With its lapses of logic and strong, almost hypnotic symbolic content, the "white hotel" journal reads like a dream. Freud in fact treats it as such and the author, it is said, wrote it during a "storm in her head." We thus have privileged entrée to Lisa's inner world and the book invites us to respond to Freud's understanding of that inner world. Freud's interpretive (and, one must add, moral) theory has, in the real world, proved attractive (if at first outré and surprising) to many people since it first appeared, and it is a merit of the book that it recognizes and expresses this enticing quality. But—as with unicorns or the Holy Grail or vitalism in the life sciences—attractive theories are not necessarily true theories. In fact, of Freudianism, as of any psychological theory, one may pose two central questions: is it valid and is it therapeutic (or otherwise useful)? These are independent criteria: the theory may possess either or both of these qualities. As for the former, there is, in fact, a dearth of rigorous evidence attesting to its validity and some clear evidence to the contrary: thus anthropological evidence strongly suggests that "Freudian conflicts" are *not* universal features of "the human condition" in the singular, and one careful study (by Alasdair MacIntyre) of the truth-claims of Freudianism concludes that it is "less well validated than witchcraft." Similarly with therapeutic value: studies using matched groups of patients, some undergoing Freudian analysis, others an entirely different treatment or no treatment at all, show no special therapeutic merit inheres in the Freudian approach. Indeed there is evidence that it may lead some patients to get worse (possibly, of course, for good Freudian reasons). Questions thus arise as to why psychoanalysis proceeds as if it were both well founded and therapeutic, and why it continues to be popular. These are questions for the sociology of knowledge, but part of the answer to the latter one may lie in Freudianism's particular appeal to a liberal individualist society, with the flattering "depth," drama, and apparent meaning it ascribes to the otherwise "homeless" individual's life. Modern America is just such a society, possibly more so than Britain (and certainly more committed to the personal therapeutic mode), and so one learns with interest that **The White Hotel** has been both better received by critics and more popular among the reading public in America than in Britain, its provenance.

We might read the book with these considerations in mind. But what *is* the meaning of the "white hotel" journal and poem? On this large theoretical issues hinge. For we may usefully compare Freudianism with the two other great idea-systems of the twentieth century: Christianity and Marxism. All three extend the frontiers of thought. All three are beguiling and have attracted singularly dedicated votaries. All three are polysemic, providing rich soil for sectarianism, yet also supplying a distinctive *nomos* that their adherents may inhabit. All three, notoriously, are "closed systems" in the sense that they offer specific reasons for the nonbelief or opposition of others. And each would propose a different interpretation of the "white hotel" sequence: to the Christian it might reveal the spirit's search for grace, even though carnality enters—hence, perhaps, the disasters in this Edenic "place without sin"; to the Marxist it would serve as an epiphenomenon of bourgeois false consciousness and "decadence"; and the psychoanalytic version—or one of them—is given in the book. How to decide between these claims? It seems one cannot, for the different traditions do not share a common epistemology. However, Freudianism and "common sense" at least accept a "sudden flash of insight" on the part of the patient to be a sign of the truth of an interpretation (a view that might be rejected by a thoroughgoing Marxist and is largely unavailable to, say, a Lévi-Straussian). So, for the record, we may note that this patient, Lisa, does accept Freud's overall exegesis of the womb-symbol as valid insight, even though she rejects his main diagnosis of her condition. But one might find this unsurprising in view of the fact that psychoanalysis was a popular way of viewing the world in middle-class Vienna in the 1920s and Lisa was presumably also impressed by Freud's distinguished status in the city. This leads one to note how modern social science would "interpret" the "white hotel." It would do so, of course, in terms of cultural rather than purely psychic symbols, detecting, for instance, an extension of the 1920s air of permissiveness (at least among the *beau monde*), the characters as disparate culture-types of the era, the early stirrings of feminism, and so on. Such an account may be partial, but it is surely just as "valid" as psychoanalysis's version—indeed, probably more so because less tied to contestable theory.

For the purposes of discussion, we have been treating the "white hotel" journal almost as though it were the real product of a real patient. It is, of course, part of a novel, a work of fiction—if serious and plausible fiction—and moreover a novel that is not written as a *roman à thèse* (and by no means as a "social novel"), but one emphasizing the ambiguities and opacity of a person's life. One of the repeated quotations of the book once used by Freud in a letter (without full approval), is from Herodotus: "The soul of man is a far country, which cannot be approached or explored." And a similar theme—of experience and events without interpretation—is found in other works of poetry and prose by D. M. Thomas. There are close parallels, for instance, with his first, award-winning novel, **The Flute Player** (1979). There the action takes place in a nameless city (and in a kind of "grey hotel") in a nameless country (which may be Russia) where social conditions are Spartan and the authorities are arbitrarily brutal and oppressive and then relatively permissive in cycles. That

book too has a central heroine, Elena, and recurrent themes of dreams, nightmares, and hallucinations, a sudden mysterious fire, a piece of psychoanalysis (by, ironically, a janitor, a retired psychologist), with which the "patient" pretends to agree, and it has the removal of Jews to a ghetto, which is "humanely" bombed because found riddled with bubonic plague. But in **The White Hotel** Thomas introduces the historical figure of Sigmund Freud (as Doctorow does, incidentally, in *Ragtime*) into a central interpretive place in the story and strives for accuracy in his portrayal of Freud, and so it is unlikely that he has *no* view himself of the validity of Freud's theory.

In fact, he comments in the preface on Freud "as discoverer of the great and beautiful modern myth of psychoanalysis. By myth, I mean a poetic, dramatic expression of a hidden truth; and in placing this emphasis, I do not intend to put into question the scientific validity of psychoanalysis." This somewhat inconsistent statement indicates at least a partial acceptance of Freud's views. But the book's story, perhaps *malgré* the author, does not in fact validate such views; nor, realistically one might say, does it show them to be therapeutic: the patient is not cured, even though she praises Freud for the self-insight she has gained. Rather, it shows, we would argue, that *social* categories are at least a necessary supplement to, if not the central means of, understanding Lisa's life and problems. Here ethnicity is crucial: much of her suffering is simply (and of course irrationally) because she is Jewish. There is also the changing social definition of sexuality: much is made of Freud's response to Lisa's writings as "obscene" and "pornographic." This is historically accurate. But were, say, Erica Jong to produce such writing today, as in effect she has done, neither would the response be so prudish nor would they necessarily be interpreted as "sublimations" of an excessive libido, as, indeed, symptoms of "illness." So a moral *and* interpretive change has occurred and we must view Lisa's analysis in terms of cultural history. Possibly such a historical approach applies to her symptoms too: reflecting on the fact that she has had sex with five men, including her first husband, she comments "How many women in Vienna were so promiscuous, outside the lowest class who sold their favours?" (*Tempora mutantur, et nos mutamur in illis.*)

What, then, of her brutal death at Babi Yar, how to "interpret" that event? Do we appeal to social or psychological categories, or both? Does this not validate Freud's discovery (or invention) of Thanatos, man's death instinct, and so confer a hidden unity on the book? We think not (whatever the author's intent here): for Thanatos is, in reified form, an essentially *self*-destructive impulse and to claim that Babi Yar, and like cases, shows it being "projected" or "externalized" on to others strikes the present writer as the most facile and evasive kind of reductionism. The broad truth is that Babi Yar and the other numerous *exempla horribilia* of the twentieth century—the Holocaust, the Gulag Archipelago, recent Cambodia, and so on—come to be treated by the mainstream of modern social science as mere "deviant" cases, anomalies, caesuras from the normal, "messy" passages to be tucked away from consciousness. What we perhaps need is a sociology of bestiality that would take them as central and, in an ideal world, would help prevent their recurrence. In the case of D. M. Thomas, Babi Yar leads him to turn away from Freud (and social science) to reflect, with Herodotus, on the opacity of man. He comments on the heap of bodies as follows: "Most of the dead were poor and illiterate. But every single one of them had dreamed dreams, seen visions and had amazing experiences, even the babes in arms (perhaps especially the babes in arms). Though most of them had never lived outside the Podol slum, their lives and histories were as rich and complex as Lisa Erdman-Berenstein's. If a Sigmund Freud had been listening and taking notes from the time of Adam, he would still not fully have explored even a single group, even a single person." To which one might add that there is, in retrospect, a particular poignant irony to Freud's valediction to Lisa after her analysis: "I told her she was cured of everything but life, so to speak."

If, as we believe, **The White Hotel** is to be recommended, it is because it threads together social and psychological issues, and moral and interpretive ones, in a particularly rich and subtle way, and because these elements neatly culminate in Lisa's surreal arrival in Palestine—for this is surely the social equivalent of Freud's womb-symbol in his interpretation of the "white hotel." The comparison is particularly apt because the country—that is, modern Israel—in actuality consciously recognizes and seeks to re-create the distant ethnic past of the Bible, while at the same time seeking to establish a secure "homeland" (physical and Bergerian) for the future. It is the natural endpoint of Lisa's wanderings, the social solution to her maladies, and, of course, the resolution of her ethnic identity. "Wonderful healing goes on over here," says her mother, and among those to be healed is Sigmund Freud, the healer himself.

The Palestine sequence, then, deftly closes the dialectic between the social and the psychological in the story. But there is another element too: the parapsychological. Lisa has correct premonitions of the deaths of Freud's daughter and grandson and of a friend's death, among others, and the possibility is raised that her "hysterical" pains are not, as with Freud, symptoms of the past but of the future, socio-somatic stigmata-in-advance as it were, for they occur at the exact sites of her eventual assault and mutilation at Babi Yar. And the "thanatic" elements in her "white hotel" writings, her desire "to poison the well of her pleasure at its source" as Freud puts it, may also be seen as an inchoate premonition of Babe Yar; indeed, in retrospect, her whole inner life may be regarded (or recognized) as an unconscious preparation for the horror of its end. All this may be fortuitous or it may be the deepest *mysterium* of all: the book, wisely, leaves the matter open. Lisa has her premonitions in dreams and the true "meaning" of dreams, it seems, despite Freud's confidence in his own codex, will ever remain epistemologically opaque. (And biological reductionism will not resolve the issue.

Even if we could, say, monitor individually all 12 million million cells that comprise the human brain and find out which ones are being activated when a person dreams and then correlate this with recalled dream content, this would still not wholly and incontestably decode the true "meaning" of the dream. Ditto with other physiological indices.) So cultural relativism has particular force here, and we may cite as examples the acceptance of dreams as prophetic by the ancient Greeks (though not Aristotle) and the Old Testament, the curious fact that in Borneo a man who dreams his wife has committed adultery has the right to ask her father to take her back, the Iroquois idea that dreams are prescriptive, to be enacted in waking hours, and the modern traditions of existentialism and behaviorism to which dreams are largely an irrelevancy bereft of meaning. Between these, and other, interpretations one must make one's choice and so it is with **The White Hotel.** It is indeed the multilayered, polysemic character of the book that is remarkable in the final analysis; and the underlying motivation of the author, primarily a poet, is, we suggest, a search for the epistemological status of poetic (or "literary") insight. Meanwhile, those still looking for the moral "message" of the book need look no further than its opening text. It is from W. B. Yeats: "We had fed the heart on fantasies, / The Heart's grown brutal from the fare; / More substance in our enmities / Than in our love. . . ."

Lore Dickstein (review date 23 April 1983)

SOURCE: "Elaborate and Perverse," in *Nation,* April 23, 1983, pp. 516-18.

[*In the following review, Dickstein offers unfavorable evaluation of* Ararat.]

The reader opens **Ararat** with a mixture of expectations. D. M. Thomas's third novel in four years, it comes in the wake of the literary and commercial success of **The White Hotel,** and the more equivocal reception accorded his translations of Pushkin's poems, **The Bronze Horseman,** which Simon Karlinsky and others have called a plagiarism of other translators. While **Ararat** will do little to dispel the doubts that hang over Thomas's literary reputation, it may help clarify what he considers to be authorship.

The question here is not that of plagiarism but of literary license and influence. It is axiomatic that translators rely on the inspiration of their original authors, but Thomas seems to have based most of his *fiction* on this premise. As a novelist, he has taken the liberties of a translator, catapulting his books on the backs of other, more brilliant writers. In **The White Hotel,** he cited his sources openly, although not the extent of his borrowings. His fictional case study of the libidinous Lisa Erdman cleverly mimics Freud's writing style, but his evocation of the massacre at Babi Yar uses Anatoli Kuznetsov's *Babi Yar* with a directness for which it was criticized in England. In the acknowledgments to **The Flute Player** (1979), Thomas notes, "Quotations ascribed in this novel to two of the fictional characters are from: Akhmadulina, Akhmatova, Baudelaire, Chapman, Dante, Emily Dickinson, Eliot, Frost, Lorca, Mandelstam, Nadezhda Mandelstam, Pasternak, Sylvia Plath, Pushkin, Rilke, Anne Sexton, Shakespeare, Gaspara Stampa, Tsvetaeva, and Yeats"—a literary pantheon which makes for some striking dialogue in an otherwise undistinguished novel. The author's note in *Ararat* mentions similar debts: the Russian poets Pushkin and Blok; the Armenian poets Nareg and Emin; the historian of Armenia Christopher Walker.

What Thomas does with his source material, how he creates a "new" work out of the works of others, is *Ararat*'s subject as well as its method. This is a novel of improvisations, a set of variations on the theme of improvisation. Reading it is like being caught in one of those elaborate and perverse boxwood mazes favored by English landscape architects. It is intricately designed, all appearances and cleverness, yet ultimately lacking in rationale. The path keeps turning in on itself; the markings are confusingly similar; the reader exits impressed but reeling.

Bracketed by a prologue and an epilogue, *Ararat* is presented from the perspective of one Sergei Rozanov, a fictional Russian poet well known for his inventiveness. Rozanov is spending the night with a student, but disenchanted with the woman's fawning admiration and bored sexually, he spins out the thread of the novel: Three writers—a Russian, an American and an Armenian—each agree to improvise a story on a common theme, improvisation. "It's just a game," Rozanov tells the student, discounting his facility "like doing crosswords."

There are three main stories within Rozanov's improvisations, two of which lean heavily on Pushkin's unfinished prose-verse work, *Egyptian Nights,* which itself is about the art of literary improvisation. Rozanov begins with the Russian, a depressed and feverish poet, Victor Surkov, who is on an ocean voyage to the United States. On board ship are an assortment of female Olympic athletes, some of whom end up in Surkov's bed, and an ancient-mariner type named Finn, a spectral figure who claims to have been involved in every atrocity of the twentieth century: the Armenian massacre in 1915, Babi Yar, Dachau, Buchenwald and more. Finn is always eagerly plucking at Surkov's sleeve, interrupting the poet's fantasies and sexual activities with graphic tales of barbarity. As in **The White Hotel,** this intermingling of sex and death creates a heightened, surreal atmosphere in which eroticism and torture, orgasms and dying, blend into one another.

In one of the many shifts of identity in the novel, Surkov imagines he is Pushkin writing *Egyptian Nights.* Thomas's translation of Pushkin's fragment is included here in its entirety. At the last line, Surkov as Pushkin is interrupted by a visitor; this is a wonderful leap into the past, to that moment when Pushkin put down his pen. "It is irritating to be interrupted like this," Pushkin/Surkov/Rozanov/Thomas remarks, "just at the point where inspiration failed before."

Written in 1835, Pushkin's *Egyptian Nights* is the story of a Russian poet, Charsky, who is visited unexpectedly by an Italian *improvvisatore,* a sort of wandering poetic entertainer. Penniless and down on his luck, the Italian asks Charsky to set up a recitation for him at a wealthy home. Impressed by the Italian's skill at composing on command a verse on the theme of poetic inspiration, Charsky agrees. At the recitation, a number of topics are submitted by the audience; the one selected by lot is "Cleopatra and her lovers." The *improvvisatore,* in verse, tells the story of how Cleopatra agrees to make love to three men, but the price for enjoying the Queen's favors is death. (Cleopatra's "bed of love and death" would be of obvious appeal to Thomas.)

In what is the best writing in this novel, Surkov picks up where Pushkin left off in *Egyptian Nights* and completes the *improvvisatore*'s verse without losing a beat. In Surkov's completed version, Cleopatra's third lover, never identified in the Pushkin, is her son by her brother Ptolemy. (This little piece of incestuous pornography is not beyond the imaginative scope of Pushkin, who wrote a scandalous poem, "The Gavriliad," in which the Virgin Mary, frustrated by the lack of sexual attention from Joseph, makes love to the angel Gabriel, God and Satan.) The *improvvisatore*'s poem completed, Surkov resumes the narrative of *Egyptian Nights;* the various turns and permutations of his plot, which mirror actual events in Pushkin's life, are a delightful sleight of hand. After this bravura performance the rest of *Ararat* pales considerably.

Surkov, dissatisfied with the way he has ended Pushkin's tale, starts again and concludes *Egyptian Nights* in just a few pages of prose. The second improvisation also uses facts from Pushkin's life, but this time the story seems arbitrary and contrived. The absurdist ending, in which the *improvvisatore* is beheaded during the Decembrist uprising (an event Pushkin fortuitously missed), feels as if the author—Thomas, Rozanov, Surkov?—had tired of the game and decided to finish his hero off quickly.

Rozanov then presents another version of Surkov's trip to America. In this utterly banal story, Surkov flies from Russia to Kennedy International Airport, where he is greeted by his hostess, an Armenian sculptor, and a goon squad of reporters. The press's inane questions—"Why do Russian poets have such good memories?" "How do you feel about being middle-aged?"—are matched by Surkov's crass answers. (One utterance by this thoroughly unlikable character, however, fairly leaps from the page. In response to a question about a novelist's supposed plagiarism, Surkov replies: "All art is collaboration, a translation if you like. But plagiarism is a different matter.")

The rest of Surkov's story and the remaining pages of *Ararat,* which, as far as I can tell, are entirely of Thomas's invention, are disappointing and lifeless. The dialogue is flat; the plot meanders aimlessly. Thomas seems to do his best work in collaboration with other authors. Rozanov's two other improvisers—the American and the Armenian—

are barely realized and are devoid of interest or motivation. The occasional allusions to Armenia and its dominant geographic feature, Mount Ararat, seem intended to hint at broader associations—a destroyed country, a people with a "problem" whose "solution" was used by Hitler as a paradigm—but they have no apparent relevance to the novel's form or content.

In *The White Hotel,* the variations of Lisa Erdman's story, presented in verse, in prose narrative and in case history echo hauntingly throughout the novel. The telling and retelling of Lisa's story is what gives the novel coherence. In *Ararat,* once Thomas leaves Pushkin, his prime source of inspiration, the writing seems tossed off, unpolished, like incomplete entries in a journal. It is as if knowing he has captivated us with his cleverness, Thomas holds us in contempt for our admiration.

Mary F. Robertson (essay date Winter 1984)

SOURCE: "Hystery, Herstory, History: 'Imagining the Real' in Thomas's *The White Hotel,*" in *Contemporary Literature,* Vol. 25, No. 4, Winter, 1984, pp. 452-77.

[*In the following essay, Robertson examines Thomas's effort to reconcile postmodern literary aesthetics, myth, and psychoanalysis with the horrific realities of twentieth-century history and female identity in* The White Hotel.]

The proper relation of art's forms to social facts has been a pressing problem for artists in this century, and so also has been the relation of psychoanalysis to political explanations of human behavior. For all their acute sensitivity to the society around them, the great modernist artists tended to give us survival by aesthetic escape into a contemplative and esoteric realm of imaginative creation. Yeats, for example, who is invoked in the epigraph of D. M. Thomas's *The White Hotel,* often worried about his poetry's responsibility for actual destruction, but he always reaffirmed, though with increasing self-irony, that the purged fantasies of art were his most adequate response to the brutal fantasies ruining the social and political life of Ireland. Likewise Freud personally experienced discrimination as a Jew both in the matter of appointment to a medical professorship and when he fled the Nazis to England, yet his psychoanalytic theory privileges intrapsychic fantasies as the source of sickness in civilization; finally he did not put much stock in social facts as the cause of neuroses and psychoses. Modernist art and psychoanalysis in its classical form share the prejudice that significant reality is to be found not in empirical fact but in a complex inference drawn from mediating and disguising signs. They do not believe that it is possible to tell the significant story "straight," the story, for example, of a person's identity or a genocidal campaign. Both typically translate from a temporal series of events into a conceptual structure of explanation which is at least one remove from empirical facts.

The postmodern artistic and historical temper is supposedly discontent with this consolation outside of history, but modernism in fact engendered two very different species of postmodern artistic reaction. On the one hand, certain "ludic" artists, or "surfictionists,"[1] dissolve the boundary of difference between sign and fact by asserting, as the modernists did not, that what usually passes as "fact" is as much a sign or "fiction" as anything else; therefore, the writer can playfully incorporate facts on the same plane of significance as fictional details into a work whose *raison d'être* is its own self-admiring game-playing rather than traditional objects of representation.[2] Whatever satirical force and social resonance this might produce is secondary to the self-reflexive purpose. Clearly this postmodern reaction is more an extension of modernism's aestheticist escapism than it cares to acknowledge. (However, the surfictionists' claim that their game-playing is also "historical" might imply that even they wish to be seen as incorporating the morality of truth to history into their art in their own way.) On the other hand, certain writers, like Saul Bellow or John Gardner, reassert the value of the representational, insisting that history's brutal fantasies result in part from art's elitist abdication of dialogue with the facts in power. If the distinction between fact and fantasy is not emphasized in this mode, it is only because art represents important social and moral content through transparent, not refractory, signs. Sometimes, as in Doris Lessing's late work, "fantasy" is given a prominent place only because the author is genuinely convinced of our untapped or evolving psychic and prophetic powers to extend the sense of the "real." Ultimately this realistic fiction is traditional enough to uphold our commonsense understanding that there is an important moral distinction between aesthetic games and worldly facts, between sanity and schizophrenia, even between good and evil. It vehemently resists the absorption of reality into the autonomous structure of art, just as Marxists resist reduction of social ills to matter for the psychiatrist's couch.

The White Hotel is an interesting test case for whether, and how, certain serious artists of the late twentieth century are able to handle authentically the inherited problem of the relation between fact and fantasy, the empirical and the mediated. This novel seems to have touched a cultural nerve in the way that books that are both best sellers and respected works of art do. I suggest it does so because it embodies the excruciating predicament facing artists as legatees of the lunatic facts of recent history, of literary modernism, and of psychoanalysis. The book does not provide a solution to this predicament, though it inherently attempts one, nor does it provide much consolation, but it does take the measure of the dilemma more thoroughly and openly than most works of recent fiction.

The White Hotel[3] opens with a series of letters among members of Sigmund Freud's psychoanalytic circle. In one letter from 1920, we learn that Freud is treating a young woman, Lisa Erdman, for "sexual hysteria" and that she has just given him an erotic fantasy poem full of the most blatant sexual imagery. The scene of this poem is an imaginary white resort hotel; the poem is written between the staves of a score of *Don Giovanni*. Freud of course counsels detachment and understanding toward this material. In the last letter of the series, written eleven years later than the others, we learn that Freud is about to publish Lisa's case history.

Next, in the first of many abrupt formal shifts in the novel, the long pornographic poem is presented to the reader, followed by another chapter that is simply an expanded prose version of the same imaginings. This version is Lisa's response to Freud's request that she annotate the poem during her therapy. In a third shift of form, we are then given Freud's case history of Lisa's "hysteria" and treatment, including his byzantine interpretive tracking of the meaning behind her symptoms. He concludes that her hysteria originated when, as a child, she accidentally witnessed her mother, her aunt, and her uncle making love on board her uncle's yacht. He also believes she has been sexually frigid with her husband because of this early trauma and because she is an unacknowledged lesbian. Subsequent to the therapy this woman resumes her musical career, which had been affected by her disease, and is able to function with only mild, undebilitating recurrences of her symptoms of breast and ovary pains.

In a fourth shift, the novel presents a chapter in the mode of mimetic realism that follows Lisa from 1929, eleven years after her therapy, through 1936, when she becomes an opera singer, marries a Russian Jew, and adopts his son, Kolya. In this section we have again a series of letters, this time between Freud and Lisa as he seeks her permission to publish her case history. At this later time, Lisa's reaction to her past therapy contains startling revelations of information she had withheld from Freud. The most important is that, as a girl and a daughter of a Jewish grain merchant in Odessa, she had been accosted in the street by sailors from her father's merchant ship and taken to the ship where, as she says, "they spat on me, threatened to burn my breasts with their cigarettes, used vile language. . . . forced me to commit acts of oral sex with them, saying all I was good for, as a dirty Jewess, was to—But you'll guess the expression they used. Eventually they let me go. But from that time I haven't found it easy to admit to my Jewish blood. I've gone out of my way to hide it" (p. 188). Ashamed of this episode and, more, of the fact that the memory of it had made her aroused, she had soon developed "asthma"—one of the symptoms of her "hysteria." Lisa also now reveals that her frigidity with her husband, whose "family were horribly anti-Semitic," was caused by her knowledge that "He said he loved me; but if he had known I had Jewish blood he would have hated me" (p. 190). Lisa explains to Freud that she had withheld this information out of delicacy about Freud's own Jewishness. On the other hand, she totally rejects these events as an explanation of her breast and ovary pains when she was a young adult. She insists that they were organic at the same time she tells Freud that in her therapy she "didn't always wish to talk about the past," being "more interested in what was happening to me then, and . . . in

the future. In a way you *made* me become fascinated by my mother's sin. . . . I don't believe for one moment *that* had anything to do with my being crippled with pain" (pp. 191-92).

Freud replies to her revelations:

> I prefer to go ahead with the case study as it stands, despite all imperfections. I am willing, if you will permit, to add a postscript in which your reservations are presented and discussed. I shall feel compelled to make the point that the physician has to trust his patient, quite as much as the patient must trust the physician.

> I call to mind a saying of Heraclitus: "The soul of man is a far country, which cannot be approached or explored." It is not altogether true, I think; but success must depend on a fair harbour opening in the cliffs. (pp. 195-96)

But of course, psychoanalysis has also always claimed the ability to penetrate masks and defenses, and so Freud comes out of this looking considerably less authoritative than when the book started.

Lisa's protestations about her pains and the relevance of her remark about her concern for the future are further vindicated when, in the novel's next and fifth chapter, the story takes her to Kiev in 1941, where, because of her widowed fostering of her Jewish stepson, she is forced into the Podol ghetto and then marched along with the other Jews there to be shot at Babi Yar. She escapes the shots and falls into the huge pit full of bodies, surviving just long enough to be finished off by the bayonet rape of a soldier checking that everyone is dead. Thirty-three thousand people died in Babi Yar on September 29-30, 1941, and Thomas concludes this chapter by explicitly remarking on the individual complexity and dignity of each of them, explaining to the reader what happened to the pit full of bodies, and generalizing such demonic horror in relation to the Holocaust exterminations elsewhere. He closes the chapter by saying, "But all this had nothing to do with the guest, the soul, the lovesick bride, the daughter of Jerusalem" (p. 253).

In a final astonishing modal shift we are then given the sixth chapter, "The Camp," which is a fantasy written in a realistic mode. In this *tour de force* Thomas imagines Lisa, Freud, her mother, and many others in the previous cast of characters, alighting after a train journey into a transit camp which has simultaneously the sensory reality of Palestine after World War II and the surreality of an imaginary place after death. It is not beatific here; people still bear the marks of their worldly wounds—Freud's cancerous jaw, Lisa's limp, the British soldier's one arm. It is a place of healing and compassion, but also a place where, as in Lisa's earlier fantasy of the white hotel, sexuality is not regulated by formal ties like marriage nor decorum respected in such matters as when Lisa drinks milk from her mother's breast. The tone is tentative and hopeful and deliberately privileges Lisa's optimism. The book ends with Lisa realizing that her pelvis and breast have not hurt that day, and, in fact, the book's last word is "happy."

Placing itself deliberately at the conceptual crossroads of all the contending factions mentioned above, **The White Hotel** takes huge risks. First, it risks the accusation that it sensationalizes both Freudian sexual themes and the pornography of Nazi violence. The charge of pornographic sensationalism is not hard to refute superficially; for Lisa Erdman is depicted overall with dignity and subjective empathy rather than reduced to an object from start to finish. Even the more subtly disquieting possibility that she collaborates in her own reduction to a psychoanalytic object[4] is refutable because the story shows her moving beyond Freud's sphere of influence and even ensnaring him in a huge interpretive trap by withholding evidence that his psychoanalytic acumen could not reach. She progresses from a pitiable "hysteric" to a competent, brave, and independent woman, and there is at least the possibility that she does it in spite of Freud rather than because of him.

The charge of using sensational and even "sacred" facts for the sake of the novel as an art work, a use that some would consider a deeper pornography, is, however, more difficult to refute. When Yeats, in what Thomas uses as the epigraph of this novel, says, "We had fed the heart on fantasies / The heart's grown brutal from the fare," he meant the Irish freedom fighters' crazy fantasies of fratricide and rebellion rather than his own poetic fantasies that were the "responsible" antidote. But by the end of Thomas's novel, we cannot be sure that the epigraph has not been turned against itself—meaning that the novel perhaps criticizes the modernist aesthetic and the psychoanalytic "solutions" as fantasies contributing to social brutality. Yet this is only speculation, since I hope to show that reading this novel as a reassertion of literary realism entails even more serious questions.

The problem this novel poses of the relation of social fact to aesthetic image is not merely one of literary history. One cannot read the grave and terrible penultimate chapter, "The Sleeping Carriage," which describes the heroine's bayonet rape and death in the pit at Babi Yar, without thinking it intends to bear historical witness to the Holocaust. If nowhere else in the book, this chapter alone would seem to argue that Thomas renounces the surfictionist approach in favor of representing facts. That is, he seems to take up the challenge described by the psychiatrist, Robert Jay Lifton, who, as a result of work with survivors from Hiroshima, the German camps, and Vietnam, believes it is essential to amend the Freudian model of the psyche from one of repression of sexual urges to anesthesia from historical trauma, and to recognize the crucial role of artists in enabling our race's psychic and physical survival. Lifton believes that contemporary culture has succumbed to "psychic numbness" as a result of peripheral or direct awareness of all such atrocities and that psychiatrists only intensify the problem by searching

for familial or intrapsychic origins when the causes really lie in political and cultural fact. Lifton believes that such numbing results in "desymbolization," an inability to reckon with and master psychologically the apocalyptic realities of the contemporary world:

> The problem is less repression of death than an impairment in the general capacity to create viable forms around it, [to bring] imagination to bear upon the unpalatable existential-historical truths, to expand the limits of that imagination on behalf of species survival . . . to overcome psychic numbing and . . ., in Martin Buber's words, to "imagine the real."[5]

In answer to those who believe that the Nazi atrocities should never be depicted in imaginative literature because one should not try to speak the unspeakable (and some object to **The White Hotel** on this ground),[6] Lifton replies that it is necessary to do the vital symbolic work enabling us to face, not only our individual death, but the imminent threat to our species. For Lifton, artists who brave such subjects touch the "mythic or formative zone of the psyche"; for, "only by creating, maintaining and breaking down and recreating viable form are we capable of experiencing vitality, and in that sense we may say that form equals life."[7] A handful of writers have taken up this challenge—Lifton discusses Camus, Vonnegut, and Günter Grass. **The White Hotel** enters this company, although it makes its task more difficult by avoiding totally the satirical bitterness that accounts for much of the energy in the work of other writers cited by Lifton.

What does Thomas's book reveal about the difficulty now of revitalizing the cultural imagination of holocaust through creative form? The predicament might be summarized thus: To "imagine the real" in our times would involve a rejection of modernism's "ritual despair" or "Olympian detachment" in autonomous forms[8] and a reassertion of the mimetic mode which requires that we respect the resistance of some facts to absorption into the purposes of self-reflexive structures. In a time when avant-garde formalism dominates high art, the really bracing gesture might be to describe the historically real with imaginative empathy governed by factual precision. Therefore, Lifton's prescription about "breaking down and creating form" should not imply modernist or surfictional escapism. However, if one does no more than portray the brutalities in a pseudo-factual style,[9] one implicitly risks reinforcing brutishness—as if to admit that the free play of imagination and the limited optimism of psychoanalytic theory are mooted by the sordid spectacles of powerful fact. The artist cannot return to modernism's transcendence of life through ironic and "despairing" art, nor the psychoanalyst to his world-renouncing myths, but neither can they adopt the moral and psychological pessimism implied by mere accurate description.

To put the predicament this way may strike some as too much either/or thinking. Instead, we should perhaps speak of a "dialectical" relation between fact and imagination. This is a familiar critical stratagem, but I think it will not do for novels like *The White Hotel* that formally pose precisely the question of whether there *can* be a dialectic between imagined detail and historical facts as horrible as the massacre at Babi Yar. In terms of Lifton's task of finding "life" for the species through form, what must be demonstrated is the ability of art—and in this novel, also psychoanalysis—to affect potently the course historical facts will take, whereas in such hopeful formulas critics too easily slide into the term "dialectic" as a refuge from this demonstration. The images in such works must seem more than compensatory, evasive, or merely decorative (as the modernists' artifices often were) in order to fulfill the moral and psychological function Lifton envisions for them. It is hard to believe that Yeats's "artifice of eternity," as described in "Sailing to Byzantium," would qualify.

Again, this issue is not confined to discussions of the role of art toward brutal facts. An observer of a recent conference that gathered survivors of the Holocaust at Yale to refute the challenge that the event never happened remarks that even there it was difficult to concentrate on the facts:

> Much of the . . . conference, in fact, was devoted to theorizing. From time to time a conference participant made a plea for memory itself—for its preservation and persistence in pure and unexplained form. But the relentless purity of memory was hard to sustain, despite the dedication of the participants to the problem of the Holocaust, despite their devotion to clinical history, and despite the fact that a number of them were survivors themselves . . . with Holocaust memories of their own. Psychological theory repeatedly intervened, studies were cited, cases were presented, and intelligence was applied. The tragic irony of the conference's limited focus was never articulated . . . the psychological damage that was inflicted upon those survivors, incomprehensibly brutal and massive as it was, was still less compelling a problem of human experience than the physical exterminations themselves.
>
> To be sure, the exterminations could not be reversed, while psychiatrists could at least hope to help, if not cure, those survivors whose lives had been so defiled and whose memories so contaminated. . . . Still, in the end, it was the reality of history rather than the god of psychoanalytic theory that brooded over the conference, at the highest level. And it was that reality that drove out the theory when, in the midst of it all, videotaped interviews from the archives of the Holocaust Survivors Film Project were shown, interviews of survivors talking not about Freud but about the black and lifeless sun of Auschwitz. That talk was about memory, its life and its death, and it stunned the group into reverent submission.[10]

Surely the readers of the chapter on Babi Yar in *The White Hotel* will agree that it portrays a "reality that drives out the [psychoanalytic] theory" which dominates the first part of the book. The rhetorical force of that chapter is greater than that of the rest of the novel put together. A hush settles over one's reading like that of the stunned conferees. And the force seems to depend a great deal precisely on that simple clear-sighted difference between fact and fantasy accepted by the modernists but rejected by the surfictionists. Yet considering the novel as a whole, we cannot be certain; fantasy, art, and theory remain in

problematic relation to history. Let us see how the problem is figured by tracing the book's rhetorical process.

For the first half of the novel, *The White Hotel* seems nothing so much as a piece of surfictionist formalist adventurism. Our reading displaces rapidly from letters to and from Freud, through a "primary process" erotic fantasy poem written by Lisa, on toward her prose version of the same events, and then to Freud's case history of Lisa's "hysteria." Thus we speculate that we might have in hand another of those verbal artifacts designed to show the arbitrariness of forms and signs as does fiction by contemporary writers like Borges or Robbe-Grillet or Coover. The freewheeling manipulation of forms seems to say that such "realistic" content can be emptied of its ordinary significance and expropriated for use in the symbolistic verbal structure that is this book. This expropriation is an especially daring move with something as supposedly objective as a case history. The construction foregrounds the forms themselves and emphasizes the gaps, as if to say that there are many ways of "writing" the reality of a person, none more or less authentic, and that the reality of a person is always "written," that is, mediated by an arbitrary discourse. The section of post cards from the different hotel guests recounting differently the same events depicts synecdochally this arbitrariness of authority in written signs. To the rather stale Faulknerian point about differential perceptions of reality is added here the typical postmodern point that such perceptions by consciousness are greatly and differently conditioned by the media through which they are expressed.[11] The first part of the novel seems to confirm the often touted idea that every piece of "fact" is always already a "fiction."

The subject matter of the Freudian hunt for the source of Lisa's hysteria seems an especially convenient peg on which to hang such a surfictionist performance, since for the classical Freudian these symptoms are signs of some deeper reality to be penetrated by always tenuous interpretive moves. The facts are not empirically available, but must be reconstructed, just as any narrative would need to be, from this displacing series of forms that Thomas uses. The game-playing spirit of psychoanalytic sleuthing correlates well with the game-playing of the novelist's art and the reader's fun. In this sense, quite apart from themes, Thomas and Freud are kindred spirits.

From early in the book when Lisa is Freud's patient, the reader feels her presence as a conventionally represented character because Freud and his correspondents discuss her that way in the opening letters; yet chapter four, in which Thomas for the first time begins the narrative account of the later period of her life, brings the reader up short because the formal emphasis shifts inexplicably from the different written forms that mediate Lisa's story to a narrative of the story itself. The earlier matter now becomes just "Lisa's past," and she assumes interest as a subject rather than as an object of someone else's discourse. This shift to something nearer Lisa's own conscious self-understanding is what prevents the book from being a pornographic exploitation, but the principal effect of chapter four is to show the reader that Freud's cleverness was almost entirely off the mark. He had interpreted her hysteria as a fixation upon a girlhood fantasy in which she had witnessed her mother and aunt having intercourse with her uncle; out of polite concern for Freud's own Jewishness, Lisa had withheld from him the crucial facts about the trauma she suffered as a half-Jewess. Still, had the novel ended here, we might easily have seen this chapter as a culmination of the surfictionist view of facts I mentioned above. That is, Lisa's correction of Freud could read as one more demonstration that mere facts do not exist undistorted by interpretation. This would have had the main satirical effect of warning the reader against overweening confidence in one's theory and especially against the misplaced confidence of the psychoanalytic model, but it would not have damaged the surfictionist theory that "all fact is fiction."

It is only with the introduction of the special subject matter of the massacre at Babi Yar that the book seems to swerve into an argument for the weightiness of the documentary discourse. The choice of subject here has the effect of making all the previous psychoanalytic sleuthing and artistic game-playing seem at the least morally frivolous, if indeed they are not somehow more directly responsible for history's nightmare. No longer are we left with Lisa's private joke on Dr. Freud and thus an affectionate swipe at psychoanalysis; we are now given a scene in which the previous mistaken interpretation of symptoms is shown to have dire public consequences. That does not mean that Freud's failure to penetrate to the ethnic trauma behind Lisa's hysteria is a direct cause of her being killed in Babi Yar. She might not have missed being sacrificed with her Jewish stepson even had she discussed the "Jewish problem" with Freud. Rather, Thomas reveals that the prescient "cause" of Lisa's "hysterical" breast and ovary pains was her premonition of something that would happen later to her in historical fact when the soldier gored her body in those places in the pit full of dying Jews at Babi Yar. Thomas seems to be arguing that Freud's larger failure to put himself in dialogue with real history is symptomatic of the failure of prominent analytical languages to make the world better by understanding what happens in history. Although Freud's failures are always treated gently in the novel, the Babi Yar chapter makes him, and implicitly anyone too caught up in such a tautological metalanguage, seem evasive of historical responsibility. In a letter early in the book, Ferenczi writes that while Jung was telling Freud about some "peat-bog corpses" in northern Germany that were "prehistoric men, mummified by the effect of the humic acid in the bog water, . . . Freud burst out several times: 'Why are you so concerned with these corpses?' . . . [and] slipped off his chair in a faint" (p. 5). When it comes, the action in the pit at Babi Yar—later filled by the Nazis with water to make a bog to hide the murders—seems designed as a brusque rejoinder: "Because, Dr. Freud, they are still there in the actual history of our own time. One should not shrink from it."

The moment of Lisa's rape in the pit takes the reader's breath away. It is difficult to descend from such a rhetorical peak of rapt horror, and many readers are annoyed that Thomas did not end there. What could possibly be left to say after such a stark reconstruction of just one of our century's many horrible facts? The best "imagination" of such facts might be only to render them accurately. To make them "heroic" in any way, to attempt consolation, might be a betrayal. How can the artist's free imagination play "dialectically" with such facts? Evidently, Thomas thinks it can because he finishes the novel in a place set beyond history, "The Camp." Since this chapter's place and action have no mimetic relation to history, the reader will treat the chapter as an example of the discourse of poetry or literature, the discourse of the poet's imagination. Up to that point realism had effaced or written over the formal games of the book, but in view of the final chapter we now must ask whether Thomas means us to have read the realistic chapter as "just one more possible discourse," no more compelling than the others, and inserted just before the poet's own special "word" on the events and meaning of Lisa's history. Has Thomas resorted to the tired idealism of the modernists in the face of history? Can the material, historical horrors really have nothing to do with the spirit and soul?

Before exploring further the problem of the book's rhetoric in "imagining the real," we must link the discussion more explicitly to the other equally major question of the book— the question of Woman. This is not just parallel to the problem of history's nightmare as embodied in the Holocaust. The two questions are deeply joined in this book, and we can justify Thomas's having joined them for at least two reasons. First, a literary reason external to this novel: woman and Holocaust victims are liable to a similar fate when portrayed in intellectual or literary history. Both tend to be pictured either as enmired or enslaved in a positivistic series of actions unassimilable to any ethos or ideology moving the real affairs and dominant spiritual preoccupations of the world, or as so sublime (in the case of the Holocaust, so sublimely terrible) that there is, again, no basis on which to join them to historically powerful ideologies or moralities. Lisa Erdman, while typical of her century, is not representative of the ideas that have dominated it. So also the Holocaust, if wrongly portrayed, appears marginal to the rest of our significant human experience. Woman as traditionally portrayed offers no image to emulate in significant action;[12] at best she inspires men in history or poetry to gather their own quite different energies in her name. She offers no such image because she has no discourse traditionally associated with public power. When not vilified or condescended to for her un-ideological, pragmatic existence at the level of daily facts, she is praised as a muse figure—*die ewige Weibliche*—in both poetry and history. While substantively this is not the problem of the Holocaust witness, formally it is homologous; the same gap between the raw "banality of evil" in the camps and the sublime resonance of the victims' suffering plagues writers who try to speak about it with meaning for the rest of our civilized world. How to make the fate of a woman or a camp inmate significant in the terms of the mainstream of civilization? For contemporary culture the oppression of women in history might seem cognate with the oppression of ethnic groups in the twentieth century; certainly there is often even a common psychological and physical brutality. But even if the Jews were more brutally treated in the Holocaust than is the fate of woman, the important thing both share is the attempt by dominant patriarchal cultures to make their sufferings seem marginal to the history of the human race, to make their historically and materially particular fates seem unrepresentative of the wider culture's depraved condition. The stories of these Jews and these women ought to matter in their representativeness as the stories of male heroes have. But *The White Hotel* shows that, although Lisa lived and suffered the social problems of her time, she had no way to speak of them or act with historical effectiveness; she was a Cassandra in the prophecy of her body's symptoms, for hysteria is not a recognized public discourse.

The second reason that the question of woman and the question of the Holocaust are inextricable is therefore internal to the novel. One of its strongest *données* is that this woman as a representative human being might have, probably does have, powers that could redeem history's horrors if she were only really heard in the civilized and material world. The revelations that, first, Freud had misinterpreted the cause of her "hysterical" sexual frigidity with her husband and, second, that the pains in her breast and ovary foreshadowed what would happen to her at Babi Yar, while "magical" in realistic terms, are surely meant to show symbolically that her discourse is more attuned to historical reality than the theories of Freud or any other political and moral metalanguage that could not foresee the coming of racist fascism. Her femaleness is thus indispensable to the theme of the book; this novel could not have had a male hero. Thomas suggests that woman has a kind of knowledge the world could use. Here is the chance to portray a female hero's effectiveness in the real terms of history. Yet Thomas lets the chance go by; he finds no way to portray woman's knowledge in other than stereotypically mythic terms or to make her death seem portentous for figures in power. Thus, Thomas does not rectify through his art, as Lifton said the artist must do, the problem of the cultural unrepresentativeness of woman and the Holocaust victim.

Interestingly, Thomas shares this problem with Lifton, who also makes an argument about "Woman as Knower."[13] Since Thomas's novel bears much resemblance to Lifton's argument, it will be useful to pause for a moment over Lifton's essay to show how the psychiatrist, like the novelist, reveals an odd inability to imagine woman as an actor for her own sake and with direct power in history. The essay shows that the predicament of "imagining the real" exists in psychiatric theory as well as literature. Lifton believes that there is a general shift in the psychology of knowing in the postmodern world:

> There would appear to be a convergence between premodern, non-Western patterns and postmodern tenden-

cies. . . . a *protean style of self-process,* characterized by an interminable series of experiments and explorations. . . . What I wish to suggest here is that feminine knowing may make specific contributions to this style. . . . [whereas the traditional world is governed by] a pair of related myths, essentially male in their theoretical absoluteness: the myth of the magnificently independent and wholly unfettered self; and the polar myth of the totally obliterated self. . . . her form of organic knowledge may humanize these harshly abstract polarities. . . .

> Much of woman's psychic potential stems from her close identification with organic life and its perpetuation; from this potential she derives a special capacity to mediate between biology and history. . . . Woman's organically rooted traditional function as informal knower can be distinguished from man's traditional explorations of ideas and symbols on abstract planes. . . . Yet her knowledge has been "informal" only in the sense that it has been relegated to a kind of social underground, as if such knowledge were not quite proper or acceptable [surely this describes Lisa's hysterical symptoms as treated by Freud in the novel]. . . . But recent developments in many fields of thought have created radical shifts in standards of intellectual acceptability, and have, in fact, placed special value on those very modes of knowing which had been previously part of the feminine informal underground. . . .

> Woman's innate dependence upon biological rhythms . . . central to her nurturing capacities . . . may provide her with psychobiological sensitivities useful for grasping the more irregular historical rhythms which confront us.[14]

This sounds very like the case Thomas seems to try to make for Lisa; yet when we follow Lifton's argument further a curious thing happens. We have just been told that woman's traditional epistemology fits well with the rapid movement in postmodern "protean" culture, but when Lifton explains exactly how this is true, he does not say that the mode of woman's protean understanding and being will substantively displace the old "male abstractions" or that she will, perhaps for the first time in the history of culture, join her knowledge to power in the social and political sphere so that the world will have a new, more "feminine" script to guide it. Rather, it turns out that the woman will function as a refuge, a crucible, a handmaiden, a muse, for the daring individuals (can we doubt they are males?) who are risking the rapid changes out in the society:

> her organic conservatism, epitomized in her nurturing, and specifically maternal, function, becomes a crucial vehicle of social change. The set of feelings and images she transmits to the infant constitute an individual basis for cultural continuity and a psychic imprint of the perpetuation of life itself. . . . But during periods of great historical pressure toward change, precisely this imagery makes possible the individual participation in change by providing a source of constancy . . . with which subsequent imagery of change can interact without threatening the basic integration of the self.[15]

The example given by Lifton of such a process is the support given to militant Japanese students from their "intense relationships with their mothers, in contrast to their distance from their quietly disapproving fathers. . . . The emotional support received from their mothers could thus often confirm the student's own sense of the nobility of their group's vision."[16] Remarkably, there is nothing here to suggest that the *content* of feminine knowing is put into the world as a direct power. Lifton apparently does not envision the feminine working in its own name or public discourse; it is merely a vehicle for something new to be born, perhaps some new set of male abstractions that her influence might humanize. The change will not be influenced by the kind of knowing woman has, but rather by the fact of it. Nothing in the above remarks by Lifton would suggest the impossibility of a group of militant young Nazis gaining support from their mothers. In fact, the use of the concept of motherhood by the Nazis is notorious.

To be fair, Thomas seems to sense that this traditional view of woman as a conservator allowing males to change the paradigms of social history will not quite do. Although she is very nurturing, Lisa Erdman is not depicted only as the classic nurturer sending men off to their projects with a kiss. Much of the book's merit lies in Thomas's effort to portray her as a powerful agent who continually transgresses the absolute dichotomies of "male" thinking, and that effort makes it all the more disappointing when he does not fully succeed, but rather, in a way slightly different from Lifton, also finally relegates woman to the status of a muse. If the effort is to portray the deep link between woman's knowledge and prevention of nightmares in history, he fails because he cannot dramatize her power changing the course of history. And since in this novel the males do not redeem history either, Thomas seems to suggest that the only hope for us who would be instructed in solutions is to celebrate Lisa's knowledge in the mythic, written poetic artifact that is the last chapter of **The White Hotel.** Thomas brought Lisa only so far before her power in history was deferred and defeated by the power of his own pen. Not that we must criticize him personally; for as we shall see below, the problem may be endemic for anyone trying to fashion new images for woman in fiction or to write in an authentic way about the atrocities of the civilized world.

For much of **The White Hotel** it seems almost as if Freud is Lisa's muse as much as she is his. He helps her to a certain extent to form a strong self. With intelligent irony this part of the book shows, under the polite veneer of the doctor-patient dialogue, a battle between Lisa and Freud for conceptual control of the facts. Freud steers the focus to a youthful "Medusa" image of maternal incest, but when Lisa in her own mind rejects that explanation of her symptoms, their battle may be seen as one involving Lifton's "re-symbolization" and addressed to the same problem that preoccupies Lifton—numbness from apocalyptic awareness—because Freud and Lisa are working on a "hysteria" that had its origins in Lisa's assault as a Jewess by the sailors, and this assault is part of the larger fabric of the Holocaust's racist apocalypse.

When Freud and Lisa correspond eleven years after her treatment because he is about to publish her case history,

this battle for control of the symbols becomes explicit for the first time in the novel. Lisa almost totally revises the perspective on the facts of her life from what they had accepted during "therapy." While amusingly she is always careful to say that she is probably only a "raving, lonely spinster," she strong-mindedly supplies new meanings for some of the key incidents they had dealt with. Ironically too, she shows that she had always been a more sexually healthy "liberated woman" than Freud had given her credit for; she reveals that the erotic fantasy Freud had taken as a sign of her disease was conceived in a deliberate and detached mood to pass the time and "to be honest to my complicated feelings about sex" (p. 183). Furthermore, she reveals that the fantasy was sparked by the very real physical "effrontery" of the waiter at her hotel. Her belated responses show that Freud had not "imagined the real" Lisa, but rather, without quite realizing it, had subordinated her to the imperatives of his own narrative.

The relation of Freud and Lisa shows three things: first, how much Freud owed to his woman "hysteric" in order to engender his psychoanalytic discourse;[17] second, how much the psychoanalytic discourse remained defensively deaf to real social facts and thus, in one way, betrayed the patient's "hysterical" insights and capacities because of faulty symbolization of the facts;[18] third, how strong a patient must be not to capitulate to this faulty symbolization and how inevitably self-doubting she will be when she ventures her own—especially when the patient is a woman trying to speak of what she knows as an actor in history rather than as part of a timeless "family romance." When we look back at the early part of the novel we see what a healthy gesture it was for a woman of her time to write frankly and spontaneously about sexual desire in a way that linked it to her nurturing capacities, and, without knowing why, to write it in the space between the lines of the libretto of *Don Giovanni*.[19] She seems symbolically to correct, or at least counteract, the archetype of the male attitude toward woman as a sexual object. Though she says in her late letter that "It shows I was crazy," we can only read that remark as Thomas's intended irony; her deference to Freud does not run very deep. She is polite to him, but she is even more resistant to his formulations than she was earlier.

Perhaps the climax of their conflict over resymbolizing spirit-numbing material comes in the passage where Lisa writes to Freud:

> What torments me is whether life is good or evil. I think often of that scene I stumbled into on my father's yacht. The woman I thought was praying had a fierce, frightening expression, but her "reflection" was peaceful and smiling. The smiling woman (I think it must have been my aunt) was resting her hand on my mother's breast (as if to reassure her it was all right, she didn't mind). But the faces—at least to me now—were so contradictory. And must have been contradictory in themselves too: the grimacing woman, joyful; and the smiling woman, sad. Medusa and Ceres, as you so brilliantly say! It may sound crazy, but I think the idea of the incest troubles me far more profoundly as a symbol than as a real event. Good and evil coupling, to

make the world. No, forgive me, I am writing wildly. The ravings of a lonely spinster! (p. 192)

The most important thing here is that Lisa reintroduces moral categories into a scene that Freud had deliberately encouraged her to think of only in psychological terms. Not that she thinks back on her mother and aunt moralistically; she is thinking about such things in broader ethical terms. Just so does the book as a whole move Lisa out of Freud's psychoanalytic realm into the realm of the ethical when she chooses to be a stepmother to Kolya and dies with him. Lisa's rewriting of this figure's meaning is, then, part of a general movement in the first two-thirds of the novel away from Freud's interpretive hegemony and toward a portrayal of Lisa as a directly ethical authoress of her life. The mode of depiction in the third, fourth, and fifth chapters is as important as, if not more important than, their reported content. Our sense of her as an ever more effective agent comes to a large extent from the formal shift from indirect to direct modes of writing about her; for, conventionally, woman is associated with oblique and indirect modes of knowing, acting, and being represented. The move from the earlier indirect portrayals to the direct, lean prose of "The Sleeping Carriage" contributes to our sense of her growing dignity in history as much as the tale of what happens to her. The depiction of Lisa as freeing herself from male modes of discourse is not long-lived, however. It is as if she escapes Freud's hegemonic discourse only to pass into that of another well-meaning male—the author. I would argue that, for all he intends a paean to Lisa in his final pages, Thomas has failed to solve the predicament at the heart of the book, which I mentioned above, for either the Holocaust or for woman.

To return to the book's rhetorical process: its success finally stands or falls according to one's reading of the last chapter, "The Camp." To have left Lisa dying shamefully in the pit would have shown her commitment to good works in the real world and her historical awareness defeated by raw political power. To have left her there in silence would have annulled any sense of triumph in the control she acquired in her life after Freud because it would be fatuous to pretend that such a death in itself is ever a victory. It was the very nature of the Nazi exterminations to prevent such an old-fashioned sense of heroism. This is one of the reasons that the Holocaust numbs our imaginations. We can make sense of Attila the Hun; he was a barbarian invading civilization. But the Nazi atrocities or nuclear war or Vietnam are so numbing to the imagination precisely because they do not respect this binary opposition. The forces of civilization are themselves barbaric, and so, how to imagine them? How fit them into the ongoing tale of culture? (Of course, Conrad's Marlow, playing on the opposition "civilized/savage," saw this many years ago.) History defeated these Nazi victims, and it is an insult to them to pretend otherwise. They did not die nobly or for a good cause. One must not make them sublime in their deaths, even if the deaths numbered millions. Of course, religious transcendence is at least theoretically a palliative, but it will not be very

credible in the twentieth century, as Thomas seems to realize in the insistent physical realism of "The Camp"'s setting. He seems to recognize that any consolation for these deaths must be depicted as coming from reform within that same real world that produced the Nazis, not from some transcendental assertion. But that would include also the transcendental assertion of the power of myth or poetry to provide the cure. In this sense, the boundary of practical conceptual difference between history and poetry needs to be reaffirmed, not removed, in reading **The White Hotel**. Has Thomas given us in the last chapter something that can overcome the conceptual paralysis induced by the numbing facts? Has he prevented a nihilistic ending and at the same time been faithful to the ethical implications of Lisa's life and death story?

One obvious way of reading "The Camp" is as a traditional dialectical effort to show that good and evil are as complementary as Lisa feared, and to induce some sense of acceptance in the reader about that. Thomas himself refers to the novel as a "synthesis of visions."[20] That statement must have an ethical force if we are to be persuaded: in other words, he must somehow make the atrocities seem inevitable. But if this book justifies itself at all, is it not because it recalls for us, through its "pseudo-documentary" elements, things that we absolutely cannot accept? It is true that empirically both good and evil exist in the world, but evil is given historical specificity here—as is the much lesser, perhaps necessary, evil of psychoanalysis—and to portray it in the mode of general philosophical pessimism is as bad as subsuming it to glorious metaphor.

The book does not seem, however, to rest in philosophical pessimism either, but to try to offer a purgatorial sense of hope. To be fair to Thomas, he has depicted not just a never-never land in which Lisa's virtues are imagined as useful, but he has also ingeniously laminated mythic poetry and historical concreteness together in this last chapter by describing the "purgatorial" camp in the sensuous terms of historical Palestine. And the fusion works literarily, even if its content seems ephemeral compared, for example, to Dante's allegory. But even though the image of Israel reminds us that there is a country on the earth politically dedicated to preventing such future nightmares, the main sense of consolation here is the way previous motifs, images, and characters are given yet another imaginative twist. In content and even more in the sheer narrative fact that Thomas adds this section, the "resolution" of the book seems to be by formal legerdemain, and all the burden falls on the poetic artifact *as such* to "answer" to the mistaken therapy and the Nazi massacre. The main reason "The Camp" does not convince us is that its sense of renewal is aesthetic rather than ethical. Here everyone's sins are forgotten in a spirit of forward-looking hope and radical tentativeness. Thomas seems to have dramatized the events in the chapter by literalizing the poet's lines quoted by Freud at the end of *Beyond the Pleasure Principle*: "What we cannot reach flying, we must reach limping." This fits well with Lisa's generous spirit, and in that sense her authority is vindicated. But moral distinctions between good and evil were essential to Lisa's "hysterical" understanding and to the force of the previous part of the book. What guarantee do we have in "The Camp" that the Gestapo will not show up a bit later, somewhat sheepish, to be nurtured by Lisa and the others?[21] One need only ask the question to see how aesthetic Thomas's answer to history really is.

If we search the chapter for ethical representations, we find at most a posture of waiting. Although Lisa is resolutely certain that "'wherever there is love, of *any* kind, there is hope of salvation . . . Wherever there is love in the heart'" (p. 271), none of the characters is shown acting upon evil through an act of moral will. Everyone here, as in most transit camps, is waiting for something better to happen to them. They are not in control of their own existences; there is something feckless about them, even though Thomas clearly wishes their hope to represent an alternative to the moral darkness of the preceding chapter. It cannot possibly look equal to the forces of actual history, whether Freud's influence or Nazi power. And waiting has always been woman's fate especially. If we read the chapter as an aesthetic closure, however, we see that the book fails to turn its toehold on "imagining the real" into a firm standing place of some new postmodern synthesis of poetry and history. It is true that Lisa's discourse refused to be bound by "male abstract polarities"—even the mind/body polarity—and therefore it is more easily compatible with the poetic license that in "The Camp" plays havoc with the usual conceptual boundaries. She is a boundary skeptic throughout the book, and that is what makes her different from Lifton's "conservator" woman. Both her poem and her subsequent life and death register her refusal to segregate female sexual pleasure from maternal nurturance, love from death, or even gender from gender. She refuses the mother's role in life, preferring the ambiguous status of stepmother to patriarchal conceptions of "family." This alternative perspective on family is emphasized in "The Camp." But, whereas the transgression of boundaries looks healthy when set against the reifications in psychoanalytic thought or Nazi ideology, it does not look healthy if it divorces moral judgment from nurturing acceptance. The merit of Lisa's body's messages was in their morality and their historical accuracy. Whatever limited significance she has as a portrait of woman's superior knowing is annulled if she can be shown to triumph only within some frankly poetic structure like this imagined place, the camp. To read the last chapter as an encomium to her woman's knowing is to betray her because she is once again thrust into a discourse not her own, making her place in the author's poetic artifact her "proper" teleology. To say that her death had "nothing to do with the soul" trivializes the mimetic significance of her gesture of dying for another as a woman and a Jew in a world where woman are raped and Jews persecuted. To allow the artifact to have the last formal word in the novel is not so different from Freud's decision to give priority to the requirements of his case history for the Goethe Centenary when he writes to Lisa, after the revisions she makes of her story, "I prefer to go

ahead with the case study as it stands, despite all imperfections. I am willing, if you will permit, to add a postscript in which your later reservations are presented and discussed" (p. 195). Both men, Freud and the author, expropriate Lisa's discourse into their own. This is conventionally woman's place as "knower," and thus represents no real advance on that front as the book had seemed to promise. The failure seems especially egregious when the problem is to redeem real historical brutalities like the Holocaust through the imagination.

The problem we have with this book as a civil war between myth and history is not really a function of the author's skill or ineptness. One can hardly imagine a more exhausting and beautiful literary attempt at synthesis than the last two chapters of **The White Hotel.** The book may well become a classic because of the powerful writing, its formal craftsmanship, and its confrontation with weighty matters in such a way that readers will return to it again and again to find some new connections and debate about its problems. The problem may be that any postmodern book that attempts to revise the image of woman or redeem historical atrocity will be subject to a double logic of reading that is "deconstructive." Jonathan Culler has described such a double logic:

> It is essential to stress . . . that there is no question of finding a compromise formulation that would do justice to both presentations of the event by avoiding extremes, for the power of the narrative depends precisely on the alternative use of extremes, the rigorous deployment of two logics, each of which works by excluding the other.[22]

The "double logic" of **The White Hotel** is that, on the one hand, the story's power hangs on showing that a woman's "hysterical" prescience about history is more politically realistic than more "hallucinatory" metalanguages like psychoanalysis. Its power, that is, derives from its pseudo-documentary witness to historical fact and its insistence that woman's knowledge is historically relevant to that fact. On the other hand, the story's power hangs on its provision of a mythic construct that resymbolizes the numbing facts and argues that the historical, material consequences are not paramount. Or—to put the predicament in formal rather than mimetic terms—by one logic the writer must set his poetic creations in the accurate footing of history's facts (so as to avoid being like Freud with his "beautiful theory"); yet by another logic the writer must create a self-reflexive literary structure in which realistic content becomes transformed in the poetic mill. Neither the Holocaust nor Woman's place in the world finish by looking different in the history of consciousness.

One may argue that in **The White Hotel** Thomas has joined myth and history as he has precisely in order to challenge the dissociated sensibility of the modern and postmodern age. In this reading, the point would be to contemplate the very problem that the failure to unify myth and history convincingly rests with our culture's reading codes, in which political realism and religious or poetic vision cannot be combined. No mythic literary product could seem to have much to do morally with the facts of the century's history, given the marginality of poets, and likewise no believable image exists for depicting woman's way of knowing as actually rather than virtually efficacious. Thus we should be content to hover in the crossfire between an aesthetic reading—the book as a necklace of discourses on which none of the different beads is privileged—or an ethical reading—the book as a limping, almost despairing, realistic portrayal of political and social evils. We should not bother to search for a more profound necessity in the link between its formal free-handedness and its particular content. However, it is important to recognize that to advocate this spirit of "negative capability" in the reader, or to imply, with Sir Philip Sidney, that "the poet, he nothing affirms, and therefore never lieth . . . and therefore, though he recount things not true, yet because he telleth them not for true, he lieth not" would itself place the reading strictly in the aesthetic mode rather than provide a true synthesis of poetry and history, aesthetics and ethics. This recognition is especially desirable in view of certain formulations now being made by critics concerning the problem. Alan Wilde, for example, has argued that postmodern writers exhibit a different kind of irony than modernist writers did. This "generative irony," he says, rejects the Olympian detachment of the modernist "reductive irony" of the abstract or mythical order in favor of a stance that recognizes that "consciousness is implicated in the world, is intentional, and that reflexivity, however ingenious, can never abrogate that relationship."[23] Surely *The White Hotel* seems written out of a wish to follow that second pattern. But in Wilde's view that is a project by which the art work "add[s] itself to the world without . . . substituting itself for it, thereby making reality, and art as well, not less but more various." He says that "generative ironists puzzle over the legacy of the modernist heroic and contrive in its place a syntax of interrogation."[24] *The White Hotel* does have such a syntax of interrogation, but it is interesting because it has a good start toward an ethical position too. "The Camp" does create what Wilde calls an "enclave of value in the face of, but not in place of"[25] the psychoanalytic and the Nazi discourses, but it is mere wordplay to think that its "interrogation" is any more efficacious toward history than the modernists' contemplative structures.

Similarly, Robert Alter says that the self-conscious novel is a type that "systematically flaunts its own condition of artifice and that by doing so probes into the problematic relationship between real-seeming artifice and reality"; it shows a "dialectic between fiction and 'reality' . . . a play of competing ontologies" which is "always simultaneously aware of the supreme power of the literary imagination within its own sphere of creation and its painful or tragicomic powerlessness outside that sphere."[26] But where is the real dialectic here? What would it be unless the artist could show art's power toward the real? And if it cannot, does it not remain in the ranks of the aesthetic, the same consolation found by the modernists, with slightly more ironic qualification? The momentum of the above

statements goes in the direction of aesthetics rather than ethics because, for example, variousness is an aesthetic value. But in cases where the stakes are as high as Lifton says they are, what is wanted is an artistic vision that *can* be a convincing model for the facts. Thomas seems to recognize this need in the way he offers "The Camp" as a frankly alternative vision and in the way he chooses Yeats's lines for the epigraph, deliberately raising the question of the usefulness of the "modernist heroic." Interestingly, the gambit of the novel does not succeed, not because Thomas fails to give a convincing literary synthesis, but rather precisely because, in succeeding in that synthesis, he necessarily fails the ethical dimension of the book, its mimesis. Necessarily, because the literary and the politically realistic codes compete with one another in our culture. Perhaps the issue is not so important for many contemporary historical facts, and so the writer's play with them is innocuous. But no one could think that about the history of the Holocaust, and, for those who recognize it as a serious problem, the history of woman in cultural discourse.

Thus one does not know by what "generic contract"[27] to read this book, yet at the same time one cannot hover between the two genres, given its content. One is reminded of the lament of one of John Barth's twins, joined to his brother belly-to-back: "To be one, paradise; to be two, bliss. But to be both and neither is unspeakable." An honest reading of the novel will not speak of "dialectic" or "synthesis" because the competing elements are not successfully resolved into a third term that escapes being wholly aesthetic. The novel shows that the culture still has a problem finding a way to "feed the heart on fantasies" that are healthy and yet have power in history. It shows that Lisa's knowledge as woman, as analysand, and as Nazi victim is literally still unspeakable in any mainstream discourse because the poet can do no more than translate, as Freud did in psychoanalysis, the discourse of her body and the insane discourse of the Nazis into a discourse foreign to the victims' own understanding of themselves, which is poetry. Unfortunately, the reason for optimism in the book's final word, "happy," is not that this woman changed history or endured it as culture's representative, but that the male poet-bird has gone bravely out on the limb in the last chapter, calling attention to his power of sympathy and poetic transmutation through his imagining of an unreal woman.

Notes

1. In *Surfiction: Fiction Now . . . and Tomorrow,* ed. Raymond Federman (Chicago: Swallow Press, 1975), pp. 7-8, Federman uses this term for the kind of experimental fiction that does not "imitate reality, but . . . exposes the fictionality of reality . . . [and] says that 'life is fiction' . . . not because it happens in the streets, but because reality as such does not exist, or rather exists only in its fictionalized version."

2. See, for example, Robert Coover's *The Public Burning* or E. L. Doctorow's *Ragtime.*

3. D. M. Thomas, *The White Hotel* (New York: Viking, 1981). References are to this edition and are indicated in the text.

4. In a review of another book involving Freud, Jung, and the patient Sabina Spielrein, Thomas remarks on the similarity of the psychoanalytic session to a classic seduction. D. M. Thomas, "A Secret Symmetry," *New York Review of Books,* 29 (May 13, 1982), pp. 3, 6.

5. Robert Jay Lifton, *The Life of the Self: Toward a New Psychology* (New York: Simon and Schuster, 1976), pp. 129-130.

6. Elie Wiesel says, for example that "a novel about Auschwitz is not a novel, or it is not about Auschwitz"; Michael Wyschograd says, "Art takes the sting out of suffering . . . It is therefore forbidden to make fiction of the holocaust . . . any attempt to transform the holocaust into art demeans the holocaust and must result in poor art"; Adorno says, "the so-called artistic representation of naked bodily pain, of victims felled by rifle butts, contains, however remote, the potentiality of wringing pleasure from it." All are quoted in Barbara Foley, "Fact, Fiction, Fascism: Testimony and Mimesis in Holocaust Narratives," *Comparative Literature* 34, No. 4 (Fall 1982), pp. 330-60.

7. Lifton, *The Life of the Self,* p. 70.

8. These are Philip Stevick's terms in *Alternative Pleasures* (Urbana and Chicago: Univ. of Illinois Press, 1981), p. 149.

9. Barbara Foley uses the term "pseudo-factual." Her article provides a sweeping, incisive review of the ideological problems raised by different modes of Holocaust writing. She prefers the "pseudo-factual" mode to the realistic or the surrealistic because it denies both the "epistemology of the realistic novel [which relies on known social] . . . analogies and congruent ethical schemes" and the "historical or epistemological skepticism [which implies] . . . the impossibility—or unimportance—of knowing what is real" (pp. 351, 354). Yet Foley's argument depends on a clear prior definition of a work's mode; *The White Hotel* tantalizes by a modal combination of extreme irrealism, ordinary realism, and pseudo-factual elements that makes history's role in the book much more than "local effects." Therefore it cannot be easily judged according to Foley's valid ideological distinctions.

10. Walter Reich, "The Enemies of Memory," *The New Republic,* 186, No. 16 (April 21, 1982), pp. 22-23.

11. The idea of the influence of the medium upon the consciousness supposedly using it finds its most general formulation in Jacques Derrida's idea that the "speech" of putatively direct consciousness is always already inhabited and disrupted by "writing," where "writing," now become a common critical term, indicates the "absence of the 'author' and of the subject-matter, interpretability, the deployment of a space and time not its [the consciousness's] own . . . and the fact that speech too—grafted within an empirical context, within the structure of the speaker-listener—is structured also as writing, that is, in this general sense, there is 'writing' in speech . . . writing is the name of what is never named." (Gayatri Chakravorty Spivak, "Translator's Introduction," in Jacques Derrida, *Of Grammatology* [Baltimore: Johns Hopkins Univ. Press, 1976], pp. lxix-lxx.)

12. Carol Pearson and Katherine Pope, in *The Female Hero in American and British Literature* (New York and London: R. R. Bowker Company, 1981), pp. 6-7, say: "With the rise of individualism, democracy, and secularism, men were expected to develop their individual identities. Women, on the other hand, continued to be taught a collective myth: They should be selfless helpmates to husband and children. Men increasingly were encouraged to achieve in the secular, pragmatic world; women were to be spiritual and not to corrupt themselves with dealings in the marketplace. In general, female independent selfhood was and still is defined by the traditional patriarchy as theologically evil, biologically unnatural, psychologically unhealthy, and socially in bad taste. Literature, therefore, tends to portray the woman who demonstrates initiative, strength, wisdom, and independent action—the ingredients of the heroic life—not as a hero but as a villain. . . ."

"When female heroism is not condemned, it often is simply ignored. It may be seen as less interesting than male heroics, such as killing bears and Germans, rescuing women from other men, and scoring touchdowns. . . ."

"Unless the heroism that women demonstrate in the world is reflected in the literature and myth of the culture, women and men are left with the impression that women are not heroic; that their heroism, when it occurs, is a reaction to the moment and that they ultimately revert to dependence on a man; and that the woman who elects a life of courage, strength, and initiative in her own behalf is an exception, a deviant, and doomed to destruction."

13. Robert Jay Lifton, "Woman As Knower," *History and Human Survival* (New York: Random House, 1970).

14. Lifton, "Woman as Knower," pp. 272, 270-71, 273.

15. Lifton, "Woman as Knower," p. 274.

16. Lifton, "Woman as Knower," pp. 274-75.

17. On this point see, for example, Dianne M. Hunter, "Psychoanalytic Intervention in the History of Consciousness: Beginning with O," *Trinity Review,* 46, No. 1 (Fall, 1980), pp. 18-23.

18. Several contemporary women critics are revealing Freud's own defensive denials toward the social

facts lived by his female patients; they argue that hysteria was an appropriate response to real social conditions such as seductions by men in their lives combined with a taboo about speaking out. See, for example, Jane Gallop, *The Daughter's Seduction: Feminism and Psychoanalysis* (Ithaca: Cornell Univ. Press, 1982) or Toril Moi, "Representation of Patriarchy: Sexuality and Epistemology in Freud's Dora," *Feminist Review,* 9 (Autumn, 1981), pp. 61-74.

19. Louise DeSalvo of Hunter College has exhumed a remark by Freud in a letter to Fliess (May 25, 1897) in which he refers to the catalogue of his own works as *il catalogo delle belle*—suggesting that perhaps he unconsciously identified with Don Giovanni since he refers to Leporello's cataloguing of his master's seductions.

20. Lesley Hazelton, "D. M. Thomas's War Against the Ordinary," *Esquire,* November, 1982, p. 100.

21. I owe this speculation to a conversation with my colleague Walter Reed.

22. Jonathan Culler, "Story and Discourse in the Analysis of Narrative," *The Pursuit of Signs: Semiotics, Literature, Deconstruction* (Ithaca: Cornell Univ. Press, 1981), p. 177.

23. Alan Wilde, *Horizons of Assent* (Baltimore: Johns Hopkins Univ. Press, 1981), p. 141.

24. Wilde, pp. 142, 149.

25. Wilde, p. 148.

26. Robert Alter, *Partial Magic: The Novel as a Self-Conscious Genre* (Berkeley and Los Angeles: Univ. of California Press, 1978), pp. x, 182, 98.

27. This is Foley's useful term, p. 340.

Boyd Tonkin (review date 6 June 1986)

SOURCE: "Russian Salad," in *New Statesman,* June 6, 1986, pp. 26-27.

[*In the following review, Tonkin offers unfavorable assessment of* Sphinx.]

A sequel to *Ararat* and *Swallow,* the third part of D. M. Thomas's planned quartet of Russian novels begins with an unlikely fantasy. In a Soviet mental hospital a tortured dissident claims to the guard that he works for the *New Statesman.* The orderly has other ideas and a cosh to support them: 'You're Kravchenko, a fucking terrorist, and a raving loonie. Learn some fucking respect.'

Ever since *The White Hotel,* Thomas has given his public Kravchenko's strange delusion in reverse: he thrills a safe Western intelligentsia with visions of persecution and massacre. What *Sphinx* in a defensive moment of self-description calls 'The author's lurid style / And themes of holocaust and lust' seem to cater to the liberal's 'hunger for absolutes'. To a doubtful culture he spins a dream of deep Slavic certainties: oppression and dissent, art and faith. Against the ambiguities of the sceptic West, Russia stand as the real thing, its Gulags crowded with a better class of poet.

At the same time, Thomas stuns his audience with a barrage of narrative twists and feints designed to teach some respect for the novelist as liar, trickster, thief and sphinx. Follow him here and you end up back in the country of the mind he calls, with a taste for stale metonymy, 'Hampstead'. In this land of interpretation there are no great truths; only versions, readings and second opinions.

As they would say in 'Hampstead', *Sphinx* puts its readers in a double-bind. Littered with people and events from the year 1982, it seems to offer a well-documented story of a gormless Welsh *Guardian* journalist in search of enlightenment among the dissidents of Leningrad.

Its geo-political nuts and bolts lock into place. Andropov takes over, Thatcher recaptures the Falklands, flight KAL 007 plunges into the Pacific. Through a dark and jaded city Lloyd George, the reporter, trails Nadia, sphinx-like in her secrets. Is she a Christian feminist actress or yet another 'swallow', planted by the KGB to trap Western visitors? And so on . . .

But, as this tangle of mutual suspicion and desire unwinds, Thomas sends out a different set of signals. These undercut the plot's claims to weight and depth with a series of spoofs, jokes, shifts of gear and rib-nudging allusions. Russia becomes 'Russia', a literary fabrication ruled by paper tigers and subverted by printer's devils. You might find Thomas's Nevsky Prospekt in a bookshop, but never on a map.

Sphinx starts with a play, *Isadora's Scarf,* which features the feckless poet Rozanov—a survivor from *Ararat* and *Swallow*—in a soapy tale of murder, adultery and Stalinist skulduggery. It finishes with a narrative poem in which the poet Pushkin dies in a duel while (in another century) Nadia gets dispatched to Rome to seduce the Pope. (She succeeds, but Wojtyla's own Jesuit spooks are 'older than the KGB' and rumble her first.)

In the novel's central prose section, Thomas once more uses his conceit of an international circuit of improvised poetry competitions dominated by the Soviets and run like gymnastics or ice-dancing. Eventually, each strand of the action fits into someone's yarn. Wait long enough and all *Sphinx*'s characters find themselves pinioned by quotation-marks and slotted into the next level of the fictional *matrushka.*

This is Thomas's Slavophilia at work, rather than a further bout of post-modernism. Mixed-media effects, the nesting of stories one inside another, the blend of fable and journalism, epic and farce: it all leads back to his beloved

Pushkin. Once a guardian angel, Pushkin has become a kind of *dybbuk* for Thomas, an obsessive demon who crouches over the typewriter and forces him time and again through the same repertoire.

As sphinxes should, the novel works well enough as a mystery and a poser of discomfiting questions. But Thomas often tries to scale a peak of myth and merely arrives at a platitude. *Sphinx* tests to destruction its stock of sloe-eyed, sad-hearted Slavic clichés: 'I flowed into her. It was like the ebb and flow of the Neva.' This naivety may be feigned, but it grows just as wearing as the genuine article.

His debt to the loose, digressive forms of Russian storytelling has saddled Thomas with another quality of traditional narrative: its tendency to clip fixed types and phrases together into a landscape of received ideas. Innocent reporters, seductive spies, boozy poets: so much invention, so few surprises. Not Leningrad, but Legoland.

Like one of his performers, Thomas can be a subtle architect but a slapdash performer. Thick with hints about the relation of knowledge to desire, and of freedom to fiction, *Sphinx* seldom finds the pressure of language or density of character to match its grand design. In the end it reminds you of a dazzling rock video whose director wraps state-of-the-art production cosmetically around brittle lyrics and lumpish acting. Loved the concept. Shame about the song.

George Stade (review date 18 January 1987)

SOURCE: "Isadora's Scarf and Other Secrets," in *New York Times Book Review,* January 18, 1987, p. 6.

[*In the following review, Stade offers positive evaluation of* Sphinx.]

American readers know D. M. Thomas best for *The White Hotel* (1981), a novel remarkable for its tragic sense of recent history, its resolute humanism, its formal virtuosity. As much may be said for Mr. Thomas's new novel, *Sphinx,* "the third of four improvisational novels," as he describes them in a note. The first of the three we have is *Ararat* (1983): the second *Swallow* (1984). Mr. Thomas dedicates the quartet to Pushkin—many of the characters are Russian, and much of the action takes place in Russia, at moments from Pushkin's time through the purges of the 1930's to the recent past.

The novels are "improvisational" in a number of senses. For one thing, most of the characters are poets or liars or spies or quick-witted scamps adroit at talking themselves out of tight corners. For another, the books are a demonstration of the way literature begets and feeds on literature, of "the mysterious way in which a word, an image, a dream, a story, calls up another, connected, yet independent," as Mr. Thomas puts it in a note to *Swallow.* Above all, the books are made up of narratives in prose and verse

of stories within stories, of stories growing out of each other at all angles, as told by improvisatrici, by professionals who improvise on given themes. The action in *Swallow,* for example, begins at an Olympiad at which improvisatrici compete. We learn only then that the earlier novel, *Ararat,* is one of their improvisations. In *Sphinx* these same characters, among new ones, continue their connected yet independent lives.

Sphinx, in fact, is a kind of trilogy within a quartet, a continuation that recapitulates the whole as we have it. Part One is an expressionist play, Part Two a prose narrative, Part Three a narrative poem. In Part One the "respectable" poet Gleb Rezanov, who lives in The House of Creativity and is writing an opus on "the theme of historical necessity," is killed in a case of mistaken identity by the lover of the mistress of the "hooligan" poet Sergei Rozanov. When he was killed, Rezanov was just about to reveal the secret of Isadora Duncan's scarf, about which. Rozanov is writing a poem. Isadora was strangled by the scarf when it became entangled in a car wheel, whereupon it passed to her husband, the poet Sergei Yesenin, who hanged himself with it. where upon it passed to his ex-wife, the actress Zinaida Raikh, who was wearing it when she was murdered by unknown hands, whereupon it passed to her husband, the great director Vsevolod Meyerhold, who was wearing it when he was shot in the neck by the K.G.B. "Its silken fabric binds together the whole glorious history of our epoch," says Rozanov.

In Part Two, Lloyd George (not the statesman of history), "an anti-smoking peace-loving left-winger," a journalist who writes "moderately radical pieces about drama, culture, disarmament, the class struggle, sexism, racism, the health service, civil rights, cricket, etc.," an obtuse and complacent pipsqueak, tells us of his visit to Russia, his bungled encounters with characters who by now have become old friends to the reader of *Ararat* and *Swallow,* his infatuation with Nadia Sakulin. Nadia is an actress, a Russian-style feminist who advocates everything American feminists reject, and a spy. Nadia hopes, in return for framing poor George, to be allowed to follow her husband, a defector—who, as it turns out, is in San Francisco, dying of AIDS. In everything to do with Lloyd George, the satire is sharp, the comedy often broad. Mr. Thomas can be a very funny writer. Like Pushkin, "He sowed confusion / Everywhere, yes; but also fun."

The concluding poem is more somber. It is in part a meditation on Pushkin's death ("It's all a mesh, a net. We're caught."). It is also an account of how Lloyd George bumbles into insanity and spends time in an institution (like Rozanov). It explains where the novel got its title ("The world's unquestionably a sphinx," and it slouches apocalyptically toward Bethlehem waiting to be reborn). There is also an account of how Nadia seduces a papal aide. "Blow the dome open!" she says, "Give us pagan / Dances and sacred orgies!"

Amen to those sentiments, and hosanna to these three novels, for their bravura art, for their rendering of the highs and depths of human imagination and their sexually charged improvisations of poetry and politics. Each of the novels pulls its own weight; each of them can be enjoyed and understood without reference to the others; but there is no doubt that, from volume to volume, Mr. Thomas's meanings, especially those he grafts onto the concept of improvisation, sprout, grow, exfoliate in all directions.

Consider, for example, the sacred text of Mr. Thomas's improvisers, the ur-text behind and within their fictions, Pushkin's "Egyptian Nights," the tale of an improvisatore who arrives in Russia out of nowhere and performs to general acclaim, although few in the audience can understand his Italian. The tale is a fragment, for Pushkin was killed in a duel before he finished it. Just the same, the main characters throughout these novels are metamorphoses of those in "Egyptian Nights," of Pushkin and the people around him.

But in the Olympiad of *Swallow,* Corinna Riznich improvises a tale about the randy and unregenerate Russian poet Sergei Rozanov, who is often linked to the real-life poets Yevgeny Yevtushenko and Andrei Voznesensky. Rozanov improvises a tale about the even more lecherous and disreputable poet Victor Surkov, who improvises a continuation of "Egyptian Nights" in which the Italian improvisatore is challenged to a duel—which is prevented, however, by news of Pushkin's death. In these tales, as throughout the trilogy, there is a demonstration of how "real" people become fictionalized in our accounts of them, how characters in fiction become real in their effects on us, how people and characters are perceived through each other, how in our accounts of them the ontological status of people and characters is indistinguishable.

Consider the Englishman Sutherland, for instance, who is another contestant at the Olympiad, who improvises a poem about the sexual awakening of an English boy during, a two-year stay in Australia. Sutherland is forced to withdraw when it is discovered that his poem has been plagiarized. ("All art is a collaboration, a translation if you like. But plagiarism is a different matter.") His source, we discover, is a first-person narration of incidents from Mr. Thomas's own childhood. The effect is to put Mr. Thomas on the same ontological plane as his characters—which is where he belongs. The tales we tell about ourselves, after all, are formally indistinguishable from fictions. We improvise ourselves, so to speak. In *Sphinx,* a "real" character with the plagiarized name of Lloyd George is reading a novel entitled *Ararat,* but

> The author's lurid style
> And themes of holocaust and lust
> On every page, aroused disgust.

The youth in Mr. Thomas's autobiographical, narrative is obsessed with Rider Haggard's "King Solomon's Mines," especially with Sheba's Breasts, those twin rounded peaks of the mountain within the womb of which lies Solomon's treasure. Similarly, the poet Rozanov, who is half Armenian, is obsessed with the twin, rounded peaks of Mount Ararat, where Noah's ark came to rest. Ararat is in Armenia, site in 1915 of one of this century's outbreaks of genocide, a country that "no longer exists" (although a portion of it crouches under Soviet dictatorship), a country that is longed for, lost, unobtainable, and unrelinquished: "In Armenia / All will be well." As a character who doesn't know the half of it observes, Ararat is at the center of "complex symbolism." Among other things, it is the symbol of an unquenchable yearning that is inseparable from sex: "The goal was Ararat, the breasts of women, both sensual and pure."

In these respects, Ararat is like poetry, which in these novels, as in life, is inseparable from sex. "Improvisation is sex," Corinna Riznich says, "and sex is improvisation. When I improvise I embrace the unknown, the dark." "I am in love with love," says the poet Surkov. "Love is laying me waste, but I want her devastation." The libidinous devastations of poetry are opposed, throughout Mr. Thomas's improvisations, to the murderous suppressions of modern politics. They are explicitly opposed, that is, to ideology, to "any *ism,* whether socialist or capitalist," to the slaughters at Babi Yar and in Armenia, of Gypsies and kulaks, to the shooting down of a South Korean jetliner and the shooting of the Pope, to gulags and to clinics in which dissidents are doped into submission, to the suppression of Poland's Solidarity, to repressions, oppressions and obsessions of all sorts. "Strangle *isms!* And continue to live with poetry," says the "hooligan" poet Rozanov, who winds up in a clinic. This opposition, in my opinion, is well worth writing a sequence of novels about.

The opposition between "the themes of holocaust and lust" is parallel to another, between manifest chaos and latent design. The physicist Masha, who lost her job because her husband, a Jewish improvisatore, wants to emigrate, has become a guide: "This is Russia, my dear!" she says. "Everything confused, shapeless, turbulent, ghostly." At the same time, her study of invisible particles and forces has convinced her that "everything in nature is implicated, involved, folded-in like a rose. A fish twisting in Lake Sevan affects a fan whirling in—in Madrid or New York." Similarly, Corinna Riznich's improvisation, says an enthusiast, has "many layers, like the inwoven petals of a rose." Mr. Thomas's novels embody this opposition not just in what the characters say, but in their very form.

On the one hand, there is the manifest chaos of styles and voices, of scrambled chronology, fractured lives, and interrupted stories, of parallactic shifts and radical juxtapositions, all of which mimic a world in which there is "No sign / Of life or meaning or design." On the other hand, there is the latent design of running motifs, recurrent symbols, and recursive patterns, all of which reflect the consolations of literature, which imposes a human shape on the void, which embraces the world like a lover. This is another opposition well worth building a sequence of novels upon, and Mr. Thomas is a master builder. *Sphinx,* alone or in context, will lift your spirits, but not by denying what weighs them down.

Richard Eder (review date 7 February 1988)

SOURCE: "The Superpower Superjoke," in *Los Angeles Times Book Review,* February 7, 1988, p. 3.

[*In the following review, Eder offers unfavorable assessment of* Summit.]

When God rested on the seventh day. He really did rest. No phone calls. No catching up on the mail. No reorganizing the files. And no fooling around with little toy worlds after working all week on the big one.

In his Soviet trilogy—*Ararat, Swallow,* and *Sphinx*—the novelist D. M. Thomas built a complex, bravura game of narrative Chinese boxes. His characters turned into characters written or related by other characters who, in turn, dissolved into the dream states of still others.

It was extravagant and sometimes out of hand, but usually fun and often thrilling. The thrill came from the seriousness to which the fun attached. The characters—poets, police spys, historical figures, and assorted Moscow denizens—tossed comically about; but what tossed them was the wind of contemporary history. They babbled absurdly in their sleep; their nightmares were real, and they were ours.

The trilogy was a work of sustained, sometimes strained imagination. And now, with *Summit,* Thomas discards the sustenance and most of the imagination. In a prefatory note, he tells us that he is reverting to what he calls "an ancient tradition in which a serious trilogy is succeeded by a farcical or satirical coda."

He is having fun, in other words. He is having most of it.

Summit is a 160-page joke, a fantasy take-off on a summit conference between a senile President O'Reilly, lavishly based on President Reagan, and the Soviet leader Grobichov, who looks like Gorbachev but departs from his austere model in picking up some of the fleshly indulgences of the late Leonid Brezhnev.

The joke is the same one that Thomas used in one section of *Swallow.* President O'Reilly suffers from a mental slowdown that causes him to respond not to a question just asked, but to the one before it. This, of course, can throw things into the greatest confusion.

Thus, when an interviewer asks O'Reilly about a call-girl's claim that he engaged in elaborate sex with her, the President's response is directed to a previous question about his supposed ruthlessness:

"If something has to be done, I don't believe in pussyfooting around." The interviewer then shifts to ask if O'Reilly would authorize a nuclear first strike, and the answer comes:

"I'll be very frank with you, Hank. There are times when you have certain fantasies. Everybody has them—we don't need Freud to tell us that. . . ."

This kind of mental Mr. Magooism spins the plot all the way. O'Reilly, counseled by two foaming-mad hawks, goes to Geneva to meet Grobichov. Through a chain of mishearings and misspeakings, the aides are convinced that a computer game designed by O'Reilly's 6-year-old grandson is a laser-beamed Star Wars device; and they want O'Reilly to press it upon the Soviets. The United States will promise to share the technology, but this will only be a promise. So go the calculations of the two: Secretary of State Mako (as in shark) and Secretary of Defense Requiem (as in death).

In discussing it with them, O'Reilly gets the subject mixed up with a remark by his wife about their daughter-in-law's contraceptive arrangements. "IUD," he mumbles. Mako and Requiem figure he means "Independent Unilateral Deterrent," and they instruct him how to present it in Geneva.

Rather puzzled, O'Reilly dutifully insists on the IUD when he meets Grobichov. Even more puzzled, the Soviet leader acquiesces. After all, O'Reilly has agreed, in return, to mutual missile removal from Europe. Furthermore, he seems to have offered to hand over California as well. Another mental blip.

The plot gets infinitely more complicated, of course, though not a great deal funnier. O'Reilly is seduced by a sexy blonde who is introduced as Grobichov's wife but who is really his daughter, and his mistress as well. Grobichov all but seduces Mrs. O'Reilly.

Two Palestinians attempt to hijack the two leaders and are gunned down by an Israeli agent who tries a spot of hijacking in turn. A project for scientific cooperation to resurrect the dead is agreed upon. The American vice president, Shrub—not Bush, of course—resigns after suspicions arise that he is a Soviet mole and Mrs. O'Reilly's lover.

And so on and on, until all these extravagant misunderstandings, through a further chain of misunderstandings, devour each other, and subside into a traditionally murky and impermeable summit communique. Nothing has happened.

What fools these world leaders be, is the theme of these Bottom-Titania capers. True enough, perhaps, and Thomas gets close to workable satire not so much of the personalities as of the processes of summitry.

The inanity of the chitchat when the U.S. and Soviet leaders go off to talk privately responds to our own skepticism of what really happens on such occasions. Thomas' wacky Geneva is within a parodist's shouting distance of the now-you-see-it-now-you-don't displacements of the Reykjavik meeting in 1986.

Summit has its clever and amusing moments, but it is not a success. The parody hovers outside the characters, instead of belonging to them. They are so frail that each joke blows them over, and the author has to prop them up again. Thomas' breath is more audible than the notes that he gets out of this toy flute of a book.

Helen Dudar (review date 2 October 1988)

SOURCE: "Canonized and Analyzed," in *New York Times Book Review,* October 2, 1988, p. 13.

[*In the following review, Dudar offers unfavorable assessment of* Memories and Hallucinations.]

The distinguished English writer D. M. Thomas interrupts the last chapter of **Memories and Hallucinations** with a brief review of his book by his cat. Kitty has complaints: there are inaccuracies and omissions, there is the absence of pattern to the narrative. "In short," concludes the cat, which is also named Thomas, "I can't recommend this book."

Clearly this was meant to be funny, a pre-emptive attack on anticipated surly notices. But employing a house pet, even an extremely literate cat, to do the work of a wit or an apologist struck me as desperate, not to say awfully cute. It's as if Mr. Thomas had leafed through his manuscript—padded out with his poems, plus his first published short story—and realized that the book had problems he couldn't fix.

"A kind of walkabout through parts of his life," is the way the cat describes it. The memoir bristles with confessions, few of them illuminating. It may well be that truth is only to be revealed in serious fiction. It is certain that, among his seven novels, Mr. Thomas has given us at least one masterful vision of good and evil in our time. **The White Hotel**—dense, experimental, erotic, an account of a woman's "journey of the soul" and descent to the hell of the Babi Yar massacre—appeared here in 1981 without warning, without the support of the English critics, without advance hyperbole. Apparently in common with other readers, I can still remember the moment I casually opened it, began reading and was swept into an extraordinary narrative.

That book eventually bestowed fame and notoriety on Mr. Thomas who, until his 46th year, had been an obscure poet, novelist and college professor. In 1982, as the paperback edition was about to appear, he accepted an academic appointment at American University in Washington, but before the term began, fled home. It was said that he was troubled by his success. Nothing of the sort. He says he loved having written a book that was widely read. It was canonization he could not endure. As he observed in a piece written that year for *The New York Times Magazine,* "I fear becoming institutionalized—made respectable."

Fat chance. Mr. Thomas was never much for conventional respectability. "Wenching," as he quaintly calls it, was a serious preoccupation. Days were spent with Maureen, his former wife, and their two children, evenings with Denise, the mistress who became another former wife, and their son. Then, when he got lucky, there were the usual dalliances with nubile young women who caught his fancy. He also found time to produce not only the novels but six volumes of poetry and several translations of Russian poets.

In 1986, Mr. Thomas suffered a severe bout of depression and, he says, began psychiatric treatment with a Viennese-trained Freudian analyst, a woman. His memoir is anchored in those sessions, careering about from childhood to adulthood to family history, but always returning to the times on the couch. Are they memories or the hallucinations of the title? I haven't a clue. Oddly, for all his artistry at translating emotion into memorable event, Mr. Thomas is not very good at conveying the dreadful burden of chronic, invasive, free-floating depression.

He is obsessed by coincidences, he has dreams that prefigure reality and he is terrific at remembering creative connections. In about two and a half pages, he tells us how **The White Hotel** was born, and the account is fascinating. From time to time, **Memories** offers recollections that are funny or sad, but the book lacks energy. It is as if, set down in print, Mr. Thomas's monumental self-absorption had drained all the drive out of a unique gift for remembering and recording.

Rowland Wymer (essay date Winter 1989)

SOURCE: "Freud, Jung, and the 'Myth' of Psychoanalysis in *The White Hotel,*" in *Mosaic: A Journal for the Interdisciplinary Study of Literature,* Vol. 22, No. 1, Winter, 1989, pp. 55-69.

[*In the following essay, Wymer examines Thomas's incorporation of classical Freudian theory, particularly themes surrounding the concept of the death instinct, in* The White Hotel, *and mythic aspects of psychoanalysis and opposing elements of Freudian and Jungian psychology in the novel.*]

D. M. Thomas's **The White Hotel** is a book which polarized the responses of its first readers and reviewers to a remarkable degree. Now that the initial controversies over alleged sensationalism and plagiarism have died down it is possible to see more clearly how richly and carefully organized the novel is and to arrive at a more certain view about what Thomas is trying to convey by means of his delicate network of cross-referenced images and allusions. A useful starting point for both a formal and a conceptual approach is the prefatory Author's Note, where Thomas speaks of Freud as the "discoverer of the great and beautiful modern myth of psychoanalysis. By myth, I mean a poetic, dramatic expression of a hidden truth; and in placing this emphasis, I do not intend to put into question the scientific validity of psychoanalysis." There is no doubt that Thomas *is* deeply responsive to "the great and beautiful modern myth of psychoanalysis" but his organization of the narrative in such a way that all of the heroine's symptoms can be explained in entirely different terms from those in which Freud analyzes them in the novel inevitably suggests the possibility that Freudianism is a "myth" in the pejorative sense. In fact I shall be arguing that Thomas presents us with both a "Freudian" and a "Jungian" critique of Freud, though his final position is tentative and paradoxical rather than strongly assertive.

The mythic pattern with which psychoanalysis, both as theory and therapy, is most easily associated, the "hidden truth" which fires Thomas's imagination, is the familiar paradigm of Fall and Rebirth. From a timeless prelapsarian world of unrepressed infantile desires in which mother and infant, subject and object, the conscious and the unconscious are not properly distinct, "the oceanic oneness of the child's first years," there is a fall into repression or, rather, a series of repressions. At the unconscious level, however, the mind never gives up its longing for that primal state so that "For Freud as for St. Augustine, mankind's destiny is a departure from, and an effort to regain, paradise" (Brown 98). Freud of course does not think that the "paradise" of early infancy can be regained but is saying only that it remains humanity's secret goal and a cause of disturbances in the psyche. For the sick patient the rebirth offered through analysis is the more limited one of a successful adjustment between one's newly revealed desires and the world as it really is. The longings which are laid bare by Freud have their close equivalents in myth and religion but the "new life" he leads his patients toward is not eternal bliss but the ability to lead a "normal" worldly existence. Although Freud often spoke of himself as having the temperament of a scientific observer rather than a doctor, it would be difficult to overestimate the regenerative hopes attached to the whole process of analysis. Without such hopes Freud would of course have had no patients and no income and, in any case, the entire enterprise would begin to look morally suspect. Dredging the unconscious, wrote Jung, "would be a thoroughly useless and indeed reprehensible undertaking were it not for the possibilities of new life that lie in the repressed contents" (*Writings* 62).

When Lisa Erdman, in Thomas's novel, comes to Freud as "a broken woman" suffering from asthmatic attacks, violent hallucinations and pains in her left breast and ovary, and asks him through the medium of her poetic fantasy "can / you do anything for me can you understand" (20), the reader cannot avoid a strong emotional commitment to her quest to be made whole again. This quest is situated within larger patterns of fall and rebirth by a series of biblical and literary allusions. The white hotel of Lisa's fantasies, which is psychoanalytically explained as the body of the mother (or even the womb itself), the lost abode of unrepressed desires, is explicitly identified with

Eden which, like the unconscious, is a place outside time: "her phantasy strikes me as like Eden before the Fall—not that love and death did not happen there, but there was no *time* in which they could have a meaning" (14-15). Like the Promised Land, the earthly type of paradise regained, the white hotel is a place flowing with milk and honey, and the mysterious orange groves which float down past the windows also suggest Palestine. Mingled with these biblical images are many echoes from T. S. Eliot, the great modern poet of regenerative longings. From *The Waste Land* comes the dusty plain awaiting rain, an escape into the mountains and the prehistoric peat-bog corpses which were perhaps victims of a sacrificial rite; from "Marina" comes the scent of pine trees and sea mist as intimations of eternal life; and from *The Four Quarters* the elemental patterning of deaths by fire, air, earth and water, together with the appearance of a mystic rose "with endlessly inwoven petals" which "though eternally still, seemed to spin within itself" (59).

It is in the context of such archetypal images and yearnings that Thomas introduces Freud's endeavors to understand Lisa and redeem her from neurosis. With great persistence and ingenuity he probes the secrets of her past, uncovering all the classic Freudian material—adultery, incest, Oedipal jealousies, lesbianism and a primal scene in which the child Lisa sees her mother and uncle naked together in the summer-house. In "The Case of Fräulein Elizabeth von R.," one of his early studies, the historical Freud wrote that "the whole work was, of course, based on the expectation that it would be possible to establish a completely adequate set of determinants for the events concerned" (3: 207). Thomas's Freud excavates an apparently more than adequate set of determinants and as a result of his treatment Lisa is freed of the worst effects of her illness, able to resume her interrupted musical career, and to find belated but genuine happiness in her marriage to Victor. Despite her real and deep gratitude to Freud, however, when he proposes years later to publish an account of her case she writes him a long letter revealing several pieces of information previously withheld and suggesting a completely different set of explanations for her symptoms.

Although brought up as a Catholic she is half-Jewish by descent and her asthmatic attacks began only after suffering anti-semitic insults as well as physical abuse from a group of sailors. The hysterical pains dated from her first marriage to a man of violently anti-semitic beliefs who was unaware of her Jewish ancestry. It was her sensitivity to this hatred and what it meant for the world that produced the hallucinations of destruction whenever she made love to him, hallucinations she had previously suffered with her Russian student lover, a political extremist who looked forward eagerly to "the coming conflagration." Her sensitive forebodings are precisely substantiated in the remainder of the novel when, after returning to Russia, she loses Victor in the Great Purges and is herself murdered at Babi Yar by the invading Germans along with her stepson and thousands of other Jews, the manner of her murder giving a new and final significance to the pains in her breast and ovary. This transformation of significance is accompanied by a similar transformation in all the key images of the book which also turn out to be "over-determined" and capable of pointing in opposite directions. The peat-bog corpses referred to in the Prologue no longer suggest a primitive fertility rite of the kind recorded by Frazer and used as a symbol of regeneration by Eliot, but now prefigure her terrible death in the mud of Babi Yar. The "emerald lake" of the white hotel now points forward to the "green, stagnant and putrid lake" which the mass grave became after the War when Russian engineers dammed up the ravine. The pattern of redemption is reversed. Lisa's painstakingly worked-for rebirth from suffering is mocked by the horrors which ensue. In one of her dreams she tried to buy a copy of Dante's *A New Life* from a station bookstall but was unable to find it. In her own life she is saved only to be destroyed.

If one asks what Thomas has achieved by setting up a psychoanalytic pattern of Fall and Rebirth only to dismantle it, the first and most obvious answer is—a lot of emotional power. Our hopes are engaged on Lisa's behalf, raised and then violently dashed. Such a sequence of aborted rebirth or canceled redemption is always particularly shocking and painful to contemplate. Suffering is more easy to accept if it appears to be meaningful and in some way progressive, but becomes unendurable when it simply negates all previous patterns of expectation. This is why the ending of *King Lear* is more terrible than those of Shakespeare's other tragedies and why the shower scene of Hitchcock's *Psycho* remains more appalling than similar and more gory episodes in later films. In *Psycho* Hitchcock uses the first third of the film to involve the audience very closely in the emotional problems and ethical dilemmas of Marion Crane (the character played by Janet Leigh). She has only just reached the apparently momentous decision to return the money she was tempted to steal when the story of her life comes to a sudden and meaningless ending. All her problems and her attempts to overcome them are washed with her blood down the bathroom plughole in the most terminal of images.

The story which approaches most closely the emotional and conceptual resonances of *The White Hotel* is in fact a true one, though one which Thomas says was unknown to him when he wrote the novel. Sabina Spielrein was little more than a footnote in the history of psychoanalysis until a bundle of her papers, including letters of hers to and from Jung and Freud, was discovered in 1977.[1] She was a Russian Jew from Rostov who was sent to Jung in 1904 suffering from what was labeled as either a schizophrenic disturbance or a severe hysteria. She was one of the first patients to be treated psychoanalytically by him, and his second letter to Freud concerns her case. Jung succeeded in curing her but she and Jung fell deeply in love and when a scandal threatened Jung broke off the affair abruptly. She turned to Freud for advice and eventually became herself a qualified Freudian analyst and member of the Vienna Psychoanalytic Society, though she remained in contact with Jung long after the great split between him and Freud. Like Lisa, she recovered sufficiently from her problems to pursue a successful professional career and eventually got married. She celebrated her regeneration by calling her first daughter "Renate." Like Lisa, she had great musical talent and dreamt prophetic dreams which really came true. The surviving extracts from her diary and letters bear witness to a passionate and highly intelligent woman with a rich inner life. Like Lisa, she returned to the town of her birth in Russia where her husband was driven insane by the pressures of the Stalinist society and her three brothers killed in the Purges. When the Germans captured Rostov in 1941 she and her daughters were shot along with all the other Jews of the town. As with *The White Hotel,* her story carries all the emotional shock of a canceled redemption. To quote Jung's comments on one of his own most famous dreams, a dream which he described as "a drama of death and renewal": "At the end, the dawn of the new day should have followed, but instead came that intolerable outpouring of blood" (*Memories* 173).

I have introduced the story of Sabina Spielrein into my discussion of Thomas's novel not only because of its uncannily similar tragic biographical pattern but because there are important links at a more conceptual and thematic level as well. As I now move on to examine some of the ideas about psychoanalysis which Thomas is expressing, it will become clear that Sabina Spielrein was responsible for creating a crucial theoretical bridge between Jung and Freud, a bridge which made it easier for Thomas himself to try and bring their opposed perspectives into a closer relationship.

The transformed meaning of all Lisa's symptoms—which Thomas's Freud had confidently traced back to a tangle of sexual desires and incidents in childhood—inevitably suggests that some critique of Freud is intended by Thomas. If this is so, I would argue first that it is partly a Freudian critique of Freud, setting the latter Freud against the earlier one. The Freud whose authority is put in question is the Freud of the early case histories, the Freud who, in "Dora," said of hysteria that sexuality "provides the motive power for every single symptom, and for every single manifestation of a symptom. The symptoms of the disease are nothing else than *the patient's sexual activity*" (8: 156). The power of the sexual instincts is not denied by Thomas but the early Freud's exclusive emphasis on them is shown to produce an inadequate account of human nature which Freud himself later endeavored to correct.

In its basic form the chapter "Frau Anna G." is closely modeled on the early investigations of hysteria (especially, Thomas has said, the case of "Fräulein Elizabeth von R." ["Freud" 1960]). Yet the date given for Lisa Erdman's first meeting with Freud, autumn 1919, means that her treatment occurs during the major reformulation of his theories that heralded the last phase of his thought (Swinden 78). Consideration of a number of phenomena, particularly the repetitive nightmares of shell-shocked soldiers, led Freud to posit that all living creatures possessed a "death instinct," a desire to return to their former inorganic state of being. This instinctual rival to Eros was most easily glimpsed in the form of aggression, whereby under the influence of self-love the primary drive towards self-destruction was turned outward against others. The new theory was first made public in 1920 in *Beyond the Pleasure Principle*.

From the very beginning of **The White Hotel** we are encouraged to believe that it is these later Freudian ideas which will provide the better explanation of Lisa's case. In one of the letters which make up the Prologue to the novel, Freud writes of his conviction "that I am on the right lines in positing a death instinct, as powerful in its own way (though more hidden) than the libido. One of my patients, a young woman suffering from a severe hysteria, has just 'given birth' to some writings which seem to lend support to my theory. . . . It may be that we have studied the sexual impulses too exclusively" (12-13). When Freud first meets Lisa her face reminds him of the victims of battle traumas (that is, of the cases who first led him to the new theory) and toward the end of her treatment he is able to write: "I began to see Frau Anna, not as a woman separated from the rest of us by her illness, but as someone in whom an hysteria exaggerated and highlighted a *universal* struggle between the life instinct and the death instinct" (116-17). Nevertheless he still goes on to summarize her case in a way which largely ignores this insight and hence becomes vulnerable to a later reorientation. The change in perspective which occurs in the novel is most economically exemplified in the changed significance of Lisa's mother and aunt—the twin sisters. In Freud's analysis of Lisa they appear as typical figures from the early case histories, part of a guilty family secret in which the sexual instincts and conventional morality are in conflict. It is the knowledge of this secret adultery which Lisa has repressed in herself, even the summer-house memory being but a screen for another occasion on which she actually witnessed her uncle, aunt and mother making love together on a yacht. Later, however, when Lisa writes her letter to Freud she presents this repressed incident in a way which, although dramatically "placed" by Thomas, powerfully suggests Freud's late myth of Eros and Thanatos, the twin immortal adversaries, rather than his earlier attempts to rattle skeletons in bourgeois family cupboards.

> What torments me is whether life is good or evil. I think often of that scene I stumbled into on my father's yacht. The woman I thought was praying had a fierce, frightening expression; but her "reflection" was peaceful and smiling. The smiling woman (I think it must have been my aunt) was resting her hand on my mother's breast (as if to reassure her it was all right, she didn't mind). But the faces—at least to me now—were so contradictory. And must have been contradictory in themselves too: the grimacing woman, joyful; and the smiling woman, sad. Medusa and Ceres, as you so brilliantly say! It may sound crazy, but I think the idea of the incest troubles me far more profoundly as a symbol than as a real event. Good and evil coupling, to make the world. No, forgive me, I am writing wildly. The ravings of a lonely spinster! (171)

From this changed perspective it is easy to see why Lisa's fantasies, despite their unrepressed and Edenic character, were so disfigured by violence. The death instinct had been present from the beginning. "It is as though, for Freud, the Creation and the Fall had been one and the same event" (Bloom 222). It is also easy to see that the violent cancelation of her redemption through psychoanalysis is something which endorses the later Freud's pessimistic view of human nature as set out in *Beyond the Pleasure Principle* and *Civilization and its Discontents*. In the latter work, particularly, his ponderings on the aggressive and destructive manifestations of the death instinct lead him to sound more and more like Hobbes or Machiavelli.

> The element of truth behind all this, which people are so ready to disavow, is that men are not gentle creatures who want to be loved, and who at the most can defend themselves if they are attacked; they are, on the contrary, creatures among whose instinctual endowments is to be reckoned a powerful share of aggressiveness. As a result, their neighbour is for them not only a potential helper or sexual object, but also someone who tempts them to satisfy their aggressiveness on him, to exploit his capacity for work without compensation, to use him sexually without his consent, to seize his possessions, to humiliate him, to cause him pain, to torture and to kill him. (12: 302)

The hypothesis of a death instinct has always been relatively ignored in post-Freudian psychoanalysis because of the therapeutic pessimism it seems to entail. Freud's earlier picture of a mental conflict in which the libidinal instincts were repressed through the agency of the self-preservative (or "ego"-) instincts, the pleasure principle bowing to the reality principle, had envisaged some sort of eventual accommodation both within the individual and between the individual and the external "reality" to which the self-preservative instincts were responsive. The contradiction between the primal forces of Eros and death, however, is described by Freud as "probably an irreconcilable one" (12: 335). If all human beings are endowed with instinctual destructiveness then all human societies will reflect this, and in *Civilization and its Discontents* Freud raises a problem which cuts the ground from under the therapeutic hopes he once entertained. The cure offered by psychoanalysis is an adjustment to reality, but "reality" in this context is largely social reality, created by other human beings who are themselves sick. What if whole communities, what if mankind itself is sick? "In an individual neurosis we take as our starting-point the contrast that distinguishes the patient from his environment, which is assumed to be 'normal'. For a group all of whose members are affected by one and the same disorder no such background could exist; it would have to be found elsewhere" (12: 338). The world in which Lisa begins her new life is a world in which Stalin and Hitler will shortly come to power. It is a world in which during the hunt for Peter Kürten, the Düsseldorf mass-murderer, "nearly a million men had been reported to the police as the Monster." It is not a world to bring children into, which is why the only times she is able to make love without suffering hallucinations of disaster are during menstruation and after her menopause. It is not a world in which one can be finally cured. Freud concludes his analysis of her by saying, "I told her I thought she was cured of everything but life, so to speak" (127).

If *The White Hotel* had ended with Lisa's death at Babi Yar it would perhaps have been possible to see it primarily as a Freudian critique of Freud, validating the later Freud's pessimism about human nature. The novel's emphasis on the relation with the pre-Oedipal mother (the womb as first dwelling-place, the breast as first love-object) is also an endorsement of late Freud rather than early Freud. After coming to terms with Otto Rank's *The Trauma of Birth* (1924), the historical Freud realized that his emphasis on the Oedipal drama had obscured a more primal relationship, one to be explored most fully by Melanie Klein and the "object relations" school, a relationship which he likened to the layer of Minoan-Mycenean civilization beneath that of Greece (7: 372). The chapter "Frau Anna G.," although dealing with an analysis which took place in 1919-20, is presented by Thomas as having been written up by Freud in 1931. In one of his pastiche editorial footnotes Thomas explains the unusual emphasis on the mother as owing something to the recent death of Freud's own mother. It is made quite clear that Lisa regards this shift in emphasis as a step toward the truth: "I think it is remarkable the way your understanding of it [the *Don Giovanni* manuscript] seems to have deepened in the intervening years. Your analysis (the mother's womb, and so on) strikes me as profoundly true" (164).

In more than one respect, then, the novel moves toward a validation of Freud's later ideas but the effect of the final chapter is to show that even these are inadequate. In the course of the book Thomas takes his readers through a whole series of different textual "layers"—the Prologue letters, poetic fantasy, prose fantasy (incorporating postcard messages from different residents at the white hotel), Freudian case history, "normal" realistic fictional narrative—layers whose very disjunctiveness draws attention to the relativity and subjectiveness of their presentation. During the penultimate chapter, however, we apparently reach a bedrock of documentary truth from which the authorial voice has disappeared—the testimony of Dina Pronicheva, the sole survivor of Babi Yar. As fiction gives way to history, "gradually the only appropriate voice becomes that voice which is like a recording camera: the voice of one who was there" (Thomas, Letter 383),[2] the change of mode being commented on within the text by the sentence "No one could have imagined the scene, because it was happening" (214). If anything is real, this surely is real; but then it turns out not to be the whole reality.

> The corpses had been buried, burned, drowned, and reburied under concrete
> and steel.
>   But all this had nothing to do with the guest, the soul, the lovesick bride,
> the daughter of Jerusalem.
>
> (222)

Rather than end the novel with the final cancelation of all Lisa's hopes in the ravine at Babi Yar, Thomas gives us a last chapter in which, along with all the figures from her past, she is resurrected in a postwar refugee camp in Palestine, a location which combines a degree of plausibility with the force of biblical redemptive myth. Like Joyce's *Ulysses*, *The White Hotel* seems to have a double ending, once within time and once outside time. A major effect of this technique is to set Freud, not against himself on this occasion, but against Jung. As a convinced materialist and rationalist who derived all psychic phenomena from an organic base, Freud could never entertain the possibility that there might be a form of mental life independent of the body and hence a possibility of life after death. Jung, however, granted the psyche a sovereignty equal to that of the body and thought that parts of the mind were not subject to the laws of space and time. In consequence he was able to speculate freely on the possibility of an afterlife and did indeed do so in Chapter 11 of *Memories, Dreams, Reflections* where, like Thomas, he imagines it as not altogether free of suffering. If Thomas's last chapter represents anything more than a delusory piece of wish-fulfilment then it must operate in part as a Jungian critique of Freud's scientific worldview. And once a Jungian influence is admitted then many other aspects of the novel fall into place.

The idea that Lisa's symptoms do not represent a personal neurosis of sexual origin but are a sensitive response to the violent spirit of the twentieth century is a very Jungian one. He himself had visions of destruction in late 1913 and early 1914 which he at first interpreted as manifestations of a personal psychic disturbance but later saw as premonitions of the coming world war. Jung also accepted the validity of more precisely precognitive experiences, such as the pains in Lisa's left breast and ovary, and gives several examples of his own in which he foresaw the deaths of friends (*Memories* 281 ff). The radical interpretive reorientation which takes place in *The White Hotel,* whereby the significance of the symptoms points forward into the future as well as backward into the past, strongly favors a Jungian rather than a Freudian perspective, and thus makes the final chapter a logical culmination rather than the gratuitous piece of whimsy which some reviewers accused it of being. Lisa's long letter to Freud also implies that she herself would have welcomed a more Jungian form of analysis: "Frankly I didn't always wish to talk about the past; I was more interested in what was happening to me then, and what might happen in the future" (171). In a Freudian analysis the past *is* the problem and hence the chief topic of investigation. In a Jungian analysis it is the present maladjustment of the patient and the prospects for a better adaptation which are more strongly emphasized.

It is a feature of Thomas's artistic strategy that the Jungian challenge to Freud should seem to arise naturally from the development of the story rather than be explicitly formulated. Nevertheless, the first three pages of the novel, which take the form of a letter from Sandor Ferenczi written during the psychoanalytic mission to America in 1909, are peppered with references to the opposition between Jung and Freud, and seem designed to provide a basis for reading the rest of the book along similar lines. Ferenczi talks of "a little tension between Jung and Freud" and of how Freud teased Jung "for being a Christian, and therefore mystical." He goes on to mention the famous incident in which Jung's repeated reference to prehistoric peat-bog corpses caused Freud to faint and later to accuse Jung of harboring a death-wish against him. Finally we are told of how Freud's refusal to "risk his authority" by elaborating on the meaning of one of his own dreams caused Jung to say that "at that moment Freud had *lost* his authority, as far as he was concerned."

Confirmation that the Freud-Jung split is central to the novel comes from Thomas himself who has said ("Freud" 1957) that the first germ of the story was a poem he wrote called **"Vienna, Zurich, Constance"** about an occasion when Freud and Jung, already beginning to fall out, failed to meet up with each other in Switzerland. The symbolic aspects of this "profound unmeeting" are brought out by introducing into the poem a young woman, dressed like Lisa in a black and white striped dress, and a young man, who are journeying by train to a hotel rendezvous.

> By a strange coincidence
> The young woman who would have been in Jung's compartment
> Had Jung been travelling, was the mistress
> Of the young man who would have been in Freud's compartment
> Had Freud been travelling. Having confused
> Their plans, they passed each other, unaware.
>
> Waiting for him in her hotel at Constance,
> The young woman stepped out of her rainy clothes.
> Her fur hat momentarily became a vulva.
> Waiting for her in his hotel at Zurich,
> The young man stared irritably out of the window
> And saw an uncanny light pass across the sky.

(***Selected Poems*** 113-14)

Freudian sexual reductionism and Jungian mysticism are polarized in the poem as they are to be in the novel which developed from it.

This major conceptual opposition is not in fact wholly distinct from the other dichotomy I have discussed, that between the early Freud and the late Freud. In simple terms the later Freud seems more valid to Thomas because he has become more Jungian. The belated recognition of the importance of the pre-Oedipal mother was a move toward a more maternally centered psychology, as Jung's had always been. The presentation of Eros and Thanatos as a pair of *a priori* absolutes with some degree of ethical significance attached to their opposition is very close to a Jungian metaphysic. Earlier I described the changed significance of the twin sisters ("What torments me is whether life is good or evil") as pointing toward the myth of Eros and Thanatos, but the connection with Jung is

even stronger. Jung wrote that "To me incest signified a personal complication only in the rarest cases. Usually incest has a highly religious aspect, for which reason the incest theme plays a decisive part in almost all cosmogonies and in numerous myths. But Freud clung to the literal interpretation and could not grasp the spiritual significance of incest as a symbol" (*Memories* 162). Similarly, in *Psychology and Alchemy,* Jung stated that "in the self good and evil are indeed closer than identical twins" (*Writings* 270).

If the idea of a death instinct eternally opposed to Eros seems to owe a lot to Jung, this is not surprising, since there is a clear though indirect path of transmission, the missing link being none other than Sabina Spielrein. As perhaps the first patient Jung treated psychoanalytically, and as his lover during the formative years of his theories, Sabina Spielrein must have shaped the direction of his ideas considerably. In one of his last letters to her, he wrote, *The Love of S. for J.* made the latter aware of something he had previously only vaguely suspected, that is, of a power in the unconscious that shapes one's destiny, a power which later led him to things of the greatest importance" (Carotenuto 190).

In return, of course, he influenced her ideas, as she developed into a theorist in her own right. In November 1911, nearly three years after the affair with Jung had ended, she read a paper to the Freudian circle in Vienna, a paper which she published the following year under the title "Destruction as the Cause of Coming into Being." The traumatic effects of the affair with Jung are clearly marked. She wrote that "A woman who abandons herself to passion . . . experiences all too soon its destructive aspect. . . . To be fruitful means to destroy oneself" (Carotenuto 151). However, she converted her personal experiences into a general psychological theory, arguing that her examples demonstrated "clearly enough that, as certain biological facts show, the reproductive instinct, from the psychological standpoint as well, is made up of two antagonistic components and is therefore equally an instinct of birth and one of destruction" (Carotenuto 142). This is very close indeed to Freud's later myth of Eros and Thanatos, and in fact Freud grants Spielrein the courtesy of a footnote in *Beyond the Pleasure Principle,* in which he says, "A considerable portion of these speculations have been anticipated by Sabina Spielrein (1912) in an instructive and interesting paper which, however, is not entirely clear to me" (11: 382n)—the last phrase being a formula he frequently employed when wishing to distance himself from someone else's insights. When the paper was first read to him in 1911, however, he was less concerned to show that he was not wholly dependent on it than to nail its Jungian tendencies. The Minutes of the Vienna meeting record Freud as objecting to the "free and easy use of mythology, which the author might have borrowed from Jung: 'The presentation itself provides the opportunity for a critique of Jung. . . .'" And years later, Jung himself wrote that it was his explanation of the death symbolism involved in the "Terrible Mother" archetype which "led my pupil Dr. Spielrein to develop her idea of the death-instinct, which was then taken up by Freud" (Carotenuto 148).

Sabina Spielrein, then, was someone who built a major bridge between Jung and Freud, and who continued trying to build bridges between them long after their final split. Her original hope had been to have a child by Jung which would unite the Jewish with the Aryan, and hence symbolically Freud with Jung. The child would have been named after the Germanic hero Siegfried, whose father was Sigmund.[3] Thomas also gives the impression of someone trying to pull opposed perspectives into some kind of unity. The **"Vienna, Zurich, Constance"** poem, despite emphasizing the differences between Freud and Jung, tells how "In their uneasy sleep the two exchanged their dreams," and in a letter to *The Times Literary Supplement* Thomas described **The White Hotel** as a "synthesis of different visions and different voices" (383). Mary Joe Hughes, the only critic so far to give proper weight to the Jungian dimension of the novel, has argued strongly that just such a philosophical merger does take place by the end of the book: "Through a synthesis of the ideas of Freud and Jung, the series of antitheses in the novel are to a large extent resolved: time past and time future; death and rebirth; Judaism and Christianity; mysticism and rationalism; body and spirit" (41). In her reading, the last chapter completes this merging process by combining the timelessness of life after death with the timelessness of blissful infantile orality: "These final pages of the novel reconcile the beliefs of Jung and Freud, whose differences were suggested in the first few pages" (44). However, as her impressive list of antitheses suggests, the kind of opposites which art, religion and philosophy try hardest to bring into relation with each other are the kind which most resist assimilation. And it is the sense of a resistance to assimilation which, I would argue, gives the novel its special tension, particularly in the closing chapters.

Jungian psychology values paradox and argues that wholeness is achieved only through the acceptance of opposites, so at one level it might seem possible for the Freud-Jung opposition to be subsumed into a Jungian world-view, Freud being taken on board as a valid part of a paradoxical totality. On another level, however, it is simply not possible. Once Freud's materialism and rationalism are let into the picture, the idea of life after death becomes nonsense and the only rebirth possible is of the modest psychoanalytic kind we have already seen canceled by the destructive operations of the death instinct. Freud's grimly physicalist view of life *cannot* be properly incorporated into a vision of eternal renewal and, in the last chapter, he appears as an awkward, lonely figure who looks ill and unhappy. During the course of the novel there are in fact a number of suggestions that death may indeed be final, suggestions which counteract the Jungian tendencies, undercut the status of the last chapter and point toward an unresolved dualism rather than a triumphant synthesis.

In the early part of the novel, Thomas uses swans as symbols of the immortal soul but then does terrible violence to this symbolism by telling how Peter Kürten, the Düsseldorf murderer, once cut the head off a sleeping swan in order to drink its blood. Lisa is haunted for weeks by the image of "a white swan nesting at a lake's edge, lost in a sleep from which it would not awake" (161). Similarly when Lisa goes to visit the famous Turin Shroud she comes away with her faith shaken, not because she disbelieves that the face is that of Christ but because it seems to her the face of a dead man, not a risen one. Her very surname Erdman, or "Man of Earth," indicates mortality and seems to prophesy her end at Babi Yar where the bodies come to resemble geological strata.

All this suggests that, despite its narratively privileged position and its seeming endorsement of Jung, the last chapter has a somewhat provisional and equivocal status. Although a vision of eternal life, it is shadowed by death and by the possibility that death may be absolute and final, and hence that Lisa's story really came to an end in the previous chapter. The actual title of the last section, "The Camp," seems vaguely ominous in a novel which deals with the Holocaust, and it begins with a train stopping in the middle of nowhere, an image previously interpreted as signifying death. The interweaving of the sinister with the redemptive which goes on in this final chapter is perhaps best conveyed by the following passage in which Lisa is conversing with her mother with whom she has been reunited.

> "Anyway," continued Lisa, "I think wherever there is love of *any* kind, there is hope of salvation." She had an image of a bayonet flashing over spread thighs, and corrected herself hastily: "Wherever there is love in the heart."
>
> "Tenderness."
>
> "Yes, exactly!"
>
> They strolled further along the shore. The sun was lower in the sky and the day cooler. The raven came skimming back, and a shiver ran up Lisa's spine. "Is this the Dead Sea?" she asked.
>
> "Oh, no!" said her mother, with a silvery laugh; and explained that it was fed by the Jordan River, and that river, in turn, was fed by the brook Cherith. "So you can see the water is always pure and fresh." Her daughter nodded, greatly relieved, and the two women walked on. (237-38)

The first point to make is that the possibility of renewal which is being dramatized here has an important ethical dimension. Whatever hopes either Freud or Jung held for humanity were closely attached to the concept of Eros (in its widest sense), and during the novel we see a number of its positive manifestations—such as Lisa's warm relationships with other women and, most notably, her decision to give up her one chance of safety at Babi Yar rather than let her stepson Kolya die alone. Both Freud and Jung recognized that Eros had its dark side too and a Jungian synthesis would involve confronting and accepting that dark side. But the image of the bayonet reminds us that there may be things too terrible to confront, aspects of Eros too appalling for acceptance. At the ethical, as well as the metaphysical level, there are elements of the novel which resist absorption and remain recalcitrantly pessimistic. The correction which Lisa quickly offers, "Wherever there is love in the heart," is no real help either since the mention of the heart takes us back to one of the Prologue letters in which Freud quotes Goethe as advising his readers not to fear or turn away from "what, unknown or neglected by men, walks in the night through the labyrinth of the heart" (15). This, Thomas has said, was the last piece of the novel actually written and it leaves unanswered the problem of exactly how the bayonet could ever be faced, accepted and recuperated.

Returning to the dialogue between Lisa and her mother, we see that its images do not unequivocally suggest eternal renewal. It is as if the last chapter were a kind of insubstantial dream vision subject to disturbing intimations of mortality, a continual return of the repressed knowledge of death's reality. The raven seems to function as a bird of ill omen, a reminder of death, but then we remember that, four pages before, it had been seen with a morsel of bread in its mouth, thus recalling the ravens who miraculously fed Elijah in the wilderness. However, the mention of the Dead Sea disturbs again because it specifically brings to mind the putrid green lake which covered the mass grave at Babi Yar after the War. It is succeeded by the life images of the river Jordan and the brook Cherith, the stream from which Elijah drank when fed by the ravens. Even here, though, there may be an intentional ambiguity since biblical commentaries explain that Cherith was not really a brook but a wadi or ravine with a small trickle of water at the bottom. Babi Yar was also a ravine with a small trickle of water at the bottom. Moreover, in the biblical episode Cherith eventually ran dry and ceased to sustain Elijah.

The images of death in the penultimate chapter prove too powerful to be easily assimilated into a pattern of renewal and continue to exert a destabilizing influence. Another way of making the same point would be to say that the historical level of the novel resists complete absorption into the mythic level (Robertson). Although enclosed by redemptive myth and fully organized into the novel's poetic pattern of archetypal images, the Babi Yar chapter has a force of actuality which refuses recuperation. History and myth, like Freud and Jung, or death and life, end up in a relationship which is more of a dualism than an integration. The first term in each pairing simply will not be swallowed whole by the second.

This means of course that any message Thomas is seeking finally to convey is highly qualified and tentative in nature. Yet the success of the novel lies as much in its emotional force as in its thematic complexity, and amidst its series of incompletely resolved dualisms one thing above all comes over very strongly, and that is Thomas's belief in the value of the individual, a belief which takes its particular form from his predominantly Jungian orientation. A sentence from *Memories, Dreams, Reflections,* a work whose influence is apparent everywhere in the novel, helps explain how, in one sense at least, Freud's "scientific" investiga-

tion of his patients can be paralleled to the Nazi terror, which in so many ways is its complete antithesis: "Overvalued reason has this in common with political absolutism: under its dominion the individual is pauperised" (280). For Thomas, every one of the nameless names who died at Babi Yar was a uniquely precious individual, possessing an inner life rich and complex enough to defy rational interpretation. "If a Sigmund Freud had been listening and taking notes from the time of Adam, he would still not fully have explored even a single group, even a single person" (220).

It is one of the real and more old-fashioned achievements of *The White Hotel* that within its disjunctive modernist structure it creates a highly distinctive, complicated, yet consistent picture of one such individual. Lisa bears many different names at different times during the novel—Erdman, Berenstein, Morozova, Konopnicka, "Frau Anna G."—yet a strong impression of both uniqueness and continuity is built up, an impression which is given great moral and emotional value by Thomas. The most eloquent expression of this value occurs when, after her marriage to Victor, she revisits the Odessa home where she spent her childhood summers. At first she feels estranged from her past,

> But suddenly, as she stood close against a pine tree and breathed in its sharp, bitter scent, a clear space opened to her childhood, as though a wind had sprung up from the sea, clearing a mist. It was not a memory from the past but the past itself, as alive, as real; and she knew that she and the child of forty years ago were the same person.
>
> That knowledge flooded her with happiness. But immediately came another insight, bringing almost unbearable joy. For as she looked back through the clear space to her childhood, there was no blank wall, only an endless extent, like an avenue, in which she was still herself, Lisa. She was still there, even at the beginning of all things. And when she looked in the opposite direction, towards the unknown future, death, the endless extent beyond death, she was there still. It all came from the scent of a pine tree. (190)

Thomas, like Christianity and Jungian psychology, here links the precious uniqueness of the individual to the possession of an immortal soul, when it is perhaps more easily inferred from a belief in the finality of death. The power of the Babi Yar chapter allows room in the novel for this response too, allows room for the feeling that the dead are most truly unique, most truly irreplaceable, when they do *not* rise again, having proved wholly vulnerable to what history could inflict on them, unredeemed by any form of myth.

Notes

1. Jung's heirs have so far refused permission to publish his letters to her, but all the rest of the material is available in the fascinating book by Carotenuto. Thomas reviewed the earlier American edition of this book in *The New York Review of Books* and commented on some of the connections with his novel. Since then new information about

Sabina Spielrein, including the circumstances of her death, has come to light and has been incorporated in the English edition of Carotenuto's book.

2. Strictly speaking, of course, what Thomas gives us is not Pronicheva's own words but a version of her testimony as mediated by Kuznetsov in his *Babi Yar.*

3. In *Memories* Jung records a disturbing dream in which he participated in the hunting down and killing of the hero Siegfried. His account concludes: "Filled with disgust and remorse for having destroyed something so great and beautiful, I turned to flee, impelled by the fear that the murder might be discovered. But a tremendous downfall of rain began, and I knew that it would wipe out all traces of the dead. I had escaped the danger of discovery; life could go on, but an unbearable feeling of guilt remained" (173). It is impossible not to connect this with his abrupt termination of the affair with Sabina Spielrein in order to avoid a public scandal, though Jung himself explains the dream in quite different terms.

Works Cited

Bloom, Harold. "Freud and the Poetic Sublime: A Catastrophe Theory of Creativity." *Antaeus* (Spring 1978). Rpt. in *Freud: A Collection of Critical Essays.* Ed. Perry Meisel. Englewood Cliffs, N.J.: Prentice-Hall, 1981. 211-31.

Brown, Norman O. *Life against Death: The Psychoanalytical Meaning of History.* Middletown, CT: Wesleyan UP, 1959.

Carotenuto, Aldo. *A Secret Symmetry: Sabina Spielrein Between Jung and Freud.* Trans. Arno Pomerans, John Shepley and Krishna Winston, London: Routledge, 1984.

Freud, Sigmund. *The Pelican Freud Library,* 15 vols. Ed. James Strachey. Angela Richards and Albert Dickinson. Trans. James Strachey. Harmondsworth: Penguin, 1974-86.

Hughes, Mary Joe. "Revelations in *The White Hotel.*" *Critique* 27.1 (1985): 37-50.

Jung, C. G. *Memories, Dreams, Reflections.* Recorded and ed. Aniela Jaffé. Trans. Richard and Clara Winston, London: Collins, 1963.

———. *Selected Writings.* Ed. Anthony Storr. London: Fontana, 1983.

Kuznetsov, Anatoli. *Babi Yar: A Document in the Form of a Novel.* Trans. David Floyd. London: Cape, 1970.

Robertson, Mary F. "Hystery, Herstory, History: 'Imagining the Real' in Thomas's *The White Hotel.*" *Contemporary Literature* 25.4 (1984): 452-77.

Swinden, Patrick. "D. M. Thomas and *The White Hotel.*" *Critical Quarterly* 24.4 (1982): 74-80.

Thomas, D. M. "Freud and *The White Hotel,*" *British Medical Journal* 287 (24-31 Dec. 1983): 1957-60.

———. Letter to *The Times Literary Supplement* (2 Apr. 1982): 383.

———. Review of Aldo Carotenuto, *A Secret Symmetry.* *The New York Review of Books* (13 May 1982): 3-6.

———. *Selected Poems.* London: Secker, 1983.

———. *The White Hotel.* London: Gollancz, 1981.

Robert D. Newman (essay date Summer 1989)

SOURCE: "D. M. Thomas' *The White Hotel:* Mirrors, Triangles, and Sublime Repression," in *Modern Fiction Studies,* Vol. 35, No. 2, Summer, 1989, pp. 193-209.

[*In the following essay, Newman provides analysis of recurring symbols, metaphors, and narrative techniques in* The White Hotel *that underscore the paradoxical dualities of truth, history, and psychic experience. According to Newman, "Through repetition of images we experience no erasure; instead we have memory and revision of memory."*]

I

When Discord has fallen into the lowest depths of the vortex concord has reached the center.

—Empedocles

The horror D. M. Thomas' **The White Hotel** is also its passion. Its narrative structure propels the reader backward and forward in an obsessive quest to explain the convergence of contraries that constitutes the novel's motifs. Sex and violence parallel and coalesce as the narrative movement conflates the pleasure of the text with its terrifying vision. The reader moves through the dizzying succession of narrative voices, each undermining its predecessor, and seeks an authoritative interpretation through repetitive clues. However, the notions of authority and repetition become attached to a death force, culminating in the Babi Yar chapter, which defies the closure of each of the previous chapters and is in turn defied by the concluding chapter. The Prologue invites us to read the text as psychoanalytic detectives, drawing on events and images from the past in our epistemological search. Freud's last letter in the Prologue advises a dispassionate attitude toward analyzing Anna G.'s poem and journal. Yet the voice of Anna's documents, matter of factly describing the rain of corpses over the landscape while the pleasures of prolific sex are tinged with violent imagery, is disconcerting. Although the scenes and events are fantastic, the tonality with which they are rendered seems strangely flat—like that of a mind in shock. This sense is reinforced in Freud's case history when he remarks that his initial encounter with Anna reminded him of the faces of victims of battle trauma (90).

Ferenczi's letter in the Prologue depicts Freud teasing Jung for his Christian mysticism, a fate he regards the Jews as having escaped (4).[1] However, Lisa's clairvoyance becomes the epistemological vector of the text that counters rational analysis. Rather than symptoms of past causes, Anna/Lisa's present torments predict the future. Here the terror of the text replicates and magnifies the terror of the events it depicts. The interpretive direction is reversed as deduction gives way to prescience and future revelation replaces a deterministic past. We discover the flat tone of Anna/Lisa's initial documents to be a repression not only of the anti-Semitism of the past but of the holocaust of the future. These are repressed in her present consciousness and disowned through the substitution of an obsessive sexuality that only partially masks, because of its place in, Lisa's persistently intrusive vision of the future.

The text itself operates within a similar psychic duplicity. Thomas directs us into Lisa's past in Freud's case history and in Lisa's modification in "The Health Resort" chapter, allowing us to reach intellectual resolutions at the conclusion of each as Freud's brilliant deductions are extended and metamorphosed through Lisa's revelations. Lisa's life appears to have reached a stable and healthy center; however, the Babi Yar chapter shatters this semblance of security. The inability of the Jews to discern the implicit meaning in the signs directing them to evacuate mocks us as readers leaning on our rational crutches. The "demon of repetition" (129) is revealed as truly demonic as the images from Anna's poem and journal are horribly realized. Repression is disclosed to be proleptic as well as historical. As Lisa indicates in the final chapter, anagnorisis—recognition—is what is wrong (261). It breaks through the metaphoric defense of repression but leaves us buried in the void.

The author's note defines myth as "a poetic, dramatic expression of a hidden truth." In plot and narrative structure, *The White Hotel* is about ways of discovering truth. By directing the reader through various revisions, it traces the mythic resonance of archetypal images. The novel functions as palimpsest where we read backward as we move forward. Through repetition of images we experience no erasure; instead we have memory and revision of memory. Mirrors and doubling imply dualities that in turn create choices for the reader. We are presented with the conflicting epistemologies of Freud and Jung, the oppositions of rationalism and mysticism, Eros and Thanatos, analysis and prescience, myth and history, Jew and Christian, Medusa and Ceres. However, the novel never comes down completely in endorsement of either side of a duality. Such absolute authorities become red herrings. Like Anna's gesture that accompanies her lies to Freud, they are the stroking of a crucifix.

In his letter in the Prologue, Hanns Sachs terms the white hotel Eden before the Fall (10), a timeless realm, and goes on to say that meaning depends on time. Although the poem and the journal are set in timelessness, as documents they enter the realm of time in Freud's and the reader's act of interpretation. By forcing the mythic into the historical, we simultaneously establish the authority of interpretation and reenact the Fall. Authority is proleptically undermined in the Prologue when Ferenczi's letter

recounts Freud's refusal to risk his authority by revealing personal feelings that would confirm or deny Jung's hypothesis regarding his sister-in-law (5-6). Thomas' footnotes to Freud's case history, which quote Freud against himself, continue to erode his authority. In contrast, the postcards from the white hotel, the excerpts from Anatoli Kuznetsov's *Babi Yar,* and Dina Pronicheva's appearance invite multiple perspectives. We are shown the limitations of the mono-myth, whether Freudian, Nazi, or hermeneutical. Essentially, the narrative structure of the novel is intentionally decentering and ultimately regenerative. Enclosures are collapsed so that expressions of truth proliferate. Through the reimposition of metaphor in the final chapter, the aesthetic transcends the historical and the text revises itself again. Repression is restored as metaphor, and the novel reveals its sublime underpinnings, igniting the reader in the purifying fire of pleasure and terror.

II

Dying each other's life, living each other's death.

—Heraclitus

Two dominant motifs, mirrors and triangles, define the narrative structure of *The White Hotel,* underscoring the Hermetic reflection of macrocosm in microcosm at the thematic heart of the novel.[2] The novel continually presents patterns of repetition and paralleling, an interweaving of details, images, and motifs. Lost or left luggage appears in Anna's journal (45), in Lisa's account of traveling by train (151), in her meeting with Victor in Milan (171), all prefiguring the confiscation of her suitcase at Babi Yar (230). The shroud of Turin is mentioned in Father Marek's sermon in the journal (71) and accounts for Lisa's rejection of Christ's resurrection in "The Health Resort" chapter (167-168). The vision of Christ with hands placed delicately over genitals is replicated in the Babi Yar chapter as Lisa views the naked Jews going to their deaths with their hands covering their genitals in a pathetic gesture at modesty (243).

The fire at the white hotel is personalized as Anna realizes that her hair is on fire (37), is picked up again when Lisa reports to Freud that Alexei singed her hair with his cigar (126), again when Anna confirms that her mother and uncle died in a hotel fire when on an illicit rendezvous (137), and is repeated in Lisa's letter to Freud when she tells him of the sailors molesting her while she viewed the burning waterfront (187). This destructive image is temporarily rendered positive when Lisa makes love with Victor and "the flashes of the lighthouse lit up her husband's white hair" (211).

Lisa's honeymoon with Victor takes place on a boat as did the incidents with Alexei, with the sailors, and with Lisa's youthful discovery of her mother, aunt, and uncle in three-way sex. These mirrorings conflate the fire/water imagery and pick up the motif of traveling that is repeated in the various train journeys throughout the novel. This conflation attains sinister proportions in the Babi Yar chapter when the Jews are told that they will be evacuated by train, itself a gruesome reminder of the thousands of Jews who were evacuated by train to death camps. In a further conflation after the massacre, the Nazi stokers construct a pyre of bodies and set the fire by igniting the hair of the dead (251). At the conclusion of the chapter, the narrator reports the continuous efforts to annihilate the dead. A dam is erected across the ravine of bodies, transforming the emerald lake of Anna's poem, which is also depicted as a red sheet, into a putrid one (252). Eventually the dam bursts, burying Kiev in mud and corpses. Again historical events coalesce, for we are reminded of Ferenczi's letter detailing Jung's fascination with mummified bog corpses, a fascination that led Freud to faint because he was convinced that Jung wished his death (5).

Blood imagery pervades the novel. Anna's lover states, "I want your blood" as they make love while she is menstruating (46). He asks her, "Can you feel the blood falling?" and she responds, "I fall ill every autumn" (45)—autumn being when her mother died and when the massacre at Babi Yar occurs. Their lovemaking is immediately followed by Anna's lover cutting his steak, an image repeated when Victor cuts up his beefsteak "tenderly and expressively" (153) and recalling the "rare and beautiful" steaks with their natural juices that the jolly chef in "Don Giovanni" cooked (28). The Dusseldorf murderer, Peter Kurten, kills because he needs to drink blood, and, out of frustration at not finding a victim one night, he cuts off the head of a swan and drinks its blood (178). Kurten desires to remain alive moments after he is executed by guillotine so that he can hear his own blood gush. The purity and innocence of the swans that conclude Chapters One and Two are contaminated by blood and death, images prefigured when Victor writes of his swan song (204). The image of Kurten's killing the swan and his wish to hear his own blood gush haunt Lisa, causing her head to spin (178). She prays that he will not be the same Peter Kurten when he enters the afterlife but believes that *somewhere*—at that very moment—someone was inflicting the worst possible horror on another human being" (179). Her prayer and belief are prophetic. Kurten is seen playing with children in the final chapter, although under the careful watch of armed guards (262-263). When Lisa looks into the ravine at Babi Yar, her head swims upon viewing the sea of bodies before she too falls into the "bath of blood" (248).

Other recurring images include oranges in the context of trees, groves, nipples, and, with water Anna's sole source of nourishment at the White Hotel, crows and ravens (symbolically birds of prophecy), corsets, cats, whales, plums, peaches, stars, and cedar and pine trees.[3] Narrative detail and inversions of detail find revelatory expression in the motif of mirrors. Freud's letter to Ferenczi characterizes Anna's hysteria as if "Venus looked in her mirror and saw the face of Medusa" (8). Freud later terms Anna's mother Medusa as well as Ceres (142).[4] In "The Health Resort" chapter, Lisa's letter to Freud introduces new facts that modify Freud's analysis. We learn that as a young girl Lisa discovered her mother (Mary) and her mother's twin (Magda)—mirrors of each other as archetypal Virgin and Whore—in a ménage à trois with Lisa's uncle. In her revision of her night on the yacht with Alexei, she recalls waking to see her reflection in the wardrobe mirror, which resurrects this traumatic discovery of "the grimacing woman, joyful; and the smiling women, sad. Medusa and Ceres" (192). Lisa distinguishes the twin sisters by the crucifix that only her aunt wears. Her mother had removed hers due to the anti-Semitic protests of her family over her intention to marry a Jew, a situation replicated in Vogel's anti-Semitic comments in Anna's journal and foreshadowed in the Freud/Jung, Jewish rationalism/Christian mysticism duality reported in Ferenczi's letter. We learn in "The Health Resort" chapter of Lisa's marriage to a Jew-hater, which causes her to deny her identity, secretly to wish that her uncle was her father, to hallucinate catastrophes when having sex with her husband, to induce a miscarriage, and ultimately to withhold significant information from Freud because he is Jewish. Lisa's suppression of her Jewish identity alters Freud's interpretation as we revise the previous chapters that have attained the status of documents within the text. However, her repression also catapults us forward to the incident at Babi Yar where she initially denies her Jewishness to escape the slaughter.

Lisa's mirror phobia coincides with her reading of Freud's case of the Wolf Man who was obsessed with intercourse *more ferarum*. Intertextual connections suggest themselves when we review this case. The Wolf Man's wife is referred to as "Tatiana" from *Eugene Onegin,* his sister is named Anna, and the color white recurs in his wolf dreams. Freud believed that evidence from this case would confirm his argument for the primacy of infantile prehistory as opposed to Jung's contention that ancestral prehistory was most influential.[5] The combination of human and savage captivates Lisa and finds expression in her attribution of Medusa/Ceres, "good and evil coupling, to make the world" (192), to her mother's and aunt's mirroring. Characteristically, it also refers us backwards and forwards in the text. In the "Don Giovanni" poem, Anna writes:

> your son impaled me, it was so sweet I screamed
> but no one heard me for the other screams
> as body after body fell or leapt
> from upper storeys of the white hotel
> I jerked and jerked until his prick released
> its cool soft flood. Charred bodies hung from
> trees (19-20)

In the Babi Yar chapter, these images are parodically paralleled as thousands of people are shot by the Nazis and fall into the ravine. Lisa jumps with Kolya before the bullets strike them. Lying amidst the carnage, her muffled movements are detected and her breast is kicked in before she is raped with a bayonet: "very gently, Demidenko imitated the thrusts of intercourse; and Semashko let out a guffaw, which reverberated from the ravine walls as the woman's body jerked back and relaxed, jerked and relaxed. . . . Demidenko twisted the blade and thrust it in deep" (249-250). Lisa's belief that the source of her breast and ovary pains was organic in opposition to Freud's contention that they stemmed from her rejection of her lesbian impulses finds disturbing confirmation in this scene. The fearful interdependence of good and evil. Eros and Thanatos, that is *The White Hotel*'s thematic design, is synecdochically expressed in the mirroring of plot details established in the poem and journal of Anna—whose name is itself chiasmic.

Triangles dominate the sexual relationships in the novel. In a version of the Oedipus conflict where the father usurps the child in the mother's affection, Madame R's mothering of Lisa ends when she marries. Lisa later forms a harmonious triangle with Victor and Vera, both of whom are Jews, and eventually takes Vera's place as Victor's wife and as mother to Kolya. She writes to Freud that she has just sung an oratorio called *Oedipus Rex,* and she performs with Victor in *Eugene Onegin,* at the center of which is a love triangle. She later accepts Victor's marriage proposal in a letter that mirrors that of Tatiana to Onegin. The initial letter of the Prologue has Ferenczi writing to his mistress Gisela whose ex-husband will commit suicide on their wedding day. And in that letter Ferenczi mentions Freud's dream regarding his sister-in-law Minna working like a peasant while his wife looks on idly, which causes the rift between Jung and him regarding his refusal to risk his authority (5). In her letter in "The Health Resort" chapter, Lisa reveals that Freud has been to Bad Gastein on vacation with Minna when Lisa, at this point a former patient, met them (182), a replication of the liaison between Lisa's mother and uncle that culminates in the hotel fire. In Anna's poem and journal, we see a triangle with Anna, her lover, and Madame Cottin, prefiguring Anna's report to Freud of Alexei's having sex with another woman on the yacht. Both events are based on Lisa's repression of the ménage à trois that she witnessed as a young girl. Anna's duplicitous report concerning Alexei has him taking the girl doggy style, replicating Anna's being mounted from behind in her poem and journal and based on Lisa's repression of viewing her mother with Lisa's uncle behind her and her aunt stroking her breast. The repression of the past is also proleptic because Lisa is raped with the bayonet from behind, and this image attains a universal dimension when linked with the Wolf Man's compulsion for intercourse with animals.

In this magic web of a novel, mirrors and triangles occur as plot details, character relationships, motifs; and triangles also define the structure of *The White Hotel.* The six chapters break down into two triangles, the details, motifs, and themes of which interlock chiasmically as mirror images—emblematically a Star of David.

The "Don Giovanni" poem, written between the staves of the libretto of Mozart's opera, implicitly warns us to read between the lines if we are to discern meaning. As Sachs indicates in his letter, we are in a timeless realm, Eden before the Fall. Freud refers to Anna having "given birth" to this material (9), a loaded image we later learn, for Anna has induced a miscarriage so that she will not give birth to the child of her anti-Semitic husband. Biblical im-

ages of flood and catastrophic fire occur in a dreamscape overflowing with breast milk and the honey of continual sex. Internal and external occurrences coalesce as the flames of the hotel fire merge with Anna's and her lover's sexual passion. Sex and catastrophe coincide, yet we witness magically restorative, regenerative, and nurturing powers. The chapter concludes affirmatively with the white purity of the swans and the snow-covered mountains as we are told that "no one was selfish in the white hotel" (28).

Like the poem, "The Gastein Journal" is a subjective fantasy that becomes a documentary object. The movement in the novel from individual to general is indicated by the shift from first to third person and from poetry to prose. The chapter begins with Anna dreaming the vision of Dina Pronicheva from Kuznetsov's account of Babi Yar, which will be realized in its mirror chapter—five. The juxtaposition of sex and violence continues as do the magical restorative powers. The white hotel is completely rebuilt ten days after the devastating fire, and guests continue to pour into its premises despite the flood, fire, landslide, and bodies falling to earth—the mirrored inversion of the sequence in which these catastrophes will occur in Chapter Five. Within the ahistorical frame of this chapter, Vogel's anti-Semitic remarks and Bolotnikov-Leskov's comments regarding violence and terrorism seem out of place except when considered as a foreshadowing of Chapter Five. The disembodied flying breast and the womb gliding over the lake also attain a realistic dimension in the mirror chapter. What emerges more clearly in "The Gastein Journal" is a sense of the community of the white hotel. The postcards provide various perspectives on the mundane and the fantastic events that occur within the hotel, often focusing on the romantic escapades of Anna and her lover. This sense of community will be reflected in the tragic community of martyrs at Babi Yar, and the statement that "the spirit of the white hotel was against selfishness" (86) will be recapitulated in Lisa's ethical decision to proclaim her Jewishness and to die with Koyla.

The third chapter, "Frau Anna G.," provides Freud's case history, his analysis of the poem and journal and his attempt to locate the source of Lisa's breast and ovary pains.[6] This case history pulls Chapters One and Two into one vision and concludes the first triangle of the novel with the authority of Freud's masculine, rational interpretation. Freud's position as a patriarchal authority is later underscored when Lisa acknowledges that he was the priest—a Father—in her poem and journal. Freud's psychoanalytic method assumes that knowledge offers release. By locating repression and by sharing repressed aspects with others, these aspects become real and unburden the self. In the final chapter Lisa will tell the young doctor that it is anagnorisis—recognition—that is the source of her pains. As Freud's epistemology moves backward, the reader reads backward, pulling together images from the poem and journal and connecting them to Anna's autobiographical revelations. White, equated with innocence in Chapters One and Two, now becomes equated with guilt. Using Lisa's stroking of her crucifix as a lie detector, Freud analyzes the source of her pains as her hatred of her disturbed femininity and comes to equate the white hotel with the womb.

However, Freud's authority, already called into doubt in Ferenczi's letter, is further undercut by the documentary footnotes that Thomas adds to the case history. We learn that "Freud's unusual emphasis on the mother's role may have owed something to the recent death of his own mother" (142n). The initial footnote tells us that one of Freud's favorite quotations was Charcot's dictum "Theory is good, but it doesn't prevent things from existing" (122n). Besides revealing Freud's capacity for self-parody, this quotation ironically adumbrates the direction of the rest of *The White Hotel,* a confirmation of mystical prescience rather than rational analysis of the past. We also learn that Freud had completed about half of *Beyond the Pleasure Principle* at the time of Lisa's analysis. This work, which focuses on the death instinct, was to revise substantially Freud's view of the unconscious. In essence then, Freud's case history of Anna G. contains the germs of revision of its own conclusions.[7] Freud's words to Lisa, that she is "cured of everything but life," turn out to be prophetic. They propel the novel into its second triangle where we move from the realm of documents for analysis (Anna's poem and journal) and a published document (Freud's case history) into an overtly novelistic treatment of Lisa's future life, the climax of which draws from Kuznetsov's document on Babi Yar.[8] The narrative voice, supplanting Anna's and Freud's personal voices, becomes omniscient so that the meaning of the white hotel in Lisa's life can be universalized.

The second triangle of the novel proceeds to revise the reader's memory of the first triangle. In effect, we have sane Lisa rereading and revising the first half of the novel, which is partially written by and partially in response to the writings of crazy Lisa. As a mirror to Chapter Three, the feminine perspective that dominates Chapter Four rivals the authority of the father offered by Freud's theories. Lisa's letter to Freud reveals her source for Don Giovanni, revises her story of Alexei, reports the incident with the sailors, and reveals her husband's anti-Semitism. We learn that her sexual escapades had been more extensive than she had admitted, and this fact and her interpretation of the girlish incident with her Japanese chambermaid counter Freud's homosexual interpretation. In response, Freud again offers a quotation that contradicts his methodology, this time from Heraclites, "The soul of man is a far country, which cannot be approached or explored" (195-196). However, Lisa's approach has paralleled Freud's; the past is dredged up and the resolution is again historical.

The white hotel becomes the health resort, and the chapter concludes with a sense of peace and resolution. Lisa marries Victor and becomes surrogate mother to Kolya. The trauma instilled by her previous experience on boats seems rectified by the domestic haven she enters on her honey-moon voyage with Victor. Inspired by the scent of a pine tree, Lisa enters a joyful epiphany in which she envisions her own perpetuity within the continuum of time (213-214). Feminine peace derives from nature, not in the timeless sense of the white hotel, but as part of time. Lisa's embracing of repetition revises Freud's view that it is a demon to be quelled. She couples male deduction with a female telluric connection to put the pieces of her life and, consequently, of the narrative memory together. Like Chapter Three and each of the subsequent two chapters, Chapter Four offers a sense of closure that, similar to all authority, is rendered ephemeral by the thematic and narrative design of *The White Hotel.* Even in this chapter, which culminates in emotional health and intellectual resolution, the death instinct haunts in Lisa's obsession with Peter Kurten, who, like the Wolf Man, incarnates the universal coupling of savage and human and, like Lisa's epiphany, is replicated backwards and forwards across the continuum of time.

In "The Sleeping Carriage" chapter, the positive resolution of "The Health Resort" is revised. Paradise in this context is only rumor, an illusory reading of signs. Sex and death are once again joined as the unconscious images of Chapter Two are realized in catastrophic history. The attention to community suggested in Chapter Two is extended to the rich human complex grotesquely massacred and buried at Babi Yar—a quarter of a million white hotels. The lack of selfishness that characterizes Anna's phantasm becomes an ethical choice, a proclamation of identity and concern in the midst of savage indifference. Again we observe the attempts of history to devour the romantic richness and complexity of the individual. The dam built over the ravine bursts as if the victims of the annihilation refuse to have their victimization repressed. Although no memorial was erected at the ravine (instead a road, a television center, and an apartment building were constructed), the novel presents a revisionist history from the inside, a commemoration of the white hotel of Lisa and of all those murdered at Babi Yar.

Lisa's mystical prescience, confirmed by the events of the chapter, is endorsed by Thomas as a viable epistemology. Tellurically centered, it presents a humanistic alternative to the material reality of linear history and to the overreliance on rational design. The epigraph of *The White Hotel,* from Yeats's "Meditations in Time of Civil War," reads:

> We had fed the heart on fantasies,
> The heart's grown brutal from the fare;
> More substance in our enmities
> Than in our love. . . .

Lisa's ethical choice, redeemed in her dream of Dina Pronicheva, counters the brutality of the heart that pervades the chapter. Following the direction espoused by the quotation from Heraclites, the last sentence of "The Sleeping Carriage" prepares us to transcend the enmity of history and the limitation of rational interpretation: "But all this had nothing to do with the guest, the soul, the lovesick bride, the daughter of Jerusalem" (253).

The title of the final chapter, "The Camp," plays on the historical concentration camp. However, the timeless realm of the first chapter is presented in this its mirror. In opposition to the conclusion of the first triangle, this conclusion is aesthetically inclusive rather than rationally exclusive. Generally, things are benign. Memory is sweet, peace and congeniality pervade, the camp is nondenominational despite the implication that this is the destination the Jews at Babi Yar had hoped for. The camp is not by the Dead Sea but is fed by the Jordan River; its water is always pure and fresh. Lisa makes contact with her father and exchanges nurturing breastfeeding with her mother. Her mother offers the final piece of the puzzle regarding the love triangle that Lisa witnessed as a young girl—that Magda was homosexual. Even Peter Kurten appears playing with children. Contrary to the interpretive direction with which the first triangle concludes, Lisa tells her mother, "it's the future that counts, not the past" (271).

Although violence and destruction have apparently ceased in this rejuvenated, albeit postlapsarian, world, the effects of Thanatos are not repressed.[9] People are still scarred and maimed; Freud's cancerous jaw continues to hurt him; and, despite Kurten's playing with children, armed guards accompany him. During her conversation with her mother, Lisa's statement, "wherever there is love, of *any* kind, there is hope of salvation" (271), is interrupted by her mental image of a bayonet flashing over spread thighs. She corrects herself with "wherever there is love in the heart." Implicitly we are returned to the epigraph from Yeats, which explains the manner in which Chapter Six revises its mirror Chapter One. Instead of Eden before the Fall, we have Eden after the Fall—more purgatory than paradise. Rather than feeding the heart on fantasies that include tragedy but repress response, the love that proceeds from the heart contains a healing impulse that both acknowledges and reacts against Thanatos. The indiscriminate breastfeeding that occurs in the first chapter is here put into context. Lisa's ethical choice in the preceding chapter is extended to the final image that we have of her in the novel as she hurries to join a group of nurses who are attending to the wounded. The telluric significance of her name, Erdmann ("Erd" is German for "earth"), and of her pseudonym, Anna G. ("G" pronounced in German becomes one of the names of the Greek earth mother, Ge),[10] are realized in Lisa's nurturing. As she goes to perform this function, she realizes that her pelvis and breast have ceased to hurt. Smelling the scent of a pine tree, her epiphany of human and temporal connection from "The Health Resort" returns. Without a system of clarity, anagnorisis, she is incapable of placing her memory of the scent, but her heart is not obscured. The pine scent "troubled her in some mysterious way, yet also made her happy" (274).

III

As soon as writing, which entails making a liquid flow out of a tube onto a piece of white paper, assumes the significance of copulation, or as soon as walking becomes a symbolic substitute for treading upon the body of mother earth, both writing and walking are stopped because they represent the performance of a forbidden sexual act.

—Freud, "Inhibitions, Symptoms and Anxiety"

In his review of *A Secret Symmetry: Sabina Spielrein between Jung and Freud* in the *New York Review of Books,* Thomas again turns his attention to a triangular relationship. Sabina Spielrein was a patient of Jung's with whom he had sex. Jung excused his breach of professional ethics on the basis that Spielrein had never paid him and was therefore technically not his patient. Spielrein went on to gain a degree in medicine and formed an intellectual alliance with Freud. Thomas writes that "Freud attempted to draw Spielrein into their shared Jewishness, against the blond Aryan" Jung. Apart from the biographical interest that this book generates, Thomas reveals that Spielrein's essay on the balance of creative and destructive forces in passion, published in 1912, was the germ of Freud's theory of the death wish, published as *Beyond the Pleasure Principle* in 1920. As already has been mentioned, Freud's fictional treatment of Anna G. occurs while he is composing this treatise. As a discourse haunted by images of catastrophe and as a movement from the authority of the empirical to that of the metapsychological, Freud's vision in *Beyond the Pleasure Principle* dovetails with that of **The White Hotel.**

Harold Bloom's discussion of Freud in *Agon* is helpful for applying Freud's psychological theories to the function of language. Bloom argues that in *Beyond the Pleasure Principle* Freud equates literal meaning to Thanatos and figurative meaning to Eros (136). Because the relationship between figurative and literal meaning in language is always a crossing over, Eros and Thanatos take the shape of a chiasmus. In his book on Freud, Paul Ricoeur stresses that Thanatos as a drive is allied to compulsions to repeat (281). As a consequence of chiasmus, repression becomes a fantasy of Eros to mask the repetitive urge within the procreative. **The White Hotel** counters the repetitive urge with a proleptic one, linking it to Eros. The dispassionate narrative voice of Chapters One and Two represses the horror of the future. However, the fantasies of proliferating sexual love ultimately are solipsistic and self-referential—taking on the repetitive dimension of Thanatos. It is only through desire of or union with another that Eros can emerge unencumbered to fight against the death instinct. **The White Hotel** presents Lisa's decision to accompany Kolya and her nurturing role in "The Camp" to counter Thanatos. The repressed narrative voice of the poem and journal is now imbued with ethical direction. Eros is restored as love from the heart and joins with reason to heal the effects of Thanatos.

After the historical documents of Anna's poem and journal and Freud's case history, the events at Babi Yar become another context of historical discourse, another form of closure. An Oedipal conflict of sorts is enacted within the narrative structure as the umbrella of male, rational authority concludes the first triangle of the novel, negating female telluric and prescient powers and foreshadowing the violation of generativity in Chapter Five. This is modified by the female interpretation that begins the second triangle before the historical dimension of Chapter Five universalizes the private history of Lisa, again undercutting Freud's individual, patriarchal interpretation. In giving us "The Camp" as future, Thomas asks the reader to reject the father and to embrace the female perspective at the conclusion. In doing so, he offers an aesthetic defense against his own created image, a restoration of metaphor to combat the demon of repetition that is the death instinct of history and of language.

Again Bloom is helpful in his linking of the sublime to *Beyond the Pleasure Principle*. Bloom draws on the Burkean notion of the sublime, which shifted the definition from loftiness of vision to terror allied with pleasure.[11] Bloom states that

> the passion caused by the great and sublime in nature, when their causes operate most powerfully, is Astonishment; and astonishment is that state of the soul, in which all its motions are suspended, with some degree of horror. In this case the mind is so entirely filled with its objects, that it cannot entertain any other. . . . Hence arises the great power of the sublime, that far from being produced by them, it *anticipates* our reasonings, it hurries us on by an irresistible force. (113; emphasis mine)

He goes on to discuss Vico's argument that the sublime poet discovers his rhetorical drive in divination, the process of foretelling the dangers to the self's survival, and equates this drive to what Freud terms the primal instinct of Eros (115). *The White Hotel* operates as a sublime text through its combination of terror and pleasure that both contributes to and is realized in its proleptic vision. As a sublime text, it defends itself against its own created image by continuously revising that creation.[12] In terms of Bloom's congruence of psychoanalytic and linguistic, it undergoes a process of unnaming akin to Freud's *Verneinung*—a psychic disavowal. Through repetition, the reader notices patterns of images that signal a center from which the reading must proceed simultaneously backwards and forwards, a collapsing of time and hierarchies that makes the text both horizontal and vertical. However, the shifting context in which these images are presented renders our interpretative centers no more than a stroking of the crucifix, another imposed and self-imposed duplicity.

Ricoeur equates repression with metaphor and, paralleling Bloom, puts repression in the realm of Eros (402). The proleptic vision that lurks through the repressions of the first four chapters of *The White Hotel* is realized in the Babi Yar chapter, which offers anagnorisis. The death force of history eradicates all metaphoric readings of signs and annihilates figurative complexity with its monomania. To end the novel at this point would be an implicit endorsement of this nihilistic vision and a negation of the narrative multidimensionality that Thomas has built. In Chapter Six, Thomas acknowledges Thanatos but restores metaphoric repression to the text so that Eros may again

prosper. Through the scent of a pine tree, fictional depth is reinstated in the imaginative life of the text.

In his "Note on a Mystic Writing Pad," Freud uses a common dime store toy, often referred to as a "Magic Slate," as a metaphor for how the unconscious works. Impressions strike the conscious mind like the writing implement on the slate, but their manifestations are eventually removed like the lifting of the plastic sheet on which the impressions register. However, the waxen slate that is underneath the plastic sheet functions like the unconscious in retaining all the marks elicited by the pressures of the writing implement.[13] *The White Hotel* functions in a similar fashion. Each chapter is so revisionary that it superficially wipes the slate clean; however, the imprints registered by all the narrative details remain in the reader's mind, sometimes superimposed on one another. The chiasmic triangles of the narrative structure constantly comment on each other as our backwards and forwards reading invites repetitive transformation, a combination of Eros and Thanatos. Psychical duplicity becomes the duplicity of fiction that is paradoxically liberating through its repressions in its sublime merger of terror and pleasure.

Notes

1. In a 1908 letter to Karl Abraham, Freud asked Abraham to forgive Jung's spirituality. It is easier for Jews to accept psychoanalysis, Freud explained, "as we lack the mystical element" (Steele 209).

2. Other critics, most impressively David Cowart, have noted some of the doubling of images and triangular relationships in *The White Hotel*. However, none has seen them functioning as an integral facet of the narrative structure of the novel.

3. Marsha Kinder thoroughly treats the image patterns of trains, swans, and pines (162-168).

4. In "Medusa's Head" (1922), Freud equates the terror engendered by the decapitated head of Medusa with castration anxiety. Medusa's head represents the female genitals, the snake encircled head suggests the public hair (105). See also Freud's "The Infantile Genital Organization of the Libido." The conjunction with Venus and Ceres in *The White Hotel* is, of course, another instance of the joining of mirrored opposites. In a different but related context, Anna recalls observing jellyfish floating just beneath the surface of the lake at her childhood home, and Freud's note tells us that she used the Russian term *medusa* for jellyfish (118). Since the jellyfish is womb-shaped, Lisa's recollection of a floating womb refers us back to the gliding womb at the white hotel and forward to the rape scene in the penultimate chapter.

5. Kinder offers an excellent discussion of the links between Freud's case study of the Wolf Man and *The White Hotel* (155).

6. The critical material on *The White Hotel* has already noted the similarities between the case history of

Anna G. and that of Freud's patient Dora in "Fragment of Analysis of a Case of Hysteria." In a letter to me dated 30 July 1987, Thomas states that he was not consciously influenced by the Dora material. "The case I studied most intensively," he writes, "mainly for style and form, was that of Elizabeth in the Freud-Breuer series." One of Jung's patients, Miss Miller, also has several parallels with the case of Anna. Miss Miller writes poetry with an accompanying prose interpretation and experiences a pain in her breast, in this case, at the sight of the dying Christian de Neurillette in *Cyrano de Bergerac*. Jung writes of her "extraordinary capacity for identification and empathy" (Jung 5: 34). In one of her poems about creation, Miss Miller puts sound before light. She explained that the pre-Socratic philosopher, Anaxagoras, "makes the cosmic rise out of chaos by means of a whirlwind—which does not normally occur without producing a noise" (Jung 5: 45). With the transmutation of a few letters, "Anaxagoras" becomes "anagornisis"—"Clarification! More light! More light! More light—and more love" (236). I am indebted to my student, Karen Riedel, for pointing out these connections to me.

7. Thomas has the fictional Freud write to Lisa, "my experience of psychoanalysis has convinced me that telepathy exists. If I had my life to go over again, I should devote it to the study of this factor" (196). The quotation comes from a letter that the real Freud wrote from Bad Gastein to Hereward Carrington, who was soliciting his support for parapsychological research (Jones 3: 419-420). Freud concluded this letter by stating, "I am utterly incapable of considering the 'survival of the personality' after death even as a scientific possibility. . . ." Cowart argues that Thomas conceived *The White Hotel* as a response to this final statement (218). In addition to being a corresponding member of the Society for Psychical Research, Freud wrote several essays on the occult: "A Premonitory Dream Fulfilled" (1899), "Premonitions and Chance" (1904), "Psychoanalysis and Telepathy" (1921), "Dreams and Telepathy" (1922), "The Occult Significance of Dreams" (1925), and "Dreams and the Occult" (1933).

8. The plagiarism controversy that emerged after the publication of *The White Hotel* is detailed by Lynn Felder. The accusations focus primarily on Thomas' use of details from Kuznetsov's novel in "The Sleeping Carriage" chapter. Using the same premise, critics might have accused Thomas of plagiarism in the "Frau Anna G" chapter because it is largely modeled on Freud's analysis of Elizabeth; however, none has. What those who accuse Thomas of plagiarism fail to understand is how much the argument inherent in *The White Hotel* hinges on the revision of documents as aspects of the multiple narrative voices.

9. Several critics, particularly early reviewers of the novel, object to the inclusion of "The Camp" after the Babi Yar chapter. See, for example, Thomas Flanagan's review. Mary F. Robertson states that "The Camp" is unconvincing because "its sense of renewal is aesthetic rather than ethical" (472). My argument holds that the sense of renewal in the final chapter, although qualified by the lingering presence of Thanatos, is aesthetic and also ethical.

10. Cowart makes these identifications (225). Robertson objects to Thomas' portrayal of his female hero's knowledge in stereotypically mythic terms. In doing so, Robertson claims, Thomas fails to rectify history's horrors through his art (465).

11. The collision between two incongruous opposites, the one terrible and the other beautiful, is also the central concern of the grotesque (Kayser passim). Certainly the frequent juxtaposition of human and animal as well as the conjunction of Venus and Medusa in *The White Hotel* contribute to a reading of the novel as a work of the grotesque. See Margot Norris' *Beasts of the Modern Imagination* for a fascinating exploration of the structural premises upon which the differences between humans and animals have been founded and the attempts to heal this breach in the "biocentric tradition" of modern thought and art.

12. A connection with Arnold Schopenhauer's view of madness as revisionary memory might be suggested here. In *The World as Will and Representation* (1: 193), Schopenhauer characterizes the madman's memory as selective, the gaps of which he fills with fictions to create a comprehensible world. Drawing in part on Harold Bloom's theory of the anxiety of influence, Daniel O'Hara links Schopenhauer's madman with revisionist theory. At the conclusion of his essay, O'Hara suggests that "revisionary madness could also be seen as an uncanny restoration to health . . . that the critic best embodies Freud's image from *Civilization and Its Discontents* of man as a prosthetic god" (47). Bloom himself deems Schopenhauer's theory of the sublime to be the precursor of Freud's in that Freud's unconscious forgetting substitutes for Schopenhauer's conscious turning away (124).

13. In "Freud and the Scene of Writing," Jacques Derrida challenges Freud's premise that there exist finite origins to repression. Using Freud's statement from "Note on the Mystic Writing Pad," "if we imagine one hand writing upon the surface of the Mystic Writing-Pad while another periodically raises its covering sheet from the wax slab, we shall have a concrete representation of the way in which I tried to picture the functioning of the perceptual apparatus of our mind" (232), Derrida agrees that "writing is unthinkable without repression" (226). However, he views that repression as ongoing rather than primal. David Hoy argues that Derrida sets up his examples after the fashion of Freud, locating

"undecidability at the syntactical rather than the semantic level" (55).

Works Cited

Bloom, Harold. *Agon: Towards a Theory of Revisionism.* New York: Oxford UP, 1982.

Burke, Edmund. *A Philosophical Enquiry into the Origin of Our Ideas of the Sublime and the Beautiful.* 1757. Ed. James T. Boulton. London: Routledge, 1958.

Cowart, David. "Being and Seeming: *The White Hotel.*" *Novel* 19 (1986): 216-231.

Derrida, Jacques. "Freud and the Scene of Writing." *Writing and Difference.* Trans. Alan Bass. Chicago: U of Chicago P, 1978. 196-231.

Felder, Lynn. "D. M. Thomas: The Plagiarism Controversy." *Dictionary of Literary Biography Yearbook 1982.* 79-82.

Flanagan, Thomas. "To Babi Yar and Beyond." *Nation* (2 May 1981): 537-539.

Freud, Sigmund. *Beyond the Pleasure Principle. The Standard Edition of the Complete Psychological Works of Sigmund Freud.* 1920. Trans. James Strachey. Vol. 18. London: Hogarth P and Institute of Psycho-Analysis, 1955. 3-64. 24 vols. 1953-1974.

———. "Fragment of an Analysis of a Case of Hysteria." 1905. *Collected Papers.* Trans. Alix and James Strachey. Vol. 3. New York: Basic, 1959. 5 vols. 13-146.

———. "The Infantile Genital Organization of the Libido." 1923. *Collected Papers.* Trans. Joan Riviere. Vol. 2. New York: Basic, 1959. 244-249.

———. "Inhibitions, Symptoms and Anxiety." 1926. Trans. James Strachey. *Standard Edition.* Vol. 20. London: Hogarth P and Institute of Psycho-Analysis, 1955. 77-179.

———. "Medusa's Head." 1922. *Collected Papers.* Trans. James Strachey. Vol. 5. New York: Basic, 1959. 105-106.

———. "Note on the Mystic Writing-Pad." 1925. Trans. James Strachey. *Standard Edition.* Vol. 19. London: Hogarth P and the Institute of Psycho-Analysis, 1955. 227-235.

Hoy, David. "Jacques Derrida." *The Return of Grand Theory in the Human Sciences.* Ed. Quentin Skinner. London: Cambridge UP, 1985. 41-64.

Jones, Ernest. *Sigmund Freud: Life and Work.* 3 vols. London: Hogarth P, 1957.

Jung, C. G. *Collected Works,* Vol. 5. *Symbols of Transformation.* 2nd ed. Trans. R.F.C. Hull. Princeton: Princeton UP, 1967. 34-38. 20 vols. 1953-1979.

Kayser, Wolfgang. *The Grotesque in Art and Literature.* Trans. Ulrich Weisstein. Bloomington: Indiana UP, 1963.

Kinder, Marsha. "The Spirit of *The White Hotel.*" *Humanities in Society* 4-5 (1981-1982): 143-170.

Kuznetsov, Anatoli. *Babi Yar.* Trans. David Floyd. New York: Pocket, 1971.

Norris, Margot. *Beasts of the Modern Imagination.* Baltimore: Johns Hopkins UP, 1985.

O'Hara, Daniel. "Revisionary Madness: The Prospects of American Literary Theory at the Present Time." *Against Theory: Literary Studies and the New Pragmatism.* Ed. W. J. T. Mitchell. Chicago: U of Chicago P, 1985. 31-47.

Ricoeur, Paul. *Freud and Philosophy: An Essay on Interpretation.* Trans. Denis Savage. New Haven: Yale UP, 1970.

Robertson, Mary F. "Hystery, Herstory, History: 'Imagining the Real' in Thomas' *The White Hotel.*" *Contemporary Literature* 25 (1984): 452-477.

Schopenhauer, Arnold. *The World as Will and Representation.* Trans. E. F. J. Payne. 2 vols. New York: Dover, 1966.

Steele, Robert S. *Freud and Jung: Conflicts of Interpretation.* London: Routledge, 1982.

Thomas, D. M. Rev. of *A Secret Symmetry: Sabina Spielrein Between Jung and Freud.* By Aldo Carotenuto. *New York Review of Books* 13 May 1982: 3, 6.

———. *The White Hotel.* New York: Viking, 1981.

Lars Ole Sauerberg (essay date Fall 1989)

SOURCE: "When the Soul Takes Wing: D. M. Thomas's *The White Hotel,*" in *Critique: Studies in Contemporary Fiction,* Vol. XXXI, No. 1, Fall, 1989, pp. 3-10.

[*In the following essay, Sauerberg examines Thomas's problematic incorporation of imaginative lyricism, psychological fantasy, and historical reality in* The White Hotel. *Sauerberg notes that, where concerning the Holocaust, the intermingling of fictive reality and historical reality raises serious moral questions.*]

In the years that have passed since the publication of D. M. Thomas's **The White Hotel** in 1981, the book has lost the best-seller status it enjoyed when it first appeared.[1] In my opinion, Thomas's **Hotel** is one of the few works of best-selling fiction from recent years that needs and deserves reconsideration. It needs reconsideration because the uproar surrounding its publication impeded a balanced assessment. It deserves reconsideration because the work is very ambitious, and it requires a critical response that discusses it on the basis of that ambition.

The book's reviewers tended to focus on its sensational aspects, the quality of its Freud imitations, and its compositional ingenuities. Although we cannot deny the presence of sensational elements, to treat the book as if it were pornography is utterly to misconstrue its intention. The imitations of Freud are cleverly done—the circumstantial and fatherly tone close to its model—and Thomas's literary acumen is well established by a textual fabric of great complexity. Few reviewers at the time of publication brought these disparate observations together.[2]

My reaction of confusion upon first reading the book is likely similar to that of other readers. Upon re-reading the book, I realized that this confusion stemmed partly from its intricate structure and partly from a feeling of uncertainty about the nature of the idea that gave rise to the book. As Thomas's virtuoso palimpsest technique of mixing fiction and reality opens itself neatly to the careful motif and structural analyst, this part of the confusion proved to be a superficial barrier. The real confusion springs from the thematic concerns.

Two possibilities for interpretation seem to arise. Either the book is to be read as an extended lyrical poem, with appreciation relying upon its suggestive qualities—which means that it must be accepted and responded to as a fact of life, whether it is understood or not—or the book is a comment on something apart from it—an attempt to come to terms with an extratextual reality. Whereas the approach based on the autonomous status of the book is a possible way of dealing with it, because the reader tuned to the lyrical experience responds to it so well, bringing together so much documentary reality in the book is a constant disturbance of the lyrical approach. *The White Hotel* insists upon bringing the text face-to-face with the reality of the issues that constitute its imaginative fabric. I contend that however admirably Thomas works his imagery, he fails to create a satisfying fictional form that contains and redeems a particularly nasty chapter in twentieth-century history.

Thomas's own comments on his book may be of initial help. The author offers two slightly different genesis stories. To *Publishers Weekly* he explained that:

> *The White Hotel* actually started as a poem. The image of a train journey had haunted him as part of a quarrel between Jung and Freud, both so convinced of their own self-importance that each felt the other should take the short train journey necessary for them to meet (in the end, neither did). Thomas wrote a poem on this idea, then worried that it seemed unfinished. Then he read Kuznetsov's *Babi Yar*, about the wartime massacre of Jews at Kiev. "I was going to the United States and wanted—needed—a long book for the flight. The account of the Holocaust suddenly connected with my poems. Everything fell into place. And I didn't go to the United States after all—I started to write the novel instead."[3]

In a later interview with Judith Thurman, he added a thematic suggestion to his account of how several originally fragmentary poetic images were brought together:

> The book began with the poem. In the Ernest Jones biography of Freud, I read that Freud had interviewed—I mean analyzed, that's a funny slip—a woman who claimed to be having an affair with his son. I thought that was a wonderful dramatic idea. So I tried to get inside the voice of the woman to whom this had happened. And the images just came to me from some very pure source. . . . But I didn't know where they were leading until I read the account of Babi Yar . . . a few years later. I realized then that the woman, almost certainly having been Jewish, could have ended

up at Babi Yar or in the camps. And that these were the poles of experience in our century: love and death, Eros and Thanatos.[4]

Asked by Laura de Coppet about his motivation for writing *The White Hotel,* he stated that:

> I could say that the motivation was to write about the real history of the Twentieth century, which flows through the humanism of Freud into the desolation of the Holocaust; from that very personal landscape where people were studied individually with great care and a good deal of insight, into the time when masses were wiped out for no good reason. But I don't actually think that the answer occurred to me at the time. It probably emerged later, as the theme of the book. What excited me at first was reading Anatoli Kuznetsov's *Babi Yar,* quoting an eyewitness account.[5]

It appears from these three interview extracts that the genesis of the book was due to a merging of seemingly incompatible material—Freud vs. Babi Yar—and that the thematic implications were realized through subsequent rationalization. Thomas's own interpretation, then, is that *The White Hotel* is the portrait of an age—an age characterized by brutalization, as suggested in the four lines from Yeats's "Meditations in Time of Civil War" that Thomas used as his epigraph: "We had fed the heart on fantasies, / The Heart's grown brutal from the fare; / More substance in our enmities / Than in our love." This interpretation is an oversimplification, however, because his portrait is both a heavily stylized likeness, with priority given to existential extremes, and the expression of a wish to transcend the reality portrayed. In other words, Thomas is committed beyond mere reflection, epistemologically as well as ethically. It is therefore necessary to describe the nature of Thomas's vision and to discuss the validity of his own interpretation.

The White Hotel is a web of two different realities: a psychological reality with its origin in a (day)dream world, and a social reality with its origin in individual and collective histories. Thomas describes the first reality in a discourse saturated with symbols and traditional poetic devices, ranging from lyrical details to apocalyptic vision. The second reality is described in accordance with the conventions of the realistic novel. The unique quality of the work arises from the tension between the poetically dreamlike and the prosaically historical. The two do not, however, appear as absolutely polarized elements, but as fading into each other during a counterpoint-like progression.

The dramatic situations in *The White Hotel* are based on death in combination with eroticism. Compared with the intensity of the love-making and monstrous scenes of death in the book, however, Thomas's moral is disappointingly anticlimatic in its modesty. Toward the end of his interpretation of Lisa's life story, Freud replies to Lisa's question about the extent of his help that "much will be gained if we succeed in turning your hysterical misery into common unhappiness" (115-16). Further on, when they part, Freud tells her that he thinks she is "cured of everything but life, so to speak" (127).

Lisa is frustrated by the nondramatic progression of her cure. She expects treatment leading to a personal revolution, but Freud offers her readjustment only. Toward the end of the book, in the camp, her mentor Richard Lyons, obviously an incarnation of Freud's son appearing in her erotic dreams, turns Freud's pragmatic observations into advice about action. On Lisa's query, "Why is it like this, Richard? We were made to be happy and to enjoy life. What's happened?" (239), he "shook his head in bafflement, and breathed out smoke. '*Were* we made to be happy? You're an incurable optimist, old girl!' He stubbed the cigarette, and took the baton from his belt. 'We're desperately short of nurses,' he said. 'Can you help?'" (239-40; Thomas's italics). Happily, Lisa then accepts her inglorious task and is instantaneously cured. Lisa's redemption is in her active participation in and service to life, but, we note, at the price of leaving ethical problems unresolved. When we do our existential sums, life comes out only slightly in the black, with Thomas falling little short of philistine stoicism in his conclusion.

"The Camp" is the concluding section of *The White Hotel,* but in a way it is also its beginning. Thomas's account of Lisa Erdman's life results in the reader's frustration if the work is read in accordance with our expectations of a realistic fictional universe. To the traditionally minded reader, who has finally found comfort when the book moves into the traditional omniscient perspective and the epic progression of the fourth section after the letters and the sexual fantasies of the first three, and who is consequently also able to see a system in these sections, the last section must seem embarrassingly out of tune.[6] Had Thomas chosen to finish the account after the blood bath of Babi Yar, he would at least have achieved a kind of tragic unity.

But the book is not written for any first reading. It unfolds in the same spatial manner as a lyrical poem beyond time and causality. The composition of the book—its structure—insists upon spatiality, which becomes clear only with the second reading. In this view, the concluding section can be seen to control our understanding of all the events, and of the structure, of the book. In his fictional letter to Freud in the prologue, Sachs writes that Lisa's fantasies seem to him Paradise before the fall: "not that love and death did not happen there, but there was no *time* in which they could have meaning" (14-15; Thomas's italics). This remark is an essential key to *The White Hotel*. Timelessness is both a condition of the reading experience and a central theme in its own right.

It should be noted that Freud is unable to cure Lisa's hysteria, or what he diagnoses as hysteria, because there are layers in Lisa's psyche deeper than or different from those reachable by Freud that stubbornly oppose the psychoanalytic probing. Freud's analysis is clearly insufficient, not only because of the technical shortcomings of his method but also, and more important, because any scientifically founded therapy is irrelevant for Thomas's purposes. Lisa's symptoms may be mitigated but not eliminated in this world. Freud's slow discovery of repressed layers in Lisa's mind, and his diagnosis of unrecognized homosexuality—that is, the psychoanalytic routine treatment with the expectation that the patient's recognition of the repression is its cure—reveal a clinical and fragmented view of man.

Freud is not to be Lisa's redeemer. In the last resort, he himself is a patient, as is emphasized by his appearance in "The Camp." Thomas's introductory author's note makes the point at the earliest possible stage: "Freud becomes one of the dramatis personae, in fact, as discoverer of the great and beautiful modern myth of psychoanalysis." Underlying the myth, which is the human attempt to meet the world by the logic of a story, is the principle of causality in the Newtonian world picture. Freud's help to Lisa is reduced to agreement with Heraclitus that "[t]he soul of a man is a far country, which cannot be approached or explored" (174).

Lisa's symptoms violate the linear concept of time and turn our accepted causality principle upside down. The pains in her breast and abdomen are proleptic stigmata stemming from the bestial treatment she receives in the mass grave. During Freud's therapy, Lisa declares that she possesses a psychic gift, a gift in whose validity Freud believes. She explains that on several occasions she has had pre-visions of events that occur later. Her explanation might be of some help on the level of symbol structure, but it is hardly a satisfactory explanation for applying the text to the reality incorporated in it. As indicated in Thomas's introductory note, Freud and psychoanalysis are given a metascientific status, and *The White Hotel* is intended as a challenge to the logic that asserts itself in the procedures of psychoanalytic therapy.

What, then, has Thomas to offer by way of challenge, apart from mythologizing? Basically, as I have argued, he offers a stoic lesson expressed in a lyrical poem of extensive length and unusual composition, victorious eros fantasies relating to a psychological reality of (day)dreaming, and a thanatos element documented as history. The problematic nature of the book is rooted primarily in the insistence of the superior value of the dream. But the reality of Babi Yar obviously resists sublimation. Thomas's acknowledgment of this problem is seen in his transition from section five to section six. After having explained in considerable detail and with the force of understatement how after the war the Babi Yar ravine was filled up and forgotten, how "progress" made its way, he claims: "But all this had nothing to do with the guest, the soul, the lovesick bride, the daughter of Jerusalem" (222). The psychoanalysis, which has been the red thread so far, is, as an essentially rationalist activity, unable to cope with an incomprehensibly cruel reality against which the highly tentative and theoretical thanatos concept has little comfort to offer. Two pages before he depicts the escape of the soul to a transcendental afterlife, Thomas describes the eventual futility of Dr. Freud's endeavors, again with the Heraclitus echo:

The soul of man is a far country, which cannot be approached or explored. Most of the dead were poor or illiterate. But every single one of them had dreamed dreams, seen visions, and had amazing experiences, even the babes in arms (perhaps especially the babes in arms). Though most of them had never lived outside the Podol slum, their lives and histories were as rich and complex as Lisa Erdman-Berenstein's. If a Sigmund Freud had been listening and taking notes from the time of Adam, he would still not fully have explored even a single group, even a single person. (220)

If we read the book not primarily for its richness of suggestive imagery but as a serious attempt to come to terms with the traumatic experiences of the twentieth century, the shift from the mass grave at Babi Yar to the "promised land" is the master fulcrum of the book; consequently, the very nature of the shift is subject to criticism. Thomas's problem is that he cannot unite persuasively the individual's wish for an afterlife with the historical certainty of the absolute, irrevocable, and *in casu* monstrous reality of death. Thomas gives expression to the instinct for survival in Lisa's jump into the mass grave just before the bullets hit her and Kolya. But the wish—the demand—for eternal life, even in a twentieth-century version of paradise reduced to a place for mere survival, must necessarily be formulated in this world, which is why the traditional literary vision—the apocalypse—presents itself as the solution.

As literary text, as postulate about its own reality, *The White Hotel* indeed has consistency. But when we begin to discuss the validity of Thomas's postulate in a broad existential context, the book's flaws appear. Suffering, both as experienced by Lisa individually and by the victims collectively, is left frustratingly unredeemed. Thomas Flanagan judges it an impossible ambition that "*The White Hotel* seeks to fuse the sufferings of an individual with the horrors of this unspeakable century, and to suggest, by radiance of image and form, that all of them can be confronted."[7] Despite the author's intention, Thomas's book makes it clear that there is a point beyond which the literary fantasy can no longer cope with the reality it transforms. It seems to be not so much a question of lack of artistic cleverness as a question of general morality, as suggested by Hermione Lee: "To give Freud an imaginary patient in 1920, and to turn her into a victim of the Nazis so as imaginatively to encompass the turning of the layers of the soul into layers of bodies, raises the question of whether the craftiness of fiction is even permissible here."[8] Fictional "reality" and experienced, historical reality are two different types. Paul Ableman has expressed the opinion that this epistemological problem is a central issue of *The White Hotel:* "A major theme of this novel is the final elusiveness of reality which must be documented before it can be scrutinised and will inevitably be distorted by the documentation."[9] Although Ableman's point is valid, I hesitate to pronounce this problem a major theme of the book. In my opinion, Mary F. Robertson is more helpful when she suggests—about the "inherited problem of the relation between fact and fantasy, the empirical, and the mediated"[10]—that Thomas's *The White Hotel* is a symptom of a widening gap between the nature of twentieth-century reality and conventional literary renderings of it. With reference to the Yeats epigraph, she concludes that:

> . . . culture still has a problem finding a way to "feed the heart on fantasies" that are healthy and yet have a power in history. It shows that Lisa's knowledge as woman, as analysand, and as Nazi victim is literally still unspeakable in any mainstream discourse because the poet can do no more than translate, as Freud did in psychoanalysis, the discourse of her body and the insane discourse of the Nazis into a discourse foreign to the victims' own understanding of themselves, which is poetry.[11]

If George Levine's *New York Review* pronouncement that "Elisabeth's heroism is unreflecting, and when she dies at Babi Yar protecting her husband's child we witness events for which no documents exist"[12] is changed modally into "for which no document *can* exist," we are, in my opinion, close to the core of the problem. Thomas is obviously aware that he is dealing with material that demands another kind of attention than that we are accustomed to in fiction. He responds with a discourse that succeeds initially in forcing the reader out of his habitual pose, but the expression of collective suffering on such a monstrous scale eludes Thomas's attempt at verbal containment. His resort to the immediacy of the eyewitness report is effective as long as it lasts, but when he chooses the metaphysical escape in his version of the human comedy, he leaves the reader with an unfulfilled sense of moral responsibility. The insane reality of mass murder will not tolerate the sublimation of poetic fictionalization.

Toward the end of his *New York Times Book Review* article, Leslie Epstein cites Freud: "To endure life remains, when all is said, the first duty of all living beings. Illusion can have no value if it makes this more difficult for us."[13] I suggest in conclusion that the way *The White Hotel* attempts to make life endurable rests on an illusion due to a general difficulty in applying a wishful literary fantasy to a repellent historical reality, a difficulty foregrounded by Thomas's choice of the Holocaust as primary subject matter. The novel format, uneasily adopted by Thomas, works optimally with reference to a reality of limited dimensions and with the moral issues that belong in our world, which is why the text succeeds so well as a case study of individual neurosis. But Thomas's total vision, which aims at nothing less than the presentation of traumatic twentieth-century history and its possible redemption through the soul's will to survive, is essentially incompatible with a generic tradition that emphasizes the individual in his social and psychological contexts. Thomas may be right in his argument that when Lisa "changes from being Lisa an individual to Lisa in history,"[14] her sudden representativeness is well reflected in the neutral and detached wording of Dina Pronicheva's eyewitness report, which has the force of anonymous and therefore collective testimony of the atrocities carried out at Babi Yar.[15] Whereas no change is felt, however, in the transformation from Thomas's own narrative into the passages adapted from *Babi Yar,* as there is no difference between the historical and the fictional on the verbal level, we might feel disturbed at Thomas's dismissal of the mass grave with the words: "But all this had nothing to do with the guest, the soul, the lovesick bride, the daughter of Jerusalem" (222). The foundation of realistic fiction in history makes us readily accept the documentary (provided there is similarity of style) but makes it difficult to accept metaphysical solutions, especially when the contrast is so cruelly marked as is the case in *The White Hotel.*

Notes

1. D. M. Thomas, born in 1935 in Cornwall, was a poet and translator of Russian poetry before he turned to fiction. *The White Hotel* is his third novel, preceded by *The Flute Player* (1979) and *Birthstone* (1980). His fiction subsequent to *The White Hotel* is a long, loosely structured improvisation novel: *Ararat* (1983), *Swallow* (1984), *Sphinx* (1986), and *Summit* (1987).

   Page references to *The White Hotel* are to the King Penguin 1981 edition and appear in the main text.

2. *The White Hotel* was, on the whole, well received everywhere. Reviewers were lavish with their praise for Thomas's brilliant narrative technique but more cautious in their interpretations, which were characterized by rather broad and noncommittal statements such as "[w]hat *The White Hotel* sets out to perform, clearly, is the diagnosis of our epoch through the experience of an individual"; (Leslie Epstein in the *New York Times Book Review,* 15 March 1981, 26); or "[i]n this bold, intellectually challenging novel, Thomas goes beyond both history and historical fiction: he explores the shadowy realm of perception and perceiver with breathtaking vision and artistry." (*Virginia Quarterly Review* 57, Summer 1981, 99). Thomas's integration in section V (entitled "The Sleeping Carriage") of material from Anatoli Kuznetsov's *Babi Yar* sparked a prolonged debate about Thomas's alleged plagiarism in the *Times Literary Supplement* in March and April 1982. Thomas's attackers felt that he had presented documentary material as his own fiction.

3. 27 March 1981, 6.

4. *Mademoiselle* (Feb. 1983) 160.

5. *Interview* (June 1982) 32.

6. I am aware that my assumption of a reading strategy along conventionally realistic lines may raise objections from those who readily place the work in a modernist or postmodernist context. But the prologue and the first five sections make sense as traditional realism as soon as the case-history pattern is realized in section three, "Frau Anna G." Until section six, "The Camp," Thomas relies upon a fragmentary technique borrowed, for instance, from suspense novels, which does not question the reality transformed into fiction or the validity of the verbal representation of that reality. It is therefore to be expected that the general reader's reaction will be based upon realistic naturalization.

7. *The Nation* (2 May 1981) 2.

8. *The Observer* (18 Jan. 1981) 31.

9. *The Spectator* (17 Jan. 1981) 21.

10. "Hystery, Herstory, History," *Contemporary Literature* 25 (Winter 1984) 453.

11. "Hystery, Herstory, History" 477.

12. 28 May 1981, 21.

13. 15 March 1981, 27.

14. Thomas's letter to the editor of the *Times Literary Supplement,* 2 April 1982, 383.

15. Thomas observes, "From the infinitely varied world of imaginative fiction we move to a world in which fiction is not only severely constrained but irrelevant" (Thomas's letter to the editor of the *Times Literary Supplement* 383).

Angeline Goreau (review date 8 July 1990)

SOURCE: "The Characters Are in Charge," in *New York Times Book Review,* July 8, 1990, pp. 3, 19.

[*In the following review, Goreau offers unfavorable evaluation of* Lying Together *and Thomas's "Russian Nights" series. Goreau finds fault in Thomas's preoccupation with theory and ideas over plot and characters in these novels.*]

In his extraordinary novel **The White Hotel,** D. M. Thomas introduced a succession of apparently disparate "documents"—an exchange of letters between analysts; the violently erotic imaginings of a young woman recorded in blank verse between the staves of Mozart's *Don Giovanni;* a prose journal written by the same woman; Sigmund Freud's (fictional) case study of "Anna G."; a traditional, third-person narrative giving the history of Frau Elisabeth Erdman, a k a Anna G.; a chilling account of the Holocaust at Babi Yar, and a surreal scene in which the resurrected heroine meets her beloved dead.

As the novel progresses, the essential connection between these perplexing fragments becomes manifest; each is, in some sense, a translation of the last: Moving from poetry, the most subjective of literary forms and that closest to the dream language of the id, to an account that assumes the objectivity of history, D. M. Thomas explores the means through which literature attempts to come to terms with experience—with the complicated meeting of self and world. How, **The White Hotel** asks, do we arrive at meaning? How do we arrive at truth?

D. M. Thomas returns to the same questions, adopting similar literary methods, in "Russian Nights," the quintet of novels written after **The White Hotel,** which **Lying Together** concludes. The sequence of novels, which began with **Ararat** in 1983, followed by **Swallow** (1984), **Sphinx** (1987) and **Summit** (1988), is unified (the author notes) by the theme of improvisation: "the mysterious way in which a word, an image, a dream, a story, calls up another, connected yet independent."

"Russian Nights" is dedicated to Pushkin, who presides over the quintet much as Freud presided over *The White Hotel,* both as progenitor and character. Mr. Thomas's improvisational novels were inspired by a narrative fragment called "Egyptian Nights," which Pushkin began in 1835, two years before he was killed in a duel. In the Pushkin story, a poet named Charsky, writing in his study, is interrupted by a foreigner whose shabby aura excites his suspicion. The stranger, it turns out, is an *improvisatore*—a performer who extemporizes verse on themes suggested by an audience—who has come to ask Charsky's help in acquiring patrons. Demonstrating his art, the *improvisatore* asks the Russian poet for a theme and the latter offers: "The poet himself should choose the subject of his songs; the crowd has no right to direct his inspiration." Obliging, the foreigner begins with these lines: "Eyes open wide, the poet weaves / Blind as a bat, his urgent way." Later on, at the evening Charsky organizes to introduce him into Petersburg society, the *improvisatore* begins a brilliant poem on the subject of "Cleopatra's Lovers." In the middle of the verses, the story breaks off.

Mr. Thomas, who is one of Pushkin's foremost translators, inserted the entire text of "Egyptian Nights" into *Ararat,* the first novel of his quintet. He framed that story, however, in a dizzying spiral of authorship. At the beginning of the book, a Russian poet named Sergei Rozanov amuses himself by improvising a story—a talent he has inherited from his Armenian grandfather. His subject is improvisation. Rozanov imagines three other writers thrown together by chance at an international conference who agree to collaborate on an improvisation of their own. They create a character named Victor Surkov, a repulsively trendy Russian poet who in his turn invents alternative endings for Pushkin's unfinished story, one of which imitates Pushkin's own real ending—a duel over his wife's honor. At one point in the narrative, Surkov seems to *become* Pushkin.

Swallow, Sphinx and *Summit* gave variations on the theme of improvisation, introducing many of the same characters and interlarding dreams, narrative, poems, a play called "Isadora's Scarf," political satire, borrowed texts (H. Rider Haggard's *King Solomon's Mines*, for example) and historical events and persons. But Pushkin and "Egyptian Nights," in one guise or another, were never far from sight. What interests Mr. Thomas in the story, from the evidence of the novels, is the paradox on which it turns: the *improvisatore* stands for creativity in its most elemental form (inspiration), but at the same time the subject of his verses is always something given to him. Literature, Mr. Thomas suggests, is a collaboration of past and present, repetition and invention, the world as given and the world imagined.

Lying Together seems at first to take a new tack. The "real" people behind the earlier fictions are unveiled: the narrator is Don Thomas, a British writer attending an international writers' conference in London. Here, he meets his Russian friends Sergei Rozanov, Victor Surkov and Masha Barash—all fictional characters in the earlier novels. The four writers discuss the novels they have improvised together—*Ararat, Swallow, Sphinx* and *Summit*—and agree to collaborate on a new one, *Lying Together.* The first four novels have been published as the work of "D. M. Thomas," we learn, because Soviet censorship made it impossible to tell the truth. Now that perestroika has arrived, however, the Russians are agitating to have their part in the novels revealed, but Don Thomas tells them that the contract with Viking Penguin forbids it.

Subsequent twists of the plot reveal still more "real" people lurking behind fictional characters—as well as fictional characters who become real people, arousing the resentment of their inventors. Each mystery solved though, seems to create several more perplexities. And all the while, the character-authors are deceiving one another, interpreting one another, and giving the reader advice on how to read the books they've improvised. Victor Surkov, discussing *Lying Together* in an interview, remarks: "There's a sexual pun there, of course: in sex there's the same combination of lies and deeper truth."

On the most intimate level, *Lying Together* insists that self-revelation is ultimately yet another form of fiction. We invent ourselves, then come to believe our own improvisations. But Mr. Thomas also intends his unfolding truths to function as a political metaphor, just as hysteria did in *The White Hotel.* Since Pushkin's time, improvisation—read disguise—has been the key to surviving the censors of both czars and revolutionaries. Where official language predominates, truth is no longer discernable.

An author's note prefacing *Summit* suggests D. M. Thomas intended that novel to conclude what he then called "The Russian Quartet." *Lying Together,* I suspect, was written as a response to the subsequent events of glasnost and perestroika. Discussing Soviet President Mikhail S. Gorbachev's speeches with his Russian friends, the fictional Don Thomas remarks that "he seemed to strike a humanistic, philosophical tone quite different from the traditional dreary, shrill propaganda jargon; a tone, moreover, to which our politicians were incapable of responding. That was because truth, in the West, had become slowly corrupted, Surkov said; whereas in the Soviet Union it had had to go underground for seventy years. Therefore when it was tapped it was still pure, like a spring."

Later on, though, Surkov tells a reporter from a London newspaper that "there is little actual censorship now, but there's something even more dangerous, in a way—self-censorship. Gorbachev is saying, Look, you guys, I'm trusting you; don't let me down! So we try not to let him down by censoring our works in our minds, or even our subconscious."

Like *The White Hotel,* the "Russian Nights" quintet is an engaging literary performance: a learned, witty, intricately constructed inquiry into the tricky relationship between art and life. Yet somehow it lacks the power of the earlier novel. In the end the quintet is more interesting to discuss than to read. This may be because, for all the fragmentation of the narrative in **The White Hotel,** that novel is still compellingly held together by a story—a story whose heroine we come to care about. This is only episodically the case with the characters in "Russian Nights"; for the most part they lack dimension. What we are left with finally is theory. Novels require something more.

T. J. Binyon (review date 7 February 1992)

SOURCE: "Dreams of Death," in *Times Literary Supplement,* February 7, 1992, p. 18.

[*In the following review, Binyon offers unfavorable assessment of* Flying to Love.]

"Ten thousand dreams a night, a Dallas psychologist told me, when I dined with her and her black lover, are dreamt about Kennedy's assassination." The journalistic flavour of the first sentence of **Flying in to Love,** with its fake numerical accuracy and hint of a prurient leer, sets the tone of the novel and also provides its form. It is to be a dream sequence about that day in November 1963, a series of random, disconnected, chronologically dislocated episodes, mingling past and present, real and fictional characters, including Lee Harvey Oswald, Lyndon Johnson and Sister Agnes, a pretty young history teacher at the Sacred Heart Convent in Dallas.

Interior monologue is the preferred mode of narration: Patrolman Tippit broods about his marital problems: Oswald contemplates life in Cuba and thinks of getting himself a Coca Cola; Marina, his wife, muses on the beauty of American bathrooms and wonders whether Lee has flushed the toilet. The characters carom against each other like billiard balls, touching but not communicating, and each break takes us back to Kennedy himself to explore a further aspect of his character. We meet him as the far-seeing statesman: "there were important things to do or think about, like what to say to Lodge on Sunday about the Vietnam situation. That was a fucking awful problem"; as the stern moralist: "A nun was a nun. There were limits. Yet her voice was as lovely as her face. Dammit"; as the deep thinker: "The world is just so crammed with beauty and heartbreak. Religion is about the only thing that makes any sense, and even that doesn't make too much"; as the diplomatic party politician, persuading Senator Yarborough to ride with Johnson: "Push him in and lock the door! Threaten to blow his fucking head off"; as the romantic poet: "I ought to have married an Irish girl. Who could sing the ballads and weave a spell of laughing words", and as the tender lover:

"You want me to put on a rubber?"

"God, no. We're Catholics."

"Oh, yes! I'd forgotten. It's OK, I'll pull out."

It is not clear that D. M. Thomas intends to turn Kennedy into such a figure of fun, largely because it is not clear what the aim of the novel itself is. After all, a dream about Kennedy is a reflection of the dreamer's psyche, not of reality. The point is made when the Dallas psychologist (a former pupil of Sister Agnes) writes: "For the British author who interviewed me during his writing of a book about Kennedy, the President stood for his father, who had been very pro-American and democratic." But putting together an inchoate mass of testimonies about the assassination is not a way of sorting out one's problems with one's parents: nor does it add up to an exploration of the collective unconsciousness.

In the end, despite its narrative pretensions, **Flying in to Love** (Love Airfield in Dallas) is just another fictionalized investigation into the circumstances surrounding Kennedy's death. It doesn't have the single-minded tendentiousness of Oliver Stone's film, *JFK:* if there was a conspiracy, it maintains, it was too complex to sort out. "The whole thing is messy, there seem to be innumerable clues, but almost all of them turn out to be red herrings, and they simply draw people deeper into a maze that has no exit." This is not a description of a conspiracy, but of a paranoiac's view of life. The novel's relentless trivialization of its characters' lives does not succeed in imbuing the event with any sense of tragedy, or showing that it had any profound effect on those involved. Thomas may not have wished to suggest that life is aleatory, sordid and meaningless, but it is difficult to find anything more positive in the book.

Robert Houston (review date 11 October 1992)

SOURCE: "Death in Dreamtime," in *New York Times Book Review,* October 11, 1992, pp. 13-14.

[*In the following review Houston offers positive assessment of* Flying to Love.]

Near the end of this novel based on the murder of John F. Kennedy, D. M. Thomas has one of his characters, a psychologist, comment on the many thousands of people who are haunted by the assassination. For all of them, she writes, it "occupies a kind of dreamtime. Kennedy is dead, he is not dead. He is being taken back for burial at Arlington; he is flying on to Austin. A physicist said to me that those few seconds carried too great a burden of event, of shock, and it was as if that weight caused time to cave in, creating a vortex, a whirlwind, in which past, present and future, and reality and illusion, became confused."

In effect, that psychologist is summarizing for us the argument of **Flying In to Love.** The novel itself is the vortex, in which Mr. Thomas dreams out the events of Nov. 22, 1963, again and again, each time from a different point of view and sometimes with a different result. In following the motorcade that departs from Dallas's Love Field, it is as if Mr. Thomas were running and rerunning the Zapruder film of the shooting, but changing the camera angles, moving backward and forward in time, adding characters, searching for a plot (in both meanings of the word), even imagining a world in which the assassination *didn't* succeed. In one sense, he is playing the what-if game long established in both historical and science fiction, but he is adding many more ifs than a less metafictionally inclined writer might dare.

Mr. Thomas, whose previous novels include **The White Hotel** and **Ararat,** assembles all of the expected cast—the Kennedys, the Johnsons, the Oswalds, J. Edgar Hoover—but he fictionalizes them with varying degrees of success. His Jacqueline Kennedy is the most sympathetic, truly in love with her husband, grieving over the baby she had recently lost, yet capable of great strength during the horror of the murder and its aftermath. Kennedy himself is a man incapable of deep affection for another individual, a man who can love only the faces in the crowds. Though there are moments when Mr. Thomas manages to make a reader feel sympathy for him, Kennedy remains too shallow, too wholly possessed by a gargantuan and amoral sexual appetite to seem fully credible, whether in a fantasy world or not. And Lyndon B. Johnson simply flops: a man who often seemed to be his own caricature can't be caricatured further, as Mr. Thomas attempts to do, without becoming merely a parody.

Of the invented characters, Sister Agnes, a young nun who was among those watching the motorcade, is the most interesting. When Kennedy stops his car and speaks to her, he sets in progress her lifelong obsession with him and his death an obsession that becomes a very complex kind of love. We stay with her through the stages of that love from the day of the assassination to the present, and see it manifest itself in dreams, fears, repressed lust, illness and finally bitterness. Sister Agnes serves Mr. Thomas well. She is both a soundly drawn character and a good vehicle for his exploration of the "vortex" caused by Kennedy's death, though her fixations on the martyred Jesus and on her father make some pretty heavy-handed symbolic connections.

Besides having difficulty creating convincing characters, Mr. Thomas sometimes runs into trouble wrapping his British tongue around the American idiom, especially the Texas variety. Although he is better at bilingualism than most writers who cross the Atlantic—in either direction—an American reader should come prepared to forgive, or not, some wooden dialogue and a few real boners. ("Nor me," exclaims a witness at one point; the novel is heavily populated with "Texan men" and "Texan Democrats.")

Despite its failings, however, **Flying In to Love** is worthwhile. Its greatest strength lies in Mr. Thomas's use of the assassination as the *occasion* for his book, rather than as the subject of it. He appears to accept the vast conspiracy theory of the killing and, in a section of the novel he calls "Historical Fictions," even expands it. Yet

the conspiracy—or its unraveling—is not what ultimately interests him. Instead, he wants to puzzle out the need so many people feel for a conspiracy to explain the assassination, a "plot" to the events, so we can believe that reasons and causality do exist in the universe, even if they're hidden. Does history seem solid and fixed, Mr. Thomas wonders, only because we're seeing it in its apparently completed form, separate from ourselves? What does it mean to us, and to our dreams, to realize that we *are* history and, even if only like particles in chaos theory, we might somehow change it? What if, what if?

On one level, Mr. Thomas's game has been played often. ("It's a Wonderful Life" comes easily to mind.) But on the level at which Mr. Thomas plays, the intellectual difference is as profound as that between checkers and chess.

Bryan Cheyette (review date 29 January 1993)

SOURCE: "A Pornographic Universe," in *Times Literary Supplement,* January 29, 1993, p. 20.

[*In the following review, Cheyette offers negative assessment of* Pictures at an Exhibition.]

The key to **Pictures at an Exhibition,** D. M. Thomas's tenth novel, can be found in the themes and content of his best-selling third novel, **The White Hotel** (1981). The earlier book generated a great deal of controversy, largely because of Thomas's shameless plundering of Anatoli Kuznetsov's account of the massacre of over 70,000 Jews in Babi Yar, on the outskirts of Kiev, in September 1941. Thomas's reworking of Kuznetsov's *Babi Yar* so as to include the sadistic rape of his fictional heroine, Lisa Erdman, caused an outcry. It was not just that Thomas rewrote an essential memoir in lurid terms, but, more worrying, that he was prepared to sacrifice the historical victims of genocide on the altar of his prevailing metaphors. In **The White Hotel,** these metaphors were part of a superficial Freudianism which united Eros and Thanatos, the life and death-instincts, eroticism and annihilation. Thomas is especially keen in his fiction to unify different realms of experience, whether they be Holocaust testimony, sexual fantasy, individual psychosis or artistic creation. **Pictures at an Exhibition** is a radical extension of this method and begins with Auschwitz death-camp, which is remade, in an act of supreme arrogance, in Thomas's own image.

Thomas's "Auschwitz" chapters are entitled "Death and the Maiden", after Schubert's *Der Tod und das Mädchen.* By taking his literary motifs and chapter headings from other art forms—especially the paintings of Edvard Munch—Thomas aims, giddily, to emulate Mussorgsky's orchestral composition based on the "pictures" of Victor Hartmann. But his version of the Wagnerian death-kiss results in an "Auschwitz" that is, above all, a place of sado-erotic pleasure. Chaim Galewski, a Jewish prisoner-doctor (whose memoirs we are meant to be reading), catches sight of a German woman in a bath towel, and records, for the reader's titillation, sexual experiments by the SS. These are associated, among others, with the figure of Irma Grese, "brandishing her whip; blonde, plump, ravishingly beautiful . . . I surmised she had a date with Dr Mengele, but meanwhile had some time to kill." Within a page of this quotation, Judith Korczak, a Jewish inmate, is practising fellatio in front of Grese and Dr Stolb. In Thomas's pornographic universe, "choking on gas" and choking on semen are no more than parallel acts. A version of this scene is repeated *ad nauseam* throughout the novel and, by eroticizing death and suffering, Thomas deliberately blurs the distinction between victim and victimizer. Thus, on hearing of his son's death, Dr Lorenz, the SS doctor whom Galewski is meant to be psychoanalysing—itself a ridiculous supposition—"wore the vacant stare of a Mussulman" (one destined for the gas ovens) and had a face as "red as the crematorium walls". On the other hand, the Jewish Galewski could "understand" why Lorenz found "most of my race unspeakable" and "admired, in a way, the SS hardness". Thomas's benign "Auschwitz" is "still quite virginal"; a "miracle" baby survives the gas ovens by sucking at her mother's breast. Later on, the death camps are characterized as a "form of repulsive art": "They had a terrible beauty of pragmatic efficiency. . . . The metaphors of purification, the bathhouses and the cleansing furnaces". Instead of a source of unknowable horror, Thomas's "Auschwitz" is a source of redemptive sado-erotic metaphors.

As with his misuse of Kuznetsov's *Babi Yar,* **Pictures at an Exhibition** ransacks the documentary record for the kind of experience, *in extremis,* around which Thomas likes to build his controlling motifs and for which it claims historical authenticity. He does this by republishing an account of starving Jewish children who try to survive by eating plaster from the walls of the house in which they are imprisoned. It is only a matter of time before one of his characters, undergoing psychoanalysis, does the same thing. In one of his most telling phrases, we learn that "we are all displaced, everyone who was touched *in any way* by Nazism" (my emphasis). Predictably, the various psychoanalytic case-studies in the novel attempt to construct the death camps as a "common home", specifically, it seems, for contemporary Londoners. According to Myra Jacobson, a Holocaust survivor, "there was more sense of spirituality at Auschwitz than there is in modern London".

If this were merely a Mel Brooks spoof, a literary "Spring-Time for Hitler", then one could simply find it unfunny. But this is a cold and calculated piece of writing, extremely self-conscious about its intentions, and designed to make its author a great deal of money. After **The White Hotel,** Thomas seems to believe that the right formula of Freud for beginners, Nazism, sadistic sex and historical revisionism will sell anything. I dearly hope that he is proved wrong.

Sean O'Brien (review date 7 May 1993)

SOURCE: "Gift with a Will," in *Times Literary Supplement,* May 7, 1993, p. 26.

[*In the following review, O'Brien offers tempered assessment of* The Puberty Tree.]

It can seem that there are two D. M. Thomases. On the one hand, there is the poet of memorable lyrics and dramatic pieces, formally various, moving readily between tradition and modernity; on the other, a writer with a broken thermostat, his poems marred by the effort to force significance on their material. The two poets can be found at work on facing pages through most of this collection.

At times, the division between the products of a gift and those of the will recalls some of the work of the late George MacBeth from the 1960s and 70s, for example in the slightly dated ingenuity of the early science fiction/ mythological monologues from *Two Voices* (1968)— **"Missionary"** ("A harsh entry I had of it, Grasud"), **"Tithonus"** and **"Hera's Spring."** The 1960s are also apparent in the social and sexual attitudes revealed in the erotic poems of schoolteaching, **"Private Detentions"** and **"A Lesson in the Parts of Speech"** Alongside these, though, is the subtler **"Pomegranate,"** one of several poems employing the myth of Persephone, in this instance, to trace the growing-up of the daughter of separated parents who is seen leaving Hades with a bag "full of books I'll expect her to know".

Mythology appeals to both Thomases. At best it's a means of understanding, at worst an auto-pilot. The most powerful myth, coming into its own in *Love and Other Deaths* (1975), is that of Thomas's Cornish family; people are so intensely present in the poet's childhood as to seem more than themselves. Aunt Cecie, for example, the taken-for-granted spinster, is disclosed in death as the real life of the house, and the poet hears her "struggle to sit up in the coffin" in order to get on with her work. The old age of the poet's mother intensifies his need of her even as he charts his self-protective detachment in **"The Journey,"** a poem which then modulates effectively from regretful matter-of-factness to submission to his own place in the story: "we are water and moor, / And far journeyers together. Whatever else we are." **"Rubble"** goes over this ground again, trying to identify the knowledge his mother seems to have attained with the approach of death: "There is / a queer radiance in the space / between us which my eyes / avoid occupying: the radium / Madame Curie found, when desolate / she returned at night to the empty table." Thomas is unafraid of emotional directness, and for the most part his grasp of the material here keeps him this side of sentimentality.

The strength of these poems (which is also present in later work such as the family portraits in **"Under Carn Brea"**) depends in part on a regard for the ordinary life through which these haunting personalities emerge. When Thomas neglects this, portentousness can be near at hand. **"Surgery,"** for example, looks at the role of a doctor in the experience of husband and wife as a marriage ends: she writes "prescriptions in a language / she herself hardly begins to know. / Something to carry her into the terrible valley. / Something to carry him into his terrible liberation." The experience may indeed be terrible, but the word, employed here as a rhetorical token, rather in the manner of Ted Hughes at his most flatly assertive, only tells what the poem ought to show. Some more baldly mythological pieces (**"Diary of a Myth-Boy," "Ani"**) seem lulled by a sense of their own credentials into language which is merely uninteresting, and when Thomas turns to the theme he is most commonly identified with—sex—the results can verge on the absurd, as in **"Flesh"** or **"Sestina: Maria Maddalena,"** which the reader seems to blunder into like a private party where the theory that eroticism and noise are directly linked is being tested to destruction.

It has been said more than once that Thomas's subjects are love and death, but literature itself should be added to these. *The Honeymoon Voyage* (1978) and *Dreaming in Bronze* (1981) contain a number of monologues in the persons of writers or characters, as well as evocations of their imaginative lives—**"Lorca," "The Marriage of John Keats and Emily Dickinson in Paradise,"** Don Juan in **"The Stone Clasp,"** Freud and Jung in **"Vienna. Zurich. Constance,"** Lou-Andreas Salomé and others in **"Fathers, Sons and Lovers."** The last two seem about to step off into prose; not simply "fictive", they need a wider space in which to operate. Since the end of the 1970s, Thomas's energies seem to have been diverted away from his own poetry, partly into translations—of Pushkin, Akhmatova and Yevtushenko—partly into his work as a novelist, the latter, by his own account in the autobiography, *Memories and Hallucinations* (1988), not quite voluntarily, though the "open hand" of fiction has clearly retained its appeal. A group of fourteen new and uncollected poems closes *The Puberty Tree*. Among them **"Persephone," "A Guide To Switzerland"** and **"In the Fair Field"** exemplify the affection, humour and musicality of which this unusual poet is capable when not distracted into oracular vulgarity.

Juliet Fleming (review date 3 October 1993)

SOURCE: "Living with Evil," in *Washington Post Book World*, October 3, 1993, p. 5.

[*In the following review, Fleming offers favorable assessment of* Pictures at an Exhibition.]

Pictures at an Exhibition is a fiercely intelligent book, and a shattering experience to read. It opens with a brilliantly bizarre therapeutic relationship. Dr. Lorenz, surgeon, administrator and expert on gassing at Auschwitz, is troubled by headaches and nightmares. Choosing a couch from the prison "stores," he instructs Chaim Galewski, a Czech prisoner, communist and Jew, with one year's psychoanalytic training, to attempt a cure.

In the novel's first instance of collusion, we find ourselves gripped by interest in the details of Lorenz's past even as, outside his comfortable room, smoke rises and trains can be heard arriving from all over Europe. Although circumstances would seem to preclude the possibility of transference between patient and therapist (when asked about his mother, Lorenz returns the question to Galewski "Did you like *your* mother?", and the silence that follows serves to indicate her fate), Lorenz is, improbably enough, cured by the fortuitous retrieval of a suppressed childhood trauma and returns to the selection ramp in full health. Meanwhile, it is dawning on us that Galewski's empathy with his patient is no simple attempt to save his own life: His admiration for Lorenz, one of the more "humane" killers in the camp, has at some point become genuine.

The scene shifts to England in 1990, where what at first appears to be a new cast of characters reveals itself as the old one dismantled and strangely reconfigured. Dreams, memories and entire identities seem to have become detached from their original owners and to be floating free in a miasma of responsibility in which guilt is everywhere, blame nowhere. The puzzle resolves itself as we realize that, in order to survive the end of the war, the SS officers, their collaborators and their victims have borrowed each others' identities, and are now caught in a web of debt and denial. Lying to each other and to us, having in part disguised and in part themselves forgotten who they are, they continue to abuse, betray and destroy one another.

Filtered through the distorted perceptions of Galewski, Thomas's Auschwitz has few heroes and none with whom we come into significant contact. Even the most innocent of the novel's characters, a baby who miraculously survives gassing, grows up under adoptive parents to sympathize with attacks on immigrant hostels in contemporary Germany: "They were youths without jobs, without hope. So one has to understand." In its slow uncovering of the unconscious truths of Auschwitz, the novel represents itself as an act of therapy offered to an entire generation, each member of which holds only a fragment of the key to the mass psychosis that bound it. But psychoanalysis itself is under the mark of deepest suspicion in the novel. Lorenz makes his reappearance in London as an eminent analyst who abuses and betrays those who consult him; his enthusiasm for the discipline suggests that the "understanding" that psychoanalysis generated does little to halt, and may indeed sanction, destructive behaviour. In a society that has forgotten constraint—where impulse is translated into action without check, and where cruelty claims to be either "necessary" or "inadvertent"—to feel the force of psychoanalytic explanation is already to have colluded.

"There is," wrote Maurice Blanchot, "no reaching the disaster." As its title suggests, *Pictures at an Exhibition* addresses itself to the ethics of its own decision to write about the Holocaust. The novel asks itself not only whether art (or for that matter science) can ethically be based on atrocity; but even whether memorials—the product of those impulses of justification and denial that comprise in part the will to remember—are not themselves open to charges of complicity. (At the novel's end a memorial is opened by a bishop who, as a military chaplain, was as he puts it "innocently involved" in the deaths of 90 children.) The fact that such charges of complicity would presumably extend even to his own book demonstrates Thomas's ethical alertness in the face of events that must not be forgotten, but can scarcely be told.

Beautifully constructed and written, *Pictures at an Exhibition* is as lucid and confusing as a dream, as strange and as compelling as the impulses that operate beneath conscious thought. Its astonishing final twist teaches us that, here at least, evil is anything but banal. Instead it is intelligent and compelling: its medium is collusion; and collusion, for human subjects, is everywhere.

Frederick Busch (review date 31 October 1993)

SOURCE: "The Man From Auschwitz," in *New York Times Book Review,* October 31, 1993, pp. 13-14.

[*In the following review, Busch offers tempered evaluation of* Pictures at an Exhibition, *which he describes as "alternately horrifying and annoying."*]

In *Pictures at an Exhibition,* D. M. Thomas returns to the world of *The White Hotel,* his third and most celebrated novel. In that earlier book, as in *Pictures at an Exhibition,* Freudian analysis figures significantly. In each, unhappy sexuality drives the dreams of patients, and in each the novel feels like a dream (or nightmare). In each, death oppresses doctors and patients (and readers) alike. And, in each, we relive a horrible slaughter of Jews—in *The White Hotel,* it is the mass killing at Babi Yar; in *Pictures at an Exhibition,* it is Auschwitz and other killing camps of the Holocaust, and the murder of 90 Jewish children in the Ukraine.

The novel opens in the 1940's, apparently in Europe. A doctor is summoned—one thinks of Kafka's story "A Country Doctor" as one reads the first pages—and he is asked to treat another doctor, who complains of headaches and nightmares and general malaise. Only gradually does Mr. Thomas let us see that Dr. Lorenz, the patient, is a physician at Auschwitz, and that Dr. Galewski, who treats him, is a Czechoslovakian Jew who is a prisoner in the camp.

This first-person section, narrated in Galewski's voice, is very skillful. Humane aspects of the Nazi are revealed, as are cruel and anti-Semitic aspects of the Jew. We learn, too, that the Jewish doctor's child has survived long enough to be adopted by a Nazi couple at the camp, and that he has saved an adolescent Jewish girl from death by coaching her through a Nazi torture—her forced incestuous coupling with her father; she survives but is used as both a whore and a partner in experiments studying prisoners having sex under duress.

This material, witnessing Nazi inhumanities and Jewish suffering, is difficult to read. It seems daring in its subtly harsh assessment of the Jewish Galewski. And Mr. Thomas's construction of a narrative puzzle that we become eager to unlock is masterly. In the prison doctor's genteel quarters, as Furtwängler's recording of *Tristan und Isolde* is played, while they eat good food before a fireplace, two intelligent men conduct witty, urgent conversation. Around them, bestiality presses at the margins of these pages and between the lines of type.

The lure of story and the cunning of the narrative drive us through the horror of the first section; we search for shape, for reason. Mr. Thomas insists that we get there, as in *The White Hotel,* by way of dream. In subsequent sections, set in the present, in England, we overhear the patients of a brilliant, beloved psychoanalyst, Oscar Jacobson, who is dying of multiple sclerosis. We almost never hear Jacobson's responses to the words of his patients; what we know comes from their repetition of what he says, and their summaries of his history and theirs.

So a patient must say this: "I've been thinking quite a lot about that dream, Dr. Jacobson. The one I had a couple of weeks ago. You know, where my sister and I were sitting with Ruth when she was dying, and Sarah admitted to me that Ruth was my child not hers." Mr. Thomas's insistence on Oscar's silence seems a comment by the author on our ability to use language truthfully. Is this the terrain of Paul de Man, a proponent of literary reasoning based upon the unreliability of language—and a quisling during the Nazi occupation of Belgium? The effect of this clumsy management of information is that one seems to be overhearing soap opera. The tension of the first section evaporates and the reader, losing dramatic involvement, declines to merely ferreting through facts.

It becomes evident from internal clues—comments by his patients, Jacobson's own letters—that he is one of the two men we met in the opening pages. It takes some good while for us to learn which, and to understand that while he seems to have become a good man, he remains a cunning malefactor. Is the Nazi a Jew? Is the Jewish turncoat reformed? We search for that truth amid the lies and dreams and clues. And we see that Mr. Thomas is drawing together the strands of the novel—the baby of the camps, the victimized girl, the two doctors—and seems to be offering a truth about human nature.

But, finally, he doesn't. He offers dreaminess, dislocated sections of narrative and the duplicity and vile cunning of Jacobson and minor characters. It's as if the story he tells is secondary to him. It's as if his paramount concern is to demonstrate to us that consciously used language, not unlike that with which we speak unconsciously to our deepest selves, will usually lie.

By itself, this is a tired truth. Poststructuralist literary theory and the book chat it has engendered have wearied us of it, and many readers seek literary art because they believe that it offers more about our humanness than that weary sophistication. Mr. Thomas has a character say to Jacobson of the complaints of his patients that it "was as if, amidst the cosmic tragedy of 'Lear,' we saw Cordelia trotting along to marriage guidance with her hubby, and complaining that he spent no time on foreplay. You said life isn't really *here,* and only survivors . . . knew where it really was." The rejection of the quotidian is by a Nazi doctor from Auschwitz. Does Mr. Thomas therefore seek to establish or invalidate the horror of the Holocaust as a higher order of truth about humanity? Does Cordelia have a right to simple happiness? Is everyone Cordelia? Should we care?

Linked to the historical documents at the novel's core, this relativism seems feeble. One section is a quotation of actual Nazi documents—from commanders and military clergy—about a house in which 90 small children of murdered Jews were locked for 24 hours without food or water. Order, secrecy, the unwillingness of any leader to be responsible for the children, and of course the war against the Jews, led to their being shot by a Ukrainian execution squad and buried in a mass grave. As the squad leader reports, "Many children were hit four or five times before they died."

Clever theories about what is written or said cannot survive juxtaposition with that sentence. Whether that is Mr. Thomas's point, or whether his novel's comment on uncertainty matters more to him, the book proves alternately horrifying and annoying, powerful as its ironic last lines, by a clergyman, may be.

While there are interesting characters and moving scenes in *Pictures at an Exhibition,* its plot is tied together in an unconvincing Freudian bundle. A second-rate detective story written by one of Jacobson's patients, a failed analyst, melodramatically mistells the truth of who the Nazi was: words lie, you see; so the unspeakable remains unspoken. Yet it is the job of the fiction writer to make art by managing to say what seems unsayable.

And there are those victims of torture and murder: their sacrifice to the plotting of a novel of middling achievement lingers disturbingly. *Pictures at an Exhibition* may be most important, then, for the questions it provokes. What shall we allow ourselves to build on the scourged soil of the killing grounds?

Rosemary Dinnage (review date 22 April 1994)

SOURCE: "Sigmund's Our Guy," in *Times Literary Supplement,* April 22, 1994, p. 21.

[*In the following review, Dinnage offers favorable assessment of* Eating Pavlova.]

Freud had no use for the Surrealists, though they thought they were his true disciples; his artistic tastes were conventional, classical, Goethean. What would he have made of the novels of D. M. Thomas? *The White Hotel,* in particular, seemed to be the first truly Freudian novel, both in subject-matter and style. Now, in *Eating Pavlova,* Thomas, in the same rich and cloudy manner, has produced a set of variations on the life of Freud himself.

An old Jewish refugee (his name never mentioned) is dying in a house in Hampstead, looked after by his dedicated daughter. Between doses of morphia, he drifts from sleeping to waking, from past to present and to future as well—since, as he once said, "time does not exist in the unconscious". The device gives Thomas the chance to let his own *plus-freudien-que-freud* unconscious run wild, with puns, jokes, obscenities, contradictions succeeding each other at speed, all of them around the theme of the life, times and character of Freud. The book may in fact have been carefully plotted, but it successfully creates the impression of absolutely free fall.

Characters move in and out of the dying man's dreams. Freud and fellow-analyst Lou Andreas-Salomé arrive with Darwin and Newton (both Fellows of the Royal Society like Freud) to discuss earthly and physical love. Victor Tausk, who committed suicide because of Freud's rejection of him, comes back for an argument, and Fleischl, whom Freud mistakenly poisoned with cocaine. Jacob Freud comes to tell his son he is a good boy but too clever for him—one day he will write books. The American poet HD, psychoanalysed by Freud in 1933, tells him he would have been a wow as analyst to a baseball team—the pretty cheerleaders would be screaming "Sigmund's our guy". "He's no goy but he's some guy", quips Freud, ready with Jewish jokes to the last. Hasn't he said, in reply to a comment on the number of suicides in his circle, "Yes, but I survived all the assassination attempts"?

Extravagant fantasy narratives loop out of the stream of consciousness: condensations of identity, convoluted incest patterns within the Freud family—which might have happened, might not. Historical events, too, hover between fact and fantasy: did Wittgenstein and Hitler really get their diplomas the same year from Linz Technical School? Was Freud's interest in dreams awakened by a book about Australian aboriginals in Manchester Public Library? Did Thomas Mann really announce the First World War as "purification, liberation and enormous hope"? Did dog-loving Freud say of Pavlov that it was easy enough to win the Nobel Prize if you were prepared to torture dogs? I don't know; and that, probably, is the point. After all, Freud muses, "The Achaeans set sail because of tall stories about how beautiful Helen was", and turns his thoughts to his colleague Helene Deutsch's paper on creative lying.

One of the most ingenious fantasies is certainly Thomas's own contribution, though Freud may have shared in its voyeurism as well as its *ben trovato* irony. Much has been made by Freudologists of whether Freud did or did not sleep with his sister-in-law, Minna. So Thomas has Freud, in a wild moment, set up an epistolary romance between

Minna and his friend Fliess. The two scarcely meet; Freud takes her letters and writes Fliess's replies, which get more and more sexual and which Minna, madly in love, always shows to her brother-in-law. Yes, she does sleep with Freud occasionally, but absent-mindedly and thinking of Fliess (as does Freud?). As good at teasing as Thomas is, Freud is cheered by the thought of future scholars poring over these Fliess-Minna letters. But: "No, of course I didn't write Fliess's letters to Minna for him! . . . A Jewish joke. . . . Or not." And then in a dream-forest he meets Rebecca, one of his father's wives, who tells him that he wrote the letters in disguise for his real love, his cool wife, Martha. In these dying fantasies Freud's women are interchangeable: hieratic and soothsaying and not very real.

Dr Tod (yes, Dr Death), an English analyst who lives in a Victorian house in Dover called The Three Caskets, has to be Thomas's own creation. She sums up Freud's character for him in a brief—very brief—analysis. "All your life you have been a prey to demons. As a result, you have tried to make your life appear orderly and rational, and you fooled everyone. Secretly, however, unknown even to yourself, you wanted everyone to be drunk on sex and poetry and fabulous internal drama. Every man an Oedipus, and every woman an Elektra. . . . That will be twenty guineas." She likes his idea, she adds that life is a paraphrase of a few important dreams. And through the book, Freud dreams and dreams. Of someone called T. S. Eliot: must be a boyhood memory of seeing the word "toilets" reflected in his nurse's spectacles, he interprets. Of a man in a prison cell accused of killing millions, named Eckermann or Eichmann; probably about his own identity, his Ich-man, and accusations that he attacked the Jewish race in his *Moses and Monotheism*. Of corpses falling from a train door and naked bodies screaming in a shower-room; puzzling, this one, reminding him of scenes of hell as depicted by early German painters. And of his daughter Anna, a quiet old woman in an immense food-store such as he never saw in Vienna, putting in her basket a few austere items.

The long love between father and daughter is at the centre of the book. Since when have you been interested in love? his wife has tartly asked him; certainly, he ruminates, love has always seemed "an unknown, as mysterious as gravity". It is Anna who has it all and returns it. Her own dream (a true one this) is of the two of them alone on a mountain. "I lean myself against him, crying in a way that is very familiar to us both. Tenderness. My thoughts are troubled."

To say that the novel is about very Freudian opposites—love/hate, truth/fiction, comedy/tragedy—is a cliché that could be slapped on many a worthy novel. Thomas is exceptional, though, in understanding and feeling such themes directly through fantasy, rather than imposing them intellectually. As its title suggests, *Eating Pavlova* is gross and elegant at once. Easy to recoil from, hard to forget.

James R. Kincaid (review date 23 October 1994)

SOURCE: "Freud Terminable," in *New York Times Book Review,* October 23, 1994, p. 28.

[*In the following review, Kincaid offers positive evaluation of* Eating Pavlova.]

In 1824 Sam Goldwyn, recognizing that "there is nothing really so entertaining as a really great love story," set out to comb the world for the really greatest love story of them all. In pursuit of this majestic quest, he resolved to call on "the greatest love specialist in the world," Sigmund Freud, and induce him to "commercialize his study and write a story for the screen." Freud responded with a one-sentence letter: "I do not intend to see Mr. Goldwyn."

Seventy years later, D. M. Thomas, who had employed Freud earlier in his novel *The White Hotel* (1981), has better luck, probably because the love story he wants Freud to write, and actually coaxes him into writing, is so much more harrowing, funny and kind than anything Mr. Goldwyn would have warmed to. In his brilliant new novel, *Eating Pavlova,* Mr. Thomas grabs Freud just in time, only a day or two before his death in September 1939, and snatches for us these final imaginary memoirs: the dreams, recollections, hallucinations, fictions and elaborate lies of the most devious and tragically generous Freud ever envisioned.

Throughout *Eating Pavlova* (the title, like everything else in this novel, carries about a dozen teasing associations—to, among others, the dancer, the dessert, Pavlov and his dogs and Freud's dear daughter Anna), Freud is in London, "finding it is harder to die than I had anticipated." His jaw is reduced to a set of cancerous perforations ("there's a hole right through to my cheek"), and out of the pain and the haze of age, morphine, guilt and fear, he recounts his life—or makes up his life. Perhaps he even starts now to live it, in the sense that he forms his life into a story with a purpose, even if that purpose can no longer avail him anything.

Responding only to his physician, Schur, and his faithful daughter Anna (who contributes an erotic short story to the stew), this Freud lets loose his memory, his analytic powers, material from his famous case studies, his libido, his storytelling craft—"I should have been Rabelais or Cervantes"—and his extraordinary generosity in order to confront and contort a moving, dangerous and funny past. In his account, time has no meaning, mistakes "inevitably creep" in and dreams are actually given priority over a very dubious "reality." Freud's very being often seems to him fictional, and the central extended story of his cuckolding is, he admits, "a Jewish joke," nothing but a pack of lies—maybe.

It is a measure of Freud's genius—and Mr. Thomas's—that as we read we become less involved with sorting lie from truth (or lie from lie) than in investigating whether lies might not be somehow more "true to life, to history," certainly more true to the needs of the human heart. Freud tells us (or tells Anna, his true audience) that he has forged a series of letters to his sister-in-law, seeking to console her for the loss of a lover. Pretending to be the preposterous (and somewhat sinister) Wilhelm Fliess, scarcely able to distinguish between noses and vaginas, Freud portrays himself as a corresponding maniac, asking Minna for erotic reveries, then nude photographs and finally a proof of her love that can be produced only if she seduces Freud.

And that's not all: Freud's wife reads these erotic forged letters years later and is so kindled by them that she begins a quasi affair with the heretofore impotent Herr Bauer (the father of the famous "Dora"), reducing Freud to hiding, with binoculars, in the shrubbery and, in the climactic scene, charging in on the lovers, being told to "beat it, Sigi," and dragging the wallowing, sweating Bauer off his wife.

Why does he concoct such a frenzied and disgraceful romp? Not, it appears, so we or Anna will believe it, exactly; but in order to explore possibilities within himself and to escape for a moment the true horrors: In the end, guilt "reaches unbearable proportions and we have no choice but to die, to escape." Also, and most important for Mr. Thomas's tragic vision, we are allowed to feel that Freud does all this as a final gift to his daughter, a way of releasing her from his power. He has seen that he and Anna were "like two climbers roped together, like those English climbers who vanished, a year or two ago, while heading for the peak of Everest," and he is trying not to take her with him as he disappears over the edge. In Mr. Thomas's version of *King Lear*, Anna—"I ask her to undo a button"—is not hauled off to prison, is not hanged as a poor fool. She is released into new life.

But maybe not. Nothing in Mr. Thomas's book is quite this smooth, as his sardonic irony keeps undercutting the simple readings we might want to impose. Like Freud, he will not minister easy consolation. Anna's feeling that life "is like a farm that I'm just visiting on holiday" is never erased; and, even more ironic, the final view we get of her makes us wonder if she was worth all the trouble: in her swan song, she grumps so vapidly about the decline in high culture that she seems to have transmogrified into William Bennett.

Besides, Freud has gone past even his daughter's needs at the end, dreaming and writing his way into the future: through the extermination of his sisters at Auschwitz, through Hiroshima, the Eichmann trial and the charges brought against "Lolita." Interestingly, these horrors are preludes to visions that ought to be utopian, visions of the untrammeled libido: gay bathhouses and, unforgettably, modern supermarkets, where anything can be taken without even asking, where "mankind is sating its libido"—and nobody is happy. Well, Freud says, it seems that, after all, "people don't want happiness."

Such stoic wit sustains Freud and this extraordinary novel as well. It was such wit, both furious and resigned, that al-

lowed the historical Freud to mock the Gestapo to their faces—"I can most highly recommend the Gestapo to everyone"—putting at risk his own escape. And it is with a similar elegant wit that Mr. Thomas escorts the novel from nightmare into high tragic compassion and then to a muted and unprotected quietness at the end, with nothing to sustain the goodbye but courage and a fiercely honest art. As Freud fades away, a friend floats into his dream and greets him, "How are you, Professor?" "Dying; otherwise, fine," he says. Not a bad way to go.

David R. Slavitt (review date 21 July 1996)

SOURCE: "So You Want to Be a Shaman," in *New York Times Book Review,* July 21, 1996, p. 9.

[*In the following review, Slavitt offers positive assessment of* Lady With a Laptop.]

The conceit is quite lovely. What D. M. Thomas apparently dreamed up was a jokey mystery he could write in which Ruth Rendell comes in as a character to reveal the motive and identity of the murderer. Meanwhile, the protagonist of *Lady With a Laptop,* Simon Hopkins, a grumpy midlist novelist, can make entertainingly snotty remarks about the holistic holiday center on Skagathos, an imaginary island in the Sporades, where he is a workshop leader. Mr. Thomas, the English novelist, has himself led workshops at the center on Skyros, which is, he says, nothing like that on the smaller, fictive island an hour's boat ride away.

While Hopkins is running his small and steadily diminishing writing group, other facilitators are leading workshops in gastric dancing, orgasmic consciousness, colonic massage and elementary shamanism, so the occasions for satire are hardly subtle. Still, Mr. Thomas's playfulness sometimes produces unobvious and pointed moments, as when Natasha, from Russia, who has been paired in the writing group with an American academic, explains that she now has a terrible choice: "Freedom or enslavement. East or West. . . . I can go back to Russia and freedom. Nowadays it's totally free there; you can say anything, believe anything. Only I was not used to freedom, and for the past two years I have a block. Well, since Priscilla has been my co-listener I have felt a craving to write, because she has maddened me with her censorships. You know, her university has 500 Sexual Harassment Officers! So like our old Political Officers, when anger made me creative! Yes, I think I must go there. . . . To the West. I choose enslavement for the sake of my writing."

There are other such grand moments, like the workshop session in which Dusky Hogmann, a not quite fictitious enough movie actor, accepts a fictitious Oscar for a starring role in "Dark Desire," the hypothetical movie version of the novel Hopkins's group is writing. Hogmann gets up and says, among other things: "This award belongs to every poor exploited Hispanic, Afro-American or Oriental, to every sexually abused child, to every gay person struggling to live productively in the midst of prejudice; to every handicapped person; to every woman enduring the daily pinpricks of discrimination. It's an Oscar for every lesbian. For every person with a weight problem. In the words of Federico Garcia Lorca, this is for all the poor beautiful dejected ones."

"Dark Desire" is a series of bizarre sexual fantasies that involve, among other characters, Issei Kagawa, a Japanese cannibal who has become a literary celebrity. (What amusing things can you do with a Japanese cannibal? You send him off with his Dutch publisher to the movies, to see *Alive*.) Kagawa is based on Issei Sagawa, who exists in the novel's real world and, through Hopkins's good or bad offices, gets invited to be (ha-ha!) a facilitator at Skagathos.

But what does it add up to? Is there any thematic target of all this hyperbole and satire? If so, I must confess that I missed it. That tourists are often silly and disagreeable, that writers can behave badly, that New Age therapists frequently say and do strange things, that there is a certain degree of risk involved in open marriages—these are not exactly dispatches from the front. The suggestion that emerges from the novel's embellishment of the title phrase is that the burdens of poor peasants are harder to bear and of a greater reality than those of "our" kind of people.

That proposition is almost impossible either to prove or to disprove, but to assert it at the conclusion of a work like this is to abandon the waspishness that was the book's main charm. It's as if Evelyn Waugh, in one of his nastier exercises, suddenly exhibited a flicker of concern for the plight of the natives. Heartlessness is what makes the liberal fetishes dance like motes in Mr. Thomas's moral airlessness. Open a window and the effect not only vanishes but changes, so that we are slightly embarrassed at having laughed before.

Which is not to deny that some of the bits, however adventitious, are pretty good. I have no fault to find, for instance, with this letter the writer receives: "Dear Mr. Hopkins, I have been command to write to you to inform your novel 'Transplanted Hearts' has be shortlist for Shalimar Prize. As you shall know, this distinguishing prize is for best and most spiritously enhancing book from non-Islamic country. The exact amount of prize varies per year, but is always suffice to relieve author of all finance anxieties for many years. Before the last judgment takes place, I have to ask you one question. Should you be award prize, we would have be sure that you shall not use occasion to propagandize on behalf of author Salman Rushdie, but on contrary express sympathy of Islamic position. May we have your assure on this? I look forward to hear from you. Your sincerely, Ibrahim Rafsanjani."

It's politically correct political incorrectness. But who's going to object?

Lesley Chamberlain (review date 15 February 1998)

SOURCE: "Homo Sovieticus," in *Los Angeles Times Book Review,* February 15, 1998, p. 8.

[*In the following review, Chamberlain offers positive assessment of* Alexander Solzhenitsyn.]

Alexander Solzhenitsyn has been an outstanding figure of the century, despite current attempts in Moscow to reduce him to a pop icon or dismiss him as a relic. He is not a joke or a legend, but a real, extraordinary man whose fate, as D. M. Thomas shows, reveals complex truths about his country. That alone would earn him a place in the pantheon of Russian writers whose art has been molded by exile, imprisonment and the experience of Russia in turmoil.

In 1945, a complaint about Stalin written in a letter to a friend earned Solzhenitsyn eight years in the labor camps. He captured his camp experience in *The Gulag Archipelago*, and the directness with which he bears witness to the deprivation and suffering around him defies aesthetic canons. The very act of reading that book induces physical shock. No one who wants to understand any aspect of Russia and the capacity for good and evil in the human heart can afford to pass Solzhenitsyn by, and it won't do to say time has moved on. His experience is one of the few remaining benchmarks of the seriousness of the age, and Thomas has written this excellent and gripping tribute: a *vade mecum* through the life of one man that captures the Russian century.

Sanya Solzhenitsyn was born in 1918 in Rostov, three months after his father died in an apparent firearms accident while serving in the White Russian Army. Sanya thrived in the young Communist state, despite his rich peasant (*kulak*) family's having been ruined by the Bolsheviks. He excelled at school, while "a kind of dignified destitution" at home taught him to disregard cold and discomfort.

If some of his drive resulted from his father's premature death, his natural ruthlessness and readiness to disregard personal needs were greatly encouraged by the Komsomol, the junior branch of the Communist Party. Courting his first wife, Natalya Reshetovskaya, he carried memory cards for the study of mathematics and physics in his pocket, so as not to waste a minute while with the woman or while waiting for a meal. Even as a boy, he imagined serving Russia with vast historical works, while a fascination with military strategy ensured that he would one day write battle scenes comparable to Tolstoy's. When Stalin's police plucked him from the front in 1945, he was an excellent Red Army officer. He was also, at 26, a consummate rationalist, believing that human nature could be more or less bullied into shape by, in Russia's case, Marxist-Leninist rules.

Prison wrought a spiritual transformation by weakening the Marxism. When he emerged at 34, Solzhenitsyn was more like Pasternak, a passionate spokesman for the non-rational integrity of man. He argued for moral decency supported by religious tradition and the rightness of a life led in poetic empathy with the world around, at odds with the Soviet impulse to dominate nature. Sanya held his new views with the same fanatical dedication that he had held the old and has not changed them since. He is, in some views, an illiberal moralizer making imperious and impossible demands on a tolerant modern consumer society. To others, he is a prophet.

Like so many writers in the Russian tradition, Solzhenitsyn made his greatest commitment to his country, with its ringing, never answered questions, posed by the tracts "What Is to Be Done?" and "Who Is to Blame?" In the Russian way, he began writing in prison and continued in exile, in Southern Kazakhstan, where he led the simple life Tolstoy only idealized. He wrote, taught and lived in a hut. Cancer he survived with the same grim strength that helped him survive hard labor, and it too entered his work, as a parallel metaphor for the metastasizing Communist evil.

In the 1960s, thanks to the Khruschchev Thaw, the world finally heard of Solzhenitsyn. Six years after *One Day in the Life of Ivan Denisovich* was published in Russian in 1962, the suppressed manuscripts *Cancer Ward* and *The First Circle* appeared in translation in the West. The Nobel Prize followed in 1970, but Solzhenitsyn's tense relationship with the Russian government precluded his leaving Russia to collect it. Implementing the renewed hard line under Khrushchev's successor, Brezhnev, the KGB even tried to murder Solzhenitsyn in 1971, but the prick of ricin, the same poison that killed the Bulgarian writer Georgi Markov in London, succeeded only in inducing near-fatal illness. Solzhenitsyn was finally deported in 1974. He led a transplanted Russian life in New England, complete with hut and snow. But this replicated second home no longer provided true inspiration. When he returned to Russia in 1994, it was too late for a new beginning.

The great personal upheaval of Sanya's life was the breakup of his first marriage to Natalya Reshetovskaya and to call it an upheaval is to say much about the man who never rated the personal highly. Their love had seemed to survive the Gulag sentence, their brief divorce and Natalya's marriage to someone else. They even married again, but it turned out that his fame and her childlessness at the onset of middle age were too much to bear. Prison was to blame, but so, writes Thomas, was a deep sexual repression evident in Sanya since his youth, which was liberated late by a powerful affair with an academic colleague, then by the love of Alya Svetlova, who became his second wife.

Readers of Thomas' novels, excessively steeped in Russian poetry and Freudian eroticism, may be relieved to hear that Thomas draws out the erotic thread tactfully and persuasively, no easy task considering that all the main characters are still alive. Reshetovskaya, the wife who found herself abandoned in middle age after years of sacrifice, became bitter and attempted suicide. Sanya accused her of irresponsibility toward him. Both of Solzhenitsyn's wives perpetuated that Russian tradition of complete dedication to the husband's political-artistic cause. (In December 1825, the wives of Russia's first insurrectionists trudged after their husbands to Siberia. Tolstoy's wife, Sonya, copied out *War and Peace* seven times. Nadezhda Mandelstam, wife of Osip, wrote her famous chronicles of life under Stalin, *Hope Against Hope* and *Hope Abandoned*.)

Solzhenitsyn's marriage with Western liberals broke up much more abruptly than his first marriage, and with no regrets, only a few years after he reached the West. Solzhenitsyn may have been anti-Communist, but he supported the Vietnam War, and he was never a democrat. In 1978, he told a Harvard audience that the West showed moral poverty and pursued the rights of man "even to excess." *The New York Times* and the *Washington Post* in reply, according to Thomas, "could only celebrate skepticism and diversity." Thomas observes that the liberalism upheld by the likes of Arthur Miller and Norman Mailer was too sure of its own exclusive rightness, but it utterly failed to grasp a single truth about Russia, which had nothing to do with Communism: that the Russian way is ambivalent toward Western "reason." Solzhenitsyn felt that Marxism was a Western straitjacket Russia had imposed upon itself, whereas its true course was to follow its Orthodox Christian traditions.

The utopia in which Solzhenitsyn's kind of intellectuals exercise public responsibility would be an authoritarian, spiritually totalitarian world, certainly not a pluralist democracy. Anti-Enlightenment, or one might say Platonic, it is not a comfortable vision for most modern minds. In essence, his vision still had much in common with the scourging, puritan aspect of Communism. Thomas suggests that the Lenin in Solzhenitsyn's difficult interior monologue, "Lenin in Zurich," is "Sanya without conscience," and that "Lenin was the dark side of his own heart," though he takes issue with the writer Tatiana Tolstaya's view that "Lenin's 'dream' and Solzhenitsyn's have something in common." At least in theory, Lenin and Solzhenitsyn share basic means toward their different ends. Each has a terrible capacity for single-mindedness and a scorched-earth policy toward intellectual dissent. The evidence is there in Sanya's personality, encouraged by a formative Communist life.

Personally, Solzhenitsyn was always egotistical, and from the hour of his fame, he became dogged. His relationship with his Soviet editor, Alexander Tvardovsky, a man so torn between art and politics that he drank himself to death, showed up his humorlessness. He demanded service and sacrifice from everyone and grew ever more miserly with his time and more peremptory and righteous in speech. In the Gulag days, he boasted that his intuition could tell a good man, but that insight deserted him once he arrived in the West. Suspicious and withdrawn, he surrounded his house with a Gulag-style fence and turned on former help-ers, one of whom said, with justice: "He is at best a Soviet character." Symptomatically, Solzhenitsyn didn't reply to Thomas' letters, which is why this biography is unautho-rized. Thomas wonders whether Sanya has been an impos-sible husband and father to his three sons but generously records that this is not so, according to them.

"At best a Soviet character." How can one explain the bulldozing cultural intransigence of which he is a supreme example? There is a kind of psychological terrorism in the Russian tradition that comes of overpowering inner convic-tion. The unswerving utilitarians and their "spiritual" op-ponents equally represent it. It has something to do with religion and accounts for extreme dedication to whatever cause and a willingness to suffer. Solzhenitsyn's creed indeed is that "he who loses his life shall gain it." But he never actually underwent religious conversion. He began referring to God and attending church when he discovered his own mission. A Christianity more Inquisitorial than compassionate perhaps has been his most useful ideologi-cal accessory.

Solzhenitsyn's art, argues Thomas, is "daylight art," often transcribed directly from experience. He is a literal writer for whom literary modernism has no relevance, and his realism, great in a short early work like "Matriona's House," has shortcomings in the later and more rambling pieces. Solzhenitsyn gives us the Tolstoyan epic without the unforgettable characters and, reflecting his own priori-ties, gives us mostly men without women and a world without erotic love. The art in the history finally expires in exile, crushed by a Stakhanovite routine. But Russian art has often seemed to subordinate aesthetic form to social mission. If something is rotten in the state of Denmark, it must be exposed.

In every pore and every weakness, Solzhenitsyn typifies what has been the Russian intellectual's responsibility for the last 200 years. Solzhenitsyn's life lends credence to the highly plausible view that Russia does not have his-tory, it has only art an art in which writers across the centuries discuss the eternal questions that endlessly recur. Thomas makes heartwarming links with the rich tradition of Russian poetry and with Yeats, Auden and Frost. He deserves our thanks for writing a marvelously readable, indispensable book about an impossibly complex man of our recent times.

Josephine Woll (review date 1 March 1998)

SOURCE: "Russia's Stern Conscience," in *Washington Post Book World,* March 1, 1998, pp. 4-5.

[*In the following review, Woll offers negative evaluation of Alexander Solzhenitsyn.*]

D. M. Thomas, prominent poet and novelist, has a long-standing interest in Russia. His early, controversial novel

The White Hotel grew out of Anatoly Kuznetsov's impas-sioned fictional account of the Nazi massacre of Jews at Babi Yar near Kiev. He has translated Russian poetry, and he loops together five of his novels under the title "Rus-sian Nights Quintet."

All the less reason, then, for him to undertake this biography. He knew the pitfalls. Solzhenitsyn's work is so patently autobiographical that a biographer has only two justifications for his own work. One is to dig up informa-tion unknown to his reader, the other is to delve deep psychologically, offering insights of which Solzhenitsyn himself and earlier biographers are incapable. Thomas does very little of the first, and absolutely none of the second.

The KGB files on Solzhenitsyn, accessible only in the last few years, do provide a few tidbits. From 1961 until his exile in 1974, Solzhenitsyn dominated Soviet intellectual life more than any other writer. His early fiction, especially *One Day in the Life of Ivan Denisovich,* overwhelmed Russian readers, and although the authorities denied him the Lenin Prize he so patently deserved, they acknowledged his importance with the dubious compliment of virtually nonstop attention.

The files contain nothing that significantly alters our understanding of Solzhenitsyn's treatment by the regime, but KGB memoranda exert their own awful fascination. Most are predictable, with their rote insults and ruthless strategies; a few demonstrate surprisingly astute percep-tions, salutary reminders that the upper echelons of the Soviet hierarchy were not as monolithic as we once thought.

These archives were collected and published two years ago as *The Solzhenitsyn Files* (edited by Michael Scammell). They are not Thomas's find, but he makes good use of them. The same cannot be said of his other sources. Three are central: Solzhenitsyn's body of published work (he ignored two requests for interviews); the memoirs and memories of his first wife, Natalya Resh-etovskaya; and *Solzhenitsyn: A Biography,* the "monumen-tal" work (Thomas's adjective) that Scammell published 14 years ago.

Thomas was bound to mine these authoritative quarries, and duplication was unavoidable, though I prefer Solzhen-itsyn's firsthand recounting of his experiences to Thomas's barely altered secondhand versions. The book's errors, however, were not inevitable. For instance, Thomas includes Khrushchev among those who, in Bertram Wolfe's classic though uncredited line, "died that most un-natural of deaths for an Old Bolshevik, a natural death." "Old Bolsheviks" designates those who were already members when the Bolsheviks took power in 1917; Khrushchev didn't get his party card until 1918. Elsewhere, Thomas takes Anna Akhmatova's bitter comment that Soviet readers lived in a "pre-Gutenberg" age as referring to the Stalin period, when in fact she was speaking of the resurrection of genuine Russian literature thanks to *samizdat* in the 1960s.

Most of Thomas's mistakes are not serious, but they exemplify his slapdash approach. What matters more, and what makes his book worse than a mere recycling of familiar facts, is his consistent simplification of complexity, his vulgarization of situations and feelings that merit subtlety, and his nearly unfailing choice of banal thought and images.

Let me illustrate. Solzhenitsyn and Reshetovskaya had a long and painful marriage, with many separations even after his time in the gulag ended. In 1956, Reshetovskaya was living in Ryazan with her second husband and two stepsons, and Solzhenitsyn was sharing a wooden house with the landlady he immortalized in the story "Matryona's House." Driven by desire, loneliness and an imperious egotism, Solzhenitsyn wrote to her encouraging a visit and, eventually, a renewal of their relationship. Thomas draws on Reshetovskaya's recollections of the visit:

"He caught his breath on seeing her step out of the train: she looked young again! Slimmer! Her whole face was aglow, as in their youth! . . . They felt, according to Natasha's account, inseparably close. Perhaps on this day they made love for the first time in twelve years; in any event they would celebrate this date as marking their reunion . . . She would make the last years of his life beautiful, ease his sufferings—or even give him the will to go on living." The cliches may be Reshetovskaya's, but Thomas borrows them wholesale, throwing in a few of his own exclamation points for soap-operatic emphasis.

Thomas relies on Scammell as much as he does on Solzhenitsyn and Reshetovskaya. Here the loss is not of detail—in a book hundreds of pages shorter than Scammell's, something had to go—but nuance. When dissident writers Andrei Sinyavsky and Iulli Daniel were tried for antistate activity in February 1965, 63 writers signed a protest. Solzhenitsyn did not. He disapproved of Sinyavsky and Daniel's decision to send their fiction abroad; he also believed such protests pointless and a distraction from his own mission. Thomas hypothesizes that Solzhenitsyn felt alien to "this tribe of Moscow intellectuals . . . he saw himself as an outsider: in him ran the peasant blood of Semyon Solzhenitsyn and Zakhar Shcherbak [his grandfathers]—individualists who had pulled themselves up by their own bootstraps." How superficial his comment compared with Scammell's:

> Behind this puritanical attitude [toward publication abroad] there seems to have stood a more purely emotional and less rational impulse . . . namely, his drive to act completely alone and his instinctive recoil from groups or factions of any description . . . At the same time, this battle was saved from sterile egoism because it was not simply for his own personal satisfaction but also on behalf of all those who had suffered unjustly and, as he saw it, of the entire Russian people . . . Signing letters on behalf of others . . . paled into insignificance in comparison with the overriding purpose of his life.

My point is not to praise Scammell at Thomas's expense but rather to wonder why D. M. Thomas, a writer of experience and skill, would produce a book that has no originality, no analysis, and no felicity of language to commend it. He tells us, in his prologue, that he thought "hard and long" about whether to accept the publisher's invitation to undertake this biography. Not, manifestly, hard and long enough.

FURTHER READING

Criticism

Batchelor, John Calvin. "The Story That Won't Go Away." *Washington Post Book World* (11 October 1992): 4, 14.
    A positive review of *Flying to Love.*

Blake, Patricia. "Collaborations." *Time* (25 April 1983): 114-15.
    An unfavorable review of *Ararat.*

Carlson, Ron. "J.F.K. and the Beautiful Democrat Nun." *Los Angeles Times Book Review* (15 November 1992): 3.
    An unfavorable review of *Flying to Love.*

Cohen, David. "On His Tod." *New Statesman and Society* (13 May 1994): 40.
    A positive review of *Eating Pavlova.*

Cowart, David. "Being and Seeming: *The White Hotel.*" *Novel: A Forum on Fiction* 19, No. 3 (Spring 1986): 216-31.
    Examines the complex interconnection of psychological processes, symbolism, myth, and Freudian analysis in *The White Hotel,* drawing attention to Thomas's provocative treatment of perception and reality in the novel.

Dalley, Jan. "A Shield Made of Words." *New Statesman* (13 March 1998): 52-53.
    A review of *Alexander Solzhenitsyn.* Dalley commends Thomas's subject though finds fault in his "free-form biographical style" and "over-heated" prose.

Eder, Richard. Review of *Sphinx,* by D. M. Thomas. *Los Angeles Times Book Review* (25 January 1987): 3, 9.
    An unfavorable review of *Sphinx.*

Freely, Maureen. "Don's Party Tricks." *New Statesman and Society* (22 June 1990): 49.
    An unfavorable review of *Lying Together.*

Gray, Paul. "Beyond Pleasure and Pain." *Time* (16 March 1981): 88.
    A positive review of *The White Hotel.*

Levy, Ellen. "A Substitute for Imagination." *The New Leader* (30 May 1983): 17-18.
   A negative review of *Ararat*.

Olcott, Anthony. "Superpower Slapstick." *Washington Post Book World* (24 January 1988): 11.
   An unfavorable review of *Summit*.

Radin, Victoria. "Jack Junk." *New Statesman and Society* (14 February 1992): 39.
   A negative review of *Flying to Love*.

Rumens, Carol. "Inviting Confusions." *Times Literary Supplement* (13-19 July 1990): 746.
   A review of *Lying Together*.

See, Carolyn. "The Underbelly of the Literary Life." *Los Angeles Times Book Review* (2 June 1996): 3, 11.
   A review of *Lady With a Laptop*.

Steiner, George. "In Exile Wherever He Goes." *New York Times Book Review* (1 March 1998): 9-10.
   A positive review of *Alexander Solzhenitsyn*.

Storr, Anthony. "D. M. Thomas' Map of Love." *Washington Post Book World* (2 October 1988): 7.
   An unfavorable review of *Memories and Hallucinations*.

Tanner, Laura E. "Sweet Pain and Charred Bodies: Figuring Violence in *The White Hotel*." *Boundary 2* 18, No. 2 (Summer 1991): 130-49.
   Examines Thomas's presentation of metaphorical violence in *The White Hotel*, which, according to Tanner, lures the reader in to an imaginative framework that suddenly becomes realistic, reflecting the reader's complicity and unconscious entanglement in acts of brutality.

Additional coverage of Thomas's life and career is contained in the following sources published by the Gale Group: *Concise Dictionary of British Literary Biography,* **1960-Present;** *Contemporary Authors,* **Vols. 61-64;** *Contemporary Authors Autobiography Series,* **Vol. 11;** *Contemporary Authors New Revision Series,* **Vols. 17, 45, 75;** *Dictionary of Literary Biography,* **Vols. 40, 207; and** *Major 20th-Century Writers,* **Editions 1, 2.**

How to Use This Index

The main references

> **Calvino, Italo**
> 1923-1985 .... CLC 5, 8, 11, 22, 33, 39,
> 73; SSC 3

list all author entries in the following Gale Literary Criticism series:

BLC = Black Literature Criticism
CLC = Contemporary Literary Criticism
CLR = Children's Literature Review
CMLC = Classical and Medieval Literature Criticism
DA = DISCovering Authors
DAB = DISCovering Authors: British
DAC = DISCovering Authors: Canadian
DAM = DISCovering Authors: Modules
      DRAM: Dramatists Module; *MST:* Most-Studied Authors Module;
      MULT: Multicultural Authors Module; *NOV:* Novelists Module;
      POET: Poets Module; *POP:* Popular Fiction and Genre Authors Module
DC = Drama Criticism
HLC = Hispanic Literature Criticism
LC = Literature Criticism from 1400 to 1800
NCLC = Nineteenth-Century Literature Criticism
NNAL = Native North American Literature
PC = Poetry Criticism
SSC = Short Story Criticism
TCLC = Twentieth-Century Literary Criticism
WLC = World Literature Criticism, 1500 to the Present

The cross-references

> See also CANR 23; CA 85-88;
> obituary CA116

list all author entries in the following Gale biographical and literary sources:

AAYA = Authors & Artists for Young Adults
AITN = Authors in the News
BEST = Bestsellers
BW = Black Writers
CA = Contemporary Authors
CAAS = Contemporary Authors Autobiography Series
CABS = Contemporary Authors Bibliographical Series
CANR = Contemporary Authors New Revision Series
CAP = Contemporary Authors Permanent Series
CDALB = Concise Dictionary of American Literary Biography
CDBLB = Concise Dictionary of British Literary Biography
DLB = Dictionary of Literary Biography
DLBD = Dictionary of Literary Biography Documentary Series
DLBY = Dictionary of Literary Biography Yearbook
HW = Hispanic Writers
JRDA = Junior DISCovering Authors
MAICYA = Major Authors and Illustrators for Children and Young Adults
MTCW = Major 20th-Century Writers
SAAS = Something about the Author Autobiography Series
SATA = Something about the Author
YABC = Yesterday's Authors of Books for Children

Literary Criticism Series
Cumulative Author Index

20/1631
    See Upward, Allen

A/C Cross
    See Lawrence, T(homas) E(dward)

Abasiyanik, Sait Faik 1906-1954
    See Sait Faik
    See also CA 123

Abbey, Edward 1927-1989 .... **CLC 36, 59**
    See also CA 45-48; 128; CANR 2, 41; DA3;
    MTCW 2

Abbott, Lee K(ittredge) 1947- .... **CLC 48**
    See also CA 124; CANR 51; DLB 130

Abe, Kobo 1924-1993 ...... **CLC 8, 22, 53, 81;
    DAM NOV**
    See also CA 65-68; 140; CANR 24, 60;
    DLB 182; MTCW 1, 2

Abelard, Peter c. 1079-c. 1142 ...... **CMLC 11**
    See also DLB 115, 208

Abell, Kjeld 1901-1961 .... **CLC 15**
    See also CA 111

Abish, Walter 1931- .... **CLC 22**
    See also CA 101; CANR 37; DLB 130

Abrahams, Peter (Henry) 1919- .... **CLC 4**
    See also BW 1; CA 57-60; CANR 26; DLB
    117; MTCW 1, 2

Abrams, M(eyer) H(oward) 1912- ... **CLC 24**
    See also CA 57-60; CANR 13, 33; DLB 67

Abse, Dannie 1923- .... **CLC 7, 29; DAB;
    DAM POET**
    See also CA 53-56; CAAS 1; CANR 4, 46,
    74; DLB 27; MTCW 1

Achebe, (Albert) Chinua(lumogu)
    1930- ...... **CLC 1, 3, 5, 7, 11, 26, 51, 75,
    127; BLC 1; DA; DAB; DAC; DAM
    MST, MULT, NOV; WLC**
    See also AAYA 15; BW 2, 3; CA 1-4R;
    CANR 6, 26, 47; CLR 20; DA3; DLB
    117; MAICYA; MTCW 1, 2; SATA 38,
    40; SATA-Brief 38

Acker, Kathy 1948-1997 .... **CLC 45, 111**
    See also CA 117; 122; 162; CANR 55

Ackroyd, Peter 1949- .... **CLC 34, 52**
    See also CA 123; 127; CANR 51, 74; DLB
    155; INT 127; MTCW 1

Acorn, Milton 1923- .... **CLC 15; DAC**
    See also CA 103; DLB 53; INT 103

Adamov, Arthur 1908-1970 .... **CLC 4, 25;
    DAM DRAM**
    See also CA 17-18; 25-28R; CAP 2;
    MTCW 1

Adams, Alice (Boyd) 1926-1999 .. **CLC 6, 13,
    46; SSC 24**
    See also CA 81-84; 179; CANR 26, 53, 75,
    88; DLBY 86; INT CANR-26;
    MTCW 1, 2

Adams, Andy 1859-1935 .... **TCLC 56**
    See also YABC 1

Adams, Brooks 1848-1927 .... **TCLC 80**
    See also CA 123; DLB 47

Adams, Douglas (Noel) 1952- .... **CLC 27, 60;
    DAM POP**
    See also AAYA 4, 33; BEST 89:3; CA 106;
    CANR 34, 64; DA3; DLBY 83; JRDA;
    MTCW 1; SATA 116

Adams, Francis 1862-1893 .... **NCLC 33**

Adams, Henry (Brooks)
    1838-1918 .... **TCLC 4, 52; DA; DAB;
    DAC; DAM MST**
    See also CA 104; 133; CANR 77; DLB 12,
    47, 189; MTCW 1

Adams, Richard (George) 1920- ... **CLC 4, 5,
    18; DAM NOV**
    See also AAYA 16; AITN 1, 2; CA 49-52;
    CANR 3, 35; CLR 20; JRDA; MAICYA;
    MTCW 1, 2; SATA 7, 69

Adamson, Joy(-Friederike Victoria)
    1910-1980 .... **CLC 17**
    See also CA 69-72; 93-96; CANR 22;
    MTCW 1; SATA 11; SATA-Obit 22

Adcock, Fleur 1934- .... **CLC 41**
    See also CA 25-28R, 182; CAAE 182;
    CAAS 23; CANR 11, 34, 69; DLB 40

Addams, Charles (Samuel)
    1912-1988 .... **CLC 30**
    See also CA 61-64; 126; CANR 12, 79

Addams, Jane 1860-1945 .... **TCLC 76**

Addison, Joseph 1672-1719 .... **LC 18**
    See also CDBLB 1660-1789; DLB 101

Adler, Alfred (F.) 1870-1937 .... **TCLC 61**
    See also CA 119; 159

Adler, C(arole) S(chwerdtfeger)
    1932- .... **CLC 35**
    See also AAYA 4; CA 89-92; CANR 19,
    40; JRDA; MAICYA; SAAS 15; SATA
    26, 63, 102

Adler, Renata 1938- .... **CLC 8, 31**
    See also CA 49-52; CANR 5, 22, 52;
    MTCW 1

Ady, Endre 1877-1919 .... **TCLC 11**
    See also CA 107

A.E. 1867-1935 .... **TCLC 3, 10**
    See also Russell, George William

Aeschylus 525B.C.-456B.C. .. **CMLC 11; DA;
    DAB; DAC; DAM DRAM, MST; DC
    8; WLCS**
    See also DLB 176

Aesop 620(?)B.C.-(?)B.C. .... **CMLC 24**
    See also CLR 14; MAICYA; SATA 64

Affable Hawk
    See MacCarthy, Sir(Charles Otto) Desmond

Africa, Ben
    See Bosman, Herman Charles

Afton, Effie
    See Harper, Frances Ellen Watkins

Agapida, Fray Antonio
    See Irving, Washington

Agee, James (Rufus) 1909-1955 ...... **TCLC 1,
    19; DAM NOV**
    See also AITN 1; CA 108; 148; CDALB
    1941-1968; DLB 2, 26, 152; MTCW 1

Aghill, Gordon
    See Silverberg, Robert

Agnon, S(hmuel) Y(osef Halevi)
    1888-1970 .... **CLC 4, 8, 14; SSC 30**
    See also CA 17-18; 25-28R; CANR 60;
    CAP 2; MTCW 1, 2

Agrippa von Nettesheim, Henry Cornelius
    1486-1535 .... **LC 27**

Aguilera Malta, Demetrio 1909-1981
    See also CA 111; 124; CANR 87; DAM
    MULT, NOV; DLB 145; HLCS 1; HW 1

Agustini, Delmira 1886-1914
    See also CA 166; HLCS 1; HW 1, 2

Aherne, Owen
    See Cassill, R(onald) V(erlin)

Ai 1947- .... **CLC 4, 14, 69**
    See also CA 85-88; CAAS 13; CANR 70;
    DLB 120

Aickman, Robert (Fordyce)
    1914-1981 .... **CLC 57**
    See also CA 5-8R; CANR 3, 72

Aiken, Conrad (Potter) 1889-1973 .... **CLC 1,
    3, 5, 10, 52; DAM NOV, POET; PC 26;
    SSC 9**
    See also CA 5-8R; 45-48; CANR 4, 60;
    CDALB 1929-1941; DLB 9, 45, 102;
    MTCW 1, 2; SATA 3, 30

Aiken, Joan (Delano) 1924- .... **CLC 35**
    See also AAYA 1, 25; CA 9-12R, 182;
    CAAE 182; CANR 4, 23, 34, 64; CLR 1,
    19; DLB 161; JRDA; MAICYA; MTCW
    1; SAAS 1; SATA 2, 30, 73; SATA-Essay
    109

Ainsworth, William Harrison
    1805-1882 .... **NCLC 13**
    See also DLB 21; SATA 24

Aitmatov, Chingiz (Torekulovich)
    1928- .... **CLC 71**
    See also CA 103; CANR 38; MTCW 1;
    SATA 56

Akers, Floyd
    See Baum, L(yman) Frank

Amis, Martin (Louis) 1949- .... **CLC 4, 9, 38, 62, 101**
See also BEST 90:3; CA 65-68; CANR 8, 27, 54, 73; DA3; DLB 14, 194; INT CANR-27; MTCW 1

Ammons, A(rchie) R(andolph) 1926- ...... **CLC 2, 3, 5, 8, 9, 25, 57, 108; DAM POET; PC 16**
See also AITN 1; CA 9-12R; CANR 6, 36, 51, 73; DLB 5, 165; MTCW 1, 2

Amo, Tauraatua i
See Adams, Henry (Brooks)

Amory, Thomas 1691(?)-1788 .... **LC 48**

Anand, Mulk Raj 1905- .. **CLC 23, 93; DAM NOV**
See also CA 65-68; CANR 32, 64; MTCW 1, 2

Anatol
See Schnitzler, Arthur

Anaximander c. 610B.C.-c. 546B.C. .... **CMLC 22**

Anaya, Rudolfo A(lfonso) 1937- ...... **CLC 23; DAM MULT, NOV; HLC 1**
See also AAYA 20; CA 45-48; CAAS 4; CANR 1, 32, 51; DLB 82, 206; HW 1; MTCW 1, 2

Andersen, Hans Christian 1805-1875 .... **NCLC 7, 79; DA; DAB; DAC; DAM MST, POP; SSC 6; WLC**
See also CLR 6; DA3; MAICYA; SATA 100; YABC 1

Anderson, C. Farley
See Mencken, H(enry) L(ouis); Nathan, George Jean

Anderson, Jessica (Margaret) Queale 1916- .... **CLC 37**
See also CA 9-12R; CANR 4, 62

Anderson, Jon (Victor) 1940- . **CLC 9; DAM POET**
See also CA 25-28R; CANR 20

Anderson, Lindsay (Gordon) 1923-1994 .... **CLC 20**
See also CA 125; 128; 146; CANR 77

Anderson, Maxwell 1888-1959 .... **TCLC 2; DAM DRAM**
See also CA 105; 152; DLB 7; MTCW 2

Anderson, Poul (William) 1926- .... **CLC 15**
See also AAYA 5, 34; CA 1-4R; 181; CAAE 181; CAAS 2; CANR 2, 15, 34, 64; CLR 58; DLB 8; INT CANR-15; MTCW 1, 2; SATA 90; SATA-Brief 39; SATA-Essay 106

Anderson, Robert (Woodruff) 1917- .... **CLC 23; DAM DRAM**
See also AITN 1; CA 21-24R; CANR 32; DLB 7

Anderson, Sherwood 1876-1941 ..... **TCLC 1, 10, 24; DA; DAB; DAC; DAM MST, NOV; SSC 1; WLC**
See also AAYA 30; CA 104; 121; CANR 61; CDALB 1917-1929; DA3; DLB 4, 9, 86; DLBD 1; MTCW 1, 2

Andier, Pierre
See Desnos, Robert

Andouard
See Giraudoux, (Hippolyte) Jean

Andrade, Carlos Drummond de CLC 18
See also Drummond de Andrade, Carlos

Andrade, Mario de 1893-1945 .... **TCLC 43**

Andreae, Johann V(alentin) 1586-1654 .... **LC 32**
See also DLB 164

Andreas-Salome, Lou 1861-1937 ... **TCLC 56**
See also CA 178; DLB 66

Andress, Lesley
See Sanders, Lawrence

Andrewes, Lancelot 1555-1626 .... **LC 5**
See also DLB 151, 172

Andrews, Cicily Fairfield
See West, Rebecca

Andrews, Elton V.
See Pohl, Frederik

Andreyev, Leonid (Nikolaevich) 1871-1919 .... **TCLC 3**
See also CA 104; 185

Andric, Ivo 1892-1975 .... **CLC 8; SSC 36**
See also CA 81-84; 57-60; CANR 43, 60; DLB 147; MTCW 1

Androvar
See Prado (Calvo), Pedro

Angelique, Pierre
See Bataille, Georges

Angell, Roger 1920- .... **CLC 26**
See also CA 57-60; CANR 13, 44, 70; DLB 171, 185

Angelou, Maya 1928- .... **CLC 12, 35, 64, 77; BLC 1; DA; DAB; DAC; DAM MST, MULT, POET, POP; WLCS**
See also AAYA 7, 20; BW 2, 3; CA 65-68; CANR 19, 42, 65; CDALBS; CLR 53; DA3; DLB 38; MTCW 1, 2; SATA 49

Anna Comnena 1083-1153 .... **CMLC 25**

Annensky, Innokenty (Fyodorovich) 1856-1909 .... **TCLC 14**
See also CA 110; 155

Annunzio, Gabriele d'
See D'Annunzio, Gabriele

Anodos
See Coleridge, Mary E(lizabeth)

Anon, Charles Robert
See Pessoa, Fernando (Antonio Nogueira)

Anouilh, Jean (Marie Lucien Pierre) 1910-1987 .... **CLC 1, 3, 8, 13, 40, 50; DAM DRAM; DC 8**
See also CA 17-20R; 123; CANR 32; MTCW 1, 2

Anthony, Florence
See Ai

Anthony, John
See Ciardi, John (Anthony)

Anthony, Peter
See Shaffer, Anthony (Joshua); Shaffer, Peter (Levin)

Anthony, Piers 1934- .... **CLC 35; DAM POP**
See also AAYA 11; CA 21-24R; CANR 28, 56, 73; DLB 8; MTCW 1, 2; SAAS 22; SATA 84

Anthony, Susan B(rownell) 1916-1991 .... **TCLC 84**
See also CA 89-92; 134

Antoine, Marc
See Proust, (Valentin-Louis-George-Eugene-) Marcel

Antoninus, Brother
See Everson, William (Oliver)

Antonioni, Michelangelo 1912- .... **CLC 20**
See also CA 73-76; CANR 45, 77

Antschel, Paul 1920-1970
See Celan, Paul
See also CA 85-88; CANR 33, 61; MTCW 1

Anwar, Chairil 1922-1949 .... **TCLC 22**
See also CA 121

Anzaldua, Gloria 1942-
See also CA 175; DLB 122; HLCS 1

Apess, William 1798-1839(?) .... **NCLC 73; DAM MULT**
See also DLB 175; NNAL

Apollinaire, Guillaume 1880-1918 .. **TCLC 3, 8, 51; DAM POET; PC 7**
See also Kostrowitzki, Wilhelm Apollinaris de
See also CA 152; MTCW 1

Appelfeld, Aharon 1932- .... **CLC 23, 47**
See also CA 112; 133; CANR 86

Apple, Max (Isaac) 1941- .... **CLC 9, 33**
See also CA 81-84; CANR 19, 54; DLB 130

Appleman, Philip (Dean) 1926- .... **CLC 51**
See also CA 13-16R; CAAS 18; CANR 6, 29, 56

Appleton, Lawrence
See Lovecraft, H(oward) P(hillips)

Apteryx
See Eliot, T(homas) S(tearns)

Apuleius, (Lucius Madaurensis) 125(?)-175(?) .... **CMLC 1**
See also DLB 211

Aquin, Hubert 1929-1977 .... **CLC 15**
See also CA 105; DLB 53

Aquinas, Thomas 1224(?)-1274 ..... **CMLC 33**
See also DLB 115

Aragon, Louis 1897-1982 .. **CLC 3, 22; DAM NOV, POET**
See also CA 69-72; 108; CANR 28, 71; DLB 72; MTCW 1, 2

Arany, Janos 1817-1882 .... **NCLC 34**

Aranyos, Kakay
See Mikszath, Kalman

Arbuthnot, John 1667-1735 .... **LC 1**
See also DLB 101

Archer, Herbert Winslow
See Mencken, H(enry) L(ouis)

Archer, Jeffrey (Howard) 1940- ...... **CLC 28; DAM POP**
See also AAYA 16; BEST 89:3; CA 77-80; CANR 22, 52; DA3; INT CANR-22

Archer, Jules 1915- .... **CLC 12**
See also CA 9-12R; CANR 6, 69; SAAS 5; SATA 4, 85

Archer, Lee
See Ellison, Harlan (Jay)

Arden, John 1930- .... **CLC 6, 13, 15; DAM DRAM**
See also CA 13-16R; CAAS 4; CANR 31, 65, 67; DLB 13; MTCW 1

Arenas, Reinaldo 1943-1990 . **CLC 41; DAM MULT; HLC 1**
See also CA 124; 128; 133; CANR 73; DLB 145; HW 1; MTCW 1

Arendt, Hannah 1906-1975 .... **CLC 66, 98**
See also CA 17-20R; 61-64; CANR 26, 60; MTCW 1, 2

Aretino, Pietro 1492-1556 .... **LC 12**

Arghezi, Tudor 1880-1967 .... **CLC 80**
See also Theodorescu, Ion N.
See also CA 167

Arguedas, Jose Maria 1911-1969 .... **CLC 10, 18; HLCS 1**
See also CA 89-92; CANR 73; DLB 113; HW 1

Argueta, Manlio 1936- .... **CLC 31**
See also CA 131; CANR 73; DLB 145; HW 1

Belinski, Vissarion Grigoryevich
  1811-1848 .... **NCLC 5**
    See also DLB 198
Belitt, Ben 1911- .... **CLC 22**
    See also CA 13-16R; CAAS 4; CANR 7,
    77; DLB 5
Bell, Gertrude (Margaret Lowthian)
  1868-1926 .... **TCLC 67**
    See also CA 167; DLB 174
Bell, J. Freeman
    See Zangwill, Israel
Bell, James Madison 1826-1902 ... **TCLC 43;**
    BLC 1; DAM MULT
    See also BW 1; CA 122; 124; DLB 50
Bell, Madison Smartt 1957- ...... **CLC 41, 102**
    See also CA 111, 183; CAAE 183; CANR
    28, 54, 73; MTCW 1
Bell, Marvin (Hartley) 1937- ...... **CLC 8, 31;**
    DAM POET
    See also CA 21-24R; CAAS 14; CANR 59;
    DLB 5; MTCW 1
Bell, W. L. D.
    See Mencken, H(enry) L(ouis)
Bellamy, Atwood C.
    See Mencken, H(enry) L(ouis)
Bellamy, Edward 1850-1898 ...... **NCLC 4, 86**
    See also DLB 12
Belli, Gioconda 1949-
    See also CA 152; HLCS 1
Bellin, Edward J.
    See Kuttner, Henry
Belloc, (Joseph) Hilaire (Pierre Sebastien
    Rene Swanton) 1870- .... **TCLC 7, 18;**
    DAM POET; PC 24
    See also CA 106; 152; DLB 19, 100, 141,
    174; MTCW 1; SATA 112; YABC 1
Belloc, Joseph Peter Rene Hilaire
    See Belloc, (Joseph) Hilaire (Pierre Sebas-
    tien Rene Swanton)
Belloc, Joseph Pierre Hilaire
    See Belloc, (Joseph) Hilaire (Pierre Sebas-
    tien Rene Swanton)
Belloc, M. A.
    See Lowndes, Marie Adelaide (Belloc)
Bellow, Saul 1915- . **CLC 1, 2, 3, 6, 8, 10, 13,**
    15, 25, 33, 34, 63, 79; DA; DAB; DAC;
    DAM MST, NOV, POP; SSC 14; WLC
    See also AITN 2; BEST 89:3; CA 5-8R;
    CABS 1; CANR 29, 53; CDALB 1941-
    1968; DA3; DLB 2, 28; DLBD 3; DLBY
    82; MTCW 1, 2
Belser, Reimond Karel Maria de 1929-
    See Ruyslinck, Ward
    See also CA 152
Bely, Andrey **TCLC 7; PC 11**
    See also Bugayev, Boris Nikolayevich
    See also MTCW 1
Belyi, Andrei
    See Bugayev, Boris Nikolayevich
Benary, Margot
    See Benary-Isbert, Margot
Benary-Isbert, Margot 1889-1979 .... **CLC 12**
    See also CA 5-8R; 89-92; CANR 4, 72;
    CLR 12; MAICYA; SATA 2; SATA-Obit
    21
Benavente (y Martinez), Jacinto
  1866-1954 .... **TCLC 3; DAM DRAM,**
    MULT; HLCS 1
    See also CA 106; 131; CANR 81; HW 1, 2;
    MTCW 1, 2

Benchley, Peter (Bradford) 1940- . **CLC 4, 8;**
    DAM NOV, POP
    See also AAYA 14; AITN 2; CA 17-20R;
    CANR 12, 35, 66; MTCW 1, 2; SATA 3,
    89
Benchley, Robert (Charles)
  1889-1945 .... **TCLC 1, 55**
    See also CA 105; 153; DLB 11
Benda, Julien 1867-1956 .... **TCLC 60**
    See also CA 120; 154
Benedict, Ruth (Fulton)
  1887-1948 .... **TCLC 60**
    See also CA 158
Benedict, Saint c. 480-c. 547 .... **CMLC 29**
Benedikt, Michael 1935- .... **CLC 4, 14**
    See also CA 13-16R; CANR 7; DLB 5
Benet, Juan 1927- .... **CLC 28**
    See also CA 143
Benet, Stephen Vincent 1898-1943 . **TCLC 7;**
    DAM POET; SSC 10
    See also CA 104; 152; DA3; DLB 4, 48,
    102; DLBY 97; MTCW 1; YABC 1
Benet, William Rose 1886-1950 .... **TCLC 28;**
    DAM POET
    See also CA 118; 152; DLB 45
Benford, Gregory (Albert) 1941- ..... **CLC 52**
    See also CA 69-72, 175; CAAE 175; CAAS
    27; CANR 12, 24, 49; DLBY 82
Bengtsson, Frans (Gunnar)
  1894-1954 .... **TCLC 48**
    See also CA 170
Benjamin, David
    See Slavitt, David R(ytman)
Benjamin, Lois
    See Gould, Lois
Benjamin, Walter 1892-1940 .... **TCLC 39**
    See also CA 164
Benn, Gottfried 1886-1956 .... **TCLC 3**
    See also CA 106; 153; DLB 56
Bennett, Alan 1934- .... **CLC 45, 77; DAB;**
    DAM MST
    See also CA 103; CANR 35, 55; MTCW 1,
    2
Bennett, (Enoch) Arnold
  1867-1931 .... **TCLC 5, 20**
    See also CA 106; 155; CDBLB 1890-1914;
    DLB 10, 34, 98, 135; MTCW 2
Bennett, Elizabeth
    See Mitchell, Margaret (Munnerlyn)
Bennett, George Harold 1930-
    See Bennett, Hal
    See also BW 1; CA 97-100; CANR 87
Bennett, Hal **CLC 5**
    See also Bennett, George Harold
    See also DLB 33
Bennett, Jay 1912- .... **CLC 35**
    See also AAYA 10; CA 69-72; CANR 11,
    42, 79; JRDA; SAAS 4; SATA 41, 87;
    SATA-Brief 27
Bennett, Louise (Simone) 1919- ...... **CLC 28;**
    BLC 1; DAM MULT
    See also BW 2, 3; CA 151; DLB 117
Benson, E(dward) F(rederic)
  1867-1940 .... **TCLC 27**
    See also CA 114; 157; DLB 135, 153
Benson, Jackson J. 1930- .... **CLC 34**
    See also CA 25-28R; DLB 111
Benson, Sally 1900-1972 .... **CLC 17**
    See also CA 19-20; 37-40R; CAP 1; SATA
    1, 35; SATA-Obit 27
Benson, Stella 1892-1933 .... **TCLC 17**
    See also CA 117; 155; DLB 36, 162

Bentham, Jeremy 1748-1832 .... **NCLC 38**
    See also DLB 107, 158
Bentley, E(dmund) C(lerihew)
  1875-1956 .... **TCLC 12**
    See also CA 108; DLB 70
Bentley, Eric (Russell) 1916- .... **CLC 24**
    See also CA 5-8R; CANR 6, 67; INT
    CANR-6
Beranger, Pierre Jean de
  1780-1857 .... **NCLC 34**
Berdyaev, Nicolas
    See Berdyaev, Nikolai (Aleksandrovich)
Berdyaev, Nikolai (Aleksandrovich)
  1874-1948 .... **TCLC 67**
    See also CA 120; 157
Berdyayev, Nikolai (Aleksandrovich)
    See Berdyaev, Nikolai (Aleksandrovich)
Berendt, John (Lawrence) 1939- ...... **CLC 86**
    See also CA 146; CANR 75; DA3; MTCW
    1
Beresford, J(ohn) D(avys)
  1873-1947 .... **TCLC 81**
    See also CA 112; 155; DLB 162, 178, 197
Bergelson, David 1884-1952 .... **TCLC 81**
Berger, Colonel
    See Malraux, (Georges-)Andre
Berger, John (Peter) 1926- .... **CLC 2, 19**
    See also CA 81-84; CANR 51, 78; DLB 14,
    207
Berger, Melvin H. 1927- .... **CLC 12**
    See also CA 5-8R; CANR 4; CLR 32;
    SAAS 2; SATA 5, 88
Berger, Thomas (Louis) 1924- .. **CLC 3, 5, 8,**
    11, 18, 38; DAM NOV
    See also CA 1-4R; CANR 5, 28, 51; DLB
    2; DLBY 80; INT CANR-28; MTCW 1, 2
Bergman, (Ernst) Ingmar 1918- ...... **CLC 16,**
    72
    See also CA 81-84; CANR 33, 70; MTCW
    2
Bergson, Henri(-Louis) 1859-1941 . **TCLC 32**
    See also CA 164
Bergstein, Eleanor 1938- .... **CLC 4**
    See also CA 53-56; CANR 5
Berkoff, Steven 1937- .... **CLC 56**
    See also CA 104; CANR 72
Bermant, Chaim (Icyk) 1929- .... **CLC 40**
    See also CA 57-60; CANR 6, 31, 57
Bern, Victoria
    See Fisher, M(ary) F(rances) K(ennedy)
Bernanos, (Paul Louis) Georges
  1888-1948 .... **TCLC 3**
    See also CA 104; 130; DLB 72
Bernard, April 1956- .... **CLC 59**
    See also CA 131
Berne, Victoria
    See Fisher, M(ary) F(rances) K(ennedy)
Bernhard, Thomas 1931-1989 ..... **CLC 3, 32,**
    61
    See also CA 85-88; 127; CANR 32, 57;
    DLB 85, 124; MTCW 1
Bernhardt, Sarah (Henriette Rosine)
  1844-1923 .... **TCLC 75**
    See also CA 157
Berriault, Gina 1926-1999 .... **CLC 54, 109;**
    SSC 30
    See also CA 116; 129; 185; CANR 66; DLB
    130
Berrigan, Daniel 1921- .... **CLC 4**
    See also CA 33-36R; CAAS 1; CANR 11,
    43, 78; DLB 5

Blom, Jan
  See Breytenbach, Breyten

Bloom, Harold 1930- .... **CLC 24, 103**
  See also CA 13-16R; CANR 39, 75; DLB
  67; MTCW 1

Bloomfield, Aurelius
  See Bourne, Randolph S(illiman)

Blount, Roy (Alton), Jr. 1941- .... **CLC 38**
  See also CA 53-56; CANR 10, 28, 61; INT
  CANR-28; MTCW 1, 2

Bloy, Leon 1846-1917 .... **TCLC 22**
  See also CA 121; 183; DLB 123

Blume, Judy (Sussman) 1938- .. **CLC 12, 30;**
  DAM NOV, POP
  See also AAYA 3, 26; CA 29-32R; CANR
  13, 37, 66; CLR 2, 15; DA3; DLB 52;
  JRDA; MAICYA; MTCW 1, 2; SATA 2,
  31, 79

Blunden, Edmund (Charles)
  1896-1974 .... **CLC 2, 56**
  See also CA 17-18; 45-48; CANR 54; CAP
  2; DLB 20, 100, 155; MTCW 1

Bly, Robert (Elwood) 1926- .... **CLC 1, 2, 5,**
  10, 15, 38, 128; DAM POET
  See also CA 5-8R; CANR 41, 73; DA3;
  DLB 5; MTCW 1, 2

Boas, Franz 1858-1942 .... **TCLC 56**
  See also CA 115; 181

Bobette
  See Simenon, Georges (Jacques Christian)

Boccaccio, Giovanni 1313-1375 ... **CMLC 13;**
  SSC 10

Bochco, Steven 1943- .... **CLC 35**
  See also AAYA 11; CA 124; 138

Bodel, Jean 1167(?)-1210 .... **CMLC 28**

Bodenheim, Maxwell 1892-1954 .... **TCLC 44**
  See also CA 110; DLB 9, 45

Bodker, Cecil 1927- .... **CLC 21**
  See also CA 73-76; CANR 13, 44; CLR 23;
  MAICYA; SATA 14

Boell, Heinrich (Theodor)
  1917-1985 ..... **CLC 2, 3, 6, 9, 11, 15, 27,**
  32, 72; DA; DAB; DAC; DAM MST,
  NOV; SSC 23; WLC
  See also CA 21-24R; 116; CANR 24; DA3;
  DLB 69; DLBY 85; MTCW 1, 2

Boerne, Alfred
  See Doeblin, Alfred

Boethius 480(?)-524(?) .... **CMLC 15**
  See also DLB 115

Boff, Leonardo (Genezio Darci) 1938-
  See also CA 150; DAM MULT; HLC 1;
  HW 2

Bogan, Louise 1897-1970 .... **CLC 4, 39, 46,**
  93; DAM POET; PC 12
  See also CA 73-76; 25-28R; CANR 33, 82;
  DLB 45, 169; MTCW 1, 2

Bogarde, Dirk 1921-1999
  See Van Den Bogarde, Derek Jules Gaspard
  Ulric Niven

Bogosian, Eric 1953- .... **CLC 45**
  See also CA 138

Bograd, Larry 1953- .... **CLC 35**
  See also CA 93-96; CANR 57; SAAS 21;
  SATA 33, 89

Boiardo, Matteo Maria 1441-1494 .... **LC 6**

Boileau-Despreaux, Nicolas 1636-1711 . **LC 3**

Bojer, Johan 1872-1959 .... **TCLC 64**

Boland, Eavan (Aisling) 1944- .. **CLC 40, 67,**
  113; DAM POET
  See also CA 143; CANR 61; DLB 40;
  MTCW 2

Boll, Heinrich
  See Boell, Heinrich (Theodor)

Bolt, Lee
  See Faust, Frederick (Schiller)

Bolt, Robert (Oxton) 1924-1995 ...... **CLC 14;**
  DAM DRAM
  See also CA 17-20R; 147; CANR 35, 67;
  DLB 13; MTCW 1

Bombal, Maria Luisa 1910-1980 ...... **SSC 37;**
  HLCS 1
  See also CA 127; CANR 72; HW 1

Bombet, Louis-Alexandre-Cesar
  See Stendhal

Bomkauf
  See Kaufman, Bob (Garnell)

Bonaventura **NCLC 35**
  See also DLB 90

Bond, Edward 1934- .... **CLC 4, 6, 13, 23;**
  DAM DRAM
  See also CA 25-28R; CANR 38, 67; DLB
  13; MTCW 1

Bonham, Frank 1914-1989 .... **CLC 12**
  See also AAYA 1; CA 9-12R; CANR 4, 36;
  JRDA; MAICYA; SAAS 3; SATA 1, 49;
  SATA-Obit 62

Bonnefoy, Yves 1923- .. **CLC 9, 15, 58; DAM**
  MST, POET
  See also CA 85-88; CANR 33, 75; MTCW
  1, 2

Bontemps, Arna(ud Wendell)
  1902-1973 ..... **CLC 1, 18; BLC 1; DAM**
  MULT, NOV, POET
  See also BW 1; CA 1-4R; 41-44R; CANR
  4, 35; CLR 6; DA3; DLB 48, 51; JRDA;
  MAICYA; MTCW 1, 2; SATA 2, 44;
  SATA-Obit 24

Booth, Martin 1944- .... **CLC 13**
  See also CA 93-96; CAAS 2

Booth, Philip 1925- .... **CLC 23**
  See also CA 5-8R; CANR 5, 88; DLBY 82

Booth, Wayne C(layson) 1921- .... **CLC 24**
  See also CA 1-4R; CAAS 5; CANR 3, 43;
  DLB 67

Borchert, Wolfgang 1921-1947 .... **TCLC 5**
  See also CA 104; DLB 69, 124

Borel, Petrus 1809-1859 .... **NCLC 41**

Borges, Jorge Luis 1899-1986 ... **CLC 1, 2, 3,**
  4, 6, 8, 9, 10, 13, 19, 44, 48, 83; DA;
  DAB; DAC; DAM MST, MULT; HLC
  1; PC 22; SSC 4; WLC
  See also AAYA 26; CA 21-24R; CANR 19,
  33, 75; DA3; DLB 113; DLBY 86; HW 1,
  2; MTCW 1, 2

Borowski, Tadeusz 1922-1951 .... **TCLC 9**
  See also CA 106; 154

Borrow, George (Henry)
  1803-1881 .... **NCLC 9**
  See also DLB 21, 55, 166

Bosch (Gavino), Juan 1909-
  See also CA 151; DAM MST, MULT; DLB
  145; HLCS 1; HW 1, 2

Bosman, Herman Charles
  1905-1951 .... **TCLC 49**
  See also Malan, Herman
  See also CA 160

Bosschere, Jean de 1878(?)-1953 ... **TCLC 19**
  See also CA 115; 186

Boswell, James 1740-1795 ...... **LC 4, 50; DA;**
  DAB; DAC; DAM MST; WLC
  See also CDBLB 1660-1789; DLB 104, 142

Bottoms, David 1949- .... **CLC 53**
  See also CA 105; CANR 22; DLB 120;
  DLBY 83

Boucicault, Dion 1820-1890 .... **NCLC 41**

Bourget, Paul (Charles Joseph)
  1852-1935 .... **TCLC 12**
  See also CA 107; DLB 123

Bourjaily, Vance (Nye) 1922- .... **CLC 8, 62**
  See also CA 1-4R; CAAS 1; CANR 2, 72;
  DLB 2, 143

Bourne, Randolph S(illiman)
  1886-1918 .... **TCLC 16**
  See also CA 117; 155; DLB 63

Bova, Ben(jamin William) 1932- ...... **CLC 45**
  See also AAYA 16; CA 5-8R; CAAS 18;
  CANR 11, 56; CLR 3; DLBY 81; INT
  CANR-11; MAICYA; MTCW 1; SATA 6,
  68

Bowen, Elizabeth (Dorothea Cole)
  1899-1973 . **CLC 1, 3, 6, 11, 15, 22, 118;**
  DAM NOV; SSC 3, 28
  See also CA 17-18; 41-44R; CANR 35;
  CAP 2; CDBLB 1945-1960; DA3; DLB
  15, 162; MTCW 1, 2

Bowering, George 1935- .... **CLC 15, 47**
  See also CA 21-24R; CAAS 16; CANR 10;
  DLB 53

Bowering, Marilyn R(uthe) 1949- .... **CLC 32**
  See also CA 101; CANR 49

Bowers, Edgar 1924- .... **CLC 9**
  See also CA 5-8R; CANR 24; DLB 5

Bowie, David **CLC 17**
  See also Jones, David Robert

Bowles, Jane (Sydney) 1917-1973 ..... **CLC 3,**
  68
  See also CA 19-20; 41-44R; CAP 2

Bowles, Paul (Frederick) 1910-1999 . **CLC 1,**
  2, 19, 53; SSC 3
  See also CA 1-4R; 186; CAAS 1; CANR 1,
  19, 50, 75; DA3; DLB 5, 6; MTCW 1, 2

Box, Edgar
  See Vidal, Gore

Boyd, Nancy
  See Millay, Edna St. Vincent

Boyd, William 1952- .... **CLC 28, 53, 70**
  See also CA 114; 120; CANR 51, 71

Boyle, Kay 1902-1992 .... **CLC 1, 5, 19, 58,**
  121; SSC 5
  See also CA 13-16R; 140; CAAS 1; CANR
  29, 61; DLB 4, 9, 48, 86; DLBY 93;
  MTCW 1, 2

Boyle, Mark
  See Kienzle, William X(avier)

Boyle, Patrick 1905-1982 .... **CLC 19**
  See also CA 127

Boyle, T. C. 1948-
  See Boyle, T(homas) Coraghessan

Boyle, T(homas) Coraghessan
  1948- .... **CLC 36, 55, 90; DAM POP;**
  SSC 16
  See also BEST 90:4; CA 120; CANR 44,
  76, 89; DA3; DLBY 86; MTCW 2

Boz
  See Dickens, Charles (John Huffam)

Brackenridge, Hugh Henry
  1748-1816 .... **NCLC 7**
  See also DLB 11, 37

Bradbury, Edward P.
  See Moorcock, Michael (John)
  See also MTCW 2

Bradbury, Malcolm (Stanley)
1932- .... **CLC 32, 61; DAM NOV**
See also CA 1-4R; CANR 1, 33, 91; DA3;
DLB 14, 207; MTCW 1, 2

Bradbury, Ray (Douglas) 1920- .... **CLC 1, 3,
10, 15, 42, 98; DA; DAB; DAC; DAM
MST, NOV, POP; SSC 29; WLC**
See also AAYA 15; AITN 1, 2; CA 1-4R;
CANR 2, 30, 75; CDALB 1968-1988;
DA3; DLB 2, 8; MTCW 1, 2; SATA 11,
64

Bradford, Gamaliel 1863-1932 .... **TCLC 36**
See also CA 160; DLB 17

Bradley, David (Henry), Jr. 1950- ... **CLC 23,
118; BLC 1; DAM MULT**
See also BW 1, 3; CA 104; CANR 26, 81;
DLB 33

Bradley, John Ed(mund, Jr.) 1958- . **CLC 55**
See also CA 139

Bradley, Marion Zimmer
1930-1999 .... **CLC 30; DAM POP**
See also AAYA 9; CA 57-60; 185; CAAS
10; CANR 7, 31, 51, 75; DA3; DLB 8;
MTCW 1, 2; SATA 90; SATA-Obit 116

Bradstreet, Anne 1612(?)-1672 ...... **LC 4, 30;
DA; DAC; DAM MST, POET; PC 10**
See also CDALB 1640-1865; DA3; DLB
24

Brady, Joan 1939- .... **CLC 86**
See also CA 141

Bragg, Melvyn 1939- .... **CLC 10**
See also BEST 89:3; CA 57-60; CANR 10,
48, 89; DLB 14

Brahe, Tycho 1546-1601 .... **LC 45**

Braine, John (Gerard) 1922-1986 . **CLC 1, 3,
41**
See also CA 1-4R; 120; CANR 1, 33; CD-
BLB 1945-1960; DLB 15; DLBY 86;
MTCW 1

Bramah, Ernest 1868-1942 .... **TCLC 72**
See also CA 156; DLB 70

Brammer, William 1930(?)-1978 ...... **CLC 31**
See also CA 77-80

Brancati, Vitaliano 1907-1954 .... **TCLC 12**
See also CA 109

Brancato, Robin F(idler) 1936- .... **CLC 35**
See also AAYA 9; CA 69-72; CANR 11,
45; CLR 32; JRDA; SAAS 9; SATA 97

Brand, Max
See Faust, Frederick (Schiller)

Brand, Millen 1906-1980 .... **CLC 7**
See also CA 21-24R; 97-100; CANR 72

Branden, Barbara **CLC 44**
See also CA 148

Brandes, Georg (Morris Cohen)
1842-1927 .... **TCLC 10**
See also CA 105

Brandys, Kazimierz 1916- .... **CLC 62**

Branley, Franklyn M(ansfield)
1915- .... **CLC 21**
See also CA 33-36R; CANR 14, 39; CLR
13; MAICYA; SAAS 16; SATA 4, 68

Brathwaite, Edward (Kamau)
1930- ...... **CLC 11; BLCS; DAM POET**
See also BW 2, 3; CA 25-28R; CANR 11,
26, 47; DLB 125

Brautigan, Richard (Gary)
1935-1984 .... **CLC 1, 3, 5, 9, 12, 34, 42;
DAM NOV**
See also CA 53-56; 113; CANR 34; DA3;
DLB 2, 5, 206; DLBY 80, 84; MTCW 1;
SATA 56

Brave Bird, Mary 1953-
See Crow Dog, Mary (Ellen)
See also NNAL

Braverman, Kate 1950- .... **CLC 67**
See also CA 89-92

Brecht, (Eugen) Bertolt (Friedrich)
1898-1956 .... **TCLC 1, 6, 13, 35; DA;
DAB; DAC; DAM DRAM, MST; DC
3; WLC**
See also CA 104; 133; CANR 62; DA3;
DLB 56, 124; MTCW 1, 2

Brecht, Eugen Berthold Friedrich
See Brecht, (Eugen) Bertolt (Friedrich)

Bremer, Fredrika 1801-1865 .... **NCLC 11**

Brennan, Christopher John
1870-1932 .... **TCLC 17**
See also CA 117

Brennan, Maeve 1917-1993 .... **CLC 5**
See also CA 81-84; CANR 72

Brent, Linda
See Jacobs, Harriet A(nn)

Brentano, Clemens (Maria)
1778-1842 .... **NCLC 1**
See also DLB 90

Brent of Bin Bin
See Franklin, (Stella Maria Sarah) Miles
(Lampe)

Brenton, Howard 1942- .... **CLC 31**
See also CA 69-72; CANR 33, 67; DLB 13;
MTCW 1

Breslin, James 1930-1996
See Breslin, Jimmy
See also CA 73-76; CANR 31, 75; DAM
NOV; MTCW 1, 2

Breslin, Jimmy **CLC 4, 43**
See also Breslin, James
See also AITN 1; DLB 185; MTCW 2

Bresson, Robert 1901- .... **CLC 16**
See also CA 110; CANR 49

Breton, Andre 1896-1966 .. **CLC 2, 9, 15, 54;
PC 15**
See also CA 19-20; 25-28R; CANR 40, 60;
CAP 2; DLB 65; MTCW 1, 2

Breytenbach, Breyten 1939(?)- .. **CLC 23, 37,
126; DAM POET**
See also CA 113; 129; CANR 61

Bridgers, Sue Ellen 1942- .... **CLC 26**
See also AAYA 8; CA 65-68; CANR 11,
36; CLR 18; DLB 52; JRDA; MAICYA;
SAAS 1; SATA 22, 90; SATA-Essay 109

Bridges, Robert (Seymour)
1844-1930 ... **TCLC 1; DAM POET; PC
28**
See also CA 104; 152; CDBLB 1890-1914;
DLB 19, 98

Bridie, James **TCLC 3**
See also Mavor, Osborne Henry
See also DLB 10

Brin, David 1950- .... **CLC 34**
See also AAYA 21; CA 102; CANR 24, 70;
INT CANR-24; SATA 65

Brink, Andre (Philippus) 1935- . **CLC 18, 36,
106**
See also CA 104; CANR 39, 62; INT 103;
MTCW 1, 2

Brinsmead, H(esba) F(ay) 1922- ...... **CLC 21**
See also CA 21-24R; CANR 10; CLR 47;
MAICYA; SAAS 5; SATA 18, 78

Brittain, Vera (Mary) 1893(?)-1970 . **CLC 23**
See also CA 13-16; 25-28R; CANR 58;
CAP 1; DLB 191; MTCW 1, 2

Broch, Hermann 1886-1951 .... **TCLC 20**
See also CA 117; DLB 85, 124

Brock, Rose
See Hansen, Joseph

Brodkey, Harold (Roy) 1930-1996 ... **CLC 56**
See also CA 111; 151; CANR 71; DLB 130

Brodskii, Iosif
See Brodsky, Joseph

Brodsky, Iosif Alexandrovich 1940-1996
See Brodsky, Joseph
See also AITN 1; CA 41-44R; 151; CANR
37; DAM POET; DA3; MTCW 1, 2

Brodsky, Joseph 1940-1996 ..... **CLC 4, 6, 13,
36, 100; PC 9**
See also Brodskii, Iosif; Brodsky, Iosif Alexandrovich
See also MTCW 1

Brodsky, Michael (Mark) 1948- .... **CLC 19**
See also CA 102; CANR 18, 41, 58

Bromell, Henry 1947- .... **CLC 5**
See also CA 53-56; CANR 9

Bromfield, Louis (Brucker)
1896-1956 .... **TCLC 11**
See also CA 107; 155; DLB 4, 9, 86

Broner, E(sther) M(asserman)
1930- .... **CLC 19**
See also CA 17-20R; CANR 8, 25, 72; DLB
28

Bronk, William (M.) 1918-1999 .... **CLC 10**
See also CA 89-92; 177; CANR 23; DLB
165

Bronstein, Lev Davidovich
See Trotsky, Leon

Bronte, Anne 1820-1849 .... **NCLC 4, 71**
See also DA3; DLB 21, 199

Bronte, Charlotte 1816-1855 ...... **NCLC 3, 8,
33, 58; DA; DAB; DAC; DAM MST,
NOV; WLC**
See also AAYA 17; CDBLB 1832-1890;
DA3; DLB 21, 159, 199

Bronte, Emily (Jane) 1818-1848 ... **NCLC 16,
35; DA; DAB; DAC; DAM MST, NOV,
POET; PC 8; WLC**
See also AAYA 17; CDBLB 1832-1890;
DA3; DLB 21, 32, 199

Brooke, Frances 1724-1789 .... **LC 6, 48**
See also DLB 39, 99

Brooke, Henry 1703(?)-1783 .... **LC 1**
See also DLB 39

Brooke, Rupert (Chawner)
1887-1915 .... **TCLC 2, 7; DA; DAB;
DAC; DAM MST, POET; PC 24; WLC**
See also CA 104; 132; CANR 61; CDBLB
1914-1945; DLB 19; MTCW 1, 2

Brooke-Haven, P.
See Wodehouse, P(elham) G(renville)

Brooke-Rose, Christine 1926(?)- ...... **CLC 40**
See also CA 13-16R; CANR 58; DLB 14

Brookner, Anita 1928- .... **CLC 32, 34, 51;
DAB; DAM POP**
See also CA 114; 120; CANR 37, 56, 87;
DA3; DLB 194; DLBY 87; MTCW 1, 2

Brooks, Cleanth 1906-1994 . **CLC 24, 86, 110**
See also CA 17-20R; 145; CANR 33, 35;
DLB 63; DLBY 94; INT CANR-35;
MTCW 1, 2

Brooks, George
See Baum, L(yman) Frank

Brooks, Gwendolyn 1917- ..... **CLC 1, 2, 4, 5,
15, 49, 125; BLC 1; DA; DAC; DAM
MST, MULT, POET; PC 7; WLC**
See also AAYA 20; AITN 1; BW 2, 3; CA
1-4R; CANR 1, 27, 52, 75; CDALB 1941-
1968; CLR 27; DA3; DLB 5, 76, 165;
MTCW 1, 2; SATA 6

Burke, Kenneth (Duva) 1897-1993 ... **CLC 2, 24**
See also CA 5-8R; 143; CANR 39, 74; DLB 45, 63; MTCW 1, 2

Burke, Leda
See Garnett, David

Burke, Ralph
See Silverberg, Robert

Burke, Thomas 1886-1945 .... **TCLC 63**
See also CA 113; 155; DLB 197

Burney, Fanny 1752-1840 .. **NCLC 12, 54, 81**
See also DLB 39

Burns, Robert 1759-1796 . **LC 3, 29, 40; DA; DAB; DAC; DAM MST, POET; PC 6; WLC**
See also CDBLB 1789-1832; DA3; DLB 109

Burns, Tex
See L'Amour, Louis (Dearborn)

Burnshaw, Stanley 1906- .... **CLC 3, 13, 44**
See also CA 9-12R; DLB 48; DLBY 97

Burr, Anne 1937- .... **CLC 6**
See also CA 25-28R

Burroughs, Edgar Rice 1875-1950 . **TCLC 2, 32; DAM NOV**
See also AAYA 11; CA 104; 132; DA3; DLB 8; MTCW 1, 2; SATA 41

Burroughs, William S(eward)
1914-1997 .. **CLC 1, 2, 5, 15, 22, 42, 75, 109; DA; DAB; DAC; DAM MST, NOV, POP; WLC**
See also AITN 2; CA 9-12R; 160; CANR 20, 52; DA3; DLB 2, 8, 16, 152; DLBY 81, 97; MTCW 1, 2

Burton, SirRichard F(rancis)
1821-1890 .... **NCLC 42**
See also DLB 55, 166, 184

Busch, Frederick 1941- .... **CLC 7, 10, 18, 47**
See also CA 33-36R; CAAS 1; CANR 45, 73; DLB 6

Bush, Ronald 1946- .... **CLC 34**
See also CA 136

Bustos, F(rancisco)
See Borges, Jorge Luis

Bustos Domecq, H(onorio)
See Bioy Casares, Adolfo; Borges, Jorge Luis

Butler, Octavia E(stelle) 1947- .... **CLC 38, 121; BLCS; DAM MULT, POP**
See also AAYA 18; BW 2, 3; CA 73-76; CANR 12, 24, 38, 73; CLR 65; DA3; DLB 33; MTCW 1, 2; SATA 84

Butler, Robert Olen (Jr.) 1945- .... **CLC 81; DAM POP**
See also CA 112; CANR 66; DLB 173; INT 112; MTCW 1

Butler, Samuel 1612-1680 .... **LC 16, 43**
See also DLB 101, 126

Butler, Samuel 1835-1902 . **TCLC 1, 33; DA; DAB; DAC; DAM MST, NOV; WLC**
See also CA 143; CDBLB 1890-1914; DA3; DLB 18, 57, 174

Butler, Walter C.
See Faust, Frederick (Schiller)

Butor, Michel (Marie Francois)
1926- .... **CLC 1, 3, 8, 11, 15**
See also CA 9-12R; CANR 33, 66; DLB 83; MTCW 1, 2

Butts, Mary 1892(?)-1937 .... **TCLC 77**
See also CA 148

Buzo, Alexander (John) 1944- .... **CLC 61**
See also CA 97-100; CANR 17, 39, 69

Buzzati, Dino 1906-1972 .... **CLC 36**
See also CA 160; 33-36R; DLB 177

Byars, Betsy (Cromer) 1928- .... **CLC 35**
See also AAYA 19; CA 33-36R, 183; CAAE 183; CANR 18, 36, 57; CLR 1, 16; DLB 52; INT CANR-18; JRDA; MAICYA; MTCW 1; SAAS 1; SATA 4, 46, 80; SATA-Essay 108

Byatt, A(ntonia) S(usan Drabble)
1936- ..... **CLC 19, 65; DAM NOV, POP**
See also CA 13-16R; CANR 13, 33, 50, 75; DA3; DLB 14, 194; MTCW 1, 2

Byrne, David 1952- .... **CLC 26**
See also CA 127

Byrne, John Keyes 1926-
See Leonard, Hugh
See also CA 102; CANR 78; INT 102

Byron, George Gordon (Noel)
1788-1824 .... **NCLC 2, 12; DA; DAB; DAC; DAM MST, POET; PC 16; WLC**
See also CDBLB 1789-1832; DA3; DLB 96, 110

Byron, Robert 1905-1941 .... **TCLC 67**
See also CA 160; DLB 195

C. 3. 3.
See Wilde, Oscar (Fingal O'Flahertie Wills)

Caballero, Fernan 1796-1877 .... **NCLC 10**

Cabell, Branch
See Cabell, James Branch

Cabell, James Branch 1879-1958 .... **TCLC 6**
See also CA 105; 152; DLB 9, 78; MTCW 1

Cable, George Washington
1844-1925 .... **TCLC 4; SSC 4**
See also CA 104; 155; DLB 12, 74; DLBD 13

Cabral de Melo Neto, Joao 1920- ... **CLC 76; DAM MULT**
See also CA 151

Cabrera Infante, G(uillermo) 1929- . **CLC 5, 25, 45, 120; DAM MULT; HLC 1; SSC 39**
See also CA 85-88; CANR 29, 65; DA3; DLB 113; HW 1, 2; MTCW 1, 2

Cade, Toni
See Bambara, Toni Cade

Cadmus and Harmonia
See Buchan, John

Caedmon fl. 658-680 .... **CMLC 7**
See also DLB 146

Caeiro, Alberto
See Pessoa, Fernando (Antonio Nogueira)

Cage, John (Milton, Jr.) 1912-1992 . **CLC 41**
See also CA 13-16R; 169; CANR 9, 78; DLB 193; INT CANR-9

Cahan, Abraham 1860-1951 .... **TCLC 71**
See also CA 108; 154; DLB 9, 25, 28

Cain, G.
See Cabrera Infante, G(uillermo)

Cain, Guillermo
See Cabrera Infante, G(uillermo)

Cain, James M(allahan) 1892-1977 .. **CLC 3, 11, 28**
See also AITN 1; CA 17-20R; 73-76; CANR 8, 34, 61; MTCW 1

Caine, Hall 1853-1931 .... **TCLC 97**

Caine, Mark
See Raphael, Frederic (Michael)

Calasso, Roberto 1941- .... **CLC 81**
See also CA 143; CANR 89

Calderon de la Barca, Pedro
1600-1681 .... **LC 23; DC 3; HLCS 1**

Caldwell, Erskine (Preston)
1903-1987 .. **CLC 1, 8, 14, 50, 60; DAM NOV; SSC 19**
See also AITN 1; CA 1-4R; 121; CAAS 1; CANR 2, 33; DA3; DLB 9, 86; MTCW 1, 2

Caldwell, (Janet Miriam) Taylor (Holland)
1900-1985 .. **CLC 2, 28, 39; DAM NOV, POP**
See also CA 5-8R; 116; CANR 5; DA3; DLBD 17

Calhoun, John Caldwell
1782-1850 .... **NCLC 15**
See also DLB 3

Calisher, Hortense 1911- ..... **CLC 2, 4, 8, 38; DAM NOV; SSC 15**
See also CA 1-4R; CANR 1, 22, 67; DA3; DLB 2; INT CANR-22; MTCW 1, 2

Callaghan, Morley Edward
1903-1990 ...... **CLC 3, 14, 41, 65; DAC; DAM MST**
See also CA 9-12R; 132; CANR 33, 73; DLB 68; MTCW 1, 2

Callimachus c. 305B.C.-c.
240B.C. .... **CMLC 18**
See also DLB 176

Calvin, John 1509-1564 .... **LC 37**

Calvino, Italo 1923-1985 .... **CLC 5, 8, 11, 22, 33, 39, 73; DAM NOV; SSC 3**
See also CA 85-88; 116; CANR 23, 61; DLB 196; MTCW 1, 2

Cameron, Carey 1952- .... **CLC 59**
See also CA 135

Cameron, Peter 1959- .... **CLC 44**
See also CA 125; CANR 50

Camoens, Luis Vaz de 1524(?)-1580
See also HLCS 1

Camoes, Luis de 1524(?)-1580
See also HLCS 1

Campana, Dino 1885-1932 .... **TCLC 20**
See also CA 117; DLB 114

Campanella, Tommaso 1568-1639 .... **LC 32**

Campbell, John W(ood, Jr.)
1910-1971 .... **CLC 32**
See also CA 21-22; 29-32R; CANR 34; CAP 2; DLB 8; MTCW 1

Campbell, Joseph 1904-1987 .... **CLC 69**
See also AAYA 3; BEST 89:2; CA 1-4R; 124; CANR 3, 28, 61; DA3; MTCW 1, 2

Campbell, Maria 1940- .... **CLC 85; DAC**
See also CA 102; CANR 54; NNAL

Campbell, (John) Ramsey 1946- ..... **CLC 42; SSC 19**
See also CA 57-60; CANR 7; INT CANR-7

Campbell, (Ignatius) Roy (Dunnachie)
1901-1957 .... **TCLC 5**
See also CA 104; 155; DLB 20; MTCW 2

Campbell, Thomas 1777-1844 .... **NCLC 19**
See also DLB 93; 144

Campbell, Wilfred TCLC 9
See also Campbell, William

Campbell, William 1858(?)-1918
See Campbell, Wilfred
See also CA 106; DLB 92

Campion, Jane CLC 95
See also AAYA 33; CA 138; CANR 87

Camus, Albert 1913-1960 ...... CLC 1, 2, 4, 9, 11, 14, 32, 63, 69, 124; DA; DAB; DAC; DAM DRAM, MST, NOV; DC 2; SSC 9; WLC
See also CA 89-92; DA3; DLB 72; MTCW 1, 2

Canby, Vincent 1924- .... CLC 13
See also CA 81-84

Cancale
See Desnos, Robert

Canetti, Elias 1905-1994 .. CLC 3, 14, 25, 75, 86
See also CA 21-24R; 146; CANR 23, 61, 79; DA3; DLB 85, 124; MTCW 1, 2

Canfield, Dorothea F.
See Fisher, Dorothy (Frances) Canfield

Canfield, Dorothea Frances
See Fisher, Dorothy (Frances) Canfield

Canfield, Dorothy
See Fisher, Dorothy (Frances) Canfield

Canin, Ethan 1960- .... CLC 55
See also CA 131; 135

Cannon, Curt
See Hunter, Evan

Cao, Lan 1961- .... CLC 109
See also CA 165

Cape, Judith
See Page, P(atricia) K(athleen)

Capek, Karel 1890-1938 ... TCLC 6, 37; DA; DAB; DAC; DAM DRAM, MST, NOV; DC 1; SSC 36; WLC
See also CA 104; 140; DA3; MTCW 1

Capote, Truman 1924-1984 . CLC 1, 3, 8, 13, 19, 34, 38, 58; DA; DAB; DAC; DAM MST, NOV, POP; SSC 2; WLC
See also CA 5-8R; 113; CANR 18, 62; CDALB 1941-1968; DA3; DLB 2, 185; DLBY 80, 84; MTCW 1, 2; SATA 91

Capra, Frank 1897-1991 .... CLC 16
See also CA 61-64; 135

Caputo, Philip 1941- .... CLC 32
See also CA 73-76; CANR 40

Caragiale, Ion Luca 1852-1912 ...... TCLC 76
See also CA 157

Card, Orson Scott 1951- ..... CLC 44, 47, 50; DAM POP
See also AAYA 11; CA 102; CANR 27, 47, 73; DA3; INT CANR-27; MTCW 1, 2; SATA 83

Cardenal, Ernesto 1925- .... CLC 31; DAM MULT, POET; HLC 1; PC 22
See also CA 49-52; CANR 2, 32, 66; HW 1, 2; MTCW 1, 2

Cardozo, Benjamin N(athan) 1870-1938 .... TCLC 65
See also CA 117; 164

Carducci, Giosue (Alessandro Giuseppe) 1835-1907 .... TCLC 32
See also CA 163

Carew, Thomas 1595(?)-1640 . LC 13; PC 29
See also DLB 126

Carey, Ernestine Gilbreth 1908- ...... CLC 17
See also CA 5-8R; CANR 71; SATA 2

Carey, Peter 1943- .... CLC 40, 55, 96
See also CA 123; 127; CANR 53, 76; INT 127; MTCW 1, 2; SATA 94

Carleton, William 1794-1869 .... NCLC 3
See also DLB 159

Carlisle, Henry (Coffin) 1926- .... CLC 33
See also CA 13-16R; CANR 15, 85

Carlsen, Chris
See Holdstock, Robert P.

Carlson, Ron(ald F.) 1947- .... CLC 54
See also CA 105; CANR 27

Carlyle, Thomas 1795-1881 .. NCLC 70; DA; DAB; DAC; DAM MST
See also CDBLB 1789-1832; DLB 55; 144

Carman, (William) Bliss 1861-1929 .... TCLC 7; DAC
See also CA 104; 152; DLB 92

Carnegie, Dale 1888-1955 .... TCLC 53

Carossa, Hans 1878-1956 .... TCLC 48
See also CA 170; DLB 66

Carpenter, Don(ald Richard) 1931-1995 .... CLC 41
See also CA 45-48; 149; CANR 1, 71

Carpenter, Edward 1844-1929 .... TCLC 88
See also CA 163

Carpentier (y Valmont), Alejo 1904-1980 ..... CLC 8, 11, 38, 110; DAM MULT; HLC 1; SSC 35
See also CA 65-68; 97-100; CANR 11, 70; DLB 113; HW 1, 2

Carr, Caleb 1955(?)- .... CLC 86
See also CA 147; CANR 73; DA3

Carr, Emily 1871-1945 .... TCLC 32
See also CA 159; DLB 68

Carr, John Dickson 1906-1977 .... CLC 3
See also Fairbairn, Roger
See also CA 49-52; 69-72; CANR 3, 33, 60; MTCW 1, 2

Carr, Philippa
See Hibbert, Eleanor Alice Burford

Carr, Virginia Spencer 1929- .... CLC 34
See also CA 61-64; DLB 111

Carrere, Emmanuel 1957- .... CLC 89

Carrier, Roch 1937- .... CLC 13, 78; DAC; DAM MST
See also CA 130; CANR 61; DLB 53; SATA 105

Carroll, James P. 1943(?)- .... CLC 38
See also CA 81-84; CANR 73; MTCW 1

Carroll, Jim 1951- .... CLC 35
See also AAYA 17; CA 45-48; CANR 42

Carroll, Lewis NCLC 2, 53; PC 18; WLC
See also Dodgson, Charles Lutwidge
See also CDBLB 1832-1890; CLR 2, 18; DLB 18, 163, 178; DLBY 98; JRDA

Carroll, Paul Vincent 1900-1968 ...... CLC 10
See also CA 9-12R; 25-28R; DLB 10

Carruth, Hayden 1921- ..... CLC 4, 7, 10, 18, 84; PC 10
See also CA 9-12R; CANR 4, 38, 59; DLB 5, 165; INT CANR-4; MTCW 1, 2; SATA 47

Carson, Rachel Louise 1907-1964 ... CLC 71; DAM POP
See also CA 77-80; CANR 35; DA3; MTCW 1, 2; SATA 23

Carter, Angela (Olive) 1940-1992 ...... CLC 5, 41, 76; SSC 13
See also CA 53-56; 136; CANR 12, 36, 61; DA3; DLB 14, 207; MTCW 1, 2; SATA 66; SATA-Obit 70

Carter, Nick
See Smith, Martin Cruz

Carver, Raymond 1938-1988 ..... CLC 22, 36, 53, 55, 126; DAM NOV; SSC 8
See also CA 33-36R; 126; CANR 17, 34, 61; DA3; DLB 130; DLBY 84, 88; MTCW 1, 2

Cary, Elizabeth, Lady Falkland 1585-1639 .... LC 30

Cary, (Arthur) Joyce (Lunel) 1888-1957 .... TCLC 1, 29
See also CA 104; 164; CDBLB 1914-1945; DLB 15, 100; MTCW 2

Casanova de Seingalt, Giovanni Jacopo 1725-1798 .... LC 13

Casares, Adolfo Bioy
See Bioy Casares, Adolfo

Casely-Hayford, J(oseph) E(phraim) 1866-1930 ...... TCLC 24; BLC 1; DAM MULT
See also BW 2; CA 123; 152

Casey, John (Dudley) 1939- .... CLC 59
See also BEST 90:2; CA 69-72; CANR 23

Casey, Michael 1947- .... CLC 2
See also CA 65-68; DLB 5

Casey, Patrick
See Thurman, Wallace (Henry)

Casey, Warren (Peter) 1935-1988 .... CLC 12
See also CA 101; 127; INT 101

Casona, Alejandro CLC 49
See also Alvarez, Alejandro Rodriguez

Cassavetes, John 1929-1989 .... CLC 20
See also CA 85-88; 127; CANR 82

Cassian, Nina 1924- .... PC 17

Cassill, R(onald) V(erlin) 1919- ... CLC 4, 23
See also CA 9-12R; CAAS 1; CANR 7, 45; DLB 6

Cassirer, Ernst 1874-1945 .... TCLC 61
See also CA 157

Cassity, (Allen) Turner 1929- .... CLC 6, 42
See also CA 17-20R; CAAS 8; CANR 11; DLB 105

Castaneda, Carlos (Cesar Aranha) 1931(?)-1998 .... CLC 12, 119
See also CA 25-28R; CANR 32, 66; HW 1; MTCW 1

Castedo, Elena 1937- .... CLC 65
See also CA 132

Castedo-Ellerman, Elena
See Castedo, Elena

Castellanos, Rosario 1925-1974 .... CLC 66; DAM MULT; HLC 1; SSC 39
See also CA 131; 53-56; CANR 58; DLB 113; HW 1; MTCW 1

Castelvetro, Lodovico 1505-1571 .... LC 12

Castiglione, Baldassare 1478-1529 ...... LC 12

Castle, Robert
See Hamilton, Edmond

Castro (Ruz), Fidel 1926(?)-
See also CA 110; 129; CANR 81; DAM MULT; HLC 1; HW 2

Castro, Guillen de 1569-1631 .... LC 19

Castro, Rosalia de 1837-1885 ... NCLC 3, 78; DAM MULT

Cather, Willa
See Cather, Willa Sibert

Cather, Willa Sibert 1873-1947 ...... TCLC 1, 11, 31; DA; DAB; DAC; DAM MST, NOV; SSC 2; WLC
See also Cather, Willa
See also AAYA 24; CA 104; 128; CDALB 1865-1917; DA3; DLB 9, 54, 78; DLBD 1; MTCW 1, 2; SATA 30

Catherine, Saint 1347-1380 .... CMLC 27

Cato, Marcus Porcius 234B.C.-149B.C. .... CMLC 21
See also DLB 211

Author Index

Chernyshevsky, Nikolay Gavrilovich
1828-1889 .... **NCLC 1**
Cherry, Carolyn Janice 1942-
See Cherryh, C. J.
See also CA 65-68; CANR 10
Cherryh, C. J. CLC 35
See also Cherry, Carolyn Janice
See also AAYA 24; DLBY 80; SATA 93
Chesnutt, Charles W(addell)
1858-1932 .. **TCLC 5, 39; BLC 1; DAM
MULT; SSC 7**
See also BW 1, 3; CA 106; 125; CANR 76;
DLB 12, 50, 78; MTCW 1, 2
Chester, Alfred 1929(?)-1971 .... **CLC 49**
See also CA 33-36R; DLB 130
Chesterton, G(ilbert) K(eith)
1874-1936 .. **TCLC 1, 6, 64; DAM NOV,
POET; PC 28; SSC 1**
See also CA 104; 132; CANR 73; CDBLB
1914-1945; DLB 10, 19, 34, 70, 98, 149,
178; MTCW 1, 2; SATA 27
Chiang, Pin-chin 1904-1986
See Ding Ling
See also CA 118
Ch'ien Chung-shu 1910- .... **CLC 22**
See also CA 130; CANR 73; MTCW 1, 2
Child, L. Maria
See Child, Lydia Maria
Child, Lydia Maria 1802-1880 .. **NCLC 6, 73**
See also DLB 1, 74; SATA 67
Child, Mrs.
See Child, Lydia Maria
Child, Philip 1898-1978 .... **CLC 19, 68**
See also CA 13-14; CAP 1; SATA 47
Childers, (Robert) Erskine
1870-1922 .... **TCLC 65**
See also CA 113; 153; DLB 70
Childress, Alice 1920-1994 .. **CLC 12, 15, 86,
96; BLC 1; DAM DRAM, MULT,
NOV; DC 4**
See also AAYA 8; BW 2, 3; CA 45-48; 146;
CANR 3, 27, 50, 74; CLR 14; DA3; DLB
7, 38; JRDA; MAICYA; MTCW 1, 2;
SATA 7, 48, 81
Chin, Frank (Chew, Jr.) 1940- .... **DC 7**
See also CA 33-36R; CANR 71; DAM
MULT; DLB 206
Chislett, (Margaret) Anne 1943- ...... **CLC 34**
See also CA 151
Chitty, Thomas Willes 1926- .... **CLC 11**
See also Hinde, Thomas
See also CA 5-8R
Chivers, Thomas Holley
1809-1858 .... **NCLC 49**
See also DLB 3
Choi, Susan CLC 119
Chomette, Rene Lucien 1898-1981
See Clair, Rene
See also CA 103
Chomsky, (Avram) Noam 1928- ..... **CLC 132**
See also CA 17-20R; CANR 28, 62; DA3;
MTCW 1, 2
**Chopin, Kate TCLC 5, 14; DA; DAB; SSC
8; WLCS**
See also Chopin, Katherine
See also AAYA 33; CDALB 1865-1917;
DLB 12, 78
Chopin, Katherine 1851-1904
See Chopin, Kate
See also CA 104; 122; DAC; DAM MST,
NOV; DA3
Chretien de Troyes c. 12th cent. - . **CMLC 10**
See also DLB 208

Christie
See Ichikawa, Kon
Christie, Agatha (Mary Clarissa)
1890-1976 .... **CLC 1, 6, 8, 12, 39, 48,
110; DAB; DAC; DAM NOV**
See also AAYA 9; AITN 1, 2; CA 17-20R;
61-64; CANR 10, 37; CDBLB 1914-1945;
DA3; DLB 13, 77; MTCW 1, 2; SATA 36
Christie, (Ann) Philippa
See Pearce, Philippa
See also CA 5-8R; CANR 4
Christine de Pizan 1365(?)-1431(?) .... **LC 9**
See also DLB 208
Chubb, Elmer
See Masters, Edgar Lee
Chulkov, Mikhail Dmitrievich
1743-1792 .... **LC 2**
See also DLB 150
Churchill, Caryl 1938- .... **CLC 31, 55; DC 5**
See also CA 102; CANR 22, 46; DLB 13;
MTCW 1
Churchill, Charles 1731-1764 .... **LC 3**
See also DLB 109
Chute, Carolyn 1947- .... **CLC 39**
See also CA 123
Ciardi, John (Anthony) 1916-1986 . **CLC 10,
40, 44, 129; DAM POET**
See also CA 5-8R; 118; CAAS 2; CANR 5,
33; CLR 19; DLB 5; DLBY 86; INT
CANR-5; MAICYA; MTCW 1, 2; SAAS
26; SATA 1, 65; SATA-Obit 46
Cicero, Marcus Tullius
106B.C.-43B.C. .... **CMLC 3**
See also DLB 211
Cimino, Michael 1943- .... **CLC 16**
See also CA 105
Cioran, E(mil) M. 1911-1995 .... **CLC 64**
See also CA 25-28R; 149; CANR 91; DLB
220
Cisneros, Sandra 1954- . **CLC 69, 118; DAM
MULT; HLC 1; SSC 32**
See also AAYA 9; CA 131; CANR 64; DA3;
DLB 122, 152; HW 1, 2; MTCW 2
Cixous, Helene 1937- .... **CLC 92**
See also CA 126; CANR 55; DLB 83;
MTCW 1, 2
Clair, Rene CLC 20
See also Chomette, Rene Lucien
Clampitt, Amy 1920-1994 .... **CLC 32; PC 19**
See also CA 110; 146; CANR 29, 79; DLB
105
Clancy, Thomas L., Jr. 1947-
See Clancy, Tom
See also CA 125; 131; CANR 62; DA3;
INT 131; MTCW 1, 2
Clancy, Tom CLC 45, 112; DAM NOV, POP
See also Clancy, Thomas L., Jr.
See also AAYA 9; BEST 89:1, 90:1; MTCW
2
Clare, John 1793-1864 ... **NCLC 9, 86; DAB;
DAM POET; PC 23**
See also DLB 55, 96
Clarin
See Alas (y Urena), Leopoldo (Enrique
Garcia)
Clark, Al C.
See Goines, Donald
Clark, (Robert) Brian 1932- .... **CLC 29**
See also CA 41-44R; CANR 67
Clark, Curt
See Westlake, Donald E(dwin)
Clark, Eleanor 1913-1996 .... **CLC 5, 19**
See also CA 9-12R; 151; CANR 41; DLB 6

Clark, J. P.
See Clark Bekedermo, J(ohnson) P(epper)
See also DLB 117
Clark, John Pepper
See Clark Bekedermo, J(ohnson) P(epper)
Clark, M. R.
See Clark, Mavis Thorpe
Clark, Mavis Thorpe 1909- .... **CLC 12**
See also CA 57-60; CANR 8, 37; CLR 30;
MAICYA; SAAS 5; SATA 8, 74
Clark, Walter Van Tilburg
1909-1971 .... **CLC 28**
See also CA 9-12R; 33-36R; CANR 63;
DLB 9, 206; SATA 8
Clark Bekedermo, J(ohnson) P(epper)
1935- .. **CLC 38; BLC 1; DAM DRAM,
MULT; DC 5**
See also Clark, J. P.
See also BW 1; CA 65-68; CANR 16, 72;
MTCW 1
Clarke, Arthur C(harles) 1917- .... **CLC 1, 4,
13, 18, 35; DAM POP; SSC 3**
See also AAYA 4, 33; CA 1-4R; CANR 2,
28, 55, 74; DA3; JRDA; MAICYA;
MTCW 1, 2; SATA 13, 70, 115
Clarke, Austin 1896-1974 ... **CLC 6, 9; DAM
POET**
See also CA 29-32; 49-52; CAP 2; DLB 10,
20
Clarke, Austin C(hesterfield) 1934- .. **CLC 8,
53; BLC 1; DAC; DAM MULT**
See also BW 1; CA 25-28R; CAAS 16;
CANR 14, 32, 68; DLB 53, 125
Clarke, Gillian 1937- .... **CLC 61**
See also CA 106; DLB 40
Clarke, Marcus (Andrew Hislop)
1846-1881 .... **NCLC 19**
Clarke, Shirley 1925- .... **CLC 16**
Clash, The
See Headon, (Nicky) Topper; Jones, Mick;
Simonon, Paul; Strummer, Joe
Claudel, Paul (Louis Charles Marie)
1868-1955 .... **TCLC 2, 10**
See also CA 104; 165; DLB 192
Claudius, Matthias 1740-1815 .... **NCLC 75**
See also DLB 97
Clavell, James (duMaresq)
1925-1994 .. **CLC 6, 25, 87; DAM NOV,
POP**
See also CA 25-28R; 146; CANR 26, 48;
DA3; MTCW 1, 2
Cleaver, (Leroy) Eldridge
1935-1998 . **CLC 30, 119; BLC 1; DAM
MULT**
See also BW 1, 3; CA 21-24R; 167; CANR
16, 75; DA3; MTCW 2
Cleese, John (Marwood) 1939- .... **CLC 21**
See also Monty Python
See also CA 112; 116; CANR 35; MTCW 1
Cleishbotham, Jebediah
See Scott, Walter
Cleland, John 1710-1789 .... **LC 2, 48**
See also DLB 39
Clemens, Samuel Langhorne 1835-1910
See Twain, Mark
See also CA 104; 135; CDALB 1865-1917;
DA; DAB; DAC; DAM MST, NOV; DA3;
DLB 11, 12, 23, 64, 74, 186, 189; JRDA;
MAICYA; SATA 100; YABC 2
Cleophil
See Congreve, William
Clerihew, E.
See Bentley, E(dmund) C(lerihew)

Clerk, N. W.
See Lewis, C(live) S(taples)
Cliff, Jimmy CLC 21
See also Chambers, James
Cliff, Michelle 1946- .... **CLC 120; BLCS**
See also BW 2; CA 116; CANR 39, 72;
DLB 157
Clifton, (Thelma) Lucille 1936- .... **CLC 19,
66; BLC 1; DAM MULT, POET; PC
17**
See also BW 2, 3; CA 49-52; CANR 2, 24,
42, 76; CLR 5; DA3; DLB 5, 41; MAI-
CYA; MTCW 1, 2; SATA 20, 69
Clinton, Dirk
See Silverberg, Robert
Clough, Arthur Hugh 1819-1861 ... **NCLC 27**
See also DLB 32
Clutha, Janet Paterson Frame 1924-
See Frame, Janet
See also CA 1-4R; CANR 2, 36, 76; MTCW
1, 2
Clyne, Terence
See Blatty, William Peter
Cobalt, Martin
See Mayne, William (James Carter)
Cobb, Irvin S(hrewsbury)
1876-1944 .... **TCLC 77**
See also CA 175; DLB 11, 25, 86
Cobbett, William 1763-1835 .... **NCLC 49**
See also DLB 43, 107, 158
Coburn, D(onald) L(ee) 1938- .... **CLC 10**
See also CA 89-92
Cocteau, Jean (Maurice Eugene Clement)
1889-1963 .... **CLC 1, 8, 15, 16, 43; DA;
DAB; DAC; DAM DRAM, MST, NOV;
WLC**
See also CA 25-28; CANR 40; CAP 2;
DA3; DLB 65; MTCW 1, 2
Codrescu, Andrei 1946- .... **CLC 46, 121;
DAM POET**
See also CA 33-36R; CAAS 19; CANR 13,
34, 53, 76; DA3; MTCW 2
Coe, Max
See Bourne, Randolph S(illiman)
Coe, Tucker
See Westlake, Donald E(dwin)
Coen, Ethan 1958- .... **CLC 108**
See also CA 126; CANR 85
Coen, Joel 1955- .... **CLC 108**
See also CA 126
The Coen Brothers
See Coen, Ethan; Coen, Joel
Coetzee, J(ohn) M(ichael) 1940- ...... **CLC 23,
33, 66, 117; DAM NOV**
See also CA 77-80; CANR 41, 54, 74; DA3;
MTCW 1, 2
Coffey, Brian
See Koontz, Dean R(ay)
Coffin, Robert P(eter) Tristram
1892-1955 .... **TCLC 95**
See also CA 123; 169; DLB 45
Cohan, George M(ichael)
1878-1942 .... **TCLC 60**
See also CA 157
Cohen, Arthur A(llen) 1928-1986 ...... **CLC 7,
31**
See also CA 1-4R; 120; CANR 1, 17, 42;
DLB 28
Cohen, Leonard (Norman) 1934- ...... **CLC 3,
38; DAC; DAM MST**
See also CA 21-24R; CANR 14, 69; DLB
53; MTCW 1

Cohen, Matt 1942- .... **CLC 19; DAC**
See also CA 61-64; CAAS 18; CANR 40;
DLB 53
Cohen-Solal, Annie 19(?)- .... **CLC 50**
Colegate, Isabel 1931- .... **CLC 36**
See also CA 17-20R; CANR 8, 22, 74; DLB
14; INT CANR-22; MTCW 1
Coleman, Emmett
See Reed, Ishmael
Coleridge, M. E.
See Coleridge, Mary E(lizabeth)
Coleridge, Mary E(lizabeth)
1861-1907 .... **TCLC 73**
See also CA 116; 166; DLB 19, 98
Coleridge, Samuel Taylor
1772-1834 .... **NCLC 9, 54; DA; DAB;
DAC; DAM MST, POET; PC 11; WLC**
See also CDBLB 1789-1832; DA3; DLB
93, 107
Coleridge, Sara 1802-1852 .... **NCLC 31**
See also DLB 199
Coles, Don 1928- .... **CLC 46**
See also CA 115; CANR 38
Coles, Robert (Martin) 1929- .... **CLC 108**
See also CA 45-48; CANR 3, 32, 66, 70;
INT CANR-32; SATA 23
Colette, (Sidonie-Gabrielle)
1873-1954 . **TCLC 1, 5, 16; DAM NOV;
SSC 10**
See also CA 104; 131; DA3; DLB 65;
MTCW 1, 2
Collett, (Jacobine) Camilla (Wergeland)
1813-1895 .... **NCLC 22**
Collier, Christopher 1930- .... **CLC 30**
See also AAYA 13; CA 33-36R; CANR 13,
33; JRDA; MAICYA; SATA 16, 70
Collier, James L(incoln) 1928- .... **CLC 30;
DAM POP**
See also AAYA 13; CA 9-12R; CANR 4,
33, 60; CLR 3; JRDA; MAICYA; SAAS
21; SATA 8, 70
Collier, Jeremy 1650-1726 .... **LC 6**
Collier, John 1901-1980 .... **SSC 19**
See also CA 65-68; 97-100; CANR 10;
DLB 77
Collingwood, R(obin) G(eorge)
1889(?)-1943 .... **TCLC 67**
See also CA 117; 155
Collins, Hunt
See Hunter, Evan
Collins, Linda 1931- .... **CLC 44**
See also CA 125
Collins, (William) Wilkie
1824-1889 .... **NCLC 1, 18**
See also CDBLB 1832-1890; DLB 18, 70,
159
Collins, William 1721-1759 . **LC 4, 40; DAM
POET**
See also DLB 109
Collodi, Carlo 1826-1890 .... **NCLC 54**
See also Lorenzini, Carlo
See also CLR 5
Colman, George 1732-1794
See Glassco, John
Colt, Winchester Remington
See Hubbard, L(afayette) Ron(ald)
Colter, Cyrus 1910- .... **CLC 58**
See also BW 1; CA 65-68; CANR 10, 66;
DLB 33
Colton, James
See Hansen, Joseph

Colum, Padraic 1881-1972 .... **CLC 28**
See also CA 73-76; 33-36R; CANR 35;
CLR 36; MAICYA; MTCW 1; SATA 15
Colvin, James
See Moorcock, Michael (John)
Colwin, Laurie (E.) 1944-1992 .... **CLC 5, 13,
23, 84**
See also CA 89-92; 139; CANR 20, 46;
DLBY 80; MTCW 1
Comfort, Alex(ander) 1920- .... **CLC 7; DAM
POP**
See also CA 1-4R; CANR 1, 45; MTCW 1
Comfort, Montgomery
See Campbell, (John) Ramsey
Compton-Burnett, I(vy)
1884(?)-1969 .... **CLC 1, 3, 10, 15, 34;
DAM NOV**
See also CA 1-4R; 25-28R; CANR 4; DLB
36; MTCW 1
Comstock, Anthony 1844-1915 ...... **TCLC 13**
See also CA 110; 169
Comte, Auguste 1798-1857 .... **NCLC 54**
Conan Doyle, Arthur
See Doyle, Arthur Conan
Conde (Abellan), Carmen 1901-
See also CA 177; DLB 108; HLCS 1; HW
2
Conde, Maryse 1937- .... **CLC 52, 92; BLCS;
DAM MULT**
See also BW 2, 3; CA 110; CANR 30, 53,
76; MTCW 1
Condillac, Etienne Bonnot de
1714-1780 .... **LC 26**
Condon, Richard (Thomas)
1915-1996 ...... **CLC 4, 6, 8, 10, 45, 100;
DAM NOV**
See also BEST 90:3; CA 1-4R; 151; CAAS
1; CANR 2, 23; INT CANR-23; MTCW
1, 2
Confucius 551B.C.-479B.C. .. **CMLC 19; DA;
DAB; DAC; DAM MST; WLCS**
See also DA3
Congreve, William 1670-1729 .... **LC 5, 21;
DA; DAB; DAC; DAM DRAM, MST,
POET; DC 2; WLC**
See also CDBLB 1660-1789; DLB 39, 84
Connell, Evan S(helby), Jr. 1924- . **CLC 4, 6,
45; DAM NOV**
See also AAYA 7; CA 1-4R; CAAS 2;
CANR 2, 39, 76; DLB 2; DLBY 81;
MTCW 1, 2
Connelly, Marc(us Cook) 1890-1980 . **CLC 7**
See also CA 85-88; 102; CANR 30; DLB
7; DLBY 80; SATA-Obit 25
Connor, Ralph TCLC 31
See also Gordon, Charles William
See also DLB 92
Conrad, Joseph 1857-1924 .... **TCLC 1, 6, 13,
25, 43, 57; DA; DAB; DAC; DAM
MST, NOV; SSC 9; WLC**
See also AAYA 26; CA 104; 131; CANR
60; CDBLB 1890-1914; DA3; DLB 10,
34, 98, 156; MTCW 1, 2; SATA 27
Conrad, Robert Arnold
See Hart, Moss
Conroy, Pat
See Conroy, (Donald) Pat(rick)
See also MTCW 2
Conroy, (Donald) Pat(rick) 1945- ... **CLC 30,
74; DAM NOV, POP**
See also Conroy, Pat
See also AAYA 8; AITN 1; CA 85-88;
CANR 24, 53; DA3; DLB 6; MTCW 1

Constant (de Rebecque), (Henri) Benjamin
1767-1830 .... **NCLC 6**
See also DLB 119

Conybeare, Charles Augustus
See Eliot, T(homas) S(tearns)

Cook, Michael 1933- .... **CLC 58**
See also CA 93-96; CANR 68; DLB 53

Cook, Robin 1940- .... **CLC 14; DAM POP**
See also AAYA 32; BEST 90:2; CA 108;
111; CANR 41, 90; DA3; INT 111

Cook, Roy
See Silverberg, Robert

Cooke, Elizabeth 1948- .... **CLC 55**
See also CA 129

Cooke, John Esten 1830-1886 .... **NCLC 5**
See also DLB 3

Cooke, John Estes
See Baum, L(yman) Frank

Cooke, M. E.
See Creasey, John

Cooke, Margaret
See Creasey, John

Cook-Lynn, Elizabeth 1930- . **CLC 93; DAM
MULT**
See also CA 133; DLB 175; NNAL

Cooney, Ray CLC 62

Cooper, Douglas 1960- .... **CLC 86**

Cooper, Henry St. John
See Creasey, John

Cooper, J(oan) California (?)- .... **CLC 56;
DAM MULT**
See also AAYA 12; BW 1; CA 125; CANR
55; DLB 212

Cooper, James Fenimore
1789-1851 .... **NCLC 1, 27, 54**
See also AAYA 22; CDALB 1640-1865;
DA3; DLB 3; SATA 19

Coover, Robert (Lowell) 1932- ...... **CLC 3, 7,
15, 32, 46, 87; DAM NOV; SSC 15**
See also CA 45-48; CANR 3, 37, 58; DLB
2; DLBY 81; MTCW 1, 2

Copeland, Stewart (Armstrong)
1952- .... **CLC 26**

Copernicus, Nicolaus 1473-1543 .... **LC 45**

Coppard, A(lfred) E(dgar)
1878-1957 .... **TCLC 5; SSC 21**
See also CA 114; 167; DLB 162; YABC 1

Coppee, Francois 1842-1908 .... **TCLC 25**
See also CA 170

Coppola, Francis Ford 1939- ... **CLC 16, 126**
See also CA 77-80; CANR 40, 78; DLB 44

Corbiere, Tristan 1845-1875 .... **NCLC 43**

Corcoran, Barbara 1911- .... **CLC 17**
See also AAYA 14; CA 21-24R; CAAS 2;
CANR 11, 28, 48; CLR 50; DLB 52;
JRDA; SAAS 20; SATA 3, 77

Cordelier, Maurice
See Giraudoux, (Hippolyte) Jean

Corelli, Marie 1855-1924 .... **TCLC 51**
See also Mackey, Mary
See also DLB 34, 156

Corman, Cid 1924- .... **CLC 9**
See also Corman, Sidney
See also CAAS 2; DLB 5, 193

Corman, Sidney 1924-
See Corman, Cid
See also CA 85-88; CANR 44; DAM POET

Cormier, Robert (Edmund) 1925- ... **CLC 12,
30; DA; DAB; DAC; DAM MST, NOV**
See also AAYA 3, 19; CA 1-4R; CANR 5,
23, 76; CDALB 1968-1988; CLR 12, 55;

DLB 52; INT CANR-23; JRDA; MAI-
CYA; MTCW 1, 2; SATA 10, 45, 83

Corn, Alfred (DeWitt III) 1943- .... **CLC 33**
See also CA 179; CAAE 179; CAAS 25;
CANR 44; DLB 120; DLBY 80

Corneille, Pierre 1606-1684 ..... **LC 28; DAB;
DAM MST**

Cornwell, David (John Moore)
1931- .... **CLC 9, 15; DAM POP**
See also le Carre, John
See also CA 5-8R; CANR 13, 33, 59; DA3;
MTCW 1, 2

Corso, (Nunzio) Gregory 1930- .... **CLC 1, 11**
See also CA 5-8R; CANR 41, 76; DA3;
DLB 5, 16; MTCW 1, 2

Cortazar, Julio 1914-1984 ... **CLC 2, 3, 5, 10,
13, 15, 33, 34, 92; DAM MULT, NOV;
HLC 1; SSC 7**
See also CA 21-24R; CANR 12, 32, 81;
DA3; DLB 113; HW 1, 2; MTCW 1, 2

CORTES, HERNAN 1484-1547 .... **LC 31**

Corvinus, Jakob
See Raabe, Wilhelm (Karl)

Corwin, Cecil
See Kornbluth, C(yril) M.

Cosic, Dobrica 1921- .... **CLC 14**
See also CA 122; 138; DLB 181

Costain, Thomas B(ertram)
1885-1965 .... **CLC 30**
See also CA 5-8R; 25-28R; DLB 9

Costantini, Humberto 1924(?)-1987 . **CLC 49**
See also CA 131; 122; HW 1

Costello, Elvis 1955- .... **CLC 21**

Costenoble, Philostene
See Ghelderode, Michel de

Cotes, Cecil V.
See Duncan, Sara Jeannette

Cotter, Joseph Seamon Sr.
1861-1949 ...... **TCLC 28; BLC 1; DAM
MULT**
See also BW 1; CA 124; DLB 50

Couch, Arthur Thomas Quiller
See Quiller-Couch, SirArthur (Thomas)

Coulton, James
See Hansen, Joseph

Couperus, Louis (Marie Anne)
1863-1923 .... **TCLC 15**
See also CA 115

Coupland, Douglas 1961- ..... **CLC 85; DAC;
DAM POP**
See also AAYA 34; CA 142; CANR 57, 90

Court, Wesli
See Turco, Lewis (Putnam)

Courtenay, Bryce 1933- .... **CLC 59**
See also CA 138

Courtney, Robert
See Ellison, Harlan (Jay)

Cousteau, Jacques-Yves 1910-1997 .. **CLC 30**
See also CA 65-68; 159; CANR 15, 67;
MTCW 1; SATA 38, 98

Coventry, Francis 1725-1754 .... **LC 46**

Cowan, Peter (Walkinshaw) 1914- .... **SSC 28**
See also CA 21-24R; CANR 9, 25, 50, 83

Coward, Noel (Peirce) 1899-1973 . **CLC 1, 9,
29, 51; DAM DRAM**
See also AITN 1; CA 17-18; 41-44R;
CANR 35; CAP 2; CDBLB 1914-1945;
DA3; DLB 10; MTCW 1, 2

Cowley, Abraham 1618-1667 .... **LC 43**
See also DLB 131, 151

Cowley, Malcolm 1898-1989 .... **CLC 39**
See also CA 5-8R; 128; CANR 3, 55; DLB
4, 48; DLBY 81, 89; MTCW 1, 2

Cowper, William 1731-1800 . **NCLC 8; DAM
POET**
See also DA3; DLB 104, 109

Cox, William Trevor 1928- ... **CLC 9, 14, 71;
DAM NOV**
See also Trevor, William
See also CA 9-12R; CANR 4, 37, 55, 76;
DLB 14; INT CANR-37; MTCW 1, 2

Coyne, P. J.
See Masters, Hilary

Cozzens, James Gould 1903-1978 . **CLC 1, 4,
11, 92**
See also CA 9-12R; 81-84; CANR 19;
CDALB 1941-1968; DLB 9; DLBD 2;
DLBY 84, 97; MTCW 1, 2

Crabbe, George 1754-1832 .... **NCLC 26**
See also DLB 93

Craddock, Charles Egbert
See Murfree, Mary Noailles

Craig, A. A.
See Anderson, Poul (William)

Craik, Dinah Maria (Mulock)
1826-1887 .... **NCLC 38**
See also DLB 35, 163; MAICYA; SATA 34

Cram, Ralph Adams 1863-1942 ..... **TCLC 45**
See also CA 160

Crane, (Harold) Hart 1899-1932 .... **TCLC 2,
5, 80; DA; DAB; DAC; DAM MST,
POET; PC 3; WLC**
See also CA 104; 127; CDALB 1917-1929;
DA3; DLB 4, 48; MTCW 1, 2

Crane, R(onald) S(almon)
1886-1967 .... **CLC 27**
See also CA 85-88; DLB 63

Crane, Stephen (Townley)
1871-1900 .... **TCLC 11, 17, 32; DA;
DAB; DAC; DAM MST, NOV, POET;
SSC 7; WLC**
See also AAYA 21; CA 109; 140; CANR
84; CDALB 1865-1917; DA3; DLB 12,
54, 78; YABC 2

Cranshaw, Stanley
See Fisher, Dorothy (Frances) Canfield

Crase, Douglas 1944- .... **CLC 58**
See also CA 106

Crashaw, Richard 1612(?)-1649 .... **LC 24**
See also DLB 126

Craven, Margaret 1901-1980 .... **CLC 17;
DAC**
See also CA 103

Crawford, F(rancis) Marion
1854-1909 .... **TCLC 10**
See also CA 107; 168; DLB 71

Crawford, Isabella Valancy
1850-1887 .... **NCLC 12**
See also DLB 92

Crayon, Geoffrey
See Irving, Washington

Creasey, John 1908-1973 .... **CLC 11**
See also CA 5-8R; 41-44R; CANR 8, 59;
DLB 77; MTCW 1

Crebillon, Claude Prosper Jolyot de (fils)
1707-1777 .... **LC 1, 28**

Credo
See Creasey, John

Credo, Alvaro J. de
See Prado (Calvo), Pedro

Creeley, Robert (White) 1926- .. **CLC 1, 2, 4, 8, 11, 15, 36, 78; DAM POET**
See also CA 1-4R; CAAS 10; CANR 23, 43, 89; DA3; DLB 5, 16, 169; DLBD 17; MTCW 1, 2

Crews, Harry (Eugene) 1935- ..... **CLC 6, 23, 49**
See also AITN 1; CA 25-28R; CANR 20, 57; DA3; DLB 6, 143, 185; MTCW 1, 2

Crichton, (John) Michael 1942- .... **CLC 2, 6, 54, 90; DAM NOV, POP**
See also AAYA 10; AITN 2; CA 25-28R; CANR 13, 40, 54, 76; DA3; DLBY 81; INT CANR-13; JRDA; MTCW 1, 2; SATA 9, 88

Crispin, Edmund CLC 22
See also Montgomery, (Robert) Bruce
See also DLB 87

Cristofer, Michael 1945(?)- ... **CLC 28; DAM DRAM**
See also CA 110; 152; DLB 7

Croce, Benedetto 1866-1952 .... **TCLC 37**
See also CA 120; 155

Crockett, David 1786-1836 .... **NCLC 8**
See also DLB 3, 11

Crockett, Davy
See Crockett, David

Crofts, Freeman Wills 1879-1957 .. **TCLC 55**
See also CA 115; DLB 77

Croker, John Wilson 1780-1857 .... **NCLC 10**
See also DLB 110

Crommelynck, Fernand 1885-1970 .. **CLC 75**
See also CA 89-92

Cromwell, Oliver 1599-1658 .... **LC 43**

Cronin, A(rchibald) J(oseph)
1896-1981 .... **CLC 32**
See also CA 1-4R; 102; CANR 5; DLB 191; SATA 47; SATA-Obit 25

Cross, Amanda
See Heilbrun, Carolyn G(old)

Crothers, Rachel 1878(?)-1958 .... **TCLC 19**
See also CA 113; DLB 7

Croves, Hal
See Traven, B.

Crow Dog, Mary (Ellen) (?)- .... **CLC 93**
See also Brave Bird, Mary
See also CA 154

Crowfield, Christopher
See Stowe, Harriet (Elizabeth) Beecher

Crowley, Aleister TCLC 7
See also Crowley, Edward Alexander

Crowley, Edward Alexander 1875-1947
See Crowley, Aleister
See also CA 104

Crowley, John 1942- .... **CLC 57**
See also CA 61-64; CANR 43; DLBY 82; SATA 65

Crud
See Crumb, R(obert)

Crumarums
See Crumb, R(obert)

Crumb, R(obert) 1943- .... **CLC 17**
See also CA 106

Crumbum
See Crumb, R(obert)

Crumski
See Crumb, R(obert)

Crum the Bum
See Crumb, R(obert)

Crunk
See Crumb, R(obert)

Crustt
See Crumb, R(obert)

Cruz, Victor Hernandez 1949-
See also BW 2; CA 65-68; CAAS 17; CANR 14, 32, 74; DAM MULT, POET; DLB 41; HLC 1; HW 1, 2; MTCW 1

Cryer, Gretchen (Kiger) 1935- .... **CLC 21**
See also CA 114; 123

Csath, Geza 1887-1919 .... **TCLC 13**
See also CA 111

Cudlip, David R(ockwell) 1933- .... **CLC 34**
See also CA 177

Cullen, Countee 1903-1946 .... **TCLC 4, 37; BLC 1; DA; DAC; DAM MST, MULT, POET; PC 20; WLCS**
See also BW 1; CA 108; 124; CDALB 1917-1929; DA3; DLB 4, 48, 51; MTCW 1, 2; SATA 18

Cum, R.
See Crumb, R(obert)

Cummings, Bruce F(rederick) 1889-1919
See Barbellion, W. N. P.
See also CA 123

Cummings, E(dward) E(stlin)
1894-1962 .... **CLC 1, 3, 8, 12, 15, 68; DA; DAB; DAC; DAM MST, POET; PC 5; WLC**
See also CA 73-76; CANR 31; CDALB 1929-1941; DA3; DLB 4, 48; MTCW 1, 2

Cunha, Euclides (Rodrigues Pimenta) da
1866-1909 .... **TCLC 24**
See also CA 123

Cunningham, E. V.
See Fast, Howard (Melvin)

Cunningham, J(ames) V(incent)
1911-1985 .... **CLC 3, 31**
See also CA 1-4R; 115; CANR 1, 72; DLB 5

Cunningham, Julia (Woolfolk)
1916- .... **CLC 12**
See also CA 9-12R; CANR 4, 19, 36; JRDA; MAICYA; SAAS 2; SATA 1, 26

Cunningham, Michael 1952- .... **CLC 34**
See also CA 136

Cunninghame Graham, R. B.
See Cunninghame Graham, Robert (Gallnigad) Bontine

Cunninghame Graham, Robert (Gallnigad) Bontine 1852-1936 .... **TCLC 19**
See also Graham, R(obert) B(ontine) Cunninghame
See also CA 119; 184; DLB 98

Currie, Ellen 19(?)- .... **CLC 44**

Curtin, Philip
See Lowndes, Marie Adelaide (Belloc)

Curtis, Price
See Ellison, Harlan (Jay)

Cutrate, Joe
See Spiegelman, Art

Cynewulf c. 770-c. 840 .... **CMLC 23**

Czaczkes, Shmuel Yosef
See Agnon, S(hmuel) Y(osef Halevi)

Dabrowska, Maria (Szumska)
1889-1965 .... **CLC 15**
See also CA 106

Dabydeen, David 1955- .... **CLC 34**
See also BW 1; CA 125; CANR 56

Dacey, Philip 1939- .... **CLC 51**
See also CA 37-40R; CAAS 17; CANR 14, 32, 64; DLB 105

Dagerman, Stig (Halvard)
1923-1954 .... **TCLC 17**
See also CA 117; 155

Dahl, Roald 1916-1990 ...... **CLC 1, 6, 18, 79; DAB; DAC; DAM MST, NOV, POP**
See also AAYA 15; CA 1-4R; 133; CANR 6, 32, 37, 62; CLR 1, 7, 41; DA3; DLB 139; JRDA; MAICYA; MTCW 1, 2; SATA 1, 26, 73; SATA-Obit 65

Dahlberg, Edward 1900-1977 .. **CLC 1, 7, 14**
See also CA 9-12R; 69-72; CANR 31, 62; DLB 48; MTCW 1

Daitch, Susan 1954- .... **CLC 103**
See also CA 161

Dale, Colin TCLC 18
See also Lawrence, T(homas) E(dward)

Dale, George E.
See Asimov, Isaac

Dalton, Roque 1935-1975
See also HLCS 1; HW 2

Daly, Elizabeth 1878-1967 .... **CLC 52**
See also CA 23-24; 25-28R; CANR 60; CAP 2

Daly, Maureen 1921- .... **CLC 17**
See also AAYA 5; CANR 37, 83; JRDA; MAICYA; SAAS 1; SATA 2

Damas, Leon-Gontran 1912-1978 .... **CLC 84**
See also BW 1; CA 125; 73-76

Dana, Richard Henry Sr.
1787-1879 .... **NCLC 53**

Daniel, Samuel 1562(?)-1619 .... **LC 24**
See also DLB 62

Daniels, Brett
See Adler, Renata

Dannay, Frederic 1905-1982 . **CLC 11; DAM POP**
See also Queen, Ellery
See also CA 1-4R; 107; CANR 1, 39; DLB 137; MTCW 1

D'Annunzio, Gabriele 1863-1938 ... **TCLC 6, 40**
See also CA 104; 155

Danois, N. le
See Gourmont, Remy (-Marie-Charles) de

Dante 1265-1321 .... **CMLC 3, 18, 39; DA; DAB; DAC; DAM MST, POET; PC 21; WLCS**
See also Alighieri, Dante
See also DA3

d'Antibes, Germain
See Simenon, Georges (Jacques Christian)

Danticat, Edwidge 1969- .... **CLC 94**
See also AAYA 29; CA 152; CANR 73; MTCW 1

Danvers, Dennis 1947- .... **CLC 70**

Danziger, Paula 1944- .... **CLC 21**
See also AAYA 4; CA 112; 115; CANR 37; CLR 20; JRDA; MAICYA; SATA 36, 63, 102; SATA-Brief 30

Da Ponte, Lorenzo 1749-1838 .... **NCLC 50**

Dario, Ruben 1867-1916 .... **TCLC 4; DAM MULT; HLC 1; PC 15**
See also CA 131; CANR 81; HW 1, 2; MTCW 1, 2

Darley, George 1795-1846 .... **NCLC 2**
See also DLB 96

Darrow, Clarence (Seward)
1857-1938 .... **TCLC 81**
See also CA 164

Darwin, Charles 1809-1882 .... **NCLC 57**
See also DLB 57, 166

Del Vecchio, John M(ichael) 1947- .. **CLC 29**
See also CA 110; DLBD 9

de Man, Paul (Adolph Michel)
1919-1983 .... **CLC 55**
See also CA 128; 111; CANR 61; DLB 67;
MTCW 1, 2

DeMarinis, Rick 1934- .... **CLC 54**
See also CA 57-60, 184; CAAE 184; CAAS
24; CANR 9, 25, 50

Dembry, R. Emmet
See Murfree, Mary Noailles

Demby, William 1922- .... **CLC 53; BLC 1;**
DAM MULT
See also BW 1, 3; CA 81-84; CANR 81;
DLB 33

de Menton, Francisco
See Chin, Frank (Chew, Jr.)

Demetrius of Phalerum c.
307B.C.- .... **CMLC 34**

Demijohn, Thom
See Disch, Thomas M(ichael)

de Molina, Tirso 1580-1648
See also HLCS 2

de Montherlant, Henry (Milon)
See Montherlant, Henry (Milon) de

Demosthenes 384B.C.-322B.C. ...... **CMLC 13**
See also DLB 176

de Natale, Francine
See Malzberg, Barry N(athaniel)

Denby, Edwin (Orr) 1903-1983 .... **CLC 48**
See also CA 138; 110

Denis, Julio
See Cortazar, Julio

Denmark, Harrison
See Zelazny, Roger (Joseph)

Dennis, John 1658-1734 .... **LC 11**
See also DLB 101

Dennis, Nigel (Forbes) 1912-1989 ...... **CLC 8**
See also CA 25-28R; 129; DLB 13, 15;
MTCW 1

Dent, Lester 1904(?)-1959 .... **TCLC 72**
See also CA 112; 161

De Palma, Brian (Russell) 1940- ...... **CLC 20**
See also CA 109

De Quincey, Thomas 1785-1859 ..... **NCLC 4,**
87
See also CDBLB 1789-1832; DLB 110; 144

Deren, Eleanora 1908(?)-1961
See Deren, Maya
See also CA 111

Deren, Maya 1917-1961 .... **CLC 16, 102**
See also Deren, Eleanora

Derleth, August (William)
1909-1971 .... **CLC 31**
See also CA 1-4R; 29-32R; CANR 4; DLB
9; DLBD 17; SATA 5

Der Nister 1884-1950 .... **TCLC 56**

de Routisie, Albert
See Aragon, Louis

Derrida, Jacques 1930- .... **CLC 24, 87**
See also CA 124; 127; CANR 76; MTCW 1

Derry Down Derry
See Lear, Edward

Dersonnes, Jacques
See Simenon, Georges (Jacques Christian)

Desai, Anita 1937- ..... **CLC 19, 37, 97; DAB;**
DAM NOV
See also CA 81-84; CANR 33, 53; DA3;
MTCW 1, 2; SATA 63

Desai, Kiran 1971- .... **CLC 119**
See also CA 171

de Saint-Luc, Jean
See Glassco, John

de Saint Roman, Arnaud
See Aragon, Louis

Descartes, Rene 1596-1650 .... **LC 20, 35**

De Sica, Vittorio 1901(?)-1974 .... **CLC 20**
See also CA 117

Desnos, Robert 1900-1945 .... **TCLC 22**
See also CA 121; 151

Destouches, Louis-Ferdinand
1894-1961 .... **CLC 9, 15**
See also Celine, Louis-Ferdinand
See also CA 85-88; CANR 28; MTCW 1

de Tolignac, Gaston
See Griffith, D(avid Lewelyn) W(ark)

Deutsch, Babette 1895-1982 .... **CLC 18**
See also CA 1-4R; 108; CANR 4, 79; DLB
45; SATA 1; SATA-Obit 33

Devenant, William 1606-1649 .... **LC 13**

Devkota, Laxmiprasad 1909-1959 . **TCLC 23**
See also CA 123

De Voto, Bernard (Augustine)
1897-1955 .... **TCLC 29**
See also CA 113; 160; DLB 9

De Vries, Peter 1910-1993 ..... **CLC 1, 2, 3, 7,**
10, 28, 46; DAM NOV
See also CA 17-20R; 142; CANR 41; DLB
6; DLBY 82; MTCW 1, 2

Dewey, John 1859-1952 .... **TCLC 95**
See also CA 114; 170

Dexter, John
See Bradley, Marion Zimmer

Dexter, Martin
See Faust, Frederick (Schiller)

Dexter, Pete 1943- .. **CLC 34, 55; DAM POP**
See also BEST 89:2; CA 127; 131; INT 131;
MTCW 1

Diamano, Silmang
See Senghor, Leopold Sedar

Diamond, Neil 1941- .... **CLC 30**
See also CA 108

Diaz del Castillo, Bernal 1496-1584 .. **LC 31;**
HLCS 1

di Bassetto, Corno
See Shaw, George Bernard

Dick, Philip K(indred) 1928-1982 ... **CLC 10,**
30, 72; DAM NOV, POP
See also AAYA 24; CA 49-52; 106; CANR
2, 16; DA3; DLB 8; MTCW 1, 2

Dickens, Charles (John Huffam)
1812-1870 .... **NCLC 3, 8, 18, 26, 37, 50,**
86; DA; DAB; DAC; DAM MST, NOV;
SSC 17; WLC
See also AAYA 23; CDBLB 1832-1890;
DA3; DLB 21, 55, 70, 159, 166; JRDA;
MAICYA; SATA 15

Dickey, James (Lafayette)
1923-1997 .... **CLC 1, 2, 4, 7, 10, 15, 47,**
109; DAM NOV, POET, POP
See also AITN 1, 2; CA 9-12R; 156; CABS
2; CANR 10, 48, 61; CDALB 1968-1988;
DA3; DLB 5, 193; DLBD 7; DLBY 82,
93, 96, 97, 98; INT CANR-10; MTCW 1,
2

Dickey, William 1928-1994 .... **CLC 3, 28**
See also CA 9-12R; 145; CANR 24, 79;
DLB 5

Dickinson, Charles 1951- .... **CLC 49**
See also CA 128

Dickinson, Emily (Elizabeth)
1830-1886 ..... **NCLC 21, 77; DA; DAB;**
DAC; DAM MST, POET; PC 1; WLC
See also AAYA 22; CDALB 1865-1917;
DA3; DLB 1; SATA 29

Dickinson, Peter (Malcolm) 1927- .. **CLC 12,**
35
See also AAYA 9; CA 41-44R; CANR 31,
58, 88; CLR 29; DLB 87, 161; JRDA;
MAICYA; SATA 5, 62, 95

Dickson, Carr
See Carr, John Dickson

Dickson, Carter
See Carr, John Dickson

Diderot, Denis 1713-1784 .... **LC 26**

Didion, Joan 1934- .... **CLC 1, 3, 8, 14, 32,**
129; DAM NOV
See also AITN 1; CA 5-8R; CANR 14, 52,
76; CDALB 1968-1988; DA3; DLB 2,
173, 185; DLBY 81, 86; MTCW 1, 2

Dietrich, Robert
See Hunt, E(verette) Howard, (Jr.)

Difusa, Pati
See Almodovar, Pedro

Dillard, Annie 1945- .. **CLC 9, 60, 115; DAM**
NOV
See also AAYA 6; CA 49-52; CANR 3, 43,
62, 90; DA3; DLBY 80; MTCW 1, 2;
SATA 10

Dillard, R(ichard) H(enry) W(ilde)
1937- .... **CLC 5**
See also CA 21-24R; CAAS 7; CANR 10;
DLB 5

Dillon, Eilis 1920-1994 .... **CLC 17**
See also CA 9-12R; 182; 147; CAAE 182;
CAAS 3; CANR 4, 38, 78; CLR 26; MAI-
CYA; SATA 2, 74; SATA-Essay 105;
SATA-Obit 83

Dimont, Penelope
See Mortimer, Penelope (Ruth)

Dinesen, Isak **CLC 10, 29, 95; SSC 7**
See also Blixen, Karen (Christentze
Dinesen)
See also MTCW 1

Ding Ling **CLC 68**
See also Chiang, Pin-chin

Diphusa, Patty
See Almodovar, Pedro

Disch, Thomas M(ichael) 1940- ... **CLC 7, 36**
See also AAYA 17; CA 21-24R; CAAS 4;
CANR 17, 36, 54, 89; CLR 18; DA3;
DLB 8; MAICYA; MTCW 1, 2; SAAS
15; SATA 92

Disch, Tom
See Disch, Thomas M(ichael)

d'Isly, Georges
See Simenon, Georges (Jacques Christian)

Disraeli, Benjamin 1804-1881 ... **NCLC 2, 39,**
79
See also DLB 21, 55

Ditcum, Steve
See Crumb, R(obert)

Dixon, Paige
See Corcoran, Barbara

Dixon, Stephen 1936- .... **CLC 52; SSC 16**
See also CA 89-92; CANR 17, 40, 54, 91;
DLB 130

Doak, Annie
See Dillard, Annie

Dobell, Sydney Thompson
 1824-1874 .... **NCLC 43**
 See also DLB 32
Doblin, Alfred TCLC 13
 See also Doeblin, Alfred
Dobrolyubov, Nikolai Alexandrovich
 1836-1861 .... **NCLC 5**
Dobson, Austin 1840-1921 .... **TCLC 79**
 See also DLB 35; 144
Dobyns, Stephen 1941- .... **CLC 37**
 See also CA 45-48; CANR 2, 18
Doctorow, E(dgar) L(aurence)
 1931- .... **CLC 6, 11, 15, 18, 37, 44, 65,**
 113; DAM NOV, POP
 See also AAYA 22; AITN 2; BEST 89:3;
 CA 45-48; CANR 2, 33, 51, 76; CDALB
 1968-1988; DA3; DLB 2, 28, 173; DLBY
 80; MTCW 1, 2
Dodgson, Charles Lutwidge 1832-1898
 See Carroll, Lewis
 See also CLR 2; DA; DAB; DAC; DAM
 MST, NOV, POET; DA3; MAICYA;
 SATA 100; YABC 2
Dodson, Owen (Vincent)
 1914-1983 .... **CLC 79; BLC 1; DAM**
 MULT
 See also BW 1; CA 65-68; 110; CANR 24;
 DLB 76
Doeblin, Alfred 1878-1957 .... **TCLC 13**
 See also Doblin, Alfred
 See also CA 110; 141; DLB 66
Doerr, Harriet 1910- .... **CLC 34**
 See also CA 117; 122; CANR 47; INT 122
Domecq, H(onorio Bustos)
 See Bioy Casares, Adolfo
Domecq, H(onorio) Bustos
 See Bioy Casares, Adolfo; Borges, Jorge
 Luis
Domini, Rey
 See Lorde, Audre (Geraldine)
Dominique
 See Proust, (Valentin-Louis-George-
 Eugene-) Marcel
Don, A
 See Stephen, SirLeslie
Donaldson, Stephen R. 1947- .... **CLC 46;**
 DAM POP
 See also CA 89-92; CANR 13, 55; INT
 CANR-13
Donleavy, J(ames) P(atrick) 1926- .... **CLC 1,**
 4, 6, 10, 45
 See also AITN 2; CA 9-12R; CANR 24, 49,
 62, 80; DLB 6, 173; INT CANR-24;
 MTCW 1, 2
Donne, John 1572-1631 .... **LC 10, 24; DA;**
 DAB; DAC; DAM MST, POET; PC 1;
 WLC
 See also CDBLB Before 1660; DLB 121,
 151
Donnell, David 1939(?)- .... **CLC 34**
Donoghue, P. S.
 See Hunt, E(verette) Howard, (Jr.)
Donoso (Yanez), Jose 1924-1996 ... **CLC 4, 8,**
 11, 32, 99; DAM MULT; HLC 1; SSC
 34
 See also CA 81-84; 155; CANR 32, 73;
 DLB 113; HW 1, 2; MTCW 1, 2
Donovan, John 1928-1992 .... **CLC 35**
 See also AAYA 20; CA 97-100; 137; CLR
 3; MAICYA; SATA 72; SATA-Brief 29
Don Roberto
 See Cunninghame Graham, Robert
 (Gallnigad) Bontine

Doolittle, Hilda 1886-1961 . **CLC 3, 8, 14, 31,**
 34, 73; DA; DAC; DAM MST, POET;
 PC 5; WLC
 See also H. D.
 See also CA 97-100; CANR 35; DLB 4, 45;
 MTCW 1, 2
Dorfman, Ariel 1942- ...... **CLC 48, 77; DAM**
 MULT; HLC 1
 See also CA 124; 130; CANR 67, 70; HW
 1, 2; INT 130
Dorn, Edward (Merton) 1929- ... **CLC 10, 18**
 See also CA 93-96; CANR 42, 79; DLB 5;
 INT 93-96
Dorris, Michael (Anthony)
 1945-1997 .... **CLC 109; DAM MULT,**
 NOV
 See also AAYA 20; BEST 90:1; CA 102;
 157; CANR 19, 46, 75; CLR 58; DA3;
 DLB 175; MTCW 2; NNAL; SATA 75;
 SATA-Obit 94
Dorris, Michael A.
 See Dorris, Michael (Anthony)
Dorsan, Luc
 See Simenon, Georges (Jacques Christian)
Dorsange, Jean
 See Simenon, Georges (Jacques Christian)
Dos Passos, John (Roderigo)
 1896-1970 ... **CLC 1, 4, 8, 11, 15, 25, 34,**
 82; DA; DAB; DAC; DAM MST, NOV;
 WLC
 See also CA 1-4R; 29-32R; CANR 3;
 CDALB 1929-1941; DA3; DLB 4, 9;
 DLBD 1, 15; DLBY 96; MTCW 1, 2
Dossage, Jean
 See Simenon, Georges (Jacques Christian)
Dostoevsky, Fedor Mikhailovich
 1821-1881 . **NCLC 2, 7, 21, 33, 43; DA;**
 DAB; DAC; DAM MST, NOV; SSC 2,
 33; WLC
 See also DA3
Doughty, Charles M(ontagu)
 1843-1926 .... **TCLC 27**
 See also CA 115; 178; DLB 19, 57, 174
Douglas, Ellen CLC 73
 See also Haxton, Josephine Ayres; William-
 son, Ellen Douglas
Douglas, Gavin 1475(?)-1522 .... **LC 20**
 See also DLB 132
Douglas, George
 See Brown, George Douglas
Douglas, Keith (Castellain)
 1920-1944 .... **TCLC 40**
 See also CA 160; DLB 27
Douglas, Leonard
 See Bradbury, Ray (Douglas)
Douglas, Michael
 See Crichton, (John) Michael
Douglas, (George) Norman
 1868-1952 .... **TCLC 68**
 See also CA 119; 157; DLB 34, 195
Douglas, William
 See Brown, George Douglas
Douglass, Frederick 1817(?)-1895 .. **NCLC 7,**
 55; BLC 1; DA; DAC; DAM MST,
 MULT; WLC
 See also CDALB 1640-1865; DA3; DLB 1,
 43, 50, 79; SATA 29
Dourado, (Waldomiro Freitas) Autran
 1926- .... **CLC 23, 60**
 See also CA 25-28R; 179; CANR 34, 81;
 DLB 145; HW 2

Dourado, Waldomiro Autran 1926-
 See Dourado, (Waldomiro Freitas) Autran
 See also CA 179
Dove, Rita (Frances) 1952- .... **CLC 50, 81;**
 BLCS; DAM MULT, POET; PC 6
 See also BW 2; CA 109; CAAS 19; CANR
 27, 42, 68, 76; CDALBS; DA3; DLB 120;
 MTCW 1
Doveglion
 See Villa, Jose Garcia
Dowell, Coleman 1925-1985 .... **CLC 60**
 See also CA 25-28R; 117; CANR 10; DLB
 130
Dowson, Ernest (Christopher)
 1867-1900 .... **TCLC 4**
 See also CA 105; 150; DLB 19, 135
Doyle, A. Conan
 See Doyle, Arthur Conan
Doyle, Arthur Conan 1859-1930 .... **TCLC 7;**
 DA; DAB; DAC; DAM MST, NOV;
 SSC 12; WLC
 See also AAYA 14; CA 104; 122; CDBLB
 1890-1914; DA3; DLB 18, 70, 156, 178;
 MTCW 1, 2; SATA 24
Doyle, Conan
 See Doyle, Arthur Conan
Doyle, John
 See Graves, Robert (von Ranke)
Doyle, Roddy 1958(?)- .... **CLC 81**
 See also AAYA 14; CA 143; CANR 73;
 DA3; DLB 194
Doyle, Sir A. Conan
 See Doyle, Arthur Conan
Doyle, Sir Arthur Conan
 See Doyle, Arthur Conan
Dr. A
 See Asimov, Isaac; Silverstein, Alvin
Drabble, Margaret 1939- ...... **CLC 2, 3, 5, 8,**
 10, 22, 53, 129; DAB; DAC; DAM
 MST, NOV, POP
 See also CA 13-16R; CANR 18, 35, 63;
 CDBLB 1960 to Present; DA3; DLB 14,
 155; MTCW 1, 2; SATA 48
Drapier, M. B.
 See Swift, Jonathan
Drayham, James
 See Mencken, H(enry) L(ouis)
Drayton, Michael 1563-1631 ..... **LC 8; DAM**
 POET
 See also DLB 121
Dreadstone, Carl
 See Campbell, (John) Ramsey
Dreiser, Theodore (Herman Albert)
 1871-1945 .... **TCLC 10, 18, 35, 83; DA;**
 DAC; DAM MST, NOV; SSC 30; WLC
 See also CA 106; 132; CDALB 1865-1917;
 DA3; DLB 9, 12, 102, 137; DLBD 1;
 MTCW 1, 2
Drexler, Rosalyn 1926- .... **CLC 2, 6**
 See also CA 81-84; CANR 68
Dreyer, Carl Theodor 1889-1968 ...... **CLC 16**
 See also CA 116
Drieu la Rochelle, Pierre(-Eugene)
 1893-1945 .... **TCLC 21**
 See also CA 117; DLB 72
Drinkwater, John 1882-1937 .... **TCLC 57**
 See also CA 109; 149; DLB 10, 19, 149
Drop Shot
 See Cable, George Washington
Droste-Hulshoff, Annette Freiin von
 1797-1848 .... **NCLC 3**
 See also DLB 133

Eckmar, F. R.
See de Hartog, Jan

Eco, Umberto 1932- .... **CLC 28, 60; DAM NOV, POP**
See also BEST 90:1; CA 77-80; CANR 12, 33, 55; DA3; DLB 196; MTCW 1, 2

Eddison, E(ric) R(ucker)
1882-1945 .... **TCLC 15**
See also CA 109; 156

Eddy, Mary (Ann Morse) Baker
1821-1910 .... **TCLC 71**
See also CA 113; 174

Edel, (Joseph) Leon 1907-1997 .. **CLC 29, 34**
See also CA 1-4R; 161; CANR 1, 22; DLB 103; INT CANR-22

Eden, Emily 1797-1869 .... **NCLC 10**

Edgar, David 1948- .. **CLC 42; DAM DRAM**
See also CA 57-60; CANR 12, 61; DLB 13; MTCW 1

Edgerton, Clyde (Carlyle) 1944- ...... **CLC 39**
See also AAYA 17; CA 118; 134; CANR 64; INT 134

Edgeworth, Maria 1768-1849 .... **NCLC 1, 51**
See also DLB 116, 159, 163; SATA 21

Edmonds, Paul
See Kuttner, Henry

Edmonds, Walter D(umaux)
1903-1998 .... **CLC 35**
See also CA 5-8R; CANR 2; DLB 9; MAICYA; SAAS 4; SATA 1, 27; SATA-Obit 99

Edmondson, Wallace
See Ellison, Harlan (Jay)

Edson, Russell CLC 13
See also CA 33-36R

Edwards, Bronwen Elizabeth
See Rose, Wendy

Edwards, G(erald) B(asil)
1899-1976 .... **CLC 25**
See also CA 110

Edwards, Gus 1939- .... **CLC 43**
See also CA 108; INT 108

Edwards, Jonathan 1703-1758 .... **LC 7, 54; DA; DAC; DAM MST**
See also DLB 24

Efron, Marina Ivanovna Tsvetaeva
See Tsvetaeva (Efron), Marina (Ivanovna)

Ehle, John (Marsden, Jr.) 1925- ...... **CLC 27**
See also CA 9-12R

Ehrenbourg, Ilya (Grigoryevich)
See Ehrenburg, Ilya (Grigoryevich)

Ehrenburg, Ilya (Grigoryevich)
1891-1967 .... **CLC 18, 34, 62**
See also CA 102; 25-28R

Ehrenburg, Ilyo (Grigoryevich)
See Ehrenburg, Ilya (Grigoryevich)

Ehrenreich, Barbara 1941- .... **CLC 110**
See also BEST 90:4; CA 73-76; CANR 16, 37, 62; MTCW 1, 2

Eich, Guenter 1907-1972 .... **CLC 15**
See also CA 111; 93-96; DLB 69, 124

Eichendorff, Joseph Freiherr von
1788-1857 .... **NCLC 8**
See also DLB 90

Eigner, Larry CLC 9
See also Eigner, Laurence (Joel)
See also CAAS 23; DLB 5

Eigner, Laurence (Joel) 1927-1996
See Eigner, Larry
See also CA 9-12R; 151; CANR 6, 84; DLB 193

Einstein, Albert 1879-1955 .... **TCLC 65**
See also CA 121; 133; MTCW 1, 2

Eiseley, Loren Corey 1907-1977 .... **CLC 7**
See also AAYA 5; CA 1-4R; 73-76; CANR 6; DLBD 17

Eisenstadt, Jill 1963- .... **CLC 50**
See also CA 140

Eisenstein, Sergei (Mikhailovich)
1898-1948 .... **TCLC 57**
See also CA 114; 149

Eisner, Simon
See Kornbluth, C(yril) M.

Ekeloef, (Bengt) Gunnar
1907-1968 ... **CLC 27; DAM POET; PC 23**
See also CA 123; 25-28R

Ekelof, (Bengt) Gunnar
See Ekeloef, (Bengt) Gunnar

Ekelund, Vilhelm 1880-1949 .... **TCLC 75**

Ekwensi, C. O. D.
See Ekwensi, Cyprian (Odiatu Duaka)

Ekwensi, Cyprian (Odiatu Duaka)
1921- ...... **CLC 4; BLC 1; DAM MULT**
See also BW 2, 3; CA 29-32R; CANR 18, 42, 74; DLB 117; MTCW 1, 2; SATA 66

Elaine TCLC 18
See also Leverson, Ada

El Crummo
See Crumb, R(obert)

Elder, Lonne III 1931-1996 .... **DC 8**
See also BLC 1; BW 1, 3; CA 81-84; 152; CANR 25; DAM MULT; DLB 7, 38, 44

Eleanor of Aquitaine 1122-1204 ... **CMLC 39**

Elia
See Lamb, Charles

Eliade, Mircea 1907-1986 .... **CLC 19**
See also CA 65-68; 119; CANR 30, 62; DLB 220; MTCW 1

Eliot, A. D.
See Jewett, (Theodora) Sarah Orne

Eliot, Alice
See Jewett, (Theodora) Sarah Orne

Eliot, Dan
See Silverberg, Robert

Eliot, George 1819-1880 ...... **NCLC 4, 13, 23, 41, 49; DA; DAB; DAC; DAM MST, NOV; PC 20; WLC**
See also CDBLB 1832-1890; DA3; DLB 21, 35, 55

Eliot, John 1604-1690 .... **LC 5**
See also DLB 24

Eliot, T(homas) S(tearns)
1888-1965 ...... **CLC 1, 2, 3, 6, 9, 10, 13, 15, 24, 34, 41, 55, 57, 113; DA; DAB; DAC; DAM DRAM, MST, POET; PC 5; WLC**
See also AAYA 28; CA 5-8R; 25-28R; CANR 41; CDALB 1929-1941; DA3; DLB 7, 10, 45, 63; DLBY 88; MTCW 1, 2

Elizabeth 1866-1941 .... **TCLC 41**

Elkin, Stanley L(awrence)
1930-1995 .. **CLC 4, 6, 9, 14, 27, 51, 91; DAM NOV, POP; SSC 12**
See also CA 9-12R; 148; CANR 8, 46; DLB 2, 28; DLBY 80; INT CANR-8; MTCW 1, 2

Elledge, Scott CLC 34

Elliot, Don
See Silverberg, Robert

Elliott, Don
See Silverberg, Robert

Elliott, George P(aul) 1918-1980 .... **CLC 2**
See also CA 1-4R; 97-100; CANR 2

Elliott, Janice 1931- .... **CLC 47**
See also CA 13-16R; CANR 8, 29, 84; DLB 14

Elliott, Sumner Locke 1917-1991 ..... **CLC 38**
See also CA 5-8R; 134; CANR 2, 21

Elliott, William
See Bradbury, Ray (Douglas)

Ellis, A. E. CLC 7

Ellis, Alice Thomas CLC 40
See also Haycraft, Anna (Margaret)
See also DLB 194; MTCW 1

Ellis, Bret Easton 1964- ..... **CLC 39, 71, 117; DAM POP**
See also AAYA 2; CA 118; 123; CANR 51, 74; DA3; INT 123; MTCW 1

Ellis, (Henry) Havelock
1859-1939 .... **TCLC 14**
See also CA 109; 169; DLB 190

Ellis, Landon
See Ellison, Harlan (Jay)

Ellis, Trey 1962- .... **CLC 55**
See also CA 146

Ellison, Harlan (Jay) 1934- ... **CLC 1, 13, 42; DAM POP; SSC 14**
See also AAYA 29; CA 5-8R; CANR 5, 46; DLB 8; INT CANR-5; MTCW 1, 2

Ellison, Ralph (Waldo) 1914-1994 .... **CLC 1, 3, 11, 54, 86, 114; BLC 1; DA; DAB; DAC; DAM MST, MULT, NOV; SSC 26; WLC**
See also AAYA 19; BW 1, 3; CA 9-12R; 145; CANR 24, 53; CDALB 1941-1968; DA3; DLB 2, 76; DLBY 94; MTCW 1, 2

Ellmann, Lucy (Elizabeth) 1956- ..... **CLC 61**
See also CA 128

Ellmann, Richard (David)
1918-1987 .... **CLC 50**
See also BEST 89:2; CA 1-4R; 122; CANR 2, 28, 61; DLB 103; DLBY 87; MTCW 1, 2

Elman, Richard (Martin)
1934-1997 .... **CLC 19**
See also CA 17-20R; 163; CAAS 3; CANR 47

Elron
See Hubbard, L(afayette) Ron(ald)

Eluard, Paul TCLC 7, 41
See also Grindel, Eugene

Elyot, Sir Thomas 1490(?)-1546 .... **LC 11**

Elytis, Odysseus 1911-1996 .... **CLC 15, 49, 100; DAM POET; PC 21**
See also CA 102; 151; MTCW 1, 2

Emecheta, (Florence Onye) Buchi
1944- .. **CLC 14, 48, 128; BLC 2; DAM MULT**
See also BW 2, 3; CA 81-84; CANR 27, 81; DA3; DLB 117; MTCW 1, 2; SATA 66

Emerson, Mary Moody
1774-1863 .... **NCLC 66**

Emerson, Ralph Waldo 1803-1882 . **NCLC 1, 38; DA; DAB; DAC; DAM MST, POET; PC 18; WLC**
See also CDALB 1640-1865; DA3; DLB 1, 59, 73, 223

Eminescu, Mihail 1850-1889 .... **NCLC 33**

Empson, William 1906-1984 ... **CLC 3, 8, 19, 33, 34**
See also CA 17-20R; 112; CANR 31, 61; DLB 20; MTCW 1, 2

Fast, Howard (Melvin) 1914- .. **CLC 23, 131; DAM NOV**
> See also AAYA 16; CA 1-4R, 181; CAAE 181; CAAS 18; CANR 1, 33, 54, 75; DLB 9; INT CANR-33; MTCW 1; SATA 7; SATA-Essay 107

Faulcon, Robert
> See Holdstock, Robert P.

Faulkner, William (Cuthbert) 1897-1962 .... **CLC 1, 3, 6, 8, 9, 11, 14, 18, 28, 52, 68; DA; DAB; DAC; DAM MST, NOV; SSC 1, 35; WLC**
> See also AAYA 7; CA 81-84; CANR 33; CDALB 1929-1941; DA3; DLB 9, 11, 44, 102; DLBD 2; DLBY 86, 97; MTCW 1, 2

Fauset, Jessie Redmon 1884(?)-1961 .... **CLC 19, 54; BLC 2; DAM MULT**
> See also BW 1; CA 109; CANR 83; DLB 51

Faust, Frederick (Schiller) 1892-1944(?) .... **TCLC 49; DAM POP**
> See also CA 108; 152

Faust, Irvin 1924- .... **CLC 8**
> See also CA 33-36R; CANR 28, 67; DLB 2, 28; DLBY 80

Fawkes, Guy
> See Benchley, Robert (Charles)

Fearing, Kenneth (Flexner) 1902-1961 .... **CLC 51**
> See also CA 93-96; CANR 59; DLB 9

Fecamps, Elise
> See Creasey, John

Federman, Raymond 1928- .... **CLC 6, 47**
> See also CA 17-20R; CAAS 8; CANR 10, 43, 83; DLBY 80

Federspiel, J(uerg) F. 1931- .... **CLC 42**
> See also CA 146

Feiffer, Jules (Ralph) 1929- ..... **CLC 2, 8, 64; DAM DRAM**
> See also AAYA 3; CA 17-20R; CANR 30, 59; DLB 7, 44; INT CANR-30; MTCW 1; SATA 8, 61, 111

Feige, Hermann Albert Otto Maximilian
> See Traven, B.

Feinberg, David B. 1956-1994 .... **CLC 59**
> See also CA 135; 147

Feinstein, Elaine 1930- .... **CLC 36**
> See also CA 69-72; CAAS 1; CANR 31, 68; DLB 14, 40; MTCW 1

Feldman, Irving (Mordecai) 1928- ..... **CLC 7**
> See also CA 1-4R; CANR 1; DLB 169

Felix-Tchicaya, Gerald
> See Tchicaya, Gerald Felix

Fellini, Federico 1920-1993 .... **CLC 16, 85**
> See also CA 65-68; 143; CANR 33

Felsen, Henry Gregor 1916-1995 ..... **CLC 17**
> See also CA 1-4R; 180; CANR 1; SAAS 2; SATA 1

Fenno, Jack
> See Calisher, Hortense

Fenollosa, Ernest (Francisco) 1853-1908 .... **TCLC 91**

Fenton, James Martin 1949- .... **CLC 32**
> See also CA 102; DLB 40

Ferber, Edna 1887-1968 .... **CLC 18, 93**
> See also AITN 1; CA 5-8R; 25-28R; CANR 68; DLB 9, 28, 86; MTCW 1, 2; SATA 7

Ferguson, Helen
> See Kavan, Anna

Ferguson, Samuel 1810-1886 .... **NCLC 33**
> See also DLB 32

Fergusson, Robert 1750-1774 .... **LC 29**
> See also DLB 109

Ferling, Lawrence
> See Ferlinghetti, Lawrence (Monsanto)

Ferlinghetti, Lawrence (Monsanto) 1919(?)- .... **CLC 2, 6, 10, 27, 111; DAM POET; PC 1**
> See also CA 5-8R; CANR 3, 41, 73; CDALB 1941-1968; DA3; DLB 5, 16; MTCW 1, 2

Fern, Fanny 1811-1872
> See Parton, Sara Payson Willis

Fernandez, Vicente Garcia Huidobro
> See Huidobro Fernandez, Vicente Garcia

Ferre, Rosario 1942- .... **SSC 36; HLCS 1**
> See also CA 131; CANR 55, 81; DLB 145; HW 1, 2; MTCW 1

Ferrer, Gabriel (Francisco Victor) Miro
> See Miro (Ferrer), Gabriel (Francisco Victor)

Ferrier, Susan (Edmonstone) 1782-1854 .... **NCLC 8**
> See also DLB 116

Ferrigno, Robert 1948(?)- .... **CLC 65**
> See also CA 140

Ferron, Jacques 1921-1985 .... **CLC 94; DAC**
> See also CA 117; 129; DLB 60

Feuchtwanger, Lion 1884-1958 .... **TCLC 3**
> See also CA 104; DLB 66

Feuillet, Octave 1821-1890 .... **NCLC 45**
> See also DLB 192

Feydeau, Georges (Leon Jules Marie) 1862-1921 .... **TCLC 22; DAM DRAM**
> See also CA 113; 152; CANR 84; DLB 192

Fichte, Johann Gottlieb 1762-1814 .... **NCLC 62**
> See also DLB 90

Ficino, Marsilio 1433-1499 .... **LC 12**

Fiedeler, Hans
> See Doeblin, Alfred

Fiedler, Leslie A(aron) 1917- .. **CLC 4, 13, 24**
> See also CA 9-12R; CANR 7, 63; DLB 28, 67; MTCW 1, 2

Field, Andrew 1938- .... **CLC 44**
> See also CA 97-100; CANR 25

Field, Eugene 1850-1895 .... **NCLC 3**
> See also DLB 23, 42, 140; DLBD 13; MAI-CYA; SATA 16

Field, Gans T.
> See Wellman, Manly Wade

Field, Michael 1915-1971 .... **TCLC 43**
> See also CA 29-32R

Field, Peter
> See Hobson, Laura Z(ametkin)

Fielding, Henry 1707-1754 ..... **LC 1, 46; DA; DAB; DAC; DAM DRAM, MST, NOV; WLC**
> See also CDBLB 1660-1789; DA3; DLB 39, 84, 101

Fielding, Sarah 1710-1768 .... **LC 1, 44**
> See also DLB 39

Fields, W. C. 1880-1946 .... **TCLC 80**
> See also DLB 44

Fierstein, Harvey (Forbes) 1954- .... **CLC 33; DAM DRAM, POP**
> See also CA 123; 129; DA3

Figes, Eva 1932- .... **CLC 31**
> See also CA 53-56; CANR 4, 44, 83; DLB 14

Finch, Anne 1661-1720 .... **LC 3; PC 21**
> See also DLB 95

Finch, Robert (Duer Claydon) 1900- .... **CLC 18**
> See also CA 57-60; CANR 9, 24, 49; DLB 88

Findley, Timothy 1930- . **CLC 27, 102; DAC; DAM MST**
> See also CA 25-28R; CANR 12, 42, 69; DLB 53

Fink, William
> See Mencken, H(enry) L(ouis)

Firbank, Louis 1942-
> See Reed, Lou
> See also CA 117

Firbank, (Arthur Annesley) Ronald 1886-1926 .... **TCLC 1**
> See also CA 104; 177; DLB 36

Fisher, Dorothy (Frances) Canfield 1879-1958 .... **TCLC 87**
> See also CA 114; 136; CANR 80; DLB 9, 102; MAICYA; YABC 1

Fisher, M(ary) F(rances) K(ennedy) 1908-1992 .... **CLC 76, 87**
> See also CA 77-80; 138; CANR 44; MTCW 1

Fisher, Roy 1930- .... **CLC 25**
> See also CA 81-84; CAAS 10; CANR 16; DLB 40

Fisher, Rudolph 1897-1934 .. **TCLC 11; BLC 2; DAM MULT; SSC 25**
> See also BW 1, 3; CA 107; 124; CANR 80; DLB 51, 102

Fisher, Vardis (Alvero) 1895-1968 ...... **CLC 7**
> See also CA 5-8R; 25-28R; CANR 68; DLB 9, 206

Fiske, Tarleton
> See Bloch, Robert (Albert)

Fitch, Clarke
> See Sinclair, Upton (Beall)

Fitch, John IV
> See Cormier, Robert (Edmund)

Fitzgerald, Captain Hugh
> See Baum, L(yman) Frank

FitzGerald, Edward 1809-1883 .... **NCLC 9**
> See also DLB 32

Fitzgerald, F(rancis) Scott (Key) 1896-1940 .. **TCLC 1, 6, 14, 28, 55; DA; DAB; DAC; DAM MST, NOV; SSC 6, 31; WLC**
> See also AAYA 24; AITN 1; CA 110; 123; CDALB 1917-1929; DA3; DLB 4, 9, 86; DLBD 1, 15, 16; DLBY 81, 96; MTCW 1, 2

Fitzgerald, Penelope 1916-2000 . **CLC 19, 51, 61**
> See also CA 85-88; CAAS 10; CANR 56, 86; DLB 14, 194; MTCW 2

Fitzgerald, Robert (Stuart) 1910-1985 .... **CLC 39**
> See also CA 1-4R; 114; CANR 1; DLBY 80

FitzGerald, Robert D(avid) 1902-1987 .... **CLC 19**
> See also CA 17-20R

Fitzgerald, Zelda (Sayre) 1900-1948 .... **TCLC 52**
> See also CA 117; 126; DLBY 84

Flanagan, Thomas (James Bonner) 1923- .... **CLC 25, 52**
> See also CA 108; CANR 55; DLBY 80; INT 108; MTCW 1

Freeman, Douglas Southall
1886-1953 .... **TCLC 11**
See also CA 109; DLB 17; DLBD 17

Freeman, Judith 1946- .... **CLC 55**
See also CA 148

Freeman, Mary E(leanor) Wilkins
1852-1930 .... **TCLC 9; SSC 1**
See also CA 106; 177; DLB 12, 78, 221

Freeman, R(ichard) Austin
1862-1943 .... **TCLC 21**
See also CA 113; CANR 84; DLB 70

French, Albert 1943- .... **CLC 86**
See also BW 3; CA 167

French, Marilyn 1929- .... **CLC 10, 18, 60;**
DAM DRAM, NOV, POP
See also CA 69-72; CANR 3, 31; INT
CANR-31; MTCW 1, 2

French, Paul
See Asimov, Isaac

Freneau, Philip Morin 1752-1832 ... **NCLC 1**
See also DLB 37, 43

Freud, Sigmund 1856-1939 .... **TCLC 52**
See also CA 115; 133; CANR 69; MTCW
1, 2

Friedan, Betty (Naomi) 1921- .... **CLC 74**
See also CA 65-68; CANR 18, 45, 74;
MTCW 1, 2

Friedlander, Saul 1932- .... **CLC 90**
See also CA 117; 130; CANR 72

Friedman, B(ernard) H(arper)
1926- .... **CLC 7**
See also CA 1-4R; CANR 3, 48

Friedman, Bruce Jay 1930- ...... **CLC 3, 5, 56**
See also CA 9-12R; CANR 25, 52; DLB 2,
28; INT CANR-25

Friel, Brian 1929- .... **CLC 5, 42, 59, 115; DC**
8
See also CA 21-24R; CANR 33, 69; DLB
13; MTCW 1

Friis-Baastad, Babbis Ellinor
1921-1970 .... **CLC 12**
See also CA 17-20R; 134; SATA 7

Frisch, Max (Rudolf) 1911-1991 ... **CLC 3, 9,**
14, 18, 32, 44; DAM DRAM, NOV
See also CA 85-88; 134; CANR 32, 74;
DLB 69, 124; MTCW 1, 2

Fromentin, Eugene (Samuel Auguste)
1820-1876 .... **NCLC 10**
See also DLB 123

Frost, Frederick
See Faust, Frederick (Schiller)

Frost, Robert (Lee) 1874-1963 ... **CLC 1, 3, 4,**
9, 10, 13, 15, 26, 34, 44; DA; DAB;
DAC; DAM MST, POET; PC 1; WLC
See also AAYA 21; CA 89-92; CANR 33;
CDALB 1917-1929; DA3; DLB 54;
DLBD 7; MTCW 1, 2; SATA 14

Froude, James Anthony
1818-1894 .... **NCLC 43**
See also DLB 18, 57, 144

Froy, Herald
See Waterhouse, Keith (Spencer)

Fry, Christopher 1907- .... **CLC 2, 10, 14;**
DAM DRAM
See also CA 17-20R; CAAS 23; CANR 9,
30, 74; DLB 13; MTCW 1, 2; SATA 66

Frye, (Herman) Northrop
1912-1991 .... **CLC 24, 70**
See also CA 5-8R; 133; CANR 8, 37; DLB
67, 68; MTCW 1, 2

Fuchs, Daniel 1909-1993 .... **CLC 8, 22**
See also CA 81-84; 142; CAAS 5; CANR
40; DLB 9, 26, 28; DLBY 93

Fuchs, Daniel 1934- .... **CLC 34**
See also CA 37-40R; CANR 14, 48

Fuentes, Carlos 1928- .. **CLC 3, 8, 10, 13, 22,**
41, 60, 113; DA; DAB; DAC; DAM
MST, MULT, NOV; HLC 1; SSC 24;
WLC
See also AAYA 4; AITN 2; CA 69-72;
CANR 10, 32, 68; DA3; DLB 113; HW
1, 2; MTCW 1, 2

Fuentes, Gregorio Lopez y
See Lopez y Fuentes, Gregorio

Fuertes, Gloria 1918- .... **PC 27**
See also CA 178, 180; DLB 108; HW 2;
SATA 115

Fugard, (Harold) Athol 1932- . **CLC 5, 9, 14,**
25, 40, 80; DAM DRAM; DC 3
See also AAYA 17; CA 85-88; CANR 32,
54; MTCW 1

Fugard, Sheila 1932- .... **CLC 48**
See also CA 125

Fukuyama, Francis 1952- .... **CLC 131**
See also CA 140; CANR 72

Fuller, Charles (H., Jr.) 1939- .... **CLC 25;**
BLC 2; DAM DRAM, MULT; DC 1
See also BW 2; CA 108; 112; CANR 87;
DLB 38; INT 112; MTCW 1

Fuller, John (Leopold) 1937- .... **CLC 62**
See also CA 21-24R; CANR 9, 44; DLB 40

Fuller, Margaret NCLC 5, 50
See also Fuller, Sarah Margaret

Fuller, Roy (Broadbent) 1912-1991 ... **CLC 4,**
28
See also CA 5-8R; 135; CAAS 10; CANR
53, 83; DLB 15, 20; SATA 87

Fuller, Sarah Margaret 1810-1850
See Fuller, Margaret
See also CDALB 1640-1865; DLB 1, 59,
73, 83, 223

Fulton, Alice 1952- .... **CLC 52**
See also CA 116; CANR 57, 88; DLB 193

Furphy, Joseph 1843-1912 .... **TCLC 25**
See also CA 163

Fussell, Paul 1924- .... **CLC 74**
See also BEST 90:1; CA 17-20R; CANR 8,
21, 35, 69; INT CANR-21; MTCW 1, 2

Futabatei, Shimei 1864-1909 .... **TCLC 44**
See also CA 162; DLB 180

Futrelle, Jacques 1875-1912 .... **TCLC 19**
See also CA 113; 155

Gaboriau, Emile 1835-1873 .... **NCLC 14**

Gadda, Carlo Emilio 1893-1973 .... **CLC 11**
See also CA 89-92; DLB 177

Gaddis, William 1922-1998 ... **CLC 1, 3, 6, 8,**
10, 19, 43, 86
See also CA 17-20R; 172; CANR 21, 48;
DLB 2; MTCW 1, 2

Gage, Walter
See Inge, William (Motter)

Gaines, Ernest J(ames) 1933- ...... **CLC 3, 11,**
18, 86; BLC 2; DAM MULT
See also AAYA 18; AITN 1; BW 2, 3; CA
9-12R; CANR 6, 24, 42, 75; CDALB
1968-1988; CLR 62; DA3; DLB 2, 33,
152; DLBY 80; MTCW 1, 2; SATA 86

Gaitskill, Mary 1954- .... **CLC 69**
See also CA 128; CANR 61

Galdos, Benito Perez
See Perez Galdos, Benito

Gale, Zona 1874-1938 .... **TCLC 7; DAM**
DRAM
See also CA 105; 153; CANR 84; DLB 9,
78

Galeano, Eduardo (Hughes) 1940- . **CLC 72;**
HLCS 1
See also CA 29-32R; CANR 13, 32; HW 1

Galiano, Juan Valera y Alcala
See Valera y Alcala-Galiano, Juan

Galilei, Galileo 1546-1642 .... **LC 45**

Gallagher, Tess 1943- ...... **CLC 18, 63; DAM**
POET; PC 9
See also CA 106; DLB 212

Gallant, Mavis 1922- .. **CLC 7, 18, 38; DAC;**
DAM MST; SSC 5
See also CA 69-72; CANR 29, 69; DLB 53;
MTCW 1, 2

Gallant, Roy A(rthur) 1924- .... **CLC 17**
See also CA 5-8R; CANR 4, 29, 54; CLR
30; MAICYA; SATA 4, 68, 110

Gallico, Paul (William) 1897-1976 ..... **CLC 2**
See also AITN 1; CA 5-8R; 69-72; CANR
23; DLB 9, 171; MAICYA; SATA 13

Gallo, Max Louis 1932- .... **CLC 95**
See also CA 85-88

Gallois, Lucien
See Desnos, Robert

Gallup, Ralph
See Whitemore, Hugh (John)

Galsworthy, John 1867-1933 .... **TCLC 1, 45;**
DA; DAB; DAC; DAM DRAM, MST,
NOV; SSC 22; WLC
See also CA 104; 141; CANR 75; CDBLB
1890-1914; DA3; DLB 10, 34, 98, 162;
DLBD 16; MTCW 1

Galt, John 1779-1839 .... **NCLC 1**
See also DLB 99, 116, 159

Galvin, James 1951- .... **CLC 38**
See also CA 108; CANR 26

Gamboa, Federico 1864-1939 .... **TCLC 36**
See also CA 167; HW 2

Gandhi, M. K.
See Gandhi, Mohandas Karamchand

Gandhi, Mahatma
See Gandhi, Mohandas Karamchand

Gandhi, Mohandas Karamchand
1869-1948 .... **TCLC 59; DAM MULT**
See also CA 121; 132; DA3; MTCW 1, 2

Gann, Ernest Kellogg 1910-1991 ..... **CLC 23**
See also AITN 1; CA 1-4R; 136; CANR 1,
83

Garber, Eric 1943(?)-
See Holleran, Andrew
See also CANR 89

Garcia, Cristina 1958- .... **CLC 76**
See also CA 141; CANR 73; HW 2

Garcia Lorca, Federico 1898-1936 . **TCLC 1,**
7, 49; DA; DAB; DAC; DAM DRAM,
MST, MULT, POET; DC 2; HLC 2;
PC 3; WLC
See also Lorca, Federico Garcia
See also CA 104; 131; CANR 81; DA3;
DLB 108; HW 1, 2; MTCW 1, 2

Garcia Marquez, Gabriel (Jose)
1928- .... **CLC 2, 3, 8, 10, 15, 27, 47, 55,**
68; DA; DAB; DAC; DAM MST,
MULT, NOV, POP; HLC 1; SSC 8;
WLC
See also Marquez, Gabriel (Jose) Garcia
See also AAYA 3, 33; BEST 89:1, 90:4; CA
33-36R; CANR 10, 28, 50, 75, 82; DA3;
DLB 113; HW 1, 2; MTCW 1, 2

Gilliam, Terry (Vance) 1940- .... **CLC 21**
See also Monty Python
See also AAYA 19; CA 108; 113; CANR 35; INT 113

Gillian, Jerry
See Gilliam, Terry (Vance)

Gilliatt, Penelope (Ann Douglass)
1932-1993 .... **CLC 2, 10, 13, 53**
See also AITN 2; CA 13-16R; 141; CANR 49; DLB 14

Gilman, Charlotte (Anna) Perkins (Stetson)
1860-1935 .... **TCLC 9, 37; SSC 13**
See also CA 106; 150; DLB 221; MTCW 1

Gilmour, David 1949- .... **CLC 35**
See also CA 138, 147

Gilpin, William 1724-1804 .... **NCLC 30**

Gilray, J. D.
See Mencken, H(enry) L(ouis)

Gilroy, Frank D(aniel) 1925- .... **CLC 2**
See also CA 81-84; CANR 32, 64, 86; DLB 7

Gilstrap, John 1957(?)- .... **CLC 99**
See also CA 160

Ginsberg, Allen 1926-1997 .... **CLC 1, 2, 3, 4, 6, 13, 36, 69, 109; DA; DAB; DAC; DAM MST, POET; PC 4; WLC**
See also AAYA 33; AITN 1; CA 1-4R; 157; CANR 2, 41, 63; CDALB 1941-1968; DA3; DLB 5, 16, 169; MTCW 1, 2

Ginzburg, Natalia 1916-1991 .... **CLC 5, 11, 54, 70**
See also CA 85-88; 135; CANR 33; DLB 177; MTCW 1, 2

Giono, Jean 1895-1970 .... **CLC 4, 11**
See also CA 45-48; 29-32R; CANR 2, 35; DLB 72; MTCW 1

Giovanni, Nikki 1943- .... **CLC 2, 4, 19, 64, 117; BLC 2; DA; DAB; DAC; DAM MST, MULT, POET; PC 19; WLCS**
See also AAYA 22; AITN 1; BW 2, 3; CA 29-32R; CAAS 6; CANR 18, 41, 60, 91; CDALBS; CLR 6; DA3; DLB 5, 41; INT CANR-18; MAICYA; MTCW 1, 2; SATA 24, 107

Giovene, Andrea 1904- .... **CLC 7**
See also CA 85-88

Gippius, Zinaida (Nikolayevna) 1869-1945
See Hippius, Zinaida
See also CA 106

Giraudoux, (Hippolyte) Jean
1882-1944 .... **TCLC 2, 7; DAM DRAM**
See also CA 104; DLB 65

Gironella, Jose Maria 1917- .... **CLC 11**
See also CA 101

Gissing, George (Robert)
1857-1903 .... **TCLC 3, 24, 47; SSC 37**
See also CA 105; 167; DLB 18, 135, 184

Giurlani, Aldo
See Palazzeschi, Aldo

Gladkov, Fyodor (Vasilyevich)
1883-1958 .... **TCLC 27**
See also CA 170

Glanville, Brian (Lester) 1931- .... **CLC 6**
See also CA 5-8R; CAAS 9; CANR 3, 70; DLB 15, 139; SATA 42

Glasgow, Ellen (Anderson Gholson)
1873-1945 .... **TCLC 2, 7; SSC 34**
See also CA 104; 164; DLB 9, 12; MTCW 2

Glaspell, Susan 1882(?)-1948 . **TCLC 55; DC 10**
See also CA 110; 154; DLB 7, 9, 78; YABC 2

Glassco, John 1909-1981 .... **CLC 9**
See also CA 13-16R; 102; CANR 15; DLB 68

Glasscock, Amnesia
See Steinbeck, John (Ernst)

Glasser, Ronald J. 1940(?)- .... **CLC 37**

Glassman, Joyce
See Johnson, Joyce

Glendinning, Victoria 1937- .... **CLC 50**
See also CA 120; 127; CANR 59, 89; DLB 155

Glissant, Edouard 1928- . **CLC 10, 68; DAM MULT**
See also CA 153

Gloag, Julian 1930- .... **CLC 40**
See also AITN 1; CA 65-68; CANR 10, 70

Glowacki, Aleksander
See Prus, Boleslaw

Gluck, Louise (Elisabeth) 1943- .. **CLC 7, 22, 44, 81; DAM POET; PC 16**
See also CA 33-36R; CANR 40, 69; DA3; DLB 5; MTCW 2

Glyn, Elinor 1864-1943 .... **TCLC 72**
See also DLB 153

Gobineau, Joseph Arthur (Comte) de
1816-1882 .... **NCLC 17**
See also DLB 123

Godard, Jean-Luc 1930- .... **CLC 20**
See also CA 93-96

Godden, (Margaret) Rumer
1907-1998 .... **CLC 53**
See also AAYA 6; CA 5-8R; 172; CANR 4, 27, 36, 55, 80; CLR 20; DLB 161; MAICYA; SAAS 12; SATA 3, 36; SATA-Obit 109

Godoy Alcayaga, Lucila 1889-1957
See Mistral, Gabriela
See also BW 2; CA 104; 131; CANR 81; DAM MULT; HW 1, 2; MTCW 1, 2

Godwin, Gail (Kathleen) 1937- ..... **CLC 5, 8, 22, 31, 69, 125; DAM POP**
See also CA 29-32R; CANR 15, 43, 69; DA3; DLB 6; INT CANR-15; MTCW 1, 2

Godwin, William 1756-1836 .... **NCLC 14**
See also CDBLB 1789-1832; DLB 39, 104, 142, 158, 163

Goebbels, Josef
See Goebbels, (Paul) Joseph

Goebbels, (Paul) Joseph
1897-1945 .... **TCLC 68**
See also CA 115; 148

Goebbels, Joseph Paul
See Goebbels, (Paul) Joseph

Goethe, Johann Wolfgang von
1749-1832 . **NCLC 4, 22, 34; DA; DAB; DAC; DAM DRAM, MST, POET; PC 5; SSC 38; WLC**
See also DA3; DLB 94

Gogarty, Oliver St. John
1878-1957 .... **TCLC 15**
See also CA 109; 150; DLB 15, 19

Gogol, Nikolai (Vasilyevich)
1809-1852 . **NCLC 5, 15, 31; DA; DAB; DAC; DAM DRAM, MST; DC 1; SSC 4, 29; WLC**
See also DLB 198

Goines, Donald 1937(?)-1974 . **CLC 80; BLC 2; DAM MULT, POP**
See also AITN 1; BW 1, 3; CA 124; 114; CANR 82; DA3; DLB 33

Gold, Herbert 1924- .... **CLC 4, 7, 14, 42**
See also CA 9-12R; CANR 17, 45; DLB 2; DLBY 81

Goldbarth, Albert 1948- .... **CLC 5, 38**
See also CA 53-56; CANR 6, 40; DLB 120

Goldberg, Anatol 1910-1982 .... **CLC 34**
See also CA 131; 117

Goldemberg, Isaac 1945- .... **CLC 52**
See also CA 69-72; CAAS 12; CANR 11, 32; HW 1

Golding, William (Gerald)
1911-1993 ..... **CLC 1, 2, 3, 8, 10, 17, 27, 58, 81; DA; DAB; DAC; DAM MST, NOV; WLC**
See also AAYA 5; CA 5-8R; 141; CANR 13, 33, 54; CDBLB 1945-1960; DA3; DLB 15, 100; MTCW 1, 2

Goldman, Emma 1869-1940 .... **TCLC 13**
See also CA 110; 150; DLB 221

Goldman, Francisco 1954- .... **CLC 76**
See also CA 162

Goldman, William (W.) 1931- ...... **CLC 1, 48**
See also CA 9-12R; CANR 29, 69; DLB 44

Goldmann, Lucien 1913-1970 .... **CLC 24**
See also CA 25-28; CAP 2

Goldoni, Carlo 1707-1793 .... **LC 4; DAM DRAM**

Goldsberry, Steven 1949- .... **CLC 34**
See also CA 131

Goldsmith, Oliver 1728-1774 . **LC 2, 48; DA; DAB; DAC; DAM DRAM, MST, NOV, POET; DC 8; WLC**
See also CDBLB 1660-1789; DLB 39, 89, 104, 109, 142; SATA 26

Goldsmith, Peter
See Priestley, J(ohn) B(oynton)

Gombrowicz, Witold 1904-1969 .... **CLC 4, 7, 11, 49; DAM DRAM**
See also CA 19-20; 25-28R; CAP 2

Gomez de la Serna, Ramon
1888-1963 .... **CLC 9**
See also CA 153; 116; CANR 79; HW 1, 2

Goncharov, Ivan Alexandrovich
1812-1891 .... **NCLC 1, 63**

Goncourt, Edmond (Louis Antoine Huot) de
1822-1896 .... **NCLC 7**
See also DLB 123

Goncourt, Jules (Alfred Huot) de
1830-1870 .... **NCLC 7**
See also DLB 123

Gontier, Fernande 19(?)- .... **CLC 50**

Gonzalez Martinez, Enrique
1871-1952 .... **TCLC 72**
See also CA 166; CANR 81; HW 1, 2

Goodman, Paul 1911-1972 ..... **CLC 1, 2, 4, 7**
See also CA 19-20; 37-40R; CANR 34; CAP 2; DLB 130; MTCW 1

Gordimer, Nadine 1923- ...... **CLC 3, 5, 7, 10, 18, 33, 51, 70; DA; DAB; DAC; DAM MST, NOV; SSC 17; WLCS**
See also CA 5-8R; CANR 3, 28, 56, 88; DA3; INT CANR-28; MTCW 1, 2

Gordon, Adam Lindsay
1833-1870 .... **NCLC 21**

Gordon, Caroline 1895-1981 . **CLC 6, 13, 29, 83; SSC 15**
See also CA 11-12; 103; CANR 36; CAP 1; DLB 4, 9, 102; DLBD 17; DLBY 81; MTCW 1, 2

Gordon, Charles William 1860-1937
See Connor, Ralph
See also CA 109

Gregory, J. Dennis
See Williams, John A(lfred)
Grendon, Stephen
See Derleth, August (William)
Grenville, Kate 1950- .... **CLC 61**
See also CA 118; CANR 53
Grenville, Pelham
See Wodehouse, P(elham) G(renville)
Greve, Felix Paul (Berthold Friedrich)
1879-1948
See Grove, Frederick Philip
See also CA 104; 141; 175; CANR 79;
DAC; DAM MST
Grey, Zane 1872-1939 . **TCLC 6; DAM POP**
See also CA 104; 132; DA3; DLB 212;
MTCW 1, 2
Grieg, (Johan) Nordahl (Brun)
1902-1943 .... **TCLC 10**
See also CA 107
Grieve, C(hristopher) M(urray)
1892-1978 ..... **CLC 11, 19; DAM POET**
See also MacDiarmid, Hugh; Pteleon
See also CA 5-8R; 85-88; CANR 33;
MTCW 1
Griffin, Gerald 1803-1840 .... **NCLC 7**
See also DLB 159
Griffin, John Howard 1920-1980 ..... **CLC 68**
See also AITN 1; CA 1-4R; 101; CANR 2
Griffin, Peter 1942- .... **CLC 39**
See also CA 136
Griffith, D(avid Lewelyn) W(ark)
1875(?)-1948 .... **TCLC 68**
See also CA 119; 150; CANR 80
Griffith, Lawrence
See Griffith, D(avid Lewelyn) W(ark)
Griffiths, Trevor 1935- .... **CLC 13, 52**
See also CA 97-100; CANR 45; DLB 13
Griggs, Sutton (Elbert)
1872-1930 .... **TCLC 77**
See also CA 123; 186; DLB 50
Grigson, Geoffrey (Edward Harvey)
1905-1985 .... **CLC 7, 39**
See also CA 25-28R; 118; CANR 20, 33;
DLB 27; MTCW 1, 2
Grillparzer, Franz 1791-1872 .... **NCLC 1;
SSC 37**
See also DLB 133
Grimble, Reverend Charles James
See Eliot, T(homas) S(tearns)
Grimke, Charlotte L(ottie) Forten
1837(?)-1914
See Forten, Charlotte L.
See also BW 1; CA 117; 124; DAM MULT,
POET
Grimm, Jacob Ludwig Karl
1785-1863 .... **NCLC 3, 77; SSC 36**
See also DLB 90; MAICYA; SATA 22
Grimm, Wilhelm Karl 1786-1859 .. **NCLC 3,
77; SSC 36**
See also DLB 90; MAICYA; SATA 22
**Grimmelshausen, Johann Jakob Christoffel
von** 1621-1676 .... **LC 6**
See also DLB 168
Grindel, Eugene 1895-1952
See Eluard, Paul
See also CA 104
Grisham, John 1955- .... **CLC 84; DAM POP**
See also AAYA 14; CA 138; CANR 47, 69;
DA3; MTCW 2
Grossman, David 1954- .... **CLC 67**
See also CA 138

Grossman, Vasily (Semenovich)
1905-1964 .... **CLC 41**
See also CA 124; 130; MTCW 1
Grove, Frederick Philip TCLC 4
See also Greve, Felix Paul (Berthold
Friedrich)
See also DLB 92
Grubb
See Crumb, R(obert)
Grumbach, Doris (Isaac) 1918- . **CLC 13, 22,
64**
See also CA 5-8R; CAAS 2; CANR 9, 42,
70; INT CANR-9; MTCW 2
Grundtvig, Nicolai Frederik Severin
1783-1872 .... **NCLC 1**
Grunge
See Crumb, R(obert)
Grunwald, Lisa 1959- .... **CLC 44**
See also CA 120
Guare, John 1938- .... **CLC 8, 14, 29, 67;
DAM DRAM**
See also CA 73-76; CANR 21, 69; DLB 7;
MTCW 1, 2
Gudjonsson, Halldor Kiljan 1902-1998
See Laxness, Halldor
See also CA 103; 164
Guenter, Erich
See Eich, Guenter
Guest, Barbara 1920- .... **CLC 34**
See also CA 25-28R; CANR 11, 44, 84;
DLB 5, 193
Guest, Edgar A(lbert) 1881-1959 ... **TCLC 95**
See also CA 112; 168
Guest, Judith (Ann) 1936- .... **CLC 8, 30;
DAM NOV, POP**
See also AAYA 7; CA 77-80; CANR 15,
75; DA3; INT CANR-15; MTCW 1, 2
Guevara, Che CLC 87; HLC 1
See also Guevara (Serna), Ernesto
Guevara (Serna), Ernesto
1928-1967 .... **CLC 87; DAM MULT;
HLC 1**
See also Guevara, Che
See also CA 127; 111; CANR 56; HW 1
Guicciardini, Francesco 1483-1540 ..... **LC 49**
Guild, Nicholas M. 1944- .... **CLC 33**
See also CA 93-96
Guillemin, Jacques
See Sartre, Jean-Paul
Guillen, Jorge 1893-1984 .... **CLC 11; DAM
MULT, POET; HLCS 1**
See also CA 89-92; 112; DLB 108; HW 1
Guillen, Nicolas (Cristobal)
1902-1989 ... **CLC 48, 79; BLC 2; DAM
MST, MULT, POET; HLC 1; PC 23**
See also BW 2; CA 116; 125; 129; CANR
84; HW 1
Guillevic, (Eugene) 1907- .... **CLC 33**
See also CA 93-96
Guillois
See Desnos, Robert
Guillois, Valentin
See Desnos, Robert
Guimaraes Rosa, Joao 1908-1967
See also CA 175; HLCS 2
Guiney, Louise Imogen
1861-1920 .... **TCLC 41**
See also CA 160; DLB 54
Guiraldes, Ricardo (Guillermo)
1886-1927 .... **TCLC 39**
See also CA 131; HW 1; MTCW 1

Gumilev, Nikolai (Stepanovich)
1886-1921 .... **TCLC 60**
See also CA 165
Gunesekera, Romesh 1954- .... **CLC 91**
See also CA 159
Gunn, Bill CLC 5
See also Gunn, William Harrison
See also DLB 38
Gunn, Thom(son William) 1929- .. **CLC 3, 6,
18, 32, 81; DAM POET; PC 26**
See also CA 17-20R; CANR 9, 33; CDBLB
1960 to Present; DLB 27; INT CANR-33;
MTCW 1
Gunn, William Harrison 1934(?)-1989
See Gunn, Bill
See also AITN 1; BW 1, 3; CA 13-16R;
128; CANR 12, 25, 76
Gunnars, Kristjana 1948- .... **CLC 69**
See also CA 113; DLB 60
Gurdjieff, G(eorgei) I(vanovich)
1877(?)-1949 .... **TCLC 71**
See also CA 157
Gurganus, Allan 1947- . **CLC 70; DAM POP**
See also BEST 90:1; CA 135
Gurney, A(lbert) R(amsdell), Jr.
1930- ..... **CLC 32, 50, 54; DAM DRAM**
See also CA 77-80; CANR 32, 64
Gurney, Ivor (Bertie) 1890-1937 ... **TCLC 33**
See also CA 167
Gurney, Peter
See Gurney, A(lbert) R(amsdell), Jr.
Guro, Elena 1877-1913 .... **TCLC 56**
Gustafson, James M(oody) 1925- ... **CLC 100**
See also CA 25-28R; CANR 37
Gustafson, Ralph (Barker) 1909- ..... **CLC 36**
See also CA 21-24R; CANR 8, 45, 84; DLB
88
Gut, Gom
See Simenon, Georges (Jacques Christian)
Guterson, David 1956- .... **CLC 91**
See also CA 132; CANR 73; MTCW 2
Guthrie, A(lfred) B(ertram), Jr.
1901-1991 .... **CLC 23**
See also CA 57-60; 134; CANR 24; DLB
212; SATA 62; SATA-Obit 67
Guthrie, Isobel
See Grieve, C(hristopher) M(urray)
Guthrie, Woodrow Wilson 1912-1967
See Guthrie, Woody
See also CA 113; 93-96
Guthrie, Woody CLC 35
See also Guthrie, Woodrow Wilson
Gutierrez Najera, Manuel 1859-1895
See also HLCS 2
Guy, Rosa (Cuthbert) 1928- .... **CLC 26**
See also AAYA 4; BW 2; CA 17-20R;
CANR 14, 34, 83; CLR 13; DLB 33;
JRDA; MAICYA; SATA 14, 62
Gwendolyn
See Bennett, (Enoch) Arnold
H. D. CLC 3, 8, 14, 31, 34, 73; PC 5
See also Doolittle, Hilda
H. de V.
See Buchan, John
Haavikko, Paavo Juhani 1931- .. **CLC 18, 34**
See also CA 106
Habbema, Koos
See Heijermans, Herman
Habermas, Juergen 1929- .... **CLC 104**
See also CA 109; CANR 85
Habermas, Jurgen
See Habermas, Juergen

Harris, John (Wyndham Parkes Lucas) Beynon 1903-1969
 See Wyndham, John
 See also CA 102; 89-92; CANR 84

Harris, MacDonald CLC 9
 See also Heiney, Donald (William)

Harris, Mark 1922- .... **CLC 19**
 See also CA 5-8R; CAAS 3; CANR 2, 55, 83; DLB 2; DLBY 80

Harris, (Theodore) Wilson 1921- ..... **CLC 25**
 See also BW 2, 3; CA 65-68; CAAS 16; CANR 11, 27, 69; DLB 117; MTCW 1

Harrison, Elizabeth Cavanna 1909-
 See Cavanna, Betty
 See also CA 9-12R; CANR 6, 27, 85

Harrison, Harry (Max) 1925- .... **CLC 42**
 See also CA 1-4R; CANR 5, 21, 84; DLB 8; SATA 4

Harrison, James (Thomas) 1937- ...... **CLC 6, 14, 33, 66; SSC 19**
 See also CA 13-16R; CANR 8, 51, 79; DLBY 82; INT CANR-8

Harrison, Jim
 See Harrison, James (Thomas)

Harrison, Kathryn 1961- .... **CLC 70**
 See also CA 144; CANR 68

Harrison, Tony 1937- .... **CLC 43, 129**
 See also CA 65-68; CANR 44; DLB 40; MTCW 1

Harriss, Will(ard Irvin) 1922- .... **CLC 34**
 See also CA 111

Harson, Sley
 See Ellison, Harlan (Jay)

Hart, Ellis
 See Ellison, Harlan (Jay)

Hart, Josephine 1942(?)- .... **CLC 70; DAM POP**
 See also CA 138; CANR 70

Hart, Moss 1904-1961 .... **CLC 66; DAM DRAM**
 See also CA 109; 89-92; CANR 84; DLB 7

Harte, (Francis) Bret(t) 1836(?)-1902 ... **TCLC 1, 25; DA; DAC; DAM MST; SSC 8; WLC**
 See also CA 104; 140; CANR 80; CDALB 1865-1917; DA3; DLB 12, 64, 74, 79, 186; SATA 26

Hartley, L(eslie) P(oles) 1895-1972 ... **CLC 2, 22**
 See also CA 45-48; 37-40R; CANR 33; DLB 15, 139; MTCW 1, 2

Hartman, Geoffrey H. 1929- .... **CLC 27**
 See also CA 117; 125; CANR 79; DLB 67

Hartmann, Sadakichi 1867-1944 ... **TCLC 73**
 See also CA 157; DLB 54

Hartmann von Aue c. 1160-c. 1205 .... **CMLC 15**
 See also DLB 138

Hartmann von Aue 1170-1210 ...... **CMLC 15**

Haruf, Kent 1943- .... **CLC 34**
 See also CA 149; CANR 91

Harwood, Ronald 1934- .... **CLC 32; DAM DRAM, MST**
 See also CA 1-4R; CANR 4, 55; DLB 13

Hasegawa Tatsunosuke
 See Futabatei, Shimei

Hasek, Jaroslav (Matej Frantisek) 1883-1923 .... **TCLC 4**
 See also CA 104; 129; MTCW 1, 2

Hass, Robert 1941- ... **CLC 18, 39, 99; PC 16**
 See also CA 111; CANR 30, 50, 71; DLB 105, 206; SATA 94

Hastings, Hudson
 See Kuttner, Henry

Hastings, Selina CLC 44

Hathorne, John 1641-1717 .... **LC 38**

Hatteras, Amelia
 See Mencken, H(enry) L(ouis)

Hatteras, Owen TCLC 18
 See also Mencken, H(enry) L(ouis); Nathan, George Jean

Hauptmann, Gerhart (Johann Robert) 1862-1946 .... **TCLC 4; DAM DRAM; SSC 37**
 See also CA 104; 153; DLB 66, 118

Havel, Vaclav 1936- ... **CLC 25, 58, 65; DAM DRAM; DC 6**
 See also CA 104; CANR 36, 63; DA3; MTCW 1, 2

Haviaras, Stratis CLC 33
 See also Chaviaras, Strates

Hawes, Stephen 1475(?)-1523(?) .... **LC 17**
 See also DLB 132

Hawkes, John (Clendennin Burne, Jr.) 1925-1998 .. **CLC 1, 2, 3, 4, 7, 9, 14, 15, 27, 49**
 See also CA 1-4R; 167; CANR 2, 47, 64; DLB 2, 7; DLBY 80, 98; MTCW 1, 2

Hawking, S. W.
 See Hawking, Stephen W(illiam)

Hawking, Stephen W(illiam) 1942- . **CLC 63, 105**
 See also AAYA 13; BEST 89:1; CA 126; 129; CANR 48; DA3; MTCW 2

Hawkins, Anthony Hope
 See Hope, Anthony

Hawthorne, Julian 1846-1934 .... **TCLC 25**
 See also CA 165

Hawthorne, Nathaniel 1804-1864 . **NCLC 39; DA; DAB; DAC; DAM MST, NOV; SSC 3, 29, 39; WLC**
 See also AAYA 18; CDALB 1640-1865; DA3; DLB 1, 74, 223; YABC 2

Haxton, Josephine Ayres 1921-
 See Douglas, Ellen
 See also CA 115; CANR 41, 83

Hayaseca y Eizaguirre, Jorge
 See Echegaray (y Eizaguirre), Jose (Maria Waldo)

Hayashi, Fumiko 1904-1951 .... **TCLC 27**
 See also CA 161; DLB 180

Haycraft, Anna (Margaret) 1932-
 See Ellis, Alice Thomas
 See also CA 122; CANR 85, 90; MTCW 2

Hayden, Robert E(arl) 1913-1980 . **CLC 5, 9, 14, 37; BLC 2; DA; DAC; DAM MST, MULT, POET; PC 6**
 See also BW 1, 3; CA 69-72; 97-100; CABS 2; CANR 24, 75, 82; CDALB 1941-1968; DLB 5, 76; MTCW 1, 2; SATA 19; SATA-Obit 26

Hayford, J(oseph) E(phraim) Casely
 See Casely-Hayford, J(oseph) E(phraim)

Hayman, Ronald 1932- .... **CLC 44**
 See also CA 25-28R; CANR 18, 50, 88; DLB 155

Haywood, Eliza (Fowler) 1693(?)-1756 .... **LC 1, 44**
 See also DLB 39

Hazlitt, William 1778-1830 ...... **NCLC 29, 82**
 See also DLB 110, 158

Hazzard, Shirley 1931- .... **CLC 18**
 See also CA 9-12R; CANR 4, 70; DLBY 82; MTCW 1

Head, Bessie 1937-1986 .... **CLC 25, 67; BLC 2; DAM MULT**
 See also BW 2, 3; CA 29-32R; 119; CANR 25, 82; DA3; DLB 117; MTCW 1, 2

Headon, (Nicky) Topper 1956(?)- .... **CLC 30**

Heaney, Seamus (Justin) 1939- ..... **CLC 5, 7, 14, 25, 37, 74, 91; DAB; DAM POET; PC 18; WLCS**
 See also CA 85-88; CANR 25, 48, 75, 91; CDBLB 1960 to Present; DA3; DLB 40; DLBY 95; MTCW 1, 2

Hearn, (Patricio) Lafcadio (Tessima Carlos) 1850-1904 .... **TCLC 9**
 See also CA 105; 166; DLB 12, 78, 189

Hearne, Vicki 1946- .... **CLC 56**
 See also CA 139

Hearon, Shelby 1931- .... **CLC 63**
 See also AITN 2; CA 25-28R; CANR 18, 48

Heat-Moon, William Least CLC 29
 See also Trogdon, William (Lewis)
 See also AAYA 9

Hebbel, Friedrich 1813-1863 .... **NCLC 43; DAM DRAM**
 See also DLB 129

Hebert, Anne 1916- ..... **CLC 4, 13, 29; DAC; DAM MST, POET**
 See also CA 85-88; CANR 69; DA3; DLB 68; MTCW 1, 2

Hecht, Anthony (Evan) 1923- ...... **CLC 8, 13, 19; DAM POET**
 See also CA 9-12R; CANR 6; DLB 5, 169

Hecht, Ben 1894-1964 .... **CLC 8**
 See also CA 85-88; DLB 7, 9, 25, 26, 28, 86

Hedayat, Sadeq 1903-1951 .... **TCLC 21**
 See also CA 120

Hegel, Georg Wilhelm Friedrich 1770-1831 .... **NCLC 46**
 See also DLB 90

Heidegger, Martin 1889-1976 .... **CLC 24**
 See also CA 81-84; 65-68; CANR 34; MTCW 1, 2

Heidenstam, (Carl Gustaf) Verner von 1859-1940 .... **TCLC 5**
 See also CA 104

Heifner, Jack 1946- .... **CLC 11**
 See also CA 105; CANR 47

Heijermans, Herman 1864-1924 .... **TCLC 24**
 See also CA 123

Heilbrun, Carolyn G(old) 1926- .... **CLC 25**
 See also CA 45-48; CANR 1, 28, 58

Heine, Heinrich 1797-1856 .... **NCLC 4, 54; PC 25**
 See also DLB 90

Heinemann, Larry (Curtiss) 1944- .. **CLC 50**
 See also CA 110; CAAS 21; CANR 31, 81; DLBD 9; INT CANR-31

Heiney, Donald (William) 1921-1993
 See Harris, MacDonald
 See also CA 1-4R; 142; CANR 3, 58

Heinlein, Robert A(nson) 1907-1988 . **CLC 1, 3, 8, 14, 26, 55; DAM POP**
 See also AAYA 17; CA 1-4R; 125; CANR 1, 20, 53; DA3; DLB 8; JRDA; MAICYA; MTCW 1, 2; SATA 9, 69; SATA-Obit 56

Helforth, John
 See Doolittle, Hilda

Hellenhofferu, Vojtech Kapristian z
 See Hasek, Jaroslav (Matej Frantisek)

Hunter, Evan 1926- .... **CLC 11, 31; DAM POP**
 See also CA 5-8R; CANR 5, 38, 62; DLBY 82; INT CANR-5; MTCW 1; SATA 25

Hunter, Kristin (Eggleston) 1931- .... **CLC 35**
 See also AITN 1; BW 1; CA 13-16R; CANR 13; CLR 3; DLB 33; INT CANR-13; MAICYA; SAAS 10; SATA 12

Hunter, Mary
 See Austin, Mary (Hunter)

Hunter, Mollie 1922- .... **CLC 21**
 See also McIlwraith, Maureen Mollie Hunter
 See also AAYA 13; CANR 37, 78; CLR 25; DLB 161; JRDA; MAICYA; SAAS 7; SATA 54, 106

Hunter, Robert (?)-1734 .... **LC 7**

Hurston, Zora Neale 1903-1960 .. **CLC 7, 30, 61; BLC 2; DA; DAC; DAM MST, MULT, NOV; DC 12; SSC 4; WLCS**
 See also AAYA 15; BW 1, 3; CA 85-88; CANR 61; CDALBS; DA3; DLB 51, 86; MTCW 1, 2

Huston, John (Marcellus)
 1906-1987 .... **CLC 20**
 See also CA 73-76; 123; CANR 34; DLB 26

Hustvedt, Siri 1955- .... **CLC 76**
 See also CA 137

Hutten, Ulrich von 1488-1523 .... **LC 16**
 See also DLB 179

Huxley, Aldous (Leonard)
 1894-1963 .... **CLC 1, 3, 4, 5, 8, 11, 18, 35, 79; DA; DAB; DAC; DAM MST, NOV; SSC 39; WLC**
 See also AAYA 11; CA 85-88; CANR 44; CDBLB 1914-1945; DA3; DLB 36, 100, 162, 195; MTCW 1, 2; SATA 63

Huxley, T(homas) H(enry)
 1825-1895 .... **NCLC 67**
 See also DLB 57

Huysmans, Joris-Karl 1848-1907 ... **TCLC 7, 69**
 See also CA 104; 165; DLB 123

Hwang, David Henry 1957- .. **CLC 55; DAM DRAM; DC 4**
 See also CA 127; 132; CANR 76; DA3; DLB 212; INT 132; MTCW 2

Hyde, Anthony 1946- .... **CLC 42**
 See also CA 136

Hyde, Margaret O(ldroyd) 1917- ..... **CLC 21**
 See also CA 1-4R; CANR 1, 36; CLR 23; JRDA; MAICYA; SAAS 8; SATA 1, 42, 76

Hynes, James 1956(?)- .... **CLC 65**
 See also CA 164

Hypatia c. 370-415 .... **CMLC 35**

Ian, Janis 1951- .... **CLC 21**
 See also CA 105

Ibanez, Vicente Blasco
 See Blasco Ibanez, Vicente

Ibarbourou, Juana de 1895-1979
 See also HLCS 2; HW 1

Ibarguengoitia, Jorge 1928-1983 ...... **CLC 37**
 See also CA 124; 113; HW 1

Ibsen, Henrik (Johan) 1828-1906 ... **TCLC 2, 8, 16, 37, 52; DA; DAB; DAC; DAM DRAM, MST; DC 2; WLC**
 See also CA 104; 141; DA3

Ibuse, Masuji 1898-1993 .... **CLC 22**
 See also CA 127; 141; DLB 180

Ichikawa, Kon 1915- .... **CLC 20**
 See also CA 121

Idle, Eric 1943- .... **CLC 21**
 See also Monty Python
 See also CA 116; CANR 35, 91

Ignatow, David 1914-1997 .. **CLC 4, 7, 14, 40**
 See also CA 9-12R; 162; CAAS 3; CANR 31, 57; DLB 5

Ignotus
 See Strachey, (Giles) Lytton

Ihimaera, Witi 1944- .... **CLC 46**
 See also CA 77-80

Ilf, Ilya TCLC 21
 See also Fainzilberg, Ilya Arnoldovich

Illyes, Gyula 1902-1983 .... **PC 16**
 See also CA 114; 109

Immermann, Karl (Lebrecht)
 1796-1840 .... **NCLC 4, 49**
 See also DLB 133

Ince, Thomas H. 1882-1924 .... **TCLC 89**

Inchbald, Elizabeth 1753-1821 ...... **NCLC 62**
 See also DLB 39, 89

Inclan, Ramon (Maria) del Valle
 See Valle-Inclan, Ramon (Maria) del

Infante, G(uillermo) Cabrera
 See Cabrera Infante, G(uillermo)

Ingalls, Rachel (Holmes) 1940- .... **CLC 42**
 See also CA 123; 127

Ingamells, Reginald Charles
 See Ingamells, Rex

Ingamells, Rex 1913-1955 .... **TCLC 35**
 See also CA 167

Inge, William (Motter) 1913-1973 ..... **CLC 1, 8, 19; DAM DRAM**
 See also CA 9-12R; CDALB 1941-1968; DA3; DLB 7; MTCW 1, 2

Ingelow, Jean 1820-1897 .... **NCLC 39**
 See also DLB 35, 163; SATA 33

Ingram, Willis J.
 See Harris, Mark

Innaurato, Albert (F.) 1948(?)- ... **CLC 21, 60**
 See also CA 115; 122; CANR 78; INT 122

Innes, Michael
 See Stewart, J(ohn) I(nnes) M(ackintosh)

Innis, Harold Adams 1894-1952 .... **TCLC 77**
 See also CA 181; DLB 88

Ionesco, Eugene 1909-1994 ... **CLC 1, 4, 6, 9, 11, 15, 41, 86; DA; DAB; DAC; DAM DRAM, MST; DC 12; WLC**
 See also CA 9-12R; 144; CANR 55; DA3; MTCW 1, 2; SATA 7; SATA-Obit 79

Iqbal, Muhammad 1873-1938 .... **TCLC 28**

Ireland, Patrick
 See O'Doherty, Brian

Iron, Ralph
 See Schreiner, Olive (Emilie Albertina)

Irving, John (Winslow) 1942- ... **CLC 13, 23, 38, 112; DAM NOV, POP**
 See also AAYA 8; BEST 89:3; CA 25-28R; CANR 28, 73; DA3; DLB 6; DLBY 82; MTCW 1, 2

Irving, Washington 1783-1859 . **NCLC 2, 19; DA; DAB; DAC; DAM MST; SSC 2, 37; WLC**
 See also CDALB 1640-1865; DA3; DLB 3, 11, 30, 59, 73, 74, 186; YABC 2

Irwin, P. K.
 See Page, P(atricia) K(athleen)

Isaacs, Jorge Ricardo 1837-1895 ... **NCLC 70**

Isaacs, Susan 1943- .... **CLC 32; DAM POP**
 See also BEST 89:1; CA 89-92; CANR 20, 41, 65; DA3; INT CANR-20; MTCW 1, 2

Isherwood, Christopher (William Bradshaw)
 1904-1986 .. **CLC 1, 9, 11, 14, 44; DAM DRAM, NOV**
 See also CA 13-16R; 117; CANR 35; DA3; DLB 15, 195; DLBY 86; MTCW 1, 2

Ishiguro, Kazuo 1954- . **CLC 27, 56, 59, 110; DAM NOV**
 See also BEST 90:2; CA 120; CANR 49; DA3; DLB 194; MTCW 1, 2

Ishikawa, Hakuhin
 See Ishikawa, Takuboku

Ishikawa, Takuboku
 1886(?)-1912 ... **TCLC 15; DAM POET; PC 10**
 See also CA 113; 153

Iskander, Fazil 1929- .... **CLC 47**
 See also CA 102

Isler, Alan (David) 1934- .... **CLC 91**
 See also CA 156

Ivan IV 1530-1584 .... **LC 17**

Ivanov, Vyacheslav Ivanovich
 1866-1949 .... **TCLC 33**
 See also CA 122

Ivask, Ivar Vidrik 1927-1992 .... **CLC 14**
 See also CA 37-40R; 139; CANR 24

Ives, Morgan
 See Bradley, Marion Zimmer

Izumi Shikibu c. 973-c. 1034 .... **CMLC 33**

J. R. S.
 See Gogarty, Oliver St. John

Jabran, Kahlil
 See Gibran, Kahlil

Jabran, Khalil
 See Gibran, Kahlil

Jackson, Daniel
 See Wingrove, David (John)

Jackson, Jesse 1908-1983 .... **CLC 12**
 See also BW 1; CA 25-28R; 109; CANR 27; CLR 28; MAICYA; SATA 2, 29; SATA-Obit 48

Jackson, Laura (Riding) 1901-1991
 See Riding, Laura
 See also CA 65-68; 135; CANR 28, 89; DLB 48

Jackson, Sam
 See Trumbo, Dalton

Jackson, Sara
 See Wingrove, David (John)

Jackson, Shirley 1919-1965 . **CLC 11, 60, 87; DA; DAC; DAM MST; SSC 9, 39; WLC**
 See also AAYA 9; CA 1-4R; 25-28R; CANR 4, 52; CDALB 1941-1968; DA3; DLB 6; MTCW 2; SATA 2

Jacob, (Cyprien-)Max 1876-1944 .... **TCLC 6**
 See also CA 104

Jacobs, Harriet A(nn)
 1813(?)-1897 .... **NCLC 67**

Jacobs, Jim 1942- .... **CLC 12**
 See also CA 97-100; INT 97-100

Jacobs, W(illiam) W(ymark)
 1863-1943 .... **TCLC 22**
 See also CA 121; 167; DLB 135

Jacobsen, Jens Peter 1847-1885 .... **NCLC 34**

Jacobsen, Josephine 1908- .... **CLC 48, 102**
 See also CA 33-36R; CAAS 18; CANR 23, 48

Jacobson, Dan 1929- .... **CLC 4, 14**
 See also CA 1-4R; CANR 2, 25, 66; DLB 14, 207; MTCW 1

Jacqueline
 See Carpentier (y Valmont), Alejo

Jagger, Mick 1944- .... CLC 17

Jahiz, al- c. 780-c. 869 .... CMLC 25

Jakes, John (William) 1932- . CLC 29; DAM
NOV, POP
See also AAYA 32; BEST 89:4; CA 57-60;
CANR 10, 43, 66; DA3; DLBY 83; INT
CANR-10; MTCW 1, 2; SATA 62

James, Andrew
See Kirkup, James

James, C(yril) L(ionel) R(obert)
1901-1989 .... CLC 33; BLCS
See also BW 2; CA 117; 125; 128; CANR
62; DLB 125; MTCW 1

James, Daniel (Lewis) 1911-1988
See Santiago, Danny
See also CA 174; 125

James, Dynely
See Mayne, William (James Carter)

James, Henry Sr. 1811-1882 .... NCLC 53

James, Henry 1843-1916 ..... TCLC 2, 11, 24,
40, 47, 64; DA; DAB; DAC; DAM
MST, NOV; SSC 8, 32; WLC
See also CA 104; 132; CDALB 1865-1917;
DA3; DLB 12, 71, 74, 189; DLBD 13;
MTCW 1, 2

James, M. R.
See James, Montague (Rhodes)
See also DLB 156

James, Montague (Rhodes)
1862-1936 .... TCLC 6; SSC 16
See also CA 104; DLB 201

James, P. D. 1920- .... CLC 18, 46, 122
See also White, Phyllis Dorothy James
See also BEST 90:2; CDBLB 1960 to
Present; DLB 87; DLBD 17

James, Philip
See Moorcock, Michael (John)

James, William 1842-1910 .... TCLC 15, 32
See also CA 109

James I 1394-1437 .... LC 20

Jameson, Anna 1794-1860 .... NCLC 43
See also DLB 99, 166

Jami, Nur al-Din 'Abd al-Rahman
1414-1492 .... LC 9

Jammes, Francis 1868-1938 .... TCLC 75

Jandl, Ernst 1925- .... CLC 34

Janowitz, Tama 1957- .. CLC 43; DAM POP
See also CA 106; CANR 52, 89

Japrisot, Sebastien 1931- .... CLC 90

Jarrell, Randall 1914-1965 .... CLC 1, 2, 6, 9,
13, 49; DAM POET
See also CA 5-8R; 25-28R; CABS 2; CANR
6, 34; CDALB 1941-1968; CLR 6; DLB
48, 52; MAICYA; MTCW 1, 2; SATA 7

Jarry, Alfred 1873-1907 . TCLC 2, 14; DAM
DRAM; SSC 20
See also CA 104; 153; DA3; DLB 192

Jawien, Andrzej
See John Paul II, Pope

Jaynes, Roderick
See Coen, Ethan

Jeake, Samuel, Jr.
See Aiken, Conrad (Potter)

Jean Paul 1763-1825 .... NCLC 7

Jefferies, (John) Richard
1848-1887 .... NCLC 47
See also DLB 98, 141; SATA 16

Jeffers, (John) Robinson 1887-1962 .. CLC 2,
3, 11, 15, 54; DA; DAC; DAM MST,
POET; PC 17; WLC
See also CA 85-88; CANR 35; CDALB
1917-1929; DLB 45, 212; MTCW 1, 2

Jefferson, Janet
See Mencken, H(enry) L(ouis)

Jefferson, Thomas 1743-1826 .... NCLC 11
See also CDALB 1640-1865; DA3; DLB
31

Jeffrey, Francis 1773-1850 .... NCLC 33
See also DLB 107

Jelakowitch, Ivan
See Heijermans, Herman

Jellicoe, (Patricia) Ann 1927- .... CLC 27
See also CA 85-88; DLB 13

Jemyma
See Holley, Marietta

Jen, Gish CLC 70
See also Jen, Lillian

Jen, Lillian 1956(?)-
See Jen, Gish
See also CA 135; CANR 89

Jenkins, (John) Robin 1912- .... CLC 52
See also CA 1-4R; CANR 1; DLB 14

Jennings, Elizabeth (Joan) 1926- ...... CLC 5,
14, 131
See also CA 61-64; CAAS 5; CANR 8, 39,
66; DLB 27; MTCW 1; SATA 66

Jennings, Waylon 1937- .... CLC 21

Jensen, Johannes V. 1873-1950 ...... TCLC 41
See also CA 170

Jensen, Laura (Linnea) 1948- .... CLC 37
See also CA 103

Jerome, Jerome K(lapka)
1859-1927 .... TCLC 23
See also CA 119; 177; DLB 10, 34, 135

Jerrold, Douglas William
1803-1857 .... NCLC 2
See also DLB 158, 159

Jewett, (Theodora) Sarah Orne
1849-1909 .... TCLC 1, 22; SSC 6
See also CA 108; 127; CANR 71; DLB 12,
74, 221; SATA 15

Jewsbury, Geraldine (Endsor)
1812-1880 .... NCLC 22
See also DLB 21

Jhabvala, Ruth Prawer 1927- . CLC 4, 8, 29,
94; DAB; DAM NOV
See also CA 1-4R; CANR 2, 29, 51, 74, 91;
DLB 139, 194; INT CANR-29; MTCW 1,
2

Jibran, Kahlil
See Gibran, Kahlil

Jibran, Khalil
See Gibran, Kahlil

Jiles, Paulette 1943- .... CLC 13, 58
See also CA 101; CANR 70

Jimenez (Mantecon), Juan Ramon
1881-1958 .... TCLC 4; DAM MULT,
POET; HLC 1; PC 7
See also CA 104; 131; CANR 74; DLB 134;
HW 1; MTCW 1, 2

Jimenez, Ramon
See Jimenez (Mantecon), Juan Ramon

Jimenez Mantecon, Juan
See Jimenez (Mantecon), Juan Ramon

Jin, Ha
See Jin, Xuefei

Jin, Xuefei 1956- .... CLC 109
See also CA 152; CANR 91

Joel, Billy CLC 26
See also Joel, William Martin

Joel, William Martin 1949-
See Joel, Billy
See also CA 108

John, Saint 7th cent. - .... CMLC 27

John of the Cross, St. 1542-1591 .... LC 18

John Paul II, Pope 1920- .... CLC 128
See also CA 106; 133

Johnson, B(ryan) S(tanley William)
1933-1973 .... CLC 6, 9
See also CA 9-12R; 53-56; CANR 9; DLB
14, 40

Johnson, Benj. F. of Boo
See Riley, James Whitcomb

Johnson, Benjamin F. of Boo
See Riley, James Whitcomb

Johnson, Charles (Richard) 1948- .... CLC 7,
51, 65; BLC 2; DAM MULT
See also BW 2, 3; CA 116; CAAS 18;
CANR 42, 66, 82; DLB 33; MTCW 2

Johnson, Denis 1949- .... CLC 52
See also CA 117; 121; CANR 71; DLB 120

Johnson, Diane 1934- .... CLC 5, 13, 48
See also CA 41-44R; CANR 17, 40, 62;
DLBY 80; INT CANR-17; MTCW 1

Johnson, Eyvind (Olof Verner)
1900-1976 .... CLC 14
See also CA 73-76; 69-72; CANR 34

Johnson, J. R.
See James, C(yril) L(ionel) R(obert)

Johnson, James Weldon
1871-1938 .. TCLC 3, 19; BLC 2; DAM
MULT, POET; PC 24
See also BW 1, 3; CA 104; 125; CANR 82;
CDALB 1917-1929; CLR 32; DA3; DLB
51; MTCW 1, 2; SATA 31

Johnson, Joyce 1935- .... CLC 58
See also CA 125; 129

Johnson, Judith (Emlyn) 1936- .... CLC 7, 15
See also Sherwin, Judith Johnson
See also CA 25-28R; 153; CANR 34

Johnson, Lionel (Pigot)
1867-1902 .... TCLC 19
See also CA 117; DLB 19

Johnson, Marguerite (Annie)
See Angelou, Maya

Johnson, Mel
See Malzberg, Barry N(athaniel)

Johnson, Pamela Hansford
1912-1981 .... CLC 1, 7, 27
See also CA 1-4R; 104; CANR 2, 28; DLB
15; MTCW 1, 2

Johnson, Robert 1911(?)-1938 .... TCLC 69
See also BW 3; CA 174

Johnson, Samuel 1709-1784 . LC 15, 52; DA;
DAB; DAC; DAM MST; WLC
See also CDBLB 1660-1789; DLB 39, 95,
104, 142

Johnson, Uwe 1934-1984 .. CLC 5, 10, 15, 40
See also CA 1-4R; 112; CANR 1, 39; DLB
75; MTCW 1

Johnston, George (Benson) 1913- .... CLC 51
See also CA 1-4R; CANR 5, 20; DLB 88

Johnston, Jennifer 1930- .... CLC 7
See also CA 85-88; DLB 14

Joinville, Jean de 1224(?)-1317 ..... CMLC 38

Jolley, (Monica) Elizabeth 1923- ..... CLC 46;
SSC 19
See also CA 127; CAAS 13; CANR 59

Jones, Arthur Llewellyn 1863-1947
See Machen, Arthur
See also CA 104; 179

Jones, D(ouglas) G(ordon) 1929- ..... CLC 10
See also CA 29-32R; CANR 13, 90; DLB 53

Jones, David (Michael) 1895-1974 .... **CLC 2, 4, 7, 13, 42**
See also CA 9-12R; 53-56; CANR 28; CD-BLB 1945-1960; DLB 20, 100; MTCW 1

Jones, David Robert 1947-
See Bowie, David
See also CA 103

Jones, Diana Wynne 1934- .... **CLC 26**
See also AAYA 12; CA 49-52; CANR 4, 26, 56; CLR 23; DLB 161; JRDA; MAICYA; SAAS 7; SATA 9, 70, 108

Jones, Edward P. 1950- .... **CLC 76**
See also BW 2, 3; CA 142; CANR 79

Jones, Gayl 1949- ..... **CLC 6, 9, 131; BLC 2; DAM MULT**
See also BW 2, 3; CA 77-80; CANR 27, 66; DA3; DLB 33; MTCW 1, 2

Jones, James 1921-1977 ...... **CLC 1, 3, 10, 39**
See also AITN 1, 2; CA 1-4R; 69-72; CANR 6; DLB 2, 143; DLBD 17; DLBY 98; MTCW 1

Jones, John J.
See Lovecraft, H(oward) P(hillips)

Jones, LeRoi **CLC 1, 2, 3, 5, 10, 14**
See also Baraka, Amiri
See also MTCW 2

Jones, Louis B. 1953- .... **CLC 65**
See also CA 141; CANR 73

Jones, Madison (Percy, Jr.) 1925- ...... **CLC 4**
See also CA 13-16R; CAAS 11; CANR 7, 54, 83; DLB 152

Jones, Mervyn 1922- .... **CLC 10, 52**
See also CA 45-48; CAAS 5; CANR 1, 91; MTCW 1

Jones, Mick 1956(?)- .... **CLC 30**

Jones, Nettie (Pearl) 1941- .... **CLC 34**
See also BW 2; CA 137; CAAS 20; CANR 88

Jones, Preston 1936-1979 .... **CLC 10**
See also CA 73-76; 89-92; DLB 7

Jones, Robert F(rancis) 1934- .... **CLC 7**
See also CA 49-52; CANR 2, 61

Jones, Rod 1953- .... **CLC 50**
See also CA 128

Jones, Terence Graham Parry
1942- .... **CLC 21**
See also Jones, Terry; Monty Python
See also CA 112; 116; CANR 35; INT 116

Jones, Terry
See Jones, Terence Graham Parry
See also SATA 67; SATA-Brief 51

Jones, Thom (Douglas) 1945(?)- .... **CLC 81**
See also CA 157; CANR 88

Jong, Erica 1942- .... **CLC 4, 6, 8, 18, 83; DAM NOV, POP**
See also AITN 1; BEST 90:2; CA 73-76; CANR 26, 52, 75; DA3; DLB 2, 5, 28, 152; INT CANR-26; MTCW 1, 2

Jonson, Ben(jamin) 1572(?)-1637 .. **LC 6, 33; DA; DAB; DAC; DAM DRAM, MST, POET; DC 4; PC 17; WLC**
See also CDBLB Before 1660; DLB 62, 121

Jordan, June 1936- .... **CLC 5, 11, 23, 114; BLCS; DAM MULT, POET**
See also AAYA 2; BW 2, 3; CA 33-36R; CANR 25, 70; CLR 10; DLB 38; MAICYA; MTCW 1; SATA 4

Jordan, Neil (Patrick) 1950- .... **CLC 110**
See also CA 124; 130; CANR 54; INT 130

Jordan, Pat(rick M.) 1941- .... **CLC 37**
See also CA 33-36R

Jorgensen, Ivar
See Ellison, Harlan (Jay)

Jorgenson, Ivar
See Silverberg, Robert

Josephus, Flavius c. 37-100 .... **CMLC 13**

Josiah Allen's Wife
See Holley, Marietta

Josipovici, Gabriel (David) 1940- ...... **CLC 6, 43**
See also CA 37-40R; CAAS 8; CANR 47, 84; DLB 14

Joubert, Joseph 1754-1824 .... **NCLC 9**

Jouve, Pierre Jean 1887-1976 .... **CLC 47**
See also CA 65-68

Jovine, Francesco 1902-1950 .... **TCLC 79**

Joyce, James (Augustine Aloysius)
1882-1941 .. **TCLC 3, 8, 16, 35, 52; DA; DAB; DAC; DAM MST, NOV, POET; PC 22; SSC 3, 26; WLC**
See also CA 104; 126; CDBLB 1914-1945; DA3; DLB 10, 19, 36, 162; MTCW 1, 2

Jozsef, Attila 1905-1937 .... **TCLC 22**
See also CA 116

Juana Ines de la Cruz 1651(?)-1695 .... **LC 5; HLCS 1; PC 24**

Judd, Cyril
See Kornbluth, C(yril) M.; Pohl, Frederik

Juenger, Ernst 1895-1998 .... **CLC 125**
See also CA 101; 167; CANR 21, 47; DLB 56

Julian of Norwich 1342(?)-1416(?) . **LC 6, 52**
See also DLB 146

Junger, Ernst
See Juenger, Ernst

Junger, Sebastian 1962- .... **CLC 109**
See also AAYA 28; CA 165

Juniper, Alex
See Hospital, Janette Turner

Junius
See Luxemburg, Rosa

Just, Ward (Swift) 1935- .... **CLC 4, 27**
See also CA 25-28R; CANR 32, 87; INT CANR-32

Justice, Donald (Rodney) 1925- .. **CLC 6, 19, 102; DAM POET**
See also CA 5-8R; CANR 26, 54, 74; DLBY 83; INT CANR-26; MTCW 2

Juvenal c. 60-c. 13 .... **CMLC 8**
See also Juvenalis, Decimus Junius
See also DLB 211

Juvenalis, Decimus Junius 55(?)-c. 127(?)
See Juvenal

Juvenis
See Bourne, Randolph S(illiman)

Kacew, Romain 1914-1980
See Gary, Romain
See also CA 108; 102

Kadare, Ismail 1936- .... **CLC 52**
See also CA 161

Kadohata, Cynthia **CLC 59, 122**
See also CA 140

Kafka, Franz 1883-1924 . **TCLC 2, 6, 13, 29, 47, 53; DA; DAB; DAC; DAM MST, NOV; SSC 5, 29, 35; WLC**
See also AAYA 31; CA 105; 126; DA3; DLB 81; MTCW 1, 2

Kahanovitsch, Pinkhes
See Der Nister

Kahn, Roger 1927- .... **CLC 30**
See also CA 25-28R; CANR 44, 69; DLB 171; SATA 37

Kain, Saul
See Sassoon, Siegfried (Lorraine)

Kaiser, Georg 1878-1945 .... **TCLC 9**
See also CA 106; DLB 124

Kaletski, Alexander 1946- .... **CLC 39**
See also CA 118; 143

Kalidasa fl. c. 400- .... **CMLC 9; PC 22**

Kallman, Chester (Simon)
1921-1975 .... **CLC 2**
See also CA 45-48; 53-56; CANR 3

Kaminsky, Melvin 1926-
See Brooks, Mel
See also CA 65-68; CANR 16

Kaminsky, Stuart M(elvin) 1934- ..... **CLC 59**
See also CA 73-76; CANR 29, 53, 89

Kandinsky, Wassily 1866-1944 .... **TCLC 92**
See also CA 118; 155

Kane, Francis
See Robbins, Harold

Kane, Paul
See Simon, Paul (Frederick)

Kanin, Garson 1912-1999 .... **CLC 22**
See also AITN 1; CA 5-8R; 177; CANR 7, 78; DLB 7

Kaniuk, Yoram 1930- .... **CLC 19**
See also CA 134

Kant, Immanuel 1724-1804 ..... **NCLC 27, 67**
See also DLB 94

Kantor, MacKinlay 1904-1977 .... **CLC 7**
See also CA 61-64; 73-76; CANR 60, 63; DLB 9, 102; MTCW 2

Kaplan, David Michael 1946- .... **CLC 50**

Kaplan, James 1951- .... **CLC 59**
See also CA 135

Karageorge, Michael
See Anderson, Poul (William)

Karamzin, Nikolai Mikhailovich
1766-1826 .... **NCLC 3**
See also DLB 150

Karapanou, Margarita 1946- .... **CLC 13**
See also CA 101

Karinthy, Frigyes 1887-1938 .... **TCLC 47**
See also CA 170

Karl, Frederick R(obert) 1927- .... **CLC 34**
See also CA 5-8R; CANR 3, 44

Kastel, Warren
See Silverberg, Robert

Kataev, Evgeny Petrovich 1903-1942
See Petrov, Evgeny
See also CA 120

Kataphusin
See Ruskin, John

Katz, Steve 1935- .... **CLC 47**
See also CA 25-28R; CAAS 14, 64; CANR 12; DLBY 83

Kauffman, Janet 1945- .... **CLC 42**
See also CA 117; CANR 43, 84; DLBY 86

Kaufman, Bob (Garnell) 1925-1986 . **CLC 49**
See also BW 1; CA 41-44R; 118; CANR 22; DLB 16, 41

Kaufman, George S. 1889-1961 ...... **CLC 38; DAM DRAM**
See also CA 108; 93-96; DLB 7; INT 108; MTCW 2

Kaufman, Sue **CLC 3, 8**
See also Barondess, Sue K(aufman)

Kavafis, Konstantinos Petrou 1863-1933
See Cavafy, C(onstantine) P(eter)
See also CA 104

Kavan, Anna 1901-1968 .... **CLC 5, 13, 82**
See also CA 5-8R; CANR 6, 57; MTCW 1

Kavanagh, Dan
See Barnes, Julian (Patrick)

Kosinski, Jerzy (Nikodem)
1933-1991 .... CLC 1, 2, 3, 6, 10, 15, 53, 70; DAM NOV
See also CA 17-20R; 134; CANR 9, 46; DA3; DLB 2; DLBY 82; MTCW 1, 2

Kostelanetz, Richard (Cory) 1940- .. CLC 28
See also CA 13-16R; CAAS 8; CANR 38, 77

Kostrowitzki, Wilhelm Apollinaris de
1880-1918
See Apollinaire, Guillaume
See also CA 104

Kotlowitz, Robert 1924- .... CLC 4
See also CA 33-36R; CANR 36

Kotzebue, August (Friedrich Ferdinand) von
1761-1819 .... NCLC 25
See also DLB 94

Kotzwinkle, William 1938- ..... CLC 5, 14, 35
See also CA 45-48; CANR 3, 44, 84; CLR 6; DLB 173; MAICYA; SATA 24, 70

Kowna, Stancy
See Szymborska, Wislawa

Kozol, Jonathan 1936- .... CLC 17
See also CA 61-64; CANR 16, 45

Kozoll, Michael 1940(?)- .... CLC 35

Kramer, Kathryn 19(?)- .... CLC 34

Kramer, Larry 1935- .. CLC 42; DAM POP; DC 8
See also CA 124; 126; CANR 60

Krasicki, Ignacy 1735-1801 .... NCLC 8

Krasinski, Zygmunt 1812-1859 .... NCLC 4

Kraus, Karl 1874-1936 .... TCLC 5
See also CA 104; DLB 118

Kreve (Mickevicius), Vincas
1882-1954 .... TCLC 27
See also CA 170; DLB 220

Kristeva, Julia 1941- .... CLC 77
See also CA 154

Kristofferson, Kris 1936- .... CLC 26
See also CA 104

Krizanc, John 1956- .... CLC 57

Krleza, Miroslav 1893-1981 .... CLC 8, 114
See also CA 97-100; 105; CANR 50; DLB 147

Kroetsch, Robert 1927- . CLC 5, 23, 57, 132; DAC; DAM POET
See also CA 17-20R; CANR 8, 38; DLB 53; MTCW 1

Kroetz, Franz
See Kroetz, Franz Xaver

Kroetz, Franz Xaver 1946- .... CLC 41
See also CA 130

Kroker, Arthur (W.) 1945- .... CLC 77
See also CA 161

Kropotkin, Peter (Aleksieevich)
1842-1921 .... TCLC 36
See also CA 119

Krotkov, Yuri 1917- .... CLC 19
See also CA 102

Krumb
See Crumb, R(obert)

Krumgold, Joseph (Quincy)
1908-1980 .... CLC 12
See also CA 9-12R; 101; CANR 7; MAICYA; SATA 1, 48; SATA-Obit 23

Krumwitz
See Crumb, R(obert)

Krutch, Joseph Wood 1893-1970 ..... CLC 24
See also CA 1-4R; 25-28R; CANR 4; DLB 63, 206

Krutzch, Gus
See Eliot, T(homas) S(tearns)

Krylov, Ivan Andreevich
1768(?)-1844 .... NCLC 1
See also DLB 150

Kubin, Alfred (Leopold Isidor)
1877-1959 .... TCLC 23
See also CA 112; 149; DLB 81

Kubrick, Stanley 1928-1999 .... CLC 16
See also AAYA 30; CA 81-84; 177; CANR 33; DLB 26

Kueng, Hans 1928-
See Kung, Hans
See also CA 53-56; CANR 66; MTCW 1, 2

Kumin, Maxine (Winokur) 1925- ..... CLC 5, 13, 28; DAM POET; PC 15
See also AITN 2; CA 1-4R; CAAS 8; CANR 1, 21, 69; DA3; DLB 5; MTCW 1, 2; SATA 12

Kundera, Milan 1929- . CLC 4, 9, 19, 32, 68, 115; DAM NOV; SSC 24
See also AAYA 2; CA 85-88; CANR 19, 52, 74; DA3; MTCW 1, 2

Kunene, Mazisi (Raymond) 1930- ... CLC 85
See also BW 1, 3; CA 125; CANR 81; DLB 117

Kung, Hans 1928- .... CLC 130
See also Kueng, Hans

Kunitz, Stanley (Jasspon) 1905- .. CLC 6, 11, 14; PC 19
See also CA 41-44R; CANR 26, 57; DA3; DLB 48; INT CANR-26; MTCW 1, 2

Kunze, Reiner 1933- .... CLC 10
See also CA 93-96; DLB 75

Kuprin, Aleksander Ivanovich
1870-1938 .... TCLC 5
See also CA 104; 182

Kureishi, Hanif 1954(?)- .... CLC 64
See also CA 139; DLB 194

Kurosawa, Akira 1910-1998 .... CLC 16, 119; DAM MULT
See also AAYA 11; CA 101; 170; CANR 46

Kushner, Tony 1957(?)- .... CLC 81; DAM DRAM; DC 10
See also CA 144; CANR 74; DA3; MTCW 2

Kuttner, Henry 1915-1958 .... TCLC 10
See also CA 107; 157; DLB 8

Kuzma, Greg 1944- .... CLC 7
See also CA 33-36R; CANR 70

Kuzmin, Mikhail 1872(?)-1936 ...... TCLC 40
See also CA 170

Kyd, Thomas 1558-1594 .... LC 22; DAM DRAM; DC 3
See also DLB 62

Kyprianos, Iossif
See Samarakis, Antonis

La Bruyere, Jean de 1645-1696 .... LC 17

Lacan, Jacques (Marie Emile)
1901-1981 .... CLC 75
See also CA 121; 104

Laclos, Pierre Ambroise Francois Choderlos
de 1741-1803 .... NCLC 4, 87

Lacolere, Francois
See Aragon, Louis

La Colere, Francois
See Aragon, Louis

La Deshabilleuse
See Simenon, Georges (Jacques Christian)

Lady Gregory
See Gregory, Isabella Augusta (Persse)

Lady of Quality, A
See Bagnold, Enid

La Fayette, Marie (Madelaine Pioche de la
Vergne Comtes 1634-1693 .... LC 2

Lafayette, Rene
See Hubbard, L(afayette) Ron(ald)

La Fontaine, Jean de 1621-1695 .... LC 50
See also MAICYA; SATA 18

Laforgue, Jules 1860-1887 . NCLC 5, 53; PC 14; SSC 20

Lagerkvist, Paer (Fabian)
1891-1974 ...... CLC 7, 10, 13, 54; DAM DRAM, NOV
See also Lagerkvist, Par
See also CA 85-88; 49-52; DA3; MTCW 1, 2

Lagerkvist, Par SSC 12
See also Lagerkvist, Paer (Fabian)
See also MTCW 2

Lagerloef, Selma (Ottiliana Lovisa)
1858-1940 .... TCLC 4, 36
See also Lagerlof, Selma (Ottiliana Lovisa)
See also CA 108; MTCW 2; SATA 15

Lagerlof, Selma (Ottiliana Lovisa)
See Lagerloef, Selma (Ottiliana Lovisa)
See also CLR 7; SATA 15

La Guma, (Justin) Alex(ander)
1925-1985 .... CLC 19; BLCS; DAM NOV
See also BW 1, 3; CA 49-52; 118; CANR 25, 81; DLB 117; MTCW 1, 2

Laidlaw, A. K.
See Grieve, C(hristopher) M(urray)

Lainez, Manuel Mujica
See Mujica Lainez, Manuel
See also HW 1

Laing, R(onald) D(avid) 1927-1989 . CLC 95
See also CA 107; 129; CANR 34; MTCW 1

Lamartine, Alphonse (Marie Louis Prat) de
1790-1869 . NCLC 11; DAM POET; PC 16

Lamb, Charles 1775-1834 ..... NCLC 10; DA; DAB; DAC; DAM MST; WLC
See also CDBLB 1789-1832; DLB 93, 107, 163; SATA 17

Lamb, Lady Caroline 1785-1828 ... NCLC 38
See also DLB 116

Lamming, George (William) 1927- ... CLC 2, 4, 66; BLC 2; DAM MULT
See also BW 2, 3; CA 85-88; CANR 26, 76; DLB 125; MTCW 1, 2

L'Amour, Louis (Dearborn)
1908-1988 ...... CLC 25, 55; DAM NOV, POP
See also AAYA 16; AITN 2; BEST 89:2; CA 1-4R; 125; CANR 3, 25, 40; DA3; DLB 206; DLBY 80; MTCW 1, 2

Lampedusa, Giuseppe (Tomasi) di
1896-1957 .... TCLC 13
See also Tomasi di Lampedusa, Giuseppe
See also CA 164; DLB 177; MTCW 2

Lampman, Archibald 1861-1899 ... NCLC 25
See also DLB 92

Lancaster, Bruce 1896-1963 .... CLC 36
See also CA 9-10; CANR 70; CAP 1; SATA 9

Lanchester, John CLC 99

Landau, Mark Alexandrovich
See Aldanov, Mark (Alexandrovich)

Landau-Aldanov, Mark Alexandrovich
See Aldanov, Mark (Alexandrovich)

Landis, Jerry
See Simon, Paul (Frederick)

Landis, John 1950- .... **CLC 26**
   See also CA 112; 122

Landolfi, Tommaso 1908-1979 .... **CLC 11, 49**
   See also CA 127; 117; DLB 177

Landon, Letitia Elizabeth
   1802-1838 .... **NCLC 15**
   See also DLB 96

Landor, Walter Savage
   1775-1864 .... **NCLC 14**
   See also DLB 93, 107

Landwirth, Heinz 1927-
   See Lind, Jakov
   See also CA 9-12R; CANR 7

Lane, Patrick 1939- ... **CLC 25; DAM POET**
   See also CA 97-100; CANR 54; DLB 53;
   INT 97-100

Lang, Andrew 1844-1912 .... **TCLC 16**
   See also CA 114; 137; CANR 85; DLB 98,
   141, 184; MAICYA; SATA 16

Lang, Fritz 1890-1976 .... **CLC 20, 103**
   See also CA 77-80; 69-72; CANR 30

Lange, John
   See Crichton, (John) Michael

Langer, Elinor 1939- .... **CLC 34**
   See also CA 121

Langland, William 1330(?)-1400(?) ... **LC 19;
   DA; DAB; DAC; DAM MST, POET**
   See also DLB 146

Langstaff, Launcelot
   See Irving, Washington

Lanier, Sidney 1842-1881 ..... **NCLC 6; DAM
   POET**
   See also DLB 64; DLBD 13; MAICYA;
   SATA 18

Lanyer, Aemilia 1569-1645 .... **LC 10, 30**
   See also DLB 121

Lao-Tzu
   See Lao Tzu

Lao Tzu fl. 6th cent. B.C.- .... **CMLC 7**

Lapine, James (Elliot) 1949- .... **CLC 39**
   See also CA 123; 130; CANR 54; INT 130

Larbaud, Valery (Nicolas)
   1881-1957 .... **TCLC 9**
   See also CA 106; 152

Lardner, Ring
   See Lardner, Ring(gold) W(ilmer)

Lardner, Ring W., Jr.
   See Lardner, Ring(gold) W(ilmer)

Lardner, Ring(gold) W(ilmer)
   1885-1933 .... **TCLC 2, 14; SSC 32**
   See also CA 104; 131; CDALB 1917-1929;
   DLB 11, 25, 86; DLBD 16; MTCW 1, 2

Laredo, Betty
   See Codrescu, Andrei

Larkin, Maia
   See Wojciechowska, Maia (Teresa)

Larkin, Philip (Arthur) 1922-1985 ... **CLC 3,
   5, 8, 9, 13, 18, 33, 39, 64; DAB; DAM
   MST, POET; PC 21**
   See also CA 5-8R; 117; CANR 24, 62; CD-
   BLB 1960 to Present; DA3; DLB 27;
   MTCW 1, 2

Larra (y Sanchez de Castro), Mariano Jose
   de 1809-1837 .... **NCLC 17**

Larsen, Eric 1941- .... **CLC 55**
   See also CA 132

Larsen, Nella 1891-1964 .... **CLC 37; BLC 2;
   DAM MULT**
   See also BW 1; CA 125; CANR 83; DLB
   51

Larson, Charles R(aymond) 1938- ... **CLC 31**
   See also CA 53-56; CANR 4

Larson, Jonathan 1961-1996 .... **CLC 99**
   See also AAYA 28; CA 156

Las Casas, Bartolome de 1474-1566 ... **LC 31**

Lasch, Christopher 1932-1994 .... **CLC 102**
   See also CA 73-76; 144; CANR 25; MTCW
   1, 2

Lasker-Schueler, Else 1869-1945 ... **TCLC 57**
   See also CA 183; DLB 66, 124

Laski, Harold 1893-1950 .... **TCLC 79**

Latham, Jean Lee 1902-1995 .... **CLC 12**
   See also AITN 1; CA 5-8R; CANR 7, 84;
   CLR 50; MAICYA; SATA 2, 68

Latham, Mavis
   See Clark, Mavis Thorpe

Lathen, Emma CLC 2
   See also Hennissart, Martha; Latsis, Mary
   J(ane)

Lathrop, Francis
   See Leiber, Fritz (Reuter, Jr.)

Latsis, Mary J(ane) 1927(?)-1997
   See Lathen, Emma
   See also CA 85-88; 162

Lattimore, Richmond (Alexander)
   1906-1984 .... **CLC 3**
   See also CA 1-4R; 112; CANR 1

Laughlin, James 1914-1997 .... **CLC 49**
   See also CA 21-24R; 162; CAAS 22; CANR
   9, 47; DLB 48; DLBY 96, 97

Laurence, (Jean) Margaret (Wemyss)
   1926-1987 . **CLC 3, 6, 13, 50, 62; DAC;
   DAM MST; SSC 7**
   See also CA 5-8R; 121; CANR 33; DLB
   53; MTCW 1, 2; SATA-Obit 50

Laurent, Antoine 1952- .... **CLC 50**

Lauscher, Hermann
   See Hesse, Hermann

Lautreamont, Comte de
   1846-1870 .... **NCLC 12; SSC 14**

Laverty, Donald
   See Blish, James (Benjamin)

Lavin, Mary 1912-1996 . **CLC 4, 18, 99; SSC
   4**
   See also CA 9-12R; 151; CANR 33; DLB
   15; MTCW 1

Lavond, Paul Dennis
   See Kornbluth, C(yril) M.; Pohl, Frederik

Lawler, Raymond Evenor 1922- .... **CLC 58**
   See also CA 103

Lawrence, D(avid) H(erbert Richards)
   1885-1930 .... **TCLC 2, 9, 16, 33, 48, 61,
   93; DA; DAB; DAC; DAM MST, NOV,
   POET; SSC 4, 19; WLC**
   See also CA 104; 121; CDBLB 1914-1945;
   DA3; DLB 10, 19, 36, 98, 162, 195;
   MTCW 1, 2

Lawrence, T(homas) E(dward)
   1888-1935 .... **TCLC 18**
   See also Dale, Colin
   See also CA 115; 167; DLB 195

Lawrence of Arabia
   See Lawrence, T(homas) E(dward)

Lawson, Henry (Archibald Hertzberg)
   1867-1922 .... **TCLC 27; SSC 18**
   See also CA 120; 181

Lawton, Dennis
   See Faust, Frederick (Schiller)

Laxness, Halldor CLC 25
   See also Gudjonsson, Halldor Kiljan

Layamon fl. c. 1200- .... **CMLC 10**
   See also DLB 146

Laye, Camara 1928-1980 ... **CLC 4, 38; BLC
   2; DAM MULT**
   See also BW 1; CA 85-88; 97-100; CANR
   25; MTCW 1, 2

Layton, Irving (Peter) 1912- .... **CLC 2, 15;
   DAC; DAM MST, POET**
   See also CA 1-4R; CANR 2, 33, 43, 66;
   DLB 88; MTCW 1, 2

Lazarus, Emma 1849-1887 .... **NCLC 8**

Lazarus, Felix
   See Cable, George Washington

Lazarus, Henry
   See Slavitt, David R(ytman)

Lea, Joan
   See Neufeld, John (Arthur)

Leacock, Stephen (Butler)
   1869-1944 .... **TCLC 2; DAC; DAM
   MST; SSC 39**
   See also CA 104; 141; CANR 80; DLB 92;
   MTCW 2

Lear, Edward 1812-1888 .... **NCLC 3**
   See also CLR 1; DLB 32, 163, 166; MAI-
   CYA; SATA 18, 100

Lear, Norman (Milton) 1922- .... **CLC 12**
   See also CA 73-76

Leautaud, Paul 1872-1956 .... **TCLC 83**
   See also DLB 65

Leavis, F(rank) R(aymond)
   1895-1978 .... **CLC 24**
   See also CA 21-24R; 77-80; CANR 44;
   MTCW 1, 2

Leavitt, David 1961- ..... **CLC 34; DAM POP**
   See also CA 116; 122; CANR 50, 62; DA3;
   DLB 130; INT 122; MTCW 2

Leblanc, Maurice (Marie Emile)
   1864-1941 .... **TCLC 49**
   See also CA 110

Lebowitz, Fran(ces Ann) 1951(?)- ... **CLC 11,
   36**
   See also CA 81-84; CANR 14, 60, 70; INT
   CANR-14; MTCW 1

Lebrecht, Peter
   See Tieck, (Johann) Ludwig

le Carre, John CLC 3, 5, 9, 15, 28
   See also Cornwell, David (John Moore)
   See also BEST 89:4; CDBLB 1960 to
   Present; DLB 87; MTCW 2

Le Clezio, J(ean) M(arie) G(ustave)
   1940- .... **CLC 31**
   See also CA 116; 128; DLB 83

Leconte de Lisle, Charles-Marie-Rene
   1818-1894 .... **NCLC 29**

Le Coq, Monsieur
   See Simenon, Georges (Jacques Christian)

Leduc, Violette 1907-1972 .... **CLC 22**
   See also CA 13-14; 33-36R; CANR 69;
   CAP 1

Ledwidge, Francis 1887(?)-1917 .... **TCLC 23**
   See also CA 123; DLB 20

Lee, Andrea 1953- ... **CLC 36; BLC 2; DAM
   MULT**
   See also BW 1, 3; CA 125; CANR 82

Lee, Andrew
   See Auchincloss, Louis (Stanton)

Lee, Chang-rae 1965- .... **CLC 91**
   See also CA 148; CANR 89

Lee, Don L. CLC 2
   See also Madhubuti, Haki R.

Longfellow, Henry Wadsworth
1807-1882 .... **NCLC 2, 45; DA; DAB; DAC; DAM MST, POET; PC 30; WLCS**
See also CDALB 1640-1865; DA3; DLB 1, 59; SATA 19

Longinus c. 1st cent. - .... **CMLC 27**
See also DLB 176

Longley, Michael 1939- .... **CLC 29**
See also CA 102; DLB 40

Longus fl. c. 2nd cent. - .... **CMLC 7**

Longway, A. Hugh
See Lang, Andrew

Lonnrot, Elias 1802-1884 .... **NCLC 53**

Lopate, Phillip 1943- .... **CLC 29**
See also CA 97-100; CANR 88; DLBY 80; INT 97-100

Lopez Portillo (y Pacheco), Jose
1920- .... **CLC 46**
See also CA 129; HW 1

Lopez y Fuentes, Gregorio
1897(?)-1966 .... **CLC 32**
See also CA 131; HW 1

Lorca, Federico Garcia
See Garcia Lorca, Federico

Lord, Bette Bao 1938- .... **CLC 23**
See also BEST 90:3; CA 107; CANR 41, 79; INT 107; SATA 58

Lord Auch
See Bataille, Georges

Lord Byron
See Byron, George Gordon (Noel)

Lorde, Audre (Geraldine)
1934-1992 ... **CLC 18, 71; BLC 2; DAM MULT, POET; PC 12**
See also BW 1, 3; CA 25-28R; 142; CANR 16, 26, 46, 82; DA3; DLB 41; MTCW 1, 2

Lord Houghton
See Milnes, Richard Monckton

Lord Jeffrey
See Jeffrey, Francis

Lorenzini, Carlo 1826-1890
See Collodi, Carlo
See also MAICYA; SATA 29, 100

Lorenzo, Heberto Padilla
See Padilla (Lorenzo), Heberto

Loris
See Hofmannsthal, Hugo von

Loti, Pierre **TCLC 11**
See also Viaud, (Louis Marie) Julien
See also DLB 123

Lou, Henri
See Andreas-Salome, Lou

Louie, David Wong 1954- .... **CLC 70**
See also CA 139

Louis, Father M.
See Merton, Thomas

Lovecraft, H(oward) P(hillips)
1890-1937 ...... **TCLC 4, 22; DAM POP; SSC 3**
See also AAYA 14; CA 104; 133; DA3; MTCW 1, 2

Lovelace, Earl 1935- .... **CLC 51**
See also BW 2; CA 77-80; CANR 41, 72; DLB 125; MTCW 1

Lovelace, Richard 1618-1657 .... **LC 24**
See also DLB 131

Lowell, Amy 1874-1925 .... **TCLC 1, 8; DAM POET; PC 13**
See also CA 104; 151; DLB 54, 140; MTCW 2

Lowell, James Russell 1819-1891 .... **NCLC 2**
See also CDALB 1640-1865; DLB 1, 11, 64, 79, 189

Lowell, Robert (Traill Spence, Jr.)
1917-1977 .... **CLC 1, 2, 3, 4, 5, 8, 9, 11, 15, 37, 124; DA; DAB; DAC; DAM MST, NOV; PC 3; WLC**
See also CA 9-12R; 73-76; CABS 2; CANR 26, 60; CDALBS; DA3; DLB 5, 169; MTCW 1, 2

Lowenthal, Michael (Francis)
1969- .... **CLC 119**
See also CA 150

Lowndes, Marie Adelaide (Belloc)
1868-1947 .... **TCLC 12**
See also CA 107; DLB 70

Lowry, (Clarence) Malcolm
1909-1957 .... **TCLC 6, 40; SSC 31**
See also CA 105; 131; CANR 62; CDBLB 1945-1960; DLB 15; MTCW 1, 2

Lowry, Mina Gertrude 1882-1966
See Loy, Mina
See also CA 113

Loxsmith, John
See Brunner, John (Kilian Houston)

Loy, Mina **CLC 28; DAM POET; PC 16**
See also Lowry, Mina Gertrude
See also DLB 4, 54

Loyson-Bridet
See Schwob, Marcel (Mayer Andre)

Lucan 39-65 .... **CMLC 33**
See also DLB 211

Lucas, Craig 1951- .... **CLC 64**
See also CA 137; CANR 71

Lucas, E(dward) V(errall)
1868-1938 .... **TCLC 73**
See also CA 176; DLB 98, 149, 153; SATA 20

Lucas, George 1944- .... **CLC 16**
See also AAYA 1, 23; CA 77-80; CANR 30; SATA 56

Lucas, Hans
See Godard, Jean-Luc

Lucas, Victoria
See Plath, Sylvia

Lucian c. 120-c. 180 .... **CMLC 32**
See also DLB 176

Ludlam, Charles 1943-1987 .... **CLC 46, 50**
See also CA 85-88; 122; CANR 72, 86

Ludlum, Robert 1927- .... **CLC 22, 43; DAM NOV, POP**
See also AAYA 10; BEST 89:1, 90:3; CA 33-36R; CANR 25, 41, 68; DA3; DLBY 82; MTCW 1, 2

Ludwig, Ken **CLC 60**

Ludwig, Otto 1813-1865 .... **NCLC 4**
See also DLB 129

Lugones, Leopoldo 1874-1938 ...... **TCLC 15; HLCS 2**
See also CA 116; 131; HW 1

Lu Hsun 1881-1936 .... **TCLC 3; SSC 20**
See also Shu-Jen, Chou

Lukacs, George **CLC 24**
See also Lukacs, Gyorgy (Szegeny von)

Lukacs, Gyorgy (Szegeny von) 1885-1971
See Lukacs, George
See also CA 101; 29-32R; CANR 62; MTCW 2

Luke, Peter (Ambrose Cyprian)
1919-1995 .... **CLC 38**
See also CA 81-84; 147; CANR 72; DLB 13

Lunar, Dennis
See Mungo, Raymond

Lurie, Alison 1926- .... **CLC 4, 5, 18, 39**
See also CA 1-4R; CANR 2, 17, 50, 88; DLB 2; MTCW 1; SATA 46, 112

Lustig, Arnost 1926- .... **CLC 56**
See also AAYA 3; CA 69-72; CANR 47; SATA 56

Luther, Martin 1483-1546 .... **LC 9, 37**
See also DLB 179

Luxemburg, Rosa 1870(?)-1919 ..... **TCLC 63**
See also CA 118

Luzi, Mario 1914- .... **CLC 13**
See also CA 61-64; CANR 9, 70; DLB 128

Lyly, John 1554(?)-1606 .... **LC 41; DAM DRAM; DC 7**
See also DLB 62, 167

L'Ymagier
See Gourmont, Remy (-Marie-Charles) de

Lynch, B. Suarez
See Bioy Casares, Adolfo; Borges, Jorge Luis

Lynch, B. Suarez
See Bioy Casares, Adolfo

Lynch, David (K.) 1946- .... **CLC 66**
See also CA 124; 129

Lynch, James
See Andreyev, Leonid (Nikolaevich)

Lynch Davis, B.
See Bioy Casares, Adolfo; Borges, Jorge Luis

Lyndsay, Sir David 1490-1555 .... **LC 20**

Lynn, Kenneth S(chuyler) 1923- ...... **CLC 50**
See also CA 1-4R; CANR 3, 27, 65

Lynx
See West, Rebecca

Lyons, Marcus
See Blish, James (Benjamin)

Lyre, Pinchbeck
See Sassoon, Siegfried (Lorraine)

Lytle, Andrew (Nelson) 1902-1995 ... **CLC 22**
See also CA 9-12R; 150; CANR 70; DLB 6; DLBY 95

Lyttelton, George 1709-1773 .... **LC 10**

Maas, Peter 1929- .... **CLC 29**
See also CA 93-96; INT 93-96; MTCW 2

Macaulay, Rose 1881-1958 .... **TCLC 7, 44**
See also CA 104; DLB 36

Macaulay, Thomas Babington
1800-1859 .... **NCLC 42**
See also CDBLB 1832-1890; DLB 32, 55

MacBeth, George (Mann)
1932-1992 .... **CLC 2, 5, 9**
See also CA 25-28R; 136; CANR 61, 66; DLB 40; MTCW 1; SATA 4; SATA-Obit 70

MacCaig, Norman (Alexander)
1910- .... **CLC 36; DAB; DAM POET**
See also CA 9-12R; CANR 3, 34; DLB 27

MacCarthy, Sir(Charles Otto) Desmond
1877-1952 .... **TCLC 36**
See also CA 167

MacDiarmid, Hugh **CLC 2, 4, 11, 19, 63; PC 9**
See also Grieve, C(hristopher) M(urray)
See also CDBLB 1945-1960; DLB 20

MacDonald, Anson
See Heinlein, Robert A(nson)

Macdonald, Cynthia 1928- .... **CLC 13, 19**
See also CA 49-52; CANR 4, 44; DLB 105

MacDonald, George 1824-1905 .... **TCLC 9**
See also CA 106; 137; CANR 80; DLB 18, 163, 178; MAICYA; SATA 33, 100
Macdonald, John
See Millar, Kenneth
MacDonald, John D(ann)
1916-1986 .. **CLC 3, 27, 44; DAM NOV, POP**
See also CA 1-4R; 121; CANR 1, 19, 60; DLB 8; DLBY 86; MTCW 1, 2
Macdonald, John Ross
See Millar, Kenneth
Macdonald, Ross CLC 1, 2, 3, 14, 34, 41
See also Millar, Kenneth
See also DLBD 6
MacDougal, John
See Blish, James (Benjamin)
MacDougal, John
See Blish, James (Benjamin)
MacEwen, Gwendolyn (Margaret)
1941-1987 .... **CLC 13, 55**
See also CA 9-12R; 124; CANR 7, 22; DLB 53; SATA 50; SATA-Obit 55
Macha, Karel Hynek 1810-1846 .... **NCLC 46**
Machado (y Ruiz), Antonio
1875-1939 .... **TCLC 3**
See also CA 104; 174; DLB 108; HW 2
Machado de Assis, Joaquim Maria
1839-1908 ..... **TCLC 10; BLC 2; HLCS 2; SSC 24**
See also CA 107; 153; CANR 91
Machen, Arthur TCLC 4; SSC 20
See also Jones, Arthur Llewellyn
See also DLB 36, 156, 178
Machiavelli, Niccolo 1469-1527 ..... **LC 8, 36; DA; DAB; DAC; DAM MST; WLCS**
MacInnes, Colin 1914-1976 .... **CLC 4, 23**
See also CA 69-72; 65-68; CANR 21; DLB 14; MTCW 1, 2
MacInnes, Helen (Clark)
1907-1985 .... **CLC 27, 39; DAM POP**
See also CA 1-4R; 117; CANR 1, 28, 58; DLB 87; MTCW 1, 2; SATA 22; SATA-Obit 44
Mackenzie, Compton (Edward Montague)
1883-1972 .... **CLC 18**
See also CA 21-22; 37-40R; CAP 2; DLB 34, 100
Mackenzie, Henry 1745-1831 .... **NCLC 41**
See also DLB 39
Mackintosh, Elizabeth 1896(?)-1952
See Tey, Josephine
See also CA 110
MacLaren, James
See Grieve, C(hristopher) M(urray)
Mac Laverty, Bernard 1942- .... **CLC 31**
See also CA 116; 118; CANR 43, 88; INT 118
MacLean, Alistair (Stuart)
1922(?)-1987 .. **CLC 3, 13, 50, 63; DAM POP**
See also CA 57-60; 121; CANR 28, 61; MTCW 1; SATA 23; SATA-Obit 50
Maclean, Norman (Fitzroy)
1902-1990 .... **CLC 78; DAM POP; SSC 13**
See also CA 102; 132; CANR 49; DLB 206
MacLeish, Archibald 1892-1982 ... **CLC 3, 8, 14, 68; DAM POET**
See also CA 9-12R; 106; CANR 33, 63; CDALBS; DLB 4, 7, 45; DLBY 82; MTCW 1, 2

MacLennan, (John) Hugh
1907-1990 . **CLC 2, 14, 92; DAC; DAM MST**
See also CA 5-8R; 142; CANR 33; DLB 68; MTCW 1, 2
MacLeod, Alistair 1936- .... **CLC 56; DAC; DAM MST**
See also CA 123; DLB 60; MTCW 2
Macleod, Fiona
See Sharp, William
MacNeice, (Frederick) Louis
1907-1963 .... **CLC 1, 4, 10, 53; DAB; DAM POET**
See also CA 85-88; CANR 61; DLB 10, 20; MTCW 1, 2
MacNeill, Dand
See Fraser, George MacDonald
Macpherson, James 1736-1796 .... **LC 29**
See also Ossian
See also DLB 109
Macpherson, (Jean) Jay 1931- .... **CLC 14**
See also CA 5-8R; CANR 90; DLB 53
MacShane, Frank 1927-1999 .... **CLC 39**
See also CA 9-12R; 186; CANR 3, 33; DLB 111
Macumber, Mari
See Sandoz, Mari(e Susette)
Madach, Imre 1823-1864 .... **NCLC 19**
Madden, (Jerry) David 1933- .... **CLC 5, 15**
See also CA 1-4R; CAAS 3; CANR 4, 45; DLB 6; MTCW 1
Maddern, Al(an)
See Ellison, Harlan (Jay)
Madhubuti, Haki R. 1942- . **CLC 6, 73; BLC 2; DAM MULT, POET; PC 5**
See also Lee, Don L.
See also BW 2, 3; CA 73-76; CANR 24, 51, 73; DLB 5, 41; DLBD 8; MTCW 2
Maepenn, Hugh
See Kuttner, Henry
Maepenn, K. H.
See Kuttner, Henry
Maeterlinck, Maurice 1862-1949 ... **TCLC 3; DAM DRAM**
See also CA 104; 136; CANR 80; DLB 192; SATA 66
Maginn, William 1794-1842 .... **NCLC 8**
See also DLB 110, 159
Mahapatra, Jayanta 1928- .... **CLC 33; DAM MULT**
See also CA 73-76; CAAS 9; CANR 15, 33, 66, 87
Mahfouz, Naguib (Abdel Aziz Al-Sabilgi)
1911(?)-
See Mahfuz, Najib
See also BEST 89:2; CA 128; CANR 55; DAM NOV; DA3; MTCW 1, 2
Mahfuz, Najib CLC 52, 55
See also Mahfouz, Naguib (Abdel Aziz Al-Sabilgi)
See also DLBY 88
Mahon, Derek 1941- .... **CLC 27**
See also CA 113; 128; CANR 88; DLB 40
Mailer, Norman 1923- ... **CLC 1, 2, 3, 4, 5, 8, 11, 14, 28, 39, 74, 111; DA; DAB; DAC; DAM MST, NOV, POP**
See also AAYA 31; AITN 2; CA 9-12R; CABS 1; CANR 28, 74, 77; CDALB 1968-1988; DA3; DLB 2, 16, 28, 185; DLBD 3; DLBY 80, 83; MTCW 1, 2
Maillet, Antonine 1929- .. **CLC 54, 118; DAC**
See also CA 115; 120; CANR 46, 74, 77; DLB 60; INT 120; MTCW 2

Mais, Roger 1905-1955 .... **TCLC 8**
See also BW 1, 3; CA 105; 124; CANR 82; DLB 125; MTCW 1
Maistre, Joseph de 1753-1821 .... **NCLC 37**
Maitland, Frederic 1850-1906 .... **TCLC 65**
Maitland, Sara (Louise) 1950- .... **CLC 49**
See also CA 69-72; CANR 13, 59
Major, Clarence 1936- . **CLC 3, 19, 48; BLC 2; DAM MULT**
See also BW 2, 3; CA 21-24R; CAAS 6; CANR 13, 25, 53, 82; DLB 33
Major, Kevin (Gerald) 1949- ... **CLC 26; DAC**
See also AAYA 16; CA 97-100; CANR 21, 38; CLR 11; DLB 60; INT CANR-21; JRDA; MAICYA; SATA 32, 82
Maki, James
See Ozu, Yasujiro
Malabaila, Damiano
See Levi, Primo
Malamud, Bernard 1914-1986 .. **CLC 1, 2, 3, 5, 8, 9, 11, 18, 27, 44, 78, 85; DA; DAB; DAC; DAM MST, NOV, POP; SSC 15; WLC**
See also AAYA 16; CA 5-8R; 118; CABS 1; CANR 28, 62; CDALB 1941-1968; DA3; DLB 2, 28, 152; DLBY 80, 86; MTCW 1, 2
Malan, Herman
See Bosman, Herman Charles; Bosman, Herman Charles
Malaparte, Curzio 1898-1957 .... **TCLC 52**
Malcolm, Dan
See Silverberg, Robert
Malcolm X CLC 82, 117; BLC 2; WLCS
See also Little, Malcolm
Malherbe, Francois de 1555-1628 .... **LC 5**
Mallarme, Stephane 1842-1898 ...... **NCLC 4, 41; DAM POET; PC 4**
Mallet-Joris, Francoise 1930- .... **CLC 11**
See also CA 65-68; CANR 17; DLB 83
Malley, Ern
See McAuley, James Phillip
Mallowan, Agatha Christie
See Christie, Agatha (Mary Clarissa)
Maloff, Saul 1922- .... **CLC 5**
See also CA 33-36R
Malone, Louis
See MacNeice, (Frederick) Louis
Malone, Michael (Christopher)
1942- .... **CLC 43**
See also CA 77-80; CANR 14, 32, 57
Malory, (Sir) Thomas
1410(?)-1471(?) .... **LC 11; DA; DAB; DAC; DAM MST; WLCS**
See also CDBLB Before 1660; DLB 146; SATA 59; SATA-Brief 33
Malouf, (George Joseph) David
1934- .... **CLC 28, 86**
See also CA 124; CANR 50, 76; MTCW 2
Malraux, (Georges-)Andre
1901-1976 .... **CLC 1, 4, 9, 13, 15, 57; DAM NOV**
See also CA 21-22; 69-72; CANR 34, 58; CAP 2; DA3; DLB 72; MTCW 1, 2
Malzberg, Barry N(athaniel) 1939- ... **CLC 7**
See also CA 61-64; CAAS 4; CANR 16; DLB 8
Mamet, David (Alan) 1947- .. **CLC 9, 15, 34, 46, 91; DAM DRAM; DC 4**
See also AAYA 3; CA 81-84; CABS 3; CANR 15, 41, 67, 72; DA3; DLB 7; MTCW 1, 2

Masaoka Tsunenori 1867-1902
　　See Masaoka Shiki
　　See also CA 117

Masefield, John (Edward)
　　1878-1967 ..... **CLC 11, 47; DAM POET**
　　See also CA 19-20; 25-28R; CANR 33;
　　CAP 2; CDBLB 1890-1914; DLB 10, 19,
　　153, 160; MTCW 1, 2; SATA 19

Maso, Carole 19(?)- .... **CLC 44**
　　See also CA 170

Mason, Bobbie Ann 1940- ... **CLC 28, 43, 82;**
　　SSC 4
　　See also AAYA 5; CA 53-56; CANR 11, 31,
　　58, 83; CDALBS; DA3; DLB 173; DLBY
　　87; INT CANR-31; MTCW 1, 2

Mason, Ernst
　　See Pohl, Frederik

Mason, Lee W.
　　See Malzberg, Barry N(athaniel)

Mason, Nick 1945- .... **CLC 35**

Mason, Tally
　　See Derleth, August (William)

Mass, William
　　See Gibson, William

Master Lao
　　See Lao Tzu

Masters, Edgar Lee 1868-1950 .... **TCLC 2,**
　　25; DA; DAC; DAM MST, POET; PC
　　1; WLCS
　　See also CA 104; 133; CDALB 1865-1917;
　　DLB 54; MTCW 1, 2

Masters, Hilary 1928- .... **CLC 48**
　　See also CA 25-28R; CANR 13, 47

Mastrosimone, William 19(?)- .... **CLC 36**
　　See also CA 186

Mathe, Albert
　　See Camus, Albert

Mather, Cotton 1663-1728 .... **LC 38**
　　See also CDALB 1640-1865; DLB 24, 30,
　　140

Mather, Increase 1639-1723 .... **LC 38**
　　See also DLB 24

Matheson, Richard Burton 1926- .... **CLC 37**
　　See also AAYA 31; CA 97-100; CANR 88;
　　DLB 8, 44; INT 97-100

Mathews, Harry 1930- .... **CLC 6, 52**
　　See also CA 21-24R; CAAS 6; CANR 18,
　　40

Mathews, John Joseph 1894-1979 .. **CLC 84;**
　　DAM MULT
　　See also CA 19-20; 142; CANR 45; CAP 2;
　　DLB 175; NNAL

Mathias, Roland (Glyn) 1915- .... **CLC 45**
　　See also CA 97-100; CANR 19, 41; DLB
　　27

Matsuo Basho 1644-1694 .... **PC 3**
　　See also DAM POET

Mattheson, Rodney
　　See Creasey, John

Matthews, (James) Brander
　　1852-1929 .... **TCLC 95**
　　See also DLB 71, 78; DLBD 13

Matthews, Greg 1949- .... **CLC 45**
　　See also CA 135

Matthews, William (Procter, III)
　　1942-1997 .... **CLC 40**
　　See also CA 29-32R; 162; CAAS 18; CANR
　　12, 57; DLB 5

Matthias, John (Edward) 1941- .... **CLC 9**
　　See also CA 33-36R; CANR 56

Matthiessen, Peter 1927- ... **CLC 5, 7, 11, 32,**
　　64; DAM NOV
　　See also AAYA 6; BEST 90:4; CA 9-12R;
　　CANR 21, 50, 73; DA3; DLB 6, 173;
　　MTCW 1, 2; SATA 27

Maturin, Charles Robert
　　1780(?)-1824 .... **NCLC 6**
　　See also DLB 178

Matute (Ausejo), Ana Maria 1925- .. **CLC 11**
　　See also CA 89-92; MTCW 1

Maugham, W. S.
　　See Maugham, W(illiam) Somerset

Maugham, W(illiam) Somerset
　　1874-1965 ... **CLC 1, 11, 15, 67, 93; DA;**
　　DAB; DAC; DAM DRAM, MST, NOV;
　　SSC 8; WLC
　　See also CA 5-8R; 25-28R; CANR 40; CD-
　　BLB 1914-1945; DA3; DLB 10, 36, 77,
　　100, 162, 195; MTCW 1, 2; SATA 54

Maugham, William Somerset
　　See Maugham, W(illiam) Somerset

Maupassant, (Henri Rene Albert) Guy de
　　1850-1893 . **NCLC 1, 42, 83; DA; DAB;**
　　DAC; DAM MST; SSC 1; WLC
　　See also DA3; DLB 123

Maupin, Armistead 1944- ..... **CLC 95; DAM**
　　POP
　　See also CA 125; 130; CANR 58; DA3;
　　INT 130; MTCW 2

Maurhut, Richard
　　See Traven, B.

Mauriac, Claude 1914-1996 .... **CLC 9**
　　See also CA 89-92; 152; DLB 83

Mauriac, Francois (Charles)
　　1885-1970 .... **CLC 4, 9, 56; SSC 24**
　　See also CA 25-28; CAP 2; DLB 65;
　　MTCW 1, 2

Mavor, Osborne Henry 1888-1951
　　See Bridie, James
　　See also CA 104

Maxwell, William (Keepers, Jr.)
　　1908- .... **CLC 19**
　　See also CA 93-96; CANR 54; DLBY 80;
　　INT 93-96

May, Elaine 1932- .... **CLC 16**
　　See also CA 124; 142; DLB 44

Mayakovski, Vladimir (Vladimirovich)
　　1893-1930 .... **TCLC 4, 18**
　　See also CA 104; 158; MTCW 2

Mayhew, Henry 1812-1887 .... **NCLC 31**
　　See also DLB 18, 55, 190

Mayle, Peter 1939(?)- .... **CLC 89**
　　See also CA 139; CANR 64

Maynard, Joyce 1953- .... **CLC 23**
　　See also CA 111; 129; CANR 64

Mayne, William (James Carter)
　　1928- .... **CLC 12**
　　See also AAYA 20; CA 9-12R; CANR 37,
　　80; CLR 25; JRDA; MAICYA; SAAS 11;
　　SATA 6, 68

Mayo, Jim
　　See L'Amour, Louis (Dearborn)

Maysles, Albert 1926- .... **CLC 16**
　　See also CA 29-32R

Maysles, David 1932- .... **CLC 16**

Mazer, Norma Fox 1931- .... **CLC 26**
　　See also AAYA 5; CA 69-72; CANR 12,
　　32, 66; CLR 23; JRDA; MAICYA; SAAS
　　1; SATA 24, 67, 105

Mazzini, Guiseppe 1805-1872 .... **NCLC 34**

McAlmon, Robert (Menzies)
　　1895-1956 .... **TCLC 97**
　　See also CA 107; 168; DLB 4, 45; DLBD
　　15

McAuley, James Phillip 1917-1976 .. **CLC 45**
　　See also CA 97-100

McBain, Ed
　　See Hunter, Evan

McBrien, William (Augustine)
　　1930- .... **CLC 44**
　　See also CA 107; CANR 90

McCaffrey, Anne (Inez) 1926- .... **CLC 17;**
　　DAM NOV, POP
　　See also AAYA 6, 34; AITN 2; BEST 89:2;
　　CA 25-28R; CANR 15, 35, 55; CLR 49;
　　DA3; DLB 8; JRDA; MAICYA; MTCW
　　1, 2; SAAS 11; SATA 8, 70, 116

McCall, Nathan 1955(?)- .... **CLC 86**
　　See also BW 3; CA 146; CANR 88

McCann, Arthur
　　See Campbell, John W(ood, Jr.)

McCann, Edson
　　See Pohl, Frederik

McCarthy, Charles, Jr. 1933-
　　See McCarthy, Cormac
　　See also CANR 42, 69; DAM POP; DA3;
　　MTCW 2

McCarthy, Cormac 1933- ...... **CLC 4, 57, 59,**
　　101
　　See also McCarthy, Charles, Jr.
　　See also DLB 6, 143; MTCW 2

McCarthy, Mary (Therese)
　　1912-1989 .. **CLC 1, 3, 5, 14, 24, 39, 59;**
　　SSC 24
　　See also CA 5-8R; 129; CANR 16, 50, 64;
　　DA3; DLB 2; DLBY 81; INT CANR-16;
　　MTCW 1, 2

McCartney, (James) Paul 1942- . **CLC 12, 35**
　　See also CA 146

McCauley, Stephen (D.) 1955- .... **CLC 50**
　　See also CA 141

McClure, Michael (Thomas) 1932- ... **CLC 6,**
　　10
　　See also CA 21-24R; CANR 17, 46, 77;
　　DLB 16

McCorkle, Jill (Collins) 1958- .... **CLC 51**
　　See also CA 121; DLBY 87

McCourt, Frank 1930- .... **CLC 109**
　　See also CA 157

McCourt, James 1941- .... **CLC 5**
　　See also CA 57-60

McCourt, Malachy 1932- .... **CLC 119**

McCoy, Horace (Stanley)
　　1897-1955 .... **TCLC 28**
　　See also CA 108; 155; DLB 9

McCrae, John 1872-1918 .... **TCLC 12**
　　See also CA 109; DLB 92

McCreigh, James
　　See Pohl, Frederik

McCullers, (Lula) Carson (Smith)
　　1917-1967 .... **CLC 1, 4, 10, 12, 48, 100;**
　　DA; DAB; DAC; DAM MST, NOV;
　　SSC 9, 24; WLC
　　See also AAYA 21; CA 5-8R; 25-28R;
　　CABS 1, 3; CANR 18; CDALB 1941-
　　1968; DA3; DLB 2, 7, 173; MTCW 1, 2;
　　SATA 27

McCulloch, John Tyler
　　See Burroughs, Edgar Rice

Mortimer, Penelope (Ruth) 1918- ...... **CLC 5**
    See also CA 57-60; CANR 45, 88
Morton, Anthony
    See Creasey, John
Mosca, Gaetano 1858-1941 .... **TCLC 75**
Mosher, Howard Frank 1943- .... **CLC 62**
    See also CA 139; CANR 65
Mosley, Nicholas 1923- .... **CLC 43, 70**
    See also CA 69-72; CANR 41, 60; DLB 14,
    207
Mosley, Walter 1952- .... **CLC 97; BLCS;**
    DAM MULT, POP
    See also AAYA 17; BW 2; CA 142; CANR
    57; DA3; MTCW 2
Moss, Howard 1922-1987 ...... **CLC 7, 14, 45,**
    50; DAM POET
    See also CA 1-4R; 123; CANR 1, 44; DLB
    5
Mossgiel, Rab
    See Burns, Robert
Motion, Andrew (Peter) 1952- .... **CLC 47**
    See also CA 146; CANR 90; DLB 40
Motley, Willard (Francis)
    1909-1965 .... **CLC 18**
    See also BW 1; CA 117; 106; CANR 88;
    DLB 76, 143
Motoori, Norinaga 1730-1801 .... **NCLC 45**
Mott, Michael (Charles Alston)
    1930- .... **CLC 15, 34**
    See also CA 5-8R; CAAS 7; CANR 7, 29
Mountain Wolf Woman 1884-1960 .. **CLC 92**
    See also CA 144; CANR 90; NNAL
Moure, Erin 1955- .... **CLC 88**
    See also CA 113; DLB 60
Mowat, Farley (McGill) 1921- .... **CLC 26;**
    DAC; DAM MST
    See also AAYA 1; CA 1-4R; CANR 4, 24,
    42, 68; CLR 20; DLB 68; INT CANR-24;
    JRDA; MAICYA; MTCW 1, 2; SATA 3,
    55
Mowatt, Anna Cora 1819-1870 ..... **NCLC 74**
Moyers, Bill 1934- .... **CLC 74**
    See also AITN 2; CA 61-64; CANR 31, 52
Mphahlele, Es'kia
    See Mphahlele, Ezekiel
    See also DLB 125
Mphahlele, Ezekiel 1919- ... **CLC 25; BLC 3;**
    DAM MULT
    See also Mphahlele, Es'kia
    See also BW 2, 3; CA 81-84; CANR 26,
    76; DA3; MTCW 2
Mqhayi, S(amuel) E(dward) K(rune Loliwe)
    1875-1945 ...... **TCLC 25; BLC 3; DAM**
    MULT
    See also CA 153; CANR 87
Mrozek, Slawomir 1930- .... **CLC 3, 13**
    See also CA 13-16R; CAAS 10; CANR 29;
    MTCW 1
Mrs. Belloc-Lowndes
    See Lowndes, Marie Adelaide (Belloc)
Mtwa, Percy (?)- .... **CLC 47**
Mueller, Lisel 1924- .... **CLC 13, 51**
    See also CA 93-96; DLB 105
Muir, Edwin 1887-1959 .... **TCLC 2, 87**
    See also CA 104; DLB 20, 100, 191
Muir, John 1838-1914 .... **TCLC 28**
    See also CA 165; DLB 186
Mujica Lainez, Manuel 1910-1984 ... **CLC 31**
    See also Lainez, Manuel Mujica
    See also CA 81-84; 112; CANR 32; HW 1

Mukherjee, Bharati 1940- .... **CLC 53, 115;**
    DAM NOV; SSC 38
    See also BEST 89:2; CA 107; CANR 45,
    72; DLB 60; MTCW 1, 2
Muldoon, Paul 1951- .... **CLC 32, 72; DAM**
    POET
    See also CA 113; 129; CANR 52, 91; DLB
    40; INT 129
Mulisch, Harry 1927- .... **CLC 42**
    See also CA 9-12R; CANR 6, 26, 56
Mull, Martin 1943- .... **CLC 17**
    See also CA 105
Muller, Wilhelm NCLC 73
Mulock, Dinah Maria
    See Craik, Dinah Maria (Mulock)
Munford, Robert 1737(?)-1783 .... **LC 5**
    See also DLB 31
Mungo, Raymond 1946- .... **CLC 72**
    See also CA 49-52; CANR 2
Munro, Alice 1931- .... **CLC 6, 10, 19, 50, 95;**
    DAC; DAM MST, NOV; SSC 3;
    WLCS
    See also AITN 2; CA 33-36R; CANR 33,
    53, 75; DA3; DLB 53; MTCW 1, 2; SATA
    29
Munro, H(ector) H(ugh) 1870-1916
    See Saki
    See also CA 104; 130; CDBLB 1890-1914;
    DA; DAB; DAC; DAM MST, NOV; DA3;
    DLB 34, 162; MTCW 1, 2; WLC
Murdoch, (Jean) Iris 1919-1999 ... **CLC 1, 2,**
    3, 4, 6, 8, 11, 15, 22, 31, 51; DAB;
    DAC; DAM MST, NOV
    See also CA 13-16R; 179; CANR 8, 43, 68;
    CDBLB 1960 to Present; DA3; DLB 14,
    194; INT CANR-8; MTCW 1, 2
Murfree, Mary Noailles 1850-1922 ... **SSC 22**
    See also CA 122; 176; DLB 12, 74
Murnau, Friedrich Wilhelm
    See Plumpe, Friedrich Wilhelm
Murphy, Richard 1927- .... **CLC 41**
    See also CA 29-32R; DLB 40
Murphy, Sylvia 1937- .... **CLC 34**
    See also CA 121
Murphy, Thomas (Bernard) 1935- ... **CLC 51**
    See also CA 101
Murray, Albert L. 1916- .... **CLC 73**
    See also BW 2; CA 49-52; CANR 26, 52,
    78; DLB 38
Murray, Judith Sargent
    1751-1820 .... **NCLC 63**
    See also DLB 37, 200
Murray, Les(lie) A(llan) 1938- .... **CLC 40;**
    DAM POET
    See also CA 21-24R; CANR 11, 27, 56
Murry, J. Middleton
    See Murry, John Middleton
Murry, John Middleton
    1889-1957 .... **TCLC 16**
    See also CA 118; DLB 149
Musgrave, Susan 1951- .... **CLC 13, 54**
    See also CA 69-72; CANR 45, 84
Musil, Robert (Edler von)
    1880-1942 .... **TCLC 12, 68; SSC 18**
    See also CA 109; CANR 55, 84; DLB 81,
    124; MTCW 2
Muske, Carol 1945- .... **CLC 90**
    See also Muske-Dukes, Carol (Anne)
Muske-Dukes, Carol (Anne) 1945-
    See Muske, Carol
    See also CA 65-68; CANR 32, 70

Musset, (Louis Charles) Alfred de
    1810-1857 .... **NCLC 7**
    See also DLB 192
Mussolini, Benito (Amilcare Andrea)
    1883-1945 .... **TCLC 96**
    See also CA 116
My Brother's Brother
    See Chekhov, Anton (Pavlovich)
Myers, L(eopold) H(amilton)
    1881-1944 .... **TCLC 59**
    See also CA 157; DLB 15
Myers, Walter Dean 1937- ..... **CLC 35; BLC**
    3; DAM MULT, NOV
    See also AAYA 4, 23; BW 2; CA 33-36R;
    CANR 20, 42, 67; CLR 4, 16, 35; DLB
    33; INT CANR-20; JRDA; MAICYA;
    MTCW 2; SAAS 2; SATA 41, 71, 109;
    SATA-Brief 27
Myers, Walter M.
    See Myers, Walter Dean
Myles, Symon
    See Follett, Ken(neth Martin)
Nabokov, Vladimir (Vladimirovich)
    1899-1977 .... **CLC 1, 2, 3, 6, 8, 11, 15,**
    23, 44, 46, 64; DA; DAB; DAC; DAM
    MST, NOV; SSC 11; WLC
    See also CA 5-8R; 69-72; CANR 20;
    CDALB 1941-1968; DA3; DLB 2; DLBD
    3; DLBY 80, 91; MTCW 1, 2
Naevius c. 265B.C.-201B.C. .... **CMLC 37**
    See also DLB 211
Nagai Kafu 1879-1959 .... **TCLC 51**
    See also Nagai Sokichi
    See also DLB 180
Nagai Sokichi 1879-1959
    See Nagai Kafu
    See also CA 117
Nagy, Laszlo 1925-1978 .... **CLC 7**
    See also CA 129; 112
Naidu, Sarojini 1879-1943 .... **TCLC 80**
Naipaul, Shiva(dhar Srinivasa)
    1945-1985 .... **CLC 32, 39; DAM NOV**
    See also CA 110; 112; 116; CANR 33;
    DA3; DLB 157; DLBY 85; MTCW 1, 2
Naipaul, V(idiadhar) S(urajprasad)
    1932- .... **CLC 4, 7, 9, 13, 18, 37, 105;**
    DAB; DAC; DAM MST, NOV; SSC 38
    See also CA 1-4R; CANR 1, 33, 51, 91;
    CDBLB 1960 to Present; DA3; DLB 125,
    204, 206; DLBY 85; MTCW 1, 2
Nakos, Lilika 1899(?)- .... **CLC 29**
Narayan, R(asipuram) K(rishnaswami)
    1906- . **CLC 7, 28, 47, 121; DAM NOV;**
    SSC 25
    See also CA 81-84; CANR 33, 61; DA3;
    MTCW 1, 2; SATA 62
Nash, (Frediric) Ogden 1902-1971 . **CLC 23;**
    DAM POET; PC 21
    See also CA 13-14; 29-32R; CANR 34, 61;
    CAP 1; DLB 11; MAICYA; MTCW 1, 2;
    SATA 2, 46
Nashe, Thomas 1567-1601(?) .... **LC 41**
    See also DLB 167
Nashe, Thomas 1567-1601 .... **LC 41**
Nathan, Daniel
    See Dannay, Frederic
Nathan, George Jean 1882-1958 .... **TCLC 18**
    See also Hatteras, Owen
    See also CA 114; 169; DLB 137
Natsume, Kinnosuke 1867-1916
    See Natsume, Soseki
    See also CA 104

Phaedrus c. 18B.C.-c. 50 .... **CMLC 25**
See also DLB 211
Philips, Katherine 1632-1664 .... **LC 30**
See also DLB 131
Philipson, Morris H. 1926- .... **CLC 53**
See also CA 1-4R; CANR 4
Phillips, Caryl 1958- . **CLC 96; BLCS; DAM MULT**
See also BW 2; CA 141; CANR 63; DA3;
DLB 157; MTCW 2
Phillips, David Graham
1867-1911 .... **TCLC 44**
See also CA 108; 176; DLB 9, 12
Phillips, Jack
See Sandburg, Carl (August)
Phillips, Jayne Anne 1952- .... **CLC 15, 33; SSC 16**
See also CA 101; CANR 24, 50; DLBY 80;
INT CANR-24; MTCW 1, 2
Phillips, Richard
See Dick, Philip K(indred)
Phillips, Robert (Schaeffer) 1938- .... **CLC 28**
See also CA 17-20R; CAAS 13; CANR 8;
DLB 105
Phillips, Ward
See Lovecraft, H(oward) P(hillips)
Piccolo, Lucio 1901-1969 .... **CLC 13**
See also CA 97-100; DLB 114
Pickthall, Marjorie L(owry) C(hristie)
1883-1922 .... **TCLC 21**
See also CA 107; DLB 92
Pico della Mirandola, Giovanni
1463-1494 .... **LC 15**
Piercy, Marge 1936- .... **CLC 3, 6, 14, 18, 27, 62, 128; PC 29**
See also CA 21-24R; CAAS 1; CANR 13,
43, 66; DLB 120; MTCW 1, 2
Piers, Robert
See Anthony, Piers
Pieyre de Mandiargues, Andre 1909-1991
See Mandiargues, Andre Pieyre de
See also CA 103; 136; CANR 22, 82
Pilnyak, Boris **TCLC 23**
See also Vogau, Boris Andreyevich
Pincherle, Alberto 1907-1990 .... **CLC 11, 18; DAM NOV**
See also Moravia, Alberto
See also CA 25-28R; 132; CANR 33, 63;
MTCW 1
Pinckney, Darryl 1953- .... **CLC 76**
See also BW 2, 3; CA 143; CANR 79
Pindar 518B.C.-446B.C. .... **CMLC 12; PC 19**
See also DLB 176
Pineda, Cecile 1942- .... **CLC 39**
See also CA 118
Pinero, Arthur Wing 1855-1934 ... **TCLC 32; DAM DRAM**
See also CA 110; 153; DLB 10
Pinero, Miguel (Antonio Gomez)
1946-1988 .... **CLC 4, 55**
See also CA 61-64; 125; CANR 29, 90; HW 1
Pinget, Robert 1919-1997 .... **CLC 7, 13, 37**
See also CA 85-88; 160; DLB 83
Pink Floyd
See Barrett, (Roger) Syd; Gilmour, David;
Mason, Nick; Waters, Roger; Wright, Rick
Pinkney, Edward 1802-1828 .... **NCLC 31**
Pinkwater, Daniel Manus 1941- .... **CLC 35**
See also Pinkwater, Manus
See also AAYA 1; CA 29-32R; CANR 12,
38, 89; CLR 4; JRDA; MAICYA; SAAS
3; SATA 46, 76, 114

Pinkwater, Manus
See Pinkwater, Daniel Manus
See also SATA 8
Pinsky, Robert 1940- .... **CLC 9, 19, 38, 94, 121; DAM POET; PC 27**
See also CA 29-32R; CAAS 4; CANR 58;
DA3; DLBY 82, 98; MTCW 2
Pinta, Harold
See Pinter, Harold
Pinter, Harold 1930- .. **CLC 1, 3, 6, 9, 11, 15, 27, 58, 73; DA; DAB; DAC; DAM DRAM, MST; WLC**
See also CA 5-8R; CANR 33, 65; CDBLB
1960 to Present; DA3; DLB 13; MTCW
1, 2
Piozzi, Hester Lynch (Thrale)
1741-1821 .... **NCLC 57**
See also DLB 104, 142
Pirandello, Luigi 1867-1936 ...... **TCLC 4, 29; DA; DAB; DAC; DAM DRAM, MST; DC 5; SSC 22; WLC**
See also CA 104; 153; DA3; MTCW 2
Pirsig, Robert M(aynard) 1928- ... **CLC 4, 6, 73; DAM POP**
See also CA 53-56; CANR 42, 74; DA3;
MTCW 1, 2; SATA 39
Pisarev, Dmitry Ivanovich
1840-1868 .... **NCLC 25**
Pix, Mary (Griffith) 1666-1709 .... **LC 8**
See also DLB 80
Pixerecourt, (Rene Charles) Guilbert de
1773-1844 .... **NCLC 39**
See also DLB 192
Plaatje, Sol(omon) T(shekisho)
1876-1932 .... **TCLC 73; BLCS**
See also BW 2, 3; CA 141; CANR 79
Plaidy, Jean
See Hibbert, Eleanor Alice Burford
Planche, James Robinson
1796-1880 .... **NCLC 42**
Plant, Robert 1948- .... **CLC 12**
Plante, David (Robert) 1940- ...... **CLC 7, 23, 38; DAM NOV**
See also CA 37-40R; CANR 12, 36, 58, 82;
DLBY 83; INT CANR-12; MTCW 1
Plath, Sylvia 1932-1963 ..... **CLC 1, 2, 3, 5, 9, 11, 14, 17, 50, 51, 62, 111; DA; DAB; DAC; DAM MST, POET; PC 1; WLC**
See also AAYA 13; CA 19-20; CANR 34;
CAP 2; CDALB 1941-1968; DA3; DLB
5, 6, 152; MTCW 1, 2; SATA 96
Plato 428(?)B.C.-348(?)B.C. .... **CMLC 8; DA; DAB; DAC; DAM MST; WLCS**
See also DA3; DLB 176
Platonov, Andrei **TCLC 14; SSC 38**
See also Klimentov, Andrei Platonovich
Platt, Kin 1911- .... **CLC 26**
See also AAYA 11; CA 17-20R; CANR 11;
JRDA; SAAS 17; SATA 21, 86
Plautus c. 251B.C.-184B.C. ... **CMLC 24; DC 6**
See also DLB 211
Plick et Plock
See Simenon, Georges (Jacques Christian)
Plimpton, George (Ames) 1927- .... **CLC 36**
See also AITN 1; CA 21-24R; CANR 32,
70; DLB 185; MTCW 1, 2; SATA 10
Pliny the Elder c. 23-79 .... **CMLC 23**
See also DLB 211

Plomer, William Charles Franklin
1903-1973 .... **CLC 4, 8**
See also CA 21-22; CANR 34; CAP 2; DLB
20, 162, 191; MTCW 1; SATA 24
Plowman, Piers
See Kavanagh, Patrick (Joseph)
Plum, J.
See Wodehouse, P(elham) G(renville)
Plumly, Stanley (Ross) 1939- .... **CLC 33**
See also CA 108; 110; DLB 5, 193; INT
110
Plumpe, Friedrich Wilhelm
1888-1931 .... **TCLC 53**
See also CA 112
Po Chu-i 772-846 .... **CMLC 24**
Poe, Edgar Allan 1809-1849 ..... **NCLC 1, 16, 55, 78; DA; DAB; DAC; DAM MST, POET; PC 1; SSC 34; WLC**
See also AAYA 14; CDALB 1640-1865;
DA3; DLB 3, 59, 73, 74; SATA 23
Poet of Titchfield Street, The
See Pound, Ezra (Weston Loomis)
Pohl, Frederik 1919- .... **CLC 18; SSC 25**
See also AAYA 24; CA 61-64; CAAS 1;
CANR 11, 37, 81; DLB 8; INT CANR-
11; MTCW 1, 2; SATA 24
Poirier, Louis 1910-
See Gracq, Julien
See also CA 122; 126
Poitier, Sidney 1927- .... **CLC 26**
See also BW 1; CA 117
Polanski, Roman 1933- .... **CLC 16**
See also CA 77-80
Poliakoff, Stephen 1952- .... **CLC 38**
See also CA 106; DLB 13
Police, The
See Copeland, Stewart (Armstrong); Sum-
mers, Andrew James; Sumner, Gordon
Matthew
Polidori, John William 1795-1821 . **NCLC 51**
See also DLB 116
Pollitt, Katha 1949- .... **CLC 28, 122**
See also CA 120; 122; CANR 66; MTCW
1, 2
Pollock, (Mary) Sharon 1936- .... **CLC 50; DAC; DAM DRAM, MST**
See also CA 141; DLB 60
Polo, Marco 1254-1324 .... **CMLC 15**
Polonsky, Abraham (Lincoln)
1910- .... **CLC 92**
See also CA 104; DLB 26; INT 104
Polybius c. 200B.C.-c. 118B.C. ...... **CMLC 17**
See also DLB 176
Pomerance, Bernard 1940- ... **CLC 13; DAM DRAM**
See also CA 101; CANR 49
Ponge, Francis 1899-1988 . **CLC 6, 18; DAM POET**
See also CA 85-88; 126; CANR 40, 86
Poniatowska, Elena 1933-
See also CA 101; CANR 32, 66; DAM
MULT; DLB 113; HLC 2; HW 1, 2
Pontoppidan, Henrik 1857-1943 .... **TCLC 29**
See also CA 170
Poole, Josephine **CLC 17**
See also Helyar, Jane Penelope Josephine
See also SAAS 2; SATA 5
Popa, Vasko 1922-1991 .... **CLC 19**
See also CA 112; 148; DLB 181

Pope, Alexander 1688-1744 .... **LC 3, 58; DA; DAB; DAC; DAM MST, POET; PC 26; WLC**
See also CDBLB 1660-1789; DA3; DLB 95, 101

Porter, Connie (Rose) 1959(?)- .... **CLC 70**
See also BW 2, 3; CA 142; CANR 90; SATA 81

Porter, Gene(va Grace) Stratton
1863(?)-1924 .... **TCLC 21**
See also CA 112

Porter, Katherine Anne 1890-1980 ... **CLC 1, 3, 7, 10, 13, 15, 27, 101; DA; DAB; DAC; DAM MST, NOV; SSC 4, 31**
See also AITN 2; CA 1-4R; 101; CANR 1, 65; CDALBS; DA3; DLB 4, 9, 102; DLBD 12; DLBY 80; MTCW 1, 2; SATA 39; SATA-Obit 23

Porter, Peter (Neville Frederick)
1929- .... **CLC 5, 13, 33**
See also CA 85-88; DLB 40

Porter, William Sydney 1862-1910
See Henry, O.
See also CA 104; 131; CDALB 1865-1917; DA; DAB; DAC; DAM MST; DA3; DLB 12, 78, 79; MTCW 1, 2; YABC 2

Portillo (y Pacheco), Jose Lopez
See Lopez Portillo (y Pacheco), Jose

Portillo Trambley, Estela 1927-1998
See also CANR 32; DAM MULT; DLB 209; HLC 2; HW 1

Post, Melville Davisson
1869-1930 .... **TCLC 39**
See also CA 110

Potok, Chaim 1929- ... **CLC 2, 7, 14, 26, 112; DAM NOV**
See also AAYA 15; AITN 1, 2; CA 17-20R; CANR 19, 35, 64; DA3; DLB 28, 152; INT CANR-19; MTCW 1, 2; SATA 33, 106

Potter, Dennis (Christopher George)
1935-1994 .... **CLC 58, 86**
See also CA 107; 145; CANR 33, 61; MTCW 1

Pound, Ezra (Weston Loomis)
1885-1972 .. **CLC 1, 2, 3, 4, 5, 7, 10, 13, 18, 34, 48, 50, 112; DA; DAB; DAC; DAM MST, POET; PC 4; WLC**
See also CA 5-8R; 37-40R; CANR 40; CDALB 1917-1929; DA3; DLB 4, 45, 63; DLBD 15; MTCW 1, 2

Povod, Reinaldo 1959-1994 .... **CLC 44**
See also CA 136; 146; CANR 83

Powell, Adam Clayton, Jr.
1908-1972 .... **CLC 89; BLC 3; DAM MULT**
See also BW 1, 3; CA 102; 33-36R; CANR 86

Powell, Anthony (Dymoke) 1905- . **CLC 1, 3, 7, 9, 10, 31**
See also CA 1-4R; CANR 1, 32, 62; CDBLB 1945-1960; DLB 15; MTCW 1, 2

Powell, Dawn 1897-1965 .... **CLC 66**
See also CA 5-8R; DLBY 97

Powell, Padgett 1952- .... **CLC 34**
See also CA 126; CANR 63

Power, Susan 1961- .... **CLC 91**
See also CA 145

Powers, J(ames) F(arl) 1917-1999 ..... **CLC 1, 4, 8, 57; SSC 4**
See also CA 1-4R; 181; CANR 2, 61; DLB 130; MTCW 1

Powers, John J(ames) 1945-
See Powers, John R.
See also CA 69-72

Powers, John R. **CLC 66**
See also Powers, John J(ames)

Powers, Richard (S.) 1957- .... **CLC 93**
See also CA 148; CANR 80

Pownall, David 1938- .... **CLC 10**
See also CA 89-92, 180; CAAS 18; CANR 49; DLB 14

Powys, John Cowper 1872-1963 ... **CLC 7, 9, 15, 46, 125**
See also CA 85-88; DLB 15; MTCW 1, 2

Powys, T(heodore) F(rancis)
1875-1953 .... **TCLC 9**
See also CA 106; DLB 36, 162

Prado (Calvo), Pedro 1886-1952 ... **TCLC 75**
See also CA 131; HW 1

Prager, Emily 1952- .... **CLC 56**

Pratt, E(dwin) J(ohn)
1883(?)-1964 .... **CLC 19; DAC; DAM POET**
See also CA 141; 93-96; CANR 77; DLB 92

Premchand TCLC 21
See also Srivastava, Dhanpat Rai

Preussler, Otfried 1923- .... **CLC 17**
See also CA 77-80; SATA 24

Prevert, Jacques (Henri Marie)
1900-1977 .... **CLC 15**
See also CA 77-80; 69-72; CANR 29, 61; MTCW 1; SATA-Obit 30

Prevost, Abbe (Antoine Francois)
1697-1763 .... **LC 1**

Price, (Edward) Reynolds 1933- ... **CLC 3, 6, 13, 43, 50, 63; DAM NOV; SSC 22**
See also CA 1-4R; CANR 1, 37, 57, 87; DLB 2; INT CANR-37

Price, Richard 1949- .... **CLC 6, 12**
See also CA 49-52; CANR 3; DLBY 81

Prichard, Katharine Susannah
1883-1969 .... **CLC 46**
See also CA 11-12; CANR 33; CAP 1; MTCW 1; SATA 66

Priestley, J(ohn) B(oynton)
1894-1984 .... **CLC 2, 5, 9, 34; DAM DRAM, NOV**
See also CA 9-12R; 113; CANR 33; CDBLB 1914-1945; DA3; DLB 10, 34, 77, 100, 139; DLBY 84; MTCW 1, 2

Prince 1958(?)- .... **CLC 35**

Prince, F(rank) T(empleton) 1912- .. **CLC 22**
See also CA 101; CANR 43, 79; DLB 20

Prince Kropotkin
See Kropotkin, Peter (Aleksieevich)

Prior, Matthew 1664-1721 .... **LC 4**
See also DLB 95

Prishvin, Mikhail 1873-1954 .... **TCLC 75**

Pritchard, William H(arrison)
1932- .... **CLC 34**
See also CA 65-68; CANR 23; DLB 111

Pritchett, V(ictor) S(awdon)
1900-1997 ...... **CLC 5, 13, 15, 41; DAM NOV; SSC 14**
See also CA 61-64; 157; CANR 31, 63; DA3; DLB 15, 139; MTCW 1, 2

Private 19022
See Manning, Frederic

Probst, Mark 1925- .... **CLC 59**
See also CA 130

Prokosch, Frederic 1908-1989 ...... **CLC 4, 48**
See also CA 73-76; 128; CANR 82; DLB 48; MTCW 2

Propertius, Sextus c. 50B.C.-c.
16B.C. .... **CMLC 32**
See also DLB 211

Prophet, The
See Dreiser, Theodore (Herman Albert)

Prose, Francine 1947- .... **CLC 45**
See also CA 109; 112; CANR 46; SATA 101

Proudhon
See Cunha, Euclides (Rodrigues Pimenta) da

Proulx, Annie
See Proulx, E(dna) Annie

Proulx, E(dna) Annie 1935- .. **CLC 81; DAM POP**
See also CA 145; CANR 65; DA3; MTCW 2

Proust, (Valentin-Louis-George-Eugene-) Marcel 1871-1922 .... **TCLC 7, 13, 33; DA; DAB; DAC; DAM MST, NOV; WLC**
See also CA 104; 120; DA3; DLB 65; MTCW 1, 2

Prowler, Harley
See Masters, Edgar Lee

Prus, Boleslaw 1845-1912 .... **TCLC 48**

Pryor, Richard (Franklin Lenox Thomas)
1940- .... **CLC 26**
See also CA 122; 152

Przybyszewski, Stanislaw
1868-1927 .... **TCLC 36**
See also CA 160; DLB 66

Pteleon
See Grieve, C(hristopher) M(urray)
See also DAM POET

Puckett, Lute
See Masters, Edgar Lee

Puig, Manuel 1932-1990 .... **CLC 3, 5, 10, 28, 65; DAM MULT; HLC 2**
See also CA 45-48; CANR 2, 32, 63; DA3; DLB 113; HW 1, 2; MTCW 1, 2

Pulitzer, Joseph 1847-1911 .... **TCLC 76**
See also CA 114; DLB 23

Purdy, A(lfred) W(ellington) 1918- ... **CLC 3, 6, 14, 50; DAC; DAM MST, POET**
See also CA 81-84; CAAS 17; CANR 42, 66; DLB 88

Purdy, James (Amos) 1923- .... **CLC 2, 4, 10, 28, 52**
See also CA 33-36R; CAAS 1; CANR 19, 51; DLB 2; INT CANR-19; MTCW 1

Pure, Simon
See Swinnerton, Frank Arthur

Pushkin, Alexander (Sergeyevich)
1799-1837 . **NCLC 3, 27, 83; DA; DAB; DAC; DAM DRAM, MST, POET; PC 10; SSC 27; WLC**
See also DA3; DLB 205; SATA 61

P'u Sung-ling 1640-1715 .... **LC 49; SSC 31**

Putnam, Arthur Lee
See Alger, Horatio Jr., Jr.

Puzo, Mario 1920-1999 .... **CLC 1, 2, 6, 36, 107; DAM NOV, POP**
See also CA 65-68; 185; CANR 4, 42, 65; DA3; DLB 6; MTCW 1, 2

Pygge, Edward
See Barnes, Julian (Patrick)

Pyle, Ernest Taylor 1900-1945
See Pyle, Ernie
See also CA 115; 160
Pyle, Ernie 1900-1945 .... **TCLC 75**
See also Pyle, Ernest Taylor
See also DLB 29; MTCW 2
Pyle, Howard 1853-1911 .... **TCLC 81**
See also CA 109; 137; CLR 22; DLB 42,
188; DLBD 13; MAICYA; SATA 16, 100
Pym, Barbara (Mary Crampton)
1913-1980 .... **CLC 13, 19, 37, 111**
See also CA 13-14; 97-100; CANR 13, 34;
CAP 1; DLB 14, 207; DLBY 87; MTCW
1, 2
Pynchon, Thomas (Ruggles, Jr.)
1937- ...... **CLC 2, 3, 6, 9, 11, 18, 33, 62,
72; DA; DAB; DAC; DAM MST, NOV,
POP; SSC 14; WLC**
See also BEST 90:2; CA 17-20R; CANR
22, 46, 73; DA3; DLB 2, 173; MTCW 1,
2
Pythagoras c. 570B.C.-c. 500B.C. . **CMLC 22**
See also DLB 176
Q
See Quiller-Couch, SirArthur (Thomas)
Qian Zhongshu
See Ch'ien Chung-shu
Qroll
See Dagerman, Stig (Halvard)
Quarrington, Paul (Lewis) 1953- ..... **CLC 65**
See also CA 129; CANR 62
Quasimodo, Salvatore 1901-1968 ..... **CLC 10**
See also CA 13-16; 25-28R; CAP 1; DLB
114; MTCW 1
Quay, Stephen 1947- .... **CLC 95**
Quay, Timothy 1947- .... **CLC 95**
Queen, Ellery **CLC 3, 11**
See also Dannay, Frederic; Davidson,
Avram (James); Lee, Manfred
B(ennington); Marlowe, Stephen; Stur-
geon, Theodore (Hamilton); Vance, John
Holbrook
Queen, Ellery, Jr.
See Dannay, Frederic; Lee, Manfred
B(ennington)
Queneau, Raymond 1903-1976 ..... **CLC 2, 5,
10, 42**
See also CA 77-80; 69-72; CANR 32; DLB
72; MTCW 1, 2
Quevedo, Francisco de 1580-1645 .... **LC 23**
Quiller-Couch, SirArthur (Thomas)
1863-1944 .... **TCLC 53**
See also CA 118; 166; DLB 135, 153, 190
Quin, Ann (Marie) 1936-1973 .... **CLC 6**
See also CA 9-12R; 45-48; DLB 14
Quinn, Martin
See Smith, Martin Cruz
Quinn, Peter 1947- .... **CLC 91**
Quinn, Simon
See Smith, Martin Cruz
Quintana, Leroy V. 1944-
See also CA 131; CANR 65; DAM MULT;
DLB 82; HLC 2; HW 1, 2
Quiroga, Horacio (Sylvestre)
1878-1937 .... **TCLC 20; DAM MULT;
HLC 2**
See also CA 117; 131; HW 1; MTCW 1
Quoirez, Francoise 1935- .... **CLC 9**
See also Sagan, Francoise
See also CA 49-52; CANR 6, 39, 73;
MTCW 1, 2

Raabe, Wilhelm (Karl) 1831-1910 . **TCLC 45**
See also CA 167; DLB 129
Rabe, David (William) 1940- .. **CLC 4, 8, 33;
DAM DRAM**
See also CA 85-88; CABS 3; CANR 59;
DLB 7
Rabelais, Francois 1483-1553 ...... **LC 5; DA;
DAB; DAC; DAM MST; WLC**
Rabinovitch, Sholem 1859-1916
See Aleichem, Sholom
See also CA 104
Rabinyan, Dorit 1972- .... **CLC 119**
See also CA 170
Rachilde
See Vallette, Marguerite Eymery
Racine, Jean 1639-1699 . **LC 28; DAB; DAM
MST**
See also DA3
Radcliffe, Ann (Ward) 1764-1823 ... **NCLC 6,
55**
See also DLB 39, 178
Radiguet, Raymond 1903-1923 ...... **TCLC 29**
See also CA 162; DLB 65
Radnoti, Miklos 1909-1944 .... **TCLC 16**
See also CA 118
Rado, James 1939- .... **CLC 17**
See also CA 105
Radvanyi, Netty 1900-1983
See Seghers, Anna
See also CA 85-88; 110; CANR 82
Rae, Ben
See Griffiths, Trevor
Raeburn, John (Hay) 1941- .... **CLC 34**
See also CA 57-60
Ragni, Gerome 1942-1991 .... **CLC 17**
See also CA 105; 134
Rahv, Philip 1908-1973 .... **CLC 24**
See also Greenberg, Ivan
See also DLB 137
Raimund, Ferdinand Jakob
1790-1836 .... **NCLC 69**
See also DLB 90
Raine, Craig 1944- .... **CLC 32, 103**
See also CA 108; CANR 29, 51; DLB 40
Raine, Kathleen (Jessie) 1908- ..... **CLC 7, 45**
See also CA 85-88; CANR 46; DLB 20;
MTCW 1
Rainis, Janis 1865-1929 .... **TCLC 29**
See also CA 170; DLB 220
Rakosi, Carl 1903- .... **CLC 47**
See also Rawley, Callman
See also CAAS 5; DLB 193
Raleigh, Richard
See Lovecraft, H(oward) P(hillips)
Raleigh, Sir Walter 1554(?)-1618 .... **LC 31,
39; PC 30**
See also CDBLB Before 1660; DLB 172
Rallentando, H. P.
See Sayers, Dorothy L(eigh)
Ramal, Walter
See de la Mare, Walter (John)
Ramana Maharshi 1879-1950 .... **TCLC 84**
Ramoacn y Cajal, Santiago
1852-1934 .... **TCLC 93**
Ramon, Juan
See Jimenez (Mantecon), Juan Ramon
Ramos, Graciliano 1892-1953 .... **TCLC 32**
See also CA 167; HW 2
Rampersad, Arnold 1941- .... **CLC 44**
See also BW 2, 3; CA 127; 133; CANR 81;
DLB 111; INT 133

Rampling, Anne
See Rice, Anne
Ramsay, Allan 1684(?)-1758 .... **LC 29**
See also DLB 95
Ramuz, Charles-Ferdinand
1878-1947 .... **TCLC 33**
See also CA 165
Rand, Ayn 1905-1982 ...... **CLC 3, 30, 44, 79;
DA; DAC; DAM MST, NOV, POP;
WLC**
See also AAYA 10; CA 13-16R; 105; CANR
27, 73; CDALBS; DA3; MTCW 1, 2
Randall, Dudley (Felker) 1914- .... **CLC 1;
BLC 3; DAM MULT**
See also BW 1, 3; CA 25-28R; CANR 23,
82; DLB 41
Randall, Robert
See Silverberg, Robert
Ranger, Ken
See Creasey, John
Ransom, John Crowe 1888-1974 .. **CLC 2, 4,
5, 11, 24; DAM POET**
See also CA 5-8R; 49-52; CANR 6, 34;
CDALBS; DA3; DLB 45, 63; MTCW 1,
2
Rao, Raja 1909- ..... **CLC 25, 56; DAM NOV**
See also CA 73-76; CANR 51; MTCW 1, 2
Raphael, Frederic (Michael) 1931- ... **CLC 2,
14**
See also CA 1-4R; CANR 1, 86; DLB 14
Ratcliffe, James P.
See Mencken, H(enry) L(ouis)
Rathbone, Julian 1935- .... **CLC 41**
See also CA 101; CANR 34, 73
Rattigan, Terence (Mervyn)
1911-1977 .... **CLC 7; DAM DRAM**
See also CA 85-88; 73-76; CDBLB 1945-
1960; DLB 13; MTCW 1, 2
Ratushinskaya, Irina 1954- .... **CLC 54**
See also CA 129; CANR 68
Raven, Simon (Arthur Noel) 1927- .. **CLC 14**
See also CA 81-84; CANR 86
Ravenna, Michael
See Welty, Eudora
Rawley, Callman 1903-
See Rakosi, Carl
See also CA 21-24R; CANR 12, 32, 91
Rawlings, Marjorie Kinnan
1896-1953 .... **TCLC 4**
See also AAYA 20; CA 104; 137; CANR
74; CLR 63; DLB 9, 22, 102; DLBD 17;
JRDA; MAICYA; MTCW 2; SATA 100;
YABC 1
Ray, Satyajit 1921-1992 .. **CLC 16, 76; DAM
MULT**
See also CA 114; 137
Read, Herbert Edward 1893-1968 ..... **CLC 4**
See also CA 85-88; 25-28R; DLB 20, 149
Read, Piers Paul 1941- .... **CLC 4, 10, 25**
See also CA 21-24R; CANR 38, 86; DLB
14; SATA 21
Reade, Charles 1814-1884 .... **NCLC 2, 74**
See also DLB 21
Reade, Hamish
See Gray, Simon (James Holliday)
Reading, Peter 1946- .... **CLC 47**
See also CA 103; CANR 46; DLB 40
Reaney, James 1926- .. **CLC 13; DAC; DAM
MST**
See also CA 41-44R; CAAS 15; CANR 42;
DLB 68; SATA 43

Rebreanu, Liviu 1885-1944 .... **TCLC 28**
See also CA 165; DLB 220

Rechy, John (Francisco) 1934- ...... **CLC 1, 7, 14, 18, 107; DAM MULT; HLC 2**
See also CA 5-8R; CAAS 4; CANR 6, 32, 64; DLB 122; DLBY 82; HW 1, 2; INT CANR-6

Redcam, Tom 1870-1933 .... **TCLC 25**

Reddin, Keith CLC 67

Redgrove, Peter (William) 1932- . **CLC 6, 41**
See also CA 1-4R; CANR 3, 39, 77; DLB 40

Redmon, Anne CLC 22
See also Nightingale, Anne Redmon
See also DLBY 86

Reed, Eliot
See Ambler, Eric

Reed, Ishmael 1938- .. **CLC 2, 3, 5, 6, 13, 32, 60; BLC 3; DAM MULT**
See also BW 2, 3; CA 21-24R; CANR 25, 48, 74; DA3; DLB 2, 5, 33, 169; DLBD 8; MTCW 1, 2

Reed, John (Silas) 1887-1920 .... **TCLC 9**
See also CA 106

Reed, Lou CLC 21
See also Firbank, Louis

Reese, Lizette Woodworth 1856-1935 . **PC 29**
See also CA 180; DLB 54

Reeve, Clara 1729-1807 .... **NCLC 19**
See also DLB 39

Reich, Wilhelm 1897-1957 .... **TCLC 57**

Reid, Christopher (John) 1949- .... **CLC 33**
See also CA 140; CANR 89; DLB 40

Reid, Desmond
See Moorcock, Michael (John)

Reid Banks, Lynne 1929-
See Banks, Lynne Reid
See also CA 1-4R; CANR 6, 22, 38, 87; CLR 24; JRDA; MAICYA; SATA 22, 75, 111

Reilly, William K.
See Creasey, John

Reiner, Max
See Caldwell, (Janet Miriam) Taylor (Holland)

Reis, Ricardo
See Pessoa, Fernando (Antonio Nogueira)

Remarque, Erich Maria 1898-1970 ... **CLC 21; DA; DAB; DAC; DAM MST, NOV**
See also AAYA 27; CA 77-80; 29-32R; DA3; DLB 56; MTCW 1, 2

Remington, Frederic 1861-1909 ..... **TCLC 89**
See also CA 108; 169; DLB 12, 186, 188; SATA 41

Remizov, A.
See Remizov, Aleksei (Mikhailovich)

Remizov, A. M.
See Remizov, Aleksei (Mikhailovich)

Remizov, Aleksei (Mikhailovich) 1877-1957 .... **TCLC 27**
See also CA 125; 133

Renan, Joseph Ernest 1823-1892 .. **NCLC 26**

Renard, Jules 1864-1910 .... **TCLC 17**
See also CA 117

Renault, Mary CLC 3, 11, 17
See also Challans, Mary
See also DLBY 83; MTCW 2

Rendell, Ruth (Barbara) 1930- . **CLC 28, 48; DAM POP**
See also Vine, Barbara
See also CA 109; CANR 32, 52, 74; DLB 87; INT CANR-32; MTCW 1, 2

Renoir, Jean 1894-1979 .... **CLC 20**
See also CA 129; 85-88

Resnais, Alain 1922- .... **CLC 16**

Reverdy, Pierre 1889-1960 .... **CLC 53**
See also CA 97-100; 89-92

Rexroth, Kenneth 1905-1982 .... **CLC 1, 2, 6, 11, 22, 49, 112; DAM POET; PC 20**
See also CA 5-8R; 107; CANR 14, 34, 63; CDALB 1941-1968; DLB 16, 48, 165, 212; DLBY 82; INT CANR-14; MTCW 1, 2

Reyes, Alfonso 1889-1959 .. **TCLC 33; HLCS 2**
See also CA 131; HW 1

Reyes y Basoalto, Ricardo Eliecer Neftali
See Neruda, Pablo

Reymont, Wladyslaw (Stanislaw) 1868(?)-1925 .... **TCLC 5**
See also CA 104

Reynolds, Jonathan 1942- .... **CLC 6, 38**
See also CA 65-68; CANR 28

Reynolds, Joshua 1723-1792 .... **LC 15**
See also DLB 104

Reynolds, Michael S(hane) 1937- ..... **CLC 44**
See also CA 65-68; CANR 9, 89

Reznikoff, Charles 1894-1976 .... **CLC 9**
See also CA 33-36; 61-64; CAP 2; DLB 28, 45

Rezzori (d'Arezzo), Gregor von 1914-1998 .... **CLC 25**
See also CA 122; 136; 167

Rhine, Richard
See Silverstein, Alvin

Rhodes, Eugene Manlove 1869-1934 .... **TCLC 53**

Rhodius, Apollonius c. 3rd cent. B.C.- .... **CMLC 28**
See also DLB 176

R'hoone
See Balzac, Honore de

Rhys, Jean 1890(?)-1979 ...... **CLC 2, 4, 6, 14, 19, 51, 124; DAM NOV; SSC 21**
See also CA 25-28R; 85-88; CANR 35, 62; CDBLB 1945-1960; DA3; DLB 36, 117, 162; MTCW 1, 2

Ribeiro, Darcy 1922-1997 .... **CLC 34**
See also CA 33-36R; 156

Ribeiro, Joao Ubaldo (Osorio Pimentel) 1941- .... **CLC 10, 67**
See also CA 81-84

Ribman, Ronald (Burt) 1932- .... **CLC 7**
See also CA 21-24R; CANR 46, 80

Ricci, Nino 1959- .... **CLC 70**
See also CA 137

Rice, Anne 1941- .. **CLC 41, 128; DAM POP**
See also AAYA 9; BEST 89:2; CA 65-68; CANR 12, 36, 53, 74; DA3; MTCW 2

Rice, Elmer (Leopold) 1892-1967 ...... **CLC 7, 49; DAM DRAM**
See also CA 21-22; 25-28R; CAP 2; DLB 4, 7; MTCW 1, 2

Rice, Tim(othy Miles Bindon) 1944- .... **CLC 21**
See also CA 103; CANR 46

Rich, Adrienne (Cecile) 1929- ... **CLC 3, 6, 7, 11, 18, 36, 73, 76, 125; DAM POET; PC 5**
See also CA 9-12R; CANR 20, 53, 74; CDALBS; DA3; DLB 5, 67; MTCW 1, 2

Rich, Barbara
See Graves, Robert (von Ranke)

Rich, Robert
See Trumbo, Dalton

Richard, Keith CLC 17
See also Richards, Keith

Richards, David Adams 1950- .... **CLC 59; DAC**
See also CA 93-96; CANR 60; DLB 53

Richards, I(vor) A(rmstrong) 1893-1979 .... **CLC 14, 24**
See also CA 41-44R; 89-92; CANR 34, 74; DLB 27; MTCW 2

Richards, Keith 1943-
See Richard, Keith
See also CA 107; CANR 77

Richardson, Anne
See Roiphe, Anne (Richardson)

Richardson, Dorothy Miller 1873-1957 .... **TCLC 3**
See also CA 104; DLB 36

Richardson, Ethel Florence (Lindesay) 1870-1946
See Richardson, Henry Handel
See also CA 105

Richardson, Henry Handel TCLC 4
See also Richardson, Ethel Florence (Lindesay)
See also DLB 197

Richardson, John 1796-1852 .... **NCLC 55; DAC**
See also DLB 99

Richardson, Samuel 1689-1761 ...... **LC 1, 44; DA; DAB; DAC; DAM MST, NOV; WLC**
See also CDBLB 1660-1789; DLB 39

Richler, Mordecai 1931- ...... **CLC 3, 5, 9, 13, 18, 46, 70; DAC; DAM MST, NOV**
See also AITN 1; CA 65-68; CANR 31, 62; CLR 17; DLB 53; MAICYA; MTCW 1, 2; SATA 44, 98; SATA-Brief 27

Richter, Conrad (Michael) 1890-1968 .... **CLC 30**
See also AAYA 21; CA 5-8R; 25-28R; CANR 23; DLB 9, 212; MTCW 1, 2; SATA 3

Ricostranza, Tom
See Ellis, Trey

Riddell, Charlotte 1832-1906 .... **TCLC 40**
See also CA 165; DLB 156

Ridge, John Rollin 1827-1867 ...... **NCLC 82; DAM MULT**
See also CA 144; DLB 175; NNAL

Ridgway, Keith 1965- .... **CLC 119**
See also CA 172

Riding, Laura CLC 3, 7
See also Jackson, Laura (Riding)

Riefenstahl, Berta Helene Amalia 1902-
See Riefenstahl, Leni
See also CA 108

Riefenstahl, Leni CLC 16
See also Riefenstahl, Berta Helene Amalia

Riffe, Ernest
See Bergman, (Ernst) Ingmar

Riggs, (Rolla) Lynn 1899-1954 ..... **TCLC 56; DAM MULT**
See also CA 144; DLB 175; NNAL

Savan, Glenn 19(?)- .... **CLC 50**

Sayers, Dorothy L(eigh)
1893-1957 .... **TCLC 2, 15; DAM POP**
See also CA 104; 119; CANR 60; CDBLB
1914-1945; DLB 10, 36, 77, 100; MTCW
1, 2

Sayers, Valerie 1952- .... **CLC 50, 122**
See also CA 134; CANR 61

Sayles, John (Thomas) 1950- . **CLC 7, 10, 14**
See also CA 57-60; CANR 41, 84; DLB 44

Scammell, Michael 1935- .... **CLC 34**
See also CA 156

Scannell, Vernon 1922- .... **CLC 49**
See also CA 5-8R; CANR 8, 24, 57; DLB
27; SATA 59

Scarlett, Susan
See Streatfeild, (Mary) Noel

Scarron
See Mikszath, Kalman

Schaeffer, Susan Fromberg 1941- ..... **CLC 6,
11, 22**
See also CA 49-52; CANR 18, 65; DLB 28;
MTCW 1, 2; SATA 22

Schary, Jill
See Robinson, Jill

Schell, Jonathan 1943- .... **CLC 35**
See also CA 73-76; CANR 12

Schelling, Friedrich Wilhelm Joseph von
1775-1854 .... **NCLC 30**
See also DLB 90

Schendel, Arthur van 1874-1946 ... **TCLC 56**

Scherer, Jean-Marie Maurice 1920-
See Rohmer, Eric
See also CA 110

Schevill, James (Erwin) 1920- .... **CLC 7**
See also CA 5-8R; CAAS 12

Schiller, Friedrich 1759-1805 . **NCLC 39, 69;
DAM DRAM; DC 12**
See also DLB 94

Schisgal, Murray (Joseph) 1926- .... **CLC 6**
See also CA 21-24R; CANR 48, 86

Schlee, Ann 1934- .... **CLC 35**
See also CA 101; CANR 29, 88; SATA 44;
SATA-Brief 36

Schlegel, August Wilhelm von
1767-1845 .... **NCLC 15**
See also DLB 94

Schlegel, Friedrich 1772-1829 .... **NCLC 45**
See also DLB 90

Schlegel, Johann Elias (von)
1719(?)-1749 .... **LC 5**

Schlesinger, Arthur M(eier), Jr.
1917- .... **CLC 84**
See also AITN 1; CA 1-4R; CANR 1, 28,
58; DLB 17; INT CANR-28; MTCW 1,
2; SATA 61

Schmidt, Arno (Otto) 1914-1979 ...... **CLC 56**
See also CA 128; 109; DLB 69

Schmitz, Aron Hector 1861-1928
See Svevo, Italo
See also CA 104; 122; MTCW 1

Schnackenberg, Gjertrud 1953- .... **CLC 40**
See also CA 116; DLB 120

Schneider, Leonard Alfred 1925-1966
See Bruce, Lenny
See also CA 89-92

Schnitzler, Arthur 1862-1931 . **TCLC 4; SSC
15**
See also CA 104; DLB 81, 118

Schoenberg, Arnold 1874-1951 ...... **TCLC 75**
See also CA 109

Schonberg, Arnold
See Schoenberg, Arnold

Schopenhauer, Arthur 1788-1860 .. **NCLC 51**
See also DLB 90

Schor, Sandra (M.) 1932(?)-1990 ..... **CLC 65**
See also CA 132

Schorer, Mark 1908-1977 .... **CLC 9**
See also CA 5-8R; 73-76; CANR 7; DLB
103

Schrader, Paul (Joseph) 1946- .... **CLC 26**
See also CA 37-40R; CANR 41; DLB 44

Schreiner, Olive (Emilie Albertina)
1855-1920 .... **TCLC 9**
See also CA 105; 154; DLB 18, 156, 190

Schulberg, Budd (Wilson) 1914- .. **CLC 7, 48**
See also CA 25-28R; CANR 19, 87; DLB
6, 26, 28; DLBY 81

Schulz, Bruno 1892-1942 .. **TCLC 5, 51; SSC
13**
See also CA 115; 123; CANR 86; MTCW 2

Schulz, Charles M(onroe) 1922- .... **CLC 12**
See also CA 9-12R; CANR 6; INT
CANR-6; SATA 10

Schumacher, E(rnst) F(riedrich)
1911-1977 .... **CLC 80**
See also CA 81-84; 73-76; CANR 34, 85

Schuyler, James Marcus 1923-1991 .. **CLC 5,
23; DAM POET**
See also CA 101; 134; DLB 5, 169; INT
101

Schwartz, Delmore (David)
1913-1966 ... **CLC 2, 4, 10, 45, 87; PC 8**
See also CA 17-18; 25-28R; CANR 35;
CAP 2; DLB 28, 48; MTCW 1, 2

Schwartz, Ernst
See Ozu, Yasujiro

Schwartz, John Burnham 1965- .... **CLC 59**
See also CA 132

Schwartz, Lynne Sharon 1939- .... **CLC 31**
See also CA 103; CANR 44, 89; MTCW 2

Schwartz, Muriel A.
See Eliot, T(homas) S(tearns)

Schwarz-Bart, Andre 1928- .... **CLC 2, 4**
See also CA 89-92

Schwarz-Bart, Simone 1938- . **CLC 7; BLCS**
See also BW 2; CA 97-100

**Schwitters, Kurt (Hermann Edward Karl
Julius)** 1887-1948 .... **TCLC 95**
See also CA 158

Schwob, Marcel (Mayer Andre)
1867-1905 .... **TCLC 20**
See also CA 117; 168; DLB 123

Sciascia, Leonardo 1921-1989 .. **CLC 8, 9, 41**
See also CA 85-88; 130; CANR 35; DLB
177; MTCW 1

Scoppettone, Sandra 1936- .... **CLC 26**
See also AAYA 11; CA 5-8R; CANR 41,
73; SATA 9, 92

Scorsese, Martin 1942- .... **CLC 20, 89**
See also CA 110; 114; CANR 46, 85

Scotland, Jay
See Jakes, John (William)

Scott, Duncan Campbell
1862-1947 .... **TCLC 6; DAC**
See also CA 104; 153; DLB 92

Scott, Evelyn 1893-1963 .... **CLC 43**
See also CA 104; 112; CANR 64; DLB 9,
48

Scott, F(rancis) R(eginald)
1899-1985 .... **CLC 22**
See also CA 101; 114; CANR 87; DLB 88;
INT 101

Scott, Frank
See Scott, F(rancis) R(eginald)

Scott, Joanna 1960- .... **CLC 50**
See also CA 126; CANR 53

Scott, Paul (Mark) 1920-1978 ...... **CLC 9, 60**
See also CA 81-84; 77-80; CANR 33; DLB
14, 207; MTCW 1

Scott, Sarah 1723-1795 .... **LC 44**
See also DLB 39

Scott, Walter 1771-1832 . **NCLC 15, 69; DA;
DAB; DAC; DAM MST, NOV, POET;
PC 13; SSC 32; WLC**
See also AAYA 22; CDBLB 1789-1832;
DLB 93, 107, 116, 144, 159; YABC 2

Scribe, (Augustin) Eugene
1791-1861 ..... **NCLC 16; DAM DRAM;
DC 5**
See also DLB 192

Scrum, R.
See Crumb, R(obert)

Scudery, Madeleine de 1607-1701 .. **LC 2, 58**

Scum
See Crumb, R(obert)

Scumbag, Little Bobby
See Crumb, R(obert)

Seabrook, John
See Hubbard, L(afayette) Ron(ald)

Sealy, I(rwin) Allan 1951- .... **CLC 55**
See also CA 136

Search, Alexander
See Pessoa, Fernando (Antonio Nogueira)

Sebastian, Lee
See Silverberg, Robert

Sebastian Owl
See Thompson, Hunter S(tockton)

Sebestyen, Ouida 1924- .... **CLC 30**
See also AAYA 8; CA 107; CANR 40; CLR
17; JRDA; MAICYA; SAAS 10; SATA
39

Secundus, H. Scriblerus
See Fielding, Henry

Sedges, John
See Buck, Pearl S(ydenstricker)

Sedgwick, Catharine Maria
1789-1867 .... **NCLC 19**
See also DLB 1, 74

Seelye, John (Douglas) 1931- .... **CLC 7**
See also CA 97-100; CANR 70; INT 97-
100

Seferiades, Giorgos Stylianou 1900-1971
See Seferis, George
See also CA 5-8R; 33-36R; CANR 5, 36;
MTCW 1

Seferis, George CLC 5, 11
See also Seferiades, Giorgos Stylianou

Segal, Erich (Wolf) 1937- . **CLC 3, 10; DAM
POP**
See also BEST 89:1; CA 25-28R; CANR
20, 36, 65; DLBY 86; INT CANR-20;
MTCW 1

Seger, Bob 1945- .... **CLC 35**

Seghers, Anna CLC 7
See also Radvanyi, Netty
See also DLB 69

Seidel, Frederick (Lewis) 1936- .... **CLC 18**
See also CA 13-16R; CANR 8; DLBY 84

Seifert, Jaroslav 1901-1986 .. **CLC 34, 44, 93**
See also CA 127; MTCW 1, 2

Sei Shonagon c. 966-1017(?) .... **CMLC 6**

Séjour, Victor 1817-1874 .... **DC 10**
See also DLB 50

Shields, David 1956- .... **CLC 97**
　　See also CA 124; CANR 48

Shiga, Naoya 1883-1971 ..... **CLC 33; SSC 23**
　　See also CA 101; 33-36R; DLB 180

Shikibu, Murasaki c. 978-c. 1014 ... **CMLC 1**

Shilts, Randy 1951-1994 .... **CLC 85**
　　See also AAYA 19; CA 115; 127; 144;
　　CANR 45; DA3; INT 127; MTCW 2

Shimazaki, Haruki 1872-1943
　　See Shimazaki Toson
　　See also CA 105; 134; CANR 84

Shimazaki Toson 1872-1943 .... **TCLC 5**
　　See also Shimazaki, Haruki
　　See also DLB 180

Sholokhov, Mikhail (Aleksandrovich)
　　1905-1984 .... **CLC 7, 15**
　　See also CA 101; 112; MTCW 1, 2; SATA-
　　Obit 36

Shone, Patric
　　See Hanley, James

Shreve, Susan Richards 1939- .... **CLC 23**
　　See also CA 49-52; CAAS 5; CANR 5, 38,
　　69; MAICYA; SATA 46, 95; SATA-Brief
　　41

Shue, Larry 1946-1985 .... **CLC 52; DAM
　　DRAM**
　　See also CA 145; 117

Shu-Jen, Chou 1881-1936
　　See Lu Hsun
　　See also CA 104

Shulman, Alix Kates 1932- .... **CLC 2, 10**
　　See also CA 29-32R; CANR 43; SATA 7

Shuster, Joe 1914- .... **CLC 21**

Shute, Nevil CLC 30
　　See also Norway, Nevil Shute
　　See also MTCW 2

Shuttle, Penelope (Diane) 1947- .... **CLC 7**
　　See also CA 93-96; CANR 39, 84; DLB 14,
　　40

Sidney, Mary 1561-1621 .... **LC 19, 39**

Sidney, SirPhilip 1554-1586 . **LC 19, 39; DA;
　　DAB; DAC; DAM MST, POET**
　　See also CDBLB Before 1660; DA3; DLB
　　167

Siegel, Jerome 1914-1996 .... **CLC 21**
　　See also CA 116; 169; 151

Siegel, Jerry
　　See Siegel, Jerome

Sienkiewicz, Henryk (Adam Alexander Pius)
　　1846-1916 .... **TCLC 3**
　　See also CA 104; 134; CANR 84

Sierra, Gregorio Martinez
　　See Martinez Sierra, Gregorio

Sierra, Maria (de la O'LeJarraga) Martinez
　　See Martinez Sierra, Maria (de la
　　O'LeJarraga)

Sigal, Clancy 1926- .... **CLC 7**
　　See also CA 1-4R; CANR 85

Sigourney, Lydia Howard (Huntley)
　　1791-1865 .... **NCLC 21, 87**
　　See also DLB 1, 42, 73

Siguenza y Gongora, Carlos de
　　1645-1700 .... **LC 8; HLCS 2**
　　See also CA 170

Sigurjonsson, Johann 1880-1919 ... **TCLC 27**
　　See also CA 170

Sikelianos, Angelos 1884-1951 ...... **TCLC 39;
　　PC 29**

Silkin, Jon 1930-1997 .... **CLC 2, 6, 43**
　　See also CA 5-8R; CAAS 5; CANR 89;
　　DLB 27

Silko, Leslie (Marmon) 1948- .... **CLC 23, 74,
　　114; DA; DAC; DAM MST, MULT,
　　POP; SSC 37; WLCS**
　　See also AAYA 14; CA 115; 122; CANR
　　45, 65; DA3; DLB 143, 175; MTCW 2;
　　NNAL

Sillanpaa, Frans Eemil 1888-1964 ... **CLC 19**
　　See also CA 129; 93-96; MTCW 1

Sillitoe, Alan 1928- ... **CLC 1, 3, 6, 10, 19, 57**
　　See also AITN 1; CA 9-12R; CAAS 2;
　　CANR 8, 26, 55; CDBLB 1960 to Present;
　　DLB 14, 139; MTCW 1, 2; SATA 61

Silone, Ignazio 1900-1978 .... **CLC 4**
　　See also CA 25-28; 81-84; CANR 34; CAP
　　2; MTCW 1

Silver, Joan Micklin 1935- .... **CLC 20**
　　See also CA 114; 121; INT 121

Silver, Nicholas
　　See Faust, Frederick (Schiller)

Silverberg, Robert 1935- .... **CLC 7; DAM
　　POP**
　　See also AAYA 24; CA 1-4R, 186; CAAE
　　186; CAAS 3; CANR 1, 20, 36, 85; CLR
　　59; DLB 8; INT CANR-20; MAICYA;
　　MTCW 1, 2; SATA 13, 91; SATA-Essay
　　104

Silverstein, Alvin 1933- .... **CLC 17**
　　See also CA 49-52; CANR 2; CLR 25;
　　JRDA; MAICYA; SATA 8, 69

Silverstein, Virginia B(arbara Opshelor)
　　1937- .... **CLC 17**
　　See also CA 49-52; CANR 2; CLR 25;
　　JRDA; MAICYA; SATA 8, 69

Sim, Georges
　　See Simenon, Georges (Jacques Christian)

Simak, Clifford D(onald) 1904-1988 . **CLC 1,
　　55**
　　See also CA 1-4R; 125; CANR 1, 35; DLB
　　8; MTCW 1; SATA-Obit 56

Simenon, Georges (Jacques Christian)
　　1903-1989 .... **CLC 1, 2, 3, 8, 18, 47;
　　DAM POP**
　　See also CA 85-88; 129; CANR 35; DA3;
　　DLB 72; DLBY 89; MTCW 1, 2

Simic, Charles 1938- .... **CLC 6, 9, 22, 49, 68,
　　130; DAM POET**
　　See also CA 29-32R; CAAS 4; CANR 12,
　　33, 52, 61; DA3; DLB 105; MTCW 2

Simmel, Georg 1858-1918 .... **TCLC 64**
　　See also CA 157

Simmons, Charles (Paul) 1924- .... **CLC 57**
　　See also CA 89-92; INT 89-92

Simmons, Dan 1948- .... **CLC 44; DAM POP**
　　See also AAYA 16; CA 138; CANR 53, 81

Simmons, James (Stewart Alexander)
　　1933- .... **CLC 43**
　　See also CA 105; CAAS 21; DLB 40

Simms, William Gilmore
　　1806-1870 .... **NCLC 3**
　　See also DLB 3, 30, 59, 73

Simon, Carly 1945- .... **CLC 26**
　　See also CA 105

Simon, Claude 1913- .... **CLC 4, 9, 15, 39;
　　DAM NOV**
　　See also CA 89-92; CANR 33; DLB 83;
　　MTCW 1

Simon, (Marvin) Neil 1927- ... **CLC 6, 11, 31,
　　39, 70; DAM DRAM**
　　See also AAYA 32; AITN 1; CA 21-24R;
　　CANR 26, 54, 87; DA3; DLB 7; MTCW
　　1, 2

Simon, Paul (Frederick) 1941(?)- ..... **CLC 17**
　　See also CA 116; 153

Simonon, Paul 1956(?)- .... **CLC 30**

Simpson, Harriette
　　See Arnow, Harriette (Louisa) Simpson

Simpson, Louis (Aston Marantz)
　　1923- ...... **CLC 4, 7, 9, 32; DAM POET**
　　See also CA 1-4R; CAAS 4; CANR 1, 61;
　　DLB 5; MTCW 1, 2

Simpson, Mona (Elizabeth) 1957- .... **CLC 44**
　　See also CA 122; 135; CANR 68

Simpson, N(orman) F(rederick)
　　1919- .... **CLC 29**
　　See also CA 13-16R; DLB 13

Sinclair, Andrew (Annandale) 1935- . **CLC 2,
　　14**
　　See also CA 9-12R; CAAS 5; CANR 14,
　　38, 91; DLB 14; MTCW 1

Sinclair, Emil
　　See Hesse, Hermann

Sinclair, Iain 1943- .... **CLC 76**
　　See also CA 132; CANR 81

Sinclair, Iain MacGregor
　　See Sinclair, Iain

Sinclair, Irene
　　See Griffith, D(avid Lewelyn) W(ark)

Sinclair, Mary Amelia St. Clair 1865(?)-1946
　　See Sinclair, May
　　See also CA 104

Sinclair, May 1863-1946 .... **TCLC 3, 11**
　　See also Sinclair, Mary Amelia St. Clair
　　See also CA 166; DLB 36, 135

Sinclair, Roy
　　See Griffith, D(avid Lewelyn) W(ark)

Sinclair, Upton (Beall) 1878-1968 ..... **CLC 1,
　　11, 15, 63; DA; DAB; DAC; DAM
　　MST, NOV; WLC**
　　See also CA 5-8R; 25-28R; CANR 7;
　　CDALB 1929-1941; DA3; DLB 9; INT
　　CANR-7; MTCW 1, 2; SATA 9

Singer, Isaac
　　See Singer, Isaac Bashevis

Singer, Isaac Bashevis 1904-1991 .. **CLC 1, 3,
　　6, 9, 11, 15, 23, 38, 69, 111; DA; DAB;
　　DAC; DAM MST, NOV; SSC 3; WLC**
　　See also AAYA 32; AITN 1, 2; CA 1-4R;
　　134; CANR 1, 39; CDALB 1941-1968;
　　CLR 1; DA3; DLB 6, 28, 52; DLBY 91;
　　JRDA; MAICYA; MTCW 1, 2; SATA 3,
　　27; SATA-Obit 68

Singer, Israel Joshua 1893-1944 .... **TCLC 33**
　　See also CA 169

Singh, Khushwant 1915- .... **CLC 11**
　　See also CA 9-12R; CAAS 9; CANR 6, 84

Singleton, Ann
　　See Benedict, Ruth (Fulton)

Sinjohn, John
　　See Galsworthy, John

Sinyavsky, Andrei (Donatevich)
　　1925-1997 .... **CLC 8**
　　See also CA 85-88; 159

Sirin, V.
　　See Nabokov, Vladimir (Vladimirovich)

Sissman, L(ouis) E(dward)
　　1928-1976 .... **CLC 9, 18**
　　See also CA 21-24R; 65-68; CANR 13;
　　DLB 5

Sisson, C(harles) H(ubert) 1914- .... **CLC 8**
　　See also CA 1-4R; CAAS 3; CANR 3, 48,
　　84; DLB 27

Sitwell, Dame Edith 1887-1964 ..... **CLC 2, 9,
　　67; DAM POET; PC 3**
　　See also CA 9-12R; CANR 35; CDBLB
　　1945-1960; DLB 20; MTCW 1, 2

Southworth, Emma Dorothy Eliza Nevitte
1819-1899 .... NCLC **26**
Souza, Ernest
See Scott, Evelyn
Soyinka, Wole 1934- .... CLC **3, 5, 14, 36, 44;**
BLC 3; DA; DAB; DAC; DAM
DRAM, MST, MULT; DC 2; WLC
See also BW 2, 3; CA 13-16R; CANR 27,
39, 82; DA3; DLB 125; MTCW 1, 2
Spackman, W(illiam) M(ode)
1905-1990 .... CLC **46**
See also CA 81-84; 132
Spacks, Barry (Bernard) 1931- .... CLC **14**
See also CA 154; CANR 33; DLB 105
Spanidou, Irini 1946- .... CLC **44**
See also CA 185
Spark, Muriel (Sarah) 1918- ..... CLC **2, 3, 5,**
8, 13, 18, 40, 94; DAB; DAC; DAM
MST, NOV; SSC 10
See also CA 5-8R; CANR 12, 36, 76, 89;
CDBLB 1945-1960; DA3; DLB 15, 139;
INT CANR-12; MTCW 1, 2
Spaulding, Douglas
See Bradbury, Ray (Douglas)
Spaulding, Leonard
See Bradbury, Ray (Douglas)
Spence, J. A. D.
See Eliot, T(homas) S(tearns)
Spencer, Elizabeth 1921- .... CLC **22**
See also CA 13-16R; CANR 32, 65, 87;
DLB 6; MTCW 1; SATA 14
Spencer, Leonard G.
See Silverberg, Robert
Spencer, Scott 1945- .... CLC **30**
See also CA 113; CANR 51; DLBY 86
Spender, Stephen (Harold)
1909-1995 .... CLC **1, 2, 5, 10, 41, 91;**
DAM POET
See also CA 9-12R; 149; CANR 31, 54;
CDBLB 1945-1960; DA3; DLB 20;
MTCW 1, 2
Spengler, Oswald (Arnold Gottfried)
1880-1936 .... TCLC **25**
See also CA 118
Spenser, Edmund 1552(?)-1599 ..... LC **5, 39;**
DA; DAB; DAC; DAM MST, POET;
PC 8; WLC
See also CDBLB Before 1660; DA3; DLB
167
Spicer, Jack 1925-1965 .... CLC **8, 18, 72;**
DAM POET
See also CA 85-88; DLB 5, 16, 193
Spiegelman, Art 1948- .... CLC **76**
See also AAYA 10; CA 125; CANR 41, 55,
74; MTCW 2; SATA 109
Spielberg, Peter 1929- .... CLC **6**
See also CA 5-8R; CANR 4, 48; DLBY 81
Spielberg, Steven 1947- .... CLC **20**
See also AAYA 8, 24; CA 77-80; CANR
32; SATA 32
Spillane, Frank Morrison 1918-
See Spillane, Mickey
See also CA 25-28R; CANR 28, 63; DA3;
MTCW 1, 2; SATA 66
Spillane, Mickey CLC **3, 13**
See also Spillane, Frank Morrison
See also MTCW 2
Spinoza, Benedictus de 1632-1677 .. LC **9, 58**
Spinrad, Norman (Richard) 1940- ... CLC **46**
See also CA 37-40R; CAAS 19; CANR 20,
91; DLB 8; INT CANR-20

Spitteler, Carl (Friedrich Georg)
1845-1924 .... TCLC **12**
See also CA 109; DLB 129
Spivack, Kathleen (Romola Drucker)
1938- .... CLC **6**
See also CA 49-52
Spoto, Donald 1941- .... CLC **39**
See also CA 65-68; CANR 11, 57
Springsteen, Bruce (F.) 1949- .... CLC **17**
See also CA 111
Spurling, Hilary 1940- .... CLC **34**
See also CA 104; CANR 25, 52
Spyker, John Howland
See Elman, Richard (Martin)
Squires, (James) Radcliffe
1917-1993 .... CLC **51**
See also CA 1-4R; 140; CANR 6, 21
Srivastava, Dhanpat Rai 1880(?)-1936
See Premchand
See also CA 118
Stacy, Donald
See Pohl, Frederik
Stael, Germaine de 1766-1817
See Stael-Holstein, Anne Louise Germaine
Necker Baronn
See also DLB 119
Stael-Holstein, Anne Louise Germaine
Necker Baronn 1766-1817 .... NCLC **3**
See also Stael, Germaine de
See also DLB 192
Stafford, Jean 1915-1979 .. CLC **4, 7, 19, 68;**
SSC 26
See also CA 1-4R; 85-88; CANR 3, 65;
DLB 2, 173; MTCW 1, 2; SATA-Obit 22
Stafford, William (Edgar)
1914-1993 .. CLC **4, 7, 29; DAM POET**
See also CA 5-8R; 142; CAAS 3; CANR 5,
22; DLB 5, 206; INT CANR-22
Stagnelius, Eric Johan 1793-1823 . NCLC **61**
Staines, Trevor
See Brunner, John (Kilian Houston)
Stairs, Gordon
See Austin, Mary (Hunter)
Stairs, Gordon
See Austin, Mary (Hunter)
Stalin, Joseph 1879-1953 .... TCLC **92**
Stannard, Martin 1947- .... CLC **44**
See also CA 142; DLB 155
Stanton, Elizabeth Cady
1815-1902 .... TCLC **73**
See also CA 171; DLB 79
Stanton, Maura 1946- .... CLC **9**
See also CA 89-92; CANR 15; DLB 120
Stanton, Schuyler
See Baum, L(yman) Frank
Stapledon, (William) Olaf
1886-1950 .... TCLC **22**
See also CA 111; 162; DLB 15
Starbuck, George (Edwin)
1931-1996 .... CLC **53; DAM POET**
See also CA 21-24R; 153; CANR 23
Stark, Richard
See Westlake, Donald E(dwin)
Staunton, Schuyler
See Baum, L(yman) Frank
Stead, Christina (Ellen) 1902-1983 ... CLC **2,**
5, 8, 32, 80
See also CA 13-16R; 109; CANR 33, 40;
MTCW 1, 2
Stead, William Thomas
1849-1912 .... TCLC **48**
See also CA 167

Steele, Richard 1672-1729 .... LC **18**
See also CDBLB 1660-1789; DLB 84, 101
Steele, Timothy (Reid) 1948- .... CLC **45**
See also CA 93-96; CANR 16, 50; DLB
120
Steffens, (Joseph) Lincoln
1866-1936 .... TCLC **20**
See also CA 117
Stegner, Wallace (Earle) 1909-1993 .. CLC **9,**
49, 81; DAM NOV; SSC 27
See also AITN 1; BEST 90:3; CA 1-4R;
141; CAAS 9; CANR 1, 21, 46; DLB 9,
206; DLBY 93; MTCW 1, 2
Stein, Gertrude 1874-1946 .... TCLC **1, 6, 28,**
48; DA; DAB; DAC; DAM MST, NOV,
POET; PC 18; WLC
See also CA 104; 132; CDALB 1917-1929;
DA3; DLB 4, 54, 86; DLBD 15; MTCW
1, 2
Steinbeck, John (Ernst) 1902-1968 ... CLC **1,**
5, 9, 13, 21, 34, 45, 75, 124; DA; DAB;
DAC; DAM DRAM, MST, NOV; SSC
11, 37; WLC
See also AAYA 12; CA 1-4R; 25-28R;
CANR 1, 35; CDALB 1929-1941; DA3;
DLB 7, 9, 212; DLBD 2; MTCW 1, 2;
SATA 9
Steinem, Gloria 1934- .... CLC **63**
See also CA 53-56; CANR 28, 51; MTCW
1, 2
Steiner, George 1929- .. CLC **24; DAM NOV**
See also CA 73-76; CANR 31, 67; DLB 67;
MTCW 1, 2; SATA 62
Steiner, K. Leslie
See Delany, Samuel R(ay, Jr.)
Steiner, Rudolf 1861-1925 .... TCLC **13**
See also CA 107
Stendhal 1783-1842 .... NCLC **23, 46; DA;**
DAB; DAC; DAM MST, NOV; SSC
27; WLC
See also DA3; DLB 119
Stephen, Adeline Virginia
See Woolf, (Adeline) Virginia
Stephen, Sir Leslie 1832-1904 .... TCLC **23**
See also CA 123; DLB 57, 144, 190
Stephen, Sir Leslie
See Stephen, Sir Leslie
Stephen, Virginia
See Woolf, (Adeline) Virginia
Stephens, James 1882(?)-1950 .... TCLC **4**
See also CA 104; DLB 19, 153, 162
Stephens, Reed
See Donaldson, Stephen R.
Steptoe, Lydia
See Barnes, Djuna
Sterchi, Beat 1949- .... CLC **65**
Sterling, Brett
See Bradbury, Ray (Douglas); Hamilton,
Edmond
Sterling, Bruce 1954- .... CLC **72**
See also CA 119; CANR 44
Sterling, George 1869-1926 .... TCLC **20**
See also CA 117; 165; DLB 54
Stern, Gerald 1925- .... CLC **40, 100**
See also CA 81-84; CANR 28; DLB 105
Stern, Richard (Gustave) 1928- ... CLC **4, 39**
See also CA 1-4R; CANR 1, 25, 52; DLBY
87; INT CANR-25
Sternberg, Josef von 1894-1969 .... CLC **20**
See also CA 81-84

Summers, Hollis (Spurgeon, Jr.)
　　1916- .... **CLC 10**
　　See also CA 5-8R; CANR 3; DLB 6
Summers, (Alphonsus Joseph-Mary Augustus) Montague
　　1880-1948 .... **TCLC 16**
　　See also CA 118; 163
Sumner, Gordon Matthew CLC 26
　　See also Sting
Surtees, Robert Smith 1803-1864 .. **NCLC 14**
　　See also DLB 21
Susann, Jacqueline 1921-1974 .... **CLC 3**
　　See also AITN 1; CA 65-68; 53-56; MTCW 1, 2
Su Shih 1036-1101 .... **CMLC 15**
Suskind, Patrick
　　See Sueskind, Patrick
　　See also CA 145
Sutcliff, Rosemary 1920-1992 .... **CLC 26; DAB; DAC; DAM MST, POP**
　　See also AAYA 10; CA 5-8R; 139; CANR 37; CLR 1, 37; JRDA; MAICYA; SATA 6, 44, 78; SATA-Obit 73
Sutro, Alfred 1863-1933 .... **TCLC 6**
　　See also CA 105; 185; DLB 10
Sutton, Henry
　　See Slavitt, David R(ytman)
Svevo, Italo 1861-1928 ...... **TCLC 2, 35; SSC 25**
　　See also Schmitz, Aron Hector
Swados, Elizabeth (A.) 1951- .... **CLC 12**
　　See also CA 97-100; CANR 49; INT 97-100
Swados, Harvey 1920-1972 .... **CLC 5**
　　See also CA 5-8R; 37-40R; CANR 6; DLB 2
Swan, Gladys 1934- .... **CLC 69**
　　See also CA 101; CANR 17, 39
Swanson, Logan
　　See Matheson, Richard Burton
Swarthout, Glendon (Fred)
　　1918-1992 .... **CLC 35**
　　See also CA 1-4R; 139; CANR 1, 47; SATA 26
Sweet, Sarah C.
　　See Jewett, (Theodora) Sarah Orne
Swenson, May 1919-1989 ...... **CLC 4, 14, 61, 106; DA; DAB; DAC; DAM MST, POET; PC 14**
　　See also CA 5-8R; 130; CANR 36, 61; DLB 5; MTCW 1, 2; SATA 15
Swift, Augustus
　　See Lovecraft, H(oward) P(hillips)
Swift, Graham (Colin) 1949- ...... **CLC 41, 88**
　　See also CA 117; 122; CANR 46, 71; DLB 194; MTCW 2
Swift, Jonathan 1667-1745 ..... **LC 1, 42; DA; DAB; DAC; DAM MST, NOV, POET; PC 9; WLC**
　　See also CDBLB 1660-1789; CLR 53; DA3; DLB 39, 95, 101; SATA 19
Swinburne, Algernon Charles
　　1837-1909 .... **TCLC 8, 36; DA; DAB; DAC; DAM MST, POET; PC 24; WLC**
　　See also CA 105; 140; CDBLB 1832-1890; DA3; DLB 35, 57
Swinfen, Ann CLC 34
Swinnerton, Frank Arthur
　　1884-1982 .... **CLC 31**
　　See also CA 108; DLB 34
Swithen, John
　　See King, Stephen (Edwin)

Sylvia
　　See Ashton-Warner, Sylvia (Constance)
Symmes, Robert Edward
　　See Duncan, Robert (Edward)
Symonds, John Addington
　　1840-1893 .... **NCLC 34**
　　See also DLB 57, 144
Symons, Arthur 1865-1945 .... **TCLC 11**
　　See also CA 107; DLB 19, 57, 149
Symons, Julian (Gustave)
　　1912-1994 .... **CLC 2, 14, 32**
　　See also CA 49-52; 147; CAAS 3; CANR 3, 33, 59; DLB 87, 155; DLBY 92; MTCW 1
Synge, (Edmund) J(ohn) M(illington)
　　1871-1909 . **TCLC 6, 37; DAM DRAM; DC 2**
　　See also CA 104; 141; CDBLB 1890-1914; DLB 10, 19
Syruc, J.
　　See Milosz, Czeslaw
Szirtes, George 1948- .... **CLC 46**
　　See also CA 109; CANR 27, 61
Szymborska, Wislawa 1923- .... **CLC 99**
　　See also CA 154; CANR 91; DA3; DLBY 96; MTCW 2
T. O., Nik
　　See Annensky, Innokenty (Fyodorovich)
Tabori, George 1914- .... **CLC 19**
　　See also CA 49-52; CANR 4, 69
Tagore, Rabindranath 1861-1941 ... **TCLC 3, 53; DAM DRAM, POET; PC 8**
　　See also CA 104; 120; DA3; MTCW 1, 2
Taine, Hippolyte Adolphe
　　1828-1893 .... **NCLC 15**
Talese, Gay 1932- .... **CLC 37**
　　See also AITN 1; CA 1-4R; CANR 9, 58; DLB 185; INT CANR-9; MTCW 1, 2
Tallent, Elizabeth (Ann) 1954- .... **CLC 45**
　　See also CA 117; CANR 72; DLB 130
Tally, Ted 1952- .... **CLC 42**
　　See also CA 120; 124; INT 124
Talvik, Heiti 1904-1947 .... **TCLC 87**
Tamayo y Baus, Manuel
　　1829-1898 .... **NCLC 1**
Tammsaare, A(nton) H(ansen)
　　1878-1940 .... **TCLC 27**
　　See also CA 164; DLB 220
Tam'si, Tchicaya U
　　See Tchicaya, Gerald Felix
Tan, Amy (Ruth) 1952- . **CLC 59, 120; DAM MULT, NOV, POP**
　　See also AAYA 9; BEST 89:3; CA 136; CANR 54; CDALBS; DA3; DLB 173; MTCW 2; SATA 75
Tandem, Felix
　　See Spitteler, Carl (Friedrich Georg)
Tanizaki, Jun'ichiro 1886-1965 ... **CLC 8, 14, 28; SSC 21**
　　See also CA 93-96; 25-28R; DLB 180; MTCW 2
Tanner, William
　　See Amis, Kingsley (William)
Tao Lao
　　See Storni, Alfonsina
Tarantino, Quentin (Jerome)
　　1963- .... **CLC 125**
　　See also CA 171
Tarassoff, Lev
　　See Troyat, Henri
Tarbell, Ida M(inerva) 1857-1944 . **TCLC 40**
　　See also CA 122; 181; DLB 47

Tarkington, (Newton) Booth
　　1869-1946 .... **TCLC 9**
　　See also CA 110; 143; DLB 9, 102; MTCW 2; SATA 17
Tarkovsky, Andrei (Arsenyevich)
　　1932-1986 .... **CLC 75**
　　See also CA 127
Tartt, Donna 1964(?)- .... **CLC 76**
　　See also CA 142
Tasso, Torquato 1544-1595 .... **LC 5**
Tate, (John Orley) Allen 1899-1979 .. **CLC 2, 4, 6, 9, 11, 14, 24**
　　See also CA 5-8R; 85-88; CANR 32; DLB 4, 45, 63; DLBD 17; MTCW 1, 2
Tate, Ellalice
　　See Hibbert, Eleanor Alice Burford
Tate, James (Vincent) 1943- ..... **CLC 2, 6, 25**
　　See also CA 21-24R; CANR 29, 57; DLB 5, 169
Tauler, Johannes c. 1300-1361 ...... **CMLC 37**
　　See also DLB 179
Tavel, Ronald 1940- .... **CLC 6**
　　See also CA 21-24R; CANR 33
Taylor, C(ecil) P(hilip) 1929-1981 .... **CLC 27**
　　See also CA 25-28R; 105; CANR 47
Taylor, Edward 1642(?)-1729 ..... **LC 11; DA; DAB; DAC; DAM MST, POET**
　　See also DLB 24
Taylor, Eleanor Ross 1920- .... **CLC 5**
　　See also CA 81-84; CANR 70
Taylor, Elizabeth 1912-1975 ..... **CLC 2, 4, 29**
　　See also CA 13-16R; CANR 9, 70; DLB 139; MTCW 1; SATA 13
Taylor, Frederick Winslow
　　1856-1915 .... **TCLC 76**
Taylor, Henry (Splawn) 1942- .... **CLC 44**
　　See also CA 33-36R; CAAS 7; CANR 31; DLB 5
Taylor, Kamala (Purnaiya) 1924-
　　See Markandaya, Kamala
　　See also CA 77-80
Taylor, Mildred D. CLC 21
　　See also AAYA 10; BW 1; CA 85-88; CANR 25; CLR 9, 59; DLB 52; JRDA; MAICYA; SAAS 5; SATA 15, 70
Taylor, Peter (Hillsman) 1917-1994 .. **CLC 1, 4, 18, 37, 44, 50, 71; SSC 10**
　　See also CA 13-16R; 147; CANR 9, 50; DLBY 81, 94; INT CANR-9; MTCW 1, 2
Taylor, Robert Lewis 1912-1998 .... **CLC 14**
　　See also CA 1-4R; 170; CANR 3, 64; SATA 10
Tchekhov, Anton
　　See Chekhov, Anton (Pavlovich)
Tchicaya, Gerald Felix 1931-1988 .. **CLC 101**
　　See also CA 129; 125; CANR 81
Tchicaya U Tam'si
　　See Tchicaya, Gerald Felix
Teasdale, Sara 1884-1933 .... **TCLC 4**
　　See also CA 104; 163; DLB 45; SATA 32
Tegner, Esaias 1782-1846 .... **NCLC 2**
Teilhard de Chardin, (Marie Joseph) Pierre
　　1881-1955 .... **TCLC 9**
　　See also CA 105
Temple, Ann
　　See Mortimer, Penelope (Ruth)
Tennant, Emma (Christina) 1937- .. **CLC 13, 52**
　　See also CA 65-68; CAAS 9; CANR 10, 38, 59, 88; DLB 14
Tenneshaw, S. M.
　　See Silverberg, Robert

Tennyson, Alfred 1809-1892 ... NCLC 30, 65; DA; DAB; DAC; DAM MST, POET; PC 6; WLC
See also CDBLB 1832-1890; DA3; DLB 32

Teran, Lisa St. Aubin de CLC 36
See also St. Aubin de Teran, Lisa

Terence c. 184B.C.-c. 159B.C. ...... CMLC 14; DC 7
See also DLB 211

Teresa de Jesus, St. 1515-1582 .... LC 18

Terkel, Louis 1912-
See Terkel, Studs
See also CA 57-60; CANR 18, 45, 67; DA3; MTCW 1, 2

Terkel, Studs CLC 38
See also Terkel, Louis
See also AAYA 32; AITN 1; MTCW 2

Terry, C. V.
See Slaughter, Frank G(ill)

Terry, Megan 1932- .... CLC 19
See also CA 77-80; CABS 3; CANR 43; DLB 7

Tertullian c. 155-c. 245 .... CMLC 29

Tertz, Abram
See Sinyavsky, Andrei (Donatevich)

Tesich, Steve 1943(?)-1996 .... CLC 40, 69
See also CA 105; 152; DLBY 83

Tesla, Nikola 1856-1943 .... TCLC 88

Teternikov, Fyodor Kuzmich 1863-1927
See Sologub, Fyodor
See also CA 104

Tevis, Walter 1928-1984 .... CLC 42
See also CA 113

Tey, Josephine TCLC 14
See also Mackintosh, Elizabeth
See also DLB 77

Thackeray, William Makepeace 1811-1863 ...... NCLC 5, 14, 22, 43; DA; DAB; DAC; DAM MST, NOV; WLC
See also CDBLB 1832-1890; DA3; DLB 21, 55, 159, 163; SATA 23

Thakura, Ravindranatha
See Tagore, Rabindranath

Tharoor, Shashi 1956- .... CLC 70
See also CA 141; CANR 91

Thelwell, Michael Miles 1939- .... CLC 22
See also BW 2; CA 101

Theobald, Lewis, Jr.
See Lovecraft, H(oward) P(hillips)

Theodorescu, Ion N. 1880-1967
See Arghezi, Tudor
See also CA 116; DLB 220

Theriault, Yves 1915-1983 .... CLC 79; DAC; DAM MST
See also CA 102; DLB 88

Theroux, Alexander (Louis) 1939- .... CLC 2, 25
See also CA 85-88; CANR 20, 63

Theroux, Paul (Edward) 1941- ..... CLC 5, 8, 11, 15, 28, 46; DAM POP
See also AAYA 28; BEST 89:4; CA 33-36R; CANR 20, 45, 74; CDALBS; DA3; DLB 2; MTCW 1, 2; SATA 44, 109

Thesen, Sharon 1946- .... CLC 56
See also CA 163

Thevenin, Denis
See Duhamel, Georges

Thibault, Jacques Anatole Francois 1844-1924
See France, Anatole
See also CA 106; 127; DAM NOV; DA3; MTCW 1, 2

Thiele, Colin (Milton) 1920- .... CLC 17
See also CA 29-32R; CANR 12, 28, 53; CLR 27; MAICYA; SAAS 2; SATA 14, 72

Thomas, Audrey (Callahan) 1935- .... CLC 7, 13, 37, 107; SSC 20
See also AITN 2; CA 21-24R; CAAS 19; CANR 36, 58; DLB 60; MTCW 1

Thomas, Augustus 1857-1934 .... TCLC 97

Thomas, D(onald) M(ichael) 1935- . CLC 13, 22, 31, 132
See also CA 61-64; CAAS 11; CANR 17, 45, 75; CDBLB 1960 to Present; DA3; DLB 40, 207; INT CANR-17; MTCW 1, 2

Thomas, Dylan (Marlais) 1914-1953 ... TCLC 1, 8, 45; DA; DAB; DAC; DAM DRAM, MST, POET; PC 2; SSC 3; WLC
See also CA 104; 120; CANR 65; CDBLB 1945-1960; DA3; DLB 13, 20, 139; MTCW 1, 2; SATA 60

Thomas, (Philip) Edward 1878-1917 .... TCLC 10; DAM POET
See also CA 106; 153; DLB 98

Thomas, Joyce Carol 1938- .... CLC 35
See also AAYA 12; BW 2, 3; CA 113; 116; CANR 48; CLR 19; DLB 33; INT 116; JRDA; MAICYA; MTCW 1, 2; SAAS 7; SATA 40, 78

Thomas, Lewis 1913-1993 .... CLC 35
See also CA 85-88; 143; CANR 38, 60; MTCW 1, 2

Thomas, M. Carey 1857-1935 .... TCLC 89

Thomas, Paul
See Mann, (Paul) Thomas

Thomas, Piri 1928- .... CLC 17; HLCS 2
See also CA 73-76; HW 1

Thomas, R(onald) S(tuart) 1913- ...... CLC 6, 13, 48; DAB; DAM POET
See also CA 89-92; CAAS 4; CANR 30; CDBLB 1960 to Present; DLB 27; MTCW 1

Thomas, Ross (Elmore) 1926-1995 .. CLC 39
See also CA 33-36R; 150; CANR 22, 63

Thompson, Francis Clegg
See Mencken, H(enry) L(ouis)

Thompson, Francis Joseph 1859-1907 .... TCLC 4
See also CA 104; CDBLB 1890-1914; DLB 19

Thompson, Hunter S(tockton) 1939- ... CLC 9, 17, 40, 104; DAM POP
See also BEST 89:1; CA 17-20R; CANR 23, 46, 74, 77; DA3; DLB 185; MTCW 1, 2

Thompson, James Myers
See Thompson, Jim (Myers)

Thompson, Jim (Myers) 1906-1977(?) .... CLC 69
See also CA 140

Thompson, Judith CLC 39

Thomson, James 1700-1748 ... LC 16, 29, 40; DAM POET
See also DLB 95

Thomson, James 1834-1882 .... NCLC 18; DAM POET
See also DLB 35

Thoreau, Henry David 1817-1862 .. NCLC 7, 21, 61; DA; DAB; DAC; DAM MST; PC 30; WLC
See also CDALB 1640-1865; DA3; DLB 1, 223

Thornton, Hall
See Silverberg, Robert

Thucydides c. 455B.C.-399B.C. ..... CMLC 17
See also DLB 176

Thumboo, Edwin 1933- .... PC 30

Thurber, James (Grover) 1894-1961 .... CLC 5, 11, 25, 125; DA; DAB; DAC; DAM DRAM, MST, NOV; SSC 1
See also CA 73-76; CANR 17, 39; CDALB 1929-1941; DA3; DLB 4, 11, 22, 102; MAICYA; MTCW 1, 2; SATA 13

Thurman, Wallace (Henry) 1902-1934 .... TCLC 6; BLC 3; DAM MULT
See also BW 1, 3; CA 104; 124; CANR 81; DLB 51

Tibullus, Albius c. 54B.C.-c. 19B.C. .... CMLC 36
See also DLB 211

Ticheburn, Cheviot
See Ainsworth, William Harrison

Tieck, (Johann) Ludwig 1773-1853 .... NCLC 5, 46; SSC 31
See also DLB 90

Tiger, Derry
See Ellison, Harlan (Jay)

Tilghman, Christopher 1948(?)- .... CLC 65
See also CA 159

Tillich, Paul (Johannes) 1886-1965 .... CLC 131
See also CA 5-8R; 25-28R; CANR 33; MTCW 1, 2

Tillinghast, Richard (Williford) 1940- .... CLC 29
See also CA 29-32R; CAAS 23; CANR 26, 51

Timrod, Henry 1828-1867 .... NCLC 25
See also DLB 3

Tindall, Gillian (Elizabeth) 1938- ...... CLC 7
See also CA 21-24R; CANR 11, 65

Tiptree, James, Jr. CLC 48, 50
See also Sheldon, Alice Hastings Bradley
See also DLB 8

Titmarsh, Michael Angelo
See Thackeray, William Makepeace

Tocqueville, Alexis (Charles Henri Maurice Clerel, Comte) de 1805-1859 . NCLC 7, 63

Tolkien, J(ohn) R(onald) R(euel) 1892-1973 .. CLC 1, 2, 3, 8, 12, 38; DA; DAB; DAC; DAM MST, NOV, POP; WLC
See also AAYA 10; AITN 1; CA 17-18; 45-48; CANR 36; CAP 2; CDBLB 1914-1945; CLR 56; DA3; DLB 15, 160; JRDA; MAICYA; MTCW 1, 2; SATA 2, 32, 100; SATA-Obit 24

Toller, Ernst 1893-1939 .... TCLC 10
See also CA 107; 186; DLB 124

Tolson, M. B.
See Tolson, Melvin B(eaunorus)

Tolson, Melvin B(eaunorus) 1898(?)-1966 .... CLC 36, 105; BLC 3; DAM MULT, POET
See also BW 1, 3; CA 124; 89-92; CANR 80; DLB 48, 76

Tolstoi, Aleksei Nikolaevich
See Tolstoy, Alexey Nikolaevich
Tolstoy, Alexey Nikolaevich
1882-1945 .... **TCLC 18**
See also CA 107; 158
Tolstoy, Count Leo
See Tolstoy, Leo (Nikolaevich)
Tolstoy, Leo (Nikolaevich)
1828-1910 .. **TCLC 4, 11, 17, 28, 44, 79;
DA; DAB; DAC; DAM MST, NOV;
SSC 9, 30; WLC**
See also CA 104; 123; DA3; SATA 26
Tomasi di Lampedusa, Giuseppe 1896-1957
See Lampedusa, Giuseppe (Tomasi) di
See also CA 111
Tomlin, Lily CLC 17
See also Tomlin, Mary Jean
Tomlin, Mary Jean 1939(?)-
See Tomlin, Lily
See also CA 117
Tomlinson, (Alfred) Charles 1927- .... **CLC 2,
4, 6, 13, 45; DAM POET; PC 17**
See also CA 5-8R; CANR 33; DLB 40
Tomlinson, H(enry) M(ajor)
1873-1958 .... **TCLC 71**
See also CA 118; 161; DLB 36, 100, 195
Tonson, Jacob
See Bennett, (Enoch) Arnold
Toole, John Kennedy 1937-1969 ..... **CLC 19,
64**
See also CA 104; DLBY 81; MTCW 2
Toomer, Jean 1894-1967 .... **CLC 1, 4, 13, 22;
BLC 3; DAM MULT; PC 7; SSC 1;
WLCS**
See also BW 1; CA 85-88; CDALB 1917-
1929; DA3; DLB 45, 51; MTCW 1, 2
Torley, Luke
See Blish, James (Benjamin)
Tornimparte, Alessandra
See Ginzburg, Natalia
Torre, Raoul della
See Mencken, H(enry) L(ouis)
Torrence, Ridgely 1874-1950 .... **TCLC 97**
See also DLB 54
Torrey, E(dwin) Fuller 1937- .... **CLC 34**
See also CA 119; CANR 71
Torsvan, Ben Traven
See Traven, B.
Torsvan, Benno Traven
See Traven, B.
Torsvan, Berick Traven
See Traven, B.
Torsvan, Berwick Traven
See Traven, B.
Torsvan, Bruno Traven
See Traven, B.
Torsvan, Traven
See Traven, B.
Tournier, Michel (Edouard) 1924- .... **CLC 6,
23, 36, 95**
See also CA 49-52; CANR 3, 36, 74; DLB
83; MTCW 1, 2; SATA 23
Tournimparte, Alessandra
See Ginzburg, Natalia
Towers, Ivar
See Kornbluth, C(yril) M.
Towne, Robert (Burton) 1936(?)- ..... **CLC 87**
See also CA 108; DLB 44
Townsend, Sue CLC 61
See also Townsend, Susan Elaine
See also AAYA 28; SATA 55, 93; SATA-
Brief 48

Townsend, Susan Elaine 1946-
See Townsend, Sue
See also CA 119; 127; CANR 65; DAB;
DAC; DAM MST
Townshend, Peter (Dennis Blandford)
1945- .... **CLC 17, 42**
See also CA 107
Tozzi, Federigo 1883-1920 .... **TCLC 31**
See also CA 160
Traill, Catharine Parr 1802-1899 .. **NCLC 31**
See also DLB 99
Trakl, Georg 1887-1914 .... **TCLC 5; PC 20**
See also CA 104; 165; MTCW 2
Transtroemer, Tomas (Goesta)
1931- .... **CLC 52, 65; DAM POET**
See also CA 117; 129; CAAS 17
Transtromer, Tomas Gosta
See Transtroemer, Tomas (Goesta)
Traven, B. (?)-1969 .... **CLC 8, 11**
See also CA 19-20; 25-28R; CAP 2; DLB
9, 56; MTCW 1
Treitel, Jonathan 1959- .... **CLC 70**
Trelawny, Edward John
1792-1881 .... **NCLC 85**
See also DLB 110, 116, 144
Tremain, Rose 1943- .... **CLC 42**
See also CA 97-100; CANR 44; DLB 14
Tremblay, Michel 1942- .... **CLC 29, 102;
DAC; DAM MST**
See also CA 116; 128; DLB 60; MTCW 1,
2
Trevanian CLC 29
See also Whitaker, Rod(ney)
Trevor, Glen
See Hilton, James
Trevor, William 1928- .. **CLC 7, 9, 14, 25, 71,
116; SSC 21**
See also Cox, William Trevor
See also DLB 14, 139; MTCW 2
Trifonov, Yuri (Valentinovich)
1925-1981 .... **CLC 45**
See also CA 126; 103; MTCW 1
Trilling, Diana (Rubin) 1905-1996 . **CLC 129**
See also CA 5-8R; 154; CANR 10, 46; INT
CANR-10; MTCW 1, 2
Trilling, Lionel 1905-1975 .... **CLC 9, 11, 24**
See also CA 9-12R; 61-64; CANR 10; DLB
28, 63; INT CANR-10; MTCW 1, 2
Trimball, W. H.
See Mencken, H(enry) L(ouis)
Tristan
See Gomez de la Serna, Ramon
Tristram
See Housman, A(lfred) E(dward)
Trogdon, William (Lewis) 1939-
See Heat-Moon, William Least
See also CA 115; 119; CANR 47, 89; INT
119
Trollope, Anthony 1815-1882 ... **NCLC 6, 33;
DA; DAB; DAC; DAM MST, NOV;
SSC 28; WLC**
See also CDBLB 1832-1890; DA3; DLB
21, 57, 159; SATA 22
Trollope, Frances 1779-1863 .... **NCLC 30**
See also DLB 21, 166
Trotsky, Leon 1879-1940 .... **TCLC 22**
See also CA 118; 167
Trotter (Cockburn), Catharine
1679-1749 .... **LC 8**
See also DLB 84

Trotter, Wilfred 1872-1939 .... **TCLC 97**
Trout, Kilgore
See Farmer, Philip Jose
Trow, George W. S. 1943- .... **CLC 52**
See also CA 126; CANR 91
Troyat, Henri 1911- .... **CLC 23**
See also CA 45-48; CANR 2, 33, 67;
MTCW 1
Trudeau, G(arretson) B(eekman) 1948-
See Trudeau, Garry B.
See also CA 81-84; CANR 31; SATA 35
Trudeau, Garry B. CLC 12
See also Trudeau, G(arretson) B(eekman)
See also AAYA 10; AITN 2
Truffaut, Francois 1932-1984 ... **CLC 20, 101**
See also CA 81-84; 113; CANR 34
Trumbo, Dalton 1905-1976 .... **CLC 19**
See also CA 21-24R; 69-72; CANR 10;
DLB 26
Trumbull, John 1750-1831 .... **NCLC 30**
See also DLB 31
Trundlett, Helen B.
See Eliot, T(homas) S(tearns)
Tryon, Thomas 1926-1991 .... **CLC 3, 11;
DAM POP**
See also AITN 1; CA 29-32R; 135; CANR
32, 77; DA3; MTCW 1
Tryon, Tom
See Tryon, Thomas
Ts'ao Hsueh-ch'in 1715(?)-1763 .... **LC 1**
Tsushima, Shuji 1909-1948
See Dazai Osamu
See also CA 107
Tsvetaeva (Efron), Marina (Ivanovna)
1892-1941 .... **TCLC 7, 35; PC 14**
See also CA 104; 128; CANR 73; MTCW
1, 2
Tuck, Lily 1938- .... **CLC 70**
See also CA 139; CANR 90
Tu Fu 712-770 .... **PC 9**
See also DAM MULT
Tunis, John R(oberts) 1889-1975 ..... **CLC 12**
See also CA 61-64; CANR 62; DLB 22,
171; JRDA; MAICYA; SATA 37; SATA-
Brief 30
Tuohy, Frank CLC 37
See also Tuohy, John Francis
See also DLB 14, 139
Tuohy, John Francis 1925-1999
See Tuohy, Frank
See also CA 5-8R; 178; CANR 3, 47
Turco, Lewis (Putnam) 1934- ..... **CLC 11, 63**
See also CA 13-16R; CAAS 22; CANR 24,
51; DLBY 84
Turgenev, Ivan 1818-1883 .... **NCLC 21; DA;
DAB; DAC; DAM MST, NOV; DC 7;
SSC 7; WLC**
Turgot, Anne-Robert-Jacques
1727-1781 .... **LC 26**
Turner, Frederick 1943- .... **CLC 48**
See also CA 73-76; CAAS 10; CANR 12,
30, 56; DLB 40
Tutu, Desmond M(pilo) 1931- .... **CLC 80;
BLC 3; DAM MULT**
See also BW 1, 3; CA 125; CANR 67, 81
Tutuola, Amos 1920-1997 ...... **CLC 5, 14, 29;
BLC 3; DAM MULT**
See also BW 2, 3; CA 9-12R; 159; CANR
27, 66; DA3; DLB 125; MTCW 1, 2

Vaughan, Henry 1621-1695 .... **LC 27**
  See also DLB 131
Vaughn, Stephanie CLC 62
Vazov, Ivan (Minchov) 1850-1921 . **TCLC 25**
  See also CA 121; 167; DLB 147
Veblen, Thorstein B(unde)
  1857-1929 .... **TCLC 31**
  See also CA 115; 165
Vega, Lope de 1562-1635 .... **LC 23; HLCS 2**
Venison, Alfred
  See Pound, Ezra (Weston Loomis)
Verdi, Marie de
  See Mencken, H(enry) L(ouis)
Verdu, Matilde
  See Cela, Camilo Jose
Verga, Giovanni (Carmelo)
  1840-1922 .... **TCLC 3; SSC 21**
  See also CA 104; 123
Vergil 70B.C.-19B.C. .... **CMLC 9, 40; DA;**
    DAB; DAC; DAM MST, POET; PC
    12; WLCS
  See also Virgil
  See also DA3; DLB 211
Verhaeren, Emile (Adolphe Gustave)
  1855-1916 .... **TCLC 12**
  See also CA 109
Verlaine, Paul (Marie) 1844-1896 .. **NCLC 2,**
    51; DAM POET; PC 2
Verne, Jules (Gabriel) 1828-1905 ... **TCLC 6,**
    52
  See also AAYA 16; CA 110; 131; DA3;
    DLB 123; JRDA; MAICYA; SATA 21
Very, Jones 1813-1880 .... **NCLC 9**
  See also DLB 1
Vesaas, Tarjei 1897-1970 .... **CLC 48**
  See also CA 29-32R
Vialis, Gaston
  See Simenon, Georges (Jacques Christian)
Vian, Boris 1920-1959 .... **TCLC 9**
  See also CA 106; 164; DLB 72; MTCW 2
Viaud, (Louis Marie) Julien 1850-1923
  See Loti, Pierre
  See also CA 107
Vicar, Henry
  See Felsen, Henry Gregor
Vicker, Angus
  See Felsen, Henry Gregor
Vidal, Gore 1925- ...... **CLC 2, 4, 6, 8, 10, 22,**
    33, 72; DAM NOV, POP
  See also AITN 1; BEST 90:2; CA 5-8R;
    CANR 13, 45, 65; CDALBS; DA3; DLB
    6, 152; INT CANR-13; MTCW 1, 2
Viereck, Peter (Robert Edwin)
  1916- .... **CLC 4; PC 27**
  See also CA 1-4R; CANR 1, 47; DLB 5
Vigny, Alfred (Victor) de
  1797-1863 .. **NCLC 7; DAM POET; PC**
    26
  See also DLB 119, 192
Vilakazi, Benedict Wallet
  1906-1947 .... **TCLC 37**
  See also CA 168
Villa, Jose Garcia 1904-1997 .... **PC 22**
  See also CA 25-28R; CANR 12
Villarreal, Jose Antonio 1924-
  See also CA 133; DAM MULT; DLB 82;
    HLC 2; HW 1
Villaurrutia, Xavier 1903-1950 ...... **TCLC 80**
  See also HW 1

Villehardouin 1150(?)-1218(?) .... **CMLC 38**
Villiers de l'Isle Adam, Jean Marie Mathias
    Philippe Auguste, Comte de
  1838-1889 .... **NCLC 3; SSC 14**
  See also DLB 123
Villon, Francois 1431-1463(?) .... **PC 13**
  See also DLB 208
Vine, Barbara CLC 50
  See also Rendell, Ruth (Barbara)
  See also BEST 90:4
Vinge, Joan (Carol) D(ennison)
  1948- .... **CLC 30; SSC 24**
  See also AAYA 32; CA 93-96; CANR 72;
    SATA 36, 113
Violis, G.
  See Simenon, Georges (Jacques Christian)
Viramontes, Helena Maria 1954-
  See also CA 159; DLB 122; HLCS 2; HW
    2
Virgil 70B.C.-19B.C.
  See Vergil
Visconti, Luchino 1906-1976 .... **CLC 16**
  See also CA 81-84; 65-68; CANR 39
Vittorini, Elio 1908-1966 .... **CLC 6, 9, 14**
  See also CA 133; 25-28R
Vivekananda, Swami 1863-1902 .... **TCLC 88**
Vizenor, Gerald Robert 1934- .... **CLC 103;**
    DAM MULT
  See also CA 13-16R; CAAS 22; CANR 5,
    21, 44, 67; DLB 175; MTCW 2; NNAL
Vizinczey, Stephen 1933- .... **CLC 40**
  See also CA 128; INT 128
Vliet, R(ussell) G(ordon)
  1929-1984 .... **CLC 22**
  See also CA 37-40R; 112; CANR 18
Vogau, Boris Andreyevich 1894-1937(?)
  See Pilnyak, Boris
  See also CA 123
Vogel, Paula A(nne) 1951- .... **CLC 76**
  See also CA 108
Voigt, Cynthia 1942- .... **CLC 30**
  See also AAYA 3, 30; CA 106; CANR 18,
    37, 40; CLR 13, 48; INT CANR-18;
    JRDA; MAICYA; SATA 48, 79, 116;
    SATA-Brief 33
Voigt, Ellen Bryant 1943- .... **CLC 54**
  See also CA 69-72; CANR 11, 29, 55; DLB
    120
Voinovich, Vladimir (Nikolaevich)
  1932- .... **CLC 10, 49**
  See also CA 81-84; CAAS 12; CANR 33,
    67; MTCW 1
Vollmann, William T. 1959- .. **CLC 89; DAM**
    NOV, POP
  See also CA 134; CANR 67; DA3; MTCW
    2
Voloshinov, V. N.
  See Bakhtin, Mikhail Mikhailovich
Voltaire 1694-1778 .... **LC 14; DA; DAB;**
    DAC; DAM DRAM, MST; SSC 12;
    WLC
  See also DA3
von Aschendrof, BaronIgnatz
  See Ford, Ford Madox
von Daeniken, Erich 1935- .... **CLC 30**
  See also AITN 1; CA 37-40R; CANR 17,
    44
von Daniken, Erich
  See von Daeniken, Erich

von Hartmann, Eduard
  1842-1906 .... **TCLC 96**
von Heidenstam, (Carl Gustaf) Verner
  See Heidenstam, (Carl Gustaf) Verner von
von Heyse, Paul (Johann Ludwig)
  See Heyse, Paul (Johann Ludwig von)
von Hofmannsthal, Hugo
  See Hofmannsthal, Hugo von
von Horvath, Odon
  See Horvath, Oedoen von
von Horvath, Oedoen -1938
  See Horvath, Oedoen von
  See also CA 184
von Liliencron, (Friedrich Adolf Axel)
    Detlev
  See Liliencron, (Friedrich Adolf Axel) De-
    tlev von
Vonnegut, Kurt, Jr. 1922- . **CLC 1, 2, 3, 4, 5,**
    8, 12, 22, 40, 60, 111; DA; DAB; DAC;
    DAM MST, NOV, POP; SSC 8; WLC
  See also AAYA 6; AITN 1; BEST 90:4; CA
    1-4R; CANR 1, 25, 49, 75; CDALB 1968-
    1988; DA3; DLB 2, 8, 152; DLBD 3;
    DLBY 80; MTCW 1, 2
Von Rachen, Kurt
  See Hubbard, L(afayette) Ron(ald)
von Rezzori (d'Arezzo), Gregor
  See Rezzori (d'Arezzo), Gregor von
von Sternberg, Josef
  See Sternberg, Josef von
Vorster, Gordon 1924- .... **CLC 34**
  See also CA 133
Vosce, Trudie
  See Ozick, Cynthia
Voznesensky, Andrei (Andreievich)
  1933- .... **CLC 1, 15, 57; DAM POET**
  See also CA 89-92; CANR 37; MTCW 1
Waddington, Miriam 1917- .... **CLC 28**
  See also CA 21-24R; CANR 12, 30; DLB
    68
Wagman, Fredrica 1937- .... **CLC 7**
  See also CA 97-100; INT 97-100
Wagner, Linda W.
  See Wagner-Martin, Linda (C.)
Wagner, Linda Welshimer
  See Wagner-Martin, Linda (C.)
Wagner, Richard 1813-1883 .... **NCLC 9**
  See also DLB 129
Wagner-Martin, Linda (C.) 1936- .... **CLC 50**
  See also CA 159
Wagoner, David (Russell) 1926- .... **CLC 3, 5,**
    15
  See also CA 1-4R; CAAS 3; CANR 2, 71;
    DLB 5; SATA 14
Wah, Fred(erick James) 1939- .... **CLC 44**
  See also CA 107; 141; DLB 60
Wahloo, Per 1926-1975 .... **CLC 7**
  See also CA 61-64; CANR 73
Wahloo, Peter
  See Wahloo, Per
Wain, John (Barrington) 1925-1994 . **CLC 2,**
    11, 15, 46
  See also CA 5-8R; 145; CAAS 4; CANR
    23, 54; CDBLB 1960 to Present; DLB 15,
    27, 139, 155; MTCW 1, 2
Wajda, Andrzej 1926- .... **CLC 16**
  See also CA 102
Wakefield, Dan 1932- .... **CLC 7**
  See also CA 21-24R; CAAS 7

Webb, Mrs. Sidney
See Webb, Beatrice (Martha Potter)

Webb, Phyllis 1927- .... **CLC 18**
See also CA 104; CANR 23; DLB 53

Webb, Sidney (James) 1859-1947 .. **TCLC 22**
See also CA 117; 163; DLB 190

Webber, Andrew Lloyd CLC 21
See also Lloyd Webber, Andrew

Weber, Lenora Mattingly
1895-1971 .... **CLC 12**
See also CA 19-20; 29-32R; CAP 1; SATA
2; SATA-Obit 26

Weber, Max 1864-1920 .... **TCLC 69**
See also CA 109

Webster, John 1579(?)-1634(?) ... **LC 33; DA;**
DAB; DAC; DAM DRAM, MST; DC
2; WLC
See also CDBLB Before 1660; DLB 58

Webster, Noah 1758-1843 .... **NCLC 30**
See also DLB 1, 37, 42, 43, 73

Wedekind, (Benjamin) Frank(lin)
1864-1918 .... **TCLC 7; DAM DRAM**
See also CA 104; 153; DLB 118

Weidman, Jerome 1913-1998 .... **CLC 7**
See also AITN 2; CA 1-4R; 171; CANR 1;
DLB 28

Weil, Simone (Adolphine)
1909-1943 .... **TCLC 23**
See also CA 117; 159; MTCW 2

Weininger, Otto 1880-1903 .... **TCLC 84**

Weinstein, Nathan
See West, Nathanael

Weinstein, Nathan von Wallenstein
See West, Nathanael

Weir, Peter (Lindsay) 1944- .... **CLC 20**
See also CA 113; 123

Weiss, Peter (Ulrich) 1916-1982 .. **CLC 3, 15,**
51; DAM DRAM
See also CA 45-48; 106; CANR 3; DLB 69,
124

Weiss, Theodore (Russell) 1916- ... **CLC 3, 8,**
14
See also CA 9-12R; CAAS 2; CANR 46;
DLB 5

Welch, (Maurice) Denton
1915-1948 .... **TCLC 22**
See also CA 121; 148

Welch, James 1940- ..... **CLC 6, 14, 52; DAM**
MULT, POP
See also CA 85-88; CANR 42, 66; DLB
175; NNAL

Weldon, Fay 1931- . **CLC 6, 9, 11, 19, 36, 59,**
122; DAM POP
See also CA 21-24R; CANR 16, 46, 63;
CDBLB 1960 to Present; DLB 14, 194;
INT CANR-16; MTCW 1, 2

Wellek, Rene 1903-1995 .... **CLC 28**
See also CA 5-8R; 150; CAAS 7; CANR 8;
DLB 63; INT CANR-8

Weller, Michael 1942- .... **CLC 10, 53**
See also CA 85-88

Weller, Paul 1958- .... **CLC 26**

Wellershoff, Dieter 1925- .... **CLC 46**
See also CA 89-92; CANR 16, 37

Welles, (George) Orson 1915-1985 .. **CLC 20,**
80
See also CA 93-96; 117

Wellman, John McDowell 1945-
See Wellman, Mac
See also CA 166

Wellman, Mac 1945- .... **CLC 65**
See also Wellman, John McDowell; Well-
man, John McDowell

Wellman, Manly Wade 1903-1986 ... **CLC 49**
See also CA 1-4R; 118; CANR 6, 16, 44;
SATA 6; SATA-Obit 47

Wells, Carolyn 1869(?)-1942 .... **TCLC 35**
See also CA 113; 185; DLB 11

Wells, H(erbert) G(eorge)
1866-1946 . **TCLC 6, 12, 19; DA; DAB;**
DAC; DAM MST, NOV; SSC 6; WLC
See also AAYA 18; CA 110; 121; CDBLB
1914-1945; CLR 64; DA3; DLB 34, 70,
156, 178; MTCW 1, 2; SATA 20

Wells, Rosemary 1943- .... **CLC 12**
See also AAYA 13; CA 85-88; CANR 48;
CLR 16; MAICYA; SAAS 1; SATA 18,
69, 114

Welty, Eudora 1909- ...... **CLC 1, 2, 5, 14, 22,**
33, 105; DA; DAB; DAC; DAM MST,
NOV; SSC 1, 27; WLC
See also CA 9-12R; CABS 1; CANR 32,
65; CDALB 1941-1968; DA3; DLB 2,
102, 143; DLBD 12; DLBY 87; MTCW
1, 2

Wen I-to 1899-1946 .... **TCLC 28**

Wentworth, Robert
See Hamilton, Edmond

Werfel, Franz (Viktor) 1890-1945 ... **TCLC 8**
See also CA 104; 161; DLB 81, 124

Wergeland, Henrik Arnold
1808-1845 .... **NCLC 5**

Wersba, Barbara 1932- .... **CLC 30**
See also AAYA 2, 30; CA 29-32R, 182;
CAAE 182; CANR 16, 38; CLR 3; DLB
52; JRDA; MAICYA; SAAS 2; SATA 1,
58; SATA-Essay 103

Wertmueller, Lina 1928- .... **CLC 16**
See also CA 97-100; CANR 39, 78

Wescott, Glenway 1901-1987 .. **CLC 13; SSC**
35
See also CA 13-16R; 121; CANR 23, 70;
DLB 4, 9, 102

Wesker, Arnold 1932- ... **CLC 3, 5, 42; DAB;**
DAM DRAM
See also CA 1-4R; CAAS 7; CANR 1, 33;
CDBLB 1960 to Present; DLB 13; MTCW
1

Wesley, Richard (Errol) 1945- .... **CLC 7**
See also BW 1; CA 57-60; CANR 27; DLB
38

Wessel, Johan Herman 1742-1785 .... **LC 7**

West, Anthony (Panther)
1914-1987 .... **CLC 50**
See also CA 45-48; 124; CANR 3, 19; DLB
15

West, C. P.
See Wodehouse, P(elham) G(renville)

West, (Mary) Jessamyn 1902-1984 ... **CLC 7,**
17
See also CA 9-12R; 112; CANR 27; DLB
6; DLBY 84; MTCW 1, 2; SATA-Obit 37

West, Morris L(anglo) 1916- .... **CLC 6, 33**
See also CA 5-8R; CANR 24, 49, 64;
MTCW 1, 2

West, Nathanael 1903-1940 .... **TCLC 1, 14,**
44; SSC 16
See also CA 104; 125; CDALB 1929-1941;
DA3; DLB 4, 9, 28; MTCW 1, 2

West, Owen
See Koontz, Dean R(ay)

West, Paul 1930- .... **CLC 7, 14, 96**
See also CA 13-16R; CAAS 7; CANR 22,
53, 76, 89; DLB 14; INT CANR-22;
MTCW 2

West, Rebecca 1892-1983 ... **CLC 7, 9, 31, 50**
See also CA 5-8R; 109; CANR 19; DLB
36; DLBY 83; MTCW 1, 2

Westall, Robert (Atkinson)
1929-1993 .... **CLC 17**
See also AAYA 12; CA 69-72; 141; CANR
18, 68; CLR 13; JRDA; MAICYA; SAAS
2; SATA 23, 69; SATA-Obit 75

Westermarck, Edward 1862-1939 . **TCLC 87**

Westlake, Donald E(dwin) 1933- .... **CLC 7,**
33; DAM POP
See also CA 17-20R; CAAS 13; CANR 16,
44, 65; INT CANR-16; MTCW 2

Westmacott, Mary
See Christie, Agatha (Mary Clarissa)

Weston, Allen
See Norton, Andre

Wetcheek, J. L.
See Feuchtwanger, Lion

Wetering, Janwillem van de
See van de Wetering, Janwillem

Wetherald, Agnes Ethelwyn
1857-1940 .... **TCLC 81**
See also DLB 99

Wetherell, Elizabeth
See Warner, Susan (Bogert)

Whale, James 1889-1957 .... **TCLC 63**

Whalen, Philip 1923- .... **CLC 6, 29**
See also CA 9-12R; CANR 5, 39; DLB 16

Wharton, Edith (Newbold Jones)
1862-1937 .... **TCLC 3, 9, 27, 53; DA;**
DAB; DAC; DAM MST, NOV; SSC 6;
WLC
See also AAYA 25; CA 104; 132; CDALB
1865-1917; DA3; DLB 4, 9, 12, 78, 189;
DLBD 13; MTCW 1, 2

Wharton, James
See Mencken, H(enry) L(ouis)

Wharton, William (a pseudonym) CLC 18,
37
See also CA 93-96; DLBY 80; INT 93-96

Wheatley (Peters), Phillis
1754(?)-1784 ...... **LC 3, 50; BLC 3; DA;**
DAC; DAM MST, MULT, POET; PC
3; WLC
See also CDALB 1640-1865; DA3; DLB
31, 50

Wheelock, John Hall 1886-1978 .... **CLC 14**
See also CA 13-16R; 77-80; CANR 14;
DLB 45

White, E(lwyn) B(rooks)
1899-1985 . **CLC 10, 34, 39; DAM POP**
See also AITN 2; CA 13-16R; 116; CANR
16, 37; CDALBS; CLR 1, 21; DA3; DLB
11, 22; MAICYA; MTCW 1, 2; SATA 2,
29, 100; SATA-Obit 44

White, Edmund (Valentine III)
1940- .... **CLC 27, 110; DAM POP**
See also AAYA 7; CA 45-48; CANR 3, 19,
36, 62; DA3; MTCW 1, 2

White, Patrick (Victor Martindale)
1912-1990 ...... **CLC 3, 4, 5, 7, 9, 18, 65,**
69; SSC 39
See also CA 81-84; 132; CANR 43; MTCW
1

White, Phyllis Dorothy James 1920-
See James, P. D.
See also CA 21-24R; CANR 17, 43, 65;
DAM POP; DA3; MTCW 1, 2

Literary Criticism Series
Cumulative Topic Index

This index lists all topic entries in Gale's *Classical and Medieval Literature Criticism, Contemporary Literary Criticism, Literature Criticism from 1400 to 1800, Nineteenth-Century Literature Criticism,* and *Twentieth-Century Literary Criticism.*

Topic Index

CLC Cumulative Nationality Index

ALBANIAN

Kadare, Ismail **52**

ALGERIAN

Althusser, Louis **106**
Camus, Albert **1, 2, 4, 9, 11, 14, 32, 63, 69, 124**
Cixous, Helene **92**
Cohen-Solal, Annie **50**

AMERICAN

Abbey, Edward **36, 59**
Abbott, Lee K(ittredge) **48**
Abish, Walter **22**
Abrams, M(eyer) H(oward) **24**
Acker, Kathy **45, 111**
Adams, Alice (Boyd) **6, 13, 46**
Addams, Charles (Samuel) **30**
Adler, C(arole) S(chwerdtfeger) **35**
Adler, Renata **8, 31**
Ai **4, 14, 69**
Aiken, Conrad (Potter) **1, 3, 5, 10, 52**
Albee, Edward (Franklin III) **1, 2, 3, 5, 9, 11, 13, 25, 53, 86, 113**
Alexander, Lloyd (Chudley) **35**
Alexie, Sherman (Joseph Jr.) **96**
Algren, Nelson **4, 10, 33**
Allen, Edward **59**
Allen, Paula Gunn **84**
Allen, Woody **16, 52**
Allison, Dorothy E. **78**
Alta **19**
Alter, Robert B(ernard) **34**
Alther, Lisa **7, 41**
Altman, Robert **16, 116**
Alvarez, Julia **93**
Ammons, A(rchie) R(andolph) **2, 3, 5, 8, 9, 25, 57, 108**
L'Amour, Louis (Dearborn) **25, 55**
Anaya, Rudolfo A(lfonso) **23**
Anderson, Jon (Victor) **9**
Anderson, Poul (William) **15**
Anderson, Robert (Woodruff) **23**
Angell, Roger **26**
Angelou, Maya **12, 35, 64, 77**
Anthony, Piers **35**
Apple, Max (Isaac) **9, 33**
Appleman, Philip (Dean) **51**
Archer, Jules **12**
Arendt, Hannah **66, 98**
Arnow, Harriette (Louisa) Simpson **2, 7, 18**
Arrick, Fran **30**
Arzner, Dorothy **98**
Ashbery, John (Lawrence) **2, 3, 4, 6, 9, 13, 15, 25, 41, 77, 125**

Asimov, Isaac **1, 3, 9, 19, 26, 76, 92**
Attaway, William (Alexander) **92**
Auchincloss, Louis (Stanton) **4, 6, 9, 18, 45**
Auden, W(ystan) H(ugh) **1, 2, 3, 4, 6, 9, 11, 14, 43**
Auel, Jean M(arie) **31, 107**
Auster, Paul **47, 131**
Bach, Richard (David) **14**
Badanes, Jerome **59**
Baker, Elliott **8**
Baker, Nicholson **61**
Baker, Russell (Wayne) **31**
Bakshi, Ralph **26**
Baldwin, James (Arthur) **1, 2, 3, 4, 5, 8, 13, 15, 17, 42, 50, 67, 90, 127**
Bambara, Toni Cade **19, 88**
Banks, Russell **37, 72**
Baraka, Amiri **1, 2, 3, 5, 10, 14, 33, 115**
Barbera, Jack (Vincent) **44**
Barnard, Mary (Ethel) **48**
Barnes, Djuna **3, 4, 8, 11, 29, 127**
Barondess, Sue K(aufman) **8**
Barrett, William (Christopher) **27**
Barth, John (Simmons) **1, 2, 3, 5, 7, 9, 10, 14, 27, 51, 89**
Barthelme, Donald **1, 2, 3, 5, 6, 8, 13, 23, 46, 59, 115**
Barthelme, Frederick **36, 117**
Barzun, Jacques (Martin) **51**
Bass, Rick **79**
Baumbach, Jonathan **6, 23**
Bausch, Richard (Carl) **51**
Baxter, Charles (Morley) **45, 78**
Beagle, Peter S(oyer) **7, 104**
Beattie, Ann **8, 13, 18, 40, 63**
Becker, Walter **26**
Beecher, John **6**
Begiebing, Robert J(ohn) **70**
Behrman, S(amuel) N(athaniel) **40**
Belitt, Ben **22**
Bell, Madison Smartt **41, 102**
Bell, Marvin (Hartley) **8, 31**
Bellow, Saul **1, 2, 3, 6, 8, 10, 13, 15, 25, 33, 34, 63, 79**
Benary-Isbert, Margot **12**
Benchley, Peter (Bradford) **4, 8**
Benedikt, Michael **4, 14**
Benford, Gregory (Albert) **52**
Bennett, Hal **5**
Bennett, Jay **35**
Benson, Jackson J. **34**
Benson, Sally **17**
Bentley, Eric (Russell) **24**
Berendt, John (Lawrence) **86**
Berger, Melvin H. **12**
Berger, Thomas (Louis) **3, 5, 8, 11, 18, 38**

Bergstein, Eleanor **4**
Bernard, April **59**
Berriault, Gina **54, 109**
Berrigan, Daniel **4**
Berrigan, Ted **37**
Berry, Chuck **17**
Berry, Wendell (Erdman) **4, 6, 8, 27, 46**
Berryman, John **1, 2, 3, 4, 6, 8, 10, 13, 25, 62**
Bessie, Alvah **23**
Bettelheim, Bruno **79**
Betts, Doris (Waugh) **3, 6, 28**
Bidart, Frank **33**
Birkerts, Sven **116**
Bishop, Elizabeth **1, 4, 9, 13, 15, 32**
Bishop, John **10**
Blackburn, Paul **9, 43**
Blackmur, R(ichard) P(almer) **2, 24**
Blaise, Clark **29**
Blatty, William Peter **2**
Blessing, Lee **54**
Blish, James (Benjamin) **14**
Bloch, Robert (Albert) **33**
Bloom, Harold **24, 103**
Blount, Roy (Alton) Jr. **38**
Blume, Judy (Sussman) **12, 30**
Bly, Robert (Elwood) **1, 2, 5, 10, 15, 38, 128**
Bochco, Steven **35**
Bogan, Louise **4, 39, 46, 93**
Bogosian, Eric **45**
Bograd, Larry **35**
Bonham, Frank **12**
Bontemps, Arna(ud Wendell) **1, 18**
Booth, Philip **23**
Booth, Wayne C(layson) **24**
Bottoms, David **53**
Bourjaily, Vance (Nye) **8, 62**
Bova, Ben(jamin William) **45**
Bowers, Edgar **9**
Bowles, Jane (Sydney) **3, 68**
Bowles, Paul (Frederick) **1, 2, 19, 53**
Boyle, Kay **1, 5, 19, 58, 121**
Boyle, T(homas) Coraghessan **36, 55, 90**
Bradbury, Ray (Douglas) **1, 3, 10, 15, 42, 98**
Bradley, David (Henry) Jr. **23, 118**
Bradley, John Ed(mund Jr.) **55**
Bradley, Marion Zimmer **30**
Brady, Joan **86**
Brammer, William **31**
Brancato, Robin F(idler) **35**
Brand, Millen **7**
Branden, Barbara **44**
Branley, Franklyn M(ansfield) **21**

Nationality Index

Nationality Index

Nationality Index

CLC-132 Title Index

Title Index

ISBN 0-7876-3207-4

90000

9 780787 632076